W9-AMV-880

THE BUILDINGS OF ENGLAND

FOUNDING EDITOR: NIKOLAUS PEVSNER

LONDON 5: EAST

BRIDGET CHERRY, CHARLES O'BRIEN

AND NIKOLAUS PEVSNER

PEVSNER ARCHITECTURAL GUIDES

The Buildings of England series was created and largely written by Sir Nikolaus Pevsner (1902–83). First editions of the county volumes were published by Penguin Books between 1951 and 1974. The continuing programme of revisions and new volumes has been supported by research financed through the Buildings Books Trust since 1994

THE BUILDINGS BOOKS TRUST

was established in 1994, registered charity number 1042101. It promotes the appreciation and understanding of architecture by supporting and financing the research needed to sustain new and revised volumes of *The Buildings of England*, *Ireland*, *Scotland* and *Wales*

The Trust gratefully acknowledges contributions toward the cost of writing, research and illustration from

ENGLISH HERITAGE

and

THE MICHAEL MARKS CHARITABLE TRUST

London
5
East

BY

BRIDGET CHERRY

CHARLES O'BRIEN

AND

NIKOLAUS PEVSNER

WITH CONTRIBUTIONS FROM

ELIZABETH WILLIAMSON

MALCOLM TUCKER

AND

PAMELA GREENWOOD

THE BUILDINGS OF ENGLAND

YALE UNIVERSITY PRESS
NEW HAVEN AND LONDON

YALE UNIVERSITY PRESS
NEW HAVEN AND LONDON
302 Temple Street, New Haven CT 06511
47 Bedford Square, London WC1 3DP
www.pevsner.co.uk
www.lookingatbuildings.org
www.yalebooks.co.uk
www.yalebooks.com
for
THE BUILDINGS BOOKS TRUST

Published by Yale University Press 2005
2 4 6 8 10 9 7 5 3 1

ISBN 0 300 10701 3

Printed in China
through World Print
Set in Monotype Plantin

London except the City and Westminster, 1952,
was dedicated

TO THE LIBRARIANS OF THE
PUBLIC LIBRARIES OF LONDON
WITHOUT WHOSE PATIENT HELP
THIS VOLUME COULD NOT
HAVE BEEN WRITTEN

This volume is dedicated to

THE LONDON HISTORIANS
OF
The Survey of London
The London County Council
The Greater London Council
The Royal Commission on the Historical Monuments of England
English Heritage

CONTENTS

LIST OF TEXT FIGURES AND MAPS

Introduction

Tower Hamlets

MAPS

PHOTOGRAPHIC ACKNOWLEDGEMENTS

We are grateful to English Heritage photographer Jonathan Bailey for taking most of the photographs for this volume (© English Heritage Photo Library) and also to the sources of the remaining photographs as shown below. We are grateful for permission to reproduce them as appropriate. Where older images have been used, every effort has been made to contact or trace copyright holders. The publishers will be glad to make good any errors or omissions brought to our attention in future editions.

Richard Kindersley: 126
John Outram: 115
Richard Waite: 125

The photographs are included in the indexes, and references to them are given by numbers in the margin of the text.

ABBREVIATIONS AND LISTS OF COUNTY COUNCIL ARCHITECTS

Area Authorities

MBW	Metropolitan Board of Works (1855–88)
LCC	London County Council (1888–1965)
GLC	Greater London Council (1965–86)
GLA	Greater London Authority (2000–)
PLA	Port of London Authority (1909–)
LDDC	London Docklands Development Corporation (1981–98)

Other Abbreviations

NMR	National Monuments Record
RCHM/RCHME	Royal Commission on Historical Monuments (of England)
RIBA	Royal Institute of British Architects
SPAB	Society for the Protection of Ancient Buildings

In order to avoid repetition, chief architects of public authorities are not mentioned on every occasion in the gazetteer. Borough architects are mentioned under individual boroughs. The chief County Council architects are as follows:

Architects to the Metropolitan Board of Works, the London County Council and the Greater London Council

Superintending Architects
Frederick Marrable 1865–61
George Vulliamy 1861–87
Thomas Blashill 1887–99
W.E. Riley 1899–1919
G. Topham Forrest 1919–35
E.P. Wheeler 1935–9
F.R. Hiorns 1939–41
J.H. Forshaw 1941–6
(Sir) Robert Matthew 1946–53
(Sir) Leslie Martin 1953–6
(Sir) Hubert Bennett 1956–71
(Sir) Roger Walters 1971–8
F.B. Pooley 1978–80
P.E. Jones 1980–6

Fire Brigade Branch
Edward Cresy 1866–70
Alfred Mott 1871–9
Robert Pearsall 1879–99
Owen Fleming 1900–

Housing of the Working Classes Branch
Owen Fleming 1893–1900
John Briggs 1900–2
Rob Robertson 1902–10

Education Branch (until 1904 architects to the School Board for London)
E.R. Robson 1871–84
T.J. Bailey 1884–1910
Rob Robertson 1910–

The Construction Division (absorbed the Fire Brigade Branch and the Housing of the Working Classes Branch from 1910, the Education Branch from 1920. Housing was placed under the Valuer's Department from 1946 until 1950, when the whole of the Architect's Department was reorganized under Sir Robert Matthew, with separate heads of department for housing and education.)

Housing
S. Howard 1946–50
H.J. Whitfield Lewis 1950–9
K.J. Campbell 1959–74
G.H. Wigglesworth 1974–80

Education
S. Howard 1950–5
M.C.L. Powell 1956–65
Schools: C.E. Hartland 1965–72
Education: M.C.L. Powell 1965–71
G.H. Wigglesworth 1972–4
P.E. Jones 1974–80

Special Works (a separate department responsible for fire and ambulance stations, magistrates' courts, civic buildings, etc.)
G. Horsfall 1960–76 (also senior architect Civic Design, 1965–70, and Thamesmead Manager from 1970)
R.A. Michelmore 1977–80 (from 1980, principal Construction Architect)

Architects to Essex County Council 1900–1965
F. Whitmore (chief assistant, H.W. Mann) 1900–14
G. Topham Forrest 1914–19
J. Stuart (chief assistant, J.W. Spence) 1920–45
H. Conolly 1945–66)

Surveyors to the Metropolitan Police
Charles Reeves 1842–66
Thomas Charles Sorby 1867–8
Frederick Caiger 1868–81
John Butler Sen. 1881–95
John Dixon Butler 1895–1920
G. Mackenzie Trench 1921–47
J. Innes Elliott 1947–74
M. Belchamber 1974–88
T. Lawrence 1988–2002
A. Croney 2002–

FOREWORD

This is the final volume to be published in the six volume series of the Pevsner Architectural Guides to Greater London.* It completes the revision of the two London books in The Buildings of England series by Sir Nikolaus Pevsner: *London, the Cities of London and Westminster* which first appeared in 1957, and *London except the Cities of London and Westminster* (1952) and expands them to cover Greater London.

The present volume, resting on the foundations established by Pevsner, includes Tower Hamlets, previously treated (as Bethnal Green, Poplar and Stepney) in *London except*, and the outer boroughs of Barking and Dagenham, Havering, Newham, Redbridge and Waltham Forest, whose constituent parts were first included in *The Buildings of England: Essex* (1954, revised 1974). It has also benefited from being able to draw on the more detailed *The Buildings of England: London Docklands* (1998), which examined the history and buildings of that fast changing area.

For the convenience of the visitor, within each borough the content is divided into smaller areas, as indicated on the maps and at the beginning of each section. In the outer boroughs these generally follow historic boundaries, in the more complex areas of Tower Hamlets and Newham there are a greater number of subdivisions. Within each subsection, arrangement follows the traditional Buildings of England order: religious buildings (Church of England followed by Roman Catholic, Nonconformist, Synagogues, Mosques, other faiths), major buildings, and perambulations (which include, as well as housing, lesser buildings, e.g. police stations, cinemas and some schools).

It should be stressed that mention of a building in no way indicates that it is open to the public. Where two dates are quoted the first is generally for the final designs, the second for completion. Failure to mention a building or feature may not imply that it is of no interest; space limits the amount of detail that can be included, and while efforts have been made to keep abreast of new information there will always be new buildings, new research and reassessments. The Pevsner Architectural Guides, as ever, will be grateful for information on errors and omissions.

*The other volumes in this London series are as follows: the centre of the capital is covered *by London 1: the City of London*, and *London 6: Westminster*. *London 2: South* deals with London south of the Thames (including the Greater London areas and the parts of Richmond across the river). *London 3: North West* consists of Brent, Ealing, Hammersmith and Fulham, Harrow, Hillingdon, Hounslow, Kensington and Chelsea, and Paddington and St Marylebone. *London 4: North* covers Barnet, Camden, Enfield, Hackney and Islington.

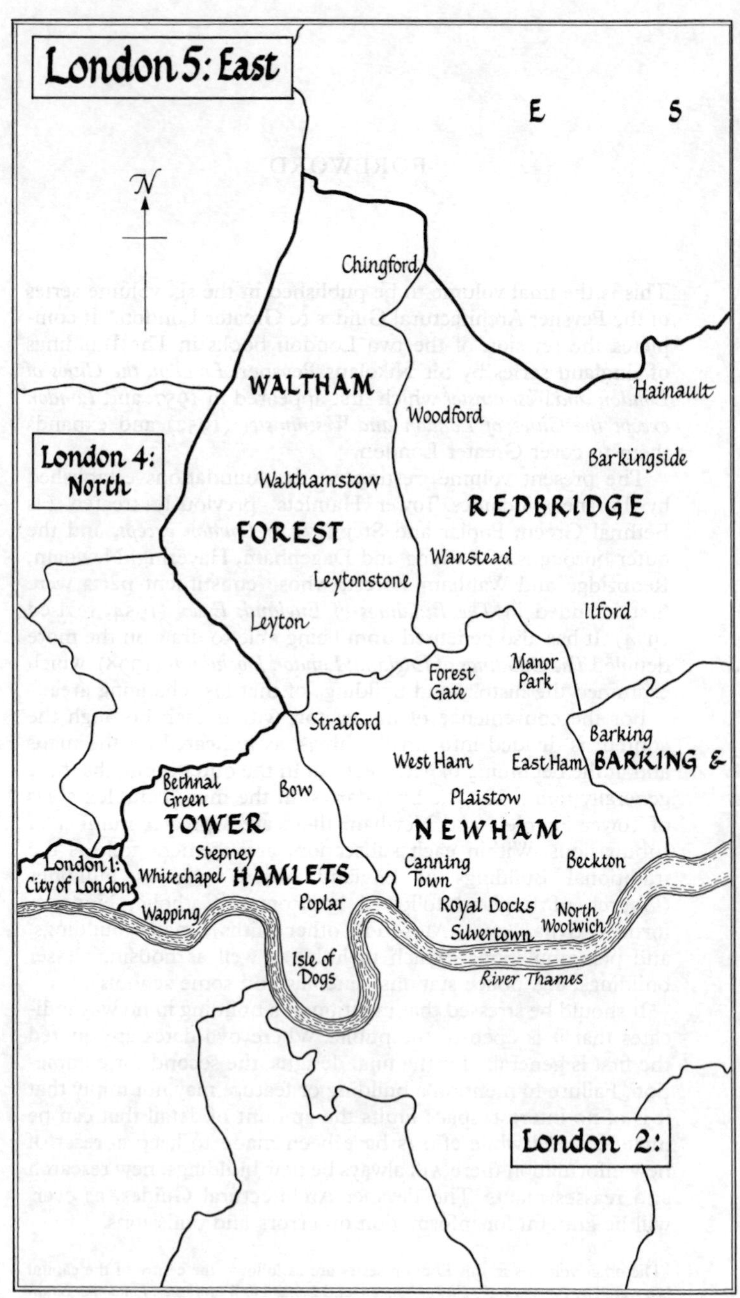
London 5: East
E
S
N
Chingford
WALTHAM
FOREST
Hainault
Woodford
London 4: North
Barkingside
Walthamstow
REDBRIDGE
Wanstead
Leytonstone
Leyton
Ilford
Manor Park
Forest Gate
Stratford
Barking
West Ham
East Ham
BARKING &
Bethnal Green
Bow
Plaistow
TOWER
HAMLETS
NEWHAM
London 1: City of London
Stepney
Whitechapel
Canning Town
Beckton
Wapping
Poplar
Royal Docks
North Woolwich
Silvertown
Isle of Dogs
River Thames
London 2:

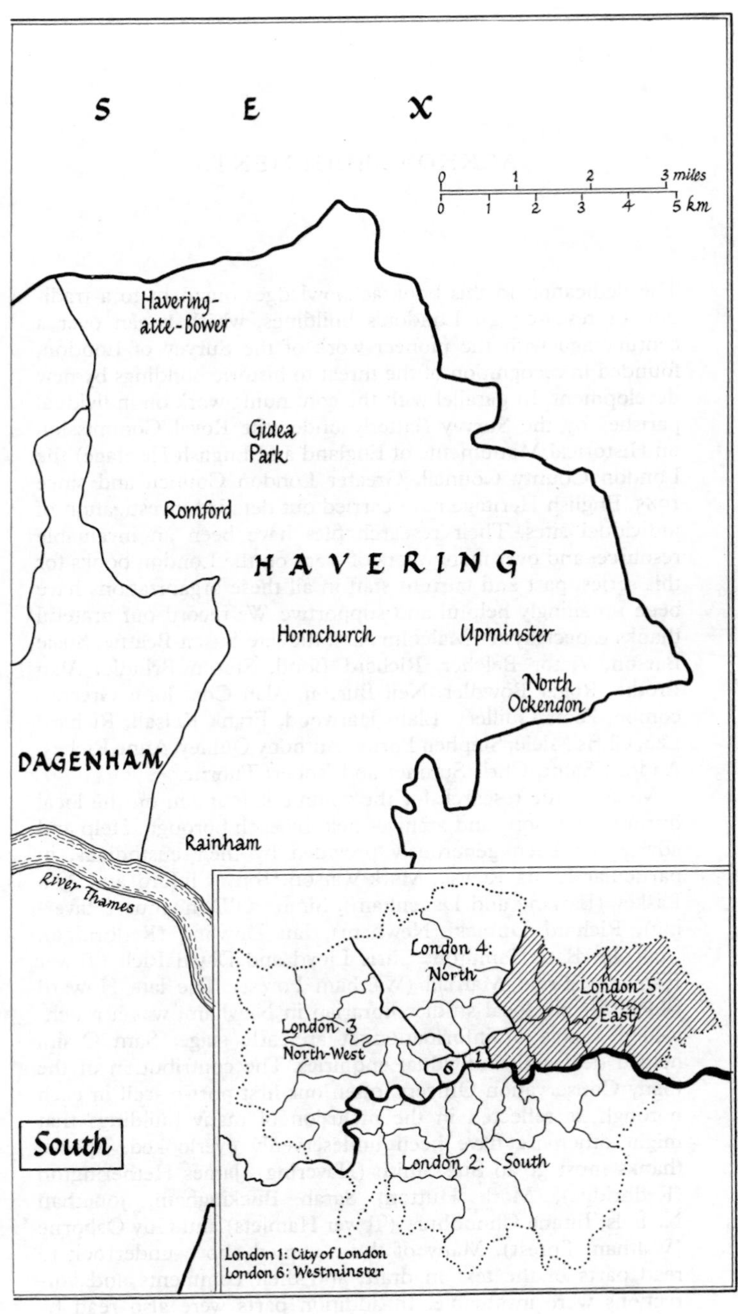

S
E
X
0
1
2
3 miles
0
1
2
3
4
5 km
Havering-atte-Bower
Gidea Park
Romford
HAVERING
Hornchurch
Upminster
North Ockendon
DAGENHAM
Rainham
River Thames
South
London 4: North
London 5: East
London 3 North-West
6
1
London 2: South
London 1: City of London
London 6: Westminster

ACKNOWLEDGEMENTS

The dedication in this book acknowledges our debt to a tradition of research on London's buildings, which began over a century ago with the pioneer work of the Survey of London, founded in recognition of the threat to historic buildings by new development. In parallel with the continuing work on individual parishes by the Survey (latterly under the Royal Commission on Historical Monuments of England and English Heritage) the London County Council, Greater London Council and since 1985, English Heritage have carried out detailed investigation of individual sites. Their research files have been an invaluable resource, and over many years of work on the London books for this series, past and current staff in all these organizations have been unfailingly helpful and supportive. We record our grateful thanks especially to: Malcolm Airs, the late Susan Beattie, Susie Barson, Victor Belcher, Richard Bond, Steven Brindle, Alan Brodie, Roger Bowdler, Neil Burton, Alan Cox, John Greenacombe, Peter Guillery, Elain Harwood, Frank Kelsall, Richard Lea, Chris Miele, Stephen Porter, Anthony Quiney, Anne Riches, Andrew Saint, Chris Sumner and Robert Thorne.

Much of the research for the volume is founded on the local history collections and archives held by each borough. Help and advice has been generously provided by their custodians, in particular Linda Rowse, Mark Watson, Tony Clifford and Ann Laskey (Barking and Dagenham), Simon O'Donoghue (Havering), Richard Durack (Newham), Ian Dowling (Redbridge), Malcolm Barr-Hamilton, Chris Lloyd and David Rich (Tower Hamlets), Brian Mardall (Waltham Forest). The late Howard Bloch, former local studies librarian in Newham, was a much-valued source of information at an early stage; Sam Orsini helped deal with individual enquiries. The contribution of the many Conservation Officers, often our first port-of-call in each borough, is reflected in the inclusion of many buildings that might otherwise have been undeservedly overlooked. Special thanks must go to Sue Smith (Havering), James Hetherington (Redbridge), Mark Hutton, Sarah Buckingham, Jonathan Nichols, Tarana Choudhury (Tower Hamlets) and Guy Osborne (Waltham Forest). Many of those named above undertook to read parts of the text in draft, and their comments and corrections were invaluable. In addition parts were also read by colleagues at English Heritage, amongst them Susie Barson, Jo Smith, Nick Antram and Peter Guillery. Elizabeth Williamson and Malcolm Tucker, authors of *London Docklands*, must be singled out for special mention, both for letting us draw on some of the text of that book and for their respective comments on Docklands and important details of industrial archaeology. Research for a revised edition of *The Buildings of Essex* has been concurrent with this volume and we have benefited much from comparisons and useful information on Essex architects from its author James Bettley. We are indebted also to the Victoria County History, in particular Diane Bolton who made available her work on Bethnal Green in advance of publication, and to the reports and notes of the Victorian Society, the Twentieth Century Society and the Spitalfields Trust. Many individuals in the planning and building control departments of the boroughs were most obliging in answering queries, and numerous architects are owed thanks for providing details of their work, especially for recent and forthcoming developments.

Expert knowledge has been willingly given and the book is much the better for the contributions of many people while others have contributed specialist knowledge on individual topics. Geoffrey Brandwood undertook much work on the churches and also let us benefit from his work on pubs for CAMRA. Peter Guillery shared with us his research for English Heritage on places of worship in Tower Hamlets, and also advised on small houses of the C18 in Bethnal Green. Stuart Foster most helpfully provided extensive details on R.C. churches in the Diocese of Brentwood. Peter Cormack of the William Morris Museum, Walthamstow, was a source of expert information on stained glass of the Arts and Crafts period. Roger Bowdler supplied details on cemeteries and churchyard monuments. We were helped also by Chris Thomas (Spitalfields Excavations), Jennifer Freeman (Historic Chapels Trust), Nick Hewett (National Inventory of War Memorials, Imperial War Museum), Dr Sharman Kadish (Synagogues and Jewish architects), Jo Smith of English Heritage (Town Halls), Geoffrey Fisher (church monuments), Richard Garnier (Sir Robert Taylor), Ursula Carlyle (Mercers' Company Archives), Christine Wagg (The Peabody Trust), Susie Barson (Metropolitan Police stations before 1920), Nicholas Long (interwar police stations), John Earl and colleagues at The Theatres Trust, Chris Sumner (London Parks and Gardens Trust), Richard Bond (timber-framed buildings), Elain Harwood and James Dunnet (post-war architecture), Jane Riches of the Public Monuments and Sculpture Association generously provided access to the database of works in East London, and the artist Brian Yale supplied details on his work.

We thank also the many people who made available their expertise on particular places. Among them we must mention Laurie Adams of the Jesus Hospital Charity, who supplied information on their developments in Bethnal Green, Isobel Watson, who provided much advice on the buildings of Stepney Green and Mile End and also on the intriguing story of Jewish speculative builders in the East End. Andrew Byrne of the Spitalfields Trust took us on an entertaining tour of Spitalfields. Tom Ridge opened our eyes to the important industrial survivals at Old

Ford and allowed us to benefit from his research on this and several other buildings. Chris Pond supplied much information on Waltham Forest and Woodford. Others who helped were Jim Connor (Great Eastern Railway buildings at Stratford), Chris Ellmers (Museum at Docklands), Neil Burton (Valentines mansion, Ilford), Julian Robinson and Anselm Nye (Queen Mary Westfield College), Rachel Boddie (Queen Elizabeth's Hunting Lodge, Chingford) and Ann Hilder (North Ockendon). Research on Eastbury Manor House was much aided by access to the files of the SPAB and a report on wallpaintings by Katy Lithgow at the National Trust. We are grateful also to Helen Kent of the London Transport Museum, Robin Winters of Thames Water for information on Abbey Mills, Sister Oonagh at St Angela's Ursuline Convent, Upton, and Cheryl St Clair at the Providence Refuge.

Many people arranged access to buildings. Among those who gave up their time to us we are especially indebted to: Kim Adams at Oxford House, H. Cleland (Woodford County Schoool), Brian Daubeny (Wiltons Music Hall), the Proof Master at The Gunmaker's Company Proof House, Jonathan Evans of the Royal London Hospital Archives, Dr Sam Everington at the Bromley-by-Bow Health Centre, Rev. Dave Gill (Mayflower Family Centre), Michael Heap (The Round House), Red Mason (Christ Church Spitalfields), Christopher Reeve and the staff of Barnardo's Barkingside, Peter Scott (Bancroft's School), Ronald Swan, Master of the Royal Foundation of St Katharine, Simon Thurley, Susie Symes (No. 19 Princelet Street), Martin Walker (Toynbee Hall), Frank Williams for information on Charles Heathcote's work for the Ford Motor Co. at Dagenham, Gerald Wright (Forest School Walthamstow).

The book could not have been written without the resources of many libraries. We are indebted to the library staff of the Bishopsgate Institute, British Library, Courtauld Institute, Guildhall Library, National Monuments Record (whose London collections are now sadly removed from London to Swindon), the Society of Antiquaries, the London Metropolitan Archives, the London Library and the British Architectural Library. We also benefited from Karen Evans' expertise at undertaking research at the National Archives.

This volume, which completes the revision of *London except the Cities of London and Westminster*, was initiated at Penguin Books and a debt of gratitude is owed to our former colleagues there and the past and present staff of the *Pevsner Architectural Guides*. We thank in particular Simon Bradley, editor of the Guides, who read and commented on parts of the text and provided both local knowledge and a ready source of useful comparisons with the City of London. We undertook most of the research ourselves but early work and the essential organization of material received since the 1950s was also provided by Helen Hills and Tye Blackshaw. Invaluable office support at Penguin was supplied by Susan Machin, while the demanding task of compiling illustrations was begun by Alison McKittrick, continued at Yale by Emily

Rawlinson and completed by Emily Lees. The final text benefitted from the careful scrutiny of Veronica Smith, Pat Taylor-Chalmers and Judith Wardman. Emily Winter patiently oversaw production of the book, endeavoured to keep the authors to schedule and accommodated their late corrections without complaint. Sally Salvesen, Commissioning Editor at Yale, has been a stalwart supporter throughout. The drawn plans are the work of Alan Fagan, the maps were prepared by Reg and Marjorie Piggott who have contributed to all the London books. Heartfelt thanks must be given to Jonathan Bailey of English Heritage who took the vast majority of the colour photos (and others for which lack of space precluded publication) and showed unfailing good humour in the face of scaffolding, parked cars and the weather. Research for the revised editions in this series is supported financially by the work of the Buildings Books Trust and we are grateful to its Secretary, Gavin Watson for all his efforts.

Bridget Cherry
Charles O'Brien
December 2004

INTRODUCTION

The scale of both the natural and man-made landscape of East London is vast, offering broad vistas and exhilarating horizons unmatched in other parts of London. The Thames is wider here than upstream. E from Canning Town, the empty sheets of water of the Royal Docks stretch for two miles to the horizon. In the old C18 suburbs, Hawksmoor's proud churches have the grandest Baroque towers in London. Further out at Wanstead the great C18 park rivalled Hampton Court, eating into the fringes of Epping Forest, relics of the ancient Forest of Essex, whose woodland still sweeps S in a broad swathe, from the higher ground on the northern borders where Greater London becomes Essex countryside. From here there is a clear view across some fifteen miles of suburban growth to the City of London and the Canary Wharf towers on the site of the West India docks.

The Thames is fundamental to the character of East London, and its tributaries form natural boundaries, even for the modern boroughs: the Lea between Tower Hamlets and Newham, the Roding dividing Newham from Redbridge and Barking, the Beam between Dagenham and Havering. Attempts to drain the Thames-side marshes began in Wapping, close to the City, already in the middle ages, and the river fringe here was busy with shipping by the C17. The enclosed docks constructed from the beginning of the C19 transformed the riverside and extended E as ships grew larger. Shipbuilding and marine engineering developed around the Isle of Dogs; beyond there were ironworks at Bow Creek and Tate & Lyle's sugar factories at Silvertown, and in the C20 Ford's motor works at Dagenham. Only at Rainham marshes and beyond are there still stretches of rough meadow.

On the gravel terraces rising above the marshes early settlements developed. Existing churches mark some early sites: St Dunstan at Stepney is of Saxon origin, while at East Ham the little Norman church still stands alone in its vast overgrown graveyard. Further N C17 and C18 merchants-turned-gentry scattered their mansions and villas around the older villages. But the gentry retreated, as C19 working-class suburbs expanded to keep pace with demands of docks and industry. A Victorian mythology of the 'East End' developed, by no means relevant for the whole area, of teeming smoggy streets with crowded workshops, squalid dust heaps and fetid undrained closes. Such living conditions scandalized those C19 journalists and philanthropists who ventured into territory untrodden by other Londoners. Gradually publicity had its effects: churches and schools were

Nova Scotia Gardens, Bethnal Green,
dust heap and St Thomas's Church, 1857

built and other amenities provided, and from the concerted campaigns of the 1880s a determination arose to tackle the problem of slum housing, a task that progressed slowly over the next half century and continued after the Second World War.

By 1914 suburban London stretched E to the established towns of Ilford and Romford. The new outer boroughs proclaimed their identity by grand civic buildings as people moved out of the old overcrowded East End to the long streets of new houses in Forest Gate, East Ham, Walthamstow and Ilford, still dense but more salubrious once the local authorities began to enforce building controls. By then the inner areas were exceptional in their concentration of industry and in the diverse origins of their inhabitants. Huguenot silkweavers, Baltic timber merchants and German sugar bakers were followed by Irish dock workers and in the later C19 by Eastern European Jewish refugees, settling on the E fringes of the City, where there had been a Jewish community from the late C17. The later C20 brought influxes of immigrants from Asia, especially Bangladesh, and from Africa.

C19 and earlier C20 industry flourished in countless small-scale enterprises: clothing and furniture amongst the houses and warehouses of Whitechapel and Bethnal Green, shipping suppliers, ropeworks, and timber merchants, engineering and chemical works, breweries and distilleries and much else along the Thames and the Lea. Further out, staid outer suburbs reached out to E and N, covering the grounds of older country mansions and transforming villages into suburban centres, though leaving scattered older buildings to recall a rural past within living memory.

In the inner areas the damage wrought by the Second World War together with poor housing prompted wholesale redevelopment. Idealistic post-war plans replaced tight and familiar street networks with clusters of flats and open spaces for a reduced population. Nostalgia for old close-knit communities, now dispersed, contributed to the potent myth of the pre-war East End. The hoped-for utopia did not anticipate the later C20 closure of the docks and the disappearance of major industry as London was transformed from a world port into a global financial centre. From the 1980s change has been rapid, with offices and private housing imposing new architectural and social patterns on an older landscape of industry and working-class flats. A different inner East End began to emerge, a diverse mix of old and new, but in contrast to its past character, quieter, greener and more spacious.

East London remains a lively focus for debate on what form suburbs should take, a question now relevant to a wider area as early C21 plans for expansion eastward along the Thames are met by concern for a wise environmental policy in the face of rising flood levels. This repeated reinvention of character, part accidental, part intentional, remains a continuing fascination for the East London explorer.

EARLY HISTORY: THE ARCHAEOLOGY OF EAST LONDON

by Pamela Greenwood

Much new information in East London has come from large-scale development, particularly in the areas of the old marshes.

Topography and Geology

Although large areas of Greater London are covered by urban sprawl and much archaeology has been destroyed, it is possible to gain a picture of the landscape and people's activities in the past. East London lies in the lower Thames valley where the river is joined by its major tributaries. A recent reinterpretation derives the place-name 'London' from a name close to *Plowonida* in Old European, thought to mean a river that is not fordable, needs boats to cross, or floods, an apt description for the lower, estuarine Thames below the ancient tidal head. *Tamesis/Tamesa*, a British or even earlier name, would then apply to the non-estuarine river upstream. The subsequent addition of *on*, often associated with locations on rivers, would complete the ancient name for a significant site, later at the meeting of four major Iron Age tribal areas and of four counties, as well as a Roman town and capital city.

For most of the ICE AGE Britain was joined to Europe and the Thames followed earlier courses through East Anglia to the North Sea, possibly joining the Rhine. About 450,000 years ago, during the period of maximum glaciation, the Anglian ice sheets reached as far S as Hornchurch, forcing the Thames S into approximately its present course. In cold periods the Thames and its tributaries cut through successive flood-plain deposits laid down in warmer periods, carving out the characteristic gravel terraces visible today; the highest are the oldest and the lowest the youngest. The chalk of the London Basin, outcropping as the Downs and the Chilterns on the outer edges, is lined by London Clay. This in turn is filled by the gravels with the lowest part of the valley occupied by the flood-plain alluvium and the river itself. Much of the higher land in East London is on London Clay.

After the end of the Ice Age, melt waters caused a rise in sea levels. This process has continued until the present day, with periods of rise and fall depending on climatic variations, exacerbated by the gradual sinking of southern Britain as the north rises, freed of the weight of the glaciers. Sea-level variations and the associated land loss and changes in marshlands have had a fundamental impact on settlement and people in the London area as has the gradual shift of the Thames into its present channel. Perhaps the best-known Ice Age fossil site finds are those of an elephant and mammoth on the Aveley-Rainham border and numerous mammals from the Ilford brick pits.

Stone Age

The earliest evidence for PALAEOLITHIC (Old Stone Age *c.* 500,000–10,000 B.C.) people in the London area is in the form of their flint tools, especially hand-axes, large numbers of which have been found redeposited in the gravels of the river terraces in north-east London. Fragments of an ancient skull from Swanscombe, Kent, are the only human remains from the region. These people were wandering hunters and foragers in conditions that varied from sub-arctic to pleasantly warm. Their prey included large mammals such as mammoths. One of the most important discoveries is that of handaxes *in situ* at Southend Road, Woodford, now under the M11, and dating to the Wolstonian Glacial, *c.* 245–300,000 years ago.

The earliest biologically modern humans, *Homo sapiens*, arrived in Britain around 40,000 B.C. but evidence for their presence is very sparse, just a few flint tools. During the last glaciation, 26,000–13,000 B.C., the soils commonly known as 'brickearth' were deposited. Around 13,000 B.C. Britain began to warm up and sea levels to rise. The treeless steppe/tundra was rapidly replaced by pine and birch forest and the large game by animals such as reindeer and horse. People returned, crossing the land bridge from the continent. Late Glacial temporary campsites near Staines and at Uxbridge in the Colne Valley are the best evidence for this period in the London area.

By around 7,500 B.C., the London area was covered by a mixed forest, predominantly of oak, lime and elm, inhabited by such animals as red deer, elk and wild cattle (aurochs), and a source of fruit, roots and nuts. MESOLITHIC (Middle Stone Age *c.* 10,000–4,200 B.C.) people, now present in sufficient numbers to leave a greater mark on the archaeological record, exploited these wild resources. They changed their toolkit to one based on the characteristic Mesolithic flint microliths. Axes or adzes for felling trees and for woodwork are commonly found; bone or antler fish spears are occasionally preserved. Hunting tactics changed too – hunters used the bow and dogs were domesticated.

Sea levels had risen, creating the English Channel and flooding more land. Around the Thames estuary these were about 30 m below the present level. Marshlands with fish, shellfish and waterfowl would have been productive areas for food. A freshwater Thames with shallow braided channels is known to have flowed S of its present course through Central London and would have been easier to cross. Towards the end of the Mesolithic it became moderately fast flowing and more meandering with fewer channels.

Despite the numbers of stray finds of axes (or adzes) and flint implements, the Mesolithic period is rather under-represented in the London area. Among the few known major sites are West Hampstead Heath, Uxbridge, and Broxbourne, Hertfordshire, and High Beech, Essex, just outside greater London. Little is known of the Mesolithic period in East London, though work along the A13 is changing that picture. Mesolithic flint implements have been found at Stratford, Barking Abbey and Brookway and nearby sites in Rainham, on high ground at Marks Warren Farm, Chadwell Heath, and in Barking along the A13. Evidence suggests that much Mesolithic settlement and activity were close to the then edge of the Thames, now buried under alluvium, and along its tributaries.

Around 6,000 years ago people began to change from hunting and gathering to raising domestic animals and crops. NEOLITHIC (New Stone Age *c.* 4,200–2,200 B.C.) people developed a new stone toolkit that included polished-stone axes. Pottery, plain at first, but eventually highly decorated, was used for cooking and storage and also in ritual deposits. The Neolithic coincided with the warmest climatic period. Wheat, barley and domestic animals are not native to Britain and so would have been imported, possibly accompanied by some newcomers. Cattle feature prominently at a number of the region's early Neolithic sites. Very gradually the previous nomadic way of life was replaced by permanent settlement in woodland clearings. More woodland was cleared for farming and stock raising, creating fields and meadows.

Sea levels continued rising and by the early Neolithic in the

London area river levels were equivalent to today's low-water mark. Although some previously usable low-lying land was now flooded and peat began forming from the Isle of Dogs downstream, large areas of alluvium-covered land were still available, perhaps explaining the riverine bias of early Neolithic sites and finds. During the later Neolithic the marshes expanded and about 2,200 B.C. the tidal head reached the Isle of Dogs. People may have built a timber trackway or platform of alder planks at Fort Street, Silvertown (3,070–2,700 B.C.) in an attempt to maintain access to the marshlands. Early Neolithic flintwork was found deeply buried at the site of the Royal Albert Dock and late Neolithic artefacts on a sandy eyot at Custom House and nearby sites. Stumps of woodland can still be seen at low tide today, mostly alder carr with some yew, which extended along the lower Thames from Southwark to Erith around 3,000 B.C.

Until recently few Neolithic sites were known in East London and the region as a whole. New sites have been discovered along the gravel terrace edge beside the river or marshes at Beckton and Movers Lane, Barking, around Brookway, Rainham, and further inland at Bow. Wheat and hazelnuts have been recovered from the A13 sites, though generally there is little evidence for agriculture. Traces of timber structures have been found at Brookway, Rainham, and Movers Lane, Barking.

Special objects, usually fine stone axes and pots, deposited in the River Thames suggest that people viewed it as sacred. This practice possibly began in the Mesolithic (many finds of adzes, 'Thames picks') and continued later, even to the present day. Stone axes were also placed in pits on dry land, for example a group of three from Temple Mills, Leyton. The only known large-scale ritual site is a 50 ft (15.25 m) diameter, early Neolithic ring-ditch at Great Arnold's Field, Rainham, with fine pottery and flintwork deposited in its ditch. A young person buried around 4,200–3,900 B.C. at Yabsley Street, Blackwall, is the oldest known 'Londoner'. Large earthen monuments, like the Stanwell cursus and the interrupted ring-ditch near Staines on the western fringes of London, have not yet been found in the E; the nearest, Orsett causewayed enclosure (an enclosure with interrupted ditches), is over the border in Essex.

There is increasing evidence for settlements of the BEAKER PERIOD (*c.* 2,500–1,800 B.C.) at the Neolithic/Bronze Age transition. Beaker pottery, characterized by large decorated drinking vessels, and a distinctive archery kit were introduced from the continent, probably accompanied by some immigrants. Settlements and finds are known at Rainham Football Ground and Moor Hall Farm, Rainham, along the A13, on an ancient sandy eyot at Custom House and at Narrow Street, Limehouse, close to a possible river crossing. Ritual activity continued at the ring-ditch monument at Great Arnold's Field, Rainham. Burial rites changed and some individuals were buried with high-status goods and beakers. A complete beaker from Gerpins Pit, Rainham, might be from such a burial.

Bronze Age

The BRONZE AGE (*c.* 2,200–800 B.C.) marks the beginning of the use of copper and bronze for tools and gold for jewellery and, by the end of the period, the earliest ironworking. It too was a period of great change, for people and the local environment. By the later Bronze Age woodland had been almost completely cleared for farming, large-scale field systems in many areas marking a major re-organization of the landscape from one dominated by monuments to one of settlements and fields. International trade increased, particularly attested to by the prestigious objects recovered from the Thames and on the continent.

In East London, as elsewhere in the region, the early part of the Bronze Age (*c.* 2,200–1,500 B.C.) is poorly represented, with most evidence so far from the Beaker phase of the Neolithic–Bronze Age transition (*see* above). There are a few finds of pottery, flint implements and arrowheads. A corduroy-style timber platform of alder and ash poles on a base mainly of yew, recently discovered at Beckton, is one of the few sites. Special objects placed in watery places include some early metalwork in rivers and the 'Dagenham Idol', a pinewood figure, dated *c.* 2,350–2,140 B.C. from the marshes near the Ford Works.

Progressive, relative sea-level rises led to the Thames rising and to flood-plain expansion. A fluctuating tidal head reached Westminster by *c.* 1,000 B.C. and retreated again, only to return *c.* 800 B.C. The Thames, now flowing in a single tidal channel, was harder to cross and so more of a boundary. Clearance of the remaining woodland and overgrazing on the gravel terraces appear to have led to greater erosion and run-off, so raising the water table. Additionally, the climate was becoming cooler and wetter. A new aspect of the archaeology of the London region is the discovery of wooden trackways in Rainham, Beckton, Barking, Southwark, Greenwich and Erith, a causeway in Dagenham with animal tracks and a corduroy-style timber platform at Atlas Wharf, Isle of Dogs. This burst of activity in the developing wetlands and peat beds of East London is characteristic of the later Bronze Age when people tried to maintain access to drier areas and grazing land in the marshlands.

In contrast, evidence for the later Bronze Age has vastly increased in the last fifteen years, possibly reflecting more archaeology and more detectable sites. Middle Bronze Age (*c.* 1,500–1,200 B.C.) settlements at the site of Uphall Camp and nearby Buttsbury Estate, Ilford, Hunts Hill Farm, Upminster, and probably at Eastbrook End and Marks Gate give the impression of farmsteads or small villages scattered across the countryside. Timber houses are of the round post-ring type. Elsewhere in London plough/ard marks are being found on the higher eyots in the flood plain. A long ditch at South Hall Farm, Rainham, may represent the earliest phase of the extensive land division so evident in the late Bronze Age.

Large middle Bronze Age cemeteries with cremation urns, typical of West London, have not been found in the E. Here the people buried their dead in small cemeteries with a few ring ditches such as the open ceremonial landscape with two ring ditches, cremation burials and the remains of pyres at Fairlop Quarry. A ring ditch at Oliver Close, Leyton, may be a ploughed-out barrow. From the middle Bronze Age onwards the practice of depositing prestigious metalwork in the Thames increases dramatically, perhaps a sign of its importance for transport and as a route to Europe. East London finds include spearheads and swords from the Lea and Barking Creek. Deposits of metalwork on dry land are usually of palstaves, for example at Hog Hill, Hainault Forest. Special pots might be put in pits, for example the jar with a quartz pebble at Hunts Hill Farm, Upminster.

In the late Bronze Age (*c.* 1,200–800 B.C.) there is greater variety in settlement types in the London region, ranging from the riverfront site at Runnymede and ring-fort sites at Carshalton, Surrey, and Mucking, Essex, to open and enclosed settlements, perhaps farms or small villages, such as at Hunts Hill Farm, Upminster, Moor Hall Farm, Rainham, Stratford and around Barking Creek. A settlement at Becontree Estate appears to have influenced boundaries from the Roman period until the C19. Small sub-square enclosures at Hunts Hill Farm and Becontree contained houses. Ring forts, clearly important foci, may be sited within larger, settled areas and field systems as at South Hornchurch. A sub-circular enclosure on high ground overlooking the Thames valley at Warren Farm, Chadwell Heath, possibly formed a pair with South Hornchurch. The typical house found was of the post-ring type. The London region was by now largely open countryside, but highly divided into settlements, fields and droveways, the latter perhaps designed for large-scale stock rearing. Waterholes within the fields often had special, ritual deposits in their lower fills. Fragmentary field systems have been identified at South Hornchurch and Whitehall Wood.

Burial evidence is rare – a few cremations, albeit token deposits, from South Hornchurch. Pots were deliberately broken and buried in pits at Hunts Hill Farm, Upminster, and South Hornchurch. The Thames, its tributaries and wetlands remained a focus for ritual activity with the peak of deposition of prestige metalwork and occasionally complete pots in the late Bronze Age. Barking Creek and the River Lea have concentrations of finds. Human skulls from the Thames and the Lea may be shadowy evidence of burial rites, perhaps associated with the metalwork. Hoards of bronze weapons, tools and fragments of a copper ingots were found on dry land at Hacton (Hornchurch), Warren Farm, Chadwell Heath, and Devons Road, Bow.

The Iron Age and Roman Periods

There is no sudden change from the Bronze Age to the IRON AGE (*c.* 800 B.C.–A.D. 50) in southern Britain – many sites and traditions continued and some major social, economic, technological and political developments of this period had Bronze Age origins. Iron became the main metal for tools and weapons, whilst bronze (and gold) remained for decorative items, prestige objects and jewellery. This period is conventionally seen as one when marginal land and heavy clays were settled in response to a rising population and worsening climate. Relative sea levels continued to rise. There is evidence of some woodland regeneration and an increase in the archaeological record of cereal crops such as wheat, barley, rye and even oats, previously thought to be a Roman introduction. In the later C2 B.C. coinage, at first gold only, was introduced from Gaul; British-made potin (tin-bronze) coins soon followed. Late Iron Age southern Britain was in regular contact and trade with Gaul and the Roman Empire and adopted wheel-made pottery during C1 B.C. Britain entered written history, one account being Caesar's invasions of 55 and 54 B.C.

The River Thames and its tributaries remained a focus for votive deposits, mainly swords, daggers, shields and pots, with fewer and richer offerings such as the Battersea Shield in the late Iron Age. Among early Iron Age ritual activities found are deliberately damaged pots placed in pits or wells at Hunts Hill Farm, Upminster, and the dumping of broken pots, possibly debris from hill-top feasts and/or termination rites at the late Bronze Age Warren Farm enclosure. Special deposits of pottery or metalwork were made in the drip gullies of middle Iron Age round houses, for example at Uphall Camp, Ilford. A rectangular triple-ditched enclosure on a spur at Moor Hall Farm, Rainham, may be a sacred enclosure similar to those found on the continent; a huge dump of broken pottery in its well probably represents a termination rite at the time of the Roman conquest.

This region, like many others, lacks an obvious burial rite for much of the Iron Age, though there are mid-C1 A.D. cremations at Corbets Tey and probable inhumations at Aveley in nearby Essex. There is, so far, a conspicuous lack of the later Iron Age elite burials found elsewhere in South-East England.

Few Early Iron Age (*c.* 800–450 B.C.) settlements are known in the London region, possibly the result of rising river levels and factors such as political changes and climatic deterioration reducing prosperity and sites being less archaeologically visible. Continuity from the late Bronze Age is shown at a number of settlements and by deposition in rivers. Early Iron Age people settled in a wide range of places from the high land at Warren Farm, Chadwell Heath, to the middle terraces at Hunts Hill Farm, Upminster, and East Ham and to the present marsh edge at Rainham Football Ground. Defensive sites, hill-forts, are known outside the area. Small-scale settlements, farmsteads dispersed in the countryside amongst field systems and trackways with occasional defended hill-fort type enclosures may be typical. These farmers grew cereals and were stock breeders as shown by an abundance of dung beetles, grassland plants and bracken from waterholes at Hunts Hill Farm, Upminster.

Settlements, farmsteads of one or more round houses and possibly small villages, are more evident in the Middle Iron Age, *c.* 450–150 B.C., for example at Barkingside (Fairlop Quarry), Stratford, Elm Park, Moor Hall Farm, Rainham, and Hunts Hill Farm, Upminster. Open settlements and small enclosures with houses are found. The standard domestic architecture was the round house, now with an external drip gully. Uphall Camp, Ilford, a massive, low-lying fortified enclosure of 24 ha, may have been a high-status regional centre, possibly for the tribe later known as the Trinovantes, sited in a strategic position for a port, guarding Barking Creek and the Thames. Hill-forts or large defensive enclosures have been found just outside the area at Caesar's Camp, Keston (LB Bromley), and possibly of the same date at Ambresbury Banks and Loughton Camp in Epping Forest. Small communities practising mixed farming with some evidence of trade and specialization, such as bronze-smithing, appear to have been the norm.

Late Iron Age (*c.* 150 B.C.–A.D. 50) settlement evidence is patchy, though at some sites occupation continued from the Middle Iron Age. During this period in Essex rectangular houses replaced round houses, though round buildings reappeared at some sites in the Roman period as outbuildings and the like. Some rectangular enclosures with ample domestic debris, for example Great Sunnings Farm and Hunts Hill Farm, Upminster, have little evidence for houses, perhaps indicating a change to sill-beam or box-frame construction. Traces of sub-rectangular houses at Corbets Tey enclosure may be of this date.

Although there is no evidence yet in the Iron Age of the extensive ditched field systems of the Bronze Age, a field system at South Hall Farm, Rainham, dates to the Late Iron Age and several in the Rainham–Upminster area span the Late Iron Age and early Roman periods.

Many enclosures, defensive or religious, were abandoned at the Roman conquest, although settlement continued. A high-status centre for the Late Iron Age, such as the extensive *oppida* (fortified 'towns') of Essex, Kent and Hertfordshire, has not been found for London, possibly because it was peripheral to several late Iron Age tribal areas. Rather, the impression is of a region of many smaller settlements scattered over the countryside, the population continuing to live there after the Roman conquest. Much of East London is within the territory of the Trinovantes, bounded by the Lea and Thames. The origins of county and hundred boundaries may lie in this period or earlier.

The Roman conquest of South-East England completed by A.D. 50 brought about a fundamental change to London, from an apparently marginal place in the Late Iron Age to the site of the largest and most important provincial town in the ROMAN period (A.D. 43–*c.* 450), both politically and economically. Londinium may have been chosen precisely because it was a boundary zone or an area of no importance, yet an ideal port and nodal point. The first trading settlement by the new river crossing was destroyed by the British rebels led by Boudica in A.D. 60/61. Rebuilt, it replaced Colchester as the provincial capital and commercial centre.

For most, if not all, of the Roman period the Thames was tidal from the City downstream, flowing in more or less its present position. River levels fell progressively for most of the period but began to rise towards the end. In the mid-C1 the tidal head was beside the present City, with high tide at *c.* 1.25 m (OD), but it then appears to have migrated downstream, dropping as much as 1.5 m until its return at the end of the Roman or early Saxon period. This would have seriously affected the Roman port, which was dismantled in the mid-C3, perhaps forcing a move downstream.

Present day East London, apart from a small part of Tower Hamlets, lay outside the Roman city and was the beginning of the countryside and of an important road network leading out of the city. The London–Colchester highway, constructed *c.* A.D. 50, has been traced at Old Ford and at least three places in Stratford where a branch forms the London–Dunmow road crossing the Roding at Chigwell. By far the most impressive Roman remains in East London are the large baths recently excavated at Shadwell, near a possible mausoleum and a cemetery, perhaps part of a relocated later Roman port complex.

Alongside these roads were cemeteries, by law outside a town's boundary: the northern cemetery around Spitalfields flanking Ermine Street, the Roman road towards Edmonton, including the rich burial of a woman in a decorated lead coffin. Straddling the Roman road towards Stepney was the very large eastern cemetery, essentially C3–C4 with some early C5 burials. A small group of burials, some high-status, lay alongside the London–Colchester road at Old Ford where a large roadside settlement spanned C1 to early C5, possibly a collection centre for cattle and other produce for the London market. Further out, burials are found along the London–Colchester road W of Romford and possibly at Harold Hill. Early Roman cremation burials are found at a number of sites including a cluster N and E of Rainham, at Barkingside (Fairlop Quarry), Goresbrook Fields and Ruckholts, Leyton. Rich, later Roman burials in stone and lead coffins at East Ham, Upney and South Hornchurch, may lie alongside a Roman precursor of the A13. Other such burials are known at Marks Gate and Valentines Park.

The countryside on the gravels E of London was well settled with roadside villages and other settlements of differing sizes and status. Old Ford and possibly Little London, Chigwell, just into Essex, are known roadside villages, and perhaps also Stratford. Durolitum, mentioned in the *Antonine Itinerary*, is an unrecognized posting station, possibly at Romford. Smaller settlements and farmsteads include Hunts Hill Farm, Upminster, Moor Hall Farm, Rainham, Manor Farm, North Ockendon, Fairlop Quarry and Tollgate Road, Beckton. Shifting settlement, but focusing on the same general area throughout the Roman period, is found in a number of places. Some sites spanned the whole period, but others faded out in the C2 or began later. The presence of some wealthier individuals and settlements in the later Roman period is suggested by the rich burials and by higher-quality rubbish at Havering Park, Moor Hall Farm, Rainham, and Church Road, Leyton. Few villas are known in Greater London; none are certainly identified in East London. Abridge, Essex, is the only apparent local candidate. A major building with mosaics at Wanstead Park may have been some kind of residence for imperial officials.

Evidence for houses or buildings of any kind at the rural settlements is sparse, possibly because a timber box-frame tradition left little trace on the ground. A shallow trench marked out the late Roman rectangular building at Corbets Tey. The only wall with a stone foundation found in the boroughs E of the Lea is at Warren Farm, Chadwell Heath. Middle Iron Age style round buildings may have lingered on in remoter areas and for non-domestic use.

Roman activity is found in and around the wetlands, as at Rainham village and its creek mouth, where ferries and shipping are documented from the medieval period onwards. Dumps of Roman pottery in wetland deposits are known from the site of the Royal Albert Dock and Milk Street, Beckton. Marshland grazing was a source of wealth in the area in historic times, notably the medieval wool trade at Rainham.

People continued to farm the gravel terraces and to grow cereals in the Roman period. New fields were laid out especially in the C2–C4, for example at Great Sunnings Farm, Upminster, and Moor Hall Farm, Rainham. Large fields and subsidiary enclosures at Fairlop Quarry include a sunken-floored building probably used for crop processing and storage. Seeds of coriander, celery and carrot, and a rare honey bee from Hunts Hill Farm, Upminster, point to kitchen gardening and apiculture. Dung beetles from waterholes at Hunts Hill Farm are clear evidence of stock raising; some of the ditch systems on the gravels were probably paddocks and stock enclosures. The gravel lands from Dagenham to Upminster were market gardens for London in recent centuries and might have supplied the Roman city.

Large dumps of tile at Rose Gate and pottery at Elm Park may be from kilns. Woodlands, especially on the London Clay, would have been exploited to supply London's massive requirements for timber and fuel. Timber linings from wells at Hunts Hill Farm, Upminster, contained rarely found elm and a reused timber, probably from a ship. The Thames and its tributaries would have been major trading routes. Pottery and other materials from as near as the Mucking–Orsett kilns in Essex and as far away as the Mediterranean are found in this area.

Identifiable religious buildings are unknown, apart from the possible mausoleum at Shadwell. A rectilinear enclosure with a small Roman road leading up to it at Warren Farm may define a sacred area. Large dumps of pottery for eating and drinking, and what appear to be disturbed burials inside the impressive Iron Age earthworks of Uphall Camp, Ilford, suggest it was reused as a sacred site. Likely ritual deposits are a complete horse buried *c.* A.D. 128–320 at Stratford Market site, holly and bramble twine from pits at Hunts Hill Farm, Upminster, and a Palaeolithic handaxe from a pit at Moor Hall Farm, Rainham.

Late Roman sites in East London date as late as C4 or early C5, but it is not known how long the people remained Roman in culture after the official Roman administration ceased in 410 and after the collapse of coin supply and pottery production. The Roman city eventually fell into disuse. Hints of continuity of population and use of property and fields are found at several sites and it is likely that people adapted to the political and economic changes.

The C5–6 is a problematic period for archaeologists, with much current debate as to the nature of the population. Conventionally called the EARLY SAXON period, it was perhaps more of a development of native culture without the Roman administration, influenced to a great degree by its close contacts with peoples from across the North Sea – Angles, Saxons and Jutes. At the end of the C6 London emerges with the later counties of Middlesex and Essex as part of the kingdom of the East Saxons. The urban focal point of London was lost until the development from 600 of the settlement and port at Lundenwic, W of the old Roman city in the Strand. During the C7 substantial trading centres developed, contact with the continent increased and Christianity and literacy flourished with the establishment of churches and religious houses. Few C5–C6 settlements are known; the largest settlement and cemetery is E of Greater London at Mucking, Essex. Rural settlements were initially small dispersed farmsteads along the Thames and its tributaries on the gravels and brickearths. A cluster of settlements in the Rainham area, South Hornchurch, and Hunts Hill Farm, Upminster (where there is also a simple, family-sized cemetery), all with late Roman occupation, show continuity of land use and of settlement areas, even if there is some shift. All are reasonably close to the Chafford Hundred meeting place and the rich C6–C7 cemetery at Gerpins Pit, Rainham. Nearby, a field system at Manor Farm, North Ockendon, dates to C5–6. Houses and buildings in the C5–C7 are post-fast, rectangular timber halls and sunken-floored outbuildings as typified by those at Mucking.

THE BUILDINGS OF EAST LONDON

Medieval Buildings: Churches and Monuments

As in other parts of England, the oldest surviving buildings are the churches, although no buildings earlier than the C12 remain above ground. Barking, a port on the estuary of the River Roding, an important early settlement, was the site of the most ancient religious foundation in the area, a Benedictine nunnery, originally a double house of monks and nuns, established by St Erkenwald, Bishop of London *c.* 666. Nothing is known of the earliest buildings, but a fragment of a C10 cross shaft remains in the parish church of St Margaret built within the grounds. The nunnery was rebuilt on a grand scale in the C12, as was revealed by early C20 excavations, and the plan is marked out on the ground, but the worked stone has disappeared. The one important C12 survival is part of a finely carved mid-C12 relief of the Crucifixion. A small and delicate late Saxon relief of the same
3 subject recalls the pre-Conquest origins of St Dunstan, the parish church of Stepney, refounded by Archbishop Dunstan in the C10 after the Viking raids.

On the fringe of the City were several establishments dating from after the Norman Conquest. St Katharine-by-the-Tower was founded by Queen Matilda in 1148 and patronized by successive English queens. It provided for a number of poor people and children. It survived the Reformation but its impressive late medieval buildings were swept away for St Katharine Docks. Nearby (on the site of the Royal Mint E of the Tower of London) was the Cistercian abbey of St Mary Graces founded by Edward III in 1350. Its unusual T-shaped plan was recovered in excavations. Also known from recent excavations is the Augustinian hospital of St Mary Spital to the E of Bishopsgate. It was founded in 1197 for the care of the sick, rebuilt in the C14, and offered
p. 386 a significant service, with 180 beds at the time when it was dissolved. The medieval traveller along the road to Colchester would have passed a sequence of other religious foundations: St Leonard's nunnery S of Bow Road close to the crossing over the Lea (Chaucer's Stratford atte Bow), founded by *c.* 1122, of which nothing is left, although a C12 building survived into the C19. A stone bridge across the Lea, built in the early C12, led to Stratford. Here the substantial Cistercian abbey of Stratford Langthorne was founded by Edward III on the edge of the Lea marshes in the 1390s, from which a few stones remain (now in the church at West Ham) together with a legacy of mills along the Lea. Further E across the Roding at Ilford, the medieval chapel still exists from a small hospital founded *c.* 1140 by the abbess of Barking. There was another hospital further S, at Hornchurch, founded in 1159 but dissolved in 1391. The place name, reinforced by the curious tradition of horns preserved on the E wall of the parish church, could suggest the memory of an even older church.

As the parochial system developed in the C11–C12, local churches became more widespread, as is evident from the number which still incorporate C12 masonry. The character of the buildings that preceded these stone churches remains shadowy. Some may have been simple timber buildings, as has been demonstrated by excavations at Little Ilford. Churches that still give a good idea of their C12 character are the tiny, atmospheric Little Ilford, with its modest Norman nave, and East Ham, 4
evocatively set within its isolated churchyard, with substantial C12 nave, sanctuary and apse, the apse with wall arcading, and, remarkably, its original timber roof structure. The most ambitious is Rainham, built in 1178 by Richard de Lucy, founder of 6
Lesnes Abbey across the Thames, and distinguished by aisles with square piers with corner shafts, ornate chancel arch and W tower, suggestive of a prosperous community at Rainham creek. C12 doorways remain at Wennington (reset) and North Ockendon, like East Ham, rural churches sited on the higher ground just N of the Thames marshes.

Later medieval church building in the area is largely unexceptional on a national level, remarkable chiefly for the surprise of finding anything of this date hidden among the C19 and C20 suburban areas. But the majority of the medieval parish churches in the area remain, and although often heavily restored, their fabric and contents are a telling reflection of concerns and tastes of successive generations.* In addition to those mentioned above, particularly rewarding, for monuments of all dates as well as fabric, are the churches of St Dunstan Stepney, West Ham, Walthamstow, Barking, Dagenham, Hornchurch and Upminster.

The trend of reconstructing chancels in the early C13 for more elaborate liturgical requirements is demonstrated at Barking, St Dunstan Stepney (sedilia) and, more modestly, at Dagenham. At East Ham, the apsed form of the chancel was retained, but a C13 piscina was added and provision was also made for a nave altar. Hornchurch also has (restored) C13 piscina and sedilia. As the population grew, extra congregational space was provided by aisles. Simple C13 examples, with arches on plain circular piers, range from the single aisle at the small Chingford old church, to the more ambitious Hornchurch, with two aisles, and the exceptionally large seven-bay nave of West Ham. Octagonal columns were popular in the C14 and C15: those at St Margaret Barking p. 221
(much altered) may date from an ambitious C14 rebuilding. Later arcades with octagonal columns, together with Perp detail are found at St Mary Bow, built as a chapel of ease within the large parish of St Dunstan Stepney. The C14 N arcade at Upminster (much rebuilt), has the widespread Perp form of quatrefoil piers, as has St Dunstan Stepney, which was impressively reconstructed

* Seventeen pre-Reformation churches survive in the area (including Ilford Hospital chapel). Four were rebuilt in the C18 or C19 (Wanstead, Woodford, Leyton, Romford). St Mary Matfelon Whitechapel was rebuilt in the C19 and destroyed in the C20; an early C16 chapel at Bethnal Green had disappeared by the C18.

in the C15 with an aisled and clerestoried nave, and chancel chapels. The chancel at Hornchurch is noteworthy as a rebuilding of 1405–8 under the patronage of William of Wykeham, as New College Oxford held the living.

As at St Dunstan, chapels flanking the chancel were frequent additions; late medieval ones were often built as chantries endowed for masses for the deceased, after the Reformation they were transmuted into commemorative family chapels. Walthamstow has two chancel chapels of the earlier C16 built by prominent local men, the brick N chapel at West Ham dates from the mid C16. A more eccentric survival is the evidence of an anchorite's cell to the N of the nave at East Ham. The parish church of Barking, exceptionally, has an outer N aisle and chapel, incorporating reused C12 material from the abbey, and so possibly post-Dissolution, although its history is not entirely clear. It has a crown-post roof, a late medieval type found also in the chancel at East Ham and the nave at North Ockendon. Good medieval tie-beam roofs survive at West Ham, Hornchurch, and Bow.

At Barking is the one upstanding remnant of the abbey, the
5 C15 Curfew or entrance tower to the precinct, whose upper floor houses the chapel of the Holy Rood with its C12 relief. Towers otherwise are in the usual position at the W end of the church. East Ham had one already in the C13 (still with a bell of this date) and so did Upminster; the latter is a remarkable structure with its heavy timber frame exposed at the end of the nave. It has a short timber spire, clad in shingles, an early example of a common Essex type. Hornchurch has a taller one originally clad in lead, a landmark visible from the Thames. The typical late medieval W tower prevalent in the London area, with battlemented top and upstanding corner turret, can be found at Walthamstow, West Ham, Barking (datable to *c.* 1490–1500), and (much altered) at Stepney and Bow. There are simpler towers without stair-turrets at Chingford and at North Ockendon (the latter with primitive ladder).

The area lacks good local stone but the Thames and its tributaries provided an easy route for bringing building materials from elsewhere. Ragstone rubble from Kent was commonly used for walling, with Reigate stone for dressings. Chalk, also from Kent, was burnt for lime at Limehouse from at least the C14. The local building stone was ferruginous gravel, widely used for rubble walling in the Thames Basin; it can be seen, for example, in the C13 W tower at East Ham, noticeably inferior to the stone walls of the C12 church, and in the churches at Hornchurch and Upminster.

Medieval FURNISHINGS have survived only occasionally. The exceptional and outstanding survivals are the later C14 STALLS from St Katharine-by-the-Tower moved to the Foundation's home in Regent's Park in 1826, and installed in the Foundation's new buildings in Ratcliffe, Tower Hamlets, in 1951. They were of the tall, canopied type which became the fashion in major cathedrals in the C14. The carving of the misericords and elbow rests is of the highest standard, and has all the delightful liveliness and variety that is associated with C14 Dec work. Also preserved from St Katharine's is some later carved WOODWORK of the C16 and C17, some of it of continental origin, suggesting that in the post-medieval period the Foundation became a haven for antiquarian collecting. The preservation of St Katharine's was an early conservation struggle; although the buildings were lost, the rescue of these remains is a tribute to the concern of early C19 antiquaries. In contrast almost nothing, apart from some fragments at Hornchurch and Upminster, remains from the timber SCREENS that would have subdivided the parish churches in the later medieval period; Rainham has the base of a rood screen; more often the rood-loft stair alone remains, as at St Dunstan and West Ham. Nor is there much to see of the stained glass and wall painting that once enlivened the interiors. WALL PAINTINGS were recorded at East Ham, but only some ashlar lining remains; Rainham has some fragments of the C13 and C14. The only notable STAINED GLASS is at North Ockendon, a late C13 panel with Virgin and child, with some C14 fragments, and at Hornchurch (panel with part of a Crucifixion). A special case is some fine C16 French and Flemish glass at Noak Hill, Havering, spoil from continental abbeys. There is also some C16 Flemish glass at Ilford Hospital chapel. A delightful and exceptional survival is a fine late medieval GRAFFITO of a ship at Rainham. At the opposite end of the spectrum is a remarkable carved stone relief at St Katharine's, showing the Adoration of the Magi, closely related to a late C15 Italian painting; its date is unclear.

Surviving MEDIEVAL MONUMENTS are few. Much has been lost. At Hornchurch there is a C13 coffin lid with cross, at Barking a more unusual incised demi-figure of a priest, †1378. At St Dunstan Stepney the much restored monument to the wealthy mercer and Lord Mayor, Henry Colet †1510, is in the form of an elaborate canopied Purbeck tomb-chest of Easter Sepulchre type. At Hornchurch there is a simple tomb-chest to William Ayloffe †1517, and at Barking a more rustic early C16 tomb recess below a brick arch. The medieval hospital chapel at Ilford has a tantalizing monument with an apparently C15 effigy under a canopy in early Renaissance style, but it seems to be largely if not entirely C19.

The best collection of BRASSES is at Upminster (figures of 1455, 1530 and later). Rainham has figures of *c.* 1480 and 1500, West Ham of 1543. At Dagenham is a brass to Sir Thomas p. 151
Urswyck †1479, notable for its depiction of the judge in his robes with his fashionably attired wife and daughters; at North Ockendon the local lord of the manor, William Poyntz †1502, is shown in armour. Little Ilford has an unusual depiction of a schoolboy, Thomas Heron †1517. George Monoux's brass at Walthamstow, 1543, was a late example of the traditional combination of chest tomb (now lost) with brasses of kneeling figures. Fragmentary inscriptions and empty matrices in many other places indicate there was once much more, and that brasses

continued to be popular into the C17. Some could be quite elaborate: the brass to William Cuttinge †1599 at St Katharine, Ratcliffe includes a coloured enamel armorial. One intriguing monument at Barking straddles the divide between the medieval and modern eras. The elegant Renaissance marble sarcophagus at Barking to William Pownsett †1553/4, is a documented work of the Italian sculptor *Nicholas Bellin* of Modena, who had worked for Henry VIII at Nonsuch. Pownsett was a wealthy Barking landowner who had been steward to the last abbess of Barking. In the uncertain religious time of the 1550s, his executors went to some trouble to ensure that traditional prayers for his soul would continue, by giving the advowson of the church to All Souls College Oxford.

Secular Buildings from the Middle Ages to the mid-C17

While most medieval parish churches survived in some form and were adapted for later use, very little remains from secular buildings of before the C17 and nothing at all of medieval buildings of high status, for example the Bethnal Green seat of the Bishop of London, who owned the whole of Stepney in the Middle Ages. Further out, moated sites survive, as at Mark's Gate, Dagnams, Havering and North Ockendon Hall, indicating medieval manor houses, later rebuilt or abandoned for more spacious settings. A frustrating gap is any knowledge of the character of Havering Palace, a royal possession which functioned from the C12 to the C16 as a hunting lodge, and from 1273 onwards as a dower house for successive queens. Building accounts and a C16 survey indicate a large irregular complex with stone buildings. The C19 parish church of Havering-atte-Bower may occupy the site of one of the royal chapels. Hunting in the Forest of Essex was indeed an important attraction for royalty, and one highly interesting
10 relic remains, the timber-framed hunting lodge on the edge of Chingford, now securely dated to the 1540s. This is an instructive example of the high standard of royal carpentry of this time:
p. 720 a robust, functional building, without frills, but displaying the latest joinery techniques.

Up to and into the C17 TIMBER provided the most commonly used material for secular building in the area around London. Excavations have shown that a tradition of timber building was established in London in the C10–C12, adopting a variety of techniques which evolved into a fully framed system of building.* The scatter of timber-framed buildings that remain in the outer areas date from the later middle ages. A significant example from the C14 was the Old Chaplaincy, Hornchurch (demolished 1970), which had evidence of an aisled hall and a storeyed wing with

* For an account covering the whole of Greater London see Malcolm Airs, 'Timber-framed building', in B. Cherry and N. Pevsner, *London 2: South*, 1983. For a summary of early developments see also Richard Bond, 'Timber-framed buildings in the London region', *Regional Variations in Timber-Framed Buildings in England down to 1550*, Conference Proceedings, Essex County Council, 1998.

crown-post. In the C15 aisled halls were superseded by halls without intermediate posts: Great Tomkyns, Upminster, is a well-preserved example of a hall house, with opposing doors. Other examples are the carefully repaired Ancient House, Walthamstow, 7
and the more altered Cross Keys Inn, Dagenham, both with crown-post roofs. In each case the hall is flanked by two-storey wings with jettied fronts roofed at right angles to the hall, a characteristic rural Essex form. The Spotted Dog, Upton, is a rare 9
and picturesque survival of the type in Newham. A more substantial example is the later C16 Upminster Hall, by this time with a ground-floor hall rather than a hall open to the roof. Rather more disguised are the substantial C16 Walnut Tree House, Leyton, its jettied timber-frame construction partly concealed by a Georgian front, and Dury Falls, Hornchurch, a picturesquely rambling C17 house elaborated in the C19. On urban sites there were more compact buildings such as the Church House in Romford Market Place, possibly a late C15 merchant's house, jettied on two sides, and with evidence for shop windows. Another urban timber building at Romford, the Golden Lion, has remains of a C16 timber inn gallery incorporated in the later structure. Hornchurch still has a little group of modest urban timber-framed buildings along the High Street, a common sight in the area up to the early C20. Jetties continued to be popular, as at the (much disguised) Essex Lodge, Plaistow; this has a late C15 or early C16 roof with queen-struts (between tie-beam and collar), a type which became common from the later C16.

For AGRICULTURAL BUILDINGS timber remained standard. The most notable survival is the magnificent Upminster Hall barn, possibly mid C15, with crown-post roof and curved braces, its traditional rural character emphasized by a thatched roof and vertically boarded walls. At Chingford, the picturesque Pimp Hall dovecote is a handsome example of the C16. 8

The rival to timber building was BRICK, the use of which became increasingly widespread during the C16. Brick had been used much earlier in East Anglia and was known in London from the C14, but its acceptance as a smart facing material in the London area followed its use at early Tudor royal seats such as Greenwich, influenced by the great Burgundian palaces of the C15. A remarkable survival in Tower Hamlets demonstrates the spread of this fashion: Bromley Hall, on the E edge of Tower Hamlets, recently re-examined after long neglect, is a brick building with octagonal corner buttresses, possibly part of an entrance range to a courtyard house. Tree-ring dating suggests it was built *c.* 1490. Its high status is indicated by moulded beams and carved timber doorway. There were other houses of the wealthy in the then pleasantly rural hamlets of Bromley and Bow, attractively sited by the River Lea; they vanished as industry grew along the river.

The so-called Old Palace at Bromley, supposed to be a retreat of James I, survived to the end of the C19, just in time to be recorded by the Survey of London. Its splendid early C17 plaster p. 600
ceilings and panelling were rescued during demolition and are

now displayed in the V&A Museum. Gentry houses also existed around Stepney Green, where in the early C16 Henry Colet and his son John lived in a grand house recorded from the C13, and at Bethnal Green, where Netteswell House is the one much-altered early survivor. This was originally built in the mid C16 by a Lord Mayor, Sir Ralph Warren, and remodelled in the mid C17, the date of the surviving shaped and pedimented gables, which link it with C17 brick buildings such as Kew Palace.

Just one large brick Tudor house survives complete, Eastbury
11 Manor House, Barking, built for a wealthy City merchant, Clement Sysley, from the mid C16. Its symmetrical H-shaped plan and lively roofline of gables and chimneys is an example of the new approach to house design, a compact plan which stressed outward show instead of the older arrangement of buildings around a courtyard, although some of the details are conservative. The interiors have been much altered but one room retains interesting fragments of early C17 wall painting. Other major houses of the C16 and C17 have vanished. At Hornchurch, in Emerson Park, a possibly mid-C16 brick well-tower remains from the manor house of Great Nelmes, built by William Roche, Lord Mayor in 1540. In much altered form the house was still standing in the 1950s. In Green Street, East Ham, Boleyn Castle survives only as a pub name and as the symbol of West Ham football club. The stadium occupies the site of a brick house with garden tower of C16 origin, which survived up to 1955. It belonged to a courtier of Henry VIII, Richard Breame, lord of the manor at East Ham, and was traditionally associated with Anne Boleyn. Further out, Gidea Hall, Romford, a medieval house enlarged by Sir Anthony Cooke, who had been tutor to Edward VI, was grand enough to receive Queen Elizabeth; it was rebuilt in the early C18 and demolished 1930.

Church monuments: mid-C16 to mid-C17

The owners and occupiers of some of these lost houses are recalled by their memorials, for although many furnishings disappeared as churches were adapted for Protestant worship, CHURCH MONUMENTS remained a significant expression of family status and identity. From the later C16 up to the 1630s a popular type was the carved wall monument with a pair of figures kneeling before a prayer desk, a Protestant adaptation of the pre-Reformation type with kneelers before a religious image (as shown on the brass to George Monoux at Walthamstow, of 1543). The creation of such monuments was in the hands of the Flemish sculptors who settled in Southwark in the C16.* One of the grandest and most accomplished, attributed to *Cornelius Cure*, is that at Romford to Sir Anthony Cooke †1576; he and his wife

*Apart from the example by Stone, none of the monuments mentioned are documented, and attributions to individual sculptors have varied. Those included here are from Adam White, *Biographical Dictionary of London Tomb Sculptors, c. 1560–c. 1660*, Walpole Society, 1999.

Romford, Gidea Hall in the C17 (visit of Marie de Medici, 1638)

kneel between Corinthian columns supporting an open pediment, their six children kneel in side compartments, with coats of arms above. The figures are all life size, and the classical detail is austere and correct, without the strapwork flourishes of later years. A more characteristic example, among some two dozen in the area, is the painted alabaster Elrington monument at 12
Woodford of 1595. Another monument of quality, attributed to *William Cure jun.*, is at Walthamstow, to Lucy Stanley †1615, a kneeling figure below an arch (the original composition altered). East Ham has a particularly elaborate early C17 group, over a tomb-chest, to Edward Nevill Earl of Westmorland and his family, rather awkwardly given pride of place in the Norman apse. A striking instance of family piety is the large number of Poyntz family monuments at North Ockendon; they include a series of eight small monuments put up by Sir Gabriel Poyntz in 1606: stiff little kneeling couples in historicising dress, set within strapwork frames. Sir Gabriel himself (†1607) and his wife have a rather grander monument, with traditional recumbent figures

lying below a charming painted wooden tester. Anne Carew †1605, at Romford, also has a reclining figure. Leyton has the only other surviving early C17 monument on a large scale, two semi-reclining figures below an arch, of Sir Michael Hicks †1612 and his wife, attributed to *Atye & James*.

At Barking is a most unusual small monument with a delicate
13 painted relief of a seated figure against a background of tents on a battlefield, to Sir Charles Montague †1625.* In the 1630s a more inventive variety of compositions developed. The Fawcitt tomb at West Ham (1636) shows William Fawcitt and his wife as kneeling figures, with her second husband reclining below. The significant influence on tomb design at this period was the sculptor *Nicholas Stone*, who produced accomplished portraits in stone and marble, without the customary painted colouring; the only
14 example of his work in the area is at Walthamstow: Sir Thomas and Lady Mary Merry (1633), two life-like busts set within a pair of ovals framed by an elaborately pedimented composition. A frontal bust in oval niche is used also for Francis Fuller †1636, Barking. Richard Blakstone †1638, Hornchurch, still has kneelers, but combined with angels drawing back a curtain. More unusual is the strange monument to Thomas Withering †1651, Cromwell's postmaster general, also at Hornchurch, showing him as a recumbent skeleton, with smaller skeleton of his son.

EAST LONDON FROM THE MID-C17 TO 1800

Church buildings and monuments from the mid-C17 to later C18

While one can trace a more or less continuous stream of church monuments through the C17 to their grand apogee in the C18 (*see* below), the story of CHURCH BUILDING is more intermittent. During this period the expanding riverside settlements of Tower Hamlets demanded their own places of worship. A chapel was built at Wapping in 1615, rebuilt in 1756. The chapel of St Paul Shadwell followed in 1656, rebuilt in the early C19. The one sur-
27 viving example from the mid C17 is the remarkable chapel at Poplar, built at the request of the local inhabitants and later supported by the East India Company, whose shipyard lay nearby at Blackwall. Disguised in C19 dress, its interior of 1652–4 survives, a close copy of the slightly earlier lost chapel at Broadway, Westminster. The plan, designed for Protestant worship, is a Greek-cross-in-rectangle with shallow sanctuary, suitable for preaching and lecturing, perhaps borrowing from Dutch precedent, and foreshadowing some of Wren's later City church designs. No original furnishings remain, and of furnishings of this period elsewhere there is little to say. A baluster font of *c.* 1635 at Barking, an elegant communion table of *c.* 1630 at St Mary Bow, a hexag-

*The composition is repeated on the monument to Martin Bond †1643, at St Helen, Bishopsgate, City of London.

onal pulpit probably of the early C17 at North Ockendon, and another at Wennington, with hourglass, represent the type of Anglican furnishings that once must have been commonplace. The exceptional marquetry pulpit in Jacobean style at St Katharine's, Ratcliffe, is now thought to be an C18 antiquarian creation.

Cromwell had been tolerant of the dissenting sects unleashed by the disruption of the Civil War. His lenience extended to Jews who were allowed to settle in England after centuries of exclusion. A Jewish cemetery, the first of many in the East End, was established at Mile End in 1657; the first purpose-built synagogue, still extant (within the City of London), was built in 1701 off Bevis Marks. By the later C17 dissenting Protestant congregations were numerous, especially in the expanding artisan suburbs close to the City. After the Restoration they at first led an uncertain life, harshly persecuted during 1660–86, but after the Act of 1689 'orthodox' dissenters – Baptists, Congregationalists, Presbyterians and Quakers – were allowed freedom of worship, although they could not hold civic office. Their early buildings are known only from records. A purpose-built Quaker meeting house at Ratcliffe was built as early as 1667, rebuilt in 1670 and again in 1798, and survived until 1935. Outside built-up London a former Quaker burial ground, first used in 1672, remains at Barking, close to the site of a house adapted for worship. Apart from home-grown Dissenters, the eastern suburbs harboured Protestants from abroad, notably Huguenots fleeing from France after the revocation of the Edict of Nantes of 1685. They too built chapels (the earliest surviving one, in Fournier Street, dates from 1743, *see* below). Danish merchants settled around the newly laid out Wellclose Square N of Wapping and built their own church, promin-ently sited in the centre of the square, designed by the Danish sculptor *Caius Cibber* in 1694–6. It was demolished in 1869, but views show that it reflected the influence of the simpler City churches rebuilt after 1666, an exterior of brick with stone quoins with round-headed and circular windows, and a plaster-vaulted interior with shallow apse. The Anglican chapel of St Mary Matfelon at Whitechapel, rebuilt in 1673, was not dissimilar: with a simple exterior of brick with stone quoins, and Venetian and oval windows. But Anglican churches did not keep pace with the rapid growth of the eastern suburbs in the later C17. The lack of suitable places of worship in Spitalfields was so acute that in 1693 the eminent theologian the Rev. George Wheler built a temporary timber tabernacle in Spital Square at his own expense.

It was against this fluid and diverse cultural background that pressure grew for an increase in the number of churches in the suburbs, a campaign supported by a new Tory government concerned to maintain the Church of England as an arm of the state. The New Churches Act of 1711 allocated funds from the Coal Tax for the building of fifty new churches, particularly in the poorer areas to the E of the city where dissenters were numerous. The first proposals for fifty churches, based on population

St Mary Matfelon, Whitechapel, built 1673, early C19 engraving

estimates (one church for *c.* 4,750 people, but allowing for *c.* 100,000 non-Anglicans), included no less than eight churches in Tower Hamlets: two in Whitechapel, five in Stepney and one in Shadwell. The guidance given by the Commissioners, no doubt aware of the disadvantages of the City churches rebuilt on awkward sites after the fire of 1666, laid stress on an impressive exterior, if possible on an island site, and an imposing entrance or portico. But churches of such ambition were expensive, and only twelve were built in all. The East End gained three, all of them magnificent works by *Nicholas Hawksmoor*: Christ Church Spitalfields, St George-in-the-East, and St Anne Limehouse, all begun *c.* 1714 and completed by *c.* 1730. Hawksmoor's style is distinctive, using classical detail in an idiosyncratic manner to express a connection with early Christian practice, in which both he and contemporary theologians were deeply interested. Hawksmoor initially explored the possibility in an unexecuted 'Basilica after the Primitive Christians' for a site in Bethnal Green. Nothing came of this, but some of the ideas expressed in his rough plan, for instance the attention paid to locations for
16, 17 baptistery, vestry and sacristy (facilities required by the commissioners), are reflected in his built churches. The three Stepney churches are all versions of a plan with strong cross-axis, emphasizing the preaching body of the church, but are very different in character. Christ Church, with an interior now splendidly restored to its original form, is the most monumental, its classical gravitas expressed by arcades on tall Corinthian columns and a strong horizontal beam across the E end, forming a mighty screen intended as an allusion to Early Christian practices. St Anne is a reworking in the grand manner of the cross-in-square plan, with central domed space (reconstructed in the C19). The
19 interior of St George, destroyed in the Second World War, also

had a cross-in-square plan. Close up, the three exteriors share
Hawksmoor's quirks: emphatic rustication and exaggerated keystones, but are all highly individual. From afar their dominant
towers in gleaming Portland stone dwarfed their original surroundings and are prominent even among today's taller buildings: St George with octagonal lantern and cluster of staircase 18
turrets; St Anne with its bold apsidal W porch below a 19
tower of receding stages; and Christ Church with its extraordi- 16
nary piling up of portico, triumphal arch and steeple. The
Gothic steeple (originally more ornate) and the surprising
detail of Roman altars crowning the pinnacles of St George,
reflects Hawksmoor's eclectic use of sources imbued with religious associations.

No other C18 church building in East London has this drama
or intensity. The survivals show a more conventional taste for
unostentatious preaching boxes: the built-up suburb of Bethnal
Green at last acquired its own church in 1743–6, St Matthew, a
dignified, rather stolid classical box by *George Dance sen.*, set in
an unusually spacious churchyard. The shell of the rebuilt St
John, Wapping also remains, of 1756, probably by *Joel Johnson*, a
simple exterior, though with a curiously eccentric Baroque
lead steeple. Johnson may also have built the modest German 28
Lutheran church in Alie Street, Whitechapel (1762–3), which
preserves its atmospheric C18 galleried interior crowded with
box pews, pulpit and florid commandment boards. For the
Huguenots, *Thomas Stibbs*, like Johnson a carpenter turned architect, built a large chapel (now a mosque) in Fournier Street, Spitalfields, and a smaller Huguenot chapel remains in Sandys Row; 30
both were originally galleried with plain brick exteriors. Further
out, in the rural villages, the medieval churches were patched
up and modified through the C17, C18 and early C19, their aisle
walls rebuilt in brick, their interiors filled with galleries. Leyton,
Walthamstow and Woodford have work of all these periods,
the best is Woodford's handsome brick W tower of 1708. At
Dagenham the old tower collapsed in 1800 and was rebuilt
together with the nave in a naïve rustic Gothic. Interior changes
of this period were almost entirely swept away in the C19, but
Dagenham still has its homely W gallery, its panels inscribed with
benefactors. The single and supreme example of a complete C18 29
rebuilding is the exquisite Wanstead, 1787–90 by *Thomas Hardwick*, paid for by the two principal Wanstead landowners, with its
elegant galleried interior, palm tree pulpit and a generous chancel
expressly designed to house the older monument of Sir Josiah
Child of Wanstead Park.

This account must now return to CHURCH MONUMENTS of the late C17–C18. The outer suburbs of East London are rich in the imposing memorials that from the later C17 became fashionable for the wealthy in the Home Counties. Merchants and City men of power and influence (Lord Mayors occur frequently) who had retired to rural country seats appear to have favoured straightforward life-size standing portraits in elaborate architectural frames rather than the type of sophisticated compositions

that filled Westminster Abbey at this time. The results could be splendid, if overpowering for small churches, with much carving of the highest quality. The sequence starts at Dagenham with Sir Richard Alibon †1688 and wife, two figures somewhat in the Flemish Mannerist tradition (attributed to *John van Nost*).
20 At West Ham, Thomas Foot †1688 and wife stand more pro-
22 saically in separate arches beneath a pediment. Sir Josiah Child at Wanstead (also attributed to Nost), †1699 but probably made a few years later, stands swagger in Roman dress (but with a wig) within a particularly exuberant architectural setting, accompanied by cherubs and allegorical figures and with his son reclining on a lower plinth beneath. At Leyton, Sir William Hicks †1702 (in Roman dress) and wife, stand in a group with a reclining father. At Walthamstow, Sigismund Trafford †1723 is also in Roman dress. At West Ham again, making a pair with the Foot monument, is an exceptionally sensitively portrayed couple:
21 James Cooper, †1743, standing with his wife within a single niche below a broad pediment. A late addition to the list is at Christ Church, Spitalfields, Sir Robert Ladbroke, by *Flaxman* 1794.

Plenty of lesser tombs merit attention, for their inscriptions as well as their sculpture. St Dunstan Stepney and Barking are memorable for their number of maritime associations; particu-
15 larly fine is the bust at Barking to Captain John Bennett †1706, with a portrait of his ship. The Buckeridge children at West Ham are an unusual group of large figures *c.* 1698–1710. Purely architectural monuments can be of high quality: Sir Francis Prujean †1666 Hornchurch; Sir James Smyth †1706, West Ham. So too is the small C18 burial chapel of the Lethieulliers at Little Ilford, with its wall of restrained memorials in a Doric frame.

Later monuments in the Neoclassical tradition are generally more routine, but occasionally have good sculpture: for example Charles Foulis †1783, Woodford, with seated woman, by *Bacon*; Richard Spencer †1784, Hornchurch, a double portrait by *Flaxman*, with two standing angels; Benjamin Kenton †1800, St Dunstan, Stepney, a fine Good Samaritan relief by *Sir Richard Westmacott*. CHURCHYARDS also have rewarding tombs; the later C18 and earlier C19 fashion for the classical sarcophagus can be studied at Old Chingford church, Leyton, Walthamstow, and Woodford; the last also has an unusual columnar memorial of 1769 by *Sir Robert Taylor*, and an austere and massive domed mausoleum in Soanian taste to the Raikes family, of *c.* 1797 by *Gibson*.

Suburban growth C17–C18

The eastward spread of London began in the later middle ages. It was encouraged by the C16 break-up of monastic property and fuelled by a rapidly rising metropolitan population (around 200,000 in 1600 rising to *c.* 575,000 in 1700). The muddle of houses and workshops that encroached on the open land E of the City, deplored by John Stow at the end of the C16, was rebuilt over the next two centuries. It is estimated that by the end of the C17 some 22 per cent of London's population lived E of the City. Gascoyne's survey of Stepney of 1703, the first accurate depiction of the area, shows the riverside built up from the Tower of London up to Limehouse, and buildings stretching E from Bishopsgate and along Whitechapel High Street, but with open land separating them from the hamlet of Mile End Old Town, where Stepney Green still provided a rural setting (for its p. 457 late C17 buildings, *see* below). Bethnal Green similarly was still a p. 544 rural retreat with large houses.

Among the survivals from this time some of the earliest in this area are the Trinity House Almshouses off Mile End Road, laid p. 466 out, as was so often the practice with almshouses, on the edge of the built-up area. They date from 1695 and are a delightful example of the domestic classical style of the time of Wren, with the chapel formally placed at the end of two rows of cottages. In complete contrast is the picturesquely haphazard string of riverside houses along Narrow Street, Limehouse, much altered and rebuilt, but with origins that go back to the later C17. They are now the sole substantial remnant of early building in the riverside hamlets.

Regularity of design remained exceptional in the East End during the C18. Spitalfields Market was laid out in the late C17, surrounded by a symmetrical pattern of streets, but the new terrace houses were generally built only a few at a time as speculations, with small amounts of capital provided by minor entrepreneurs, and erected by small carpenters and bricklayers. A good early example is the surviving pair of houses at Victoria Park Square, Bethnal Green, of the 1690s. Many streets in Spitalfields and Whitechapel were laid out haphazardly, their siting conditioned by tenter grounds, brickyards and an artillery ground. Industry mixed with residential development: in Brick Lane there was a brewhouse from the 1660s, the kernel of the much bigger enterprise developed by Benjamin Truman in the C18. The pow- p. 478 erful entrepreneur Nicholas Barbon was involved in the development of Wellclose Square, N of Wapping, but this and its neighbour Prince's (later Swedenborg) Square were also built up slowly and irregularly, as was Spital Square (so called, though not a true square), which emerged from the ruins of the monastic buildings of St Mary Spital. From these three squares only one older house remains, No. 47 Spital Square, now the offices of the Society for the Protection of Ancient Buildings. It was built in the 1740s and occupied by a Huguenot silk-weaving family, a relatively late example of how the generation succeeding the Huguenot refugees of the 1680s could afford comfortable middle-class accommodation.

The replacement of humbler hovels and workshops in Spitalfields had indeed begun earlier, as the area prospered. A variety of three-storey houses of the 1720s remain in Elder Street, and in the same decade a more uniform sequence sprang up close to Hawksmoor's new church, in and around Fournier Street, the 25 most coherent surviving area of this date. Some more remain in

Mile End Road: Nos. 107–13, of 1717. The restrictions of the post-Fire Building Acts concerning external timber detail were not widely observed in East London, nor had the aesthetic conventions of the Palladians yet taken hold, and the houses of the 1710s–20s were built with an attractive variety of carved doorcases, and with windows of similar height to each floor, their frames flush with the outer walls. Some have the long attic windows associated with weaving lofts.* Unlike many C18 terraces in other parts of London interiors are not to a uniform plan, but are characterized by panelled timber partitions, and good quality joinery. At around the same time the Mansell Street neighbourhood, which had been laid out in the 1680s S of Whitechapel High Street, was rebuilt with substantial houses, also still in the free Baroque manner, but of these almost nothing is left.

The greater stylistic consciousness that began to affect house façades can be demonstrated by No. 5 White's Row (off Commercial Street) of the 1730s and by Nos. 133–9 Mile End Road of 1741–2, their superior status in both cases indicated by their five-bay width. The finest survivals are the two adjoining houses in Artillery Lane, Nos. 56–8, rebuilt in 1756–7 for two silk merchants in the characteristic refined style of the City architect *Sir Robert Taylor*. They have elegant interiors, and the Rococo shopfront of No. 56 is the best of its kind in London, echoing the sophisticated taste of luxury retailing at this time. Taylor may also
26 have been involved in improving the house of Sir Benjamin Truman's brewery in Brick Lane, a composite C18 creation with some lavishly decorated interiors, including a corridor with a typically Taylorian vaulted ceiling. High quality detail is also characteristic of the buildings of another local business, the long established Whitechapel Bell Foundry; its C18 premises in Whitechapel Road include a fine early C19 shopfront.

In the later C18, uniform rows of three-storey, three-bay houses for the middle classes became more commonplace, invading former centres of earlier housing. A pair remains from a group of the 1760s on Stepney Green, and a substantial number, though much altered, on the S side of Mile End Road. In Old Ford Road, Bethnal Green, Nos. 2–5 date from 1787–91. An individual house from the 1790s of unusual interest is No. 2 Butcher Row, Ratcliffe, now part of St Katharine's Foundation. It was built after a disastrous fire had destroyed much of the hamlet in 1794, for Matthew Whiting, sugar refiner, perhaps by *Thomas Leverton*. It is a rare example within the inner East End of the type of elegant detached house found more commonly beyond built-up London (*see* below). Its interior painted with landscapes reflects a taste that has been associated with commercial rather than aristocratic patronage.†

*The date of these lofts is unclear. Some at least may be later alterations when silk weaving declined and working conditions became more cramped.

†See M. Galinou, ed., *City Merchants and the Arts*, 2004.

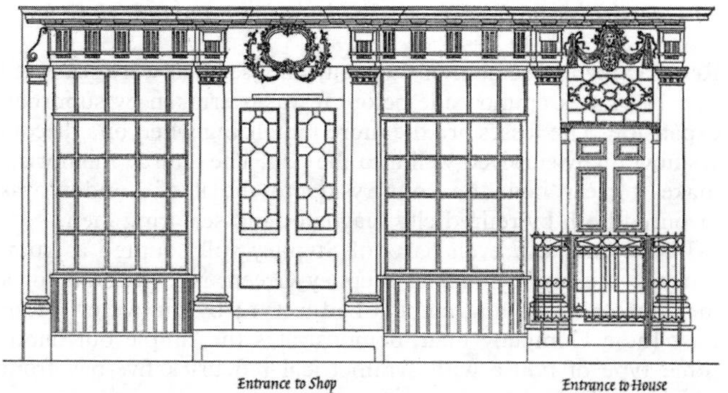

Shopfront, No. 56 Artillery Lane, Spitalfields, 1756–7, attributed to Sir Robert Taylor

The pattern of development changed at the end of the C18, coinciding with the building of the Docks and the population explosion of the C19. But the more standard, repetitive streets of the earlier C19, both two and three storeyed, built to house artisan and labouring families, did not become universal in Tower Hamlets. Old views and records show that especially in the riverside hamlets a miscellany of minor C17 and C18 buildings remained, including timber-framed and weatherboarded houses. Variations in internal planning catered for workshops and multi-occupation. The interiors of some of the Spitalfields houses fall within this local vernacular tradition, so do some odd survivals in Bethnal Green (Bethnal Green Road, Brick Lane and Sclater Street).* The variety of older houses around Rainham Creek perhaps gives some impression of what might once have existed further E.

Apart from churches and houses, few other types of buildings remain from the C18 eastern suburbs. In Raine Street, Wapping, 24
is the former Raine's School, a fine Baroque front of 1719 with giant pilasters and niches with figures of charity children. The former St John's School, Wapping, rebuilt 1756–60 together with the church, also has niches for this purpose. The most ambitious C18 institution in the area is the Royal London Hospital, founded 2
by a group of doctors in the 1740s and built on Whitechapel Road during 1752–7 by *Boulton Mainwaring*. Although much extended, its plain symmetrical mid-C18 core is still recognizable. It stood on the edge of the built up area, with extensive grounds to the S.

*For the wider picture of this subject, with many illustrations of lost buildings, *see* P. Guillery, *The Small House in Eighteenth Century London*, 2004.

Secular architecture in the countryside: late C17 and C18

Remarkably few remain of the gentry houses that were scattered over the Essex countryside before it was overtaken by suburban expansion. The losses are the more tantalizing when one discovers how many survived well into the C20. The church memorials make it clear how the countryside to the E of London was favoured both by retired city magnates and seafaring men.

In the later C17 even parts of Stepney still counted as rural
23 retreats: the finest house at Stepney Green, No. 37, built for a
merchant *c.* 1694, and embellished *c.* 1714 by the widow of an East India Company man, demonstrates the simple but handsome type of house with symmetrical red brick five-bay front which, with some modifications, remained a standard basic recipe for the smaller rural gentry house through much of the earlier C18. The Stepney house has a timber cornice, C18 examples have brick parapets. More ambitious houses of the earlier C18 might be of seven bays and also sport giant pilasters, as at Reydon Hall, Wanstead, and Hurst House, Woodford (*c.* 1714). A major loss from this Baroque phase was Leyton Great House, demolished in 1905. It was built by 1712 by Fisher Tench on the estate acquired by his father, Sir Nathaniel Tench, one of the first directors of the Bank of England, a characteristic example of City merchant turned country gentleman. The rich interiors included a painted stair hall. The cupola on Leyton church is said to come from its roof. The tall Baroque front with emphatic quoins, cornice and parapet, appears as late as 1729 as a feature of an
31 especially attractive and complete smaller house, Rainham Hall,
built next to his counting house for Captain John Harle, owner of Rainham wharf. The house is old-fashioned for its date but with excellently crafted detail both inside and out, a compact design of three full storeys and basement, with attention paid to the three-bay flanks as well as to the five-bay front and rear. Two
p. 187 staircases are squeezed into the slightly irregular layout. A telling
32 contrast is Bower House, also of 1729, built for John Baynes, a
lawyer, at Havering-atte-Bower. It is by *Henry Flitcroft*, his first independent building, a neat essay in the Palladian manner: two storeys, the ground floor raised over a basement, and a demure
33 central pediment. The fine interiors in the manner of Kent
include a small but accomplished staircase; its walls are painted with arcadian scenes and grisailles.

Of an entirely different order was Wanstead House, begun in
p. 353 1715 by *Colen Campbell* for the fabulously wealthy Sir Richard
Child, son of Sir Josiah, who had acquired the Wanstead estate in 1667. The new house, of seventeen bays with six-column portico, was the first in England to establish a pattern for the grand Palladian country house, its fame spread by its publication in *Vitruvius Britannicus*, but its palatial scale and extravagant interiors remained atypical in the area. It lasted for only a century. The other two larger houses that still exist are smaller fry, so much altered and added to that they are difficult to classify. Valence House, Becontree, is a confusing fragment of a house of

medieval origin, the much altered existing parts with some good C17 panelling. Valentines, Ilford, is partly of the late C17 but enlarged in the C18 and early C19: the garden side, formerly the entrance, has a nine-bay show front of the 1760s, the present entrance side has an elegant semicircular port cochère of the early C19.

Smaller houses up to the 1760s compromise between the domestic Baroque of Rainham Hall and the polite Palladian of Bower House. Walthamstow and Woodford, providing attractive locations on the fringe of the forest, preserve the largest number of these brick 'citizens' villas'. Superficially similar, they vary in both detail and plan. Such houses often changed hands and were improved by a succession of new owners. Refacing was common; sometimes staircases appear older than frontages, closed-string staircases with thick balusters of late C17 type, for example, are to be found at Manor House, Woodford, and at Bretons, Hornchurch, which otherwise appear later in date. Water House (William Morris Gallery), Walthamstow, is an example of a good mid-C18 house, with a front smartened by later bows. It has its original staircase, which rises from the back of an unusually broad central hall. Chestnut House, Hoe Street, Walthamstow is a characteristic, less altered, larger house of the 1740s: red brick, seven bays with central pediment, also with original staircase, here given its own space opening off the hall, with decorative plasterwork on the walls. Good Rococo plaster ceilings remain in two other Walthamstow houses built as a speculation *c.* 1762, Thorpe Combe and Walthamstow House. The latter was enlarged by the addition of a large bowed dining room, a typical later C18 requirement, in this case for the extensive family of Sir Robert Wigram, a director of the East India Company. Bower House, Havering, and Langtons, Hornchurch, were similarly given wings with canted bays in the later C18. Among minor later Georgian improvements to older houses, the most charming are those to two adjacent mid-C18 houses now occupied by Forest School, 36
Walthamstow: one has an elegant small circular ground-floor room of the 1790s, its neighbour has a remarkably Soanian first-floor drawing room with bowed ends and starfish ceiling.

These earlier C18 houses are only rarely associated with a known architect. The 1760s mark a change: during this decade the area began to be affected by the fashion for the mature Palladian villa, of the type developed elsewhere from the 1750s by Sir Robert Taylor. The earliest survivor appears to be Hactons, Upminster, of 1762, but its pedimented Palladian front with one-storey pavilions has been so altered and added to that it is barely recognizable. Two examples are preserved rather better as part of school complexes. Hare Hall (Royal Liberty School), now in p. 195
the eastern suburbs of Romford, was built in 1768–9 for John Wallinger, a Colchester merchant, by *James Paine*, one of his relatively few country houses in southern England. It is a compact Palladian villa on a grand scale, equipped with side pavilions, smartly dressed in rusticated stone with an attached giant portico, and with a top-lit oval stair hall. Of similar date is

Highams (Woodford High School) on the E edge of Waltham Forest. It was built for an M.P. in 1764, an early work by *William Newton*. It has a more restrained front, its centre simply marked by giant pilasters. The interior has a handsome square entrance hall; the staircase opens off the end of a spine corridor. Highams was given an additional floor in the later C18 together with a prospect lantern on the roof. This latter feature was an asset in an area where an elevated view across the flat landscape could take in the Thames with its shipping. An old view shows another such lantern on Little Ilford Manor House (demolished in the C19). There was a second villa by *James Paine*, Gaynes, at Corbets Tey, Upminster, built in 1771 for the principal landowner of Upminster, Sir James Esdaile, but rebuilt in the C19. An attractive lodge remains, classical with Gothic windows, and two bridges from the former grounds (*see* below). In 1782 Esdaile built another villa in the area for his son-in-law, Harwood Hall, now a school; a compact house with canted bay, altered later.

The most intriguing among smaller houses of the late C18 is
37 the Round House, Havering-atte-Bower, an oval house of *c.* 1792,
p. 172 most ingeniously designed on geometric principles, and plausibly attributed to *John Plaw*. This has been excellently restored. Others of this period have been more altered: Claybury Hall, of 1790–1 by *Jesse Gibson*, now apartments, has a Neoclassical exterior with bowed centre, and fine top-lit central hall with cantilevered stair. The handsome vicarage at Barking of 1794 is now offices. Slightly later is the former Gwynne House, Woodford Bridge, now a hotel, of 1816 by *J.B. Papworth*, with a small but good top-lit staircase. Around 1800 larger and plainer houses became more common, often rendered or of pale brick rather than the red brick used earlier, such as Harts, South Woodford with Ionic colonnaded entrance, and Leytonstone House, which has a severe front but an unexpected little projecting bow at the back. Occasionally a playful Gothic is found, the prettiest is the frontage (all that remains) of No. 669 Leyton High Road; the early C19 Etloe House, Church Street, Leyton, is another. Bower Farm Cottage, Havering-atte-Bower, is an attractive cottage orné in Tudor style. The Essex villages do not appear to have attracted the C18 speculative middle-class urban-terrace-in-the-country that are features of prosperous villages both N and S of built-up London (Hampstead, Clapham, etc). An exception is Leytonstone, where a late C18 terrace remains, set back from the High Road, testifying to the late Georgian appeal of the area. But in general it was the detached house with its own grounds that remained the distinctive type in the countryside E of London.

From many of these houses as well as from others that have been lost, a surprising amount remains from their GROUNDS. What survives is not always obvious, but the remnants demonstrate how attractive this part of the Essex landscape must once
p. 354 have been. The surroundings of Wanstead were as ambitious as the great mansion itself, incorporating a formal layout from the grounds of its predecessor, which were embellished in the later C18 with a string of picturesque lakes together with a grotto and

View from my Own Cottage, watercolour by Humphry Repton, 1816

temple, which still remain (the grotto sadly ruinous) in the extensive public park. Fragments of these characteristic phases of C17–C18 landscaping, the formal succeeded by the picturesque, can be found in many other places. From the other major house at Wanstead, Wanstead Grove, now lost, there are remains of a straight canal, and an C18 temple and a gazebo now in suburban gardens. Valentines at Ilford is a rare case of a house surviving together with its park, which retains remnants of an interesting formal layout with water feature and shelter. The grounds of the lost mansion of Gidea Hall (rebuilt in the early C18, demolished in the early C20) are partly preserved as Raphael Park. Here too the site is visible of an early C18 long canal, now dry, and a later C18 serpentine lake remains, with bridge by *James Wyatt*. From Gaynes there is also a serpentine lake and a major and a minor bridge from *Paine*'s time. Highams was landscaped by *Humphry Repton* in 1793–4. He produced one of his famous Red Books for the estate. In order to integrate the house with its surroundings he created a lake with an island, some way off, which could be viewed from the first-floor veranda that he added to the house. The substantial lake, originally an encroachment into the royal forest (deer had to be allowed access), is no longer visible from the house and comes as a surprise in its present suburban setting. Repton was much employed in the area, for he was a local man, living in the little hamlet of Hare Street, E of Romford. Nothing now remains there from this time, but the view from his cottage onto the high road is well known from his picturesque depiction of the scene. His taste can still be enjoyed on a miniature scale in the grounds of Langtons, Hornchurch, with its small lake, orangery, gazebo and shelter planting (*c.* 1805). His name is recalled by the modern Repton Park, Woodford Bridge, now largely housing on the hospital site occupying the grounds of Claybury, for which he produced a Red Book in 1791. At Stubbers, North Ockendon, some crinkle-crankle walls remain from his work (the Red Book dates from 1796). Other estates where he worked included Dagnams, Harold Hill (1802), from which Dagnam Park remains, Woodford Hall (1801), and Wallwood House, Leytonstone (*c.* 1810), both now built over. In 1813 he was engaged to report on the grounds of Wanstead. He recommended reinstating the formal layout, by then much neglected, and some planting was carried out, but the estate was already bankrupt and he was never paid.

Other changes to the countryside in the C17–C18 were concerned more directly with agriculture and industry. Drainage of the marshes remaining alongside the Thames continued in the C17, securing the Isle of Dogs for grazing, and enabling the building of windmills along the exposed western marsh wall, the 'mill wall'. At Dagenham, longstanding efforts to cope with the flooding of the River Beam met with success in 1716–20, following the work of the harbour engineer *Captain John Perry*. The C18 engineering project most visible today is the Limehouse Cut, a straight channel created in 1767–70 by *Thomas Yeoman* linking the River Lea Navigation to Limehouse (*see* further below). The River Lea had a long history of industrial activity. In the C17 and C18 dyeing and calico industries used the clean waters at Bow. Milling goes back to the medieval watermills of the abbey of Stratford Langthorne. Gunpowder was produced in the area and in the C16 and C17 many tide mills were located between Stratford and Bromley-by-Bow. The one significant relic from the C18
35 is the remarkable group on the Lea at Three Mills. The large timber-framed House Mill, worked by the ebb tide, which milled grain for distilling, still has its water wheels and much of its milling machinery. Its later companion, the Clock Mill, has been more altered; it also was built with some show, and retains its attractive corner tower, faced in brick in the early C19 and smartened up by Gothic windows. In the early C19 there was also a water-powered oil-seed mill, later a copper mill, at Walthamstow. The one surviving windmill in our area is at Upminster,
34 built in 1802–3 by a local farmer, a traditional smock mill complete with its original wooden machinery.

As with the gentry houses, much MINOR RURAL BUILDING of the C18 has disappeared or has been so altered that its original character is only superficially preserved. The outermost villages are the best hunting grounds: Upminster, North Ockendon, Noak Hill, Havering-atte-Bower, Woodford and Chingford – isolated examples remain elsewhere, though often disguised. The most recognizably distinctive vernacular feature is the use of weatherboarding, which was common both in Essex and in the London region. It could be used to conceal older timber framing (as at The Spotted Dog, Upton) but also for covering the timber-framed constructions which continued to be built, often combined with brick, through the C18 and into the C19. The House Mill on the Lea is an unusually large example of a timber building with a brick front and boarded rear. The Old Dispensary, Romford Road, Stratford, of *c.* 1700 is timber-framed and weatherboarded, but the five-bay house adopts plan and proportions similar to its polite brick contemporaries. Humbler houses reflect a variety of vernacular plans. One which became widespread in the earlier C17 was the lobby-entrance house, with its front door placed in line with a central chimney-stack heating rooms on either side. Among still quite numerous C17 examples are Dagenham Vicarage, Rainham Vicarage, Berwick Manor Rainham, and some smaller two-room cottages such as Kilbro, North Ockendon, The Ship, Main Road, Romford and No. 195 High Street, Hornchurch. Later smaller houses adopted the plan with end chimneystacks common through the C18 and C19.

ALMSHOUSES on the edge of London have already been mentioned. Further out in the country the best examples are at Walthamstow: the two-storey Monoux almshouses originally established in 1527, together with a schoolroom, much reconstructed since, and Squire's almshouses of 1795, a low but polite composition with very large pediment. There were a number of rural C18 charity schools, such as Dame Tipping's at Havering-atte-Bower, but all have been rebuilt later. At Walthamstow the Vestry House (now museum) was built as a WORKHOUSE in 1730 and enlarged in 1756 to provide a vestry room for parish business; it is entirely domestic in appearance. Upminster has a simple poorhouse of 1750.

EARLY C19 EAST LONDON

The C19 was the greatest period of change in East London's history. Within a century the old Tower Hamlets had been transformed into an intensely industrial suburb with severely overcrowded streets and houses, giving rise not only to squalid slums but also the migration E of many of its inhabitants into new suburbs within Essex. The transforming moment arrived with the new century and the opening of the first, enclosed secure docks.

*The Docks and the riverside up to 1850**

The docks' history belongs to the story of the growth of trade on the Thames, which began in earnest with the founding of Londinium soon after A.D. 43 on a site with sufficient deep water for a port serving Europe. After the building of the first stone London Bridge, completed in 1209, the port was divided into two parts: below the bridge there was deep-water anchorage, but

* Much of this account is adapted from Malcolm Tucker and Elizabeth Williamson's longer introduction to *The Buildings of England: London Docklands*, 1998.

only small craft could venture upriver through its arches. Imports and exports of dutiable goods were regulated by the Legal Quays established below the bridge on the N bank from 1558. All foreign goods had to be landed there. By the C18, London had 1,400 ft (430 m) of Legal Quays, still only a third of the space available at Britain's second port, Bristol. The river was so jammed with ships that unloading a cargo could be delayed for weeks. Pilfering was rife from ships and quays, especially the East India and West India cargoes of sugar, rum, coffee and hardwoods. Secure trading docks were the solution, with high walls or moats to keep out thieves, and lock gates to allow unloadings at any time. Liverpool had developed the first in 1710–17 and by 1795 had an extensive system. In London, pressure was applied by a committee of merchants (formed in 1793) and in 1796 a Select Committee of the House of Commons agreed to docks in principle, to be financed by private capital. The West India Docks, established on the then almost deserted Isle of Dogs (1799–1806), were quickly followed by the London Dock in Wapping (1880–5), the East India Docks at Blackwall, formed from the Brunswick fitting-out dock (1803–6), and St Katharine Docks (1825–9), again in Wapping, built in an attempt to capitalize on the ending of the original monopolies granted to dock companies for certain classes of goods. It was a greedy speculation that displaced hundreds of people as well as the medieval foundation of St Katharine.

The excavations for the docks were remarkable, three-quarters of a million cubic yards of soil being dug from the West India Import Dock in little more than a year. Steam engines drained the ground, mixed mortar for the brickwork and, in the London Docks, hauled waggon loads of spoil up inclined planes. Infilling and redevelopment of the docks since 1970 (*see* below) has left only selected survivals of their original layout and engineering. Preserved sections of the very high brick boundary walls remain at the London Docks and East India Docks, though few of their grand gateways, which were deliberately constricting, have survived into the C21. Better preserved are the original fine brickwork and masonry QUAY WALLS, which partly survive at the West India Import and Export Docks, where the engineer *William Jessop* introduced elegantly curved walls, leaning gently backwards (they later earned the nickname 'banana walls' from a propensity to slip if a dock was hastily drained). These were the model for the quay walls of *Rennie*'s London Docks, where substantial sections, with stone rubbing bands, are still preserved. Jessop also introduced LOCK CHAMBERS with substantial inverted-arch bottoms, among which the disused western entrance to the City Canal (West India South Dock) of 1805 remains intact. Most docks were built with TIDAL ENTRANCE BASINS (examples survive at St Katharine's, the London Docks and West India Docks), which served as reservoirs to fill the entrance locks and were replenished at high tide. The water level at the quays was held constant by communicating locks, which separated the docks from the basins. This system continued in

St Katharine Docks, Wapping, after 1860

use until impounding stations with powerful pumps were provided in the early C20. The St Katharine Docks, with their restricted space, used a pumping engine from the start. To cross the locks, double-leaf SWING BRIDGES were introduced at West India in 1802 and the first of cast iron were devised by Rennie at the London Docks in 1804. The only early bridge surviving is the unusual retracting footbridge of 1829 *ex situ* at the St Katharine Docks.

WAREHOUSES dominated the upriver docks and the riverside from the City down to Limehouse until the late 1960s and took much of the trade from the Legal Quays. They stored mainly imported goods and commodities of a seasonal character. The major dock and wharf companies applied high standards of architecture to their warehouses, with formal compositions and details generally in a classical idiom. Portland stone or, later, stucco was widely used for cornices, string courses and other embellishments. Except in the almost blind boundary walls, windows were generally large to light the deep interiors without the risk from
oil lamps. *George Gwilt & Son* at West India Docks from 1802 65
made the windows broader than tall, with secure cast-iron frames (often supplemented by spikes), in what became a universal style. Granaries, however, used wooden shutters in small openings. Walls were pierced by tiers of loading doors or 'loopholes', with robust wooden jambs and hinged platforms, accompanied by swivelling wall-cranes, the smaller ones often of elegantly forged iron. At St Katharine Docks in 1828, *Philip Hardwick* introduced giant blind arcades, pilaster strips and Doric colonnades of cast iron. There, cramped quays were tucked under the warehouses and goods hoisted directly from ship into warehouse, the model for the surviving Albert Dock in Liverpool. Of the river warehouses Old Aberdeen Wharf, Wapping (1843–4), is unique in

having a grand stucco frontage to the river with attached columns. Italianate modillioned cornices were used from that time.

p. 671 The early dock warehouses set the pattern of CONSTRUCTION for the rest of the C19. Timber floors kept down costs and loads on foundations, but cast-iron columns were introduced for their load-bearing capacity, first inserted in 1810 in the London Docks South Stacks (demolished) and in 1814 in the surviving West India No. 2 Warehouse. *Daniel Alexander*'s surviving Tobacco Dock Warehouse of 1811–14 in Wapping is particularly innovative in its use of iron for a series of branching stanchions. In London, cruciform-section columns were preferred throughout the C19 where extra strength was required. The London and St Katharine Docks had magnificent groin-vaulted cellars, still seen at Tobacco Dock and beneath the so-called Ivory House. The roofs of the earliest large warehouses remaining, at Free Trade Wharf, Ratcliffe (1795), and the Dickens Inn at St Katharine, have queenpost trusses steeply pitched for common tiles. Welsh slate roofs and shallow pitches soon became the norm, although the exceptionally long roof trusses at West India No. 2 Warehouse (1802) supported upper slopes of copper. Trusses of over 50 ft (15 m) span were once common – some remain in the Pennington Street sheds at News International, Wapping (1811–13).

Security against theft and fire were the primary considerations, balanced against economy and convenience. The London Building Act of 1774 extended to the eastern parishes the rules already existing in the City for external walls and party-walls of brick, carried up as parapets above roof level. The dock companies were exempted but were keen to adhere because of the value of the goods stored. However, only the so-called Ivory House, St Katharine Docks (1858–60) wholeheartedly adopted incombustible, 'fireproof' construction with brick arches, here on wrought-iron beams, as newly advocated by Sir William Fairbairn. The same architect, *George Aitchison sen.*, used an early and very prominent plate girder in the now demolished 'H' warehouse of 1852.*

DOCK OFFICIALS' HOUSES overlooking the entrances to the London Docks, St Katharine Docks and the West India Docks are all roughly contemporary with the construction of the docks and share a restrained Neoclassical style with many London houses of the early to mid C19. Their distinguishing characteristic is the use of full-height bows on one or two façades, to overlook the river and to monitor the dock entrance. Those that flank
49 the former entrance to the London Docks at Wapping Pier Head are the terminal blocks of substantial terraces designed by *D. A. Alexander* in 1811–13 to make a fine gateway to the docks. The

*Transit sheds, now all demolished, used for temporary shelter of goods, did use early forms of iron roof from 1810 in the London Docks (details unknown) and 1813 at West India Docks, commissioned by *Rennie*. Corrugated-iron roofing was developed by *Henry Palmer* at the London Docks in 1829.

dockmasters' houses erected by the *Rennies* during the 1820s at Coldharbour and Manchester Road, Isle of Dogs and St Katharine Docks take the form of individual villas under pyramidal roofs.

Earlier C19 urban developments

New MAIN ROADS followed the Docks as their owners sought to improve the transport of valuable goods from the ships into the City. The Commercial Road (including the West India Dock Road) of 1802–4 and its tributary East India Dock Road (1806–12) conveyed so much traffic that the Commercial Road stoneway was laid along it in 1828–30, with slabs of granite to reduce the wear from heavy road wagons. To the E, an iron bridge by *John Rennie* spanned the River Lea in 1814 (replaced in a major road scheme of 1929–35) to ease access to the river port at Barking. Dock Street linked the London Docks to Whitechapel, enlarged after Commercial Street was opened in 1843 to provide access from the docks to N and W London. In the intervening years water transport was revolutionized with the development of CANALS. The Regent's Canal arrived at Limehouse in 1820, with its own dock entered from the river, now preserved as Limehouse Basin marina. It provided a direct connection to the Midlands and was for long the distributor of much seaborne coal and timber. Providing a link between the canal and the Lea Navigation from 1830 was the Hertford Union (or Duckett's) Canal skirting the N edge of Bethnal Green and Bow. The Lea Navigation was improved from the 1850s.

Though most of the docks were carved out of virgin land, the London and St Katharine Docks displaced the existing inhabitants who crowded into surviving houses, which quickly degenerated. Handsome properties soon became slums and the riverside hamlets burst their bounds and spread into new neighbourhoods N of Commercial and East India Dock Roads. Part of this area's development preceded the Docks and had been prompted by the cutting of New Road, through the estate of the London Hospital, to create a N–S link between Whitechapel and Wapping. The hospital began laying out new streets on the W side of the road in the 1790s but developed the area to its E only after 1810. The greatest tracts of land in Stepney and Ratcliffe belonged to the Mercers' Company. They exploited land cleared by the Ratcliffe fire in 1794 and started to build anew on the open land N of Commercial Road as far as the parish church of St Dunstan, E to Limehouse and W to Whitechapel. From 1814, their surveyor *George Smith* maintained control over the general character of the development and designed churches and schools for the estate, but the work was done by a myriad of local builders. Some, such as John Barnes, spawned a dynasty of builder–developers who were active in Mile End from the late C18 to the 1860s. Smith's pupil and partner *William Barnes* may have been a member of the same family. The best houses lay along the

principal roads. Three-storey terraces with decorative iron balconies still survive along parts of Commercial Road close to Limehouse and Ratcliffe, but the general character was more suited to a respectable artisan's pocket with streets and small
52 squares of modest terraces as at Arbour Square and Albert Gardens off Commercial Road. The freer vernacular of C18 housing was now replaced by considerable uniformity as similar houses were built on smaller estates throughout the East End. Small terraced houses frequently opened directly onto the street,
50 as can still be seen at Cyprus Street, Bethnal Green (*c.* 1850), and the Jesus Hospital Estate, Bethnal Green, built up in the 1860s. These were better than average and have survived; most of the early C19 East End's burgeoning populace were housed in cruder terraces and cottages, swept away in later clearances.

Superior PLANNED DEVELOPMENTS of the early C19 were few. Newby Place and Mountague Place, laid out round the new church of All Saints, Poplar, were modest imitators of the wealthier parts of late Georgian London. The only grand scheme, and the high point of this period, is the planned development of
51 *c.* 1830 around Tredegar Square, N of Bow Road on the estate of Sir Charles Morgan. It follows the West End fashion for terraces in a classical style. The houses are of three storeys above basements, three sides of the square are of brick with stucco trim, the fourth side is a grandiose palace frontage in the Nash manner, in stucco, with a giant Ionic order. This ambitious scheme came too late to create a lasting select residential district in East London and a similar effort to create a desirable enclave around Victoria Park in the 1840s was similarly ill-fated.

Earlier C19 religious buildings

For the Church of England at the start of the C19 religious inspiration came from the Evangelical movement, crystallized by the campaigning Clapham Sect; its interests, encompassing both the anti-slavery campaign and global missionary activity, drew in rich and influential figures. Anglican missions on the home front were spurred by the growth of Dissent and particularly the New Dissent of Methodism, especially in the rapidly expanding industrial areas where churches were thin on the ground. While Dissenting congregations were free to set up their chapels, until 1843 new Anglican churches needed an Act of Parliament to enable the raising of rates for the purpose. The difficulties that could be encountered are illustrated by the struggle to rebuild the C17 church of St Paul Shadwell, a local campaign begun in 1810, but opposed by the local ratepayers, including the London Dock Company. A special Act was eventually passed in 1817 and the church, together with schools and rectory, rebuilt in 1820–2 by *John Walters*, an architect trained by D.A. Alexander (architect to the London Dock Company). The church survives, its exterior in conservative classical style with a W spire in a Baroque tradition, the interior originally galleried, with shallow arches

on four sides. An Act was also passed in 1817 for an entirely
new church in Poplar, the fast expanding hamlet closest to the
new enclosed docks. All Saints Poplar, 1820–3 by *Charles Hollis*, 38
forming an ambitious centrepiece to the superior middle-class
quarter mentioned above, is a grand Grecian version of the
St Martin-in-the-Fields formula of tower and steeple set back
behind a pedimented portico. N and S porches with giant columns
in antis match the main W entrance. The church cost £35,000,
an unusually ambitious building for the East End, benefiting
from Poplar's rising prosperity. The dignified parsonage opposite the large, railed churchyard is also by *Hollis*. Church and
gatepiers make use of Devon granite, a novel feature, heralding
the import of the wider range of building materials available in
the C19. The building of clergy accommodation together with the
church also became common in the C19, when funds allowed.
But the amplitude and grandeur of the setting of All Saints
remained exceptional in the C19 East End.

The third church of this period, St Philip Stepney, 1818–20,
was rebuilt in the later C19. It was also by *Walters*, but pinnacled
Perp in style, built initially as a chapel for the newly developed
London Hospital Estate in Whitechapel. The costs were met by
William Cotton (†1866), partner in a cordage works at Limehouse and a future Governor of the Bank of England, who played
a significant role in the story of C19 church building in East
London. Cotton lived in Leytonstone, where he supported the
rebuilding of his local church, a traditional role for a wealthy
landowner, but his involvement with new churches in the poor
inner suburbs marked a new trend. William Cotton and his father
Joseph, a wealthy mariner, merchant and Deputy Master of
Trinity House, were among the influential lay churchmen associated with Joshua Watson, who provided evidence to the government for the need for new churches in 'populous parishes'. The Churches Act of 1818, which was the result, made
£1,000,000 available, and a further £500,000 added in 1824. But
the Church Commission only gave grants when a parish provided
a site, and their activity remained limited in the East End. One
of the few buildings which benefited from a substantial grant
(£17,346 out of the total coat of £18,226) was St John, Bethnal 42
Green, of 1826–8, a severe, impressive design by *Sir John Soane*, p. 553
with his idiosyncratic classical detail, but compromised by the
omission of the middle storey of the W tower on grounds of cost
and the later unsympathetic rebuilding of the interior after a fire.

A further source of funding, which appears also to have been
an initiative of William Cotton, was the Church Building Society
founded in 1818, incorporated in 1828, which collected voluntary
contributions and gave grants on certain conditions, among them
the undertaking that a number of seats would be free. The Society
contributed to many of the numerous churches built in the
1830s–40s in expanding centres of population that lay some way
from their parish churches, some of them also receiving small
parliamentary grants. In the outer areas these buildings ranged
from St John, Stratford, in relatively grand lancet Gothic, by 44

Edward Blore, 1832–4, to the tiny rural Noak Hill in an eclectic Tudor by *George Smith*, of 1841–2. The prolific Blore also provided new churches at Leytonstone, Plaistow (demolished), and Barkingside as well as two in Tower Hamlets. Blore's churches are mostly in an economical version of Gothic, although Barkingside and St Peter Stepney have Norman details. Whatever the style, the model at this time remained a preaching space with plenty of seating, and a minimal sanctuary. As requirements changed during the C19, none of these churches have stayed unaltered. But the towers that were a feature of this period remain distinctive, their spires and pinnacles skinny in comparison with later Victorian buildings, but at least with the merit of having been completed. The interiors of the most ambitious of Blore's buildings have a restrained elegance, visible in the impressive spare Gothic arcades of St John Stratford. A similar long-aisled interior, but a rather odd W front, was provided for the very large (former) Holy Trinity Bow (1834–9), by the local surveyors *D. & J. Austin*, which was begun with private funds as a proprietary chapel. Another ambitious effort is *Lewis Vulliamy*'s St Peter and St Paul Chingford, of 1844, paid for by the rector and lord of the manor, Robert Boothby Heathcote; it has an unusually elaborate exterior, making use of flint chequerwork and flushwork, an early example of the revival of traditional local building materials. To provide sufficient seating many of these churches were given galleries in the C18 tradition, invariably removed in the later C19; the barn-like interiors that could result, as at Chingford and Leytonstone, give a misleading impression of their original character. The much altered St Mary Ilford, 1829–31 by *James Savage*, has an interior which has suffered similarly, so has *John Shaw*'s St Peter in the Forest Walthamstow of 1840, which once must have been an unusual and appealing building, square and compact, with Lombard Romanesque detail. Shaw also built a major church in Tower Hamlets, Christ Church Watney Street, 1840–1 (lost in the Second World War), the only one which was fully funded by the Church Commissioners. It was a serious exercise in Romanesque with apse, twin W towers, and stone arcades to nave and gallery.

Church building in Tower Hamlets was encouraged by Charles Blomfield, Bishop of London 1828–56. Blomfield was a reformer who firmly believed that the solution to Anglican apathy was the redirection of diocesan resources to the building of more parish churches. His Metropolis Churches Fund was established in 1836 (William Cotton became treasurer) with an offshoot for building churches in Bethnal Green, one of the most deprived districts in London, whose population of *c.* 70,000 was hard hit by the decline of the London silk trade. The building campaign was successful; by 1850 Bethnal Green had ten buildings to supplement St Matthew and St John (the last, St Thomas, given by Cotton in memory of his son). Providing them with adequate clergy and filling the churches with congregations was another matter. Church attendance was in decline in the area from the 1880s, and decreased further with the influx of Jewish refugees. By the

end of the century it was recognized that the experiment had not been a success. Today only the first two of the new Bethnal Green churches remain in use: both designed by *Vulliamy* in the eclectic Norman style that was briefly popular in the 1840s: St Peter 43
of 1840–1, and St James the Less of 1842, much altered since Second World War damage. *Blore*'s more ambitious cruciform St James the Great, in red brick with Gothic lancets (1842), remains a major landmark in Bethnal Green Road, but like *William Railton*'s St Bartholomew (1843), it has been divided into flats.

From other religious buildings of the earlier C19 almost nothing is left, as the Roman Catholics and the Nonconformists were vigorous rebuilders in the later C19. Out in Havering are a couple of minor examples: at Upminster is a small Independent chapel of 1800 with classical front of 1847 (now part of an R.C. girls' school); at Romford the sober Salem Baptist Chapel, also 1847, is given a little style by its tapering Egyptian W window. Other distinguished buildings have gone, such as the Independent chapel on East India Dock Road by *William Hosking*, 1840–1, 'an unusual blend of Grecian and Italian Renaissance styles' (Colvin) paid for by a local philanthropist, the shipbuilder George Green (his almshouses of 1849 remain nearby). The earliest remaining example of the chapel with classical portico, a type which continued to be popular among nonconformists after it had been abandoned by the Anglicans, is the former chapel
(later synagogue and now Sikh temple) of 1854–5, at Bow, an 39
appropriate complement to the grand terraces of the nearby Tredegar Square.

VICTORIAN AND EDWARDIAN EAST LONDON

*The Railways, Docks and Riverside**

The second half of the C19 was dominated by new technologies and freedom of trade, heralded by the arrival of the RAILWAYS from the 1830s. The first was the London & Blackwall (earlier Commercial) Railway of 1836–40, which ran past the docks to the Brunswick Wharf steamer quay. The Eastern Counties Railway (later Great Eastern) opened in 1839–40 with a terminus at Shoreditch. Its works at Romford, partly preserved, were superseded by colossal repair shops and engineering works established slightly later at Stratford (demolished). It was concerned at first with long-distance traffic and less with the growing class of commuters into the city. Both the Blackwall and the Eastern Counties lines crossed the then built-up area from W to E upon distinctive, elliptical arched viaducts, with some grander arches across the canal dock at Limehouse. Over the years,

* Part of this account is adapted from Malcolm Tucker and Elizabeth Williamson's fuller introduction to *The Buildings of England: London Docklands*, 1998.

various goods stations, now gone, were built adjacent to them including the large two-level station at Bishopsgate (1881). Some late C19 railway warehouses remain in the Spitalfields area. The North London Railway of 1846–51 provided a necessary northward connection for goods and particularly coal from its small Poplar Dock, which was the first railway dock in London. From 1850 middle-class residents of Bow could use the North London's early commuter services to Fenchurch Street in the city via the new viaduct of the London & Blackwall Extension railway of 1849. Other stations were later opened in that area. The more proletarian, horse-drawn tramways started with a line from Whitechapel to Stratford opened in 1870. From 1874 the Great Eastern Railway (successor to the Eastern Counties), opened its terminus at Liverpool Street: its approaches displaced 7000 people in Bethnal Green, Spitalfields and Bishopsgate. For its impact on outer suburban development, *see* below. The underground railway system reached Whitechapel from the City in 1884, was extended via Mile End to Bromley-by-Bow in 1902 linking these with the London, Tilbury & Southend Railway, and was electrified through to East Ham in 1905.

Rail transport of goods made it possible to carve new docks out of cheap farmland miles from the City and drove the second boom in DOCK BUILDING, which began *c.* 1850. The speculative line from Stratford to the steam ferry at North Woolwich (1844–7) opened up a large new area for dock and industrial development. Its elegant Italianate terminus at North Woolwich (1854) and adjoining pleasure gardens were designed to promote the area. More importantly it unlocked the distant marshland of West Ham for the cheap and speculative promotion of the Victoria Dock in 1850–5 to accommodate the growing number of larger, longer ships and wide paddle steamers. Foreseeing further growth, the dock had the largest area of impounded water (94 acres) of any dock in the world. The Victoria Dock started a trade war, which culminated in its amalgamation with the London and St Katharine Docks in 1864–5. Further large docks proved worth developing, including the Millwall Docks, excavated out of the still-empty centre of the Isle of Dogs in 1863–9, and the Royal Albert Dock, adjoining Victoria Dock, in 1875–80. These dealt primarily in bulky imports from Europe and the growing Empire, such as foodstuffs and meat (in the Royals), timber (at Millwall) and grain. Parts of the older docks became rail-connected. The London & Blackwall Railway was extended down the Isle of Dogs mainly for goods traffic in 1865–72 and its link to the main-line system, first made in 1849, was strengthened by the Limehouse Curve of 1880. However the Royal Albert Dock's efficient layout for transfer direct to rail provoked the East and West India Dock Company to open a similar dock for still larger ships fifteen miles further down river at Tilbury in 1886, served by the London, Tilbury & Southend Railway. Such cut-throat overinvestment put a brake on further improvements until the Port of London Authority, created in 1909, began the King George V dock (completed 1921).

As works became larger, new CONSTRUCTION TECHNIQUES improved the economics. For the steamboat quay at Brunswick Wharf, Blackwall in 1832–4, *James Walker* had used cast-iron piles and sheeting, anchored by iron rods and backed with lime concrete, a development of the traditional timber wharf walls. *George Bidder* repeated the principle for the Victoria Dock, where his 80ft wide entrance lock, with wrought-iron lock gates, was almost twice as long and wide as previously seen in London. Mass concrete using Portland cement was incorporated in quay walls from then onwards, at first behind protective facings of brickwork. *J.M. Rendel*'s quay wall at Shadwell New Basin, 1854–8 (the London Docks' tactical response to the Victoria Dock), had piers of concrete and relieving arches below the water line, saving on brickwork while improving the balance of the wall. The Royal Albert Dock, 1875–80, used walls with a mechanically efficient stepped back and a projecting toe. By then concrete had improved sufficiently to be left exposed on the face. The Royal Albert also used steam-powered excavators for the first time.

Changes were made to the layout of quays in the new docks. The Victoria Dock not only had the usual long ranges of warehouses on broad quays, of which the surviving K–R warehouses (1859) are notable survivors, but also finger jetties, supporting small warehouses, to maximize the length of quayside within the plan area. These jetties were cramped and turntables had to be used for access by railway wagons; they also restricted the length of ships. They were abolished in the 1930s. The Royal Albert Dock returned to long quays on which cranes and railway wagons could readily travel, backed by transit sheds for the sorting of cargoes. They set the pattern for the King George V Dock and later improvements.

The cranes, capstans, swing bridges and lock gates of the early docks were entirely manually powered. HYDRAULIC POWER, the use of high-pressure water pumped through mains to drive mechanical equipment, swept through the London docks in the early 1850s, as soon as the weight-loaded accumulator had been invented. Accumulator towers to hold this pressure-regulating device may be seen in several places, notably the Regent's Canal Dock (Limehouse Basin) and Poplar Docks, while hydraulic pumping station buildings remain at Wapping, Blackwall, East India Dock. While the dock companies had their independent systems, the London Hydraulic Power Company at Wapping provided hydraulic mains under the Central London streets from 1893, and to the great benefit of riverside wharves and the area to their N.

While the dock companies struggled financially, the later C19 was a boom time for riverside wharves after duties had been removed from most imported goods and all exports, the corn trade freed of import restrictions and regulation of the remaining dutiable goods simplified. Large WAREHOUSES now spread along the waterfront, housing goods such as grain and spices, though the dockside warehousing maintained a hold on wool, tobacco, sugar and spirits. These could be handsome buildings, such as Metropolitan Wharf, Wapping of the 1860s. Oliver's Wharf, Wapping (1869–70) has contrasting coloured brick dressings with Gothic ornament but this was a rarity. Jetties were added to allow ships to berth, from the late C19. Powered cranes were used on the waterside and goods then passed through the warehouse and were lowered to road vehicles on the landward side. As wharves expanded and landside warehouses added, the streets were bridged by tiers of iron gangways for goods to be wheeled across on barrows. Once widespread, they have been preserved N of the river only at Dundee Wharf, Wapping High Street.

Massive warehouses grew up in the hinterland of the docks and along the City fringe, not only along new roads, such as Commercial Street (1843) but also the railways. Most important was the London, Tilbury & Southend railway's colossal warehouse of 1886 (demolished) in Goodman's Fields, E of Leman Street, where hydraulic power was used to lower wagons from the high level viaduct. Its pumping station survives. Close by, in Back Church Lane, are contemporary wool warehouses by *Holland & Hannen* for Brown & Eagle. In the same decade the Co-operative Wholesale Society built the first of its mighty warehouses along Leman Street and Prescot Street, Whitechapel, creating a canyon-like scale in a once residential district. Many other smaller warehouses grew up around Dock Street, Commercial Road and Commercial Street, while others remain along Middlesex Street, the heart of the second-hand clothing market.

Manufacturing and Industry

As SHIPBUILDING started to move from wood to iron in the 1830s, shipyards were established in the Isle of Dogs, notably the Millwall Ironworks. There the engineering workshop where parts of *I.K. Brunel*'s Leviathan *ss Great Eastern* were built still remains, together with part of the special slipway built in 1854 to launch it sideways into the Thames. Shipbuilding crashed in the 1860s and moved elsewhere. The last big shipyard, the Thames Iron Works on Bow Creek, closed in 1912. The old riverside dry docks continued in use until the late C19 in Wapping and Limehouse, with later ones on the Isle of Dogs. Remains may be seen at Orchard Dock, Blackwall, and at the site of Blackwall Yard – the latter in use until the 1980s. The curious Pontoon Dock (1858) at the Victoria Dock, where ships were lifted hydraulically on to floating platforms, was the first of several repair facilities within the trading docks added as attractions to dock users. Dry docks can be seen at Millwall Dock (1868) and Blackwall Basin, West India (1878). There were three dry docks with major workshops in the later Royal Docks, where repairs to big ships continued until closure in 1980. The workshop for smaller repairs in the London Docks is now the John Orwell Sports Centre, Wapping.

London's ENGINEERING interests spread far wider than shipbuilding, and there were numerous works, particularly in Millwall, making equipment such as anchor chains, screw propellers, grain elevators and swing bridges and serving also the wider construction needs of London and the Empire. Rope walks had earlier been a common feature of the back lands, while remains of sailmaking factories survive at No. 11 West India Dock Road and No. 777 Commercial Road, Limehouse. The latter was adapted after 1889 for Caird & Rayner who made salt-water distillation plant for ships. Their additions include the rare survival of a galleried workshop. The Trinity House yard where buoys and lightships were maintained, at Orchard Place, Leamouth, has the unexpected feature of an experimental lighthouse. 66

MANUFACTURING of every sort continued, as commonly in the home and small workshops as in factories, and the products of the C19 East End – from furniture to sweets – were startling in their variety. Some continued the traditions of earlier centuries: many of London's arms makers, for example, kept workshops in Whitechapel and St George's to be close to the armouries at the Tower and the Proof House of the Gunmakers' Co., which still stands in Commercial Road behind a smart frontage of 1820. Silk weaving had been on the wane from the late C18 and mutated into a mass clothing industry of immense size but grinding impoverishment for a large proportion of Whitechapel, Spitalfields and Bethnal Green's population. Bootmaking and second-hand clothing were associated with Jewish businesses, so too cigar manufacture. Godfrey Phillips's cigarette factory, in Commercial Street from the 1840s, was rebuilt and extended stylishly over the course of a century. Furniture makers occupied small workshops S of Hackney Road.

Many process industries were also carried on in downwind East London. Foremost among these were major BREWERIES and DISTILLERIES. Most have been demolished and none survive in production. The brewing trade entered a period of unparalleled expansion with the removal of Beer Duty in 1830 and the improved transport of hops and grain from East Anglia and Kent. Major expansion began almost at once at Truman's Black Eagle Brewery in Brick Lane, now the one brewery to retain buildings from the C18–C20. From Charringtons at Mile End only their Baroque-style former offices survive. Mann Crossman & Paulin's Albion Brewery, Whitechapel, retains its frontage including an energetic relief of St George and the Dragon. The compact building of the St George's model brewery of 1847 remains in Commercial Road. Of the once colossal Ind Coope brewery at Romford, only meagre parts of the 1850s rebuilding remain.

Noxious industries were progressively moved further E to the fringe of the built-up area, especially after 1844 when the Metropolitan Building Act proscribed such activity within the metropolis. Sugar refineries survived in Whitechapel until the

1870s when the business went into decline. The smaller works were replaced by warehouses while larger firms now set up within Essex at West Ham and East Ham: Tate's were at Silvertown from 1878 and Lyle's nearby from 1881. It was in such areas along the Thames and N into the Lea Valley that industry now flourished. Imported raw materials and local coal-gas by-products gave rise to numerous works in the late C19 and C20. The Isle of Dogs, Bow Creek, Silvertown, Bromley-by-Bow, Old Ford and Stratford had soapworks, vegetable-fat processors, tar works, oil works, paint factories, dye works chemical works, fertilizer works, sugar refineries, sweet factories, food preservers, metals processors, telegraph-cable works and many others.

The most important surviving industrial complex in the whole of East London is the former Bryant and May match factory at Bow, founded in 1860 and extended after 1874. It was supplied by a wharf on the Lea and the adjacent railway. The construction of a new factory in 1909–11 by *Holman & Goodrham* with fire-precautionary water tower gave it a silhouette reminiscent of an Italian hill town. The company was highly progressive for its date, its production based on Swedish models and with exceptional standards of accommodation, including picturesque groups of cottages for senior employees, but was made notorious by the match girls' strike in 1888. Within its sight is the area known as Fish Island at Old Ford, built up in the late C19 with a mixture of industry and housing, the latter now gone.

From *c.* 1880–1900 industrial buildings began to make use of mild STEEL for construction although building regulations in inner London did not allow independent steel frames before 1909 (even after that date steelwork had to be clad for fire protection, see for example the printworks, Smeed Road, Fish Island). Early C20 factories increased in size, for example Spratt's Dog Biscuit factory at Limehouse Cut, often processing imported raw materials. REINFORCED CONCRETE was increasingly used from 1900; the surviving jetty at Dagenham Dock is an early example and the PLA made bold use of it in the Docks, although almost nothing survives. The more widespread use of the material was in private warehouses and factories where until 1916 it has to be concealed by brickwork.

Service industries developed prodigiously in the C19. The early WATERWORKS at Shadwelled from the C17 and West Ham, from the mid C18, were superseded by the East London Water Works Company's large establishment of 1807–9 at Old Ford on the Lea. Theirs was the first waterworks to adopt the Cornish type of steam engine, in 1838. From 1834, an aqueduct brought sweeter water from Lea Bridge, but treatment at Old Ford ceased after the 1836 cholera epidemic was traced to its reservoirs. The Lea Bridge works of 1852 continued until the 1970s; the magnificent Italianate engine houses have gone but the filter beds are preserved. The first of many reservoirs at Walthamstow were opened in 1863, and during the C20 the Metropolitan Water Board extended them N to beyond Chingford. Among the company's other scattered pumping stations are an Italianate tower of 1864 at The Coppermill, Walthamstow, and lively work of 1890–1903 commissioned by the engineer *W.B. Bryan* – variously Arts and Crafts of Germanic styling, with shapely roofs at Chingford Mill and Ferry Lane, a domestic gabled grouping at Wanstead, and English Baroque at Greaves Pumping Station, South Chingford. The neighbouring South Essex Water Company perpetuated the Italianate style at Dagenham and Roding Lane.

The cholera outbreak of 1866 convinced health reformers that the disease was water-borne. Previous outbreaks were London-wide but in 1866 only East London remained unconnected to the new system of SEWERS designed in 1859–68 by *Sir Joseph Bazalgette*, engineer to the Metropolitan Board of Works. Large-diameter interceptor sewers run deep underground from W to E. Those to the N of the river, originally three in number, collect all the sewage from inner North London. They convey it to the Northern Outfall Sewer, which crosses East London within a raised embankment (now the Greenway) from Old Ford to treatment works at Beckton, East Ham, where it originally discharged into the Thames. The drainage from the lowest of the interceptor sewers, and from such low-lying areas as the Isle of Dogs and 67
West Ham, must be pumped to the level of the outfall sewer. Particularly is magnificent Abbey Mills pumping station close to Stratford. The original building of 1865–8 by *Charles Driver* of the MBW remains one of the greatest sights along the flat marshy land of the Lea in a hybrid Gothic–Byzantine style with a lantern lighting the ornate cast-iron interior.

The world's first GAS company, the 'Chartered' Gas Light and Coke Co. of 1812, failed to supply the districts E of the City, so other enterprises stepped in at Whitechapel in 1815 and more particularly the Ratcliffe Gas Co. in the Wapping area from 1823 and the Commercial Gas Co. at Stepney from 1837. Yet other companies exploited East London's advantages, including a tolerance of air pollution, to make gas for sale elsewhere. Among them, the Imperial Gas Company built its Bromley works on Bow Creek from 1870. While waterside sites were favoured, for delivery of coal by barge, the Gas Light and Coke Co. went one better, developing from 1868 a huge site on the East Ham marshes where sea-going collier ships discharged directly to the works at riverside jetties. The area was named Beckton after the company's governor. With modernization, this was to remain the world's largest gasworks until the making of coal gas finished there in 1969. The chief reminder of this industry is the GASHOLDERS, with their prominent guide frames, and East London retains a lion's share of elegant examples. The Imperial Gas Company pioneered the type with classical cast-iron columns arranged in two superimposed orders in 1857–8 at Bethnal Green. One of 1866 remains there and seven of 1872–82 are clustered at Bromley-by-Bow, all with guilloche-patterned girders. At Beckton, one holder of 1876–9 has distinctive buttress-like columns in latticed cast iron. Latticed wrought iron then came in, of which there are exquisitely tapered columns and girders in one holder at the Poplar gas works, South Bromley. Much taller holders with lattice frames of sophisticated design and mostly of steel are seen at Bethnal Green (1889), Beckton (1892) and Poplar (1929) together with C20 replacements of the spiral-guided, frameless type.

Crossing the Thames was assisted by several notable engineering endeavours. Ferries had been the chief mode of crossing E of London Bridge but the expansion of the docks and the eastern suburbs soon required a proper road crossing. This was finally achieved with TOWER BRIDGE in 1885–94, which became the symbolic gateway to the City and, eventually, a much-loved London landmack. Only Victorian engineering – a steel structure and hydraulically-powered bascules – made possible a crossing that could still allow passage of large ships. Earlier subaqueous experiments had culminated in the first THAMES TUNNEL, achieved against all odds through the ingenuity and heroic perseverance of *Sir Marc Brunel,* 1825–43. Intended as a road crossing from Rotherhithe to Wapping, it was opened to pedestrians only. It subsequently served the East London Railway (now East London Line), of 1865–76 by *Sir John Hawkshaw*. The publicly financed Blackwall Tunnel followed in 1891–7 (Act of 1887), built with the aid of compressed air. It was duplicated in 1960–7. Following its success, the LCC built another road tunnel from Limehouse to Rotherhithe (1904–8) and foot tunnels accessed by stairs and lifts at Greenwich (1897–1902) and Woolwich (1909–12). By then Woolwich also had a Free Ferry, managed by the LCC from 1889, with floating landing stages, as a balance to the freeing of toll bridges in W London.

Housing and Urban Improvements after 1840

With increasing industrial activity in the East End, and the expansion of its population through increased immigration, its appeal as a residential area diminished. Some industrial expansion was accompanied by speculatively built WORKERS' HOUSING, often of a deplorably low standard. On the Isle of Dogs from *c.* 1840, several landowners exploited the land between docks and riverside wharves for unexceptional terraced housing (largely demolished after Second World War damage). Similar terraces were also built in the communities planted as new industrial settlements, such as Cubitt Town, begun on the Isle of Dogs by William Cubitt in 1842, and Silvertown, started in West Ham by the rubber manufacturer Abram Silver in the 1850s. Hallsville and Canning Town were brought into being to serve the Thames Iron Works of C.J. Mare & Co. at Bow Creek and grew further to serve the Victoria Dock after 1850. Their reputation was appalling. At Stratford in the 1840s a whole new town of mean cottages was created to serve the massive works of the Eastern Counties Railway and named after its boosterish chairman, Hudson. It was entirely rebuilt after the Second World War. Housing for the Gas Light and Coke Co.'s new township of Beckton was laid out complete with institute and chapel from 1868: the handsome Italianate terraces along Winsor Terrace are the only remains.

The slum conditions of the new industrial districts provoked immediate condemnation from writers such as Dickens but it was the continued existence of squalid tenemented C17 and C18 property that inspired the first generation of IMPROVED HOUSING in the East End. The earliest venture was by the self-explanatory Metropolitan Association for Improving the Dwellings of the Industrious Classes, established in Spitalfields in 1841. Its approach was primarily commercial and intended to assuage the housing shortage by producing small profits sufficient to satisfy shareholders and fund the next venture. The first scheme at St Pancras paid for buildings in Spicer Street, Spitalfields, in 1848–50 with large blocks for family dwellings and a lodging house, the Artizan's Home, which also contained communal facilities of a library, kitchen and reading room to serve the estate. The design was by *William Beck*, who later added the surviving rows of two-storey cottage flats (Victoria Cottages, 1857 60
and Albert Cottages, 1865). These sweet buildings, with doorways paired under shared brick lintels are divided by a pathway between tiny gardens. At a time when the imperative was to build high, this homely, low-rise layout was unique for a profit-minded building company. It must, however, have fitted neatly with the small scale of their surroundings. Private (i.e. entirely charitable) schemes started with considerable ambition at Nova Scotia Gardens in Bethnal Green, where Miss (later Baroness) Burdett-Coutts created Columbia Dwellings in 1859–62 (demolished 1958). Her adviser for an appropriate site was Dickens, her architect *H.A. Darbishire*, who created a formal layout of grimly functional Gothic five-storey blocks set around a courtyard. The buildings had shared lavatories and sculleries with drying yards-cum-playgrounds in the attics. These features, including rows of shaped gables along the upper floor, reappeared in Darbishire's experimental design for the newly established Peabody Trust in 1863–4 at Commercial Street, Spitalfields, on a corner site with ground-floor shops. Thereafter Gothic was eschewed and formal, plainly designed, four- to five-storey blocks became standard for all Peabody's estates, which quickly became famous for the spartan, unplastered interiors where wallpaper was forbidden. The design for their estates scarcely varied in forty years (estates at Shadwell 1866, Royal Mint 1880 and Bethnal Green 1910 have only minor stylistic variations).

The commercial ventures continued with greater success from 1862 with Sydney Waterlow's Improved Industrial Dwellings Co., which became the major provider of housing in the East End for two decades, setting out to provide a return of 5 per cent to investors and affordable homes for artisans. In collaboration with his builder *Matthew Allen*, Waterlow developed a standard design from a 'cottage-dwelling' shown by *Henry Roberts* at the Great Exhibition in 1851. This basic symmetrical unit could be adapted laterally as a continuous terrace and vertically as a tall block.

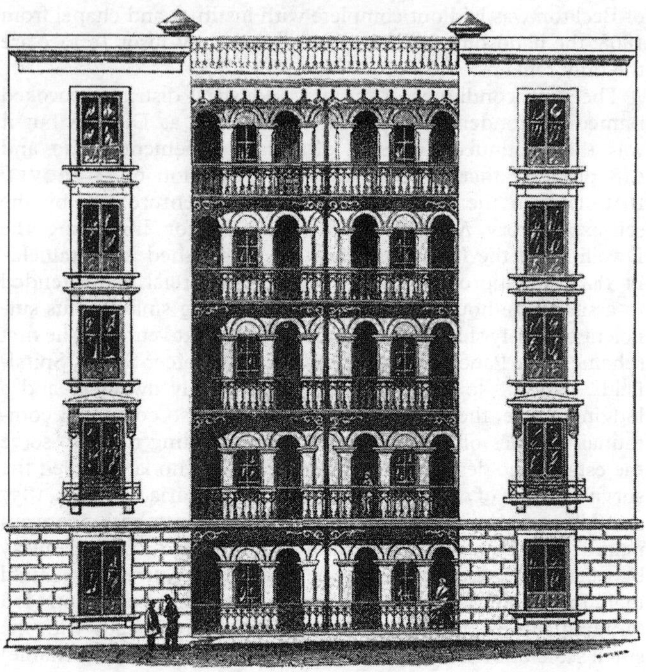

Typical tenement by the Improved Industrial Dwellings Co.

The first block was in Shoreditch and the identical group at Wapping (1864) demonstrates this principle and has the company's standard feature of a central, recessed, open staircase with small access balconies in front, serving flats on the upper floors. These were considered more hygienic than the enclosed stairs and corridors of the Peabody blocks and more dignified in having self-contained flats with private lavatories and sculleries projecting at the rear. From 1867 government loans made it possible to build on a grander scale. Series of blocks appeared at Columbia Road, Bethnal Green in 1872 and as a complete urban scheme of several entire streets (Corfield Street, Wilmot Street), also in Bethnal Green, up to 1890. Their visual treatment was varied, the earlier buildings are flat fronted, soon superseded by dwellings with increasingly decorative bay windows (using pre-cast components), iron railings and, eventually, semi-enclosed staircases. Ready-made sash windows imported from Sweden were another innovation.

The 1880s produced far reaching changes in the scale and ambition of new housing as other building companies began to appear with an ambition to reach the poorest class of tenant for whom the rents of the earlier companies were too high. An important spur was the 1875 Artisans' and Labourers' Dwellings Act, which for the first time made it possible not only for local authorities to purchase and demolish whole streets of unfit housing but also required them to rehouse as many people as had originally occupied the site. In London this responsibility for clearance fell to the Metropolitan Board of Works with the job of rehousing to be undertaken by private developers or building companies. But few were willing to pay the prices for acquisition and far fewer schemes were completed than was deemed necessary. The East End Dwellings Co. was founded by Samuel Barnett, Vicar of St Jude, Whitechapel, in 1884. He experimented at first with management of existing houses in nearby Wentworth Street, on the model of direct contact between landlord and tenant espoused by Barnett's mentor Octavia Hill. They were eventually replaced by model tenements designed by *Elijah Hoole*, Hill's architect for housing schemes elsewhere in London. Lord Rothschild's Four Per Cent Jewish Industrial Dwellings Co. was founded in 1885 and attempted to address the squalid overcrowding experienced by the increasing number of Jewish immigrants to Spitalfields, Whitechapel and Stepney. Both companies were actively involved in the first two East End slum clearances after 1875. The first was a notorious site behind the Royal Mint in 1884, followed by building on a more extensive scale at Flower and Dean Street, Spitalfields, from 1885, where Rothschild employed *N.S. Joseph* to erect staggeringly austere and tall six-storey blocks of tenements with sparing detail (demolished). The only surviving EEDC dwellings of this period is the uncharacteristically plain Museum House, Roman Road, Bethnal Green, of 1888 by *Davis & Emmanuel*, who designed all the company's buildings. Much friendlier red brick and terracotta were used to mellow the appearance of the large tenements erected by both companies during the 1890s at Stepney Green, where *N.S. Joseph*'s Stepney Green Court, and *Davis & Emmanuel*'s Dunstan Houses vie for importance across the verdant setting of the Green. Each was generously planned; they share imaginative rooflines of gables and turrets with stucco decorative embellishment. The greater-attention architectural character is clearly influenced by the LCC's Boundary Street Estate (*see* below). At Globe Road, Bethnal Green, the last major development of the EEDC accompanied its tenements with delightful rows of cottages. By 1900 numerous smaller schemes had also been undertaken by the Guinness and Sutton trusts.

Tenants of improved housing were often subject to highly restrictive management, which discouraged not only those for whom regular wages were rare but also those whose work had to be carried out in the home. There was therefore plenty of opportunity for private developers to take advantage both of small slum clearance areas considered unprofitable by the building companies and land where buildings leases were falling in. This was the case of the London Hospital Estate, Whitechapel, where late C18 properties were cleared and replaced by unadorned red brick tenements built by *Hyman & Israel Davis*, part of an extended family of speculative builders who were active throughout Whitechapel, Spitalfields and Bethnal Green from the 1890s. They, and their relations, usually employed architects and their buildings are often distinguished by good detail, as in the stepped-gabled terrace at Hanbury Street, Spitalfields, by *J.R. Moore-Smith*. Several of their buildings are indistinguishable from model housing. The tenements with open staircases at Fieldgate Mansions, Whitechapel, were designed for the firm by *Rowland Plumbe & Harvey*. Private developers often included attic workrooms or separate ranges for workshops as at Mansford Street, Bethnal Green, by the Hackney builder *Charles Winckley*.

The setting of an agreeable architectural stamp on mass housing was given its greatest boost by the advent of the LCC as the London-wide authority to replace the MBW. The Housing Act 1890 extended its power to carry out wholesale slum clearance and rehousing itself, for which it established a Housing Branch in 1893. In the same year it began work on the Bound-
78 ary Street Estate at Bethnal Green. This was a watershed in
p. 587 housing design and set out with the avowed intention of provid-
ing a type of housing not only more attractive than earlier improved housing but also comparable to middle-class mansion flats of the same decade. Its layout of asymmetrical blocks arranged around a circus with terraced gardens and a bandstand as its focal point was a notable departure in planning. Above all, visual interest was created by individual designs for each block, with a variety of shaped gables and façades enlivened by patterned and coloured brick. A wash house, shops, schools and rows of workshops completed the estate as a self-sufficient district. The enterprise was ambitious and costly and, though Westminster's similar Millbank Estate followed before 1900, nothing else of this sophistication was attempted again in the East End. The large blocks of the LCC's Solander Gardens Estate, Shadwell, of 1901 are far simpler, but the refined aesthetic can be seen on a smaller scale elsewhere: at the row of cottages at Goldsmith's Row off Hackney Road (for the overspill from Boundary Street) and the small cottages in Cranford Street, Ratcliffe. The Housing Act of 1890 also paved the way for municipal housing by other local authorities. West Ham built cottage flats soon after the formation of the County Borough, East Ham followed suit in 1902 – a survivor is Brooks Avenue, East Ham by *A.H. Campbell*. But of the three East London boroughs created in 1900 within the LCC area, only Stepney erected housing in the years before 1914, on a limited scale with small groups of flats, e.g. Potter Dwellings, Limehouse Causeway of 1904. Poplar and Bethnal Green failed to build any housing until the 1920s.

The creation of PARKS and preservation of OPEN SPACES is as important an aspect of Victorian and Edwardian urban improvements as new housing. In the earlier period this meant the government's creation in 1841 of the spacious Victoria Park, to provide an essential 'green lung' at the heart of the East End, picturesquely laid out by *James Pennethorne* with lakes, a gravelled drive and varied planting. For the rest of the East End, efforts were concentrated on protecting what survived of ancient greens and common land. Bethnal Green had first been protected by the foresight of its C17 inhabitants entrusting it for the poor. An Act of 1868, passed at the time of the building of the Museum (*see* below) secured part of it as ornamental gardens. The remainder was finally saved in 1895 by the LCC. Elsewhere the pickings were meagre. The Metropolitan Gardens Association acquired for public recreation the remains of Stepney Green in 1872, a small burial ground in Vallance Road (1880), the large churchyard of St Dunstan in 1887, and the former Victoria Park Cemetery, Bethnal Green, which was reopened as Meath Gardens in 1893. The LCC's creation of Edward VII Memorial Park at Shadwell from 1910 was the first new park for the East End in fifty years.

In the new suburbs there was pressure to open formerly private parks of older mansions to the public – West Ham Park in 1874, Valentine's Park, Ilford, in 1896, Raphael's Park, Romford, in 1904. They were usually adapted with the familiar amenities of Victorian parks: boating lakes, bandstands and refreshment pavilions. Only rarely have the mansions, as at Valentine's, survived to serve as community buildings. From *c.* 1890 numerous small parks and recreation grounds were also laid out to add diversity to the emerging suburbs and as an incentive to prospective buyers. Of wider importance and as a preventative to the onward growth of East London were the efforts to preserve the remains of the Forest of Essex, reduced by encroachment from the late C18 and partially cleared and enclosed during the mid C19. A campaign led by Edward North Buxton of Knighton House, Woodford, secured its transfer in 1878 to the Corporation of London, who opened it to the public as Epping Forest in 1882. Small parts of forest at Highams Park, Woodford and Chingford were added later and still penetrate deep into the edges of the suburbs. Buxton followed this in 1902 by encouraging the LCC to acquire the remains of Hainault Forest and adjoining farmland, which was returned to forest and heathland and opened to the public.

Religious Buildings in the Inner Suburbs from the 1840s to 1914

In the overcrowded East End social welfare generally was of greater concern than architectural embellishment. St Paul Dock Street, by *Henry Roberts* (1846–7), is a typically plain, minimally Gothic building, founded as a chapel connected with the nearby seamen's hostel. It took some time for the churches of the East End to be affected either by Pugin's advocacy of correct medieval Gothic, taken up by the Cambridge Camden Society (founded 1839), or by the revival of ritual which followed on from the Oxford Movement, both of which were to transform much future Anglican church building. An early example of more consciously medievalizing Gothic, with walls of ragstone and E.E. plate tracery windows, is St Mary, Cable Street, Ratcliffe, a mission church built through the efforts of William Quekett, the energetic vicar of Christ Church, Watney Street, with donations from Lord

Haddo. It dates from 1848–50, an early work by *F. J. Francis*. The extensive mission work of the East End clergy and their helpers, which included not only church services but children's schools and adult evening classes, more often took place in makeshift accommodation for many years, while spare funds went towards women's and convalescent homes and other social benefits. This was the pattern in the case of the pioneering work of Father Charles Lowder in the slums of Wapping. He began as a curate at St George-in-the-East in 1856, but his church, St Peter London Docks, was not built until 1865 and was still incomplete at his death in 1881. Lowder believed in the value of ritual, inaugurating services with vestments, street processions and outdoor preaching, and despite initial hostility, won over the local population through his dedication during the cholera outbreaks. The clergy did not have an easy task. The Low Church suspicion of ritual practices (given some support by the sympathies of Blomfield's successor, Bishop Tait) gave rise in 1859–60 to regular riots at St George-in-the-East, which for nearly a year became 'the zoo and horror and coconut-shy' of London.*

Meanwhile the churches of the Roman Catholics, who had a strong following among the numerous Irish immigrants of the East End, were beginning to make an impact. Soon after the Roman Catholic hierarchy was re-established in 1850, earlier chapels began to be replaced by confidently ambitious Gothic buildings. *William Wardell*'s fine cruciform St Mary and St Joseph, Poplar, 1851–5 in Puginian Gothic, replaced a chapel of 1818. This church was destroyed in the Second World War, but two significant landmarks remain: St Mary and St Michael, Commercial Road, Shadwell, of 1856, also by *Wardell*, for a congregation which traced its origins to a mission of 1762; and St
47 Anne, Mile End New Town, built in 1853–5 by *Gilbert Blount* in serious E.E. Gothic, replacing a chapel of 1848. In both cases their E ends are not as originally conceived, but they retain their impressively long Gothic naves, anticipating huge congregations. St Anne is supplied with an unusually large number of built-in confessionals to accommodate the Marist fathers who served the church from 1850, based in the adjacent large and severe Gothic presbytery.

What was the nature of the Anglican churches after 1850? Architecturally most of the survivors in Tower Hamlets are minor, compared with mid-Victorian churches elsewhere in London, though one must remember that many have vanished and that the survivors often suffered badly in the Second World War.† Christ Church, 1852–4 by *Frederick Johnstone*, given by the

* *See* Owen Chadwick, *The Victorian Church*, I, 1966, 499.

† For a complete account of the churches of Stepney see Gordon Barnes, *Stepney Churches*, 1967. In both Stepney and Poplar the disappearance of churches was speeded by the Second World War, although a limited number were rebuilt. Stepney had 34 Anglican churches by the 1870s, 26 of them new in the C19, from which a dozen survive, not all in Anglican use. Of the borough of Poplar's 23 Anglican church buildings existing in 1901 (all except four dating from after 1830), 7 remain in some form.

developer William Cubitt as the focal point (and now almost the sole survivor) of his Cubitt Town on the Isle of Dogs is unexciting in its detail, but has a good spire and the features demanded by the Ecclesiologists: a long chancel and lofty open roof. The notable collection of furnishings (now a rarity in the East End), which includes some from other churches in the Isle of Dogs, are a reminder of the popularity of the trappings of High Church ceremonial by the end of the C19. A similar witness is the memorable interior of Charles Lowder's church, St Peter London 46
Docks, Wapping by *F.H. Pownall*, 1865, but completed only from 1884 by *Maurice Adams*, without much of the intended carving. The church is a forceful and individual work, its dynamic internal polychromy as daring as in Butterfield's buildings. The group which surrounded it, Clergy house, Sisters' house and school survive only in part, but enough to underline the aspirations of such a centre. Elsewhere one may find only fragments of these groups, for example the tough Gothic vicarage of the demolished St Stephen, Commercial Street, 1860–1 by *Ewan Christian*.

As industrial London spread eastward so did the Victorian churches, providing new focal points in the spreading suburbs. St Michael, by the local *R.W. Morris*, 1864–5, now flats, is not specially distinguished but its funny clock tower-cum-spire is a cheering sight in a monotonous part of Poplar. But it cannot quite compete in eccentricity with *W.M. Teulon*'s curious recasting of the old Poplar chapel as St Matthias, which wrapped the C17 building in ragstone, added clumsy tracery windows and crowned it with a very curious lead-covered spire. St Saviour, one of the few older buildings to remain in this part of Poplar, is another Gothic church by *Francis*, 1873–4, once part of a mighty group with school (demolished) and vicarage, towering above a sea of small streets. It was funded with help from the Wigram family of Walthamstow, associates of the Cottons.

Across the Lea are some of the most outstanding among later Victorian churches. Two now have other functions. St Mark 45
Silvertown, of 1860–2 (adapted as a music hall) is one of *S.S. Teulon*'s dramatically individual buildings, with a powerful tower and spire rising over the chancel behind its apsed end. The melancholy poetry of the blackened and deserted structure in a desolate setting has vanished, but recent cleaning has revealed Teulon's virtuoso detail with its exotic brick and terracotta polychromy. At Canning Town an even mightier apse rears up among post-war housing: *Giles & Gane*'s St Luke (1873–5). An ingenious conversion allows glimpses at E and W end of its dramatically tall interior and mosaic-clad apse. Further E at Plaistow is the powerful St Andrew by *James Brooks*, remaining in use though insensitively divided, built 1868–70 in the sturdy French Early Gothic that was a popular source at this time, complete with vicarage and school. At Old Ford is St Paul with St Stephen, 1873–8 by *Newman & Billing*, an impressive example of the economical church designed for maximum capacity, with long, broad nave, passage aisles, and clerestory, which became a standard later C19 type and continued in modified form into the C20.

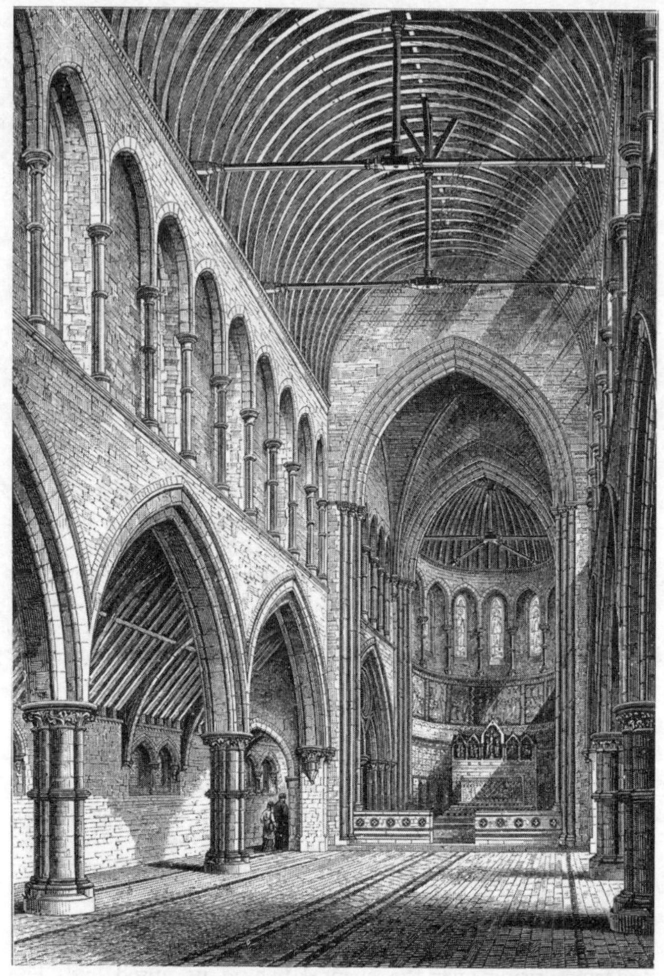

St Andrew, Plaistow, by James Brooks, 1868–70, interior

Few Anglican churches were built in Stepney in the late C19, for the area was by then well supplied. The distinguished exception is the former St Philip (well converted as the library of London Hospital), rebuilt in 1888–92 by *Arthur Cawston*. It is easily overlooked, lacking the intended tower, as happened so often at this time. The tall expanses of exterior orange brickwork conceal a splendidly accomplished interior, serious vaulted Gothic on a cathedral scale, reminiscent of Pearson.

Roman Catholic churches of the later C19 are varied: Our Lady and St Catherine, Bow, by *Blount* 1869–70, is rather pedestrian ragstone Gothic, the more original English Martyrs, Prescot Street, by *Pugin & Pugin*, is a galleried Gothic building crammed into a tight site, and the most unexpected St Patrick, Wapping, by *F.W. Tasker*, 1877, is in the form of a grand classical Roman basilica with austere pedimental gable.

Some of the NONCONFORMIST ARCHITECTURE of the second half of the C19 was grander than ever before, but little remains of its buildings. The figures revealed by a survey of 1902–3 showed that in East London total Nonconformist attendance exceeded that of the Anglicans.* In Tower Hamlets on a single day the three biggest Baptist chapels each drew in over one thousand people. Attendance at the Shoreditch Tabernacle in Bethnal Green, the Poplar and Bromley Baptist Tabernacle, and the Berger Hall, Poplar was rivalled only by a handful of Anglican and Roman Catholic churches.† But the grand chapels suffered badly in the Second World War and their only substantial C19 relic, though a most interesting one, is the Sunday School p. 558
building of the Shoreditch Tabernacle, built by *George Baines* in 1890–1, on a horseshoe plan with classrooms on two levels opening off a central hall. On quite a different scale, one of the most attractive survivals is the chapel built for Scottish Presby- 41
terian shipworkers on the Isle of Dogs (now The Space), 1859 by *T.E. Knightley*, a tiny exercise in Italian Romanesque polychromy, with innovative roof trusses of laminated timber. Drawing on similar Italian sources is the handsome chapel in Bethnal Green built for Congregationalists by *W.D. Church* in 1880, but soon 40
sold to Unitarians. Other chapels turned to Gothic already in the mid C19: for example, the former Wesleyan Mission church in Hackney Road, 1841, and Pott Street Chapel, Bethnal Green by *John Tarring*, 1849 (once a fine building but now much mutilated). But apart from a few minor buildings of the end of the C19 in Bow, little remains in Tower Hamlets from the dozens of places of worship of different Christian sects listed in Mudie-Smith's book. They included a number of churches for foreign congregations, some of which had a long history; all have disappeared or been rebuilt; the oldest building now in this category is the R.C. Lithuanian Church of St Casimir, Bethnal Green, of 1912 by *Benedict Williamson*, plain but with interior decoration reflecting its Baltic connections, and furnishings including an enormous Rococo-style Oberammergau reredos.

By the end of the C19 Christian places of worship were matched by a huge number of SYNAGOGUES in Spitalfields and Whitechapel. Earlier synagogues on the E fringe of the City had been built for the Sephardic congregations established from the late C17. The newcomers, some of them tiny, were built for the Jewish Ashkenazi refugees escaping persecution in Eastern Europe, who settled in the area in the later C19. Top-lit galleried

* R. Mudie-Smith, ed., *The Religious Life of London*, 1904. East London here refers to the metropolitan boroughs of Poplar, Stepney, Bethnal Green, Shoreditch and Hackney.

† Those with the highest attendance (over 1,000) were St Anne, Limehouse, St Peter London Docks and St Mary Matfelon, Whitechapel, and among the R.C. churches: St Mary and St Joseph, Poplar, St Mary and St Michael, Stepney, St Anne Spitalfields and English Martyrs, Whitechapel.

halls were built out over the yards behind close-packed terrace houses. A couple of this type remain, the atmospheric example
48 in Princelet Street (now the Museum of Immigration) built for a Polish prayer group in 1869–70, and another (rebuilt in the C20)
30 behind a house in Fieldgate Street. Former Huguenot chapels were also taken over, as in the case of the well-known chapel in Fournier Street. Best preserved and still with its fittings is the chapel which became the Sandys Row Synagogue, converted in 1870, and given a discreet new frontage by *N.S. Joseph*. The first large synagogue to be built in the East End rather than the City was in the then Jewish area around Stepney Green, 1876–7 by *Davis & Emmanuel*. Its exterior in a polychrome round-arched style only hints at the former splendour of the interior, now converted to flats. Synagogues continued in traditional styles into the C20: the Sephardic synagogue of 1923 by *Lewis Solomon & Son* in Nelson Street has a formal classical interior; the Congregation of Jacob in Commercial Road, 1920–1 by the same firm, has a top-lit interior of a more vernacular character, a remarkable survival.

Development in the outer suburbs up to 1914

As the squalor of the East End increased, the outer areas provided a refuge for its better-off inhabitants. But unlike the more favoured areas of N and W London few major early C19 houses were built, and fewer remain. An exception is the rather serious and awkward Neo-Elizabethan Friday Hill House, Chingford by *Vulliamy* for the local lord of the manor and rector in the 1840s.

The Eastern Counties Railway, opened in 1839, had stations at Stratford, Romford and Ilford and a branch line via Low Leyton, Leytonstone, Snaresbrook, and Woodford in 1856. Barking, East Ham and Plaistow were served by the London, Tilbury & Southend railway by 1858. But at that date commuter traffic was not a priority and only small numbers of villas had grown up in some of these areas by the 1870s. Cheap workmen's trains were then introduced on some lines by the Great Eastern Railway, a *quid pro quo* for creating the terminus at Liverpool Street in 1874. The opening in 1870 of its branch to Walthamstow (soon extended to Chingford and attracting Epping Forest day trippers) was the signal for a rapid spread of artisan housing in Walthamstow, Leyton and Leytonstone, through which the Tottenham & Forest Gate Railway threaded its viaducts and cuttings in 1890–4. Urbanization was helped by the horse trams, appearing from the 1870s. Some of the first suburbs of larger houses appeared E of Stratford at Forest Gate and Manor Park where the Gurney Estate and the Woodgrange Park estates were laid out from the late 1870s to 1890 with comfortable houses for a well-to-do Jewish population moving out from the East End. Woodgrange Park, with its rows of houses with iron verandas, was begun by Thomas Corbett and com-

pleted by his son A. Cameron Corbett, Scots with a reputation for quality. The younger Corbett went on to develop Seven Kings and Goodmayes, near Ilford, by the end of the century. The principal developers elsewhere were usually local figures who subsequently achieved prominence as benefactors and worthies. J.H. Bethell, later Lord Bethell, a local surveyor, oversaw the building of small artisan terraces from the 1880s at East Ham. In the same decade at Walthamstow, the local landowner Thomas Courtenay Warner began to develop his own estates with extensive housing of a varied character with a mixture of terraced houses and cottage flats by *John Dunn*, all with uniform English domestic motifs and brick decoration of the type revived by Norman Shaw after 1870. At Leytonstone the sale in 1873 of the estate of the East End philanthropist William Cotton (*see* p. 41) also paved the way for superior houses. At Ilford, where a large town was created in twenty years, W.P. Griggs M.P., the head of a family of builder–developers, laid out the estate around his own house with typical medium-sized Edwardian houses during the 1890s. He later moved to Upminster for further developments, where he is commemorated by a splendid window in the former Congregational church. From the 1890s, suburbs of larger villas set in formal rows developed on high ground close to Epping Forest, where the tide of building was held back by the 1878 Act.
Examples are The Drive, South Woodford, with their roof-top 84
viewing platforms, and the smart houses along Broomhill Road, Woodford Green, including an expertly handled essay in Old English by *J.A. Gotch*. The less authentic Tudor revival of The Drive, Chingford, is by *Edmond Egan* of Loughton.

The spirit of the GARDEN SUBURB ideal of spacious, often secluded plots for large houses in wooded avenues is apparent at Emerson Park, Hornchurch (begun 1900), and in some of the later Warner housing at Highams Park, but only Gidea Park, Romford set out to emulate the tradition of Hampstead Garden Suburb and Letchworth. It began in 1910 as an exhibition of small houses by different architects and still betrays that in its slightly rigid layout and absence of community buildings. Among
the mixture of Arts and Crafts and Neo-Georgian styles, the most 87
notable is a group by *M.H. Baillie Scott*. It is an oddity in East London. So too are a pair of Edwardian houses, The White House at Woodford Green, based on designs by *C.F.A. Voysey*, 1906, and Upminster Court, a solid English Renaissance mansion by *Charles Reilly*, 1906, for the engineer and industrialist A.E. Williams, whose family business at Dagenham Dock paid for its erection.

That is the picture of the urban and suburban scene by 1914. What then of the RURAL BUILDINGS of the Essex countryside into which these developments now encroached? In the S parts E of the River Roding where the impact of the railway was little felt until the C20, East London was still countryside with farms, manor houses and rural inns amongst the market gardens that served the metropolis. The marshland villages of Dagenham, Rainham and Wennington were mere handfuls of houses, while further inland at Cranham and North Ockendon the grouping of manor house and church had barely altered since the Middle Ages. Indeed the amount of agricultural land increased in the rural E during the C19 with the clearance of Hainault Forest in 1851 and the division of Crown land between small farms. New farmhouses and cottages, each stamped with the Crown badge, survive at Aldborough Hatch, Hainault, in London Road, Romford and elsewhere. An attractive row of cottages was built for farm workers at Tanners Lane, Barkingside, in 1863, and the appearance of farms also began to alter as progressive methods of farming were introduced. At Havering-atte-Bower, the McIntosh family, who had enriched themselves as contractors for the London and East India Docks at the dawn of the C19, built two large complexes in the 1860s at Bower Farm and Park Farm for the efficient commercial management of dairy herds, following experiments at Havering by Collinson Hall, a progressive agriculturalist who helped to invent the steam plough.

COUNTRY HOUSES engulfed by suburbia were increasingly taken into institutional use. Only in the sub-rural fringes were they still home to the gentry. Older mansions or their replacements continued to provide, as they had done in the C17 and C18, homes for London businessmen. Their wealth often derived from industrial and speculative ventures in the East End, for example the Barnes and Pemberton-Barnes clan, who had begun as builders in Mile End and Stepney in the C18, by the early C19 were living at the curious Round House and the Hall at Havering-atte-Bower.

Religious buildings in the outer suburbs c. 1850–1914

The transformation of the rural areas into new suburbs was accompanied at first by CHURCH BUILDING on a modest scale. *George Gilbert Scott*'s Emmanuel, Forest Gate, 1850 is a country church in ecclesiological Gothic; Christ Church, begun by *Scott* in 1860 for the village of Wanstead (though completed later by others), is a little more ambitious (the vicar and the diocesan bishop were both sons of Sir Robert Wigram, a family noted elsewhere for its church building involvement). *Scott* also built a new chancel for All Saints, West Ham, which remains complete with its furnishings. Most of the other architects involved are of less distinction. The centre of the growing town of Romford was provided with quite a showy Gothic church, St Edward the Confessor, 1849–50 by *John Johnson*, who ten years later also built St Andrew, a substantial building paid for by the local brewers for the working-class area of New Romford. Romford also has one of the earliest C19 R.C. churches in the area, also dedicated to St Edward, a ragstone Gothic building by *Daniel Cubitt Nichols*, 1856.

In the still rural areas Woodford Bridge had its own church from 1850 (by *Charles Ainslie*). Older buildings began to be replaced: as at Aldborough Hatch, with a little church of 1863 by

Arthur Ashpitel, and at Cranham, in 1873 by the Essex architect *Richard Armstrong*, an example of a serious Early Gothic building, complete with tower and spire, provided by a landowner next door to his solitary country house. At Woodford Wells, still in the 1870s a straggle of hamlets, a new accent with tall spire appeared at the N end of the green, All Saints, by *F.E.C. Streatfeild* (1874). The most appealing example of a rural church is an early work by *Basil Champneys* at Havering-atte-Bower (1875), an engaging 1
building with sweeping tiled roofs and original open tower with carved detail, perhaps consciously recalling the site of the medieval royal palace. Quite different in spirit is the chapel at the Forest School, Walthamstow, enlarged in 1875 by *William White*, an intense spiky affair for a school with High Church leanings. At the other end of the scale is the simple rural mission church, as for example, Ascension, Collier Row, 1883 by *E.C. Lee*.

From the 1870s churches proliferated in the newly built suburban areas of 'London over the border'. A start was made in rapidly expanding Walthamstow, with St Saviour by *F.T. Dolman* 1873, the first of three in the area to be paid for by Richard Foster, a munificent supporter of new London churches, who had been associated with the campaign for new churches in Haggerston, Hackney. St Saviour has a fine tower and is on a grand scale, but plainly detailed and now somewhat altered. Foster's second involvement was with St Michael Walthamstow, 1884 *by J.M. Bignall*, a very ambitious but somewhat eccentric building with huge clerestory. *A.W. Blomfield* was responsible for two large, safely conservative buildings of the 1880s, the dauntingly austere, flint-faced All Saints Manor Park (1886), and the stone St Andrew Leytonstone (1887), built for the new suburb laid out on the late William Cotton's estate, with a chancel given by his family as a memorial. Private donors were still significant: the three Misses Nutter contributed to several local churches in Wanstead and Woodford and themselves built Holy Trinity, Woodford, an unusual, rather gaunt exercise in Transitional Gothic, by *James Fowler* (1886). It never received its intended S aisle; on its site a temporary tin tabernacle remains as a hall. Some churches never raised the money to build more grandly. Walthamstow has humble examples, still in use, of mission buildings combining church with hall or school: St Gabriel (1882), St Luke (1901). An unusually grand survival of High Church magnificence in a working-class area (again without its intended tower) is St Margaret Leytonstone, 1892 by *Newman & Jacques*. It marks the end of an era. Progressive Anglican architecture of the turn of the century was developing in new ways.

But before turning to this, the buildings of the Nonconformists should be considered. Both East and West Ham were noted for the strength of their nonconformity, which was fortified by competitive mission work by the different sects. In the 1902–3 survey the Congregationalist figures in these areas overtake the Baptists. Forest Gate still has two large former Congregational churches of the 1880s: a former one in Romford Road with a particularly massive Gothic exterior, 1880–5 by *T. Lewis Banks*; the other, in

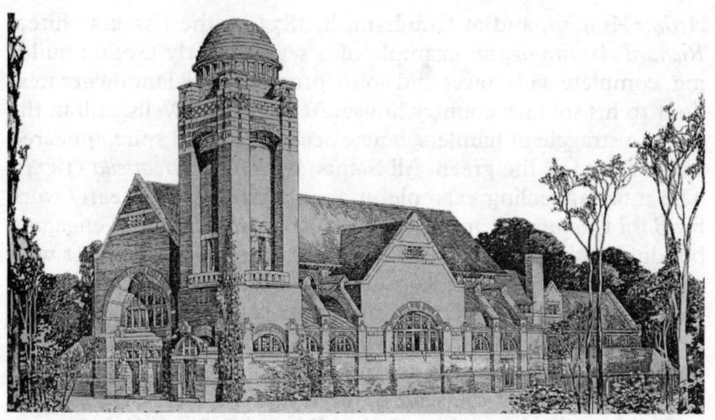

Woodford Green, United Free church, by Charles Harrison Townsend, 1904. Original design, not as built

Sebert Road, large and less accomplished, but still with its galleried interior. At East Ham the Methodists' Elizabeth Fry Memorial Church, 1889 by *William Dartnell*, is unusually elaborate. The Primitive Methodists church at Leytonstone, 1900 by *Clark Hallam* in a debased mixed Renaissance, is an example of the imposing effect achieved by piling the church above a ground-floor hall, the equivalent of the multistorey board school.

Nonconformist churches of the early C20 remain plentiful in the outer boroughs, although mostly on a minor scale, and generally by architects who made a speciality of such buildings. Around the turn of the century the Free Churches adopted a new and more lively style, borrowing from the Anglicans an interest in late Gothic detail and deploying it vigorously to create spirited street façades, characteristically with a big traceried W window and playful, asymmetrically placed turret. The Methodist Church, Highams Park, 1903, is a good example by *G. & R.P. Baines*, who were the leaders in promoting the type. Their Baptist church at Ilford, 1907, is the centre of a pretty group with schools etc. Other examples are the former Congregational church, Cranbrook Road, Ilford, by *Smee & Houchin* 1906–7, in elaborately detailed free Gothic, and the Congregational Church (now Trinity U.R.) at Upminster, 1911 by *T. Stevens* of Bournemouth, which keeps its good interior. Larger buildings continued the older Nonconformist tradition of galleries on three sides facing
93 a pulpit, as in the former Fetter Lane Congregational Church by *Morley Horder* at Leytonstone, 1900, raised high above a lower hall, an unusual building with restrained Arts and Crafts detail and a Scottish vernacular flavour. The former Methodist church at Goodmayes of 1904 (now R.C.) is another large galleried example in more conventional free Perp. The outstandingly original building of these years is the United Free Church, Woodford Green, 1904 by *Harrison Townsend*, which adopts a free Byzan-

tine style on a noble scale, although carried out less elaborately than intended. At Chingford, the former Congregational church of 1910 by *J.D. & S.T. Mould* is a late example of the Nonconformist polygonal auditorium of the type that was developed in the later C19, as is the Baptist church at Aldersbrook, Wanstead, of 1908. The architects of Roman Catholic churches also turned to free versions of late Gothic at this time, as in two Tower Hamlets examples provided by wealthy donors, the attractive
Guardian Angels, Mile End of 1901–2 by *F.A. Walters*, and the 89
noble Our Lady of the Assumption, Bethnal Green, with a fine, lofty interior, by *E. Goldie*, 1911–12.

How did the Anglican building of the early C20 respond to these challenges? From the 1890s the general trend favoured the late Gothic period, but exteriors were less flamboyant than those of the Nonconformists. Interiors are well lit, gentler and quieter than the lofty basilican structures of the C19. St Barnabas, Little Ilford, by *Bucknall & Comper* 1900–9, is an accomplished effort in pleasant straightforward Perp; St Barnabas, Walthamstow (another Richard Foster gift), 1902–3 by *W.D. Caröe*, is in the architect's distinctively eclectic late Gothic with plenty of unusual Arts and Crafts touches, as well as a fine collection of furnishings. The attractive St Gabriel, Aldersbrook, by *Charles Spooner* 1914, spacious Perp with reticent brick-and-tile detailing, points the way towards the simpler churches of between the wars.

Despite the experience of Bishop Blomfield, the recipe of a large number of new churches for the new suburbs was repeated by the Bishop of St Albans' fund for 'London over the Border' churches. A Perp version of the plain long-naved church became the speciality of the firm of *J.E.K. & J.P. Cutts*, who built some ten churches of this type in our area, including four in the suburbs of Ilford between 1898 and 1914. Not all survive; St Alban, Ilford, one of the first, retains a dignified unaltered interior. Their Ascension, Custom House (now subdivided), was paid for by Felsted School, an example of one of several involvements of public schools in East End missions. A similar Perp formula was adopted by *Richard Creed* for the former St Catherine, Leytonstone (and for the unexpectedly large dining hall at Forest School, Walthamstow). Rather more original, and built only after a struggle with the planners, are two more vaguely Perp churches in East Ham and Leyton, of 1914 by *E. Douglas Hoyland*, low buildings with walls of terracotta blocks set in a steel frame. Inside there are timber arcades, a feature of some other very modest buildings such as St Matthew Stratford (1903 by *E.P. Loftus Brock*). Some of the mission activity of the pre-1914 years only came to fruition in permanent churches of between the wars; others were built in stages, such as St Paul, Goodmayes, a characterful Perp church by *Chancellor & Son* 1903–29; and many remained incomplete, as in the case of two promising examples *by E.T. Dunn*: St Luke, Ilford and St Barnabas, Woodford Wells.

Notable additions to earlier buildings are *Blomfield & Son*'s new chancel at Chingford (1903), a sympathetic addition to

Vulliamy's church, and *Caröe & Passmore*'s S aisle at Leytonstone (1909) which transformed Blore's rather plain building. A reference should be made here to the concern with sensitive repair of medieval churches, which took off in the 1890s, increasingly under the auspices of SPAB. *J.T. Micklethwaite* rescued East Ham from proposed demolition; *C.C. Winmill* and *William Weir* worked at West Ham and Barking. Rainham was tactfully restored by Rev. *Ernest Geldart* from 1897. A much publicized case was St Mary Bow, rescued from threatened total rebuilding and repaired under the eye of *C.R. Ashbee* from 1900.

Good CHURCH HALLS are a feature of the Edwardian period, less tied to convention and often with attractive domestic Arts and Crafts detail. St Mary Woodford (1902 by *J. Kingwell Cole* and *K. Wood*), Havering-atte-Bower (also 1902), St Saviour Forest Gate (1904 by *F. Danby Smith*) and Emmanuel, Leyton (1906 by *E.C. Frere*) are all worth seeking out.

CHURCH FURNISHINGS of the C19 and early C20 have been mentioned only occasionally so far. It will already be obvious that most churches could not afford the lavish fittings to be found in other parts of London. Much was lost in the Second World War, especially stained glass windows, so often a principal focus of C19 donations, as they superseded sculpture as personal memorials. A few highlights can be mentioned. Individual WINDOWS of the 1850s include a fine enamelled glass window by *Clutterbuck* in St Anne, Limehouse, and unusual stained glass by *James Powell* at the German Lutheran church, Stepney. There are good individual windows by some of the larger firms. By *Clayton & Bell*: All Saints West Ham, 1866. By *Morris & Co.*: Ilford Hospital Chapel; Forest School Walthamstow. By *Heaton, Butler & Bayne*: St Peter Bethnal Green; St Matthew Stratford. By *Hardman*: All Saints Cranham; St Antony R.C. West Ham; St Michael Walthamstow; Our Lady R.C. Bethnal Green. St Luke Canning Town has unusual pictorial mosaics in the apse, the Unitarian Church Bethnal Green a fine *opus sectile* panel attributed to *Holiday*. Victorian and Edwardian fittings have rarely been preserved complete, although there are plenty of individual items deserving of appreciation; the most notable ensembles are those gathered together at the Walthamstow churches of St Michael and St Barnabas, at St Margaret, Leytonstone and at St Peter London Docks.

Public Buildings and Institutions of the C19

The spread of legislation from the 1830s onwards brought into existence a wealth of new buildings designed for an expanded public realm, and provision for the relief of poverty and ill health, and for improved education. Previously these tasks had been the responsibility of the local parish, supplemented by charities for the sick and infirm.

The spectre of the residential WORKHOUSE always loomed large for the destitute in need of parish relief, but the Poor Law

City of London Union Workhouse, Bow Road, 1849 by Richard Tress

Act of 1834 paved the way for a new class of workhouse buildings designed to be a visible deterrent to the 'idle' poor. A remarkable number of these dismal buildings survive in East London; Romford (now Oldchurch Hospital) is of 1838–40 by *Francis Edwards*, the nearly contemporary group at Leytonstone was built for the West Ham Union by *A.R. Mason* 1839–42. Their uncomfortable accommodation was usually hidden behind a polite public face, as in the attractive Italianate block for offices and receiving rooms designed by *Richard Tress* for the City of London Union's workhouse, Bow Road, of 1849 (now St Clement's Hospital). INFIRMARIES, added after the 1867 Metropolitan Poor Act, have their legacy in several existing hospitals. An example is St Andrew's Hospital, Bromley-by-Bow, a grim design for the Poplar and Stepney Sick Asylum, 1868 by *A. & C. Harston*, chiefly novel for adopting the pavilion plan of ward blocks within a year of its appearance at St Thomas's Hospital, Lambeth. Only the much larger and later Whipps Cross Hospital, Leyton (1900–3 by *F.J. Sturdy*) takes architecture as a serious concern, sporting a striking silhouette of ogee domes that can be seen for miles around.

For the children of the poor, the Victorians also offered INDUSTRIAL SCHOOLS. Forest Gate Industrial School was built in a bare Italianate by the Whitechapel Guardians in 1852–4. It is typical in having been built in the open rural areas of Essex far beyond the London slums. Part of Bethnal Green industrial schools also survive, added behind Leytonstone House in 1881–9 by *A. & C. Harston*. This was a typical fate for many large mansions in the area. Also placed in open countryside, but with buildings of a far grander sort, are a pair of private ORPHANAGES: the Snaresbrook Infant Orphan Asylum (now Snaresbrook Crown Court) of 1841–3 is late Tudor in inspiration with gatehouse centrepiece and ogee turrets, an early work by *George Gilbert Scott* of

Scott & Moffat, who specialized in such buildings, while the mag-
59 nificent Wanstead Merchant Seamen's Orphan Asylum by *George
Somers Clarke sen.* 1861–71, is in a Ruskin-inspired Venetian
Gothic and distinguished by a dramatized scene of shipwreck and
other carved decoration by *Thomas Earp*. Dr Barnardo espoused
a more sympathetic attitude towards the care of children, founding his first home in Stepney in 1870 and creating groups of
village homes at then-rural Barkingside. The distinctive 'col-
86 lecting-box' cottages by *Ebenezer Gregg* were arranged around
greens, with their own church and schools. Barnardo was not
the first to plan on such principles but was highly influential on
the state-provided institutions. St Leonard's Cottage Homes at
Hornchurch, built by the Shoreditch Poor Law Union in 1886–9,
follows a similar village model but with homes on a larger, more
institutional scale facing each other across a private street.

Smaller, private institutions also looked for sites outside the overcrowded East End; the most civilized were numerous small ALMSHOUSES provided for the elderly poor. Many were originally established in the East End by City Companies or merchants; the neat and commodious Weavers Almshouses, Snaresbrook, of 1857 by *Joseph Jennings*, brought together two older institutions founded in Spitalfields and Shoreditch. The Bakers Almshouses, Leyton, by *T.E. Knightley* 1859–66, is on a more lavish scale, in rustic Italianate.

Free DISPENSARIES were an C18 phenomenon which grew
with the early C19 cholera epidemics and the reports of health
reformers such as Chadwick and Southwood Smith. Institutions
55 providing rudimentary health care included the Eastern Dispensary, Whitechapel (founded 1782), a smart stuccoed Italianate
56 palazzo of 1858–9, and the former Queen Adelaide Dispensary,
Bethnal Green, a lavish Free Renaissance design by *Lee & Long*
1865–6. The London Hospital had its beginnings in a dispensary,
and other HOSPITALS appear from the mid C19. Some were
specialized: for example, the London Chest Hospital, Bethnal
Green, which was founded 1848 by City merchants but given
purpose-built premises in a Baroque style by *F.W. Ordish* in
1850–1. Set within the unpolluted surroundings of Victoria
Park, it followed the example of Brompton Hospital, Chelsea.
Quakers founded the former Children's Hospital in Goldsmiths
Row, Bethnal Green, in 1867, designed by *William Ward Lee* in a
Gothic style. The Mildmay Mission Hospital is another philanthropic medical institution, established by Anglican evangelicals
in the slums of the notorious 'Nichol' in Bethnal Green and
rebuilt in 1890–2 by *R.H. Hill* to serve its replacement, the
Boundary Street Estate (*see* above). There were numerous others,
and the growing immigrant communities of C19 East London
also developed their own institutions or pioneered the expansion
of existing ones: there had been separate Jewish wards at the
London Hospital from the C18 and even allowance for the provision of kosher food, later replaced by proper kitchens for
preparing according to ritual. By the later C19 a separate Jewish

Hospital existed at Mile End, rebuilt in 1919 at Stepney Green (demolished).

Much further out, at the rural fringes, lay large ASYLUMS for the mentally ill, none more impressive than *G.T. Hine*'s Claybury p. 374
Asylum begun for Middlesex County Council at Woodford Bridge, which was set on high, wooded ground (now Repton Park) with a colossal water tower, lavishly decorated recreation hall and chapel at the apex of an echelon plan of homes for patients. Such planning, designed to provide maximum light and air, was followed at Goodmayes Asylum, built for West Ham by its surveyor, *Lewis Angell* in 1897–1901. Isolation and fever hospitals also required sites at some remove from built-up districts, for example, the Plaistow Fever Hospital in a Free Style by *E.T. Hall.*

The cholera outbreaks in an already overcrowded area urged reform of the repositories of the dead. Resurrectionist (i.e. grave robbing) scares were a major concern in the late C18 and early C19, reflected in the appearance of watch houses close to some of the graveyards – a sturdy example remains at St Matthew, Bethnal Green, and a small 'sentry box' at Wanstead. But the rank and odorous state of the overcrowded churchyards was an equally pressing problem. New CEMETERIES were opened, laid out either by private companies or local boards: the earliest was Tower Hamlets Cemetery in 1841, one of seven privately owned cemeteries to serve the metropolis from the 1830s. The absence of significant funerary monuments reflects the area's lack of wealth in comparison with its more fashionable counterparts in the rest of London. The private Victoria Park Cemetery, Bethnal Green, was opened in 1845 but closed due to overcrowding in 1874. The largest cemetery in East London was opened at Aldersbrook by the City of London in 1853; it has a characteristically Victorian layout of winding avenues and pathways, and Gothic ragstone chapels by the City surveyor, *William Haywood.* MONUMENTS at the City of London aspire to a higher sophistication with several major memorials marking the reinterred remains from the old City churchyards, but elsewhere the cemeteries are full of more pedestrian examples of the monumental mason's art. There are only a few mausolea to display family pride in the departed; the most notable example is the Evelina de Rothschild
mausoleum at the Jewish Cemetery, West Ham, by *Sir Matthew* 81
Digby Wyatt 1866.

Civic Buildings

The development of an architectural identity for local government in the second half of the C19 was promoted by the Metropolitan Management Act of 1855, which gave new powers to the vestries of the Tower Hamlets parishes to manage rates and drainage. Some small parishes were grouped together under the authority of District Boards of Works. Both required

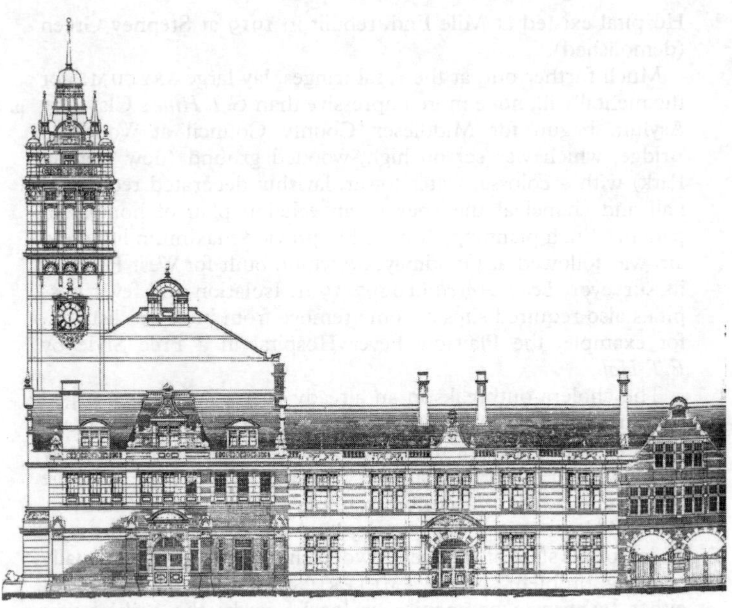

East Ham Town Hall complex, selected design by Cheers and Smith, 1898

PUBLIC OFFICES, usually containing a board room, offices and occasionally a hall for public use. Bethnal Green was notable in building its Town Hall early, preceding the Act in 1851, in a Tudor style by a local surveyor *G.H. Simmonds* (demolished). Most buildings date from the 1860s onwards and are eclectic, often crude interpretations of the polite civic architecture of the mid-C19 metropolis: St George's, Cable Street, is the earliest, of 1860 by *Andrew Wilson*, emulating the solid Italianate popularized by Charles Barry's Travellers Club in the 1840s. Liberal interpretations of Italian Renaissance styles are found at the former District Board of Works office, White Horse Road (Ratcliffe), of
53 1862–4 by *C.R. Dunch*, Mile End Vestry Hall, Bancroft Road, by *J.M. Knight* 1862–5 and Bromley-by-Bow of 1868–71 by *A. & C. Harston*. The same firm, with *Hills & Fletcher*, were responsible
54 for Poplar District Board of Works offices; here the style is different, an elaborate but unsophisticated example of High Victorian Gothic eclecticism. The Harstons return to their palazzo style at Limehouse Town Hall in 1869–71.

By the end of the century the growth of local authorities in the suburbs gave rise to far grander types of TOWN HALLS, reflecting in their planning and construction the assumption of power over a wide sphere of public provision. These might incorporate not only a Board Room but also offices for rate paying and space for the local fire brigade or coroner's court. West Ham's Town Hall by *Lewis Angell* and *John Giles* 1867–8 still provides the

dominating landmark at the centre of Stratford, monumentally
self-confident with striking tower and clusters of allegorical sculpture. Particular attention was lavished on the public hall, designed
for meetings and social events, which in later buildings was treated
with ever increasing importance. The following decades brought
a rush of similar buildings, sometimes requiring rebuilding or
extension within a matter of years as urban districts and boroughs
replaced boards. At Leyton, the local Board's offices of 1882–3
(by *J.M. Knight*, architect of Mile End Vestry Hall two decades
earlier) were superseded by *John Johnson*'s outrageously High
Renaissance Town Hall in 1895–6. Barking's Public Offices of 74
1893 by *C.J. Dawson* are in an equally free Flemish Renaissance,
while Ilford Town Hall is Baroque by *Benjamin Woollard*, 1901,
with a colossal public hall, later adapted with an orchestra pit.
East Ham Urban District commissioned a pointedly showy Town
Hall by *Cheers & Smith* (won in competition 1898, built 1901–14) 73
to rival West Ham. Dominated by a 150-ft tower and richly flamboyant decoration, it marked the zenith of Edwardian civic pride,
incorporating within a single complex not only Hall and offices
but also courts, library, fire station, swimming pool, technical
college, tram depot and (a sign of the times) electricity offices and
substation. East Ham was early with its electric tramways. This
form of transport inspired other buildings of distinction: tram
offices survive at Plaistow and Walthamstow, an LCC depot (now
bus garage) at Bow. The Act of 1899 created the County of

London and three boroughs for the Tower Hamlets: Bethnal Green, Poplar and Stepney, but only Bethnal Green marked this event with a new building, its handsome Baroque Town Hall by *Percy Robinson & Alban Jones*, 1909–10.

The early Victorian vestries and boards of works were famed for their cheese-paring attitude to public provision of badly needed amenities to serve the overcrowded inner areas. From the 1850s private philanthropic enterprise introduced new building types to the East End and by extension to London as a whole. In Old Castle Street, Whitechapel, the façade is preserved from the BATHS and WASHHOUSE, a pioneering example of provision paid for by the Committee for Promoting the Establishment of Baths and Washhouses for the Labouring Classes. The designer was the engineer *P.P. Baly*, using an early example of iron roof truss. Further public baths were built after the 1890 Washhouses Act made it easier for local authorities to erect their own premises. The best surviving example is the gorgeously striped building in Cheshire Street, Bethnal Green, carried out in a strictly non-institutional domestic Queen Anne style by *R.S. Ayling*, 1891.

The provision of FREE LIBRARIES by local authorities was possible after 1855 but London's vestries were slow to respond until the 1890s when voting to adopt the Libraries Act became a simpler matter. The building of such establishments in the East End, however, would have been unthinkable without the largesse of J. Passmore Edwards, proprietor of the *Building News*. He took the lead in 1891 with funds for the Whitechapel Free Library. The style is a friendly Free Renaissance with decorative terracotta by *Burmantofts*. The design had already been won in competition by *Potts, Sons & Hennings*. Elsewhere Passmore Edwards took a close personal interest in promoting architects of his own choosing. *Maurice B. Adams*, editor of *Building News*, designed the library in Cable Street in Shavian Queen Anne (demolished by bombing) while the Cornishman *Silvanus Trevail* executed the Library (and cottage hospital) at East Ham in a mixed Renaissance style. The domed Plaistow Library by *S.B. Russell* (1902–4) was funded by Edwards but opened by Andrew Carnegie, the émigré Scots industrialist whose wealth funded libraries nationwide. He made no prescription over design and the task usually fell to the local surveyors of the newly formed local authorities, outstanding among them the works of *A.H. Camp-*
75 *bell* of East Ham. His Manor Park Library of 1904 is Neo-Baroque in a furious red brick and terracotta while his extension for the library at the Town Hall is in an eclectic Jacobean. Allegorical decoration was often included, but Bethnal Green's library of 1922 has a unique series of portrait reliefs of Marx, Morris, Darwin and Wagner.

London's growth required authorities to oversee and manage different aspects of the entire metropolis. In 1855–88 this was the responsibility of the Metropolitan Board of Works. In East London its authority extended as far as the River Lea. It was predominantly concerned with street improvements and slum clearance. There was little new building except for FIRE STATIONS, of which a single example survives as the London Buddhist Centre, Bethnal Green, by *Robert Pearsall* 1888, in his characteristic picturesque Gothic. This style was later eschewed by the MBW's successor, the LCC's Fire Brigade Branch, which favoured a Free Style with domestic 'Queen Anne' elements, as at East Ferry Road, Isle of Dogs (1904–5). In the outer suburbs fire stations were often incorporated within civic complexes, but a very domestic building survives at Wanstead, fitting neatly into its village setting.

POLICE STATIONS were quick to appear in the apparently lawless districts of the East End after the Metropolitan Police was established in 1829 to cover an area within a seven mile radius of Charing Cross (roughly equivalent to the boundaries of Greater London today). Early stations, for example Bow Road, 1854, the work of the Met's surveyor *Charles Reeves,* are simple Italianate with quoins and dentilled cornices. Reeves also acted as Surveyor to the County Courts in England and Wales: the colourfully polychromed palazzo of the former courthouse in Prescot Street, Whitechapel, betrays Ruskin's influence on public buildings by 1858. Most stations were built or rebuilt from the 1880s by *John Butler* and his son, *John Dixon Butler*. Unique to the Thames are the river police stations, built for a force founded in 1798 to combat piracy and pilfering from ships. The Blackwall (Isle of Dogs) and Wapping stations, by father and son respec- 76
tively, have striped façades, in the manner of Norman Shaw's New Scotland Yard (where Butler Sen. had worked for Shaw), oriels to take in views up and downriver, and police barge entrances beneath. *J.D. Butler* rose to Baroque drama for a new station at Bow Road in 1903. It sports his trademark, elongated consoles above the entrance, which are seen in many suburban stations such as Plaistow, East Ham, Walthamstow and Barking. At these, the style is consciously domestic, the semi-rural stations at Chadwell Heath and Woodford Bridge even have half-timbered upper storeys.

Educational and Cultural Buildings

By 1800 SCHOOLS usually comprised little more than a schoolroom and a home for the teacher. The National Society for the Education of the Poor in the Principles of the Established Church was founded in 1811 to establish schools in each parish for religious and moral education. Earliest surviving of these are those close to St Paul, Shadwell, which look like a late Georgian terrace. Plain buildings of 1825 and 1828 survive at Walthamstow. The schools at St Matthew, Bethnal Green (1820), and the village school at Dagenham (1830) have simple pointed Gothic windows, while Tudor Gothic was used at Plaistow (1831) and at Wanstead where the teacher's house remains, of 1840 by *Blore*. Gothic, appropriate for church schools, was taken increasingly seriously, as is seen at the school in Granby Street, Bethnal

Green, 1874 by *Joseph Clarke*. Nonconformists provided schools through the British and Foreign Schools Society after 1814. An example survives in Ramsey Street, Bethnal Green (1849).

Much larger BOARD SCHOOLS appeared after the 1870 Education Act. Their gabled rooflines are still a dominant presence amongst streets of small houses and make clear their purpose. Tower Hamlets come under the London School Board, which had its own architect, *E.R. Robson*, from 1871 but demand in the early years saw many designs put out to competition: Harbinger School, Isle of Dogs, by *R. Phené Spiers*, 1872–3 and the well-detailed Olga Street School, Old Ford, 1874 by *Hammack & Lambert*, belong to the first generation of Gothic-style schools built before the secular Queen Anne style was generally adopted, with its limited decoration provided by moulded brick pilasters and gables and the glazing patterns of large sash windows. A good example is Bonner Street, Bethnal Green, by *Robson* with *J.J. Stevenson*, 1876. Where space allowed the schools were given open sites with playgrounds but this was often precluded in the densely built-up East End where buildings had to be tailored to
70 narrow plots, for example the Durward Street Board School, Whitechapel, by *Robson* 1876–7, a tight square plan with roof playground. In the later 1880s the classic 'three deckers' became the norm, with infants, girls and boys stacked one above the other and with separate entrances. An early experiment at Johnson Street School, Stepney, by *T. Roger Smith* (1872, demolished) used the 'Prussian' plan of a central hall on each floor opening to all the surrounding classrooms but was considered expensive and not favoured until after 1884 under Robson's successor *T.J. Bailey*. Smaller ancillary buildings added to the earlier schools presented opportunities for one-off designs of outstanding quality, such as the cupola-topped Cookery School at Henriques Street. Bailey otherwise developed an increasingly formulaic plan for all large schools, usually with a symmetrical frontage to the street animated by the tall windows to the halls on each floor and flanking stair towers, but treated in a variety of styles including rich confections of voluted gables and cupolas (Southern Grove, Bow) and mannered Baroque (Marion Richardson School, Senrab Street, Stepney and Myrdle Street, Whitechapel). By 1900 even church schools had accepted the essential form of the secular institutions: Guardian Angels R.C. School, Mile End by *Leonard Stokes*; *Joseph & Smithem*'s red brick Jewish Infants School, Stepney Green; and St Antony's R.C. Schools, Upton.

Where London had led, London-over-the-Border was quick to follow. The publication in 1874 of Robson's *School Architecture* set down principles that were followed dutifully as the eastern suburban districts established their own boards in the 1890s and employed private architects. All erected large three-deckers but
71 with a distinctive stamp: from West Ham's perfunctory efforts by *Newman & Jacques*, to East Ham's excellently varied compositions by *R.L. Curtis*, the well-detailed yellow- and blue-brick schools designed by *C.J. Dawson* in a Free Jacobean for the populous districts of Barking and Ilford after 1897, and the charac-

terful rooflines of *H. Prosser*'s schools for Walthamstow. In the rural areas the greater availability of land made it possible to achieve the single-storey ideal until surburbia encroached. COUNTY SECONDARY SCHOOLS for girls were built in the early C20. At Romford, by *Hickton & Farmer* of Walsall, 1909–10, and Walthamstow, by *C.J. Dawson*, 1911–13, they are in a dignified English Baroque; Leytonstone, by *W. Jacques*, 1911–13, adopts a more inventive Free Style. Among COLLEGES notable buildings are the LCC's School of Marine Engineering at Poplar (now Tower Hamlets College) by *Percy Ginham* 1902, and West Ham Technical Institute (now UEL), opened in 1899, a pioneering effort by a local authority to provide technical education, and a uniquely ambitious essay by *Gibson & Russell* in their eclectic Free Style, marrying classical details with the sinuous forms 72
of Art Nouveau. East Ham and Leyton also provided technical schools as part of new civic complexes.

The East End had large numbers of GRAMMAR SCHOOLS that started as charitable foundations. Most were given new buildings after 1870 or moved from the cramped inner city to new sites in the less populated suburbs. Bancroft's School (run by the Drapers' Company) moved from Mile End to Woodford in 1889 to new buildings by *A.W. Blomfield*, in a Neo-Tudor collegiate style, complete with gatehouse, central quad and chapel. George Green's Grammar School at Poplar of 1883–4, was rebuilt by *Sulman*, an architect well-known for his Congregational churches, in an old-fashioned North German idiom, while *T. Chatfeild Clarke*'s Parmiter's Foundation School at Bethnal Green (now Raine's Foundation), 1887, is in an eclectic Domestic Revival. In contrast, only ten years later at the Davenant Foundation School, Whitechapel, *F. Pouler Telfer* added a large Free Jacobean hall with dramatic external covered stair trimmed in terracotta. Coborn School, Bow, by *George Elkington*, uses an asymmetrical Free Style with stripy stonework. The Coopers' Company, which had taken over C18 schools at Ratcliffe, rebuilt in 1909 on a new site adjacent to Tredegar Square, Bow. The buildings by *Figgis & Munby* are full-blown Baroque revival, also realized at Raine's Foundation School (now Tower Hamlets College) in Arbour Square, Stepney, of 1913 by *H.O. Ellis*.

MUSEUMS, ART GALLERIES and CULTURAL INSTITUTES provided education and entertainment of a morally improving sort. The Bethnal Green Museum, 1868–72, was the first phil- 69
anthropic initiative in this area, importing (literally) the culture of Albertian South Kensington by dismantling the iron structure of the first museum in Brompton Road and re-erecting it within a brick casing by *J.W. Wild*, decorated with mosaic panels designed by *F.W. Moody* and students of the Art Training Schools at South Kensington. Its frame is one of the earliest surviving examples of the Crystal Palace era. A more lavish and even more ambitious plan for enriching the East End's cultural life was The People's Palace at Mile End, 1888–91, for which *E.R. Robson* at first produced a series of fantastical Orientalizing designs before settling on a no less eclectic Grecian-cum-Moorish style. The Palace was

underpinned by a serious commitment to technical education with classes funded by the Drapers' Company, who eventually assumed control of the whole institution and established the college as part of London University (now Queen Mary Westfield College). Another enduring legacy is the famous
82 Whitechapel Art Gallery, whose roots lie in the annual exhibitions organized by Samuel and Henrietta Barnett at St Jude's Church from the 1880s, and for which the Barnetts' circle of artist friends, amongst them Watts, Rossetti and Morris, would provide loans. The commission for a permanent gallery went to *C.H. Townsend*, architect of the recently completed Bishopsgate Institute, and was executed in 1898–1901 in his highly personal and distinctive form of Art Nouveau, although sadly denied the
p. 399 mosaic frieze designed for its façade by *Walter Crane*. More unusual opportunities for learning were provided at St George-in-the-East, where the tiny former mortuary was converted into a Natural History Museum in 1904.

The People's Palace and the Whitechapel Art Gallery were the legacy of the SETTLEMENTS, an East London phenomenon from the 1880s onwards. The dynamic Samuel Barnett, Vicar of St Jude, Whitechapel, from 1874, established Toynbee Hall in 1884 as a residential centre for social and educational work amongst the poor, staffed by University students. The building by *Elijah Hoole* was inspired by English architecture of the C16 and C17 centuries and deliberately combined the collegiate style of the Universities with the domestic architecture of the Elizabethan manor house, expressing a characteristically Victorian relationship between the poor of the district and the obliging 'gentry' at the hall. Interior decoration was executed by *C.R. Ashbee* who established his Guild of Handicraft here before moving to permanent premises at Essex House, Bow, in 1891 and from there to the Cotswolds. An alternative to the predominantly secular ethos of Toynbee was provided by the Anglican Oxford House in Bethnal Green, established in the same year. Both sought to extend their influence by nurturing other similar clubs and institutions. Oxford House spawned, amongst others, the women's settlement at St Margaret's House, Bethnal Green, and University House, a non-political workingmen's club. There were numerous others founded before 1914, including St Hilda's (established by Cheltenham Ladies College) and Kingsley Hall at Bromley-by-Bow, rebuilt in the 1920s by *C. Cowles-Voysey*. All have laid the foundations for active community centres in the C21 East End. Within the East End, philanthropic endeavours by established Anglo-Jewry extended beyond improved housing in an attempt to ameliorate the suffering of the poorest immigrants.
79 Most handsome of all is the former Soup Kitchen for the Jewish Poor in Brune Street, Spitalfields, by *Lewis Solomon* 1902, with its flamboyant terracotta decoration. It included a shop and tailors' workrooms. Slightly later, St George's Settlement, Henriques Street (now flats), was founded by Basil Henriques as a Jewish settlement on the Toynbee model, with new buildings in the 1920s. Several other clubs flourished, including Boys' and

Girls' Clubs, the latter the origin of the Brady Centre, Spitalfields. Settlements and clubs of this sort also emerged in the poor area of Canning Town. Of Mansfield College's settlement in Barking Road, only the building of the boys' club survives. The Mayflower Family Centre, founded as a mission in 1894 by Malvern College, survives as an impressive group of Neo-Tudor buildings of the 1920s by *Geoffrey Raymond*. It was intended as the first of a network of settlements in Britain's ports.

The building type special to the environs of the docks was the SEAMEN'S MISSION. These usually had a strong religious or national bias but provided accommodation superior to the common lodging houses along with chapels, reading rooms, recreation rooms, banks, offices and refreshment rooms. The first, still partly preserved, was the Sailors' Home opened in Well (later Ensign) Street close to London Dock in 1830, probably p. 488
designed by *Henry Roberts*. This was organized by the Rev. George Smith, a midshipman turned Baptist minister, one of the founders in 1818 of the Port of London Society for Promoting Religion among Merchant Seamen, forerunner of the British and Foreign Sailors' Society. Several other missions were prominently sited on the Commercial and East India Dock Road and employed architectural devices to attract the passing sailor. On the East India Dock Road, the earliest was *George Green*'s Sailors' Home of 1839–41, which had a grand Greek Revival portico; the Methodist Queen Victoria Seamen's Rest (by *Gordon & Gunton*, 1901–2) has an entrance tower and cupola; and the Missions to Seamen Institute by *Blomfield*, begun in 1892, a friendly, obviously English exterior. The Sailors' Palace, Com- 77
mercial Road, of 1901 by *Niven & Wigglesworth*, the former headquarters of the British and Foreign Sailors' Society, is the most original, Art Nouveau in spirit, a welcoming gateway in form, and fluently carved with maritime symbols. The missions continued on an even larger scale after the First World War with Limehouse's austere Empire Memorial Sailors' Hostel by *Daniel & Parnacott*, 1923–4, and The Flying Angel, Victoria Dock Road, of 1934–6 by *Petch & Fermaud*, crowned with a tower and a flashing beacon to distinguish it from the many other, less edifying sailors' lodging houses ranged along the Royal Victoria Dock.

The embellishment of public spaces by MONUMENTS and SCULPTURE began in earnest in the C19. The few East London examples are eclectic in style, ranging from the plain obelisk memorial to Samuel Gurney at Stratford by *J. Bell* (1861) to the ornate Gothic–Moorish drinking fountain at Victoria Park 80
by *Henry Darbishire* 1862, given by Baroness Burdett-Coutts. Equally eccentric is the terracotta Martyr's Memorial at St John's, Stratford, of 1878. Conventional memorials include the paternal figures of Richard Green, shipbuilder, at East India Dock Road, by *E. W. Wyon* 1865–6, and Gladstone by *Albert Bruce Joy* 1881, placed prominently outside St Mary Bow. The affectionate memorial to Dr Barnardo, 1910, at Barkingside is by *George Frampton*, one of the sculptors associated with the liberated, sensual forms of the 'New Sculpture' after 1890. The movement

had a profound effect on ARCHITECTURAL DECORATION. The firm of *Gibson & Russell* employed *W. Birnie Rhind* at West Ham
72 Technical Institute for intricate, allegorical figure sculpture and pictorial friezes. Numerous other sculptors provided excellent detailing on a smaller scale: the piscatorial figures around the entrance to the LCC's School of Marine Engineering, Poplar by *Bertram Pegram*; panels on a memorial at Stepney Green by *Gilbert Seale* and *W.S. Frith*'s memorial to Edward VII (1911) in Whitechapel Road; of the same date is the seated female figure sculpture above the entrance to Bethnal Green Town Hall by *Henry Poole*, one of the most successful architectural sculptors of his generation. Modelling for architectural terracotta was highly skilful, notably *R. Caldwell Spruce* of *Burmantofts* whose gambolling cherubs decorate the Whitechapel Free Library (1892).
82 Next door, the Whitechapel Art Gallery (1901) has a terracotta façade incorporating stiff foliage, possibly to designs by *William Aumonier*, made by *Canning & Gibbs*.

Buildings for Entertainment and Commerce

In the C18, when Garrick made his debut at Whitechapel, THEATRES were a fashionable attraction, free from the regnlations imposed on West End theatres. The creation of the docks and influx of new inhabitants at first sustained the business. As late as 1840, *G.H. Simmonds* built the Royal Pavilion Theatre, Whitechapel, to seat 3,000 (demolished). The influx of Yiddish-speaking Jews created an entirely separate form of theatrical entertainment that thrived into the later C20 but has left no permanent memorials. The only surviving suburban theatre of the later C19 is the Theatre Royal, Stratford, by *J.G. Buckle* 1884. Its interior is a reworking of 1902, to a West End standard, by *Frank Matcham* for the Fredericks family, who had commissioned Matcham to design their nearby Borough Theatre in 1895 (since remodelled).

An alternative, sometimes more bawdy, form of entertainment was to be had in scores of MUSIC HALLS, of which only two survive in London. The best is the celebrated and atmospheric
61 Wilton's Music Hall, Grace's Alley, a purpose-built hall of the 1850s with supper rooms and bars.* The halls became far grander in the 1890s but lost their popularity in the C20 and were soon replaced by cinemas. Music halls had their beginnings in PUBS, the traditional centre of working-class entertainment. They grew in number and extravagance throughout the C19. The
63 Commercial Tavern, Commercial Street, 1865 is notable for its elaborate debased stucco decoration. The Star of the East, Commercial Road, unusually has a fancy polychromed Gothic frontage, no doubt intended to attract drinkers from the nearby docks. The larger, fancier pubs are mostly the product of the boom-time of the 1890s, built by the major breweries and distilleries to compete with each other. They are often found in the

*The other is Hoxton Music Hall, Hackney.

new suburban town centres of that period. East Ham is a particularly good hunting ground for well-preserved frontages with work by several pub specialists: *Shoebridge & Rising* at The Boleyn 64
and *F.W. Ashton* at The Duke of Fife (1890s) and Denmark Arms (1903). His trademark buxom female caryatids reappear at the smaller Britannia, Church Road, Barking. The internal division into socially distinct compartments has not survived the C20 although the separate entries often remain, as at the lavish Earl of Essex, Manor Park by *H. Poston* and *W.E. Trent*, 1901–2. Little is left of the once ornate interiors sparkling with engraved glass and coloured tiles. The Ten Bells, Commercial Street, has an intact tiled scheme of the 1890s by *W.B. Simpson & Sons* with a pictorial panel of 'Spitalfields in ye Olden Time'.

Rebuilding was often intended to present an outwardly more respectable appearance in the face of the TEMPERANCE MOVEMENT which grew in strength from the 1870s. Its adherents provided their own establishments, competing in grandeur for an inebriated public's attention: the most magnificent (since demolished) was erected at Mile End by Frederick Charrington, rebellious heir to the brewery. The former Red House Coffee Palace by *E. Burgess* still stands out amongst the decayed frontages along Commercial Road. Larger pubs doubling as hotels were a speciality of Chingford, catering for trippers to Epping Forest: the Royal Forest Hotel of 1899, the less altered and more fanciful Queen Elizabeth, both by *Edmond Egan*, and the Bull & Crown at the Green with its fancy Chambord roofline. An equally distinct group are the Queen Anne style pubs and hotels along the N side of the Royal Albert Dock by *Vigers* and *Wagstaffe*, 1881–3, for the London and St Katharine Dock Co., built to serve passengers for the steamships.

Shopping in much of Victorian East London was centred on

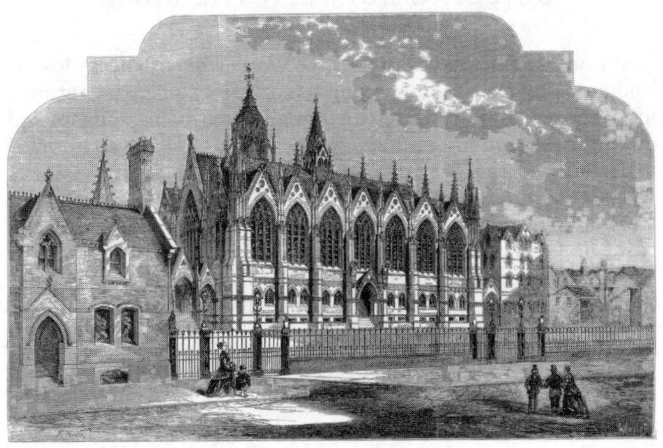

Columbia Market, Bethnal Green, Market Hall, 1866
by Henry Darbishire

2 the numerous STREET MARKETS which survive into the C21. The inner East End was characterized not only by the general food markets but also those specializing in particular goods: live birds in Club Row and later Sclater Street; flowers (still) at Columbia Road, second hand clothes in Petticoat Lane (Middlesex Street). A lone alternative was the extravagant Gothic fantasy of the ill-fated Columbia Market, 1866–8, founded by Baroness Burdett-Coutts next to her improved housing in Columbia Road (*see* above). It was the first enclosed and covered (and therefore controllable) market for the East End. In contrast, in the 1890s, domestic vernacular was the style used for the rebuilt Spitalfields Market by *George Sherrin*. Other wholesale covered markets existed at Stratford and Shadwell (both demolished). Smaller, speculative enterprises for covered markets included a Jewish market established by *Abraham & Woolf Davis* in the 1890s s of Commercial Road. They carried on with flair but without success with the brightly polychromed Moorish-style Fashion Street market of 1905 in Spitalfields. In some of the larger suburban centres, SHOPS and STORES for firms of drapers were once dominant. Gardiner's at Whitechapel (destroyed by fire in 1974) provided a landmark at the junction of the newly extended Commercial Road from 1870, while Stratford boasted an impressive series of late Victorian and Edwardian frontages, mostly thoughtlessly done away with in the 1970s. More permanent commercial buildings with their own distinct architectural character are the many small BANKS, in the late C19 usually in classical or Free Baroque style.

THE TWENTIETH CENTURY: BUILDING BETWEEN THE WARS

East London emerged from the First World War with heavy losses, evidenced by the strikingly long list of names of its young men inscribed not only on church memorials but also the poignant and unique East End street memorials, of which two have survived in Bethnal Green (Cyprus Street and Bonner Street). Official WAR MEMORIALS were erected by most of the boroughs and local councils. Good examples are at East Ham, Wanstead and Newbury Park. Plaistow's war memorial, unusually, was a large YMCA in Greengate Street by *T.B. Daniel*, with faience decoration incorporating the emblems of the allied powers.

Domestic Building

The SUBURBAN GROWTH of outer London as a whole had slowed in the first decade of the C20 but gained new momentum after 1918 when the metropolis doubled in area and spilled further into the Home Counties. About 860,000 houses were

built in Greater London, but the slowest change was in the E. Nevertheless the opening of the Eastern Avenue (A12) in the late 1920s prompted further development in the northern districts of Walthamstow and the areas N of Ilford: Barkingside, Gants Hill and Newbury Park, while Chingford grew from a small suburb of 10,000 to 40,000 by 1939. The character of the development followed the general London pattern with genteel semi-detached houses in orderly roads and crescents, built to a lower density than before the war. Houses are tacitly vernacular in appearance but the builders added often inventive and peculiar applied-timber decoration. What Osbert Lancaster memorably called 'bypass variegated' still forms the dominant impression of the outer ring of suburbs for the car traveller to and from London: bows or canted bays, tile-hung walls and coloured glass to the windows and front door. Their little front gardens are sadly too often sacrificed to crazy paving and asphalt. Good examples are to be found in Chingford, Wanstead, Woodford and Barkingside. Nods towards a jazzy Art Deco style are rare and more progressive styles in architecture after 1930 made little impact on private housing at this time. A uniquely suburban type of this date is the small complexes of serviced flats. Redbridge has two splendid examples, both of 1935–6: Hermitage Court, South Woodford, in a streamlined Deco style and The Shrubbery, Wanstead, with Modernist trappings. An exhibition of 1934 at Gidea Park, Romford, promoted 'Modern Homes' but most have been unsympathetically altered and only No. 64 Heath Drive, by 101
Francis Skinner with *Tecton*, still evokes the purity of the forward-looking designs of the Modern Movement on the continent.

A major part of East London's growth was accounted for by PUBLIC HOUSING, in particular the LCC's mammoth Becontree Estate, built on cheap farmland between Barking and Dagenham as the first and largest of the council's 'out-county' estates, which were conceived as a solution to the housing shortage in London. It followed the low-density Unwinian ideal of the garden suburb, providing homes for over 120,000 people. In the inner suburbs a more successful, smaller-scale effort of this type is the 'Homes for Heroes' Chapel House Estate laid out by Poplar borough in 1919–21 on undeveloped land on the Isle of Dogs. The design, like the contemporary Bethnal Green estate and elsewhere in London, was by the *Office of Works* under *Sir Frank Baines*.

Most interwar public housing in Tower Hamlets was built as a result of slum clearance. An unrealized scheme by *T.H. Mawson* in 1919* proposed major reconstruction within the Borough of Stepney, replacing Cable Street with a wide boulevard, new civic centre and tall campanile at the centre of a Beaux-Arts axial plan that linked to parks along the river. It remained an optimistic fantasy,† but all over the East End, jerry-built courts of houses

* *The Builder*, v.116, 1919.

† Although the widening of Cable Street was still considered desirable in the 1943 County of London plan.

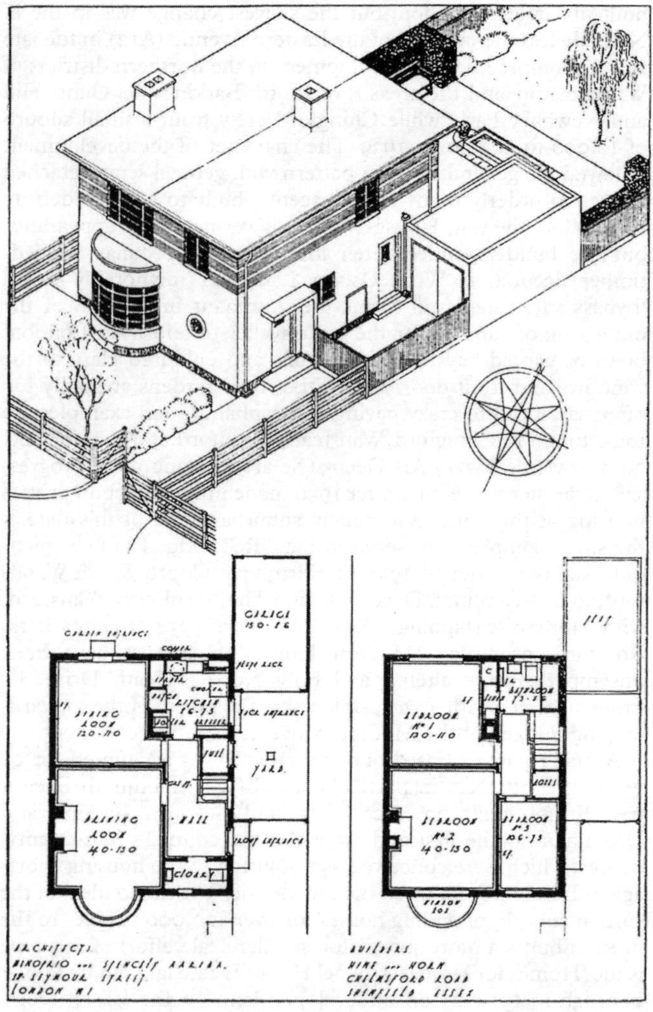

Gidea Park, Romford, No. 18 Brook Road by *Minoprio & Spencely* for the 1934 exhibition. Plan and elevation

and the wrecked remains of C17 and C18 property were swept away for flats. The pattern of brick, Neo-Georgian walk-up flats of four or more storeys with rear access balconies was set down by the LCC in the early 1920s at the Wapping Estate and Collingwood Estate, Bethnal Green, and continued with minor variations (e.g. more streamlined balconies) up to 1939. Independent housing trusts were also active, sometimes in

partnership with local authorities. St Hubert's House, Isle of Dogs, by *Ian. B. Hamilton* (1935–6), has decorative work by *Gilbert Bayes*. Of the same date is an attractive group provided for retired ship-repairers at Jubilee Crescent, Isle of Dogs. The 88
cubic forms of Continental Modernism with rendered walls and metal windows appear in several small schemes for private landlords in the East End, all of 1934–6. Turnour and Chapman Houses, Bigland Street, are severe blocks by *Joseph Emberton*, so too a small block in nearby Henriques Street by *Burnet, Tait & Lorne*. Gwynne House, Turner Street, Whitechapel, by local 102
architect *H. V. Kerr*, makes a feature of its curved staircase tower. It was built on the estate of the London Hospital where standards of new housing were strictly maintained. A go-ahead streamlined style was the keynote of the Socialist Poplar Borough Council in the 1930s. It took pride in demonstrating what it could do for its residents, with large blocks of flats, luxurious public baths, clinics and new libraries. Housing for the other boroughs tended to be less inspired.

Religious Buildings

There was much church building between the wars, both in the new suburbs of the 1920s and 30s and in those older areas that acquired long-intended permanent churches at this time. These lower, generally towerless, buildings are no longer as dominant as their predecessors. The greater simplicity of the churches of between the wars had already been adumbrated before 1914. Charles Spooner, writing on modern churches in *The Builder*, 1911, recommended 'largeness and simplicity, good proportions and sound building', precepts which were generally followed. He also advised against the use of revival styles, though this message seems to have had less effect; the reduction of detail that is general at this time may be due as much to economy. Planning generally remained conservative, continuing forms established by the late C19: a long, usually aisled nave, the chancel often with side chapel and vestries. The outstanding church of this period is the great brick basilica of St Andrew, Ilford, 1923–4 by *Sir Herbert Baker*, built as a memorial to Bishop Edgar Jacob of St Albans, who established the fund for 'London over the Border churches', and was instrumental in the creation of the new diocese of Chelmsford (1913) which embraced the spreading outer suburban areas. The church is memorable for its unexpected combination of grandeur with exquisitely crafted brick- 92
and-tile detail, and for furnishings by distinguished artists: these include excellent stained glass by *Karl Parsons* and others, and 91
work by two artists who collaborated with Baker elsewhere, *Sir Charles Wheeler*, whose bronze figure of Peace surmounts the domed W Baptistery, and *Laurence Turner*, who was responsible for the woodwork. The tradition of local patronage remained strong: the church has a separate chapel devoted to the family of the local builder, A.P. Griggs. Baker used a neutral round-arched

style, and the search for alternatives to Gothic is demonstrated by others at this time. St Paul, East Ham, by *Charles Spooner* (1933), is also in a simple round-arched style but with the novelty of a colonnade instead of an arcade, and innovative also for its use of concrete for beams and columns. The enormous West
90 Ham Baptist Central Mission at Plaistow has a centrally planned auditorium fronted by a Byzantine façade with two square domed towers (1921–2 by *W. Hayne*). A version of Romanesque, adopted by some R.C. churches already before 1914, appears at St Joseph Leyton, built as a war memorial, and prefaced by a grand, angular westwork (1924 by *Sandy & Norris*). Romanesque is used more ornately at St Peter Becontree by *W.C. Mangan*, 1937. In contrast, *Mangan*'s chapel for St Mary's R.C. Convent, Canning Town 1929, has a gloriously festive Italian Renaissance interior in coloured marbles. Our Lady Immaculate R.C., Limehouse (*A.J. Sparrow* 1925–34) has an elegant classical interior, quite unexpected from its rather dour outside. *Caröe & Passmore* also turned to classical sources, but in this case via late C17 England, for the Anglican St John the Divine, Romford (1927).

But Gothic was by no means dead: it was used confidently by *Geoffrey Raymond* for the chapel of the Mayflower Centre, Canning Town (1923–30), Our Lady of Lourdes R.C., Wanstead (1928–40), and St Vincent R.C., Becontree (1931), and a version of Perp was also adopted for the most lavish of the Becontree churches, St Alban, by *Milner & Craze*, funded by Violet Wills of the tobacco family. Restrained, carefully detailed examples of C14 Gothic by architects who specialized in churches of this kind are *H.P. Burke-Downing*'s St John, Walthamstow 1924–5 (sadly subdivided), and *Newberry & Fowler*'s St Martin, Becontree 1931–2, and Good Shepherd, Collier Row, 1934–5. The latter firm also built St George and St Ethelbert, East Ham, 1935–7, not in their usual late Gothic but with lancets and crossing tower inspired by the cathedral at Hereford, whose diocese contributed to the costs. An individual and particularly attractive building is Our Lady of Grace and St Teresa R.C., Chingford, 1930–9 by *G.W. Martyn*, Gothic but with much unusually good detail in a by then old-fashioned Arts and Crafts tradition. Two older churches have tactful additions in a subtle and restrained late Gothic idiom: Ilford (*J.H. Gibbons*) and Upminster (*Sir Charles Nicholson*), both of 1928. *Nicholson*'s two suburban churches, St Elisabeth, Becontree, and St George, Gants Hill (both 1931), are in a friendly, sturdy Jacobean brick Gothic, a not inappropriate compromise style for the Church of England. Emmanuel, Leyton, by *Travers & Grant* is also in a rough kind of vernacular Gothic, but with some quirky 1930s touches. Art Deco makes its appearance most blatantly in the intriguing little chapel at Chadwell Heath Cemetery (1933).

The most original church architect of this period is *N.F.*
94 *Cachemaille-Day*. St Mary, Becontree (1934–5) belongs with the more innovative of his buildings. It has his favourite device of a tall lantern tower lighting the sanctuary, with keeled shafts to emphasize verticality; the motif is repeated on the furnishings.

The exterior is rendered and despite some stylized Gothic detail also appears untraditional. Quite different is his St Edmund Chingford (1938–9); it also has a sanctuary tower, but has overtly Gothic tracery, and is clad in vernacular Essex manner in flint and brick. The shift in the late 1930s towards more traditional cladding materials was typical of some progressive architects. His third church, St Laurence, Ilford (1939), is faced in brick, again with a lantern tower but in a simple round-arched style. The most unusual church of the end of the decade is St Patrick, Barking, by *A.E. Wiseman* (1940), built of concrete with an E end in the form of a streamlined tower, but now much altered inside.

Nonconformist churches of these years are modest: the *Baines* firm carried on the tradition of a Gothic street front and broad auditorium, but with simplified detail, as at the Methodist churches of North Chingford and Ilford (both 1927); the former retains its original, nicely finished simple fittings. South Chingford Methodist Church of 1930 turns to a plain Neo-Georgian.

Among the FURNISHINGS of the earlier C20 the most noteworthy are STAINED GLASS windows by artists working in the Arts and Crafts tradition, which stand out among the more routine productions by the established firms. Those at St Andrew, Ilford, already mentioned, by *Karl Parsons* and *William Aikman*, 91
are unusual in forming a complete scheme. English Martyrs R.C., Whitechapel, has ambitious windows by the Dublin firm of *William Earley*, 1930. Other notable windows on a more intimate scale are those by *Veronica Whall* at Our Lady and St Teresa, Chingford; by *Heywood Sumner* at North Ockendon; by *Margaret Chilton* at St Andrew, Leytonstone; and by *M.E. Aldrich Rope* at St Peter, Wapping. At All Saints, West Ham, there is an unusual war memorial window by *W. Reynolds Stephens*, at St Margaret Barking a window and rustic carved chapel screen by *George Jack*. St Margaret, Leytonstone has a huge and more solemn rood of 1921 by *Sir Charles Nicholson*.

Public Buildings

The expansion of the suburbs required new TOWN HALLS for recently created boroughs. They express the confident prosperity of East London's suburbs between the wars. At Ilford, the 98
Town Hall was extended after 1931 with an unusually richly fitted council chamber in an exuberant classical style. The late 1930s was an especially fertile period. Dagenham Civic Centre, by *E. Berry Webber* 1937, is a moderne spin on traditional Georgian forms with pride of place given to the entrance portico and grand stair leading to the council chamber. Similar in approach is Walthamstow Civic Centre by *P. D. Hepworth*, also begun in 1937, but here the spirit is more daring, classical in its formal composition, but clearly inspired by Scandinavian architecture in its use of simple, geometric forms eschewing ostentatious ornament. The influence is also evident to a lesser degree in the plain asymmetry of the contemporary Romford Town Hall by *Collins &*

Geens of Bournenouth. In the East End, Poplar built a large modernistic Town Hall (with a public theatre) by *Clifford Culpin* at Bow, decorated with excellent Socialist Realist reliefs of its builders. By contrast, Bethnal Green stuck to stripped classicism for its Town Hall extension by *E.C.P. Monson* (begun 1939) but fitted it out with a moderne interior of great panache. Also traditional was Barking's Town Hall, planned at this date but executed in the more austere decade after the war with a downgrading of its intended extravagance.

Genteel Neo-Georgian was the overwhelming preference for lesser public buildings of the period, especially for SCHOOLS and other educational buildings throughout the area. Essex County Council's architect *John Stuart* gave the lead, and with wearying dullness. Symmetrical frontages to the street with wings flanking a higher central block topped by a cupola became the norm, employed for primary schools, the new county secondary schools and even the technical colleges. Two buildings, both built by Ilford borough in the late 1930s, show an awareness of the new styles emerging from the continent: the flat-roofed Uphall
99 Nursery School, Ilford, and Parkhill Junior and Infants School, Barkingside, by *D. Edleston*. The LCC built far fewer new schools in its area (the consequence of generous provision since the 1870s). Libraries and other institutions are generally conformist during this period, with the exception of the jazzy interior of
100 Leytonstone library by *J. Ambrose Dartnall*. An unexpectedly pure example of Modern Movement style is the police stables at Bow by *G. Mackenzie Trench* 1934.

Industrial, Commercial and Transport Buildings

Employment for the inhabitants of the suburbs was increasingly provided by new, local INDUSTRIES, particularly electrical engineering, which accounted for much of London's success between the wars and was hardly affected by the Depression after 1929. There was much expansion along the Lea Valley, but the most important large industrial concern was the Ford Motor Co. (begun 1929) on the Thames at Dagenham, which helped sustain the new Becontree Estate and much of the surrounding area. Its early factory buildings and offices by *Charles Heathcote & Sons* survive only in part but impress by their scale. The motor age also produced an attractive showroom and garage in High Road, Ilford, designed in an appropriately streamlined style by *Cameron Kirby*, 1934. Other commercial concerns were quick to adopt new styles, as in the case of the Co-operative Wholesale Society which continued to be an enlightened patron, with striking Expressionist-style offices of 1930–3 by their architect *L. G. Ekins*
96 in Prescot Street, Whitechapel. Sadly, the creation of Eastern Avenue failed to produce a memorable sequence of opulent Art Deco FACTORIES in the way that the Great West Road had done for West London's suburbs. An isolated example is Woodcraft, Newton Industrial Estate, by *Fuller, Hall & Foulsham*: an all white

factory with a stylish streamlined tower to the fore. *Wallis Gilbert*'s
formal brick and stone Forest Works, Walthamstow, is a superior
example, while still prominent on Stratford High Street is the
former Yardleys box factory, seriously modern in style for 1937
but with a sentimental tiled panel of lavender pickers. Jazzier
detail appears in new buildings for the expanding textile trades
centred on Whitechapel and Spitalfields, as at Cheviot House,
Commercial Road, built as a woollen warehouse by *G.G. Winbourne* and the former sequin factory, Brody House, in Brody
Street, Spitalfields. The Second World War boosted expansion
for many industries: at Dagenham, *Edward Mills'* buildings for 103
May & Baker (now Aventis) pharmaceuticals included very early
examples of structures with shell-concrete roofs (1943–4) –
designed for economy in the absence of steel beams, and widely
used in the ration-burdened post-war years.

Most of the new suburbs were served by Neo-Georgian style
shopping parades of little or no character. In the larger town
centres one looks in vain for good commercial styles. The most
obvious buildings are frequently the Deco-style Burtons stores,
either in white faience or with exotic cast-stone decoration.
Romford built its first covered arcade in this period and its centre
also has a good group of small 1920s banks, but the larger type
of DEPARTMENT STORES are rare. Wickhams, Mile End Road
of 1925–7, has a pompous Beaux Arts frontage of West End pretension but is comically undermined by the survival of an older
shop in its midst. In the outer suburban towns, at Stratford,
Barking and Ilford were other large stores (mostly now replaced).
At Ilford (Bodgers) and at Upminster (Roomes) are remarkable
survivors of family-owned department stores.

Buildings for popular entertainments were more conscious of
passing fashion. CINEMAS are far fewer in number today than in
1939 and rarely survive unaltered. The best preserved have often
survived through conversion for bingo halls. A very early type,
the former Grove Picture Palace at Stratford of 1911 by *Gilbert
& Constanduros* is little more than a shed with a decorative brick
frontage, and the Coronation Cinema, Manor Park, 1921, by *Clifford Aish*, uses a watered down classicism. From 1930 the buildings grew in ambition and size, often doubling as theatres, and
have cafés and even ballrooms to enhance their appeal. Architects specializing in cinema design are also prevalent, employing
a variety of exotic styles such as Moorish in Hoe Street, Waltham- 95
stow, by *Massey & Komisarjevsky*; the latter also designed the
interior of the Granada, East Ham (with *W.E. Trent*, 1936). Art
Deco gained popularity in the early 1930s and was enthusiastically employed at the Troxy, Commercial Road, whose designer
George Coles dominated in this field, with cinemas at Mile End,
Stratford and Barkingside. He also designed the interior of the
multi-purpose New People's Palace, Mile End Road, 1934, done
in a stripped-classical style with exterior reliefs by *Eric Gill*. The
architect for the Odeon chain, *Andrew Mather*, produced a Modernist design for the Boleyn cinema, East Ham, in 1935. GREY-
HOUND STADIUMS were an entirely novel form of entertainment

and also adopted up-to-date styles. The best preserved in the whole of London is at Walthamstow, a streamlined group of 1932 with arresting neon signage.

PUBS continued to provide centres of recreation. Much rebuilding and improvement took place of the smaller street pubs of the inner East End, particularly by Truman's in-house architect *A.E. Sewell*, whose pubs usually sport attractive faience decoration and domestic architectural motifs, for example The Royal Oak, Columbia Road, Bethnal Green. Larger pubs were built to serve the new suburbs and estates, deliberately conceived to reduce 'perpendicular drinking' by including diversions such as bowling alleys, and appealing to women by providing tearooms etc. The Becontree estate has many of this type; the style varies from homely Olde English to Neo-Regency. The Neo-Georgian Doctor Johnson, Barkingside, of 1937 by *H. Reginald Ross* has a well-preserved Art Deco snug bar.

UNDERGROUND STATIONS, a notable feature of some parts of London's interwar suburbia, are less well-represented in East London. The Central Line extension from Liverpool Street to Ongar (partly incorporating existing branch lines) was begun in the 1930s. Only the stations at Bethnal Green and Mile End by *Holden & Heaps* were finished by the outbreak of war during which parts of the tunnels were used as factories. Bethnal Green, quickly taken over as an air raid shelter, was the scene of a terrible civilian disaster. The progressive style associated with *Charles Holden* is shown best by his stations at Wanstead, Redbridge and Gants Hill, completed in 1947 to pre-war designs. Above ground they have characteristically clean detailing and simple massing of geometric forms derived from Dutch and Scandinavian architecture but show the austerity of the times in which they were eventually built. The rest of the extension, incorporating the existing stations of the LNER, was mostly given exceptionally plain new buildings in the late 1940s. At Newbury
104 Park, the station was integrated with a new Bus Station by *Oliver Hill*, also conceived before the war but opened in 1949, with an elegantly plain curving roof on concrete arches.

POST-WAR EAST LONDON

Planning and Housing 1940s–80s

Many problems faced the post-war planners. The war had interrupted the progress of extensive slum clearance plans. Bomb damage in Tower Hamlets and in the docklands areas of Newham had been severe and the housing problem was acute. Vast numbers of prefabricated buildings covered Stepney and Poplar, built in the 1940s by the government (a pair of Orlit concrete-panel prefabs remains in Tiller Road, Isle of Dogs). Many bombed-out families had moved away, but it was expected that they would return. Neither the overall decline in London's population, which was to sink from 8.6 million in 1939 to below seven million by 1981, nor the total closure of the docks, was anticipated. The recent outer suburban areas were less affected, but lacked amenities, especially secondary schools. Concern over suburban sprawl before the war had eventually achieved the declaration of a green belt around London (1938), with the intention of limiting further growth. Now in contrast to a general pre-war distrust of planning, there was a new enthusiasm for the official creation of post-war utopias. The planning backbone was provided by Forshaw and Abercrombie's *County of London Plan* of 1943, consolidated in the official plan adopted in 1951. The *Greater London Plan*, also by Abercrombie, was published in 1944, although the areas covered by the present outer London boroughs (in this volume Newham, Waltham Forest, Redbridge, Barking & Dagenham, Havering) only became an official part of Greater London in 1965. Until then these five consisted of boroughs or districts within the county of Essex, with facilities such as libraries and most of their secondary schools and colleges provided by the Essex County Council.

The *County of London plan* provided a framework for rebuilding in Tower Hamlets which survived up to *c.* 1970: basic principles were an agreed density (136 people per acre in the inner areas), combined with a much greater provision of open space, requiring the removal of surplus people to outer suburbs or new towns. Zoning of land use was recommended, so that wherever possible housing was to be separated from industry and commerce. This meant a radical rethinking of the traditional dense mix of activities in the historic East End. The solution proposed was the most ambitious rebuilding programme in London:

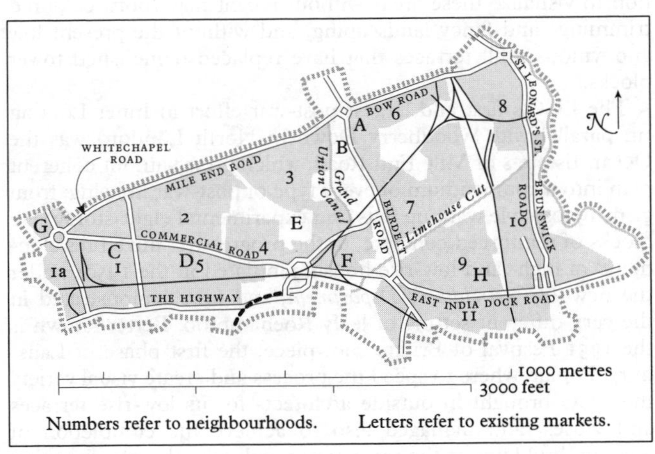

Stepney-Poplar Reconstruction Area

comprehensive redevelopment of a core of 1,321 acres, stretching from Whitechapel to Poplar, which was to be rebuilt as eleven inward-looking 'neighbourhoods', with housing turning away from the main roads and focused on schools, parks and community buildings. In execution this approach was rarely wholly successful because piecemeal land acquisition made coherent planning difficult. Providers of other amenities did not always cooperate; government cuts removed proposed nursery schools and health provision, while all or parts of old traffic routes, shopping streets and other buildings remained and were not integrated into the new layouts. The situation was not helped by division of responsibilities between the LCC and the boroughs of Stepney and Poplar. By 1962, 7,900 new homes had been provided in the area, just under half those built in the whole of Tower Hamlets, roughly two thirds by the LCC and the rest by the boroughs. Although the original vision was undermined by lack of resources for maintaining both buildings and open spaces, and by the unanticipated rise of car ownership, the concept of the 'neighbourhood' was humane; it is still recognizable in a few of the LCC's early and best-coordinated efforts (e.g. the Lansbury and Locksley estates), and there have been efforts to reinforce it in recent years by new amenity buildings. There was extensive rebuilding outside the reconstruction area, following on from earlier slum clearance plans, notably in Bethnal Green, mostly by the local borough, and on the Isle of Dogs, initially by Poplar but then largely by the LCC. West Ham adopted the neighbourhood principle for its borough plan of 1946, which included the total rebuilding of the savagely damaged area of Canning Town, and subsequently of Stratford New Town.

What are the highlights for the architectural visitor from the thirty years of post-war reconstruction? A warning here is needed: much has been transformed in recent years, and the visitor in search of the 1950–60s needs some creative imagination to visualize these areas without recent new roofs, coloured trimmings and fancy landscaping, and without the present low anonymous infill terraces that have replaced demolished tower blocks.

The LCC's first and largest post-war effort in Inner London (in parallel with Woodberry Down in North London) was the Ocean Estate s of Mile End Road, which grew without coherent plan into a compendium of every type of post-war housing, from grim 1930s-style walk-up flats and experimental eight-storey slab blocks of reinforced concrete, to the progressive 'mixed development' of high- and low-rise housing initiated in the 1950s under the new *LCC Architect's Department*, and first demonstrated in the very different setting of leafy Roehampton. Better known is the 1951 Festival of Britain showpiece, the first phase of Lansbury, Poplar, where to speed the process and create visual variety the LCC brought in outside architects for its low-rise terraces and closes, and managed also to achieve the completion of amenity buildings at the same time – schools, church, shopping centre – a feat which proved difficult to repeat. The best of the

Poplar, Lansbury, housing of 1951

LCC work of the later 50s produced some picturesque grouping of buildings and landscape, as at the Avebury Estate, Bethnal Green and at Park View Estate, 1953–5, by *de Metz & Birks* for the LCC, where a tactfully oblique array of flats was created beside Victoria Park.

Meanwhile the Borough of Bethnal Green, unconvinced by the LCC's approach, pursued its own original path, employing radical private architects to experiment with housing layouts which would be both humane and high density. The most original was the housing by the two offshoots of the pre-war firm of Tecton, following its early post-war work in Finsbury: *Denys* p. 595
Lasdun's forceful cluster blocks in Usk Street and Claredale Street (1955–9) re-created backyards in the air, and the lively and spirited estates of mixed heights by *Skinner Bailey & Lubetkin*, 111
Dorset, Lakeview and Cranbrook (1955–68), are full of the quirky patterning so beloved by Lubetkin. The Borough of Stepney took a more traditional approach, using the 1930s formula of brick walk-up blocks, for example for early parts of the Tarling and Limehouse Fields estates, the latter with a larger than usual proportion of 'cottages'. The early blocks (now nearly all transformed or demolished) were drearily austere, though in the later 1950s Stepney developed a more stylish streamlined style, as in their brick flats on the Sidney Street Estate. Stepney's change to more up-to-date Modernism came with the Clichy Estate of the early 1960s, by *Riches & Blythin*, with its neat medium-rise ranges with coloured cladding panels around a tall slab and pedestrian court, the planning reflecting the newly-acknowledged need to consider car ownership.

From the late 1950s the LCC architects revelled in transforming the traditional low East End skyline through the expressive concrete forms of increasingly ambitious and dominant tower blocks, centrepieces of their 'mixed development' estates. They made a dramatic appearance on the edge of the enlarged Stepney Green, a typically Corbusian siting: three 17-storey towers of 1958–64 (all now demolished). Their significance was emphasized further by a nearby sculpture by *Henry Moore* (now removed). This was an example of the LCC's idealistic post-war aim of bringing modern art to the people: other examples in the East End, which have survived more happily, are *Franta Belsky*'s Mother and Child at the Avebury Estate and *Elisabeth*
111 *Frink*'s Blind Beggar on the Cranbrook Estate, both in Bethnal Green.

The heights of tower blocks increased over the next decade.* The success with which they are integrated in their settings varies. On the Chicksand Estate, Mile End New Town, the single tower fits neatly at the apex of a well-planned group of varied heights; the three horrendously bleak giants at Crossways, Bow,
113 stride over unkempt wasteland; at St George's the chunky concrete of the towers complemented by bold use of concrete detail for the lower buildings, with landscaped space at different levels. The pressure for housing was such that the most unappealing sites were pressed into use, beside main roads, gasworks and railway lines. Some of the worst sites were beside the enlarged Blackwall Tunnel approach, a challenge that inspired both *Ernö*
112 *Goldfinger*'s impressive Balfron Tower on the Brownfield Estate, 1965–7, given a distinctive profile by its semi-detached lift shaft, similar to his better known Trellick Tower in West London, and the *Smithsons*' more rebarbative but ingenious pair of inward-looking barrier slabs at Robin Hood Gardens, Poplar (1966–72), both commissioned by the LCC. On the Isle of Dogs, badly bombed but outside the comprehensive redevelopment area, the Borough of Poplar built Lansbury-type low-rise housing immediately after the war, but later sites were developed by the GLC with mass housing of a depressingly routine kind, which continued into the early 1970s. Tower Hamlets built equally uninspiringly on its NE fringes at Old Ford.

The story of post-war housing in the outer areas is less dramatic. Soon after the war the LCC continued with its policy of low-rise estates outside its boundaries, building from 1947 at
110 Hainault, where its steel-framed prefabricated houses have survived well. Harold Hill, an LCC estate for 25,000, was laid out on the edge of the green belt on more formal garden-city lines (1947–54), and low LCC housing spread down Friday Hill, Chingford, where land had been acquired before the war. The

*For example (nearly all still standing): Lincoln Estate, Bow Common, two 19-storey towers, 1958; Chicksand, Mile End New Town, a single tower of 21 storeys, 1961; Bigland and Glamis, one tower each of 22 storeys, 1963–5; Watney Market, two of 25 storeys, 1966; Crossways, Bow, three of 25 storeys, 1968–70; St George's, three of 28 storeys, 1968–70.

local authorities were also active: examples from the 1940s–50s, designed with some care and worth singling out here, are the unusually elegant groups of suburban houses at Ropers Avenue, Chingford, by *Reginald W. Lone*, housing of mixed heights at *Norman & Dawbarn*'s Heath Park Estate, Dagenham, and the formally composed Thames View Estate, Barking (*C.C. Shaw*, borough architect) 1953–60. There were a few early high-rise developments, which stood out as innovative and original at the time: Priory Court, by *C.H. Doody* of East Ham, 1953, and a group of eight-storey blocks (also called Priory Court) at Walthamstow by *F.G. Southgate* (now much altered and refurbished). West Ham, badly affected by bombing, built much more, under the borough architect *T.E. North*. Canning Town at first had quite spacious low housing on garden-suburb principles, but the borough soon adopted a mixed development programme, turning to system-built towers to speed the process. Two dozen towers over twelve storeys had been built by 1965, and the new Borough of Newham added a further two dozen in the later 1960s. The policy came to an alarming end with the partial collapse in 1968 of Ronan Point, one of eight 23-storey towers on Canning Town's Freemasons' Estate.

In the 1960s the outer boroughs varied in their approach. The more middle-class areas avoided tower blocks; Redbridge and Havering built only a handful, but Leyton had thirteen by 1965, and after it became part of Waltham Forest the new borough continued the policy, with eighteen blocks of twelve storeys and over planned from 1965–8. Major public housing schemes, never popular in the more conservative outer suburbs, ceased in these areas with the decline of government funding in the 1970s.

The drawbacks of high-rise for family accommodation were becoming clear well before the collapse of Ronan Point; among experimental alternatives was a small government-sponsored group at Canning Town of 1961–4 by *A. W. Cleeve Barr* and *Oliver Cox*, which provided low, tightly knit housing in a friendly weatherboarded idiom, a precursor of future trends. Other alternatives to high-rise were being explored by the end of the 1960s. One unusual group in Redbridge, offering a novel form of low-rise, deserves mention: the tight clusters by *Derek Stow* at Anworth Close, Woodford, 1967, built on the fringe of a large clearance area. *Shepheard, Epstein & Hunter*'s dense medium-rise scheme at Gough Grove, Lansbury, of 1970, included segregated car and pedestrian routes.

A greater concern with context became apparent in new housing schemes of the 1970s. The GLC combined complex three-dimensional layered planning on the sloping site of the Glamis Estate, Cable Street (1976–7), with low frontages along Cable Street in keeping with older survivals in the area. One of the most attractive examples of the rediscovery of a vernacular idiom for new housing is the pretty group of canal-side cottages added in the early 1980s on the fringe of the Ocean Estate, a final fling by the GLC shortly before its abolition in 1985. After this date responsibility for the old GLC sites passed to the boroughs, but with the decline in government funding the future for social housing now lay with housing associations.

Post-War Education

Next to housing, the provision of new SCHOOLS was a principal focus of architectural activity after the war, to cope with bomb damage and to realize the aims of the 1944 Education Act. Only a few can be singled out here among the dozens built. Tower Hamlets came under the London School Plan (1947) that required the reorganization of secondary education on comprehensive lines; the boroughs of East and West Ham built their own schools (at first with separate grammar and secondary moderns), the outer areas came under Essex County Council. The ideal of the light and airy PRIMARY SCHOOL of modern materials was illustrated by *Yorke Rosenberg & Mardall*'s ingeniously planned Susan Lawrence School (now Lansbury Lawrence), 1950–2, a showpiece of the Lansbury exhibition in 1951, and followed by their adjacent nursery school. *Cecil C. Handisyde*'s Old Palace Primary, Bow, of 1952 is in a similar spirit. These primaries were of two storeys. There was more space in the outer boroughs; under *Harold Conolly* of the ECC low, 'finger plan' schools of standardized units were quickly built on the new estates, for example at Hainault and Friday Hill, Chingford. Priory Junior, Harold Hill (1953), was unusual in being built of prefabricated timber parts. Sympathetically designed SPECIAL SCHOOLS were also a post-war ideal, realized by the Phoenix School, Bow, 1951–2 by *Farquharson & McMorran*, and later by the GLC/ILEA's Bromley Hall School, Poplar, 1967–8. SECONDARY SCHOOLS adopted a variety of models: an early example is *Yorke Rosenberg & Mardall*'s friendly, well-detailed Hainault Forest High School, 1951. Another is *George Whitby*'s Secondary Modern (now part of Plashet School), East Ham, 1953–4, which responded to the small site with an eight-storey building on an interesting cross-shaped plan. In contrast, Langdon Secondary, by *J. W. Taylor* of East Ham (1953–64), spreads over a generous riverside site: a group of three schools (boys' and girls' grammars and secondary modern) in a trim pre-war-modern brick and glass idiom. The large LCC comprehensives were generally more compact; Stepney Green, with its overpowering eight-storey classroom slab (1961–3) is typical. Most of these older secondaries today are composite groups, their neutral brick and curtain-walled classrooms extended with specialized buildings for drama, music, sports, sixth forms, etc. The results seldom make for architectural distinction, and private schools are similarly accretive. Individual components can be impressive, such as the polygonal concrete theatre at the Forest School (*Ove Arup & Partners*, 1963–5), or the additions by *van Heyningen & Haward* at the George Monoux College (1990–7) (both Walthamstow).

A rare case of a unified secondary of the 1970s is the GLC's George Green School, Isle of Dogs; its long four-storey stepped ranges of concrete blocks respond creatively to the site, and it was innovative, too, in including community facilities. Some of the GLC/ILEA primaries of the 1970s (ceasing with the dissolution of the GLC in 1985) also have a new liveliness, with friendly exteriors and experimental layouts reflecting new teaching approaches (among them the short-lived fashion for open planning), for example the earlier part of Cyril Jackson, Limehouse, and Hermitage, Wapping. St Paul's Primary, Bow Common, by *Maguire & Murray* 1972, is another example, tucking everything under a big sloping roof. In contrast, Shapla, off Wellclose Square, Stepney, one of the last of the GLC's buildings, 1983–5, is arranged around two courtyards. Newham also built distinctive and colourful open-plan primaries in the 1980s: Cleves in East Ham, and three schools on generous sites for the new housing in Beckton (North Beckton, Ellen Wilkinson and Winsor). Waltham Forest was unusual in the 1970s in building nursery schools (e.g. Low Hall, Walthamstow). Queen Mary College remained East London's only UNIVERSITY until 1992. Its post-war enlargements by *Playne & Lacey* on a tight site are memorable chiefly for the little domed, circular chapel of 1962–3, which must also be considered in the context of religious buildings.

Religious Buildings: Mid C20–Early C21

Religious buildings will be considered here over the span of the entire half century. Despite a decline in church attendance compared with the start of the century, mid-C20 CHURCH BUILDING was a busy activity. Although a large number of bombed churches were not replaced, war-damage money made rebuilding or repair possible for many. The Nonconformists produced the least traditional buildings. Early replacements of major lost buildings include the determinedly modern Congregational church on the Lansbury Estate, by *Handisyde* and *Stark* (1949–51), the dignified Methodist church, Bow Road (1951), and the straightforward Methodist group at Forest Gate (1955–64) both by *Paul Mauger*. The latter, like the Lansbury church, illustrates the continuing Nonconformist practice of including integrated halls and schoolrooms. Of the same period is the austere but capacious East London Baptist Tabernacle by *Hubert Lidbetter* and the little Stepney Meeting House with concrete-shell roof by *Felix Goldsmith* (both 1955). Rebuilding for other groups in the 1960s included a large synagogue complex at Ilford, 1960–1 by *N. Green,* and an ingenious cluster plan for the Friends Meeting House, Wanstead, by *N. Frith* 1968.

Anglican buildings of the 1950s were a varied bunch: they range from *Seely & Paget*'s St Nicholas and All Hallows, Poplar, quietly progressive in its avoidance of Gothic detail (and memorable for its painted ceiling by *Brian Thomas*), and the modest, timidly modern St Paul Stratford, 1953–4 by *Humphreys & Hurst*, to churches by older architects who continued to build in a Gothic style, such as *J.H. Gibbons'* St Philip and St James Plaistow, and *J.J. Crowe*'s St Nicholas Elm Park, Hornchurch. R.C. churches of this time are an even odder mixture; 1950s examples in the outer suburbs are dull, but *Adrian Scott*'s extraordinary St Mary and St Joseph, Lansbury (1950–4), is in a category all of its own, arranged round a mighty crossing tower, with fanciful Gothic/Deco detailing. Particularly intriguing is the German R.C. church of St Boniface, Whitechapel; ostensibly it is by *D. Plaskett Marshall*, but owes its modern look to the incumbent, who was advised by a German architect. The small (former) Danish church at Limehouse by *Holger Jensen* 1958–9, is another example of invigorating Continental Modernism.

Remodelling older churches often included removal of C19 fittings, but where only the shell remained after bombing, more radical change could be introduced. St George-in-the-East was rebuilt by *Ansell & Bailey* with courtyard and smaller church contained within Hawksmoor's massive outer walls. *J. Anthony Lewis* recast three damaged churches in Bethnal Green without their
106, 107 aisles. Of these St Matthew is especially interesting for its wealth of new furnishings by young artists, while at the remodelled St James-the-Less the new W wall was filled with Modernist glass by *Keith New*. Stepney Meeting House has good slab glass by *Pierre Fourmaintreaux*, 1955. Generally 1950s stained glass is disappointingly conservative, but it includes some evocative pictorial period pieces, such as the dramatic E window at St Dunstan, Stepney, by *Hugh Easton*, and the colourful work by *Celtic Studios* in the Welsh church at Leytonstone.

The most significant break with tradition was created through the Liturgical Movement, with its emphasis on bringing altar and priest into closer contact with the congregation. Before the war Cachemaille-Day had been interested in greater integration of the chancel and the rest of the church but, generally, conservative planning had prevailed. An important pioneer in the East End was the furnishing of the simple new chapel at St Katharine's Foundation Ratcliffe in 1954 by *Keith Murray* and *Robert Maguire*, with a centrally placed freestanding altar carved by *Ralph Beyer*, emphasized by a hanging corona. In 1958
108 *Maguire & Murray* went on to build St Paul Bow Common, radical both in its central planning and in its use of industrial-looking plain brick and concrete surfaces, relieved outside only by *Beyer*'s lettering and inside by mosaics by *Charles Lutyens*. St Paul was too extreme a statement to have direct progeny, but its inward-looking character is echoed elsewhere, for example by the small circular St Benet's chaplaincy at Queen Mary College, 1962–4, which has striking sgraffito murals by *Adam Kossowski*. A defensive exterior (considered essential in a tough area), was adopted for a rare purpose-built shared church at North Woolwich, of 1968 by *Laurence King & Partners*, a plain, modern design with top-lit sanctuary and nave in a single space, which replaced older Anglican and R.C. buildings. *Gerard Goalen*'s Holy Trinity Leytonstone (1973–4) also has a tough shell but an attrac-

tive interior, with a subtly lit cross-in-square nave and small sanctuary.

From the 1960s, as the tenets of the Liturgical Movement were accepted more widely both by R.C. and Anglican churches, free-standing altars became more general; chancels were used less and sometimes ruthlessly stripped of their furnishings; elaborately composed R.C. High Altars were split up and subsidiary altars removed. The fashion among the numerous new R.C. churches that sprang up in the outer suburbs, most of them at this time by *John Newton* of *Burles, Newton & Partners*, was for light, modern materials and a single well-lit space, as at St Michael, East Ham (1959), Our Lady of La Salette, Rainham (1967), and St John the Baptist, Ilford (1966–7). The last is notable for its bold semi-abstract windows by *Patrick Reyntiens*.

By this time appreciation of the impractical dim and lofty naves and remote chancels of High Victorian Anglican churches was at its nadir; neglect followed by demolition or crude subdivision were the solutions adopted in many cases. The old parish of East Ham was notable for a more constructive approach, based on a study of local needs by *Martin Purdy* in the 1970s. One result was that the vast cemetery attached to the medieval church became a nature reserve (one of the first such examples), another was that Purdy's firm *APEC* was engaged to replace churches on other sites. The first was St Bartholomew, East Ham, where a large Edwardian church patched up after war damage was replaced by a block containing a small new church, health centre and old people's flats (1979–83); the idea caught on and other multi-purpose groups followed (St Mark, Forest Gate, 1986, St Mark, Beckton, 1989, St Michael, Manor Park, 1990, St Matthias, Canning Town, 1991). The *APEC* groups have deliberately friendly, domestic-looking exteriors, with small, ingeniously lit worship spaces, often flexibly planned to open up to a larger hall. Flexible use was also the aim of the reordering of the small post-war Congregational church at Bromley-by-Bow by *Wyatt MacLaren* 1991–2, the start of exceptionally enterprisng activity which led to a series of neighbouring community buildings. In Tower Hamlets conversion of churches to housing or other uses was more common, retaining only the outward form as a piece of townscape. A more imaginative approach developed in the later 1990s, with adaptations which endeavoured to retain some vestige of the spatial quality of the interior, as at St Luke, Canning Town (by *Peter Eley* 1998) and St Paul, Old Ford (by *Matthew Lloyd* 2003). A move in favour of more formal liturgical space, created in a strikingly modern style, is evident in *Cottrell & Vermeulen*'s remodelling of St Martin, Plaistow (1991–7). Examples of quieter, dignified refurnishings giving a new look to older buildings include St Nicholas and All Hallows, Poplar (reopened after a period of closure), and All Hallows, Devons Road, Bow, both by *Tom Hornsby* of *Keith Harrison Architects*, Our Lady of Grace and St Teresa Chingford, by *Richard Hurley Associates*, and the chapel at St Katharine's Foundation, Ratcliffe, transformed in 2004 by *Christopher Smallwood Architects*. The

most striking among the few completely new recent churches is the large R.C. church of Our Lady and St George, Walthamstow,
109 by *Plater Inkpen Vale & Downie* 1995, memorable for its gentle curves and brightly-lit vaulted interior.

Prominent buildings and large congregations are not synonymous. The Afro-Caribbean charismatic churches, drawing in hundreds of people, plainly accommodated in former cinemas, halls and warehouses, rarely make an architectural mark. The same was true until recently of MOSQUES, but today it is these rather than churches which are beginning to provide the new landmarks. The first mosque in London opened in Commercial Road in 1941, but from the 1970s large numbers of places of worship were established by immigrant Islamic communities in temporary or converted buildings. From the 1990s the change to purpose-built premises began to be evident.* The new buildings are cultural centres, including teaching and community spaces as well as prayer rooms. They adopt traditional Islamic features such as arched openings and glazed tiles as defining signatures, incorporated in plain, modern structures, as in the mosque whose neat symmetrical brick frontage faces Lea Bridge Road, Leyton. The more ambitious examples have domes and minarets: the major example is the East London Mosque, Whitechapel Road, of 1982–5 by *John Gill Associates*, next to the still larger London Muslim Centre by *Robert Klashka* of *Markland Klashka*, 2003–4.

Public Buildings 1950–c. 1985

Apart from housing and schools, government restrictions limited other types of buildings until 1954. In 1951 Lansbury was provided with shops around *Frederick Gibberd*'s modest and friendly pedestrian Market Square (the first post-war pedestrian square to be built in England), with a clock tower as an extra flourish; but this was an exceptional display for the Festival of Britain. Walthamstow also made a special effort, under *F.G. Southgate*, rebuilding its bombed town centre crossroads at Hoe Street in a cheerful Festival spirit; its E side remains. The occasional rebuilt pubs, low key and domestic (the Artichoke in Stepney Way, Princess Alice at Forest Gate), now appear as period pieces of these early post-war years.

1954 saw the start of the long delayed Town Hall at Barking, its formal pre-war design by *Jackson & Edmonds* simplified, but

*English Heritage recorded 23 mosques in Tower Hamlets in 2003, in accommodation ranging from prefabricated cabins and railway arches to former pubs, shops, community halls and synagogues. Only two were in new buildings: the Bow Muslim Community Centre in Roman Road and the East London Mosque in Whitechapel Road. The latter traces its origins to the first mosque in Commercial Road of 1941, all the others were established from 1975 onwards. F. Gailani, *The Mosques of London*, 2000, lists 15 mosques in Newham, 8 in Waltham Forest, many of them in private houses.

appearing old-fashioned amidst the post-war enthusiasm for new architecture. In the 1960s cultural amenities began to be provided for the outer suburbs. Essex County Council led the way, providing a series of light and attractive modern branch libraries, each one slightly different (Upminster, Hornchurch), and a larger central library at Romford, forming a strong accent at the end of the market place. After 1965 the new boroughs took over. Havering built an ambitious swimming pool at Harold Hill (1966); the 105
same year Redbridge built a library at Wanstead, in a rather tougher idiom than those by the ECC. It also commissioned *F. Gibberd, Coombes & Partners*, whose cheerful circular domed library and nearby swimming pool of 1968 provide notable landmarks at Barkingside, their surfaces a mild reflection of the concrete Brutalism fashionable by this time.

Apart from St George's swimming pool, by *R.H. Uren* 1965–9, little in the way of amenities was built in Tower Hamlets, which had to make do with its remaining patched-up older buildings. Outside the housing estates there was a dearth of interest in producing attractive townscape in the 1960s. The novel flatted workshops of concrete (Adler Street, Whitechapel, by *YRM* 1963–4), built as part of the drive to relocate industry, attracted interest, but were austerely functional. Less distinguished buildings on a large scale began to invade the outer areas, not to their aesthetic benefit. Romford developed the first of a succession of pedestrian shopping centres from 1967, and high-rise commercial towers appeared at Ilford and Barking following the government's encouragement of the dispersal of offices from central London (the best of them at Barking, by *Owen Luder* 1973–5, but not up to the firm's better offices). The transport improvements that accompanied this growth, for example the ring roads around Romford and Ilford, also did little for architecture, with the exception of Barking's robust, well-designed Eastern Region station (1959–61). The arrival of the new Victoria Line at Walthamstow (1968) was unspectacular.

Although shopping patterns changed, the East London tradition of street markets continued. Their importance had been acknowledged by the post-war planners, but with the proviso that it would be desirable to separate them from traffic. Lansbury's pedestrian market square set a new pattern, but its progeny were less successful. At the GLC's Watney Market (1966–76) and the similar smaller development at Bromley-by-Bow the markets dwindled, moved off the road and sandwiched between shops, within a rigid layout of deck access housing. Elsewhere, despite the explosion of large covered shopping centres in the 1970s, the older open markets continued along the main roads (some eventually made partly pedestrian from the 1980s) as can be seen in their vigorous survival, for example at Whitechapel, Roman Road 2
(Old Ford), Walthamstow, Barking and Romford. At Stratford the market continued within the covered shopping area of 1971–3, part of a dreary mammoth redevelopment that destroyed many of the town's good Victorian buildings.

The best buildings of the 1970s–80s reflect the wide range of architectural styles and materials current at the time. Walthamstow Magistrates' Court, 1972–3, was a mature, carefully designed production of the GLC Special Works Department, its austere concrete horizontals a counterpoint to the older Town Hall by its side. It set the model for later courts, including those at Barkingside, 1974–7. Also by GLC Special Works Department is the boldly functional Refuse Transfer Station at Barking. Another aspect of the GLC's work was flood prevention. This produced both the Barking Flood Barrier and the Thames Barrier. The latter, by *Rendel Palmer & Tritton* 1974–82, was the most ambitious piece of engineering of these years, impressive for its grand sculptural forms as well as for its foresight in tackling an issue that was to become of increasing concern by the end of the century.

Among other novel approaches of these years is *Arup*'s frontage to Truman's Brewery in Brick Lane, demonstrating the potential of sleek mirror glazing as a neutral mask between older buildings (1973–7). Minor buildings include Libraries and Health Centres, post-war ideals deferred by economy. Woodford's red brick group by the borough of Redbridge, unusually combining the two functions (1972–5), is an irregular Modernist composition but uses scale and materials appropriate to a historic area. The later central library at Ilford (1983–6), although large, is more consciously vernacular in its detail. A variety of ingenious modern designs for health centres were produced, typically enlivened by top-lit central waiting areas: by *Aldington, Craig & Collinge* at North Woolwich 1981, and by *John Allan* (later *Avanti Architects*) at Brick Lane Spitalfields, Florida Street Bethnal Green and Cleveland Road Ilford. The Brick Lane Health Centre was built together with the new housing by *Shepheard, Epstein & Hunter* (*see* below).

A surprise in the outer boroughs is the appearance of theatres built by the local authorities: at Barking built together with the Town Hall (1960–1), at Ilford neatly slotted into the town centre (1972–4) and at Hornchurch, more pompously isolated (1975). But nearly all these buildings, serviceable and for the most part unostentatious, are small fry in comparison with what followed in East London over the last fifteen years of the C20. Only the large New Spitalfields Market, by *EPR*, built in the 1980s on derelict railway land near Stratford, heralded the scale and ambition of what was to come in Docklands (*see* below).

New approaches from the 1970s

Comprehensive redevelopment and mass housing fell out of favour as interest in CONSERVATION gathered force from the 1970s. The campaign to save the Georgian houses of Spitalfields focused attention on the East End, and the realization that there was still older fabric elsewhere that could have a useful future as social housing led to the restoration of early C19 remnants in Cable Street and elsewhere (Arbour Square, York Square).

Revival of interest in the traditional close-knit character of the East End is witnessed by the powerful Cable Street Mural of 1979–82, depicting the street as it was before the war, at the time of the famous 'battle'. An inspirational reaction against mass housing was the picturesque group on the Isle of Dogs commissioned from *Stout & Litchfield* by a local doctor, Michael Barraclough, 1975, who took advantage of the final years of the declining docks to instigate the building of a group of houses for himself and other like-minded people. He was able to acquire a site on the Isle of Dogs with a view of Greenwich Hospital, as well as timbers, slates and other handsome materials from warehouses in the process of being demolished. It inspired a self-build scheme nearby, Maconochie's Wharf, designed by the same firm (1985–90). Nearby, *Levitt Bernstein*'s reticent riverside housing at Midland Place, 1979–83, is likewise a reaction in favour of more homely low-rise vernacular townscape, a trend which can be seen in one of its more extreme forms, making play with picturesque rooflines, in the rebuilding around Flower and Dean Walk, Spitalfields, by *Shepheard, Epstein & Hunter*, 1983–4. By this time the rigid principles of zoning and density laid down in the post-war plans had been largely abandoned. 114

The small developments on the Isle of Dogs belong to spasmodic efforts in the 1970s to make use of derelict land when the docks and their associated industry were in terminal decline. Conservation of dock buildings was a low priority at this time. Those that had survived bombing were unappealingly smoke-grimed, shabby and patched, and the deep plans of the warehouses were considered impractical for reuse, except by a few unconventional pioneers. They included artists, who seized upon them as studios but who also frequently turned them into unofficial homes as well. Peter Sedgeley and Bridget Riley were instrumental in securing the retention of the so-called Ivory House at St Katharine in 1968 during the period before the dock's commercial development. Where artists go, the more conventional follow. Oliver's Wharf, Wapping, was an early conversion to flats for sale in 1970–2 by a young architectural practice, *Goddard & Manton*.

At Wapping an effort was made in the 1970s by Tower Hamlets to find new uses for both the St Katharine Docks and the London Docks (the latter mostly filled in by the PLA). St Katharine was sold to Taylor Woodrow and developed for mixed use as a marina (but losing nearly all its original buildings). For London Docks, *Shepheard, Epstein & Hunter* produced a community-based masterplan in 1971 for low-rise social housing, although it was only patchily implemented before the London Docklands Development Corporation took over. It included conversion of a former maintenance shed to the John Orwell Sports Centre, bounded by an original dock wall. Elsewhere the PLA transformed an early C20 warehouse at the Isle of Dogs into the New Billingsgate Fish Market, and created workshops from early C19 stores at West India Dock basins. But these efforts now appear minor compared with what was to follow.

DOCKLANDS*

The Decline of the Riverside and Docks 1945–80

The international importance of the Port of London had been under threat from the beginning of the C20 but repairs, improvements and even some expansion had taken place between the wars. The devastation caused by bombing in the Blitz – at the Millwall and Surrey Docks especially – was followed by a revival of activity and at Silvertown and North Woolwich industry developed on an even bigger scale despite extensive bomb damage. Increasingly mechanized handling methods, some learned from the Americans during the war, such as the use of pallets and fork-lift trucks, were now adopted. These rendered obsolete most of the traditional warehouse accommodation. The already partly infilled East India Docks closed in 1967, quickly followed in 1968–70 by the St Katharine Docks, the London Docks, and the Surreys on the S side of the river. But the remaining docks, modernized, were themselves overtaken by the container revolution, which eliminated the handling of individual pieces of cargo and required vast open quays. In 1968 the first container terminal opened downstream at Tilbury, where the PLA's huge grain terminal was opened in 1969. The roll-on-roll-off ferries also took away much European passenger traffic. The riverside warehouses and industries from Wapping to Bow Creek became redundant, were deserted or demolished, concluding centuries of trading history on the Thames.

In the 1970s no models existed for regeneration on this scale and developing a strategy was protracted. Only in 1976 (nearly a decade after the first closure) did the Docklands Joint Committee, composed of representatives of the GLC and the boroughs, publish their Strategic Plan, with ideas for providing new jobs, housing and amenities, and for opening up the dock areas and riverside with green spaces. Developments were slow and little happened at first apart from plans for social housing at the London Docks, the commercial development of St Katharine Docks and a few minor building activities and conversions.

Docklands 1981–98

The piecemeal, gradualist approach towards the revival of the post-industrial riverside and docks was transformed in 1981 with the creation of the London Docklands Development Corporation (LDDC). This was the first of its kind in Britain, with powers to acquire all the PLA's land and much of the adjoining hinterland (an area of $8\frac{1}{2}$ sq.m.) stretching from Wapping to Beckton on the N side of the river and including Bermondsey, Rotherhithe and the Surrey Docks on the S bank. Around this area a new

*This section has been adapted from the Introduction to *Buildings of England: London Docklands*, 1998, by Elizabeth Williamson.

boundary was tightly drawn, in several instances creating anomalous divisions within historic riverside parishes. From 1981 to 1998 the LDDC acted as the planning authority within this zone and received money for regeneration direct from central government with which to instigate programmes of improvements in transport, housing, employment and training.

Commercial and industrial redevelopment was slow to develop until the formation of the LDDC and was characterized at first by small industrial and business estates, cheaply built for rent and slotting into existing suburban settings. Attention was heavily focused on the Isle of Dogs with the establishment of the ENTERPRISE ZONE* in 1982, a band of land bordering the West India and Millwall docks and covering the infilled area of the East India Docks at Blackwall. In this zone developers were granted tax and planning concessions in an effort to attract new enterprises. The best of the business parks was Heron Quays by *Nicholas Lacey, Jobst & Hyett* 1981–9, on the quayside between the West India Export Dock and South Dock, a model that many thought should be pursued, small-scale mixed development closely related to the water. But success soon spawned a new generation of larger buildings, when in 1985–6 events conspired to stimulate a frenzy of activity. The promised deregulation of the trading of stocks and shares in 1986 ushered in a short period when huge dealing floors were demanded so that dealing could be done from offices via computer. Anticipating this change, the Americans saw that Docklands had the space which the City of London lacked. Canary Wharf was born in 1985 when the North American developer G. Ware Travelstead obtained a huge acreage of the zone for a consortium of North American banks, having failed to acquire land within the City. Other American companies followed suit and by December 1986 nearly 1,500,000 sq. ft (457,000 sq. metres) of office space had been created on the Isle of Dogs, even before development had begun at Canary Wharf.

CANARY WHARF changed the face of Docklands. It shifted decisively the focus of Docklands from light industry to the burgeoning financial sector, creating a need to attract highly skilled white-collar workers from outside the area and initially relegating most local people to support jobs. In turn this contributed to the demand for new housing of a more luxurious type than low-cost family houses. Perhaps most importantly, it brought dramatic changes to the infrastructure: the developers were so important to the government and the LDDC that they could demand, and get, the extension of the Jubilee Line (*see* below). Above all, the new development provided the landmark by which Canary Wharf and the whole of Docklands came to be recognized and marketed.

Architecturally Canary Wharf had a major impact on London and introduced the British to the speed and efficiency of American fast-track construction on a huge scale, and to the size,

*Modelled on an idea published by Paul Barker, Peter Hall and Cedric Price in *New Society*, 1969.

eclecticism and luxury of North American Postmodern commercial architecture. Its first phase (1987–91) included work by the famous *Skidmore Owings & Merrill*, by the Chinese-American *I.M. Pei* and by the Argentinian-American *Cesar Pelli*, who designed the gleaming skyscraper, No. 1 Canada Square, which acted as an inescapable reminder of Canary Wharf all over
121 London. This tower set its own records: at 800 ft (244 metres) it was the tallest in Europe when completed in 1991. Its challenge was taken up not only by a vogue for a new generation of tall buildings in the City of London but in the later phases of commercial development at Canary Wharf. This began after the recession and property crash of the early 1990s, with further work by the earlier teams but now accompanied by 'signature' buildings by well-known architects, including two towers by *Norman Foster*. In these later phases the influence of Postmodern eclecticism has been replaced by a return to the traditions of Modernism and its High-Tech offspring. An exception is the humorous Neo-Egyptian hotel by *Philippe Starck* in a prominent position on the riverside.

Beyond Canary Wharf there was little large-scale office building of architectural consequence. Numerous, superficially flashy, offices appeared in the Enterprise Zone, many replaced after less than two decades. At East India Dock appeared a new building type – stimulated by expanding information technology – the telecommunications centre, blank-faced boxes housing more equipment than people. Both the *Richard Rogers Partnership*'s for Reuters and *YRM*'s for KDD managed to turn this unpromising type into two of the best and most dramatic buildings in Docklands. Nearby the former *Financial Times* printing works, built by *Nicholas Grimshaw & Partners*, is in the spirit of the most famous printing works of the C20; the transparent boxes designed by Sir Owen Williams for the *Daily Express*. This followed a series of huge and ugly printworks in Docklands which started with Rupert Murdoch's printworks, the so-called Fortress Wapping begun 1979, which marked the end of the traditional newspaper trade in Fleet Street.

Housing and Public Amenities in Docklands

With the advent of the Conservative government in 1979 the change in policy from publicly financed to private housing was instantly implemented by the LDDC. In 1981, 80 to 90 per cent of housing within Docklands was in public ownership: in 1997 the proportion (43 per cent in owner occupation) was closer to the Greater London average. The operation of the market soon took effect and SOCIAL HOUSING was almost squeezed out. Although from the mid 1980s the LDDC funded many rehabilitation schemes, most social housing was concentrated in the areas remote from those of greatest commercial activity, in particular at Beckton and the better than average estate of Britannia Village at the Royal Docks. Here groups such as Peabody continued a tradition of providing quality low-cost housing for the East End, with a small component of more adventurously designed social housing and amenities.

In the riverside areas of Wapping and Limehouse speculative housing came to dominate and WAREHOUSE CONVERSIONS became desirable as changes of use from industrial to residential became generally acceptable after the strict zoning policies of the GLC and local authorities had been abandoned. The new concept of internal atriums, introduced to bring light to the deep plans, could have a dramatic effect, as at *Terry Farrell & Partners'* Miller's Wharf (Wapping), but in other attempts to increase accommodation, rooflines were spoilt with clumsy additional storeys. Successful small-scale conversions combined frankly modern insertions with imaginative but conservative treatment of new upper storeys. Retention or reproduction of timber or cast-iron windows and hinged loading platforms became common, but other external features, such as iron bridges, hoists and wall-cranes (e.g. Metropolitan Wharf, Wapping) survived only sporadically. A rare example of a romantic treatment is Sun Wharf, Limehouse, transformed for the film director David Lean by *Scott, Brownrigg & Turner* in 1983–5. But the warehouse theme soon became ubiquitous in new housing and seems to be the last refuge of the unimaginative.

Burrell's Wharf at the tip of the Isle of Dogs is an example of old interwoven with new build, combining the rehabilitation of one of the most historically important industrial complexes in the area, a former iron and shipbuilding works, with monumental new blocks of flats by *Jestico & Whiles*. The *Gwilts'* West India Dock warehouses proved the most intractable conversion due to sensitivity to their historic importance, their huge scale and floor areas and, in the case of No. 2 Warehouse, their very shallow floor-to-ceiling heights. Conservatively restored in 1984–5 by *Feilden & Mawson*, they now contain a successful mixed development of retail units, 'loft' spaces on the upper floors and the Museum in Docklands.

Amongst the wealth of NEW HOUSING, good examples include the tidy group of housing around Shadwell Basin, Wapping, by *MacCormac Jamieson Prichard & Wright* and, on the Isle of Dogs, Compass Point by *Jeremy Dixon* with *BDP*. Their asset was the relationship with waterside settings. Each conformed closely to the manner and principles used by these architects elsewhere. They create a strong sense of place, drawing on historical, and especially London, precedent. An underlying theme was also the narrow-fronted, gabled brick houses of Dutch or Scandinavian origin, no doubt chosen for canalside associations and much in evidence along the canal in the former Western Dock of the London Docks. A Postmodern spirit was also evident, for example, in the planning of *BUJ*'s Timber Wharves village on the Isle of Dogs and in Beckton N of Tollgate Road, with the organization of standard spec housing into monumental compositions, under the influence of architects such as Rob Krier. In Beckton, a selection of standard London housing types: mansion block, paired villa, terraced cottage, are organized in axial avenues, crescents and gardens, emphasized by obelisks and columns, layouts that at least give some urbanity and form to an otherwise amorphous suburb.

116 More obviously Postmodern was the wedge-like Cascades on the Isle of Dogs, commissioned by Kentish Homes from the adventurous practice of *CZWG*. Its play with geometry, symbols and colour established a taste for landmark blocks of luxury flats that read dramatically in the wide watery landscape. This proved influential for the next generation of housing, built after the property crash of the early 1990s when the priorities in Docklands changed towards high-rise residential development and even conversion of surplus office space. From 1996 CZWG completed two further theatrical schemes, Dundee Wharf at Limehouse and Millennium Wharf, Isle of Dogs. Amenities such as health clubs and swimming pools and, of course, car parking have become commonplace since the mid 1990s in new housing developments aimed at a more affluent market. In 2004 further high-rise residential buildings were planned for the area around South Quay and the Millwall North Dock on the Isle of Dogs, where the small-scale business parks of the 1980s once dominated. The ersatz historic styles of the early 1990s have become period-pieces of speculative style, superseded in recent years by High Tech styles (Hermitage Wharf, Wapping) or a return to clean, white Neo-Modernism, as at Pierhead Lock, Isle of Dogs, and Barrier Point overlooking Thames Barrier Park, both by *Goddard Manton Partnership* for Barratts. There is much else that is banal and even the most exciting exteriors conceal dull plans and small and boxy rooms.

The predominance of housing throughout Docklands, unleavened by shops, offices and amusements, threatened to turn the area into a huge exclusive suburb and was much criticized by members of established Dockland communities. Under the LDDC, public buildings and amenities were slower to emerge than offices and housing, with only a handful of well-designed recreational centres such as the sailing centre by *Kit Allsopp Architects* on the Millwall Docks, the dynamic Regatta Centre at the Royal Albert Dock by *Ian Ritchie Architects* and the Limehouse Club for local activities by *Michael Squire & Partners*. Only one exceptionally good conventional public building makes a strong contribution to the townscape: the Isle of Dogs Neighbourhood Centre, originally designed in 1988 by *Chassay Architects*. By the end of its period of influence, the LDDC had provided an enduring, if mixed, legacy for East London. The conservation of surviving buildings and dock structures, particularly the quay walls, cranes, locks and bridges, some in a working condition, others, such as hydraulic pumping and impounding stations, converted for new uses, remains as one of its indisputable successes.

Enhancement of the riverside and improved access also showed the LDDC to be an enlightened patron, delivering a series of buildings that quickly became emblematic of Docklands,

not least the thrilling array of BRIDGES commissioned to complete the Thames Path and span the docks. These are subtle pieces of engineering, dramatic in their sculptural form and effective as works of art. Younger architects and engineers skilled in High Tech architecture, such as *Lifschutz Davidson* (high-level crossing at Royal Victoria Dock), *Chris Wilkinson* and *Future Systems* (at West India Dock) amongst others, established a tradition which has continued in the post-LDDC era. A purely practical preparation of potential sites had been land drainage. Here, a necessity was turned into an architectural advantage by the employment of architects to design the superstructures of PUMPING STATIONS. The contrast between the 1970s GLC pumping station at Gallions Reach, close to the Royal Docks, 115
and those commissioned by the LDDC is striking. *John Outram*'s primitive temple is a wonderful surprise in a back street on the Isle of Dogs; *Richard Rogers Partnership*'s colourful cylinders make a sculptural incident in the open space by Royal Victoria Dock, while *Nicholas Grimshaw and Partners*' station at North Woolwich is discreetly clad in profiled aluminium.

Remarkably little consideration was given to shopping facilities and in areas such as Wapping, there is still a palpable sense that the shopping street serves the established community rather than the inhabitants of the warehouse conversions. The most ill-fated scheme was the conversion of *Alexander*'s magnificent former Tobacco Dock warehouse in Wapping, modelled on the GLC's earlier transformation of Covent Garden Market, but without the necessary tide of tourists to ensure its success. In contrast, the inclusion of large underground shopping malls helped transform Canary Wharf in its later phases from the private preserve of a financial elite to a commercial centre with the potential to serve thousands of people in East London, on both sides of the river. Further out, at Beckton, major shopping centres on the out-of-town model provide competition with the suburban town centres.

By the 1990s the effect of the redevelopment of the docks was evident throughout the LDDC area. Wapping and Limehouse were reborn as gentrified enclaves while the remodelling of the Isle of Dogs and Blackwall wrought far more dramatic changes. The commercial heart at Canary Wharf, the centrepiece of the West India Docks, was on a scale and with a visual impact intended to rival the City of London. It had its own suburb on the rest of the Isle of Dogs where private housing had replaced riverside industry. Further E, the vast basins of the Royal Docks remained eerily quiet until the 1990s as several elaborate schemes foundered, before the colossal Excel exhibition centre, business parks, recreational amenities, hotels, new housing and the University of East London were begun. In 2004 it remained the only part of the former dock system to be exploited further. To its N an entirely new suburb was created on former industrial land at Beckton. Only along the river fringe of Silvertown and North Woolwich did heavy industry continue to dominate into the early C21.

Improved access to the Isle of Dogs included construction of new roads and the costly Limehouse Link road tunnel of 1989–93. The extension of PUBLIC TRANSPORT to serve the new commercial and residential areas was vital to the success of Docklands and provided many of the most eye-catching new buildings for visitor and resident alike. Plans for extension of the Jubilee Line, through South London to Thamesmead, had been shelved in 1980. The Docklands Light Railway was conceived as a cheap alternative and opened from Tower Gateway to the tip of the Isle of Dogs in 1987. It was extended W to Bank in 1991 (to appease developers who required a direct connection to the heart of the City), E to Beckton in 1994, N to Stratford in 1999 and S to Lewisham in 2001. In 2004 work was underway for extension to North Woolwich as the riverine industrial fringe E of Canning Town became available for development. The first sections used existing viaduct (e.g. the former London and Blackwall) or new raised track, and the DLR STATIONS were perfunctory, but the extensions produced a series of elegant High Tech stations on the Beckton branch assembled from a recognizable kit of parts designed by *Ahrends, Burton & Koralek*. The interchange between West India Quay and Poplar stations looks arresting by night and day while Prince Regent Station has
117 splendid artwork by *Brian Yale* as an integral part of the design. The new generation of stations of the C21 are discreet and unfussy, with the exception of Heron Quays station, a typically bold design by *Will Alsop*, 2004, a cheeky intruder amongst the corporate sleekness of South Canary Wharf.

Demand quickly outgrew the capacity of the DLR and demanded an alternative, complementary commuter transport system. The JUBILEE LINE EXTENSION (1993–9) was revived but now running from Westminster to Stratford for connection to the anticipated International Station. The stations, under strong direction from the commissioning architect, *Roland Paoletti*, were by leading designers with a penchant for technology. Those within our area were all purpose designed for their
119 sites: *Sir Norman Foster & Partners*' Canary Wharf bubbles are designed to be seen from above and to be discreet at ground level but with monumental spaces below. *Troughton McAslan* designed new platforms at Stratford, brought together with various local railway lines beneath the vast roof of *Wilkinson Eyre*'s station
118 (1991–4), its sheer glazed frontage turned to face a new plaza with a jaunty fabric-roofed bus station (by *Soji Abass* and *YRM*, 1994). Wilkinson Eyre also built a huge, exquisitely detailed High Tech shed as a depot for London Underground at Stratford Market (1994–8). Conversely, *Troughton McAslan*'s tiered design for Canning Town station dramatically advertises a major transport interchange (with a consciousness of local history in the display of a section of iron ship's hull atop a plinth inscribed by
126 *Richard Kindersley*). High-Tech was the dominant tone except at West Ham where *van Heyningen and Haward* look back in homage to the brick and glass suburban stations of Charles Holden in the 1930s.

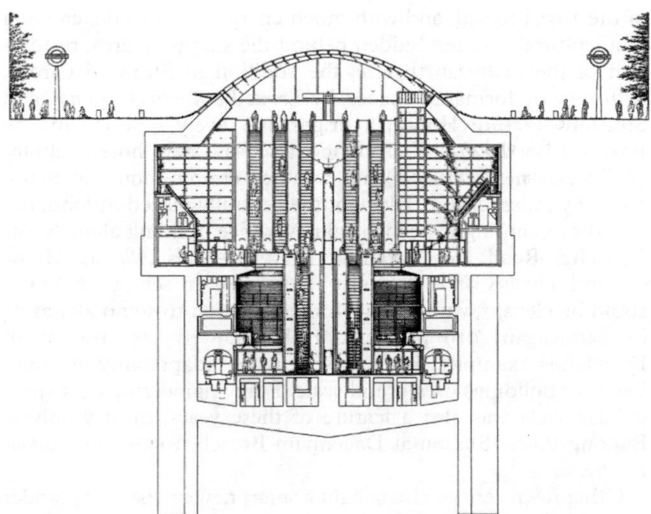

Canary Wharf Underground Station. Section, 1991–9

A final word is required upon the role played by PUBLIC ART in the new developments from the 1980s. The LDDC commissioned several pieces to provide drama along the new roads, for example *Allen Jones'* Aerobic figure on the Leamouth roundabout. Developers were also persuaded to contribute, with mixed results and too often lacking in originality. Inevitably much of the best work is to be found at Canary Wharf where, on the American model, it plays an integral part in the public spaces provided by the developers: from street furniture, to Neoclassical pieces by *Igor Mitoraj* and *Ron Arad*'s abstract Big Blue, Canada Square. 125
Non-conventional modes of sculpture since the late 1990s include integrated light sculptures by *Martin Richman*, and *Constance de Jong*'s highly original *Speaking of the River*, an audio installation at Canary Wharf riverside, commissioned by the Public Art Development Trust.

EAST LONDON FROM THE MID-1980s

Improvements to the transport infrastructure, including the new Jubilee Line (*see* above) transformed the centre of Stratford, where ambitions were heightened by the prospect of the channel-tunnel rail link,* and by a more temporary flurry of excitement over the connection to the mammoth Millennium Dome at North Greenwich.

The town began to be brightened from the late 1990s for its new role as a regional centre, with its lumpen commercial legacy

*Under construction 2001–6, with long tunnels eastward through water-laden ground, a major civil engineering achievement.

of the 1970s reclad, and with much energy put into the creation of a 'cultural quarter' hidden behind the shopping area: restoration of the Victorian theatre, the addition of Stratford Circus, with new performance spaces, by *Levitt Bernstein Associates*, and Stratford Picture House, a bright and lively new cinema by *Burrell Foley Fischer*. This period also saw new hotels, library (*Miller Bourne Partnership*) and even new church rooms, in tactful mode by *Purcell Miller Tritton* for the centrally placed St John, but also disappointingly mechanical new office building along Stratford High Road. Near Stratford, at Abbey Mills, *Allies & Morrison* and *Thames Water* demonstrated that even sewage buildings could be elegant, with a new pumping station to stand alongside its extravagant C19 predecessor. It followed the triumphant Docklands examples that had shown the adaptability of High-Tech for buildings on a grand scale. Pure engineering on a spectacular scale was also a feature of these years, most visibly at Barking Power Station at Dagenham Breach, 1992–5 by *Balfour Beatty*.

Other town centres also sought a smart new image on a grander scale than previously, the styles indicative of their dates: at Ilford, The Exchange, 1988–91 by *Chapman Taylor*, has bombastic Postmodern entrances (but quite successful galleried covered malls); the same firm used a sleek version of High-Tech for the remodelling of Romford's shopping precinct, 2002–3, while in 2004 Walthamstow chose a stridently attention-seeking design by *Colman Partnership* for its new library and other facilities.

A sense of showmanship also pervades some other buildings despite their variety of styles and materials: the fortress-like Magistrates Courts at Bow Road (*Phillip Arrand* of the Metropolitan Police 1990) adopts a glossy Postmodern idiom with colourful facing materials, a staider example (*Roughton & Partners* 1994) was built at Stratford. *Rock Townsend*'s lively Fire Station, Leyton 1992, provides a light, transparent home for its engines. Transparency is also a dominant feature of the Ideas Stores by *Adjaye Associates*, 2004, at Poplar and Whitechapel, where Tower Hamlets' reincarnated libraries are contained within colourful glass envelopes.

In the face of the daunting scale and anonymity of much architecture of the mid to later C20, much effort was made in the 1990s to create educational buildings of distinctive character that could foster a sense of local identity. Their diversity is remarkable. Swanlea, Whitechapel, the first secondary school in London for ten years, by *Colin Stansfield Smith* and *Percy Thomas Partnership* 1993, drew on the former's experience with the Hampshire schools service. Its spine is a dramatic glazed central mall connecting the different parts. A similar focus is provided at Newham's Royal Docks Community School, 1999, by the central glazed atrium linking the four wings, which has a spiral ramp emphasizing its commitment to access for the disabled. Emphasis on improved communication was also the starting point of the
127 quite extraordinary bridge linking the two parts of Plashet School, East Ham, by *Birds Portchmouth Russum* and *Techniker* 2000. Shared use of school buildings by the wider community

was a continuing theme, as in the case of the well-provided Sports Centre added at Langdon, East Ham.

In Tower Hamlets, post GLC primary schools, no longer standardized, often by private architects, and in some cases assisted by LDDC finance, have more individual character than in previous decades. The curiously angled Cyril Jackson, Limehouse, by *Robert Byron Architects* 1991–5, and the dramatic rooflines of Bluegate Fields, Cable Street, 1993 by *GHM Rock Townsend*, both make their mark in the streetscape. A quieter example is Mowlem, Bethnal Green, 1997 by *Paul Irons*, with pitched roof and broad eaves. Increased concern over the importance of preschool experience is reflected in some innovative nursery schools and play centres, for example Playarc, Plaistow 1991, one of several by *Hawkins Brown*, and John Perry, Barking, by *Deborah Saunt David Hills Architects*, distinctive for its translucent cladding. The imaginatively designed East London Childcare Institute at Stratford, incorporating a nursery, by *Cazenove Architects* 2002–4, can also be grouped here. Training and resource centres were another development of these years: the Urban Learning Foundation, East India Dock Road, by *Paul Hyett* 1992, is restrained and delicately detailed; the City Learning Centre, Walthamstow, by *Austin-Smith:Lord* 2001, appealingly curved and colourful. Stephen Hawking School, Limehouse, is a sensitively designed Special Needs School by *Haverstock Associates* 1997. Outside the conventional educational spectrum are the Jagonari, Whitechapel, a Women's Educational Resource Centre by *Matrix Feminist Design Co-Op* 1987, with attractive use of Indian motifs, The Click, Leytonstone, an eye-catchingly modern internet café and training centre by *van Heyningen & Haward* 2001, at the entrance to the new Langthorne Park, and the Online Centre and Crèche at Sydney Russell School, Becontree, by *Cottrell & Vermeulen*, 2003.

Much happened on the University front. In 1992 Queen Mary College united with Westfield College, Hampstead, and the University of East London was formed from three older Technical Colleges. At QMWC, the numerous additions include a memorably brusque brick and concrete Library by *Colin St John Wilson* (1988–92), providing a focus for the central square of the campus, together with the Arts Faculty building by *RMJM*
(1992). Cheerfully colourful student lodgings along the canal by 120
MacCormac Jamieson Prichard (1991) formed the start of a student village continued by *Feilden Clegg Bradley*. Even more striking is the new campus for UEL beside the Royal Docks, supplementing their centre in Stratford. This has an arresting combination of buildings by *Edward Cullinan Architects* (1998–9): drum-shaped student lodgings beside the quayside in front of a lively group of academic buildings notable for their concern with energy efficiency and recycled materials. On a more cramped site, off Whitechapel Road, the Women's Library, part of London Metropolitan University, 2001–2 by *Wright & Wright*, with carefully crafted brick-faced interiors, is ingeniously fitted into the footprint of an early washhouse, incorporating its C19 frontage. Not far off, and arrestingly outré among the London Hospital's

buildings, is *AMEC* and *Alsop Architects*' glass box with hanging pods, for the School of Medicine and Dentistry, 2004. Among Further Education buildings, for long a poor relation in the education family, the Bramley block is a crisply elegant addition to Barking College, Dagenham, by *Perkins Ogden* with *Hampshire County Architects*, 2002–3.

Housing and townscape from the 1980s

The number of tower blocks mentioned earlier suggests drastic changes to the street pattern and skyline, but in many cases these were short lived. Throughout East London refurbishment programmes from the 1980s onwards, carried out piecemeal through a number of agencies, led to some remarkable transformations, disguising the austere aesthetic of post-war Modernism by pitched roofs, rewindowing, decorative metalwork and colour, sometimes, but not always, to visual advantage. The principal fairy godmother was *Hunt Thompson Associates* who, for example, reclothed two towers in Walthamstow in bold Postmodern dress in 1989, and gave Watney Market, Stepney, a makeover in 1994, removing one of its towers and giving its reclad twin a formal approach. Many more towers have been demolished, others refurbished, and new amenities such as health centres, community centres, new schools and improved landscaping are beginning to fill the gaps left by earlier cheeseparing. The loose-knit landscape of mixed development with its ideal of towers in parkland has given way to more traditionally aligned terrace housing and private spaces, as can be seen for example around Stepney Green Park. From the 1980s there were efforts to consult residents (something that was not done in the 1950s–60s). On the Ocean and Limehouse Fields estates preferences were for a return to street architecture; in 1998–2003 parts were rebuilt to designs by *PRP Architects* in a vaguely Georgian or Regency idiom (although acknowledging the need to make space for car ownership). Even the nearby gasworks has disappeared. It is as if the gritty Victorian East End and its aftermath never existed. But this level of attention to layout and detail remains exceptional. Rare exemplars of innovative social housing are two small groups of 2003–4 for Peabody at Britannia Village, Royal Docks.

C20 PRIVATE HOUSING is barely a subject in the inner areas until the 1980s, when with the regeneration of Docklands the East End started to attract a wider social mix. By 1998 the figure for private housing was close to half the housing stock in Tower Hamlets.* An early example outside Docklands is *CZWG*'s Eaton Terrace, off Bow Road, for Kentish Homes, 1983–5 which declares its character by playful Postmodern trimmings. At the same time the 'right to buy' introduced by the Conservative Government began to break down the monolithic local authority ownership of rented housing, as is clear from the often idio-

*31,600 out of 76,000, *Focus on London 2000*.

syncratic alterations made by new home owners. Away from the older housing estates, the LDDC's pattern of superior urban waterside flats and houses on old industrial sites, in a mixture of modern and warehouse-revival styles, continues into the C21, filling in gaps around the Limehouse Basin and between Blackwall and Leamouth, and expanding along the inland waterways of the Limehouse Cut, the Lea and the Hertford Union Canal. There have also been noteworthy conversions of major C19 industrial and institutional complexes to precincts of private housing, ranging from Bryant & May's match factory at Bow to the seamen's orphanage at Wanstead. Largest of all, right on the fringes of Greater London, is the huge former asylum at Claybury, Woodford Bridge, now reborn as Repton Park. At the other extreme, occasional quirky architects' houses enlivened Tower Hamlets in the first years of the new century, among them Elektra House, Ashfield Street, with blank windowless street front, and Dirty House, Chance Street, both by *David Adjaye*, a
concrete and steel house in Bacon Street by his former partner 124
William Russell and the joky Blue House, Garner Street, by *Fat*. 123

A trend which emerged in the 1990s, developing out of the tradition of artists' studios in older buildings, was an enthusiasm for 'live-work' units, responding to the desire to create new employment opportunities. Their character ranges from *CZWG*'s bold group for Peabody at West Ferry, with its consciously industrial balconied courtyard, to a discreet combination of old and new, as on the old Poplar Library site on the edge of the industrial wasteland by the Lea. The Lea Valley is a focus for major regeneration, stimulated by the bid for the Olympic site for 2012 (masterplan by *EDAW* with *Allies & Morrison* and *Foreign Office Architects*). A C21 spirit of rapid transformation is encapsulated on the site between Gillender Street and the river, in the temporary low-cost offices (by *Containerspace Ltd*, *Nicholas Lacey &* 128
Partners 2004), made from recycled containers, on the model of their colourful prototypes at Trinity Buoy Wharf, Leamouth.

Open Spaces: the second half of the C20

A final word needs to be said about the spaces in between the buildings.

The effects of the policy in the County of London Plan, 1943 to provide 3.6 acres of OPEN SPACE per thousand people took long to mature, but flowered remarkably by the end of the C20 when money was also found for much relandscaping of older sites, with an increasing emphasis on ecological value. The results can be seen in the inclusion of small local parks within the rebuilt housing areas of Tower Hamlets, in the extension of Stepney Green and in the grand concept which became Mile End Park, intended to stretch from Victoria Park to the Thames and for long fragmentary, but in 2000 united by *Piers Gough*'s bold 'green bridge' across Mile End Road. N of the bridge *Tibbalds Monro*'s imaginative masterplan provides for a range of different users;

earth-covered buildings, water, planting and landscape are happily blended. An even more ambitious linear park was sketched out in the Greater London plan 1944 for the industrialized Lea Valley, stretching from the Thames into Hertfordshire. This too took shape in the later C20 under the Lea Valley Regional Park Authority, with footpaths, nature reserves and recreational facilities fitted among reservoirs and intriguing relics of industry. It links up with the Greenway, a landscaped footpath made in the 1980s along the raised bank of Bazalgette's sewer through Tower Hamlets and Newham.

A large informal district park was created as part of the Docklands efforts at Beckton, and on the Isle of Dogs a park of considerable size was created from the 'mudchute' in the centre of the island, and a city farm established (there is another at Stepney Green). The Thames itself (now so much cleaner) has been opened up by footpaths along much of its length, an ideal which also goes back to the 1940s, and presents a very different picture from the closed off quays and wharves of the C19 and earlier C20. Beside the river, still remote when first created in its then desolate setting S of the Royal Docks, is the entirely new
122 Thames Barrier Park, an exquisite geometric layout by the French *Groupe Signes*, 1997–2000, with a dramatic, green sunken garden to recall past docks. A similarly geometric aesthetic informs the hard landscaping by *Patel Taylor* at the Royal Docks, which has the added asset of *Lifschutz Davidson*'s exciting transporter bridge. In contrast, Eastbrookend Country Park at Dagenham is ecologically inspired, reclaimed from derelict land, and provided with an energy-efficient Millennium Centre by *Penoyre & Prasad*. Similar aims inspire the centre by *van Heyningen & Haward* for the bird sanctuary on Rainham Marshes.

The urban landscaping at Canary Wharf began with a formal Beaux Arts layout on the axis of Cesar Pelli's tower, embellished with much art work; the later Jubilee Park to its S (2000–2 by *Jacques & Pieter Wirtz*) is more relaxed, with undulating paths. On a more homely level, Langthorne Park in Leytonstone is a good example of a new community park, divided into 'zones' for a mixture of specific uses.

Further out, existing open spaces, preserved after the green belt had been declared in 1938 in the face of encroaching suburbia, were later consolidated more formally as country parks: for example at Hainault Forest and Fairlop Waters. Havering Park was retrieved as part of the green belt in the 1970s after being carved up into plotlands in the 1920s, initially for East Enders' self-built weekend retreats, a rare case of this kind of haphazard development reverting to public space. Whether a healthy balance between open land and building can be maintained in the face of government pressure for new housing in the SE, especially in the vulnerable marshlands along the Thames, remains an open question.

GAZETTEER

BARKING and DAGENHAM

The boroughs of Barking and Dagenham were brought together in 1965 as the London Borough of Barking, an implicit recognition of the historic importance of the medieval abbey and town over surrounding settlements, including Dagenham and Chadwell Heath. Dagenham only reasserted its identity in 1980. Until the 1920s much of the borough was open fields and market gardens but the creation by the LCC of the immense 'township' of the Becontree Estate irreversibly changed the largely rural area into a densely populated suburb. The estate creates a uniform district at the heart of the modern borough, relieved only by the variety of its many churches, but the older settlements maintain a distinct identity. The area's earlier history is now represented by only a handful of buildings. The borough's flat terrain is a visual disadvantage and architectural highlights are few in number but compensated for by their significance: at Barking, the medieval church of St Margaret and the splendid Eastbury Manor House; St Peter and St Paul, Dagenham; and Valence House at Becontree. These are worth the visit alone. Barking and Dagenham's riverside, unlike the regenerated docklands of Tower Hamlets and Newham, is still blighted by industrial endeavours, although in 2004 work had begun on reclamation of land around Dagenham's famous Ford Motor Works and major reconstruction for a new town at Barking Reach.

BARKING

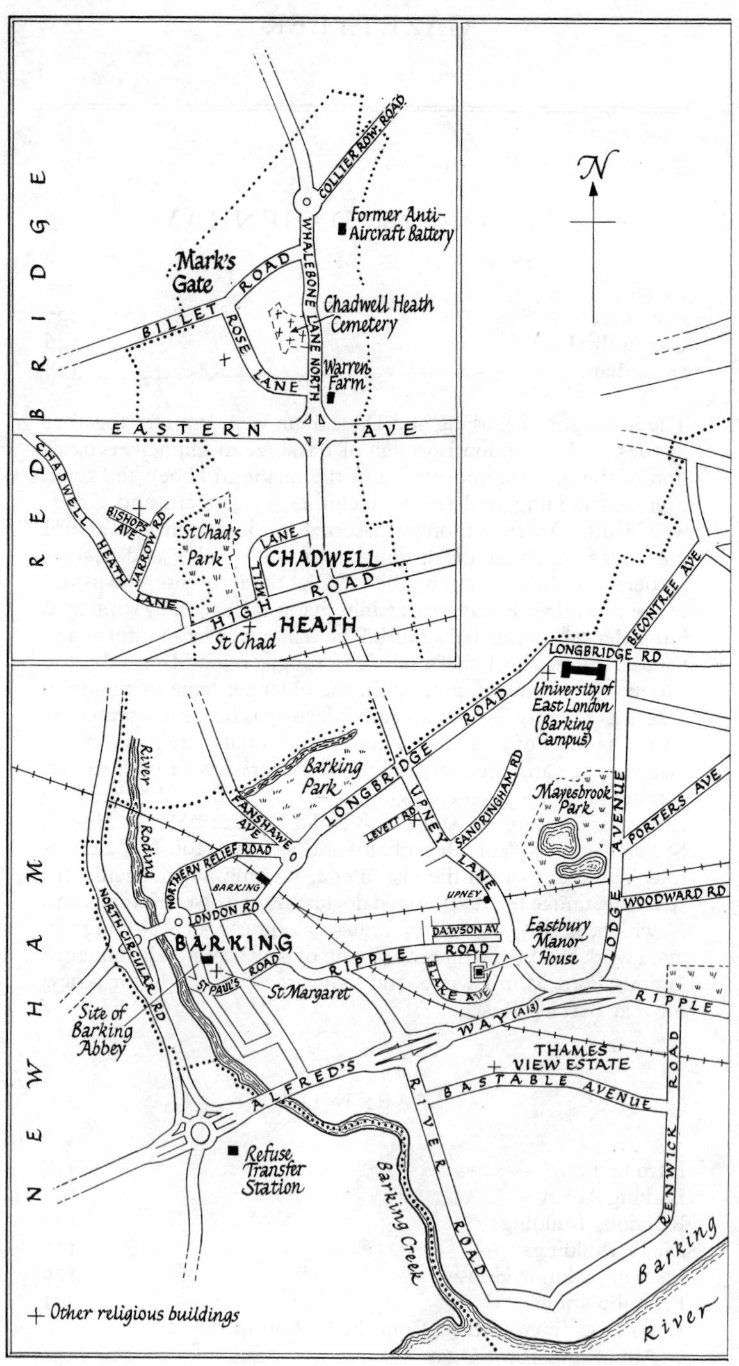
N
REDBRIDGE
NEWHAM
COLLIER ROW ROAD
Former Anti-Aircraft Battery
Mark's Gate
BILLET ROAD
WHALEBONE LANE NORTH
ROSE LANE
Chadwell Heath Cemetery
Warren Farm
EASTERN AVE
CHADWELL HEATH LANE
BISHOPS AVE
JARROW RD
St Chad's Park
MILL LANE
CHADWELL
HIGH ROAD
HEATH
St Chad
LONGBRIDGE RD
University of East London (Barking Campus)
BECONTREE AVE
LONGBRIDGE ROAD
Barking Park
River Roding
FANSHAWE AVE
UPNEY LANE
LEVETT RD
SANDRINGHAM RD
Mayesbrook Park
LODGE AVENUE
PORTERS AVE
NORTHERN RELIEF ROAD
BARKING
UPNEY
WOODWARD RD
LONDON RD
DAWSON AV.
Eastbury Manor House
NORTH CIRCULAR RD
BARKING
RIPPLE ROAD
ST PAUL'S ROAD
St Margaret
BLAKE AVE
RIPPLE
Site of Barking Abbey
WAY (A13)
THAMES VIEW ESTATE
ALFRED'S
RIVER ROAD
BASTABLE AVENUE
RENWICK ROAD
Refuse Transfer Station
Barking Creek
Barking
River
+ Other religious buildings

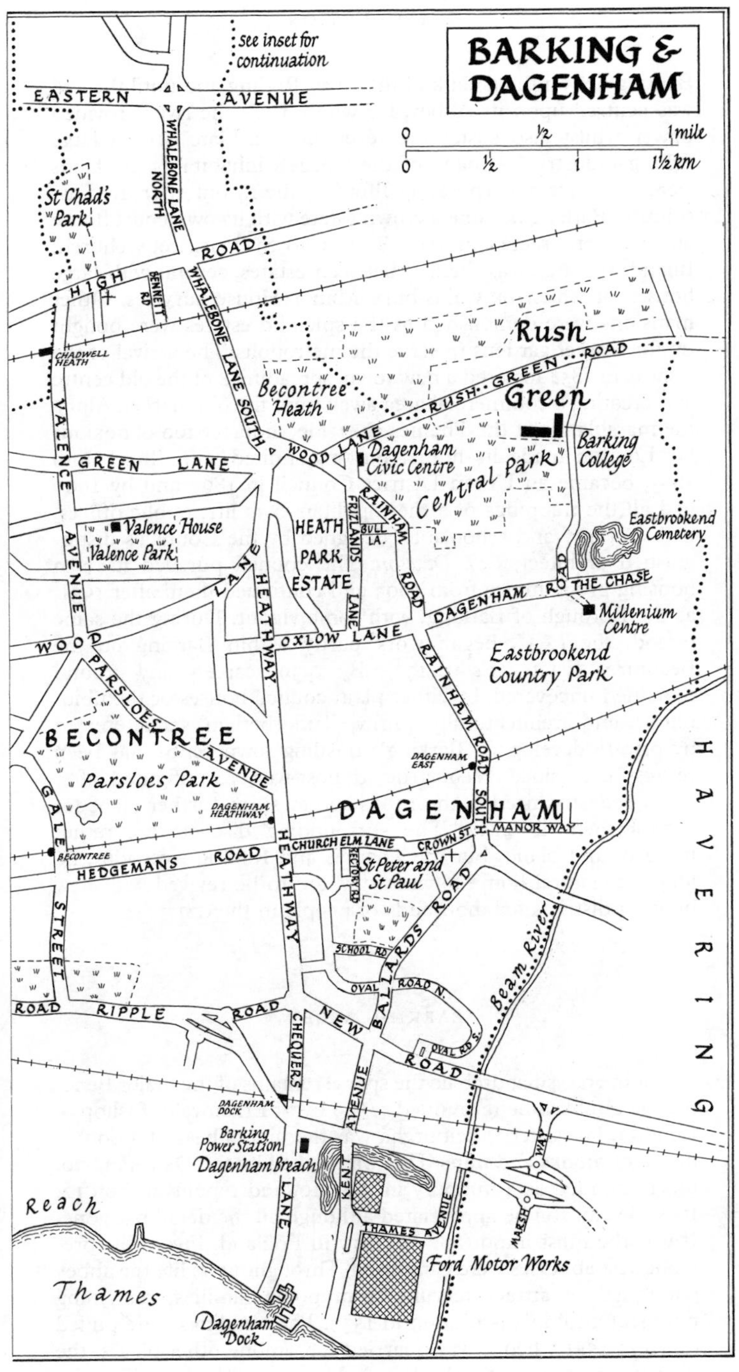
BARKING &
DAGENHAM
see inset for continuation
EASTERN AVENUE
WHALEBONE LANE NORTH
St Chad's Park
HIGH ROAD
BENNETT RD
WHALEBONE LANE SOUTH
CHADWELL HEATH
Becontree Heath
Rush Green
RUSH GREEN ROAD
WOOD LANE
Dagenham Civic Centre
Central Park
Barking College
VALENCE AVENUE
GREEN LANE
Valence House
Valence Park
HEATH PARK ESTATE
FRIZLANDS LANE
RAINHAM ROAD
BULL LA.
Eastbrookend Cemetery
THE CHASE
DAGENHAM ROAD
Millenium Centre
LANE
HEATHWAY
OXLOW LANE
WOOD
Eastbrookend Country Park
PARSLOES AVENUE
BECONTREE
Parsloes Park
DAGENHAM EAST
RAINHAM ROAD SOUTH
DAGENHAM
MANOR WAY
DAGENHAM HEATHWAY
GALE STREET
BECONTREE
HEDGEMANS ROAD
CHURCH ELM LANE
CROWN ST
RECTORY RD
St Peter and St Paul
BALLARDS ROAD
SCHOOL RD
OVAL ROAD N.
OVAL RD S.
Beam River
HAVERING
ROAD RIPPLE ROAD
NEW ROAD
CHEQUERS LANE
DAGENHAM DOCK
Barking Power Station
Dagenham Breach
KENT AVENUE
THAMES AVENUE
MARSH WAY
Ford Motor Works
Reach
Thames
Dagenham Dock

INTRODUCTION

Barking lies on the E bank of the River Roding and until the C16 was centred upon its Abbey, for whose mills the river provided power whilst also sustaining (even into the late C19) a large fishing industry for many of the village's inhabitants. Its lands were extensive, incorporating Ilford to the N, but after the Dissolution Barking became a crown estate with its own court house and market, erected in 1567–8 close to St Margaret's church. Inland, the area was divided between estates, several with large houses of which only Eastbury Manor House survives. Other mansions were demolished as the splendid estates were bought up for market gardens to serve the metropolis. The arrival of the railway in 1854 fostered a new town, spreading E of the old centre and creating a commercial area away from the old market. Along the marshlands of the Thames riverside, industry too obnoxious for London made its home. Barking, united with Ilford until 1883, became an Urban District Council in 1897 and by 1900 had all the trappings of a metropolitan civic life: public offices, baths, library and schools; all designed by the Council's distinguished architect, *C.J. Dawson*. The council pursued its own housing programmes from 1903 and continued them after 1931, as the Borough of Barking, with some vigour. During the same period, the LCC, began work partly within Barking on the Becontree Estate (*see* p. 137). By 1939 scarcely any ground remained uncovered, by either plain council houses or the ubiquitous, and architecturally quirky, 'Tudorbethan' semis erected by private developers. Barking's bustling town centre has been restless ever since: reconstructed post-war, reconfigured after 1968, pedestrianized in the 1990s and awaiting further plans for enhancement in 2004. The surrounding districts are rather uniform and bland, but the Thames and Roding riversides, no longer a natural home for industry, are to be revived with new housing districts for thousands of people in the C21.

BARKING ABBEY

NW of the parish church lie the sparse remains of the major Benedictine establishment founded *c.* 666 by St Erkenwald, Bishop of London. His sister Ethelburgha was the first abbess of a double house of monks and nuns. This was sacked by the Danes in 870, but refounded as a nunnery in the C10, and rebuilt in the C12. Its scale can still be appreciated although all the detail has gone. It was the most important nunnery in England. Five of its pre-Conquest abbesses were canonized. Throughout its life the abbey continued to attract recruits from noble families, remaining powerful until its dissolution in 1539. The buildings were pulled down in 1541 when it was quarried for, among other places, the 'fairest quoin stone for the King's Manor at Dartford'. The site

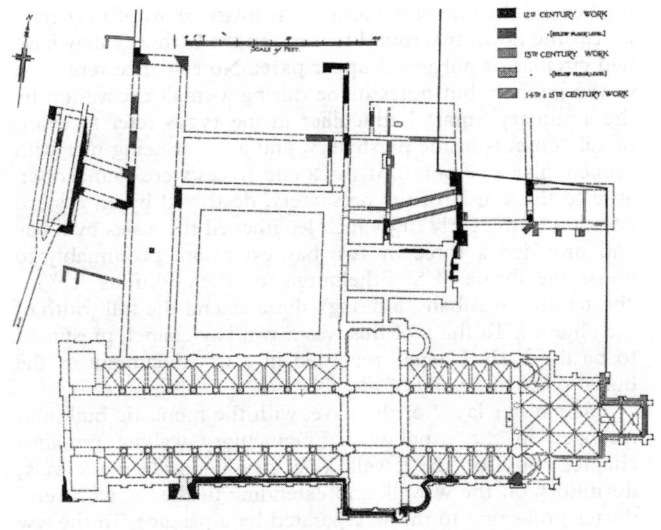

Barking Abbey plan, based on excavations in 1910

was excavated in 1910 by A.W. Clapham and C.J. Dawson.* The plan of the church deduced from this evidence is inscribed in stone lines in the grass.

The E gate or CURFEW TOWER, built *c.* 1460, is now the entrance 5
to the parish churchyard, the only abbey building to remain complete. Two storeys, with battlements and an octagonal NW stair turret. Four-centred archway with ogee niche above on both E and W sides. Blocked windows on the N and S sides to the upper floor, which was the chapel of the Holy Rood. Within, built into the E wall, is a large mid-C12 ROOD, worn and damaged, but of excellent quality. Three figures in relief, built up of oblong blocks, like the more famous reliefs at Chichester, but with more delicate carved detail. St John on the r. has clearly defined stylized drapery with angular folds, reminiscent of C12 manuscript painting. The crucifixion figure has been scraped back, but the drooping arms and the S-shape of the body are still readable. The background has diaper ornament. Other fragments of this reused in the tower suggest the rood may have been part of a larger composition.

The C12 ABBEY CHURCH of St Mary and St Ethelburgha was just under 300 ft long, with five-bay presbytery, transepts, ten-bay nave and W towers, on a scale comparable to St Albans or Peterborough. All that remains visible is some low buttressed walls: chiefly the N transept apse and N wall, the N aisle wall of the nave with an entrance in the seventh bay, and a W end with corner towers with clasping buttresses, project-

*Report in *Trans. Essex Archaeol. Soc.* vol 12, 1913.

ing beyond the line of the aisles. The instructions of 1541 refer to 'casting down two round towers', so the W towers may have had circular or polygonal upper parts. No evidence remained of the interior, but notes made during a small excavation by the antiquary Smart Lethieullier in the 1720s refer to cylindrical columns in the presbytery, and a NE crossing pier with semicircular E respond. At the E end traces were found of an apse to the S aisle of the presbytery, destroyed by an eastern addition of the early C13 which lengthened the aisles by a bay and provided a three by two bay extension, presumably to house the shrine of St Ethelburga (cf. the additions at Winchester and St Albans, although these extend the full width of the church). To the E of this was a two bay chapel, presumed to be the Lady Chapel, recorded in a C15 document as the burial place of several of the abbesses.

The cloister lay N of the nave, with the monastic buildings arranged in the usual way. Fragmentary walling remains: chapter house off the E walk, refectory alongside the N walk, dormitory off the W walk and extending further N, with reredorter projecting to the W separated by a passage. To the NW was the infirmary with its separate chapel.

RELIGIOUS BUILDINGS

ST MARGARET, Broadway. A church of proper town size, not small like the nearby churches of East Ham and Dagenham. The present building developed from the C13 to the C16. It lies within the abbey precincts, SE of the site of the abbey church, and may have started as a small chapel; it became a parish church *c.* 1300. It consists of chancel and chancel chapels, nave and aisles, W tower with taller stair turret, and more unusually, an outer N aisle and chapel. The story is complicated by the existence of C12 fabric in the outer N aisle and chapel, probably taken from the abbey after the Dissolution. The rest is rag and flint except for the C15 stone tower of roughly squared Reigate stone. The windows are mainly restorations by *C.J. Dawson* in 1889 and 1907, attractive if mostly inauthentic interpretations of their medieval predecessors, albeit reusing some original tracery. Perp N porch with crown-post roof. The N doorway with quatrefoils in the spandrels. Further E an early C18 N doorcase. The SE vestry is C15, with wainscoting of 1698, reroofed by *C.C. Winmill* in 1930.

The church is entered through the CHURCH CENTRE on the S side, 1991 by *K.C. White & Partners*. Parallel ranges of roughly squared stone with tiled roofs, entirely sympathetic. Some BENEFACTORS' BOARDS displayed inside.

Inside the church the medieval fabric is extensive but the building history is confused by late C18 alterations, 1840s restorations by the vicar, Robert Lidell, and extensive white-

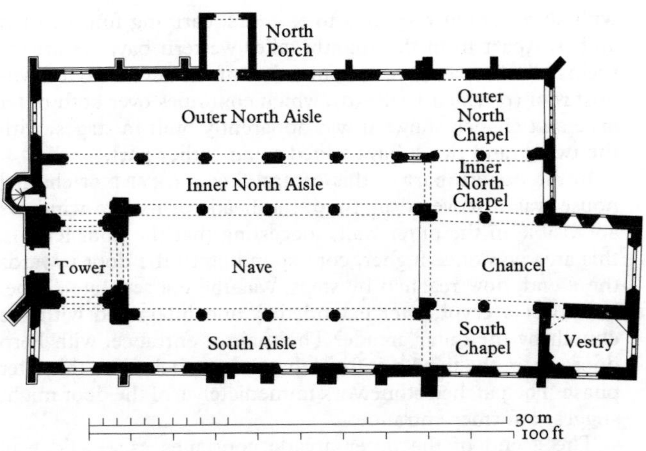

St Margaret, Barking, plan

washing. The long chancel is early C13, with a PISCINA in the S wall, and N and S lancet windows, the latter revealed in 1928–30 during restoration by *C.C. Winmill*, but the E window is clearly C16. The prettily enriched stucco vault, panelled with large foliage bosses, is all that survives of major refurbishment in 1770–1, paid for by Sir Bamber Gascoyne, possibly employing *William Hillyer* (who refurbished Gascoyne's house Bifrons at this date).

The nave arcades now look very similar, due to their C19 restoration, when the octagonal capitals were restored after C18 defacing; minor differences suggest a complicated history, although precise dating is difficult. The slimmer octagonal piers of the S arcade rest on large footings, possibly the remains of an older arcade. Of the present arcades, the N one looks the earlier, with sturdier piers, chamfered bases and simple chamfered arches, details which would fit the C13 or early C14. The S arcade arches have hollow double chamfers, a feature which occurs also on the chancel arch and on the broader eastern arch of the N as well as the S nave arcade. This suggests a remodelling of this part of the church as well as the rebuilding of the S arcade in the C14 or early C15. The chancel arcades have similar mouldings. The only part that can be dated more precisely is the W end, where both N and S aisles were extended to embrace the tower: the responds of the arches below the tower have carefully moulded capitals and bases. Bequests indicate the tower was begun after 1490 and under way in 1500. The nave clerestory and shallow pitched roof look C15. Traces of a painting remain on the spandrels over the chancel arch. Below the clerestory is a string course with large ball flower, its uniformity suggesting the C19.

The most puzzling area is that of the outer N aisle and chapel. The outer aisle is divided off by irregular piers, each with slim shafted responds to N and S, carrying four-centred arches. Apart from the slightly taller western bay, the arcade seems all of a piece, yet examination of the seven-bay crown-post roof (revealed 1928–30), which continues over both outer aisle and chapel, shows it was apparently built in stages, with the two W and two E bays added to an earlier part.*

In the eastern part of this central area a CRYPT or charnel house was discovered in 1929; the heads of its two windows are visible in the outer wall, suggesting that the floor level in this area was once higher, corresponding to the door towards the E end, now reached by steps. Was there a separate chapel here over a crypt, later extended W and integrated with the church by the outer arcade? The main N entrance, with Perp doorway, in the third bay from the W, must belong to this later phase. The patched stonework immediately E of the door might suggest a former entrance.

The E end of the outer arcade continues as a solid wall pierced by a small Perp window, presumably a reused piece inserted as a squint. The NE chapel has further puzzles: it is divided from the N chapel by a slim C12 drum pier and responds, with scalloped capitals (found by Dawson to be of plaster and so probably restorations). The most likely explanation is that these are spoil from the abbey after the Dissolution, used to create the NE chapel. Its E wall also is made up of C12 material, and the chapel roof includes reused timbers. Could this area have been intended as a chantry chapel for William Pownsett (see also below)?

FURNISHINGS. – FONT. Bowl on baluster stem, with ornate scrolly ornament, just going gristly, i.e. *c.* 1635. Wooden cover by *W.G. Rogers*, *c.* 1842, painted in the C20. – PULPIT. 1727, by *Thomas Marchand* and *Thomas Humphreys*, originally double-decker but cut down. Hexagonal on an elegant pedestal with inlaid panels. Staircase railing of finely twisted balusters. REREDOS. Late C18. Screen with paired Temple of the Winds half columns. – ORGAN CASE in the N chancel chapel. 1770 by *Byfield and Green*; incorporated with the instrument by *J. W. Walker & Sons* in 1913. – ALTAR. Table by *C.C. Winmill*, 1928, from a design by Philip Webb. Openwork panels. CHANCEL SCREEN. Dec with ogee-shaped centre and frieze of vines etc., 1893. – SCREEN. S aisle chapel, with carved and painted figures associated with Barking, including Captain Cook and Elizabeth Fry. By *George Jack*, a pupil of Philip Webb and friend of Winmill, *c.* 1930. – PEWS. The church was reseated in 1842. – C19 wrought iron screen above the W door, originally part of the sanctuary rail. ROYAL ARMS. C18 (?) painted wood, unusually shown with a lion above the crown. Good collection of C17 and C18 BENEFACTORS' BOARDS. – SCULPTURE. In a

* *See* Bond and Lea, *Post-fire survey of St Margaret, Barking, English Heritage report* (1994) and *Victorian restoration and St Margaret's Church, Barking* (AA essay) by Thomas Cromwell. Winmill's Survey of 1928 is published in *Charles Canning Winmill, an architect's life by his daughter*, 1946.

case by the N door: fragment, *c.* 12 in. high, of Saxon cross shaft with close thin interlace ornament. Perhaps C10. In the NE tower pier an elaborate Perp NICHE with canted traceried sides, one with a recess, and lattice vault. Curved embattled top. STAINED GLASS. E window, the Last Supper, spread across three lights; canopy work above and angels below. – N chapel E: 1913, crucifixion; – N aisle W: 1896 Ascension. – S aisle: two local maritime scenes and pretty quarries with shells etc., contemporary with the nearby screen, designed by *Winmill* and *Jack* *c.* 1930.

MONUMENTS. A fine collection, described topographically. Chancel: tomb recess, S wall. Depressed brick arch with small rosettes. C16. – Incised slab to Martin, first Vicar of Barking, †1328, large demi-figure, an important work of its type. – Sir Charles Montague †1625. Painted alabaster. A beautiful and 13
unusual design, attributed to *Maximilian Colt*, a small seated figure in a tent, musketeers l. and r. outside, and many more tents in the distance. Sir Charles seems to muse on the next day's destinies, and there is a great deal of suspense in the eve-of-battle atmosphere. – Francis Fuller †1636, with frontal bust in oval niche, attributed by Adam White to *John Colt the younger*, an assistant of Le Sueur. – Alice Bertie †1677, severe classical aedicule, and Elizabeth Bertie †1712 with fine drapery and putti heads.* S chancel chapel: Robert Bertie †1701. Ionic aedicule with arms, books etc. N aisle E respond: Sarah Fleming †1765. Inscription on feigned drapery, with putti heads. N chapel: Brass of Richard Malet †1485, demi-figure of Priest. Outer N chapel: Black marble slab with figures and inscription referring to Maurice, Bishop of London †1105 and Alfgive, Abbess of Barking. – John Bennett, sea captain, †1706, a spec- 15
tacular monument with a frontal demi-figure in an elegant attitude between two fluted pilasters carrying an open segmental pediment. It bisects, to l. and r., a warship in relief with globes (terrestrial and celestial) set below: the detail of the utmost refinement. Outer N aisle: William Pownsett of Loxford †1553/4, a local landowner who, according to Lysons, was the last steward of Barking abbey. White marble sarcophagus with elaborately moulded profile, by *Nicholas Bellin* of Modena 'image graver to the Queen's majesty' as he is called in the account. The sole known example of such work by an artist who had been employed as painter and carver of Renaissance work for the French and English courts. The black marble top slab probably dates from 1784 when the tomb was repaired by All Souls College. Pownsett's executors had acquired the advowson for the college in 1557, as a means of securing the continuation of prayers for Pownsett's soul, an indication of the uncertain times. The vicar of Barking was indeed imprisoned in 1559 as a suspected papist. – Robert Westley Hall †1839, bust on Grecian base. – John Bamber †1753, a bust

* Geoffrey Fisher attributes Alice Bertie's monument, 1677, to *William Stanton*; Eliz. Bertie 1712 to *Thos. Stayner*.

(attributed to *Roubiliac* by Bindman and Baker), set on a lion-footed sarcophagus on a plinth. – Sir Crisp Gascoyne †1761, Lord Mayor of London, elegant with weeping putto and marble urn against a grey obelisk. – Captain Joshua Banaster †1738, broken pediment with trophies and putti. S aisle: Sir Orlando Humphreys †1737, standing wall-monument with detached Corinthian columns carrying a far-projecting broken segmental pediment. Between them the bust of Sir Orlando; outside the columns cherubs. Original iron railings. – Many other lesser wall monuments and ledgers, also matrices of lost brasses.*

CHURCHYARD. Among many tombstones a few more elaborate monuments: Captain John Bennett †1706. Sarcophagus with acanthus leaves and relief panels on either side, one depicting his ship, *The Lennox*, the other with arms. Nearby, two-tier pedestal carrying an obelisk, originally set on four skulls; one survives. Panels with putti.

ST ERKENWALD, Levett Road. 1954–5 by *R.C. Foster* (*Tooley and Foster*), successor to a building of 1934, which now serves as its hall. Red brick, saddleback N tower and projecting porch with cast-stone relief over the door of St Erkenwald with the Saxon King, Sebbi, by *Philip Lindsay Clark*. Restrained interior, with the concrete frame of the roof structure plainly exposed above the nave and chancel. Low aisles and S transept (Lady Chapel). FURNISHINGS in oak by *Foster*. Of far greater interest, an important set of GLASS by *John Hutton*. Eight lancets of 1955, tinted in soothingly watery blues, greens and gold, with figures in tense drapery engraved with fluid lines; the style strongly evocative of Henry Moore's drawings and similar to Hutton's work at Coventry Cathedral (completed 1962). A second set installed in the nave aisles in 1968 is as vivid as the earlier work is gentle. Bonded sections of glass provide an abstract frame to the symbols of the Passion.

ST PATRICK, Blake Avenue. 1940 by *A.E. Wiseman* of Chelmsford. The donor was Mrs Lavinia Keene. 'An odd attempt at modern church architecture,' remarked Pevsner in 1954, 'with a circular tower housing the apse and ending in bell-openings of somewhat streamlined appearance.' Without the intended fleche, the effect is rather like Holden: apart from the cross in the E face, the tower might be taken for a part of an underground station. Two low transeptal projections, S for the Lady Chapel; N for the vestries. Buff brick surrounds a reinforced concrete frame. Flat roofs. Inside, more reinforced concrete in the tapering piers between the nave and passage aisles, and in the rood beam. The semi-dome of the apse has vertical bands of coloured relief decoration that look as though they belong to a 1930s cinema. The W end has been partitioned off and divided horizontally, and the windows have been insensitively bricked in.

*Not on view: BRASSES of Priest *c.* 1480, of Thomas Broke †1493 and wife, and of John Tedcastell and wife †1596.

ST MARY AND ST ETHELBURGA (R.C.), Linton Road. 1979 by *John Newton* of *Burles, Newton & Partners.* Low, unobtrusive and domestic but distinguished by careful massing. Large circular E window with coloured glass from the previous church of 1869 and a monopitch roof lighting the altar. Bare brick interior, pine roof and small recessed sanctuary. Reset memorial stones from its predecessor. In the doorway, a Gothic tablet to Rev. James Gilligan †1887. Adjacent, the Presbytery and the former school of 1862, still with its bell. In the courtyard, a massive carillon.

ST THOMAS MORE (R.C.), Longbridge Road. 1991 extension by *Gerald Murphy* of *Burles, Newton & Partners* to a 1935 hall. Red brick Neo-Perp with straight gables echoing the earlier building. Plainly treated interior entered on the diagonal with a spine lantern over the line of the processional approach. Shallow pitched roof sloping down to N and S corner chapels. FURNISHINGS: green marble and Portland stone. In the S chapel a large vividly coloured STAINED GLASS corner window of St Thomas and St Vincent flanking a panel depicting the Descent of the Holy Spirit. By *John Lawson* of *Goddard & Gibbs.*

BAPTIST TABERNACLE, Linton Road. 1893. *Holliday and Greenwood*, builders. Renaissance-style, the façade in the form of a big segmental pediment with pedimented centre and Lombardic windows. Inside, a large hall with raked pews and galleries, added in 1905 when the hall was re-roofed; mighty timber trusses carried on iron columns. At the E end is a large ORGAN, rebuilt in 1952. Its case has a modicum of Gothic decoration. The first organ, installed in 1911, was built in 1825 for the Trinity Chapel, Mare Street, Hackney.

METHODIST CHURCH, London Road. 1958–9 by *George Baines & Syborn*, replacing the Central Hall, East Street, destroyed by a bomb in 1945. Brick with shallow-pitched pantiled roof; gable end with projecting stone buttresses to the centrepiece, and mullioned window over the entrance. Along the flanks, rectangular windows framed in stone. The church is behind a low foyer and meeting room. A light interior with flat ceiling, narrow passage aisles. Tall rectangular side windows high up, leaded, with a piece of coloured glass in each. Shallow sanctuary with blind end wall faced in brick, with a wooden and brass cross.

NEW PARK HALL EVANGELICAL CHURCH, Axe Street. 1929–31 by *C.J. Dawson, Son and Allardyce.* Plain brick with gabled centre and low wings with mullioned windows. Hexagonal roof over the centre.

UNITED REFORMED CHURCH, Upney Lane. Former Congregational. 1929 by *John S. Broadbent.* Red brick, dull but with attempts at Arts and Crafts detailing.

GURDWARA SINGH SABHA (LONDON EAST SIKH TEMPLE), North Street. Former Friends Meeting House, 1908, by *C.J. Dawson.* In Dutch C17 style with big scrolled and shaped gables on each side. Central cupola. Brick, now overpainted and rewindowed to bright but ill effect. The Quakers' first meeting house in Barking was founded here in 1673. The former Burial Ground, acquired one year earlier, stands opposite. Now cleared.

RIPPLESIDE CEMETERY, Ripple Road. 1886, extended 1903. One chapel of ragstone and with Perp details by *C.J. Dawson*. The low tower and higher stair turret make it looks like a diminutive parish church. Many memorials with anchors, including that for Samuel Hewett (†1904) of the family who founded the Barking fishing fleet in the C18.

MAJOR BUILDINGS

TOWN HALL, Town Square. By *Herbert Jackson and Reginald Edmonds*. The design was won in competition in 1936 but not built until 1954–8, omitting some elements. The grandly stepped entrance was replaced by a more modest and democratic-seeming archway beneath the mayor's balcony. In spite of this, the Neo-Georgian style must have seemed distinctly *retardataire* by contemporary standards. Topping the hall is a soaring clock tower, an enduringly popular motif in pre-war public buildings, crowned by a domed cupola. Folding gates in the entrance were (reputedly) made from oak rescued from the Elizabethan Leet Hall demolished in 1923. Marble-faced entrance hall with staircase on each side. Travertine-clad walls and dark Ashburton pillars with concave fluting are the limits of ostentation. Attached at the rear, facing Gascoigne's Road, is the flat-roofed BROADWAY THEATRE, not completed until 1960–1. Its unshowy municipal classical façade has been replaced by an exciting new entrance in brick and glass by *Tim Foster Architects*, 2004.* Inside, a flexible performance space for 320-seat theatre with suspended balconies and rectractable seating.

MAGISTRATES COURT, East Street. Originally Public Offices and Free Library. 1893–4 by *C.J. Dawson*, Surveyor to Barking Local Board. A jolly, Flemish Renaissance design in brick with warm terracotta and stone dressings, much carved and decorated. Prominent porch decorated with strapwork, first-floor oriel windows and slightly projecting wings with high gables. Cupola clock turret. At the rear, where Dawson intended a public hall, an entrance tower has been abruptly inserted by *Essex County Council* since conversion in 1960. The royal coat of arms, dated 1588, which hung in the original court house in Broadway is now in the Borough Museum (Valence House, *see* Becontree).

* Circular reliefs of Barking Abbey and a medieval fishing smack by *A. John Poole* have been removed.

CENTRAL LIBRARY, Town Square. 1974. Rectangular, concrete framed with brick-faced upper storey and ranks of vertical windows. The interior originally had a galleried upper floor, now floored. Abstract, heavily-textured wall decoration is continued into a small light well with a pond. SCULPTURE by *George Muller*. Scheduled for refurbishment in 2004.

FIRE STATION, Alfred's Way. 1938 by *C.C. Shaw*, Borough Architect. Conservatively modern, with a flat parapet and pitched roof but streamlined projecting wings flanking the engine bays. At each end, a single L-shaped cottage.

POLICE STATION, Ripple Road. 1910 by *John Dixon Butler*. A text book design, two-storeys, attic and basement in red brick and Portland stone with bay windows and tall roof-dormers.

BARKING HOSPITAL, Upney Lane. Red brick clinic and ward blocks, grouped around a central garden and linked by glazed atriums with tubular steel trusses. To the W, the Hedgecock Centre was designed as a Nurses' Education Centre by *Sebire Allsopp Architects*, 1983–5. Single storey, covered by a broad pitched roof, and lit along the spine corridor. A few older two-storey ward blocks were built in the 1930s for the Borough's infectious disease hospital. The rest of the site was cleared for housing in the 1990s.

BUS GARAGE, Longbridge Road. 1920s Neo-Georgian with an extension of 1958 by *M. Maybury*, Borough Architect, spanned by 70-ft (21.3 metres) wide pre-cast concrete bowstring trusses.

REFUSE TRANSFER STATION, Jenkins Lane. *c.* 1978 by the *General Works Department* of the *GLC Department of Architecture*. Very similar to the station at Brentford (1977), with the same clustering of chimneys and steel-clad tipping hall atop a concrete podium which holds the compactor.

BARKING FLOOD BARRIER, at the mouth of the River Roding: 1979–83 by *Binnie and Partners*, engineers with *G.T. Bone*, architect. A tall drop-barrier like a portcullis spanning 125ft (38.1 metres) between 193-ft-(57.9 metres)-high towers.

BARKING POWER STATION (*see* Dagenham p. 157).

BRIDGE, over the River Roding, London Road. 1902–4 by *P.J. Sheldon* for Essex County Council. Cast-iron balustrade of rosette-centred quatrefoils.

BARKING PARK, Longbridge Road. Laid out in 1898 to designs by the Council Architects, *C.J. & C.F. Dawson*. By the dome-capped gatepiers is a small Arts and Crafts LODGE, dated 1912: square plan with thick chimneystacks, hipped and dormered roof, shallow bow window and corner porch set back under the eaves. Along the N edge of the park, lined by avenues of lime trees, runs a long meandering lake. In the midst of ornamental gardens and arboretum is a WAR MEMORIAL, erected in 1922. Portland stone, curved and stepped with a raised centre. Restored and rededicated in 2001, with polished granite name panels. The park's recreational amenities have gone to seed, including the defunct Lido by *R.A. Lay*, Borough Engineer, 1931, but happily refurbishment is planned.

Schools

Barking's schools up to 1945 reflect the characteristic pattern of school planning and design of a 'go-ahead' council. In the period after 1870 provision was poor but expanded in the 1890s with three large BOARD SCHOOLS each by *C.J. Dawson*. NORTH STREET (now Northbury) of 1897 and WESTBURY (now Westbury Centre), Ripple Road of 1904 typify the designs: three storeys with central halls on each floor. Less heavily fenestrated than the London Board Schools but impressively detailed in red and yellow brick with ranks of big Flemish gables, crenellated stair towers and cupolas giving architectural zip to the necessary bulk. – The ubiquitous 'bungalow' designs, favoured in the suburbs where land was available, appear in Barking as early as 1912. At RIPPLE SCHOOL, Suffolk Road, *Dawson* practised an undidactic and friendly Neo-Georgian, with hipped-roof classroom blocks symmetrically linked to a central hall block with a cupola; near identical to the design by Essex County Architect, *John Stuart* for the Borough's first secondary school (now BARKING ABBEY COMPREHENSIVE), Longbridge Road.

Barking quickly adopted the 1926 'Hadow' division into elementary and senior schools and embarked upon a major building programme, in part prompted by the demands of the new Becontree housing estate. The style remained Neo-Georgian, the planning conventional for the period, with symmetrical quadrangular plans on the open-air system of classrooms opening onto courtyards with covered walkways. The former Park Modern (now EASTBURY COMPREHENSIVE), Rosslyn Road, 1926 (which included the Education Committee's offices) and the former EASTBURY SENIOR SCHOOL, Dawson Avenue of 1929–32 show the approach in the larger schools, with boys and girls separated around adjoining courtyards. An interesting variation in planning terms, FAIRCROSS SPECIAL SCHOOL, Hulse Avenue of 1922, is a single block with inclined wings to the playground and classrooms open on both sides, a form subsequently used for several infants schools e.g. the former EASTBURY INFANTS SCHOOL, Dawson Avenue. MANOR SCHOOLS and BARKING ABBEY COMPREHENSIVE, Sandringham Road of 1939 are two-storey and in a more imposing Baroque style, by *C.C. Shaw*, Borough Architect. But the persistence of the Dawson tradition continues in the buildings of the Sixth Form Centre at EASTBURY COMPREHENSIVE, Rosslyn Road, completed in 2002, which has yellow brick wings with cupolas.

Pre-war provision meant few new schools were built after 1945, except in the new housing areas, e.g. Thames View Estate (*see* perambulation 2). ST MARGARET'S C.E. PRIMARY SCHOOL, North Street by *K.C. White & Partners*, 1968, is designed to be discreet and respectful to its medieval neighbours, with a nod towards ecclesiastical design in the triangular-headed windows of its upper storey. Extended 1995.

UNIVERSITY OF EAST LONDON, BARKING CAMPUS (since 1992), Upney Lane/Longbridge Road. The former South West Essex Technical College of 1935–6 by *John Stuart*, Essex County Architect. Symmetrical, large H-plan, with projecting wings and a seven bay centre with a solid stone cupola. Three-storeyed, pale brick, with some good cast-stone decoration by *E.J. & A.T. Bamford*. Over the entrance doors in the main front, keystones with beasts of the British Empire: from l. to r. Springbok, Elephant, Bear and Kangaroo. Balconies at first floor are carved with the canon of the great architects, artists and engineers of Western civilization; at parapet level are the trades and industries of the world. – Undistinguished extensions. CIVIL ENGINEERING, a three-storey reinforced-concrete-frame block raised above a low podium, by *Harold Conolly*, the Essex County Architect, *c.* 1965. At the rear, linked to the main building by an enclosed bridge, is the LEARNING RESOURCE CENTRE, by *Sidney J. Harris*, Borough Architect, 1978. Faceted pre-cast panels of exposed aggregate and slit windows. Contrasting dark brick base and lecture theatre block on the N side. Timid STUDENT RESIDENCES of 1992–3 by *Team Design and Build*.

EASTBURY MANOR HOUSE

Eastbury Square

A good example of a medium-sized late C16 manor house, providing an air of mystery and interest in an area of extensive and bland interwar borough council housing.

Eastbury Manor House was almost certainly erected for Clement 11
Sysley, a wealthy City merchant, *c.* 1556–73: the earlier date indicated by dendrochronology, the latter by a date on a rain-water head (no longer visible but noted by Pevsner in 1954). Described by Defoe as 'now almost fallen down' in 1724, the house was saved from destruction in 1841 by the interest of local antiquarians but only to be preserved for further mal-treatment and to be threatened again when the surrounding estate was sold for development in 1918. After a campaign to save it led by the Society for the Protection of Ancient Buildings and the London Survey Committee, who had published a monograph on the house in 1917, it was acquired by the National Trust and used as a club. Major repairs were undertaken with characteristic sensitivity by *William Weir* between 1928 and 1935 when it was opened as a museum by the Borough of Barking. Further work in 1964, and restoration of the W wing completed in 2003 by *Richard Griffiths Architects*.

The house is impressive, of red brick with a lively roofline of gables and big diagonal chimneys. The PLAN is an H-shape with short wings in front and larger wings behind, framing a S

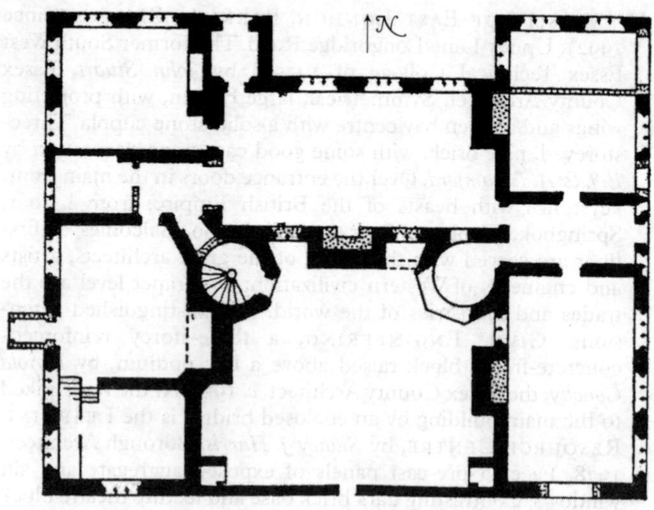

Eastbury Manor House, Barking, plan

courtyard enclosed by a high brick wall. This means that the house is outward facing, a reversal of medieval practice that is consolidated by the regular arrangement of the (restored) windows on the main elevations. Each of three lights with one transom, and moulded brick surrounds rendered to imitate stone, they give no indication of the hierarchy of rooms within. The symmetry, enhanced by placing the large chimneystacks (with fine groups of octagonal chimneys) on the courtyard side, is only broken on the N FRONT by a three-storey porch set against the W wing. It has a moulded brickwork pediment with attached pinnacles above a four-centred arch. Such detail, along with polygonal angle shafts to the gables and diapering in the brickwork must certainly be considered backward-looking for the 1570s and Eastbury retains other curiously outmoded features, including the original stairs housed in octagonal angle turrets in the COURTYARD, an unusual if not unknown combination in England (e.g. Plaish Hall, Shropshire). The E tower was demolished *c.* 1814 and *Weir* advocated sympathetic replacement. Instead a steel stair has been inserted within the shell, but the original handrail is still visible: its fine brick moulding good evidence of its higher status than the W tower at the service end of the house. This retains its stair, with a massive but plain oak newel and oak treads, which spirals upwards to a small octagonal parapet room.

Although the INTERIOR was greatly altered after 1841, when much of the house was made to serve as farm buildings, the planning of the Elizabethan house is easily discernible to the contemporary visitor. The N porch originally led into a screens passage dividing the hall from the W service wing. The staircase is an early C19 insertion, superseding the original main stair in the E tower. The screen was replaced by a partition, through which one enters the single-storey HALL, with a broad fireplace in the S wall. At its E (dais) end, a bulging chimney-breast intrudes awkwardly into the space, perhaps exaggerated by the removal of a wall which once extended across the present E door. Behind, in the E parlour wing, are two large rooms separated by a passage, much repaired by *Weir* after use for stabling and storage in the C19. At this level in the refurbished W wing were the kitchen, sculleries, pantry etc. (Small trefoil headed niche in the hatch connecting the kitchen and buttery. The SW room has C16 or C17 panelling, probably reset. On the first floor, further chambers.)

Above the Hall is the PAINTED ROOM, originally two chambers, the W one reduced by the creation of the C19 staircase and since thrown together with its neighbour. On the E and S walls are fragments of an important series of *a secco* wall paintings showing brightly coloured sea- and landscapes, Dutch in character, glimpsed through a series of arched panels divided by Solomonic columns. These stand on panelled plinths with classical busts. Croft-Murray points to this arrangement as comparable to Tarris' panoramic seascapes of 1617–23 at Palazzo Lannellotti, Rome. A date of *c.* 1603 is suggested, however, by the incorporation of the arms of John Moore, tenant from that year. The paintings on the E wall appear to have originally included a third panel and overdoor, removed in the C19.

The first floor of the E wing is presented as a LONG GALLERY, though may have been subdivided originally. At the S end, a C16 stone fireplace with a frieze of alternating foliated circles, lozenges and shells. The second floor is open to the queenpost roof, its joists carried on the tie-beams: substantially repaired by *Weir*. There is no trace of wall paintings, recorded by the Survey of London, which showed figures in C17 dress. – KITCHEN GARDEN. Planned to a C16 design. WALLED GARDEN on the E side with openings in the E wall, possibly former bee-boles.

PERAMBULATIONS

Barking is undemanding on the tourist's feet and only the town centre demands perambulation. The area S of the A13, covered in perambulation 2, is best approached by bus or car.

1. Barking Town Centre: from the Station to the Abbey and Town Quay

Most visitors on foot to Barking will need to pass through the town centre to reach the Abbey and church, and this route takes

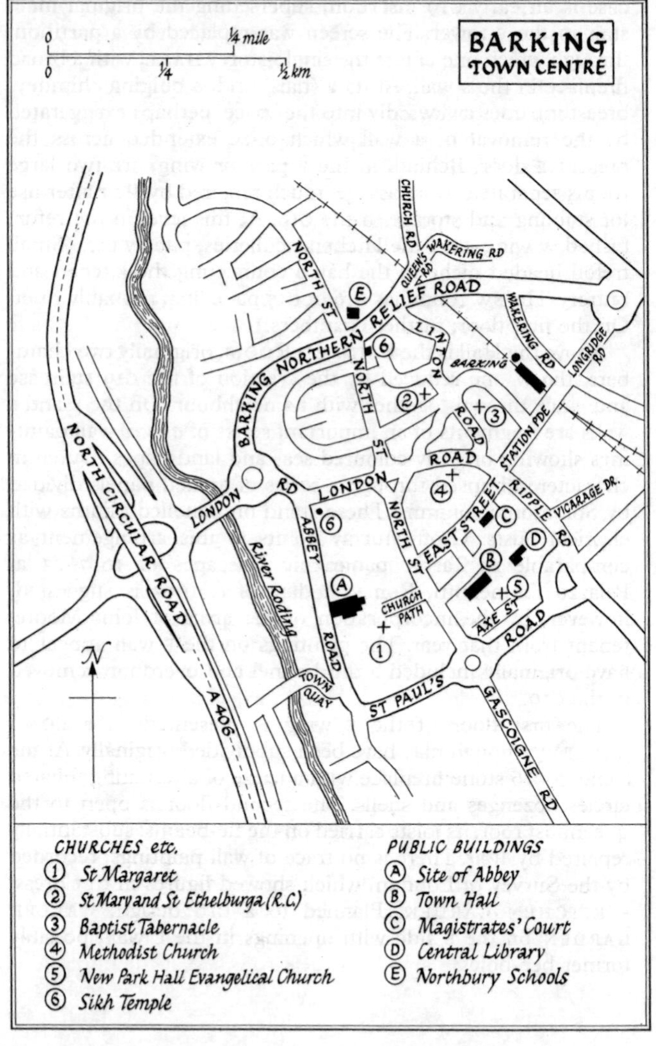

in the town's principal buildings. The centre still retains its medieval street pattern. Unlike other major towns in East London (e.g. Stratford, Ilford, Romford) Barking did not grow up around a river crossing or road junction. The London road crossed the Roding before halting at North Street by the parish church. Travellers continuing E would pass along East Street and then S along Ripple Road and this wiggly pattern is still preserved today for the pedestrian.

The tour begins at BARKING STATION, opened on the Tilbury line in 1854. To the street, the booking hall of 1959–61 by *John Ward* of British Railways Eastern Region; its design an echo of Montuori's entrance to Rome station (1956). Erected to coincide with electrification of the railway, it is commensurately modern in outlook and unquestionably one of the best English stations of this date. Pre-cast concrete beams, forming an undulating roof, project forward and upward as a broad canopy carried on a frame infilled on all sides by glass; its transparency only mildly affected by the encroachment of shops inside.

The commercial centre of Barking is a patchwork of periods, from the two-storey shops of the C19, through 1930s Neo-Georgian to concrete and glass of the 1960s and since. Close to the station is THE SPOTTED DOG, rebuilt *c.* 1910, in red brick with corner chimneystacks and half-timbered gables. Ground floor and interior remodelling by *F.M. Kirby*, 1925, the panelled bar still part preserved. Earlier buildings associated with the pub since 1870 adjoin at Nos. 15a–b and in the garden behind. Otherwise the interest is confined to the compact shopping area at the junction of East Street and Ripple Road, pedestrianized *c.* 1998 for the busy street market. At the crossroads is the anachronistic addition of a bandstand. The big SW corner block at the crossing was an Edwardian Baroque landmark, Blake's ironmongers and furnishers. Its grandiose clock tower was destroyed by bombing. The replacement corner block is entirely out of scale. S on this side of RIPPLE ROAD is the POLICE STATION (*see* above), adjoined to the r. by a tall, five-bay frontage in the style of an early C18 house, red brick with channelled quoins, cut brick window labels and a stone cornice. Dated 1914. Ground floor pilasters with cherubs heads and garlands. The E side is dominated by the VICARAGE FIELD SHOPPING CENTRE, bland Neo-Victorian of 1990 in brick banded with reconstituted stone. Gabled bays with big round arched windows above first floor. The mall extends over the site of the old football ground. At its heart a tall atrium with sub-Italianate arcaded galleries, linked at the upper level to Station Parade. Further S along Ripple Road the scale suddenly becomes domestic with Victorian terraces on both sides with shops to the ground floor. On the r. PESCI BROS., the presumably punning name of a 1950s fish and chip shop, which has sub-aquatic scenes engraved on the glass door.

In VICARAGE DRIVE to the E is the former Vicarage, a handsome house of 1794 whose gardens originally fronted Ripple Road. Built with a legacy from Dr Ralph Freeman, Fellow of All Souls College. It replaced an earlier house, owned by Jeremy Bentham, father of the philosopher. Brick, three bays with a dentilled pediment to front and back. Round-arched ground floor openings. Sensitively converted to offices in the 1990s with sympathetic additions linked to the main house by Doric arcades.

EAST STREET was the medieval route to and from the Abbey

but now lined by the variegated forms of late Victorian and early C20 frontages above shops. The only major incident is the impressive former Public Offices of 1893, now Magistrates Court (*see* above). Immediately S, the dismal TOWN SQUARE provides a singularly undistinguished setting for the TOWN HALL and CENTRAL LIBRARY (*see* above). Their dislocation from their surroundings promises to be repaired by plans by *Allford Hall Monaghan Morris*, 2004, which propose a grand axial approach from Ripple Road set between new buildings, and refurbishment of the Library, with housing above.

At the W end of EAST STREET, S, is a wildly jazzy former Burton's showroom of *c.* 1931, faced in cast stone with the full gamut of chevroned and scalloped Art Deco styling including big elephant heads. On the opposite corner is THE BULL, an ancient establishment, rebuilt in 1925 by *S.A.S. Yeo*. Angled corner entrance (with large plaster bull above), faux gabled crosswings to the end bays, and big chimneys. The upper storey has moulded brick window surrounds with pulvinated heads.

The junction with BROADWAY brings us to what was the heart of the old village. Immediately ahead is the CURFEW GATE
5 to ST MARGARET'S CHURCH and, just beyond, the site of the ABBEY with, on its N side, ST MARGARET'S (C.E.) PRIMARY SCHOOL (*see* above). Until the 1930s a narrow street, Church Lane, approached the Curfew Gate between rows of houses. Slightly S stood the open market place with the Leet Hall (Court and Market House) in the centre. Erected in 1567–8, its demolition in 1923 heralded the undoing of the interesting late medieval context for the church and abbey. Clearance of the narrow lanes and closely packed houses began in the 1930s along the E side of Broadway to make way for the proposed Town Hall (*see* above) and what was left of the enclave around the churchyard was removed in 1971–4 to provide a broad open setting for the medieval remains. This purported enhancement now seems mistaken, and the informal landscaping, by *Professor G. Peter Youngman*, decidedly timid. Close to the roadside stands a single granite block rescued from *Rennie*'s London Bridge (1831; demolished 1968).

S of Broadway, GASCOIGNE ROAD leads into a massive mixed estate developed in 1963–70 by the Borough. Unworthy of detour except perhaps for THE HOPE public house, 1898.

Instead, continuing W of Abbey Road, one reaches the River Roding at the historic TOWN QUAY, where waterside industry is being gradually superseded by housing developments and the ubiquitous sheds for commercial outlets. At the approach to Town Quay, three inscribed granite plinths by *Harry Gray* allude to Barking's past. The only trace of the town mill is the 1870 granary on the wharf: four storeys with a five storey tower at the E end. Hoists and loft doors have been preserved.

The old LONDON ROAD across the Roding was improved in 1810 for better access between the West India Docks and Tilbury. Historically, it halted at Barking's main street, NORTH STREET, but was extended E after 1937 to connect with Ripple

Road. Thus along both streets are contemporary developments for flats: one in North Street has a sculptural panel on the corner. Furthest N, close to the relief road, are two buildings of greater interest: the former FRIENDS MEETING HOUSE and NORTH STREET SCHOOL (*see* above).

E along London Road, however, the pickings are fewer. Close to the centre, at LINTON ROAD, the scale is suddenly altered by the presence of high-rise office blocks of the 1960s, built as part of the drive to create offices in suburban towns close to transport interchanges. No. 1 (MARITIME HOUSE) is a grim slab of aggregate facing; CROWN HOUSE on the opposite side is altogether odder, a wilfully angular tower in reinforced concrete with brick infill and a glazed stair tower as its spine. In its shadow is the BAPTIST TABERNACLE (*see* above) and further on, to the l. the CHURCH OF ST MARY AND ST ETHELBURGA (*see* above). The view N is closed by the largest block of THE LINTONS estate, a sixteen-storey slab of 1960–3 by *M. Maybury*, Borough Architect, reclad to dubious effect. The estate was an early example of using totally precast factory-made components (by *Concrete Southern Ltd*). Across the railway, along CHURCH ROAD, some old-fashioned entertainment is provided by THE BRITANNIA pub, 1898 by *F.W. Ashton* with his trademark buxom termes. Half-timbering and turrets with pargetting to the walls. In 2004 new housing by *Jestico & Whiles* is under way.

S back to the Station along WAKERING ROAD, first, standing tall, WIGHAM HOUSE, by *Owen Luder Partnership*, 1973–5, possibly by *Rodney Gordon* who designed several of this firm's out-of-town offices at this period. Tough and uncompromising, of ten storeys with big pre-cast window panels with inward sloping reveals and characteristically brutal detached service and stair towers of windowless channelled concrete. Good quality but unloveable. Rather in its shadow, PHOENIX HOUSE (Job Centre) is equally representative of its period, the late 1980s, in a highly coloured mix of pale brickwork and blockwork covered by a roof with exposed steel trusses.

2. *S of the A13: Thames View Estate and Barking Reach*

The London–Tilbury Road (A13) lies as a grim belt across the borough and is as unpleasant as any major urban thoroughfare can be. In spite of this a dedicated effort by architect *Tom de Paor*, in association with Barking & Dagenham, has been under way since 1996 to drastically enhance its environment as the A13 ARTSCAPE. The plan is seen as an integral feature of the wider regeneration of the area along the N side of the Thames. Artist-designed landscapes and earthworks, major light works, new sculptural commissions and street furniture have been introduced, including HOLDING PATTERN (Lodge Avenue Roundabout), by *Graham Ellard and Stephen Johnstone* with *Tom de Paor*. Slim beacons of light. At the Goresbrook Road

Junction, two mysterious concave-sided cones covered in black tarmac, by *Thomas Heatherwick Studio*, erupt from roundabouts either side of the flyover. Other works are less obtrusive, quietly knitted into the overall landscaping.

S of the A13 lies an area which was historically reserved for some of the more noxious and unneighbourly industries lining RIVER ROAD and beyond. It is a staggering mess, a hinterland of factories and warehouses, so it is a surprise to find in its midst the leafy and quiet THAMES VIEW ESTATE, created 1953–60 to designs by *C.C. Shaw*, the Borough Architect and his assistant, *M. Maybury* with *C. Harper*, the Borough Engineer. The demands of post-war reconstruction led the Borough to identify the traditionally uninhabitable Ripple Marshes for housing in 1949. 160 acres required reclamation and the driving of piles for concrete foundations. The remote location means it is a self-contained neighbourhood with its own shopping centre, schools, pubs and church.

The dominant tone is that of the interwar cottage estate but mixed with elements of strongly formal planning, particularly along the central E–W axis of BASTABLE AVENUE (named after the Ministry of Local Govt. housing officer; all the other streets also take the names of officials). This has the plain, unaisled CHRIST CHURCH of 1958–9 which doubles as a hall. Porch beneath a high buttressed bell-tower with honeycomb belfry and sloping roof. E of the church the road widens and opens on the S side to an open recreation ground, with schools, clinic and community centre grouped close by. THAMES VIEW INFANTS SCHOOL is flat roofed and unremarkable but with some interest created by the school keeper's house with its big square clock tower, something of an Essex County Council trademark but also in tune with the Festival style of 1951.

Facing the open ground on the avenue's N side is the shopping parade, with two-storey flats above shops with covered arcades around three sides of a precinct. Relandscaping in 1998–9 by *Jason Cornish* and *Phil Power* introduced benches and new lighting. Closing the view N is Maybury House, a nine-storey block of flats, one of three which act as markers at the edge of the estate amongst the low- and medium-rise elements. Each is placed as a visual full-stop at the end of an avenue. A late addition to the estate in 1957 but technically innovative as the first in London, and only the second in Britain, to use load-bearing large-panel pre-cast concrete for rapid construction by *Concrete Ltd.* Each tower is tripartite, with a rectangular central block attached to skewed end blocks. Four one-bedroom flats per floor with balconies paired in the centre within a slightly projecting grid. Extensions with squat towers, to the W end of the estate in 1967, are mundane and damaging to the earlier coherence.

Even further SE, at BARKING REACH, plans are under way to create an entirely new town, on the largest brownfield site in London, as part of the wider plans for development of the Thames Gateway. The 2003 masterplan by *Maxwan Architects and Urbanists* for English Partnerships and Bellway Homes envisages a series of visually distinctive neighbourhoods, linked by a network of open spaces and with a park along the riverside. More than 10,000 homes are to be built over a 130-acre site. Completion is expected in 2020.

BECONTREE

Becontree was the largest of all the interwar London County Council's out-county estates and at its creation bestrode the borders between Barking, Dagenham and Ilford. Its size and history justify treating it separately from its neighbouring settlements. Indeed in the revival of a name used for the area in the Domesday Book, its planners at the Council consciously wished to distinguish it as a 'township complete in itself'.*

THE ESTATE

The LCC was permitted to build outside the County of London by the Addison Housing Act of 1919 and in that year recruited *G. Topham Forrest*, from Essex County Council, as Chief Architect expressly to draw up and implement the estate plans. These were completed by his successor, *E. P. Wheeler*. At the outset the LCC planned to house 120,000 in 24,000 terraced houses on a 3,000-acre site. This was largely arable land and market gardens punctuated by a handful of older manor houses, notably the ruinous Parsloes (demolished in 1925) and Valence House. The latter was respectfully kept, first as council offices, now as a museum (*see* below). In the peak years 1922–3 and 1926–9 between 2,000 and 4,000 houses per annum were built. Officially complete in 1935, when the population was over 167,000, the estate expanded after the war with later phases designed by Dagenham Borough.

The earliest PLANS, published in 1921, were radial, with three main avenues leading to a Civic Centre at the heart of the estate (the junction of Parsloes Avenue and Porter Avenue) and the

* This account is much indebted to *'A Township complete in itself': A Planning History of the Becontree/Dagenham Estate* by Dr Robert Home, London Borough of Barking & Dagenham, 1997. The phrase was used by the LCC.

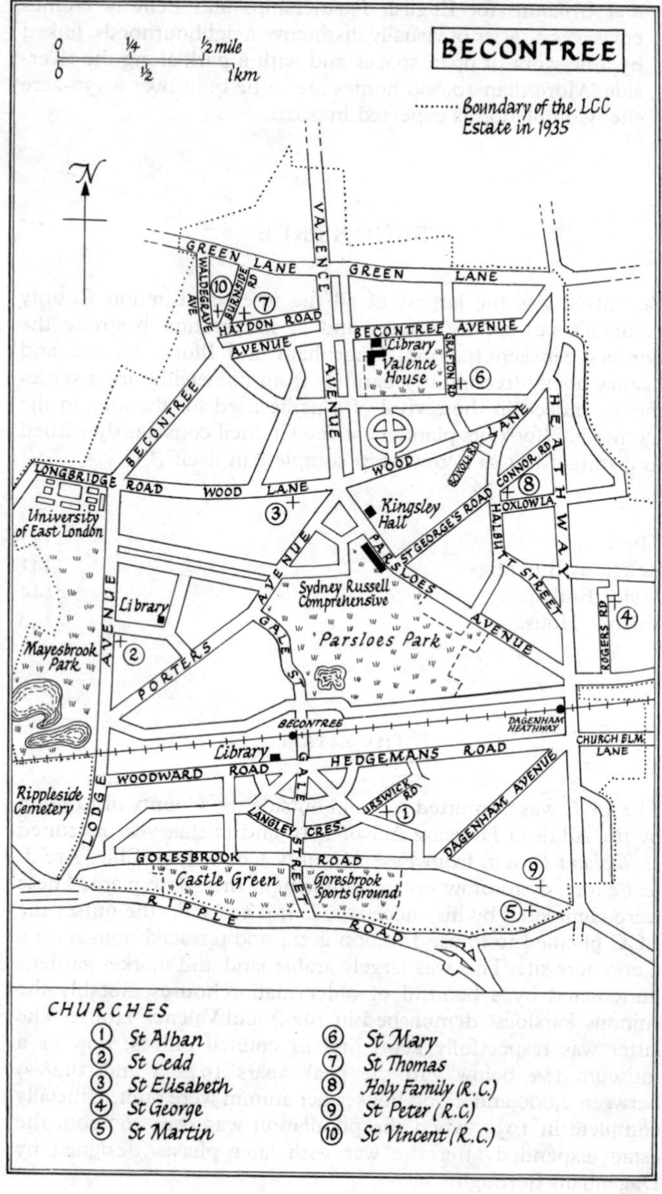

housing surrounded on all side by strips of open land and planned public parks. This element was retained in the executed plans in which the existing lines of country lanes were also observed and new arterial roads of considerable width introduced with Valence Avenue and Heathway as the central N–S spines. Railway tracks were laid down the centre of these avenues to transport building materials on to the estate from the river, their line still represented by the generous grass verges of the completed design. Rigid linearity was offset by the use of circuses and crescents. *Cul-de-sacs*, perhaps the most characteristic feature of the inter-war housing estate, whether public or private, were a new experiment, here referred to by the planners as 'banjos' for their distinctive shape. This made for an economy in road building but limited easy passage of residents from one part of the estate to another.

To begin with, socially mixed development was the ambition but the percentage of planned private housing was minimal and concentrated in the area of the estate within already well-to-do Barking. A few old buildings were retained (e.g. No. 39a Wood Lane and Pettits Farm, Halbutt Street) but the overall architectural character of the HOUSING was firmly the responsibility of the council's architects, and in the earlier phases, particularly in the NW (close to Ilford) and SE (by Dagenham village), they attempted to maintain a degree of variety. Decorative use of brick and tile was combined with nods to the Essex vernacular in the use of pantiles, weatherboarding and even, to a very limited degree, timber framing (e.g. Nos. 233–53 Wood Lane). Thereafter the dictates of rapid provision saw endless repetition of basic types, details and motifs with the result that the different parts of the estate are scarcely distinguishable to the visitor. Everywhere at the junctions of streets are to be seen the customary semi-detached pairs angled to the street with gable ended 'cross-wings', set back behind triangular greens, many of which retain the original admonishing signs forbidding ball games. Concrete construction was employed alongside more traditional brick, and roughcast rendering became the norm. Gardens back and front (now mostly paved over) were viewed as an essential component of the creative atmosphere of the planned community but equally an encouragement to refrain from more traditional working class pursuits provided by the pub. Blocks of flats in larger mansard-roofed blocks with open arched entrances at street level were only introduced in the early 1930s.

The forging of a strong community life presented greater difficulties than the provision of mass housing but was arguably discouraged by shortcomings in the LCC's provision of amenities, an attitude which later ran contrary to its own post-1945 principles. It was best expressed by Pevsner in 1954 who identified some of the key problems of an 'estate . . . characterized by winding roads, cottages in terraces (neither detached nor semi-detached), pubs in a genteel Neo-Georgian taste ("not conducive to inebriety"), and a lack of accents. It is impossible to plan for such a large number of people without planning on urban principles.' The most startling omission, still strongly felt, is the lack of a proper commercial and civic centre to serve the estate. Interestingly the Council chose instead to observe the centres of the old hamlets as the foundation for the new corner SHOPPING PARADES, e.g., at Broad Street, Five Elms and elsewhere. In the

S of the estate, the Dagenham UDC attempted to rectify this deficiency by creating a commercial centre along HEATHWAY, close to Dagenham Heathway station (opened 1934). In 1978–80 it was expanded again to answer the lack of large shops with THE MALL, a covered shopping centre beneath a multi-storey block of flats. Brown brick, but its architectural language is quite alien to the estate.

Community centres and other major buildings (*see* below) were almost non-existent until many years after the estate was completed. PUBS are of more than passing interest. In Heathway, at the corner with Church Elm Lane, THE CHURCH ELM, an existing plain brick beer house, was much expanded and 'improved' by *Edward Meredith* in 1931 to provide public and private bars, an off licence and, most tellingly, a tea room and lounge (now remodelled for shops). This was the customary treatment for established houses that could be remodelled. New pubs had to follow stringent planning restrictions set down by the LCC to encourage less 'perpendicular' drinking and to give greater emphasis to family space. They were criticized by planners and residents alike for their scarcity and for their immense size. On the W side of the estate, close to Mayesbrook Park on a triangular site between Porters Avenue and Lodge Avenue, THE ROUNDHOUSE, a highly unusual design by pub specialist *Alfred W. Blomfield*, 1936. A circular plan bisected by a T-plan upper storey and, in the centre, a fat square tower. The residual classical detailing and Neo-Regency window shutters are unaggressively modern when compared to the tidy-minded estate aesthetic. It originally had a large oval lounge, tea room and a wing containing an indoor bowling green along Lodge Avenue. In the same spirit of 'improved' leisure, the Neo-Tudor half-timbered and gabled ROBIN HOOD, Longbridge Road, by *T.F. Ingram*, *c.* 1930 included a concert hall, winter garden, tea room and children's playground. THE CHERRY TREE, Wood Lane by *C.C. Winmill* and *F.G. Newnham*, 1933, evokes a late C17 double pile house in red brick with low wings and steeply pitched roof with big square dormers.

Landscaping was minimal, even in the larger green spaces. The LCC only provided PARSLOES PARK, reserved from the grounds of the (demolished) Parsloes, as the central open space. MAYESBROOK PARK was laid out by Barking Borough on the W side of the estate. Both have lakes created from gravel pits. GORESBROOK PARK (Castle Green) on the S edge is a straight band of green space acting as a buffer to the A13.

Dagenham Council, with authority over the majority of the estate, was forced to use Valence House (*see* below) for its offices, and when eventually built, the civic centre was placed outside the estate's border on Becontree Heath (*see* Dagenham). For post-war architects and planners Becontree seemed to exemplify an unsatisfactory conclusion to the late C19 'garden city' ideal in the creation of a low-density, monolithic working class town (composed of 89 per cent manual workers in the 1920s) of a type which was anathema to the creators of the New Towns. But today the enduring popularity of the terraced house and the advent of owner-occupiers after the sales of council housing has tempered the once monotonous vernacular of Becontree with multifarious 'improvements'.

A tour of Becontree is demanding even for the enthusiast. The churches and Valence House (*see* below) remain the principal buildings of interest and *en route* to these one can readily appreciate the general character and layout of the streets.

RELIGIOUS BUILDINGS

Becontree's churches were allocated space in the LCC's plans and, as Pevsner observed, 'help locally and timidly'. Permanent buildings, the first consecrated in 1927, quickly succeeded temporary churches but ten sites were reserved by the Bishop of Chelmsford and an appeal launched in 1930 for new Anglican buildings. Each soon established its own distinct character, from High Church to Evangelical.

ST ALBAN, Urswick Road. 1933–4 by *Milner and Craze*. The donor was Miss Violet E. Wills of the Wills tobacco family. An expensive work in beautifully cut ashlar. Neo-Perp with a striking W tower with a pyramid roof, clasping corner buttresses and flattened Gothic pinnacles. Extremely long aisleless nave and chancel in one with big capped buttresses along the flanks and huge sloping buttresses at the E end. The E window is a liberal interpretation of the Dec style; the tall rectangular windows along the nave have Deco-style leading and clear glass. Inside, buff brick walls. Soaring, spacious nave under a massive roof with trusses carried low on stone corbels. Immensely tall tower arch, convincingly Perp. Low screen walls incorporating two ambos divide off the narrower chancel which has stone columns. N chapel and S organ loft over the vestry, which has good solid wooden doors, late Arts and Crafts in feel. REREDOS. Stone, with corner posts carrying angels and figures of the evangelists. FONT. Octagonal stone font with foliage band and supporting angels. – STAINED GLASS. E window scenes of the Nativity, Feeding of the Five Thousand and Ascension.

ST CEDD, Lodge Avenue. 1964 by *Thompson & Whitehead*. Cruciform, in pale brick with octagonal copper roof and flèche.

ST ELISABETH, Wood Lane. 1931–2 by *Sir Charles Nicholson*. Red brick Neo-Jacobean, an interesting mix of Gothic and classical traditions. C17 Gothic W window, round-headed lights to the square aisle windows. Tall Italianate bellcote over the NW entrance. Basilican interior with four bays of round-headed arches on Doric columns. White plastered walls. Segmental ceiled barrel vaults; gilded bosses over the sanctuary. N chapel, now glazed off, with unmoulded round-arched arcade and flat ribbed ceiling with bosses. COMMUNION RAIL with turned balusters. Octagonal PULPIT with lacy panelling and carvings of dolphins and lilies. FONT with elaborate carved cover. Classical LECTERN. On the N wall small memorial with Virgin and Child to Lilian Hamilton Inskip of the Diocesan Mothers Union 'by whose energy and devotion the church was built'.

S of the church, the Vicarage, also by *Nicholson*(?).

ST GEORGE, Rogers Road. 1935 by *Milner and Craze*. Brick basilica with low passage aisles on each side. Blind E wall with brick cross. Bare brick interior with square piers to the arcades and heavy roof trusses carried on stone corbels over the nave; cf. St Alban. Brick cogging to the nave windows and a narrow chancel.

ST MARTIN, Goresbrook Road. 1931–2 by *J.E. Newberry and C.W. Fowler*. Large, red brick, with a single roof sweeping down over nave and aisles. Perp windows with brick tracery. Flèche between the nave and chancel. Restrained, traditional interior of buff brick, octagonal piers and open timber roof. Circular E window set high up, and below it a painting of the Crucifixion by *Hans Feibusch*, 1949. Expressive style, finely toned in blues and greens. N chapel and S aisle with ORGAN LOFT above. 1932 with fretwork screen. Donated by Mary Ann Bowett. PULPIT donated by Charles Bowett: cords and arrowhead relief. STAINED GLASS. N chapel. St Michael, 1945.

94 ST MARY, Grafton Road. 1934–5 by *Welch, Cachemaille-Day and Lander*. A distinctive and important work. From the SE it is reminiscent of a fortified French church with an imposing crenellated tower over the chancel. The large semicircular projection at the SE corner mirrors the tower stair-turret which is topped by a belfry formed of eight concrete columns. To the W a nave and N aisle. The fabric is brick but entirely rendered; the windows have stylized reticulated tracery and surrounds are bare, dark brick. The tower is surrounded by an ambulatory, windowless on the S. Three two-light windows on each face of the tower with prominent projections between. Interior with buff brick walls; the dominant elements are the tall, steeply keeled nave roof with bays marked by transverse timber arches on stone corbels, and the climax created by the open tower over the sanctuary. Above a gallery, pointed vertical brick fins lead the eye upward to a glazed lantern. Narrow arches open to the shallow ambulatory on the E and S sides, thrillingly top-lit through coloured glass. The baptistery is unusually placed on the N, where a Lady Chapel might be expected. Instead there is a huge FONT with concrete bowl, reflecting the ideas of the evangelical Protestant Church Pastoral Aid Society, the patrons of the living. Little decoration but the motif of keeled shafts is repeated elsewhere, to excellent effect, notably on the semicircular PULPIT with graceful bronze rail and on the ORGAN CASE in the N aisle. The organ came from Ram's Chapel, Hackney. The ALTAR RAIL is in a different spirit, with gorgeous turned balusters of diminishing section, the ALTAR TABLE solid with seats at either end and side lecterns. STAINED GLASS. E window by *Christopher Webb*.

ST PETER, Warrington Road. Temporary church by *Edward Meredith*, erected 1931. Its nave (now roughcast) was retained when a brick chancel, lady chapel and vestry were erected in 1958–9, by *J.J. Crowe* of Romford. Bellcote.

ST THOMAS, Burnside Road. By *Arthur C. Blomfield & A.J. Driver*, 1926–7. The first permanent church on the estate. Large and brick. The exterior is dominated by two turrets at the W end and three large transverse gables on the sides, each containing three stepped lancets. Inside, the impression of an earlier era persists, even down to the mid-Victorian capitals with their prominent volutes. The wide nave is flanked by passage aisles with strangely arranged arcades. The transverse gables are mirrored by tall arches and the walling in between by low ones, hence a disconcerting high-low-high-low rhythm. The W parts were partitioned off for parish rooms in 1985. VICARAGE, dated 1926. Gable over the door and tilework.

HOLY FAMILY (R.C.), Oxlow Lane. 1934 by *W.C. Mangan*. Brick with steeply gabled front inset with a tall round-arched window. Mosaic panel over the W door. On the S side an apsidal baptistery. Lady Chapel.

ST PETER (R.C.), Goresbrook Road. 1937 by *W.C. Mangan*, founded by the 'La Salette Missionaries', a French Alpine order. A brick basilica, with narrow passage aisles. Lombardic Romanesque. Pairs of arched windows inset with stone columns with elaborate Byzantine capitals. Lavish Romanesque doorway. Inside, a spacious nave with narrow side aisles. Deeply coffered ceiling and six-bay arcades with stone columns with cast stone capitals. Circular W window. Coffered chancel arch and apse with a deep cornice, dominated by an immense cream-painted baldacchino over the stone altar. Four columns with lavish capitals, fantastic tasselled fringe and scrolled pediment. N chapel with an apse decorated with highly coloured mosaics of Our Lady of Salette, whose cult originated in 1876. A second shrine at the W end depicts the same story against a photo of an alpine scene. Separate baptistery added in the 1960s. The church was reordered and reorientated in 1985, with a worship space in the centre of the nave. Simple cast stone lectern, altar and font. SCHOOLS by *T.H.B. Scott*, 1935. Very plain, brown brick. Scott lost the competition to design the church.

ST VINCENT (R.C.), Waldegrave Road. 1932–3 by *Geoffrey Raymond* of *Scoles & Raymond*. Large, of dull red brick. Perp style with crowstepping. Sheer, windowless E wall. The nave is one large hall with broad W gallery and ceiled hammerbeam roof. Narrower chancel, partly screened off to create a chapel. Two shallow N and S chancel chapels with ribbed vaulting. The central worship space was created in 1989 by *Richard Hurley* of *Tyndall, Hogan Hurley*, of Dublin. ALTAR carved from a single piece of Bath stone, and other furnishings, by *Angela Godfrey*. TABERNACLE, surround, and CROSS by *Dom Benedict Tutty*. Bronze LECTERN in the form of a realistic eagle. Side altar with figure of St Vincent against a gold mosaic. Mosaic REREDOS with a crucified Christ on a Gothic pinnacle visible above the new chapel in the chancel. Old fashioned STATIONS OF THE CROSS in Gothic frames. SCHOOLS. Waldegrave Road, 1929; extended with an entrance block with exposed portal frame and glazed upper storey. Colourful nursery extension by *Cottrell & Vermeulen*, 2000.

BAPTIST CHURCH, Wood Lane. 1932 by *C.J. Haines* in the estate style of red brick with pointed gable end and two low aisles. Arched fanlight over the door.

ELIM PENTECOSTAL CHURCH, Green Lane. Former Regent Cinema, 1930 by *Lewis Solomon & Son*. Entrance framed beneath an ebullient faience pediment with gargantuan urns.

ST JOHN THE DIVINE, Goresbrook Road. Demolished.

MAJOR BUILDINGS

LIBRARIES. Provision of libraries for the estate was divided between Barking and Dagenham. The latter's enlightened policy sought to provide a library within walking distance of all residents, but many were in temporary accommodation. Becontree's first purpose built library, WOODWARD, Woodward Road, by Barking's architects *C.J. Dawson, Son and Allardyce*, 1934–5, is traditional. Brick with two low close-set projecting wings flanking a central block with stepped central parapet and cupola clock tower. Semicircular lending library at the rear. – VALENCE LIBRARY, Becontree Avenue, of 1937 by *F.C. Lloyd*, Dagenham Council Engineer and Surveyor is still Neo-Georgian but with a Moderne spin in the straight plan, broad windows and curved hood over the entrance, but not foregoing a little whimsy in a pair of relief panels of book-ends. – MARKYATE LIBRARY, Markyate Road, 1938–40 by *C.C. Shaw*, Barking Borough Architect, takes advantage of a corner site with an octagonal reading room between two short, splayed wings and the entrance in the angle. Refurbished and raised to two storeys in 2002 to dubious effect.

POST OFFICE and SORTING OFFICE, Boxoll Road. 1934 by *F.A. Llewellyn* of *H.M. Office of Works*, in quiet Tudor. Restored in 2004. Brick and tile with moulded brick mullion windows, dormers, a round-arched entrance to the l. beneath a big pointed gable and flat roofed office to the r. (cf. Post Office, New Road, Dagenham).

BECONTREE DAY HOSPITAL, Becontree Avenue. 1930 as Dagenham UDC's clinic for the estate. Probably by *T.P. Francis*, the Council Surveyor. Domestic late C17 style, with the main block set back between two gabled wings, and a lychgate to the street.

KINGSLEY HALL SCHOOL, CHURCH AND COMMUNITY CENTRE, Parsloes Avenue. A branch of the settlement founded in Bromley-by-Bow (*see* p. 632) and established by residents of the estate who had been moved from there. – NURSERY SCHOOL. 1930–1 (designs 1925–6) by *C. Cowles-Voysey*, who also designed the nursery school in Bromley-by-Bow, but in a quite different style. Single storey with central block and lower classroom wings E and W, with hipped, pantiled roofs. Arched windows and open veranda. – CHURCH. 1938–9. Strictly austere in pale brick, low lying with projecting fins. – Big extension for COMMUNITY CENTRE by *Edward D. Mills and Partners*, 1957–8. Anonymous, with a curiously emphasized boiler chimney in the centre. Concrete with a polygonal glazed base.

SCHOOLS. – The new estate required a burst of school building. The designs were divided between *C.J. Dawson*, Barking Borough Architect (for which *see* p. 128), and the Essex County Architect, *John Stuart*. There is little to distinguish between them, both being equally committed to symmetrical, hipped-roof 'bungalow' designs with classrooms grouped around internal courtyards, e.g. HENRY GREEN PRIMARY, Green Lane, the first school for the estate in 1923. The larger schools are typified by SYDNEY RUSSELL COMPREHENSIVE, Parsloes Avenue, the former County High School, by *John Stuart*, 1936–7. Symmetrical with powerfully massed two-storey entrance block, buttressed by stair-towers. Later additions, including a striking Online Centre and Crèche by *Cottrell & Vermeulen* 2003. Transparent screen overlaying a brick base and panelled cladding. Steel screen by *Simon Patterson* with a map of the world, manufactured at Ford, Dagenham.

VALENCE HOUSE

Valence Park, Becontree Avenue

The one building of genuine historic and architectural interest in Becontree, now a museum and local studies centre. It was co-opted by the LCC as their headquarters during construction of the estate* and extended in 1928–9 by Dagenham UDC for its offices and council chamber. It might reasonably have been a focus for Becontree but it seems too remote now, set within a flat park of disappointing dullness and its immediate surroundings grossly abused by thoughtless siting of a Council depot and plastic window factory!

A moated manor house existed on this site from at least the C13 but it takes its name from early C14 tenants Agnes and Aylmer de Valence. No detailed record is given until 1649 when a survey for the Bonham family details a nine room house that must have been larger than the present L-shaped building. After a period of expansion, the building was reduced progressively in the C18 and C19, before extension to its present form in 1928–9. Although rendered and even in appearance, the house is very obviously an accumulation of phases, the understanding of which is somewhat conjectural.

*Who, it has been claimed, refused entry to the Surveyor of the Royal Commission on Historic Monuments in 1921.

The entrance is in the centre of the S side of the E–W wing. To the l. is the older part of the house, to the r. extensions of the C17 and C20. The shorter SW wing is probably C17 in date, note the S dormer on this side. Inside is a cross-passage through the depth of the wing. To the l. is a small room (now shop), with a large brick chimneystack in the W wall, which is contained within a two-storey timber-framed structure, possibly of the C15. The frame is partly exposed in the rear corridor. This structure may have been jettied on its N side at first floor. A bracket is preserved, but obscured by later extensions.*

The room to the r. of the lobby (THE FANSHAWE ROOM) has early C17 raised and fielded panelling, apparently rearranged in the early C18 when the present fireplace was inserted. This has a bolection-moulded surround. Beyond is the C20 extension. Off the N side of the entrance lobby, the staircase compartment, added in the late C17, with a fine well stair with twisted-oak balusters on vase bases. W of this at ground floor are service rooms (possibly added in the C16 but now set out with displays of C19 domestic life), and the C17 SW wing.

On the first floor the rooms are used for exhibition displays. The PERIOD ROOM retains later C17 panelling with reset C15 panels and a firegrate from Belhus, Essex (demolished 1958). At the far end is an entertaining reconstruction of a typical kitchen and living room of one of the houses on the Becontree Estate. The room in the E wing (now O'Leary Gallery) was extended and heavily remodelled as the Council Chamber in 1928.

GARDENS. To the E, the remains of the moat have been reduced to a pond, rather stagnant but enthusiastically fished. It seems likely that the filling in of the moat and landscaping took place in 1863 when the drawbridge was removed. To the W of the house is an attractive Herb Garden, laid out by *Virginia Nightingale* in 1992 with a chinoiserie gazebo at the centre. Late Georgian wrought-iron gates, previously at Dagenham parish church.

CHADWELL HEATH

(and Mark's Gate)

Chadwell Heath was a medieval settlement within Dagenham parish on the Romford Road but closer to Ilford, whose parish church served it from 1830. It expanded with the arrival of the Great Eastern Railway in 1864 and was progressively built up from the end of the C19, partly within the Borough of Ilford. It

*English Heritage, 1992, suggested that this may have been a cross-wing for a hall-house, the hall subsequently replaced by the SW wing, but the evidence is inconclusive. Some early painted decoration was discovered in the roof of the older part.

became a parish in 1895. Proximity to the Becontree Estate means its present character is predominantly of the interwar period. Close by, to the N, lay the medieval manor of Marks and the small hamlet of Marks Gate which remained wholly rural in character into the mid C20. Even now, the open Essex countryside lies just beyond its edges.

ST CHAD, St Chad's Road. Founded as a chapel-of-ease to St Peter and St Paul, Dagenham. 1895–8 by *Frederic Chancellor*. Red brick with stone dressings, large plate tracery W window. Embattled NW clock tower, added 1897–8 to commemorate the Diamond Jubilee.

ST MARK, Rose Lane. 1956. The district church for the Marks Gate Estate, doubling as a church hall. Brown brick with low, pitched roofs and bellcote with criss-cross patterning.

ST BEDE (R.C.), Bishop's Avenue. 1963 by *Purcell & Johnson*. Hexagonal, brick, with large glazed gables. Light, plain interior; coloured GLASS in a room l. of the foyer.

CHADWELL HEATH BAPTIST CHURCH, High Road. 1905 by *Frederick Faunch*. Red brick and stone with a crenellated porch and gable with crocketted pinnacles: a fancy mask to a utilitarian hall.

UNITED REFORMED CHURCH, Mill Lane. 1911 by *C.H. Gurney*. Ungainly stripped Perp.

CHADWELL HEATH CEMETERY, Whalebone Lane. Laid out by Dagenham UDC in 1933–4. Close to the gates is the CHAPEL, a good design by *T.P. Francis*, the Council Surveyor. Quite austere, in brick and reconstituted stone with a semi-octagonal apsed E end set beneath a kneelered gable with a cross. The main elevation is most striking, with a cenotaph-like tower in brick and stone. At the base, an arched entrance with a sarcophagus over the door. Charming interior fittings, including 'sunburst' patterns to the doors and slightly whimsical silhouettes of children over the doorway to the chapel. In the apse, painted plaster relief of angels at Christ's tomb.

WHALEBONE LIBRARY, High Road. 1998–9 by *Laing Homes* as a *quid pro quo* for the right to develop the adjoining site. Square plan with projecting, ball-finialled gable at the front and pyramidal lantern roof.

FURZE INFANTS SCHOOL, Bennett Road. 1949 by *Harold Conolly*, Essex County Architect. Single-storey classroom blocks with an asymmetrically set rectangular water tower.

PERAMBULATION

The centre is the long and busy HIGH ROAD. This has a few scattered buildings of interest: from W–E along the S side, the former Police Station (now pub) of 1892 by *John Butler*. Brick and stone with half-timbered gables. Much further E stand the Baptist Church (*see* above) and the WHITE HORSE pub, recorded in 1602 but rebuilt *c.* 1899, when it had splendid gardens with pergola walks and rockeries of the type beloved of the Edwardians. Behind in ST CHAD'S ROAD is the parish church.

WHALEBONE LANE takes its name from a pair of whalebones recorded at the crossroads in the C17. The manor of Marks lay to the N and bordered the edge of Hainault Forest. Indeed, until the 1950s this area was still entirely rural with a scattering of farms. Several stood along ROSE LANE which became the central road for Dagenham's MARKS GATE ESTATE, planned *c.* 1951–6 as a joint enterprise with Ilford Borough Council, to designs by *A.E. Stickland*, Dagenham Borough Engineer. A self-contained community with its own church and schools, e.g. INFANTS SCHOOL, 1957, accented by a pronounced concrete water tower. Mixed housing, mainly low-rise but at a higher density than pre-war estates so with greater use of maisonette blocks in concert with the usual terraced houses. In advance of the laying out of the estate, a site at the corner of Rose Lane and Hatch Grove was reserved for a small L-shaped group of bungalows for the disabled, erected as Dagenham's War Memorial to designs by *Graham Dawbarn*, 1956. Pretty modest, only three dwellings around a sunken garden. A single seventeen-storey tower block, by *M. Maybury*, was added at the E end of the site, *c.* 1965.

On the fringes are some remnants of rural life. Off BILLET ROAD, N of the Marks Gate Estate, FURZE HOUSE FARMHOUSE, 1839–40 with modest later extensions. Three bays with round-arch windows to the ground floor and pilastered Tuscan doorpiece. In Whalebone Lane, WARREN FARM has a large C17 barn with a long gambrel roof and mighty cart entrance. It was associated with the old manor house of Marks, which was acquired *c.* 1461 by Sir Thomas Urswyck. He may have rebuilt the house, described *c.* 1796 by Lysons as 'a very ancient structure of timber and plaster forming a quadrangle. It is surrounded by a moat at two corners of which are square towers embattled'. Of this the moat partly survives, NE of Warren Farm; the house was demolished 1808.

In open land N of Warren Farm is a relic of London's earlier C20 defences, a well-preserved and substantial ANTI-AIRCRAFT BATTERY erected in 1935–9. Concrete semicircular emplacements for eight guns, accommodation blocks and shelters.

DAGENHAM

Dagenham, a Saxon hamlet with a parish church from the C13, remained an Essex village into the early C20, in spite of a population of over 9,000 in 1921. No other settlements of significance existed within the parish except the hamlet around Chadwell Heath to the NW. Modest expansion of the village was encouraged by extension of the Tilbury railway in 1885, but it was the compulsory acquisition of the smaller hamlets within the parish and the ancient manorial estates for the LCC's Becontree Estate after 1919 that forced its absorption into suburban London. In 1926 an area which only twenty years earlier had been almost entirely rural was designated an Urban District, although on the N and NE fringes the *timbre* of rural life was maintained for longer in the hamlets of Rush Green and Marks Gate (*see* p. 148) which became part of the Borough of Dagenham in 1938. Contemporary with the shift from rural to suburban, agricultural Dagenham became industrial, beginning with the establishment of the deep-water Dagenham Dock in 1887 and confirmed by one of the largest industrial enterprises of the C20, the Ford Motor Works. This bewildering expansion, incorporating an area stretching from the Thames riverside to Hainault Forest, left Dagenham with little identifiable heart, although new civic buildings were symbolically placed at its geographic centre on Becontree Heath in 1937. After 1965, Dagenham temporarily lost its identity as part of the London Borough of Barking but reasserted it in 1981. Even so, the absence of a proper town centre remains its most evident deficiency, and the closure of vehicle assembly at Ford in 2002 has presented an opportunity for major and much needed regeneration.

CHURCH AND CEMETERY

ST PETER AND ST PAUL, Crown Street. A true village church, in a village street, surprising between the Becontree Estate and the Ford Motor Works. Long, early C13 chancel, rendered, with lancet windows, a group of three stepped lancets in the E wall. Late C15 N chapel. The rest was rebuilt by *William Mason*, 1801–5, after the tower and spire collapsed on to the nave in 1800. Old material was reused for the walls, with dressings in brown stone which emphasize the flat corner buttresses of the tower and the parapet of the nave. S wall of three bays with projecting centre. Pevsner found the W tower 'of the most ignorant and entertaining Gothic' and the curly battlements especially noteworthy. The tower had a spire, removed in 1921. Set against a recess in the tower is a semicircular W porch with Gothick quatrefoil shafts and shaft rings. Inside, the nave is a single space with a W gallery on quatrefoil columns; benefactions are listed on the gallery front. The nave floor was raised in 1801, but lowered in a restoration of 1878, probably by *J. T. Lee*, when the church was reseated. Stucco decoration to the chancel arch and plaster ceilings to chancel and N chapel, presumably also of *c.* 1801, but the chancel retains a C13 PISCINA with arched head. Between chancel and chapel, late C15 two-bay arcade with flattened arches and pier with four shafts and four hollows. – FONT. Fluted bowl on baluster stem. – MONUMENTS are gathered together in the large N chapel, which is contemporary with the earliest, to Sir Thomas Urswyck †1479, Chief Baron of the Exchequer and Recorder of London. Plain tomb chest with BRASSES on a Purbeck marble slab: Urswyck in his judicial robes, his wife Anne turning sideways to display an elaborate headdress, and a group of nine daughters, the eldest shown as a nun (a group of four sons and three out of four shields are missing). – James Hervey †1627. Wall monument with flanking Corinthian columns. – Jonathan Lloyd †1652, rector of Dagenham, oval cartouche, a skull below and arms above. – Sir Richard Alibon †1688, large standing figure in judge's robes, holding a scroll, and his wife Barbara, elaborately draped, resting an arm against a tall pedestal with an urn. On the base a Latin inscription translated into English, and relief of scales of justice. Ascribed by Esdaile to *John van Nost*. – Jacob Uphill †1662 and wife Ann †1667, erected 1707, white marble, with long inscription. – Maria Massingberd †1777, tablet and urn against streaky dark marble. – Many good LEDGERS including one to Richard Uphill, royal standard bearer, †1717/18. In the nave, smaller tablets, one with two cherubs recording the foundation of a charity school in 1825 by William Ford, farmer; another to William Stone, farmer, †1849 with mourning woman and urn.

Large CHURCHYARD, managed as a wildlife centre, with coffin-shaped tombs in the typical Essex manner. Some CHEST TOMBS close to the E end, one with quasi-fluted pilasters, another to the N, with gadrooned baluster-shaped corners.

EASTBROOKEND CEMETERY, The Chase, off Dagenham Road. Opened 1914. Neo-Tudor chapel.

MAJOR BUILDINGS

CIVIC CENTRE, Rainham Road South/Wood Lane. 1936–7 by *E. Berry Webber* with *F.C. Lloyd*, Borough Engineer. Dagenham's best building by far and a good inter-war example of the traditional language of civic architecture absorbing a more go-ahead modern style. Long, shallow symmetrical range with glazed semicircular staircase projections at the ends, their curved form originally echoed in lily ponds. The centre has a portico of four thin square pillars, elegantly carved on the outer

St Peter & St Paul, Dagenham. Brass to Sir Thomas Urswyck, died 1479

face, with panels in the frieze of Engineering, Local Government and Navigation by *W. Aumonier and Sons*. At the back a semicircular projection for the council chamber. Inside, a glazed staircase hall lavishly faced in marble and much incised decoration leads to the public gallery. An assembly hall was planned at the rear but unbuilt. On the site, and linked by a two storey bridge, a three-storey office extension of 1964, also by *Berry Webber* and respecting his own work. Slightly S, FIRE AND AMBULANCE STATION, also 1937 by *Berry Webber*. Brick, with five engine bays. Flat roofed and patterned brickwork. Monumental practice tower at rear.

RECTORY LIBRARY, Rectory Road. 1935 by *F.C. Lloyd*, Council Engineer and Surveyor. Classically minded Art Deco in brick, heavily dressed in stone with a shallow bowed porch.

DAGENHAM SWIMMING POOL, Wood Lane, close to the civic centre. Monstrous and ugly, by the Borough Architects, *S.J. Harris and M. Maybury*, 1972.

SCHOOLS. No schools from before 1918. All designs before 1965 are by the *Essex County Architect*. The interwar schools are either the usual Neo-Georgian e.g. EASTBROOK SCHOOL, Dagenham Road, of 1935 or of the larger sort with Deco styling e.g. DAGENHAM PARK COMMUNITY SCHOOL, School Road. Better are the post-war primaries e.g., BEAM PRIMARY SCHOOL, Oval Road South, of 1951. Pleasant and humane, in brick and concrete with linear ranges of single-storey classroom blocks contrasted with an asymmetrically set rectangular water tower. The introduction of greater standardization from the mid 1950s can be seen at e.g. WILLIAM BELLAMY INFANT and JUNIOR SCHOOLS, Frizlands Lane, with steel-frame windows and flat roofs, informally grouped with gardens.

JOHN PERRY PRIMARY, Charles Road, off Manor Way, of 1952 has a distinguished Nursery School of 2003–4 by *Deborah Saunt David Hills Architects*. Walls of render and dark engineering brick with translucent cladding pierced by irregularly placed openings. Cantilevered canopy.

ALL SAINTS' (R.C.) SCHOOL AND TECHNOLOGY COLLEGE, Terling Road, off Wood Lane. 1954 by *Sterret and Blouet* and progressive for its date. Long two-storey range in concrete, glazed staircase hall and upper floor carried on pilotis, in the centre, creating a *piano nobile* effect. Functional curved roof classrooms adjoining Science Centre of 1991 by *Living Architects*. Music and Drama Centre by *Curl La Tourelle Architects*, 2003.

BARKING COLLEGE, Dagenham Road, Rush Green. Facing the street, the former buildings of the College of Further Education. 1961 by *H. Conolly*, Essex County Architect. A three-storey reinforced concrete-framed teaching block with slightly recessed ground floor. Single-storey range, to the l., originally for workshops. Extending to the rear over a spacious campus are buildings of several later phases. The best is BRAMLEY BLOCK of 2002–3 by *Perkins Ogden Architects* with *Hampshire County Architects*; an exemplary design for technical workshops (plumbing, carpentry, design etc.) in three blocks projecting from a spine 'mall' corridor. Yellow brick facing with continuous glazing above and profiled metal roofs carried on columns to form narrow arcades around the sides. Central lobby with full height glazing to front and back. Inside, the light steel structure and services are exposed. Block D, 1993, looks tired by comparison, anonymous boxes clad in a grid of grey, red and green panels. The whole is tied together by excellent hard landscaping by *Hyland Edgar Driver*.

PERAMBULATIONS

1. Dagenham Village

There is not much left of Dagenham village but what survives is focused around the Church and the green with the WAR MEMORIAL, a stone cross on an octagonal tapered shaft and buttressed plinth. This open space, for all modern wishful thinking, had no medieval precedent but was created after 1968 by *W.E. Outterside*, Borough Engineer and Planning Officer, to improve the setting for the village's few historic buildings. First, facing CROWN STREET, the CROSS KEYS INN: an early C15 hall house with two gabled cross-wings. W wing always two storey, originally with a S jetty, now underbuilt, and cased in brick *c.* 1952. The hall is of two bays horizontally subdivided in the later C16. Wider E wing. (The roof, much damaged by fire in 1995, was recorded as having collar-purlin and crown-post braced laterally and longitudinally over the hall; queen-struts in W wing. Some C17 panelling. Fireplaces, *c.* 1500.) Later additions on the N side. To the E is the former VICARAGE, a bizarre concoction, probably erected in the early C17, but the S front rebuilt 1665 (dated on the projecting two-storey porch). Timber-framed and rendered with bargeboarded eaves. Many later additions, including low canted bay windows on the E elevation. S of the church, in CHURCH LANE, the former NATIONAL SCHOOL of 1835, the earliest school building in Dagenham. Extremely simple, with one central pointed arch window and entrances of similar form to each side. Iron roof. The other older village buildings were demolished after 1968 to allow for new groups of housing. This completed the absorption of old Dagenham into the new, yet the character of this enclave cannot be denied.

2. North: Rainham Road to Becontree Heath

RAINHAM ROAD links the old village with Dagenham East station and N to the Civic Centre. S of the station is the former POLICE STATION, No. 621, 1850. Two storeys with round-headed gauged brick arch window reveals in recessed bays.

Its successor, of 1962, lies N of the railway. Plain, brick with concrete frame exposed at S end, glazed in the upper floor. E across Rainham Road is AVENTIS, an extensive complex established for pharmaceutical production by May and Baker Ltd before the Second World War. From 1943 they expanded their premises to designs by *Edward Mills*, who created here some
103 of the first shell concrete structures in Britain. The Canteen, of 1943–4, with its wavy roof and full glazed façade is of principal interest. Prior to that the land was used to grow fruit for Tiptree's jam, and mired in the midst of the site is an early C19, but much altered, farmhouse. There is little else memorable until further N, beyond Dagenham Road, WOODLANDS, a C18 brick mansion with a plain three-storey and five-bay façade, arched windows in the ground floor and Adamesque doorway. Short wings to either side. Much extended at the rear *c.* 1900.

Housing in this area is varied, much of it developed post-war by Dagenham, e.g., along BULL LANE, two parallel blocks of terrace form with maisonette blocks flanked by individual houses at each end. W of FRIZLANDS LANE, N and S of RUSHOLME AVENUE, is the HEATH PARK ESTATE laid out by *Norman & Dawbarn* for Dagenham in 1951, and firmly in the Festival spirit. It marks the introduction of a truly urban character of housing, of a type practised by this firm at Lansbury (*see* p. 651), and consists of cottages as well as slab-shaped blocks of flats of three, four and five storeys, with a great deal of variety of both types of housing and design, although shabby now. At the N end, on LISTOWEL ROAD, is a staggered screen of four-storeyed maisonettes, with a small group of old people's cottages around a green in front. At right angles to these are five blocks of three-storey flats and in the centre one group of five-storey flats with S facing balconies angled out from the W side (and with the Festival badge). Close to these is the low, spreading social centre. Further S again on WYTHENSHAWE ROAD, one slab of five storeys at r. angles to the others and three of three storeys, with 'bicycle-basket' balconies.

To the N, either side of Wood Lane, close to the civic centre, the BECONTREE HEATH ESTATE marks the progression towards a more avowedly urban scale with the introduction of three H-shaped seventeen-storey towers by the Borough Architect *M. Maybury*, 1966–70. In Wood Lane, THE THREE TRAVELLERS, an attractive pub of *c.* 1899 with half-timbered gables and a domed corner turret.

3. *North-East: Eastbrookend and Rush Green*

DAGENHAM ROAD leads to and through EASTBROOKEND COUNTRY PARK, nearly 350 acres of once derelict land, reclaimed since the early 1990s. The park is contiguous with the featureless Central Park and the Chase Nature Reserve. At its heart, by the entrance off Dagenham Road, is the

MILLENNIUM CENTRE, 2000, by *Penoyre & Prasad*. A showcase for energy efficient design powered by light and wind. Timber-clad with profiled metal roofs swept up at the upper floor and down low over the exhibition centre at the front. Between the two blocks an off-centre, windowless, stair tower. Slightly further on, by Eastbrookend Cemetery, HOOKS HALL FARMHOUSE, C17 timber-framed with a C19 brick front and a cross-shaped chimneystack.

Close to the entrance to the park on Dagenham Road, stands the FARMHOUSE TAVERN (originally Eastbrook Grove House) of *c.* 1840 with early C20 additions at the W end. Slightly N, at a bend in the road, BELL HOUSE, early C18, but remodelled and stuccoed. Distinctly pretty with the eponymous bell on the roof ridge: was it added when it was a farmhouse or when it was a school? Further N, beyond an expanse of flat open space, the campus of BARKING COLLEGE (*see* above) in the area of the old hamlet of Rush Green.

4. *Dagenham Dock and the Ford Motor Works*

Until the C19 the marshy ground S of Dagenham village served little purpose other than as a destination for travellers from London to DAGENHAM BREACH, a lake first formed by the breaching of the River Beam's bank in the C14. The breach was the subject of repeated repair efforts including that by *Cornelius Vermuyden* in 1621 and, finally, the harbour engineer *Captain John Perry** in 1716–20 who closed the 400 ft gap and drained the land in a spectacular example of early civil engineering. The remaining 55-acre lake became a popular destination for anglers but was greatly reduced in size as the area was adopted for industrial expansion. In 2004 it has been restored and re-established as a wildlife reserve, part of the rehabilitation of this area after decades of industrial ravaging. The first event in that story was the creation in 1887 of DAGENHAM DOCK (although efforts had been made to create a dock here from the 1840s) by Samuel Williams and Sons who quickly exploited their estate (served by its own station from 1908). They built a 500 ft (150 metre) reinforced concrete jetty, appropriate for unloading heavy cargoes, in 1899–1903. It survives as JETTY NO. 4, one of the oldest concrete structures of its kind in Britain (by *M. Gerard* of *L. G. Mouchel Partners*). A further jetty was built upstream in 1910–11 (*A.E. Williams*, engineer) where the Dreadnought 'Thunderer', the largest warship built on the Thames, was fitted out after construction at the Thames Ironworks in Canning Town. But the single greatest effect on the industrial development of the riverside was the decision of Ford Motor Company Ltd to move from Manchester's Trafford Park to Dagenham (the preferred choice had been Southampton) in the late 1920s.

*John Perry, *An account of the stopping of Dagenham Breach*, 1721.

The FORD MOTOR WORKS were erected in 1929–31 to designs by *Charles Heathcote & Sons* of Manchester. Heathcote recommended himself on two counts: not only had he adapted the Trafford Park factory, but he had also already designed four factories at Dagenham Dock for Samuel Williams and Sons, *c.* 1909–14. Encouraged out of retirement specifically to work on the Dagenham site, Heathcote also designed the company's showrooms in Piccadilly. With *Sir Cyril Kirkpatrick* as consulting engineer, and the general layout of the site developed by Ford's 'Cast Iron Charlie' Sorensen, it was intended as a counterpart to the massive plant in Dearborn, Michigan and on a scale unprecedented in Britain. 22,000 concrete piles, cast on site, were driven into the soggy marshland to carry buildings over 66 acres on the riverside E of Dagenham Dock. In the 1930s Ford was the largest works in Europe, employing 40,000 workers by 1953, many of them residents of the Becontree Estate. The fully integrated plant included its own power station, foundry (the only blast furnace in southern England, which ceased production 1978), coke ovens and gas plant, plus the largest private wharf on the Thames, with dedicated railway for transporting material from the dock. An associated industrial estate was also planned by Ford's future chairman Lord Perry and modelled on his experience as co-founder of the Slough Trading Estate. Other motor companies established works here, their premises ultimately suborned to Ford's own use. Major redevelopment and expansion of the N end of the site in 1954–9 created a new paint, trim and assembly plant by *Martin Hutchinson* with *Posford, Parry & Partners*, engineers.

The site, now over 473 acres, is contracting for the first time in its history. Car production at Ford ceased in 2002. By this time over 11 million vehicles had been made. Today, the works are dedicated to design and assembly of diesel engines, with demolition of redundant buildings under way in 2004. At its heart, the Breach has been restored and wider regeneration is planned in the area N of New Road. A partnership of *Shillam + Smith, Maccreanor Lavington, S333* and *West 8* was formed in 2002 to develop plans. These propose redevelopment of the entire area between New Road and the railway, with the exception of the 1950s Body Plant, between Chequers Lane and Kent Avenue, and the creation of a new residential area grouped around newly created lakes and canals between Kent Avenue and Thames Avenue.

Most of the site is of little interest to the casual architectural visitor but the scale of the operation is still awesome, worthy of its nickname 'Fordsville'. It is announced along THAMES AVENUE in a characteristically American way by two tall water towers emblazoned with the iconic company logo. This is the main road into the complex and leads towards the river and the original ASSEMBLY PLANT buildings by *Heathcote and Sons*, 1929–31. Nine parallel two-storey ranges, 1000 ft long, of steel framing clad in brick with modest classical pilasters dividing bays of large glazing. Double canted roofs. At the S end, single-storey ranges. Although inevitably modified for changing methods of car production, their significance cannot be under-rated as the earliest surviving relics of the revolutionary Fordian process. At the E end stood the power house and foundry, feeding raw materials into the northernmost range and thus progressively through the conveyor system until the completed vehicles could be driven under their own power onto the quayside, the exit marked by a square two-storey pavilion. Here the large JETTY built for importing iron ore and coal survives. Behind it on the quayside, the Deco style former HEAD OFFICES (including hospital and training centre) by *Heathcote & Sons*. The rest of the site has less historic or aesthetic value and especially in the area towards Chequers Lane, W of the main plant, is gradually being cleared in 2003. The exception to this trend is the DIESEL ENGINE ASSEMBLY PLANT by *Austin-Smith:Lord*, splendidly situated on the Breach, E of Kent Avenue. Sleekly silver sheds in rows with raised spine roofs and apsidal ends.

On the W side of the Breach, powerfully impressive by the waterside, stands BARKING POWER STATION. 1992–5 by *Balfour Beatty Projects and Engineering Ltd* for Thames Power Services Ltd. It uses 'combined cycle gas turbines clean technology to efficiently generate electricity from natural gas or oil with a minimum effect on the environment'. A 345 metre turbine hall and to the fore, a pair of Herculean chimneys, wrapped serpent-like with pipes, ducts and vents.

On NEW ROAD is an original car SHOWROOM, announced by a tall square clock tower. Enticingly large glass windows and curved corners lend an appropriately streamlined air. New Road in the 1930s must have been a good centre for this part of Dagenham, but only relics can be singled out, e.g. the former POST OFFICE (No. 36, S side) of 1939 in the *H.M. Office of Works:* stripped down, dark brick Neo-Tudor with round-arched doorways and moulded brick mullions (probably by *F.A. Llewellyn*, cf. Post Office, Boxoll Road, Becontree). Further E, the former National Provincial Bank, is a neat Neo-Georgian design with scooped corner and curved porch. On the N side the former Princess Cinema by *Robert Cromie*, 1932. Neither can do anything to alleviate the sense of decrepitude.

Further E, along MARSH WAY close to Rainham (within Havering), is CEME (Centre for Excellence in Manufacturing and Engineering) a training and business centre by *Sheppard Robson*, 2001–3, funded by Ford and local colleges. Campus style with a graceful curved plan overlooking a pond, and two eyecatching features, a central cedar-clad drum and a bulbous pod containing lecture theatres.

DAGENHAM DOCK and the area W of CHEQUERS LANE await clearance of its industrial sites for redevelopment as part of the Thames Gateway regeneration. In 2004 the atmosphere is dystopian.

HAVERING

Havering is the furthest E of the London boroughs and the character of its buildings is shared equally between the suburbia of its western neighbours and the rural vernacular of the Essex countryside. This mix is unique in East London, comprising still remote medieval parish churches along the Thames marshlands, tiny rural villages, farmhouses set in open fields, a scattering of mansions, leafy Edwardian suburbia and, at its heart, the brash commercialism of Romford. Its topography is equally varied, ranging from the flat plains at Rainham to the sloping, wooded hills at Noak Hill. The formation of the Borough in 1965 from Romford Borough and Hornchurch Urban District not only drew these diverse settlements together but revived the name of the medieval Royal Manor and Liberty of Havering to which they had once belonged. Though long since defunct the Liberty's name had persisted in memory through the survival of the bucolically named village of Havering-atte-Bower, high up on the ridge of ground N of the London road, where the royal palace or hunting lodge had once existed. The manor was roughly coterminous with the medieval parish of Hornchurch whose village church and priory, founded by Henry II, stood close to the Ingrebourne river. To its E, outside the medieval manor, were a series of smaller agricultural parishes: Upminster and Cranham in the N, North Ockendon, Wennington and Rainham to the S. The last three had churches by the C12, best preserved at Rainham whose life and trade was centred on its little port by the Thames.

For most of its history the villages and manors of Havering
were part of the agricultural life of Essex. Early maps show a
series of large manor houses, many of them on moated sites, set
within parkland. More substantial properties included Gidea p. 21
Hall, Dagnams and Pyrgo Park (all since demolished) which lay
in the N, close to the London road, but in the remoter parishes
there were also smaller houses, several of which survive. With the
expansion of London from the late C17, Havering began to enjoy
increasing favour as a rural retreat from the metropolis for successful merchants who bought up older properties and in the following century even began to build new country houses. These
were often of the villa-mansion type more suited to owners with
interests elsewhere. Their taste generally lagged behind contemporary C18 fashion, even in the case of lavish houses such as
Rainham Hall, but there are notable exceptions: the Palladian 31
Bower House at Havering-atte-Bower, an early work by *Flitcroft*,
James Paine's Hare Hall, E of Romford, and the extraordinary late 32
C18 Round House, also at Havering-atte-Bower. In several places 37
the houses have gone but their ornamental and landscaped
gardens are preserved, as public gardens and parks. Several are
testament to the skills of the landscape designers, *Richard Woods*
and, later, *Humphry Repton* who was a resident of Hare Street, p. 23
the little hamlet (now Gidea Park) E of Romford. Even into the

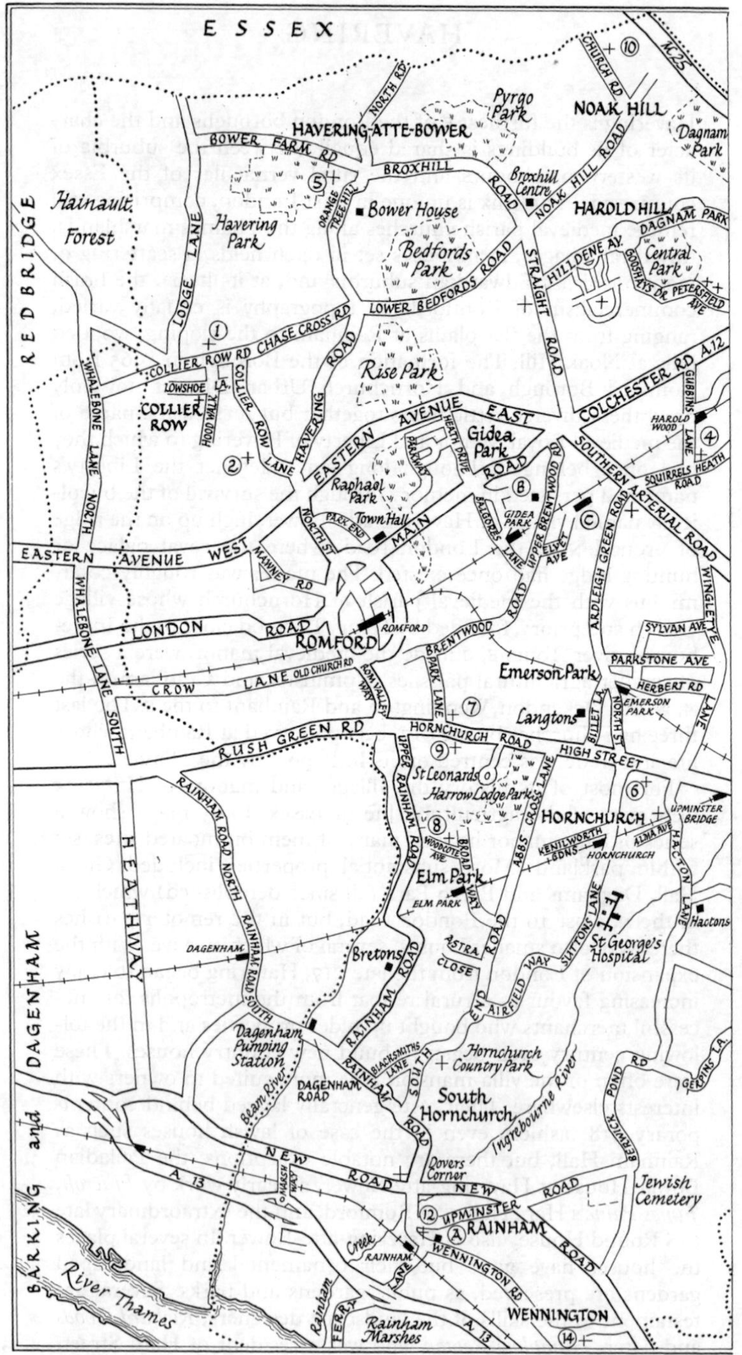
ESSEX
REDBRIDGE
DAGENHAM
BARKING and
HAVERING-ATTE-BOWER
NOAK HILL
HAROLD HILL
COLLIER ROW
ROMFORD
HORNCHURCH
Elm Park
South Hornchurch
RAINHAM
WENNINGTON
Hainault Forest
Havering Park
Pyrgo Park
Dagnam Park
Bedfords Park
Central Park
Rise Park
Gidea Park
Raphael Park
Emerson Park
Langtons
St Leonards
Harrow Lodge Park
St George's Hospital
Hactons
Bretons
Dagenham Pumping Station
Hornchurch Country Park
Jewish Cemetery
Dovers Corner
Rainham Marshes
Bower House
Broxhill Centre
Town Hall
River Thames
Beam River
Ingrebourne River
Rainham Creek
BOWER FARM RD
BROXHILL ROAD
NORTH RD
CHURCH RD
M25
NOAK HILL ROAD
STRAIGHT ROAD
HILLDENE AV.
DAGNAM PARK
GOOSHAYS DR
PETERSFIELD AVE
ORANGE TREE HILL
LODGE LANE
BEDFORDS ROAD
LOWER BEDFORDS ROAD
CHASE CROSS RD
COLLIER ROW RD
LOWSHOE LA.
HOOD WALK
COLLIER ROW LANE
HAVERING ROAD
EASTERN AVENUE EAST
COLCHESTER RD A.12
GUBBINS LANE
HAROLD WOOD
SOUTHERN ARTERIAL ROAD
SQUIRRELS HEATH ROAD
HEATH DRIVE
PARKWAY
MAIN ROAD
BALGORES LANE
GIDEA PARK
UPPER BRENTWOOD ROAD
ELVET AVE
ARDLEIGH GREEN ROAD
WINGLETYE LANE
SYLVAN AVE
PARKSTONE AVE
HERBERT RD
EMERSON PARK
BILLET LA.
NORTH ST
WHALEBONE LANE NORTH
WHALEBONE LANE SOUTH
EASTERN AVENUE WEST
MAWNEY RD
PARK END
NORTH ST
LONDON ROAD
BRENTWOOD ROAD
CROW LANE
OLD CHURCH RD
ROM VALLEY WAY
PARK LANE
RUSH GREEN RD
HORNCHURCH ROAD
HIGH STREET
UPPER RAINHAM ROAD
ABBS CROSS LANE
UPMINSTER BRIDGE
ALMA AVE
HACTON LANE
KENILWORTH GDNS
WOODCOTE AVE
BROADWAY
ELM PARK
ASTRA CLOSE
SOUTH END ROAD
AIRFIELD WAY
SUTTONS LANE
HEATHWAY
RAINHAM ROAD NORTH
RAINHAM ROAD SOUTH
RAINHAM ROAD
BLACKSMITHS LANE
DAGENHAM ROAD
BERWICK POND RD
GERPINS LA.
NEW ROAD
A 13
UPMINSTER ROAD
WENNINGTON RD
FERRY LANE
RAINHAM
DAGENHAM
HORNCHURCH
ROMFORD
1
2
4
5
6
7
8
9
10
12
14
A
B
C

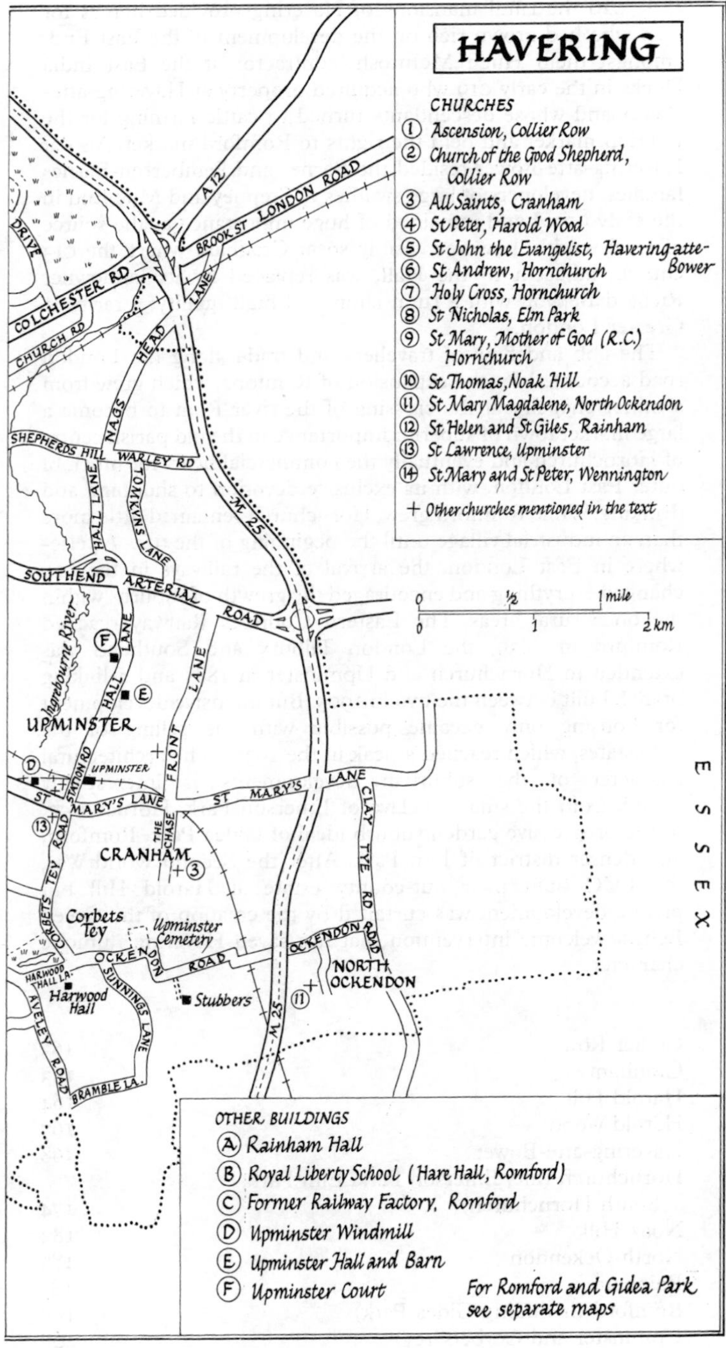
HAVERING
CHURCHES
① Ascension, Collier Row
② Church of the Good Shepherd, Collier Row
③ All Saints, Cranham
④ St Peter, Harold Wood
⑤ St John the Evangelist, Havering-atte-Bower
⑥ St Andrew, Hornchurch
⑦ Holy Cross, Hornchurch
⑧ St Nicholas, Elm Park
⑨ St Mary, Mother of God (R.C.) Hornchurch
⑩ St Thomas, Noak Hill
⑪ St Mary Magdalene, North Ockendon
⑫ St Helen and St Giles, Rainham
⑬ St Lawrence, Upminster
⑭ St Mary and St Peter, Wennington
+ Other churches mentioned in the text
0 ½ 1 mile
0 1 2 km
A12
LONDON ROAD
BROOK ST
COLCHESTER RD
CHURCH RD
DRIVE
NAGS HEAD LANE
SHEPHERDS HILL
WARLEY RD
HALL LANE
TOMKYNS LANE
SOUTHEND ARTERIAL ROAD
M25
Ingrebourne River
HALL LANE
FRONT LANE
UPMINSTER
UPMINSTER
STATION RD
ST MARY'S LANE
THE CHASE
CLAY TYE RD
CRANHAM
TEY ROAD
CORBETS TEY
Corbets Tey
Upminster Cemetery
OCKENDON ROAD
OCKENDON ROAD
NORTH OCKENDON
HARWOOD HALL LA.
Harwood Hall
SUNNINGS LANE
Stubbers
AVELEY ROAD
BRAMBLE LA.
ESSEX
OTHER BUILDINGS
Ⓐ Rainham Hall
Ⓑ Royal Liberty School (Hare Hall, Romford)
Ⓒ Former Railway Factory, Romford
Ⓓ Upminster Windmill
Ⓔ Upminster Hall and Barn
Ⓕ Upminster Court
For Romford and Gidea Park see separate maps

early C20 the rural mansions of Havering provided homes for men who had grown rich on the development of the East End, amongst them Hugh McIntosh, contractor at the East India Docks in the early C19 who acquired property at Havering-atte-Bower and whose descendants turned to cattle farming for the London market and held the rights to Romford market. Also at Havering-atte-Bower resided the Barnes and Pemberton-Barnes families, developers of large swathes of Stepney and Mile End in the early C19. Land remained of huge importance as the source of local wealth, however, visibly so at Cranham where the C13 church, adjacent to the Hall, was replaced by its landowner Richard Benyon with a rural church of high quality: a rarity in Greater London.

The ebb and flow of travellers and trade along the London road accounted for the expansion of Romford, which grew from a minor chapelry at the crossing of the river Rom to become a large market town of superior importance to the old parish centre of Hornchurch and eventually the commercial heart for much of outer East London, with its exclusive devotion to shopping and drinking. While Romford grew, Hornchurch remained little more than an industrial village until the beginning of the C20. As elsewhere in East London, the arrival of the railways in the C19 changed everything and encouraged the growth of suburbs within the once rural areas. The Eastern Counties Railway reached Romford in 1839, the London Tilbury and Southend was extended to Hornchurch and Upminster in 1885 and a linking branch built between the two in 1905. But intensive development for housing only became possible with the selling of the old estates, which reached a peak in the 1930s. The architectural character of the suburban developments is interestingly varied: from the smart enclave of Emerson Park, Hornchurch, to the progressive garden suburb ideal of Gidea Park, Romford, and denser district of Elm Park. After the Second World War, the LCC built their out-county estate at Harold Hill but private development was curtailed by the creation of the Green Belt, a welcome intervention that has saved Havering's unique character.

COLLIER ROW

A hamlet named from charcoal burners which grew into a suburb between the wars, with an indifferent hilltop shopping centre along Collier Row Road.

ASCENSION, Collier Row Road. 1884 by *Ernest C. Lee*, 'quaintly designed' as *Building News* reported.* A humble mission church built for a largely agricultural area. Red brick with dressings of red stone; chancel with lancets, nave with pairs of transomed lights. Shingled two-tier flèche between nave and chancel. A parish church from 1928.

CHURCH OF THE GOOD SHEPHERD, Collier Row Lane, 1934–5 by *Newberry & Fowler*. Conservative late Gothic, elegant and refined. Pale brick, with a simple battlemented NE tower. Good interior, simply but subtly detailed. Nave arcades with double-chamfered arches on octagonal piers, no capitals. Clerestory and tall scissor-braced open roof. Narrow aisles with lean-to roofs and windows in long bands of five lights. Deep splays to all the windows. Traditional sanctuary with REREDOS with carved stone panels, carved openwork altar frontal and stained glass E window, a contrast to the now cleared and carpeted chancel and the reseated nave. FONT supported by four carved angels. Plans (2003) for extensions to link the church to the hall to the W.

VICARAGE to the S, roughcast upper floor, doorway with tiled arch.

CORPUS CHRISTI (R.C.), Hood Walk and Lowshoe Lane. A late work by *W.C. Mangan*, 1964–5. Very plain. Buff brick exterior with pantiled pitched roof. Red brick arcades. Paired windows with stained glass figures against clear glass.

CRANHAM

In The Chase, hall and church stand on their own.

ALL SAINTS CHURCH, 1873 by *Richard Armstrong* for Richard Benyon of Cranham Hall. A rarity in Greater London, a C19 rural church of high quality donated by the local landowner. It replaced a humbler building of C13 origin. Serious Gothic, just a nave and chancel, S porch and NE tower with spire, in neat dressed random rubble. A curved E stair turret to the tower, with conical cap, an unusual, slightly French touch. Big three-light geometric-traceried E and W windows. Expensive detail inside: well carved capitals and corbels, chancel arch with marble shafts. The W gallery was added in the 1960s, its front made from choir stalls damaged by a fire.

* We owe this reference to Geoff Brandwood.

REREDOS. Last Supper, relief in cast stone. – STAINED GLASS. E and W windows by *Hardman*: Crucifixion (E); Old Testament figures and creation scenes (W), finely drawn and brilliantly coloured. Later nave windows, some also by *Hardman*. – MONUMENTS. Samuel Wright and three older generations, C18; James Oglethorpe †1785, the founder of Georgia; a long epitaph. He married a daughter of the manor.

In the CHURCHYARD, railed tomb to Thomas Woodroffe †1746: square tapered sarcophagus on feet, with vase.

CRANHAM HALL. Rebuilt 1789, possibly incorporating C16–C17 parts of the house of General Oglethorpe. Three storey, five-bay E front, stuccoed; dentil cornice below shallow hipped roof. Wide four-column Doric porch. Later additions: N, 1904; W, 1970s. Extensive, much patched C16 GARDEN WALLS to the S.

BOYD HALL, St Mary's Lane. Built as Cranham Boyd School 1870 by Richard Benyon. Schoolroom with teacher's house on the l., yellow brick with spare red brick dressings, small bellcote.

Suburban Cranham lies N of St Mary's Lane around FRONT LANE, a place to study variants of bungalows.

ST LUKE, Front Lane. 2002 by *John Marsh* of the *MEB Partnership*, replacing a church established 1957. A rather muddled brick exterior with small clock turret. A spacious foyer opens into a large and light flexible interior in an evangelical tradition, rather like a concert hall. Curved glass-fronted gallery on three sides, on thin steel columns; raised E end with immersion font below communion table, lit by rooflights behind a shallow arch. The foyer is linked to a two-storey 1960s block with hall and meeting rooms.

HAROLD HILL

Before 1947 Harold Hill was farmland, woodland and parkland, which surrounded the medieval manor of Dagnams. This is shown on a map of 1633 as a moated site but by 1748 the moat had been filled in and a park laid out. The house was rebuilt *c.* 1772 by Sir Richard Neave, overseas merchant and later Governor of the Bank of England. *Repton* was employed in 1802 to make picturesque alterations to the landscape, which then consisted 'of a park, wooded sufficiently, and the distance presents a pleasing offskip; but the most conspicuous feature is a large circular pond, or pool with naked banks, from which the cattle are excluded by a hurdle'. The pond survives at the centre of DAGNAM PARK, but the house, acquired by the LCC to serve their new estate (*see* below), was demolished in 1950. Within the park's boundaries, close to the SE entrance, is a heavily overgrown MOAT enclosing a square site. It is shown on the 1633 estate map as planted with an orchard and adjacent to a second mansion, Cockerels (demolished).

Most of the Dagnams estate was sold off in 1919. Abercrombie's *Greater London Plan* of 1944 recommended a 'quasi-satellite town' in this area for deliberate overspill from London and in 1947 the remaining 850 acres of Dagnams Park Farm was acquired for the HAROLD HILL ESTATE, one of the largest LCC housing enterprises after the Second World War. Designed by the Valuer's Department (Housing Architect: *S. Howard*), and in essence a small 'new town'. It began as an estate of prefabs in 1947, proper construction began in 1948, slightly after the similar Hainault Estate (*see* Redbridge) and was largely complete by 1954. 7,631 houses provided space for over 25,000 people.

The undulating character of the site lent itself well to the Council's aim of maintaining variety over such a large area – 'the greatest possible use of the physical conditions has been made' it boasted. Mature trees were retained, and housing laid out around the existing woods and spinneys. Part of the park was retained at the centre, the rest as green belt. Planning was on the neighbourhood principle with one large and two smaller shopping centres dividing the housing into two neighbourhoods, and industry reserved for an area to the SE. Such provision represents a departure from design of pre-war estates and, moreover, included community buildings. But the planning is still recognizably of the pre-war garden suburb type, with avenues, crescents and *points-de-vue* arranged along a principal N–S axis, punctuated by circular greens on high ground. In the centre of these, churches were to act as eye-catchers, surrounded by formal arrangements of three-storey blocks of flats. In practice far less consideration was given to variety with the result that architecturally not much of special interest can be discovered. The houses are of the expected type, mixtures of brick terraces and semi-detached houses with a few blocks of flats. Permanent types of prefabricated housing were all employed but less visibly than at Hainault and the dominant tone remains entirely traditional. Larger types of houses, intended to produce a greater social mix, were provided on the higher ground.

The focus for the estate is the SHOPPING CENTRE at the N end of the main axis along Hilldene Avenue. Begun in 1952, its design marks the change wrought by the younger members of the *LCC Architect's Department* at this date. Four-storey brick blocks on each side with maisonettes and flats above shops expressed within boxy concrete surrounds. Spacious arrangement, the central avenue perhaps deliberately suited to a street market. At the N end, the blocks overlook a small green (with an anonymous granite-boulder War Memorial of 1998, marking the estate's fiftieth anniversary). Slightly N uphill, sites were reserved on either side for a clinic (not built) and LIBRARY, the latter a simple flat-roofed box by *Essex*

County Council, 1959, with decorative tiling. Closing the view, housing for the elderly: a continuation of the entirely pedestrian type of pre-war council housing with inset round-arch porches. Answering this at the S end of Hilldene Avenue is the anticlimax of ST GEORGE'S CHURCH of 1952–3 by *J.J. Crowe*. A plain, dual purpose church and community hall, altered 1984–5. The original plans for the estate placed this further uphill behind a grassy approach, where some purposeful effect might have been achieved. Instead, on the top are three-storey blocks of FLATS arranged without any sense for the natural contours of the site, as if the planners had never seen it.

W of here, GOOSHAYS ROAD skirts the edge of CENTRAL PARK. Gooshays Farm, a plain, red brick C18 building was preserved in the early days of the estate as a community centre but destroyed by fire in 1958. Of about that date, the purpose built COMMUNITY CENTRE. The other amenities provided for the estate are, alas, in 2004 due for replacement. These include the nearby HEALTH CENTRE, of 1955, a rarity on post-war estates. Festival style. Something of that spirit, though blunted by neglect, also informed the SWIMMING POOL set in spacious surroundings by the park. 1966 by *L.C. Dando* of the Havering Borough Architect's Dept. Large hall with N gallery, expressed as a cantilevered glazed balcony with wavy roof. E and uphill along DAGNAM PARK DRIVE, the natural advantages of the site can be best appreciated as the ground rises sharply NE over wooded slopes lined by mature trees. Here, in the area close to the green belt, larger houses were provided but the effect is monotonous.

The estate has a few other CHURCHES. In Petersfield Avenue: ST PAUL, 1953 and MOST HOLY REDEEMER (R.C.) 1963–4 by *Donovan Purcell*, brick, with largely glazed W front. ST DOMINIC (R.C.), Straight Road. 1956 by *Burles & Newton*. Romanesque style, with SE campanile. Mr Evinson writes 'Unobstructed view provided by omitting the columns forming the aisle and carrying the clerestory lighting on longitudinal lattice trusses.'

Of greater interest are the SCHOOLS. Eleven were provided, each in large open spaces which created an informal green link through the estate i.e., on the neighbourhood principle. BROXHILL CENTRE, Noak Hill Road, was built as Harold Hill Grammar School by *Harold Conolly*, Essex County Architect, 1958–60. Curtain-walled. 'Friendly and naturally decorative', Ian Nairn called it: not a fair assessment today. – PRIORY JUNIOR SCHOOL, Settle Road, also by *Conolly*, 1953, is of prefabricated timber construction, made in Austria and imported by rail to Harold Hill in an effort to meet the needs of the estate as quickly as possible. Mixture of brick and boarding. Refurbishment has altered its windows and with it much of its character. – DYCORTS SCHOOL, former Harrowfield Secondary Boys' School, Sheffield Crescent. By *Richard Sheppard*

& Partners in collaboration with *H. Conolly*, County Architect, 1952–4.

HAROLD WOOD

Harold Wood was part of the Gubbins estate, the site of the manor house is now occupied by Harold Wood Hospital. It was the first suburban development within Hornchurch, made possible by the opening of a station on the Great Eastern Railway line in 1868, but was overtaken by the smarter developments in Emerson Park and only saw much house building, of a modest nature, after 1918; a permanent church was not erected until 1939. In the meantime, however, small industries had settled here for access to the railway, notably the milling business of James and George H. Matthews Ltd and brickworks in Church Road (now Bates Industrial Estate).

ST PETER, Gubbins Lane. By *J.J. Crowe*, 1938–9. Successor to an iron church erected in Church Road in 1871 to serve the newly expanding suburb. A typically unfussy piece of work in brick with Crowe's trademark of a tower topped by a flèche. Inside, calm and spare, just a broad nave and chancel under a single barrel-vaulted and panelled roof, with very narrow passage aisles beneath round-arch cross-vaults. Lancets of two and three lights along the flanks. N transept, and chancel chapel with corresponding vestry on the S side. Foundation stone laid by the Matthews brothers, local millers,* the church is at least in part a memorial to Frederick Lawson Matthews, killed in 1916. In the N transept a wall MEMORIAL placed here from the earlier church and STAINED GLASS E window of 1939. Nice oak staircase, with arrow-loop detail, to the former ORGAN LOFT on the S side, which has a timber screen. Over the altar an inscribed stone 'Come unto Me'. The church has had a long evangelical tradition, so the recent reordering looks well thought out. A single-storey annexe at the W end, of 1963, is less so.

HAROLD WOOD LIBRARY, Arundel Road. 1960 by *Essex County Council*. Very simple and attractive, on a triangular site, with its own shady forecourt. Double height with much glazing between brick piers. Projecting entrance under a light canopy, which continues across the width of the front. The taller outer bays splay slightly forward.

HAROLD WOOD HOSPITAL, Gubbins Lane. The manor house of Gubbins was demolished in the C18 and replaced by a farmhouse. On its site is THE GRANGE (now offices) built for William Compton, owner of the Gubbins estate. Dated 1883.

* The Matthews were millers and seedsmen with business across Essex and Suffolk.

Free Renaissance with thickly mullioned windows, tile-hung gables and stamped terracotta decoration. It became a children's convalescent home in 1909 for West Ham County Borough who made extensions. The main HOSPITAL, rebuilt in 1986–7, is low, in red brick with broad, low-sloping slate roofs and cantilevered timber-faced upper storeys. Quadrangular plan, with courtyard gardens. Ward blocks with two-storey bay windows along each side. Striking 1960s MATERNITY BLOCK. Stone clad, five storeys with grids of inset windows along the flanks and a higher central service tower. The hospital is scheduled for closure in 2004.

STATION, Gubbins Lane. 1868. Neo-Tudor, in grey brick with coped gables and diaper-pattern brickwork. Stone dressings around the entrance and parcel office doorway, possibly alterations made by the LNER. In STATION ROAD, of the same date, the KING HAROLD pub, with bargeboarded gable.

HAVERING-ATTE-BOWER

1 The village lies on a ridge of high ground, a pleasant spot, more rural Essex than Greater London, with a few older houses around the green. The Royal Liberty of Havering, which existed from the Middle Ages (roughly coterminous with the modern borough), took its name from the palace, or royal hunting lodge, of Havering-atte-Bower, which lay W of the present church. This had a continuous use as a royal residence from the C12 to the time of Henry VIII. Nothing remains, although the medieval building accounts give a tantalising picture. In the C13 much was spent by Henry III on embellishing the chapel and on the queen's lodgings, which included a second chapel. The main chapel was rebuilt in 1374–7. The palace was held as a dower house for the queen mother from 1273, and subsequently by successive royal consorts, the last being Henry VIII's third wife, Jane Seymour. The infant Prince Edward had a household here in 1538; Elizabeth I and James I visited several times, but by the early C17 the palace was falling into decay. The buildings are shown on a survey of 1578, an irregular straggle with prominent buttressing, which suggests C13 and C14 structures. By 1650 they were in ruins, and in the early C19 nothing remained apart from a building then in use as the parish church. The royal estate included the area which later became Pyrgo Park, where there was another substantial house, rebuilt as a classical villa in 1851–2 by *Salvin* for Thomas Allason, remodelled in Italianate style by *E.M. Barry* in 1862, and demolished in 1938. From the numerous gentry mansions that once existed in the area there are still the excellent C18 Bower House down the hill and the unusual Round House hidden away to the E.

ST JOHN THE EVANGELIST. 1875–8 by *Basil Champneys*, an early work of this Arts and Crafts architect, showing an accomplished mastery of both massing and Dec detail. Flint with stone dressings, Dec windows, and a S aisle; in the Essex tradition, but with a surprisingly elaborate tower porch. The Victorian church replaced a simple building with thatched nave, tiled chancel, small W bellcote and Perp windows, reputedly on the site of one of the chapels of the royal palace.* Was Champneys (with the assistance of the local gentry) deliberately aiming to recreate some medieval royal grandeur? The three-stage, SW tower porch has open arches on three sides. Above the E arch three gabled and crocketed empty niches. The building committee expressly asked that these should be made in such a way that it would be impossible to put statues in them. Other instructions given to the architect (removal of credence table and of a step up to the altar) also suggest anti-ritualist attitudes. The porch interior has a vault on three bold lion's-head corbels. The stair turret in the fourth corner rises above a delicate openwork parapet. Rewarding detail elsewhere as well: windows with varied flowing tracery, the S chancel buttresses with playfully curved copings, and a dramatic sweep of big tiled roofs on the N side where there is no aisle.

Inside, a correctly Dec N arcade of three bays; filleted quatrefoil piers, moulded capitals, and boldly moulded arches. Tall chancel arch; below the SE window SEDILIA with three crocketed gables, and some foliage carving at the base of the arch to the organ chamber. The chancel has a ceiled barrel, with small carved bosses, the nave has an open crown-post roof. Furnishings and monuments evoking the C18 and C19 gentry fit uncomfortably with a spartan late C20 reordering. The choir stalls have gone. REREDOS with painting of the Last Supper, Gothic figures against gold background. Given in memory of Ann Pemberton Barnes †1912. It presumably displaced the plain flanking TEXTS in Gothic frames. – Simple C19 COMMUNION TABLE and RAILS. – FONT. Late C12, octagonal Purbeck marble bowl, two arches in shallow relief on each face; C19 Perp pedestal and cover. – STAINED GLASS. E window, replacing one of 1891 lost in World War Two. Late Arts and Crafts: small figures with scenes from the life of Christ in a hard-edged style against pale glass. Chancel SE 'King of Kings' 1926, signed by *Percy Bacon* (Davies family). Chancel SW, Christ with Mary and St John (Pemberton-Barnes family), both with florid Gothic canopy work and stodgy figure drawing. Two more of the 1920s in the S aisle (McIntosh and Jessops families).

MONUMENTS, partly from the old church. Some good C18 LEDGERS at the E end of the N aisle, and a restrained series of wall monuments and tablets, tidily displayed. – John Baynes †1736 of Bower House: 'having built and beautified a Neat Seat in Havering he lived not to enjoy it long, Leaving this life

*Was it the remains of an undercroft to the C14 chapel? The C16 survey shows the chapels at first-floor level. *See* H.M. Colvin, *The King's Works*, vol. IV.

for a better'. A fine classical aedicule; Ionic columns, broken pediment with cartouche, three putti heads below. – Sir John Smith Burges †1803 'of Havering Bower', by *James Wyatt*. Plain pedimented tablet. He was a director of the East India Company and married the daughter of Ynyr Burges of East Ham. – Several monuments to the Fields of Pyrgo Park: Michael Field †1836 and Caroline Field †1828. Two marble scrolls against an elegant pair of Gothic arches in black marble; animal-head corbels below. – Robert Field †1855. – Eleanor Charlotte Kerr †1864; with simpler Gothic arches. – Isabel Alderson of Havering Grange †1839, tablet with urn. – John Barnes 'of the Round House and Mile End' †1849, classical tablet above another to four of his children †1834–41, both set against black marble. – William Pemberton Barnes of the Hall, †1872. Marble scroll. – Octavius Mashiter †1875. Sarcophagus with large marble urn with drooping bayleaves. – Collinson Hall, †1880. Signed by his daughter-in-law *C.C. Hall*, 1883. Unusual, especially for this date: portrait bust and mourning figure of agriculture, farming implements below, and a harvest scene with mechanical reaper and traction engine. Hall, who leased Manor Farm until 1849, was a progressive agriculturalist who helped to invent the steam plough and developed commercial dairy farming.

CHURCH HALL. Two buildings now linked. The E one is an attractive design of 1902, given by the Pemberton Barnes family. Pale brick with stone dressings; round-arched openings, the windows with wooden mullions and arched lights. Stonework with delicately tooled patterns. Interior now floored and subdivided.

On the green to the SE, STOCKS and WHIPPING POST, quite a rarity, restored 1966. On the N side, a group of weatherboarded cottages of three and two bays, the eastern one with the former one-storey forge attached. Across the road the OLD VICARAGE, of several dates, partly C18: front range with eagles on the parapet and early C19 tripartite window at the r. end; a steep-roofed range behind, perhaps earlier. Down NORTH ROAD, ROSE COTTAGE, another carefully restored small timber-framed weatherboarded cottage (its substantial roof timbers suggest a possibly early C18 date). IVY HOLT is early C19, rendered, with bay windows and an attractive veranda along the whole front. Beyond is DAME TIPPING INFANTS SCHOOL, with informative plaques: founded 1724, rebuilt 1837, rebuilt again 1891. The Tudor schoolhouse to the r. looks 1837: yellow brick with dripstones.

W of the green are the remains of HAVERING PARK. The dock contractor Hugh McIntosh acquired the former royal estate in 1828. His son David McIntosh, who inherited in 1840, built a substantial house *c.* 1850–70, Italianate with a tower, which was demolished in 1925. The SOUTH LODGE on Orange Tree Hill remains from this era, one storey, white stucco, with pairs of arched windows in the projecting wings. Enlarged in the 1980s. The estate buildings were rebuilt from the 1860s. Close to the green an estate cottage, and a riding school which occupies the former STABLES, a substantial U-shaped building; both with polychrome brick trim to windows and eaves.

Beyond the stables are scrappy C20 buildings, including an uninspired village hall not making the best of a magnificent view N. The extensive grounds to the W, heavily planted by the McIntoshes, were sold off in one-acre plotlands in 1925. In 1961 Essex County Council decided to implement the green belt policy for the area. The small plotland houses were cleared in the 1970s, by the GLC, to local protest, and the land reunited as HAVERING COUNTRY PARK, opened 1976. An avenue of Wellingtonias still runs along the high ground, with other C19 planting, now somewhat overwhelmed by later woodland. On the avenue, a single surviving plotland bungalow remains as a park office.

BOWER FARM, Bower Farm Road. Part of the Havering Park estate. A bailiff's house, cottage, and between them a substantial group of cattle sheds (now converted to stables), as at Park Farm (*see* below). Coloured brick trim to the windows. Other buildings include a small gas house with chimney.

PARK FARM, Lodge Lane. Another farmhouse with unusually complete C19 farm buildings on the same pattern as those of Bower Farm: a connecting series of five long ranges, of the type that became popular for progressive large-scale dairy farming in the later C19. The production of milk for the London market on the Havering Park estate had begun in the 1840s, pioneered by Collinson Hall; see his monument in the church. Behind a walled enclosure the front cattle shed has the date 1869 and DM for David McIntosh jun. in a central gable. Broad segment-headed openings on either side of a central passage which leads to a lower, hipped-roof shed behind; beyond this a larger building with cart entrances in the gable ends; another hipped-roof range and large barn beyond. On the other side of the farmyard two-storey open cart-shed with hayloft.

ROUND HOUSE, Broxhill Road, E of the green, well concealed. 37
A remarkable oval villa built *c.* 1792 for William Sheldon, a London entrepreneur, restored with much care in 1980–1 by *Julian Harrap*. Convincingly attributed by Neil Burton to *John Plaw*, the architect of St Mary Paddington, who was specially interested in central plans, and who designed the circular Belle Isle, Windermere in 1775.* Sheldon was a subscriber to Plaw's *Rural Architecture* published in 1785.

Three storeys with rendered walls and a far-projecting shallow conical roof covered with Westmorland slates. The curving walls are neatly divided by four pairs of giant pilasters rising to a string course, with further pairs to the top storey. Porch of two pillars and two Ionic columns. Front doorway below a delicate iron fanlight. Between the pilasters three windows on N and S sides, to E and W a broader single window

*See *Georgian Group Journal*, 1991.

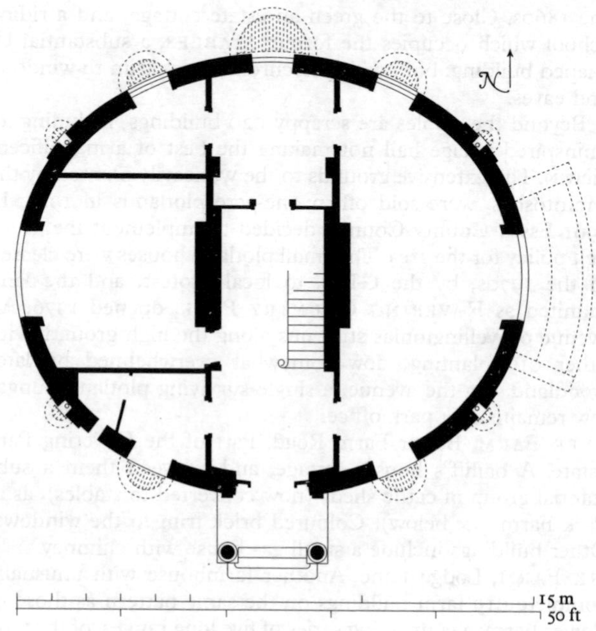

Round House, Havering-atte-Bower, plan

on ground and first floor takes advantage of the views. The larger first floor windows have simple iron balconies, formerly canopied. The house stands on a mound which cleverly conceals the service basement and an encircling outer covered passage lit by gratings in its vault. This can be reached on the E side by a tunnel which starts close to the DAIRY, a tiny brick building with rendered front, four pilasters and pediment.

Inside the neat geometrical subdivision of the plan (the oval is 30 ft by 40 ft) is ingenious and successful, with hall and staircase on the short axis, allowing for comfortably deep rooms on either side. The E room on the ground floor and the W room on the first floor fill a half circle, the others are smaller; it is uncertain whether all the present subdivisions are original. The central stair, with slim straight banisters, winds elegantly up to the top floor through a roof-lit oval drum which contains the chimney flues and is concentric with the outer walls. By a further stair one can enjoy excellent views from the roof.

Throughout the house the joinery is consistently minimalist, with windows, doors and fireplaces set in rectangular framing with little squares at the corners. Few later alterations of note: the large first-floor bedroom was aggrandized in the later C19, repeating the detail but on a bigger scale. Some unusual French panoramic wall paper of *c.* 1820 is now in the Victoria and Albert Museum. The basement stair formerly rose to a separate lobby but in 1930 was relocated beneath the main staircase.

Also in Broxhill Road, THE THATCH, a one-storey thatched cottage, early C19.

ORANGE TREE HILL runs SW from the green. On the E side BOWER FARM COTTAGE, a pretty Tudor cottage orné with lozenge-patterned glazing, spiky bargeboards and fish-scale tiles. BLUE BOAR HALL is a timber-framed house of the C16–C17 behind a C19 refronting.

BOWER HOUSE, Orange Tree Hill, is set back in its own grounds 32
with a splendid view S. A great treasure for this area, an excellently preserved C18 house with fine interior detail. It is *Henry Flitcroft*'s first house, built in 1729 for John Baynes, a lawyer. Used by Ford Motors as a training centre until 2003, and well cared for. The original house was quite small; a sober Palladian composition, as one would expect from Flitcroft, of five bays and two storeys over a basement, with slightly advanced three-bay centre with pediment. Doorway also with pediment. On the S side another pedimented doorway with rusticated Doric pilasters and triple keystone. The material is red brick, not generally a Palladian choice. Was it originally rendered? It was enlarged by one-storey wings, *c.* 1800, which have elegantly canted S ends and tall arched windows, providing an additional large room on each side. Entrance hall and the central S-facing Saloon preserve fine interiors in the manner of Kent. In the hall, pedimented door to the saloon, other doors with enriched mouldings, and an elaborate fireplace with flanking tapering scrolls and swan-neck pediment to the overmantel. On the pediment is placed a medieval corbel: an angel bust bearing the arms of Edward III, presumably from the royal hunting lodge. The Saloon is equally lavish, with enriched woodwork and a fireplace flanked by terms; its small but grand overmantel is treated as a pedimented Ionic aedicule. Stairhall off 33
to the W, a small but handsome space entirely decorated with dark wall paintings of arcadian scenes: shepherds and maidens and a bacchic group. Croft Murray suggests an English artist, but doubts the traditional ascription to Thornhill. There are also grisaille busts and medallions with classical scenes. The stair is of mahogany, with symmetrical balusters of the Inigo Jones type, as approved by the Palladians. In the big room in the added E wing a brought in and much restored fireplace in earlier C16 style, but with the date 1659.

STABLES, NE of the house. Red brick, large alternatingly rusticated archways on l. and r., now blocked; a lantern in the centre. Altered for offices and reception centre. The grounds were reputedly laid out by *Bridgman*.

To the N of LOWER BEDFORDS ROAD, UPPER BEDFORDS FARMHOUSE. A three-storey crenellated tower with stair turret; built between 1792 ands 1816 as an eyecatcher by John Heaton, owner of a now demolished house called Bedfords. S of the road, BELLEVUE, in origin a late C18 weatherboarded lobby-entry house.

HORNCHURCH

Hornchurch is the chief settlement in the S of the borough. It developed on the main road along the gravel terrace N of the Thames marshes, but was little more than a village until overtaken by suburban development in the earlier C20. The medieval church lies up the hill to the E. The site of the priory founded by Henry II in 1159 probably lay nearby; it functioned as a hospital for the poor, but was dissolved in 1391 when its lands were acquired by Willliam of Wykeham as an endowment for New College Oxford. Expansion came with the railway: the station at Hornchurch, on the London, Tilbury & Southend line opened in 1885, followed by Emerson Park on a line from Romford in 1905, and Elm Park in 1935. There was minor industry as well: Hornchurch brewery which flourished from 1789–1930, and the Fairkytes iron foundry and engineering works founded in the early C19. All that has gone and the general impression now is of an indifferent crossroads shopping centre surrounded by C20 housing. In the centre almost nothing recalls the attractive Essex village visible on early C20 photos, although there are still some good houses to seek out on the fringes. The borough's intention is to encourage the development of Hornchurch as a cultural centre, but the individual attractions so far fail to add up to coherent townscape.

RELIGIOUS BUILDINGS

ST ANDREW, High Street. A large townish church sited on a knoll, the highest point between Romford and Upminster, the prominent W tower and spire a landmark visible from the Thames. The church is C13 in origin, but externally appears Perp, though the remodelling was not all of the same date. Rubble walls of Septuaria and ragstone. The chancel was rebuilt in 1405–8, soon after the benefice was acquired by William of Wykeham as an endowment for New College Oxford. The E window dates from an extensive restoration of 1869. The E gable has an oddity, a (restored) bull's head with horns, its origin unclear. The horns are recorded already in 1610 and the place name existed by the C13 when the priory was called the 'horned monastery'. The N and W doorways in square-headed surrounds, clerestory and E chapels are all later C15 or early C16. S aisle and chapel walls were rebuilt in brick in 1802, probably by *John Johnson*, Essex county surveyor. The tower is also later C15, of three stages, with diagonal buttresses, hexagonal corner pinnacles and higher SW stair turret. On the W side a carved figure of a bishop. The recessed spire, completed in 1491–2, was formerly clad in lead, replaced in copper in 1805. Structural repairs by *Sir Charles Nicholson*, 1918, and more extensive ones, with concrete ring-beam, in the 1960s.

The interior is light, because of the later medieval clerestory, but the nave arcades are C13, possibly related to a grant of 1243; circular piers with moulded capitals and double-chamfered arches. A carved roundel in the spandrel between third and fourth bay. Fine late medieval nave roof with moulded tie beams and carved heads at the feet of the central braces. The C15 chancel chapels have octagonal piers. Chancel and S chapel arches of 1869–71, when the late C13 PISCINA and SEDILIA were uncovered and restored: tall five-cusped arches on slim shafts. There is a squint in the back wall of the westernmost seat. Remnants of an early C16 SCREEN given by William Ayloffe, whose monument is in the N chapel. In the tower original DOOR to the turret stair. This leads to the W gallery ringing chamber, enlarged eastward in 2001 when the peal was increased from eight to ten bells. Early C19 BELL BOARDS and two inscribed ALE JARS of 1732 and 1815 celebrate the ringers' prowess.

STAINED GLASS. N chapel E: medieval fragments of a Crucifixion, headless, and coats of arms. E window by *Gerald Smith*, 1954, made by *Nicholson Stained Glass Studios*. N aisle centre, by *John Lawson* of *Goddard & Gibbs*, 1991, with contemporary detail.

Remains of a once large number of BRASSES (some now under a carpet). The most complete are to Thomas Drywood †1591 and wife, and Thomas Hone †1604 and wife, each with two figures and two groups of children below (the later ones cruder). – Small group of five sons, from a brass to Thomas Crafford †1508. – Two hatted wives from brass of William Drywood, †1602. – More fragmentary remnants: slab with remains of a Lombardic lettered inscription, formerly with cross and two half figures, dated to *c.* 1330–40, i.e., early for a brass. – Shield from brass to Thomas Scargill †1475 and wife. – Two shields from a brass to Katherine Powlett, 1510. – Inscriptions only from brasses of 1530 (George Reede, vicar), 1587 (James Pollexfen), 1595 (Humphrey Drywood).

MONUMENTS. C13 coffin lid with floriated cross. – Chancel N: William Ayloffe †1517, of Bretons. Tomb chest with three panels of quatrefoils and arms, plain Purbeck marble slab. – Tower S: Francis Rame and wife †1617, 1613, alabaster wall monument, pilasters with ribbon work framing two kneeling figures, ten children in relief below. – N chapel: Richard Blakstone †1638, two kneelers and two angels drawing back a curtain, a popular motif in the 1630s. – More unusual is the wall monument to Thomas Withering †1651, the first postmaster general; a classical frame with ribbon work decoration and flanking obelisks, and at the foot a recumbent skeleton; perched oddly above it is a smaller skeleton representing a son who died aged five. Attributed to *William Wright* of Charing Cross (GF). – Sir Francis Prujean †1666, attributed to *Thomas Burman* (GF). Large architectural frame with broken and scrolled pediment. – Richard Spencer of Hornchurch Hall, †1784, by *Flaxman*. Two standing angels, medallion with double portrait. – William Mashiter and wife †1871, 1834, urn with drooping bay leaves. Many other minor tablets.

To the S, linked to the church, octagonal HALL by *Thompson, Whitehead & Partners*, 1969–70. Large CHURCHYARD with C18 headstones and railed tomb chests.

ALL SAINTS, Ardleigh Green Road, Squirrels Heath. 1957 by *Tooley & Foster*. Very simple, brick with tiled roof, small bellcote. Small, richly coloured E window.

HOLY CROSS, Park Lane and Hornchurch Road. 1932–4 by *Pite, Son & Fairweather*. A cruciform church in grim dark brick, isolated on a lawn. A large oculus in the W gable, crocketed lead spirelet over the crossing. Small rectangular windows high up, under tiled arches. Interior in a simplified Romanesque, with plaster groin vaults and round-headed arcades on brick piers. S transept window 1933.

ST NICHOLAS, Woodcote Avenue, Elm Park. A late work by *J.J. Crowe*, 1956. Red brick nave and chancel under one roof, N and S chapels, the latter partly under the tower, which has a louvred top and copper roof. Cheerful well-lit interior with rendered walls above brick dado, segment-arched arcades and narrow aisles. The chancel has a shallow barrel vault. Three-light E window by *Terence D. Randall*, 1966.

ST JOHN AND ST MATTHEW, South End Road, South Hornchurch. Simple building of 1957, successor to a mission church of 1864, refurbished by *Ronald Wylde Associates*, with funding from landfill tax.

ST MARY MOTHER OF GOD (R.C.), Hornchurch Road. 1931–3 by *D.H. Burles*. Red brick, Perp, with SW tower and turret. Good traditional interior in minimal Gothic, arcades with pointed chamfered arches on octagonal columns without capitals. Blind E wall with three statues. Main altar and other furnishings removed when reordered, the tabernacle from it now in a side chapel, on a square, polished stone base. Bronze FONT, a shallow bowl on curved stand. STATIONS OF THE CROSS, carved wood. S chapel. WINDOW by *Goddard & Gibbs*, 1980.

ENGLISH MARTYRS (R.C.), Alma Avenue (off Hacton Lane). 1954–5 by *D.R. Burles* of *Burles, Newton & Partners*. Broad nave, elliptical panelled ceiling. Bold abstract STAINED GLASS by *Goddard & Gibbs*, 1981; colourful creation theme around the apse.

ST ALBAN (R.C.), Langdale Gardens, Elm Park. 1959 by *D.R. Burles* of *Burles & Newton*. Steel portal frame, brickfaced, with T-shaped bell tower.

CHURCH OF JESUS CHRIST OF THE LATTER DAY SAINTS (R.C.), Ardleigh Green Road. 1962–4, extended 1986. Timber and yellow brick, with odd detached, gilded spire in the shape of an arrow. A large cluster with an open porch to the road, the worship area lit by a clerestory with close-set mullions, surrounded by lower rooms.

MAJOR BUILDINGS

LIBRARY, North Street. One of Essex County Council's post-war decent, straightforward modern boxes. SOUTH HORNCHURCH LIBRARY, Rainham Road, has a zigzagging roof as its special feature.

HAVERING SIXTH FORM COLLEGE, Wingletye Lane. Buildings of 1996 by the *Borough of Havering Architects' Department*, incorporating Dury Falls school (opened 1935, enlarged, 1963–4, 1974). The latest parts are a postmodern concoction: reconstituted stone with some corbelling under the cornice, angular bronze bay windows of tinted glass and a glazed double-height entrance atrium. Steel-framed library block and sports hall.

ST GEORGE'S HOSPITAL, Suttons Lane. Psychiatric hospital designed for 1050 patients, 1932–8 by *John Stuart*, Essex County Architect, on the site of an older private institution. Impressively large but not fearsome and thoughtfully laid out. The individual blocks are done in Stuart's sparingly detailed Neo-Georgian with the principal buildings arranged in line W–E: to the fore the administration building, with projecting wings and canted bays, then wards, large dining hall block and at the rear of the site a power house with a monumental tower. Flanking this core on each side are the two-storey ward buildings, creating a series of open courts, and at the outer edges were originally staff residences (S), isolation wards (N) and, set apart at the NW corner, a nicely treated children's ward. Bungalow, cranked plan with verandas overlooking a broad playing field.

PERAMBULATIONS

1. The centre of Hornchurch, starting at the church

Outside the churchyard gate, a graceful WAR MEMORIAL by *Sir Charles Nicholson*, 1921; a cross rising from a base with niches, on a hexagonal plinth with marble name tablets.

Opposite the church an C18 garden wall remains from the Old Chaplaincy, built by New College for the parish priest. The two-storey solar wing of a timber-framed aisled hall, datable to *c.* 1400, survived until 1970. Its significance was discovered only during demolition after a fire. Replaced by flats. The adjacent manor house, Hornchurch Hall, was destroyed in the Second World War.

Downhill in HIGH STREET on the S side is the pretty WYKEHAM COTTAGE, originally a pair (Nos. 218–20), C18 Gothic, with thin applied timbers on the front elevation. Four bays, with a Gothic window with arched head on the r.; the door is not in its original position. The rest of the S side was largely occupied by Hornchurch Brewery until the 1930s. The N side of the road has just a little to remind one of the traditional Essex village that survived until the C20. The group of timber-framed buildings here are rare survivals in the area of once common types. No. 197 is late C17, probably two dwellings in origin; roughcast and plastered, one door with pedimented hood. Its neighbours may be earlier C17: No. 195 is a tiny two-bay house, just two rooms on each floor, with inserted brick stack; No. 191–3 has the ground floor rebuilt in brick and a big central stack. Then No. 189, the King's Head Inn, low, with rendered front, and rear wing, but much altered.

The town centre at the junction with North Street is an undistinguished mess. The traffic now circles round the former White Hart inn, rebuilt in a stodgy, angular, classical style and deprived of its gardens when the road layout was changed in 1935. Burton's store, on the blunt-nosed NE corner is the only building with presence, it replaced the picturesque Britannia Inn in 1939; its ornate upper storeys now seem a welcome contrast to its indifferent post-war neighbours. Further W, CINEMA (Mecca Bingo), a symmetrical faience-clad frontage by *Kemp & Tasker*; opened 1935 as 'The Towers', including a café and ballroom. The spacious foyer and auditorium to seat 1,800 remain.

In NORTH STREET, CHURCH HOUSE, Gothic, yellow and red brick, built as teacher's house for the church school provided by New College in 1855. Taken over by the school board formed 1886, and superseded by LANGTONS SCHOOL, around the corner in Westland Avenue. This is of 1902 by *S.I. Adams* of Southend; quite an impressive composition: a long, gabled building in three sections, striped brick and stone, a ventilator turret over each of the wings. The paired central entrances have fat columns with Art Nouveau foliage, under a Venetian window. Original gatepiers and railings. Rear additions of 1932.

The civic centre of Hornchurch was to have been along NORTH STREET, but energy petered out when the focus moved to Romford with the creation of Havering in 1965. The one big effort is the THEATRE, standing in isolation between North Street and Billet Lane. By *R.W. Hallam*, Borough Architect (*N.W.T. Brooks*, project architect), opened 1975, a new home for a repertory theatre established in 1948. A tough-looking box on a recessed basement. Slate-clad fly tower, floor-to-ceiling glazing to the generous but bland foyer which is wrapped round three sides of the auditorium, with bar tucked awkwardly down steps beneath – a change after a planned studio theatre was not included. Auditorium seating 560, with thrust stage.

Off NORTH STREET in BILLET LANE are the best buildings. LANGTONS, down a lane to the W, is a good C18 house with grounds to the S, used as council offices from 1929–65, but now restored and used for weddings. Seven-bay entrance front facing N. The early C18 S front has a tall five-bay centre with straight-headed windows, moulded brick strings between the three storeys, and parapet. The lower projecting canted wings are later C18 additions. They have little oval windows above the first floor. Much altered in the early C20, the date of the large entrance hall and stair hall filling the centre of the house. At the W end a one-storey billiard room with coved ceiling, extended later. The grounds, small but attractive, were remodelled for the Massu family, Huguenot silk merchants, by *Repton*, according to Peacock's *Polite Repository*, 1805. The serpentine lake and lawn with trees flanked by shrubberies may be his work. W of the house, ORANGERY, the five bays and ends all fully glazed. A GAZEBO to the SE overlooks the lake, probably contemporary. Timber-canted front with sashes (at the back is a plunge bath lined in Portland stone). Walled kitchen garden. Former STABLES to the N, a long two-storey, hipped roof range with pediment over the centre three bays, and cupola above.

Adjoining are the grounds of FAIRKYTES (Havering Arts Centre from 1972). Five bays, a much-altered house of the mid-C18, refronted *c.* 1830, the older parts concealed from the road by a seven-bay Neo-Georgian frontage. Mid-C18 staircase, altered.

2. *Emerson Park*

EMERSON PARK is a suburb of superior housing developed by William Carter of Parkstone, Dorset, after parts of the Great Nelmes estate were sold for building in 1895. Large plots, with detached houses of varied design (Parkstone Ave, Herbert Rd etc.). The second phase, further N, took place after another sale in 1901 (Woodland Ave, Elm Grove, Sylvan Ave). After the First World War, the estate was expanded by E.A. Coryn & Son with houses by individual architects (Coryn's own house is on the corner of Ardleigh Green and Ayloff's Walk). The mansion of Great Nelmes was regrettably demolished in 1967. It was a substantial manor house of C16 origin, built by William Roche, Lord Mayor in 1540, with a S front of *c.* 1720. It lay to the N of SYLVAN AVENUE, near the road called The Witherings, where a lawn with cedar trees remains. Beyond are remains of a moat, now an adjunct to a group of lavish Neo-Georgian houses. In the garden of No. 3 Sylvan Avenue is the curious WELL TOWER, a conduit house, with 9 ft square lower part of red brick with small round-headed openings, possibly of the C16 (comparable to the conduit houses at Kingston serving Hampton Court). The upper part of brick, with lookout platform, may be C18, perhaps built as a dove house. The timber-framed top and slated spire probably date from after 1875. Nearby, set back, CAPEL NELMES, a composite creation: later C19 parts tile hung with brick-mullioned windows, timbered Tudor-style range behind of *c.* 1930 and later. (It incorporates a late C17 staircase of three flights from Great Nelmes.) The C16 red brick rear wing was formerly stables, but is much altered.

3. *South West including Elm Park*

ST LEONARDS, S of Hornchurch Road. An unusual group which originated as Hornchurch Cottage Homes, 1886–9 by *F.J. Smith* for the Guardians of Shoreditch Poor Law Union on the farmland of Harrow Lodge. The principle of separating children from the environment of the workhouse was a progressive move at the time. The original housing lies along THE MALL. It was planned as a village of eleven cottages, each housing thirty children, with school, chapel and infirmary. The site was sold in 1984, and the surviving buildings converted to private housing from 1993. The houses are of yellow brick with red trim, carved pendants on the gables providing sparse ornament. A larger pair at the N end, with stone doorcases, was the Lodge. Near the centre, the Hall, dated 1887, has an entrance with brick niche above. This formerly housed an early C19 sculpture of a woman with boy and girl, signed by the pottery manufactory 'Van Spangen and Powell, Mile End'. It came from the parochial school, Kingsland Road, Shoreditch and is now at Bethnal Green Museum.

HARROW LODGE. Former farmhouse; stuccoed front of 1787, with two full-height bow windows, much altered and extended. Converted to offices *c.* 1970.

HARROW LODGE PARK runs from S of Hornchurch Road through the northern part of Elm Park along the line of the River Ravensbourne, a recreational centre created from the 1940s on land given by Costains, the developers of Elm Park (*see* below). At the N end SWIMMING BATHS, by *V. Williams*, Council Surveyor and *D. Pearcy*, Council Architect, 1957–8, extended by a large SPORTS CENTRE of the 1980s. Rainham Road entrance gates 1952–3, boating lakes 1954–6, walled garden 1959–60.

ELM PARK. A large suburb SW of Hornchurch, with its own station. It was farmland until developed by Richard Costain Ltd with a master plan of 1933 for a 'country town of 7,000 houses', the largest private housing enterprise in Britain at the time, intended for a population of *c.* 25,000. Modest, closely set houses. The centre is the unassuming BROADWAY PARADE, with shops, running N and S of the station; one side was built by 1936, but other facilities were slow to arrive. Expansion S took place after the Second World War, with 3000 council dwellings built by Hornchurch UDC, mostly low-rise, but including their first high-rise block, on the Mardyke Estate (1962), followed by six more of twelve storeys (Wates system).

SOUTH END ROAD leads to remnants of an older area, already populated enough to require a mission church in 1864. A BOARD SCHOOL was built in Blacksmith's Lane in 1899, enlarged 1912 and 1929. A long composition (cf. Langtons, above). Gabled centre, wings with half-timbering and roughcast.

ALBYNS, South End Road. Very trim former farmhouse; an L-shaped timber-framed house of the C16–C17 with C18 brick-faced S entrance front. Central doorway with fanlight and pediment on brackets. Attractive outbuildings, weather-boarded with pantile roofs, including an C18 timber-framed barn.

HORNCHURCH COUNTRY PARK, Airfield Way, off South End Road, created 1980 on the site of Hornchurch Airfield. Hornchurch's air history goes back to the First World War, when an airfield at Suttons Farm was constructed as a base for protecting London against the Zeppelins. A new airfield was laid out in 1924–8 off South End Road and in the Second World War was an important centre for Fighter Command. Much was demolished after the site was sold in 1962 for gravel extraction. A fighter pen, gun posts and pillboxes are visible along the eastern pathway, and remains of an air raid shelter and aircraft dispersal bay at the northern car park. The remaining buildings lie W of South End Road. The former officers' mess building in ASTRA CLOSE is now a medical centre, a formal one-storey building with Tuscan columned porch and small cupola. Two-storey residential quarters on either side; other married quarters survive among new housing. The reticent Neo-Georgian mode was characteristic of interwar military aircraft buildings, designed to fit discreetly into the suburban scene.

BRETONS, W of Rainham Road near the boundary with Dagenham. A surprising survival of an isolated gentry house, now a community centre, still with open land around it. Curved wrought-iron C18 screen and gates, a cedar tree on the front lawn. An imposing red brick front of five bays and three storeys, with parapet. The centre bay projects full height, incorporating a columned Doric porch in front of a rusticated doorway. The projecting bay has a pediment and wooden modillioned cornice and a rather crude arched, first floor window. The date is a puzzle. The front appears to be a remodelling of *c.* 1740, the windows at back and sides have been crudely altered or remade. But inside a black and white paved entrance hall and archway with cartouche leads to a robust staircase of typical late C17 type: closed string, twisted balusters and square newels. The simpler upper flight is C18. Four-room plan, the interiors plain and much altered; a modillion cornice in the SE room; the NE room has simple full-height panelling of *c.* 1740. To the SE two C16 brick barns and some stretches of C16 garden wall.

4. West

DURY FALLS, Upminster Road and Wingletye Lane (No. 35). C19 detail, but an early C17 timber-framed house. Five-bay front, the three E bays the oldest. Extended W in the mid-C17, the western bay a cross wing with two-storey canted bay window. Brick stack with diagonal shafts. Timber-framed rear wing with stair turret on W. C19 and C20 extensions. Behind are fish ponds or a moat.

In WINGLETYE LANE, No. 272 (Lilliputs). Attractive red brick C18 front, four windows wide. Older behind, with two cross-wings. Evidence for a moat suggests a medieval site.

NOAK HILL

A straggly Essex hamlet in the green belt, just within the borough boundary, on the northern fringe of the Harold Hill estate.

ST THOMAS, Church Lane. Built as a chapel of ease in 1841–2 by the London architect *George Smith*, for Lady Frances Neave of Dagnams (*see* Harold Hill). A modest and attractive red brick building with shallow transepts and octagonal SW turret. Eclectic detail in a Tudor spirit; one- and three-light windows under flattened arches, the main windows with transoms. Inside, timber arcading and an open roof. The small W gallery carries an C18 chamber organ brought from Dagnams. Painted metal REREDOS with texts. Interesting collection of fragments of old GLASS, presumably given by the Neaves. E window with six panels, the upper three with Crucifixion, early C16 Flemish. Lower lights are later C16: the centre (St Mary and St Elizabeth) said to come from Brussels, the outer two (St John the Baptist and St Peter) from Rouen. In the side windows other French and Flemish pieces and C17 armorial glass (Charles II and Manners, Earls of Rutland). In the trim churchyard, monuments to the Neaves, including a Neo-Grecian pedestal to Charlotte Mary Neave, with relief of mourning woman.

Former SCHOOL, 1848 on the W side of Church Lane.

NOAK HILL ROAD still gives an impression of the pre-suburban Essex countryside. Along the N side a scatter of C19 timber-framed and weatherboarded cotttages: (from W–E) Old Keeper's Cottage, Thatched Cottage and Rose Cottages. On the S side, set further back (E–W) two pairs, both of brick: Orchard Cottages, C18 and Meadow Cottages, C19, then Holly Tree Cottage, timber-framed and tarred weatherboarding, late C18, with classical doorcase and fanlight, and the larger C19 group of Manor Farm and its outbuildings.

NORTH OCKENDON

The parish is crossed by the M25. The main centre is along the secluded Church Lane near the church, with some more houses ¼ m. further E, along the road to South Ockendon over the Essex boundary. North Ockendon became part of Hornchurch Urban District in 1935 and hence is within Greater London, although seventy years later it still had nothing urban about it.

ST MARY MAGDALENE. A neat flint-faced exterior with two E gables and lower N vestry, the latter and the flintwork dating from a restoration of 1858 by *Richard Armstrong*, paid for by the lord of the manor, Richard Benyon of Cranham Hall. To the N an extension by *John Glanfield & Partners*, 2003. The windows are of various dates, but the nave and chancel wall are later C12; S doorway with three orders with zigzag, one column with scalloped and one with a foliated volute capital. C15 W tower of ragstone with diagonal W buttresses and battlements. Inside, the N arcade is an early addition, though altered. Two double-chamfered arches in the centre, E.E., one circular pier and one octagonal. Simpler western arch with one chamfer. The easternmost arch is a C15 alteration, similar to the chancel arch. C15 nave roof with tie beams and crown-posts with four-way struts. Early C14 N chapel with two-bay arcade to the chancel, its quatrefoil pier with carved foliage capital.

In the tower, stairs, steep and of elementary construction with solid treads and chamfered runners, probably contemporary with the building.

REREDOS 1879, Last Supper in alabaster, supplied by *Farmer & Brindley*. – PULPIT. Hexagonal, Elizabethan type with delicate decoration, though probably C17. – FONT, 1842. – ROYAL ARMS, also 1842, of *Coade* stone. – STAINED GLASS. E window. Made up from medieval pieces (reset after the Second World War): a fine late C13 female saint (St Helena?), and much tabernacle work, perhaps a little later. N chapel E, three C14 shields. Chancel S, Road to Emmaus. By *Heywood Sumner*, 1907. Two lights, a distinctive drawing style with much hatching, heavily leaded, with pale, translucent colours.

BRASSES. – Thomasyn Badby, †1532, stiff frontal figure in furred gown, with part of an inscription and three shields. William Poyntz (†1502), in armour, and his wife Elizabeth, turning sideways, two groups of children below, and three (formerly four) shields. – John Poyntz †1547, inscription and shields (interesting palimpsest details). – Rev. Edward Foley Evans, †1933, kneeling figure in flowing robes by *Culn Gawthorp & Sons*.

MONUMENTS. A rewarding collection to the Poyntz family. The earliest, all put up in 1606 by Sir Gabriel Poyntz, are eight small monuments to his forbears, himself and his son: kneeling couples in appropriate costume, within frames. – Sir Gabriel Poyntz (†1607) and his wife Ætheldreda are commemorated by recumbent effigies on a large, alabaster tomb chest. Attributed to *Gerard Johnson*. Back panel with typical Southwark school ribbon work. The unusual feature is a wooden tester unsupported by columns, its underside delightfully painted with clouds, sun, moon and stars. – Pair of almost identical wall monuments, one erected by Sir Gabriel Poyntz to his daughter and son-in-law, early C17, the other to Sir James (†1623) and Richard Poyntz †1643. – Sir Thomas Littleton (Poyntz) †1709. Large, standing wall monument with bust high up, one hand elegantly on his breast. Weeping putti and Corinthian columns l. and r. supporting an open segmental pediment with reclining putti. – John Russell of Stubbers †1825, bust by *William Behnes*, opposite a medallion of his widow, Elizabeth †1838, by *Thomas Smith*. A tablet of 1996 commemorates the botanist William Coys (†1627) of Stubbers.

In the CHURCHYARD a well traditionally associated with St Cedd.

Garden walls and a moat W of the churchyard remain from North Ockendon Hall, the Poyntz seat from the C15–C18. The C16 house was destroyed in the Second World War. S of the church, brick outbuildings of Hall Farm, tactfully incorporated within a housing complex of 2002–3. Further up Church Lane is the former SCHOOL, rebuilt 1902 by James Benyon, now converted to residential use, and to its S a PARISH READING ROOM, the gift of Richard Benyon.

Along OCKENDON ROAD a rural group of mixed dates: KILBRO (The Old Bakehouse) C17, timber-framed, central chimney stack. RUSSELL COTTAGE, early C19, rendered, central door with fanlight. THE FORGE, C17 timber-framed, weatherboarded wing to N, lower rear wing. No. 7 Castle Cottages, *c*. 1700, is timber-framed with rendered front and flush frame sashes.

STUBBERS, 1 m. W. Now an outdoor leisure and wildlife centre. The C16–C18 house was demolished in 1960. Fishponds, a crinkle-crankle wall and other garden walls remain. The walls probably date from after 1796, when *Repton* advised the Russell family on the landscaping, sweeping away the four walled gardens of the C17 botanist William Coys. Here in 1604 the first Yucca flowered in England.

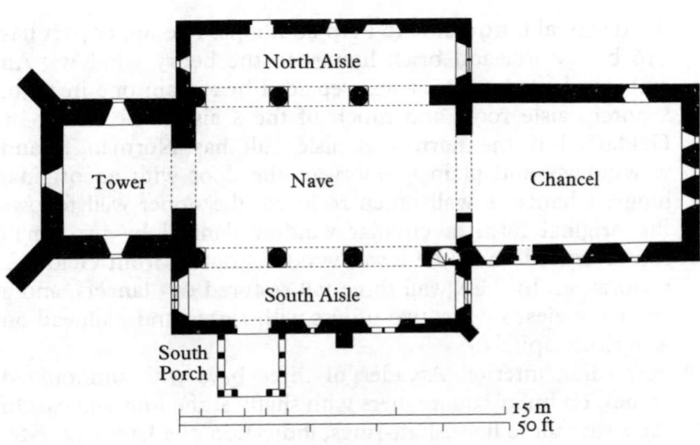

St Helen and St Giles, Rainham, plan

RAINHAM

Rainham still feels remote, an ancient settlement on the N edge of Rainham Marshes, by the creek formed by the once navigable River Ingrebourne. The medieval wharf was improved *c.* 1718 by its owner John Harle, builder of Rainham Hall, and used for importing coal and building materials. In the later C19 Rainham was still the shipping point for the produce of the market gardens that surrounded the village, but this had ceased by the mid-C20.

The centre of the village is a triangular area at the junction of Broadway, Wennington Road and Upminster Road South, with the C12 church and the C18 Rainham Hall close by. The railway arrived in 1854. There was expansion to the E from *c.* 1880, and to the N from *c.* 1920 when smallholders' plots were sold around New Road. The marshes, formerly used for grazing, are now carved up by the railway (doubled 2003 for the Channel Tunnel link) and the A13. Around Ferry Lane is the beginning of a Thames Gateway business park (2003), nearer the river a vast landfill refuse disposal area. Riverside industry was established from the later C19 (chemical and fertilizer works from 1869, Murex iron founders from 1917) but has disappeared, as has the small hamlet which grew up around the former ferry across the Thames.

ST HELEN AND ST GILES. A complete late Norman church with aisles and W tower, a rarity among Essex parish churches, and a building of some sophistication. Built *c.* 1178 by Richard de Lucy, justiciar, who married a daughter of Henry II and was founder of Lesnes Abbey in Kent, just across the river, to which the church passed after his death. Its medieval character was recovered in a sensitive restoration by the Rev. *Ernest Geldart*, 1897–1910. Walls of Essex Septaria and flint rubble. The tower is short and broad with small Norman windows;

the diagonal buttresses are Perp additions. The upper part has C16 brickwork, and brick linings to the belfry windows. An embattled brick parapet was replaced by a plain one in 1959. S porch, aisle roofs and much of the S aisle wall rebuilt by Geldart, but the narrow N aisle still has Norman N and W windows and plain N doorway, the door with an original hinge. Chancel E wall much restored; the upper wall follows the original form: a circular window flanked by two small round-arched ones, the lower windows dating from Geldart's restoration. In the S wall three tall restored C13 lancets, and a late C12 priest's door: two orders with zigzag and nailhead on waterleaf capitals.

6 A rewarding interior. Arcades of three bays with unmoulded arches, on bulky square piers with shafts at the four angles. On the S side these have shaft-rings, indication of a later C12 date. Many-scalloped capitals, continuing from the W respond as a frieze to connect to the tower arch. The chancel arch has an outer order with three-dimensional zigzag, on plain responds. Its awkward shape suggests a later widening. To its l. two pointed C13 wall arches, facing W and S, for an additional altar. Curiously shaped clerestory windows, perhaps C18 enlargements. The chancel has a C15 roof with crown-posts with four-way struts on tie-beams. The form is imitated by Geldart's nave roof.

Foliate head of a pillar PISCINA (S aisle). – Base of ROOD SCREEN *c.* 1500, and ROOD LOFT STAIRS. Near the foot of the stairs unusual GRAFFITO of a ketch at anchor, probably also *c.* 1500. – Chancel SEATING 1901 by *Geldart*, made by *Jones & Willis*. – CHAIR made up from C15 bench ends. – Iron-banded oak CHEST, C16. – Remains of ornamental C13 and C14 PAINTING in the chancel and on the nave N and S and especially W walls, the latter discovered when a W gallery was removed. – STAINED GLASS. E windows and two in S aisle by *Percy Bacon Bros*, *c.* 1898. BRASSES (not on view), lady with butterfly headdress *c.* 1480, small. Civilian and wife *c.* 1500. Both with two shields. Katherine Hollden †1612, inscription and achievement.

OUR LADY OF LA SALETTE (R.C.), Dovers Corner. 1966–7 by *John Newton* of *Burles, Newton & Partners*. Church and presbytery and school next to a C19 parish hall. The church has as a steep steel portal A-frame roof in a diagonal pattern embracing the glazed N entrance foyer front, and a glazed W gable. The interior is a single space with gallery and side chapel. PARISH HALL by *W.C. Mangan*, 1939, converted from a barn.

CEMETERY, Upminster Road North. Chapel 1899, E.E, rose window over five lancets on the front to the road.

JEWISH CEMETERY, Upminster Road North. Enclosed by high walls. Buildings by *Lewis Solomon & Son*, 1937–8. Central hall linked by curving Tuscan colonnades to hall and office.

PRIMARY SCHOOL, Upminster Road South. Gabled wing dated 1872 with bellcote, and tripartite window. Enlarged 1926 and

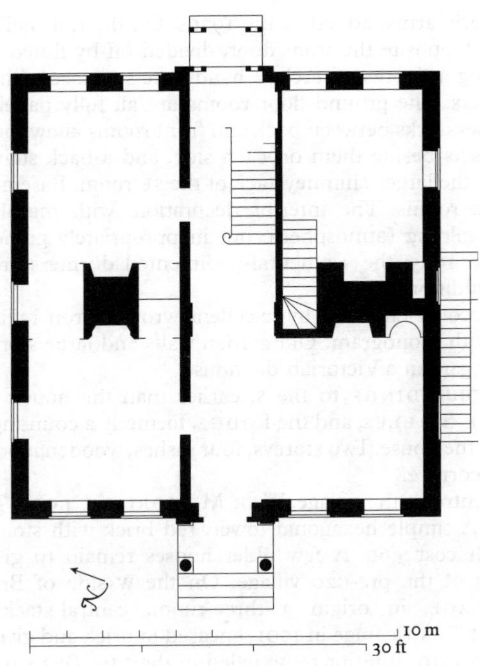

Rainham Hall, plan

later. Long one-storey part with slightly Art Deco detail to the eaves line and over the end window.

RAINHAM HALL, Broadway. Sumptuous though small house of red brick in the tradition of English domestic baroque of the early C18, an old-fashioned design for 1729, when it was built by Captain John Harle, a sea-captain from South Shields who had married a Stepney widow, and was the owner of Rainham Wharf. Restored *c.* 1920 by Colonel H.H. Mulliner, given to the National Trust in 1949. Five by three bays, three storeys divided by brick string courses, above a basement. Parapet above an enriched cornice, not only to front and back, but carried round the sides as well. It breaks forward at the corners and over the slightly projecting centre bays, a liveliness that is accentuated by stone quoins at the corners and by stone keystones to the segment-headed windows. Splendid doorway with open scrolly pediment, carved with deeply undercut flowers, framed by a far-projecting porch on Corinthian columns carrying an entablature and open segmental pediment. Another porch on the garden side. Above it the tall 31
arched staircase window is slightly off centre to match the stair inside, the only external note of asymmetry.

The entrance hall, with black and white marble floor, takes up the r. three bays of the house. Over the fireplace, oval with the Harle arms, added in the 1920s. On the r. a shell-headed niche. Opposite the front door, divided off by fluted pilasters carrying a depressed arch, a handsome staircase with twisted balusters. The ground-floor rooms are all fully panelled. Big chimneystacks between back and front rooms allow for lobbies or closets beside them on each side, and a back stair tucked beside the larger chimneystack of the SE room. Basement with service rooms. The interior decoration, with marbling and faded gilding (atmospheric but inappropriately grand) dates from *c.* 1965; the segmental-pedimented dormers are also a later addition.

Forecourt enclosed by excellent wrought-iron railings and gate with monogram. Old garden walls and large stone vases. In the garden a Victorian doghouse.

OUTBUILDINGS to the S, earlier than the house: COACH HOUSE, STABLES, and the LODGE, formerly a counting house, facing the house. Two storeys, four sashes, wooden modillioned eaves cornice.

In the centre of the village, WAR MEMORIAL CLOCK TOWER, 1920. A simple hexagonal tower, red brick with stone dressings. It cost £60. A few older houses remain to give some feeling of the pre-C20 village. On the W side of Broadway, VICARAGE, in origin a three-room, central-stack house, bought for a vicarage in 1701, encased in brick and given a rear stair in 1710. Interior remodelled in the C19. Two storeys and attic, doorway with wide hood on brackets; lower SE weatherboarded extension.

REDBERRY HOUSE, No. 29 Broadway, was associated with a wharf behind. Exterior of *c.* 1800, doorcase with fanlight; earlier inside. At the back an oriel window looks out over a yard with early C19 coach house and stables. Then THE ANGEL, rebuilt 1906, roughcast above brick, replacing a one-storey inn. To its NW a fragment of the creek has been preserved in landscaping of *c.* 2002. On the E side of Broadway, S of the intrusive Tesco, a more ambitious pub, THE BELL, *c.* 1900, with half-timbered gable and boldly coved cornice over an angled porch. NE of the churchyard UPMINSTER ROAD SOUTH starts with Nos. 2–8, a picturesquely irregular group of timber-framed cottages of *c.* 1700.

To E and N of the village several buildings on ancient sites.

SOUTH HALL FARMHOUSE, Wennington Road. Possibly late C16, hall and cross-wing, attractively brick-cased in C18 style. One of the manors mentioned in Domesday Book.

Off the road N to Hacton in Berwick Pond Road, on another ancient manor site, BERWICK MANOR COUNTRY CLUB, a C17 timber-framed farmhouse with three-room plan and central stack. Restored after a fire. Now rendered and with stucco porch. Early C19 stables. Further N the late C18 gate and piers come from the demolished Rainham Lodge, an C18 house on the estate.

W of GERPINS LANE, garden wall of *c.* 1700 from the manor house of Gerpins.

DAGENHAM PUMPING STATION, Dagenham Road. Built as a substation of the South Essex Water Co. *c.* 1910. Handsome Italianate, with heavy cornice and round-headed openings. ENGINE HOUSE and BOILER HOUSE, chimney demolished. Converted to offices, with exterior well restored.

On RAINHAM MARSHES, a bird sanctuary since 2000, ENVIRONMENT CENTRE, by *van Heyningen & Haward* for the RSPB, 2003–5. A sensitive lightweight design, timber boarded and on stilts, making use of solar power and recycled rainwater.

ROMFORD

Romford is the largest town within Havering and the borough's commercial centre. Until the C19 it was a dependant of Hornchurch. Although its position on the London–Colchester road may have given it a significance during the Roman occupation it only developed as a town in the Middle Ages. The village probably grew up close to the River Rom (in the SW part of the town known as Oldchurch) where there was a chapel in 1147, but by 1247, when Romford received permission to hold a market, the settlement was focussed along the main road. A new chapel was built *c.* 1410 (rebuilt 1850) on the N side of the market place, which continues to be the town's centre today. Surrounding the town were agricultural estates and manor houses, the most prominent of which, Gidea Hall, lay to the E of the town close to the hamlet of Hare Street. All but one, Hare Hall (*see* p. 194), were demolished by 1960, their estates long since consumed by suburban development. That process began in 1839 with the opening of the Eastern Counties Railway (the line was extended to Brentwood a year later), transforming Romford from Essex market town into London commuter suburb. Estates of housing sprang up to E and W of the centre followed by commercial and industrial expansion, in particular for Ind Coope's brewery. Suburbanization, in common with so much of East London, grew apace after 1890, most notably for the Gidea Park Garden Suburb but less memorably elsewhere. Romford Urban District, formed in 1900, was expanded to include the rural villages of Havering-atte-Bower and Noak Hill in 1934 and became a Borough three years later. Romford's decline as a market town began with the closure of the cattle market in 1958, followed by a comprehensive plan of 1965–70 by *F. Chadderton*, the Borough Planning Officer, which enclosed the town centre within the tight embrace of a ring road and redeveloped much of the central area for a shopping precinct. Since then, Romford's role has been to provide an ever-expanding shopper's paradise, strong enough to resist the threat of the out-of-town mega-malls of the 1980s and since.

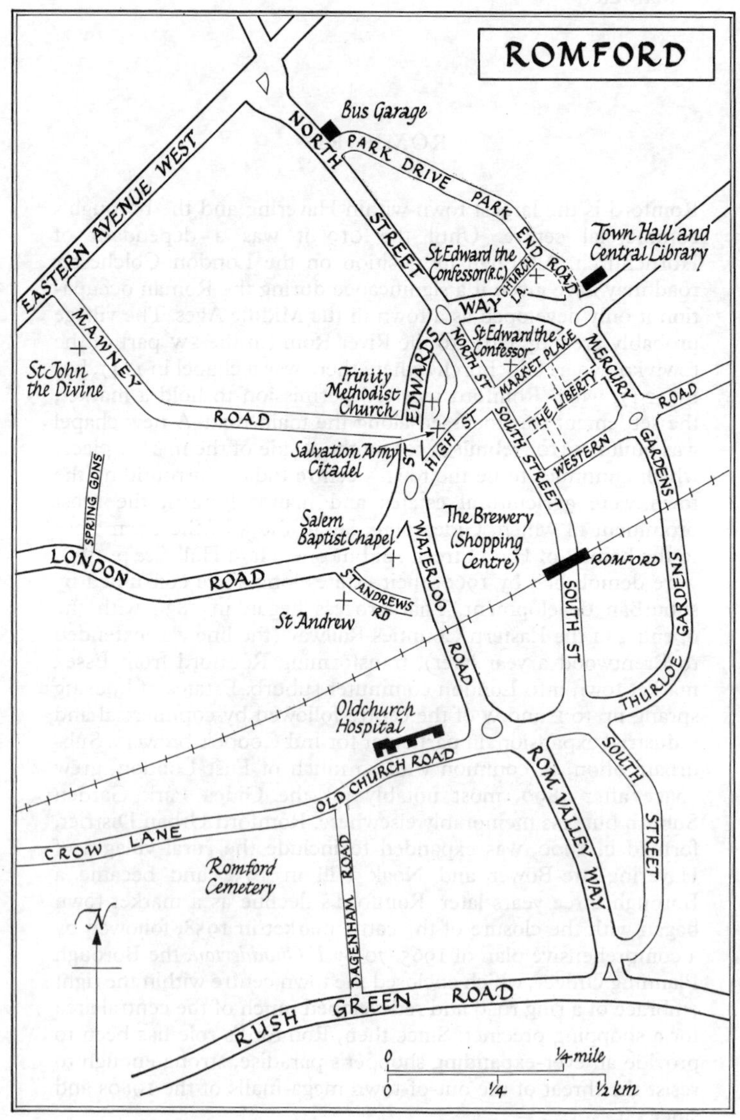

ROMFORD
Bus Garage
EASTERN AVENUE WEST
NORTH STREET
PARK DRIVE
PARK END ROAD
Town Hall and Central Library
St Edward the Confessor (R.C.)
CHURCH LA
WAY
MAWNEY ROAD
St John the Divine
St Edward the Confessor
NORTH ST
MARKET PLACE
MERCURY
ROAD
THE LIBERTY
Trinity Methodist Church
ST EDWARDS
HIGH ST
SOUTH STREET
WESTERN
GARDENS
Salvation Army Citadel
SPRING GDNS
Salem Baptist Chapel
The Brewery (Shopping Centre)
ROMFORD
LONDON ROAD
WATERLOO ROAD
ST ANDREWS RD
St Andrew
SOUTH ST
THURLOE GARDENS
Oldchurch Hospital
OLD CHURCH ROAD
ROM VALLEY WAY
SOUTH STREET
CROW LANE
Romford Cemetery
DAGENHAM ROAD
N
RUSH GREEN ROAD
0
¼ mile
0
¼
½ km

RELIGIOUS BUILDINGS

ST ANDREW, St Andrew's Road. 1861–2 by *John Johnson*. Built for the working-class district of New Romford with support from the Ind and Coope brewery families. Ragstone, Dec detail, a small W spirelet and octagonal NE vestry. Very tall nave; chancel arch and S arcade with quatrefoil piers and moulded capitals, aisleless N side with taller windows. The chancel is embellished by four corbels with angel musicians. A High Church tradition was established by 1900 and many of the original C19 fittings remain.* Stone FONT with foliage carving, PULPIT linked to low stone SCREEN with open ironwork *c.* 1893; carved REREDOS. Painted panels of 1915 on the altar frontal. STAINED GLASS. Major E window, Dec tracery with highly coloured window of 1993. Transfiguration, in an effective graphic style with much hatching on light colours. The C19 upper lights with evangelists and St Peter and St Andrew survived war damage. N aisle windows, †1878 by *Westlake*, †1883, seems to incorporate an older piece. Octagonal vestries by *E.D. Lewinston* of Brentwood. The CHURCH CENTRE, St Andrew's Road, was built on the site of the National Schools of 1843.

ST EDWARD THE CONFESSOR, Market Place. 1849–50 by *John Johnson*, replacing a chapel consecrated in 1410.† Large and ambitious, built of ragstone, a tower porch with tall spire on the S side facing the market place. Some of the building materials came from the colonnade of Nash's Quadrant in Regent Street, pulled down the year before. *The Ecclesiologist* was critical, describing it as 'bristling with gable-crosses, copings, gurgoyles, cornices and ridge-crests'. 'Fussy enough to impress' was Pevsner's comment. Five-bay nave, aisles, chancel and Lady Chapel, all separately roofed, in the ecclesiological manner. Two N vestries, 1885. Elaborate Dec tracery, the clerestory with spherical triangles. Spacious interior with alternating arcade piers (quatrefoil and concave octagonal); foliage capitals. W gallery. Reordered 1976 with nave altar; new moveable seating 1988. STAINED GLASS. E of the S doorway by *Lavers & Westlake*, 1891. MONUMENTS. Sir Anthony Cooke of Gidea Hall, tutor to Edward VI, †1576, and his six children. Alabaster and marble. A very handsome broad tripartite composition with Corinthian columns, pediment over the centre with arms above. Husband and wife kneeling before a prayer desk in the centre, two sons and four daughters in the side parts. Attributed to either *William* or his son *Cornelius Cure*. – In the porch two incomplete monuments: Anne Carew †1605, semi-reclining effigy, head propped up in elbow, and her

* Plans for reordering by *Fergusons* of Chelmsford, 2003, with nave altar and reduced number of pews.

† *E. Blore*'s plans of 1840 for a new church at the other end of the market place were begun in 1844 but aborted for lack of funds.

brother Sir George Hervey †1605 and wife (figures in store), with Corinthian columns.

ST JOHN THE DIVINE, Mawney Road. An unusual Byzantine and classical-inspired design, begun 1927 to a scheme by *W.D. Caröe*, who built the sanctuary. A large basilican church was intended, but the rest was completed in 1932 to a simplified plan by his partner *Herbert Passmore*. N chapel 1948, choir vestry 1966–8. The W wall, replacing a temporary one, is by *Laurence King & Partners* 1979. The church is of brick with tiled heads to the arched windows; a tower rises over the chancel (its top added 1980). The well-lit white-plastered interior borrows elements from London City churches. Stone Tuscan columns carry a heavy straight entablature and concrete barrel vaults pierced by clerestory windows. The five-bay aisled nave has a central cross axis of barrel-vaulted transepts with tripartite N and S windows. Above the chancel the surprise of a dome on pendentives, lit by windows in the tower.

ST MICHAEL AND ALL ANGELS, Main Road, Gidea Park. 1938 by *J.J. Crowe* (*Crowe and Careless*), and unfortunately playing no particular role in the garden suburb. Red brick, Neo-Tudor. Nave, chancel and aisles under a continuous roof. S chancel chapel divided from the S aisle by a tall, square tower with louvred and shingled roof, a typical Crowe feature. Projecting S porch. (Plain interior, four-bay Neo-Perp arcades with a pointed, timber-lined vault.)

ST EDWARD THE CONFESSOR (R.C.), Park End Road. A good group of church, former schools and presbytery. Of some significance as one of the first post-Reformation R.C. churches in South Essex. The church, replacing a building of 1852, is an early work by *Daniel Cubitt Nichols*, 1856. The major donor was the twelfth Lord Petre. Ragstone, with late C13 tracery, and a prominent timber turret over the nave. Inside, an aisleless nave under a scissor-truss roof, and a narrow, lower chancel with a smaller version of the same. N chapel toward the W end, added 1934, when the W gallery of 1917 was rebuilt and the chancel roof panelled. Octagonal stone FONT. – Carved stone REREDOS by *Boulton & Harris*, given by Agnes Clifford, sister of Lord Petre, with high pinnacled canopies over scenes of the Nativity and Deposition, flanked by figures of St Edward the Confessor and St Agnes. – ALTAR FRONTAL with Crucifixion. – Other FURNISHINGS of 2000.

SCHOOLS of 1891 by *George Sherrin*, a secularized version of the church. PRESBYTERY more overtly Domestic Tudor, coursed ragstone with coped gables and cross-windows.

Plans in 2004 by *Anthony Delarue Associates* for flats and community hall at the rear along St Edward's Way. Very ambitious: the hall like a Wren church, including a tall spire and Baroque towers at the corner of the flats. It could be very effective.

Former SALEM BAPTIST CHAPEL, London Road. 1847, replacing an earlier building erected contemporary with the development of this part of Romford. Two shades of stock brick and stucco. Good proportions. Central dooway with stucco pilasters; over it an Egyptian-style window.

TRINITY METHODIST CHURCH, Angel Way. 1888. Schools, 1899. Extended 1923 and 1936. Broad front of red brick with Perp windows.

UNITED REFORMED CHURCH, Western Road. 1965. Polygonal, red brick, spirelet lantern. Halls at rear.

SALVATION ARMY CITADEL, High Street. 1967 by *Ernest T. Lipscombe*. Tall, two-storey polygonal building for Sunday school, with coloured glass and concrete fins. Rectangular hall, with staggered street frontage.

ROMFORD CEMETERY, Crow Lane. Opened 1871, with a pair of identical Gothic ragstone chapels linked by an arch. Only one is still in use, both of exceedingly plain design inside.

MAJOR BUILDINGS

TOWN HALL, Main Road. 1937 by *H.R. Collins* and *A.E.O. Geens*, marking the graduation of Romford to Borough status. Plain square modern building with entrance projection asymmetrically placed. Flat roof, unmoulded window frames and heavily raked joints to the pale brickwork. Not very distinguished and economically detailed. Plain but attractive interior, with a marble-faced stair rising to a broad landing, slightly Scandinavian in feel. Small council chamber, arranged like a courtroom with councillors' chairs in a horseshoe and public gallery on one side as if for a jury. In common with schemes of this date, this was to have been the first stage of a planned civic centre including an unbuilt Assembly Hall. Brown brick rear extensions.

CENTRAL LIBRARY, St Edward's Way. By *H. Conolly*, Essex County Architect (project architect *N.P. Astins*) 1962–6, and forward-looking for its date. Three storeys, concrete frame faced with stone panels, the bands of glazing set between thin mullions. Semi-open ground floor, part of the upper floor carried on stilts. Good detailing to the ground floor entrance, including a serpentine walled cloakroom, faced in mosaic, which carries the Librarian's office above. The children's library projects out behind a circular glass wall. Airy double-height lending library and galleried reference library on the first floor.

OLDCHURCH HOSPITAL, Oldchurch Road/Waterloo Road. Expansive general hospital built around the core of the former ROMFORD UNION WORKHOUSE, whose yellow brick, two-storeyed buildings face Waterloo Road. 1838–40 by *Francis Edwards*, a long façade of twenty-five bays, with bowed centre. Smaller ranges of workshops behind originally enclosed a central court containing the cruciform workhouse (dem. *c.* 1993); a standard design of this date, which allowed for segregation of inmates and their observation from the master's house in the centre. A separate gate lodge and two-storey block of similar date and style served the casual wards. The Infirmary, built to the E in 1893 by *Frank Whitmore*, has been engulfed by C20 additions, tacked on in *ad hoc* and thoughtless fashion.

N of the workhouse, a former Nurses Training School and residences of 1924–36 by *Harrington and Evans*. An ambitious and well-ordered group in a late Baroque style with projecting mansarded wings, a channelled stone work, segmental pediment, *œil-de-bœuf* windows and garlands. The site is to be redeveloped for housing once the new hospital for Barking, Redbridge and Havering opens in 2005, on the adjacent Oldchurch Park site to the S. A PFI scheme by *Jonathan Bailey Associates* for Catalyst Healthcare.

PRIMARY SCHOOLS. – MAWNEY PRIMARY SCHOOL, Mawney Road. 1896 by *Charles Bell*. Nicely scaled with pitched roofs, tile hanging, two-bay arcaded entrance. – CROWLANDS INFANTS SCHOOL, London Road. Former Elementary Schools by *Cecil Sharp* and *A.S.R. Ley* in an attractive Arts and Crafts style. The Infants building, 1908, has a porch beneath an octagonal tiled roof with sprocketed eaves, and classrooms flanking a gabled hall with a central cupola. Immediately behind, Junior School of 1912, many gabled with a central hall. – CLOCKHOUSE PRIMARY, Clockhouse Lane of 1936 is weatherboarded and pantiled, something of a rarity for *Essex County Council*. GOBIONS PRIMARY, Havering Road, of 1952–3, is a typical design by *H. Conolly*, the Essex County Architect.

ST EDWARDS (C.E.) SCHOOLS. Founded as a charity school in 1711, with new buildings erected in Market Place in 1728. Its successor is the PRIMARY SCHOOL, Havering Drive, of 1976, a series of flat-roofed classrooms, linked by lantern-roofed halls. The COMPREHENSIVE SCHOOL, London Road by *J. W. Hammond*, 1964, is utterly conventional for its date. Five-storey curtain-walled teaching block in the centre, the lower blocks grouped informally around.

FRANCES BARDSLEY LOWER SCHOOL, Heath Park Road. Built as Romford County High School for Girls in 1909–10 by *Hickton and Farmer* of Walsall. Renamed in 1974 in honour of its founder, a prominent campaigner for education of girls. Wrenaissance, red brick with stone dressings and a square central cupola over the hall and wings with moulded arched hoods. Richly carved decoration around the entrance.

ROYAL LIBERTY SCHOOL, Upper Brentwood Road. Opened 1921 as the County High School for Boys. The core is HARE HALL, the most ambitious surviving mansion, or more correctly villa, of Romford. By *James Paine*, 1768–9 for John Wallinger, a cork and stone merchant of Colchester. W facing front, ashlar-faced, five-bay, two-and-a-half storey centre connected by, originally one-storey, short colonnades to a pair of low two-storey pavilions – what Muilman's *History of Essex**

*Vol. 6, 1772.

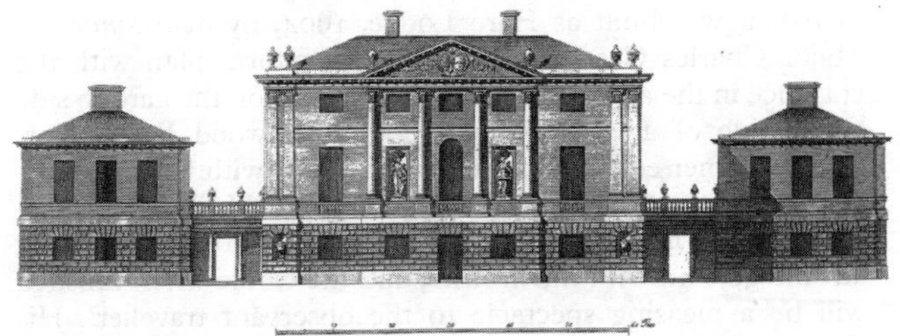

Hare Hall, Romford. Elevation by James Paine, 1768–9

described as 'an elegant house of stone, with proper offices on each side'. The house has a crisply rusticated ground floor. The semicircular Tuscan porch is an addition of 1896 by *Howard Seth-Smith* who remodelled the house for the Castellan family and moved the family rooms to the ground floor, a reversal of the Palladian ideal. Above this, as Paine liked it, a giant attached portico of Adamish columns and a pediment decorated with coats of arms, separating this elevation into his preferred 1-3-1 rhythm. At the angles of the house coupled giant pilasters, also a characteristic Paine device (cf. Heath House, Wakefield). The rear of the house is in plain brick but obscured by later additions. Across the ground floor *Seth-Smith* added a pair of garden rooms, with slightly bowed fronts, and a vestibule behind a Doric colonnaded porch. This is done with some sensitivity, not so the deplorably crass 1960s upper storey. The house now forms the N block of a quad created in 1929–30 by *John Stuart*, Essex County Architect. His Neo-Georgian classroom blocks harmonize effortlessly, with seven-bay arcades around the garden, *œil de bœuf* niches and a large hall on the S side, with a big coffered ceiling. Good stained glass war memorial window.

Inside, few decorative embellishments are preserved. The low entrance hall has its original black and white chequered floor, but a patterned plaster ceiling of the 1890s. To either side are rooms that originally served as cellars and domestic offices linked to the kitchens etc. in the pavilion wings. Directly behind, in the centre of the plan, a central top-lit oval staircase with iron balustrade rises to first floor. Gallery above. Enfilade of rooms along the W front, the former Dining Room (NW, now offices) with plaster panelling and Adamesque (C19?) fireplace, the Breakfast Room in the centre (Headteacher's office) and the former Drawing Room (SW). This occupied the depth of the building until subdivided in 1896. Lugged window architraves and a large cornice with acanthus leaf moulding. The attic floor contained the C18 bedchambers. – SOUTH LODGE, 1898. Queen Anne, with sleepy-eye dormers in red tiled roofs; half timbering and tapered chimney. Two ranges around a courtyard. South Drive was the original approach to the house, now built up with interwar houses. At the N end, HARE PARK

SCHOOL was built as Hare Lodge, 1904, by *Seth-Smith* for Major Charles Castellan, a curious cruciform plan with the entrance in the angle and wings splayed out on the garden side either side of a veranda. In Upper Brentwood Road, Nos. 450–2, former estate cottages (dated 1868) with blowsy doorcases. In 1772 Wallinger was described by Muilman as 'disposing the grounds about [the house] to the greatest advantage, and with much taste; and the whole when finished will be a pleasing spectacle to the observant traveller'. His designer for this enterprise was the landscape gardener *Richard Woods* (see also Raphael Park) who provided such curious features as a 'petrified' stone tree and cork tree in recognition of Wallinger's trades. Nothing much remains of this, the result of encroachment after 1921, except for the drained basin of a pond, with the overgrown and much damaged relic of a cascade and a brick and flint bridge. The line of Woods' 'Elysian walk' laid out along the E side of the estate, is also still discernible.

Former RAILWAY FACTORY, Elvet Avenue. An early and rare group of engineering and engine repair works. 1841–2 by *John Braithwaite*, the Chief Engineer of the Eastern Counties Railway. The railway opened in 1839 with a line between Mile End and Romford, extending to Brentwood by 1840. This required purchase of the Hare Hall estate and its villa (*see* Royal Liberty School), where Braithwaite lived for the following years, the open land ideal for construction of the railway's works. It comprises two large parallel brick ranges and a smaller power house with a chimney. The N range, closest to the railway, has a two-storey front block with central archway (for engines to enter the building), this bay distinguished by a raised pediment and a square tower, originally with a clock. Single-storey former workshops at rear, the interior originally divided by rows of cast-iron columns and lit by ranks of round-arched windows. The broader S range, with a two-storey centre and single-storey pavilion blocks, contained the engineering works. A notably early example of a galleried workshop, its cast-iron internal frame (the columns drain the roof gulleys) dividing the interior into an aisled space with galleries on four sides. The works were moved to Stratford in 1847 (*see* p. 239), the buildings here easily adapted for production of sacks and tarpaulin. In 2004 surrounded by anonymous new flats and being converted to housing. The ECR also built two rows of terraces for its workers along Elvet Avenue, cleared 1963–5 for a group of large towers by *Romford Metropolitan Borough Council*.

CORONATION GARDENS, Main Road. An unsatisfactory setting for the town's war memorials: the consequence of a chequered history. In 1844 it was to have been the site for the church (designed by *Blore*), but when that was instead built in Market Square this became a burial ground. Its chapel was demolished in 1953, the date of its present naming. The dull but large WAR MEMORIAL, *c.* 1921, was placed here in 1970 to make way for the ring road. Later memorials are equally mild and inadequate in this setting. C19 gravestones have been placed at the back out of sight (and mind?).

RAPHAEL PARK, Main Road. Opened 1904. The C18 landscaped gardens and parkland of Gidea Hall (demolished 1930). Acquired by Sir Herbert Raphael in 1897 in advance of the laying out of Romford Garden Suburb (*see* Perambulation 2). The W parts were donated to Romford in 1902, the remainder acquired by the Council. The late medieval Hall was rebuilt in 1720 by Sir John Eyles, Sub-Governor of the South Sea Co. who 'also formed the lake and greatly improved the park' and of the formal gardens of this period survives the SPOON POND at the N end of the park, now drained and with tennis courts laid out along its length and terminating in a circular basin with a children's playground, surprisingly effective in its own way. This straight channel was aligned precisely with the short N–S axis of the house, no doubt a tremendous formal effect when viewed from within. The estate was sold in 1745 to Richard Benyon who enlarged the park *c.* 1776 and began to deformalize it, perhaps with the advice of *Richard Woods*, who, like Repton, was a tenant of the estate and had worked at Hare Hall (*see* Royal Liberty School). The lake was widened from a straight canal to one of serpentine form, and *James Wyatt* employed to design a new BRIDGE to carry the main road to Romford over its S end. Three elliptical arches with oculi. Now known as Black's Bridge, after the next owner, Alexander Black. At the main entrance, a LODGE, *c.* 1904 rather in the style associated with the later Garden Suburb. Minor municipal additions, e.g refreshment house and bandstand.

N and S of Raphael Park, undeveloped land on the Gidea Park estate was acquired to create a 'green lung' between Romford and Havering-atte-Bower, the vision of Thomas England, local trader and councillor. The first addition was LODGE FARM PARK, S of Main Road, acquired in 1927. RISE PARK (Golf Course), N of Eastern Avenue, was acquired in 1937, linking up with BEDFORDS PARK, sold to Romford Council in 1933 (*see* also Havering-atte-Bower).

PERAMBULATIONS

1. Town Centre

The centre of Romford is entirely embraced by the ring road and into this tight pen have been poured almost all its commercial and office buildings, principally exemplars of the drearier styles of the last thirty years. There are almost no buildings of before the C19, little sense of relationship between town centre and residential areas and none with its public buildings, which are strung out with very little effect along Main Road to the E.

Visitors, by train or car, thus find themselves confined to the shopping streets, but this is Romford's *raison d'être*. It has no less than five shopping centres, developed over the course of the C20. In spite of this the traditional street market continues to prosper and is still held, as instructed in 1247, on Wednesdays. For the student of consumerism and its buildings, from covered market to corporate mall, there is much to divert one; for the architectural traveller commensurately less.

The characteristic feature of Romford is its spacious MARKET PLACE, about 365ft long and 50ft wide. At its W end, until 1933, stood the court house and gaol; now its only old relics are on the N side with St Edward's church (*see* above) and close around it a few individual buildings of distinction. First, opening onto the churchyard, is CHURCH HOUSE. Suggestions that it may have been a chantry house seem unfounded; most likely it was a merchant's house, possibly one of three identical gabled and jettied fronts along the Market Place. It claims, plausibly, a date of *c.* 1480, though possibly altered in the C16, when it became an inn. Jutting upper floor on the W side, also originally over the street (massive dragon beam inside) but underbuilt with two canted bays in the C19(?). (Inside, a two-cell plan, with close studding. The room towards the street has exposed beams and evidence for medieval shop windows. C17 staircase. Crown-post roof and wainscotted upper room.) W of the church, HSBC was built by *W.E. Westgate*, 1905, for L.F. Makins, grocer, and still proudly wears his badge. Brick and Bath stone, Free Renaissance with bay windows along the first floor and a gable with diagonal colonnettes. Then THE LAMB, an old inn rebuilt in 1852–3, in plain fashion with two pedimented gables.

In 1954 Pevsner noted 'much rebuilding is likely in the Market Square area in the next few years'. This came to pass with depressing inevitability,* typified on the N side by T.J. HUGHES, 1960 by *North & Partners*, a big store with textured-tile facing. The S side is of even less quality and ever greater scale e.g. the grim-faced DEBENHAMS. The N side of Market Place is being redeveloped in 2004 with a scheme by *Maslen Hennan Brenshaw Partnership* for flats above shops to replace partly the 1930s covered market, RUMFORD SHOPPING HALL. The E end of the square is to be closed by a three-storey 'market hall' of early C18 type with an attic roof and solid cupola, flanked by two-storey asymmetrical wings, the southern of which will have an open, arcaded ground floor. This will finally reinstate the necessary sense of enclosure which was removed in the 1960s by the destruction of Laurie Hall. It was intended as a court house but never used as such; Pevsner described it as having 'a portico on the upper floor and debased classical detail'. Erected by John Laurie *c.* 1850

*Demolished since 1954: No. 33, early C18, five bays, segment-headed windows, doorway with pediment on carved brackets and two other early C18 houses.

as part of his development of the E end of town with smart semi-detached villas arranged around Laurie Square.* Romford has had thirty years to repent.

W of the Market Place, on the N side of HIGH STREET stands the GOLDEN LION, perhaps Romford's best building. A three-storey early Victorian frontage with original lettering hides a C16 house with jettied wing along North Street. Inside, moulded beams and on the upper floor, the remains of a window indicate that this was a galleried inn. Notwithstanding this, plans to demolish in the 1950s were only just averted. The remaining interest is concentrated on the S side. THE FORD AND FIRKIN† was originally The White Hart, rebuilt in 1896 in English Domestic Revival style with a symmetrical upper floor of big bay windows and dormers breaking the eaves. The adjoining frontage served the former ROMFORD BREWERY; founded by Edward Ind at the Star Inn in 1799, but rebuilt along High Street for Ind Coope & Co. in 1850–2, by *Charles Dyson*. This work survives in part, an irregular, gabled group with later alterations above ground floor of arched windows linked by stone imposts, beneath pairs of oculi, of varied date and style, mostly of stock brick. Archway to the brewery yard, with (replica) gates decorated by wrought-iron hop vines. The brewhouse stood behind the offices to the l. Three-bay front, probably late C19, with broadly spaced windows and a large doorway. The Rom flows beneath the brewery site. Inset into the wall is a stone from the old bridge 'Georg ii Regis Anno Imperii Decimo Reaedificatus', rebuilt in 1738. Closed in 1993, the buildings converted with big stripy brick blocks of flats behind.

The rest of the 26-acre site was cleared for THE BREWERY complex of supermarket, multiplex cinema, leisure complex and shops by *Chetwood Associates*, 2002. Two immense blocks along the S side, clad in profiled aluminium sheeting and accessorized by brightly coloured clip-on detail. Similar free-standing canopies are scattered across the site, a modish and slightly garish motif. Lower block to the E, with roof car park served by a ramp sleekly wrapping around the totemic 180ft chimney, built in 1974 of lozenge-section pre-cast concrete units. Close to the entrance from London Road is a copper boiler from the brewhouse, by *R. Ramsden & Son*, 1850.

The junction of High Street and Market Place with North and South Streets is marked by commercial buildings of the inter-war years. The banks were quick to colonize sites where display could be achieved: LLOYDS TSB, NE, red brick, Bath stone and lotus leaf columns, has an extravagant panelled ceiling with acanthus leaf moulding over the banking hall. The CO-OPERATIVE BANK, SE, built as the National Provincial Bank

*Mostly demolished in the 1960s. A final relic, a small, three-bay Italianate in Park End Road, was demolished in 2004.

†The Angel, 'a narrow house with a pretty Gothick oriel filling the width of the upper floor', has been demolished.

in 1932 by *Palmer & Holden* is crisply detailed in Portland stone with anthemion leaf detail over the corner entrances and arcaded ground floor. The SW corner (Prudential Buildings) was rebuilt in comparable classical style in the late 1930s. Next to it, the immense frontage of NATWEST, with extruded mullions in highly polished black and grey granite shows the way banks could accept the precepts of post-war Modernism without ceasing to be conservative.

The rest of SOUTH STREET is a poor affair. It was widened in the 1930s and took precedence over the High Street as the principal commercial street from that time. The first event in that story was the building in 1935 of the QUADRANT ARCADE, an L-plan arcade linking South Street and Market Place behind the street frontages, with a ballroom on the upper floors. Cheap Art Deco in brick (a good horizontal roof light with curved mouldings survives inside), typical of the low quality of frontages along the rest of the street. What once was good has been compromised: e.g. the former POST OFFICE (W side), now Brannigans, of 1913 by the *Office of Works*, its Beaux Arts detail fighting to be appreciated above the crassly rebuilt ground floor. Further on to the Station the stock depreciates further with the TIME & ENVY nightclub, conversion of the Havana of 1936 by *Kemp & Tasker*, one of the better firms of cinema architects. Another characteristic piece of Moderne style is KINGSLEY FURNITURE, the former Times Furnishing Warehouse of 1936. Small windows between close-set mullions and broad pilasters with the company's 'T' logo emblazoned above the parapet. Unrecognizable beside it, an 'improved' pub of the 1930s, once in a hygienic modern style with curved and glazed walls. Almost opposite, at the corner with Eastern Road, former GAS SHOWROOMS AND OFFICES (now a bar) of 1937; pompous Neo-Georgian with doorways beneath segmental-headed pediments on acanthus leaf consoles. Flank of round-arched windows.

On the E side of SOUTH STREET, STEWARDS WALK, with tacky clock tower, is a mock-Victorian arcade of the 1980s, following the line of the 1930s Romford Arcade. It connects to THE LIBERTY, originally an enormous redevelopment of 1967–72 by *Bernard Engle & Partners* to create an open shopping precinct on the backlands behind South Street and Market Place, contemporary with the ring road. To WESTERN ROAD, large podium blocks faced in white mosaic with paired uprights between pre-cast window panels with sloping reveals, and an office tower (Lambourn House). The open precinct, entered from Western Road and Market Place, has been elegantly enclosed as a curved mall beneath a glass roof, supported on tree-like columns, part of extensive and highly successful refurbishment in 2002–3 by *Chapman Taylor and Partners* with *Arup*, structural engineers. The broad and spacious mall links under the ring road to LIBERTY TWO, opened 1990, showing that period's delight in shiny surfaces and 'traditional' forms: in this case walls of grids of mirror glass and a tall glass dome over its galleried atrium. Serving these, big multi-storey car parks, towards the ring road, revamped and overlaid with curtains of steel mesh.

S of the railway are big interwar shopping parades, e.g. STATION PARADE and MILL PARADE (in Victoria Street) of a type seen all over the suburbs. Close by, at the junction of South Street and the ring road, are the former premises of PAGE, CALNAN & CO., timber merchants (now a restaurant). Deco style, *c.* 1933 with lovely mosaic work to the parapet.

2. *W and N of the Town Centre*

Romford expanded W in the 1840s between London Road and Waterloo Road for the development of New Romford, a district of small-scale artisans' cottages, built on the site of cavalry barracks established during the Napoleonic Wars. The church of St Andrew (q.v.) was erected in its midst in 1861, but the area largely redeveloped post-war by Romford Borough.

In LONDON ROAD, THE SUN public house, probably by *A.E. Sewell* for Truman's, turning his hand to the big scale and more inviting style of a suburban pub, rich with good Neo-Regency-cum-Art Deco detailing, its sun motif liberally emblazoned. The former Salem Chapel (q.v.) is the only 1840s survivor in the neighbourhood. Further W, close to Crowlands Infant School (see above), ROMFORD STADIUM was opened in 1931, a reminder of the huge working class enthusiasm for greyhound racing in London of that period. Its stands are later and of little consequence. N of the road off SPRING GARDENS is an industrial enclave with AB Electronics, a remarkable factory of *c.* 1959–60 by *J. W. Hammond* of Romford for Colvern Ltd, one of a number of electrical engineering firms established in the prewar suburbs. Four storeys with patterned aggregate cladding to the ends and nascent curtain walling with once colourful yellow panels beneath the windows. Low projecting entrance carried forward on piloti and a fascinating rooftop pavilion under an angled concrete roof. Much further W along London Road's N side, beyond the built-up area, are earlier relics. CROWN COTTAGES are one of the many improved dwellings built on Crown lands after the clearance of Hainault Forest in the 1850s. Typically straightforward, brown brick with the 'VR AR' badge. The handsome CROWN FARMHOUSE, in the fields immediately N, is earlier. C16 behind a Georgian refronting in white render. The tall and muscular cluster of chimneystacks is a clue to its true age. Barns and late C18 brick granary.

NORTH STREET was the main route from Romford to Havering-atte-Bower and Collier Row. Nos. 96–102 (E side) is late C17 in part, timber-framed with a tile-hung gable, recently discovered garderobe overhanging the street, much altered on this side. The big event here is the BUS GARAGE. Built 1953 by *Thomas Bilbow*, Architect to the London Transport Executive. A considered asymmetrical composition in buff brick with a slightly curved stair-tower breaking the long horizontal lines of two-storey offices. Those on the l. have windows inset between columns, the floors divided by pale blue spandrels. Plain walls of the rooflit garage beyond, entered from the side. Furthest N of the W side Vine Cottage, Nos. 215–17. 1799. Brick, three bays.

3. Gidea Park (*)

Gidea Park, the Romford Garden Suburb begun in 1910, is neither as large, as well-known nor as well-regarded as the other artistically-minded garden suburbs in London. Indeed, surprisingly, it found no mention at all in Pevsner's *Buildings of Essex*. Its uncelebrated status is in part deserved, for its conception and execution were less complete than might have been hoped: there is for example none of the focus provided at Bedford Park by the church and inn, nor the consistency of style and sense of communality found at Hampstead. Architecturally, there is nevertheless much worth consideration and the designers of the houses comprise most of the influential figures of the late Arts and Crafts movement.

The story of its development begins with Gidea Hall, a late medieval mansion and residence of the Cooke family during the C16 and C17, but rebuilt in the C18 and set within formal land-
p. 21 scaped gardens (*see* Raphael Park). The house stood N of Hare
Street, the main road from Romford, where a small hamlet was
p. 33 home to *Humphry Repton* in the early 1800s. Sir Herbert Raphael
M.P., who had leased 90 acres for a golf course only a few years earlier, acquired the Hall and its estate in 1897. In 1909 he formed Gidea Hall Development Co. (later Gidea Park Ltd), in association with Charles McCurdy and John Tudor Walters, with the express intention of developing a garden suburb, along the lines of Hampstead, in the area around Gidea Hall between the golf course and Raphael Park.

Plans for its layout, possibly by *Parker & Unwin*, were published in 1909. *Lutyens* was also commissioned to produce the layout for the area E of the golf course but this was subsequently put out to competition, won by *Gibson & Dann* but never executed. Clearly indebted to Hampstead and Letchworth, it made much of a series of formal squares and avenues and placed the church in an axial arrangement with Gidea Hall. By contrast the plan of the completed section is essentially a grid, with the line of each of the roads deliberately varied to prevent uninterrupted straight avenues and retaining existing landscape features. Almost immediately after work began in 1910 a further 60 acres S of Main Road were acquired to secure access to the newly

*This account is indebted to the publications of the Gidea Park Society and notes prepared by Roderick Gradidge for the Twentieth Century Society.

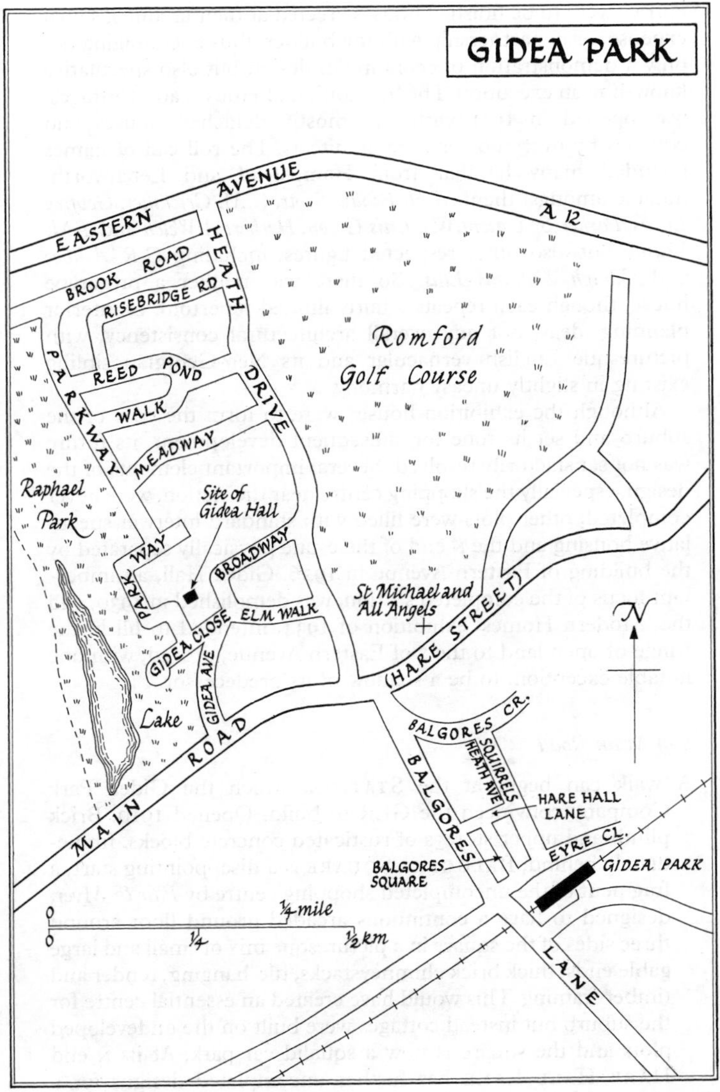

opened station at Squirrels Heath. In this area the planning was more formal but in both parts the overall provision of space was decidedly generous so that along the side roads, the houses are set well back and spaced out from their neighbours, an effect only slightly diminished by later infill.

The design for the houses was also organized as a competition with two classes: £500 houses and £375 cottages. The aim was a commercial one and unlike earlier competitions, the submitted entries were to be finished houses erected at their architect's own expense, or in partnership with the builder, thus encouraging not only a demonstration of economy in design but also speculative know-how in execution. The 'Exhibition of Houses and Cottages' was opened in 1911 with 140 mostly detached houses and cottages by over 100 separate architects. The roll-call of names included many familiar from Hampstead and Letchworth, notable amongst them *M.H. Baillie Scott, C.M. Crickmer, Geoffry Lucas, Parker & Unwin, W. Curtis Green, Herbert A. Welch* and *T.M. Wilson* but also other respected figures, including *C.R. Ashbee* and *Clough Williams-Ellis.* So there was neither a prototype house, though each repeats a fairly limited repertoire of interior planning ideas, nor any overall architectural consistency, with picturesque English vernacular and its Neo-Georgian sibling existing in slightly uneasy harmony.

Although the exhibition houses were to form the core of the suburb and set its tone for subsequent development, its future was not satisfactorily resolved. Several important elements of the design, especially the shopping centre near the station, were never completed; other plots were filled with standard interwar speculative housing and the N end of the estate physically separated by the building of Eastern Avenue in 1926. Gidea Hall, an important focus of the completed section, was demolished in 1930, and the 'Modern Homes' exhibition of 1934, intended to fill in the fringe of open land to the S of Eastern Avenue, proved, with one notable exception, to be a shadow of its predecessor.

S of Main Road

A walk can begin at the STATION, which the Gidea Park Company convinced the GER to build. Opened 1910. Brick plinth and upper storeys of rusticated concrete blocks. Immediately behind, BALGORES SQUARE is a disappointing start, a fragment of the uncompleted shopping centre by *Fair & Myer*, designed to have a continuous arcaded ground floor around three sides of the square in a picturesque mix of small and large gable ends, thick brick chimneystacks, tile-hanging, render and timber framing. This would have created an essential centre for the suburb but instead cottages were built on the undeveloped plots and the square is now a squalid car park. At its N end HARE HALL LANE has further uncompleted designs for a terrace of shops and flats: a notable late work by *C.R. Ashbee* and *Gripper & Stevenson* consciously pursuing the Queen Anne Revival of twenty years before, with subtle variation. High end block with hipped roof, big cornice and a satisfying variety of windows: arched, rectangular, circular and Venetian with tiled surrounds. To the fore, a narrow semicircular oriel with a band of decoration including the eponymous hare. Entrance to the flats is at the rear, the elevation evocative of Ashbee's Chelsea work. The composition is rudely divided in two by Hare Court, a completely spiritless block of flats of 1937. E in SQUIRRELS HEATH AVENUE, *Ashbee* and *Gripper & Stevenson* also collaborated on a formal design for houses around an elliptical green in the centre of the road. Only the E side was completed: a group of four Neo-Georgian houses, with corner cottage blocks joined to a pair of set back semi-detached houses by arcaded links. Paired chimneystacks. The W side was built in conventional speculative Moderne fashion in the 1920s. On the same side, No. 26 by *E. Willmott* has big ungainly labels, but the neat Nos. 28 and 30 by *Ernest Mager* have pretty panelled doors beneath bracketed hoods. Paired chimneystacks feature again at *Gripper & Stevenson*'s No. 3. The same firm's No. 5 is another variation on C18 revival with two-storey porch entrance in Gibbsian surround.

BALGORES CRESCENT is mostly infill of the interwar years, mainly vernacular except Nos. 1–3 with Crittal-type curved bay and corner windows.

BALGORES LANE has lesser examples of the 1911 exhibition houses on its E side (Nos. 17, 32 and 33, 35, 39, 47, 49, 51 and 57), intermingled with the standard suburban mix. At the N end, the grey and yellow brick BALGORES HOUSE of the 1850s (now Gidea Park College), served as refreshment rooms for the exhibition. Almost next to it, and still standing in 1911, was *Repton*'s cottage. From here he depicted both his well-known view of the beggar at his gate and his own idealized response. The little plaque on Lloyds Bank can scarcely make up for such an unnecessary loss.

Main Road and North

MAIN ROAD was the historic Hare Street. Some way off to the E stands the parish church of St Michael and All Angels (*see* above) of 1937, its remoteness from the suburb meaning it plays no role in the townscape, in the way that the plans of 1910 intended. Closer to the junction are a few reminders of the old hamlet including THE SHIP, one of the only ancient buildings in this area but, ironically, masked behind a C20 façade of applied half-timbering. Inspired no doubt by the vernacular, if not the Arts and Crafts ethics, of the suburb. The centre, with hipped tiled roof, is probably C17 but the offshoots to either side are later (C18?) additions. Inside, what appears to have been a lobby entry house with a central stack and single room to either side. That on the l. has an immense Tudor-arch fireplace and close-studded partition with a window, presumably the original outer wall. Panelling. On the S side of the road, also possibly C17 but extensively altered, Nos. 198–200. Then, the first of the suburb buildings, although completed after the exhibition in 1912. Shops with flats above; a varied gabled roof line, with steep pitch roofs, diagonal stacks and oriel windows. On the N side, No. 75, timber-framed with panels of pargetting in the upper floor, was built allegedly for the 1910 Japan–British Exhibition at White City and placed here in 1913 as the estate office. Atrocious underbuilding of its jetty, and extension at the rear in bright red brick.

HEATH DRIVE leads into the suburb proper, the tone strictly

kept to half-timbering, but on a big scale at Nos. 3, 5 and 7 by *Bunney & Makins*, then a pair of houses on the other side by *T.M. Wilson*, with colour-washed gables, catslide roofs and huge triplets of diagonal chimneystacks. Indeed, the scale of houses in this part is rather larger than the standard: neither those by *Bunney & Makins*, nor Nos. 3, 5 and 7 ELM WALK by *W. Curtis Green*, for example, were exhibition houses. Further N, the houses along Broadway have gardens backing down to the former fishponds of the Gidea Hall estate.

Beyond these in HEATH DRIVE former entrance gates and section of wall, dated 1750. Gidea Hall stood to the W. The first of the representative, if not the most superior, exhibition houses begins with No. 41 HEATH DRIVE, by *Parker & Unwin*. Double-height bows to the front light the principal rooms. Along the S flank of the double-depth drawing room, panels of Art Nouveau stained glass. (Inside, moveable partitions and inglenook fireplaces.) The house was designed with all its furniture. Then No. 43 by *Curtis Green*, with diaper brickwork on the gable end.

MEADWAY has some of the smaller cottage houses sold for £375, e.g. Nos. 34 and 36 both by *C.M. Crickmer*. Facing on the N side, No. 27, by *Van't Hoff & Maxwell*, with a cruciform plan, central chimneystack (in fact a pair divided internally by a passage) and the upper storey contained in the roof. Beautifully detailed tile work and forward sweeping eaves. On the other side, the prize-winning No. 16 by *Philip Tilden*, a square two-storey cottage with short, hipped roof wings designed for box room and stores. No. 7, by *Percy Houfton* is Neo-Georgian, red brick banded with grey. No. 4 by *Gripper & Stevenson* has a central two-storey porch, and arched entrance with tile work surround.

PARKWAY provides the W boundary of the suburb with views over the park and its pond (*see* Raphael Park). Unsurprisingly, these plots were reserved for the more expensive Class I houses. Nos. 46–62 were all exhibition houses. No. 54, Neo-Georgian by *Geoffrey Lucas*, took 1st prize, a surprise given its style. Three bays beneath an immensely steep roof with big end stacks and box dormer. No. 42 by *Fair & Myer* has a beamed ceiling and inglenook.

Parallel with Meadway, REED POND WALK has an overgrown central green and perhaps the best variety of houses. Along the S side of the green No. 32 stands out. By *Cecil A. Sharp*, nicely composed with a long range to the street, the junction with its cross-wing marked by a thick chimney stack. Colour wash and brick mixed with tile work and even Ham Hill stone. On the other side of the Green, No. 23 by *Clough Williams Ellis* bucks the vernacular trend with whimsical Regency Revival of tiled quoins, a pantiled platform roof and shuttered windows. Its horizontality was originally offset by a pair of chimneystacks. Then at the bend in the road, an attractive ensemble of three houses. No. 29, by *Edwin Gunn*, square with a steep hipped roof peppered with gablet dormers. Good solid doorcase.

Designed for 'the typical suburban family with one servant', the chimney is thus set off to one side to allow for a bedroom in the centre of the attic floor. Old English at No. 31, by *Reginald Longden*, then No. 33, another excellent design by *Parker & Unwin*, here with double-height canted (rather than bowed) bay windows with thick stone mullions and casements, a late Voysey motif. Moveable panelled partitions allowed for the subdivision of the main room on the street side. On the S side, Nos. 36 and 38 by *M.H. Baillie Scott* make a non-identical pair, 87
linked by a low wall, unfortunately differentiated by repainting. No. 36 has pargetting of grape vines etc. Inside, firegrates with similar motifs 'modelled by Mr Bankart'. These were amongst the furnished houses and included 'wall hangings and other fabrics specially made by the Deutsche Werkstatten',* cottage furniture by *Heal's* and other pieces designed by *Scott*. In the front garden is the base of a small sundial, also by *Scott*, an octagonal shaft faced in colourful geometric tiles, distinctly German Arts and Crafts in style.

Returning to Heath Drive, and by way of contrast, Nos. 45–8, four large Neo-Georgian houses by *Ronald P. Jones*, an able practitioner of the emerging style. The centre pair are set back slightly, but otherwise identical with brick corner quoins, large eaves cornice and pedimented doorcases.

The last of the 1911 houses are in Risebridge Road but further N are the houses built in the 1934 'Modern Homes' exhibition, along Brook Road and Eastern Avenue. Initiated by Raphael's son, the ambition was the same – economically built, architect-designed houses capable of challenging the speculative competitors and demonstrating the benefits of rational design – but the achievement fell short of 1911. The one clear exception is the prize-winning No. 64 101
Heath Drive by *Francis Skinner* and *Tecton*, one of their first works and built for only £900. Two storeys of reinforced concrete, L-shaped with the service range overlooking the street and the main rooms towards its garden. Strip windows on the garden side and a sun terrace carried on pilotis, all distinctive modernist motifs. The terrace has been partly built over and the garage truncated by the addition of a room. The house was designed for repetition along Heath Drive to form a continuous white-walled frontage, a daring concept and one alive to ideas of new forms of social housing rather than the one-off villa. But it is the latter concept that characterizes the other houses, e.g. along Brook Road where the houses are closer in spirit to the homegrown modern of Crittal's Silver End tradition than the full-blooded Modernism of Tecton. No. 18 by *Minoprio & Spencely* was flat-roofed with continuous glazing p. 82
in the upper floor and a glazed bay window. Facing Eastern Avenue, Nos. 328–30, a pair of semi-detached houses by *Holford, Stevenson & Yorke* (the first house design by *F.R.S.*

* Baillie Scott had commissions from the Werkstatten at this time so these may well have been executed to his own designs.

Yorke), designed as a rectilinear concrete box with slightly projecting upper storey on steel columns covering the kitchen entrance. Of the remaining houses, some brick some concrete, none have escaped 'customization' by later owners with Neo-Georgian porches, plastic windows and even pitch roofs: something which has scarcely affected the earlier houses. This speaks of the reluctance to accept the modernist style of the mid-C20 as appropriately 'domestic', but also perhaps the timidity with which it was introduced to the suburbs.

UPMINSTER and CORBETS TEY

Upminster lies in the SE part of the borough, divided from Hornchurch by the Ingrebourne river. Before the C20 it was just one long village street running E–W along the high road (St Mary's Lane), with the church in the centre, and a separate hamlet, Corbets Tey, to the S. Gentry houses and farms were scattered over open countryside. The railway came in 1885, but suburban growth only began after 1901, proceeding rapidly in the 1930s as the large estates came onto the market. The population doubled between 1931 and 1951, but expansion was halted by the green belt and the Second World War. So suburbs and rural life coexist, with the happy survival of a complete windmill, a scatter of farmhouses and barns, and relics of buildings and landscaped grounds from the larger houses.

ST LAURENCE, St Mary's Lane. Remarkable C13 tower, rubble-walled, four-square and sturdy, with clasping buttresses only at the foot. Short leaded and shingled spire, an early Essex example. Inside the first floor is carried on two massive posts standing against the middles of the N and S sides and a big beam. Arch braces connect post and beam. Braces on corbels carry the beams along W and E walls. A fine piece of C13 construction. All the timbers are straight, and are connected by secret notched lap joints, a type which Cecil Hewett considers was developed in the earlier C13. DOOR to tower with C13 ironwork. The rest of the church was much rebuilt in 1862–3 by *W. G. Bartleet*, retaining the C14 N arcade with short quatrefoil piers, moulded capitals and double-chamfered arches. The old chancel became part of the nave when choir and sanctuary were built in 1928 by *Sir Charles Nicholson*, who also added the S chapel and a Lady Chapel beyond the older Gaynes chapel on the N side. Nicholson's work is characterized by reticent dying arches; the elaborate foliage capitals on the N side of the chancel are perhaps reused from the C19 chancel arch. SE vestries of 1937.

SCREEN to the N chapel, incorporating C15 fragments. STALL, N chapel, with moulded rail and one poppyhead. (PULPIT carved by *Violet Pinwill* of Devon.) FONT C15, octagonal, with quatrefoil panelling, from the chapel at Upminster Hall. STAINED GLASS. E window, 1927, standing figures below Renaissance canopies. N aisle: good armorial, dated 1630 and other fragments, mostly C16. BRASSES. One of the better collections surviving in Greater London. Several of the C16 and C17 ones are palimpsests (i.e. with remains of older brasses on the back).* Elizabeth Dencourt †1455, female effigy (husband missing); civilian *c.* 1530; Nicholas Wayte †1545 and wife, figures and long inscription. Lady holding a book, *c.* 1553, possibly Elizabeth Latham. Geerardt D'Ewes, in armour, 1591, traditional pose with dog at his feet, unusual at this date. Grace Latham, 1631, small figure.

MONUMENTS. Elizabeth Dugdale †1701, small tablet with broken pediment. – Many memorials to the Branfills of Upminster Hall and the Esdailes of Gaynes. – Andrew Branfill †1709; demi-figure on large tablet against marble back. – Champion Branfill †1792, draped tablet and urn. – Sir James Esdaile †1793 attributed to *R. Westmacott*. – James Esdaile †1812 by *Sir Richard Westmacott*. Very plain, sarcophagus-shaped. – (Brydges Robinson Branfill. Inscription *by Eric Gill*, 1906).

ST JOSEPH (R.C.), Champion Road. 1939 by *Marshall & Archard*. Dark brick precisely detailed, with rectangular framed windows and a cornice; octagonal turrets flanking a steep W gable. Plain interior with cruciform piers and straight-headed openings to narrow aisles, a shallow barrel vault over the nave. Stone-faced apse; reredos with projecting canopy, the reticent mood contrasting with the more recent brightly coloured abstract STAINED GLASS to N and S. W window, also abstract. STATUE of St Joseph by *Joseph Cribb*, above W entrance.

TRINITY UNITED REFORMED CHURCH, Station Road. A Congregational church of 1911 by *T. Stevens* of Bournemouth. Sober Perp, stone, with tiny corbelled-out corner pinnacles to the front and side gables. A tower was intended at the SE corner, a W gallery also remained unbuilt. A spacious, unified interior with arcades on four clustered columns, well lit by tall side windows, and complete with original furnishings. Organ installed 1912. STAINED GLASS. Grand window commemorating the local developer W.P. Griggs, †1920 by *Percy Bacon*. The Nonconformist virtues of Education, Industry, Religion and Benevolence are represented by four angels. MONUMENTS. Several tablets in the entrance lobbies: Rev. George Clayton †1862, classical with urn. – James Nokes †1838, a founder of the Independent chapel which preceded this one (*see* perambulation 1). At the back, halls of 1914–23 by *W.D. Key*, given by Griggs, extended 1947 and 1992.

* See illustrations in W. Lack, H. Martin Stuchfield and P. Whittemore, *The Monumental Brasses of Essex*, 2003.

UPMINSTER CEMETERY AND SOUTH ESSEX CREMATORIUM, Ockendon Road, Corbets Tey. The latter of 1956–7, enclosed by red brick walls. Formal gardens around a central L-shaped complex with two chapels and a smaller conical-roofed Chapel of Meditation, all surrounded by Tuscan colonnaded verandas.

PUBLIC LIBRARY, Corbets Tey Road. By *H. Conolly* of Essex County Council, 1962–3. Two storeys, with the original touch of a full-height inset entrance below a roof punched with circular lights (refurbished in 2004).

COOPERS' COMPANY AND COBORN SCHOOLS, St Mary's Lane. 1974 by *Laurence King & Partners*. Informally composed flat-roofed blocks, concrete framed with a dirty brown brick face. Functional and tasteful, but lifeless. In the centre, the principal accent is the theatre, rising up behind a sheer aggregate-panelled wall bearing the foundation's arms. Close to the entrance and inside, a good group of foundation stones associated with earlier schools, which began as two separate charitable foundations in the East End. The Coopers' Company School was founded first, in 1536 in Ratcliffe; the Coborn Girls School in Bow in 1701. Amalgamated in 1891. Inside the foyer, the school's lineage and its buildings are shown in one of two large MURALS. The second, by *Glyn Owen Jones*, a former pupil, depicts the intellectual and sporting activities of the present school. Brightly coloured and slightly super-realist. On the first floor, stained glass WAR MEMORIAL WINDOW, 1948, with the Coopers' arms (reset from the earlier school at Bow). Fine display of the tools of the coopers' trade. Recent extensions for MUSIC SCHOOL, pale brick with cut away corners, 2000.

UPMINSTER DEPOT, Front Lane. 1958–9 by *A. W. Manser*, Chief Mechanical Engineer (Railways) London Transport and *T.R. Bilbow*, Architect, for the District Line. High-Tech Signalling Control Centre, 1994.

UPMINSTER STATION. 1885. An intact example by the London Tilbury & Southend railway. A pleasant irregular group; two-storey station house on the l. and a one-storey building on the r., both of red brick with blue brick dressings to their angular windows.

PERAMBULATIONS

1. The centre of Upminster

STATION ROAD, which links the station to St Mary's Lane, the old high road, developed in the earlier C20 as the shopping centre for the new suburbs. A terrace with quirky bay windows in a debased Mannerist style bears the date 1907 and the brewery name of Taylor Walker & Co. The showpiece is ROOMES DEPARTMENT STORE, a rare survival of the once common suburban phenomenon of the independent family-run store. James Roome, who founded a successful drapery store in Upton, West Ham in 1888, moved his family to Upminster in 1907. The store here was established by his son in 1927. The main building on the W side of Station Road, with façade of cream tiles, dates from 1937, incorporating the 1927 building in its three-storey centre, with an extension of 1974 to the N, heightened 1989. Further N is the furniture store, on a site acquired in 1939 but not built until 1952–3. Its style marks a shift toward a pre-war Scandinavian modernism, with brick exterior and framed windows with zigzag glazing. Opposite (undaunted by competition from Lakeside), is a bland new furniture store of 2001, red brick and gabled.

W of Upminster Church in its large churchyard at the SW corner of the crossroads is the former RECTORY, now offices, an attractive H-shaped house of *c.* 1735, whitewashed brick with segment-headed windows. An old-fashioned plan, with single-depth centre; good staircase (three balusters to the tread) between the rooms on the E side. Plain fielded panelling in the NE room.

Further W along ST MARY'S LANE, the CONVENT OF THE SACRED HEART OF MARY occupies HILL PLACE, a house of 1790 reconstructed in 1871–3 for Temple Soanes in serious domestic Gothic by *W.G. Bartleet.* Diapered brick and mullioned windows, the gabled S front with asymmetrical bay windows; the N front facing the road with a staircase tower, and timber porch of *c.* 1900 in front of a jettied and pargetted entrance bay. Well preserved interior: a spacious, atmospheric stairhall with plenty of Gothic detail, hooded fireplace, carved corbels and robustly detailed mahogany open-well staircase. The landing window has stained glass by *Morris & Co.* designed by *Burne-Jones*: five standing musicians, and roundels of women; more roundels and figures of Lancelot and Elaine in a side window. The SW room (used as a chapel) has carved dado panelling, the SE room an elaborate plaster ceiling. Additions from 1927 when the house became a convent.

Adjacent to the W is SACRED HEART OF MARY GIRLS' SCHOOL. Main building of 1930–9 by *Marshall & Archard*: Neo-Georgian with an East Anglian or Dutch tinge. Hall range with shaped gable over the entrance, projecting two-storey classroom wing with mansard roof. Brick toothing shows a matching wing was intended. The post-war additions are at the back, of the 1950s, 1970s and 1990s.

Facing onto the main road is a former Independent CHAPEL (destined for use by the school). Built 1800 by James Nokes of Hunt Farm, enlarged 1827, refronted 1847. Rendered front, Tuscan porch, pediment with semicircular window.

N of St Mary's Lane, standing back, is Upminster's most unexpected treasure, a WINDMILL of 1802–3, a smock mill com- 34
plete with sails, boat-shaped cap and fantail, a beacon for miles around, the only survival of the many windmills that were once in the area. Built by James Nokes. The octagonal timber and

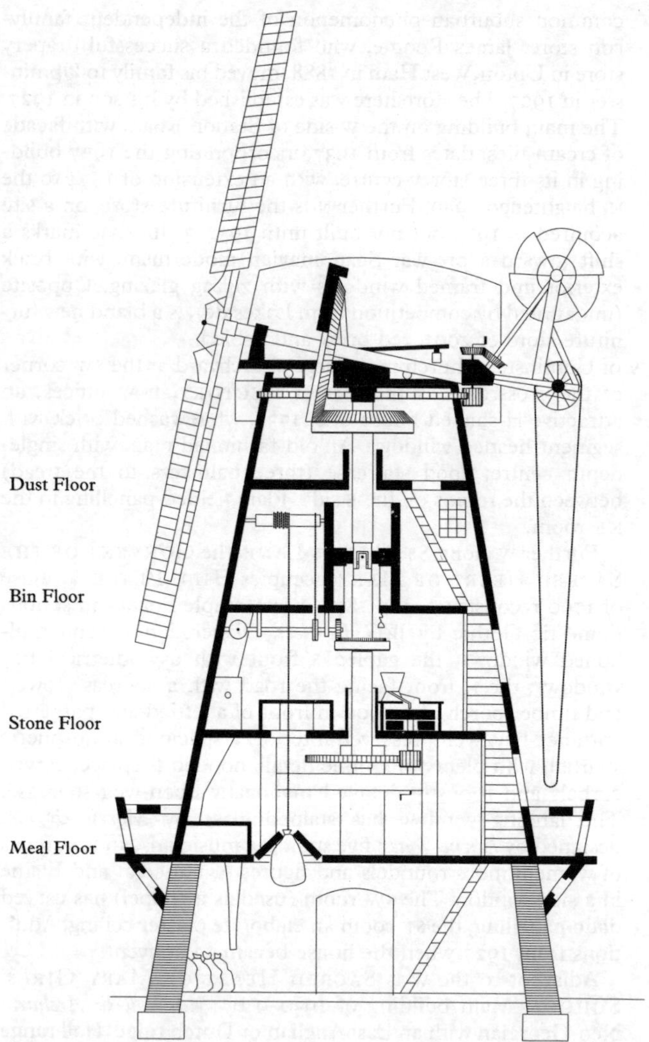

Windmill, Upminster, section

weatherboarded upper part stands on a brick base There are three pairs of millstones; and a fourth probably added *c.* 1850. The highly sophisticated original wooden machinery survives, a great rarity. Additional power was provided by steam in 1811, an early example, with a boiler house behind, but this has disappeared, as have the mill house and outbuildings, demolished by the County Council in 1960. The mill, which was working until 1927, has been preserved through much local effort.

Essex CC were owners from 1940 followed by Havering from 1964; it was opened to the public in 1968. New sails were installed in 1970 and the fantail rebuilt in 1983. The present Trust hopes to restore the mill to full working order.

Lower down on the N side, toward Upminster Bridge, INGREBOURNE COTTAGES, a plain two-storey row built as a poorhouse in 1750 and extended in 1787. Converted to six cottages after the Romford Union workhouse was built in 1836.

There is less to see in St Mary's Lane E of the church. On the S side, CLOCK HOUSE, formerly stables, remains from NEW PLACE, built *c.* 1775 for Sir James Esdaile, a City banker of Huguenot origin who was Lord Mayor in 1777, and the principal C18 landowner in Upminster. Red brick. The main front of 1-3-1 bays with pediment faces W and is difficult to see. The clock cupola now faces N to the road, with clock dated 1774. The mansion, which had a grand ballroom used for public assemblies, lay W of the stables; it was demolished in 1924, after much of the estate had been developed for housing by W.P. Griggs (*see* below) from 1909. Part of the grounds, with a substantial MOAT, remain as a public park. On the N side of the road, Nos. 265–7, originally a pair of hipped-roof weatherboarded cottages; early C19 doorcase with (restored) hood on brackets.

2. *Hall Lane and North*

On higher ground to the N of the station was the Upminster Hall estate, which W.P. Griggs developed as a select garden suburb from 1906, on the pattern of Emerson Park, Hornchurch, although not quite so spaciously laid out. His architect was *George Verlyck*. As at Emerson Park, many of the houses are detached (Waldegrave Avenue, Engayne and Ashburnham Gardens etc.). They sport a range of vernacular and Norman Shaw-derived trimmings, and are noticeably superior to those S of the railway. The showpiece was No. 28 HALL LANE, a long frontage with three bay windows.

UPMINSTER HALL, E of Hall Lane, was retained as the clubhouse for the golf course laid out in 1927. A substantial timber-framed house, probably of the C16, with gabled and jettied cross-wings, some old timber-mullioned windows, and stacks with diagonal shafts. Much altered, especially the S wing, and with many rear additions, but the RCHME report a roof with cambered tie beams over the hall range, and queenpost truss roof to the N wing. Two-storey porch with carved bargeboards to a jetty on moulded beam. The porch opens into the former screens passage. The adjoining ground floor hall has a C16 ceiling with moulded beams. The enriched cornice and plain fireplace perhaps date from an early C18 remodelling, as does the good early C18 stair off the NE corner (somewhat rearranged), with three different balusters to each tread. It rises to a curved landing with coved cornice. Further N a two storey range with C18 sashes.

HALL BARN, E of Hall Lane. Opened as an agricultural museum in 1976 operated by the Hornchurch & District Historical Society. On an impressive scale. Timber-framed, thatched and weatherboarded, with central cart openings. The original weatherboarding consisted of vertical boards, some of which remain. Aisled interior, the aisles carried round the ends. Crown-post roof; tie beams with curved braces, further bracing provided by curved shores at the back of the main posts, a Kentish feature. The mixture of constructional techniques, with the older 'reversed assembly' (aisle plate above the tie beam), used at eaves level but not at the main tie beam level, suggests a possibly mid-C15 date when the estate was owned by Waltham Abbey.

UPMINSTER COURT, on the W side of Hall Lane, by *Charles Reilly*, 1906–8 for A.E. Williams, of Samuel Williams & Son, Dagenham Dock. Now an education centre. A handsome villa on a grand scale, in a free English Renaissance style. Entrance front of red brick, two storeys and dormers with a big, hipped slate roof. Projecting ends of three bays with steep, rendered gables treated as pediments. Giant Ionic columns at the angles. In between, a long one-storey Doric colonnade, balustraded, with three pairs of windows above. The garden front uses the same motifs, omitting the colonnade. Here there is only a central gable, anchored by two tall, slim chimneys. To the N, an attractive group of outbuildings, with clock turret over carriage archway. Walled garden to the S.

Further N a scatter of vernacular buildings remain, still in a rural setting. In Hall Lane, APSE TREE COTTAGES, late C18, timber-framed and weatherboarded. GREAT TOMKYNS, Tomkyns Lane, is a good example of a C15 yeoman's hall house with exposed timber framing; two-storey jettied wings to W and E, the earlier E one with arched braces. (Inside, a full-height hall with original window in the E part, and two service doors at the lower end.) Thatched weatherboarded BARN to the NE, datable to the C13 or C14, aisled, with passing braces to aisles and collar-rafter roof. Unusually, it has a complete set of carpenters' marks which follow a circuit round the building, suggesting the order of assembly.

Other rural survivals include: TYLER'S HALL, Nag's Head Lane, a nice timber-framed and weatherboarded group with early C18 farmhouse and outbuildings; PAGE'S FARM, originally C13, altered and raised by a storey in the C17, timber framing concealed by render. Three-room plan with rear gabled staircase projection. In the room l. of the cross-passage brackets with the date 1663 and initials of the Witham family. The roof has reused older timbers. PARK CORNER FARM, Park Farm Road, has a mid-C18 brick BARN. BRAMBLES, Brambles Lane is a farmhouse probably of the C18. Rendered front, three irregular bays. Three storeys, with three rooms on each floor. Possibly originating as a two-room lobby-entrance house with central stack, the third room being an addition. A lone survival in an area much altered by gravel extraction.*

3. Corbets Tey and South

The principal estate of this hamlet S of Upminster was GAYNES, the largest manor in the parish. The house was demolished in 1930. It dated from 1846, and stood on the site of a Palladian villa built for Sir James Esdaile in 1771 by *James Paine*, who also laid out the grounds. These were largely built up from 1930 with singularly unexciting straight streets of dull houses, but some remnants survive from the later C18. In CORBETS TEY ROAD, LITTLE GAYNES LODGE, probably by *Paine*. Delightful small house with formal Palladian massing: pedimented front and lower flanking wings with half pediments, but enlivened by Gothic detail: a quatrefoil window above a trefoil-headed doorway, and small flanking arched windows. TADLOWS, No. 251, named after a Gaynes head gardener, is a two-storey late C18 house, with mansard roof and curiously quirky double-arched windows with central keystone and intersecting glazing bars. S of Parklands Avenue, PARKLANDS OPEN SPACE preserves part of Gaynes Park with attractive walks beside a serpentine lake, crossed by a BRIDGE with curved approach walls, of brick, rendered, originally with balustraded parapet (to be restored). Large central arch with stepped keystones, smaller blocked side arches. In THE GROVE (invisible from the public path) a FOOTBRIDGE remains at the rear of Nos. 52 and 54, a single-span arch of red brick, formerly rendered; rusticated with splayed voussoirs.

The centre of the hamlet of Corbets Tey is at the junction with Harwood Hall Lane, where HIGH HOUSE faces boldly up Corbets Tey Road. A strangely proportioned frontage of *c.* 1700: three bays and two storeys over a basement, with a very tall central door, partly glazed, with shell hood, flanked by tall windows (9 + 9 sashes). The garden front similar but with simpler doorcase. It looks like an incomplete fragment, but was perhaps just a polite addition to an older house. (Unusually complete original interior, with panelled rooms on two storeys, corner fireplaces to the front rooms, staircase with twisted balusters, and a plaster ceiling in the ground floor front room.) Low timber-framed wing to the E. Opposite, THE OLD COTTAGE, with old tiled roofs, and two former doorcases with pediments.

Along HARWOOD HALL LANE a pleasingly rural group: the OLD ANCHOR, timber-framed, roughcast, of the C18, with C19 Gothic windows and Nos. 1–8, a row of C17 and C18 cottages, Nos. 1, 2 and 3 with exposed timber framing, the rest weatherboarded. Further on, set in its own grounds, HARWOOD

*Details on the rural buildings of Upminster come from research by the GLC Historians (now English Heritage).

HALL (Montessori school). Castellated front with raised central canted bay. Built 1782 by Sir James Esdaile for his son-in-law, George Stubbs. Enlarged *c.* 1840 and given its castellations in 1881.

In SUNNINGS LANE, SULLEN'S FARMHOUSE, a former timber-framed hall house; rendered exterior, early C19 cross-wing. Airfield hangar installed in the 1950s for storing crops. GREAT SUNNINGS is C17, timber-framed and rendered, but externally too restored to reveal its history.

HACTONS, Hacton Lane. A once fine Palladian villa, horribly mangled. Built *c.* 1762–5 by William Braund, Portugal merchant. Five bays; three-bay, projecting, pedimented centre emphasized by quoins, with Venetian window above a porch, flanked by one-storey pedimented pavilions. Converted to flats 1954 with new attic storey.

WENNINGTON

Lonely marshland village with a few houses along the road by the church. The marshes to the S are now a bird sanctuary.

ST MARY AND ST PETER. An appealing rural church; flint and rubble stone exterior with chequerwork parapet, C13 chancel and S aisle, C14 N aisle and W tower. A Norman doorway with three bands of saltire-crosses, reset in the E wall of the S organ chamber, points to an even older origin. Simple whitewashed interior. Thin lancets in the chancel N wall, a wider one on the S side with sedilia below. S arcade of two bays with circular pier and double-chamfered arches, the aisle itself a C19 rebuilding by *Rev. E. Geldart*, having been destroyed earlier. In the nave W wall a lancet looking into, and thus earlier than, the W tower. The tower windows indeed look C14, although its low, unbuttressed appearance is of the earlier Middle Ages. Inside, steep timber tower stairs of primitive construction, difficult to date. There is a bell of 1662 in original frame. N arcade with slim octagonal pier and double-chamfered arches, C14 or C15. Perp chancel arch and chancel roof: tie beams, short, moulded crown-posts with four-way struts; simpler crown-post roof in the nave. STAINED GLASS, E window †1911, Resurrection etc. – MONUMENT. Henry Bust †1624. Small alabaster tablet with father and son at prayer desk. – Flat Jacobean FONT COVER. – Jacobean PULPIT. Next to it, HOURGLASS STAND, wrought iron. – CHEST, C13, of hutch type.

In the churchyard, railed tomb E of the chancel. – Small obelisk to Henry Perigal †1888, geometrician, recording his work on the laws of compound circular motion.

NEWHAM

Newham lies across the River Lea to the E of the old boundary of the London County Council. The borough was created in 1965 from the County boroughs of East Ham and West Ham, both of which were local authorities within the county of Essex. The mutual pride of each ensured that neither could take precedence in the naming of the new Greater London borough in 1965.

West Ham and East Ham had origins in medieval parishes and hamlets which grew rapidly in the C19 at a time when industrialization brought entirely new districts into existence along the Thames and its marshlands. The formation and expansion of the Royal Docks in the C19 and C20 and contemporary growth of London's eastern suburbia led first to the creation of the County borough of West Ham in 1886 and of East Ham in 1901. The C20 was catastrophic for the buildings of both boroughs: bombing in the Second World War destroyed 14,000 homes in West Ham alone and the inexorable decline of the major industries and the docks compounded the gloomy picture. The combined populations of West and East Ham in 1901 was approximately 313,000, in 1951 291,829 and by 2001 was estimated at 237,900. In that time its ethnic identity has been transformed: in the earlier period with Jewish migration from the inner East End and more recently by immigrants from around the world (over 100 languages are spoken in Newham's schools and there are nearly 200 different religious congregations within the borough). To an increasing degree such diversity is making a visible difference to the borough's built environment, evident, for example, in the shopping centre of Green Street. In the last decade of the C20, major opportunities for wider renewal presented themselves, not only with the continuing redevelopment of the Royal Docks (*see* p. 290) and its hinterland, but also in the culturally led regeneration of Stratford. Major changes are promised in 2004 with plans for development of the Lower Lea Valley along the borough's western edge, including the possibility of the 2012 Olympic village and the creation of an entirely new town N of Stratford. This will replace the depressed industrial fringe along the river valley and, perhaps, finally remove the division between London and London-over-the-border.

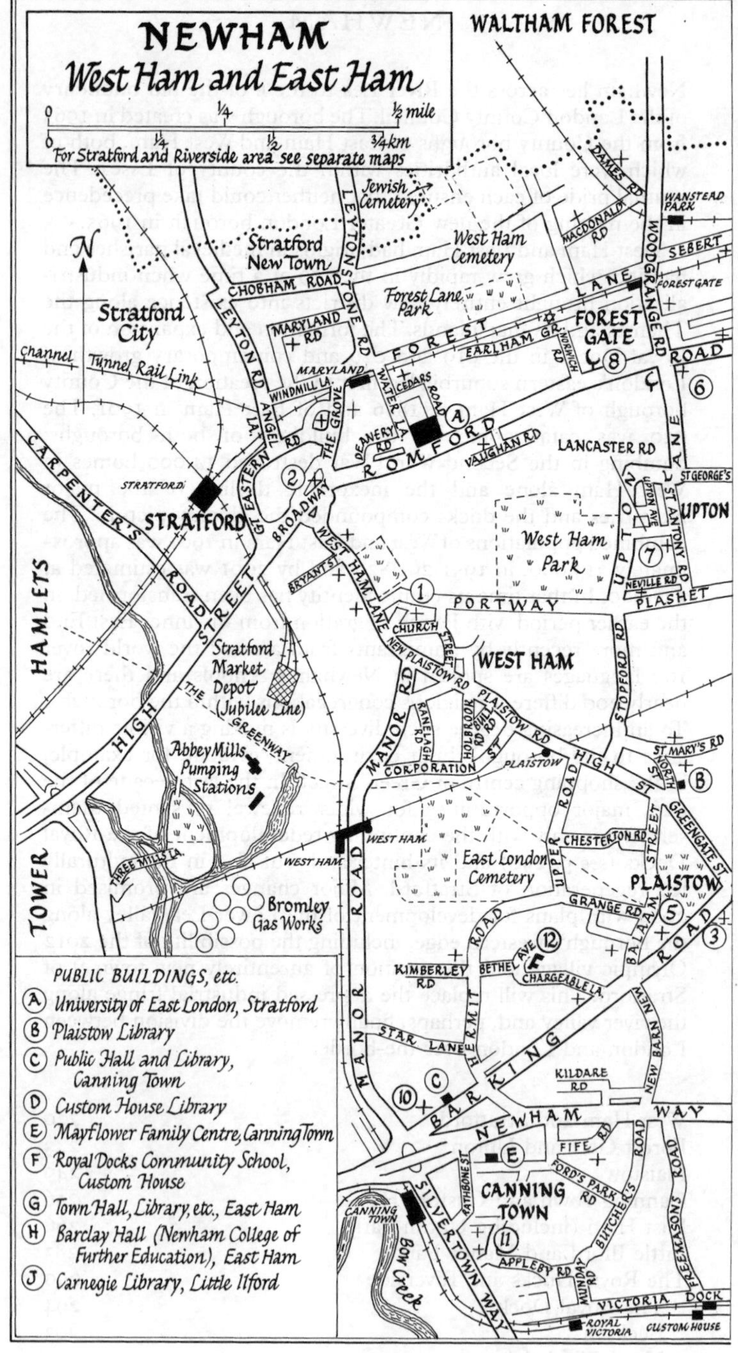
NEWHAM
West Ham and East Ham
0 1/4 1/2 mile
0 1/4 1/2 3/4 km
For Stratford and Riverside area see separate maps
WALTHAM FOREST
N
Jewish Cemetery
Stratford New Town
West Ham Cemetery
CHOBHAM ROAD
Stratford City
Forest Lane Park
MARYLAND RD
FOREST GATE
WANSTEAD PARK
SEBERT
FOREST GATE
DAMES RD
MACDONALD RD
WOODGRANGE RD
EARLHAM GR.
NORWICH
ROAD
Channel Tunnel Rail Link
MARYLAND
WINDMILL LA.
CEDARS
WATER LA.
ROAD
LEYTONSTONE RD
LEYTON RD
ANGEL LA.
THE GROVE
DEANERY RD
ROMFORD
VAUGHAN RD
LANCASTER RD
STRATFORD
STRATFORD
GT EASTERN RD
BROADWAY
ST GEORGE'S
UPTON
UPTON AVE
ST ANTONY RD
UPTON LANE
West Ham Park
CARPENTER'S ROAD
WEST HAM LANE
BRYANT ST
NEVILLE RD
PORTWAY
PLASHET
HAMLETS
TOWER
HIGH STREET
CHURCH STREET
NEW PLAISTOW RD
WEST HAM
STOPFORD RD
Stratford Market Depot (Jubilee Line)
THE GREENWAY
MANOR RD
RANELAGH RD
HOLBROOK RD
BULL RD
PLAISTOW RD
ST
HIGH ST
ST MARY'S RD
NORTH ST
Abbey Mills Pumping Stations
CORPORATION
PLAISTOW
UPPER ROAD
GREENGATE ST
WEST HAM
WEST HAM
THREE MILLS LA.
East London Cemetery
CHESTERTON RD
STREET
PLAISTOW
Bromley Gas Works
GRANGE RD
BALAAM
MANOR ROAD
ROAD
KIMBERLEY RD
BETHEL AVE
CHARGEABLE LA.
HERMIT ROAD
NEW BARN ST
STAR LANE
BARKING
KILDARE RD
NEWHAM WAY
FIFE RD
CANNING TOWN
RATHBONE ST
SILVERTOWN WAY
FORD'S PARK RD
BUTCHER'S ROAD
FREEMASONS ROAD
CANNING TOWN
Bow Creek
APPLEBY RD
MUNDAY RD
VICTORIA DOCK
ROYAL VICTORIA
CUSTOM HOUSE
PUBLIC BUILDINGS, etc.
A University of East London, Stratford
B Plaistow Library
C Public Hall and Library, Canning Town
D Custom House Library
E Mayflower Family Centre, Canning Town
F Royal Docks Community School, Custom House
G Town Hall, Library, etc., East Ham
H Barclay Hall (Newham College of Further Education), East Ham
J Carnegie Library, Little Ilford

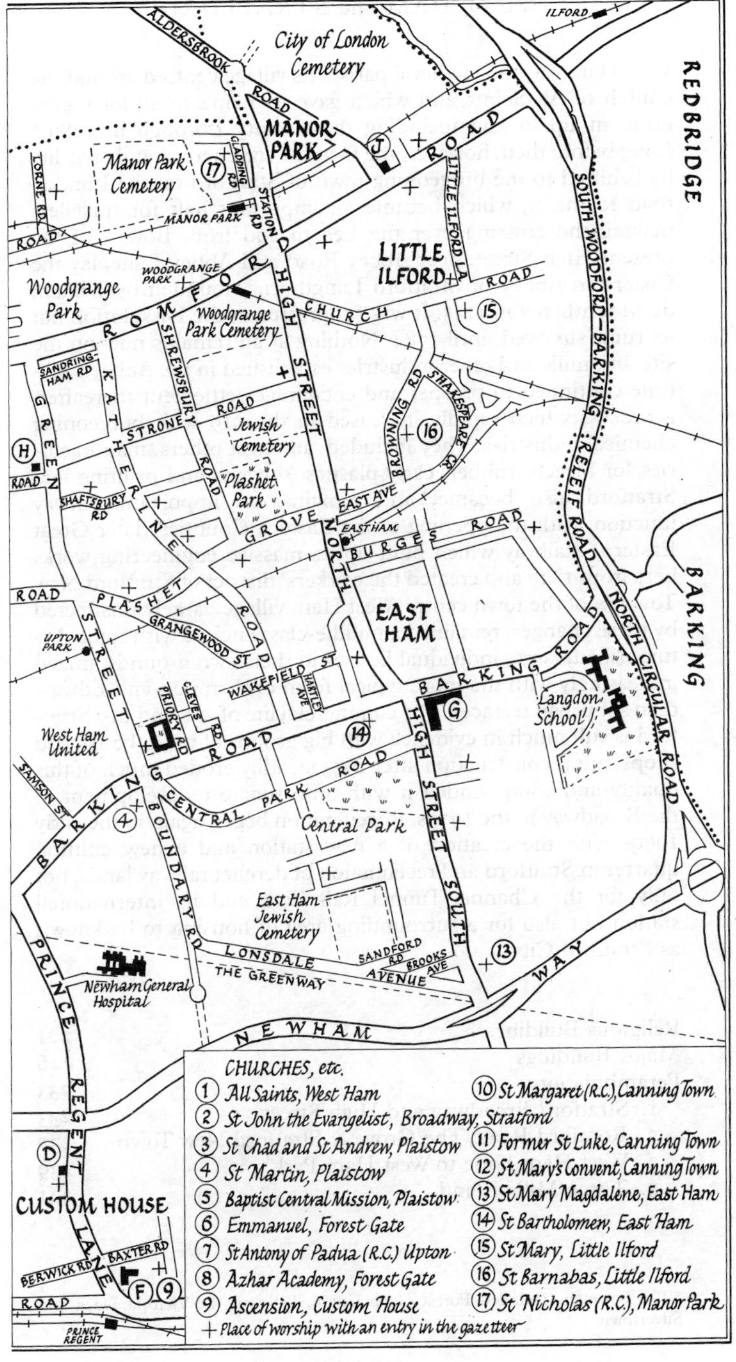
City of London Cemetery
ALDERSBROOK ROAD
ILFORD
REDBRIDGE
MANOR PARK
Manor Park Cemetery
MANOR PARK
GLADDING RD
STATION RD
LITTLE ILFORD LA
ROAD
SOUTH WOODFORD–BARKING RELIEF ROAD
TORNE RD
ROAD
LITTLE ILFORD
WOODGRANGE PARK
Woodgrange Park
ROMFORD ROAD
HIGH STREET NORTH
CHURCH ROAD
Woodgrange Park Cemetery
SANDRINGHAM RD
KATHERINE ROAD
SHREWSBURY ROAD
GREEN STREET
STRONE ROAD
Jewish Cemetery
BROWNING RD
SHAKESPEARE CR
Plashet Park
EAST AVE
SHAFTSBURY RD
GROVE
EAST HAM
BURGES ROAD
BARKING
ROAD
PLASHET ROAD
GRANGEWOOD ST
EAST HAM
NORTH CIRCULAR ROAD
UPTON PARK
WAKEFIELD ST
HARTLEY AVE
BARKING ROAD
Langdon School
PRIORY RD
CLEVES RD
West Ham United
ROAD
SAMSON ST
CENTRAL PARK ROAD
HIGH STREET SOUTH
BOUNDARY RD
Central Park
East Ham Jewish Cemetery
SANDFORD RD
BROOKS AVE
LONSDALE AVENUE
THE GREENWAY
WAY
Newham General Hospital
NEWHAM
PRINCE REGENT LANE
CUSTOM HOUSE
BERWICK RD
BAXTER RD
ROAD
PRINCE REGENT
CHURCHES, etc.
1 All Saints, West Ham
2 St John the Evangelist, Broadway, Stratford
3 St Chad and St Andrew, Plaistow
4 St Martin, Plaistow
5 Baptist Central Mission, Plaistow
6 Emmanuel, Forest Gate
7 St Antony of Padua (R.C.) Upton
8 Azhar Academy, Forest Gate
9 Ascension, Custom House
10 St Margaret (R.C.), Canning Town
11 Former St Luke, Canning Town
12 St Mary's Convent, Canning Town
13 St Mary Magdalene, East Ham
14 St Bartholomew, East Ham
15 St Mary, Little Ilford
16 St Barnabas, Little Ilford
17 St Nicholas (R.C.), Manor Park
+ Place of worship with an entry in the gazetteer

WEST HAM and STRATFORD

West Ham was the medieval parish, its village centred around the church of All Saints and which gave its name to all local government up to and including the County Borough in 1889.* Long before then, however, the focus of commercial and civic life had shifted to the burgeoning town of Stratford on the London road to the N, which became an important halt for travellers making the crossing over the Lea to and from Bow. S of the present High Street, near Abbey Road and Abbey Lane, lay the Cistercian Abbey of Stratford Langthorne, founded by William de Mountfichet in 1135. It was suppressed at the Dissolution but its ruins survived until 1784. Nothing at all remains now on the site, but mills and other industries established in the Abbey's lifetime continued to prosper and encourage settlement thereafter, a process which rapidly increased in the C19 with burgeoning chemical industries. They included, amongst others, manufactories for bleach, rubber, early plastics, solvents and printing ink. Stratford also became, and remains, an important railway junction, with the opening of the Eastern Counties (later Great Eastern) Railway which built up its massive engineering works here from 1847 and created the workers' district of Stratford New Town, N of the town centre. West Ham village, largely unaffected by these changes, remained a middle-class enclave with some distinguished, large, individual houses in their own grounds, mixed increasingly with the more typical form of Victorian and Edwardian suburban terraces. The commercial life of C18 and C19 Stratford is still much in evidence with big groups of pubs, banks and shops, but reconstruction after 1945 steadily eroded much of this quality and compounded it with unfortunate redevelopment of the Broadway in the 1970s. Regeneration began again in the early 1990s with the creation of a new station and a new cultural quarter in Stratford and reclamation of derelict railway lands, not only for the Channel Tunnel Rail Link and its international station but also for a surrounding area of housing to be known as Stratford City.

*The boroughs included Forest Gate, Upton, Plaistow, the Victoria Dock and Silvertown.

RELIGIOUS BUILDINGS

ALL SAINTS, Church Street. The medieval parish church of West Ham. A long, low, aisled building with a complicated history, of older origin than the apparently Perp exterior. Sturdy C15 W tower of the usual Thames valley type, with clasping buttresses and upstanding SE stair turret. Built of large, irregular blocks of Kentish rag, with a sprinkling of red tile repairs dating from conservation in the approved SPAB manner by *William Weir*, 1904–5. W doorway under a square head, with quatrefoils in the spandrels. On the N side, rubble aisle walls with C19 Perp windows. Further E a N chapel of *c.* 1550, red brick with blue diapering, incorporating an earlier rood stair turret. Windows with brick mullions and three or four arched lights below four-centred arches. Apparently the chapel was built from the proceeds of the sale of church property before it could be confiscated by the Crown. From the S the church is approached by an extraordinary covered way, a C19 replacement of a classical colonnade in existence by 1799. It incorporates a few older timbers but the roof members are cast-iron resembling C17 work. E end, S chapel and aisle were refaced in buff stock brick, 1803. Renewed S aisle windows 1892–4, early work by the Arts and Crafts architect *C.C. Winmill*. Winmill's SW vestry was demolished in 2002 as part of a major refurbishment by *Purcell Miller Tritton*, planned by *Martin Ashley* from 1992 and continued under *Brian Anderson*. New church rooms are intended on the S side.

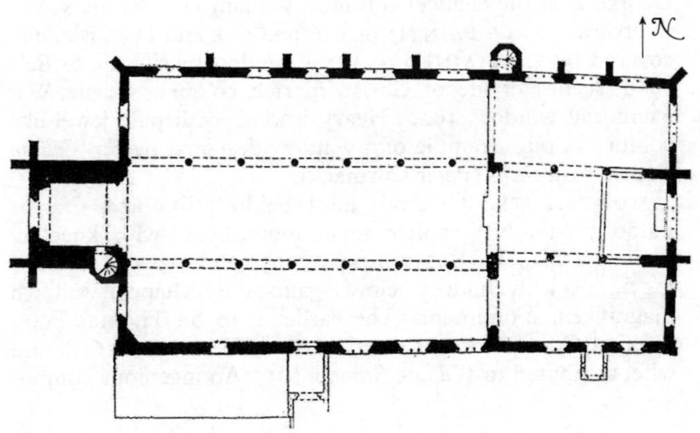

All Saints, West Ham, plan

Inside, blocked round-arched windows high up above second, third and fourth arches from the W are evidence of a C12 building, which was given aisles and enlarged to E and W in the C13 to provide a nave of seven bays, an exceptional length for a parish church. Arcades with circular piers, double-chamfered arches and drastically renewed capitals. The concave-sided W responds were rebuilt with the tower. Perp chancel, encroaching slightly on the E bay of the nave, flanked by late C15 S chapel and mid-C16 N chapel, each divided off by three-bay arcades with four-centred arches on octagonal piers. Nave roof with late C15 cambered tie-beams on curved braces. Moulded tie-beams in the chancel, *c.* 1500. N chapel roof with simpler C16 tie-beams. Plaster ceilings in the aisles, the E end of the N aisle with a wagon roof. Post-medieval changes included dormer windows in the nave (gone) and the N aisle (altered). The two dormers and hipped ends to the S aisle roof probably date from 1800–3. The 1847–9 restoration by *George Dyson* and *G.G. Scott* reseated the church and probably introduced the unusual little windows and arches high up in the nave. W gallery and the wall plaster were removed in 1865. The planned reordering includes dividing off the W ends of the aisles by glass screens.

FURNISHINGS. – Sanctuary fittings remain from *G.G. Scott*'s work of 1866: REREDOS, four elaborate nodding-ogee arches above mosaic figures of Moses, St John, St Peter and David; TILED FLOOR. – ALTAR, S chapel. Made up in 2002 from fragments of a Perp tomb chest: quatrefoils with coats of arms. – FONTS. C19 Perp, octagonal on marble stem. Its predecessor is dated 1707; plain octagonal but inscribed with three churchwardens' names. Another, medieval, plain octagonal and much worn. – SCULPTURE, below tower. From Stratford Langthorne Abbey. A stone with skulls behind bars, a vivid piece of carving, early C16. Also a two-light window (S aisle).* – ROYAL ARMS. George II at the chancel entrance. William IV over the S aisle doorway. – WALL PAINTING. C16 text at E end of S aisle, discovered 1977. – STAINED GLASS. E window by *Clayton & Bell*, 1866, scenes of life of Christ, in rich colours. N aisle, War Memorial window, 1920. Heavy leading with pale jewel-like colours. A rare example of a window designed by *Sir William Reynolds-Stephens* (Peter Cormack).

MONUMENTS.† Chancel: John Faldo †1613 and Francis Faldo †1632, two similar small monuments with kneeling figures. N chapel: – Robert Rooke †1630 and two wives; kneeling figures with children below. Against the N chapel E wall two magnificent monuments. The earlier is to Sir Thomas Foot,
20 the first Commonwealth Lord Mayor of London, †1688, and wife, attributed to *William Stanton* (GF). An ingenious compo-

*In store at time of writing, likewise royal arms of William IV.

†The BRASS to Thomas Staples †1592, shown with his four wives, on a rectangular plate, with verses below, was transferred to the Passmore Edwards Museum and has disappeared.

sition: gadrooned sarcophagus divided by the base of a large inscription plate. On each side of the inscription a niche with life-size standing figure, the whole under a pediment with large cartouche of arms, an urn above. – James Cooper †1743 and 21
wife. Two wonderfully natural life-size standing figures together in one niche under a pediment. The quality of the pair is excellent, and it is a great pity they are not signed. S chapel: – William Fawcitt †1631 and wife, and her second husband William Toppesfield, erected 1636. Large monument with two kneeling figures, facing each other as usual but with the first husband semi-reclining below. – Six children of the Rev. Nicholas Buckeridge, † between 1698 and 1710. Apparently a composite memorial. A kneeling daughter above, probably the daughter who died 1698, with a corbel of three cherubs' heads, perhaps the children who died in infancy. Below are kneeling figures of a young man and woman (†1709–10). Two small busts on pedestals, which look like additions. By *Edward Stanton* (according to Mrs Esdaile but Fisher disagrees). – Sir James Smyth, Lord Mayor, †1706 and family, attributed to *Grinling Gibbons* (GF). Very restrained; purely architectural, of a fine grey-veined marble, with Tuscan columns on a high base. S aisle: James Spearman †1725. Wall tablet with skulls and fleshy ornament. (W end N aisle, not *in situ*. – Rev. John Finch †1748 signed by *Robert Taylor*).* – Many other C18 and early C19 wall tablets and some fine ledger stones.

Large CHURCHYARD with several chest tombs, also some coffin-shaped tombs and a handsome chunky obelisk on a square base with convex sides (in need of repair).

ST JOHN THE EVANGELIST, Broadway, Stratford. 1832–4 by
Edward Blore. A prominent town centre site facing a graveyard 44
enclosed by decorative railings (restored on the model of the original *Blore* railings at St John Leytonstone). This was the second new church to be built in the old parish of West Ham, and like the earlier St Mary Plaistow, another Blore church, was assisted by parliamentary grant. Stately W front in pale brick with Dec Gothic detail, more ambitious than many of this date. SW tower with papery arcading and ogee arch below a steep gable; two sets of crocketed pinnacles linked to a broach spire by flying buttresses. The roofline then descends from the nave W gable with Geometric window to a lower N aisle with plain parapet; the effective *finale* is the gabled lobby to the church rooms in matching brick, added in 1998, by *Chris Betts* and *John Burton* of *Purcell Miller Tritton*. The S side has triplets of lancets below a high parapet; transept with two lights and a roundel. Slightly projecting chancel of 1884, with five-light traceried window.

The light and airy interior of this early C19 version of Gothic is in telling contrast to the old parish church. Broad five-bay nave, tall clustered piers carrying stilted shallow arches of three chamfered orders. Clerestory windows in pairs; roof trusses

*Attention was drawn to this by Dr John Physick.

with bold openwork. Minimal ornament: carved stops to the hoodmoulds and tiny figures below the tie-beams. Broad E arch originally framing a small pre-ecclesiological sanctuary, recast in 1884 into a full-blown chancel, with wall arcading and pointed ceiled barrel vault. Traceried wooden panelling and REREDOS with mosaic, late C19. – SCREEN. Tall, with metal openwork, 1900. – FONT and PULPIT, with marble columns, *c.* 1884, the font with nice openwork metal COVER – LIGHTING. Attractive hanging coronas, converted from gaslights. – STAINED GLASS. E window signed by *Gerald Smith*, 1955, Crucifixion panel against plain glass; the only replacement for windows blown out in the Second World War.

CHURCH ROOMS. The W lobby, cleverly lit from an E gable, leads S into the church and E into rooms tucked neatly along the N side of the church, with taller gabled hall at the E end. An exemplary extension.

MARTYRS' MEMORIAL in the churchyard, dated 1878, by *J.T. Newman* and erected under the influence of the fervent Protestant vicar, William Bolton, in memory of Marian martyrs, thirteen of whom were reputed to have been burned on this spot. A large, ungainly affair with polygonal angle-shafts and top-heavy spire. It is of terracotta, made and erected by *Johnson & Co.* of Ditchling, Sussex.

ST MATTHEW, Dyson Road and Vaughan Road. 1894–6 by *E.P. Loftus Brock* who died before its completion. It was finished by his chief assistant, *James Richardson*, and *George Patrick* who took over his practice. Of knapped flint with stock brick and stone detailing. Late C13 windows. Double transepts and an octagonal turret between nave and chancel (sadly its openings filled in). An unusual interior: nave and transept with slender columns and arches of timber, supporting an elaborate roof with thin tie-beams. The W three bays have been partitioned off as a hall, with seating now spread across the spacious crossing and transepts. Original chancel furnishings and openwork timber pulpit. The whole rather dim because of the ambitious STAINED GLASS windows. W window 1898, commemorating Rev. Armitage and the philanthropist Thomas Fowell Buxton; ten scenes in rectangular panels, quarries above and below. E window: Ascension, rather busy. S transept S by *Heaton, Butler & Bayne*, 1903, Christ preaching, pictorial.

ST PAUL, Maryland Road. *Humphrys & Hurst*, 1952–3. The church for Stratford New Town, rebuilt as the focus of the post-war rehousing programme, replacing a bombed church by *E. Bassett Keeling* of 1861–4. Reinforced concrete arched frame, clad in dark brick with flint panels below the closely-set rectangular windows along the side. These have concrete lozenge-shaped transoms which alternate in a rhythm of two and three (the effect now diminished by their fortress-like protective mesh). The W front attempts a little Festival of Britain gaiety, with tall curved porch on thin supports, and a broad open bellcote (now empty) with curved balcony below a gabled roof. Foundation stone taken from the reredos of St Paul's Cathedral. CHURCH HALL to the E, 1986 by *K.C. White & Partners*.

ST FRANCIS OF ASSISI (R.C.), Grove Crescent Road. 1868 by *E.W. Pugin*. Originally St Vincent de Paul; its dedication changed by the Franciscan Friars Minor in 1873. Classical brick façade with the stuccoed centre brought forward under a spired bell turret in the centre of the pedimented gable. The church is raised above street level to accommodate a school below; the entrance has a prominent doorcase with open and broken pediment and stucco decoration. Confident and appealing if not particularly competent. Clerestory-lit; no side windows; flat ceiling. Panelled walls incorporating confessionals. The sanctuary was added 1931–2 by *W.C. Mangan*, the awkward transition from the nave framed by a depressed arch, and new furnishings added (Stations of the Cross). Restored and redecorated in pale colours in 1996–7 by *Tooley & Foster Partnership*. Marble ALTARPIECE of 1931–2 incorporating a Spanish painting of St Francis by *Bartolommeo Carducci*, a pupil of Federigo Zuccari (looted from Spain by Napoleon, given to the Franciscans in 1926).

THE FRIARY, The Grove. Extended 1876 by Brother *Patrick Dalton* from two houses. L-shaped, two storeys, Gothic, in red brick with blue dressings and diapering. In the gable a canopy with figure of St Francis.

CENTRAL BAPTIST CHURCH, The Grove. *c*. 1854–5 (?). Single long nave with square corner buttresses supporting stone octagonal pinnacles (tops removed). The W window replaced. Adjoining to the l., the Sunday school, 1861. Plate tracery in the gable.

METHODIST CHURCH, Bryant Street. *c*. 1965. Yellow and blue brick, pitched roof. Centrepiece with concrete mullions and glass with flashes of colour. Pebbly panels above and below. Joined by later buildings to the attractive JUBILEE HALL of 1897, dark brick with red brick dressings and a central window with Art Nouveau glass. The congregation originally met at the Conference Hall in West Ham Lane (destroyed 1941), erected in 1884 by the YMCA and an evangelist group, the Mizpah Band. In the boundary wall a foundation stone from a demolished cottage erected in 1890: 'Built with their own hands by members of the Mizpah Band as a work of love. The materials being the gift of the council. The love of Christ Constraineth Us.'

UNITARIAN CHURCH, West Ham Lane. 1869 by *T. Chatfeild Clarke*. Brick with faint hints of Lombardy. Oblong W tower with raised brickwork at the corners. Restored 1946.

WEST HAM TABERNACLE, West Ham Lane. 1903, Baptist. Tall and gaunt with school below. Plain; five grouped lancets under gable.

RADHA KRISHNA TEMPLE, Cedars Road. A converted chapel

with plain gable and blocked window. Inside, a single windowless space; on the raised E end colourful sacred statues within tabernacles. (New building with a frontage with parabolic arches planned by *Rihman Design Consultants*, 2002.)

MAJOR BUILDINGS

OLD TOWN HALL, Broadway. 1867–8 by *Lewis Angell*, engineer and surveyor and *John Giles* architect, for the West Ham Local Board of Health. Enlarged by *Angell* in 1884–5 (builder *Thomas Ennor*). Damaged by fire in 1982, reopened 1986 following refurbishment by *Kenneth Lund*, *Roy Mizen*, *Peter Revell* and *Kevin Hagger* of *Newham Architect's Dept.*

The style is a confidently Victorian version of arched Cinquecento; rusticated stone ground floor with square-headed window openings beneath an upper range of round-arched windows divided by granite Corinthian columns. Two-storey entrance porch and loggia and curved two-storey return to West Ham Lane. All this is carried off with considerable panache, especially in the asymmetrical 100 ft high fishscale-slate domed tower, in which Angell's own office was accommodated. Assembled along the balustraded parapets are five allegorical figures by '*Mr Bromfield of Kennington*':* of an original ensemble of Arts, Science, Agriculture, Commerce, Industry, Justice, Mercy, Prudence, Fortitude and Temperance; the upper parapet has figures of St George and Britannia. At the far end of the high but plain brick S range is *Angell*'s two-storey extension of 1884–5, providing a further public room on the ground floor and separate offices.

Inside, a spacious entrance hall. On the ground floor were accommodated the boardroom, vestry and other parochial offices. A grand stair ascends to a landing running around three sides with decorative metal banisters, behind which, occupying almost the entire upper floor, is the magnificent public hall. 50 ft by 75 ft by 30 ft and surprisingly opulent decoration by *Messrs Boekbinder* with fluted Ionic pilasters between the windows, beneath a deep panelled frieze of shields and musical instruments. Ceiling of octagonal coffers.

The contemporary FIRE STATION stood alongside in Broadway. All that survives is a small section with a carved inscription. The rest was rebuilt in 1877–8. Italianate, of four bays and two storeys above four wide engine entrances (two blocked). In the rear courtyard is a *c.* 1900 block with a high tower. Closed 1964. The street block was refurbished after 1986 as a restaurant. In the courtyard, a square pool with SCULPTURE, Bird and Monkey, 1986 by *Judith Conan*. The new fire station in Romford Road, 1964, is plain brick and concrete.

* *Illustrated London News* 18.9.1869.

Former POLICE AND CORONER'S COURT, West Ham Lane. 1884 by *Lewis Angell*, extended by *John G. Morley* in 1901. The first phase, contemporary with Angell's Town Hall extension (*see* above), was in the latest classical style usual for courthouses, the material is yellow brick, the windows are arched. Its narrow symmetrical façade and long thin plan were seamlessly repeated in mirror-image for the Coroner's Court and Mortuary. Above each of the entrances are large coats of arms.

BOW COUNTY COURT, Romford Road. *c.* 1957–9 by *H.M. Office of Works*. Very dull, flat-roofed with unrelieved walls of pale brick framed by Portland stone dressings. Recessed entrance in the centre beneath a large stone panel of the Royal coat of arms.

MAGISTRATES COURT, High Street. 1994 by *Roughton & Partners*; project architect *Paul Mantripp*. One of a new generation of courts with a traditionally-minded exterior. Long asymmetrical façade in soapy reconstituted stone, dominated by a high projecting, gatehouse-like tower with an arched entrance at the base, the Royal arms on the face, and an Egyptianized cornice. Tall projecting windows and smaller towers flanking to l. and r. Inside, a mall-like top-lit central corridor with courtrooms placed on either side.

POLICE STATION (Stratford), West Ham Lane. 1969. Three storeys, with pairs of windows grouped between thick concrete crosswalls, floorbands and thin mullions.

POLICE STATION (West Ham), Manor Road. 1990s. L-shaped, two storeys in pale brick with light profiled aluminium curved roofs. Glazed stair and entrance hall implies transparency of purpose but the design is tough enough to evoke a sense of authority.

WEST HAM MUNICIPAL BATHS, Romford Road. 1932 by *Arthur H. Roe*, Deputy Architect and *T.V. Griffiths*, Borough Surveyor. Typical interwar civic Neo-Georgian of red brick with Portland stone trimming.

STRATFORD LIBRARY, The Grove. 1999–2000 by *Miller Bourne Partnership* with brightly coloured interior by *Faulkner Browns*. A cylindrical drum, containing entrance lobby, elevator and staircase, opens to the reading rooms behind.

Stratford's cultural centre is provided by a group of major buildings arranged around GERRY RAFFLES SQUARE, created under a masterplan devised by *Levitt Bernstein Associates* from 1999: the focus is the THEATRE ROYAL, a building of considerable local importance with, for a suburban theatre, a distinguished dramatic tradition. Erected in 1884 for Charles Dillon, actor-manager, who with typical ebullience bestowed the unwarranted regal title on the theatre. It is the sole surviving work of *J. G. Buckle* who extended it in 1886, and again in 1891, for its new owners, the Fredericks family. They engaged *Frank Matcham*, architect of their Borough Theatre (*see* below), to refurbish it in 1902. Major refurbishment and extension in 1993–2001 by *Levitt Bernstein Associates*.

The exterior is extremely unpretentious, brick above a

channelled stone plinth with raised central parapet and canted oriel window. To the r. the main entrance. Set back and facing W is the pilastered bar entrance, added by *Buckle* in 1891. Filling the angle, polite extensions of 1998–2001 in steel, glass
62 and coloured render. The interior, beautifully restored in 1993 by the architects with *Jenny Tiramani*, the theatre's associate designer, maintains its rambling Victorian pomposity. The tiled foyer runs, somewhat oddly, alongside the auditorium. At the far end, at right angles is the bar, once narrow like a train carriage but opened up and extended during refurbishment. The splendid auditorium is a rare survival in suburban London, retaining the original iron-columned tiers of horseshoe balconies and boxes. Reconstruction has restored the stalls boxes and the lavish red and gold painted plasterwork decoration created in 1902 by Matcham with the decorators *De Jong*.

The character of the theatre's exterior embellishments is echoed in *Levitt Bernstein Associates*' STRATFORD CIRCUS, designed in 1997–2001 for small-scale performances. Exposed steel frame with broad areas of glazing above ground floor, offset by the blank, aluminium-clad exterior of the main performance space on the l., and a public balcony at first floor. Polite, modern and a little dull. Inside, three colour-coded auditoria (or 'circuses') of varying sizes, flexibly designed for rehearsal and performance. Especially good is the dance rehearsal room on the upper level. Light sculptures on the exterior and in the bar by *Ron Hazeldon*.

Completing the group, STRATFORD PICTURE HOUSE by *Burrell Foley Fischer*, 1997. One of a series of new-generation picture houses, all by this firm, to revive the adventurous spirit of cinema architecture. Angled two-storey glazed façade beneath an overhanging roof carried on thin columns. Along the spine of the building a cylindrical section (containing the projection rooms) provides a hinge for the four small blank-walled auditoria, their raking roofs with projecting eaves of convex section. At the corner, a free-standing steel column supports a prow-like 'marquee' reminiscent of a 1950s 'drive-in'.

BOROUGH THEATRE, High Street. 1895–6 by *Frank Matcham* for the Fredericks family as a superior and successful competitor to their Theatre Royal. Reconstructed as a cinema in 1933–4 by *George Coles* and *Arthur Roberts*. A lively asymmetrical Neo-Jacobean frontage, with tripartite first floor windows, decorative oculi (one containing a bust of Beethoven) and openwork balustrade above. The fly-tower, in striped brick and stone to the l., has lost its top. Corner entrance, reconstructed by *Coles* with a rendered façade, subtly ornamented by pilasters with scrolling capitals dividing slim windows with Art Deco ironwork. The interior, restored after a fire in 1997, by *Barry Reynolds Associates*, has the usual 1930s swank, with wavy and scrolled decoration.

STRATFORD STATION, Great Eastern Road. Opened 1839 on the Eastern Counties Railway, with an entrance in Station

Street. Of this little survives except offices etc. on platform ten. Major reconstruction in 1991–9 turned the station to face Stratford town centre for the first time and created a large transport interchange for five railway lines and buses. In the first phase, 1991–4, platforms for the Jubilee Line extension were designed by *Troughton McAslan* in an unfussy combination of concrete, glass and aluminium, leaving the flourish to *Wilkinson Eyre Architects'* design for the main station, com- 118
pleted 1995–1999. Reconciling the different levels between the lines was achieved by creating a vast, curving, aluminium-clad roof over the concourse, its steel ribs anchored into the railway embankment. From this canopy sheer glazing is hung, enclosing the side elevations and angled at a steep inward slope along the face.

In the forecourt, a SCULPTURE, Time Twist by *Malcolm Robertson*, 1996; a dramatically contorted steel clock-tower. Also, 'Robert', a 1933 industrial tank locomotive built by the *Avonside Engine Co. Ltd*, Bristol.

STRATFORD BUS STATION. 1994 by *Soji Abass*, of London Transport Bus Passenger Infrastructure. Engineered by *YRM*. Twenty-two steel masts arranged in pairs, suspending canvas canopies like inverted umbrellas: the form of Hopkins' stand at Lords in reverse. Boxy passenger amenities shelter beneath.

STRATFORD MARKET DEPOT, Burford Road. 1994–8 by *Chris Wilkinson Architects* for London Underground. One of the most poetic essays of the cool High-Tech tradition. The 19,000 sq.m train maintenance and repair facility, capable of holding eleven whole trains at one time, is on an angled parallelogram plan to allow easy access from the adjoining railway. Wide span, with thin steel columns supporting its low curving roof structure. Across the roof, seam-like rooflights double as emergency air-vents. Metal and glass walls. The depot replaced the Great Eastern Railway's wholesale fruit and vegetable market (demolished 1992), established in 1879 as a rival to Spitalfields Market (*see* Tower Hamlets).

WEST HAM STATION, Manor Road. Opened on the London Tilbury & Southend Railway, 1901. Rebuilt in its present form in 1999 by *Van Heyningen & Haward*, as the first of the new stations for the Stratford extension of the Jubilee Line. By contrast with the High-Tech sleek machine aesthetic of Canning Town and Stratford, the materials used here – exposed precast concrete trusses, glass-block glazing and ruddy-red brick – hark back to Underground designs of the Holden era, further evoked in the tall, brick clock tower.

ABBEY MILLS PUMPING STATIONS, Abbey Lane. One of the most splendid sights along the flat, marshy, creeks and channels between the rivers Lea and Channelsea, with exciting architecture applied to the most foul purposes. The first station (Station A) is by *Charles Driver*, architect under the engineer 67
Sir Joseph Bazalgette, 1865–8 (the third of four including Deptford, 1864; Crossness, 1865 and Western, 1875) for the Metropolitan Board of Works' Main Drainage project. It was

Abbey Mills Pumping Stations, Stratford, 1868

designed to raise London's sewage to the high level of *Bazalgette*'s Northern Outfall Sewer (which runs beneath the 'Greenway' path between Old Ford and the river at Beckton). The Greek-cross plan, which accommodated eight beam engines (two in each of its mansarded 'transepts'), has earned it the nickname 'the cathedral of sewage'. An unorthodox mix, vaguely Italian Gothic in style but with tiers of Byzantine windows and a central octagonal lantern that adds a gracious Russian flavour. The exotic appearance was originally enhanced by two huge octagonal chimneys with Moorish minarets. Their stepped bases survive, like ruined mausolea. The expensive treatment of the exterior seems subdued compared with the interior where *Driver*'s florid cast-iron arcades and galleries demonstrate the outrageous hybrid art of the Victorian architect/engineer. Some conservation work in 1998–9; project consultants: *Dearle and Henderson Design*.

The verdant surroundings of Station A, originally laid out as formal gardens, are contrasted sharply by the siting of STATION F which stands dramatically on the flat open marshland to the S. 1994–7, by *Thames Water* and *Allies and Morrison*. A sleek Hi-Tech barn, 56 metres long by 29 metres high, its steel A-frame clad entirely in aluminium and louvred panels with a curving roof punctured by drum-like air vents and spiky exhaust pipes.

Along ABBEY LANE, set close to the sewer's embankment, Nos. 116–130 are a striking, and for their date generous, group of paired cottages of *c.* 1865 for the Works' employees. Grey brick with round-arch windows and pointed headers in red and black brick. In spite of their desolate surroundings, they have the look of love about them.

Former WEST HAM SEWAGE PUMPING STATION, Canning Road/Abbey Lane. 1895–7 by *Lewis Angell*, to bring the borough's sewage to the Northern Outfall Sewer. Brick engine house, deceptively like a classical Nonconformist chapel with high pedimented gables. The adjoining boiler house retains its cast-iron roof, window frames and composite roof trusses. Two beam engines, of 1895–1900 by *Lilleshall Co.*, Shropshire.

BROMLEY GAS WORKS, Twelvetrees Crescent. Developed from 1870 as a major works of the Imperial Gas-Light and Coke Company. A remarkable array of seven (originally nine) cast-iron framed gasholders erected 1872–82 to the design of *Joseph Clark*, engineer under *Thomas Kirkham* chief engineer, but the later ones with some modifications by *Vitruvius Wyatt*. Large diameter versions of the ones at Pritchard's Road, Bethnal Green, each with 24 or more double order columns mostly retaining their heavy entablatures. No. 1 was raised to three tiers in 1927. BRIDGE across the River Lea erected 1872 by *Peter William Barlow*, engineer; two wrought-iron plated girder arches on handsome stone piers. Balustrade of interlacing arches and cast-iron gas lamps. Restored 2002.

MEMORIAL RECREATION GROUND, Memorial Avenue, off Manor Road. Opened 1897. Improvements planned in 2004, including the daring Woodlands Community Resource Centre by *Eger Architects* with *Ove Arup & Partners*, designed to be sunk into the parkland with its roof covered by turf and access via a series of ramps.

Educational Buildings

UNIVERSITY OF EAST LONDON (Stratford Campus), Romford Road. West Ham's finest C19 building, comprising the former Technical Institute, Public Library and Museum. By *Gibson & Russell*, the Institute and Library completed 1895–8, the Museum 1898–9. The Institute's buildings were partly destroyed by fire in 1899 but re-opened in 1900. Since then it has formed the basis for what became the University of East London in 1992.

The main building is quadrangular in plan divided into two courts by a central E–W cross-block containing the Great Hall, with its own public entrance on the W side. The Library, also with its own entrance, occupies the N part of the plan, its reading rooms extending into the N court. The Institute, entered from Romford Road occupied the rest of the building on both floors.

Pevsner's description in 1954 is still pertinent: 'Every conceivable motif is used which was available at that peculiar moment in the history of English architecture when the allegiance to forms of the past was at last thrown to the winds. Giant columns and Gibbs surrounds of windows are still permitted, but the turret and cupola shapes for instance are without any period precedent. Besides the grouping of masses is completely free. Altogether the architects have certainly enjoyed being fanciful and have not minded being a little vulgar. But the whole is of a robust vitality which seems enviable today. The carved exterior sculpture is by *W. Birnie Rhind* and its plentiful long trailing-out tendrils and scrolls are especially characteristic of the 1890s.'

72 The INSTITUTE faces Romford Road, an asymmetrical composition with a long screen of giant columns across the upper floors with a second screen, half its size, set behind to frame the second floor. Two flanking turrets with figures inset in the niches anchor this at either end, their vertical emphasis echoed by a pair of towers with cupolas at the gable ends. At first floor a long frieze carved with cherubs engaged in different crafts and sciences. To the entrance, figures of Truth and Beauty carry the arched canopy. At the W façade are large round-arched gables, each originally articulating one of three entrances and adorned with sculpture. From r. to l., figures representing engineering (originally over a separate entrance for women students), then over the entrance to the GREAT HALL, representations of music. Emblazoned on its columned porch (reconstructed after war damage) is a curious emblem of an eagle with two figures, possibly art and industry, that strikes the one discordant note in the otherwise entirely consistent melody of the decoration. Inside the hall is more soberly treated, but repeating some of the exterior's less orthodox architectural detail of Gibbs surrounds on the panelling and pilasters and windows divided by short pairs of columns. At the N end the entrance to the former public LIBRARY is set back, but emphasized by a tower with a turret of odd and playful shape set against a gable carved with figures of children representing Literature. Inside, most of the decorative whimsy has survived intact. In the main reading room tendrils creep up the octagonal columns and the barrel-vault roof, braced by decorative carved trusses, has panels inset with Tree of Life plasterwork, almost certainly designed by *Gilbert Seale*. On the round-arch tympana are a pair of outstanding painted gesso panels by *H.C. Fehr* depicting allegorical scenes of Romantic and Serious Literature. Restored in 1950. At the rear, in the top-lit former Reference Library is a beautiful glazed bookcase by *Messrs Garne and Son*, with attached colonnettes and inscriptions in the frieze of improving character: 'Knowledge is essential to Freedom', 'No furniture so charming as books', 'Speech is great but silence is greater'.

SCULPTURE. In front of the Library entrance a *Coade* stone figure of Shakespeare, 1846. Reputedly originally at the Opera House in the Haymarket but presented to the Borough in 1923 (Alison Kelly).

The PASSMORE EDWARDS MUSEUM (now STUDENTS UNION) projects on the r. of the main façade to Romford Road, a lower domed block with an identical roof finial to the Institute and big round gables at the axes. Over the entrance a bronze panel, by *H.C. Fehr*, with a portrait of J. Passmore Edwards on a shield held by an ethereal female figure. Inside, beneath the dome, is a charming circular space with a gallery carried on columns. At the rear, stairs to the first floor. To l. and r. of the entrance, small vestibules retained original display cabinets in 2002. Until 1994 the Museum housed the important collection of the Essex Field Club, now dispersed. The building was allowed to sink into neglect before restoration in 2003.

EAST LONDON CHILDCARE INSTITUTE, Mark Street. By *Cazenove Architects*, 2002–4. Four storey L-shaped building with teaching rooms above a ground floor nursery. Compactly designed on a tight site, but spatially inventive inside, with generous communal foyer and stair. The nursery has a double height main space and smaller rooms opening off. Lifted out of the ordinary also by clever natural lighting, ingenious detailing and lively use of colour.

SCHOOLS are generally disappointing. SARAH BONNELL SCHOOL, Deanery Road/Water Lane, provides a fair summary of typical school architecture in West Ham Borough over the two main periods of building. Facing Water Lane, the former WATER LANE BOARD SCHOOL of 1897. Big and plain, three storeys with pointed gables. To its NE, the school for the deaf and dumb of 1900 by *W. Jacques*, with shaped gables. At the S end, towards Deanery Road, the former WEST HAM TECHNICAL SCHOOL FOR GIRLS, 1949 by *T.E. North*, Borough Architect, with *R.B. Padmore*, Assistant Architect. Yellow brick, flat-roofed, a freely grouped composition typical of the date.

THREE MILLS PLAY CENTRE, Abbey Lane by *Hawkins Brown*, 1997. A more conventional successor to the firm's earlier modular structures for nursery schools, the Playarc (Plaistow) and Playbarn (Canning Town). Steel frame and barrel roof. Timber facings and glass blocks provide good foils to the metallic tones.

PERAMBULATIONS

1. Stratford Broadway and High Street

The centre of Stratford is the Broadway, which divides on either side of St John's church and retains much of the flavour of the commercial and civic centre, with lots of C18 and C19 pubs, banks and shops. At its W end the Broadway becomes the High Street which extends to the river crossing to Bow.

The tour starts in the BROADWAY, the old market area of Stratford. In the centre, between the covered market and the main road is St John's Church (*see* above). In front of it is the GURNEY MEMORIAL of 1861, a plain tall obelisk of granite by *J. Bell* to Sir Samuel Gurney (†1856), resident of Ham House and one of the many Quakers to contribute to West Ham's civic and charitable life in the C19. The N side of the

Broadway is decidedly mixed architecturally. At its W end it is dominated by the rebuilding of 1971–3 by *T.P. Bennett* which provided office towers, multi-storey car parks and the STRATFORD SHOPPING CENTRE. The dark brick and glass frontage along the Broadway is sadly drab and monotonous in comparison with what was there before, although the recently revamped interior with its cross-plan of airy malls is not unpleasant. The only interesting older survival on the N side is No. 58–62, a tripartite composition with four-bay side parts with large first floor show windows, flanking a taller gabled centrepiece. Built *c.* 1900 for Thomas & Williams drapers, whose emblem is visible in the pediment of the gable window. At the end of this range are the late 1950s former London Co-operative Society Stores with a long subtly concave façade. Eleven bays, each recessed between stone-faced mullions, the windows set at angles between mosaic panels. The Q BUILDING by *Buckley Gray*, 2002–3 strikes the first significant contemporary note, and exemplifies encouragement of residential developments in the C21 town centre. Four storeys of flats above a bar with modish layered façades of expansive glazing, sliding timber-louvred shutters and aluminium cladding. Cranked façade along Salway Place behind a tight grid of aluminium blades.

On the other side of the church, the S side of BROADWAY has fared better. No. 63 is a tall tower-like Edwardian building, *c.* 1904, on a narrow site, with mullioned windows and a steep hipped roof with little lantern. Striped brick and stone. Beyond, the former London and County Bank of 1867 by *Frederic Chancellor.* Italianate, three storeys, with engaged columns to the ground floor, six close-set pediments to the first floor windows, and a heavy cornice. One-bay addition (No. 49) of 1904, probably by *Brown & Barrow.* Red brick and Portland stone with canted oriel with column mullions. It makes a serious contrast to the humble EDWARD VII pub (former King of Prussia, renamed, unsurprisingly, in 1914); an C18 establishment, remodelled in the early C19 with ornate and bumptious doorcases. The entrance to the Saloon Bar has excellent late C19 tiling and engraved glass. On an island between Tramway Avenue and Town Hall is THE SWAN, the historic coaching halt for traffic to and from London. Established here by 1631, rebuilt in the C18 and again in 1925 in stately later C17 style, three storeys and dormers, five bays framed by sturdy chimneystacks. Its gardens were built up with shops in the C19, including one in West Ham Lane with giant fluted stucco pilasters. At the rear is the QUEEN'S HEAD, single storey, Wrenaissance of *c.* 1925.

The BROADWAY continues with the OLD TOWN HALL and FIRE STATION (*see* above), the start of a lively sequence of tall urban frontages that include the former TWO PUDDINGS, an early C20 pub with three stilted-arched windows in the first floor and the upper floor set back. Then Nos. 21–3, a façade with weird half timbering. To the corner, YE OLDE BLACK BULL, 1892. Busy brick and stone with a shallow oriel and open attic under a gable. Fairly lavishly ornamented including an ornate corner entrance with painted stucco bull set in a niche. Dull brick.

HIGH STREET continues W, but only its E end is worthy of exploration. BURROWS HOUSE, at the corner with Chant Street, is the former Parr's Bank of *c.* 1897–8, probably by *Frederick Pinches.* Stock brick with stone ground floor and corner entrance beneath a swan-neck pediment on columns. Dormers with shaped gables. Banking hall with panelled ceiling and big composite column with a medallion portrait of Queen Victoria. More Victorian buildings follow, including Nos. 411–13, the former Post Office by the *Office of Works,* with coronets in the tympana of the windows. No. 403 is crumbling cut-price Ruskinian Gothic; then more financial probity at Nos. 399–401, 1913 by *C.J. Dawson* for the London and South Western Bank. Polished granite ground floor, stone dressings and pointed dormers. The MAGISTRATES COURT, 1994 (*see* above) provides the major incident before, further W, the DISCOVERY CENTRE. Built as the Alexandra Temperance Hotel, a residence for London workers employed in Stratford's expanding industries. By *S.B. Russell,* 1901. Disastrously over-painted ground floor with large moulded arches; upper windows separated by brick piers with stone band, flat parapet. The absence of sculptural detail, so tantalizingly visible in the original design, and a Russell trademark, must have been the inevitable victim of economy. Nos. 379–81 was a furnishing warehouse, with large arched display windows on first floor. Then ESSEX HOUSE, tremendous Northern Renaissance of *c.* 1901 in brick and terracotta, with griffins between the high pointed gables, and panels with impish figures beneath the shallow bow windows of the upper floors. Possibly by *J.H. Gladwell* who had offices here. Finally the BOROUGH THEATRE (*see* above).

Across Bridge Street, the former STRATFORD MARKET STATION erected in 1891–2 for the Great Eastern Railway (Chief Engineer, *John Wilson*) to serve their fruit and vegetable market (*see* Stratford Market Depot, above). Arched windows and paired doorways, a big hipped roof with two gabled dormers and a covered passage over the street. Just beyond in BURFORD ROAD are two- and three-storey ranges of workshops in blue engineering brick with red trim, erected for the railway's printworks. At the foot of the road, stood the market depot, since rebuilt (*see* above). Between these, a large and smart development of STRATFORD SOUTH CENTRAL by *Stock Woolstencroft*, 2003, characteristic of early C21 development in Stratford. Five blocks of offices and flats, subtly varied with broad areas of glazing, timber-boarding and black tile facings. Dramatically stepped façade to the S block.

Some way W of here along the noisy High Street, THE LOG CABIN (No. 335–7); its core is *c.* 1740, with a closed-string stair, but much altered. Prominent on the N side of the bridge crossing is WARTON HOUSE, the former Yardley's box factory. Good straightforward Modern of 1937 by *Higgins & Thomerson*. Tiled façade with a curved end, the character now reduced by unsympathetic reglazing and overpainting. On its W face a whimsical panel of lavender pickers.* The Edwardian main factory was in CARPENTERS ROAD, N of the High Street, a former area of industry and small works, surrounding the fearsome system-built slabs of the CARPENTERS ESTATE built *c.* 1967–8.

Back along the N side of the HIGH STREET: THE BUILDER'S ARMS, at the corner of Lett Road, revealed by road widening in the 1950s. Interwar free Tudor of 1937; pretty gutters with foliage trails and hoppers marked 'BB' (Bow Brewery?). Then the WEST HAM LABOUR PARTY offices, an odd 1930s façade with faience-clad projecting cross-walls. Across the railway, BROADWAY HOUSE and JUBILEE HOUSE (Council Offices), 1980s. Nasty curtain-walled blocks, with grids of yellow and blue trim and triangular roofline. At the junction with GREAT EASTERN ROAD a SCULPTURE: Railway Tree by *Malcolm Robertson*, 1996, a vertical cluster of

* Based on primrose sellers from Wheatley's *Cries of London*.

curved steel rails. Beyond lie the spectacular BUS STATION and STRATFORD STATION (*see* above).

2. *Romford Road, The Grove & Stratford New Town*

Until the C19, Stratford's E expansion halted beyond the Broadway at Stratford Green, the common land. Along its S side ran the London–Ilford Road, now ROMFORD ROAD, well established by the late C16. It starts with No. 2 (S side), ST JOHN'S HOUSE, a good late Georgian villa with a restrained front of three bays, slightly projecting centre and end panels, Doric porch and pedimented centre window. Earlier and still in the Essex vernacular, No. 30, THE OLD DISPENSARY, is a rare survival of a weatherboarded, timber-framed house of *c.* 1700. Five bays, two storeys. Restored in 1989–90 by *Julian Harrap Architects* (new shutters and rebuilt brick wing at rear). Original plain panelling in two rooms: on the l. of the entrance (glazed cupboard and simple marble fireplace) and on the first floor at the front. Used as a dispensary from 1861–79 by Dr William Elliott of the West Ham Union. Now a heritage centre.

Further on, on the N side, the former WORKING MEN'S CLUB, founded 1865 in the church deanery, and rebuilt 1904–5 by *W. Henden Winder*, builders *E.M. Thomas & Co.* Modest eclectic Baroque, its centre emphasized by a curved pediment on Ionic pilasters; attic with angled volutes and a small dome. Flanking shopfronts below corbelled-out bays. In the lobby, several tablets record the club's development. Refurbished in 2001–3 conserving much of the fabric including terrazzo floors and the staircase. The hall retains its ribbed and vaulted tin ceiling with dainty decorative bosses for light fittings. In DEANERY ROAD to the N, SYSTEM HOUSE, former Public Offices of 1910, probably by *John G. Morley*, Borough Engineer. Late C17 style, nine bays in channelled grey and red brick with a high mansard. Opposite, Lyon House looks like a post-war prefab canteen.

The S side of Romford Road has a familiar main road mix of C19 villas and terraces: some on quite a grand scale, e.g. the refurbished group at Nos. 54–8. Nos. 60–2 are a typical pair of medium-size early C19 villas with deep first floor windows below arches. Tucked in behind is a small but distinguished scheme of flats, faced in cedar panelling, and set around a courtyard, by *Stock Woolstencroft c.* 2000. Vicarage Terrace (Nos. 64–82), is a seamless group of *c.* 1820, three-storey and basement houses with depressed arch windows in the ground floor. No. 82 has a Greek Doric prostyle portico. On the W corner of Vicarage Lane are the former Borough Electricity Offices and Showrooms of 1927–30, early Georgian Revival in brick and stone with a deep rusticated ground floor of broad display windows. Size and lavish treatment are a measure of local pride in the borough's electrification. Now flats, with an offensively disrespectful attic storey above the big stone cornice. Just beyond, BOW COUNTY COURT (*see* above) and, at the corner of Maitland Road, THE PIGEONS, a large public house by *Henry Poston*, 1898 with an openwork iron 'tower' at the corner. Much further on, on the N side, the former MUNICIPAL BATHS (*see* above). But the unmissable highlight on the N side of Romford Road is the magnificent group of the former WEST HAM TECHNICAL INSTITUTE and PASSMORE EDWARDS MUSEUM (University of East London), at the corner with Water Lane (*see* above).

Opposite the Institute, in DEANERY ROAD, NEWTEC, an education and training centre for women. A single-storey 1960s block, reclad and book-ended by extensions of 1994–6 by *Cazenove Architects Co-operative*. Exposed timber framing, the walls faced in plywood panels. Taller block at the E end covered by a curved stainless steel roof. N in WATER LANE the SARAH BONNELL SCHOOL (*see* above) and facing E, GREEN POINT, a reminder, in name only, of Stratford Green: twenty-two-storey tower by *T.E. North*, Borough Architect, 1961. The first of such height in West Ham and the highest in Essex at the time. Further N on the W side, THE MANBEY ARMS, an early C19 pub with classical pilasters and pediments to the ground floor. At the corner with Manbey Road, No. 43a is a former butcher's shop with stucco cow-head keystones.

At the top of Water Lane, the road crosses the railway into LEYTONSTONE ROAD. Immediately ahead, flats of 2003 stand on the site of Holy Trinity Church, a major landmark destroyed by fire in 1952. On the opposite curve, a group of poorly maintained but striking mid-C19 paired houses, with later shopfronts. Hipped roofs, stucco fronts, one pair retaining its gigantic chimneystack. Just beyond, some crudely preserved pilasters incorporated within a new section of wall are the sole evidence of the distinguished Whitehall Distillery. This little area first developed as Maryland Point, described by Defoe as 'new' in the 1720s. There is nothing of this date to see but the name is maintained for the short stretch of road which begins with the CART AND HORSES, an early pub which moved to this site in 1805 and was rebuilt *c.* 1880.

In THE GROVE, S of the railway, No. 121 (Surgery) was the GROVE PICTURE PALACE of 1910 by *Gilbert & Constanduros*, the most important firm of pre-1914 cinema architects. Red brick with stamped terracotta detailing and Renaissance-style frieze along the front. Also preserved, the central timber kiosk window, a most unusual and rare feature in British cinemas of any date. Behind the parapet, a segmental pedimented gable conceals the auditorium. Next to this the Central Baptist Church; opposite is the Friary attached to the Church of St Francis of Assisi in Grove Crescent Road (*see* above). Set back from the line of the road behind shops, a paired early C19 villa with central pediment and pilasters.

In GROVE CRESCENT ROAD, the former MARYLAND WORKS. Pedimented front with a clock dial in the centre spelling out its name. Erected for Young and Marten, builders' merchants, whose main premises originally distinguished the junction of The Grove with the Broadway and Romford Road by a notable Victorian domed cornerpiece. Shortlived but striking council offices in the form of a ziggurat were built on the site in the 1970s but replaced in 2000 by *Miller Bourne Partnership*'s scheme for a supermarket, hotel and the STRATFORD LIBRARY (*see* above). They exhibit the late 1990s enthusiasm for streamlined motifs, e.g. rounded corners and circular towers with angled flat roofs. As a group, too bland to create a varied townscape. In front of the library, two MEMORIALS: Gerard Manley Hopkins, born at No. 87 The Grove: large granite boulder; and social activist Edith S. Kerrison (†1934), copper relief by *Christine Gregory*, 1936, on an Art Deco plinth.

Beyond the junction with GREAT EASTERN ROAD lies Stratford's cultural centre, focused around GERRY RAFFLES SQUARE, relandscaped in 2002 by *Art2Architecture* and *Newham Council Environmental Services*. A circular steel ring is set into the paving. Grouped around this, the Picture House, Theatre Royal and Stratford Circus (*see* above). Towering above the square, an early 1970s office block has been completely revamped for flats, with superimposed balconies and three floors of sleek and transparent stepped penthouses.

The walk may conclude here, but the indefatigable explorer can penetrate N along ANGEL LANE into the area developed in 1839–40 by the Great Eastern Railway as Hudson Town (named after the company's founder), later known as STRATFORD NEW TOWN. Once characterized by rows of small houses for the company workers but redevelopment in the early 1950s by *T.E. North*, the Borough Architect and Town Planner, almost entirely eradicated the Victorian streets in favour of low-rise flats and terraces in yellow brick. In Maryland Road, St Paul's Church (*see* above) was built to serve the new neighbourhood. Close to the railway at the corner of ANGEL LANE and WINDMILL LANE are some C19 survivals. First the substantial RAILWAY TAVERN, designed by *Henry Poston*, 1897, and opposite ANGEL COTTAGE, a sweet double-fronted cottage, with a front garden and path to the door. Dated 1826. It looks most out of sorts here. To the W, the former railway lands are in upheaval for construction of the Channel Tunnel Rail Link, International Station and associated developments to create Stratford City (due to begin in 2004) masterplan by *Arup Associates* and *Fletcher Priest Architects* for 5,000 homes.

3. *West Ham Lane to West Ham Park*

WEST HAM LANE was the medieval route between Stratford and the church at West Ham. S of Stratford on the E side, the UNITARIAN CHURCH (*see* above), then No. 43, the former district office of the Transport and General Workers' Union, by *R.S. Bowers*, 1939. A prominent faience-faced corner building with a black plinth, pale tiles above and bands of windows divided by green tiled mullions. Over the entrance an octagonal and domed clock tower with openwork globe finial, originally designed to be illuminated. Beyond East London Childcare Institute, *see* above. Further behind, in Elliot Close, is a ten-storey tower, built in load-bearing brick by *ATP Group Partnership*, 1971–8, for small families and single people. Reclad in the late 1990s and renamed Focus E15.

On the W side of West Ham Lane housing on the site of West Ham (later Queen Mary's) Hospital. Its gateway, to Bryant Street, is preserved, a classical arch in Portland stone and brick with an inscribed parapet. S of Bryant Street is the POLICE STATION (*see* above). It succeeded *J. Dixon Butler*'s station at No. 94 (now Park House) of 1895. Three storeys with big cornice over first floor and Butler's typical elongated consoles over the door. Further on, the HEALTH CENTRE, 1963 by *T.E. North* with *Alan Dicken, Kenneth Lund and John Hume*. T-shaped, a long three-storey wing with higher block at the S end. Brick and curtain walling. Just beyond is the WEST HAM TABERNACLE (*see* above). These buildings face WEST HAM RECREATION GROUND, municipal gardens laid out 1899–1903 by the Borough, as part of a campaign to create green spaces for the developing area. Half-timbered lavatories with pointed gables. Railings with big spiky finials.

At the junction with CHURCH STREET, the layout of roads was radically reconfigured after 1945 so that the Parish Church of All Saints (*see* above) now sits back in a quiet close. On the N side of the street, an Edwardian parade of shops, close by the KINGS ARMS, rebuilt in 1885 in red brick with pale gault brick dressings, lots of unrefined terracotta detailing and big triangular gables inset with cogged brickwork. Its relationship with the church is good, but the atmosphere is soured by the characterless post-war flats, shops and car park on the S side. E of the church it is difficult to recapture much ancient flavour, although two buildings have long histories within West Ham. First, THE ANGEL, rebuilt in a rather cheap half-timbered style in 1910. Its ground floor, with attached columns, suggests it may have been retained from an earlier building. Almost opposite, facing along GIFT LANE, HARRIS COTTAGES of 1939 by *W.H. Ansell*, successors to a group of almshouses erected for the poor by Roger Harris in 1633. Refurbished 1987. Attractively done, quiet Neo-Georgian, of three ranges around an open court. Stone architraves, pantiled roofs and sash windows.

N of the churchyard is PORTWAY, the ancient route between West Ham village and its neighbouring hamlet of Upton (*see* p. 248). The main attractions are on the N side including the PARK TAVERN, in a striking palazzo style, with ranks of arched windows and a bracketed eaves cornice. A two-storey extension to the rear has a separate entrance beneath an ornate stucco pediment decorated with garlands and a comedic mask, perhaps denoting entertainments. The pub is probably *c.* 1874, no doubt capitalizing on the opening of nearby WEST HAM PARK in that year. The park was created from the former grounds of Rooke Hall (later Ham House, demolished 1872), bought in 1762 by Dr John Fothergill who established extensive botanic gardens. From 1812 the house and gardens belonged to the Quaker philanthropist Samuel Gurney, whose donations enabled this to become a public park under the ownership of the Corporation of London. Overtly municipal intervention has been relatively limited, apart from a simple bandstand. Fine ornamental gardens. On the terrace above the tennis courts are *Coade* stone urns rescued from Wanstead House. At its gates are a series of pleasing lodges of various dates, the best at its SW entrance on Portway, PARK COTTAGE: a truly delightful L-shaped cottage orné, with deep sloping roof, mullion windows with Gothic heads and drip moulds. The one unwelcome intrusion, also on Portway, is the TA Centre of *c.* 1960, built on the site of The Cedars, a large house belonging to the Fry family, one of several such houses built by Quaker families in West Ham, but mostly demolished. Along Portway's S side, extensive speculative late C19 housing.

4. *Three Mills Island*

THREE MILLS ISLAND provides one of the most surprising sights along the River Lea and a forcible reminder in the C21 that 'London-across-the-Border' was once rural Essex. The core is the historic buildings of two former mills, later converted for distilling, now film studios and a museum.

The first mills along Bow Creek were established on the abbey lands at Stratford Langthorne in the medieval period to supply grain to the bakeries of Stratford-atte-Bow but fell into disuse after the Dissolution. Milling remained an industry on the bank of the tidal Lea and by the early C18 was harnessing the ebb tide to power the machinery. The mills here were erected, originally on a man-made island, precisely to gain maximum advantage. They were purchased in 1727 by Huguenots, Peter Lefevre, Daniel Bisson and John Debonnaire for gin distilling. By the early C19 the mills had seven waterwheels and drove eighteen pairs of millstones. Both milling and distilling continued until after 1945. The House Mill was retained as a museum and information centre by the River Lea Tidal Mill Trust. Restoration or conversion of all buildings by *Julian Harrap Architects*, 1989–97. Much of the rest of the site was converted to film studios from *c.* 1994.

The island is reached by footpath over the bridge from THREE MILLS LANE on the W bank of the Lea, close to Bromley-by-Bow station. Owing to the foreground of water, the setting is picturesque and the atmosphere tranquil. First, bestriding six channels and tributaries of the Lea and Channelsea, is the mighty HOUSE MILL. Its date plate 'DSB 1776', indicates rebuilding for Daniel Bisson, though the present mill was reconstructed after a fire in 1802. Three storeys, ten bays, with brick faced front and weatherboarded rear concealing a massive timber-framed structure. Steeply sloping roof, double-ridged and containing two attic storeys, lit by twelve dormers. Inside, timber floors carried on tie-beams, using long beams of Scandinavian timber to span its great width. Some C19 and C20 cast-iron columns.

Four undershot waterwheels (the oldest surviving one of timber), drove eight pairs of millstones, later increased to twelve. The tidal energy also powered the hoists which raised the grain to the top floor. Restored from 1989 by the River Lea Tidal Mill Trust. The House Mill was so called from its position between manager's and miller's houses. The former has gone, but the 1763 façade of the miller's house was rebuilt in facsimile in 1992–3 by *Julian Harrap Architects* as the Visitor and Interpretation Centre. The original black and white hall floor remains. At the rear the centre appears as a striking glazed box with copper roof. Next to it, the early C19 CUSTOMS HOUSE, with bowed brick front.

Opposite, across the cobbled courtyard is the CLOCK MILL, now housing. At its W end, the clock tower, erected first, *c.* 1753 but its wooden base later rebuilt in brick. Square in plan, surmounted by an octagon in its upper stage beneath an octagonal timber cupola. Pointed Gothic windows. The adjoining mill was probably erected in the mid-C18 but destroyed by fire and rebuilt in 1817 by Philip Metcalfe, his initials on a lead plaque on the flanking wall. Four storeys high with two drying kilns (that to the N, pre-1817, that to the S *c.* 1840) with dentilled eaves cornices, conical slated roofs (added in the late C19) and cowls of recent date. On its S side, set high in the attic is a loft winch in the roof for hoisting grain from the river to the stores. Eight bays, cast-iron columns and kingpost roof. To the E, later buildings including still houses and bonded warehouses associated with Nicholson's distillery from 1836. The main warehouse has a date plaque, 1836, 1872, 1950. On the site of the granary, a large shed for the film studios with blank façade to the river.

NE of the island, a small square has been created with a GATEWAY and BRIDGE by *Peter Fink* of *Art2Architecture* with *Clash Associates*. This links to part of LEE VALLEY PARK, a linear green space gradually being created along the entire valley from former industrial lands. Close to the canal towpath, by the N gate, a MEMORIAL to workers killed in 1901 in a well on the site when overcome by the noxious gases. The original memorial cross was replaced in 2001 by a sculpture: Helping Hands by *Alec Peever*, and two angled brick walls inset with carved panels and fragments of the earlier memorial. Views E from the park are to the Abbey Mills Pumping Stations and S to Bromley Gas Works (*see* above).

FOREST GATE and UPTON

Forest Gate began as a hamlet to the E of Stratford at the entrance to the Forest of Essex. Just N of the Romford Road lay Woodgrange Farm, recorded in 1189 and attached to the Cistercian abbey at Stratford. Woodgrange Road is shown on Rocque's map in 1744 and a station for the Eastern Counties Railway opened here in 1841. This promoted development of new housing on land N of the railway, where Forest Gate Industrial School and the West Ham Cemetery were established by 1860. Forest Gate assumed its reputation as a slightly superior suburb in the 1870s, with the laying out to E and W of Woodgrange Road of, respectively, the Woodgrange and Gurney Estates. These are distinguished by large houses and a series of grand Nonconformist churches. But this character has been only fitfully maintained up to the present day and the focus of its commercial life much dissipated.

The neighbouring hamlet of Upton lay S of Romford Road around Upton Lane. Even as Forest Gate was developing, Upton could still claim to be a rural retreat from London with several large houses, many owned by West Ham's Quaker elite, set in their own grounds. Of this there is now almost nothing to be found, the consequence of unbridled suburbanization which spread S from Forest Gate and NW from East Ham to form the new suburb of Upton Park in the 1890s, and the gradual demolition of the older mansions during the C20. Absorbed into the County Borough of West Ham in 1885, both Forest Gate and Upton struggle to maintain their identity.

RELIGIOUS BUILDINGS

EMMANUEL, Upton Lane and Romford Road. Built for the growing suburb on the border between East and West Ham. 1850–2 by *G.G. Scott*, in his favourite Middle Pointed, and really a country church come to town. Ragstone, with three gables to the E. Steep roofs, originally with patterned tiles. At the junction of nave and chancel an attractive timber steeple with tiled base, and an open, traceried tier below a spire with splayed foot. The nave has a lean-to S aisle, the N aisle was enlarged by *W.A. Coombs* in 1890–1 in a rather fussy Perp, with NW porch and turreted N transept. Six-bay nave with round piers; capitals and corbels with grossly luxuriant naturalistic foliage, roof with close-set rafters. Crudely subdivided in 1980, with a flat suspended ceiling over the W part. Raised two-bay chancel with pointed wagon roof, divided off by a large stone arch and openwork SCREEN. – Sanctuary with TILES. – Feeble STAINED GLASS by *A.L. Wilkinson*, 1952. – MONUMENT. William Jones †1910; colourful alabaster and mosaic tablet.

Former INSTITUTE N of Romford Road, 1882 by *Habershon & McDonall*, brick with stone dressings. Gable with wheel window.

ST MARK, Lorne Road. A small cluster by *APEC Architects* (*see* East Ham), 1986, for multi-purpose use, replacing, after much local consultation, a church of 1893–8 by *E.P. Loftus Brock* and hall of 1905. Single storey and smaller than other community centres by APEC in Newham. Typical of the firm the sweeping slate roof at the front and bands of windows under the eaves with taller monopitch clerestory-lit roof over the E–W spine. Light and pleasant interiors. Lobby and corridor with hall to the r., the church behind linked to it by folding doors. The church is white-walled, with movable furnishings. A low baptistery projects from the NE corner, with a timber and copper basin over a covered immersion font. – STAINED GLASS. War Memorial window from the old church, 1920 by *Herbert Hendrie* of *Lowndes & Drury*: a crowded design, Crucifixion and soldier with sword of justice, angels above.

ST SAVIOUR, MacDonald Road. 1904 by *F. Danby Smith*. Formerly the hall to a now-demolished church. A striking and original building in an Arts and Crafts manner. Low front with four brick buttresses; the entrance under a broad, stone moulded arch. Rising behind is a gable with shaped top and carved kneelers. Interior with slim stone columns and plain round-headed arches; clerestory above.

ST ANTONY OF PADUA (R.C.), St Antony's Road. A church, school and Franciscan monastery complex founded by Franciscans from Stratford. By *Pugin & Pugin*, 1884–91. The church is large, aisled, E.E. and frankly quite dull. The intended NE belltower was not built. Clerestory. Wide seven-bay nave, aisles with lean-to roofs, incorporating confessionals on the S side. Reordered by *Campling and Iliffe*, 1967–8 (their prominent false ceiling now removed), when the furnishings were simplified. S transept divided off for a sacristy. LADY ALTAR by *Boulton* of Cheltenham to designs by *P.P. Pugin*. – Much STAINED GLASS. E rose (with Franciscan saints) restored after war damage. Good windows by *Hardman*: S aisle (Passion of Christ), 1902–3, N aisle quatrefoils, 1922, S aisle W, 1933.

The buildings to the S have alternating projecting and recessed bays and, like the church, are built of buff stock brick with stone and black brick trim. Plain and large. Monastery addition of 1908, also ST ANTONY'S SCHOOLS in Lancaster Road, 1903, a bulky, Board-school type elementary school.

BAPTIST CHURCH, Romford Road. 1881–2 by *J.W. Chapman*, extended 1901. Quite a striking asymmetrical façade with a sheer brick wall, large entrance arch and big rose window over. To the l. an octagonal timbered lantern. Sunday school (hall) to the rear, 1899.

BAPTIST CHURCH, Neville Road. 1885. Single-storey hall with wheel window in the gable and low Romanesque entrance with nook-shafts and florid capitals.

CONGREGATIONAL CHURCH (now MIRACLE MINISTRY MISSION), Sebert Road. 1884 by *Francis J. Sturdy*. Yellow and red brick, large. In a flabby Italianate style with two orders of pilasters. Two octagonal towers, one finished off with a dome, the other stubby yet apparently completed. Grand interior with galleries on three sides, on iron columns.

METHODIST CHURCH and HALL, Woodgrange Road: 1955–64 by *Paul Mauger* and evincing his conviction that post-war Methodist churches should be more explicitly community-minded. In contrast with its bombastic predecessor of 1890, the group is low-key and domestic, in light brick with pitched roofs. The hall opened first, in 1956. The church is equally simple, with a steep pantiled roof and an angular porch of concrete with chamfered sides. Above, a sculpture leaps forward: 'The Preacher', modelled in concrete (or more accurately 'Pericrete') by *Peter Peri*. *See* also p. 246.

CHURCH OF GOD, Dames Road. Small, with plain brick pediment projecting above the roof. Built 1894–5 for Christian Israelites (VCH), repaired after war damage, 1952, with further work in 2002.

AZHAR ACADEMY, Romford Road. Built as Romford Road and Stratford Congregational church. Hefty E.E. work of 1880–5 by *T. Lewis Banks*. Knapped flints with red brick and sandstone dressings. Square SW tower with slated spire and corner pinnacles. W front with grouped lancets, double transepts, each with a triplet of lancets. After war damage a smaller church was constructed within the original shell, completed 1958. Former CHURCH HALL to the N. All under conversion, 2003–4.

MINHAJ-AL-QURAN MOSQUE AND CULTURAL CENTRE, Romford Road. A former Odeon cinema by *Andrew Mather*, 1937. Brick with grey ashlar facings, three narrow windows. Recent adornments reflect its current use; some of the original decoration, including a figure of Pan, has been concealed or removed.

WEST HAM SYNAGOGUE COMMUNAL HALL, Earlham Grove. 1927–8 by *Bertie Crewe*, the theatre specialist, who had designed the Romanesque-style synagogue in 1911. It stood to the rear of the hall but was destroyed by fire in 1984. The commission for both buildings must have come through the Abrahams family, for whom Crewe had designed a number of London theatres; A.E. Abrahams appears on the foundation stone. Stone or cement faced with a pedimented gable and Star of David window.

WEST HAM CEMETERY, Cemetery Road. Founded 1857 by the local Burial Board. Gothic ragstone chapel with polygonal transeptal projections by *T.E. Knightley*. The Nonconformist one has gone. No notable monuments.

JEWISH CEMETERY, Buckingham Road. Contiguous with West Ham Cemetery and founded in the same year by the congregations of the New and Great synagogues. Its monuments are

largely undistinguished, with the noble and notable exception of
81 the Rothschild MAUSOLEUM erected for Evelina de Rothschild †1866 by her husband Ferdinand. A domed building on a circular plan with Baroquizing Renaissance details, by *Sir Matthew Digby Wyatt*. The deceased's initials cleverly entwined.

MAJOR BUILDINGS

Former POLICE STATION, Romford Road. Derelict. 1888 by *John Butler*, Metropolitan Police Surveyor. Funded by residents of the Woodgrange Estate, after complaints about 'the throwing of bricks and brick bats at the windows of properties careless of the safety of tender ladies therein'. Red brick with terracotta dressings, mullioned windows, and diagonal chimneys; reassuringly domestic. Its successor on the corner with Green Street is pseudo-Victorian, with long ranges to the street, wavy parapets and corner entrance beneath a slated mansard. 1992 by *Property Services Department* of the Met.

DURNING HALL COMMUNITY CENTRE, Earlham Grove. 1957–64 by *Shingler & Risdon Associates*. A settlement originally founded in Limehouse in 1884 by Unitarians, and now managed by the Aston Mansfield charity. Informally composed with the flat-roofed Church of the Holy Carpenter to the fore and hall and residential block set behind at right angles. This has a large Aston Charities coat of arms on its gable end. The church has a fine *dalle-de-verre* stained glass behind the altar. A new building for the Trust in Woodgrange Road, by *van Heyningen & Haward*, attached to the Methodist Church (*see* above), is planned in 2004.

ST ANGELA'S URSULINE SCHOOL (R.C.), St George's Road. Convent girls' school founded in 1862, in houses in Upton Lane, by the Ursuline order of nuns. New buildings erected in the gardens in 1871–2. Yellow stock brick with Portland stone dressings, arcaded windows a steep mansard roof, and an unexpected Franco-Flemish flourish in the centre of the façade of a slim, projecting stair-tower with witch's hat roof. Set into a niche is a figure of St Joseph and Christ by *Philip Lindsay Clark*, 1962. On the first floor an attractive apsed CHAPEL with original oak stalls. Small gallery. Refurbished *c.* 1948, of that date, the Virgin and St John the Baptist by *Michael Lindsay Clark* and stained glass by *John Trickett*.

Many later additions, first *c.* 1880 for a SE wing, then W along St George's Road, a block, added 1889, for assembly hall and classrooms. Superficially Italianate with round-headed windows, stucco sill bands and bracketed eaves. Dull C20 extensions, and *c.* 1950 stripped classical along Upton Lane.

STRATFORD SCHOOL, Upton Lane. 1958 by *T.E. North*, Borough Architect. One of the few notable post-war schools in Newham. Cruciform tower with staircase in the main axis, four-storey curtain-walled teaching blocks with brick gable-ends.

FOREST LANE PARK. The park surrounds the former INDUSTRIAL SCHOOL. Erected in 1852–4 by the Whitechapel Guardians, to provide, as was the norm, schools at some remove from of the choked inner districts from which their children sprang. Converted to a workhouse in 1897 and extended as Forest Gate Hospital from 1929–86. The original school building faces Forest Lane. Originally E-plan, with three wings behind, but now reduced to a single block. Italianate, symmetrical three storeys in red brick with round-arched windows on the ground floor and a slightly projecting, towered centre bay. Entrance in a square porch beneath a shallow bow window. LODGE and INFIRMARY in similar style.

PERAMBULATION

Forest Gate

The tour begins in WOODGRANGE ROAD at FOREST GATE STATION, opened in 1841 on the Eastern Counties Railway. Five bays, round-arched windows and entrance, tiled roof. In front stands a curious ogee-roofed cylindrical kiosk with mullioned windows, originally part of a later extension. Just to the N, at the junction with Forest Lane is an 1890s polished granite drinking fountain donated by A.C. Corbett, developer of the Woodgrange Estate (*see* Little Ilford). From its centre rises a later cast-iron column supporting a clock, by *James Rowly and Parkes Co.* of Clerkenwell, with trefoil cresting around the face. This was the C19 suburb's market place, indicated on the side of the road by an Italianate range with 'The Market' inscribed in its parapet. All of the E side was developed with the Woodgrange Estate and is unremarkable, punctuated only by the EAGLE AND CHILD pub, recorded by Rocque in 1744 but rebuilt *c.* 1896. The ground floor has five funny, carved, wooden reliefs of 'Merrie England' subjects of drinkers, musicians, Henry VIII and Elizabeth I. These must be later, perhaps of the 1920s when 'Brewer's Tudor' was in vogue. The S end of Woodgrange Road was greatly enhanced *c.* 2002–3 by some thoughtful investment by the Council in restoration of the shopfronts on the W side. They are now in appropriately C19 uniform style and look good with the former Public Hall of 1902 in a debased Italianate. On the E side stood the major landmark of the Methodist Church but its successor (*see* above) is shy and retiring.

Detours E and W of Woodgrange Road are scarcely worthwhile except for enthusiasts for the larger type of late Victorian suburban housing. Amongst this repetitive streetscape, however, there are a few isolated highlights: in SEBERT STREET (E), the former Congregational Church (*see* above); in FOREST LANE (W), the Tudor-style Jabez Legg Almshouses of 1858, extended 1863, and the former Industrial School (*see* above). The streets to the W of Woodgrange Road and S of the railway were laid out on the Gurney Estate, *c.* 1870–90. The larger houses in EARLHAM GROVE are typical. On its N side beyond DURNING HALL (*see* above), is the Holy Order of Cherubim and Seraphim Church, formerly EARLHAM HALL. From *c.* 1879 this was the Forest Gate School (later Metropolitan Academy) of Music founded by John Curwen, pioneer of the Tonic-Sol-Fa method of teaching. To the fore is a low hall, of 1897, with pedimented gable. Behind this the earlier building, brick disguised under later rendering, of two storeys with pointed windows and an octagonal tower, stunted by the loss of its slated spire. By the early C20 much of Forest Gate's population was Jewish, dispersed from the inner East End. They worshipped at the West Ham Synagogue whose Communal Hall (*see* above) survives further W.

E of Woodgrange Road, the CLAREMONT ESTATE, between Claremont and Windsor Road, is a textbook mixed estate of the late 1950s, designed by *T.E. North*, Borough Architect and Planning Officer, and the first in West Ham to incorporate a point block, of eleven storeys. The rest is a mix of cottages, flat and maisonette blocks.

At the crossroads of Woodgrange Road and Romford Road, a tall block of FLATS converted from former offices in 2001 by the Peabody Trust. Reclad with vivid pink panels and a wavy-roofed single-storey block in front. On the opposite corner is THE PRINCESS ALICE, by *Donald Hamilton, Wakeford & Partners*, *c.* 1951, replacing an earlier pub destroyed by bombing. Curved façade of careful brickwork, the ground floor set behind concrete mullions with curving window above. Set-back top floor, presumably for the publican, with projecting flat roof carried forward from the wall on piers.

In ROMFORD ROAD, the few buildings of interest are scattered. On the S side, W of the crossroads, the NATWEST BANK was the London & County Bank, 1900, by *Zephaniah King and Co.* Respectable stone-faced classicism in yellowish limestone. Five bays, the outer ones advanced with pilasters, rusticated ground floor and balustrading. Then the MINHAJ-AL-QURAN Mosque and Cultural Centre (*see* above). The LIVE AND LET LIVE pub, interwar Queen Anne, carries the only echo of the pre-C19 street line of houses with front gardens. Further W, No. 224, a very large house of *c.* 1880 with stamped terracotta details, hipped roofs and closely stacked octagonal chimneys, set within a large garden. E of the junction (N side), beyond the Emmanuel Church Institute (*see* above), is a series of small three-bay houses of the mid C19: No. 35 has single-bay wings, one of which has a nice timber Gothic porch and, more peculiarly, a Victorian iron lamp standard glass with lights depicting bodybuilders.

Upton

UPTON LANE begins on the E side with Emmanuel Church (*see* above) but the rest of this C19 shopping street is less inspiring. Further S, the road bends W. At the corner with ST GEORGE'S

ROAD, the buildings of ST ANGELA'S URSULINE SCHOOLS (*see* above), one of a group which reflects the importance of the Roman Catholic Church in this neighbourhood from the mid-C19. Further along Upton Lane, the St Antony's Catholic Club was based at No. 13 UPTON AVENUE, a substantial Neo-Jacobean villa also known as The Red House. It is the only surviving example of the many large houses which existed in Upton before the last decades of the C19. Two-storey frontage, 5+1 bays, the end bay on the r. broad with a shaped gable. Ground floor canted bay with openwork balcony incorporating a little terracotta relief of fishermen; similar panels are inserted beneath the oriel window at the N façade. Openwork balustrades also to the porch and to the roof, which carries an array of urns. Its present appearance is probably *c.* 1865, a remodelling for the Tuthill family whose crest is shown in armorial glass above the door. The interior too is exclusively C19 or later but the core is evidently of the C18. A bell, taken from the cupola, is dated 1762 but the house is perhaps rather earlier if the flush sashes to be seen at the rear are taken as evidence. Modest rear additions *c.* 1933 for St Antony's Catholic Club.

Further W, UPTON LANE bends S by THE SPOTTED DOG, the one other reminder of rural Upton and a surprising survival. C16 timber-framed weatherboarded house, much altered but still atmospheric, despite later additions at the back. Hall range in centre, open roof with crude tie-beams; inserted chimney at r. end. Storeyed wings at each end, formerly jettied, now underbuilt; their internal partitions partly replaced by C19 iron columns. Its attractions in the C18 were enhanced by pleasure grounds and in the C19 by playing fields, especially for cricket. Picturesque Victorian additions are testament to its growing popularity. But its gardens have gone, now occupied by a hideous early C20 factory, the road is too busy and any memories of the quiet hamlet long forgotten. On the opposite corner, a former Methodist Chapel, now builder's yard and Stratford School (*see* above). Further S, facing West Ham Park (*see* Stratford and West Ham) the MEGGS' ALMSHOUSES, founded in Whitechapel in 1850 but rebuilt here in 1893 by *William La Riviere* for the Whitechapel Guardians. Brick and stone dressings with timber and slate pentices to the ground floor windows between three gabled projections.

PLAISTOW

Plaistow lay at the very edge of the marshes towards the Thames. First recorded in the C15, it appears on later maps as the third settlement besides Stratford and West Ham and by the 1740s was probably the largest hamlet in the parish. Its triangular layout of High Street, Balaam Street and Greengate Street is still discernible and may suggest that the village was centred on a large green. Several large houses, in particular Essex House, are noted, and some pubs still survive of the fourteen listed in 1742, but today Plaistow has almost no ancient building stock. The development of London in the C18, and the requirements of its markets, made Stratford far more important than Plaistow, which had no direct route across the Lea. This was corrected in 1812 when the Commercial Road Co. extended their route (now Barking Road) from the West India Docks to the river port at Barking. A chapel of ease, St Mary's, was established close to the centre of the village in 1829, but the focus of commercial life was now concentrated on the Barking Road to the S, with new streets of houses laid out in the wake of the Royal Docks (*see* p. 290) and since. Plaistow was absorbed into the County Borough of West Ham in 1899 and lost much of its identity in the C20, disadvantaged by rebuilding after 1945 and by the creation of the busy A13 road (Newham Way) to supersede Barking Road. In 2004 plans for regeneration of the High Street and its neighbourhood are under consideration.

RELIGIOUS BUILDINGS

ST CHAD AND ST ANDREW, St Andrew's Road. Originally St Andrew. Founded 1862 as a mission of St Mary Plaistow; built 1868–70 by *James Brooks*. Part of a fine group with the vicarage, schools and hall. The church is one of the series of monumental yet cheap buildings that Brooks made his speciality in poor areas of London. But unlike the brick St Chad and St Columba, Shoreditch, this is all of ragstone, the detail inspired by French C13 Gothic. Mighty apsidal E end, windows almost entirely lancets throughout. The S side has a transept, the N side only a chapel with big flying buttresses above. A crossing tower with spire and corner turrets, derived from Angers Cathedral, was intended but never completed. W entrance with two doors, divided in French Gothic manner by a statue under a canopy, lancets and plate-tracery roundel
p. 58 above. The power and height of the interior are no longer apparent as the church was subdivided in 1982–5 after some ten years of neglect. Brooks's four-bay arcades – now beneath a depressing flat ceiling – have thickly moulded arches on short circular piers with attached shafts in the cardinal directions, all with shaft rings, and a variety of foliage capitals. The upper walls were designed with a continuous arcade on colonnettes with shaft rings, which was carried across the transepts as open arcading, and around the tall apse. There was a large REREDOS made to Brooks' design by *T. Nicholls*, and a timber chancel

screen with carved figures above. The FONT remains. Of coloured marbles; a robust design by *Brooks*, made by *Burke & Co.* Square bowl on a massive drum, small colonnettes at the corners. – FONT COVER. An octagon with trefoiled niches below and spire with small gables and circular lucarnes above. – PULPIT. Timber, with a painted panel, on a stone base. – STAINED GLASS in the aisles by *Clayton & Bell*. In the divided-off E end STENCILLING with architectural motifs remains around the apse.

Brooks's VICARAGE of 1876–7 is an inventive Gothic building, with a symmetrical façade to the space in front of the church. Three storeys and three bays, each with a hipped roof over. Between these hips a couple of squeezed-in attic dormers. In the main front the windows are varied and original and form a large proportion of the wall surface. In the two lower tiers they are set within a pattern of linked stilted and round-arched hoodmoulds.

SE of the church, SCHOOL of 1873 and a HALL of 1883 and additions of 1894, all in keeping with the overall scheme.

ST MARTIN and NEWMARTIN CENTRE, Boundary Road. A cheap mission church of 1894, adventurously adapted and expanded by *Cottrell & Vermeulen*, 1991–7. The most overtly Modernist among Newham's many church conversions. The old building, with gable to the road, red and black brick details, wooden side windows and open timber roof has been transformed inside by clear glazing, white walls and bright colours. ALTAR and FONT of polished concrete, each raised on a red platform. The font, faced with glass mosaic, is divided into three compartments (for holy water, traditional baptism and immersion). The E window is screened by white fabric; when the sun is in the E the stained glass is mysteriously back-projected onto the screen. At the W end of the nave is a simple timber-and-glass box with counselling room and store, with a gallery above; a sacrament chapel is tucked into the NW corner, with CANDLE SCREEN of metal mesh alongside.

Adjoining is a hall shared with the Newmartin Community Youth Trust, and on the S a wing with youth facilities, with an arresting metal-clad projecting stair. The courtyard garden behind was designed to be shared by church and community: it has a pool and a site for a fire used to light candles for the Easter Mass.

ST MARY, St Mary's Road. *c.* 1981. A feeble focus in an almost entirely post-war area. A long, low, brick rectangle with shallow, split-pitched roof covered in pantiles. Windows only on the S side rising clumsily into the roof. It replaced *Blomfield*'s large E.E. church of 1889–94, itself a successor to the chapel of ease designed by *Edward Blore* in 1828–9. In May Road, and much more attractive than the present church, are the church schools, now GIVEN WILSON INSTITUTE, the oldest surviving school buildings in Newham. 1831 by *George Russell French* (who exhibited drawings at the RA that year). Tudor Gothic, with mullioned window and pointed gables. Extended N 1836.

ST PHILIP AND ST JAMES, Whitwell Road. 1954–5 by *J. Harold Gibbons*. On an ample corner site, contemporary with the rebuilt housing of the area. An assured building of stock brick; long, continuous roof over nave and chancel, twin transverse gables and a quasi-Italian NW tower with pyramid cap. Reminiscent of Gibbons's interwar work in NW London, especially St Barnabas, Northolt. The patterned tiling beneath the eaves and the simple square-headed windows are favourite Gibbons devices. On the E wall a carved roundel with the Crucifixion in low relief. Inside, whitened walls throughout and utterly plain, mostly round arches. Half arches across the aisles. At the W end a mixture of arches of different shapes, recalling the work of Temple Moore for whom Gibbons worked briefly fifty years before and whose designs he so much admired.*

HALL, also by Gibbons and contemporary with the church, repeating the patterned tiling under the eaves. Single long room with low vestibule at the front entered through a round arch. Small hall added 1960 by *P.J. Tucker*. Improved entrance and landscaped courtyard planned by *Ronald Wylde Associates* *c.* 2003.

90 WEST HAM (BAPTIST) CENTRAL MISSION, Barking Road. 1921–2 by *William Hayne*. An ambitious Byzantine front to the street with a battery of door and window openings, the big round-arched entrance flanked by two short, domed towers. The array of foundation stones testifies to Baptist strength at this time. Reddish orange brick sharply contrasting with white glazed terracotta details. Plainer side elevations of grey brick. Inside an impressive open central space but the overall effect marred by partitions under the gallery and the painting of the woodwork. The theatre next door began as a Baptist youth centre.

GLORY HOUSE, Barking Road, an independent Pentecostal church in a large group of cream-painted buildings, converted in 1997. Architecturally anonymous outside. The front is disguised by a shop although tall, arched windows along the flank to Tabernacle Road reveal an earlier life as a Baptist chapel of 1876, predecessor to Central Mission, funded by James Duncan, a Silvertown sugar refiner. It was originally set back from the road with steps up to two large porches which flanked a large round-headed window. This building is now subdivided as church offices; the present entrance is at the N end, with foyer leading to the church seating *c.* 1000, in a vast, plain one-storey converted warehouse. Behind is a multi-purpose hall, in a former cinema.

EAST LONDON CEMETERY, Grange Road. A private cemetery opened in 1872. Fine gate piers. Two Gothic chapels faced with crazy-paved ragstone but marred by modern additions. The one on the l. (or W) converted to a crematorium in 1954.†

*We owe these comments, and some others on West Ham churches, to Geoff Brandwood.

†One had windows by *A.J. Davies* of the *Bromsgrove Guild*, 1930–2.

Between the gate and the chapels a granite cross with a tall, rugged base to commemorate Britain's allies in the Great War – yet dating from as early as 1917. There are no single monuments of great merit but the post-1945 ones include a remarkable array of individualistic, often touching memorials that are so characteristic of E London cemeteries. Popular types include the overt symbolism of half-open doors, open arches and heart shapes, while footballs, a lorry, teddy bears, dogs and even a dart-board provide highly personal mementoes of the deceased. They are a far cry from the dreary lines of headstones usual in modern English burial grounds.

MAJOR BUILDINGS

PLAISTOW LIBRARY, North Street. 1902–3 by *S.B. Russell*. Single storey, in brick with concave inset corners banded in stone. Paid for by Passmore Edwards. A reduced, less decorative version of Russell's design for the Passmore Edwards Museum in Romford Road (*see* p. 232). The principal borrowed-key motif is the big open-segmental pediment over the entrance bay which is set within a full-height stone centrepiece with canted sides and Gibbs surround. The arched form reflects the cross-in-plan interior, where barrel vaults on square piers support a shallow saucer dome.

PLAISTOW FIRE STATION, Prince Regent Lane, 1931 by *Arthur H. Roe*, Deputy Architect and *T.V. Griffiths* Borough Surveyor. Neo-Georgian going modern, with three vehicle entrances set between brick pavilions with Venetian windows. The flat parapet hides a pitch roof.

PLAISTOW POLICE STATION, Barking Road. 1912 by *John Dixon Butler* in his mature phase, the domestic concerns of his earlier stations now overridden by increasing scale. Four storeys, in red brick with stone-banded ground floor and large bow window. Attic dormers and two large segmental pediments.

NEWHAM GENERAL HOSPITAL, Glen Road. 1979–83 by *North East Thames Planning* team with *The Hospital Design Partnership*. A large hospital, of two storeys in reinforced concrete, faced in brick with aggregate-faced band at first floor. Spine plan entered from W and E, with units set at right angles to the corridor around internal courtyards. The modular design was intended as a prototype for 'nucleus' hospital design, in essence allowing a phased development with the ground floor facilities in use before the first floor was complete. Profiled aluminium pitch roofs were added in the 1990s.

PLAISTOW DAY HOSPITAL, Samson Street. Built 1899–1902 as Plaistow Fever Hospital, by *Edwin T. Hall*. Hot red brick with terracotta dressings and ornament by *James Stiff & Sons* of Lambeth. Pavilion plan of ward blocks, originally with open-arched basements. The essential element of separation (which included no access between floors within the individual blocks) is now rendered scarcely visible by progressive enlargement and later additions. The Nurses' Home has a cut brick panel of the West Ham Borough arms.

NEWHAM SIXTH FORM COLLEGE, Prince Regent Lane. Adapted from the buildings of the former Plaistow municipal secondary school of 1926–30. The earlier buildings are brick, stripped classical, mainly dull, laid out as single storey N and S quadrangles behind the main elevation. New N entrance, created in 1992 by *Newham Technical Services* with *Nick Evans Architects*. Spirited, a variation on the mall idea of a covered street, complete with mature trees. Glass roof on arched braces.

9 PLAYARC, Plaistow Park. A generic play centre designed by *Hawkins Brown*, 1991 as a self-contained unit, constructed of an arched, timber frame clad in profiled metal. Secure sliding shutters open along one side. One of a group of four designed for Newham by this firm (cf. the Playbarn, Hermit Park, Canning Town; Three Mills Play Centre, West Ham; Major Road Playcentre, Stratford).

PERAMBULATION

Plaistow Station to Barking Road, a circular tour

PLAISTOW STATION, in Plaistow Road, opened on the London Tilbury & Southend Railway, 1858 (District Railway after 1902). Rebuilt 1903–5. Tripartite composition of symmetrically placed entrances set slightly back from the main façade. Its pierced parapet has been lost. LTSR benches and cast-iron brackets on the W platform canopy.

In PLAISTOW ROAD S of the station, the first building of note is housing, of the live/work type, by *Stock Woolstencroft*, 2001–2. Primary colours, timber facings and projecting windows clad in aluminium. Interesting more for novelty than character. Otherwise the scene is one of unrelieved housing estates of the 1950s and later, with almost nothing to divert interest. In HIGH STREET, at the corner with Grasmere Road, one lonely physical reminder of old Plaistow is THE BLACK LION public house, a concatenation of buildings with an appealingly varied façade and roofline. It was recorded in 1742 but refaced in 1875 and later altered in 1892. At the S end is a narrow two-bay house with a cranked gable and tiled roof. Then a four-bay section with stucco quoins and window architraves, perhaps of 1875. The range beyond is also early and incorporates the carriageway to the yard. The rest of the High Street is exclusively post-war and with little feeling of a commercial centre except for a short, covered parade of shops set into the podium of RICHMOND COURT, a fifteen-storey tower of 1962–5 by West Ham Borough.

THE BROADWAY is the junction of several streets that are shown on the early maps. To the l., in NORTH STREET is the excellent PLAISTOW PUBLIC LIBRARY (*see* above). On the SW corner of the Broadway is the COACH AND HORSES, here by 1742 but rebuilt in the C19. Three-bay brick front with lower wings flanking. BALAAM STREET continues SW, its name a corruption of Balun, a family recorded in Plaistow from the C12. Its once fashionable status is now long forgotten, although No. 197 is a large house of the 1880s with Kentish ragstone facing. Big gables and bay windows, quite the largest house in the neighbourhood. Further on, in CHESTERTON ROAD stood Chesterton House, the late Georgian residence of the Quaker meteorologist Luke Howard, and described by Pevsner as of 'seven bays, two storeys, yellow brick with porch of Roman Doric columns'. The house was demolished in 1960 but a fragment survives of a scheme, laid out in its gardens *c.* 1838, for a crescent of paired stucco villas. The road continues E as an avenue of lesser houses of similar date.

The E side of BALAAM STREET is open to the featureless Plaistow Park (partly created from land vacated by the tram depot) and slightly S the entrance to THE GREENWAY, a pedestrian footpath from Bow to Beckton following the line of Bazalgette's Northern Outfall Sewer. The rest is a mixture of dilapidated Victorian shops mixed with 1950s housing, which extends over a large area to the W around the church of St Philip and St James (*see* above). Of the Georgian terraces which once lined Balaam Street only Nos. 42–4 survive: *c.* 1760, with a fine modillioned, broken-pedimented Doric doorcase. Extended 1816. The original sash windows have gone. (Interior work of both periods survives, including panelling and the staircase.) Owned by the Franciscan Society of the Divine Compassion since the 1890s. Glowering alongside is the Borough's monstrous LEISURE CENTRE and swimming baths, which superseded *A. Saxon Snell*'s Plaistow Baths of 1894. Two long blocks in dark engineering brick, covered by broad monopitch roofs, with expressively treated brickwork patterning at the gable ends.

BARKING ROAD crosses E–W from the junction with Balaam Street. On the S side, the very large ABBEY ARMS, another old pub, rebuilt 1882 for Taylor Walker & Co., their name inscribed in the frieze. Tall and wide Italian palazzo with big recessed entrances to the bars with surviving ironwork. To the E the sights are few in number apart from the Baptist Mission Church, Police Station and further E by the Greenway, the Church of St Andrew (*see* above).

GREENGATE STREET completes the triangle of Plaistow's old streets with a handful of notable buildings. THE GREENGATE pub, long established but rebuilt in 1953–4, is not one. Its sign carries a bucolic scene, quite divorced from the grimy reality of its surroundings. Further on, at the entrance to the park stands ESSEX LODGE (now Essex Lodge Surgery). Towards the street, it appears as a charming gabled cottage orné of 1836, in the typical Tudor style with hoodmoulds and decorative bargeboards. But attached to the rear of the three-storey front block, and entirely disguised, is a two-storey timber-framed structure of the C16 with jettied upper floor and queen-strut roof with arched windbraces: an almost unique survival (*see* also The Spotted Dog, Upton) in Newham. The 1830s wing contains older fragments, including, over the N entrance, a *c.* 1700 shell hood. Inside, a stone chimneypiece with elongated voussoirs and keystone (perhaps cut down from an early C18 doorcase) bears the crest of the Willyams family, which suggests these fragments may have been salvaged from their residence, Essex House, which stood nearby (demolished 1836). A new wing added for a surgery by *Freeman Ankerman and Hickling*, 1994, the rest over-vigorously restored. Next, the former WEST HAM TRAMWAYS offices. 1905–6 by *John G. Morley*, Borough Engineer, in his trademark Free Style of red brick with stone banding and terracotta dressings. Tall and narrow, two big arched windows in the ground floor and shaped gables. The depot lay to the rear. To the street, the WAR MEMORIAL to its employees, a plinth with a small obelisk under a flat canopy on four columns. Opposite, raised up above steps, is the former PLAISTOW RED TRIANGLE CLUB, erected in 1920–1 by *Thomas Brammall Daniel* as a youth club for the YMCA and YWCA. Steel frame, clad in pale brick and glazed faience. Prominent centre flanked by tall window bays. Vaguely Art Nouveau detail, but with lavish ornament more American in spirit, perhaps explained by Daniel having spent much of his early career there. The façade also serves as Plaistow's WAR MEMORIAL, with decorative emblems of the allied powers (cf. Daniel's Empire Memorial Hostel, Limehouse). Plans for conversion to flats by *Herzog & de Meuron* in 2004.

CANNING TOWN and CUSTOM HOUSE

By contrast with the hamlets and villages of West Ham, which vanished under the engulfing sprawl of late Victorian London, the story of Canning Town and Custom House belongs entirely to the industrial age. In 1777 this area was part of the Plaistow marshlands, separated from Poplar to the W by the Bow Creek. But in 1810–12 an iron bridge crossing was erected and Barking Road was formed, linking the West and East India Docks to the river port at Barking. Settlement began only after 1846 when the North Woolwich Railway and Mare and Co.'s (later Thames Iron Works) shipbuilding yards were opened, followed by the Victoria Dock in 1850–5. In 1857 Dickens mentioned Hallsville, a small group of streets close to the Bow Creek, and Canning Town with its 'new streets of houses without drains, roads, gas or pavements'. Built below the river's high tide level, only an embankment prevented its regular inundation. The poor housing and sanitation brought the area to the attention of health reformers

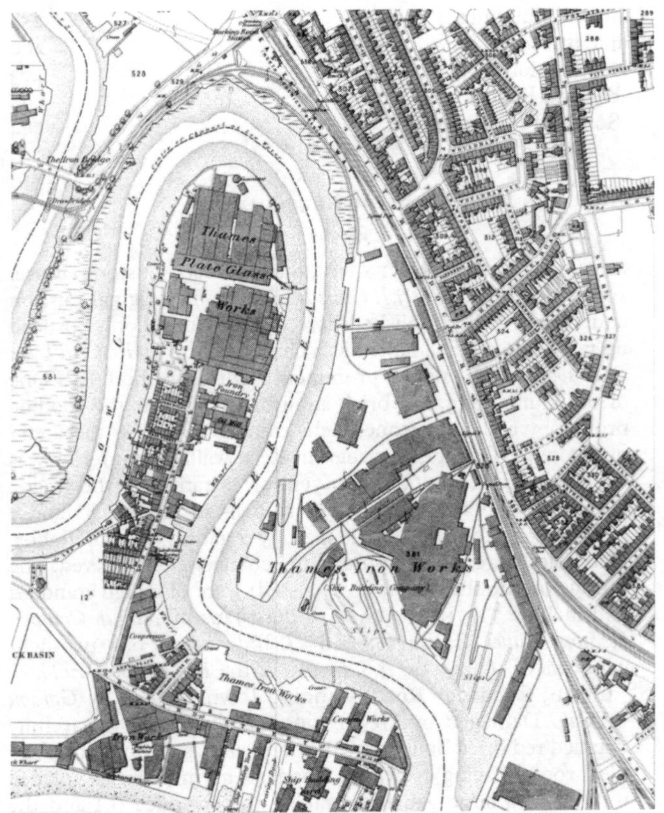

The Thames Iron Works, Canning Town and Bow Creek, 1867

and, like the inner East London districts, it became the focus for social settlements and religious missions from the 1880s onwards, several of whose buildings survive. Housing continued to spread S and E over the remaining marshland in the later C19 and early C20 to form a district, centred upon Prince Regent Lane, and known increasingly as Custom House. By the early C20 four parishes had been created. Proximity to the docks inevitably brought some of the heaviest destruction experienced in East London during the Blitz and consequently massive reconstruction for the Keir Hardie Estate. The A13 (Newham Way) has superseded Barking Road as the main E–W route and cut the district in half. The exclusion of the area from the Docklands Development zone after 1986 further served to create an isolated district on which the major new developments of the 1990s to the S of Victoria Dock Road now firmly turn their back. A masterplan for the regeneration of Canning Town and Custom House by *Shillam + Smith* was approved in 2003 for 7,000 new homes and a new town centre on Barking Road.

RELIGIOUS BUILDINGS

ASCENSION CHURCH CENTRE, Baxter Road, Custom House. 1903–7 by *J.E.K. and J.P. Cutts*, replacing the original mission church and hall established here by Felsted School. Spruced up in 1995–6 when adapted as a church centre by *Richard Lyon & Associates*, and now a prominent sight from the DLR. One of the Cutts' long, red brick suburban churches; the roofline broken by a slender stone flèche over a bellcote at the E end of the nave. Grouped lancets in the E wall. The interior was subdivided in 1995–6: a new central entrance on the N side leads into a lobby giving access to halls in the W part and a worship area to the E, overlooked by a gallery over the lobby. The aisles were divided off and the chancel floor lowered. The fittings (no doubt paid for by Felsted) were of a high standard and include STAINED GLASS of the 1920s by *Ninian Comper, Heaton, Butler & Bayne*, and *H. Wilkinson*. Four two-light windows of 1924–7 by *A.J. Davies* of the *Bromsgrove Guild*.

ST CEDD, Chadwick Road, Canning Town. 1938–9 by *Gordon O'Neill*. Damaged by fire in 1995, derelict 2003. A carefully detailed red brick building with round arches throughout. Pantiled roofs. Facing Newham Road an asymmetrically placed tower and a large gable embracing the entrance (l.) and the baptistery (r.).

Former ST LUKE'S, Jude Street. Now St Luke's Centre. Virtually the only old building remaining in this part of Canning Town. 1873–5 by the little known *Giles & Gane*.* Deconsecrated 1985 and vandalized, but saved from demolition by a local group, and converted for community uses in 1998–2000 by *Peter Eley* (engineers: *Alan Baxter Associates*). The building epitomizes the Victorian ideal of the imposing town church rising above its surroundings both physically and metaphorically. Continuous nave and chancel with flèche between the two, tall clerestory rising above the aisles, and a precipitous apse, a demonstration of the type of French Gothic introduced to London by Pearson at St Peter, Vauxhall and taken up to such good effect by James Brooks. The transepts are doubled. Simple, economic materials and details: yellow stock brick with window arches of red brick and some stone dressings. Lancets except at the W end, which has a grand window with geometric tracery and a double portal under a diapered gable. The intended SW tower was never built.

*Probably Charles Edmund Giles and Richard Gane, both of whom worked in the West Country and elsewhere (GB).

Externally the evidence of conversion is restricted to pointed dormers and roof lights. Inside, although one may lament the loss of the original space, the subdivision is thoughtful and ingenious. Five floor levels are provided within an inserted steel frame, but retaining the drama of the full height at E and W ends. The lofty western bay of the nave, used as a café, is splendidly lit by the W window and overlooked by new undulating glazed galleries on each side. White plastered inserted walls contrast with the exposed yellow brick of the original interior, carved stone capitals add character to the new spaces, and on the top floor, the crown-post roof is left exposed. The original arrangement, otherwise now concealed, was a five-bay nave, the arcades with alternating round and square piers with shaft rings, divided from the chancel only by a pair of elongated wall shafts. The apse (sadly only used as a store) has three tiers of stone arcading, filled with unusually fine MOSAICS of *c.* 1893 in a pictorial style, by then rather old fashioned; the centre row with the Twelve Apostles and the Ascension, with angels above and foliage below, all against a gold ground. STAINED GLASS. Three apse windows with strongly leaded figures against clear patterned glass, 1950 by *Patience Hallward*. War Memorial tablets and other fittings are now at St Mary, Wethersfield, Essex.

ST LUKE'S PARISH CHURCH AND SCHOOL, Ruscoe Road, Canning Town. 1999–2000 by *Ronald Wylde Partnership.* A replacement for the Victorian church. Neatly planned but with clumsily detailed exterior. A shared octagonal central foyer, top lit with thin spire containing a bell. Small chapel on the r., which can open up to a hall used by the school. Low spreading classroom blocks behind. In chapel and hall, six STAINED GLASS windows from the Royal Marine Chapel, Deal.

ST MATTHIAS, Kimberley Road, Canning Town, 1991 by *APEC*. Another replacement, this time a chapel and community rooms attached to a U-shaped block of flats for residents with special needs, under a descending sequence of pitched roofs; with vicarage to match.

ST ANNE (R.C.), Berwick Road, Custom House. 1980–1 by *Francis Weal*, replacing a war-damaged church. Brick, octagonal, with steel-framed roof, a glass lantern over the sanctuary. Parish room above the foyer. White marble furnishings. The entrance archway remains from the original church of 1898–9 by *R.L. Curtis*.

PRESBYTERY by *John E. Sterrett*, 1953–4.

ST MARGARET AND ALL SAINTS (R.C.), Barking Road, Canning Town. Founded 1859, built 1875–6 by *F.W. Tasker*, repaired 1949–51 by *T.G. Birchall Scott* after war damage to the E end. An austere stock brick front with tall narrow gable with saddle roof and a large circular window, a favourite motif of Tasker's; the unusual Star of David tracery appears to be original. Side entrance on the l., originally connecting an adjacent school destroyed in the war. The surprise is the dignified vaulted interior, in a Transitional Gothic, the passage-aisle plan without clerestory and with arches through internal buttresses is reminiscent of western France. The three-bay nave has brick arcades and some carved stone capitals, moulded cross ribs and pointed transverse arches. Flat-roofed passage aisles with round-arched arcading and lancet windows high up. Vaulted apse with two lancets, the lower wall lined with marble panels. These were added after war damage in place of more elaborate fittings. Other walls now painted cream. W gallery added 1899, extending over the aisles of the W bay.

Adjoining the church, three-storey later C19 PRESBYTERY, 1884 by *Tasker*, with added floor of 1899. CHURCH CENTRE by *Ronald Wylde Associates*.

ST MARY'S CONVENT (R.C.), Bethell Avenue, Canning Town. Founded 1897 by Franciscan missionaries of Mary and later partly used as an Old People's Home. Convent buildings of 1902, with new wing of 1909; gutted by fire in 1941 and rebuilt 1946–55. To be replaced by a smaller convent, 2004.

CHAPEL OF THE SACRED HEART OF JESUS, 1929–31 by *W.C. Mangan*. Unusually ambitious. The exterior is an Arts and Crafts version of Lombard Romanesque. Mixed red and purple brick with bands of tilework and pantiled roofs. NW entrance at an angle, with mosaic tympanum by *Gabriel Pippett*. A most impressive and attractive Renaissance interior, with a festive use of Italian coloured marbles all carried out to Mangan's design by Art Marbles, Stone & Mosaic Co. The large nave, built for public use, has a barrel vault springing from a cornice, above five-bay arcades on marble columns with Corinthian capitals. Well lit by lunette clerestory windows cut through the vault. Apsed E end with round-headed windows, flanked by low side chapels. Lavish marble HIGH ALTAR and canopy. Another marble altar from a Franciscan convent in The Boltons, Kensington, installed 1996–7. W organ gallery, now glazed. There was formerly a screen dividing off the Nuns' choir from the nave. Sacristy to the N, converted to a chapel.*

KEIR HARDIE METHODIST CHURCH, Fife Road, Canning Town. 1960. Contemporary with later phases of the Keir Hardie Estate. A modest portal-framed building with shallow copper-covered pitched roof; yellow brick, the gable end with concrete panels.

CUSTOM HOUSE BAPTIST CHURCH, Prince Regent Lane. 1927, low and domestic looking.

MAJOR BUILDINGS

PUBLIC HALL and LIBRARY, Barking Road. A single composition of 1891–4 by *Lewis Angell*, Borough Engineer. The Public

*We are grateful to Marilyn Johnson for details on St Margaret and St Mary's Convent.

Hall (now community centre) is a grandiose Baroque affair, in brick and stone with a massive pediment and balustrade. Arcaded entrance of three bays with much lively carved detail. Tall windows in the centre and *œils de bœuf* to the sides. The ground floor was intended for swimming baths (later erected elsewhere), but built instead with a small hall-cum-police court and offices. The subdivided main hall retains its ebullient decorative ceiling and proscenium arch. The Library, to the W, is in the same red brick and Portland stone. J. Passmore Edwards contributed to its erection. Retrograde Italianate. Seven bays, divided by thin pilasters at first floor, of round-arched windows with stone dressings, aprons and carved friezes in alternate bays. Asymmetrical entrance in the second bay from the l. with prominent stone surround, open pediment and consoles carrying obelisks. Indifferent interior, reconstructed after bombing which destroyed a notable array of technical gadgetry, devised by the Chief Librarian, including an automated indicator and automated steps.

CUSTOM HOUSE CARNEGIE LIBRARY, Prince Regent Lane. 1905 by *John G. Morley*, Borough Engineer. A lighthouse in a gloomy sea, set back from the street behind railings with terracotta-faced gatepiers. Square plan, single storey with a central two-storey tower in the centre with a timber roof-lantern. Delightful Free Style detail of terracotta panels, decoration and dressings, especially the scooped parapets of the wings with badge decorations.

THE HUB, Star Lane. Multi-functional Community Resource Centre by *Eger Architects* and *Ove Arup & Partners*, 2003–4. The first of a series planned for Newham and incorporating a nursery, business units and recreational facilities. Energy efficient with blue solar panels in strips along the straight frontage; curved steel roof behind descending towards a garden and a glazed section to the r. revealing a café.

Former FAIRBAIRN HALL, Barking Road. 1898–9 by *H.C. Lander*. Built as a boys' club associated with the Mansfield House university settlement.* Now flats. Free Style, but outwardly symmetrical. Of three storeys, with two large round-arch windows at the ground floor and projecting square bays rising through the height of the building to l. and r. Mullion windows with terracotta dressings and pressed-steel windows. Entrance in the r. bay, beneath a corner bartizan with shallow dome roof. The plan of the original building was an angled L-shape, with a single-storey wing containing a gymnasium. The latter was demolished for remodelling and extension in 1929–30 by *Louis de Soissons* and *G. Grey Wornum*. Of this period survive only a commemorative tablet by *Eric Gill*, inlaid terrazzo floors and the staircase, with curly iron balustrade by *Cashmore Art Workers*. Other interiors have not been retained:

* Mansfield House, a social settlement founded by Mansfield College, Oxford under F.W. Newland. The main building, of 1897–8 by *F.W. Troup* was also in Barking Road but since demolished.

they included a café with decorative work by *Miriam Wornum* (wall paintings) and *Ronald Grierson* (etched glass) and a galleried gymnasium. An upper floor containing theatre, chapel and workshop was added in 1939 by *Philip G. Freeman* and *G. Grey Wornum*.

MAYFLOWER FAMILY CENTRE, Vincent Street. By *Geoffrey Raymond* 1923–30, extended and remodelled by *Stillman & Eastwick Field c.* 1977–80. Founded as the Malvern College Mission in 1894 in a row of terraced houses but expanded after 1918 by *Sir Reginald Kennedy-Cox* as Dockland Settlement No. 1 (the first of a national network in Britain's major ports), and after 1958 under its present name. It was far larger than contemporary settlements elsewhere in East London, with Tudor-style buildings for residences, club rooms and chapel arranged around a quadrangle which was originally closed on its W side by terraced housing. War damage was, amazingly, only superficial.

The main entrance is on Vincent Street in a two-storey range, originally for residential workers, with close-studded upper storey, attic dormers and red brick ground floor, extended at the W end by *Stillman & Eastwick Field* who also added the adjoining Youth Centre. By contrast with the Old English invocations of the early buildings, this is entirely attuned to inner city reality; robustly executed in brick with a broad recessed entrance and a continuous roof. An oppressively spartan, but undoubtedly vandal-proof, interior. On the r. of the main block is the gabled S wall of the CHAPEL OF ST GEORGE AND ST HELENA (1929–30), with a large six-light Perp window. Beneath this the entrance, framed by a Tudor arch with nook shafts, leads to an ante-chapel beneath the gallery; on the r. was the baptistery, divided by a Gothic screen. Dividing it from the chapel is a panelled screen with four-light openings. The chapel is breathtaking, in character like a great C16 unaisled hall, covered by a broad hammerbeam roof with angels on the beam ends. Eight-bays long with big Perp windows on both sides in alternate bays. At the N (liturgical E end), the chancel is created by low wooden screens, by *Maile and Son Ltd*, extending forward to form passages to l. and r. of the altar and a 'minstrels gallery' behind. Linenfold panels with bands of carved vines. Stone FONT by *Maile and Son Ltd.* In front of the altar steps, a piece of stone from the Roman amphitheatre at Carthage, inscribed 'the Blood of Martyrs'. STAINED GLASS. In the E and W windows, shields of Malvern College, the City, Diocese and the chapel's benefactors. Also emblems of Christ's Passion (E wall) and the Stations of the Cross by *Jessie M. Jacob*. N wall. Rose window. Large S window by *Reginald Bell*, showing Christ's triumphant return to Earth. In the lower tier, scenes of 1930s dockworkers and their families with Christ against a background of the Thames dockside. Flanking on each side, windows replaced after war damage: a medieval wharfinger and a Second World War airman (l.); the Abbess of Barking and a soldier (r.).

Damaged glass was re-assembled in two windows in the ante-chapel which also has windows of St George and St Helena (both by *Bell*) to l. and r. of the entrance.

Towards Cooper Street, the second residential range, dated 1930, with close-studded upper floor, brick below with Tudor hoodmoulds to the windows and doors and a projecting, gabled cross-wing to the right. In Burke Street, the former swimming pool, erected with funds from Bernhard Baron, the philanthropic American tobacco magnate. Classical front with pedimented gable, big thermal windows along each side and the chimney disguised as slender *campanile* with open bellcote.

CUMBERLAND SCHOOL, Barking Road, Alexandra Street and Morgan Street. 1951–2 by *T.E. North* with *R.B. Padmore* and *H.C. Macaree* as the South West Ham County Technical School for Boys. A good big asymmetrical building in the Modern style of 1951. Flat roofs and a successful distribution of the various wings.

ROYAL DOCKS COMMUNITY SCHOOL, Prince Regent Lane. 1999 by *Property and Design Consultants of the Borough of Newham*. The most significant recent secondary school in the borough. Designed for shared community use and an exemplar for accessibility and inclusiveness, in particular the top-lit central rotunda which has a spiral ramp to first floor for disabled students. From this central feature the wings are arranged in a cruciform plan.

ST LUKE'S CENTRE AND SCHOOL (*see* Religious Buildings, above).

CANNING TOWN STATION, Silvertown Way: 1996–9 by *John McAslan & Partners*, who won the job as *Troughton McAslan* in 1991. An admirable design in glass, concrete and aluminium providing a link for three rail lines and bus interchange. Conceived as two stations set in parallel, but kept to a tight area by using double-deckered train platforms raised on huge pre-cast V-shaped concrete pillars above a submerged third storey, for ticket halls, where ingenious use of top-lighting creates a luminous interior.

The staircase to the underground ticket hall supports a 126 wrought-iron panel from the hull of HMS *Warrior*, the first iron-clad warship, built on this site in 1860 at the Thames Iron Works. This provides the centrepiece for an elegant tribute to Canning Town, the Ironworks and the formation by its workers, symbolized by their hammers, of West Ham United F.C. The unfurling inscription, carved directly into the concrete facing panels, is by *Richard Kindersley*.

PERAMBULATIONS

Canning Town is not a rewarding area for extensive perambulation. Its buildings of individual note are scattered and only the W end of Barking Road has any coherence as a centre.

1. Barking Road

The tour begins close to Canning Town Underground Station (*see* Public Buildings) at the W end of BARKING ROAD, laid out in 1810–12. With the development of the adjoining land for workers' housing it soon became the centre for the district. Its present appearance is very decayed. On the N side, Nos. 51–53 (Rathbone Clinic) the former London and County Bank by *Cheston & Perkin*, 1897; red brick with a large pedimented roughcast gable, and six bays of windows with cut brick aprons, an Essex domestic architectural motif. The modest landmarks are the former ROYAL OAK, a big but decrepit 1880s pub with a tiled entrance depicting the eponymous tree in an oval frame, ST MARGARET'S CHURCH and PRESBYTERY of 1919 (*see* above), and ANCHOR HOUSE (No. 81), a Roman Catholic seamen's mission, erected in 1962 by the Roman Catholic Apostleship of the Sea. Six-storey residential slab to the road with flanking single-storey wings under zigzag roofs. Further E, the LIBRARY and PUBLIC HALL (*see* above) make the only architectural statement of note. Beyond Bethell Avenue is TRINITY GARDENS, built on the bombed site of Trinity Church designed by *Banks & Barry* in 1867. A good example of West Ham's post-war housing. Eight storeys slab, mixed with four and six storey blocks with balconies and pitched roofs. On the S side of Barking Road is CUMBERLAND SCHOOL (*see* above) of similar date.

To its W, beyond Beckton Road (the old route to the river), C19 shops were cleared for the dismal RATHBONE MARKET of 1961–3 by *T.E. North*, the Borough Architect. A wedge- shaped market place, with covered stalls, enclosed by low flat-roofed shop and a ten-storey slab at its E end, THOMAS NORTH TERRACE: reinforced concrete frame with concrete cross walls, infilled with brick, all painted a sickly yellow. Plans for redevelopment are under consideration in 2004.

2. South of Barking Road

The creation of Rathbone Market was part of the major replanning of the entire area to the S of Barking Road after 1945. C19 Canning Town (between Silvertown Way and Freemasons Road as far as the edge of the Royal Docks) was destroyed by bombing, and plans by *T.E. North*, West Ham Borough Architect, were prepared for rebuilding as early as 1944, when they were published in Forshaw and Abercrombie's *Greater London Plan*. Under the 1946 West Ham Development Plan, the area to the E, known as Custom House, was incorporated to create Neighbourhood Unit 15, later renamed the Keir Hardie Estate in honour of West Ham's, and Parliament's, first Labour M.P. At 230 acres (with a planned density of 100 persons per acre) it was one of the largest redevelopment areas in Britain and showed up most of the successes and failures of post-war planning. As elsewhere, the neighbourhood idea involved the incorporation (where they survived) of existing churches, e.g. St Luke, community centres such as the Mayflower Family Centre (*see* above) and schools. Pubs were also retained, or newly built, but few are worthy of note except perhaps for the Hallsville Tavern, Hallsville Road, a picturesque pub of *c.* 1840 with curly bargeboards, possibly the sole survivor of the earliest developments in Canning Town. Attempts were made to retain the traditional shopping centres of the old districts, e.g. along Freemason's Road but these were never as generous as envisaged and are still surprisingly few in number. Green spaces were to be created for the first time in this district, and industry zoned to the edges along Silvertown Way, where it remains.

Perambulation is neither easy nor particularly desirable other than for serious enthusiasts for public housing. A walk can begin at ROYAL VICTORIA DLR at the S side of the estate. The dominant tone in the earlier parts is that of the pre-war Garden Suburb ideal, demonstrated in the terraces and semi-detached houses, for large families, of MUNDAY ROAD, APPLEBY ROAD, MONK DRIVE and BOWMAN AVENUE, streets named after local ARP wardens killed during the Blitz. This pattern is repeated over such a large area that Pevsner was correct to call it 'a town of terraced housing in the Council Estate style'. Density was kept to seventy persons per acre but in the later phases, undertaken in the mid-1950s, higher-density housing was introduced with flats and maisonettes in four-storey blocks grouped around green spaces. This phase followed the LCC mould of loose planning on the ground, but also preserving some C19 street patterns and introducing mixed heights and patterns to enliven the streetscape. Examples are visible around BUTCHER'S ROAD and in FIFE ROAD. Later still, point blocks were introduced, first by West Ham Borough Council *c.* 1961–4 around RATHBONE STREET and at the N end of BUTCHER'S ROAD, all of eleven storeys. These were followed from 1966 by the notorious FREEMASONS' ESTATE, with eight 23-storey towers built for the London Borough of Newham, using the Larsen–Neilsen system. The 1968 disaster, in which a gas explosion caused partial collapse of Ronan Point, marked the beginning of a two-decade campaign to remove the towers, achieved only after 1986. Today only a single example of this type remains in FORDS PARK ROAD, but the smaller Borough Council designed towers have been retained.

An alternative approach to high-density housing of the same period is demonstrated N of Newham Way (A13) in the small scheme of thirty-nine houses around RAVENSCROFT ROAD and KILDARE ROAD. These used an experimental timber and steel composite frame grid (known as 5M) developed by the *Ministry of Housing and Local Government.* Designed by *A. W. Cleeve-Barr* and *Oliver Cox* in association with *T.E. North* in

1961–4, these low-rise houses were expressly intended to illustrate what could be achieved with the new Parker Morris standards. There are six types of houses, faced in brick and weatherboard, with an interesting stepped layout. Their planning, with greater provision of single bedrooms, two living rooms and emphasis given to access for cars, reflects consultation with residents over the design.

Recent housing has maintained the low-rise terrace ideal, mixing with C19 and early C20 housing stock around Custom House and extending E of Prince Regent Lane to form an irregular fringe around the edge of Beckton District Park (*see* Beckton).

EAST HAM

The parish of East Ham stretched from the Thames to just N of the Romford Road. Its transformation into an urban borough was rapid. Up to the later C19 the medieval church lay on its own just to the N of the flood levels of the Thames marshes. About a mile further N, Barking Road, an eastward continuation of Commercial Road, was laid out in 1812 and the principal settlement grew around this, expanding from the 1870s to engulf scattered hamlets and farms and the sites of gentry houses sold up for development. Growth during the 1890s was the fastest of any urban area in Britain. The population rose dramatically from 32,713 in 1891 to over 96,000 by 1904, when the borough was incorporated, having by then taken in the small parish of Little Ilford to the NE (*see* below).

Much of East Ham is dull. But the long straight streets of two-storey bay-windowed houses N and S of Barking Road represented order and respectability for those who could afford to escape the squalor of the East End. They have survived remarkably complete, for the local authority established in 1878, with *William J. Savage* as surveyor, was efficient, creating main drainage from 1886, and ensuring that most houses were well built. There was less Second World War damage in the centre of East Ham than close to the Thames and in West Ham. In the northern area extensive post-war rebuilding took place only on the western borders around Green Street and on the poor eastern fringes of Little Ilford. Minor accents of the turn of the century are still provided by a scatter of imposing board schools (by *R.L. Curtis*), churches of all types (Nonconformists were strong here), and a few good corner pubs (though few and far between in comparison with the old East End). The architectural highlight is the extensive group of flamboyant civic buildings of 1901–14 by *Cheers & Smith*, a confidently urban statement by the new borough, in conscious competition with longer established West Ham. Recreation grounds, council housing, libraries and cottage hospital were also provided, under the leadership of *A.H. Campbell*, Borough Surveyor from the 1890s. Many of these amenities owed much to the negotiating skills of J.H. Bethell (1861–1945), a local surveyor and developer who progressed from radically minded ratepayers' leader in the 1880s to mayor in 1904–5 and local M.P. from 1906, becoming Lord Bethell, first Baron Romford, in 1922.

On the southern fringe of the Victorian suburb the small Norman church remains, an extraordinary survival, built on the fringe of the marshes, and now on the edge of a vast burial ground which still gives it the semblance of rural setting. But beyond, the busy A13 marks off a different world of retail parks and late C20 housing. The story of the southern part of East Ham is told in more detail in the Royal Docks and Riverside section below (p. 294). In this area is North Woolwich, a riverside hamlet by the crossing to Woolwich across the Thames, which remained part of Woolwich until 1965. The Royal Docks, created from 1850, encouraged development here, and at the adjacent Silvertown in West Ham. Further E Beckton gasworks was opened in 1870 with a small settlement at its gates; it remained isolated until the whole area was transformed from the 1980s as part of the docklands redevelopment.

RELIGIOUS BUILDINGS

ST BARTHOLOMEW, Barking Road. A tall block in dark red brick incorporating church, day-care centre and surgeries, with three storeys of old people's flats above. Planned from 1975, built 1979–83 by *APEC* with joint funding from Newham and the health authority. The radical plan for mixed use was the first of this firm's church work in Newham, and an early example of such an approach among Anglican churches in Greater London. It arose out of the diocese of Chelmsford's special study of East Ham churches carried out by *Martin Purdy* (of APEC) in the 1970s. The new building replaced an imposing red brick church with E.E. and Dec detail (1901–10 by *Micklethwaite & Somers Clarke*, gutted 1941, restored 1949–52), the principal church in the centre of East Ham, successor to St John in High St North. The new church retains a presence on the main road, but a reticent one (contrast the firm's later St Michael, Little Ilford). Against a plain, red brick wall, SCULPTURE of a family group by *John Bridgeman*. A side window allows a peep into the church, which is approached through a low shared foyer, rather dark because of the flats above. The church itself is a broad and light white-walled space which can be opened up to the hall behind. Lit from high up, with tall roof sloping down towards the altar. Pale ash wood fittings. Side chapel with Crucifixion figure by *John Bridgeman*. From the old church the fine polished-marble FONT, dark grey with big fossil shells.

ST EDMUND KING AND MARTYR, No. 464 Katherine Road. The former church by *Cutts*, 1901–34, which stood at the corner of Halley Road, was replaced in 1989 by flats for Springboard Housing association, by *APEC*. The vicarage, a large house with hipped gables, was adapted by *APEC*, 1988, into a multi-use centre with a chapel. Later additions of 1993–4 are by *Cottrell & Vermeulen* (architects of the conversion of St Martin, Plaistow). They aimed to emphasize the sacred character of the building, with roadside cross and bell, and a figure of Christ Triumphant from the old building placed against the side wall. Within the simple white-walled worship space, a new SCREEN was added, of white panels and coloured perspex, with small, carved wooden Crucifix. Some fittings and glass from the old church.

ST GEORGE AND ST ETHELBERT, Burford Road. Hidden among the neat, uneventful streets S of Barking Road, a quiet but carefully detailed brick building of 1935–7 by *Newberry & Fowler*, which succeeded a mission church of 1912. Over half the cost was raised through an appeal by the Bishop of Hereford to his diocese, hence the dedication to St Ethelbert, the Herefordshire martyr who came from Essex. The lancet windows and the cruciform plan with weighty crossing tower were loosely inspired by Hereford Cathedral, but the simplified Gothic detail is decidedly of the 1930s. Low W entrance porch (windows have replaced N and S doors). A light, impressive interior; sandy-coloured brick walls, passage aisles with chamfered Gothic arches dying into octagonal brick piers. Single lancet clerestory windows below a lofty open roof with arched trusses. Low SE Lady Chapel.

FURNISHINGS. Hardly changed from the 1930s layout (quite a rarity now), the long nave with chairs facing a formal sanctuary with high altar. Plain stone octagonal FONT. Early C20 CHOIR STALLS from the demolished church of St Alban, Upton. STAINED GLASS. E window 1957, a powerful figure of Christ in red drapery; SE, 1963, Virgin and child; S, 1969, St Francis; W, St George, signed G&G (for *Goddard & Gibbs*). Figures set in clear leaded glass. VICARAGE to the N, a pleasant brick and pantiled house of 1957. 1960s HALL to the S, concrete, with barrel roof.

ST MARY MAGDALENE, High Street South. The medieval parish church stands away from the centre of East Ham in an evocative setting, a vast overgrown churchyard on flat land

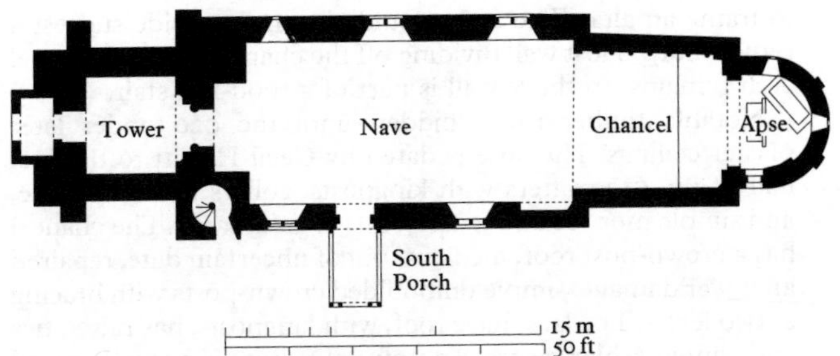

St Mary Magdalene, East Ham, plan

stretching S to the embankment of the outfall sewer. The church is remarkable in retaining its C12 Norman form complete – apse, chancel and substantial unaisled nave, with the addition only of a W tower and some later windows. The ancient building in its romantically isolated position appealed to early antiquaries. William Stukely (†1765) chose to be buried in the churchyard, as did many other Londoners. By the later C19 the burial area was huge but the church was dilapidated; it was rescued from proposed demolition after a report by *J. T. Micklethwaite* and restored 1891–6. Further repairs by *P.M. Johnstone*, 1930, after war damage in 1940, 1965–6 and in the 1980s.

The stumpy, unsubdivided tower is of rough gravel conglomerate with thick, flat buttresses. It may be C13. Later belfry with arched windows of two lights, and an added SE stair turret rising only half way. All much repaired in brick. The rest of the building is of roughly coursed ragstone rubble. One tiny original window remains in the N wall of the nave, another on the S side (and a third is visible inside). The apse has two 4
single-light windows, the S one enlarged, pilaster buttresses, and an inserted C13 S priest's door.

The Norman S door, within a Victorian porch, has an arch of two orders, the outer one roll-moulded, and one original shaft with scalloped capital. The W door now within the vestry inside the tower is a little grander, but similarly plain, three orders, one of them moulded, with cushion capitals to the shafts. The interior is quite light, as the deeply splayed Norman windows are supplemented by Victorian tracery windows of 1844–5 and a C17 window of three uncusped lights in the chancel S wall. In the chancel, intersecting wall arcading with chevron mouldings but no capitals, details which suggest a date after *c.* 1130. The apse has a plain, unmoulded W arch, and one internal pilaster, indicating an intended vault. Early C13 liturgical elaboration is suggested by a double PISCINA with pair of trefoil arches below a pointed arch, with lamp bracket on a head corbel with trumpet-scallop capital. In the nave S wall a pointed arch with another piscina below, presumably intended to frame an altar. The arch mouldings on the E side suggest a return along a lost wall dividing off the chancel, but no chancel arch remains. In the N wall is part of a rood-loft stair.

Notable timber roofs, hidden until the C20 under later plaster ceilings. The apse is dated by Cecil Hewitt to the first half of the C12: rafters with kingposts, collars and wall plate, and simple mortice and tenon joints, a great rarity. The chancel has a crown-post roof, medieval but of uncertain date, repaired after war damage: simple unmoulded crown-posts with bracing at two levels. The later nave roof, with kingposts, has raised ties and canted ashlar pieces. An unusual feature is a small arched window low down in the N chancel wall, assumed to be for an anchorite's cell. Excavations outside revealed two burials here.

Early C13 WALLPAINTING in the chancel and apse: red outline masonry lines, the upper part including five-petal flowers, thin foliage frieze above. Discovered in the C19, whitewashed over in the 1960s, the remains uncovered in 2003. No sign now of the figural subjects visible in the C19, or of a head and foliage seen on the apse arch soffit. – Marble FONT. Bowl of 1639 given by Richard Heigham, on later baluster stem. – Brass FONT COVER, 1898. – Two CHURCHWARDENS' PRICKERS of 1805. – SCULPTURE. Small wooden figure of St Mary Magdalene, Flemish, given in the 1930s. – In the tower, an iron circular staircase of 1908, when an extra floor was added and the vestry moved here from the S porch. The tower has a medieval tenor BELL, dated 1380, a great rarity. – Under the tower is PANELLING recording charity bequests, from the gallery removed 1891–6, now placed above neat late C20 vestry cupboards. – STAINED GLASS. Brightly coloured apse window, 1980, a mosaic of slab glass.

BRASSES. Hester Neve †1610, figure with shield and inscription, the costume well depicted. – Elizabeth Heigham †1622, smaller figure with two shields and inscription. – Inscriptions of 1585, and 1631 with indent of a swaddled infant, William Johnson. MONUMENTS. Pride of place is given to the early C17 standing wall monument to Edward Nevill, Earl of Westmorland, his wife Jane (†1647) and daughter Katherine (†1613), placed awkwardly against the NE part of the apse, and lit by the C17 window opposite. Alabaster, with painted figures of good quality. The Earl and his wife kneel at prayer desks; six (originally seven) kneeling children against the tomb chest below. Two allegorical figures on top. The small flanking obelisks are C20. – Giles Bream †1621, kneeling figures also facing one another, smaller than the Nevill tomb. – William Heigham †1620 and wife Anne †1612. Good alabaster monument with two standing cherubs, no effigies. – Mary Heigham †1621. Small alabaster tablet with cherub below. The Bream and Heigham families were lords of the manor and held the advowson. – Neoclassical tablets to Ynyr Burges †1792, paymaster of the East India Company, and to his daughter Margaret, Countess Powlett, †1838.

CHURCHYARD. The vast churchyard covering $9\frac{1}{2}$ acres was treated as a nature reserve from 1976, an example of the more imaginative approach to burial grounds that took off in the 1970s. By the entrance a simple NATURE INTERPRETATION CENTRE by *APEC*. Among the many memorials a number of C18 tomb chests and headstones.

ST PAUL, Burges Road. On part of the Burges Estate on the eastern fringe of East Ham, developed in the 1890s. A cluster consisting of church hall (the former mission church), 1907, church of 1933, a late work by *Charles Spooner*, and a linking foyer of 1993 by *Raymond Hall* of *Peoples and Places Architects*. The two-storey hall is exuberantly Edwardian, with timber framing to the gable and fancy woodwork to the porch. The church is more sober; brown brick, in a simple round-arched style; no decoration apart from bands of tiles up the W buttresses. It straddles an angular site, hence the S porch and W bellcote at the end of a S aisle shorter than the nave. The entrance is now through the foyer which neatly fills the triangular space between church and hall. Low timber open porch, gable with wooden relief of worshippers by *Jane Quail*. Inside the church, plastered walls and unusually, a colonnade with plain tapered columns, which Spooner chose instead of an arcade in order to produce a more spacious effect. Columns and beams are of concrete. Open roofs; side lit sanctuary, framed by a plain round-headed arch concealing the windows behind. Reordered 2002 by *Raymond Hall*: chancel platform extended, choir stalls and pulpit removed, seating rearranged. Redecorated in pale yellow, white and deep red.

OUR LADY OF COMPASSION (R.C.), Green Street, Upton Park. Successor to the C19 R.C. chapel at Boleyn Castle (*see* below). 1911 by *R.L. Curtis*. Red brick. The Italian Romanesque style was the choice of Archbishop Bourne. Small SW tower, central doorway with recessed orders on stone columns neatly set into the unusual feature of a western apse. This forms a foyer beneath a deep W gallery. A carefully detailed interior: five bays with emphatically striped piers of brick and stone, continued as wall arcading to the square chancel, where they frame large lunette windows. Lean-to aisles with triplet windows. Carved and painted STATIONS OF THE CROSS in baroque frames. Reordered 1991–3 reusing original alabaster and stone fittings with the addition of a relief Crucifixion of clay on the E wall, 1991 by *Stephen Scully*. Lady Chapel in N aisle; carved pietà on base of altar.

ST MICHAEL (R.C.), Tilbury Road (off High Street South). 1959 by *A.J. Newton* of *Burles & Newton*. Bold and bright, with a thin, detached, brick bell tower and a steeply pitched roof with patterned tiles over welded-steel portal frames. A zigzag of dormer windows high up, and another of aisle windows. Projecting sanctuary with side windows of coloured glass panels; former baptistery with *dalle-de-verre* glass. Inside, the ceiling was lowered in 1983, concealing the dormers. STATUES by *M. O'Brien.* To the E the Presbytery and an older hall; to the N a primary school; its main buildings with two gables, dated 1931.

ST LAZARUS AND ST ANDREW (Greek Orthodox), Rutland Road. Built as St Michael and All Angels (C. of E.), 1910–12 by *E. Douglas Hoyland.* One of the more unusual churches of the 1900s. A broad front of biscuit-coloured terracotta with half-timbered gable, a wide roof spanning both nave and aisles. The terracotta blocks are set in a steel frame (permitted only after an appeal against the Borough Council's bye-laws). The interior has timber arcades.

ASSEMBLIES OF GOD, Plashet Grove and Whitfield Road. Built as the Methodists' Elizabeth Fry Memorial Church, 1889 by *William Dartnell.* Broad gabled front of red and yellow brick, faintly Lombard Romanesque. The church, raised above a basement, is approached up steps to a wide arched entrance (the doorways altered). Carved stone foliage capitals to the windows and to the paired columns of the entrance, an unusually elaborate touch.

CONGREGATIONAL AND METHODIST CHURCH, Pilgrim Way. A rebuilding of 1956 by *A.D. Cooke*, replacing a Congregational church of 1900. Portal frame, the end wall with pattern of projecting bricks, W side glazed with tinted frosted glass, not appealing externally. Inside, the altar is set against a tall diapered wooden panel. Attached to the S is a hall of 1910, an attractive interior, aisled, with timber piers, clerestory and open trussed roof. Its frontage to Market Street has pilasters and arched openings with red brick dressings.

EAST HAM BAPTIST CHURCH, Plashet Grove. 1900–1 by *Edgar Stones.* Bulky and quite imposing, with round-arched entrance up steep stairs. Orange brick with some pale brick stripes. Big, arched window, small octagonal buttresses, broad domestic-looking canted staircase bay on each side.

METHODIST CHURCH, High Street South. Rudimentary classical; centre with pediment and four plain pilasters. Built for Primitive Methodists, 1885.

TRINITY COMMUNITY CENTRE, East Avenue. Spare, Free Gothic front of red brick, with a short tower on the l.; 1903 by *John Wills* for Presbyterians. Church hall 1905 by *T.J. Jones.* Subdivided inside.

TEMPLE, Shaftesbury Road (Shree Kutch Satsung Swaminarian). 2001–3; orange brick front with arched windows, small stupas rising behind. A single, large, windowless worship area inside.

JEWISH CEMETERY, Sandford Road. Founded 1919. Crowded with tombstones. Plain white-walled prayer hall and cloisters in a round-arched style, 1924 by *H.W. Ford.*

MAJOR BUILDINGS

TOWN HALL, Barking Road and High Street South. 1901 by *Henry Cheers* of Twickenham and *Joseph Smith* of Blackburn,

with additional buildings by the Borough Engineer *A.H. Campbell.* The supreme London example of the power and confidence of the Edwardian local authority, transforming an indifferent crossroads into an urban centre. The 150 ft tower at the large crossroads site announces not only the Town Hall, 73
but a conglomeration of buildings serving the new borough: Assembly Hall, public offices, Police Courts, Library, Education and Public Health offices, Fire Station, Swimming Pool, Technical College, Tram Depot, Electricity Offices and substation, all built between 1903 and 1914. The bold thinking behind this owed much to J.H. Bethell (1861–1945), first mayor of East Ham in 1904–5. The flamboyant architectural character was established by Cheers and Smith's successful competition design of 1898 for a civic group; initially this was to have consisted of Town Hall and Assembly Room, with separate library and technical school, but as built, the group differs from the original scheme, which had placed the library in the tech- pp. 70–1
nical school block, and further buildings were added as the ambitions of the borough expanded.

The L-shaped group of public hall along Barking Road and lower offices with frontages along the High Street is recessed from the street and anchored by a commanding clock tower close to the corner, with receding tiers of pinnacles, topped by a tall dome and a spike. The materials throughout are bright red Accrington brick and biscuit-coloured Doulton terracotta. They are employed to provide much lively detail – Tudor mullioned windows, playful blocked columns and shaped gables, and touches of Loire chateaux in the decorative balustrading – a carefree mixture typical of the 1890s before it was overtaken by the fashion for more monumental Baroque. *Building News*, writing in 1898, already considered the detail 'overwrought' and the 'rococo' ornament 'in questionable taste'. Cheers had some earlier experience with lesser civic buildings and went on to build others: his slightly later Town Hall at Hereford has similar detail. But East Ham was an exceptionally large commission (the total costs for the Town Hall group came to £80,000); for inspiration in handling such a large site he perhaps looked to E.W. Mountford's Sheffield Town Hall, completed 1897, comparable both in its eclecticism and in its corner clock tower.

At the corner facing Barking Road an asymmetrically placed arched entrance invites one up the stairs to the Assembly Room. Along the High Street the different functions are clearly distinguished: a low but richly adorned three-bay front has a lesser entrance to the Town Clerk's and Treasurer's departments (their names on the glazed doors within). The more pompous entrance in the adjoining block to the r., a doorway with prominent segmental pediment over an arch with emphatically blocked voussoirs, leads to former police courts, committee rooms, and the first-floor council chamber.

The interiors are notable for the quality of the interior fittings: glazed tiling, mosaic floors, Devonshire-marble columns and elaborate ironwork and carpentry throughout.

The Assembly Hall, with stage and large W gallery, planned to seat 1200, is a festive space with curved fibrous-plaster ceiling and three colossal hanging lights, well lit by large windows on each side. The windows have small busts, above the radiators are relief panels with ships. A semi-octagonal ticket-booth is at the entrance. The Council Chamber is top-lit with a dome with coloured glass, original horseshoe seating and panelling. Committee rooms have coved ceilings and sliding partitions. The police courts (now divided) were on the ground floor, with cells beneath.

The LIBRARY, 1907–8, like the earlier one at Manor Park, was funded by Andrew Carnegie and designed by *A.H. Campbell*, Borough Surveyor, very much in the spirit of Cheers and Smith. It occupies a prestigious site S of the Town Hall, originally intended for the Fire Station. Shaped central gable, and a S end with octagonal top and dome. The large mullion-and-transomed windows with arched lights, slightly collegiate in feel, distinguish it from its neighbours. Extended 1910 for Public Health and Education Departments. The FIRE STATION, 1913–14, was displaced to the corner of Nelson Street; a less elaborate red brick and stone frontage with a good corner feature. A row of firemen's cottages behind. Further along Nelson Street are the BATHS, originally of 1911–12, designed by *Campbell*, extended 1933, but reconstructed as part of the Leisure Centre of 2001. The new back parts mix pinkish brick and yellow stone, distinct from but sympathetic to the surrounding buildings. On the new wall a tile relief commemorates the borough's trams. Adjoining are three big gables, the frontage of the former TRAMSHED. They have sparing terracotta decoration, and two pairs of arched entrances with bold brick voussoirs. Also by *Campbell*, 1901, when East Ham introduced both electric trams and electric street lighting. A power station behind the Town Hall was built at the same time.

The entrance to the LEISURE CENTRE of 2000–1 is approached from the N. On this side it confidently proclaims its character as a modern building, a sleek all-glazed wall with projecting sunblind eaves. The spacious double-height foyer and café in front are separated by a glass wall from an L-shaped swimming pool lit by clerestory and circular rooflight. Gym and other facilities are in brick buildings on the tramshed site. The approach to the leisure centre is a welcome move towards improving the public spaces around the buildings, hitherto dominated by car parking.

Finally, the former TECHNICAL COLLEGE on Barking Road (now offices, but built to house both a secondary school and an evening college). By *Cheers & Smith* 1903–4, designed to complement the Town Hall, and equally bombastic in its detail, especially in the W entrance facing the Town Hall with its attendant terracotta lions. This leads to a grand imperial stair of off-white Doulton-ware, the end newels carrying griffins. The other entrance, with a porch, faces Barking Road. The main hall has a glazed barrel roof decorated with pretty

Renaissance ornament. An elaborate ventilating system drew cool air through the building by means of a very large, still extant fan.

POLICE STATION, High Street South. 1901–4 by *J. Dixon Butler*, surveyor to the Metropolitan Police. His characteristic combination: domestic detail given presence by Free Baroque elements. Brick with stone bands. Two mannered, rather ungainly, segmental gables crown the projecting end bays, a steep triangular-headed dentilled gable rises over the centre. Tall plain post-war addition behind.

NEWHAM COLLEGE OF FURTHER EDUCATION, High Street South. The replacement for the technical college next to the Town Hall. A big, sheer curtain-walled slab of 1962 by the *Borough of East Ham*. Eight storeys, pale mosaic-faced spandrels to the upper floors. On the blind wall of the S wing, an abstract mosaic mural on a curved panel.

BARCLAY HALL, Green Street (now part of the College of Further Education). 1905 by *Frederick Rowntree*. Built for the first branch of the Quaker Bedford Institute to be established beyond Inner London, five years after it started in an iron shed on the adjacent site. Unusually ambitious, with classrooms, hall to seat 400, and space for a variety of activities 'for those untouched by other churches'. Two tall storeys and attics, brick on a stone base, in a simple Free Classical style. The front has a dentilled cornice, with attic window above in a stone surround, the name nicely carved below. The original curly gable has been clumsily replaced by a straight one. Main entrance under a segmental stone arch, glazed when renovated by Newham in 1996. Smaller entrance in a two-bay wing on the r., with its original door, two leaves of vertical planks in rustic Quaker tradition. Plain walls to W and N suggest further extensions were intended. The building commemorates Joseph and Jane Barclay of Knotts Green, Leyton, one of several eminent Quaker families in the area.

REGISTRY OFFICE, Plashet Grove. Built as East Ham's first purpose-built Library, funded by Passmore Edwards, one of his several involvements in East Ham, through the efforts of J.H. Bethell. 1898–9 by Passmore Edwards's protégé, the Cornish architect *Silvanus Trevail*. A pleasant building in a mixed Renaissance style, red Ruabon brick with Bath stone dressings, mullion and transom windows, clock turret over the central gable. Decorated with prominent lettering and reliefs of a man and woman reading in the spandrels of the Venetian entrance. Recessed porch with mosaic floor behind fat marble columns. Behind is the original screen (reset) leading to a central hall. Now much altered inside. Originally the reference library lay to the l. (now marriage room), with lending library behind (now subdivided), on the r. a committee room and newspaper room. Part of the latter, with decorative open timber roof, now forms the registry office, with a new side entrance. The first floor had storage rooms and a librarian's flat.

SHREWSBURY CENTRE, Shrewsbury Road. A cottage hospital was first suggested as early as 1887. At first conversion of Shrewsbury House, an existing building on the site, was proposed, but a new building to the S was made possible through a contribution of £5000 from Passmore Edwards, built 1899–1901, by *Silvanus Trevail*. It had the standard cottage hospital plan of a two-storey domestic-looking central block with gables and bow windows, flanked by one-storey wings (r. wing rebuilt). Central doorway under a hooded arch, windows with a little Art Nouveau glass. Extended in 1926–9 by *Mennie & Smith* with a separate MEMORIAL HOSPITAL wing to the N, which replaced Shrewsbury House. (Now closed and with an uncertain future.) A confident composition in early C18 style, brick and stone, still domestic in character, but more formal, with a stone-columned main entrance, pedimented centre and steep tiled roof above a timber dentilled cornice. Lesser entrances have thickset Baroque doorcases with swan-neck pediments on fat consoles. Three wings behind linked by a central spine. Behind the cottage hospital, the SHREWSBURY CENTRE for outpatients, 1997, with neat, angled foyer connecting older extensions. Further additions to the S.

WEST HAM STADIUM, Green Street. On this site from 1904. A mighty, local landmark with an interesting history (see p. 281), though hardly a visual asset. The W side, to Green Street, has the most recent grandstand, Dr Martens, 2003, a two-tier stand seating 15,000, part of a grand rebuilding scheme intended to provide accommodation for 40,500. It incorporates hotel, conference rooms, and a museum. The entrance is flanked by the club's emblems, giant, toytown castles in strident yellow.

EAST HAM UNDERGROUND STATION, High Street North. The London Tilbury & Southend Railway line was opened 1858; the station was rebuilt 1902 for the District Line. Red brick bridge frontage with rusticated pilasters and Baroque gable, well preserved platform canopies with good ironwork incorporating the LTS monogram. UPTON PARK, Green Street, has a similar station building.

Schools

Schools form some of East Ham's most striking buildings. The East Ham School Board's sense of importance in coping with the burgeoning school population is conveyed by its offices in Wakefield Street. It expanded to include Little Ilford; but after the Education Act of 1902 its functions were reluctantly taken over by the local authority. The East Ham Board adopted the London School Board's precedent of compact buildings on tight sites. Many of the capacious three-storey schools, each planned for *c.* 1300 children, still tower over the surrounding streets, and continue in use as primary schools. The most impressive are those of the 1890s by *Robert L. Curtis*, who gave his large compositions some dignity by skilful massing and sparing ornament. Penny-pinching after 1902 produced more austere results, but both the post-Second World War period and the late C20 produced some imaginative buildings.

Former SCHOOL BOARD OFFICES, Wakefield Street, 1899 by *Robert L. Curtis*. In the form of a grand overblown villa, with bowed windows set back between piers, an entrance with marble columns, and a carved panel with St George and the dragon. The E wing marked 'girls entrance' was a pupil teachers' centre.

SHAFTESBURY SCHOOL, Shaftesbury Road. 1893 by *Robert L. Curtis*. A fine composition with four large and two smaller gables, creating a lively rhythm below the central cupola. Vestigial classical ornament in red brick, in the form of disconnected pilasters and sketchy window pediments. Carved stone lintels to the playground gateways, an indication of the Board's generosity at this time.

SANDRINGHAM SCHOOL, Sandringham Road. 1895 by *Robert* 71
L. Curtis. A three-decker on a magnificently palatial scale. The formal twenty-window-long front avoids monotony through projecting ends and a two-bay gabled centre, with windows grouped in threes on either side. Entrances at the side and back. The long roof has a cheerful cupola with spike and no fewer than six ventilating turrets. Minimal ornament, as at Shaftesbury.

LATHOM JUNIOR SCHOOL, Clements Road. 1897. Three-decker with projecting staircase towers. Long side with central shaped gable. Upper floor with striped brick and stone pilasters. Originally quite colourful. Main entrance in Clements Road where there are also caretaker's house and cookery centre. Central hall with classrooms each side.

HARTLEY PRIMARY, Hartley Avenue. 1901–2 by *Robert L. Curtis*. Three-decker with fat domed corner turrets for the cloakrooms.

NELSON PRIMARY, Nelson Road 1901, is a grimly plain three-decker. MONEGA, Monega Road, 1904, has coped gables with just a suspicion of decoration; at VICARAGE LANE SCHOOLS, 1910, two storeys, and 1912, one storey, ornament is confined to nice decorative ridge tiles. On these later schools dates in large metal letters provide a little extra interest.

ST STEPHEN'S SCHOOL, Whitfield Road. Built 1951, pleasant example of an infant school on a generous site, reflecting new post-war standards. Brick with the lightweight porches and circular windows popular at the time; an airy glazed hall on the r., low classrooms extending in wings to N and E.

WILLIAM DAVIES, Stafford Road. The more compact, blocky type of the 1970s; with one-storey classrooms clustered around a hall.

CLEVES, Cleves Road. An irregular one- and two-storey line of buildings in a curve around Priory Park, brightened by touches of colour and made distinctive by shallow pitched roof with deep eaves projecting over external walkways. Similar to the borough's 1980s schools in Beckton.

LANGDON SCHOOL, Langdon Crescent. Designed 1946, built 1953–64, by *J. W. Taylor*, of East Ham's engineer's department, the first to be built as part of the borough's post-war education plan. Low brick and glass buildings in a pre-war Modernist tradition, spread over former marshland by the river, before compact planning for schools became general. Built as three linked schools, sharing dining hall, library and other facilities. These are in a symmetrical central block, with a tall, plain water tower as a focal point. The boldest feature is at the rear, where two fully glazed curved staircase towers project on either side of the dining room. The two-storey classroom wings on either side are linked by covered ways, all similar, and extend W with long bands of windows. The two ranges on the N were for the Boys' Grammar school, the four on the S for the Girls' and Boys' Secondary Moderns. Tucked behind to the SE, a large, neat SPORTS CENTRE of the 1990s, with curved roof and ribbed horizontal cladding. Designed for shared community use.

PLASHET SCHOOL, Plashet Grove, for 1400 girls. One is struck
127 first by the cheerfully whacky FOOTBRIDGE of 2000 by *Birds Portchmouth Russum*, with *Techniker* as engineers. It crosses the road supported on single, tapering struts and consists of a snaking ribbon of blue metal with perky fabric roof on hooped trusses. Their shape at first seems arbitrary but inside is a visibly logical alternation of skewed hoops. The delight in avoiding the purely utilitarian is apparent too in the angular window which provides a view midway across the road at the point where the two curving sections meet. Drainage and lighting are ingeniously built into the structure. The bridge links the buildings of two formerly separate schools; to the S the Grammar School for Girls, 1932 by *Essex County Council*, plain and compact, on a courtyard plan; to the N the bridge plunges into the first floor of the former secondary modern school. This was planned in 1951 by *George Whitby* for 680 girls, and built in 1953–4 on a confined site, hence the exceptional cross-shaped plan with seven upper storeys above a ground floor, and gymnasium and hall extending W and E. Central staircase, a mezzanine for offices tucked below the upper floors of classrooms. The construction was innovative at the time: steel shortages in 1952 encouraged the use of *in-situ* concrete with pre-cast main beams and posts, but the cladding panels proved unsatisfactory and were renewed when the building was refurbished from 1984. It is now clad neatly in mottled brick, the floorbands picked out in red brick, with rough stone blocks on the ground floor. (Cold war air raid shelter below.)

BRAMPTON MANOR SCHOOL, Boundary Road. In a re-landscaped setting just S of Greenway. Large secondary school, the earlier flat-roofed parts by *J. W. Taylor*, 1957, extended and refurbished by *Initiatives in Design*, 1992; pale brick with white cladding around a five-storey block with shallow curved roof.

PERAMBULATIONS

1. From East Ham station to Plashet Grove and Katherine Road

In HIGH STREET NORTH, to the N of the station, the BURNELL ARMS marks the corner with Plashet Grove by a late C19 gabled front, not yet with the exuberance of the pubs of *c.* 1900. Extended by *Yetts, Sturdy & Usher*, 1901. PLASHET GROVE was the old route to the hamlet of Plashet, whose centre lay near Katherine Road. It still retains an echo of its earlier existence when this was a select area with gentry houses. It is worth a visit for the public buildings which have replaced them (*see* above). First the large C20 GIRLS' SCHOOL with its eyecatching bridge, then close to PLASHET PARK (made from the grounds of Wood House), the handsome Registry Office, built as East Ham's first purpose built LIBRARY.

Further E, the HOSPITAL, built in the grounds of Shrewsbury House. Another house was Plashet House, the home of Elizabeth Fry, the prison reformer. At the corner of Plashet Grove and Katherine Road, the GREEN MAN, a mid-C19 pub with brick and terracotta extension of *c.* 1900, is a reminder that KATHERINE ROAD (named after Elizabeth Fry's daughter) began as a pre-suburban route. Further N the DUKE OF FIFE, *c.* 1890s by *Frederick W. Ashton*, adorned rather oddly with a profusion of Ashton's favourite terracotta caryatids around a corner turret and above the doorway, and with cherubs and foliage panels below the upper windows. At the corner of Rutland Road St Lazarus and St Andrew (*see* above). Opposite, at the corner of Shaftesbury Road, former TREBOR SWEETS factory, functional four-storey white-walled buildings of 1931 and 1947 by *Higgins & Thomerson*, converted in 1999–2001 to live–work units by *Stock Woolstencroft Architects*, with a new penthouse floor. A tall brick chimney is preserved as a freestanding monument behind. Yet more variety beyond: a towering Board School and a small distinctive Temple (*see* above).

2. From East Ham station S via Barking Road to Upton Park station

HIGH STREET NORTH had few houses until the 1880s. Development as a town centre shopping street was at first modest, and is still so, for grander buildings have come and gone: they included a large Edwardian music hall close to the railway, of 1905 by *Wylson & Long*, demolished after the Second World War, and by Market Street where there is now a car park, a commanding Co-operative Stores of 1929 (its urns are now in Central Park). The most notable survival is on the W side: a cinema, now bingo hall, with thin tower, black fins and black-tiled frame. Formerly the Premier Electric. The long foyer had its origin as a theatre of 1912, it was rebuilt as a cinema by

W.E. Trent in 1921 with an auditorium seating 2409. At the S corner of Pilgrim Way a former Post Office (George V monogram) in *Office of Works* Free English Baroque: striped brick and stone with pedimental gable. Shopping activity is concentrated in Market Street, with a recent SAINSBURY'S on the S side, and at the end, a MARKET HALL of 1922, low but extensive, with pedimented entrance.

The junction of the High Street and Barking Road is dominated by the TOWN HALL (*see* above) and one can sense its impact on local architectural standards. The DENMARK ARMS commands the NW corner with fussy late C19 frontage with terracotta ornament and a corner turret, possibly by *F.W. Ashton*. The Free Classical additions to the N are of 1903 by *C.J. Dawson*, who also remodelled the inside and added the grand pedimented High Street entrances to hotel and new saloon bar. Good interiors: an arabesque frieze above deep-red Art Nouveau tiles in the public bar; Ionic columns and another frieze in the saloon. Rising architectural ambitions can be gauged also by the contrast between the mean NE corner, dated 1887, and the attractive Free Style gabled terrace (Nos. 383–91) with chequerwork gables and plain windows linked by long stone bands, which continues E along Barking Road. On the SW corner a confident former bank, dated 1902.

Now to the W along BARKING ROAD. On the S side, ST BARTHOLOMEW, with church, day-care centre, surgeries and flats, planned from 1975, built 1979, by *Martin Purdy* of *APEC* (*see* above). The flats look S toward the former vicarage, now FELLOWSHIP HOUSE, St Bartholomew's Road, which began as a detached villa of *c.* 1850. Regency style on an inflated scale; two storeys with very large Greek Doric porch and ground-floor windows recessed under arches.

On the N side of Barking Road, further W, the former GRANADA CINEMA (Gala Clubs Bingo) Hall, 1936 by *W.E. Trent*. Striking faience-clad Art Deco front with taller l. side and curved end. Classical interior by *T. Komisarjevsky*, Granada's preferred designer. Large, well preserved foyer; at r. end an iron-railed stair up to balcony. Square piers with Ionic capitals. First-floor café in front. Auditorium for 2468.

THE CENTRAL on the S side, by Macaulay Road, an ample pub with half-timbered gables above green-tiled ground floor, belongs with a clutch of superior, well preserved streets around Central Park (*see* below); note the houses with two-storey bay windows. This was part of the estate developed from 1887 on land built up in the C18 by Ynyr Burges of the East India Company. His house stood in High Street South until the mid-C19. Further on, on the N side, the story was different. The streets named after Henry VIII's wives, laid out on the Boleyn estate, were built up with indifferent housing in the 1870s–80s and rebuilt after the Second World War. Along Barking Road STONDON WALK of the 1970s is a late addition, by Newham, a long, yellow brick, three-storey range with flats and maisonettes over garages. On the N side each upper pair is approached up its own staircase; a reaction against the communal access of earlier decades. The blank walls which shield the houses from Barking Road have been cheered up by panels of text and attractive cut-out metalwork designs of *c.* 2000. Further E, in PRIORY ROAD is the earliest post-war rebuilding phase, PRIORY COURT, architect-in-charge *C.H. Doody*, of the Borough of East Ham, 1949–53. Three eight-storey, Y-shaped clusters, an impressive design, the first East Ham flats of over four storeys. Long frontages broken up by panels of inset balconies. Further N a mixture of low terraces and one fifteen-storey tower, around the edge of the snaking form of PRIORY PARK, laid out on the site of a C19 gravel-working area with lake. Here too Cleves Primary school (*see* above).

The junction of Barking Road, Green Street and Boundary Road lies on the boundary between East and West Ham. The corner with Green Street is marked by THE BOLEYN, rebuilt by the 64
pub architects *Shoebridge & Rising* in 1898, one of the first examples in the area of the florid Free Baroque detail which became popular for pubs *c.* 1900. Good interiors with plenty of cut-glass screens and mirrors: top-lit billiard room and another top-lit smaller area. Next door is the BOLEYN CINEMA, 1938, by *Andrew Mather*, built as the New Odeon. Plain Modernist exterior with broad foyer window inset between end piers, the overhanging roof in front of the window dotted with lights. Big double-height foyer originally with pink walls painted with animals in brown, green and gold. The auditorium (now divided for three screens) had abstract ornament in the form of streamlined grilles of silver louvres below wavy patterns in red, purple and blue. Opposite, a mean, oddly detailed late C19 terrace with skyline of squashed urns and angular gables. On an island opposite the pub, a sculpture: 'We are the Champions' by *Philip Jackson* 2003: Bobby Moore held aloft by three team-mates. Over life-size, super-realist figures, a prelude to the clumsy gigantism of West Ham United's STADIUM in Green Street (*see* above). S of the stadium the R.C. church of Our Lady of Compassion (*see* above) and, displaced by the stadium to a site to its N, ST EDWARD'S R.C. PRIMARY SCHOOL, by *Ronald Wylde Associates*, 2002–3, a symmetrical composition with low pitched roofs, blue cladding panels and red window frames.

The castle allusions of the stadium, the Boleyn name and the unexpected presence of a R.C. church and school hard by the huge grandstand are a legacy of the history of the site, although, regrettably, nothing remains of its old buildings. In the C16 Richard Breame, a servant of Henry VIII, owned an estate at Green Street. It was claimed (on no reliable evidence) that Henry VIII visited the house to court Anne Boleyn. Old views show an irregular red brick house with Tudor chimneys, apparently of C16 origin, much enlarged later. The name Boleyn Castle which became attached to the site derived from a detached octagonal brick tower in the grounds. The estate was bought in 1869 by Cardinal Manning and used for a reformatory school until 1906. From 1904 the grounds were rented to West Ham United Football club, which had been formed from a number of amateur clubs, notably one at Thames Iron Works founded in 1895. The R.C. church was built in 1911 for the worshippers displaced from the chapel of 1901 attached to the school. The house was let to a social club, and finally demolished in 1955.

GREEN STREET suffered badly in the Second World War. Piecemeal rebuilding of shops and houses began in the late 1940s, but the West Ham side was radically reconstructed from the late 1960s. An unappealing tall slab of flats rises behind the dismal Queens Market and multi-storey car park, the latter not improved by the borough's garish cosmetic recladding of 1992, reminiscent of cheap bedroom furniture. The contemporary PUB is by *Covell, Matthews & Partners*, 1968. Perched on the railway bridge UPTON PARK STATION, with brick Baroque frontage of 1902, and white-walled STATION PARADE opposite, mirror images of the station buildings at East Ham. N of the railway Green Street is scrappy architecturally, but more enjoyable, with dazzling displays in a long string of Asian shops occupying the low-key post-war buildings which were put up after serious bomb damage. Efforts to brighten the street include a MILLENNIUM PAVEMENT, with mosaic decorations and Gaudiesque seating, created by local communities (lead artist *Peter Dunn*, seats by *Anne Thorne* and *Rachel Silver*). This lies in front of ST STEPHEN'S PARADE, one of the few taller post-war groups, on the site of a bombed church of 1887. Post-war Infant School to its E (*see* above). Further N on the E side, the WHITE HART, a crowded late C19 front with elongated windows in two tiny turrets which have lost their caps, and on the W side Barclay Hall (*see* p. 275).

3. *East Ham, S and E of the centre*

BARKING ROAD E of the High Street has only scattered items to note. On the S side beyond the town hall, Nos. 330–54, TOWN HALL ANNEXE, 1938–9 by *A. T. Bridgewater*, Borough Engineer; austere, stripped classical with a slightly Deco stepped central cornice, opposite a more homely Neo-Georgian EMPLOYMENT EXCHANGE of similar date ('employers' above the front entrance, now disused). Further on, the DUKE'S HEAD, rebuilt 1900, striped brick and stone, with relief busts on carved panel. The area to the N was part of the Burges estate, built up with a dull grid of streets in the 1890s. On the S side of Barking Road, built on open land near the river, DUKE'S COURT, three-storey flats of 1947–50 by *Howes & Jackman*, in groups of three. Attractive fencing of *c.* 2000 incorporates shiny etched-metal panels with historical scenes (including the eclipse of the sun, 1999), an effort intended to provide a welcome at the E boundary of the borough.

HIGH STREET SOUTH runs S from the Town Hall towards CENTRAL PARK, opened 1898; the grounds were those of the early C18 Rancliffe House. Rusticated gatepiers of 1905 at the SE corner. Nearby is the WAR MEMORIAL, designed gratis by *Robert Banks-Martin*, mayor of East Ham during the First World War. A Lutyens-type composition in Portland stone; aedicule with two bronze wreaths suspended within open arches. Bronze plaques below with a vast number of names. Near the N entrance, formal garden with small three-tier fountain, and four large iron urns of *c.* 1929 from the Co-operative stores in the High Street, demolished 1989.

At a bend on High Street South, FIRE STATION, recent parts adjoining a grand formal composition of the 1920s, tripartite, with angular classical detail. To the r. a large archway with triple keystone. Further S at the fringe of the built-up area, the vast burial ground around the ancient church (*see* above), and BROOKS AVENUE opposite, which has a long row of early municipal dwellings of 1902 by the borough engineer *A.H. Campbell*, contemporary with and similar to those built at Savage Gardens, Beckton. Named after John Brooks, chairman of the committee. Cottage flats (since converted to houses) with canted bays and low projecting roofs over the entrances, given a little variety by three types of gable: half-timbered, tiled and brick.

LITTLE ILFORD and MANOR PARK

Part of East Ham from 1886, but Little Ilford has a separate early history. The small medieval parish between East Ham to the W and the River Roding to the E, possibly older in origin than Ilford on the other side of the river, had its centre around the tiny C12 St Mary's church, a remarkable survival. Excavations have shown that a timber building predated the existing church. No other older buildings remain apart from a manor house, now flats, in Gladding Road, N of Romford Road. The vast City of London Cemetery, laid out in the 1860s on the edge of the open lands of Wanstead flats, covers the site of the manor of Aldersbrook. In the C18 this was famous for its fine grounds, the home of the Lethieullier family whose monuments survive in their burial chapel attached to the parish church.

Suburban expansion around Romford Road was encouraged by more frequent trains to Manor Park, on the line to Ilford, and by the opening of a station at Woodgrange Park in 1894. Manor Park was the name given to the suburban centre at the junction of High Street North and Romford Road; Woodgrange Park, further W, was developed as a superior residential area, and attracted wealthier Jewish residents moving out of the East End. S of Romford Road development was more dense, following the pattern of much of East Ham. Around the existing N–S routes of Little Ilford Lane, High Street North and Katherine Road, relentlessly straight streets were laid out fringed by repetitive two-storey terraces made respectable by minute front gardens and stuccoed bay windows. Little has changed, except on the E fringes where multi-storey blocks replaced the poorest quality housing in the 1960s–70s. Architectural highlights are scattered thinly; most reflect the social needs of the expanding population of *c.* 1900: a handful of pubs, a scatter of modest churches and chapels, huge Board schools and a magnificently florid public library.

RELIGIOUS BUILDINGS

ALL SAINTS, Romford Road, and Hampton Road, Manor Park. 1886 by *A. W. Blomfield.* Economically detailed, but on an ambitious scale. Long nave, the continuous roof broken only by a shingled spirelet at the start of the chancel. Dark knapped-flint facing, with flat brick edgings to the windows and sparse use of Bath stone. Lean-to aisles, transepts and a short chancel; lancet and plate tracery windows. The interior is similarly plain, with brick walls and clerestory above arcades with octagonal piers painted white. Stepped brick arches without mouldings. Only the sanctuary is a little more lavish, divided from the chancel by a stone arch, and with especially rich encaustic TILES. Did the money run out after this? Simple FONT and PULPIT, with marble colonnettes. A few later embellishments: three *opus sectile* mosaic panels set in brick recesses in the E wall, Risen Christ with Angels, presumably by *James Powell & Sons* of Whitefriars. The two side panels, with more static angels, were a gift of 1936, the central panel with livelier drapery perhaps earlier. STAINED GLASS. E window, 1901, Worship of the Lamb, a crowded composition across three lights. Probably by *Heaton, Butler & Bayne*, who signed a number of the aisle lancets; these have standing figures above inscriptions, 1895 onwards. In the N aisle one more adventurous light, Bread of Life, by *A. J. Davies* of the *Bromsgrove Guild*, 1931. MONUMENT. Percy James Carr †1900, the standard City of London Volunteers bronze plaque, an attractive Arts and Crafts design by *F. Wheeler*.

ST MARY, Church Road. A surprising survival, a tiny medieval church in an ancient churchyard, some way S of the modern centre along Romford Road. As Pevsner said, not impressive, though lovable. The fabric of the nave is C12, the chancel was rebuilt in the early C17 and the chapel N of the nave added in the C18.* Nave of rubble stone, with timber bell turret and brick S porch. Small, slightly pointed S and W windows with thick rendered surrounds. Broad arched windows with Y-tracery. The chancel is of brick above stone foundations. The E wall with dentilled pedimental gable was probably built after 1724, when the Lethieulliers of Aldersbrook sought a faculty for a burial vault with chapel above. Their brick chapel projects N of the nave, slightly overlapping the N window, with circular windows to E and W.

The simple interior retains some of its Georgian character (Victorian fittings have been removed). Cream-painted plastered walls, the nave and chancel divided off by a rough chamfered beam with another above, linked by vertical struts, perhaps the remains of a timber-framed partition. Low W gallery on rough posts, the front with simple grained panels and painted wood, and Hanoverian ROYAL ARMS. Organ, installed in the later C19, in a new case of 2000. From the C12 church visible remains include a string course on the nave S wall, interrupted by an enlarged S window, continued round the E side of the round-headed S doorway. This has a slightly segmental lintel with blank tympanum above. The N doorway (now opening into the chapel) is also round headed, possibly heightened. To its W a tiny, deeply splayed C12 window.

The blind N wall of the LETHIEULLIER CHAPEL is given a restrained Doric architectural composition: central pediment on columns; pilasters at the back and at the ends, frieze with triglyphs and metopes. It frames a small red-marble sarcophagus in the centre, to Elizabeth Lethieullier (†1724 in a carriage accident) and John Lethieullier †1737. Urns to l. and r., to the antiquary, Smart Lethieullier †1760 and his wife Margaret †1753. The former has a long inscription extolling his virtues and noting that he did not want a long eulogy; was the plain tablet above originally intended for his name alone? Similar larger tablets on S and W walls commemorate other members of the family (his brother Charles †1759 and wife Mary †1777, and Benjamin Smart, some time treasurer of the Middle Temple, †1761. Fragments of old GLASS in the chapel E window: crowned Tudor rose, crowned red rose and a tiny quarry with a heron, perhaps associated with the Heron family, C16 owners of Aldersbrook. The burial vault below is approached by steps at the W end of the nave.

STAINED GLASS. Chancel N, †1887, two figures with elaborate detail; E window: memorial to Queen Victoria, 1901, Christ the King and two angels. Both by *A.J. Dix*. Nave S, Presentation in the Temple, in similar style. BRASSES mounted on N wall of nave. Thomas Heron †1517, schoolboy with inkhorn and pen-case. Two children of Barnard and Anne

*Excavations in 1984 found postholes suggesting an earlier timber church with apsidal E end, and foundations for a later stone chancel, possibly never completed. Existing monuments and a reference to a communion table in the chancel in 1638 suggest the chancel was rebuilt in the early C17.

Hyde: William †1614 and Ann †1630, the infant boy in swaddling clothes, the daughter standing, with verse inscription in English and Latin composed by her brother.

MONUMENTS. William Waldegrave and wife †1619 and 1599, kneeling figures facing across a prayer desk. Seven children below, not large. Strapwork frame. Francis Osbaston, High Sheriff, and infant sons †1678. Architectural frame with segmental pediment, Corinthian columns, cherub heads below; black marble and other stones. Anne Brisco †1739. Framed by marble pilasters, armorial above. Nathaniel Lambert †1745, simple classical tablet with open pediment and armorial. Several other plain tablets to the local gentry, also to Miguel Yglesias †1868 'a kind and liberal benefactor formerly of the parish at whose cost the church was repaired and presented with pulpit and reading desk'.

The small CHURCHYARD is a rectangle enclosed by a wall of blackened brick kiln wasters. Several railed chest tombs, including a large chest to Thomas Smith and family, and a small late C18 sarcophagus bearing an urn with lions' feet, to the family of James Hatch of Claybury Hall, Woodford Bridge. Several headstones with the device of a soul borne by a flying angel.

ST BARNABAS, Browning Road, by *Bucknall & Comper*, built in three stages, 1900–9. The most appealing of the area's suburban churches. Fine, quiet three-gabled brick and stone front set back from the road, simpler than Comper's first plans which included a turret and projecting triple entrance. Perp windows, the central one only slightly larger. The interior is a well lit hall church, cool and competent, with tall stone arcades, wide aisles, timber ceilings and parquet floor. NE Lady Chapel, attractive SE vestries 1904, the choir vestry with low Perp windows and barrel ceiling. Riddle posts with angels remain from *Comper*'s high altar. PULPIT with fielded panelling, C17, brought from Rayleigh, Essex. STAINED GLASS, E window, 1954 by *Comper*. VICARAGE to S, 1908 by *Bucknall*. L-shaped with slate-hung gable.

To the N, 1920s church halls, now a GURDWARA.

FROUD CENTRE, Romford Road and Toronto Avenue, with ST MICHAEL, replacing a church of 1897–8 by *Charles Spooner*. The new church, community centre and flats, named after Rev. Jimmy Froud of Forest Gate, are of 1990 by *APEC* (see also St Bartholomew East Ham and St Mark Beckton). The Luncheon Club at the corner juts forward with two layers of slate roof. The lower roof continues as porch to a common entrance. To the r. the church is announced by a freestanding bell-frame and a figure of St Michael slaying the devil, by *Robert Crutchley*, against a chamfered wall of red and purple brick. The church is a light, intimate space, lit by a clerestory below a roof sloping down towards the altar. Furnishings by *Bill Tromans*. The tall main area is flanked by lower spaces to N and W, which house a reused Gothic window with stained glass of 1906 (SS Mary and John, from a Crucifixion), and a small wooden triptych War Memorial with names on its hinged doors.

ST NICHOLAS (R.C.), Gladding Road. 1869–70 by *Gilbert Blount*. The church originated as a chapel attached to R.C. industrial schools in the adjacent Manor House (1868–1925), established by Cardinal Manning. Repaired after bomb damage, 1949–50. Gothic, grey brick with sparing black brick ornament, tall and gaunt. An apsed aisleless nave over a hall, thin paired lancets, circular W window with bold pastry-cutter tracery over a small porch with carved niche. Homely interior with painted walls and timber barrel vault, E end with shafts on carved corbels, W organ gallery.

ST STEPHEN (R.C.), Church Road. 1958 by *D.R. Burles* of *Burles Newton*. Steel-framed, faced in grey brick, with pinnacle spire. Large W choir gallery. STATIONS OF THE CROSS by *Rev. H. Buckley*.

METHODIST CHURCH, Romford Road and Herbert Road. The church of 1964 by *Stevens, Scanlan & Co.* was burnt out in 2003 and demolished, a sad loss of a bold landmark on the main road. It had a steep green-tiled roof of inverted-V profile, with big laminated-timber trusses and sharply angled gables. There remains WESLEY HOUSE to the S, 1937 by *R.J.L. Slater*, a fortress-like exterior concealing generous provision for Sunday school and functions; entrance hall with an elegant staircase, an intimate oak-panelled chapel upstairs.

SALVATION CHURCH OF CHRIST, High Street and Strone Road (former Congregational). 1903 by *G. and R.P. Baines*. Cheerful late Perp detail, tower on the l., church hall on the r.

CELESTIAL CHURCH OF CHRIST, Romford Road and Sixth Avenue. 1901, built as a Methodist church. Small, but with bold use of stone dressings with emphatic voussoirs. Arresting corner tower in striped stone and brick, with circular windows and small lead cap.

CITY OF LONDON CEMETERY, Aldersbrook Road. Founded in 1856 by the Corporation of London to provide an alternative to the desperately overcrowded city churchyards. The large site was acquired in 1853, and laid out by *William Haywood*, surveyor to the Commissioners of Sewers, with landscaping by *Robert Davidson*. Unlike too many London cemeteries, well cared for, and a good place to appreciate the original character of the trim Victorian cemetery on a grand scale, complete with its original buildings. The mood is disturbed only by the presence of cars and a C20 crematorium. Straight tree-lined avenues lined with tombs fan out from the entrance, providing vistas of the chapels, while a more relaxed winding route hugs the northern periphery. To S and E are later memorial gardens and regrettably dull extensions. The approach is through archways in a curved screen wall which links two Gothic LODGES, picturesquely roofed with patterned slates. The ANGLICAN CHAPEL, of ragstone, has a steeply gabled front with large traceried window under an ogee arch, a pretty crocketed spire on the left, and thin pinnacled buttresses. The

French Flamboyant Gothic detail is an unusual choice. The more sober NONCONFORMIST CHAPEL is octagonal, with a rose window to its entrance foyer. Further S is a Gothic, arcaded crescent of CATACOMBS, partly converted to columbaria with etched-glass entrance doors. The ceremonial approach to this is now awkwardly interrupted by the CREMATORIUM of 1971, a low building with patterned-concrete screen walls and an overbearing flat roof. An older crematorium lies to the S, 1903 by *D.J. Ross*, the second to be built in London. Lancet style, with chimney disguised as a tower.

The most prominent MONUMENTS are those erected for remains reinterred from City churchyards. They are pleasingly various in design; beside Central Avenue, running SE from the entrance, the grandest is a Gothic tower with upper stage and tall cross on top (for remains from St Andrew and St Sepulchre), 1871 by *Haywood.* Probably also by him the large Gothic structure with gabled arches (All Hallows Bread Street and St John Evangelist). In Forge Avenue beyond the Anglican church a Classical aedicule (St Olave Jewry and St Martin Pomeroy), 1889. By Anchor Road two mausolea of the 1860s in Grecian style (Pedley and Hasluck families) in a mixture of stone and granite; Haywood's own monument is a Gothic mausoleum near the entrance gates (†1894). But mostly obelisks and angels on pedestals provide the principal accents. An eccentricity is the memorial to Gladys Spencer †1931 with piano and reclining figure.

MANOR PARK CEMETERY, Sebert Road. Founded 1874. Stripped Gothic, red brick chapel, rebuilt after bombing; crematorium added 1955.

WOODGRANGE PARK CEMETERY, Romford Road. Established 1890; near the entrance a desolate ruined Gothic chapel with small tower and canted apse, flanked by the grander urns, angels and red-granite columns. The crowded bramble-covered wilderness behind contrasts sharply with the neat railed-off territory of the Muslim Patel Burial Trust. To the E WAR MEMORIAL with cross of sacrifice.

MAJOR BUILDINGS

75 CARNEGIE LIBRARY, Romford Road and Rabbits Road. 1904 by the borough engineer *A.H. Campbell.* Red brick and terracotta, bristling with blocked columns and Baroque detail, in the manner established locally for public buildings by Cheers' East Ham Town Hall and Gibson & Russell's West Ham Institute. The foundation stone was laid by Passmore Edwards, but it was Andrew Carnegie who was persuaded by J.H. Bethell (mayor when the library opened in 1905) to fund the building. Names of literary luminaries along the front: Dickens, Longfellow, Milton, Shakespeare, Tennyson, Carlyle; on the

side Burns and Scott, in deference to the Scottish origins of Carnegie, whose bust is placed below the gable. Large porch on the l., leading to hall and charming, domed circular lobby, from which doors with Art Nouveau glass lead to three library rooms (now united). On the first floor a former public hall.

RECTORY MANOR SECONDARY SCHOOL, Browning Road. 1955–7 by *J. W. Taylor*.

PERAMBULATION

N of Manor Park station in GLADDING ROAD is the only surviving older house in the area, MANOR HOUSE, apparently of *c.* 1810, built by the lord of the manor of West Ham on his Hamfrith estate. Occupied by the R.C. St Nicholas industrial Schools, *c.* 1868–1925 (whose chapel remains, *see* above), and later by the London Co-operative Co. as a milk depot. Now flats and much altered. Two and a half storeys, five bays, stuccoed, with big cornice, rusticated end pilasters and C19 clock turret.

The Edwardian commercial centre is concentrated around High Street North and Romford Road. From Manor Park Station, STATION ROAD leads to the junction, past the BLAKENEY ARMS, 1887, with much overpainted terracotta detail. At the SW corner the EARL OF ESSEX. A jovial Baroque composition 1901–2 by *Henry Poston* and *W.E. Trent*, typical of complex pub design of this date. Two grandiose entrances, each with a balconied superstructure, the corner one rising to a finialed dome. The corner entrance was to the public bar, the larger one facing the High Street combined entrances to saloon and private bars, with 'bottle and jugs' door in the centre. The roofline is augmented by triple dormers with central pediments and a lesser, corbelled turret at the W end, with names of the architects and 'Coronation year 1902'. The other corners fail to live up to this.

First to the S. HIGH STREET NORTH has little except for the CORONATION CINEMA (now snooker hall). 1921 by *Clifford Aish*. An exceptionally sumptuous 'suburban palace' (*East Ham News* 1921), a rebuilding of a cinema opened in 1911. The plan is old fashioned, a long barrel-vaulted auditorium seating *c.* 2000, but the decoration was unusually lavish. The confidently classical exterior, with paired pilasters along the front is in a quite sober taste (but inside, a riot of elaborate plasterwork, now partly concealed by a suspended ceiling). Some way further S, RUSKIN ARMS, with half-timbered gables at the corner of Ruskin Avenue. 1901 by *Yetts, Sturdy & Usher*.

Now to the W along ROMFORD ROAD, past SALISBURY PRIMARY SCHOOL, squeezed onto a small triangular site. Built by East Ham School Board, *c.* 1893, by *R.L. Curtis*. Large three-decker with a cluster of gables, gauntly picturesque through being set at an angle to the road. Minimal red brick trim: windows with aprons and the suggestion of pediments, a Curtis hallmark (*see* East Ham). Further W, close to Woodgrange Park Station, No. 544, LUMIERE BUILDING, lone example so far in this area of a block of private flats, *c.* 2000, crisp and confident with projecting red vertical panels to E and W, and recessed corners to the top floor. Further W at Shrewsbury Road, the RISING SUN, dated 1896, broad-arched windows; curly foliage and sun in the tympana.

WOODGRANGE PARK, N of Romford Road on the edge of Forest Gate is announced by the big church of All Saints on its fringe (*see* above). The estate, extending W to Forest Drive, was largely built up 1877–80 and completed 1892. By then it had 1160 houses. It was begun by Thomas Corbett and continued by his better known son, A. Cameron Corbett, who went on to build extensively in Ilford and elsewhere, gaining a reputation for reliable quality. Staid two-storey houses, laid out along an unexciting grid of streets, but notable for the generous size of the plots which allowed for double-fronted detached houses as well as terraces, and for some variety of porches, iron verandas and windows.

ROMFORD ROAD E of High Street North is an indifferent shopping street, but with some good individual buildings. On the N side the CARNEGIE LIBRARY, and then the FROUD CENTRE with St Michael's church (*see* above). The far end tails away with little of note until a sudden change of scale close to the borough boundary. On the S side an array of tall flats, with lower housing behind, built in the 1960s by East Ham to replace poor quality 1900s housing erected (despite contemporary criticism) on the Roding flood plains. Cheerful landscaping and trimmings of the 1990s. Beyond, the mighty flyover of the North Circular marks the boundary with Ilford. Further S, the low-lying land beside the river remains open, with parks and playing fields.

LITTLE ILFORD LANE is the old route leading S from the main road to the tiny medieval church of St Mary (*see* above), now in undistinguished surroundings. Some way to the S of this beyond the railway, a tall group at HATHAWAY CRESCENT, a triangular area between railway lines: one fifteen-storey and five eight-storey H-shaped towers, 1963 onwards, grouped quite pleasantly around an open space.

THE ROYAL DOCKS and RIVERSIDE*

The Royal Docks were the last group of docks to be built in London, between 1850 and 1921, and the last to close, in 1981. Compared with their predecessors they are vast, stretching along

*This section draws on part of the text by Elizabeth Williamson and Malcolm Tucker published in *London: Docklands*, 1998.

the river for over three miles E of the River Lea. The huge cargo ships and liners which the docks were built to accommodate have gone, together with the warehouses and transit sheds that lined the seven miles of quay. What remains are the great shining stretches of water, silent and still except for the dwarfed pleasurecraft to which the docks are now devoted.

The docks were made in the virtually uninhabited stretches of the flood plains between the Thames and the higher ground further N. Hammarsh had been owned by Westminster Abbey. There was a medieval chapel and hamlet here, but after flooding the area remained empty marshland used for grazing until it was transformed by rail transport from the mid-C19. Development began through the enterprises of the railway engineer and promoter G.P. Bidder. First came a freight line from the Eastern Counties line at Stratford to a new wharf on the Thames at Bow Creek, opened in 1846, extended to the ferry at North Woolwich in 1847. The Metropolitan Building Act of 1844, which proscribed noxious industries within the metropolitan area, made the riverside of West Ham and East Ham a magnet for many insalubrious trades from India-rubber manufacture to carcase rendering. Dickens' account of this area in 'Londoners over the border', from *Household Words* (1857), is a classic piece of Victorian *grand guignol*, describing it 'as a place of refuge for offensive trade establishments turned out of town, those of oil boilers, gut-spinners, varnish makers, printer's ink makers and the like'. Communities grew up rapidly around them: Canning Town (*see* p. 256) for the workers at the Thames Iron Works at Bow Creek, Silvertown at Silver's rubber works, established 1852, North Woolwich around ferry, railway and local telegraph cable works, and furthest E, after 1868, Beckton, for the huge gasworks of the Gas Light and Coke Co. The poor quality Victorian housing has now gone, either destroyed in the Second World War or rebuilt since.

Meanwhile Bidder joined in promoting the Victoria Dock, to be linked by railway and designed to be large enough for the new iron steamships. It was constructed by 1864 and sold to the London and St Katharine Dock Co., who went on to build the Royal Albert Dock to its E in 1875–80. Following its opening they provided passenger facilities along the railway line, all designed by *George Vigers & T.R. Wagstaffe*, of which three examples survive. The newly created Port of London Authority added the King George V Dock in 1912, with an entrance large enough for, exceptionally, the 35,000 ton liner S.S. *Mauretania*.

The railway links and the ample storage space available put increasing emphasis on goods in transit, especially food, assisted by developing technology: hydraulic power from 1855, arc lighting from 1880, electric and mechanical handling equipment from the early C20. At the Royal Albert Dock the world's largest cold store was built *c.* 1914. The Royal Victoria had a large complex for tobacco, and major C20 dockside flourmills. There were also important ship-repair facilities, notably at the Pontoon Dock of the Royal Victoria.

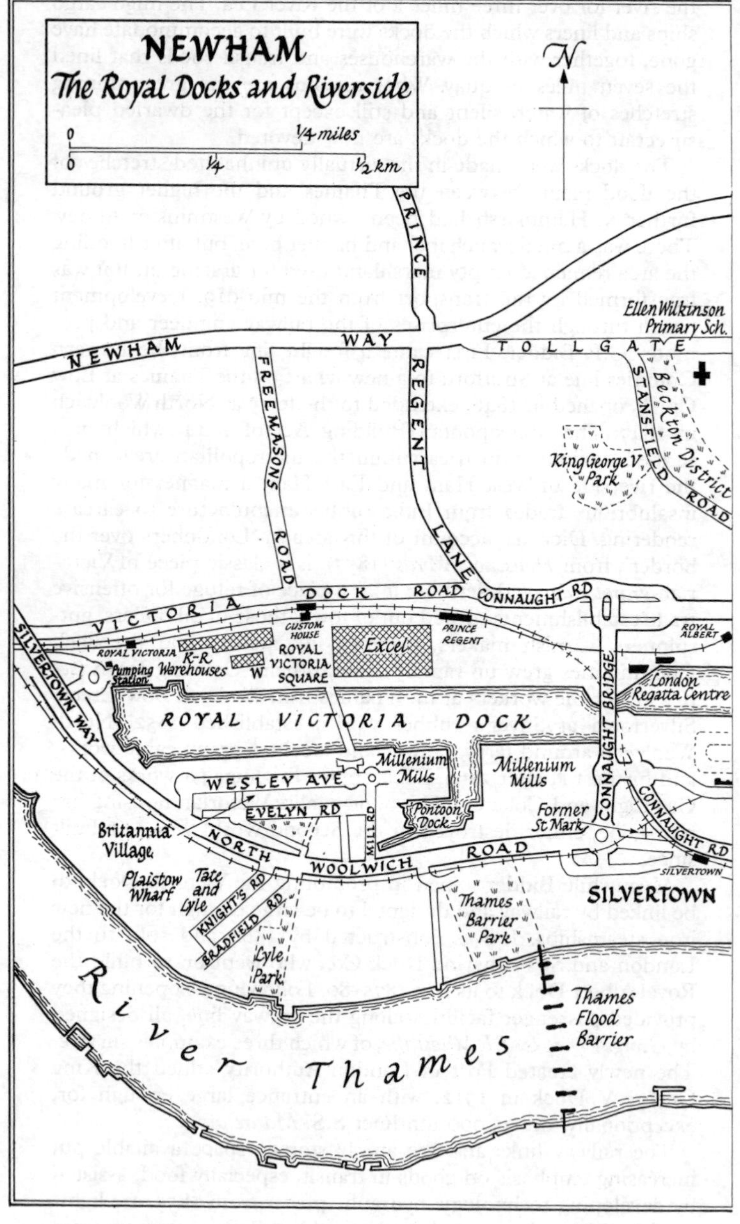
NEWHAM
The Royal Docks and Riverside
0 1/4 miles
0 1/4 1/2 km
N
PRINCE REGENT LANE
NEWHAM WAY
TOLLGATE
Ellen Wilkinson Primary Sch.
FREEMASONS ROAD
STANSFIELD ROAD
Beckton District
King George V Park
VICTORIA DOCK ROAD
CONNAUGHT RD
CUSTOM HOUSE
PRINCE REGENT
ROYAL ALBERT
ROYAL VICTORIA
Pumping Station
K-R Warehouses
W
ROYAL VICTORIA SQUARE
Excel
CONNAUGHT BRIDGE
London Regatta Centre
SILVERTOWN WAY
ROYAL VICTORIA DOCK
Millenium Mills
Millenium Mills
WESLEY AVE
EVELYN RD
MILL RD
Pontoon Dock
Former St Mark
CONNAUGHT RD
Britannia Village
NORTH WOOLWICH ROAD
SILVERTOWN
Plaistow Wharf
Tate and Lyle
KNIGHT'S RD
BRADFIELD RD
Thames Barrier Park
SILVERTOWN
Lyle Park
River Thames
Thames Flood Barrier

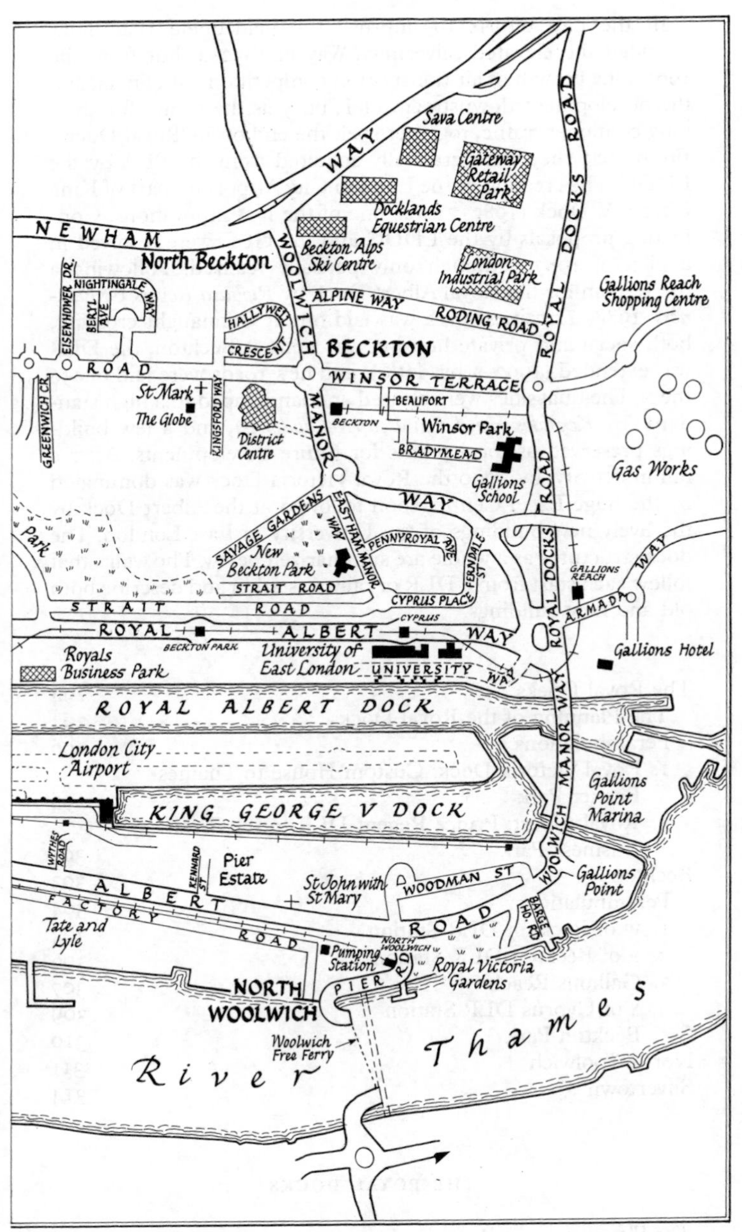
NEWHAM WAY
North Beckton
Sava Centre
Gateway Retail Park
Docklands Equestrian Centre
Beckton Alps Ski Centre
London Industrial Park
Gallions Reach Shopping Centre
ROYAL DOCKS ROAD
WOOLWICH MANOR WAY
ALPINE WAY
RODING ROAD
BECKTON
NIGHTINGALE WAY
EISENHOWER DR.
BERYL AVE
HALLYWELL CRESCENT
ROAD
WINSOR TERRACE
BEAUFORT
St Mark
The Globe
KINGSFORD WAY
GREENWICH CR.
District Centre
BECKTON
Winsor Park
BRADYMEAD
Gallions School
Gas Works
WAY
SAVAGE GARDENS
EAST HAM MANOR WAY
PENNYROYAL AVE
FERNDALE ST
New Beckton Park
Park
STRAIT ROAD
CYPRUS PLACE
GALLIONS REACH
ARMADA WAY
STRAIT ROAD
ROYAL ALBERT WAY
CYPRUS
BECKTON PARK
Royals Business Park
University of East London
UNIVERSITY WAY
Gallions Hotel
ROYAL ALBERT DOCK
London City Airport
Gallions Point Marina
KING GEORGE V DOCK
WYTHES ROAD
KENNARD ST
Pier Estate
St John with St Mary
WOODMAN ST
Gallions Point
ALBERT ROAD
FACTORY ROAD
BARGE HO. RD
Tate and Lyle
Pumping Station
NORTH WOOLWICH
PIER RD
Royal Victoria Gardens
NORTH WOOLWICH
Woolwich Free Ferry
River Thames

In the C20 efforts to improve the inadequate road links included the elevated Silvertown Way of 1932–4, but from the 1960s, the growth of air transport in competition with liners, and the development downstream of Tilbury as the centre for shipping container traffic, together spelt the end of the Royal Docks. From 1981 they were gradually acquired from the PLA by the LDDC. The creation of the London City Airport on part of King George V Dock (1982–7) was one of the first innovations. Conflicting proposals by the LDDC and the GLC were resolved in a plan of 1987, although only partially realized. Following a masterplan for the Royal Albert Dock by *Richard Rogers & Partners*, 1988, a business park was laid out at Connaught crossing, both social and private housing was built at Beckton, the DLR was extended (1992–4 by *ABK*), and new roads were laid out to the N. The quaysides were cleared and landscaped to a high standard (by *Keysides Hard Landscapes–Gillespies*), and a few buildings preserved as focal points for future developments. After a lull in activity, by 2000 the Royal Victoria Dock was dominated by the huge Excel Centre, soon followed at the Albert Dock by the lively new buildings of the University of East London. The dock structures as a whole are summarized below. The walks that follow each start from a DLR or railway station and describe both old and new buildings.

THE ROYAL DOCKS

The Planning of the Royal Docks

The ROYAL VICTORIA DOCK was built 1850–5 by the Victoria Dock Co. formed by the railway contractors, Samuel Morton Peto, Edward Ladd Betts and Thomas Brassey with the engineer *G.P. Bidder*. Their aim was to sell it quickly, but it was not until 1864 that the newly amalgamated London and St Katharine Dock Co. bought the dock, spurred on by lack of space in the

Victoria Dock, view of excavations, 1850

old docks and by the fact that the Victoria Dock had taken much of the tobacco trade away from the London Docks.

The dock was an advance on earlier docks in several ways, apart from size ($1\frac{1}{4}$m. long, 94 acres of water): it had its own railway system, connected to the main railway system by marshalling sidings on the N side; hydraulic power from the start, with machinery by *W.G. Armstrong & Co.*; and a novel construction with, on the N side, five finger jetties (previously experimented with at the London Docks) to increase capacity. It was built economically with earthen banks, but the entrance lock and some other parts used cast-iron piled and panelled walls backed with concrete, a technique used before by Bidder at Brunswick Wharf (*see* Blackwall). The finger jetties were extensively reconstructed from 1935 into the 1940s when the river entrance from the W into the Tidal Basin was closed. When work on the main dock was already well advanced, *Bidder* promoted the building of the Victoria Graving Dock, later known as the PONTOON DOCK. Here there was a revolutionary hydraulic ship lift, first used in 1858 and invented by *Edwin Clark*, who had hydraulically lifted the tubes of the Britannia Bridge over the Menai Straits, 1850. Each ship was lifted out of the water on pontoons that were raised by hydraulic jacks. Drained of its ballast water, the pontoon then floated the ship into one of the eight finger docks for repair. Run by the Thames Graving Dock Co. until 1896, by which time the size of ships had exceeded the capacity of the lifting equipment.

The Victoria Dock was renamed when the ROYAL ALBERT DOCK was built in 1875–80 for the London and St Katharine Dock Co. to provide a new E entrance to the Victoria Dock to accommodate the larger ships developed during the previous twenty years. 85 acres of water, the main dock, of 71 acres, being 1 mile long. It was initially intended to be a ship canal with a quay along the N side to allow ships to berth. Only during construction was it decided to wharf the S side as well. The engineer was *Sir Alexander Rendel*. There was electric light, by arc lamps, from the beginning. The dock was used chiefly for transit and it was efficiently laid out for transfer to rail. Railway sidings lining the quays were almost entirely built up with large single-storey metal sheds. Built in 1882, these twin-span structures made by *Westwood, Baillie & Co.* had frames of wrought-iron trusses on cast-iron columns and corrugated-iron sheet cladding, and were linked by covered areas into six groups. They represented the important change in dock warehousing from long-term storage to transit facilities. Cold stores were later added at the NW corner for the large frozen meat trade. Nearly all the buildings were cleared in the 1980s.

Two docks were planned for N and S of the Royal Albert Dock, by the London and India Dock Co., who obtained an Act in 1901. The PLA took over the proposals when they were established in 1909 and built only the KING GEORGE V dock in 1912–21. Begun by (*Sir*) *Frederick Palmer*, the Port of London Authority's first Chief Engineer, completed by (*Sir*) *Cyril Kirkpatrick*. Its 64 acres of water are only five-eighths the size of the Royal Victoria Dock. It has concrete quay walls, some original capstans dated 1916. On the N side were two-storey transit sheds, of reinforced concrete with brick infill. The whole N side and the W dry dock, as well as the integral graving docks at the SW end of the Royal Albert Dock, were obliterated by the formation of the City Airport (*see* below).

PERAMBULATIONS

1. Royal Victoria Dock to the Thames Barrier, beginning at Custom House Station

The walk begins at CUSTOM HOUSE STATION opened on the Eastern Counties Railway in 1855 as Victoria Dock station on the 'avoiding line' to North Woolwich made necessary by the construction of the dock. The DLR station by *ABK* now shares the site and its footbridge links Victoria Dock Road and the dock. On the N side of the road: THE FLYING ANGEL, No. 287, of 1934–6 by *Petch & Fermaud* to house the Anglican Missions to Seamen Institute which moved here from Poplar (*see* Poplar, Perambulation). Big, eight-storeys of seamen's accommodation in red brick and white render. Tower-like blocks to N and S. Centrepiece of tiered attics carrying a hint of 1930s commercial buildings such as Joseph's Shell-Mex building, Victoria Embankment, Westminster. On the top there is a square-arched lantern that originally housed a flashing light. Centre of the building, including the originally irregular E side, reorganized in the conversion to shared serviced flats for single people by *Jefferson Sheard*, 1985–8.

SE of the station stood the CUSTOM HOUSE (properly called the Dock Directors' Access Centre) built in 1920–4 by *Sir Edwin*

Cooper for the PLA. They intended it as a warehouse and office premises for letting to the railway company and tobacco importers. The landward ground floor contained a refreshment room and canteen. In spite of restoration in 1994–5 it was demolished to make way for the gargantuan and dazzlingly white EXCEL exhibition and conference centre. This dominates the area around the station and links to it via a footbridge with tensioned canopies. 1999–2000 by *Moxley Architects* (won in competition 1990 by *Moxley Jenner & Partners*). 90,000 m^2 on three storeys with an attention-seeking roofline of sixteen white tubular-steel roof hangers. These allow for a column-free interior covered by the largest (87 metre wide) single-span roof in the UK. The supporting columns also carry the first-floor lorryway that serves the entire building. Three storeys with ground-floor services and exhibition halls at first floor, separated by an anonymous 96 ft (35 metre) wide internal mall, top-lit at the centre. On the upper floor are smaller rooms around the perimeter. Functionally impressive but another waste of a peerless waterside setting (admittedly useful for hosting the annual Boat Show). Its W end has a big pyramidal glass entrance from where steps lead down to the dockside. Proudly erect along the quay is a row of *Stothert & Pitt* portal quay CRANES (1962 design in welded tubular construction) at the front of ROYAL VICTORIA SQUARE, created by *Patel Taylor* with landscape architect *EDAW* in 2000. Japanese-style, i.e. geometric mix of hard and soft landscaping, superbly planted with tight diagonal rows of beech trees and a pergola on the main axis. Light-wands sprout, like bulrushes, from the hard paving.

The N quay of the dock is now as rebuilt in 1937 but the 'W' WAREHOUSE represents its original line. 1883 by the company engineer *Robert Carr*. Narrow and four storey, with three-storey giant arcades in the style of the earlier St Katharine Docks warehouses (*see* Wapping p. 504). The warehouse has its S wall on brick arches supported on cast-iron screw piles, revealed by the reintroduction of a small area of water in front. Timber floors on cast-iron columns, queenpost roof. Restored for the LDDC by *Feilden & Mawson*; converted to flats in 2004. Behind are the enormous 'K–R' WAREHOUSES, an original bonded store for tobacco of 1859 by *Bidder*. Attached to it W, but now demolished, was another warehouse of similar length divided by a central firebreak wall. Two storeys with round-arched windows and pilaster strips above a basement ventilated by arched brick areas. The E part (K) with tall loading bays under hipped roofs was restored for the LDDC by *Rees Johns Bolter Architects*, 1994–5. Internally of two storeys plus loft, with timber floors on cruciform cast-iron columns. Its trussed timber roof was of unusual design, with iron hanger rods to reduce weight, and of large central span. Warehouses O–R were reconstructed internally after a fire in 1925 as single storey sections under hipped-roofs. Each has steel trusses on tall steel or concrete columns carrying crane rails. They were enlarged at the rear, towards Seagull Way, to form a continuous range with a pitched-roofed warehouse added at the back of 'K' in 1919 by the PLA. Yellow stock brick, with tall upper windows above a row of smaller ones, lighting a single large hall used for the high stacking of tobacco casks.

The C21 developments now extend almost continuously along the N quay, designed principally to serve the Excel centre: closest to the warehouses is an attractive NURSERY SCHOOL and CRECHE by *Walters & Cohen* 2001–2. Three parallel timber-clad ranges, under steel butterfly roofs, with courtyard gardens between. This strikes an exceptional note of quality against its neighbours to the E, banal designs for apartments and a series of chain hotels: NOVOTEL, HOLIDAY INN and IBIS. They employ the usual repertoire of light-weight cladding, primary-coloured walls and the odd streamlined corner.

The W end of the Victoria Dock basin was extensively remodelled in the 1930s to incorporate its former tidal entrance basin after the building of SILVERTOWN WAY (1932–4 by *Rendel Palmer & Tritton*) closed the original entrance from the river. The name lives on at this end of the quayside in the derelict TIDAL BASIN TAVERN, Neo-Elizabethan with coped gables, and the colourful piece of sculpture that is the TIDAL BASIN PUMPING STATION. 1986–90, designed to handle drainage for the Royal Docks area. Engineers *Sir William Halcrow & Partners*. Two circular chambers, a main chamber and a screen chamber behind. The main chamber has two concentric drums rising about 39 ft (12 metres); inside, an 82 ft (25 metre) shaft lifts waste water from underground channels to a high-level discharge from where it runs into the Thames. What we see is by the *Richard Rogers Partnership* in a characteristically industrial manner. White polycarbonate sheet as semi-opaque curtain walls are encased in an external steel grille. Royal-blue-rendered drums and steelwork in primary colours; now rather weathered.

Now across the Dock by the thrilling BRIDGE, 1997–9 by *Lifschutz Davidson* and *Techniker* who won an LDDC competition for a transporter bridge to connect housing development on the Dock's S side with the DLR. The design was for a cable-stayed bridge, high enough to allow the passage of yachts below, with lifts up the masts to a transporter car suspended from the 418 ft (127 metre) main span, supported by an ingenious succession of cable-stayed cantilevers, each springing from the previous one. The transporter car, omitted in the final stages, can be introduced in the future. The apparent folly is more than compensated for by the outstanding views to E and W, laying out the entire Royal Docks in a panorama, silent except for the hum of activity at London City Airport on the quay between the Royal Albert and King George V docks.

At the bridge's S end, CRESCENT, a curved block of flats by *Tibbalds Monro*, 1998, for Peabody. Shops with flats above including provision for the disabled. Italian Postmodern garb, in plan rather similar to old-fashioned access balcony flats but fully glazed in on the N side. An archway leads through to a mix of private and social housing in BRITANNIA VILLAGE which extends S from the quay to North Woolwich Road. Conceived by the LDDC as a self-contained community within an urban setting, with shops, pub, a village common, village hall and a primary school. The masterplan was devised by the *Tibbalds Colbourne Partnership* (later *Tibbalds Monro*) in 1989. Building began in 1995–7 with housing along the quayside by *Tibbalds Monro* for Wimpey. The layout follows the masterplan: pavilions of flats along the quay and conventional streets of terraced houses leading from a central crescent. The buildings themselves, in yellow brick, are unexceptional, encompassing variations on the theme of the London terrace house or warehouse block but with lots of unnecessary tricks.

To the S the village common, developed from the late 1990s, picks up the original intention of the plan, enhanced by changes in level which create a sloping site for the surrounding low-rise housing. This replaced an unmourned pair of twenty-two-storey tower blocks of 1966, linked by crescents of shops, community rooms etc. Near the common are two innovative commissions by Peabody, won in competition, 2001. In EVELYN ROAD No. 117, 2003–4 by *Niall McLaughlin*. Timber-framed construction, clad in red cedar, with novel glass-cladding system to the S wall, devised with the light artist *Martin Richman* to contain light boxes which change colour and opacity. Loft-style interiors, with tall L-shaped living rooms. In BOXLEY STREET, four timber-framed flats by *Ash Sakula*, 2003–4, with cladding of gold and silver foil, and unconventionally large kitchens and halls. Completing the picture on the W side, in WESTWOOD ROAD, the PRIMARY SCHOOL, a large but friendly example of Newham's recent work, and VILLAGE HALL and CLINIC built into the slope with a dark brick plinth, timber-clad upper storeys and a curved roof.

S of here, a detour can be made across NORTH WOOLWICH ROAD to the industrial riverside, still busy but experiencing redevelopment and soon to be served by the DLR (under construction in 2004). Plaistow Wharf was first used for oil storage but in 1881 Abram Lyle & Sons began to make Golden Syrup here before amalgamating with Tate's (*see* Silvertown) in 1921. The 1930s factory survives in KNIGHT'S ROAD, but the offices (built in 1946–50) were demolished *c.* 2001. They bore the firm's trademark of the lion killed by Samson surrounded by bees and, from Judges XIV, the answer to Samson's riddle 'Out of the strong came forth sweetness'. Just S stood a wharf manager's villa of pre-1860, also demolished, the home of James Lyle in 1891. E of the factory, off Bradfield Road, is the well-hidden pocket of LYLE PARK, provided by Lyle's for the Borough of West Ham in 1924 and still an oasis of green. It has an expansive playing field surrounded by paths and at the S end steps rise to a platform planted with mature trees, overlooking the river. Placed here in 1994, in the form of a screen at the head of the steps, the Adamesque iron gates of the Harland and Wolff shipyard at North Woolwich (closed 1971). In the NE corner of the park, a drinking fountain. Modern plinth with cavetto mouldings, inset with a tile memorial to the First World War dead of West Silvertown – 'erected by public subscription'.

E of Britannia Village, on the N side of North Woolwich Road, lies the undeveloped area around the Pontoon Dock (*see* above), scheduled to become Silvertown Quays, under a masterplan by *Urban Strategies* for housing, offices, shops and leisure facilities including a massive aquarium by *Terry Farrell & Partners*. Within this scheme will be retained a few historic structures associated with the grain and flour mills that occupied the area around the Pontoon Dock after 1896 when it was used for the transhipment of grain. In Mill Road, the tall mid-C20 brick CHIMNEY of Rank's Empire Mills. Prominent behind this, Spiller's Millennium Mills remain a major landmark on the dock side. Gabled W wing dated 1933: formal N side of 1954.* Immediately S, visible from the landscaped pathway along North Woolwich Road, a former grain silo ('D' Silo) built in reinforced concrete in 1920 to replace a group of corrugated-iron silos built by the London Grain Elevator Co., 1898, but damaged in the Silvertown explosion of 1917. Planar, white-painted walls with small windows, some of them circular, distinctly symmetrical with octagonal plant rooms on top. Bulk grain was lifted from ships and barges into the central cube of silos and the two side towers, both by bucket and by suction elevators, and loaded through weighing machines into other barges.

The development of Silvertown Quays will link up with the Thames Barrier Park, S of North Woolwich Road, and achieve the necessary physical continuity between the docks and river. The park was the result of an international competition held by the LDDC in 1995 (though plans for a park here had been put forward by the GLC shortly after completion of the barrier) and completed in phases 1997–2000. The landscape architects were *Groupe Signes*, the architects *Patel Taylor Architects*. *Alain Provost* of Group Signes was a consultant to the Parc Citroën, developed on a similar riverside industrial site in Paris from 1972. Like the Parc Citroën it has been designed on a bold framework with strong diagonal routes shooting through the underlying geometry, and incorporating a series of cultural references. The approach from the N is immediately striking with steep, sloping walls of plain concrete framing a paved area dotted with spouting water fountains.
122 These herald the beginning of the 'Green Dock', a 1312 ft (400 metre) channel hollowed out of the central plateau with deep concrete retaining walls designed to carry creeping lonicera. Its floor is a strip of lush planting with undulating yew hedges

*Three other mills, including the striking horizontal-banded C.W.S. Mills, 1938–44 by *L. G. Ekins*, were mostly demolished in the early 1990s.

driving between beds of herbaceous plantings. Long steel bridges cross at diagonals above. The exceptional minimalist approach is shared by the few buildings, most successfully by the café and visitor centre, of almost pure Miesian simplicity: a glass box, oak-framed at one end. Its transparency contrasts with the solid concrete walls of the rear section. At the S end of the park, by the river, a Tadao Ando-esque PAVILION, designed as a memorial to civilians killed in the Blitz. Flat roof, carried on slender tubular-steel columns which are clustered together in the centre, and pierced by a circular opening. It shelters benches in polished granite whose wavy forms echoes the hedges of the 'dock'. Formal plantings over the E plateau.

The perimeter of the park on each side is residential. On the W side, BARRIER POINT by *Goddard Manton* for Barratt, 2000–1, comparable in character to their Pierhead Lock on the Isle of Dogs in its evocation of the pure white modernism of the 1930s. A continuous group, stepping down in storeys towards the park and terminated at the riverside by a fifteen-storey tower. On the E side, employing the same stepping effect but without the fluency or the cool materials, TRADEWINDS by *Denning Male Polisano*, also for Barratt.

The THAMES BARRIER itself, between here and Charlton on the S bank, is one of London's most ambitious civil engineering works, mostly hidden below water, but with the sculptural, silver, shell-like roofs of the machinery rooms making a memorable visual impact. It was designed to protect London from catastrophic flooding caused by surge tides in the Thames estuary. By *Rendel Palmer & Tritton* for the GLC Department of Public Health Engineering, 1974–82. The barrier was anticipated to close twice a year but it has been used on eighty-eight occasions since opening, with as many as fourteen closures in 2002 alone.

There are four navigation openings each of 200 ft (61 metres; the same width of opening as Tower Bridge), two subsidiary openings of 103 ft (31 metres), and four side spans also of 103 ft. While the side spans have radial gates which fall from above, the navigation openings have the novel feature of pivoted D-shape welded-steel gates which lie flat on the river bed and rotate into a 66-ft high vertical position to close the barrier. Beneath the gates and shaped to their curve, cellular pre-cast concrete sills span between the piers which are capped with boat-shaped roofs of laminated timber clad with stainless steel. On the S bank a tall control building with sculpted roof and viewing galleries, by the *GLC Architect's Department*.

2. *Royal Albert Dock: Prince Regent DLR to Royal Albert DLR*

PRINCE REGENT DLR is one of *ABK*'s distinctive 1990s stations for this line. To Connaught Road, a fine piece of popular art, a stainless steel FRIEZE with lively silhouettes of docklands scenes and figures from British history (including the artist's 117 mother) by *Brian Yale*, 1995. Walking E from the station, at this point the elevated track of the line can be appreciated in isolation as it crosses Albert Way and snakes E along the N side of the docks. Startlingly simple in its elegance, just a series of H-frame supports in smooth concrete. The viaduct passes between two new arrivals to the Docks in 2003, chain hotels built to serve the EXCEL exhibition centre and in time the Royals Business Park (*see* below). RAMADA (by the dockside) by *BUJ Architects*, with a ten-storey towered section topped by a wavy-walled glass lantern and sleek cladding, and TRAVEL INN, vividly coloured with a crude delight in varied textures and materials. Neither is distinguished.

Sitting back from these towards Connaught Road is their C19 predecessor, the CONNAUGHT TAVERN of 1881 by *George Vigers & T.R. Wagstaffe*; the first of their buildings for the London and St Katharine Dock Company. Wagstaffe was appointed surveyor to the dock company in 1881, Vigers had been a student at the Royal Academy Schools when Norman Shaw taught there. Shaw's influence is obvious. Tall (the published designs show it a storey lower) and made taller with high ribbed chimneystacks. Tile-hung gables, a central Dutch gable, and canted bays rising from a ground-floor projection with timber balustrade, extended later to form a terrace. Brick ship relief to the side. Restored by the *Brian Clancy Partnership* (1996); the ground floor has been built out on the W side creating the false impression of the upper storeys resting on a podium. Inside, two iron columns with cruciform caps. Just E of here lay the former Great Western Railway goods station of 1900, of very early reinforced concrete.

The junction between the Victoria and Albert Docks is marked by the CONNAUGHT CROSSING, a swing road bridge, by *Sir William Halcrow & Partners*, 1990 for LDDC. Cable-stayed, steel box girder, with control cabin perched on the central pylon. Concrete approach spans on pilotis. A two-leaf swing FOOTBRIDGE echoes the main bridge with the curved soffit of its box girders. The old SWING BRIDGE of 1879 was one of the largest such bridges (90-ft, 27.5 metre, span) and took two rail tracks and a single-lane road between three hog-backed plate girders. Its main cross-girder and hydraulic operating gear are preserved. The crossing spans the CONNAUGHT PASSAGE, linking the docks; 1880, deepened 1935–7, widened 1958 except through the bridge. The concrete copings belong to the excellent 1990s landscaping by *Keyside-Gillespies* designed to show off the dockside relics. The creation of the passage required diversion of the North Woolwich railway through a steep TUNNEL beneath. Dated 1878 on the tunnel portal. It is marked by two brick circular ventilation shafts and a lantern-roofed octagon over the pumping shaft.

W of the crossing the expanse of the ROYAL ALBERT DOCK is fully revealed. The DOCK WALLS are 40-ft (12 metres) high, mostly of concrete; 18–19 ft (5.5 metres) thick at the bottom, reducing to 5 ft (1.5 metres) at the top, with an up-to-date and technically efficient stepped rear face and projecting toe at the base. Entirely of Portland cement concrete, one of the first occasions that this was used for quay walls without a protective brick facing. From here the view S takes in the King George V Dock and London City Airport (*see* Silvertown, below), whose runway occupies the intervening quay. Two of the Albert's major dry docks for ship repairs are now beneath the airport.

The recreation of the crossing was partly needed to allow for an Olympic-standard continuous rowing course between the two dock basins. In the NW corner of the dock, the REGATTA CENTRE. By *Ian Ritchie Architects*, 1999. A fiercely angular and tough design for the Clubhouse with sharp 'prow' on the S side, aligned to the dockside for viewing balconies from the first-floor bar. Flanking on both sides, tall gabions of granite fragments encased in steel mesh anchor the building to its site. Inside, the clubhouse has an innovative powered rowing tank for training designed by *Arup*, engineers, to reproduce as closely as possible the experience of rowing on open water. Separate BOAT STORE protected behind a gabion wall, simple steel structure of three bays with an undulating steel catenary roof.

The NW corner of the Albert Dock was historically the site of cold stores for the large frozen-meat trade, and is now ROYALS BUSINESS PARK. The only relic is the former cold-store compressor house, a handsome red brick building of one tall storey, with a bold stone cornice and the PLA badge, built *c.* 1914–17 to serve a store for 305,000 carcasses. Unusual concrete lattice-beam roof structure, supporting a concrete water-retaining roof for the cooling process. The trusses dominate the single-volume interior, retained in the restoration by *Rees Johns Bolter Architects*, 1994–5. By the dock, new buildings for the business park, planned by *Aukett Associates* for the London Development Agency since 1997. BUILDING 1000, completed 2004, achieves a scale appropriate to its setting. Two five-storey office blocks, with internal malls linked by glass winter gardens, under a continuous roof supported on Y-shaped props. Heavily glazed on all sides. Phase Two will continue E along the dock and complete the development. For the derelict Central Buffet and Dock Manager's Office (1881–3) and University of East London to the E, *see* Beckton Park and Cyprus, below.

BECKTON

Beckton owes its existence to the Gas Light & Coke Co. which in 1868 bought 540 acres of land for new works to serve much of the Metropolitan area N of the Thames, and was named after Simon Adams Beck, governor of the company. The gasworks on the marshes, opened in 1870, became the largest in Europe, at their peak serving 4.5 million customers. Coal came from northern England via the company's site by Barking Creek, which had riverside piers, its own steam colliers and its own railway with 42 miles of track. From 1877 by-products such as tar, coke, fertilizers and dyes were also manufactured on the site. A private road (now Winsor Terrace and Tollgate Road) was laid out to the W, on axis with the main gate; terraces of houses remain along the S side, those on the N side and the church, chapel and institute have gone. A railway line from Custom House (leased to the Great Eastern Railway) brought workers from further afield. There were two other early settlements, both now rebuilt: New Beckton, known as Cyprus, developed from the late 1870s, and some equally isolated housing, of better quality, provided in 1903 by East Ham, next to an embryo park named Savage Gardens (*see* p. 308). The rest of the marshy farmland was reserved for dock expansion until the 1960s. E of the gasworks the MBW's Northern Outfall Sewer, constructed 1859–64, poured untreated sewage into the Thames until sewage treatment works were begun here in 1889. One small C19 pumping station remains; the present works date from 1959, 1975 and 1998.

The transformation of Beckton in the late C20 was triggered by the closure of the docks and the replacement of 'town' gas by natural gas. Coal-gas manufacture ceased at Beckton in 1969. The 1976 Docklands Strategic Plan, drawn up by a joint committee of the GLC and the boroughs, proposed an increase of population from 6,500 to 28,000. Newham's District Plan of 1976 proposed development in the garden city tradition, with low-density housing interspersed with open space around a district centre, and light industry on the gasworks tar-distillery site. The infrastructure, largely put in place by Newham, was continued under the LDDC in 1981–98. Some grand schemes came to nothing, but one success was the creation of Beckton District Park (*see* p. 310), a broad green swathe running S from the A13 down to South Beckton, linking up with New Beckton Park at Cyprus and King George V Park at Custom House. The inspiration, as at Milton Keynes, is the low-rise, low-density, car-dependent but very green North American conurbation rather than the English garden-city model of the original plan. The district centre is nothing special; in contrast some of the private housing is self-consciously monumental. Much of it is private, a tribute to the power of market forces in the 1980s. The borough had intended a greater proportion of social housing, although Beckton has more than elsewhere in Docklands.

PERAMBULATIONS

1. W of Beckton DLR Station

The prospect from the station is not enticing. Opposite is BECKTON DISTRICT CENTRE, a mediocre agglomeration of buildings beyond a vast car park and bus stand, its presence announced at the crossroads by a feeble little brick tower. ASDA, opened 1983, takes the form of a would-be-vernacular envelope, brown brick with pantiled roofs, enclosing a large shopping shed with amorphous covered mall behind. To the W of this, facing an empty paved square, are later buildings by Newham. THE GLOBE, council district offices and library, 1997, has as its distinguishing feature a large, white funnel-shaped projection to the library, open to two storeys inside, but of unclear purpose. S of the Square the long range of KINGSFORD COMMUNITY SCHOOL, 2002, a three-storey classroom block of brick with lower white-walled part in front, and a recessed, curtain-walled entrance, but as with the Globe, the mixture of textures and colours is not enough to leaven the bulk. To the N, facing Tollgate Road, TOLLGATE HEALTH CENTRE.

ST MARK, Tollgate Road, lies to the N of the Globe, an interdenominational church, 1989 by *APEC Architects* of Birmingham. The most distinguished building in the centre, the exterior deliberately unchurchy. Planned so as to integrate church and other functions, like the firm's earlier St Bartholomew, East Ham. The building was planned to form the NE corner of a town square, with an access route running through its centre, but the wider context was not built as intended. Large, sweeping roofs at different levels and windows in long bands along the main road. The golden brick of the walls is repeated inside with extensive timbering and top lighting, creating a warm and attractive interior. The church lies E of a central corridor, the liturgical centre tall and brightly lit. In the E wall a brick niche with statue of the Virgin. Baptistery with immersion font in the NE corner. The lower hall behind can be opened up to the church. W of the corridor is a large sports hall, and elsewhere, shop, refreshment bar, meeting rooms etc.

Between Tollgate Road and the A13 to the N is a collection of housing developments of the 1980s onwards. Some are arranged around formal crescents, squares and courts, surprisingly urban schemes with echoes of the type of monumental Neo-Classicism championed by some Postmodernist architects. Much of the architectural detail is crude, and generally of less note than the planning. The variants on historicist themes appear uncomfortably contrived, but perhaps may acquire the appeal of period pieces. The mid-1980s was the most fertile time; most of the later building is more routine.

Going E–W, first HALLEYWELL CRESCENT, 1994 for Southern Housing Group, rather cramped, Neo-Victorian, up to four storeys with steep gables of different heights picturesquely clustered. At the N end NORTH BECKTON PRIMARY SCHOOL, low spreading wings and shallow-pitched roofs. AMBASSADOR GARDENS is the centre of a development by *Form Design Group*, 1987, a long garden square with three- and four-storey terraces in formal compositions; stripy brick ground floors and red brick trim, reminiscent of Edwardian mansion flats. NIGHTINGALE WAY and EISENHOWER DRIVE (the latter by Newham Borough Council) have semi-detached houses with shared pedimental gables, an early C19 suburban type. Red brick with cast-stone detail; curved front-garden walls allow for circles of paviours intended for trees. Another group along GARNET WALK are set back from Tollgate Road behind a green with an obelisk: bleak buff-brick frontages with mannered giant brick arches; the smaller houses, e.g. in BERYL AVENUE, have large lunette windows to the first floor.

S of Tollgate Road details are less eccentric and the effect is more relaxed (the contrast between N and S curiously reminiscent of Hampstead Garden Suburb). Good examples down SWAN APPROACH: to the E GREENWICH CRESCENT has Regency-style cottages with central chimneys, grouped round a green, by *George F. Johnson Associates*, 1984. The planning is by *Neylan & Ungless*, who also devised the pleasant informal grouping to the W, with footpaths and courts around MAVIS WALK. Running through this area E–W is a raised landscaped walk (along an old railway line), which links up with Beckton District Park. On the edge of the park ELLEN WILKINSON PRIMARY SCHOOL, a striking group: long, tiled roofs with overhanging eaves and prominent white gable ends edged with yellow. Taller main block with a row of circular windows.

For the District Park *see* p. 310.

2. *E of Beckton DLR Station*

A good way E down WINSOR TERRACE, named after Friedrich Winzer, who founded the Gas Light & Coke Co. in 1812, is the C19 group on the S side that survived the Second World War: three dignified terraces of the 1870s in blackened stock brick: simple two-storey brick houses with round-arched doorways and segment-headed ground-floor windows; three-storey gabled houses for senior staff at the end of each row, dignified by fretted bargeboards. The street ends at the iron gates of the gasworks. A scruffy little park now lies behind, beside the new Royal Docks Road.

S of Winsor Terrace, BEAUFORT leads over the DLR to WINSOR PARK, built 1987–95 on former gasworks land. The first of 1,500 social housing units planned for the Royal Docks area, by *Chris Wilkinson Architects*. Conventional streets with two-storey terraces flanked by taller flats; variety provided by boldly striped brickwork in different combinations. The most formal street is BRADYMEAD, leading E to GALLIONS SCHOOL, by the Borough of Newham: *c.* 2000, with a profile of low-pitched roofs broken by complicated roof lights. It is flanked by social club and resource centre; a single corner shop opposite.

N of Winsor Terrace other developments on gasworks land. The most prominent is Beckton Alps, at the junction of Woolwich Manor Road and Newham Way, a conical hill with dry ski slope, created in the 1970s from the waste material for the purification of gas augmented by spoil from the basement of the new British Library. Between it and Winsor Terrace: London Industrial Park. On Alpine Way, Workshops by *Nicholas Grimshaw & Partners* 1984–5, designed for haulage contractors, moved here from West India Docks in 1986. Silver steel-clad shed with mezzanine offices, supported from six red masts to free the internal area and minimize piling.

On Newham Way, next to the Alps, as part of a fringe of recreational centres, Docklands Equestrian Centre, an indoor arena and barn for twenty horses. Appropriately simple and rustic, in blockwork, timber and metal roofing. 1994–5 by *Aukett Associates,* also responsible for Sava Centre in the adjacent Gateway Retail Park, a sleek steel-framed, white-clad shed of 1992–3. Curved aerofoil roof sailing out on angled struts to make a shady canopy all round.

E of Royal Docks Road is Gallions Reach shopping centre, *c.* 2004. Crisp sheds in silver and white cladding with attention-seeking roofline of blue fins and a slender tower with a blue-glazed top and needle mast. The centre adjoins the Gasworks, which still has some prominent gasholders. No. 8 by the engineer *Vitruvius Wyatt*, 1876–9 has unusual buttress-like columns in cast iron with very fancy latticework and ogee finials. No. 9, by the engineer *George Trewby*, 1890–2 with a capacity of 8 million cubic ft was the third largest holder then built in Britain. Its lattice steel, six-tier guide frame is soberly rational. A dramatic landscape of mid-C20 coke-ovens, conveyors and coal bunkers was mostly cleared away in the 1980s. On the river, the W jetty is the original one of *c.* 1870, with later alterations. Heavy plate girders on cast-iron caissons. E jetty of 1895.

3. *Gallions Reach*

This part of the DLR uses a railway line running E from Custom House, built by the London and St Katharine Dock Company for the use of dock workers and ship passengers at the Albert Dock. The line originally continued E from Gallions Reach DLR station to the Gallions Hotel, intended for liner passengers. Originally surrounded by railway tracks, it stood alone and boarded up in muddy wasteland until 2004, when a start was made on Furlong developers' Royal Quay housing. The hotel dates from 1881–3, and like the Connaught Tavern (p. 302) is by *George Vigers & T.R. Wagstaffe*, fully in the Norman Shaw tradition. Long, rendered front with a jettied upper storey, an ogee-capped tower and 'Ipswich' windows as at Shaw's Tabard Inn, Bedford Park, of two years earlier. The rich plaster frieze, originally blue and white, is by *Edward Roscoe Mullins*. The first-floor billiard room opened on to a balcony over the station platform canopy. Cast-iron columns on ground and first floors.

Plans for business parks around the Albert Dock were made in the 1980s but little happened for twenty years apart from IVAX pharmaceutical works; long grey buildings, partly on pilotis over the end of the Albert Basin, now GALLIONS POINT MARINA.

PUMPING STATION, Gallions roundabout. 1975–8 by *Mason, Pittendrigh & Partners*, engineers, built to drain surface water from Beckton marshes before redevelopment. An innovative layout within a reinforced-concrete diaphragm wall set in the Thanet sand. Brick-clad steel superstructure with distinctive pre-cast pleated roof and travelling crane spanning the diameter.

EAST LONDON RIVER CROSSING. A crossing between Gallions Reach and Thamesmead, to link the M11 with the A2 in Kent, was debated from the 1940s. Proposals in 1990 included an imaginative design by *Santiago Calatrava*; an alternative scheme gained planning permission, but came to nothing as a result of environmental objections. A scheme on a different alignment was being developed by *Marks Barfield Architects* in 2004, as part of the government's Thames Gateway project.

4. *Cyprus*

N of the Station

Almost nothing remains of the C19 hamlet of New Beckton (named Cyprus from the colonization of that island in 1878). It never progressed further than a few streets, pubs and shops, built on the marshes without drainage and soon in poor condition. After the Second World War the area became a city of prefabs for those made homeless by bombing. Those too have gone. The only Victorian remnant is the FERNDALE pub in Ferndale Street.

New low-rise housing was begun by Newham in the late 1970s. The old cottages were replaced by a Radburn-type layout between PENNYROYAL AVENUE and CYPRUS PLACE, with a landscaped pedestrian path between rows of closes. Timber-framed terrace houses and flats with projecting square bays. In East Ham Manor Way a group of shops and WINSOR PRIMARY SCHOOL, by the Borough of Newham, one of Newham's low, spreading schools of the open-plan era. To the W, off STRAIT ROAD along the S side of New Beckton Park, dark-brown brick terraces with monopitches and diagonal boarding.

NEW BECKTON PARK now appears as an informal village green, but began as an early C20 amenity created by the borough of East Ham to the S of SAVAGE GARDENS, where the Borough Surveyor *W.J. Savage* laid out East Ham's first council housing in 1903, in an effort to bring a better standard of housing to this deprived area. This has gone; the present buildings all date from after 1981. At the E end of Savage Gardens an inward looking group, 1981 by *Neylan & Ungless*, built when the whole area was still derelict and inhospitable. STAPLES HOUSE, for the elderly, has big white-clad gables, then a horseshoe-shaped court followed by an imitation stable court, in a comfortably domestic Arts and Crafts meets Frank Lloyd-Wright style. Wright-inspired common room, with hollyhock glass murals by *Bill Ungless* in the horseshoe-shaped court, another glass mural in Staples House. The scheme was intended to continue W, but instead was followed by Beckton's first LDDC-period private housing, on garden suburb lines.

S of Cyprus DLR Station

The UNIVERSITY OF EAST LONDON has the most arresting new buildings in the Royal Docks area. A new university campus; the first in London for fifty years, for a university created in 1992 from three technical colleges.* The master plan, for a campus with 7,000 students, and the first phase, 1998–9 are by *Edward Cullinan Architects* (project architect *John Romer*). Rapidly built on a tight budget to fulfil the government's requirement for a fast-track 'develop and construct' contract,† and built on green principles, using recycled materials and an energy-efficient heating and cooling system.

The buildings are squeezed onto a narrow but enviable site between the DLR Beckton line and the Albert Dock. The first phase is for 2,400 students in eight departments, with accommodation for 384. The approach from the station is dramatic, over a bridge towards a formal entrance between tall red walls, a prelude to a sheltered open square between the two academic buildings. Beyond on the dockside are the five student 120
halls. These steal the show. Five pairs of stumpy drums with jaunty butterfly roofs, from a distance looking mysteriously industrial, until one takes in the four floors of neat square windows (small, to avoid aircraft noise) alternating with circular vents. The drum shape was chosen for its economy, rather than for its visual allusions, but the effect seems happily appropriate. Each pair consists of one white drum and one brightly coloured, standing out against the white cliff of the teaching building behind. They inject much cheerfulness into the still barren surroundings of this part of the Docks. Each drum is compactly planned, with two groups of five small rooms on

*These were West Ham Technical Institute, South East Essex Technical College and NE London Polytechnic. UEL has two other campuses, at Longbridge Road, Barking, and at Romford Road, Stratford.

†A contract which allows for more detailed design drawings than 'design and build' but not for the architects' supervision during building.

each floor radiating from a central lobby. The lively and angular academic blocks also have character, white-walled, with elegantly swooping north-light roofs. These are poised on slender exposed-steel supports, which project out to sharp points on either side of the central square. Freestanding rainwater pipes with shiny conical hoppers meet the roof valleys. The W block has library, lecture theatre and administration, and will become the central focus when the campus extends further W. The larger E block has studios and workshops for the art, design and engineering departments on either side of a full-height central mall; here also colour is used to distinguish the different parts. To the N a wing with business start-up units has been incorporated, and the building also houses the Thames Gateway technology centre. Car parks to the NE, arranged so that everyone approaches the campus through the main pedestrian entrance. NE of the railway line a space proposed for a sports centre. Disappointingly, the original architects were not selected for Phase 2 (begun 2003), whose plain buildings lie further W.

5. Beckton Park

The DLR station lies near the W end of the ALBERT DOCK (*see* further p. 302–3, and Gallions Reach, above). Immediately S of the station, in ROYAL ALBERT WAY is the CENTRAL BUFFET AND DOCK MANAGER'S OFFICE.* 1881–3. The plain, apparently conventional Domestic Revival exteriors conceal the largest known use of a concrete system of construction patented by the builder *W. H. Lascelles* in 1875, and first used at his house at 266 Sydenham Road Croydon. The system, which involves walling slabs screwed to timber uprights, was recommended by *T.R. Wagstaffe*, surveyor to the Dock Company. The buffet has a bold central bow and is very plain, although published drawings show lavish pargetting. The use of concrete is most obvious at the base of the concrete blocks, the rest is rendered. Inside, some concrete and some timber joists; cast-iron columns helped to support the upper floor. The office looks more domestic, like an H-shaped manor house with jettied wings and central cupola. Basement of rough concrete covered with concrete bricks; chimneys of brick and narrow, concrete bricks laid in an Arts and Crafts way. Moulded-concrete details on both buildings, also some concrete imitating brickwork. The panels were mostly through-coloured with a red iron pigment but in the restoration have been painted for economy.

To the N of the station lies BECKTON DISTRICT PARK, a green swathe stretching N to the A13, created by the LDDC in the 1980s–90s from the fields and derelict industrial land left between the old settlements and the new developments. The

*At present disused and accessible only from the road.

overall effect is informal and semi-rural, though there are strong links, such as the cycle track, between the communities and to older open spaces: New Beckton Park to the SE (*see* Cyprus), and King George V park to the W. The amenity buildings of 1982 are designed to read clearly in this flat landscape. In the S part of the park, SPORTS PAVILION by *Carr, Goldsmith & Fallek*, with a pyramid roofscape (incorporating a heat recovery system). Another pavilion near a children's play area, by Newham, with low tower and colonnade. Near the E end of the main bridleway and cycle track, three sculptures by *Brian Yale*: HORSES in stainless steel appear to walk elegantly through a paved paddock, enclosed by a SCREEN of stylized trees; further W a kinetic group of BIRDS poised on a branching pole.

NORTH WOOLWICH

North Woolwich is a small but distinct neighbourhood. Although now in Newham, it belonged to the South London borough of Woolwich from 1889–1965, and previously was part of Kent. 'Kent in Essex' probably had its origin in the land around East Ham creek held in 1086 by Hamon, Sheriff of Kent. Its development began in 1847, when the Stratford to Bow Creek railway line was extended to North Woolwich, together with a new steam ferry across the Thames, promoted by the engineer *G.P. Bidder*. The route was supplemented by a direct line to London in 1849, and the railway company opened a pleasure garden by the river to encourage visitors. However the rural appeal soon disappeared with the creation of the Royal Docks and the spread of industry along the riverside, and workers' housing filled the area between the docks and the rail and ferry termini. In 1889 the newly formed LCC established a free passenger and vehicle ferry to transport workers from Woolwich, part of a number of efforts made to improve the amenities of the area, as Woolwich fell within the LCC's province.

The railway ferry declined, closing in 1918. The old railway station is now a museum, but there are few other C19 buildings now. North Woolwich, like the Royal Docks, was badly bombed in the Second World War and the part away from the river was almost completely rebuilt with public housing in the 1960s. The river front was relandscaped by the LDDC in the 1990s with a path alongside the flood barrier, a prelude to the inclusion of this once isolated area in the redevelopment of the surroundings of the Royal Docks. Private housing now fills the riverside E of the ferry; to the N the DLR branch to the City Airport and North Woolwich was under construction in 2003–4.

NORTH WOOLWICH OLD STATION MUSEUM, Pier Road. 1854, terminus of the Eastern Counties and Thames Junction railway. Bombed in the Second World War, restored 1984–5 by *Julian Harrap* and converted to a delightful transport museum. Small but quite elaborate. Richly detailed two-storey Italianate front, U-shaped, with central single-storey ticket office, possibly originally set back behind an open arcade.* Its parapet is continued as a balustrade across the wings, above columned and rusticated archways which look quite Baroque. Inside, the ticket office has been returned to its interwar form. Plain seven-window rear with round-headed openings, the platform canopy in front has iron columns with characteristic GER openwork spandrels, brought from Goodmayes station (Redbridge). Remains of an unusual axial locomotive turntable, within a walled enclosure. Alongside the track, small station of 1979, beside the former goods yard.

Across the road, remains of the covered RAILWAY PIER to the former ferry, rebuilt 1900.

The WOOLWICH FREE FERRY lies W of the railway pier. Maintained free of toll from 1889, successively by the LCC, GLC, and the Borough of Greenwich. Terminals by *Husband & Co.*, 1964–6, with steel-trussed ramps adjustable to a 30-ft tidal range, replacing floating landing-stages of 1889.

WOOLWICH PEDESTRIAN TUNNEL, Pier Road. 1909–12 by the engineer *Sir Maurice Fitzmaurice* for the LCC. Similar to the Greenwich Foot Tunnel (Isle of Dogs), but with a smaller entrance rotunda. Red brick, segmental-headed paired sash windows, wrought-iron grilles. Copper dome with little conical-roofed lantern on top. Entrances with glass canopies on cast-iron columns with foliated caps, decorated bargeboards. An earlier subway here, begun 1876 by *J.H. Greathead*, was not completed.

PERAMBULATION

The hub of the settlement is the junction of PIER ROAD, the former High Street, with ALBERT ROAD. On the N side, NORTH WOOLWICH POLICE STATION, 1904 by *J. Dixon Butler*, an enterprising example of his Free Style, striped brick and stone, with shaped gables, an unusually ample hooded stone porch, and a pretty and no doubt useful corner bow window with a domed cap. Opposite, The ROYAL STANDARD, a tall late C19 pub with simple Baroque details, all in brick. Lush ironwork overthrow to the saloon entrance.

Now E through the ROYAL VICTORIA GARDENS, between the river and Albert Road, created 1890 by the LCC from the railway company's older pleasure gardens, by then in decline. A long avenue of plane trees parallel to the river and a recent espalier walk at right angles. Near the SE corner a small steam-

*As shown on a model inside based on an early OS map.

hammer from the blacksmith's shop of the ship-repair yard in the Royal Albert Docks, by *R. Harvey* of Glasgow. On the N side of Albert Road the CALIFORNIA at the corner of Milk Street, 1914 by the East Ham architect *Robert Banks-Martin*; two colours of brick with flat Baroque detail and Art Nouveau lettering.

Just E of the gardens in WOOLWICH MANOR WAY, NORTH WOOLWICH PUMPING STATION, 1895–7, another LCC improvement, built for main drainage. Red brick with pedimental gabled ends, arched windows with large stone keystones. Next to it a manager's house, THE LODGE, three bays and two storeys, now cement-rendered. Round the corner in BARGE HOUSE ROAD, the Borough of Woolwich provided a row of early council housing in 1901; a nicely detailed two-storey terrace, with segment-headed windows and shaped gables. The terrace opposite of *c.* 2000 copies the general form but not the detail. Across the road, curved C19 building in striped brick, now flats, formerly the ROUND HOUSE pub, at the corner of Woodman Street.

Dominant at this end of N Woolwich is GALLIONS POINT, a self-contained housing estate by Fairview developers, 2003. In a sea of hard landscaping for cars, short terraces of plain brick houses, thickly detailed butterfly-roofed flats along the river and a twelve-storey tower at the far end by the entrance to George V Dock.

KING GEORGE V DOCK, built 1912–21 SE of the Royal Docks, has the oldest operational lock in unaltered state in the Port of London. ENTRANCE LOCK with three pairs of steel gates, some of which remain. Hydraulic machinery, removed 1989, on display alongside. Single-storey brick CUSTOMS HOUSE, 1948. Small Lock Keeper's OFFICES by the PLA. A LIFTING BRIDGE takes Woolwich Manor Way over the lock. Attractive classical red brick and stone abutments of *c.* 1920. Steel box-girder bridge of *c.* 1990 (replacing a pair of steel-trussed bascule bridges), named after the Olympic rower Sir Steve Redgrave. It continues over the entrance to the Albert Dock. Gently curved soffits, with footways elegantly cantilevered on raking struts. From here there are spectacular views W toward the City Airport and the Royal Docks. In the distance are the colourful drums of the University of East London and the spiky roof of the huge Excel building, dwarfed by the vast expanse of water. For the area N from here *see* Gallions Reach and Beckton. This tour returns W.

The narrow strip of North Woolwich between Albert Road and the City Airport is all post-war public housing. From E–W, first the housing around WOODMAN STREET, by the Borough of East Ham, completed 1965. Parts still in an approachable 1950s idiom: traditional streets with a mixture of low Lansbury-type terraces, butterfly-plan eight-storey cluster blocks, clad in brick, and some later tall slabs. In Woodman Street DREW PRIMARY SCHOOL NURSERY, in a long, low school building of 1915. PIER ROAD was rebuilt as a shopping street, the shops with flats above refurbished in the 1990s with new cladding and bold barrel-vaulted roofs.

W of Pier Road is the LCC's PIER ESTATE. Mixed development, mostly of 1962–4, a more radical approach, similar to their 1960s estates in Tower Hamlets. Housing grouped round informal open spaces, linked by tree-lined pedestrian routes. Three nineteen- and twenty-storey tower blocks, quite sculptural, with corner balconies to offset the Brutalist exposed concrete and dark brick cladding. The dark brick of the lower houses and flats is diluted by some later groups built of pale blockwork with heavy arched porches. The materials meet in GRENADIER ROAD, a three-storey block with bold drum-stair tower and odd arched arcade in the manner of de Chirico.

ST JOHN with ST MARY and ST EDWARD, Albert Road and Manwood Street. C. of E. and R.C. combined. 1968 by *Laurence King & Partners*. Planned as part of the Pier Estate, and like the housing, of dark brick. A forbidding exterior, the lower part without windows, with square lantern supporting a thin white flèche. Simple white-walled interior, the lantern lighting a spacious sanctuary floored with black slate; the large square ALTAR of green stone sits beneath a spiky octagonal metal corona. Above a broad low aisle, four pairs of narrow clerestory windows with abstract, coloured glass signifying the seasons. FONT. Moveable. A copper cooking pot from Africa set in a wooden frame, given by the architects. Painted STATUES of St Mary and St Edward from the former R.C. church.

The entrance is through a glazed link to the community centre to the W, another dark brick box. Small paved garden in between.

NORTH WOOLWICH HEALTH CENTRE, Kennard Street, by *Aldington Craig & Collinge*. 1981. Concrete-block walls, with sloping top lighting (to avoid vandalism) creating a pleasantly lit waiting area in the centre. Interior remodelled in the 1990s.

S of the railway line at the E end of Factory Road, an array of large satellite dishes: a BT SATELLITE STATION established in the 1990s, on the site vacated by Henley's, an offshoot of the Silvertown rubber industry. Opposite in STORE ROAD, large Thames Water SEWAGE PUMPING STATION, designed by *Grimshaw Architects* in the late 1980s, built 1995–8. A large and a small shed; steel portal frames with concrete walls and deliberately dramatic, lopsided curved roofs.

SILVERTOWN

Silvertown originated with the creation of the Victoria Dock (1850–5) and the establishment of the rubber and telegraph works of S.W. Silver & Co. founded 1852, demolished in the 1960s. It was known as Silvertown by 1859, with St Mark (1862) and a station on the North Woolwich line (1863) soon built close to the works. In 1867 there were still only *c.* 360 houses, but by 1900 the narrow strip between dock and Albert Road had been built up with plain terraces. A separate area of housing known as West Silvertown grew up further W near Pontoon Dock off Victoria Dock, now largely replaced by Britannia Village (*see* p. 299).

Chemical, engineering and food-processing industries quickly extended E and W along the Thames, attracted by the lack of restrictions on noxious industries, and by the river, docks and railway which brought in bulk raw materials and distributed goods to a world-wide market. Chemical manufacturers came from Germany after 1870 and several of the food processors from the W of Scotland. They included Abram Lyle & Sons, who began to make golden syrup at Plaistow Wharf in 1881 (see p. 299). Henry Tate & Son, whose firm began in Liverpool, established themselves at Silvertown in 1878 to manufacture the recently patented cube sugar; the firms amalgamated in 1921, retaining the two sites, and are now one of the few older industries still present.

Silvertown was badly damaged in both the World Wars. In 1917 the terrible Silvertown explosion, caused by a fire in the TNT plant at Brunner Mond, damaged 60–70,000 properties throughout West Ham and killed seventy-three people. In the Blitz of 1940 the industrial plant all along the river was badly damaged or wiped out and houses destroyed. Most of the few surviving industrial premises are post-war, and only a few terraces near St Mark still date from the C19.

Former St Mark, North Woolwich Road and Connaught Road. 45
Now Brick Lane Music Hall. 1860–2 by *S. S. Teulon*. Built on a site given by the dock company together with a now demolished vicarage and school; confident, massive, and exotically decorative, in deliberate contrast to its industrial setting. By the time Pevsner visited in the early 1950s it stood grimy and alone 'of a pathetic self-assertion in its surroundings'. For years it stood empty and vandalized; meticulous restoration after a fire, by *Julian Harrap*, 1984–9, included the cleaning of the exterior, which revealed the extent and intricacy of Teulon's polychrome detail, 'a triumph of decorative brickwork' as it was described by Matthew Saunders, Teulon's biographer.

The design shows how by 1860 the Gothic Revival, drawing on continental sources, favoured bold geometry combined with original detail. The dominant features are the hefty tower over the chancel (an idea imported from Normandy, as at Butterfield's St Matthias Stoke Newington of 1849–53), and the equally continental apse. At the SE angle of the tower a Germanic turret combines staircase and chimney. The steep roofs of both nave and apse are covered in patterned slates, the walls make extensive use of hollow bricks of buff terracotta and stock brick, with red and black brick supplying decorative detail. The aisles are lean-to, but above them rise three large clerestory windows with Dec tracery that break dramatically through the eaves with gables of their own. On the tower the louvred belfry windows likewise are forced up into the gables set against the spire. The window treatment is varied throughout: square heads in the aisles, pointed elsewhere, and an amazing display of exotic tracery in the tower, with a distinctly Islamic feel.

Inside, the character is set by the exposed materials which are the same and as strong as outside. Their force is diminished by the present muted lighting, which accentuates the power of the lofty hammerbeam roof (restored by *Harrap* after the fire). Nave arcades with octagonal piers, chancel framed by corbelled arches and with twinned piers. Conversion in 2003 to a music hall, by and for *Vincent Hayes*, has been tactful, with a reversible, non-interventional structure, creating a stage within the chancel, with fly tower for tumbling cloths in the tower above. The W bays are screened off, with lively art work by *Chris Floyd*, but the building is still legible as a whole.

PERAMBULATION

Little remains of the old Silvertown. Apart from St Mark the defining monument is TATE & LYLE's huge sugar refinery, established here at Thames Wharf in 1878. It stands due S of the Silverlink railway station, along FACTORY ROAD. Mostly rebuilt post-war. In the style of the 1950s, a bulky tower and a long frontage with decorative tiles and canopies over the lower windows. Further W is the restored remains of the monumental gateway to Tay Wharf, dated 1900, the site of Keiller & Sons jam factory (1880–1997). From here a landscaped footpath by the road leads towards Thames Barrier Park (*see* p. 300). It follows the line of the Silvertown Tramway, the old line of the Eastern Counties railway, taken over by the docks after the line was rerouted around the E end of the Victoria Dock in the 1850s.

N of the Silverlink railway line, at the corner of ALBERT ROAD and WYTHES ROAD, the former Tate & Lyle SOCIAL CLUB 1887, designed by a Mr *Lewis* as the Tate Institute, with amenities such as a reading room, billiard room and hot baths for the local inhabitants. Tile-hung upper floors, sgraffito panels with sunbursts. In Wythes Road Newham's DREW PRIMARY SCHOOL, 2002–3, replacing a former Board School demolished for the DLR extension. Compact plan with long barrel-vaulted spine, two storeys of classrooms on each side with barrel vaults at right angles. A few late C19 and early C20 terraces remain; further E informal groups of 1970s council housing, some with white boarding, merge with the fringes of North Woolwich (q.v.).

LONDON CITY AIRPORT. Created on the quays between Royal Albert and George V Docks, 1982–7, approached from Hartmann Road, off Connaught Road. A STOL (short take off and landing) airport aimed particularly at business travellers to European airports. Extended after 1990 to allow the use of small jets. TERMINAL by *Seifert Ltd*, completed 1987, little more than a dreary shed clad in grey-blue coated metal panels with grey fascia and blue-tinted glazing. Control tower on one side. Minimal landscaping, car parking and other facilities; no rail link until the DLR extension of 2003–4. The King George V Dock OFFICE BUILDINGS, 1931 by *Sir Edwin Cooper*, is now the airport transit office. Rather Soanian, in yellow brick with mostly blank walls and top lighting. Round arches and round windows away from the dock. Also by Cooper the tiny DOCKMASTER'S OFFICE 1922–4.

REDBRIDGE

The Red Bridge was an ancient crossing over the River Roding in the centre of the present borough, now superseded by the Eastern Avenue crossing. The Roding, a quite substantial tributary of the Thames, links the disparate N and S parts of Redbridge which were united in 1965: Wanstead and Woodford in the N; Ilford in the S. In the northern part where the North Circular Road and the M11 now run high above the flood plain, the area remained rural into the C20. S of Eastern Avenue the river meanders through the lakes of Wanstead Park, relics of an exceptionally ambitious piece of C18 landscaping. Further S the Roding forms a decisive boundary between the densely built-up suburbs of Ilford and East Ham before it enters Barking and an industrial setting of wharves and industry close to the Thames.

In the Middle Ages Ilford belonged to Barking Abbey, and until the C19 it formed part of the huge parish of Barking, which stretched N for seven miles, from the Thames marshes to the edges of Hainault Forest. Ilford, named from the Hile, an old name for the Roding, was a small crossroads settlement on the road to Colchester, distinguished by a medieval hospital, which partly survives on Ilford Hill E of the river crossing. Further N Wanstead and Woodford were separate parishes with their own churches, and N of the church at South Woodford a scatter of settlements in forest clearings marked the route to Epping and Newmarket. From the C18 this picturesque area on the forest fringe, conveniently accessible to the City, was increasingly populated with smart houses for merchants and gentry. Elsewhere there were a few hamlets, farms and gentry houses, some with their own chapels; a rare vestige of such a chapel remains at Aldborough Hatch. By far the grandest of the C18 houses was Sir Richard Child's Wanstead House, but this Palladian mansion on a palatial scale lasted only to the early C19. Valentines, deep in suburban Ilford, is the best surviving major house; others are recalled by fragments of grounds and a few garden and estate buildings preserved among the all-enveloping repetitive streets of respectable suburbia.

The C19 brought changes. Hainault Forest was cut down in 1851, replaced by farms and market gardens which sent their produce to expanding London. The Eastern Counties Railway was laid out in 1839, but development only took off from the 1870s, when suburban trains became more frequent. By this time 'London-over-the-border' had expanded over most of East Ham and was beginning to stretch further E. In 1881 Ilford's population had reached 7,645. By 1911 it was 78,188. Streets of houses and, gradually, new churches and other amenities sprang up outside the old centre together with the new stations further E at Goodmayes and Seven Kings, to be followed between the wars by suburbs further N at Gants Hill and Newbury Park. This was almost entirely private housing. Compared with the inner

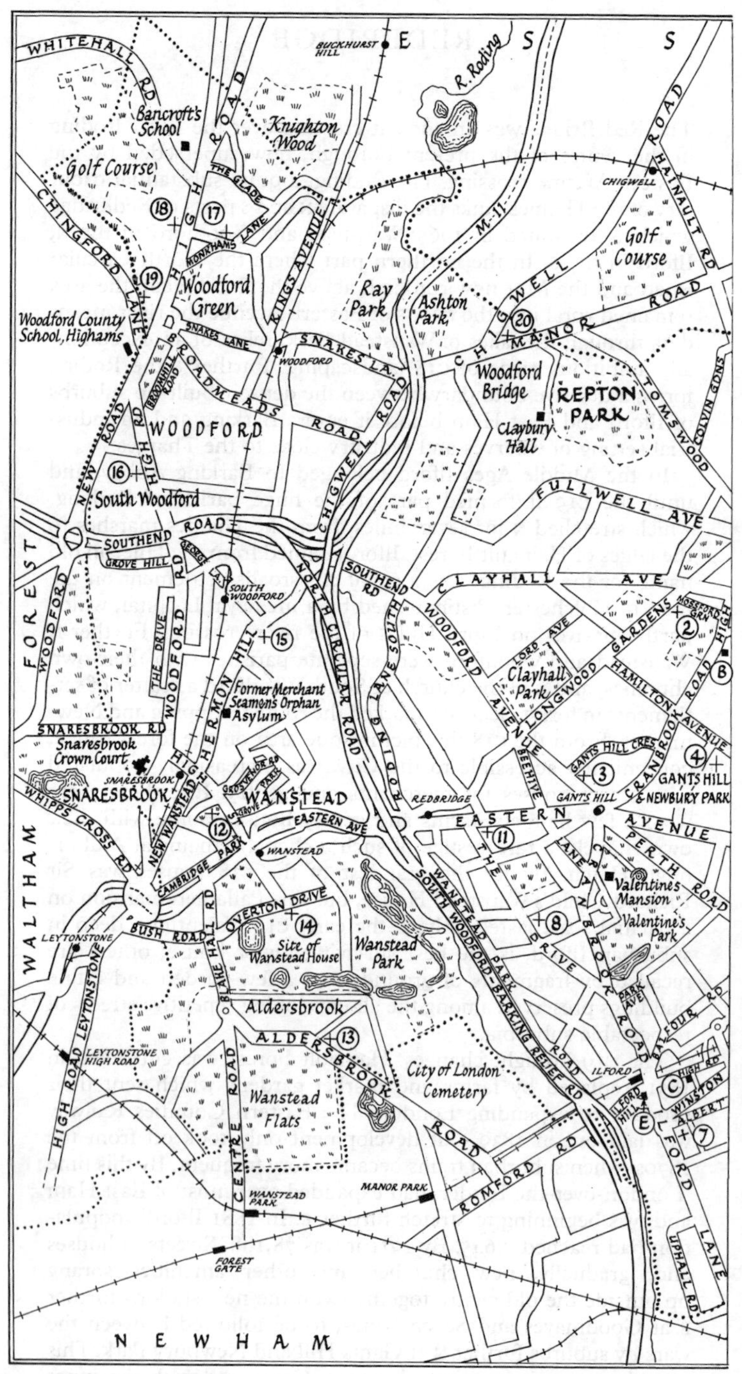

Whitehall Rd
Bancroft's School
Knighton Wood
Buckhurst Hill
R. Roding
Golf Course
Chingford Lane
High Road
The Glade
Monkhams Lane
Kings Avenue
Woodford Green
Woodford County School, Highams
Snakes Lane
Woodford
Broadmeads Road
Broomhill Road
Chigwell
Hainault Rd
Golf Course
Ray Park
Ashton Park
M-11
Chigwell Road
Manor Road
Woodford Bridge
Repton Park
Claybury Hall
Tomswood
Colvin Gdns
Fullwell Ave
South Woodford
New Road
High Rd
Southend Road
Grove Hill
George Lane
Forest
Woodford Rd
The Drive
Woodford Road
South Woodford
Hermon Hill
Former Merchant Seamen's Orphan Asylum
North Circular Road
Roding Lane South
Southend Rd
Woodford Avenue
Clayhall Ave
Lord Ave
Clayhall Park
Longwood Gardens
Mossford Grn
Hamilton Avenue
Cranbrook Road
High
Snaresbrook Rd
Snaresbrook Crown Court
Snaresbrook
High St
Grosvenor Rd
Grove Park
Wanstead
Redbridge
Beehive
Gants Hill Cres
Gants Hill
Gants Hill & Newbury Park
Whipps Cross Rd
New Wanstead
Eastern Ave
Eastern Avenue
Perth Road
Cambridge Park
Wanstead
The Drive
Lane
Valentine's Mansion
Valentine's Park
Waltham
Leytonstone
Bush Road
Blake Hall Rd
Overton Drive
Site of Wanstead House
Wanstead Park
South Woodford-Barking Relief Rd
Park Ave
Cranbrook Road
Balfour Rd
Aldersbrook
Aldersbrook Road
City of London Cemetery
Leytonstone High Road
High Road Leytonstone
Centre Road
Wanstead Flats
Ilford
High Rd
Ilford Hill
Winston
Albert
Ilford
Romford Rd
Manor Park
Wanstead Park
Forest Gate
Uphall Rd
Lane
Newham

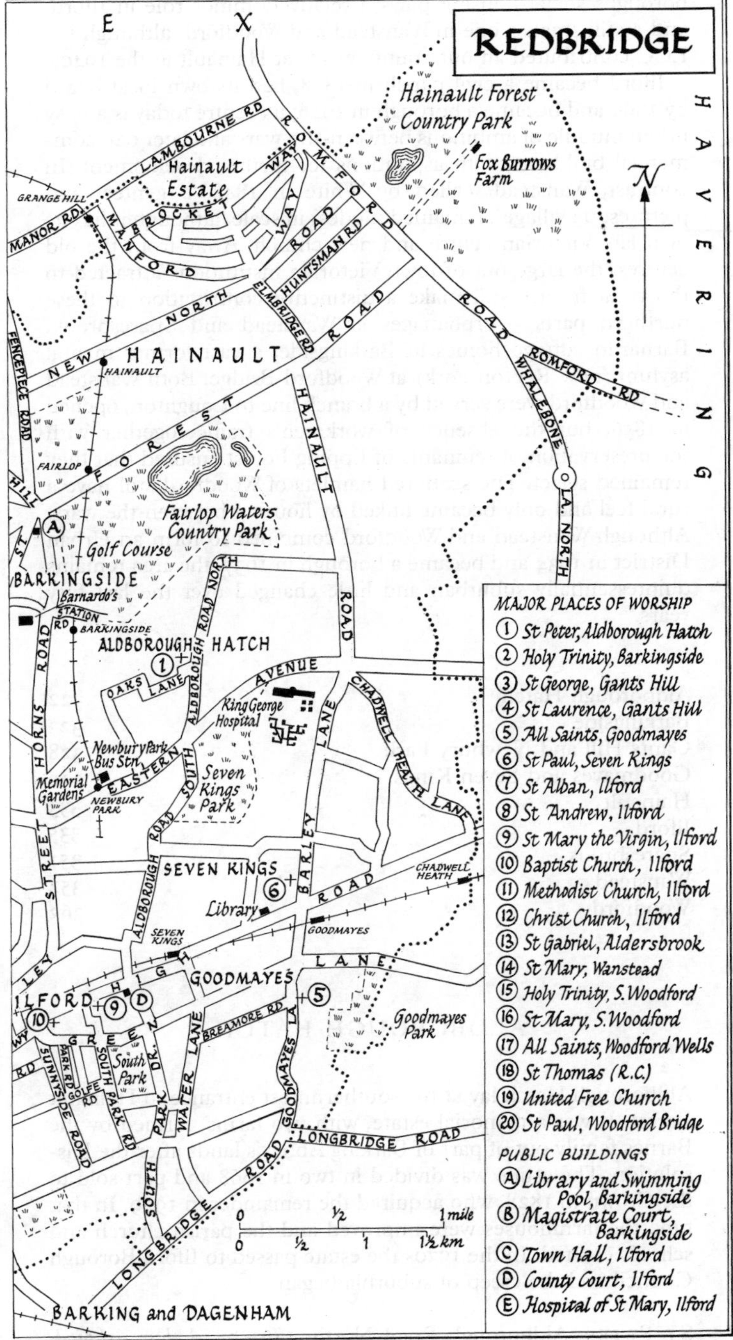
REDBRIDGE
E X
H A V E R I N G
Hainault Forest Country Park
Fox Burrows Farm
Hainault Estate
LAMBOURNE RD
ROMFORD ROAD
BROCKET WAY
MANFORD WAY
GRANGE HILL
MANOR RD.
HUNTSMAN RD
NEW NORTH ROAD
HAINAULT
ELMBRIDGE RD
HAINAULT ROAD
WHALEBONE LA. NORTH
ROMFORD RD
FENCEPIECE ROAD
FOREST
FAIRLOP
Fairlop Waters Country Park
Golf Course
BARKINGSIDE
Barnardo's
STATION RD
ALDBOROUGH HATCH
ALDBOROUGH ROAD NORTH
OAKS LANE
AVENUE
King George Hospital
CHADWELL HEATH LANE
Newbury Park Bus Stn
Memorial Gardens
NEWBURY PARK
EASTERN
Seven Kings Park
ALDBOROUGH ROAD SOUTH
HORNS ROAD
SEVEN KINGS
Library
BARLEY LANE
ROAD
CHADWELL HEATH
GOODMAYES
LANE
ILFORD
HIGH
GREEN
BREAMORE RD
Goodmayes Park
South Park
PARK RD
GOLFE RD
SOUTH PARK RD
SUNNYSIDE ROAD
SOUTH PARK DR.
WATER LANE
GOODMAYES LA.
GOODMAYES ROAD
LONGBRIDGE ROAD
0 ½ 1 mile
0 ½ 1 1½ km
BARKING and DAGENHAM
MAJOR PLACES OF WORSHIP
① St Peter, Aldborough Hatch
② Holy Trinity, Barkingside
③ St George, Gants Hill
④ St Laurence, Gants Hill
⑤ All Saints, Goodmayes
⑥ St Paul, Seven Kings
⑦ St Alban, Ilford
⑧ St Andrew, Ilford
⑨ St Mary the Virgin, Ilford
⑩ Baptist Church, Ilford
⑪ Methodist Church, Ilford
⑫ Christ Church, Ilford
⑬ St Gabriel, Aldersbrook
⑭ St Mary, Wanstead
⑮ Holy Trinity, S. Woodford
⑯ St Mary, S. Woodford
⑰ All Saints, Woodford Wells
⑱ St Thomas (R.C.)
⑲ United Free Church
⑳ St Paul, Woodford Bridge
PUBLIC BUILDINGS
Ⓐ Library and Swimming Pool, Barkingside
Ⓑ Magistrate Court, Barkingside
Ⓒ Town Hall, Ilford
Ⓓ County Court, Ilford
Ⓔ Hospital of St Mary, Ilford

boroughs social housing plays a relatively minor role in Ilford, and a still smaller one in Wanstead and Woodford, although the LCC contributed an out-county estate at Hainault in the 1940s.

Ilford became a civil parish in 1888, had its own local board by 1890 and became a borough in 1926; its centre today is a busy urban muddle of ambitious between-the-wars and later C20 commercial buildings, with aspirations for further development. In contrast, Wanstead, called by White in 1848 'a genteel and picturesque village', remained modest in scale, although it has its own late Victorian centre and new church. Away from the old centres, the large out-of-town Victorian institutions attracted to the rural fringes still make a distinctive contribution to these northern parts – orphanages at Wanstead and Snaresbrook, Barnardo cottage homes at Barkingside, a vast former mental asylum (now Repton Park) at Woodford Bridge. Both Wanstead and Woodford were served by a branch line to Loughton, opened in 1856, but the absence of workmen's trains together with the preservation of remnants of Epping Forest ensured that they remained select. The scattered hamlets of Woodford still have a rural feel and only became linked by housing between the wars. Although Wanstead and Woodford combined to form an Urban District in 1934 and became a borough in 1937, the area remains quintessentially suburban and little changed over the last fifty years.

ALDBOROUGH HATCH

Aldborough Hatch lay at the southernmost entrance to Hainault Forest. It was a manorial estate, with two farms, formed by the Barnes family out of part of Barking Abbey's lands after the Dissolution. The estate was divided in two in 1668 and part sold to the Crown in 1828, who acquired the remainder in 1929. In that time the farmhouses were improved and the parish church and schools erected. In the 1930s the estate passed to Ilford Borough Council and the creep of suburbia began.

ST PETER, Aldborough Road North. 1863 by *Arthur Ashpitel.* Truly a country church. It served this tiny rural parish long before the surrounding housing was built up and still looks out over open farmland on the N side. Of ragstone. Small and simple with only a nave, chancel and tower with shingled turret N of the chancel. Timber S porch. Plain interior. ORGAN. Beautifully decorated by *N.H.J. Westlake*. The pipes richly treated in mainly blues and yellows; angels in the panels below. It was shown at the International Exhibition of 1862 and was the model for the organ in Sir Frank Dicksee's painting 'Harmony'. – STAINED GLASS. Some by *Hardman*. CHURCH HALL. Former School, 1867, closed 1912. Plain with single-storey C20 extensions on each side.

ALDBOROUGH HATCH FARM and ALDBOROUGH HOUSE FARM, in Oaks Lane, were two substantial houses in the C18, both demolished in the C19 and replaced *c.* 1855–7 by modest successors built by the Crown, whose badge they wear. Of principal interest is the BARN at Aldborough House Farm, formerly its chapel (and a chapel of ease for the farm labourers), perhaps built in 1728 at the same time as the farmhouse to which it was attached at its E end. Red brick, with a narrow pedimented W front in bright red brick with rubbed surrounds. Gibbsian door, similar to one shown on the farmhouse in drawings of *c.* 1800. The chapel had a gallery in the C19, lit by a row of oculi in the flanks. Later used as a fowl house, it has been converted, extended and over restored. Services were held here until 1863 when St Peter's Church was built.

BARKINGSIDE

(including Fairlop)

This was literally the Barking side of Hainault Forest. Besides cottages for forest workers and a few farmhouses, there was also a handful of larger mansions around Mossford Green and Cranbrook Lane (now Road). Prominent amongst these in the C18 were the old mansions of Gayshams, Clay Hall (also medieval but rebuilt 1763), and Great Gearies but none of these have survived. It was enough to justify the building of a church in 1840. Mossford Lodge was given to Dr Barnardo, who from 1873 began to develop the first of his children's cottage villages on his estate. Barkingside had no railway until 1903, so suburban development was insignificant until the creation of Eastern Avenue in 1925. After that date the farmland of Clay Hall was built over, the house demolished in 1935 and its grounds preserved as a public park for the new suburb. Much commercial development took place along the High Street, where in 1967–8 the recently formed Borough of Redbridge considered creating a new civic centre in this historically neutral and central location. Plans remained unrealized.

HOLY TRINITY, Mossford Green. 1839–40 by *Edward Blore*. Built with funding from the Church Commissioners as a result of a local appeal, and still with the character of a simple, earnest country church of the earlier C19. Plain Norman in yellow brick. Starved tower-porch on the N side, with recessed top ending in a spirelet rising behind large gables. Wide nave with long Norman lancets, three exceedingly long ones in the W gable. Chancel, 1867 by *J.P. St Aubyn* with a little Gothic detail, including a panelled sedilia and STAINED GLASS with medallions with family portraits and quarries, old-fashioned for the 1860s. S nave glass of 1905, busy; W lancets, 1993, with big, brightly coloured figures, designed by *John Lawson*, made by *Goddard & Gibbs*.

Large burial ground. CHURCH HALL. 1969 by *A.E. Head*.

ST FRANCIS OF ASSISI, Fencepiece Road. 1956 by *J.J. Crowe*. Of brick. The distinguishing feature is the W tower with broad offsets N and S which create a spreading structure; it contains a balcony. Low aisles.

ST AUGUSTINE OF CANTERBURY (R.C.), Cranbrook Road. 1953–4 by *D.R. Burles*; red brick in plain round-headed Early Christian style. Reordered 1980 by *Austin Winkley* with new stone furnishings; a weekday chapel made within the chancel. The first church, by *T.H.B. Scott*, 1928, is now the parish hall.

ST TERESA (R.C.), Eastern Avenue, Newbury Park. 1951–2. Plain brick, Early Christian round-arched style.

METHODIST, Fremantle Road. 1956 by *Francis Lumley*. Red brick. W tower. Plain.

POLICE STATION, High Street. 1964. Concrete and glass. Extended 1993 in yellow brick with battered plinth.

MAGISTRATES COURT, Cranbrook Road. 1974–7 by *GLC Dept of Architecture and Civic Design*. A characteristic example of new court design after 1970, outwardly tough but considered in its internal planning. A series of low blocks, for Magistrates and Youth Courts, clad in big square panels of channelled concrete. Originally planned as part of the borough's unrealized Civic Centre scheme of 1967.

105 FULWELL CROSS LIBRARY and SWIMMING POOL, High Street. 1968 by *Frederick Gibberd, Coombes & Partners* in association with *H.C. Connell*, Borough Architect. A distinctive group and enjoyable in parts. The circular LIBRARY dominates at the N end, not in bulk but in character. Raised central dome, sixteen-sided with big arched clerestory windows: the form determining the wavy roof vaults, tapering towards the apex and drawn tight at the centre like a parachute. Outer single-storey ring of reading rooms and offices with staggered slit windows. Inside, the effect is expectedly light and airy. The low link on the S side behind a paved court contains the entrance to the POOL. One mighty hall, spanned by a pitched roof, and clad, like the library, in slim, vertical, concrete panels, omitted as required for slit windows on the street façades. On the other sides, the building is fully glazed, opening to a garden

terrace with paddling pool, now defunct. Inside, light-green mosaic facings and gallery seating along one side. At one end, a glass box cantilevered out for the café.

FAIRLOP PRIMARY SCHOOL, Colvin Gardens. 1933 by *L.E.J. Reynolds*, Architect to the Ilford Education Committee, and *J.F.A Cavanagh*, Senior Architectural Assistant for Schools. Conventional Neo-Wren, of the type which was practised consistently for interwar suburban schools.

PARKHILL JUNIOR AND INFANTS SCHOOLS, Lord Avenue. A one-off by a junior member of the Borough Architect's Dept., *D. Edleston*, *c.* 1939–40, and a definite break with conservative earlier designs. Flat-roofed, Modernist single-storey finger plan for the junior school classrooms, designed on the open-air principle with their own entrances to the playing field. Separate Nursery block with big bow-ended wing. Some recent additions and replacement of the original hinged, full-height glazing on each side of the classrooms.

IIFORD COUNTY HIGH SCHOOL, Fremantle Road. 1932–3 by *John Stuart*, Essex County Architect. The big Free Baroque produced for all of the Essex designed grammar schools between the wars.

PERAMBULATION

A tour of Barkingside can start at the STATION, worth the visit in itself. 1903 by *William Burgess* for the GER, originally on the branch line from Woodford but later incorporated with the Central Line. A sublime combination of late Arts and Crafts with a Free Style sensibility. A long frontage with the central ticket hall set forward, and lower wings stepping back. Hipped and tiled roofs, in the centre a charming octagonal lantern cupola. Refined detail: especially the generous limestone dressings to the segmental-headed hoodmoulds, the staggered quoins, the rugged granite plinth and Doric half columns in the windows.

Close to the entrance to STATION ROAD, cottages of similar date, with a porch on bulbous columns. The superior design of the station for a village of such modest size must surely be the consequence of the presence here of the BARNARDO'S VILLAGE HOME. Thomas Barnardo opened his first boys' home in Stepney in 1870 and on his marriage in 1873 was presented with Mossford Lodge, Barkingside, part of which he planned to adapt as a home for girls. The barrack system of dormitories was soon dispensed with and instead a village of separate cottages was developed, where each group of girls would be trained for domestic service under the guidance of a house 'mother'. This was not the first of such experiments in the institutional care of children,* but Barnardo's is the earliest surviving example, albeit in part. The design of the cottages and the layout of the village around a green was the work of the otherwise apparently obscure *Ebenezer Gregg*. Each of the first ten homes was funded by individual donors and erected 1875–6. Further cottages were gradually added, eventually creating three greens surrounded by sixty cottages and served by a church, hospital and schools on the 60-acre site. A second village, for boys, was established at Woodford Bridge (*see* p. 374).

The entrance (now closed) was on HORNS ROAD, close to the Village Church (*see* below). At the gates, a small LODGE, half-timbered with a jettied and tile-hung upper storey. This sets the tone for the seventeen surviving cottages (the model for the early collecting boxes) which are laid out in a long, narrow horse-shoe around a green, still planted with Victorian
86 specimen trees. The cottages are half-timbered, slightly funny and squat with pairs of gables sitting heavily, and central porches with carved brackets. Each had differently coloured doors for the illiterate children. The S range is closed by the big accent of the CAIRNS MEMORIAL COTTAGE: added 1887 in memory of 1st Earl Cairns, the charity's first president. It reprises the cottagey tone but in a major key, two storeys with a curiously elongated octagonal corner clock tower with gabled faces and a spire.

The green was originally open at its W end towards Mossford Lodge (since demolished, its site occupied by the Magistrates Court, *see* above). At the opposite end of the green stood the Governor's House, rebuilt in the 1960s. The second of the three greens was laid out N–S with cottages on its E side towards Horns Road. At the head was placed Dr Barnardo's grave (†1905), beneath an outstanding MONUMENT by *George Frampton*, 1908. A tender group of charity (a nurse) cradling infants on a plinth above a bronze relief portrait of Barnardo above three girls in contemporary dress, their faces apparently modelled on residents of the home. Integral with it are two outward-curving granite benches, nicely modelled.

At the NE corner, THE VILLAGE CHURCH, also by *Gregg*, built in 1892 'with a single donation'. Brick with a small, SW tower, battlemented and buttressed in stone with ogee-arched entrances. Aisled and clerestoried nave of five bays, octagonal piers and chamfered arches. Panelled ceiling and wide chancel arch. Trussed roof over the chancel. Colourful, sentimental STAINED GLASS by *Caroline Townshend*. E windows, 1936: Christ with children and the Nativity below. On either side windows of appropriate subjects, eternal and temporal: St Francis, St Catherine, Joan of Arc and Florence Nightingale. In the aisle windows single subjects, mostly well executed.

*The Princess Mary Village Homes at Addlestone, Surrey were opened in 1872 and included, as here, cottages around a green with a church, schools, laundry etc.

Beyond the church, OFFICES built to succeed the Stepney headquarters, by *Ian Fraser and Associates* with *H. Hall*, Chief Architect to Barnardo's, 1969: not a good moment to expect buildings of sympathetic scale and materials. Deep floor bands of roughly textured concrete and glazing set back. A lower block to one side. Near the NW entrance on Tanners Lane: half-timbered stores, then ATHLONE HOUSE, the former technical school of 1920, Neo-Georgian with segmental-pedimented doorway on the S side. The principal school building, rebuilt in 1892, stood immediately to the W. The village other buildings stood S of the green. Demolished except for QUEEN VICTORIA HOUSE (now Registry Offices) on Cranbrook Road, built as the entrance house in 1903.

N of the village in SANDRINGHAM GARDENS are two straight rows of labourers' cottages associated with Barkingside's development after the disafforestation of Hainault. Erected 1851–60, almost certainly by William Ingram, farmer and owner of Clay Hall. They are of the model type, decent if not luxurious, and still look well enough today. Tudor style with thick diagonal chimney stacks in pairs, Tudor-arch doors and leaded windows. The second group is less well detailed. Restored 1981. On the W side of CRANBROOK ROAD, facing the sub-vernacular sheds of Tesco, is another mid-Victorian relic, a Tudor-style cottage with shouldered dripmoulds and bargeboards. N the road becomes HIGH STREET, mostly interwar and characterized by the tedious Neo-Georgian commercial style beloved of the suburbs. Only at its N end are there buildings of more than passing interest. On the E side, the Library and Swimming Pool (*see* above).

The area of Hainault Forest E of Barkingside was known as FAIRLOP and famed for the annual fair which took place around the massive Fairlop Oak. It blew down in 1820 (the fair continued until 1856) but is commemorated at the head of the High Street by the NEW FAIRLOP OAK pub, early C20 William and Mary Revival. The eponymous 'new' oak, replanted in 1951, stands in the centre of the Fulwell Cross roundabout.

W of the HIGH STREET, in FAIRLOP ROAD is the former STATE CINEMA (Gala Bingo), 1938 by *George Coles*. Slightly curious composition with a tall, streamlined rectangular tower and a lower drum, which contains the entrance, jostling together against the auditorium whose buttressed flank is left exposed to the street. Inside, a characteristically light-hearted decorative scheme, the tall circular foyer has little balconies set halfway up behind frothy ironwork balustrades (large auditorium, richly coved ceiling and closely grouped half columns rippling along the wall).

Further SW are some scattered sights in an area largely composed of suburban houses, which display an impressive variety of builder's mock-Tudor detail or (if more ambitious) jazzy Art Deco, e.g. Lord Avenue. Best of all, at the corner of LONGWOOD GARDENS and Rushden Gardens, is the DOCTOR

JOHNSON pub, a surprisingly intact piece of Moderne Neo-Georgian by *H. Reginald Ross*, 1938. Over the entrances, portraits in relief of the good Doctor by *Arthur Betts*. Domestic but big, the scale one associates with the interwar suburbs, with separate rooms on four sides of the bar. Snug corner bar, Deco style with exceptionally well-preserved bar fittings in teak with concealed lighting and illuminated pelmet. Walnut-veneered dadoes.

FAIRLOP WATERS, S of Forest Road. Open ground created by clearance of part of The King's Wood in 1853. The Crown divided the land between three farms – Hainault Farm, Forest Farm and Foxburrows Farm (*see* Hainault County Park). Its preservation from development (unlike Hainault) seems to have been an accident. Forest Farm's land became a balloon station in the First World War. An RFC landing ground was established at Hainault Farm. Part of the land was sold in 1938 to the Corporation of London who intended it for City Airport.* It became RAF Fairlop, 1941–5, as a base for fighter squadrons but sold to Ilford Borough Council after the War. Pits dug for gravel extraction were flooded as boating lakes and the ground opened as a country park and golf course. Plans in 2001 for the London City Racecourse (design by *Foster & Partners*) were refused. The preservation of Fairlop means that one may still walk ½m. SE of Barkingside station across open countryside to the handful of outlying farms, associated with Aldborough Hatch (*see* p. 323).

GANTS HILL and NEWBURY PARK

Interwar suburbs promoted by the creation of Eastern Avenue in 1925 and the subsequent extension of the Central Line from the late 1930s. Neither has any true centre.

ST GEORGE, Woodford Avenue. 1931–2 by *Sir Charles Nicholson*. Mottled brick with a broad and square W tower with copper-covered spire rising in two tiers, intended as a reference to the low belfries of old Essex churches. The church is low and broad, with no clerestory and no structural division between nave and chancel. The detail suggests the C16 or C17: simple round-arched windows in twos and threes, dressed in red brick; E window with five ascending lights. Pleasant white-walled interior with Nicholson's typical panelled ceilings, the ribs painted in black and white. Arcades with simple-chamfered arches on octagonal columns. C19 FONT carved with symbols. STAINED GLASS. E window by *William Aikman*, 1952; five figures, three in deep-red drapery, nicely detailed scenes below, with much use of pale blue and white glass.

*Plans were prepared by *Norman & Dawbarn*.

Above the W gallery in the tower, ENGRAVED GLASS screen by *John Hutton*: the Good Samaritan.

ST LAURENCE, Hamilton Avenue and Donnington Avenue. 1939–40 by *N.F. Cachemaille-Day*; an interesting example of his work; in a pared-down round-arched idiom omitting period references. Of light-brown brick. The exterior is dominated by the powerful, broad crossing tower with solid diagonal buttresses, and a spire with tall, narrow lucarnes. Round-arched windows: the three-light ones with concrete mullions. Five-bay, round-arched arcades on circular concrete piers; narrow aisles. The tower buttresses appear inside, cut through by openings between the various parts surrounding the crossing. As in other churches by *Cachemaille-Day*, this area is brightly lit, both from the transept side windows and by the tower windows between the big, blocky squinches. The spaces E of the crossing were intended to be replaced by a true chancel at a later time.

ST JOHN VIANNEY (R.C.), Stoneleigh Road. 1966 by *Donald Plaskett Marshall*. A severe concrete and brick cruciform church. Reordered 1983 by *Austin Winkley* of *Williams & Winkley*, when the S transept was made into a narthex and an altar placed under the crossing. New stone furnishings (sculptor: *David John*): the square altar with bronze reliquary beneath, the TABERNACLE enclosed in stone with bronze panel. Lady Chapel in the S transept, former sanctuary screened off as a morning chapel. STATIONS OF THE CROSS, mosaic in concrete, by *Mrs Furneaux-Wood*.

METHODIST, Gants Hill Crescent. 1928. A busy Neo-Wren front with pediments, pilasters and some circular windows. Copper dome on the low tower to the r. Broad barrel-vaulted interior with gallery.

METHODIST, Oaks Lane. Church now in the former school. 1934. Flint chequerboard patterning in the gable head. Low vestibule.

UNITED REFORMED (formerly Congregational), Woodford Avenue. 1931 by *Percy Brand*. Of light-brown brick. Sideways to the road, and set back, offering a varied composition of NW tower-porch with copper spirelet, long tiled roofs broken by big transeptal gables, a row of little gabled vestries, and a polygonal apse. All the windows with distinctive angular brick heads dying into splayed reveals. Interior of some individuality with pointed roof sweeping down low and penetrated by the windows. Adjacent HALL with bellcote.

GANTS HILL LIBRARY, Cranbrook Road. 1937–8 by *L.E.J. Reynolds*, Borough Surveyor, with *H.B. Nixon*, Architectural Assistant. Sober municipal Neo-Adam, in brick with a Portland stone column porch, distyle in antis beneath a Neo-Grec pediment with acroterion. Plainly treated wings with projecting ends. Top-lit reading rooms. Separate entrance to the children's library at the S end.

GANTS HILL STATION, Eastern Avenue. Submerged beneath a roundabout and reached by subways. By *Charles Holden*,

1937–8, although not built until 1947. The recently completed Moscow metro reputedly inspired its planning, including the uniquely tall tunnel vaulted hall opening to the platforms. Refurbishment in 1994 by the *Rogers Partnership* reinstated panelled ceilings, modelled on the originals.

104 NEWBURY PARK BUS STATION, Eastern Avenue. 1937 by *Oliver Hill*, built 1947–8, contemporary with the incorporation of the existing railway station into the Central Line extension. Of hangar type and open on the roadside to reveal seven semi-circular concrete arches supporting a tunnel-vault roof of 60-ft span, clad in copper sheeting. Austere but gracious. Festival of Britain plaque bearing the *Abram Games* logo, awarded for merit, 1951.

NEWBURY PARK PRIMARY SCHOOL (former Horns Elementary), Horns Road. By *C.J. Dawson*, 1904, for Ilford Council. Two storeys. Assured Anglo-Dutch with segmental hood-moulds, stripy end gables and pyramidal-roofed stair towers with crenellated parapets. Earlier building of 1895, now Bet Tikvah synagogue.

WILLIAM TORBITT SCHOOL, Aldborough Road North/Eastern Avenue. 1937 by *L.E.J. Reynolds*, Architect to the Ilford Education Committee, and *J.F.A. Cavanagh*, Senior Architectural Assistant for Schools. Long symmetrical front, with jagged Dudokian brickwork to the central and end towers.

OAKS PARK HIGH SCHOOL, Oaks Lane. 2003 by *Watkins Gray International*. Massive X-plan principal block, the angled wings on the N side framing the playing fields. Sweeping curved roofs, sheet-metal-clad upper storeys with brick below.

MEMORIAL GARDENS, Eastern Avenue. Opened 1922. At the entrance, the First World War Memorial. Tapering stone Celtic cross with a moulded base, set on a plinth. In front, a bronze infantryman in battledress, by *N.A. Trent*, standing at attention above the names of the dead. Immediately NE, just outside the gardens, is a small octagonal building of 1927 by *C.J. Dawson, Son and Allardyce*, originally a Memorial Hall attached to the children's wing of the King George V Hospital (dem. 2002). On its own the hall looks convincingly like a mausoleum. Stripped classical in brick and stone with upper stages stepped back. (Glass dome, lighting memorial panels on the walls.)

GOODMAYES and SEVEN KINGS

The suburbs of Goodmayes and Seven Kings were described in 1901 by the local historian George Tasker as having become 'a town without going through the preliminary stages of hamlet and village'. Indeed, they simply continue Ilford's suburban development about 1 m. E along the High Road. The driving force behind their creation was the indefatigable developer, A. Cameron

Corbett, who sought to make his estates more attractive to commuters by actively promoting new stations on the GER. The rapidity and consistency of development ensures a character of inescapable uniformity. From 1898 most of the building was done at Seven Kings, N of the High Road, with the parish church of St Paul in Barley Lane after 1903, but soon spread S to Goodmayes with development of the Mayfield Estate in 1900. This was sufficiently built up by 1913 for a second church, All Saints, to be erected in Goodmayes Lane. Corbett provided Seven Kings Park in 1902, the smaller Goodmayes Park in 1905.

ALL SAINTS, Goodmayes Lane. 1912–13 by *P.K. Allen* of Tunbridge Wells. Quite a striking exterior, with SW bellcote and a shingled flèche rising through a corona. Brown brick with stone dressings, tapering buttresses, big sweeping roofs, broken by two pairs of transverse gables with thick Perp tracery in large windows. A distinctive if slightly clumsy interior: a very broad nave with square stone piers carrying painted brick arches with dying mouldings, below a roof with heavy tie-beams. Some good FURNISHINGS. Arts and Crafts LAMPS; REREDOS (War Memorial) and the ORGAN CASE in the S chancel arch, reputedly brought from Sandringham. High Gothic painted decoration on the pipes and flowing ironwork. PULPIT, timber, with open trefoil-headed arcading on three sides. Brought from the earlier church, which used the adjoining hall from 1909. Alabaster FONT, octagonal on a stone base, carved with tracery. LADY CHAPEL, furnished 1937, with a rather cramped Old English altar, and STAINED GLASS of the late 1930s and 1947.

N of the church the pebble dashed HALL of 1909. Arts and Crafts; large roof and many gables. Thick sloping buttresses. Extended E, 1924. To the E, VICARAGE, broad, hipped-roof house with angled bay windows and offset door.

ST JOHN THE EVANGELIST, Aldborough Road South. Chancel and two bays of nave 1902–3 by *J.E.K. & J.P. Cutts*. W part of nave 1906, aisles finished by *Cutts, Davis & Boddy*, 1913–14. A brick, Perp, clerestoried church: the quite grand, spacious interior is now subdivided.

ST PAUL, Barley Lane. By *Chancellor & Son*. A large, airy Perp church in red brick with stone dressings, a chequerwork pattern in the E gable. Built gradually: S chapel and S aisle 1903, nave 1917; the N aisle, W baptistery, vestry and chancel were complete for the consecration in 1929, but the intended tower over the S porch only reached two storeys. Four-bay nave with stone piers and arches, nave roof with kingposts, chancel roof arch-braced. The STAINED GLASS is the chief interest, late *Morris & Co.* work in E and W windows, 1929 (the E, badly repaired after war damage, commemorating Emily Randall, whose family were significant donors). Figures in deep colours; the W window with nice leafy backgrounds. The best of the later glass are two windows in the S chapel by *L.C. Evetts*, 1975, lively designs in pale colours. Other windows by *Whitefriars*

(N aisle NW, 1920s); Jesus the carpenter window (signed with a monogram 1957); S chapel E (signed with Trilby hat, 1955). HALL of 1908.

ST CEDD (R.C.), High Road. Former Methodist church on a large scale, 1904, taken over by the Catholics in 1966. Free Gothic in red brick with lively Dec window above a projecting stone porch with ogee top, whose form is repeated in the gable. A typically ample Nonconformist interior: raked gallery on short iron columns, fine hammerbeam roof. Reordered, with new granite FURNISHINGS, 1983, in front of the organ across the end, by *Gerald Murphy* of *Gerald Murphy, Newton & Partners*. Six bay side flanks with pointed gables and buttresses. An incomplete tower on the l. Large presbytery in Blythswood Road.

METHODIST, Seven Kings Road. 1904–5 by *George Baines & Son*. The usual turn-of-the-century free Perp. NW tower with a shingled spire set idiosyncratically behind an open parapet.

SIKH TEMPLE, High Road. Former 1930s Telephone Exchange, an austere closed brick box.

Former CARNEGIE LIBRARY and PUBLIC HALL, High Road. 1907–9 by *Herbert Shaw*, the Ilford Borough Engineer. Brick with stripy stone banding and a corner entrance beneath a broad, segmental-arched stone canopy with elongated consoles and exaggerated voussoirs above the door. The central block, sitting slightly back and higher than the two flanking wings, is finished by a cupola. Lower ranges at either end: to the r., a cottage in matching style (for the librarian?), to the l. a single range with separate entrance for the Public Hall.

FIRE STATION, High Road. 1987. Yellow brick striped in courses of red. Lively.

KING GEORGE HOSPITAL, Barley Lane. General hospital built in 1990–3 by *YRM* (*Wimpey Construction Limited*). Groups of two-storey, yellow brick blocks around a court. Flexibly planned for expansion. Later phases to the S for acute services by *Architects Design Partnership*. Chapters House completed 2002 for mental health patients previously accommodated in the adjacent GOODMAYES HOSPITAL. This was built as the West Ham Asylum by *Lewis Angell*, West Ham Borough's Engineer, in 1897–1901, when it was well-situated in open country. Echelon plan, the form perfected a decade before at nearby Claybury (*see* p. 374), with patients accommodated in cottages linked by walkways (male to W, female to E, with communal buildings – chapel and recreation hall – in between). The principal reception blocks and some of the ward buildings have been retained as offices. Strong red brick, domestic Baroque in style: gables, *œil de bœuf* windows and cupola to the main block; two-storey bay windows to the cottages and some decorative elaboration. Along Barley Lane, rows of villas, houses and cottages for hospital staff and workers in similar style.

CANON PALMER CATHOLIC HIGH SCHOOL, Aldborough Road South. 1961 by *Essex County Council*. Mother Teresa

Sixth Form Centre: 1998 by *Redbridge Architectural Consultancy*.

NEWTON INDUSTRIAL ESTATE, Eastern Avenue. WOODCRAFT (Ebbes House). A striking, white-rendered streamlined factory with a tall Art Deco tower – one of the few examples of the style to be built along the new arterial road. 1936 by *Fuller Hall & Foulsham* for Frederick King & Co. Ltd, preserved provision merchants.

PERAMBULATION

GOODMAYES STATION in Goodmayes Road, opened in 1901, is neat and small, in an appropriately domestic style of red brick with steep roof and gable ends banded in stone but with a broad, segmental pediment over the entrance. S of the station, at the junction of GOODMAYES LANE and the old thoroughfare of Green Lane, is a CLOCK TOWER erected by All Saints in 2000. Railed enclosure, stepped base and brick pier carrying a bracketed clock stage and swept roof with ball finial and cross. The church is to the S on the E side. Facing is BREAMORE COURT, chunky Deco flats by *H. W. Binns*, 1935. They stand out as something of a rarity in an area largely composed of terraced houses.

W along BREAMORE ROAD to Water Lane is an intriguing interwar development, chiefly bungalows with canted bay windows and half-timbered gables, mostly well-preserved and retaining their leaded lights, by the builder developers *W.H. Knox* and *J. W. Moore*, 1919–39. WATER LANE leads N back to Green Lane. On the W side, SOUTH PARK PRIMARY, large elementary and junior schools of 1913 with chequerboard-patterned gables to each of the bays. Close by, SOUTH PARK CHAPEL of 1905, a plain hall with a decorative inscription over the entrance – 'And the word of the Lord endureth for ever'. N of Green Lane, SEVEN KINGS ROAD leads to SEVEN KINGS STATION, a similar design to that at Goodmayes. The larger houses of Corbett's Seven Kings development are laid out in streets to either side of Aldborough Road South.

HAINAULT

HAINAULT FOREST COUNTRY PARK, Romford Road, was opened in 1906. The forest (i.e. that part of the Forest of Essex which lay E of the River Roding) was in the possession of Barking Abbey until the Dissolution, after which the Crown acquired 2,800 acres of woodland. These were cleared in 1851 leaving only small sections of woodland in the area near Chigwell, Grange Hill and Lambourne, the remainder divided up for arable land. 800 acres, the land of Fox Burrows Farm and the surviving woodland, were preserved in 1902–5 by the efforts of Edward North Buxton, Verderer of Epping Forest. He encouraged the LCC to purchase the land, oversee its re-afforestation and replanting for grass and heathland, and to open it to the public. The buildings of Foxburrows Farm, rebuilt by the Crown in 1856, were used for refreshment buildings and park offices. Similar cottages can be found scattered over a wide area, including those s along Hainault Road.

In 1943, the LCC acquired land for the Hainault Estate, one of their 'out-county' cottage estates. Development was undertaken 1947–53, by the Valuer's Department under *Cyril H. Walker* (Housing Architect, *S. Howard*). It was thus too early to display the more imaginative and radical tendencies of the council's architects of the 1950s, nevertheless the result was a more varied and interesting group than pre-war Becontree. The planning was rather simple, roughly parallel roads running E–W and curving over the contours of the site, each with names relating to the Forest's history. An area on the s side was reserved for industry to prevent the estate becoming a dormitory satellite for London. A mixture of housing was also aimed for, partly to encourage higher income families to the estate, but of 2,779 houses built, the vast majority are of the permanent prefabricated construction favoured in the late 1940s. Brocket Way has the most common house type, the BISF
110 steel-frame houses with pressed-steel-sheet cladding on the upper floors. Many of these remain largely intact, and quite surprisingly, retain much of the colouring introduced by the council to avoid monotony but elsewhere the structures have also lent themselves to wholesale brick recladding. At the centre of the estate is Manford Way, with a large shopping centre begun in 1949, close to the church and community centres. A long three- and four-storey block, designed to accommodate large 'multiples' and small stores alike, with balcony-access flats and maisonettes above. Light-brown glazed tiling.

The Assumption (R.C.), Manford Way, is of 1952–3 by *D.R. Burles*, red brick, with pedimented front and plain arcaded interior, reordered in the early 1980s.

Two schools merit mention: Manford Way Primary School, a particularly good design of 1948 by *Harold Conolly*, the Essex County Architect, set back behind a spacious lawn. It has the trademark tower at the junction of the single-storey classroom block (open to the playground on the N side), offices and the separate nursery (with its own garden) at the W end. Hainault Forest High School (former Kingswood County Secondary), Huntsman Road, by *Yorke, Rosenberg & Mardall*, 1951, is a typically excellent design with the sort of friendly detail so attractive in schools of that date. Linear plan, with two-storey teaching block and offices either side of a hall, divided down its centre by a screen of mosaic-clad columns. Geometric-pattern tiles by *Peggy Angus* (cf. Lansbury Lawrence, Poplar *see* p. 656). On the S side is the Assembly Hall and on the N, the Dining Hall at a higher level. Both have simple steel roof trusses with wavy bracing. Over the N playground, a slender chimney with drum water tower faced in blue mosaic. Somewhat compromised (but not too much) by later extensions.

ILFORD

Ilford was part of the parish of Barking until the C19 and apart from Barking itself was the only medieval settlement within the parish. It centred on the London–Colchester Road close to the River Roding where the medieval hospital of St Mary was established in the C12 by the Abbess of Barking. Houses first sprang up around the junction of the High Road, Cranbrook Road and Ilford Lane but expansion of Ilford was slow until the late C18 when the hospital first allowed development of its lands. Even so, until the end of the C19 the village was predominantly rural with a few large houses and villas, of which only Valentines survives. Ilford became a parish from 1830 with its church placed slightly E of the centre, on land given by the owner of the Clements estate, strategically sited to serve also the small village of Chadwell Heath (Barking and Dagenham). The Eastern Counties Railway arrived in 1839 but significant suburban development was not begun until after 1879 when the Clements estate, S of the High Road, was sold off. It was quickly developed, not only by local builders but also by A. Cameron Corbett whose work on the Woodgrange estate in nearby Manor Park was also just beginning (*see* Newham). The Ilford Lodge estate and the Cranbrook estate to the N of the High Road were developed during the same period by the Griggs family. In 1891 Ilford's population was 10,711, ten years later it had grown to 41,235 and the shape of the present town centre had been created, with a new station and its own impressive Town Hall for the Urban District Council. The pace of expansion increased after 1918, spurred on by the success of developing light industries which were served by the new suburbs at Gants Hill, Newbury Park and Barkingside. These were incorporated in the new Borough of Ilford in 1926. Expansion of Ilford's commercial centre in the same decades was equally marked, particularly along Cranbrook Road. Since the 1980s there have been efforts to re-establish the primacy of the town centre as a commercial and residential area by diverting traffic from the High Road and planning for the creation of Unity Square, a new public space at the heart of the town and focus of its major buildings.

RELIGIOUS BUILDINGS

ST ALBAN, Albert Road. The first and best preserved of four churches built for Ilford's rapidly growing suburbs between 1892 and 1912, supported by the Bishop of St Alban's fund for 'London-over-the-border' churches. Characteristic work by *J.E.K. and J.P. Cutts*, planned 1899, built in stages: chancel and first bay of nave 1900, W parts and narthex 1906, vestries 1910. A big, competent, brick Gothic church. W bellcote and corner pinnacles. Five-bay clerestoried nave with stone piers and red brick arches. Interesting scissor-braced roof. Rich High Church fittings: ALTAR, Gothic, with painted figures against gold, 1900. Hanging ROOD from St Edmund, Edmonton with symbols of evangelists. Hexagonal PULPIT *c.* 1700, given by All Souls Oxford in 1949. STAINED GLASS, N chapel 1913, N window, 1915.

ST ANDREW, The Drive. 1923–4 by *Sir Herbert Baker*. An exceptional church in a C20 suburban area, on a scale that one associates with the later C19 rather than between the wars. Built as a memorial to Bishop Edgar Jacob of St Albans (†1920), promoter of the diocese of Chelmsford and of the fund for building churches in 'London-over-the-border'. The detail was supervised by Baker's assistant *C.A. St Leger* and the building work carried out at cost by Albert Philip Griggs, local builder, churchwarden (and mayor of Ilford in 1933–4), who built the N chapel at his own expense. His father developed much of the surrounding district.

The plan is conventional: a long, very tall, aisled nave roofed in one with the chancel, with a western flèche, a polygonal E apse, and a small, apsed W baptistery, but both detail and furnishings are out of the usual run. Red brick throughout, including the small traceried windows, and much carefully crafted tilework. On the copper semi-dome of the baptistery a fine bronze figure of Peace by *Sir Charles Wheeler*. The apse is
92 neatly embraced by low lean-to porches. The interior is dark and lofty, reminiscent of medieval Italy. Simple round-arched arcades to vaulted passage aisles, an open hammerbeam roof over the nave, brick vault over the sanctuary cleverly tucked in around the windows. The detail repays study: brickwork of

exceptional quality, tiled patterns in the aisles, different in every bay, and in the baptistery apse, where they surround a coloured Poole-pottery ceramic panel of dove and flowers by *Phoebe Stabler*, given by Baker. FONT with traceried COVER, Perp PULPIT and other WOODWORK by *Laurence Turner* (who, like Wheeler, worked with Baker elsewhere). REREDOS: triptych with paintings by *Colin Gill*. Most memorable is the STAINED GLASS glowing jewel-like in the tiny aisle windows, especially the beautifully drawn figures by *Karl Parsons*: N aisle: St Andrew and St Peter (1929–30); S aisle: St Ruth, St Agnes,
woman crowned with stars, and Remembrance (1929); 91
baptistery: St John Baptist (1930). Parsons, a pupil of Whall, had worked with Baker in South Africa. Other windows by *William Aikman*, some of them post-war: N aisle: St John, St James, St Philip; S aisle: Lydia, St Luke, St Barnabas, St Paul. Chancel windows also by *Aikman*, apart from the possibly older central light and two by *John Hardman Studios*, 1965–6.

The N chapel is a Griggs family memorial. The three E lights by *Herbert Hendrie* commemorate H.E. Griggs, †1915, showing him as student and soldier. N and W windows by *Parsons*, with Christ the carpenter, Solomon's temple, and the Virgin Mary, plainer than his other work. Many nicely lettered tablets to the Griggs family, including A.P. Griggs †1953. Tablet in a classical frame to Stanley Wilson, vicar 1923–5.

CHURCH HALL, to S, 1907, with shaped gable. VICARAGE to E. By *Baker*, 1924. Unusual. Vernacular but formal. One-storey symmetrical front, with dormers in a very big, hipped roof with two tall chimneys.

ST CLEMENT, Park Avenue. The former church hall by *C.J. Dawson*, 1907, used following the demolition *c.* 1977 of the *Cutts* brothers' church of 1889–96. Vaguely Arts and Crafts, with dormers breaking the eaves. Built as Cecil Hall, with classrooms, kitchen, games room and first-floor hall. The entrance front has been reconstructed to some degree and window bays inserted.

ST LUKE, Baxter Road. 1914–15 by *Edwin T. Dunn*, with the promise of a very imposing building had the chancel been completed. Nave, aisles and transepts, built of orangey brick with a tall, clerestoried nave and varied late Dec tracery. A diagonally-set bellcote on the NW corner. The lofty, well-proportioned nave is simply detailed with square piers with chamfered corners and stone shafts rising to the wall-plate. It was burnt out by a bomb 1940 and was not reconsecrated until 1954. In 1982–3 the orientation was turned through 180 degrees, and offices, a kitchen and other rooms were built under the transepts.

W of the church a most attractive hall of 1903–4 with a shingled turret.

ST MARGARET OF ANTIOCH, Perth Road and Balfour Road. 1913–14 by *Edwin T. Dunn*. A pleasing exterior with subtly varied dark-red brick laid in English bond. The tracery, mainly Perp, of brick too. S aisle under its own gable, the N aisle with a lean-to roof. Four-bay nave with square piers with chamfered corners and no capitals, as at St Luke.

ST MARY THE VIRGIN, High Road. The curious appearance is due to an uncompleted scheme to rebuild early in the C20 which produced the towering chancel, grafted on to an existing building. The first church was by *James Savage*, 1829–31, of brick, with an immensely wide galleried nave, paired lancets and an emaciated W steeple. A remodelling in 1865–6 by *Arthur Ashpitel* produced a polygonal apse, W tower (with a spire, demolished 1950) and the present windows with their thin, quasi-Dec tracery. In 1883 *E.C. Lee* removed the N and S galleries, put in new seating and lowered the floor to its present level. Edwardian proposals to rebuild lapsed and the present chancel was not built until 1919–20 by *Edwin T. Dunn*. It is high and wide and, had the scheme continued W, the whole would have been most impressive. S chapel, 1928–9, by *J. Harold Gibbons*, an associate of Temple Moore whose influence is reflected in the small passage pierced through the internal window jambs, and the twinning of the S windows. It has an elaborate REREDOS with vine scroll decoration. – STATIONS OF THE CROSS. 1916 by *A.E. Fellowes Prynne*. Also by him ALTAR PAINTING, 1919.

ST MARY & ST ERCONWALD (R.C.), Ilford Lane. 1971–2 by *Burles, Newton & Partners*. A low, red brick, industrial-looking building with the worship area on the first floor. ALTAR and TABERNACLE, 1979.

ST JOHN THE BAPTIST (R.C.), Wanstead Park Road. 1967 by *John Newton* of *Burles, Newton & Parners*. A prominent but ungainly exteior: a large slab of red brick, flanked by large windows; at the side a low glazed foyer (porch added 1978) linked to a slim triangular tower. Baptistery and Lady Chapel open off the foyer. The interior is pleasing, a cool white space with clerestory windows and shallow-pitched timber ceiling, the sanctuary lit by concealed side windows. The very large rear windows facing the road have striking STAINED GLASS by *Patrick Reyntiens*, two similar designs in pale colours, with subtle differences, representing the Tree of Knowledge and the Tree of Life. Reyntiens devised a complete scheme for the whole church, not executed for lack of funds, intended to modify the excessively light interior. STATIONS OF THE CROSS, small glazed ceramic squares, delicately drawn and coloured. Carved stone FURNISHINGS brought from the old Brentwood Cathedral in 1990, the ALTAR with the Last Supper in a slightly Romanesque mode, by *John Poole*, 1974.

ST PETER & ST PAUL (R.C.), High Road. 1898–9 by *R.L. Curtis*. Stone Perp front to the road, brick flanks. Aisles added 1904–12; the arcades have strange capitals that look as if they have been stretched – 'very horrid' Basil Clarke called them. Pinnacled tower 1906–7.

CLEMENTSWOOD BAPTIST CHURCH, Ilford Lane. 1927. Of purple and red brick. Pedimented gable and two flanking projections.

BAPTIST, High Road. 1907 by *George Baines & Son*. Large and frothy free Perp design with a big window to the street and a tower at the side. School and institute in the same style to the S by the same firm, 1908.

METHODIST, The Drive and Eastern Avenue. 1927 by *George Baines & Son*. Freely-treated Perp (similar to Chingford Methodist church, p. 713), but more restrained than the firm's pre-First World War work. W window sliced by two mullions, tower with flèche, polygonal apse. Large HALL to the E, 1927, and separate SUNDAY SCHOOL, 1931, with quite a fancy frontage, the part behind very plain.

METHODIST, Ilford Lane. 1961, brick with a tower, replacing a church of 1902 by *F.W. Dixon* (VCH). Adjacent hall of 1932 in Neo-Tudor style with faience dressings.

ILFORD SYNAGOGUE, Beehive Lane. 1960–1 by *Norman Green*. Substantial; a pale brick exterior with clerestory, set back behind a large porch with a tapering corner column and marble-faced entrance. Galleried interior with central Bimah, marble-faced Ark recess, and clerestory windows with Star of David motif. Sliding doors open to a hall, lit by a curtain-walled gable wall. At the opposite end offices of 1977.

ILFORD ISLAMIC CENTRE, Nos. 52–6 Albert Road. On this site from 1977, red brick, with a rhythm of 1-3-1 tall arches to the road, and a minaret.

HOSPITAL OF ST MARY AND ST THOMAS OF CANTERBURY
High Road

A very charming sight behind its high brick wall, so detached from the suburban bustle of Ilford. The hospital was founded *c.* 1140 by Abbess Adelicia of Barking. From the C13 it catered for lepers, with lodgings for thirteen men. It passed into private ownership at the Reformation, but continued as a chapel of ease for the local population. The chapel is set back behind a court, flanked by two short wings for pensioners' lodgings and chaplain's house, sensitively rebuilt to allow for road widening in 1927, by *F.W. Speaight* with *W.J. Kieffer* and *H.S. Fleming*. *The Builder* described them as a 'quiet and restful design of Jacobean character'. One storey, roughcast, with hipped roofs and dormers, each with a central gable. The windows have heavy wooden casements.

The foundations of the CHAPEL and its very thick N wall must date from the original building. The E wall with Perp E window may have replaced an apsed E end. Nave and chancel were remodelled in the C14, the division marked only by a shingled bell turret. C19 S aisle, a six-bay arcade of dark stone with simple roll mouldings and no capitals, on thick octagonal columns, part of a major reordering and restoration of 1889–90 by *J.M. Brooks*, which also added Lady Chapel, organ loft and vestry. The two-light nave windows, though much restored, are of the original early C14 shape, those of the S aisle no doubt reused, likewise the PISCINA in the S wall.

FURNISHINGS mostly of the later C19. The chapel was the first in the area to adopt High Church practices under James Reynolds, chaplain in the 1860s, continued by Rev. Arthur Ingleby, who supervised the restoration, sweeping away box pews and W gallery. Ingleby provided the REREDOS of Caen stone, with the Last Supper, a carved tableau behind cusped ogee arches. – FONT. 1882, octagonal with carved panels, given by Ingleby's father Dr Clement Ingleby of Valentines. – COMMUNION RAIL. Early C20, tapered balusters. – SCREEN, wrought iron with concealed gas lighters along the top. – STAINED GLASS. Chancel N, two lozenge-shaped panels, the arms and merchants' mark of John Gresham on the l., Norfolk arms on the r. Displaced from the E window, which has two panels with St Thomas à Becket and the Virgin by *Gibbs & Co.* commemorating James Reynolds (†1866). They flank a pictorial Crucifixion. Chancel S with nine roundels of Flemish glass, one dated 1550, brought from All Saints Epping Upland, Essex. Mostly armorial, but also three good roundels with Visitation and Old Testament scenes. The outstanding windows are by *Morris & Co., c.* 1891: S aisle W, St Clement and St Valentine, designed by *Burne-Jones*, figures against rich blue-damask backgrounds, in memory of Clement Ingleby of Valentines. Nave W, a rose window with musical angels in mouchettes, gold, pink and white. According to Sewter designed by *Dearle*, but an attribution to *Henry Holiday* has been suggested. – MONUMENT. John Smythe, master of the hospital; †1475. Between chancel and Lady Chapel. A puzzle. Effigy of priest in vestments set below a double-sided canopy in Early Renaissance style. Inscription to Smyth, copied from a lost brass, above the canopy, but the style of the latter, with its finely carved pilasters, is of the 1520s. Effigy and canopy are of dark stone like the nave arcade, and look entirely C19, although both have been claimed as reworking of older material.* On the S aisle wall another panel with Renaissance arcading; was it intended as a back panel, or for the front of the tomb chest? – The Lady Chapel was furnished as a war memorial, with REREDOS by *J.N. Comper*, 1922, with painted carved figures, and small AUMBRY in the window reveal.

MAJOR BUILDINGS

TOWN HALL, High Road. Ilford became a separate Board of Health in 1893. Plans for public buildings were won in com-

*Smythe's brass included a half-effigy of a priest. It is unlikely he had a carved effigy as well.

petition by *Clark & Hutchinson* but unrealized.* The present group is of 1901 by *Benjamin Woollard*, with sympathetic additions in 1926–7, for the central library, and 1931–3 for new offices and council chamber. The original building faces the High Road. Bath stone, symmetrical with a mighty central tower, turrets over the outer bays and lots of free classical detailing. Entrance to the town hall on the l., through a porte-cochère, the entrance to the public hall on the r., where the central feature is a semicircular porch with bay window above: forming a subordinate entrance to the gallery of the public hall. The later extensions along Oakfield Street are entirely in keeping, but in a slightly darker Ancaster stone. At the S end, and built first, is the former Central Library (now offices) of 1926–7 by *Herbert Shaw*, the Borough Engineer. Narrow, with elongated open pediment above the end bays, a tall round-arched entrance and Venetian windows beneath the cornice. Between this and the town hall, extensions of 1931–3 by Shaw's successor, *L.E.J. Reynolds* with *H.B. Nixon*, Architectural Assistant, in matching style. Symmetrical, with towered end bays and tight oriel windows at first floor. Civic classicism with Neo-Grec guilloche banding and seated lions on the ground floor. Parapet with acroterion and pantiled mansard roof set back.

Inside, on the High Road side, is a small but lavishly finished vestibule to the public hall, with apsed recesses at each end, a shell design in the semi-domes. Mosaic floor. Above the inner entrance is the relatively uncommon feature of a Boer War Memorial. Bronze, signed *Sterling Dudley* (?) and *E. Hirch*. Doors with stained glass with Ilford coat of arms. Behind is the PUBLIC HALL, built for 700. Large, rectangular, an impressive space. Balcony at N end, stage with proscenium arch at S end. Narrow passage aisles at sides behind square chamfered piers. Bulgy curved consoles above these support the ribs of the partly glazed and barrel-vaulted roof. Loose, free classical decoration. Relief plasterwork on balcony front and above, also around the proscenium arch. Enlarged in 1931–3, when an orchestra pit (now covered in) was created.

The main entrance to the Council Offices leads into a grand but narrow stairhall, well lit by a glazed barrel vault supported by a deep cove. Imperial stair, lush but cramped, with broad, sinuously moulded grey-marble rail and fat balusters. Curved landing (allowing more light down to ground floor). The 1930s extension is linked by a corridor at each level. At first floor this is oak panelled, stripped classical and grand, but subtle compared to the COUNCIL CHAMBER. Extravagant – indeed 98
amazingly old fashioned for its date – and not in the least redolent of the Depression years. Rectangular room with engaged giant Ionic columns around the walls, these are fluted, in veined Sienese yellow marble, with bronzed (iron) bases and

* *Building News* June 23, 1893 p. 883.

capitals; a lavish American Beaux Arts style. Beautiful burr-walnut panelling and, in the centre of the floor, an elaborate parquetry sunburst pattern by *Hollis Bros.* in walnut, mahogany and oak. Ceiling with central glazed barrel vault and original lighting, more obviously Moderne than the rest, likewise the illuminated clock. Council seats in a semicircle, partly 1933 by *Hampton & Sons*, chunky with Neo-Grec detail, some more ornate ones presumably of 1901. Public gallery in tiers at the W end. – MEMBERS' ROOM. Oak-panelled, quite cosy. – MAYOR'S PARLOUR, posher, with bow window; laurelwood panelling and plaster ceiling, by *Waring & Gillow*, with enriched ribs in late C17 style. These two rooms face S and E respectively. The S block containing the former library is less well cared for. A sequence of top-lit rooms with a large square main room with glazed octagonal lantern; upper lunette windows.

Former POLICE STATION, Ilford Hill. 1906 by *John Dixon Butler*. Recognizable Butler design in red brick with stone dressings. Entrance beneath a canopied porch with elongated consoles.

POLICE STATION, High Road. 1995. Large, in brown brick with blue metal trim. Heavily glazed with big roofs. Unattractive.

COUNTY COURT, High Road and Buckingham Road. 1931–2 by *J.H. Markham* of the *Office of Works*. Stripped Wrenaissance. Central block with cupola, an arched public entrance with channelled brickwork and scrolled keystone. Lower courtroom wings to l. and r., the latter with attached judges' chambers, facing High Road. Little altered inside. Vestibule faced in pinkish 'granolite' panels. Lunette window in the W wall.

CENTRAL LIBRARY, Clements Road. 1983–6 by *D.J. Restick* and *T. Lawrence*, Borough Architects. On an island site created by the ring road but strong enough to hold its own. Dark brick with fully glazed upper storeys under copper-clad pitch roofs with projecting eaves, moderately vernacular but on a big scale. On the N side, behind a projecting grid, two-storey glass curtain walls light the reading rooms. Sensibly planned inside, atrium-style with central free-standing stair between ground and second floors. Full-height glazing on the S side with abstract STAINED GLASS by *Goddard & Gibbs*.

ILFORD SWIMMING POOL, High Road/Highbury Gardens. 1929–31 by *L.E.J. Reynolds*, Borough Engineer, working it seems to a design of 1914 by his predecessor *Herbert Shaw*. The style is Edwardian, stripy red and yellow brick, obscured by a later steel and glass entrance block set hard across its face. Inside was the expected myriad of facilities from Turkish baths to tea rooms.

JOHN TELFORD CLINIC, Cleveland Road, off Albert Road. 1989 by *Avanti Architects*. Cruciform plan with a tubular-steel frame, exposed internally. The closely spaced uprights carry pitched roofs with spine rooflights. Each arm serves a separate element of the clinic, with waiting rooms at the crossing. Flexibly planned, with partitions independent of the frame.

FAMILY DAY CENTRE, Albert Road, 1983 by *Redbridge Architect's Dept.* (project architect: *Norman Turner*). For disabled children. Single-storey pavilions, grouped around courts, in yellow brick with hipped and gableted roofs.

KENNETH MORE THEATRE, Oakfield Road, Ilford. 1972–4 by *Redbridge Architect's Dept* (project architect: *Jack Lewis*). A well-detailed design for a small suburban theatre of this period, behind a slightly dreary exterior, with vertical panels of aggregate facing a concrete frame. This is left fair-faced where exposed, e.g. at the recessed entrance beneath its glazed upper storey. Copper-clad auditorium roof and short fly tower. The interior is more engaging, designed for a 365-seat theatre and 50-seat studio. Lobby and former restaurant area with dark brick floor, and slatted fronted box-office and shop set like pods on one side.

REDBRIDGE STATION, Eastern Avenue. By *Charles Holden*, 1937–8, although not built until 1947. It repeats, on a diminished scale, the circular ticket hall and tower composition of Southgate and Chiswick Park.

RODING PUMPING STATION, Roding Lane South. 1904, probably by *Bernard W. Bryan* of the South Essex Waterworks Co. Engineer's Italianate, the mid-Victorian style for such buildings still in fashion in the early C20. Engine house with tall, arched windows and bracketed cornice. Smaller boiler house adjoining.

BOARD SCHOOLS: a distinguished group comparable to the London School Board. The architect for the Ilford Board (established 1893) was *C.J. Dawson* of Barking. The first new building, CLEVELAND ROAD SCHOOLS, opened 1896 for 1,800 pupils, is identical to Dawson's North Street School, Barking. Three storeys in yellow stock brick with big Flemish Renaissance gables and central cupola. This was the largest school but far more impressive are CHRISTCHURCH SCHOOLS, Balfour Road, 1899. Three storey E-plan in buff stocks and blue brick. High and mighty with five stripy Flemish gables and big central cupola. Lodge and Domestic Science block adjoining in the same lively style. Dawson continued to design on this scale e.g. the handsome HIGHLANDS SCHOOL, Highlands Gardens, of 1910, reflecting the lack of available space in the expanding suburb.

UPHALL NURSERY SCHOOL, Uphall Road, is outstanding. 99
Built as a Domestic Science building *c.* 1937 in a forward-looking and properly Modern style (cf. Parkhill Primary, Barkingside). Single storey with bands of metal-frame windows, bowed sections and splendid glazed lantern over the stair to the roof playground. Excellent refurbishment by *Tooley & Foster Partnership*, 1999, who added little porthole windows at child-head height.

VALENTINE'S SCHOOL, Cranbrook Road. Former County High School for Girls. 1927 by *John Stuart*, Essex County Architect. Classical with projecting wings, in brick and Bath stone. Segmental pediment over the entrance.

VALENTINES
Cranbrook Road

Ilford's last surviving mansion of significance, preserved within its own grounds, now a public park. For a house of this size and importance, its building history remains tantalizingly obscure.*

Traditionally, the house is said to have been built in 1696–7, apparently by Elizabeth Tillotson, widow of the Archbishop of Canterbury. Nothing of this date is visible externally, the consequence of several phases of enlargement: first by Robert Surman, a City banker, *c.* 1724, who it is claimed 'greatly improved the house and gardens';† *c.* 1769 for Charles Raymond,‡ also a banker and ship-owner, and once more in 1809–11 by Charles Welstead. The last owners were the Ingleby family who first sold part of the grounds (*see* below) to the Council and in 1912 the house. Exterior restored by *Richard Griffiths Architects* in 2002.

The N side of the house probably became the entrance front in the early C19 when a semicircular porte cochère was added, with an elegant barrel-vaulted roof carried on Ionic columns. Beautifully floored in a herringbone pattern of tough red 'Adamantine Clinker' bricks and with a linking porch with turret light. The irregular arrangement of windows on this side is perhaps indicative of the planning of the late C17 house, but the Palladian stair window to the l. of centre must have been added in the 1720s. Closely set windows to the r. for the service stair. At the NE corner is a two-storey addition of 1871, partly masked by extension of the porte cochère.

The show front, however, is the S side of nine bays with three-storey bows at either end and stucco modillion cornice; evidently part of a refronting of the entire house by Charles Raymond *c.* 1769 (dated rainwater heads on the N side) in yellow stock brick with red brick dressings. The central first-floor window, distinguished by a pediment and an aedicule surround, is shown in an early C18 engraving set above an Ionic portico but now has an early C19 balcony. The E front has a big canted bay in purplish brick, very obviously of a different

*We are grateful to Neil Burton and James Hetherington for their analysis of the house's development.

†According to the antiquary Smart Lethieullier, of Aldersbrook, writing in 1759.

‡In 1765 Raymond built a second mansion, Highlands, to the S and the bizarre triangular folly Ilford Castle as a mausoleum.

date from the rest of the house and probably of *c.* 1723–4 (dated on panelling inside this room), when it would have overlooked the formal gardens laid out by Surman (*see* below). Associated with the same period is the service wing to the W with the red brick former Orangery. Big arched window reveals on the S side, partly filled in. Originally of seven bays, truncated when it was converted into a Dairy and Pantry. On the N side, a late C19 catslide roof on thin columns provides a covered walk.

The interior of the house has been extensively remodelled and in spite of good survivals of panelling and early C18 fireplaces, a clear understanding of its planning and dating is elusive. The ENTRANCE HALL with a floor of chequerboard slabs must have been larger, until the insertion of a service stair between it and the Drawing Room to the S. The spare slabs appear to have been relaid along the S front. The fireplace is a curious hybrid design with a swan-neck pediment terminating in eagles' heads and bulbous console bracket, possibly late Baroque but most likely a C19 confection of parts. The STAIRCASE HALL to the E was evidently much rebuilt in 1871 when the NE room of the house was added and the hall enlarged to serve it. Only the twisted balusters of the stair look genuine C17 but the ceiling with enriched circular border is Victorian, in a late C17 manner. The Palladian window has brightly coloured early C19 glass.

Along the S front from E–W, the bow-ended DINING ROOM (SE) must have been remodelled in the 1760s but the character of the panelling and box cornice is early C18. Particularly good fireplace in the Adam style with inset coloured stones. Narrow ante-room adjoining, later the BILLIARD ROOM, with a corner fireplace (now concealed) in the customary fashion of the late 1690s. C19 display cabinets. The DRAWING ROOM must have been the main entrance hall to the house until the early C19; the cornice with egg-and-dart moulding is of that date. The LIBRARY (SW) has good 1760s panelling and original glazed shelving around the door. The Servants' Hall (NW) was evidently once larger. It may have served as the early C18 kitchen.

The first-floor rooms were extensively refurbished in the C19 and several fittings appear to have been brought in, most obviously the over-scaled doors to rooms along the S front. Immediately W of the stair landing, however, is the original service stair to the attic floor with characteristic late C17 urn and baluster rails. The two rooms in the NW corner, possibly a bedroom and closet, also possess features of the late 1690s; fielded panelling, coved cornices etc. The large central room of the S front was the Drawing Room in the early C19. In the E window, coloured glass of some quality; romantic painted scenes, one a moonlit castle, in the style of Sebastian Pethers. This room became the Library in the late C19. Original bookcases and a fireplace inscribed *non immane benefice*, the motto of the Ingleby family. At the E end, two large chambers both with simple early C18 fireplaces, one with fishscale pattern decoration.

The Gardens and Park

Early C18 GATEPIERS at the S entrance to the park on Emerson Avenue: curve-fronted pedestals with stone urns with gadroon edges and acorn finials. These are shown in 1771 on the main axis to the S entrance from Cranbrook Road, opposite Beehive Lane. SUNDIAL in the forecourt. Most of the garden buildings are associated with Surman's improvements of the 1720s. Close to the N side of the house, a WALLED GARDEN with a two-storey octagonal DOVECOTE. Stock brick with ogee-headed windows in its upper storey. Immediately parallel a smaller, walled flower garden, quartered by box and with arched openings at each corner. The bones of the attractive formal GARDENS also survive. N of the walled gardens, a single long brick-lined CANAL, fed at its head by a reservoir, which once poured its water through a scenic CASCADE of three arches, all in brick and rockwork. A second cascade, in parlous condition, feeds the canal at its E end into an ornamental pond in the informal parkland. On the S side of the canal, close to its source, a charming little GROTTO, of tripartite form, with Gothic gables over each bay and flint quoins. The outer arches are blind, perhaps once the bearer of *trompe l'œil* pictures to create a picturesque effect. The central recess has a seat, artfully skewed so that it would appear correct when seen at an angle from the avenue which leads away on the other side of the canal, and which was terminated by a similar feature at its N end. This and other features of the C18 park are now obscured, but restoration is planned. E of the house, in the later C18 the garden was separated from its wilderness by a HA-HA, still visible.

Informal plantings of trees, largely Victorian, distinguish the parkland close to the house from the open spaces of the PUBLIC PARK. This retains its late Victorian municipal character. The council acquired the land in 1896 and named it Central Park. The design by *Herbert Shaw*, the Council Surveyor, included the adaptation of the existing lake into a boating pond, fed by the Cranbrook. At its W end, close to the road, a charming octagonal CLOCK TOWER and shelter, donated by W.P. Griggs, the local builder/developer and owner of Cranbrook Hall, from whose stables the clock was appropriated. The clock tower was originally accompanied by two rustic shelters with lattice screens of bent wood. Their replacements pay no particular compliment. Half-timbered BOATHOUSE. BANDSTAND: an open octagonal platform with iron railings. The same railings surround the stylish CAFÉ: a rebuilding in 1959 of the original refreshment pavilion. Firmly in the optimistic spirit of the Festival of Britain, especially the cantilevered zigzag concrete roof. DRINKING FOUNTAIN of polished granite. LIDO. Opened 1926. Filled in.

PERAMBULATIONS

1. *Ilford Town Centre and the High Road*

Begin at the crossroads, originally the Broadway, slightly S of the Station. Downhill towards the Roding in ILFORD HILL is the medieval Hospital (see above), the former Police Station (*see* above) and Conservative Club (No. 42) of 1930. Competent Neo-Georgian with big, canted bay windows each side of the entrance and dentilled string course. Genuine C18 but greatly altered *c.* 1850, the former Red Lion on the N side of the hill. At the crossroads, a landmark bank (NATWEST) takes the whole of the corner. Neo-Jacobean, with lots of display. Octagonal columns rise through the height of the façade to domed cupolas. Attached Doric columns to the ground floor, visually animated by heavy blocking.

The HIGH ROAD, to the E, was pedestrianized in 1987 after the creation of the ring road. That cannot compensate for its disappointingly ragged and mixed character. Only a few buildings stand out: on the S side, a former Burtons, early 1930s, recognizable by the grey stone façade and Deco styling of the pilasters with Neo-Grec detail. On the N side, the former ANGEL HOTEL, an ancient inn rebuilt in 1897. Neo-Jacobean, with Dutch gables over broad two-storey curved oriels. Angels' heads with garlands in the bays of the ground floor. In the yard to the side is a column, faced in colourful faience tiles, Quattrocento style, with masks to the Ionic capital. Slightly surprisingly, the S side has another former Burton's store of 1930, this time streamlined Moderne in white faience, with vertical fins between the windows and chevron-patterned floor bands.

Off to the S in CHADWICK ROAD is a rare survival of a small and very early TELEPHONE EXCHANGE, 1911 by *Edward Cropper* of *H.M. Office of Works*. Domestic Neo-Georgian with segmental hood over the door on console brackets. Grey brick dressed with rubbed, red brick quoins, aprons and surrounds to the windows. The TOWN HALL (*see* above) is the High Road's saving grace and challenged only for self-assertiveness by THE EXCHANGE shopping centre, by *Chapman Taylor Partners*, 1988–91. Its main façade is presented as a vast Italian Baroque temple mixed with the flamboyant and colourful classical revival of Bofill. Inside, malls on three levels link between here and Cranbrook Road. The rest of the buildings of High Road must necessarily play second fiddle, with the exception of HARRISON GIBSONS furniture store by *Forrest and Barber*, 1961. A compellingly horrible behemoth, clad in dreary grey aggregate panels. Floor beam-ends are exposed in a staggered pattern on the side walls, reflecting the arrangement inside where the showroom floors are syncopated to create an overlapping effect, with double-height voids between each storey. This is designed to ensure the shopper is always aware of what lies above and below; an interesting psychological device but one which creates oppressive low spaces. On the roof, the former restaurant (now nightclub). Harrison Gibsons began in the adjoining terrace, built in 1902. Upper floors of bay windows in buff terracotta beneath stripey Dutch gables, originally topped with segmental pediments. The firm's furniture depository stands close to the railway in HAINAULT ROAD. Here too some housing developments in high-rise blocks, part of a plan to bring more people to live in the town centre. SPECTRUM 67, twelve-storey slab by *ATP Group Partnership*, 2002–3 raised on a plinth of vivid blue tiling, the upper storeys in vertical bands of red, blue and yellow brick. Wavy rooftop. Across the railway, by the bus station, REDBRIDGE FOYER by *ATP Group Partnership* for East Thames Housing Group, designed to provide small flats and an integrated training centre for disadvantaged young people. Similarly lively, two ranges in yellow brick with metal-clad upper storeys linked by a turreted stair tower. Curved section towards the main forecourt.

Back in the High Road, THE GENERAL HAVELOCK is the last entertaining building on the N side, *c.* 1900 Arts and Crafts with a corner tower with pointy roof squeezed between big roughcast gables. On the S side, calm and dignified, BARCLAYS BANK, a highly distinguished temple front with elongated Doric columns set *in antis* to the high banking hall, short upper storeys and a small pediment. 1913 by *L.T. Moore*. The bank originally stood, like its neighbouring houses, within a small garden, a measure of how much the leafiness of this suburb has been degraded since. Harder to love, the thirteen-storey council offices (LINTON HOUSE) of the 1960s. Reinforced concrete with floor bands faced in rough, dark aggregate.

2. *High Road East*

The pedestrian precinct of the High Road is bluntly brought to a close by the ring road which is carried on an overpass across the railway. Beyond this barrier are a scattering of buildings along the S side which nevertheless belong to the town centre. First the huge Police Station (*see* above), then, hemmed in by traffic, the former Regal Cinema, now a bar. By *W.E. Trent*, 1937. Plain façade, its tiles overpainted. Much smaller but twice as characterful, is the former Billiard Hall (now CITY GATES CHRISTIAN CENTRE). A curious concoction, elaborately enriched in glazed terracotta with Greek detail including acroterion crest. Then in quick succession, the Methodist Church and the Church and schools of St Peter and St Paul.

Further E the sights are strung out, from the County Court and the parish church of St Mary, to the former ELECTRICITY OFFICES AND SHOWROOM on the corner with Clarks Road. This is of 1931 by *L.E.J. Reynolds*, Borough Surveyor. Commonplace stripped commercial classicism. Steel framed, faced in Portland stone. Deep window bays to the ground-floor showrooms. Splayed corner. Then the Swimming Pool and, on the opposite side a CAR SHOWROOM AND GARAGE: 1934 by *Cameron Kirby*. An early example for England of the Modern style in architecture, and characteristic of the snappier inter-war suburb. Over-painted and unsympathetically altered, but with a continuously glazed showroom along the front with a curved return. Concave corner inset with a half-height convex projecting section, originally for the petrol station. The workshop was located behind, designed for drive-in service as well as more essential repairs. Finally on this side, THE CAULIFLOWER pub, *c.* 1900. Big, flashy and immensely tall with a polished-granite plinth, but brick above with fussy stucco decoration in a typically Victorian ragbag of Jacobean/Flemish motifs. Inside, not quite the unaltered 'gin palace' that it claims to be but still lots of good engraved glass in the screens and bar. The individual bars, once subdivided are now thrown together. At the back, the largest space is the former billiard room, originally top-lit.

3. *South of the High Road*

S of the High Road there is little of interest. Development of the Loxford Hall Estate was largely complete by 1899 when the council acquired SOUTH PARK. Opened in 1902: a typical Edwardian park with a long lake, varied landscaping and plantings of specimen trees, but now largely stripped of its more picturesque amenities. Close to the entrance in SOUTH PARK ROAD, a single larger house, dated 1907, with mullioned Tudor windows and doorway, quite atypical in a street of mainly 1930s houses with two-storey bow windows beneath gables. PARKSIDE, in GOLFE ROAD, is a refreshing alternative to the endless terraces. Built as rest homes in 1910 by *Arthur C. Russell* for the Sons of Temperance Friendly Society. Like almshouses, with a two-storey projecting centre bay in brick and render, its facing gable steeply pitched with dentilled eaves and cupola above. Flanking bungalows to l. and r. each with recessed porch, that in the centre with characterful round arch continued as a curved wall. Mosaic panel in the centre of the gable. The streets to the W were laid out on the Clements Estate, sold in 1879 and quickly developed over the next two decades. In PARK ROAD is a rather splendid former corner pub, THE HULSE ARMS, of 1905 by *Foulsham & Riches* in red brick and terracotta, the moulded surrounds of the upper-floor windows with broken-pedimented heads. Balustraded parapet and a tiny Dutch gable over the splayed corner.

4. North: Cranbrook Road and The Drive

CRANBROOK ROAD, the N expansion of the town centre, is most rewarding in the area immediately around the STATION. Above ground, a rebuilding of the 1980s, with a big spreading hipped roof and glazed sides, behind, platforms of the 1890s with distinctive GER ironwork brackets to the awnings. The E side of CRANBROOK ROAD is a good C20 commercial mix. First, a local landmark, BODGERS department store, established in 1890 and rebuilt here in 1914 as an arcade. Of that date, the range facing Station Road with a screen of fluted columns. The end to Cranbrook Road is a rebuilding, with an unattractive sloping corner. Next to this, and set back is the entrance to THE EXCHANGE shopping centre (*see* above), through a gigantic Serlian arch, a typical Postmodern joke, inflating a Venetian-window form to triumphal arch proportions. On its l. WOOLWORTH'S, originally C&A, 1950s, with a tall, angled corner tower faced in fluted panels, and open top storey. The main range behind is long and convex with small windows. Just beyond, Nos. 28–32, a corner block with a dome, liberally ornamented with carved decoration of garlands and fruit. Built *c.* 1900 with a remodelled ground floor of coupled fluted Ionic columns for the National Provincial Bank. Then several examples of the variety of styles favoured for large stores between the wars e.g. No. 46, formerly WEST'S department store. Sober Neo-Classicism, Greek in flavour. Tripartite upper storey with giant columns.

On the W side, LLOYDS BANK with a curved corner, by *Johnson & Astbury*, 1932. Portland stone, stripped classical with the barest traces of incised detailing. Further N, CRANBROOK HOUSE, 1924. Steel frame, faced in faience, with wide bays and much glazing. The rest of Cranbrook Road's buildings are spaced out, e.g. the splendid former WYCLIFFE CONGREGATIONAL CHURCH of 1906–7 by *Smee & Houchin*. Unusually lavish Free Gothic in red brick with terracotta detail, low tower and a huge window to the road. Some Art Nouveau details. Converted first to a theatre, then to offices in the 1980s.

A short detour down PARK AVENUE gives a little flavour of mid-C19 Ilford, with Nos. 4–14, 1840s terraces with pedimented porches and Grecian detailing, no doubt part of an isolated speculative scheme capitalizing on the close proximity of the parkland around Valentines. Nos. 16 and 18 typify the more picturesque Tudor cottage villa of similar date. Brick and stucco with decorative bargeboards.

Further N, Cranbrook Road's E side is open to VALENTINES PARK (*see* above). Close to the Mansion (see p. 344), E along BETHELL AVENUE, is a scheme of seventy houses laid out by *H.C. Lander* for the Town Planning and Garden City Co. Ltd, *c.* 1910, with larger than average individual dwellings.

The more customary type of Edwardian terraces characterize the area to the W around THE DRIVE. This was the drive to

Cranbrook Hall, owned by the local builder/developer, W.P. Griggs, who demolished the house in 1901 and built up the estate with housing. Near the N end, past St Andrew's Church (q.v.), the former PORT OF LONDON AUTHORITY'S SPORTS GROUND, badly neglected and needing rescuing if only to save the excellent PAVILION of 1923 by *Edwin Cooper*, architect of the PLA's majestic headquarters on Tower Hill in the City of London. Identical N and S elevations with Tuscan porticos, the pavilion appropriately simple. Steward's LODGE of the same date, also by *Cooper*. 1950s Club House.

SNARESBROOK

Snaresbrook is the area just W of Wanstead on the road to Epping, a mixture of woodland, a few older buildings, and stretches of superior Edwardian housing, served by a station on the Eastern Counties branch line to Loughton. The principal feature is the former orphanage and its grounds, now the Crown Courts.

SNARESBROOK CROWN COURT, Hollybush Hill. Used as law courts from the 1970s, but built as an INFANT ORPHAN ASYLUM (founded in Hackney, 1827), later known as the Royal Wanstead School. It was planned for *c.* 500 children. An early work by *Gilbert Scott*, then of *Scott & Moffat*, 1843, illustrated in vol. 1 of *The Builder*. Scott was responsible for the external appearance. An impressive but rather dull symmetrical Jacobean composition, of grey limestone from near Whitby, with Bath and Caen stone dressings. Projecting gatehouse-like centrepiece with oriel between a pair of tall turrets. Boldly treated entrance doorway with faceted voussoirs linked by two bands. A similar centrepiece on the N front. The flanking ranges look quite domestic, in contrast to the later, more monumental Seamen's orphanage at Wanstead. They are two-storied with attics, with mullioned windows and shaped gables, broken by projecting gabled bays. Inside, spare detail, the grandest feature a double staircase with columns rising above the balustrades. Much altered for the present use, after the school closed in 1971. Additional courts in a steel-framed building behind were added by *Mayell, Hart & Partners* for the P.S.A., 1972–4, with underground link to the old buildings; further additions in 1988 brought the total to twenty courtrooms.

The CHAPEL remains, a broad, rather ungainly space, the roof timbers supported on stone angel-corbels. Wide chancel arch, canted apse. STAINED GLASS, including several good panels with scenes from the Life of Christ and Acts of Mercy. E window by *William Morris* of London *c.* 1920.

STATION. The original station house of 1856 survives. Other buildings of 1883, 1893 (downside platform canopy), 1915 (upside canopy extended). Ticket office 1947, when the line was electrified.

N of the Crown Court, at the junction with Wanstead High Street, a little drinking FOUNTAIN of 1872 with shingled spirelet. Further N, opposite the Eagle Pond, the EAGLE HOTEL, a coaching inn of C18 origin, with nice early C19 tented balcony across the front. N of Eagle Pond, beyond Snaresbrook Road, SNARESBROOK HOUSE, now flats, a white-stuccoed house in its own grounds. It looks early C19 but has been much altered.

Further S in NEW WANSTEAD, WEAVERS' ALMSHOUSES, 1857 by *Joseph Jennings.* A most attractive group, given presence by prominent Vanbrughian chimneystacks linked by arches. Simple two-storey ranges broken by a taller stucco-trimmed centrepiece, with a pair of canted bays, openwork balustrading and slim clock turret. Segmental centre pediment; below are the weavers' arms with their motto 'weave truth with trust', and reset plaques of 1824 and 1851. The buildings replaced foundations at Shoreditch (1670) and at Spitalfields (1729). Stairs within the centre block lead to rear balconies giving access to the upper flats. Threatened demolition was averted in the 1970s, and instead, interiors were remodelled 1975–6 by *F.G. Dobson* and *H.M. Grellier & Son*, who also added a parallel range behind, similarly arranged, with a central community room.

WANSTEAD

Wanstead has two parts: the delightful C18 church and large park remaining from Wanstead House, which lie enshrined in suburbia to the E of Blake Hall Road, and the village which developed further N, along the High Street to the N of Eastern Avenue. Here there are some remnants – though fewer than fifty years ago – from the substantial C18 houses built by London merchants attracted by the combination of attractive countryside and frequent coaches along the Colchester Road. Suburban development took over in the later C19, but as at Woodford, absence of workmen's trains kept the area select.

1. *Wanstead Park and Church*

The architectural fame of Wanstead was WANSTEAD HOUSE, a very large classical mansion built by *Colen Campbell* for Sir Richard Child (†1750), who became Viscount Castlemaine and

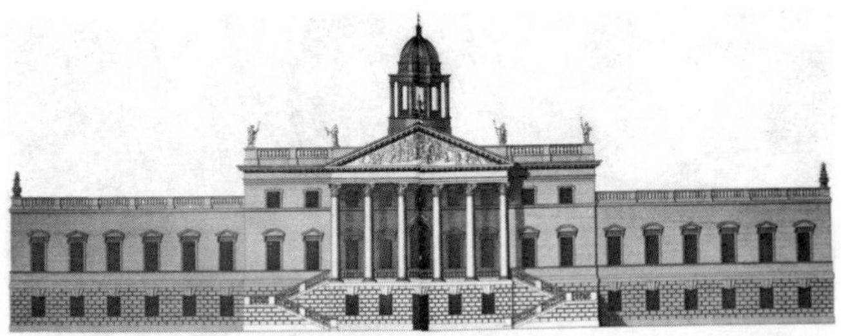

Wanstead House, elevation from *Vitruvius Britannicus*, 1717–25

first Earl Tylney after inheriting the Tylney estate from his wife. His house replaced an older one on the same site, which had been acquired in 1667 by Sir Richard's father, Sir Josiah Child, chairman of the East India Company, 'a suddenly monied man' as John Evelyn said in 1683. The new house was begun in 1715 and was thus the earliest major building in the revived pure Palladian style, and by far the largest to be found in the countryside around London. It is illustrated in the first volume of *Vitruvius Britannicus*. It was 260 ft long, 6+9+6 bays, the centre with a six-column pedimented portico. The house continued to flourish under the second Earl. It fell on hard times in the early C19, after the substantial fortune of the heiress, Catherine Tylney-Long, had been frittered away by her husband, the spendthrift William Pole-Wellesley, nephew of the Duke of Wellington. The contents were sold in 1822 to help pay debts of over a quarter-of-a-million pounds. The house failed to find a buyer, and was demolished; fragments were acquired as building materials; capitals from the portico for example, are now at Hendon Hall, Barnet. Two rusticated GATEPOSTS with carved panels and balls remain at the entrance to OVERTON DRIVE, and E of the church are the former stables, now a GOLF CLUB established 1893. Main building with central, shallow gable over a brick arch, one storey ranges to l. and r., all of red brick with dark pantiles. The golf course includes the site of the mansion, of which nothing remains, and a hollow defines the octagonal basin which lay on its western axis.

To the S and E of the golf course lies the present WANSTEAD PARK, opened 1881. 140 acres of the grounds were acquired by the Corporation of London from the Tylney-Longs, as part of the campaign to save Epping Forest from further enclosures. The park is now largely a natural landscape of grass and woodland, but something can still be seen of the formal grounds begun by Sir Josiah. Their vast extent is shown on a Kip view of the early C18. Running E from the site of the house is a broad AVENUE which ended in a formal canal, later enlarged to form a string of lakes. On either side of the avenue, now hidden by trees, two MOUNTS for viewing the grounds

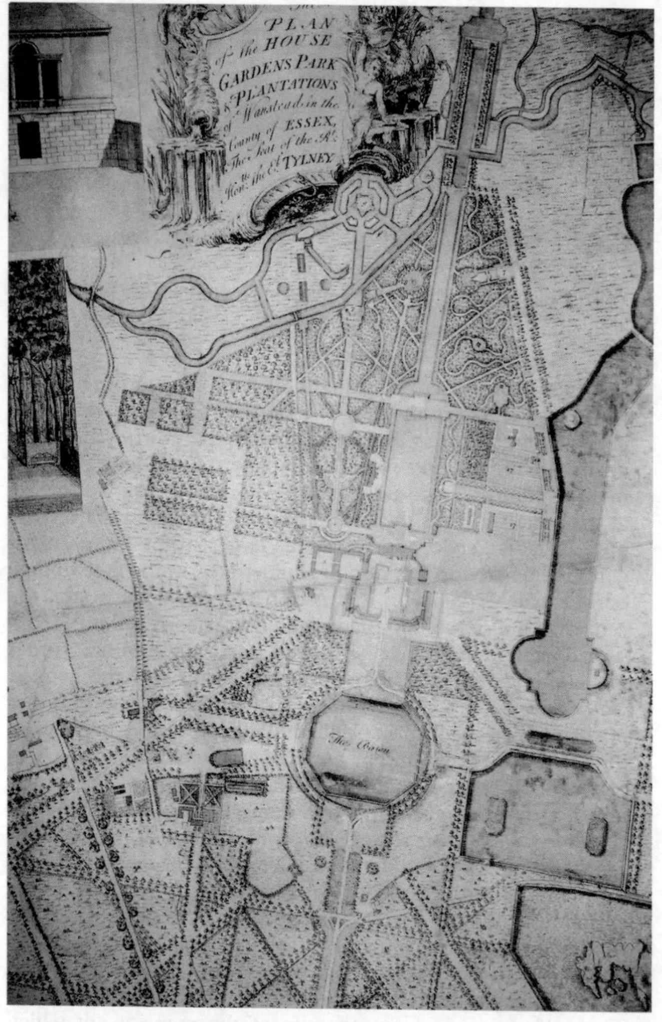

Wanstead Park, detail from Rocque's survey 1735

also belong to the early work. Rocque's survey of 1735 shows them surrounded by woodland crossed by snaking paths. Further N was an amphitheatre with stepped grass banks, which overlooked the island 'fortification' in the lake, where mock battles and entertainments could be held. These features and the creation of the chain of informal lakes were added for the first Earl, Sir Richard Child (†1750), possibly by *George London*. The elaborate water engineering was carried out by *Adam Holt*. The northern lakes were fed from the River

Roding, the southern ones, Shoulder of Mutton pond, the large Heronry pond and Perch pond, from the basin W of the house to which water was brought from Snaresbrook.

In 1761–2 the second Earl added a GROTTO by the lake S of the main avenue. It contained a boathouse below a lavishly decorated, domed upper chamber. Now a fenced off ruin, after a fire in 1884 and later vandalism. Happily the TEMPLE to its W, of the same date, was repaired in 1992–7, after being occupied by Forest keepers from 1882–1960. It is placed on a mound which makes it more visible in the flat landscape, and which conceals a basement floor accessible at the rear. Centrepiece with four-column Doric portico forming an entrance to an upper room, reinstated with the original blue and white colour scheme. The simple two-storey brick wings with pantiled roofs were added later. Within the Temple is displayed a lead figure of Andromeda, formerly outside the grotto. To the W an avenue of sweet chestnuts has recently been recreated. Elsewhere trees survive from work by *Humphry Repton*, in the final Tylney-Long phase. His report of 1813 respected the grand formal tradition of the grounds: 'it must be classed with those royal and princely residences which form the retreats of the great from court or city'. His work (for which Tylney-Long failed to pay) included a parterre to the W of the house, and a partly surviving avenue of sessile oaks S of the Temple, some of them surprisingly massive due to Repton's practice of 'bundle planting'.

ST MARY, Overton Drive. Pevsner wrote rightly that the church is 'worthy in its appearance of the noble aspiration of the mansion'. It was built in 1787–90 by *Thomas Hardwick*, as directed by the two principal landowners, Sir James Tylney-Long, and George Bowles of Wanstead Grove, on a site given by Tylney-Long just to the N of the old church. The building, faced with finely jointed ashlar throughout, is in a restrained classical style, clearly of Gibbs derivation. Tall porch with two pairs of Doric columns. W front with central pediment, and set back, a fine timber bell turret: a clock storey with rustication, and an upper storey with paired Ionic columns set diagonally, crowned by a little cupola. The flanks have two storeys of windows, segment-arched below, round-headed above, corresponding to galleries inside. An excellent, beautifully proportioned and unaltered interior. Five bays, the arcades with tall 29
Corinthian columns, each with its own entablature. They are set on high pedestals to allow for the BOX PEWS. The main ceiling is flat, the galleries and chancel have groin vaults with a little plaster adornment. PULPIT. Lovely, hexagonal on an elegant fluted stem, with sounding board carried on two palm-tree columns, its top curving up to a carved knop and pinnacle. The steps have an attractive wrought-iron balustrade similar to the fine curved COMMUNION RAILS and CHANCEL RAILS. Substantial chancel, planned to accommodate the huge monument of Sir Josiah Child, with family pew opposite. The sanctuary is panelled, with large E window treated in Venetian

manner, but with blind side lights. ALTAR PAINTING: Burial of Christ.

N of the chancel a lobby with separate external door, leading to the VESTRY, which has a marble fireplace and a BOARD in an early C19 frame listing 'customary dues and surplice fees'. STAINED GLASS. Roundels in the E end of the galleries, contemporary with the church; arms of George III and the Tylney-Longs.

Very few later additions: E window 1890, Ascension, with Renaissance borders; some pictorial aisle windows by *Mayer* of Munich, from 1889, a later one by *A.F. Erridge* (N aisle). Also the FONT, a marble bowl with swags, *c.* 1880. MONUMENTS.
22 The monument to Sir Josiah Child †1699 dominates the chancel. One of the show pieces of the period, glorifying the father who was the source of wealth for the creator of the great house. Attributed to *John van Nost.* (Esdaile). On the pedestal the reclining figure of the son, and two allegorical women. Higher up stands Sir Josiah in Roman vestments and a wig, two cherubs with symbols of mortality at his feet, a canopy with swagged drapery over his head. He stands within a grand aedicule with fluted Corinthian columns l. and r. carrying an open, broken-segmental pediment. Trumpeting Fames recline on top, a flaming urn on either side. All the ornamental carving is very fine. The inscription suggests a date after 1704. Among lesser monuments, on the W wall, David Petty †1745, signed by *P. Scheemakers*: flat obelisk above a gadrooned sarcophagus of dark marble. – Barlow family, *c.* 1770, delicate Neo-Grecian stele in coloured marbles. – George Bowles of Wanstead Grove †1817 by *Chantrey* (S gallery), mourning woman seated by a bust on a pedestal.

Large, wooded churchyard with many chest tombs, the site of the earlier church to the S marked by several C18 ledger stones. – Fine classical monument to Robert Pamplin, Vice Admiral, †1824. Pedestal with naval trophies, with strigillated column and urn. – WATCHING HUT (against bodysnatchers); a stone sentry box with tapered sides, domed vault, pediment and acroteria, built 1831 in memory of the Wilton family.

2. *Aldersbrook*

Between Wanstead Park and the City of London Cemetery is the suburb of Manor Park, ALDERSBROOK, on the border of Wanstead and East Ham. It was developed from 1899–1910, with gabled and bay-windowed middle-class villas in a variety of styles, and a parade of shops of 1904 provided by the ubiquitous J.H. Bethell of East Ham. SCHOOLS in Ingatestone Road and Harpenden Road: 1908 by *C.H. Brassey*, two storeys, with shaped gables, one-storey Infants School with classrooms around a central hall, added 1911.

ST GABRIEL, Aldersbrook Road. By *Charles Spooner*, completed

1914, with funding from the Misses Nutter (see also Holy Trinity Woodford). Attractive Perp building of thin red bricks, reticently detailed with pretty tile decoration. Continuous pantiled roof over nave and chancel, a small W flèche and embattled aisles. Inside, a big W arch supporting the flèche marks off a baptistery. Refined, light interior with wide nave, stone octagonal piers, boarded keeled ceiling with painted ribs, and a N chapel broadening out from the N aisle, defined by stone rere-arches. Simple Perp windows with diamond leading.

BAPTIST CHURCH, Aldersbrook Road, 1908 (future uncertain). Crude but expressive Free Perp. Thin corner tower with copper spire. Spreading square interior with octagonal roof carried across the corners. Beams with texts, large carved pulpit, immersion font in the canted E end.

3. *Wanstead Village and Hermon Hill*

CHRIST CHURCH, Wanstead Place. In a leafy corner of the green, W of the High Street. An 1860s chapel of ease, built by the rector of Wanstead, Rev. W.P. Wigram, brother of the Bishop of Rochester, whose diocese included this area at the time.* Ragstone, with sturdy C13 Gothic detail; plate tracery apart from the E window, which is a little more elaborate. Nave and N aisle, with simple timber porch, 1860–1 by *G.G. Scott*, no doubt planned with enlargements in mind. Matching S aisle added by *D.A. Cobbet*, 1867, vaulted N tower-porch and broach spire by *J.T. Bressey*, 1868–9, all built with donations from Lady Morrison of the Hermitage, Snaresbrook. Wide aisles under separate gables, circular windows in their E walls. Spacious, dignified interior, quite light because of the loss of much glass in the Second World War. Plain nave with low quatrefoil piers, the moulded capitals with octagonal moulded abaci, no clerestory. In contrast the chancel arch has luscious foliage capitals and two layers of carved corbelling. The chancel retains characteristic enrichments of the later C19. These date from 1895, the gift of Elizabeth Bangs: elaborately Gothic arcaded STALLS and COMMUNION RAILS, PULPIT in similar style. Old English ALTAR, 1956, with Baroque posts, carrying angel candlesticks from Ely Theological College added 1974. Gothic ORGAN CASE. ROOD installed 1990, from Salisbury Teacher Training College. STAINED GLASS. E window, Christ and angels, in memory of Jessie Nutter †1919, given by her sisters (see also Holy Trinity South Woodford). Plain CHURCH HALL, *c.* 1970.

OUR LADY OF LOURDES (R.C.), Cambridge Park. 1927–8 by *Geoffrey Raymond* of *Scoles & Raymond*, the aisles completed 1934 and 1940. Red brick with stone dressings, conventional Perp, the interior with rendered walls and white-painted open

* Sons of Sir Robert Wigram of Walthamstow House (*see* p. 758–9).

roof. Five bay arcades with dying arches, on stone columns with shafts attached to E and W. No clerestory. Sanctuary flanked by side chapels. Traditional furnishings: elaborate canopied REREDOS in grey stone with carved figures, 1929. Carved STATIONS OF THE CROSS. Reordered 1972 with nave altar and reading desk, simple blocky forms. At the W end, FONT, in stripes of polished and rough granite, on a patterned marble floor, 2002. Attached on the r. side, PRESBYTERY, 1931, and large but tactfully designed PASTORAL CENTRE, 2002, gabled, red brick with rendered panels. Stained glass by *Michael Lassen* in entrance lobby.

METHODIST CHURCH, Cambridge Park. Built as a Methodist Free Church by *Frederick Boreham*, 1875, small but quite elaborate. Central triplet of windows; plate tracery. Glazing in small squares with little roundels. A pair of entrances under porch arches on lush capitals. Hall behind, much rebuilt 1964.

HERMON HILL METHODIST CHURCH. 1876 by *J.T. Bressey*. Ragstone front with Geometric tracery windows above a doorway with red sandstone columns. E wall with rose window; floral patterns in quatrefoils.

UNITED REFORMED CHURCH, Nightingale Lane and Grosvenor Road. 1864–7, built for Congregationalists, the strongest C19 Free Church in Wanstead. It made use of stone from St Luke, Kings Cross, a Gothic church by *John Johnson* demolished for St Pancras station, an example of how Anglican and Nonconformist styles of architecture had to some extent become interchangeable by this time. Three-gable stone front; elaborately Dec windows and carved doorway. But the clerestory was omitted, and the side walls look incongruous with their spiky tracery windows set in austere brick. Inside, moulded arcades on octagonal columns and an open timber roof on carved stone corbels. The tall chancel arch frames the organ. At the E end, GROVE HALL, 1895–6 by *E.M. Whittaker*; Perp with open timber roof.

FRIENDS MEETING HOUSE, Bush Road. Four linked hexagons of white brick, 1968 by *Norman Frith*, with the main meeting room set back from the busy road. It replaced a meeting house on the same site, adapted in 1870 from Becontree Assembly Rooms, bought by Joseph Gurney Barclay for the use of the Quaker families who had moved E from Plaistow.

LIBRARY, Spratt Hall Road; off Cambridge Park, 1966–9 by *D. Meyer* and *B. Ettridge* (*Redbridge Architect's Department*). Single storey. An offputting entrance front with rather grim, unrelieved dark brickwork, but large staggered floor-to-ceiling windows along the N side. The interior is much better: the strong ceiling grid with raised northern roof light echoed by the regular lines of book stacks, with a well-lit reading area by the N windows. To the S, CHURCHILL HALL, a plain, top-lit meeting room.

59 Former MERCHANT SEAMEN'S ORPHAN ASYLUM, Hermon Hill. 1861–71 by *George Somers Clarke sen*. A magnificent group

on an eminence, visible from afar, dominated by a tall, asymmetrical tower. Used as a convent and refuge after the orphanage moved to Bearwood, Berks in 1920, and later as a hospital for the care of the elderly. Converted to flats *c.* 2000. The asylum was founded in 1827 in Wapping, moved to Bow Road in 1834, then, like so many Victorian institutions of this kind, sought space and fresh air in the London countryside. Funding came from the major shipping companies. Built in stages: the foundation stone was laid by Prince Albert in 1861, the S range (for boys) and W range (for girls) were completed in 1862. The ground floor was used for schoolrooms, the upper floors for dormitories. The *Illustrated London News* called the style 'a lovely Venetian Gothic'. (Pevsner commended the detail, although he found the ensemble more like St Pancras Station than the Doge's Palace.) Stock brick, enlivened by a Ruskinian polychromy of red and black Ewell bricks contrasted with white Ancaster stone. Strong horizontal bands of black brick bind the composition together. Ground- and first-floor windows are paired below trefoil arches. The steep roofs are broken by angular dormers. The entrance tower (housing servants' bedrooms and water tanks) is a tour de force, with fanciful North Italian battlements, a slated spire above bold windows in Venetian style, and a portal with pointed arch on grey marble columns with elaborate capitals. Tympanum with pathetic scene of children orphaned by a shipwreck. All the carving is by *Thomas Earp. The Builder* of 1863 described the reception hall with Devonshire marble columns, brick vault and alabaster and marble chimneypiece. The boys' schoolroom lay beyond, with covered playground below. The Dining Hall, added to the N in 1866–7, was a lofty space with windows high up, below a boarded wagon roof canted out on struts, with decorative tie-beams. In front, a lower range with nautical reliefs over window and door was the entrance to the girls' wing. Further N is the former Infirmary, 1901 by *Arnold Mitchell*, surveyor to the Asylum. On a gently canted plan, of brick, stone and terracotta, with stepped gables, in the pleasant free Queen Anne style characteristic of Mitchell.

SUKKAT SHALOM SYNAGOGUE is the former Chapel of 1863, paid for by Lady Morrison. Converted to its present use by *Ronald Wylde Associates*, *c.* 2000. This too is elaborately Gothic. Triplets of lancets below arches in alternating brick and stone, a wheel window over the entrance. Formerly with a flèche as well as corner turrets. Inside, furnishings and stained glass brought from the synagogue at the Jewish Hospital, Tottenham.

WANSTEAD PUMPING STATION, Eastern Avenue, by the Roding. 1901–3 by *W.B. Bryan*, engineer, of the East London Waterworks Co. Red brick, Tudor style. Set in its own grounds like a country house. Big square central tower with ball finials on the corners of the parapet. Lower pumping hall behind with kneelered gables and ball finials. A Tudor style gatehouse, Water Works Cottage, completes the domestic ensemble.

PERAMBULATION

WANSTEAD STATION, George Green, was built for the Central Line extension. A good design of 1937–8 by *Charles Holden*, completed after the war with the original intentions, it has a crisp box-like exterior faced with grey tiles. At the corner of the green an 1897 Jubilee DRINKING FOUNTAIN, a small, charming, triangular composition with three brick arches over two water taps and a trough, under a steep shingled turret. Across Eastern Avenue, the GEORGE HOTEL, on the site of an C18 inn, 'rebuilt 1904 by A.J. Bywater', as a plaque explains. It marks the start of the HIGH STREET with three copper ogee turrets on polygonal corner bays. Tablet dated 1752, and a portrait medallion of George III. Curly ironwork at the entrance. Some engraved glass, the interiors now a single space.

The two best C18 houses of Wanstead, both divided into flats in the 1920s, are on an unenviable site just E of the High Street, directly N of Eastern Avenue. ELM HALL, now with rendered front, is of seven bays, and three storeys (the top one a later alteration from former attics). At the back of the central entrance hall a good earlier C18 staircase, somewhat reconstructed, with triplets of twisted and straight balusters and contemporary panelling. Some remodelling *c.* 1820–30, including the front door with arched fanlight. Around this time a tall room with canted bay was added to the rear and an attic stair at the front. REYDON HALL, also of seven bays, is on a larger scale and has a more showy early C18 brick front with giant Corinthian fluted pilasters of stone at either end. Segment-headed windows above inset panels to each floor, and a tall parapet. Doorway also with fluted pilasters. Railings with iron overthrow.

Set back from the E side of the High Street was the Mall, which had another good group of C18 houses of which only a few remain. The most complete is MANOR HOUSE. Formerly the Conservative Club, hence the twice-life-size bronze head of Churchill (the local M.P.) in front, by *Luigi Fironi*, 1968, presented by French and Italian admirers and inscribed 'the giant of England'. It emerges incongruously from a rough stone plinth brought from old Waterloo Bridge. The house is C18 in general appearance, though upper parts are much rebuilt. Seven bays and two storeys on a basement, brick plat band and parapet. Five dormers, the centre one with segment-headed pediment. The windows with poor segment-headed arches now have blank Victorian sashes. The central door has a shell hood with monster face, which looks C18, but seems pinched for its setting. Later Gothic fanlight below. The back, more convincingly early C18, has a grander doorcase with scrolled pediment, staircase window above, and straight-headed windows. The staircase is old fashioned for *c.* 1700, rising around a well from basement to top floor, with closed string, thick spiral balusters with knops, and wall panelling.

Some panelling remains in the NE room. All in a bad state, under repair in 2003. Two C18 houses remain adjacent to the S, they have shops built out in front, but at the rear is a nice early C18 doorcase with carved brackets.

Opposite is No. 50, a new block with six apartments, by *PCKO Architects*, 2002–3, discreetly set back from the High Street, with a pool in the forecourt. Timber-framed construction, unashamedly modern with its mixture of steel, glass bricks and wooden cladding, and a shallow roof with deep eaves, a pioneer in this conservative neighbourhood. Glazed and top-lit central stairhall, porthole windows to a basement, designed (a sign of the times) as IT rooms.

Off to the W in WOODBINE PLACE is a school of 1912 by *Frank Whitmore*, Essex County Architect, now TREE HOUSE NURSERY SCHOOL. Single storey; two adjacent classrooms with big windows, roughcast gables at each end.

At the corner of the High Street and GROVE PARK to the E, No. 2, a house of 1890 with much sgraffito decoration, and with a plaque commemorating the astronomer royal, James Bradley (†1762), whose research was encouraged by his uncle, the rector of Wanstead. Bradley set up his telescope in a house on the Wanstead Grove Estate. The present house belongs with the development of GROVE PARK and THE AVENUE, laid out from 1889 with comfortably large houses by *Potts, Sulman & Hennings*. The big house of Wanstead Grove, demolished the same year, stood near the junction of the two roads. It was first built *c.* 1690 by Sir Francis Dashwood, and rebuilt in 1822. The extensive formal grounds included a long canal from which a remnant survives as a pond off Grove Park. Two C18 garden buildings remain in The Avenue. At No. 20 a square, early C18 GAZEBO may be the summerhouse referred to in a lease of 1713. Red brick with straight-headed sash windows. Panelled interior with corner fireplace. It is built on a mound, with a grotto beneath, its brick vault originally decorated with shells and iron slag. Behind No. 14 is an elegant TEMPLE with four-column timber Ionic portico which originally looked down the canal. Interior with apse and stucco ceiling. Possibly built in the 1730s by the then owner, Matthew Wymondesold, when he extended the gardens. His connections with the Childs might support an attribution to *Colen Campbell*.

WANSTEAD PLACE to the W of the High Street leads to the Victorian CHRIST CHURCH (*see* above). On the l., No. 47, a nice late C19 tile-hung house with gable, and Nos. 39–41, a modest pair, of *c.* 1840. The former Town Hall, now WANSTEAD HEALTH CLINIC, was built as the local Board of Health offices in 1881 by its surveyor, *J. T. Bressey*. Grey brick, with small superimposed Doric and Ionic pilasters as rather skimpy decoration. Three bays and a l. addition in the same style. Further on, the Red Cross Centre is the former FIRE STATION of 1913. Yellow brick, red terracotta decoration. Projecting front with doors for two engines, the fire hose tower at the side looking like an overblown chimney. On the far side of the green in SPRATT HALL ROAD, simple POLICE STATION of 1886 by *John Butler*, standing out here because of its red brick and three storeys.

Further N in the HIGH STREET, a pair of rural cottages, Nos. 6–8, at right angles to the street, brick and weatherboarded. Then the CHURCH SCHOOL, founded 1796, the unassuming buildings now mostly of 1980, but with the attractive Tudor-style teacher's house remaining, 1840–1 by *Edward Blore*, the gabled N end with a bellcote. Nearby, WAR MEMORIAL. Tall plinth with bronze angel of Victory holding a palm, signed by *N.A. Trent*.

In GROSVENOR ROAD to the E, THE SHRUBBERY is an eye-catching formal group of flats, around a cedar tree, *c.* 1935 by *Cockett, Henderson & Gillow* for North East London Property Co. Horizontal cream bands between red brick, with the Modernist trappings of projecting balconies and curved corner windows, a slighty jerky composition. It is given Art Deco panache by pedestrian entrances through two exotic catenary archways. Opposite, a stately pair of stucco-trimmed villas with Tuscan porches recall C19 aspirations here, but the rest is plainer and much rebuilt.

WOODFORD

Woodford does not feel like part of Greater London. It still reflects its origins as a straggle of settlements which grew up along the high road to Newmarket among the pleasant woodland and greens of the Essex Forest, and retains a few survivals from a once plentiful sprinkling of larger houses occupied by City merchants. Thorne's *Environs of London* in 1876 called it 'a district of citizens' villas'. By then more concentrated growth was under way, following the arrival of the Loughton branch of the Eastern Counties Railways in 1856. But the railway company sought to keep this line for lucrative season ticket traffic, refusing to grant workmen's fares, and the local council underpinned the middle-class nature of Woodford by refusing to allow trams and later trolley buses into their area. Thus Woodford developed as the prime superior suburb of North East London. New centres grew around the station at George Lane, SOUTH WOODFORD, some way S of the old parish church on the High Road, and around Woodford station, ½ mile E of WOODFORD GREEN, the largest of the old hamlets. Further N is WOODFORD WELLS, where medicinal springs had a brief popularity in the C18. The more remote WOODFORD BRIDGE lies away to the E, across the River Roding, now also separated by the great gash of the M11. Here on the higher ground close to the borough boundary is the late C18 Claybury Hall, which was surrounded by a *Repton* landscape, taken over for a vast County Asylum at the end of the C19 and transformed a century later into the select urban village of Repton Park.

SOUTH WOODFORD

HOLY TRINITY, Hermon Hill. 1886–7 by *James Fowler*. An ambitious, plain limestone building for the new middle-class suburb, in a precisely detailed late C12 Transitional style, rather old-fashioned for the time. Nave, N aisle, base of the NW tower and chancel were built 1887–90. The chancel was paid for by the Misses Nutter, benefactors of several local churches, but there were inadequate funds to complete the tower and intended spire, and there is only a brick wall in place of the S aisle. The tower has a bold sloping plinth, the W doorway red sandstone columns and trumpet-scallop capitals. Wide nave of five bays with circular piers, three clerestory windows to each bay, and semicircular apse with tall lancets and a dado of intersecting arcading. Interior walls originally plain brick, plastered later. Lady Chapel REREDOS in N aisle by *Laurence King*, *c*. 1950. STAINED GLASS. Three E lights by *Hugh Easton*, 1950.

To its S the temporary iron church remains, acquired from St Michael, Camden Town and erected in 1882. HALL to the W, 1907, domestic.

ST MARY, High Road. There was a church here from the C12. The appearance from the street is confusing. The present entrance is through the E front of 1888, after rebuilding following a fire in 1969. The oldest part is away from the road, a sturdy brick W tower, 1708, with broad corner buttresses rising to stumpy polygonal pinnacles (these and the parapet rebuilt 1899). Round-arched openings, the doorway of fine red brick; circular windows at the third stage, originally for the clock. The outer walls of the church survive from a minimal Gothic rebuilding by *Charles Bacon* in 1817. Broad lancet windows, the brickwork stripped of its original stucco in 1899. The orange brick and stone Perp chancel, 1888–9 by *W.O. Milne,* now forms the entrance hall, with a room inserted above. Within, the remodelling of 1971–2 by *John Phillips* removed the early C19 nave arcades, creating a spare late C20 space with new furnishings, white plastered walls, and boarded ceiling. The altar stands forward on a platform, with functional rectangular lighting frame above. Windows with clear glass, each enlivened by a small panel of rescued coloured fragments. The windows flanking the new 'E' end have abstract patterns by *Alan Younger*, 1983–4. Beside the entrance hall, parish office, and a rather dark brick-faced chapel.

MONUMENTS, a fine collection, restored after the fire and
12 tidily displayed between the windows. Rowland Elrington †1595 and wife, small, with the usual kneeling figures, in a frame with delicate ribbonwork; alabaster, with some colour. – Elizabeth Elwes †1625, a small figure kneeling frontally in a niche with draped curtains. Naïve Corinthian columns and open pediment. – Anna Holbech †1666, attributed to *Thomas Burman* (GF). Inscription in sober black and white classical frame. – Richard Bayly †1694, attributed to *William Stanton* (GF). Inscription on a feigned scroll with cherubs' heads and drapery. – Charlotte Crowe †1720. Quite imposing; a delicate medallion below with a weeping woman, thick drapery and foliage detail above. – David Bosanquet †1741. Frame with Corinthian columns and weeping cherub. – Drigue Olmius †1753 by *Sir Robert Taylor* (who was born in Woodford). Elegant urn in relief (restored in wood) against marbled background. – Charles Foulis of 1783, signed by *J. Bacon*. Urn on pedestal with relief of a seated woman holding an oil lamp. – John Popplewell †1829. Inscription with coarse drapery, by *G. Teague* of Leytonstone.

BRASSES: inscriptions of 1585, 1616, 1638 (with verse), 1652.

In the CHURCHYARD, sensitively redesigned by *John Phillips* with *Julian Litten*, many good table tombs, as well as C18 gravestones carved with the usual devices of skulls, angels etc. Near the tower a tall Corinthian marble COLUMN of jasper, with entablature formerly carrying an urn, to Peter Godfrey †1769, erected by *Sir Robert Taylor* in memory of his early patron. – Thomas North †1747 (erected after 1761), obelisk and urn on a bulging sarcophagus, probably also by *Sir Robert Taylor*. – Edward Keepe †1781, by *Samuel Robinson*, made of *Coade* stone; a refined podium, formerly with angels at the corners, carrying a Neoclassical urn. RAIKES MAUSOLEUM. First interment Martha Raikes †1797. A hefty structure roofed with a shallow dome with very Soanian segmental arches, a strigillated sarcophagus on top. According to Soane's notebook, he inspected the monument in 1800, which was by *Gibson,* and oversaw the cutting of the inscription in 1801; did it influence Soane's later tomb for his wife? – William Morris of Woodford Hall †1847, father of the famous William Morris. Large Grecian-style table tomb with draped urn on top.

MEMORIAL HALL to the NW. 1902 by *J. Kingwell Cole* and *Kenneth Wood*. The gift of Sir John Roberts, a local benefactor (*see also* Woodford Green). Rough-cast and half-timbering in an Arts and Crafts manner. Pretty inscribed corner stone with cherub's head. Timber arcades and open roof inside. W extension, brick and roughcast, 1904.

ST ANNE LINE (R.C.), Grove Crescent, off Grove Hill. 1965–6 by *D.M. Blouett*. Square, steel-frame building with a broad, low octagonal lantern. Walls of brick and, on two sides, pre-cast stone pierced by small rectangular windows. It is laid out diagonally inside with free-standing altar in the NW corner. Main illumination from the lantern. STATUE of St Anne Line by *Joseph Cribb*, 1967.

WOODFORD BAPTIST CHURCH, George Lane. 1895–6. Red brick, rather crude Dec tracery. Pleasant interior, a single space flowing into shallow transepts, unified by a bold, ceiled roof rising in a series of coves. W gallery with openwork panels on slim iron columns. Reordered with seating angled towards a music platform in the S transept. Rooms to the N, 1933.

WOODFORD NATIONAL SPIRITUALIST CHURCH, Craig Road and Grove Crescent, off Grove Hill. Dominated by a mono-pitch roof; windowless, rounded projections below. Internal lighting chiefly from the long, high clerestory above a lean-to roof.

LIBRARY and HEALTH CENTRE, High Road. By *C.A. Stok* and *J. Hockley* of *Redbridge Architect's Department*, 1972–5. A C20 intrusion in an C18 setting, but on a friendly scale. Bright-red brick. Crisp, ingeniously interlocking multi-level buildings, including some council offices and flats. The main library space flows down into a lower mezzanine with children's library, and up to a reference area above.

PERAMBULATIONS

1. South Woodford, from the railway station to Woodford Road

The railway line cuts rudely across the old route of GEORGE LANE. The level crossing was replaced in the 1940s by a curved concrete viaduct when the Central Line took over this route. The STATION was opened in 1856 but its buildings are largely of 1910, red brick, in domestic-revival style; platform canopy with curvy valences, supports with pierced spandrels. On the up platform, waiting room and canopy of 1880–1. Alterations for electrification, 1947–8.

A few modest stucco terraces of *c.* 1860 to the S, more stylish turn-of-the-century shopping parades to the N; the best building is the NATWEST BANK dated 1905. Red brick over a stone ground floor, with nicely carved detail over its corner entrance. Further N the lane broadens, with THE SHRUBBERIES set back on the E side, a cheerful series of late C19 villas with pretty white-painted verandas. Then ELECTRIC PARADE, 1925 by *H.H. Dartnell*, a predictable faintly Georgian terrace with shops, curving round to the HIGH ROAD. Immediately to the N, hidden behind Electric Parade and incongruously attached to a huge Waitrose supermarket, is GROVE LODGE, an attractive pattern-book-Gothic villa dated 1835. Tall, of yellow brick, with two daintily bargeboarded gables of uneven size, stone mullioned windows, and clustered chimneys. It deserves a better setting.

THE GEORGE, on the HIGH ROAD at the corner of George Lane, appears early C18 in origin, with an appealing spread-out two-storey front, and big hipped roof on coved eaves. Eight bays, brick, with broad sash windows, the two r. bays a later addition. The columned porch looks early C19. The interior is now a single room. The ODEON just to the S was built as the Majestic, 1934 by *S.B. Pritlove*, a formal, symmetrical, streamlined front of faience, with banded cornice above five tall windows. Designed with neon lighting on the pilasters in between. The interior, now with six screens, included a café and ballroom. Further S on the W side, Nos. 37–41, an elegant group of the earlier C19 with nice iron balconies with swept roofs, and on the E side a much altered C18 range (Nos. 32–44). In GLEBELANDS AVENUE to the E, Glebelands Home is a remnant of Glebelands House, demolished in the 1930s. Then exemplars of different phases of suburban development. To the
84 W and parallel to Woodford Road, THE DRIVE has a particularly sumptuous array of half-timbered and turreted turn-of-the-century villas (e.g. No. 38, dated 1899, and No. 43), some with viewing platforms on the roof. Opposite at the S end is the period piece of HERMITAGE COURT, 1936 by *A. Duckworth* for Suburban Real Estates: three storeys of flats on an E-plan, brick with white-rendered bands, curved balconies and Art Deco detail. Pantiled entrance gateway and front walls to match. Nos. 23–5 WOODFORD ROAD are a later C18 pair of five-bay houses with pedimented Doric doorcases. For the area further S *see* Snaresbrook.

2. *South Woodford* N *of the North Circular Road*

In the neighbourhood of St Mary's church, several C18 mansions remain along the HIGH ROAD, although too spread out to form a coherent group. The oldest is ELMHURST, set back in its own grounds on the E side. A tall mid-C18 three-storey front of five bays, with three-bay pediment. Yellow brick, with a stone frontispiece: doorway with vermiculated quoins linked to the window above; first-floor windows distinguished by false balconies. Three-bay extension to the S. Basement at the back. A large room on each side of central hall, the r. one panelled, the l. one with early C19 cornice and doorcases. Converted by *Edward Playne* as a hostel for Queen Mary College from 1926. The grounds (to be redeveloped, 2004) were filled with further college accommodation: first the conservative brick Old Lynden Hall of 1938 by *Playne*, then in 1962–9 three concrete towers with one-storey glazed link buildings by *Playne & Lacey*, and POOLEY HALL by *Feilden & Mawson*, 1975.

N of the Health Centre and Library (*see* above) No. 140, HOLMLEIGH, a neat three-bay, three-storey later C18 house, with parapet; doorway with fanlight.

On the W side, among a roadside group of shops, the WHITE HART, later C18 altered. Next to the church, THE OLD RECTORY, also later C18, seven bays and three storeys, carefully proportioned, with the first floor defined by two stone bands in the Palladian manner. Attractive arched entrance with fanlight; a later, originally two-storeyed, bow window to the S. Converted to offices after council occupation, with further flats in the grounds. Behind the church were the grounds of the principal manor house, Woodford Hall, designed by *Thomas Leverton*, 1771, and home of the elder William Morris (*see* churchyard), before the family moved to Water House, Walthamstow. The grounds were developed from 1869 by the British Land Co. and the house demolished *c.* 1900.

WOODFORD GREEN AND WOODFORD WELLS

ALL SAINTS, Inmans Row. 1874 by *F.E.C. Streatfeild.* The church with its SE tower and splayed and shingled spire forms a fine landmark, closing the N end of Woodford Green. Ragstone, rather severe. Low, narrow S aisle, but a wide N one of 1876 under its own gable. Quatrefoil clerestory, E end with five stepped lancets. Wide, five-bay nave with circular piers. Timber floor and W gallery 2004. Stone FONT and PULPIT. STAINED GLASS. Chancel E. Small scenes between patterned bands, to Alice Barclay †1867. N aisle, 2nd from W, Works of Mercy, to Henry Ford Barclay †1891 and his wife 'much esteemed for their charity and benevolence'. N aisle W and 1st from E, First World War memorials. Elaborately lettered bronze memorial plaque near the latter. S aisle W, *c.* 1943, by *Reginald Hallward*, in an attractively naïve drawing style, gently coloured, with St Cedd and Bradwell chapel.

Behind and to the E, CHURCH HALL and VICARAGE, both of 1907, with attractively homely detail, arch heads of tile and tile-hung walls.

ST BARNABAS, Snakes Lane East. 1910–11 by *Edwin T. Dunn.* Perp. Of red brick with touches of black brick and stone to vary the texture. Tall N chapel. Refined interior; moulded stone arches without capitals. *Laurence King* added the W façade to the incomplete Edwardian church in 1963–4. WAR MEMORIAL. Calvary by *Sir Charles Nicholson*, 1921. BRASS. Rev. Ernest Wheeler †1948, first vicar, standing figure in vestments.

ST THOMAS OF CANTERBURY (R.C.), High Road. 1895–6 by *Canon A.J.C. Scoles.* E.E., the W wall with plate tracery. Large, of bright red brick with long pantiled roof. Plain six-bay nave with octagonal columns. Reordered 1976 when elaborate furnishings were removed; the stained glass high up in the aisle walls is now the principal ornament. Sanctuary now with glass doors to the Blessed Sacrament chapel. This was originally used by the adjacent Franciscan convent. Carved roundel of St Francis in the S aisle; in the SE chapel a slab to the foundress, Henrietta Pelham-Clinton, Dowager Duchess of Newcastle, †1913. She is represented as St Mary Magdalene in the life-size Calvary. The Duchess occupied a neighbouring later C18 house called The Oaks, used as the convent from 1920. Convent buildings of 1898 are now the Science Dept. of Trinity R.C. School, Mornington Road.

p. 64 UNITED FREE CHURCH, High Elms, W of High Road. Built in 1904 for Woodford Union church, a flourishing congregation formed in 1875 from members of Congregational, Baptist and Methodist churches. Joseph Hocking, who became minister in 1901, insisted on a new church, which was designed in 1904, by the Arts and Crafts architect *Harrison Townsend*. A large and unusual building in a free Byzantine style, boldly detailed, but alas much simplified from Townsend's original designs. Brick with stone banding. W gable with a deep, round-headed arch with stone bands, enclosing a big lunette over two stone doorways. Smaller entrance on the r. in the base of Townsend's unbuilt tower. This was a highly unusual design drawing on symbolic geometric forms: a domed top over an upper part with curved core recessed behind square corner piers. A meeting hall beyond the main church was also planned, but economy prevailed. The church was repaired and remodelled by *Craig Hall & Rutley*, 1991. Inside, the W bay was divided off, with an inserted floor. The impressive main space lies beneath a domical vault supported by broad, unmoulded brick arches with stone bands, springing from marble-faced piers. Shallow transepts and sanctuary with transverse arches. Big lunette windows in the transepts, smaller ones at clerestory level in the sanctuary. Memorial chapel off the S transept by *Michael Farey*, 1963, with abstract window and glass mural by *Laurence Lee*. Of the same time five small ceiling paintings on the main vault, by *Jean Manson Clark*, inadequate in this grand setting. Small alabaster and green marble War Memorial, a delicate tablet.

BROADMEAD BAPTIST CHURCH, Chigwell Road. On this site from 1957. Eyecatching frontage, a foyer with pink-painted, cast-concrete abstract reliefs. Church behind with polygonal roof and glazed lantern. Plain hall at the back.

BANCROFT'S SCHOOL, High Road, Woodford Wells. 1889 by *A. W. Blomfield*; collegiate Tudor on a grand scale. The school, originally in Mile End Road, Tower Hamlets, was part of a foundation of 1728 from the bequest of Francis Bancroft, an official of the City of London, for an almshouse and school for 100 boys, with the Drapers' Company as Trustees. Its original buildings were replaced by the People's Palace.

Red brick with stone dressings. E-facing gatehouse tower

with corner turrets, in the centre of the main classroom range. To the W the range incorporates a cloister, now glazed, overlooking a spacious quadrangle, with dining hall and assembly hall (now Library) in ranges to the N and S. The cloister continues, more simply detailed, in front of the S range. Above the entrance arch facing the quadrangle, inscription and white stone medallion with coat of arms, 1728, the latter rescued from Bancroft's tomb in St Helen, Bishopsgate by *George Dance*, destroyed in 1892. WAR MEMORIAL in the centre of the quadrangle, 1920 by *Sir Reginald Blomfield*. Opposite, off centre, is the chapel, leaving the S side of the court partly open. The plan had originally included both a chapel and a lecture hall, but the present asymmetry provides a pleasantly relaxed touch. Later additions around the edges have tactfully avoided encroaching on the main court, but are consequently in cramped settings: large new Assembly Hall to the NW, 1937 by *E.N. Clifton*, linked by a new cloister past 1960s classrooms; gym and swimming pool behind, 1972. S of the present library, art rooms developed from 1987, science block of 1910 further E. Across the playing fields, 1990s Prep School; two pitched-roof blocks for hall and classrooms.

The long, narrow CHAPEL interior, with pews arranged stallwise, is bleak apart from a dominant STAINED GLASS E window with pictorial scene (Ascension) across five lights, commemorating John Edward Symns, headmaster 1889–1906. The present LIBRARY is a clever conversion, using the upper half of the original assembly hall. Impressive open-timber roof combining all the tricks: arch braces, scissor braces and hammerbeams with pendants. A good roof also in the adjoining computer room (former lecture room): tie-beams and braces.

In front of the entrance tower, iron WAR MEMORIAL GATES, 1950. To the S, the HEADMASTER'S HOUSE, tall and double-gabled in a pleasant Tudor domestic style. To the N a row of tile-hung cottages.

PERAMBULATIONS

1. *From Woodford Station to the Green*

The Eastern Counties Railway line of 1856 cuts across the old route of SNAKES LANE which linked Woodford Green to Woodford Bridge. The level crossing was replaced by a brutal subway; the line was electrified in 1947 and became part of the Central Line. The first STATION, of 1856 remains, a plain two-storey house with bracketed eaves and late Georgian-style windows. Extended 1888, the date also of waiting room and canopy on the down side. New entrance, booking office and canopy on the up side, 1892. 1980s booking hall for London Underground.

To the N, the modest BROADWAY, with two matching PARADES of *c.* 1900, fussily decorated, and a BANK with bowed window. The surrounding roads, e.g. Monkhams Avenue to the N, are archetypal early C20 high-class suburbia: houses in a variety of sedate vernacular styles set in trim gardens.

To the W SNAKES LANE leads toward Woodford Green, formerly a road of Victorian Gothic mansions. Much of the S side was cleared by the council for comprehensive redevelopment from 1966. At the W end of this site is an interesting example of novel planning: ANWORTH CLOSE, an unusual low-rise pedestrian layout with tightly grouped clusters of four butterfly-plan houses, each with distinctive circular window, by *Derek Stow Associates*, 1967. On the N side a discreetly Neo-Georgian Telephone Exchange, 1938, large additions behind.

Around the large GREEN the rural character is still evident despite intermittent efforts to create a suburban centre. The tour proceeds clockwise. The grandest houses lie on the E side. A decorative stuccoed Italianate LODGE in Hart's Grove announces the approach to HARTS, the largest surviving mansion, now a nursing home with housing in the former grounds. The large, plain-stuccoed house is a rebuilding of 1816. Three storeys with recessed centre, the entrance within a six-column one-storey Ionic colonnade with balustrade above. To the garden seven bays with pediment over the central three. An additional bay and extension on the l., on the r. there is a curved link to a low service building. The grounds were famous in the C18 for the botanical garden of Richard Warner (†1775); restored fragments remain from a sham ruined abbey of flint and brick.

BROOMHILL ROAD, S of Snakes Lane, has grand suburban mansions of the 1890s. First the ungainly No. 19 with shaped gables, tall chimneys and belvedere on the roof, then two trim white brick and stone villas of 1893, flanking Glebe Road. No. 34 at the corner of Grange Avenue, in a well-handled Old English style, gabled with a big mullioned stair window at the back, is by the expert in Elizabethan architecture, *J.A. Gotch*, 1894. NEW JUBILEE COURT, housing of 1988, has a plaque of Queen Victoria, reset from the Jubilee hospital built on this site by *J.R. Roberts* in 1897.

HURST HOUSE, Salway Hill, at the S end of Woodford Green, *c.* 1714, is striking from a distance, but much restored. Grand six-bay front with giant Corinthian pilasters and a parapet with vases. The doorway also has Corinthian pilasters, an entablature rising to a point in the middle, a typical early C18 motif, and a big segmental pediment. Wrought-iron garden railing and gates. The interior was much rebuilt after a fire in 1935, but retains its staircase with daintily twisted balusters. Bay windows to the garden. Formerly with outbuildings and later wings, demolished by the 1930s.

On the green opposite, 9ft bronze STATUE of Churchill (M.P. for the area from 1924 to 1964) by *David McFall*, 1959. From here the High Road continues S to South Woodford (*see* above).

Bunce's Lane leads W from the High Road to Woodford New Road, past ST AUBYN'S SCHOOL, formerly Pyrmont House. The school (founded 1884) moved here *c.* 1918. Large N facing C19 stucco villa with two-storey canted bay. Behind, a long plain range, four bays with a further five bays, and later additions. Baronial sytle STABLES of 1890. To the W, up to the corner of Chingford Lane, are the former grounds and C18 mansion of HIGHAMS, now Woodford County High School for Girls (*see* Highams Park, Waltham Forest, p. 722.

Further N the buildings around the green still keep to a village scale. On the S side of JOHNSTON ROAD small POST OFFICE with mullioned windows and busy Edwardian detail. No. 8 is an C18 timber-framed house with weatherboarded upper floor, built as a butcher's shop; pilastered shop-front of *c.* 1840. The W side of the green has an informal mix of shops and pleasant small houses. From S to N: No. 383, late C18, with arched ground-floor windows and rusticated doorway; Nos. 387–9, a pair with shared pediment and blind Venetian window below; then a grander inn, THE CASTLE, three storeys, late Georgian. Stuccoed, with six irregular bays, parapet and canted bay windows. Porch with Doric columns. Opposite, on the Green, No. 352, a suburban interloper, a former MIDLAND BANK, 1920 by *T.B. Whinney*, still in the Midland's pre-First World War Italian Renaissance style; only one storey but given pomp by corner dome and balustraded parapet. Further on traces of a haphazard rural hamlet remain, with No. 403, an C18 five-bay house set at an angle to the road, and more cottages to the W, especially off MILL LANE and around THE SQUARE, where the small-scale character has been preserved by some sympathetic late C20 infilling. In Mill Lane a former temperance coffee house probably converted from a British School. ELM TERRACE, partly stuccoed and a little grander, is dated 1873; HIGH ELMS, three storeys with cornice, looks early C19. Past the United Reformed church (*see* above), WOODFORD GREEN SCHOOL. Gabled one-storey building with lancet windows, built as a National School, 'erected by voluntary subscription 1820'. Taken over by the School Board, enlarged 1889 and later. On the W side of the High Road, Nos. 455–7, shops in an Italianate mode, and No. 449, Harris's, with well-preserved butcher's shop interior, disused.

The landmark at the NE end of the green is a former Methodist Free Church, built in 1869, originally in Gothic style. After Townsend's church was built (*see* above), it was adapted as a MEN'S CLUB and presented in 1904 by the local benefactor J.R. Roberts, 'for the benefit of the inhabitants of the neighbourhood'. The Gothic window was replaced by a roughcast gable wall and balcony, and the spire to the corner tower by a domed cap. Repaired 2004 by *Hibbs & Walsh Associates*.

2. N *of Woodford Green*

WOODFORD WELLS, once a little C18 spa, now has miscellaneous later C19 and early C20 housing. In INMAN'S ROW a few modest, stuccoed houses near All Saints (*see* above). Further N there were scattered mansions on the fringe of Epping Forest. Their large grounds were built up rapidly in the earlier C20. E of the High Road, WOODLAND WAY is a typical road on the KNIGHTON estate, developed from 1931 with spacious houses on the woodland edge. From Knighton House, home of Edward North Buxton, a leading campaigner for Epping Forest, there remains only the consciously picturesque LODGE HOUSE, built after 1866, when Buxton had the main road moved W, away from his house. The lodge is at the corner of THE GLADE opposite Bancroft's School, a thatched cottage, busily detailed with half-timbered gables, latticed windows and diagonal chimneystacks. KNIGHTON WOOD remains to the N. Around Buckhurst Hill, the MONKHAMS estate, owned by Henry Ford Barclay from 1864–91, was built up with cosy half-timbered houses from 1903; the house was demolished in 1930. E of MONKHAM'S LANE, No. 9 PRINCE'S AVENUE is the former bailiff's house, *c.* 1845, stock brick in Regency style, with broad sash windows, a canted bay, and a wide door with arched fanlight.

3. *East of Woodford station*

E of the railway line suburban development is much humbler. SNAKE'S LANE EAST leads from the station to RAY PARK, beside the River Roding and now sadly close to the noisy M11. The municipal park was made from the grounds of an early C19 villa, on an estate of medieval origin. Large polygonal WALLED GARDEN with high brick walls in Flemish bond (now Parks Dept nursery). RAY HOUSE nearby, now pathetic and disused, was much rebuilt in the early C20 after a fire, and used from 1924–58 as Bryant & May's sports club. The three-bay S front looks early C19: castellated, faced in Roman cement, with canted bay windows; another projecting bay to the E. Plain parts behind, with stables and service wing. Within the grounds, now demolished, was Ray Lodge, built 1796–7, an early work by *J.B. Papworth*, for George Wright, son of Sir James Wright of Ray House.

WOODFORD BRIDGE and RAY LODGE SCHOOLS, Snakes Lane East, 1904 by Woodford School Board, are ultra-plain two-storey gabled ranges, the Boys' school in front dignified by red brick, Girls' and Infants' building behind.

WOODFORD BRIDGE

ST PAUL, Manor Road. Nicely set on a sloping green. 1853–4 by *Charles Ainslie* but damaged by fire in 1880 and restored by *W.G. Bartleet & Son*, 1886. Gothic church of ragstone, in a straightforward Early Middle Pointed style. NW tower porch, the steeple with broach spire. Aisled, four-bay nave. Alabaster and mosaic REREDOS; WAR MEMORIAL of the same materials, with figure of St George, 1920. In the S aisle, standing out from the later C19 STAINED GLASS, a delightful roundel in clear glass, the border with tiny animals; 1987 by *Alan Younger.*

Former POLICE STATION, in the fork of Chigwell Road and Manor Road, 1900 by *J. Dixon Butler*, small but carefully detailed, brick with stone dressings to the ground floor bay; upper floor corbelled out, tall chimneys. The entrance has been moved. Tiny outbuilding behind.

ASHTON PARK, Chigwell Road. Playing fields close to the river, made after draining the water meadows, with pavilion and community centre of 1937, a fresh, modern design by *Herbert Welch*: simple rendered walls, octagonal clerestory-lit centre and low wings. Given by H.S. Ashton of Ingatestone 'to encourage the right use of leisure', as is noted on a nicely lettered tablet. A matching one records his death in 1943 and that of his son in 1942.

PERAMBULATIONS

1. *Around the greens*

Woodford Bridge has two linked greens, the upper green with St Paul's church. The red brick CHURCH HALL to its W was built in 1860 as school and schoolhouse. To the S, pleasant gabled pairs of council houses, and THURLBY HOUSE, now flats, the cream-stucco exterior concealing a complicated history, as the irregular window arrangement shows. Five-bay centre perhaps late C18 in origin; given tripartite windows, porch, and W extension in the early C19; a Victorian service wing to the E. Present entrance hall with elegant stair and an Ionic pilaster. Further N on Chigwell Road, a late C19 inn at the borough boundary, THREE JOLLY WHEELERS, red brick above rendered ground floor, the r. end with a Norman Shaw-like oriel.

The village centre is around the lower green at the junction with Manor Road. Two-storey Victorian terraces, dated 1867–8, and the WHITE HART, a coaching inn rebuilt *c.* 1900, quite an elaborate half-timbered effort with three gables. Opposite, a row of older cottages, much altered: Nos. 637–641, 643, 645 (with central stack) and 647–9. Further S along Chigwell Road a Victorian shopping terrace with Gothic upper windows.

2. *North of the greens along Manor Road*

PRINCE REGENT HOTEL, Manor Road. Formerly Gwynne House. 1816 for Henry Burmester by *J.B. Papworth*, a rebuilding of an older house. A restrained Neoclassical front; seven bays, two storeys, with 6 + 6 sashes, low parapet and Greek Doric porch with entablature. The interior much changed *c.* 1980 for hotel use, but a handsome curving top-lit stair remains, its minimal stick balusters typical of *c.* 1800. Garden front with trellis porch. The house was used as a centre for Dr Barnardo's Homes from 1910 to the 1970s (*see also* Barkingside, p. 325). To the E is a substantial hotel extension by *John Brunton Partnership*, on a curve, brick with slated roof, quite tactfully done, with car park below. It forms a link to the former Barnardo's chapel, now hotel bedrooms. This is of 1932 by *W.H. Godfrey*, a long brick building. Stone windows with Perp tracery, prominent flying buttresses above the low aisles. A little stained glass remains in the E windows. The grounds, formerly extensive, were built up with cottage homes for boys, now replaced by housing known as Gwynne Park.

Further uphill, opposite the pond, 'the Cottages', a pair with hipped roof, pastel-blue-painted weatherboarding, and two tiny bay windows, so immaculate that they appear pastiche. GUIDE DOGS LONDON CENTRE, built on part of the Barnardo's site in 1984–6 by *Hanson Rowe & Partners*, is a dark brick monopitch-roofed cluster, discreetly set back. At the top of the green, the mansard-roofed CROWN AND CROOKED BILLET, late C18 in origin.

REPTON PARK, Manor Road. An estate with three layers of history. The park belonged to Claybury Hall, which dates from *c.* 1790; *Humphry Repton* advised on the grounds, one of his many jobs in the area around his home at Hare Street, Romford. He praises the 'profusely beautiful situation' in his Red Book. A century later it was developed for CLAYBURY ASYLUM, a mental hospital designed by *G.T. Hine* in 1887–8, originally for the county of Middlesex, but taken over by the newly formed London County Council. Building took place in

Claybury Asylum (Repton Park), Woodford Bridge, 1889

1890–3, on the flattened-out summit of the hill, to the N of the C18 house, which was adapted for private patients. The new buildings were on a grandly conceived échelon plan, the first of many such plans used for mental asylums. The asylum was designed to accommodate 800 men and 1,200 women, the first to be built for such large numbers, with sexes and types of patient strictly segregated. As was the practice with asylums, the establishment was intended to be self-sufficient, with its own laundry, farm and workshops, and was notable at the time for being entirely lit by electricity. Vast institutions, however enlightened in their planning or impressive in their architectural effect, were not favoured as an approach to mental health by the later C20, and Claybury closed in 1996. The estate was developed for private residential use by Crest Nicholson, 2000–3, converting some of the existing buildings and adding others.

CLAYBURY HALL. Rebuilt 1790–1 by *Jesse Gibson* for James Hatch on a bluff at the S end of the estate, with a spectacular view S. Built of white brick from Woolpit, Suffolk. Simple seven-bay entrance front, two storeys with parapet. Central doorway with fanlight and restored porch with paired columns. The entrance was moved to the N front on *Repton*'s advice. The garden front has a bow window surrounded by a colonnade of Adamish Roman Doric columns. At the side, a well-detailed Venetian window. The interior, damaged in a fire, was restored in 2002. It has a central top-lit stair hall with some Neoclassical plasterwork panels and cornice with paired brackets; a stone cantilevered stair with iron balustrades rises through three storeys. An elaborate cornice and doorcase remain in the Saloon, which extends S into the centre bow.

THE MANOR, a neighbouring range of apartments, laid out on a curve, is by Ripley Homes, 2001.

The échelon plan of the HOSPITAL is still clearly visible, respected by the new development, which has found new uses for many of the buildings. Originally the hospital looked S, approached by a perimeter road which ran from the lodges and entrance on Manor Road. The main access is now from the N along a formal avenue on the site of the service buildings. It leads to the massive WATER TOWER with Gothic detail at the top, and to the grand RECREATIONAL HALL beyond, which has been given a new entrance. This is a building of quality, reflecting the concern at the time to provide amenities for mental patients. Free Jacobean style, the interior with good panelling and frieze, and a magnificent barrel-vaulted elliptical ceiling, its fibrous-plaster panels decorated with geometric panels. At one end is a highly ornate proscenium arch with bust of Shakespeare above. A bold new mezzanine for a gym has been inserted into part of the hall, but without destroying the sense of the total space. Attached to the hall is the CHAPEL, now transformed into a swimming pool. Exterior of red brick, with well-detailed stone dressings: aisled, with a clerestory, and a canted apse with Dec window tracery above a band of arcading. Side turret with stone spire. The elaborate S-facing bay-windowed villas flanking the chapel were for the Medical Superintendent (E) and Administration (W).

Stepping out to l. and r of the central hall is the accommodation for the inmates, now converted to apartments: plain, red brick clusters of three-storey ranges with canted bay windows, designed to provide a maximum amount of S-facing rooms. The extreme E and W ends are each marked by a polygonal tower with steep slate roof rising from a corbelled-out parapet. Lower ranges within the complex accommodated epileptic and chronic patients. The new private housing along the centre tree-lined boulevard echoes the materials of the older buildings, smartened by stuccoed ground floors: formal rows of quite dignified three-storey houses in the form of linked villas with canted bays, hipped roofs and gables. More informal new groups fill the leafier outer areas.

TOWER HAMLETS

The borough created in 1965 adopted an ancient name. In the C16 Tower Hamlets was the term for the suburbs E of the Tower of London which owed military service to the Tower; in 1832 it was used for the much larger new parliamentary constituency.* Much of the area of the present borough lay within the vast medieval parish of Stepney, which stretched from the City fringe to the banks of the River Lea. Stepney (Stebunheath or Stebba's landing) may first have referred to the riverside landing at Ratcliffe, but came to denote the whole medieval parish centred on the church of St Dunstan, N of the river at Stepney Green.

Gascoyne's map of the parish of Stepney, 1703, the first detailed survey, shows a scatter of still distinct settlements. The old Roman road to Essex started in the suburb of Whitechapel, built up and with its own church (the 'white chapel') by the C13. A mile further on, Mile End, until the C19 a select retreat for merchants and gentry, was an extension along the main road from the village to its S at Stepney Green. Further E was Bow, at the crossing over the Lea, and a little to its S was the small village of Bromley which had grown up around a medieval nunnery. Quite distinct from these and separated from them by open land until the C19, were Bethnal Green to the N, and the hamlets along the Thames: Wapping, Ratcliffe, Shadwell, Limehouse and Poplar, linked by a road (the Highway) along the higher ground above the riverside marshes.

In the C16 and C17 the inner suburbs expanded over land once occupied by two major religious houses, the Cistercian St Mary Graces, near the Tower on the site of the later Royal Mint, and a hospital, St Mary Spital, which gave its name to Spitalfields. Their sites are known from excavations (*see* pp. 384, 483) A third, also near the Tower, the Royal Foundation of St Katharine, which remarkably survived the Dissolution, was displaced for St Katharine Docks, though preserved some of its fittings (*see* p. 519). The 'Tower Liberties', E of the Tower of London, later developed as a crowded, insalubrious area with a lawless reputation; in contrast Spitalfields flourished from the later C17 as the centre of the silk weaving industry, encouraged by the skills of Huguenot refugees, one of the successive waves of immigrants to find employment in the area. Spitalfields still has not only some of its C18 houses but also the mighty Christ Church, one of three new Stepney churches designed by *Nicholas Hawksmoor*, as a result of the 1711 Churches Act, part of a campaign to combat the Nonconformity prevalent in the E end. The other Hawksmoor churches were St Anne at Limehouse, and St George-in-the-East,

*The Tower of London lies within Tower Hamlets, but is described in *London I: The City of London*. The parliamentary constituency in addition to the part forming the present borough included Shoreditch and Hackney, now both within the borough of Hackney.

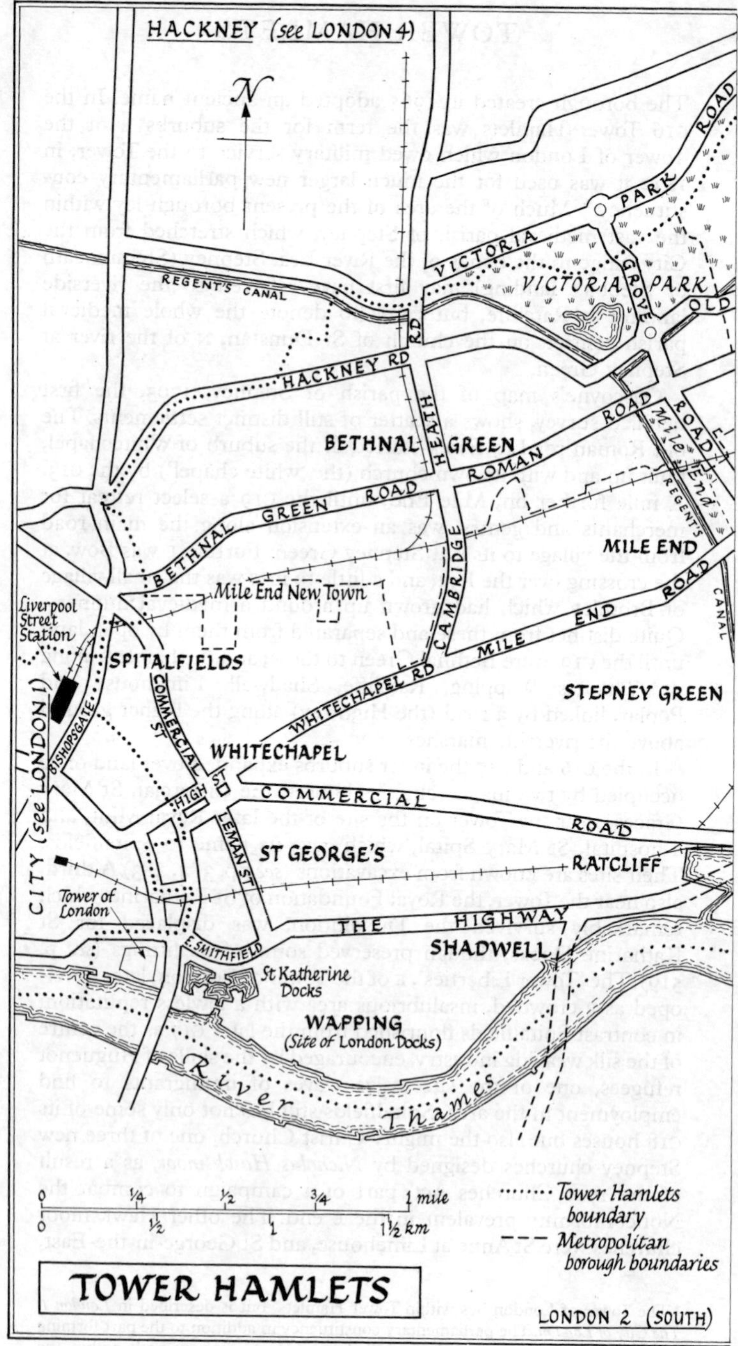
HACKNEY (see LONDON 4)
N
REGENT'S CANAL
VICTORIA PARK ROAD
VICTORIA PARK
GROVE RD
OLD
HACKNEY RD
HEATH
BETHNAL GREEN
ROMAN ROAD
MILE END ROAD
REGENT'S
BETHNAL GREEN ROAD
CAMBRIDGE
MILE END
Mile End New Town
MILE END ROAD
CANAL
Liverpool Street Station
SPITALFIELDS
WHITECHAPEL RD
STEPNEY GREEN
BISHOPSGATE
COMMERCIAL ST
WHITECHAPEL
HIGH ST
COMMERCIAL ROAD
CITY (see LONDON 1)
LEMAN ST
ST GEORGE'S
RATCLIFF
Tower of London
THE HIGHWAY
SHADWELL
E. SMITHFIELD
St Katherine Docks
WAPPING
(Site of London Docks)
River Thames
0 1/4 1/2 3/4 1 mile
0 1/2 1 1 1/2 km
Tower Hamlets boundary
Metropolitan borough boundaries
TOWER HAMLETS
LONDON 2 (SOUTH)

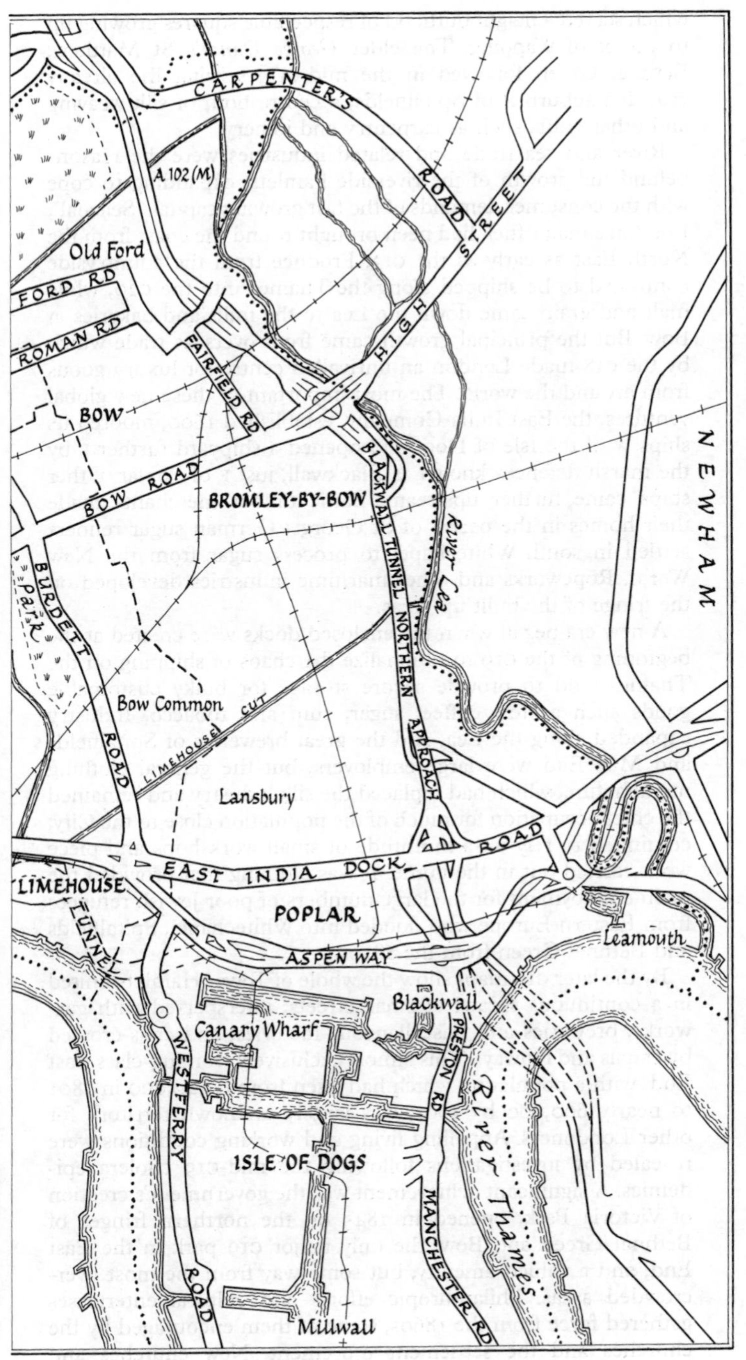
CARPENTER'S ROAD
A 102(M)
HIGH STREET
Old Ford
FORD RD
ROMAN RD
FAIRFIELD RD
BOW
BLACKWALL TUNNEL NORTHERN APPROACH
NEWHAM
BOW ROAD
BROMLEY-BY-BOW
River Lea
BURDETT ROAD
Park
Bow Common
LIMEHOUSE CUT
Lansbury
EAST INDIA DOCK ROAD
LIMEHOUSE
TUNNEL
POPLAR
ASPEN WAY
Leamouth
Blackwall
Canary Wharf
WESTFERRY ROAD
PRESTON RD
River Thames
ISLE OF DOGS
MANCHESTER RD
Millwall

which served a neighbourhood of respectable squares growing up to the N of Wapping. The elder *George Dance*'s St Matthew, Bethnal Green followed in the mid-C18, serving the already crowded suburb N of Spitalfields, a centre both of silk weaving and other crafts such as carpentry and joinery.

River and sea trade and related industries were the reasons behind the growth of the riverside hamlets, expanding to cope with the consumer demands of the fast growing capital. 'Seacoal', London's major fuel, had been brought round the coast from the North East as early as the C13. Produce from the countryside continued to be shipped along the Thames into the C20, while malt and grain came down the Lea to the mills and bakeries at Bow. But the principal growth came from overseas trade which by the C18 made London an unrivalled centre for luxury goods from around the world. The most important of these new global ventures, the East India Company, established 1600, moored its ships W of the Isle of Dogs and opened a shipyard further E by the marsh defences known as Blackwall, just E of Poplar. Other ships came further upstream. Baltic timber merchants made their homes in the parish of St George; German sugar refiners settled in south Whitechapel to process sugar from the New World. Ropeworks and other maritime industries developed on the fringe of the built up areas.

A new era began when the enclosed docks were created at the beginning of the C19 to rationalize the chaos of shipping on the Thames, and to provide secure storage for bulky customable goods such as tea, coffee, sugar, rum and tobacco. Industry expanded along the Lea, and the great breweries of Spitalfields and Mile End were large employers, but the general clothing manufacture, which had replaced the silk industry and remained the chief occupation for much of the population close to the City, continued to rely on a multitude of small workshops and piece work carried out in the home. It was clothing that provided the main employment for the large numbers of poor Jewish refugees from Eastern Europe who flooded into Whitechapel, Spitalfields and Bethnal Green from the 1870s.

By the later C19 maps show the whole of Tower Hamlets united in a continuous sprawl of small streets, interspersed with gasworks, breweries and miscellaneous factories, and criss-crossed by canals and railways. This almost exclusively working-class East End, with a population which had risen from *c.* 142,000 in 1801 to nearly 600,000 by 1901, was largely unknown territory for other Londoners. Appalling living and working conditions were revealed by investigations following the mid-C19 cholera epidemics. A significant achievement was the government's creation of Victoria Park, opened in 1845 on the northern fringes of Bethnal Green and Bow, the only major C19 park in the East End, and a valued amenity, but some way from the most overcrowded areas. Philanthropic efforts and cultural enterprises gathered force from the 1860s, some of them encouraged by the churches and the settlement movement. New churches and chapels sprang up and numerous synagogues in the Jewish areas.

Tenements of improved housing began to replace the worst terrace houses and slum courts, with attention focused on the overcrowded riverside areas, but effective provision of better living conditions started only towards the end of the C19, galvanized by the publicity generated by Andrew Mearns' *Bitter Cry of Outcast London* (1883), with its passionate account of slum life.

The old hamlets were grouped into three metropolitan boroughs in 1899: Bethnal Green became a borough in its own right, Poplar embraced not only the old hamlet, including the Isle of Dogs, but also the parishes of Bow and Bromley to its N, the rest fell within the new borough of Stepney. They formed the easternmost of the boroughs within the area of the London County Council, created in 1888. Bethnal Green soon built its own Town Hall, Poplar followed in the 1930s but Stepney's grand plans remained unrealized.*

The youthful LCC, energetic and idealistic, and with greater resources than the boroughs, took the lead in providing new housing, starting with the replacement of a notorious set of slums at Bethnal Green by the exemplary Boundary Street Estate. After the Second World War the existing slum clearance programme was combined with radical reconstruction after extensive war damage following the principles outlined in *Forshaw & Abercrombie*'s County of London Plan of 1943 (*see* p. 89).

By the 1970s, as elsewhere in Britain, disillusion with comprehensive development had set in, and the remaining fragments of an older, livelier East End came to be valued. Saving the C18 houses of Spitalfields became a much publicized conservation campaign and elsewhere refurbishment of surviving C19 terraces gradually became official policy. Housing as well as warehouses and workshops left empty by retreating industry were converted for artists,† before price rises put them out of reach of all but the rich. New housing once again respected the older street pattern, often in modern versions of the vernacular stock brick terrace. Although the population had declined the need for housing did not disappear, for the East End, ever fluid and volatile, continued to attract immigrants, notably the Bangladeshis who settled in Spitalfields from the 1970s. After the demise of the GLC in 1986 responsibility for housing (and for other matters such as schools) passed to Tower Hamlets. Bleaker mid-century flats were modernized and smartened up, often to unrecognizable effect, by new private owners or a variety of housing agencies.

Late C20 concern with environmental improvements was manifested in other ways. The Liberal Democrats, in power in the 1980s, introduced neighbourhood authorities which

*The Town Hall appears in a formal Beaux Arts plan by *T.H. Mawson* for rebuilding of Stepney with a major E–W boulevard, on the line of Cable Street, called Stepney Greeting (see *The Builder*, 1919) and a big civic centre marked by a tall campanile.

†Assisted by such organisations as SPACE (founded 1968) and ACME (founded 1972).

encouraged the distinctiveness of different areas by a diversity of street embellishments. Government funding became available to improve the open spaces which had been part of the post-war vision: footpaths were opened up along waterways now largely clear of noxious industry, and Mile End Park, envisaged in the post-war plans, was completed as a grand millennial project, a green swathe linking the Thames riverside to Victoria Park.

Later C20 developments of this kind were not unique to Tower Hamlets, but what gave them special motivation and publicity, and in some cases provided additional funding, was the concurrent transformation of what became known as Docklands (*see* p. 102). Post-war rebuilding had not envisaged the closure of the docks, but it was this that provoked the most eye-catching changes of the later C20. The London Docklands Development Corporation, created in 1981, was responsible for providing a new infrastructure. The 'Enterprise Zone' on the Isle of Dogs, in existence from 1982–92, encouraged investors by simplifying planning procedures. The West India Docks were transformed as Canary Wharf developed with office towers for international business, set in an imaginative new land- and waterscape, challenging the commercial hegemony of the City of London. Private housing followed along the abandoned wharves and industrial sites by the river. Improved transport suddenly made the area attractively accessible (Docklands Light Railway, 1987, extended 1991 and 2004–5, City Airport 1987, Jubilee Line 1998).

For many Canary Wharf appeared an interloper which had little to do with the life of the rest of the borough. With improved transport and a wider range of jobs, a broader social mix is becoming evident in other areas, though in 1998 Tower Hamlets was still ranked as the sixth most deprived district in England. The long tradition of lively cultural diversity continues (ethnic minority groups account for 46 per cent of the population of 181,300), reflected in the variety of places of worship and social centres. Further change is under way: City offices are ruthlessly intruding into Spitalfields and Whitechapel, while regeneration projects for the Lea Valley, a spearhead of eastward-looking Thames Gateway schemes, are starting to transform the desolate aftermath of retreating industry.

SPITALFIELDS AND WHITECHAPEL

INTRODUCTION

Whitechapel developed as a medieval suburb on the E fringe of the City, deriving its name from a stone chapel first recorded in the C13, which lay beside the main road to Essex. By the late C17 the area had *c.* 3000 houses and had begun to be settled by Jewish immigrants. The wealthier houses lay to the S of the High Street around Leman Street. Spitalfields, further N, stretching from the eastern fringe of the City to Brick Lane, referred to the fields belonging to the hospital of St Mary, which was attached to a house of Augustinian canons just to the E of Bishopsgate, founded in 1197 by Walter and Rose Brown, and refounded in 1235, when the buildings were rebuilt on a larger scale. The foundations of the hospital were uncovered in excavations in the 1990s. The church was aisled, with an eastern Lady Chapel added *c.* 1400; the C13 infirmary, also aisled, adjoined it at right angles (cf. St John Canterbury). It was adapted for chantry chapels after a new two storey infirmary was added to the W *c.* 1280. By the C14 there was a series of buildings around several cloisters or courts, as well as almshouses along Bishopsgate. According to Stow, when the hospital was closed in 1538 it had 180 beds for the poor. Discoveries in the large churchyard to the S confirmed Stow's account of Spital Cross, which survived the Reformation and was rebuilt as an outdoor pulpit in 1594, continuing in use for annual sermons attended by the Lord Mayor and his retinue. They were accommodated in a 'fair built house' which lay against a charnel chapel built *c.* 1391. Remarkably, the

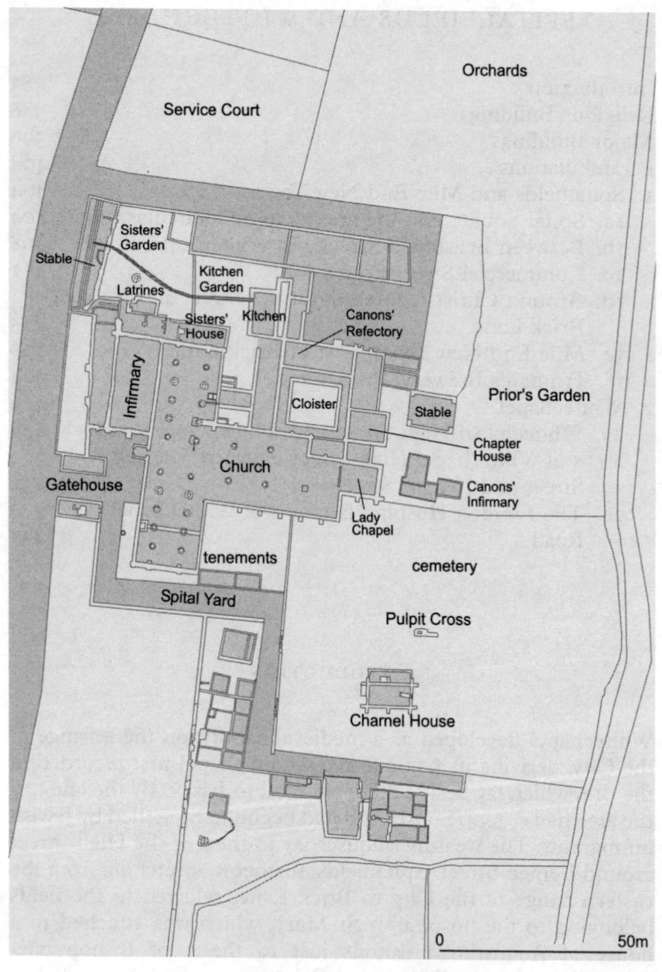

St Mary Spital, plan of church and precinct as excavated in the 1990s

walls of the undercroft of this chapel survived, with springers for a stone vault reusing C12 ribs. The building is preserved in a basement below the offices built on the site in 2004, its W end visible in an area reached by steps from Bishops square.

In the C16 and C17 Spitalfields became a fashionable address, close to the City yet outside it, comparable to the former monastic precincts of Clerkenwell. The buildings of the priory were adapted, the suburb expanded and a market was established in 1682 to the S of the hospital site. The part of the precinct which lay S of this was leased to the Guild of Artillery, enclosed by a wall, and used as a practice ground by archers and gunners. The

Artillery Ground was built up after 1682, when a building licence was granted to associates of Nicholas Barbon. The enclave of new streets was approached at first only via Artillery Lane, until Brushfield Street (then called Union Street) was extended W to Bishopsgate in 1784–5.

Spitalfields was never a purely domestic suburb: the area flourished as a centre of high quality silk weaving, introduced here in the early C17 and strengthened by Huguenot refugees who had fled from France after 1685. By 1700 there were nine Huguenot churches in Spitalfields, and a charity called La Soupe to help poor families. The early cottages have gone, but the prosperity of the area by the C18 can be seen from the handsome early Georgian houses which were developed in the streets around the market. A monumental centrepiece was provided by Hawksmoor's Christ Church, built as a counter-offensive to the Nonconformity prevalent in the area. E of Brick Lane more scrappy development took place from the C17, in the area which became known as Mile End New Town. Further E, S of Whitechapel Road, the London Hospital was established in 1750, and modest but respectable suburban development sprang up around it. To the S the area around Leman and Alie Streets enjoyed a fashion in C18 London society for its theatres, which were unrestricted by the censorship of the West End.

By the C19 silkweaving could not compete with foreign imports and factory processes elsewhere, the industry fell on hard times, many of the larger houses were subdivided or multi-occupied. The weaving lofts in the attics which are such a celebrated feature of some of the C18 Spitalfields houses probably date from this period of decline. Commercial Street was cut through from the 1840s to provide a route to the Docks and S of Whitechapel High Street the smart enclave of the C17 and C18 became increasingly industrial. The area continued to attract immigrants; two surviving German churches in this area testify to the German community whose speciality was sugar refining. In the C19 this activity gave way to warehousing, especially after the arrival of railways linked to the docks.

By the later C19 both Spitalfields and Whitechapel had sunk into extremes of destitution and overcrowding, following the later C19 influx of Ashkenazi Jewish refugees from eastern Europe. Around Artillery Lane a population of 2,516 people in 176 houses was recorded in 1881. The clothing trade dominated, dependant on sweated labour in small workshops, although there were many other industries, including tobacco works, breweries and engineering. The poverty-stricken streets and alleys became a prime focus for Victorian philanthropic endeavour, galvanized by the indefatigable Canon Samuel Barnett of St Jude's Whitechapel, founder of Toynbee Hall and Whitechapel Art Gallery. Some of the evidence can still be seen: model housing, churches and synagogues, clubs and soup kitchens, built in attempts to alleviate the lot of the poor.

Whitechapel was drastically affected by bomb damage in the Second World War and the part S of the High Street and

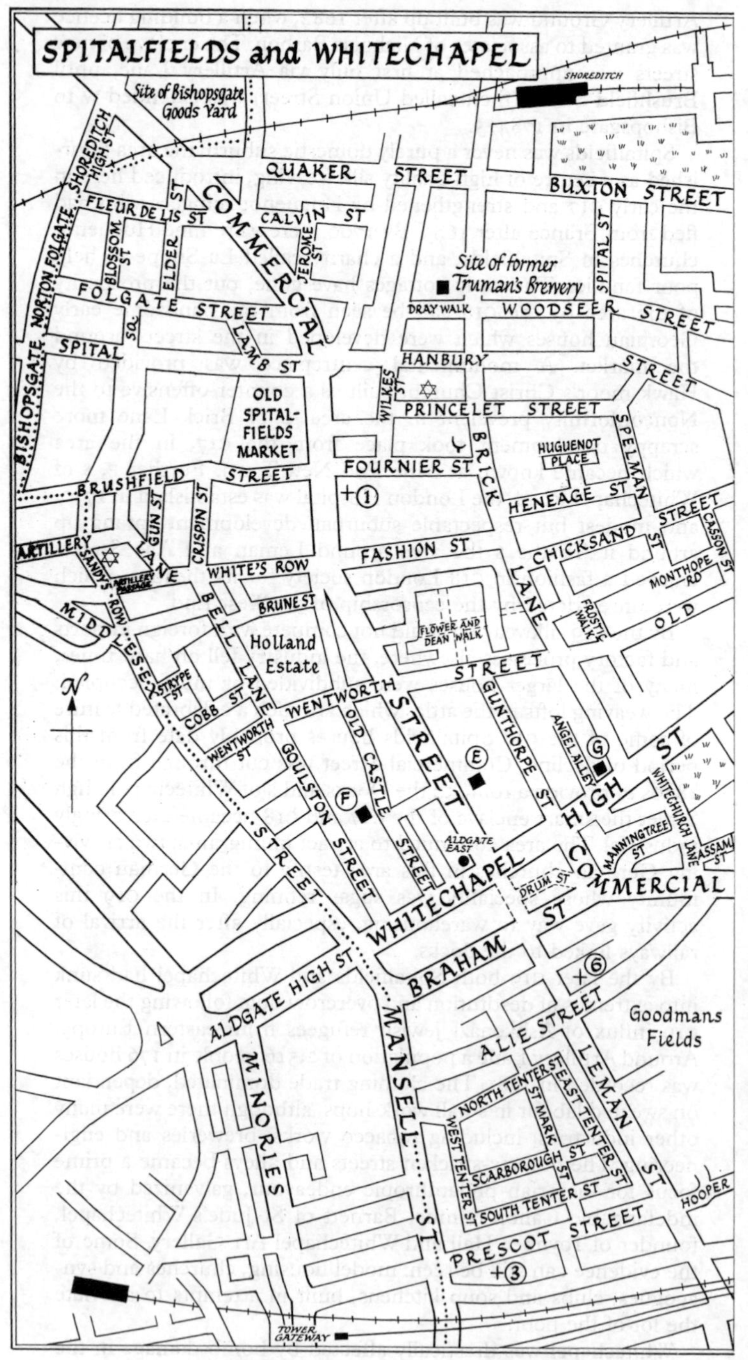

SPITALFIELDS and WHITECHAPEL
SHOREDITCH
Site of Bishopsgate Goods Yard
SHOREDITCH HIGH ST
QUAKER STREET
BUXTON STREET
FLEUR DE LIS ST
COMMERCIAL
CALVIN ST
NORTON FOLGATE
BLOSSOM ST
ELDER ST
JEROME ST
Site of former Truman's Brewery
SPITAL ST
FOLGATE STREET
SQ.
DRAY WALK
WOODSEER STREET
BISHOPSGATE
SPITAL
LAMB ST
HANBURY STREET
OLD SPITALFIELDS MARKET
WILKES ST
PRINCELET STREET
BRICK
HUGUENOT PLACE
SPELMAN
FOURNIER ST
BRUSHFIELD STREET
HENEAGE ST
STREET
CASSON ST
ARTILLERY
GUN ST
CRISPIN ST
FASHION ST
CHICKSAND
LANE
SANDY'S ROW
ARTILLERY PASSAGE
WHITE'S ROW
MONTHOPE RD
MIDDLESEX
BELL LANE
BRUNE ST
FLOWER AND DEAN WALK
FROSTIC WALK
OLD
Holland Estate
STREET
N
STRYPE ST
COBB ST
WENTWORTH
WENTWORTH ST
OLD CASTLE
GUNTHORPE
ANGEL ALLEY
GOULSTON
STREET
HIGH ST
WHITECHURCH LANE
ALDGATE EAST
MANNINGTREE ST
ASSAM ST
WHITECHAPEL
DRUM ST
COMMERCIAL
ST
BRAHAM
ALDGATE HIGH ST
ALIE STREET
Goodmans Fields
MINORIES
MANSELL
NORTH TENTER ST
EAST TENTER ST
ST MARK ST
LEMAN
WEST TENTER ST
SCARBOROUGH ST
SOUTH TENTER ST
HOOPER
PRESCOT STREET
TOWER GATEWAY

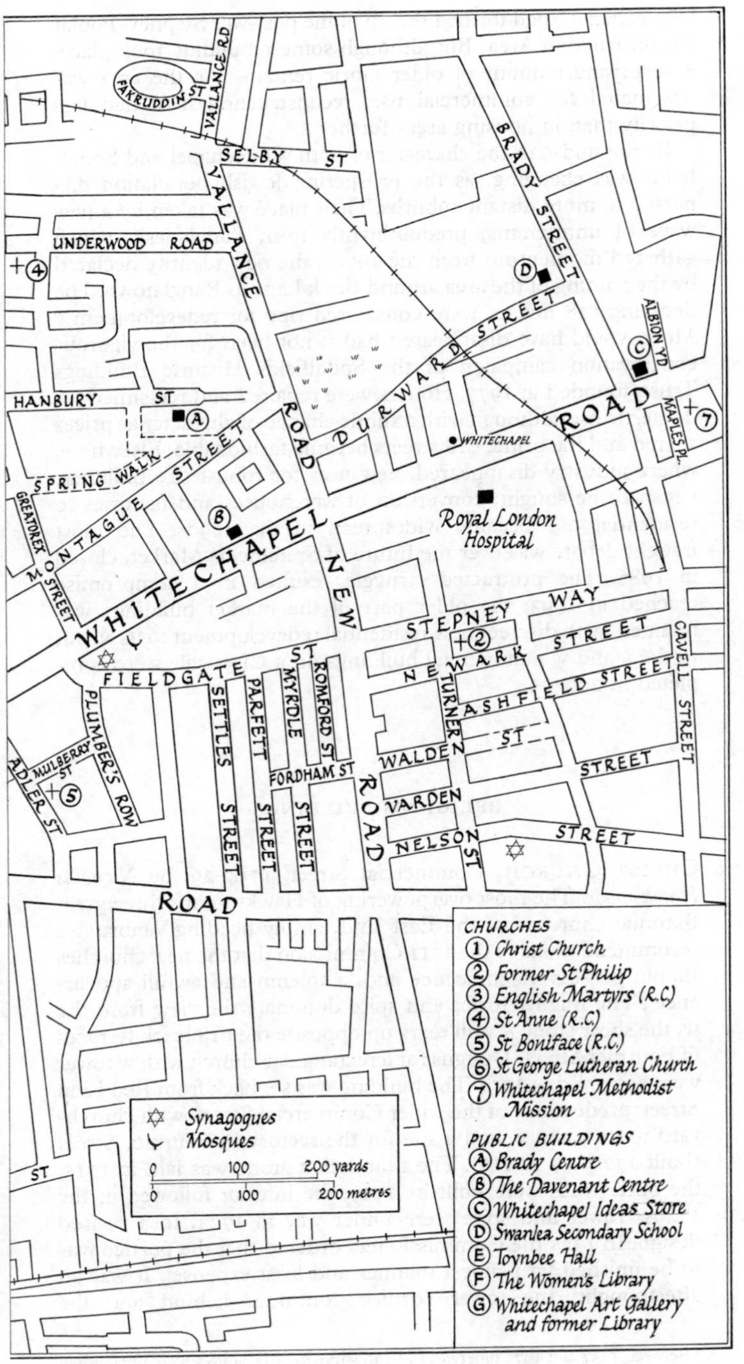
FAKRUDDIN ST
VALLANCE RD
SELBY ST
BRADY STREET
UNDERWOOD ROAD
VALLANCE ROAD
DURWARD STREET
ALBION YD
HANBURY ST
WHITECHAPEL
ROAD
MAPLES PL.
SPRING WALK
STREET
GREATOREX STREET
MONTAGUE STREET
WHITECHAPEL
Royal London Hospital
NEW ROAD
STEPNEY WAY
NEWARK STREET
CAVELL STREET
FIELDGATE ST
SETTLES STREET
PARFETT STREET
MYRDLE STREET
ROMFORD ST
TURNER ST
ASHFIELD STREET
ST
WALDEN STREET
FORDHAM ST
MULBERRY ST
PLUMBER'S ROW
ADLER ST
VARDEN STREET
NELSON ST
ROAD
ST
Synagogues
Mosques
0 100 200 yards
0 100 200 metres
CHURCHES
1 Christ Church
2 Former St Philip
3 English Martyrs (R.C.)
4 St Anne (R.C.)
5 St Boniface (R.C.)
6 St George Lutheran Church
7 Whitechapel Methodist Mission
PUBLIC BUILDINGS
A Brady Centre
B The Davenant Centre
C Whitechapel Ideas Store
D Swanlea Secondary School
E Toynbee Hall
F The Women's Library
G Whitechapel Art Gallery and former Library

Whitechapel Road formed the tip of the post-war Stepney–Poplar Reconstruction Area. But although some rebuilding took place, a surprising amount of older fabric remains. As the area was designated for commercial use, reconstruction here had less priority than in housing areas further E.

By the mid-C20 the character of both Whitechapel and Spitalfields was changing, as the prospering Jewish population dispersed to more distant suburbs. Their place was taken by a new wave of immigrants, predominantly from Bangladesh, which gathered momentum from the 1970s; the new identity declared by the naming of the area around Brick Lane as Banglatown. The decaying C18 houses were considered ripe for redevelopment.* More would have disappeared had it not been for the vigorous conservation campaign of the Spitalfields Historic Buildings Trust, founded in 1977. Houses were repaired and reclaimed for domestic use, although with a subtle change of character as prices soared and the prime C18 streets became fashionable. Elsewhere, where industry disappeared, new uses for robust C19 buildings began to be sought; conversion of warehouses and factories to residential use became widespread in the 1990s. The most fraught debate was over the future of Spitalfields Market, closed in 1986. The protracted struggle resulted in a compromise reached in 1993; the older part of the market buildings was retained, with discreet new residential redevelopment to its N; but to the S and W commercial buildings on a City scale were completed in 2004–5.

RELIGIOUS BUILDINGS

16 CHRIST CHURCH, Commercial Street. 1714–29, by *Nicholas Hawksmoor*. The most overpowering of Hawksmoor's three great Baroque churches of the East End, amply heeding Vanbrugh's recommendations to the 1711 Commission that the new churches should possess magnificence and 'a solemn and awfull appearance'. The mighty tower and spire dominate the view from the W, the sheer stone N wall rears up opposite the C18 brick terraces of Fournier Street. Designs for a rectangular church with W tower were approved in 1714. The building was set back from Red Lion Street, predecessor of the wider Commercial Street, with churchyard to its S and E, and a site for the rectory in Fournier Street (built 1726, *see* p. 416). The foundation stone was laid in 1715, the outer walls were built by 1719, the interior followed in the 1720s. Tower and spire were under way in 1724, to a revised design. In 1725 the Commissioners ordered that the portico was to be finished 'in plainest manner and least expense'. It was an afterthought: the tower cornice continues behind and the

*Between 1957 and 1975 ninety out of 230 surviving C18 houses were demolished (M. Girouard, *Huguenot Soc. Proc.* 23, 1980).

pilasters were cut back for the portico. The church was ready for consecration in 1729. The principal craftsmen were *Thomas Dunn*, mason, *James Grove* and *Samuel Worrall*, carpenters, *Isaac Mansfield*, plasterer, *Thomas Derby* and *Gervas Smith*, carvers.

The spire was stripped of its ornament in 1822–3 and the proportions of the interior were drastically changed by *Ewan Christian*'s removal of the galleries and box pews, and alterations to the windows in 1851 and 1866. The church was closed as unsafe in 1958. The crypt was converted by the Spitalfields Crypt Trust in 1966, but a major restoration programme began only in 1976, inaugurated by the Friends of Christ Church, coinciding with the start of the Spitalfields conservation campaign. Exterior work was completed in 2000, restoring S entrance and N and S windows to their original form, the interior, with replacement of the galleries, was completed in 2004.

The project architect throughout was *Red Mason* (for *Whitfield Partners* to 2001, then *Purcell Miller Tritton*). Completion became a reality after major Heritage Lottery funding was granted from 1996.

EXTERIOR. The W tower rises behind the oddest of porticoes. It is approached up steps, to allow for the crypt beneath, and consists of four Tuscan columns, the outer ones carrying a straight entablature, the inner ones a semicircular arch. It is a bolder version of the Roman *Serliana* motif of St Alfege Greenwich, transforming the Venetian-window shape into a monumental statement, made the more severe by the choice of the plain Tuscan order (the only example among Hawksmoor's London churches). It was Hawksmoor's own eccentric alternative to the pedimented temple front that was becoming the accepted form for London churches of the 1720s. The tower is even stranger. Seen from the W, it is a structure of stupendous width, exactly as wide as the four-column portico. From the front the effect is of a triumphal arch raised up on high, with central opening breaking through a heavy cornice, flanked by arched niches, but the side views show that this broad tower front is a sham, gained by especially deep buttresses which project to N and S. In a most Baroque manner, on N, S and E sides they curve back to form concave hollows with windows set in. Above is a smaller stage, with an arched window on each side (clock added 1866) then from a base with a row of arcading rises a decidedly medieval-looking broach spire; the total height is 225 ft. 'Ugly' was Pevsner's verdict on both tower and portico 'in spite of all one's admiration for Hawksmoor's originality'. The present smooth profile of the tower was not Hawksmoor's intention. Until 1822 the outline was enlivened by a classical finial, crockets and small dormer windows, uniting classical and medieval precedent. The railings which curve out in front of the portico are late C20, devised to compensate for the loss of the forecourt.

The monumental body of the church is of smooth ashlar brusquely punched by openings. Most are entirely unmoulded or have the plainest of bands. N and S walls have two rows of windows within blind arches with big triple keystones, with oculi above, below a heavy dentilled cornice. On the S side, facing the churchyard, Hawksmoor's favourite device of a cross-axis is expressed by the slight projection of the central five bays, with doorway approached by a double stair. Here the flanking windows are given moulded sills and aprons. A corresponding N doorway was removed in 1743 when Fournier Street was extended W. The E wall is plainer; the advanced centre has a Venetian window, with large lunette above the cornice, flanked by two small-arched sacristy windows, with porthole windows above. At the corners the aisle walls are terminated by giant Doric pilasters.

17 INTERIOR. After the austere exterior the interior is richly theatrical, and since its restoration, the best church to appreciate Hawksmoor's original intentions. The nave is entered from a low vaulted vestibule beneath the tower. On either side is a majestic five-bay arcade with tall Composite columns on high bases (to allow for box pews), the arches springing from individual fragments of entablature. It is well lit by a clerestory, with a flat ceiling divided in a grid plan. The three central bays are defined by clustered corner piers, and enriched by elaborately coffered transverse barrel vaults over the aisles, emphasizing cross-axis created by the S door. The chancel is separated by a straight architrave carried right across from N to S, supported by the last aisle columns and two more free-standing columns forming a screen. Hawksmoor was aware of contemporary theological interest in the evidence for such screens in Early Christian churches. Behind this giant screen is one further bay and then the narrower chancel with its large Venetian window. The space on either side of the chancel is filled by sacristies and (formerly) stairs to the galleries. The W end has a similar motif, but the architrave is not carried right over. The galleries, restored in 2000–4, are set back from the columns, each level lit by its own aisle window. The 5-ft thick walls are of brick behind their outer stone skin. The W galleries

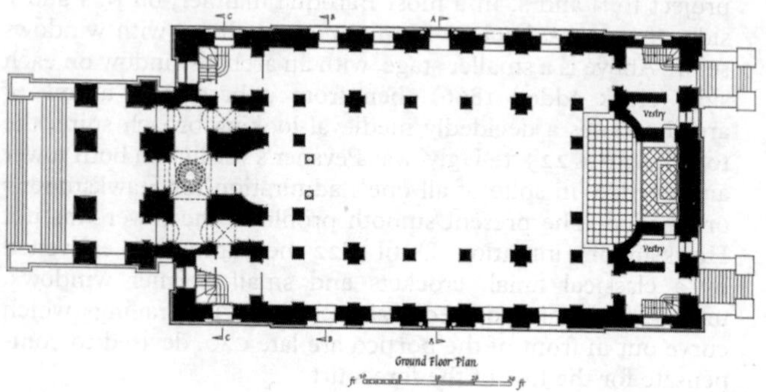

Christ Church, Spitalfields, plan

have a complicated history. In the centre is the ORGAN, in a magnificent case, by *Robert Bridge*, installed 1735 on a W gallery probably enlarged for the purpose, supported on two fluted-timber Corinthian columns. There were originally small balustraded upper galleries on either side. The lower W galleries were added by Christian, using old material. A deep niche with a door to the vestry room, now blocked by the organ, suggests that early plans intended the organ to be placed elsewhere.

FURNISHINGS. Stone FONT, rectangular shaft, oval bowl with gadrooning. – Another FONT, later and more classical, also oval, from the Jewish Episcopal Chapel in Palestine Place, Bethnal Green. – PULPIT, the former reading desk; curved front, with exquisite pierced scroll and foliage carving, and a large sounding board. – Fine COMMUNION RAIL of wrought iron with pilasters and scrollwork. – ROYAL ARMS. Over the E screen, by *William Croggan*, of *Coade* stone, *c*. 1822. – In the chancel, fragments of C19 decoration, with marbled walls, and STAINED GLASS. E window of 1876 by *Ward & Hughes*.

MONUMENTS. Two prominent monuments flank the entrance to the chancel: Edward Peck †1736, by *Thomas Dunn* (the chief mason of the church), standing wall monument with bust on sarcophagus and cherubs l. and r. Peck laid the foundation stone and was the vestry member most active in promoting the church. – Sir Robert Ladbroke, by *Flaxman*, 1794. Standing wall monument, with free-standing statue in robes. Sir Robert had been Lord Mayor of London and president of Christ's Hospital. In the vestibule, ten tablets commemorating members of the London Society for Promoting Christianity among the Jews, brought here in 1895 from the Episcopal Jews Chapel.

Sturdy staircases on either side of the entrance lobby, with urn balusters and square newels, lead to the VESTRY ROOM on the first floor of the tower, a fine space with barrel-vaulted ends, and a plaster wreath around the central bell hole. A fireplace at each end, charity board above the N one. Below the church, the CRYPT, the E part converted and subdivided in 1966. Originally approached by doors below the N and S doors. Below the centre of the nave a row of square piers. Despite the original intention of the 1711 Act that intramural burials should not be allowed, burials took place from 1729–1857, and the vaults below the tower were also divided up for this purpose. In preparation for conversion of the W crypt, excavations in 1984–6 removed 983 burials whose analysis revealed an exceptional quantity of information about Spitalfields inhabitants.

CHURCHYARD. S of the church. Until the later C19 this stretched E as far as Brick Lane. It was enlarged in 1791 and in 1859 when it was extended W to Commercial Street, closed for burials and made into a garden. The outdoor pulpit on the S wall of the portico dates from 1899. Most monuments were removed in 1950.

Former ST PHILIP, Newark Street. By *Arthur Cawston* 1888–92, made redundant in 1979 but sensitively converted in 1988 as the London Hospital's Medical School library by *Fenner & Sibley*, who restored the exterior and adapted the Chapter House for office space. Refined, C13 Gothic, in bright orange brick with stone dressings. Improbably large and magnificent for an East End parish church, even though the intended W tower was not completed. Commissioned by the Rev. Sidney Vacher to replace an unsatisfactory church of 1818–23 by *John Walters*. A lofty nave, in the spirit of Pearson, whom Cawston admired. On a cathedral scale with triforium and clerestory, double aisles to N and S with quadripartite vaults carried on quatrefoil piers with plain moulded capitals. Huge transepts and apsed choir with ambulatory, all in buff London stocks. Clustered piers at the crossing and soaring vaults of brick with stone ribs. W baptistery, organ loft and deep crypt. Eight STAINED GLASS windows, on medical themes, by *Johannes Schreiter* commissioned in 1996. Lift tower, by *Surface Architects*, 2004, dramatically placed at the centre of the crossing. Stainless steel, etched to resemble slate.

ENGLISH MARTYRS (R.C.), Prescot Street, 1875–6 by *Pugin & Pugin* (begun by *Edward Pugin* †1875, completed by his brothers), for the mission of oblates of St Mary Immaculate who came to Tower Hill in 1865. Tall street front, striped brick and stone; an octagonal turret with spire on the l., balanced by a r. buttress. Eclectic Gothic tracery, French rather than Perp, above a double entrance. Over the doors C20 mosaics by *Arthur Fleischmann*. Inside the flat E end with big Gothic window is an inset polygonal apse, with a triplet of arches under gables. Transepts, each with a rose window. The constricted site enforced a short nave, supplemented by galleries on stumpy polished-granite columns with lush foliage; the aisles have depressed arches and low, flat ceilings, but the upper areas are spacious and dignified, with rib vaults to the galleries and extra lighting from a clerestory. Rich FURNISHINGS. The final addition was the High Altar by *J.S. Gilbert*, 1930, designed as a shrine to the English Martyrs; wrought-iron grilles, corbelled tabernacles with statues to l. and r. – Older carved altars: Sacred Heart (N); Pentecost, especially elaborate (S). – Off the N transept, apsed chapel with the shrine to Our Lady of Graces, given by Susanna Rachel Walker †1883. Above the carved alabaster altar, and lit from behind to theatrical effect, is a white-marble statue of the Virgin by *Boulton*, surrounded by angels, within a grotto-like setting. Later mosaics by *Arthur Fleischmann*. – STAINED GLASS. E window with Crucifixion and martyrs, a fine display of richly coloured glass, 1930 by *William Earley* of Dublin. The deep red and yellow mosaic glass and small roundels in the side chapel roses are of the same time, but funds allowed for only a dull floral design in the S transept. In the nave, stone and alabaster MEMORIAL to Father Robert Cooke, †1882, founder of the mission.

ST ANNE (R.C.), Underwood Road. A stone group in grey Kentish rag, once among the crowded streets of Mile End New Town, now in an entirely later C20 setting. The church is successor to one built in 1848 for Irish immigrants, served by French Marist Fathers from 1850. By *Gilbert Blount*; nave 1853–5, apsed E end completed 1894 to a less ambitious plan, omitting Blount's intended transepts and crossing tower with steeple. The W end has a rose above a triple gable, W doorway with capitals left uncarved. Within is an impressive, seriously Gothic interior. Five-bay nave with clustered columns with well-carved foliage capitals; steeply pointed multi-moulded arches with angel headstops; clerestory below a tall arch-braced roof with two sets of wind-braces, the principals on corbels with musical angels. The carving is by *Farmer & Brindley*. The aisles have paired lancets with rere-arches on slim colonnettes; below are groups of three arches for confessionals neatly tucked between the buttresses. After this accomplished richness the E end is weak, with thin-plaster rib vaults to apse and side chapels. HIGH ALTAR, marble reredos with gabled niches, 1901 by *Edmund Sharp* of Dublin to designs by Rev. *M.J. Watters*. In front, altar with arcaded brass frontal. In the Lady Chapel (S), stencilled Ms on the S wall, all that remains of a more elaborate scheme by *Joseph A. Pippet* of 1904. STAINED GLASS was largely destroyed in the war. Two windows in the N aisle; S aisle, to Mary Potter †1913, founder of the Little Company of Mary, showing a local scene, 1952 by *Goddard & Gibbs*. 47

To the E a substantial gabled PRESBYTERY with mullioned windows.

ST BONIFACE German Church (R.C.), Adler Street. Planned 1957, built 1959–60, replacing a church of 1875 destroyed in the war. The new church reflects the influence of its initiator, Father Felix Leuschacke, advised by *T. Hermanns* of Cleve; the architects were *D. Plaskett Marshall & Partners*. Leuschacke wanted a discreet building, but the desire to reuse the old bells resulted in a tall, slim tower, an arresting sight when seen across the former churchyard of St Mary Whitechapel. Its austere modern form looks as if it could have strayed from Berlin's post-war Hansaviertel. Rectangular with the top cut away as a bell cage. The church is a straightforward portal frame faced in silver-grey bricks with shallow-pitched copper roof rising behind a lower 'westwork' clad in mosaic, with a pattern of tiny windows with coloured glass. Tall, light interior, with bands of windows under the eaves, and a glazed W gable rising above the W choir gallery. White plastered walls set off carefully chosen fittings. Along the gallery front, STATIONS OF THE CROSS, Oberammergau work of 1912 from the old church, restored (with three replacements) by the original workshop, *Lang-selige-Erben*. – STATUE of Virgin and Child, modern copy of a late Gothic Rhineland figure, Leuschacke's only other concession to tradition. – ALTAR and FONT of dark-green marble, the font of rounded triangle shape. – Bronze FONT COVER, *c.* 1976. – Sturdy TABERNACLE decorated with beaten copper and silver emblems and rock crystals, by *Paul van Oyen*. – ALTARCROSS and CANDLESTICKS by *Willi Polders*. – On the blank E wall above the altar, sgraffito MURAL in coloured and textured plaster, by *Heribert Reul* of Kevelaer, Christ in Glory with St Boniface, somewhat Romanesque in inspiration. – Unusual WROUGHT IRONWORK by *Reginald Lloyd* of Bideford with subjects in outline: screen to SE gallery with Marriage of Cana; Communion rails (now against E wall) with religious symbols. – Also by Lloyd the STAINED GLASS in the W gable, Pentecost, in vivid red, blue and yellow. – In the foyer, bronze TABLET by *Joseph Welling*, to the association of the church with the Pallotine brothers from 1903–96; reliefs of their founder and two churches.

Small brick-faced MANSE attached to the S. Adjacent in Mulberry Street is a German HOSTEL, 1972 by *Plaskett Marshall & Partners*; entrance hall with window of coloured glass. Later upper storey.

ST GEORGE, German Lutheran chapel, Alie Street. A remarkable, atmospheric survival. 1762–3 probably by *Joel Johnson*, carpenter turned architect. The oldest surviving German church in Britain, funded chiefly by Dederich Beckman, a wealthy member of the local German community of sugar bakers. Taken into the care of the Historic Chapels Trust in 1998, restored 2003–4.

Only the entrance front is visible from the street, a modest classical composition, three bays with pediment. Two entrances with arched windows above flank a slightly advanced central bay. This has a Venetian window below a lunette. The superstructure was removed in the 1930s: a panel with a clock against the pediment, surmounted by a little classical bell-turret, its three receding tiers topped by a cupola with weathervane (a design similar to Johnson's St John Wapping of 1756). Little-altered interior, complete with C18 furnishings. The whole space is filled by numbered, grained box pews; galleries on timber Doric columns around three sides, also with pews, in three raked rows. The original coved ceiling was restored in 2004.

28 At the (liturgical) E end, an assemblage of FURNISHINGS in the Lutheran tradition. – Behind the COMMUNION RAILS with turned balusters, placed centrally and approached by elegant stairs on either side, a high PULPIT of bulbous shape, tester with dove above. On each side lower reading desks. – On the wall above, two large COMMANDMENT BOARDS, in German, in ornate carved frames with scrolled tops, cherubs' heads and garlands, and a large gilded ROYAL ARMS of George III. – STAINED GLASS, W window, an early work by *James Powell & Sons*, 1855. Crucifixion, originally with jewelled borders, some of the latter now in the side lights. Made as one of a pair (displaced by the present E windows of 1912). Other windows with coloured margin lights, also 1855–6, when the church was 'renovated and beautified'; as is recorded on a

tablet. – ORGAN in W gallery, 1886, remodelled 1937, when the space below was divided off. – MONUMENTS. Plain tablets to Dr Gustavus Anthony Wachsel, the first pastor †1799 and his son J.C. Wachsel, surgeon †1819.

Adjoining to the NE is the two-storey VESTRY built 1765–6, domestic looking; red brick aprons below the windows, one with brick dated 1766, the windows with grooves and catches instead of sliding sashes. Panelled vestry room on the ground floor; the fitted cupboards in the room above housed a distinguished theological library started by Wachsel, now in the British Library. The vestry looks across a secluded courtyard to the buildings of the former GERMAN INFANT SCHOOL, 1859, cheerful red and yellow brick, two tall storeys with pointed upper windows.

WHITECHAPEL METHODIST MISSION, Whitechapel Road. By *Lee Reading Associates*, *c.* 1971. Dark brick. Carefully planned with much packed into a small site. Ground-floor shops with double-height top-lit church above, under a sloping boarded roof. Behind are assembly and meeting rooms, a residential hostel for thirty boys and, in the crypt, accommodation for the homeless.

EAST LONDON CENTRAL SYNAGOGUE, Nelson Street. A Sephardish synagogue of 1923 by *Lewis Solomon & Son*. Discreet brick exterior with two tiers of windows beneath round-headed arches with stone keystones. Fine classical interior. Galleries with iron railings between Ionic columns; coved ceiling above a big cornice, the recess for the Ark up curved steps, framed by a Venetian arch on Doric columns. Above the Ark, scrolled pediment with tablets of the law and Lions of Judah. Panelled pews and Bimah.

GREAT SYNAGOGUE, Fieldgate Street. Rebuilt 1959–60 after war damage, replacing the Great Synagogue of 1899. Typical of the Federation's small synagogues. Plain domestic street front; a passage along the E wall leads to a full-height room behind, a long galleried space lit by a skylight in the concrete roof, with centrally placed Bimah in the Ashkenazi tradition, benches facing each other and Ark at the end. Marbled cast-iron columns, which must be reused from the older building.

SYNAGOGUE, Sandys Row. Built as a chapel, 1763–6, for a French congregation, formerly entered from Parliament Court to the E. Consecrated as a synagogue 1870, for a Friendly Society of Dutch Ashkenazi Jews, when *N.S. Joseph* added a new entrance from Sandys Row, a reticent three-storey front with round-arched windows for offices and caretaker's flat. The meeting room behind, raised over a basement, is a reduced version of the Fournier Street chapel (*see* below); with large round-arched windows at gallery level, and a coved ceiling. Gallery on three sides, on plain Doric columns with triglyph frieze. Plain panelled central Bimah of 1870. A more elaborate Ark recess framed by Corinthian pilasters and pediment, probably 1904 by *Lewis Solomon*. Seating and lighting of the 1950s.

Former SYNAGOGUE, No. 19 Princelet Street, *see* Museum of Immigration, p. 400.

LONDON JAMME MASJID (GREAT MOSQUE), Fournier Street and Brick Lane. The building encapsulates the immigrant history of Spitalfields. Built 1743–4 as a Huguenot chapel with minister's house at No. 39 Fournier Street, by the French church in Threadneedle Street, the architect probably their surveyor, *Thomas Stibbs*. From 1815–19 used as a chapel by the Society for Propagating Christianity among the Jews; from 1819 a Methodist chapel. In 1897 converted to a synagogue by Messrs *Maples* for an orthodox congregation from eastern Europe. The vestry had been used for Talmud Torah classes from 1895. It became a mosque in 1975. Large, plain and unadorned, but sound and solid. Pediments on both sides above a stone cornice, with stone band dividing the two floors. The main entrance was originally on Fournier Street. Slightly projecting centre with two doors, windows above in a rhythm of 1-4-1, all with stone keystones; sundial in the pediment. The side to Brick Lane has three broad bays with central Venetian window and oculus above. The present entrance is through No. 59 Brick Lane, the former vestry and school, also by *Stibbs*, a plain three-bay domestic front. The original interior followed the practice of C18 chapels, with reredos and pulpit on the long N wall facing the entrance. Formerly there was a coved ceiling, and three galleries on Tuscan columns with triglyph frieze. Part of the E gallery was removed in 1897 for the Torah shrine. The interior was largely stripped out in 1986. Vaults below, leased to brewery and wine merchants through the C18 and C19.

EAST LONDON MOSQUE, Whitechapel Road. 1982–5 by *John Gill Associates*. The golden glass-fibre dome and cluster of minarets make a striking landmark. Asymmetrical street frontage in red brick, with a row of tall Islamic arches to the l. of the main entrance. Spacious top-lit entrance hall; large prayer hall at an angle, approached up steps. To the r., on a much larger scale, the LONDON MUSLIM CENTRE, 2003–4 by *Robert Klashka* of *Markland Klashka*, with broad, glazed entrance inset below a curved canopy faced with patterned tiles. The main building, of six storeys, has a series of large halls, classrooms and offices; around the corner in Fieldgate Street, MOSQUE TOWER is earlier; eight storeys of sheltered housing, and a four-storey terrace.

JEWISH CEMETERY, Brady Street. *See* Bethnal Green.

MAJOR BUILDINGS

TOYNBEE HALL, Commercial Street. 1884–5 by *Elijah Hoole*. An institution of national, if not international, importance but its significance belied by the rather depressing appearance of its buildings. Partly destroyed during the war, the Hall has several undistinguished post-war additions.

Founded in 1883 by Rev. Samuel Barnett, vicar of St Jude's Commercial Street, as a residential 'Settlement of University men' to carry out educational and social work in the East End. Named in memory of the young Oxford historian Arnold Toynbee, who had undertaken such work in Whitechapel during the 1870s. In time Barnett hoped that Toynbee would form the foundation of an East London university college. The impulses behind the settlement are partly expressed in the design, firstly in its role as a Hall, with its inevitable Old English associations of hospitality, and secondly as a scholastic college.

The 1880s buildings are set back from Commercial Street's E side behind gardens and appear quite insignificant at first. Originally, however, the Hall was screened by tall warehouses which created a narrow and secluded inner quad entered through a tall gatehouse (completed 1892; destroyed 1941). The surviving part is Neo-Tudor with paired kneelered gables and robust chimneystacks. Diaper-patterned red brick with stone dressings. Two large mullioned windows with leaded panes light the Hall's principal rooms, the Dining Room and Lecture Hall (Gothic doorway with dogtooth brick moulding). A shorter N elevation originally provided a link to a similar Library. S of the quadrangle is a single-storey wing, originally for the Drawing Room and now separated by mid-C20 additions. A low open arcade with octagonal clock turret (now blocked) linked it to the gatehouse. SCULPTURE. Small, attenuated bronze Woman & Child by *Claire Winsten*. A memorial to Jane Addams, founder of Hull House, Chicago. On the clock tower a profile relief of Alfred, Viscount Milner of 1936 by *Gilbert Ledward*, a copy of his relief in Westminster Abbey.

Inside, the Lecture Hall has Neo-Jacobean panelling and a fireplace with arched niche and columns of 1890. The Dining Room is of greater interest, with a partly-preserved decorative scheme of 1887–8 by *C.R. Ashbee*, undertaken by his students at Toynbee. Gilded-plaster roundels, embellished
with Ashbee's stylized motif of a tree in the form of a 'T', 83
were originally part of a larger design (now overpainted), possibly as the faces of large sunflowers. Above, a frieze of painted- and gilded-plaster shields of the Oxford and Cambridge colleges. Delicate glass lamps of a suitably Arts and Crafts character were introduced during refurbishment in 1984 by *Caröe and Martin*. On the N wall, a profile portrait relief of Arnold Toynbee, set within a circular surround, its author unknown. Over the fireplace, a portrait of Samuel Barnett and his wife Henrietta, later founder of Hampstead Garden Suburb (*see London 4: North*). By *Hubert von Herkomer*, 1908, donated by H.H. Asquith.

TOYNBEE STUDIOS in the SE corner of the quad was the first major C20 extension, for a School of Music & Drama.

1939 by *Alister G. MacDonald* (son of Ramsay). Starkly modern, of steel-frame construction, clad in white brick with a high N stair tower. On the ground floor a small theatre in a Deco style reminiscent of MacDonald's interwar cinemas. Flanking the stage, a pair of excellent wall-paintings of 1939 by *Clive Gardiner*.* On the r. Tragedy; Orestes Pursued by the Furies, on the l. Fancy and Comedy, both showing the artist's predilection for mythological subjects at this date. The first-floor Music Room, with book-back panelling, doubled as juvenile court. On the third floor a lattice frame girder is deliberately exposed, almost as a sculptural form.

Toynbee Hall's post-war recovery was driven by its energetic warden, Jimmy Mallon, who put forward plans for major rebuilding. The gatehouse was only rebuilt in 1965–7 by *Martin & Bayley*. Very uninspiring; flat roof, dark brick panels and first floor over a covered walk. On the N side of the courtyard, on the site of the demolished Library, ATTLEE HOUSE of 1971 by *David Maney & Partners*. Respectful but dull, in orange brick, of four storeys with cut-away corner and a large decorative concrete panel. The identical SUNLEY HOUSE, flats of 1976 by the same firm, stands to the rear of the Hall towards Gunthorpe Street on the site of C19 tenements. COLLEGE EAST, flats of *c.* 1984 by *Shepheard, Epstein & Hunter*, face Wentworth Street and retain a single bay of the brick-and-terracotta Gothic façade of College Buildings. This was an experimental tenement design by *Hoole*, a precursor of Barnett's East End Dwellings Co. buildings, and planned as the first stage in a comprehensive redevelopment of the neighbouring slums (*see* perambulation *1d*). The building also appears to have incorporated student hostels, Wadham House: opened in 1887, and Balliol House, opened in 1891.

82 WHITECHAPEL ART GALLERY, Whitechapel High Street. 1898–1901 by *Charles Harrison Townsend*, one of the architect's remarkable trio which includes the Bishopsgate Institute and the Horniman Museum. Pevsner called it 'wonderfully original and quite an epoch making building in spite of its moderate size', recognizing it as 'original as any Art Nouveau on the continent'.

The gallery was an effort to establish an art institution of national standing in the East End. Its promoter was the indomitable Henrietta Barnett who founded a series of exhibitions at St Jude's School in the 1880s, mostly with gifts of work by the Barnetts' circle of friends, including Watts, Morris and others. The gallery's founding spirit was Ruskinian in tone, declaring that 'Life without industry is guilt, Industry without Art is brutality.' J. Passmore Edwards bore much of the cost and published Townsend's first design in his *Building News* in 1896, a broad, vaguely Romanesque front with an arcaded upper storey, flanked by tapered towers with shallow domes.

* Son-in-law of Jimmy Mallon, Warden of Toynbee.

The executed composition, revised to fit the narrow street-frontage, is similar to Townsend's Bishopsgate Institute (1892–4): buff-terracotta lower storey dominated by an asymmetrical double doorway under a massive keyed arch, which springs from the string course. Above, a low frieze of square windows, then two squat towers (originally designed with domed spirelets). These are clasped at their bases by realistically layered foliage, possibly by *William Aumonier*, made by *Canning & Gibbs*. In the centre a dark, painted panel, originally intended to hold a mosaic by *Walter Crane* representing Art, attended by Labour, Time, History, Poesie, Truth & Beauty. It was excluded when Barnett refused to allow the gallery to bear Passmore Edwards' name. Significantly, the *Building News* gives only a minor reference to the building's opening and its reception elsewhere was rather mixed given its incomplete appearance. The confined site also made the interior spaces unsatisfactory, with the smaller upper gallery placed directly over that below so that the lighting is confined to the walls. Refurbished in 1988 by *Colquhoun Miller Partners* when acquisition of adjoining property allowed space for additional galleries at first floor, lecture room and café. Externally of buff brick but inside an elegant all-white treatment sympathetically detailed in a geometric style evocative of Mackintosh and the Vienna Secession.

The gallery acquired the adjoining LIBRARY in 2003. Won in competition in 1891–2 by *Potts, Son & Hennings* but its construction paid for by J. Passmore Edwards, the first of the free libraries provided by him in East London. Renamed in 1896, just as Edwards was beginning to fund the neighbouring Art Gallery (*see* above). Free Queen Anne, red brick with buff-terracotta dressings and frieze with putti at first floor. Sculpted spandrels of putti, signed by *R. Spruce* of *Burmantofts*. Oriel windows and an asymmetrical roofline, originally more varied with gables either side of a central tower with cupola (now removed). In the lobby, a tile tableau of 'Whitechapel Hay Market, 1788' by *Charles Evans and Co.*, 1888, allegedly removed from a local pub. Major remodelling of the

Whitechapel Gallery, mosaic by Walter Crane (unexecuted), 1901

interior, by *Robbrecht en Daem Architecten*, will be completed in 2007.

WHITECHAPEL IDEAS STORE, Whitechapel Road. The third and largest of the C21 successors to the borough's public libraries. *See also* Bow, p. 613, and Lansbury, p. 649. By *Adjaye Associates*, 2003–4. Five storeys, concrete frame with cladding of vertical glazing panels, many of them in bright translucent colours, intended to evoke the spines of books.

THE DAVENANT CENTRE. No. 179, Whitechapel Road. Former Davenant Foundation School, a late C19 amalgamation of two older charitable schools in Whitechapel. The five-bay stucco frontage to the road is dated 1818, of two storeys above a basement with central three bays projecting and 'Whitechapel School' engraved in the frieze above. Windows with flat gauged brick arches. Remodelled 1896 by *F. Pouler Telfer* when the large new hall and classroom block were erected at the rear of the site on the former workhouse burial ground. Splendid Neo-Jacobean in rich red brick with terracotta dressings, of five bays with gables over the second and fourth bays. Mullion and transomed windows, pointed at the E and W ends, all with coloured leaded lights. The hall is raised over a covered playground (later enclosed) with piers faced in blue brick and served by a striking and unusual covered stair with a stepped, open, arcade. Inside, a barrel-vaulted timber roof on arch-braced trusses with tie-beams and king posts.

Now attached to the JAGONARI, a Women's Educational Resource Centre. 1987 by *Matrix Feminist Design Co-Op*. A considered four-storey design combining a mix of motifs drawn from Indian architecture, including fretted screens to the windows within recessed panels and an elaborate mosaic door surround, with more traditional gable and cupola.

SWANLEA SECONDARY SCHOOL, Brady Street. By *Sir Colin Stansfield Smith* in association with *Percy Thomas Partnership* 1993, when it was the first new secondary school in London for a decade. Swanlea demonstrates the ideas of humane school design developed from the late 1970s by the Hampshire County Architects under Smith. Large and spreading, planned around the central spine of a glazed two-storey mall covered by an exciting and showy glass roof, supported by three tensely braced struts with radiating trusses of tree-like form, that cascades over the entrance as a porch. Yellow brick classrooms with curved roofs are set at right angles on the S side and open to courtyard gardens. Inside the mall are stairs to galleries serving the classrooms on the higher N side.

48 Former synagogue, NO. 19 PRINCELET STREET, now a Museum of Immigration.* One of the most evocative interiors of the East End. The exterior of the brick terrace house of *c.* 1718 gives little away, distinguished from its neighbours only by the rusticated stucco ground floor with arched entrance, added by *Lewis Solomon* in 1892–3. The house retains many of its C18 fittings.

* Open on selected days or by arrangement.

It was used as a school for the attached synagogue, with lodgings on the upper floors (made famous by the strange story of the reclusive tenant on the top floor*). Built out over the back garden is the synagogue itself, constructed by a Mr *Hudson* in 1869–70 for a Polish *hevra* (prayer group), the Loyal United Friends Friendly Society founded 1862. A long, narrow space, top-lit by a clerestory and tinted roof lights. Galleries on three sides supported on twisted iron posts. Simple iron gallery railings above varnished wood panels with gilt inscriptions. The fourth wall has an arch framing the site of the Ark. Originally there was a raised central reading platform, or Bimah, of which parts survive. Below is a large meeting room.

ROYAL LONDON HOSPITAL, Whitechapel Road. Remnants of 2
the plain, balanced composition of the Georgian hospital designed by *Boulton Mainwaring* in 1752 are still just traceable in the agglomeration of buildings extending along Whitechapel Road. The hospital was founded in Featherstone Street in 1740 by professional doctors, in contrast to other London hospitals, before moving to Prescot Street a year later as the London Infirmary. A new site was required as early as 1744 and open land leased from the City. The new hospital, for 200 patients, was largely complete by 1757 but building continued until 1771. The original design was plain, in stock brick, of three storeys and twenty-three bays with a simple pedimented five-bay centre. It is shown in an C18 print next to the curious Mount, the remains of a Civil War defence (removed *c.* 1808). The planned two-storey wings attached at right angles to the main block, each accommodating a double or 'back-to-back' ward on each floor, were completed in the 1770s by *Edward Hawkins* and extended to their present length by *A.R. Mason* in the 1830s, partly to incorporate wards for the increasing number of Jewish patients. Changing attitudes to hospital design and sanitation encouraged the building of two pavilion wings in the 1860s and 1870s by *Charles Barry Jun.* with better-ventilated 'Nightingale' wards. This made it the largest hospital in the country with 650 beds. Minor additions were made in the 1880s by *Rowland Plumbe* prior to his major extension and rebuilding from 1896–1906 when the hospital spread S for the first time in its history. The coherent planning of this period has not been replicated since. Post-war plans for complete rebuilding were never carried out, but from 1966 *T.P. Bennett & Son* developed radical plans for the creation of a 1,300-bed hospital which would have required destruction of most of the main site. As a result the pre-Plumbe buildings were listed but in spite of this the Alexandra Wing was destroyed in 1974 and replaced. Subsequent building has been in small units but in 2004 major redevelopment is planned by *Skanska/Innisfree* with *HOK International*; glass towers are to replace most of the late C19 and C20 parts while the historic range to Whitechapel Road will be restored.

*R. Lichtenstein and I. Sinclair, *Rodinsky's Room* (1999).

EXTERIOR: *Mainwaring*'s original building has been heightened and so engulfed by its later extensions that only the stone cornice, a few bays either side of the entrance and a single surviving door to the E can give much sense of its appearance. The projecting pedimented porte-cochère, flanked by turreted towers, was added by *Plumbe* in 1889–90. The round-headed traceried windows of its upper floor lit the chapel. At the E end of the frontage, the stately GROCERS' COMPANY WING of 1875–6 by *Charles Barry Jun.*, three storeys over a basement, stone band below second floor, stone dentilled cornice. On the site of Barry's W pavilion, the colossal ALEXANDRA WING, of 1978–82 by *T.P. Bennett*. This has projecting stock brick piers with a canted face dividing the windows in a forceful vertical rhythm. Roof-top helicopter pad. On the S side of the main building is a small courtyard garden, flanked by the rear wings. These are much altered but retain the three-bay central pediments added in the 1830s. The rest is a crude remodelling and infill of 1958–62 by *Watkins Gray & Partners* after war damage. The garden has a bronze SCULPTURE of Queen Alexandra by *James Wade*, 1908. A relief panel on the plinth shows Edward VII, Frederick Treves, Sydney Holland and others at a demonstration of the Finsen light treatment for 'tuberculosis of the skin'. Providing the backdrop to this, GARDEN HOUSE, a two-storey cruciform plan for the paediatrics dept of *c.* 1996 by *T.P. Bennett*.

The hospital INTERIOR has been extensively remodelled but cheered up since 1996 by artworks commissioned by *Vital Arts*, including brightly coloured floors in Children's Services by *Sarah Hammond*, 1998, a glass ceiling in the Endoscopy Unit by *Kate Maestri*, 1999 and windows in the multi-faith CHAPEL by *Amanda Townsend*. In 1999, a MOSQUE was opened in the Alexandra Wing. The first of its kind, comprising two small prayer rooms decorated with hand-stencilled Islamic patterns by *Areen Design*.

THE HOSPITAL PRECINCTS: The Hospital began to exploit its estate for its own expansion in the late C19. A tour can begin in TURNER STREET, with the first building of importance: the MEDICAL COLLEGE, built 1886–7 by *Plumbe* on the site of an earlier college of 1854 by *A.R. Mason*. Tall, but rather uninspiring, of seven bays divided horizontally by moulded strings and vertically by paired brick pilasters originally with low pediments over the penultimate bays and a central bellcote. *Plumbe* reconstructed the S front in 1898 with a ground-floor loggia and decorative pediment. Inside, an open-well stair of some quality, rising through three storeys carried on plain Ionic columns with fluted bases. Arcaded upper floors. The old Library at the rear is a long double-height room with tall windows and an arched recess on the E side. N and W galleries, with bookcases beneath. Sumptuous deocration, the panelling liberally decorated in C18 style and with a fine plasterwork ceiling, divided into three octagons with bulbous pendant drops. Bust of Sir William Blizard (†1835), surgeon and founder of the first medical school in 1781.

In STEPNEY WAY, a succession of C19 and C20 extensions. First, W of the College, the OUTPATIENTS DEPARTMENT of 1903 by *Plumbe*. Shaped gable over the entrance adorned with terracotta name plaque and garland festoons. Corner towers to the flanks with pyramidal roofs and ball finials, a Plumbe motif. The largest building of its type in Britain at the time of construction and instrumental in pioneering a flow system of treatment whereby patients would be registered and seen in succession. Trapezoidal plan, three floors organized around a rectangular top-lit waiting hall for 1,000 patients with subsidiary entrance and registry hall on one side, dispensary and exits on the other. Remodelled 1963. Artworks include LIGHT LADDER by *Jon Bjarnesson* and LIVING TREE by *Nathalie Joiris*. Facing New Road is the ANNEXE, originally Dept of Massage and Medical Electricity, 1936 by *Adams, Holden & Pearson*, in a blockish, modern style with bands of brick and concrete. Chamfered corners with Crittall-type windows. On the S side of Stepney Way, the DENTAL INSTITUTE is a defiant podium block and slab of 1965 by *Stephen Statham & Associates* (due for demolition in 2004).

Filling most of the site S of NEWARK STREET, a major extension of 2003–4 for the SCHOOL OF MEDICINE AND DENTISTRY by *AMEC & Alsop Architects*. In two parts with a linking bridge. The public face is a sheer glass box along Turner Street with brightly-coloured abstract patterns on the glazing. For open-plan research laboratories, over which are to be suspended coloured organic pods shaped like human cells, designed for meeting rooms and an exhibition space. Taller block behind clad in profiled metal sheeting, for lecture theatre and services. It incorporates an earlier block of 1997 by *Llewellyn-Davies* at its W end.

The buildings E of St Philip's Church (*see* above, now the Medical College library) on both sides of STEPNEY WAY are scheduled for demolition in 2004. Of these only perhaps the NURSES' HOMES at the E end deserve mention for reflecting the hospital's enlightened and pioneering attitude to the training and accommodation of staff. Despite their grim, barrack-like appearance, they were generous in their provision. OLD HOME was the earliest, 1886–7 by *Rowland Plumbe*, overlooking the hospital garden and incorporating an existing Matron's home of *c.* 1873. Long with a projecting centre under a pyramidal roof surmounted by ball finial. Iron balconies, corbelled cornice and strings. Covered iron bridges link this to the later homes: ALEXANDRA HOUSE, 1894 on N edge of Stepney Way, a lofty six storeys with the minimum of detail and the more ambitious EVA LUCKES HOME of 1905–6 designed around a courtyard with small frontage to the street with shallow-bow windows lighting the library and drawing room. The larger accommodation block overlooks Newark Street with oriel windows, shaped gables and diaper-pattern brickwork. EDITH CAVELL HOME, East Mount Street, 1916 is handsome and classical with a stone porch on columns beneath a balcony and broken pediment. S of Eva Luckes Home is the large, five-storey PATHOLOGY and PHARMACY BUILDING, begun in 2004 by *Capita Percy Thomas*. Red tile cladding. (For other buildings *see* Perambulation 2C: The London Hospital Estate.)

PERAMBULATIONS

1. *Spitalfields and Mile End New Town*

1a. *Spital Square and the area to its N; a circular tour*

Spital Square, just E of Bishopsgate, owes its name to the priory and hospital of St Mary (*see* p. 384). Some of the medieval buildings survived, partly rebuilt by later occupants, until the early C18, when the area began to be developed more systematically by its owner, Sir Isaac Tillard, with houses for wealthy merchants. Spital Square, occupying part of the site of the S transept of the medieval church, was laid out as a cross-shaped arrangement of streets rather than a square. It remained a secluded enclave until extensive demolition for the expanding market in the earlier C20.

The entrance to SPITAL SQUARE from Bishopsgate, which was the original entrance to the priory, is now flanked by late C20 buildings, glass-fronted to the S, hard red brick on the N. No. 37 on the S side is the only C18 survivor, sensitively converted in 1981 by *Julian Harrap* as offices for the Society for the Protection of Ancient Buildings. The house probably dates from *c.* 1740; one of the last to be built in the square, apparently on the site of an earlier building. The following year it was occupied by the Huguenot Ogier family. Three storeys of straight-headed windows over a low basement, the front door reached by steps, the doorway with good carved brackets. The well-preserved interior is a good introduction to the C18 houses of the area, not one of the richest or most elaborate, but with details demonstrating the hierarchy of decoration characteristic of Georgian houses. The panelled ground floor has a dentilled cornice; a handsome staircase with carved tread-ends leads to the grander first-floor front room, which is distinguished by a modillion cornice. Snug back rooms with corner fireplaces. The upper flight of the stairs is treated more simply, with a closed string. A back extension on different levels (perhaps older) contained a kitchen, and perhaps a counting house; it now has an upstairs meeting room of 1981, with new bay window to the back court.

To the E is ST BOTOLPH'S HALL, built 1891 and used by the Central Foundation School for Girls whose other buildings here have disappeared. They were on the site of a mansion occupied by the Earl of Bolingbroke in the C17 and then by the Tillard family. The northern arm of Spital Square is largely a rebuilding of the 1990s. On its NW corner, Eden House, a low, faience-clad streamlined 1930s warehouse built for the Co-operative Wholesale Society by *L. G. Ekins*. To its N C18 houses were demolished in 1952 and 1961 for the expanding market; the exteriors of No. 15 and the adjoining No. 20 Folgate Street are replicas, initiated by the Spitalfields Trust in 1985 to restore the street corner to its C18 form.

FOLGATE STREET (formerly White Lion Street) existed with modest houses already in the C17. The S side was rebuilt as part of the development of the area by the Tillards: Nos. 10–18 are a fine, tall row of 1724; four storeys above low basements (the street level has risen); a moulded brick cornice above the second floor, and segment-headed windows throughout, as was popular in the 1720s. No. 18* was discreetly modernized in the Regency period, with a new round-headed doorcase, and enriched window reveals to the first floor. Nos. 12 and 14 are rebuildings of 1983, with a carriage entrance, returning the group to an almost uniform appearance. No. 10 was designed as one of a mirrored pair. It retains its original wooden Doric doorcase with rusticated pilasters. Nos. 6–8 are a lower, early C19 pair in buff brick. This side of the street retained its respectability into the later C19, occupied in 1860 by silk manufacturers and ladies' schools. In contrast, at the same date the opposite side had a pub, cowkeeper, and humbler tradesmen. The existing Nos. 5–11 on the N side are a rebuilding of 1904 with an Arts and Crafts flavour; the dormers to the houses have arched glazing bars, the PEWTER PLATTER pub has an arresting, angled corner stack and lively mixture of red-and blue brickwork. Nos. 17–21 are small C18 houses, No. 17 of two-and-a-half bays, No. 21 with dentilled cornice remaining from a projecting Regency shopfront.

For the parts of Folgate Street further E, *see* below.

BLOSSOM STREET leads N into a different world, reflecting the significance of the nearby Bishopsgate goods station. On the W side, after C20 offices, a long range of four-storey grey brick warehouses of 1886 onwards; loading entrances faced with blue bricks, cranes above, the premises of Nicholls & Clarke, builders' merchants. In 1860 they were trading as lead and glass merchants and manufacturers in Shoreditch High Street, directly to the W, on the site of their present interwar, Deco-style showrooms. They occupied Nos. 12–13 in 1887, Nos. 14–15 by 1900. On the E side a further range dated 1927.

FLEUR DE LIS STREET was laid out on the northern part of the Tillard Estate and built up in the 1720s, but nothing remains from this time. The S side, much rebuilt *c.* 1812, now has vaguely Neo-Georgian offices of the 1970s, taking in LOOM COURT behind, once a squalid court of early C19 weavers' dwellings. E of Elder Street Newlon Housing Trust

*Open to the public.

flats, 1980 by *R.E. Bousell*, also minimally Georgian, on the site of a corner pub.

ELDER STREET, leased for building from 1722, is the most complete of the C18 streets in this part of Spitalfields, its survival the result of a preservation campaign in 1977 which routed the developers through occupation of the partly demolished Nos. 5–7.* The pair were repaired and resold, followed by others in the street. The general effect of the surviving C18 houses is uniform, buildings of four floors with segment-headed windows and flush window frames, mostly of dark red brick with rubbed brick dressings, but there are plenty of minor individualities to pick out in both planning and detail. Many have original surviving interior features. Nos. 5 and 7, each of three bays, are quite modest houses with low ceiling heights, originally with a very simple plan, only one room deep, with newel stair. No. 5 has a broad, single second-floor window, probably rebuilt for workrooms in the C19, and 'weavers windows' to the attic (the pantiled roof is visible behind, from a yard off Folgate Street). Nos. 9–13 were built as two houses of five and four bays, for some time divided into three (hence the extra door). Two good doorcases with Doric pilasters and rustication, of the kind found elsewhere in the area. Nos. 15 and 17, another pair, date from 1727, similarly detailed, but with four storeys over basements, and lower floors. Both were originally only one room deep, but No. 15, probably during building, was given a timber extension with staircase, also an extra, elaborate Doric doorcase. Another pair, Nos. 19–21, have fluted keystones, and end pilasters slightly projecting. No. 23, adjoining No. 29 Folgate Street has later stucco with pilasters and some Greek key decoration. Four bays, only one room deep, with newel stair to the upper floors, a plan type that is frequent near street corners where there is less space at the back. On the W side the N end of the street was rebuilt with Fleur de Lis Street; Nos. 24–36 remain from the 1720s. A varied group: No. 24 with carriage entry, No. 26 only two bays wide; Nos. 28 and 30, originally one room deep, with later, stucco ground floor. No. 30, although a small house, has an especially fine Ionic doorcase, columns against rustication, and a pediment. Restored by *Erith & Terry*, *c.* 1973. Nos. 32–36 form a continuous range but are of different sizes. No. 34 has an archway to a rear yard. No. 36, five bays, one room deep with return to Folgate Street, was given a fashionable doorcase in the later C18.

The N side of FOLGATE STREET, E of Spital Square, is largely C20: the long range of offices, given some character by a glazed ground floor recessed between chunky brick-faced piers, is a reworking of a 1960s block, by *Murphy Philips*, 2001. For the Peabody buildings further E *see* Commercial Street (p. 412). The S side was entirely rebuilt after heated debate in the 1980s on appropriate form and function for the area after the depar-

* See Spitalfields Historic Buildings Trust, *The Saving of Spitalfields*, 1989.

ture of Spitalfields Market, involving a galaxy of well-known architects. The retention of the main market building meant that only the surrounding fringes were available. The Folgate Street area, designated for residential use, was rebuilt by *Lawrence & Wrightson* with 201 apartments for the developer St George's in 1995–9, according to a masterplan agreed in 1993 which established the principle of a contemporary rendering of Georgian character. Conservationist pressure resulted in a conscientious re-creation of Georgian detail near Elder Street. The four-storey block between Spital Square and Nantes Passage (where there were C18 house up to the 1960s) has a frontage of early Georgian type, although the three doorcases all numbered 32 betray that these are flats not houses.

To the S, facing ELDER GARDENS, the whole group is overtly C20, plainly detailed, with iron balconies and alternating brick and render to provide some variety. E of Nantes Passage a late C18-to-Regency style is adopted for the Folgate Street frontage, yellow brick with honeysuckle balconies. Further E adjoining Commercial Street, on the site of Spitalfields Flower Market (built 1935, demolished 1995) a warehouse idiom appears, enlivened by stone bands and vertical strips of blue cladding on the side to LAMB STREET. In the landscaped area in front, *Vortex*, sculpture by *Barbara Sandler*, 1999. At the opposite end of Lamb Street next to the E branch of Spital Square, the final stage, six storeys, and entirely modern, in the spirit of the encroaching commercial architecture of the City.

S of Lamb Street, facing Commercial Street, is the old SPITALFIELDS MARKET. Licensed in 1682 by Charles II, the fruit-and-vegetable market was expanded immediately by Edward Metcalfe but entirely rebuilt in 1883–93 for Robert Horner, a former market porter and the market's last private owner. Purchased by the Corporation of London and expanded in 1926–9, the market closed in 1986 and moved to Leyton (*see* Waltham Forest). New and imaginative uses were found for the old market stalls and warehouses while a long campaign raged, heavily resisted locally, for commercial redevelopment.

The C17 market was centred on a cruciform market building with a central clock tower and Doric portico to each of its faces. Rocque's map of 1746 shows axial streets leading off the market square, between blocks of houses. This pattern was partly retained in the C19 rebuilding. At a cost of £80,000, *Henry Lovegrove*, surveyor, demolished the market building and covered the market square with an iron and glass roof of lattice girders carried on tall columns (*Oswald Garner & Co.*, engineers). The buildings around the market place were replaced by six blocks of shops and warehouses designed by *George Sherrin*, in an attractive, if slightly mechanical, Queen Anne style of tile-hung gables and half-timbering. The first block on Lamb Street has good cut-and-rubbed brick detailing; the NE block, facing Commercial Street adds decorative pargetting of human figures and fruit. Less domestic in character, the adjoining former Flower Market with a lantern roof and an arresting upper storey of giant rusticated gauged brick arches with windows in shaped and panelled surrounds. The principal entrance on Commercial Street (following the line of the C17 East Street) has a high archway between two blocks with high dormer gables, cut-and-rubbed dressings and floral frieze.

On BRUSHFIELD STREET, C20 expansion of market business is emphasized by the appearance of branch banks: a classical stone façade for the Westminster Bank, by *Septimus Warwick*, 1929. Channelled rustication, bays of arch windows with gorgeously curved keystones. It incorporates the entrance to the market Superintendent's Office with radial fanlight. Mirroring it, set into the central S block, but with carved keystones of wheat and sugarcane, is the former National Provincial Bank of 1930 by *F.C.R. Palmer* with *J. Reeve Young*.

Facing, on the S side of Brushfield Street, the former FRUIT AND WOOL EXCHANGE of 1929 by *Sydney Perks*, the City Surveyor. Bold and showy. Five storeys with a grand five-bay Portland-stone centrepiece crowned by a segmental arched attic window, a deferential nod to the portico of Hawksmoor's Christ Church. Brick and stone wings. Show rooms were placed on the ground floor with offices on three floors above overlooking the central auction rooms, laid out theatre-style with tiers of seats. The massive basement, designed for warehousing, was adopted as a huge air-raid shelter during the Blitz.

Sydney Perks erected extensions to the C19 market to the W between Crispin and Steward Streets in 1926–8. (Displaced residents moved into a small estate in Adelina Grove, Stepney.) These respectful Neo-Georgian blocks were partly demolished, after nearly twenty years of proposals for the site, to make way for BISHOPS SQUARE, colossal glass offices of up to thirteen storeys by *Foster & Partners*, 2003–5. The baleful effect of this cannot be overemphasized and marks the continued, and doubtless irresistible, empire building of the City of London in place of the domestic and social needs of the East End. The 1920s buildings along Brushfield Street have been retained as a superficial sensitivity to historic fabric, and excavated remains have been preserved below Bishops Square, but the cherished contrast in scale between high-rise W of the City boundary and the intimate domesticity of Spitalfields is lost for ever.

1b. Between Brushfield Street and Whitechapel Road

16 BRUSHFIELD STREET provides a magnificent vista of Christ Church from the W. Near the Bishopsgate end the N side was all rebuilt from the end of the C20 (*see* above). The S side still has a scatter of later C18 houses. Nos. 8–10 are a facsimile rebuild after a fire in 1983, old shop signs lending a period feel. Nos. 14–16 are genuine C18, as are Nos. 40–42, with No. 11

Gun Street. No. 52 was altered *c.* 1784 when the street was extended to Bishopsgate, but has early C18 fabric and panelling in the wing facing Crispin Street.

S of Brushfield Street, the cramped mix of Georgian and Victorian houses in narrow streets has been much smartened, but still conveys something of the character of the poorer parts of C19 London. Down GUN STREET near the junction with ARTILLERY LANE is DOME HOUSE, filling an awkward trapezoidal site. This began as a chapel, probably in the mid-C18, and was used as a synagogue from 1896–1948. The stucco frontage is a replica of the original destroyed *c.* 1950: seven bays with three sturdy, pedimented wooden doorcases; segment-headed windows in between, arched windows to the upper floor. The interior has been subdivided but the top-lit oval dome remains, oddly off centre to the front. Originally the central space had galleries on three sides; it is now subdivided, with staircase added below the dome. A glance to the W can take in ARTILLERY PASSAGE, a narrow, atmospheric pedestrian route to Bishopsgate, lined with Victorian (or Victorian-looking) shops. The buildings mostly have C19 fronts; No. 9, although a crudely detailed replica, indicates the type of late C17 house that may have existed here. PARLIAMENT COURT, running S, is a rare survival of the tiny passages that were once common; it provides a glimpse of the E end of the Sandys Row Synagogue (*see* p. 395).

The gem of ARTILLERY LANE is the pair further E, Nos. 56–58, a generously scaled front in pale brick, 3+3 bays with blind window in the centre, stone modillioned cornice above three floors, and full attic floor above. They date from 1756–7, when the site was redeveloped by Nicholas Jourdain, a silk merchant. The design is convincingly attributed to *Sir Robert Taylor.** Jourdain occupied No. 58; Francis Rybot, another silk merchant, was at No. 56. The elegantly ebullient shopfront to No. 56 is the best surviving example of its date in London. Two curved-bay windows, the central shop door and the house door on the r. each flanked by Doric columns. The Doric entablature curves forward to run above the windows, an unusually p. 29 elaborate architectural treatment for a shopfront. The shop door has octagonal-patterned glazing and a Rococo cartouche above, both fashionable mid-C18 features. Above the house door a delicate Rococo fanlight with festooned mask above. The continuous iron balcony above is an early C19 addition. Also of the early C19 is the unassuming flat shopfront to No. 58, with Doric pilasters.

The interior detail has the refinement associated with Taylor. In No. 56, in the ground floor room, three arched recesses against the party wall, divided by pilasters. The entrance hall has a tripartite ceiling, with pendentives in the centre, cross-vaults at the ends. The front first-floor room has an enriched cornice, pedimented doorcases, and cupboards flanking the

*Richard Garnier, *Georgian Group Journal* XII, 2002.

fireplace, and above this a Rococo fruit and flower garland. The back room had a most elaborate Rococo chimneypiece (removed 1927 but to be replaced). In No. 58 a Rococo ceiling remains in the first-floor front room.

Opposite, with main front to Crispin Street, is the former R.C. CONVENT OF MERCY and PROVIDENCE NIGHT REFUGE, eloquent of the needs of the area in the C19 in contrast to the prosperity of the C18. Founded 1860 by Rev. Daniel Gilbert in Providence Row, Finsbury, and opened here (on the site of a Jewish fairground) in 1868. Designed by *Messrs Young*. A large, bleak four-storey range in low-key Gothic, with pairs of arched windows, distinctly ecclesiastical in tone, with a figure of the Virgin over the entrance to the Convent of the Sisters of Mercy. The refuge offered accommodation for 300 women and children and 50 men, with separate entrances under bracketed inscribed panels. The male wing was extended in similar fashion along Artillery Lane in 1885. Each range had large ground-floor reception halls; the top floor of the female wing accommodated women training for domestic service. The Convent, N, was extended in 1895–8 by *William Patrick Ryan*, with a memorial chapel to Gilbert (†1895). Four bays with windows beneath arched dripmoulds; pilasters with foliage caps mildly leaven the austerity. Associated buildings, including schools and hostels in Gun Street, were demolished in 2002, leaving only the frontage and the façade of a corner pub.

WHITE'S ROW runs E towards Commercial Street. Here it is the C20 which intrudes, with brash multi-storey car park with façade-cum-crash barrier of rolled-steel sections by the *Corporation of London Architect's Department*, *c.* 1969–71. Opposite, No. 5 dates from *c.* 1733–5, a large five-bay house with painted brick front, segment-headed windows (the pairs on the ground floor probably altered); three storeys with attic, over a high-railed basement. Pretty pattern-book wooden doorcase with mask and scrolls. (Good staircase, centrally placed at the back.) Further on a characterful assortment of late C19 warehouses and C20 infilling. The largest warehouse, No. 8, five storeys and six bays, is boldly articulated by pilasters with arches at the top and heavy cast-iron grilles; its other side in Brune Street has the same treatment. Brune Street is reached by TENTER GROUND, the name recalling the use of this area for hanging out cloth before it was irregularly built up from the mid-C17 onwards. On the W side three-storey workshops of *c.* 1900, with colourful detail: white stone, red, blue and yellow brick. At the corner, a stiffly classical three-storey Stepney Borough Council building of the 1920s.

79 In BRUNE STREET the most striking building is the SOUP KITCHEN FOR THE JEWISH POOR, 1903 by *Lewis Solomon*. It shows the splendid effect that could be created in a philanthropic building whose function was mundane but humane. Rich, red brick dressed with mouldings of warm terracotta by Edwards of Ruabon. Asymmetrically composed with mullion

windows through three storeys, and gables with volutes. Over the length of the ground floor a tiled fascia heavily inscribed in flowing lettering with names and dates in English and Hebrew. Beneath the central three bays, an entrance, originally to the Committee's offices, with curved pediment inset with relief of a soup tureen. The entrance and exit to the kitchen area are placed on either side to allow for circulation. The W range was originally independent, with ground-floor shop beneath classrooms, reading rooms and workshops. Converted to flats in 1997 by *Duncan Thomas*. Nearby, until 1939, was the Jews' Free School, with buildings of 1820 onwards, a major complex on the W side of Bell Lane. By the C20 it catered for 3,500 children; demolished after the school moved to Camden Town.

Further S, the streets N of Whitechapel High Street were rebuilt from the later C19. They had been haphazardly built up from the C16, and by the mid-C19 had some of the worst overcrowding. The pre-war parts of the HOLLAND ESTATE, by the LCC, 1927–36, fill much of the area between Brune Street, Bell Lane, and Wentworth Street, part of a continuing effort to clear the squalid C19 slums of this area. Three four-storey ranges in the LCC's usual Neo-Georgian (rewindowed, alas) around a grassed court facing Bell Street, with a three-storey block, Barnett House, in the centre. Behind is a two-storey range of workshops in Toynbee Street (Toynbee Hall, *see* above, is across the road in Commercial Street.) WENTWORTH STREET was mostly rebuilt from the 1880s, but on the N side by Ann's Place No. 9 survived, a former mid-C19 pub used in 1859–90 as a ragged school. Italianate stucco trim; S and E sides each of three bays with pedimented upper windows. On the S side post-war housing at the E end, then bleak five-storey tenements of 1888 onwards, built by Wentworth Dwelling Co., following some of the first clearances by the MBW made possible by the Act of 1875.

S of Wentworth Street is the remnant of a pioneering improvement created in the notoriously insalubrious alleys leading off Whitechapel High Street. In OLD CASTLE STREET the front wall of a WASHHOUSE planned 1846, the year of the first Baths and Washhouses Act, and completed in 1851 as a charitable enterprise by the Committee for Promoting the Establishment of Baths and Washhouses for the Labouring Classes. It followed an earlier experiment in Ratcliffe. The architect/engineer was *P.P. Baly*. Seven bays of simple round-headed windows, completely unadorned except for 'Washhouse' and the date in Portland stone. The building also included baths, and was of fireproof construction, with an iron roof. The remains were incorporated in THE WOMEN'S LIBRARY, 2001–2 by *Wright & Wright*, part of London Metropolitan University. Office, exhibition space and library are housed within a muscular red brick case. Inside, exposed red brick and a staircase winding around a cage that is lit from within, producing dramatic *chiaroscuro* effects. Curious exhibition space with lecture theatre inserted awkwardly into its midst, with a mezzanine on its roof. The University also occupies CALCUTTA HOUSE, a warehouse built for Brooke Bond in 1909 by *Dunk & Bousfield.* A bridge over Old Castle Street links it to the former workers' welfare centre, 1932 by *A.L. Abbott*, a progressive concept at the time, but too early in Britain to look modern. Five storeys of dark brick with panels of steel-framed windows and end stair-tower.

MIDDLESEX STREET, thus named from 1830, is the old boundary between the City and Stepney. This was the centre of the famous Sunday clothes market known as Petticoat Lane, in existence from the early C17. The name is commemorated by Petticoat Square, the centre of the City of London's forbidding Middlesex Street Estate of 1965–75, just to the W. On the E side the array of warehouses dates from after the 1883 widening of the S end of the street by the MBW. Especially showy are Nos. 38–48, which have giant pilasters spaced in pairs, interspersed with no less than twelve loading bays. At the corner of New Goulston Street, a pub, the MARKET TRADER, with terracotta plaque of a bell on the canted face. Further N, No. 84, at the corner of COBB STREET, a handsome warehouse, four storeys below a cornice, with a crane. Another former warehouse dated 1901, with shaped gables and loading bays with cranes, at the corner of STRYPE STREET (which commemorates the birthplace of the antiquary John Strype, son of a silk throwster). This area was cleared in the late C19; the S side has mean dwellings by *James Hood & Son*, *c.* 1900. At the end, BRODY HOUSE, Leyden Street, a smart all-white revamping and extension by *ORMS Architects* of a streamlined sequin warehouse built for the firm of Brody in 1938. An adjacent lower block of flats of 2002. Further N a new link was cut to join Middlesex Street to Widegate Street in the City of London. The borough boundary continues N to Artillery Lane along the narrow SANDYS ROW, named for its C18 builder, past the stark front of the SYNAGOGUE (*see* p. 395). At the corner of Widegate Street is the KING'S STORES pub, by *W.M. Brutton.*

1C. *Commercial Street from S to N*

A busy route slicing through Spitalfields, one of the schemes put forward as part of the metropolitan improvements advocated by *Sir James Pennethorne*; the purpose was to connect the Docks with N and W London. Built in two parts: the S part up to Christ Church was laid out 1843–5, the extension to Shoreditch High Street 1849–57, although parts were not built up until the 1870s. The link to the City Road was not achieved until the building of Great Eastern Street through Shoreditch in 1872–6. The new road provided the opportunity for a few blocks of model dwellings, but most of the new buildings were commercial and industrial in a variety of styles; less uniformity was required by the Commissioners in this poor neighbourhood than in the contemporary creation of New Oxford Street. Activities here in the C19 were various; the clothing trade became pre-eminent only after 1900, but by the end of the C20 was giving way to offices and residential conversions.

After the SE corner building (*see* Whitechapel High Street) the E side starts with a decent stucco-trimmed four-storey terrace with shops, typical of the scale of the street's earliest buildings. Then come buildings associated with the Rev. Samuel Barnett, which were clustered around the church of St Jude, where he was vicar from 1873–94. The church, built 1845–8 by *F.J. Francis*, with a mosaic by *G.F. Watts*,* commissioned by Barnett, was demolished in 1925, rendered redundant by the then predominantly Jewish character of Whitechapel. Behind its empty site, CANON BARNETT PRIMARY SCHOOL, built as Commercial Street Board School, with a pair of prominent towers with hipped roofs. Nearby is the plain postwar entrance and low garden wall of Toynbee Hall which Barnett founded (*see* p. 396), set back in a secluded position until wartime destruction opened up the front to Commercial Road.

At the corner of Wentworth Street an ornate three-storey pub, built as the PRINCESS ALICE by 1850, but rebuilt by *B.J. Capell* for Truman's Brewery in 1883; the paired first-floor windows have shouldered heads on banded columns; the top floor has two-light Gothic windows set in a band of quatrefoil-patterned tiles. Nos. 44–52 are a handsome continuous warehouse range: below a pronounced cornice the four storeys are divided by string courses. Ground and top floors have arched openings in contrast to the other windows with segmental hoods over straight heads. Cranes and loading bays remain on the restored N part. No. 58 has stucco surrounds to third-floor windows; first storey altered later for large show windows. Three bays were premises of an iron tube maker, John Russell, whose name is faintly visible on the pediment to the fourth floor. C19 four-storey warehouses follow, of brick, partly painted.

The W side starts with a dour grey brick and concrete complex of LCC housing of the 1960s, the twenty-two storey centrepiece flanked by shops with rooftop maisonettes. The unprepossessing rear faces Toynbee Street, where it becomes clear that this is a late cuckoo in an older LCC nest, a post-war addition to the pre-war Holland Estate (*see* perambulation 1b, above). From the corner of Wentworth Street, No. 43 was built as six shops and thirty dwellings by the Jewish and East London Model Lodging House Association, 1862–3 by *H.H. Collins*. Centre part rebuilt. The adjoining Nos. 45–55 was built as the Jews' Infant School, 1858 by *Tillot & Chamberlain*. Substantial, symmetrical composition of 1+5+1 bays, the centre distinguished by stone quoins, with linked arches to the first-floor

*Now in St Giles, Holborn.

windows. Plainer end bays, the entrance on the r., the l. bay altered.

N of Fashion Street the road follows the line of the older Red Lion Street, the W side entirely rebuilt in several stages for Spitalfields Market (*see* above). After Christ Church there are smaller properties on the E side: at the corner of Fournier Street, the TEN BELLS, mid-C19, on a site of a C17 pub: four bays, stucco trim with pediments to the upper windows. Good, tiled interior by *Wm. B. Simpson & Sons*, including a picture in the Commercial Street entrance of 'Spitalfields in ye olden times'. Then a taller C19 brick group, four storeys, Nos. 88–90 with giant arcading. Beyond is PUMA COURT, formerly Red Lion Court, with Almshouses of 1860 by *T.E. Knightley*, a pair of close-set two-storey cottages built to replace the Norton Folgate almshouses in Blossom Street destroyed for the new road. N from here a plain mid-C19 terrace, much altered, up to No. 104. A terracotta plaque on a frontage of 1890 announces the entrance to Stapleton's repository 'established 1842'. Prominent at the canted corner with Hanbury Street, THE GOLDEN HEART is an interwar Neo-Georgian pub, probably by *A.E. Sewell*, with stone-faced centre of three bays; two brick bays either side.

N from Hanbury Street a large stretch of the E side is taken up by the former tobacco works of Godfrey Phillips & Son, who was trading as cigar manufacturer at No. 116 by 1865. Rebuilt and extended by *W. Gilbee Scott* and *B.W.H. Scott* between Jerome Street, Corbet Place and Hanbury Street in 1922–5, and along Commercial Street, with faience facings, in 1927. *B.W.H. Scott* went on to rebuild the corner with Jerome Street in 1935–6, linking it to a new, much showier factory to the N, on the site of the Cambridge Music Hall. A sleek composition of five storeys, faced in buff faience. Above the central entrance, raised attic with Art Deco fluting and clock. Top storey added 1998–9 when converted to apartments. Immediately behind in JEROME STREET, a TELEPHONE EXCHANGE of 1928 by the *Office of Works*. Neo-Georgian with peculiar carved stone rosettes.

On the W side, at the corner of Lamb Street, a former Lloyds Bank, with giant pilasters and large ground-floor windows, 1935 by *Victor Wilkins* (contemporary with Spitalfields extensions to the market). On the triangular site at the corner
57 of Folgate Street, PEABODY BUILDINGS, the first of the Peabody Trust's model housing, built 1863–4 by *H.A. Darbishire*, before the Trust had developed its standard style and layout. An awkward site, with two four-storey wings at an angle. Red brick, with slightly Jacobean-shaped gables. Channelled brick ground floor with shops, upper windows given a little variety by arched, ogee or segmental heads. The quicker rhythm of narrow attic windows reflects the laundry, drying rooms and bathrooms at this level. The flats were later much criticized because they were not self-contained; lavatories were grouped by the staircases, and there were fireplaces only in the

living rooms. Converted to apartments for sale, 1999. N of Fleur de Lis Street, former Police Station, 1874–5 by *F.H. Caiger*. Austere but dignified: ground floor with channelled masonry, upper parts brick, with angular stone window heads. Top storey added 1906.

The COMMERCIAL TAVERN of 1865 makes a show on the E 63
side, at the curved corner to Wheler Street, with its name on a raised central parapet. Three storeys, with rusticated pilasters to the upper floors and paired brackets below eaves. More unusual is the very fancy stuccowork: small heads in fruity wreaths over the arched windows, and jambs with leafy mouldings. A little to the N, No. 152 is recognizable as a former vicarage: a tall urban house in muscular Gothic, with some polychrome brickwork, arched doorway and gable, its appearance compromised by reglazing. Its curved N end echoed St Stephen's church next door, which had the unusual feature of an apsed W end to the street. Both built 1860–1 by *Ewan Christian*. The church was replaced by a cinema in 1933; the church schools in Wheler Street have also gone. Remaining in Wheler Street at the junction with Quaker Street is BEDFORD HOUSE, formerly the Bedford Institute, a Quaker mission named in memory of Peter Bedford, Spitalfields silk merchant, and established here in 1865. The first buildings, in a Gothic style, were by the Quaker architect *William Beck*. Rebuilt in 1894 by *Rutland Saunders*, at a time when the Institute was at its most active, establishing branches in outer East London. Main front to Quaker Street, steeply gabled, in a Dutch mid-C17 style: red brick enlivened by stone bands and keystones, arched windows, and a curious little curved oriel tucked above the pedimented entrance. Two rows of large arched windows along the flank wall and another gable at the W end.

1d. Around Christ Church: Fournier Street and Brick Lane

The development of the area around Christ Church began in the early C18 when two Somerset-born lawyers, Charles Wood and Simon Michell, acquired a tenter ground and market garden to the N of the church site, by that time one of the few areas of Spitalfields not yet built over. Fournier Street, Wilkes Street and Princelet Street were laid out to the S of the already existing Hanbury Street; plots were leased from 1718, mostly to carpenters, and built up with houses superior to most of the existing development in the area. The three streets retain a remarkable number of their original buildings. As the area declined into poverty in the C19, little was rebuilt, although the houses suffered from multi-occupation and industrial use. From the later 1970s, through the endeavours of the Spitalfields Historic Buildings Trust (*see* Elder Street, above) many were gradually reprieved from decay, repaired to a meticulously high standard, and returned to single occupation. By the 1990s the replacement of later ground-floor shops by shuttered windows and replica doorcases was beginning to create an illusory sense of quiet domestic existence and continuing prosperity from the time of building. Old photos tell another story.

FOURNIER STREET, originally Church Street. The S side has the latest and grandest houses, with basements lit by railed areas, unlike the cellars opposite just peeping above the pavement. Directly E of the great cliff of Christ Church, No. 2, the RECTORY, an exceptionally fine, austere design, 1726–9 by *Hawksmoor*. An expensive building, costing the Commissioners £1,456. The three-storey street front matches the scale of its neighbours, but is distinguished by its sober and solider detail. Four bays, segment-headed windows whose deep reveals show the thickness of the walls, rubbed brick dressings, a heavy dentilled cornice of stone, topped by a parapet. At the back, two full-height canted bay windows, early for such a feature, taking advantage of the southward views over the churchyard, which was laid out on the tenter ground extending to Brick Lane. Inside, fielded panelling on two floors; the stair hall occupies the two r. bays, its showpiece a well staircase rising to the attic, with the flight from ground to first floor embellished by carved treads. Leases for the neighbouring houses were granted in 1726, soon after the rectory was begun. No. 4–6 is also a stylish effort, built by *Marmaduke Smith*, carpenter. Five bays, with the Baroque feature of broad Doric end pilasters, and a grand doorcase with rusticated surrounds, carved brackets and a deep hood. Rooms on either side of a central hall with staircase of mahogany, an early use of the material, lit by a large window in the rear. Nos. 8–10 were built by *Samuel Worrall* and Nos. 12–18 by *William Tayler*, both carpenters, and are of the more usual design, three bays each with segment-headed windows. No. 10 has a doorcase with fluted pilasters and upturned arch to the lintel, a popular 1720s pattern, repeated in replica at No. 8. No. 12 was refronted in the early C19, see the arched doorway with fanlight. No. 14, four bays, is more elaborately detailed: doorcase with Ionic columns carrying a curved hood; windows with rubbed brick triple keystones below moulded brick bands. An unusual plan, with well staircase in the SE corner, separated from the entrance hall by a columned opening. A large, panelled first-floor room runs the whole width of the house. Nos. 16–18 have paired doorcases with good carved brackets, No. 20, also leased 1726, has a doorcase like No. 10, and thick early C18 glazing bars (elsewhere such glazing has often been replaced by thinner sashes of the later C18).

The N side starts with the stuccoed Ten Bells at the corner of Commercial Street (*see* above), then Nos. 1–3, a tall pair, built *c.* 1755 when this end of the street was widened. No. 3 has good, panelled interiors, and an upstairs fireplace lined with C18 Delft tiles. At No. 5 the homely Market Café remains as part of a frontage of the early C20, but the house itself dates

from *c.* 1722, built together with Nos. 7–11. E of Wilkes Street, Nos. 15–25 were built under leases of 1725. Nos. 17–25 are all of three bays, No. 17 with an original doorcase with fluted pilasters and hood on elaborate carved modillions. Most have typical upper windows of the early C18: segment-headed openings with rubbed brick surrounds and flush sashes. This group also has a sequence of boarded attics with long windows, probably later additions for weaving lofts. The five-bay No. 27 is 25
distinguished by stone keystones and a doorcase with carved brackets. Built in 1725 for Peter Bourdon, an eminent silk-weaver; used from 1829–1946 as the London Dispensary. Nos. 29–37 is a uniform range of three-bay houses, with the standard type of doorcase with lintel with upturned arch. Built in 1725 by *Samuel Worrall*, carpenter. The entry to his yard lay between Nos. 33 and 35. No. 39 was built in 1744 as minister's house for the adjacent chapel, now London Jamme Moasjid (*see* p. 316).

Continuing past the mosque along Brick Lane one arrives at PRINCELET STREET, parallel to Fournier Street, but less ostentatious (no area railings). The N side has a nearly complete sequence of unassuming three-bay houses. Nos. 21–27, distinguished by brick bands, was built by 1705–6 for the brewer Joseph Truman, together with houses in Brick Lane and Hanbury Street. Nos. 17–19 were built as a pair, *c.* 1718, but No. 19 (now a museum of immigration, *see* p. 400) is now distinguished by a stucco ground floor with arched openings, an alteration made after the house became an adjunct to the former synagogue built out at the back in 1869.

On the S side, at the W end, Nos. 2 and 4, each of four bays with segment-headed windows, by *Worrall*, 1723–4. Near the E end, Nos. 12–22, with straight-headed windows, some with brick keystones 1721, also by *Worrall*, backing on to his yard (*see* Fournier Street). In between, Nos. 8–10, a boldly-scaled boot manufacturer's brick warehouse with some decorative brick detail; 1931–2 by *W.C. Inman*; converted to apartments in 1999. No. 24 provides further variety: an unapologetic red-painted modern house, a 1990s refurbishment of a 1950s building.

WILKES STREET, running N–S, begun 1721, looks at first sight consistently C18, but the street was damaged in the war and its present appearance owes much to late C20 repair and rebuilding. Houses of varying widths: No. 6, one-room deep, has a fine array of five segment-headed windows with rubbed heads, No. 13 has ancient shutters, the model for many replicas; Nos. 23 and 25 have good, Doric doorcases with rusticated pilasters. The street leads N to HANBURY STREET, which existed already in the mid-C17. Disappointingly, the N side was destroyed in 1970 for the C20 buildings of the Brewery (*see* p. 424). On the S side scrappy remains of the later C18 and early C19. Further E, Hanbury Community Project, a former chapel of 1719, extended to the street in 1864 by *C.M. North*, and adapted for use as Christ Church Hall in 1867–8. An odd, broad front with arched windows and oculus above, some red and black brick decoration.

Nos. 24 and 26 date from *c.* 1717–18, a pair with unusual detail: shaped brick lintels and inset brick keystones to the central first-floor windows. Nos. 34–8, with straight-headed windows and stone bands, were built in 1705–6, together with the similar houses behind in Princelet Street.

Brick Lane and its neighbourhood

Brick Lane, busy and narrow, the centre of today's 'Banglatown', has much character but little that stands out architecturally. The street was strongly Jewish in the early C20, but has since become a centre for the Bangladeshi immigrants who settled in the area in large numbers from the 1970s. Its name came from the nearby claypits used for brickmaking. It was first built up haphazardly during the C17, and much rebuilt around 1900. To the N the lane leads into Bethnal Green (*see* p. 584) past the extensive former brewery buildings of Truman, Hanbury, Buxton & Co., of 1700 onwards (*see* perambulation *1f*). The dominant visual impression of the southern part, described below, is of the consistency of scale of the three-storey buildings contrasted with the colourful multitude of small Asian shops and restaurants.

BRICK LANE, at the NE corner with Hanbury Street, has the date 1903, on a neat red brick terrace, possibly by *H.H. Collins* for Jewish builder developers H. & I. Davis. To the S, Nos. 114–122 are a group of two-bay houses; above a C20 ground floor, they are early C18, with a frontage renewed *c.* 1795. Here Spitalfields Soup Ladling Society was founded in 1797 at a time of great food shortages during the Napoleonic wars. It is commemorated by a plaque with date over a passage next to No. 116. On the W side a few other C18 houses are recognizable above shopfronts (Nos. 75, 67, both with brick bands.) In between is the former Laurel Tree, probably by *B.J. Capell* for Truman's, with terracotta plaque dated 1901. After the Mosque (*see* above), No. 57 at the S corner of Fournier Street is also early C18.

CHRIST CHURCH PRIMARY, 1873–4 by *James Tolley & D. Robert Dale*, the successor to charity schools established in 1708. The school provides a low interlude on the W side, set back from Brick Lane between projecting wings originally designed as houses for the master and mistress. Red brick with blue brick diapering and stone dressings, steep slate roof with ornamental ridge tiles. The centre range of two storeys and four half-dormered windows contained classrooms over a Gothic-arcaded covered playground (now filled in), constructed on arches in order to avoid disturbing graves. Stairs at either end, one in a bay-fronted lobby, the other open. The plaque on the S wing shows the first purpose-built parochial schools of 1782.

On the street front a sturdy DRINKING FOUNTAIN with octagonal cap. The Seven Stars, a tall pub with pantiled roof, is of 1937 by *William Stewart*.

FASHION STREET W of Brick Lane. The name is a corruption from Fossan, its C17 builder, but suits the strangely exotic-looking range on the S side. This dates from 1905, erected by the builder/developers *Abraham* and *Woolf Davis* as a market arcade in Moorish style (perhaps inspired by the similar style of the Cambridge Music Hall of 1898 in Commercial Street, now demolished). Lively patterning of red brick, terracotta and cream render, restored 2003–4. The long frontage is punctuated by pyramid-roofed former entrance pavilions with pairs of arches and terracotta frieze. Upper floor with a busy rhythm of close-set horseshoe arches. The arcade was a commercial failure; part was converted to industrial uses in 1909.

Back in Brick Lane, on the E side, the black-painted Café Naz, a smart refurbishment of the 1990s, occupies the shell of the former Mayfair Cinema, 1935 by *Leslie Kemp & F.E. Tasker*. On the W side the Sheraz restaurant, formerly the Frying Pan, 1891 by *S.W. Grant*. Terracotta plaque.

SPITALFIELDS HEALTH CENTRE makes a prominent show on the W side of Brick Lane. 1984 by *Shepheard Epstein & Hunter* with *John Allan Architects*. An example of the new type of the light and airy health centre of the 1980s, incorporating several clearly defined health facilities. An awkward site with a narrow frontage. An impressive prow-like front to Brick Lane: a sharply raked roofline descends down to the domestic scale of the entrances, flanking a double-height window. Inside, informally planned with small waiting areas opening off a top-lit staircase.

The health centre heralds the rebuilt area around FLOWER AND DEAN WALK, named from two mid-C17 bricklayers who first built up the area. In the late C19 Flower and Dean Street became notorious for its common lodging houses; twenty-eight in 1882. The street was rebuilt with 'model dwellings' by several different companies from 1886–1908, following a MBW slum-clearance scheme of 1877. In reaction against these severe, close-set tenements, the area was radically reconstructed a century later for the Toynbee Housing Association, by *Shepheard, Epstein & Hunter*, 1983–4. Low brown brick housing, densely grouped around quiet pedestrian cul-de-sacs. A mix of staggered two- and three-storey terraces and less formal catslide roofs creates some visual variety. The central walk emerges in WENTWORTH STREET, through a decorative brick and terracotta archway dated 1886, a survival from the tenements built by *N.S. Joseph* for the Four per cent Industrial Dwellings Company founded by Nathaniel Rothschild in 1885 for the benefit of Jewish artisans.

The S side of Wentworth Street mostly has buildings for Toynbee Hall (*see* above). On the E corner of Gunthorpe Street, the DELLOW CENTRE (Providence Row Housing Association) incorporates the convent formerly in Crispin

Street (*see* perambulation *1b*). Neat, unassuming pale brick, four storeys, broken by three glazed staircase bays; projecting bows at N and S ends. The S bow has a chapel on the top floor with window by *Patrick Reyntiens*. To the S one-storey range with six sharp gables along the curve of Gunthorpe Street, refurbished in the 1980s with new build by *Shepheard, Epstein & Hunter* for Toynbee Hall.

1e. Mile End New Town, E of Brick Lane: a circular tour from S to N

The area E of Brick Lane, known in the C18 as Mile End New Town, was patchily built up from the C17 onwards. Its old centre lay around Greatorex Street. It became industrial from *c.* 1800, and was badly overcrowded and poverty-stricken by the early C20, when the area was filled with Jewish immigrants. Parts of the area close to Brick Lane still have a close-knit mix of commercial and domestic building, but further E the tight pattern of small streets was simplified by the rebuilding which began between the wars. More sweeping comprehensive redevelopment took place after the district was added to the official Stepney–Poplar reconstruction area in 1960. Piecemeal replanning over fifty years helps to explain the incoherent mixture that resulted: older schools and welfare buildings once slotted into the old network of streets were left stranded among unrelated schemes of social housing. More recent building following the old street lines is beginning to re-create the urban character destroyed in the mid-C20.

The tour starts in the centre of Brick Lane opposite Christ Church school. HENEAGE STREET leads E. On the S side, No. 2, now flats, was a synagogue called Ezrat Haim (Life's Work). Opposite is an informal group whose adaptation in the 1980s demonstrates the growing concern to preserve existing character. A low pub, THE PRIDE OF SPITALFIELDS, has a C20 front concealing an older building which belonged to the White Lion brewery. Then Nos. 5a and b, new houses discreetly set back, and No. 5, Brewer's House, with plain, early C19 street front. No. 7 was discreetly converted to architects' offices for *MacCormac Jamieson Prichard*, 1982. More office conversions in industrial buildings around HUGUENOT SQUARE, reached through a carriageway.

Further E, bounded by Casson Street, Spelman Street and Chicksand Street, a survival from the dense urban pattern of *c.* 1900: close-set tenement housing, 1901 by *H. Chatfeild Clarke*, given some architectural pretension by terracotta trim and gabled roofline. S of this is OLD MONTAGUE STREET, which until the 1960s had an array of small Jewish shops and businesses. All that remains of its pre-war character is a tall L-shaped block of private flats, the front in Moderne style with corner windows; the back with cramped, iron access balconies.

By *Edgar Tanner*, 1936. At the corner of Old Montague Street and GREATOREX STREET, formerly Great Garden Street, are the buildings associated with the Great Garden Synagogue, a model synagogue built in 1896 for the Federation of Synagogues by *Lewis Solomon*. It lay back from the street with associated halls and youth centre occupying Nos. 9–11. The low range with mosaic-clad upper floor is a rebuilding of 1962, the adjoining buildings added in 1974 housed the head offices of the Federation and a Kosher Luncheon Club. They closed in 1992 when the Federation moved to NW London. Converted to offices and studios and deftly united by white-walled passages in 1999 by *Ankur Architects*. Within a small courtyard are preserved the foundation stones of 1962, and of synagogues of 1914 and 1896. Part of the site of the galleried synagogue area remains as a top-lit space.

At the NE corner of OLD MONTAGUE STREET is a cheerful effort to reinvigorate the street scene: a striking bowed front in striped brick, part of an L-shaped group by *Hunt Thompson*, 1993, with advice centre and three storeys of balconied workshops along Greatorex Street. The site was originally reserved for a synagogue, to replace those cleared for the Chicksand Estate in 1960. Further N in Greatorex Street, a three-storey yellow brick terrace of houses and flats by *Hunt Thompson* for the Spitalfields Co-operative Housing Association.

The LCC's CHICKSAND ESTATE illustrates half a century of urban renewal, extending on either side of Greatorex Street up to Spelman Street and Vallance Road. In the earlier, W part, Chicksand House is the centrepiece, completed 1937; the start of clearances which simplified the C19 street pattern. The usual five-storey ranges, laid out in the LCC's routine formal manner, set back from the street on three sides of a grassed area. Plain Neo-Georgian fronts, long brick access balconies behind, curving round corners. Close by at the corner of Greatorex Street is a nod to neighbourhood conviviality, the QUEEN'S HEAD, a corner pub now sad and disused.

The post-war part of the estate, E of Greatorex Street, is in a quite different spirit. Here a triangular wedge of small streets dense with synagogues (four in this area alone) was swept away for a classic example of the LCC's mixed development of the 1960s, with buildings of different heights and types composed around a landscaped pedestrian area. Its landmark at the far end, the nineteen-storey point block, Pauline House, 1960–1 (architect-in-charge *R. Jackson*, job architect *G.B. Finch*), was the first part to be built, on the site of a bombed Board school; the rest followed from 1964. Along Greatorex Street and HANBURY STREET powerfully dour ranges of six-storey maisonettes enclose the precinct, of sober dark brick relieved by pebbly concrete bands; strong enough in character not to be diminished by the cheerfully personalized ground floors and front gardens which have developed along Hanbury Street. Within the precinct the effect is gentler and visually more varied; the maisonettes with light-coloured balconies look out over an attractively quiet and spacious green; a path, SPRING WALK, runs past low old people's housing to a row of staggered two-storey houses on a friendly scale. The name pays homage to a row of humble cottages on the site, built 1813–19.* Nearer the tower paved spaces contrast with the grassed area. All this has a coherence and quality lacking in the later parts of the estate N of Hanbury Street: W of Deal Street: later 1960s maisonettes in dark brick with a former corner pub gloomily rebuilt to match, and further E, unappealingly lumpy six-storey blocks in white brick of 1974.

In Hanbury Street at the corner of Deal Street, a towering BOARD SCHOOL of 1895–6 with handsome red-and-yellow brick front; end pediment with the motto *Lux Mihi Laus*; on the N side two more pediments and a broad projecting bow. The roof playground indicates the former shortage of open space. Further E is No. 192–6, the BRADY CENTRE, 1935 by *Ernest Joseph*, on the site of a C19 Salvation Army Hostel. Now an arts centre, but formerly a Jewish girls' club, an offshoot of the boys' club established nearby in 1896 in Durward Street. A period piece, three storeys with faience-clad base, Crittall-type windows. The splayed canopy is a later addition. Extended E for a gymnasium in 1959 on land freed by the clearance for the Chicksand Estate. Later extension to the W. Remodelling by *Wallbank Architects* 1996–9, created a roof extension with art rooms and a pleasant top-lit exhibition foyer.

VALLANCE ROAD, formerly Baker's Row, was named after the late C19 clerk of the Whitechapel Union, responsible for the Workhouse Infirmary, later St Peter's Hospital, which dominated the E side of the road until after the Second World War. To its S (and overlooked in Corbusian fashion by the tower of the Chicksand Estate) a small RECREATION GROUND was laid out for the Whitechapel District Board in 1880 on the site of a burial ground, at the suggestion of Canon Barnett. A chipped marble fountain given by the Metropolitan Association remains, but, alas, not the 'rockwork entrance' and the decorative panels donated by the Kyrle Society. Vallance Road is now scrappy. Near the S end the street is still late C19: Nos. 3–11 have unusually eclectic stucco and sgraffito decoration. N of the recreation ground the hospital, damaged in the war, was replaced by Lister House and Treves House, nine and four storeys, built 1956 for the LCC by *Stillman & Eastwick Field* (associate-in-charge *R. Smorczewski*). Two trimly modern blocks with horizontal bands of windows, behind a nicely landscaped forecourt. LISTER HOUSE, designed 1955, attracted attention as an early example of a plan with central corridor and maisonettes on a 'crossover' plan, enabling each to have rooms facing both E and W. Its compact streamlined appearance contrasts with the adjacent post-war flats of HUGHES MANSIONS, 1952–4 by the Borough of Stepney, with whose

*A few survived to the 1960s, but were not deemed worthy of retention.

old-fashioned ways the LCC became so irritated. The red brick cluster is grouped quite cleverly on a staggered plan, providing some visual variety between the horizontal lines of the access balconies, a vertical curved bow and the more broken effect of private balconies (in the early 1950s still a novel amenity). The pre-war block of HUGHES MANSIONS makes a show to Vallance Road, 1928 by *B.J. Belsher*, Borough Architect, as a plaque proudly declares; five storeys with some red-tile ornament in front above ground-floor shops, the frontage broken by two projecting gabled bays. The flats are named after the social worker Mary Hughes (1860–1941), who lived at No. 71a Vallance Road next to the pub which she converted as the Dewdrop Inn, a centre for the homeless.

Between Selby Street and the railway line are desolate cleared areas. A few patches of new housing suggest a transition to uneventful domesticity. To the E, filling the site of the Spitalfields Coal Depot, a quiet traditional suburban enclave of well-grouped buildings in red and yellow brick, 1992 by *Feilden & Mawson*. To the W, FAKRUDDIN STREET, a self-contained close of neat two-storey 1990s Neo-Regency houses by the Spitalfields Housing Co-operative. S of this in Buxton Road, ROBERT MONTEFIORE SCHOOL, a low post-war primary.

This tour returns W along UNDERWOOD ROAD, which has a succession of older buildings providing for the needs of the neighbourhood. First the large OSMANI SECONDARY SCHOOL, of the 1930s. Further on, the MARY HUGHES CHILDREN'S CENTRE, formerly the Jewish Maternity Home, which was established behind Nos. 24–26 in 1911. A crow-stepped gabled house faces the street. Extended by *Messrs Joseph* in 1927–8, with an attractive three-storey range in Early Georgian style with big coved cornice and pretty tiled window-heads in an Arts and Crafts tradition. After some later C20 low-rise housing comes the stately stone-clad group of St Anne's R.C. church and presbytery (*see* above), now facing play-grounds instead of C19 terraces. The one notable survivor of C19 housing in the area is a little further S down DEAL STREET. VICTORIA COTTAGES (E), 1857, and ALBERT COT- 60
TAGES (W) 1865, are sweet paired two-storey terraces with little gardens, late additions to a pioneering housing scheme by the Metropolitan Association for Improving the Dwellings of the Industrious Classes. The earlier buildings further N (now dem.) were a lodging house for single men (1848) and a five-storey block of 'family dwellings' (1849–50) by *William Beck*, winner of a competition in *The Builder* of 1848. The two surviving groups provided thirty-two and thirty-six dwellings, with a separate flat on each floor, intended for those who could not afford the higher rents of the family dwellings. Pairs of doors face the path between each of the two rows.

Deal Street continues N to BUXTON STREET where demolition has left little to see. On the edge of a featureless open space, the post-war THOMAS BUXTON INFANT SCHOOL, one storey, stepped back symmetrically, and further on a solitary group associated with the church of All Saints of 1839, the first Anglican church to be built in Mile End New Town (demolished 1951). Near its site, a two-storey C19 school, then a taller gabled building (Old St Patrick's School). To their W the demure three-storey former Vicarage, a three-bay house in late Georgian style but with Tudor hoodmoulds and Gothic panelled door. The park has the welcome diversion of a CITY FARM; the isolated building by the railway viaduct is Weaver House, Stepney flats of 1929.

Back S by SPITAL STREET past Stepney Borough flats of 1956–63, and the long nine-bay frontage of the COOPERAGE of Truman's Brewery. Finally the very urban part of HANBURY STREET which runs towards Brick Lane. On the N side large warehouses (Nos. 49–59), opposite, Nos. 40–66, 1906 by *J.R. Moore-Smith* for Maurice Davis, builder/developer. Shops with three storeys of flats above, crowned by flamboyantly Netherlandish crow stepped gables with ball finials.

1f. Truman's Brewery, Brick Lane

The former buildings of Truman, Hanbury and Buxton's Black Eagle Brewery divide the N and S ends of Brick Lane; a wonderfully complete example of a brewery with distinguished survivals from the C18–C20.

A brewhouse was built on land W of Brick Lane by Thomas Bucknall *c.* 1666 and purchased by Joseph Truman in 1679. Expansion began *c.* 1730 under Sir Benjamin Truman who enlarged the premises further in 1742–3, possibly with *John Price* as surveyor. The E frontage to Brick Lane measured 156ft, that to the S, 163ft, extending N to Westbury (now Quaker) Street by 1779. Sampson Hanbury and Thomas Fowell Buxton joined the firm in 1800, heralding the first of two phases of major expansion up to 1858, when Truman, Hanbury, Buxton & Co. was the third largest brewery in London. Records suggest that *James Young* and *James Brodie* were surveyors for several of the surviving early C19 buildings with *Robert Davison*, a major innovator in brewery design, making important extensions E of Brick Lane after 1830, when Beer Duty was abolished. The brewhouse was rebuilt in 1924–7 by *A.R. Robertson*, but replaced in the programme of large-scale modernization by *Arup Associates c.* 1970–7. The brewery closed in 1988 and since 1991 has been imaginatively redeveloped and refurbished as a multi-faceted arts, media and commercial enclave.

The buildings lie on either side of Brick Lane, between Hanbury Street and Quaker Street, centred on the cobbled former brewhouse yard on the W side. Set back is the former BREWHOUSE, rebuilt for the final time *c.* 1973–7 by *Arup Associates* who screened the functional concrete and brick structure with a daring stepped façade of mirrored glass, its silvered panels reflecting the surrounding buildings. Contemporary railings and gateway, traditional in spirit.

S of the courtyard is the DIRECTORS' HOUSE, facing Brick Lane. Nine bays and two storeys with a flat parapet and cornice. Its present appearance probably of *c.* 1745. *John Price*, who had recently rebuilt the brewhouse for Benjamin Truman, is thought to have enlarged an early C18 counting house; visible vertical joins in the brickwork mark the additional bays on this side. At the ends are narrow, slightly projecting, pilastered features set with Venetian windows in the upper floors (also on the S face). Round-headed windows in the second and eighth bays of the upper floor, probably later than the flat-headed sashes. The short N façade to the courtyard was remodelled, *c.* 1970 by *Arup Associates*.

Inside, the original layout can only be guessed at but comprised offices on the ground floor with Truman's residence above. The entrance is now from the yard but the staircase is placed at the S end of the house. Good C19 cast-iron balustrade, curved return, and lit by an oval lantern. On the first floor, the S rooms were originally for use of the directors. Some still have moulded skirtings, dados and cornices and, in several rooms, good Rococo fireplaces, evidently inserted in the 1740s. The rest of the first floor was much remodelled for Sir Benjamin Truman in the 1770s. According to his will, these improvements were undertaken to encourage his great grandsons 'to spend some part of their time in Spitalfields, especially during the winter season'. This may explain why the several surviving fine (though restored) interiors are reminiscent of a wealthy country mansion rather than a town house. The design of the N CORRIDOR strongly suggests the involvement of *Sir* 26
Robert Taylor. Five bays of circular arched vaults rise alternately into domes between fluted Ionic pilasters. Fluted and pedimented doorcases and much formalized floral decoration. By contrast, the former DINING ROOM on the N side of the corridor has simple mid-C18 panelling with a dentilled cornice. At its W end is a cupboard, probably once connected to the small ante-room adjoining. SW of the corridor, the *tour de force* is the former DRAWING ROOM, added to the house in 1745. Of that date, the heavily moulded plaster panelling, floreted-modillion cornice and richly decorated ceiling with birds holding festoons and putti as the Four Seasons in each corner. The decoration of sphinx and lyre on the marble chimney-piece is similar to one at the Bank of England by *Taylor*. A screen of marbled Corinthian columns must also be of the 1770s.

Closing the N side of the courtyard, the former HEAD BREWER'S HOUSE of *c.* 1834–7, probably by *Robert Davison*, with a regular two-bay front with staircases in quadrant curved wings to its side. The building to its rear was converted in the 1920s for use as the Experimental Brewery, a small-scale working brewhouse for the testing of ingredients and plant, an innovation reflecting the increasingly scientific methods applied to brewing by this date. Its five-storey, five-bay round-arched yellow brick flank was retained and restored to its original form in the 1970s. To Quaker Street, four bays of new brickwork, all in keeping.

On the E side of Brick Lane, early C19 expansion led to the erection of the VAT HOUSE, *c.* 1803–5, probably by *James Young* and *John Brodie*. A charming three-bay front of simple classical design, rather like a meeting-house, with open-pediment, clock and hexagonal cupola (containing a bell of 1803). Central pedimented entrance, a remodelling of the 1840s, beneath three large round-arched iron-framed windows to the vat room, its floor carried on iron columns with capitals supporting I-beam girders to sustain the great weight of the beer. Truncated N façade with twin gables over the remaining two bays. The neighbouring three-storey, four-bay ENGINEER'S HOUSE *c.* 1831–6, presumably by *Davison* for himself, is subdued late Georgian with a side entrance and round-headed ground-floor window set between Doric pilaster strips. Partially tile-hung to the rear. Following on, *Davison*'s STABLES of 1837, reflect the might of Truman's by the mid-C19. Blank ground floor, beneath a striking arcaded upper floor with circular windows and a stucco pediment surmounted by the eponymous black eagle. Designed to house 114 horses but accommodating nearly twice that number in double-decked boxes by 1891. From its N end sprouts a towering chimney in red brick with the company name inset in white tiles, dating from conversion to a boiler house and canteen in 1929 by *A.R. Robertson*. Behind is the former cooperage, with a grand entrance from Spital Street (*see* perambulation *1e*).

C20 expansion vastly increased the extent of the brewery. S of the Directors' House, a former bottling store of 1929, its deep loading bays in DRAY WALK have been successfully converted to retail use, extended S to HANBURY STREET by *Gordon Smith & Partners*, 1970. Brick with crenellated metal roof. The same firm constructed the warehouse on the E side of Brick Lane and numerous large stores and warehouses, now derelict, W towards Commercial Street, linked high over street level by a series of enclosed bridges.

2. *Whitechapel*

2a. *Whitechapel High Street and Whitechapel Road*

Whitechapel High Street is the beginning of London 'East of Aldgate' and here the contrast between the prosperity of the City and its eastern neighbour is decidedly marked. Until the later C20 buildings on the High Street, and its continuation Whitechapel Road, remained predominantly three and four storeyed, with a plentiful supply of inns, a mixture of narrow C18 and C19 frontages, and narrow alleys leading off, typical of an ancient street pattern. War damage and indifferent later redevelopment have left only scrappy remains and the gradual creep of the City further threatens the intimate scale.

The tour can begin from Aldgate East Underground station in WHITECHAPEL HIGH STREET. On the S side the SEDGWICK CENTRE of 1986–8 by *Fitzroy Robinson Partnership* continues the overweening scale of the City. Eight storeys of offices, behind mirror glazing within a grid of chamfered mullions and floorbands faced in polished granite. A lean-to glazed W canopy over the entrance to an underground shopping mall. E of this is a building site in 2004. On the N side, at the corner with Goulston Street, the Students' Union of London Metropolitan University occupies a building which had already broken the mould in 1939. By *Philip S.B. Nicolle*, company architect to Price's Tailors Ltd, built as workshops and showrooms. A handsome block, seven storeys with set-back attic. Brick, with Moderne details: ribbon windows wrapping around the corner and faience-faced first floor with chevron band, but in the classical tradition it has a stone cornice above the sixth floor. The rest of the N side maintains an older scale. No. 130, NATWEST BANK, has a restrained Neo-Georgian frontage, with pediment over all three bays, and a tripartite window above a black marble-faced ground floor. Surprisingly late for this treatment, rebuilt *c.* 1959 after bomb damage to the original bank of 1864. Narrow-fronted houses follow: No. 129, late C19, stucco trim; two bays, four storeys and dormers. Big keystones of first-floor windows rise into the aprons of the windows above, a Baroque touch. Then No. 128, C18, but much altered; brick; two bays, four storeys. Nos. 122–5 were demolished *c.* 1890 to widen the entrance to Old Castle Street in the wake of the last of the notorious murders of 1888, shortly after the overcrowded alleys to the N had been cleared by the Metropolitan Board of Works. Flanking Tyne Street, a group of three houses with terracotta leaf frieze over first-floor windows and monogram WHW; *c.* 1880–3, the date of the narrow alley's realignment. To the corner with Commercial Street, offices and hotel begun in 2004 by *John Seifert Architects*.

The junction of the High Street, Commercial Street and Commercial Road was busy even in the C19 and replaced by a daunting gyratory system in 1976. Stranded in its centre on the S side of the High Street is the SUMMIT SPORTS AND CONFERENCE CENTRE of 1985 by *Frederick Gibberd, Coombes & Partners*. One of the first awkward intrusions on the E fringe of the City, for which its facilities were clearly intended. A white-panelled exterior, tall, with silo-like corner towers; its faux-industrial appearance made even more ludicrous by the giant globe lanterns suspended on arms from the roof. Then, LLOYDS BANK with brick piers and glazed vertical panels, only three storeys, in deference to the older group which follows. CENTRAL HOUSE (London Metropolitan University), dominates the next stretch. 1963–4 by *Lush & Lester*, intended for flatted factories above warehouse and shops (although the N blocks were almost immediately taken over by the Sir John Cass School of Art). This was one of the few post-war efforts in the area to provide new working conditions in multi-purpose buildings. Four blocks, each of six floors, with an internal service road. A bold asymmetrical composition with central open staircase, exposed concrete floors and precast panels (overpainted).

On the N side of the High Street, E of Commercial Street, FAIRHOLT HOUSE, *c.* 1910 by *J. Wallis Chapman and Shepherd* for Atkinson's clothing store. Arched mezzanine and two upper storeys on W side rebuilt after war damage. Further on, after some indifferent buildings, the WHITE HART. Only one bay wide, but its C19 front with tripartite window grandly flanked by giant Corinthian pilasters. The rear with (done up) sign 'established 1721' is visible from a passage to Gunthorpe Street. Incorporating the passage entry, ALBERT'S (No. 88) was reconstructed for the short-lived *Jewish Daily Post*, the first Anglo-Jewish daily newspaper, in 1935 by *H.P. Sanders*. Deco-style shopfront with black marble fascia bearing an elaborate badge of Jewish symbols set within the Star of David, by *Arthur Szyk*, the Polish Jewish artist. No. 87 was the headquarters of the George Yard Mission established in 1856 by George Holland. The Mission erected several buildings as it expanded, including Sir George's Home for Girls of 1886, which survives behind in Gunthorpe Street. No. 85 is a crumbling former public house by *Bird & Walters*, 1900. Alongside, in the atmospheric ANGEL ALLEY, is a mural of radical writers and anarchists by *Anya Patel* for the Freeform Arts Trust and the Freedom Press, whose left-wing bookshop here is an East End institution. The George Yard Ragged School on the opposite side of the alley was demolished for the extension of the Whitechapel Art Gallery (*see* above).

p. 24 WHITECHURCH LANE runs S of the High Street skirting ALTAB ALI PARK, the former churchyard of St Mary Matfelon. The original 'white chapel' began as a C13 chapel of ease to St Dunstan Stepney (q.v.). It was rebuilt in the C14 by the Matfelon family, in the later C17, and again, in C13 style, by *Ernest C. Lee* in 1875–7. Demolished in 1952 after war damage; its outline traced by stones laid out on the grass. In the wall at the corner with Whitechapel Road a DRINKING FOUNTAIN of 1860, moved here in 1879, quite elaborate, with Norman arch under a coped gable now sheltering a shapeless stone lump on a polished-granite plinth. Its inscription is mysterious: 'Erected by one who is known yet unknown'. In 1989 the churchyard was renamed in memory of a local Bangladeshi youth murdered in 1978. The C19 Gothic GATEPIERS have an iron overthrow by *David Petersen*, 1989, symbolically combining motifs of Bangladeshi and English Perp architecture. A few tombstones to the NE. To the SE, a fine tapered sarcophagus to the Maddock family (†1770s–†1801), armorial panel on the W end, a damaged urn on the pyramidal top. The sides are decorated with Vitruvian scroll and gadrooned band. In the SW corner is the MARTYRS' MONUMENT (Shaheed Minar), a copy of that erected in Bangladesh to the memory of five students killed in 1952. Each is represented by a narrow free-standing steel screen with inclined head set on a semicircular platform and grouped in front of a large blood-red circular panel. Installed in 1999, to designs by *Freeform Arts Trust* with *Arts Fabrications*.

The small streets around the churchyard, WHITECHURCH LANE, MANNINGTREE STREET and ASSAM STREET still convey something of the chaotic character of pre-war Whitechapel, with domestic terraces overtaken by the rag trade, interspersed with modest industrial building of between the wars, such as Nos. 29–33 Whitechurch Lane, with curved windows. Also in Whitechurch Lane, former ST MARY'S CLERGY HOUSE, 1894 by *Herbert O. Ellis*, a deliberately picturesque exception, red brick with stone dressings, three gabled bays of mullioned windows and a corner turret. The neatest of the older houses is No. 17, the standard early C19 type with first-floor windows within arches. A bomb damaged gap S of the park was filled *c.* 2000 by the large blocks of flats in render and engineering brick by *Squire & Partners*. To its S in ASSAM STREET the back of the former St George's Brewery (*see* Commercial Road, p. 491); three giant arches with big stone keystones extending through three floors.

On the park's E side, ADLER STREET suffered badly from a flying bomb and was entirely rebuilt, with the austere tower of St Boniface R.C. German church on the corner of Mulberry Street providing a landmark. In this small area before the war there was a Jewish reading room and two synagogues and a tiny street of houses off Mulberry Street. The reconstruction plans decreed that this should be an industrial and commercial zone, so opposite the church in Adler Street Nos. 1–13 are four-storey flatted workshops by *YRM* for the LCC, 1963–4. They form a bold Brutalist composition in concrete, with inset first floor behind an aggregate-faced balcony rail and piloti at one end.

Mulberry Street leads to PLUMBER'S ROW and the famous WHITECHAPEL BELL FOUNDRY, recorded in Whitechapel from the C15. It has been on this site from 1738, when it took over the Artichoke Inn, and was enlarged after *c.* 1805 under Thomas Mears to undertake bell hanging. Facing Plumber's Row a workshop range with sturdy jib crane above a broad gated carriageway, leading into the yard. This has early C19 workshops built around it with further workshops added to the S in 1981. No. 2 is a three-bay early C18 domestic front: doorway with rusticated surround, straight-headed windows with flush frames. Round the corner in WHITECHAPEL ROAD, the foundry continues with No. 34, C18 in reddish-brown brick, of two bays, with a beautiful early C19 timber shopfront that has ingenious sliding vertical shutters and Soanian incised detail. Inside, painted and grained fittings and access to the cellar of the former inn. No. 32, of the same build, is five bays wide and handsome: it must have served as a home for the foundry's master. Pedimented and pilastered doorcase and original railings. Two rooms at the front (now the foundry's offices) retain polite C18 fittings including arched recesses either side of the fireplace in the room to the r. of the entrance. Then Nos. 28 and 30, two bay, each with C20 shopfronts.

WHITECHAPEL ROAD N side is all post-war up to Greatorex Street. Prominent is No. 45, Black Lion House, large and unappealing offices of the 1980s, seven storeys high, faced in polished brown stone. The l. part set back. On the courtyard, four plain brick plinths carry some insignificantly small sculptures, Les Naïades by *Ivor Abrahams*, 1985. Further E, altered three-storey terraces over shops, and the OLD BLUE ANCHOR, an elaborately stuccoed frontage of *c.* 1860, three storeys with attic above cornice. A varied mix on the S side begins E of Plumber's Row with the LONDON MUSLIM CENTRE of 2004 and the East London Mosque (*see* above). No. 120, the former ROYAL OAK, *c.* 1870, has an elaborate five-bay front; window surrounds with curved corners and moulded detail; cast-iron balconies to the second floor, and a pedimented centre. Then Nos. 128–30 with two tall gables and the date 1901.

Back on the N side: a fairly varied but interesting group. First, BOOTH HOUSE, a Salvation Army hostel by *Fraser Brown McKenna*, 2000–2, re-using the structure of the previous building by *H.M. Lidbetter* but replacing the façade with light steel framing panels of unbonded red brick. William Booth founded his first headquarters in Whitechapel Road in 1866. Further on the Davenant Centre and Jagonari Centre (*see* above). E of Vallance Road, the busy street market opposite the London Hospital (*see* above) has as its backdrop a terrace with some much altered C18 houses. In the midst of the market, DRINKING FOUNTAIN, 1911 by *W.S. Frith*, bronze angel of peace on a tapering stone pillar with low-relief bronze plaques of Justice, Liberty, cherubs and a portrait head of King Edward VII, in whose honour the fountain was 'erected from subscriptions raised by Jewish inhabitants of East London'.

Further along a few pubs with good fronts; the LORD NAPIER, and the GRAVE MAURICE, 1874, three storeys with Gothic overtones, and Nos. 271–3, 1920s Neo-Georgian, three bays between giant pilasters under arched pediment. Next to Whitechapel Underground Station, Nos. 279–81 (now flats), were built as the Working Lads Institute by *George Baines*, 1884–5, extended 1886–8 for lecture hall and swimming bath. Working Lads Institutes were first proposed in 1876, by J.E. Saunders of the Corporation of London, to provide distractions for boys over thirteen in between work and home. The institute at Whitechapel was to have been the first of several in London with reading room, library, classroom, bank and clothing club. A single Arts and Crafts stained glass window of the Tree of Life survived conversion in 1997. Probably by *A.O. Hemming & Co.* who provided windows for the Lecture Hall depicting Art, Religion, Industry and the Seasons.

Opposite is the London Hospital Tavern, grotesquely and unsympathetically repainted, then the very dull 1960s EAST LONDON MAIL CENTRE and POST OFFICE (originally linked by underground railway to Paddington via Mount Pleasant and St Martin le Grand. *H.H. Dalrymple-Hay*, engineer). Closing the S side, No. 234; former London & South Western Bank. 1889 by *Edward Gabriel*. Deep, three-bay arcaded windows, with mask keystones. Upper floors of mullioned windows in Bath stone. Off-centre pediment. Strapwork decoration beneath first and third floors.

E of Brady Street on the N side is the Ideas Store (*see* above) and ALBION YARD, the remaining buildings of the Albion Brewery, closed 1979 and converted to flats in 1993–4 by *Peter Brooks Associates*. The first brewhouse was established in 1808 by the landlord of the Blind Beggar public house and acquired by James Mann in 1826. Rebuilt 1860–8, probably by *E.N. Clifton*, for Mann, Crossman & Paulin whose name still graces the arched iron overthrow above the gates. W of the entrance, the former Head Brewer's House (NatWest), a four-storey block in plain yellow brick with windows in relieving arches. To its rear, a lower range originally for stores and fermenting rooms, with a rooftop water tank dated 1864. Balancing to the E, the former Brewery Offices and stores of 1863–4; now Health Centre. Four-storeys with six bays of recessed windows; C20 upper floor. Ground-floor hall with plaster ceiling, decorated with bands of entwined hops and barley. Within the courtyard a later two-storey porte cochère in Portland stone. Probably contemporary with the expansion of the brewery, *c*. 1902–5 by *William Bradford & Sons*. At about this date, the 1860s fermenting house at the rear of the courtyard was remodelled and liberally embellished in show-off Baroque style, dominated by a high pedimented gable between huge carved volutes, a clock and a splendid carved relief of St George & the Dragon, its sculptor sadly unknown. Much carved detail of hops and barley.

The brewery's engineer, *Robert Spence*, rebuilt the adjoining BLIND BEGGAR pub in 1894. Workmanlike Queen Anne with gables, stamped terracotta detail and two wide four-centred arch doorways. A worker's canteen and billiard room were added on the E side of Cambridge Heath Road (Nos. 2–12), *c*. 1930 by *Stewart and Hendry* in a very regressive style of red and brown brick with mullioned windows.

The Brewery's extensive works, extending N along BRADY STREET were cleared for SAINSBURY'S in 1993–4. By *D.Y. Davies Associates*, in brick with curved Perspex canopies to the fore. W of Brady Street is the more inspiringly innovative SWANLEA SECONDARY SCHOOL (*see* above), dominated by its graciously curving roof. It extends along DURWARD STREET where the contemporary spirit continues with the WHITECHAPEL SPORTS CENTRE, by *Pollard Edwards*, 1998. A low, wide plan, defined to the street by a long curving wall

of rusty-red brick enlivened by bands of cogging. Three profiled metal monopitch roofs over the main sports hall. Oppo-
70 site, the admirably restored former BOARD SCHOOL of 1876–7 by *E.R. Robson*, now flats. Though not amongst the earliest, it is unique in plan and design: four-square and compact, the consequences of a very cramped site. It has a roof playground and may originally have had one at ground floor under an open arcade (now infilled). Vermiculated stone banding and minimal dressings give it a measured distinction. From here, a bridge leads back over the railway to Whitechapel Road.

2b. South of Whitechapel High Street between Mansell Street and Leman Street

The area S of Whitechapel High Street was open ground in the C16, known as Goodman's Fields, which was partly divided into garden plots. By the early C17 it was also in use as tenter grounds for the pinning of cloth. The land was bought by Sir John Leman, Lord Mayor of London, whose great-nephew, William Leman, first laid out four streets around the tenter grounds in the 1680s; each given the family name of his relatives, Mansell, Prescot, Ayliff and Leman. Strype described these 'fair streets of good brick houses' in 1717 but most were replaced by Richard Leman and his builder Edward Hawkins in the late C18, when the area was still fashionable. Its social decline was promoted by the noxious sugar refining industry and completed by the encroachment of large warehouses in the late C19, which now compete against the scale of new buildings associated with creeping development from the City.

The tour starts at the junction of Aldgate High Street and Whitechapel High Street in MANSELL STREET, a busy traffic artery since the late 1890s when it was extended S to join with the new Tower Bridge Approach. The W side lies in the City. The N end is unprepossessing: large 1980s offices dominate, the majority in rudimentary developers' Postmodern. The first buildings of interest on the E side are Nos. 57 and 59, lone relics of the area's well-to-do character in the early C18, much restored in 1988 by *Trehearne & Norman* after long neglect. Five bays and three storeys each, the wider central bays broken forward. No. 57, *c.* 1720, is late Baroque in style but self-assured, speaking of a mercantile prosperity at some distance from the newly fashionable Palladianism of the West End. Red brick and Portland stone; frontispiece with wide round-headed entrance with double doors, and broken pediment on full-fluted Doric columns; the rest of the ground floor all restoration. Surprisingly, No. 59 is a façsimile refronting of *c.* 1880, in stock brick with red brick trim, dressed in poorer stone. By the C20 both houses were multi-occupied and the upper floors in use as workrooms. No. 63, Neo-Georgian of 1930 by *Lewis Solomon,* was the Jews Shelter. Prominent stone cornice.

Further S, INSIGNIA HOUSE, by *Elana Keats and Associates* and *John Winter & Associates* with *Jonathan Ellis Miller*, 1990–1 (engineers *Ove Arup*). An early manifestation of the cool minimalism that returned to favour in the 1990s. Transparent full-height atrium, formed by a projecting glass box, jointed and braced in the High-Tech manner, projecting from a white panelled frontage. To the corner, flats of *c.* 2000, indicative of developers' changing priorities in the C21 City fringe.

PRESCOT STREET, to the E, is ragged with insignificant commercial premises and flashy offices muscling in on older fabric. On the S side, No. 30 is early C19. Then the R.C. Church of the English Martyrs (*see* above), reminder of the Irish workforce which served the docks. It lost its presbytery for JUNO COURT, brashly unpleasant 1980s offices. No. 23, a single house, four storeys in yellow brick with fine pedimented doorcase on engaged columns with fluted capitals, is a sole reminder of the redevelopment of the Lemans' estate in the 1770s. In the adjoining houses (now demolished) the London Infirmary (later the London Hospital) was established in 1740. On the site, crude offices with a tall arcaded front self-consciously echoing Victorian warehousing. Across Magdalen Passage, the former WHITECHAPEL COUNTY & POLICE COURT, 1858–9 by *Charles Reeves & Lewis G. Butcher*, displays Ruskinian influences at an early date. Confident, three-storey Venetian palazzo with heavy eaves cornice and tall chimneys with decorative caps, richly polychromed in red, black, white and blue brickwork. Six bays with ground floor of large round-arched windows and asymmetrical entrance. Smaller groups of paired windows within arches and an upper range of square-headed lights are divided by slender iron columns. The court-room block is visible at the rear. Squeezed in next to the Co-operative Bank (*see* below), is the PRINCESS OF PRUSSIA, a *c.* 1880s public house. Neat and narrow with a projecting bay, coloured glazed dressings and tablet gable with broken scrolled pediment. The N side of Prescot Street has the overpowering KINGSLAND HOUSE, gargantuan Postmodern offices in the Stirling vein with pink and beige striped cladding and a curved corner tower.

N of Prescot Street lay the tenter grounds. An encircling roadway had been laid out by 1829 with access to streets N and S. Backfilling of garden plots with housing followed. St Mark's Church by *Wyatt & Brandon* was built in 1838–9 (demolished 1927), the remaining space was filled with short rows of terraces either side of ST MARK'S STREET by 1855. The only survivals of that period are the SCARBOROUGH ARMS, a public house with rounded corner and Nos. 31–3; small two-bay houses with stucco cornice. On the site of the church, a warehouse by *Moore-Smith & Colbeck*, 1927, incorporated the Neo-Tudor vicarage for its offices. Now flats. Fitful post-war rebuilding produced three dismal 1970s pitched-roof terraces in SCARBOROUGH STREET and Nos. 36–60 of 1989 by *Hastwell Associates*, rather better; in a Neo-Wrightian manner with broad overhanging eaves, rendered facings, timber balconies and stairs. W of St Mark's Street, behind smart railings, the pleasant ENGLISH MARTYRS R.C. SCHOOL, 1969 by *Broadbent, Hastings, Reid & Todd*. Two- and three-storey flat-roofed buildings in concrete and brick with timber facings, set into landscaped surroundings of well-planted gardens.

Around the square are the four TENTER STREETS, mostly dominated by the backs of offices but with a few earlier buildings. In WEST TENTER STREET, Nos. 29–31, a three-storey clothing warehouse with central loading bays, 1899 by *Dunk & Bousfield* for Moses Bros. Refurbished for offices in 1988 by *Trehearne & Norman* and linked to No. 58 Mansell Street (*see* above). Moses Bros also owned No. 18 NORTH TENTER STREET of *c.* 1888 by *Dunk & Geden*. Tall four storeys, brown brick with blue and red trim, converted to apartments by *Yeates Design & Architecture*, 1995. No. 6 is a small C18 house of three storeys, then in EAST TENTER STREET, tenements by speculative builders *N. & R. Davis*, *c.* 1900 of five storeys with attic workrooms; pedimented dormers rising above swept parapets. The N end of St Mark's Street (built as Alie Place) is flanked on either side by a pair of *c.* 1820 three-storey houses with windows in arched recesses. Four-storey versions of the same face Alie Street where No. 28 has been carefully restored.

ALIE STREET is a mix, suffering under a weight of pompous commercial overspill from the City at its W end. Opposite St Mark's Street on the N side, however, Nos. 17–19 are a late C18 symmetrical pair of two storeys with sash windows, stuccoed ground floor and entrances in Half Moon Passage. The rear looks earlier, with brick plat band. The WHITE SWAN is early C19, a slim two bays, the ground floor with curved window, console brackets and fancy iron lamp bracket. Facing on the S side, Nos. 30–44, *c.* 1720 three-storey houses under sloping tiled roofs, largely altered. No. 32 has an unusual projecting C19 shopfront (restored) with coloured glass and originally a lantern roof. No. 34 had a finely carved doorcase (recorded by John Summerson in the 1950s*) but the rest have shopfronts, reconstructed in 2000 with channelled-masonry facings. Alie Street's E end, across Leman Street towards Commercial Road, has a small group of buildings for the C18 and C19 German community. First, the discreet St George's Lutheran Chapel of 1762 (*see* above), built by a wealthy sugar boiler. Next to it, the lofty German and English Voluntary Schools of 1877 by *E.A. Gruning*, son-in-law of the chapel's pastor. Three storeys of ruddy brick with pairs of classrooms on each floor. Ranks of large elliptical-arch windows to ground floor with smaller pairs above and central gable and dormers in the attic. At its back, invisible from the street are the earlier church schools (*see* chapel, above).

Alie Street's S side opens to a vast complex of buildings, collectively known as GOODMAN'S FIELDS, of 1975–8 by *Elsom*

*J. Summerson, *Georgian London*.

Pack Roberts Partnership for Natwest. It stands in spacious landscaped grounds on the site of the massive London, Tilbury & Southend Railway's Goods Depot (1886, demolished). Two large blocks, originally for computer services and management, in heavily modelled bright-red brick, of five and seven storeys with boldly expressed vertical sections and recessed windows. Its spirit is transatlantic but for all its impressiveness it lacks sympathy for the local grain.

LEMAN STREET, a main N–S thoroughfare, was entirely built up with brick houses by the 1740s but now is mostly C19 and C20. At the N end, on the E side, No. 17 was the former German Mission Day School, 1863. Gothic with black and red brick headers and moulded stucco keystones. Established in 1861, possibly in the small building to the rear facing Buckle Street, but rebuilt by Lutheran pastors as part of their Mission to German labourers. Then No. 19a, the grandiose two-storey former EASTERN DISPENSARY of 1858–9 by *G.H. Simmonds*, 55
local surveyor and the dispensary's secretary. Built by *John Jacobs* of Leman Street. Repair and refurbishment by *Ronald S. Hore* c. 1997–8 restored much of its appearance after long neglect. Mannered Italianate with channelled-stucco plinth, round-arched entrance under a balcony and upper storey of five bays of windows beneath segmental and pointed pediments. Founded 1782 by City doctors, it was amongst the first to provide free healthcare to the poor of East London.

The W side of Leman Street begins at the N end with BEAGLE HOUSE, by *R. Seifert & Partners*, 1976. A nine-storey tower with angled profile, an echo of the firm's earlier Centre Point at Tottenham Court Road with thin bays composed of faceted H-shaped pre-cast units faced in mosaic. Ground floor with Seifert's typical tapered piers at the end, and a purple engineering brick wall continuing as a single-storey extension along Braham Street. S of Alie Street, Leman Street still has a domestic scale and character. No. 40, The Black Horse, is low-key 1840s with extended ground floor. Then Nos. 42–50, offices by *C.A. Cornish* 1988–9, the round-arch windows making an effort to harmonize with the C19 frontages. Nos. 52–60, high-fronted red brick tenements of *c.* 1901, display the poor character of the district at the end of the C19. Narrow entrances and windows under moulded elliptical headers. Built back-to-back with the group in East Tenter Street (*see* above) by *N. & R. Davis*, Jewish builder developers. Then a mixture of early house fronts, the majority substantially reconstructed in recent decades. No. 62 is late C18 but its open-pedimented stone doorcase with attached Ionic columns and entablature has been imported. No. 66 is genuine 1760s town house of a type once common in the area. It stands slightly back from the railed basement area. Big pedimented doorcase with Ionic columns. Bracketed cornice to the third floor. Photos of 1914, when it was a dosshouse, show a grand panelled interior and staircase, with thin carved balusters. No. 68 is a small, much repaired house of *c.* 1780. No. 70, MR PICKWICK'S, was known as the Garrick Tavern from the early C19, in homage to David Garrick who performed in the Goodman's Field Theatre, Alie Street, in the 1740s. Rebuilt 1854 by *Joseph Lavender*, who added the large Garrick Theatre behind (demolished *c.* 1889). Adjoining, the former Police Station of 1960 by *A. Dunand* of the *Scotland Yard Chief Architect & Surveyors Dept.* A very large, plain, six-storey Portland stone block over a ground floor of dark brick. On the site of one of the first of Peel's watch houses, rebuilt in 1890–1.

The magnificent, cliff-like group lining the E side of Leman Street is testament to the enlightened architectural patronage of the Co-operative Wholesale Society, who were established in the Minories in 1874, moved to a former sugar refinery in 1881 for access to the railway and local markets and quickly expanded. Their buildings should be studied from S–N. First, No. 99 at the corner with Hooper Street, of 1885–7 by the CWS's architect, *J.F. Goodey*. Six storeys in red brick and Portland stone, rising from a granite plinth with broad windows to the lower floors and paired arched openings above set within giant arches. Over the entrance a four-storey canted bay, lighting the central staircase, has modestly carved emblems of the Society and the cities of Manchester and London. Stressing the vertical is an octagonal, corner oriel carrying the lofty, square clock tower. Goodey erected tea warehouses immediately behind (dem.), with an open wagon road running between the two blocks to serve the ground-floor stores. Offices were on the first floor, then three floors of large workshops with concrete vaults carried on iron columns. The top floor Assembly Room (now subdivided) still retains part of its ceiling with ribbed vaulting and decorative plasterwork. Lengthy N extension of 1910 by *F.E.L. Harris*. Poorly scaled in exaggerated Baroque style. Wide and high entrance, under an open-segmental pediment and oriel window, and stodgily enriched open pediment over its penultimate bays. Beyond Nos. 53–5, the drapery warehouse of 1929–30 by *L.G. Ekins*, the Society's architect from 1916–45. Classy commercial classicism; steel frame, clad in moulded-faience tiles with bronze panels to floor sections. Slightly bowed three-bay centre framed by pilasters with inset detail of giant reeds scaling the full height of the façade and terminating as fasces. The last of the CWS group is the corner block on the W side (No. 1
96 PRESCOT STREET, originally offices, flats since 1999). 1930–3 by *Ekins*, extended to his design in the 1950s. Rugged Amsterdam School-style Expressionist brick work with piers dividing four floors of windows with fluted bronze panels under a stylized frieze of pendant motifs and a two-storey stepped-mansard roof in green pantiles. Artificial granite plinth with rough and square entrances. Attractive bronze gates, by the Society's own craftsmen, with lozenge insets of the CWS emblem. Over the N entrance, a carved relief of figures symbolizing 'Co-operation' by *J.C. Blair*, brother of one of the Society's directors. A second, lesser, block for the Co-

OPERATIVE BANK was added in 1936–8 in matching style. On the opposite corner the dark brown tone is picked up by No. 100 Leman Street, 1978–80 by *Brian Shaw & Co.* (stone-faced ground floor remodelled 1999–2000), which replaced CWS buildings by *Heythrop* of 1897.

The E side of Leman Street continues S with a low range of earlier C19 flatted shops with regular bays defined by flat brick pilasters. No. 137 is *c.* 1800; an attractive three-bay house, its first-floor windows set within wide arched recesses springing from stone bands. The Brown Bear Public House, *c.* 1830, is also well preserved, its three N bays with giant, rendered pilasters.

Just off Leman Street in HOOPER STREET is the ENGINE HOUSE of the (demolished) LTSR's Goods Depot, designed by the railway's Chief Engineer, *L.A. Stride* in 1885–6, to power the depot's hydraulic cranes and hoists. Church-like, with high brick tower, slightly off-centre from the 'nave', the flanks of which are detailed in red and blue brick with stone dressings over the arch windows. For the area to the S and E *see* St George's.

2c. *The London Hospital Estate, S of Whitechapel Road*

The London Hospital (*see* p. 401) was one of several large private landowners in Stepney up to 1945 but now almost the only one to retain a substantial part of its estate. The hospital acquired the land of Red Lyon Farm in 1755 and 1772 but only began to develop it after 1790, in an undisciplined fashion. A second burst of activity got under way 1808–30 with the building leases more closely controlled by the estate's surveyor. By the end of the C19 the entire area was composed of houses interspersed with chapels, schools and numerous corner pubs. Some of the older parts characterized by cramped cottages, courts and alleys were cleared for street widening and the construction of 'improved' tenement housing. Good management, like that of the Mercers' Company's estates in Stepney, ensured the survival of much of the C18 and C19 stock into the present. But the hospital's own expansion after 1895 and the progressive encroachment of inter-war clothing factories created a more mixed architectural character that still obtains today.

The estate is divided into two parts by New Road laid out *c.* 1772. The tour begins on the W side in FIELDGATE STREET which is shown as a trackway from Whitechapel to St Dunstan's on early C18 maps. It is a scrappy mix now but dominated since the beginning of the C20 by the monstrous, looming, derelict red brick mass of TOWER HOUSE, one of the largest of Lord Rowton's hostels, providing lodgings for 816 single men. By *H.B. Measures*, 1902. Long derelict, but due for refurbishment as flats. Six storeys with a central gable and a turret at each end, the oppressive effect increased by the ranks of diminutive windows, which lit the individual rooms.* It overlooks the grid of streets laid out on the hospital estate from the 1790s. The earliest terraces, in SETTLES STREET, were swept away in the 1890s and replaced by high-fronted tenements, e.g. at the N end (E side) DAVIS'S TERRACE, 1891, by *Israel & Hyman Davis* of Bishopsgate. Austere, bare yellow brick. Also by them, but slightly later Nos. 39–55 and Nos. 10–28, in a more humane red brick with mouldings and pointed dormers, but with the same narrow proportions. Facing on the W side, behind a high wall, penetrated by louvred portholes, the KOBI NAZRUL SCHOOL. A solid 1990s design in brick with strong massing of one- and two-storey buildings under deep-pitch roofs and echoes in the detailing of Victorian schools. Just beyond, the JOB CENTRE, built as the Stepney Employment Exchange, 1934–6 by the *Office of Works*, a particularly well-composed Neo-Georgian design. Symmetrical block in good brick with pantiled pitch roof and a pair of monolithic chimneystacks. Squat brick porches to the outer bays; set forward at both ends are gabled bays with Venetian windows. Curved rear block.

St Augustine's church (1879 by *Newman & Billing*) stood between Settles Street and Parfett Street, its tight site occupied by a clothing warehouse by *Batir Associates* (*A. Tekvar*), 1970–3, with steeply-raked curtain-walled lower floors. It has a narrow frontage to COMMERCIAL ROAD where E of Parfett Street, Nos. 111–125 have tall red-terracotta upper storeys with mullioned windows and a gable. Built *c.* 1900 as the Red House Coffee Palace, a temperance establishment founded by the vicar of St Augustine, Harry Wilson. By *Edward Burgess*, who designed similar establishments during the 1880s in his native Leicester. It once bore an inscription: 'A good pull-up for Bishops'.

PARFETT STREET was created in the 1890s when the hospital cleared a dense group of courts and alleys and replaced them with sturdy, three-storey model dwellings (the first of their kind on the estate) by their surveyors, *Newman & Jacques*. Small windows with colonette mullions and entrances under segmental and pointed pediments. A larger scheme for rebuilding along Settles Street and Myrdle Street with identical blocks was unrealized. The street's N end still has three-storey terraces of the 1790s on both sides, several with their original fanlights and doorcases. Renovated when the model dwellings were erected and reflecting the estate's preference for individual houses, seen also in Myrdle Street to the E.

In FORDHAM STREET, a colourful group of flats with covered entrances and high, central arch windows mimic the tenements of FIELDGATE MANSIONS in ROMFORD STREET, designed by the hospital surveyors, *Rowland Plumbe & Harvey* at the request of the builders, Davis Brothers, 1905–6. Ruddy-

*Its reading room had painted panels of 'The Seasons' by *H.F. Strachey* (*Building News*, 1902).

coloured square blocks with hipped roofs and open central staircases to three floors set in an arched frame. Plumbe originally planned individual three-storey houses N and S of Fordham Street but the LCC purchased the land to the S forcing a revision to higher-density flats. These were not the hospital's preferred housing type, concerned that it was too redolent of the architecture of charity and therefore undesirable to 'respectable' tenants. The LCC used the land to build GRENFELL SCHOOL in MYRDLE STREET, one of the first of their higher-grade Central schools. A unique, outstanding design by *T.J. Bailey*, 1905. Although shallow and compact, it shows off with two semicircular corner staircase towers with copper domes flanking the central hall.

NEW ROAD was laid out *c.* 1772 by the Commissioners of the St George's Turnpike to provide a route to Ratcliffe and Wapping. Its line roughly marks that of the City's civil war defences of 1642 and at the N end on the E side is Mount Terrace, built by the Corporation of London, *c.* 1808, after they had cleared the Mount, part of the defences. New Road's W side is an incongruous mix of housing and industry typified by No. 101 (SHIV HOUSE), a large clothing factory of 1930 by *H. Victor Kerr* whose Moderne style is much in evidence in this area. The buildings between Fieldgate Street and Fordham Street were built by several hands, as Gloucester Terrace *c.* 1793–9, but mostly refronted or replaced from the later C19 onwards. No. 81 has brashly ornamented upper floors, indicating its origins as the Duke of Gloucester Public House, 1887. Nos. 77–9 are an uneven pair with pedimented doorcase with Doric pilasters. EMPIRE HOUSE (No. 67–75), is 1934; again by *H. Victor Kerr*. Concrete, square-cut Deco parapet and steel-frame windows. Nos. 63–5, three storeys with vermiculated rusticated quoins and keystone heads, pastiched as flats at Nos. 55–61, are contemporary with the houses S of Fordham Street. Facing, Nos. 10–16 have good C19 shopfronts, e.g. No. 12, fussy Italianate by *William Wigginton*, 1864.

The estate E of New Road was built up from 1808, apparently prompted by the London Dock Company's attempt to purchase the land. NELSON STREET is typical: terraces of two-bay, two-storey houses with arched fanlights over narrow doorways raised sharply off the street. TURNER STREET, crossing N–S, has three interwar buildings by *H. Victor Kerr*: first, at the corner with Nelson Street, a factory and showroom of 1932 for gown manufacturer M. Levy (for whom Kerr also designed No. 101 New Road, above). White rendered, with tall square-cut stair towers on either side, sharp angled corner and slightly projecting bands of windows with curved ends. Further N, the Neo-Georgian No. 47 was built for the Ophthalmic Centre for the Hospital Savings Association, 1933; finally (beyond the School of Medicine and Dentistry, *see* Royal
London Hospital above) GWYNNE HOUSE of 1934, a 102
forward-looking and exemplary white-walled Modernist block of flats with prominent curved stair-tower to the fore and

narrow balconies. Next to it, facing Stepney Way, the GOOD SAMARITAN, one of *A.E. Sewell*'s excellent pubs for Truman's, 1937. Neo-Georgian with flashes of Art Deco detail.

E along NEWARK STREET, in the shadow of the former St Philip's church (*see* p. 392), the character of the C19 has been retained, beginning with Nos. 28–34; early C19 with upper windows in arched recesses. Nos. 30–2 have fluted jambs to the doorcases. Slightly later and more sophisticated is No. 34 with light cast-iron balconies. The buildings of the former St Philip's National Schools form the centrepiece of this range. A sandy-painted Tudor-Gothic design by *Alfred. R. Mason*, the hospital's surveyor, 1842. Central stepped gable over a high Gothic arch window framed between two high octagonal turrets. End pavilions for schoolmaster and mistress with straight-edge gables. This abuts the former Vicarage for St Philip's, 1864 by *A.W. Blomfield*. Ecclesiastical dourness with tile-hung insets to the pointed arch windows. Once the home of J.R. Green, historian and incumbent of St Philip's (1865–8). Then, Nos. 40–2 of *c.* 1839. Three storey with recessed arch to first floor and rubbed headers. Coved stucco architraves to doors and round-arched ground-floor window.

PHILPOT STREET was pedestrianized in the late C20 in an attempt to draw together the hospital's various residential buildings. On the E side are houses erected *c.* 1839 as Philpot Terrace. They were the largest houses on the early C19 estate and deliberately built for private lettings. Architecturally, they show greater flair in the fluted pilasters, round-arch windows and deep sashes above. The interlacing tracery of the windows is echoed in the arched fanlights of the doors and windows of FLOYER HOUSE opposite, the former Medical College Students' Hostel, by *E. Maufe*, 1934. Nice brick building with arched ground-floor loggia and projecting window frames. S of this, the SCHOOL OF NURSING & MIDWIFERY (City University), 1965–7 by *T.P. Bennett & Son*. A crisp, five-storey box with blue horizontal banding between glazed sections. Immediately in front of the entrance, a circular concrete 'pill-box' lecture theatre. This makes an effective group with JOHN HARRISON HOUSE, staff residences of 1963 by *Bennett*. Y-plan tower with canted balconies to the centre of each block and roof terrace.

Immediately opposite, WALDEN STREET has on its N side a recently restored group of terraced houses, truncated to create a courtyard around which on three sides are grouped a series of nurses' homes in six blocks of flats and bedsits. Completed 1972–6. Domestically scaled, brick and weatherboarded with generous balconies behind blank-painted metal panels. They give a more suburban feel and the character of a modest, low-scale housing estate.

Philpot Street's S end crosses Varden Street, the S boundary of the hospital estate. On opposite corners of the crossing, JOSCOYNE HOUSE, 1934 and PORCHESTER HOUSE, designed in 1936, built in 1951, make a clumsy pair by *Lee &*

Dickins. Also here, several blocks of the LCC's DORIEN ESTATE. Brick and concrete flats of 1957–9. At the S end of Philpot Street, facing COMMERCIAL ROAD, is the prominent tower of CHEVIOT HOUSE. By *G.G. Winbourne*, 1937 for Kornberg and Segal, woollen merchants. It has the flashiness which one associates with modernistic interwar commercial buildings. Sleekly curving window sections, towered corner and a splayed cornice. Now council offices. Almost opposite, the tall LORD NELSON of 1892 by *Bird & Walters* (No. 230).

MILE END and STEPNEY GREEN

INTRODUCTION

There was largely open land N and S of Mile End Road until the early C19, traversed by a field track, now Stepney Way, leading from Whitechapel to Stepney village. At the heart of the village stood the medieval parish church of St Dunstan, surrounded by several large houses for the gentry including the mansion known variously as Worcester House or King John's Palace. The hamlet of Mile End was so named for its distance along the road from London and comprised small clusters of houses grouped around the manorial common land of Mile End Green, where Wat Tyler and his followers assembled before marching on London in 1381. The common survived longer at Mile End than in Whitechapel whose restless expansion in the C17 saw most of the 'waste' taken for building, even E of the Whitechapel turnpike where good brick almshouses for City livery companies colonized the N side of Mile End Road.

Speculative development of Mile End also began in the late C17 and progressed rapidly in the early C18, fostering the creation of a smart suburban enclave inhabited by a newly wealthy class of merchants and mariners. The best new houses, of which some still remain, lay off the main road on the part of the Green

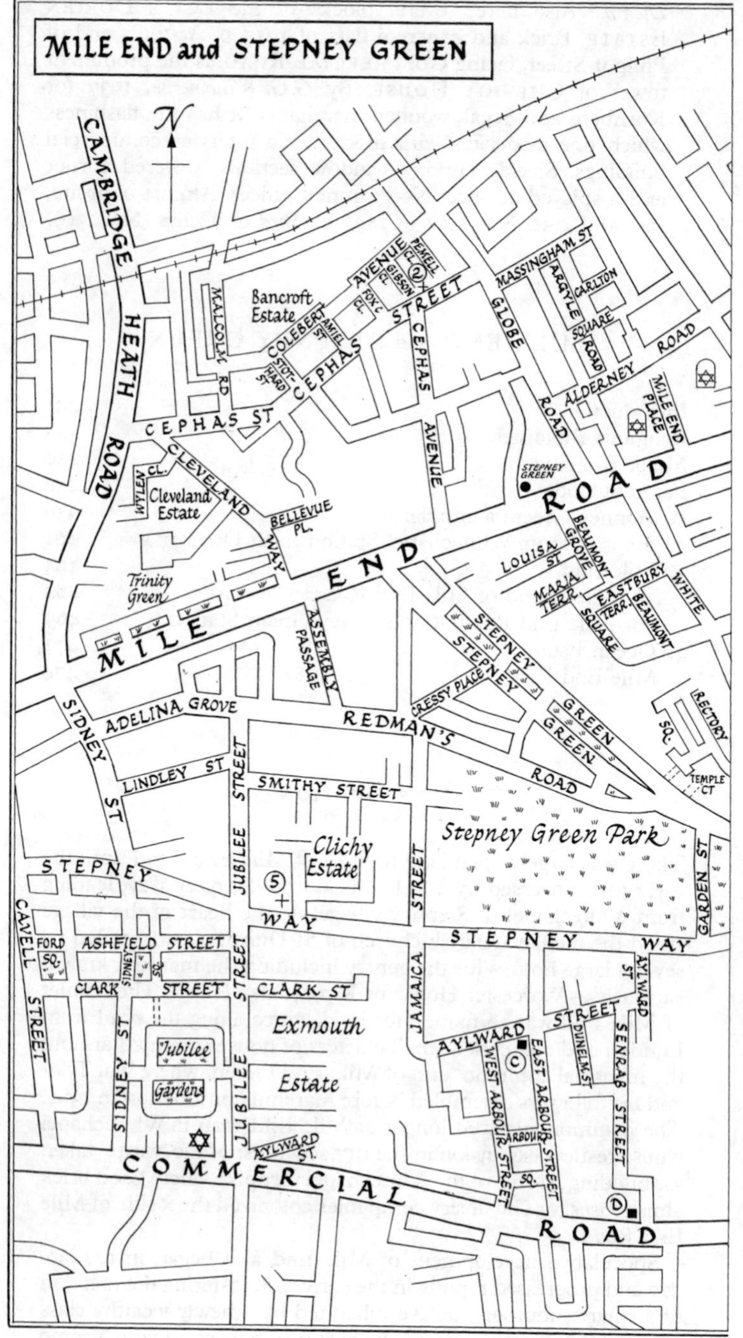
MILE END and STEPNEY GREEN
N
CAMBRIDGE
HEATH
ROAD
Bancroft Estate
MALCOLM RD
COLEBERT AVENUE
AMIEL ST
STOT-HARD ST
FOX C CL.
GIBSON CL.
PEMELL CL.
CEPHAS STREET
CEPHAS AVENUE
CEPHAS ST
MASSINGHAM ST
ARGYLE SQUARE
CARLTON SQUARE ROAD
GLOBE ROAD
ALDERNEY ROAD
MILE END PLACE
STEPNEY GREEN
WYLEN CL.
CLEVELAND WAY
Cleveland Estate
BELLEVUE PL.
Trinity Green
MILE END ROAD
ASSEMBLY PASSAGE
BEAUMONT GROVE
LOUISA ST
MARIA TERR.
EASTBURY TERR.
SQUARE
BEAUMONT
WHITE
STEPNEY GREEN
CRESSY PLACE
RECTORY SQ.
TEMPLE CT
SIDNEY ST
ADELINA GROVE
REDMAN'S ROAD
LINDLEY ST
SMITHY STREET
JUBILEE STREET
Stepney Green Park
Clichy Estate
JAMAICA STREET
GARDEN ST
STEPNEY WAY
CAVELL STREET
FORD SQ.
ASHFIELD STREET
SIDNEY SQ.
CLARK STREET
CLARK ST
AYLWARD ST
Exmouth Estate
AYLWARD STREET
DUNELM ST
SENRAB STREET
WEST ARBOUR STREET
EAST ARBOUR STREET
ARBOUR SQ.
Jubilee Gardens
SIDNEY ST
AYLWARD ST.
COMMERCIAL ROAD

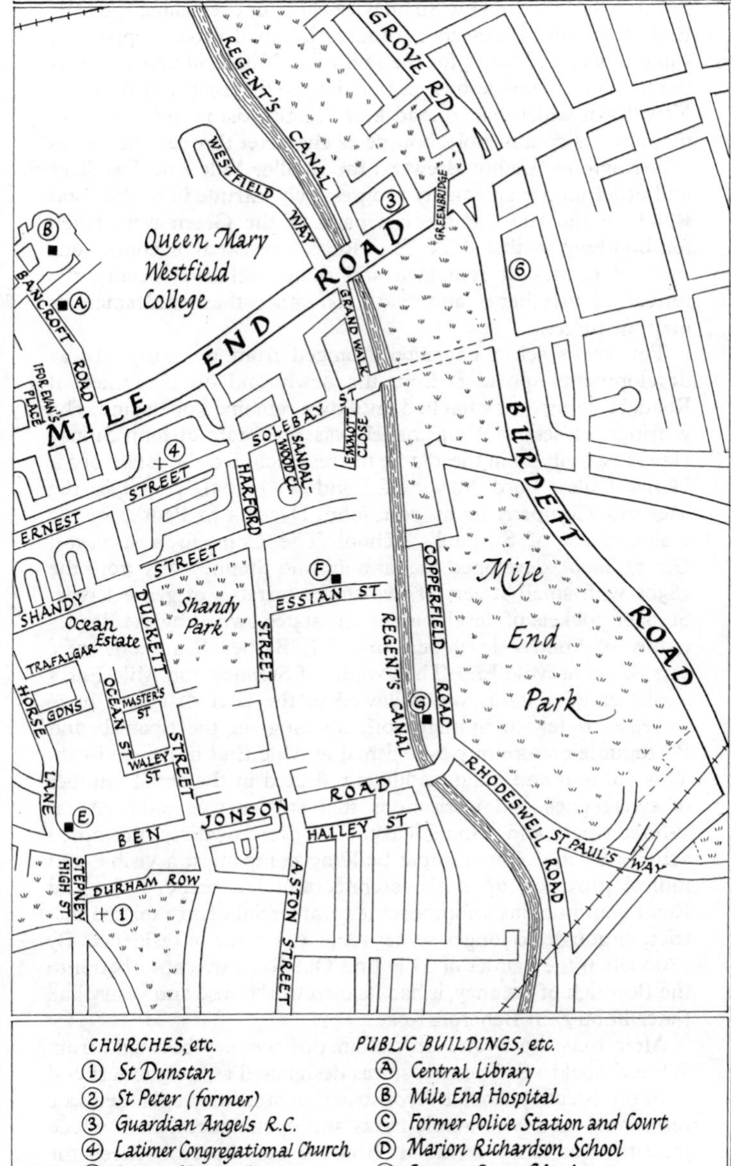
REGENT'S CANAL
GROVE RD
WESTFIELD WAY
GREENBRIDGE
Queen Mary Westfield College
MILE END ROAD
BANCROFT ROAD
IFOR EVAN'S PLACE
GRAND WALK
SOLEBAY ST
SANDALWOOD CL
EMMOTT CLOSE
BURDETT ROAD
STREET
ERNEST
HARFORD
STREET
SHANDY
Shandy Park
Ocean Estate
DUCKETT STREET
STREET
ESSIAN ST
COPPERFIELD ROAD
REGENT'S CANAL
Mile End Park
TRAFALGAR GDNS
HORSE LANE
OCEAN ST
MASTER'S ST
WALEY ST
BEN JONSON ROAD
HALLEY ST
RHODESWELL ROAD
ST PAUL'S WAY
STEPNEY HIGH ST
DURHAM ROW
ASTON STREET
CHURCHES, etc.
① St Dunstan
② St Peter (former)
③ Guardian Angels R.C.
④ Latimer Congregational Church
⑤ Stepney Meeting House
⑥ East London Tabernacle
Congregation of Jacob Synagogue
PUBLIC BUILDINGS, etc.
Ⓐ Central Library
Ⓑ Mile End Hospital
Ⓒ Former Police Station and Court
Ⓓ Marion Richardson School
Ⓔ Stepney Green School
Ⓕ Ben Jonson Primary School
Ⓖ Ragged School Museum
0 ¼ mile
0 ¼ ½ km

23 towards the church, now Stepney Green, but even along the Mile
p. 457 End Road smart clusters of houses in small groups appeared, some of terraced form, for the first time. Mile End Old Town, as the hamlet became known at this time to distinguish it from the New Town which had spread E of Spitalfields, found it hard to maintain its comfortable, bourgeois character through the C18 as Charrington's Anchor Brewery, the smaller Mile End Distillery and other industrial activity progressively intruded on Mile End Road. In the late C18 the last parts of the Green were taken for building so that Mile End Road consisted of continuous rows of houses. It remained still quite exclusive socially, the retreat of merchants and mariners rather than tradesmen or manufacturers.

The area's select character changed from the early C19 as developments spread N from the newly laid out Commercial Road, building over what had until then remained open land. The W fringe, closest to Whitechapel, was the estate of John Sidney Hawkins, built up in the 1820s; the rest included the estate of Sir Henry Colet, Lord Mayor of London (†1505), vested in the Mercers' Company by his son, John, Dean of St Paul's, for the maintenance of St Paul's School. The Company's surveyor, *George Smith*, developed the land around Stepney Way from the 1830s with small streets of two-storey terraces of genteel type. Smaller pockets of development on estates owned by the Barnes family of builder-developers and J.T. Barber Beaumont were carried on at Mile End. The exodus of Stepney and Mile End's wealthier inhabitants was followed in the later C19 by a huge increase in Jewish immigration, building on the Spanish and Portuguese community established in Mile End in the mid-C17. This cultural and religious life is reflected in the small number of synagogues and institutions that still survive today. As at Whitechapel and Spitalfields the overcrowding prompted activity by the philanthropic building companies, a visible and radical intrusion upon the architectural landscape. Mile End Road continued as an important commercial centre for the district, although no longer so desirable as a place of residence. By 1899 when the hamlet of Mile End Old Town was absorbed into the Borough of Stepney, it had its own workhouse and vestry hall (later library) in Bancroft Road.

After 1945 the W and central area of Stepney borough, from Whitechapel to St Dunstan's, was designated as 'neighbourhood 2' of the Stepney–Poplar reconstruction area and replanned as a residential area with ample parks and open spaces, from which industry was to be excluded. Housing was shared between the LCC and Stepney. E of the church between Mile End Road and Ben Jonson Road, limited slum clearance had been undertaken in the 1930s, but post-war the LCC set to work on the massive Ocean Estate – 'neighbourhood 3' of the reconstruction area. Further W, close to Whitechapel, Sidney Street Estate was initiated by the Borough of Stepney, which also began work N of Mile End Road on the large and dull Bancroft Estate. The new blocks of mixed heights turned away from the main streets with the consequent loss of any coherent townscape except where scattered fragments of the old terraces survived. A few scattered community buildings were provided, but are minor incidents. Redevelopment was hampered by lack of coordination between the LCC and Stepney, economies which affected the landscaping, and the lengthy building period, during which the initial concept of neighbourhoods shrank to more prosaic individual building projects. In the 1970s, larger and clumsier blocks were crammed in as remaining pockets of land became available. In the same decade, the tide turned towards conservation, and what survived of the good early C19 terraces began to be rescued and refurbished. At Stepney Green and Mile End Road, the remaining smart C17 and C18 houses were revived after decades of decline. From the 1990s the stark contrast between old and new began to be reduced by the elimination of some tower blocks and infilling with bland low-rise housing in yellow brick, while amorphous open spaces created by post-war planning began to be transformed by new landscaping, reclaiming some of Mile End and Stepney Green's distinctive and genteel character.

RELIGIOUS BUILDINGS

ST DUNSTAN and ALL SAINTS, Stepney High Street. The principal medieval church of East London, standing in a spacious churchyard by Stepney Green. In medieval times its parish extended over the whole of the present borough of Tower Hamlets. The church appears now as a much restored late medieval aisled building with a commanding W tower, but its origins are more ancient: St Dunstan rebuilt the church in 952, according to Matthew Paris, and the rare survival of a pre-Conquest carving is a reminder of a venerable history. Surviving evidence suggests there was a substantial C13 and C14 church, remodelled in the later C15 when the aisles were rebuilt and extended E. Post-Reformation alterations were swept way in the successive C19 restorations which have given the buildings its present appearance: 1806–8, porches removed, monuments repaired; 1846–52, general repairs under *Benjamin Ferrey*, E wall rebuilt in brick; 1871–2, exterior refaced, new porches and vestry by *Newman & Billing*; 1885–6, choir reordered by *Basil Champneys*; 1899, galleries removed, stonework scraped, by *J.E.K. & J.P. Cutts*. In 1901 the interior was gutted by fire; new E windows of chancel and S aisle were installed, roofs and furnishings were restored by Cutts and the church reopened 1902. Further repairs after war damage, 1946–52 by *A. Wontner Smith*, included rebuilding of the upper part of the tower and reroofing of the aisles. Reordering of the interior took place in 1967–8; recent repairs by *Julian Harrap*.

EXTERIOR. Victorian impressions dominate, hardly surprising after such a catalogue of repairs. Flint battlements throughout, with lively Victorian gargoyles in place of the crude water-spouts visible on C18 views. Elsewhere the stonework is Kentish rag. Perp three-light aisle windows, on the S side, of two types, all restored, but following the earlier designs, divided by the projecting rood loft stair. Those to the E are two-centred with six slim upper lights; the simpler windows further W resemble those of the N aisle, three lights below a flattened arch. One Dec window (N 2nd from E) with two ogee lights and mouchettes above, perhaps reused. Small Perp S chancel doorway, its height showing the original ground level before this was lowered in the C19. Perp N and S doors to the nave are concealed by C19 porches (the N door, with four-centred archway with shields in spandrels, was uncovered in 1899). The E wall has a weak post-war window in a wall refaced in stone in 1901, to its N is the crisp outline of *Newman & Billings'* polygonal flint-faced vestry with steep tiled roof.

The sturdy W tower is C15, with angle buttresses and NW stair turret, is of three stages; the tall belfry stage is a post-war rebuilding, its three-light Perp windows and pinnacles copying C19 restorations. In the C18 there were simpler two-light windows, plain battlements and a little bell turret, and also, until the C19, a classical W porch in the elaborate style favoured by early C17 City bricklayers. The W door was widened in the post-war repairs: Perp style with spandrel carvings of a ship and the devil with tongs (for St Dunstan).

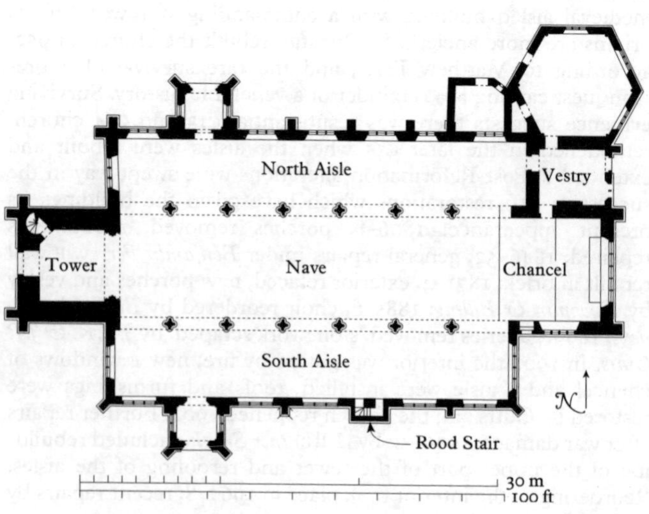

St Dunstan, Stepney, plan

INTERIOR. Sadly scraped stonework, now whitewashed. The loss of the division between chancel and nave has destroyed the medieval proportions, but emphasizes the impressive 150-ft length of the building. Seven bays in all, one of the largest surviving medieval churches in the London neighbourhood. Typical Perp detail of the undatable C15 kind common around London: broad, two-centred tower arch with attached shafts: arcades with piers of moderate height, the standard form of four attached shafts and four hollows in the diagonals; moulded polygonal capitals, moulded arches of two orders, with deep hollows. At the E end no responds, but a corbel with devil (N side) and recarved monster in foliage (S side). The second N arch of a different shape suggests adjustments had to be made when an older chancel arch was removed, and the second N pier has additional shafts, perhaps to strengthen the wall above with passage for access to the rood screen. Two phases of rood-stair doorways. Clerestory and roofs also Perp, the windows low and square-headed, the nave roof shallow pitched (traces of an older, steeper roofline visible outside). Flat aisle roofs, all much restored after the 1901 fire, but with C15 moulded timbers remaining in the N aisle, and stone shield bearing angel corbels in the S aisle. The E part of the S aisle is slightly taller, to allow for its more elaborate windows, and was no doubt built as a separate chapel. Brick-lined squint from N aisle to chancel. The chancel is older: on the S side is a fine triple SEDILIA with paired shafts, the middle arch with C13 foliage, and the restored E window retains slim C14 shafted jambs and rere-arch.

STONE CARVINGS. Rood, i.e. a small stone panel, a rare survival, 3
with Crucifixion, the Virgin and St John (39 × 27 inches; 99 × 68.5 cms). Late Anglo-Saxon, perhaps early C11, and very different in style from post-Conquest work. Particularly characteristic the indistinct modelling of the bodies within the plane of the frame, the unsystematic criss-cross of the draperies, and the dancing pose of the figures. Robed busts represent the sun and moon. The heavy frame with palmette ornament is reminiscent of C11 manuscripts and heralds the more formal C12 Romanesque style. – Annunciation: small C14–C15 panel above N chancel door; figures under a crocketed gable. CARTHAGE STONE (S aisle) quaintly inscribed to explain it came from the walls of Carthage, with the name Thomas Hughes 1663. Formerly in the N porch. – FONT. Square basin, C12 style; the spandrel carving looks convincing but the intersecting arches on the side appear recarved, on a C19 base. – ALTARPIECE. Triptych, C19 (?), now in N porch memorial chapel (not seen, under restoration). – STATIONS OF THE CROSS. 1960s. – ORGAN, C19, from St Augustine Haggerston, installed W end of the N aisle in the 1960s. – STAINED GLASS. Three disturbingly dominant windows by *Hugh Easton* replace the older glass, all lost in the war. E window, 1949, a notable period piece: a muscular Christ (said to be based on the then Rector) rises above ruined Stepney (note St Dunstan's tower without

pinnacles). – N aisle, 1951, 'to the Men of the Sea'; SE window, 1952: the Virgin and Jesus as carpenter; insistent realism in hard, bright colours.

MONUMENTS. Coffin lid with tapering sides and carved cross, C13. The C16–C19 monuments form an interestingly representative collection of wealthier Stepney residents – Sir Henry Colet †1510, father of John Colet, and twice Lord Mayor of London, who had a mansion close to the church and was an important Stepney landowner. N chancel wall. Not at all showy. An important example of the early C16 London fashion for a simple but prominently placed tomb doubling as Easter Sepulchre. Large Purbeck tomb chest with three quatrefoils in square panels, recess above with blank panelling and pretty mini-fan-vault. The present form of the straight top with small cusped pendant arches and quatrefoiled parapet must be a restoration, later than the repairs by the Mercers' Company which gave the tomb a classical frame (illustrated in the *Gentleman's Magazine* 1793). – Thomasine Brewster †1596, arms and inscription in brass, within a Purbeck panel. – Sir Thomas Spert †1541, founder of Trinity House, erected by Trinity House 1723, according to an inscription, but the style recalls the early C17. Repaired 1806. Inscription flanked by Corinthian columns; ship on panel below. – Jane, Lady Detheck †1606, painted wall monument with inscription under arch flanked by Doric columns, arms in a circlet above. – Robert Clarke †1610 and Frances his infant daughter: wall monument with kneeling figures of husband and wife facing each other, strapwork behind – Elizabeth Starture †1620, painted alabaster and marble, a similar type but in two tiers, with the lady above, daughter and son-in-law below. – Admiral Sir John Berry †1689, black and white marble, with bust in a classical aedicule (N aisle). – Rebecca Berry †1696, wife of the above. (S aisle, formerly outside on the chancel E wall). Fine bold cartouche with winged cherub head and a long verse. – Captain Nathaniel Owen †1707/8 and his two wives, finely carved small cartouche with draped cherubs' heads and skulls below. – Dr James Blondel †1734, physician of Ratciffe, Latin inscription between fluted pilasters, two oil lamps above. – Alex Weller, citizen and silk thrower †1738, cartouche with feigned drapery. – Rev. Henry Leche †1742, simple elegantly lettered tablet with skull below. – Benjamin Kenton †1800, 'a conspicuous example of commercial prosperity' by *Sir R. Westmacott*; SE corner of chancel. Small, standing wall monument with two short Roman Doric columns on convex base with convex entablature. Relief of Good Samaritan between the columns and an epitaph worth reading, recording Kenton's philanthropic work. – John Charrington †1815, plain but handsome neo-Grecian table. – Joseph Somes, shipowner †1855, big Neo-Gothic wall monument with relief of three-masted ship in a harbour (W end N aisle, partly obscured by the organ).

The CHURCHYARD is enclosed by handsome Gothic railings and gatepiers, inscribed *R. Mason* surveyor, 1844. Small mortuary chapel in NE corner. The churchyard had been enlarged in the C17 for plague burials but was desperately overused by the early C18, when Strype records that over 2,000 were buried in a single year. He noted many 'fair and costly' late C17 altar monuments, as did Sir Richard Steel (*Spectator* 24 Oct 1712), who commented that he knew no other place with so many remarkable verse inscriptions. The few surviving tombs form but a fraction of those that once filled the huge seven acre space. It was cleared and tidied in 1802 and in 1887 opened as an 'open air sitting room' or park by the Metropolitan Public Gardens Association. Nine-tenths of the 650 monuments were swept away, mainly in the late 1950s. What remains is disappointing. Lysons, in 1795, listed forty-four tombs to naval officers alone. Of them only two survive. The best commemorates Rear Admiral Sir John Leake †1720, Portland stone chest, much repaired, with heavy scrolled angles and a marble panel relating his nautical triumphs. – Matthew Mead †1699: a weathered chest tomb with angles enriched by cherubs' heads and gadrooning, a surprisingly lavish monument for a noted Independent divine. – Thomas Ward †1847: a heavy sarcophagus of Portland stone with delicate garlands of oak leaves on each end, massive railings with pyramid spikes. The present dog area in the SW marks the site of a huge plague pit. Its emptiness is bleakly eloquent.

Former ST PETER, Cephas Street. 1838 by *Edward Blore* for the Metropolis Churches Fund. Declared redundant in 1986; converted to housing 2001–2. The former church and later vicarage form a good landmark, a nice group in grey Suffolk brick, with bellcote on the projecting transept-like S gable facing the approach from Mile End Road. Plain, with pairs of round-arched windows in a slightly Norman style. Pinnacles along the roof have disappeared.

GUARDIAN ANGELS (R.C.), Mile End Road, 1901–2 by *F.A. Walters*, built by the family of the Duke of Norfolk as a memorial to Lady Margaret Howard, who had worked in the East End. The church is oriented N, with a nice red brick front to the road with large seven-light Perp window and polygonal turret to its r., a distinctive landmark rising beyond the Green Bridge of Mile End Park. Entrance porch below the turret. Spare, angular interior with minimal ornament (cf. Walters' earlier Holy Name, Bromley, *see* p. 449). Tall nave with narrow aisles of three bays, arches without capitals, pairs of tall clerestory windows with varied tracery. Lofty open roof with scissor trusses and hammerbeams with carved angel corbels. Chancel arch flanked by a niche with bishop on each side. The proportions of the narrower chancel differ: two bays with lower arcades and taller clerestory. Traceried REREDOS without sculpture. STAINED GLASS in the E window above. 89

Neo-Tudor brick Presbytery to the E, and big three-decker school of 1896 at the back by *Leonard Stokes*.

EAST LONDON TABERNACLE BAPTIST CHURCH, Burdett Road. 1955 by *H. & H.M. Lidbetter*, replacing a building of

1871. A large complex running N–S beside the busy road, with entrance between the church on the l. and three floors of community rooms on the r. Stock brick, austerely detailed apart from angled brick decoration around the main windows. Tall, spacious interior, stark but impressive, with steeply raked floor and W gallery, well lit by large rectangular windows and a clerestory. Rendered walls, the sanctuary emphasized by walls of dark brick and a wavy canopy.

STEPNEY MEETING HOUSE (U.R.), Stepney Way. 1955 by *Felix Goldsmith*, on the corner of the Clichy Estate, replacing a destroyed Presbyterian church of 1844. Small but enterprising. Faced in pale brick, with shell-concrete dome; shallow sanctuary with narrow side windows of coloured glass set in concrete, by *Pierre Fourmaintreaux* of *Whitefriars*. Good quality FURNISHINGS, communion rails, elders' seats, font. JOHN KNOX HALL behind, of the same date; Manse of 1952.

LATIMER CONGREGATIONAL CHAPEL, Ernest Street. 1951. Plain, with tower-porch between the hall on the l. and the manse at an angle on the r. In the porch STAINED GLASS with a ship, to Frederick Albert Homan, 1995.

CONGREGATION OF JACOB, Nos. 351–3 Commercial Road. A rare survival of a traditional small synagogue still in use. By *Lewis Solomon & Son*, 1920–21, probably a conversion of an older building, for a congregation founded in 1903 of Eastern European Hassidic origin. The exterior has a simple classical frontage. The synagogue is a traditional narrow galleried room, with fittings which provide an echo of the folk art traditions of an immigrant community. Lighting comes from the pitched glazed roof over the centre, rising from sloping roofs over the galleries. In the end wall a lunette with coloured glass above a painted panel with seven-branched candlestick and other symbolic objects. Below this a lively pair of gilded lions of Judah support the tablets of the law, above the enclosure with the Ark. Central railed Bimah with corner lights.

JEWISH CEMETERIES, Mile End Road and Alderney Road. The Velho cemetery of the Spanish and Portuguese congregations is the oldest Jewish cemetery in London, opened 1657, the year after Cromwell allowed Jews back to England. Burials took place from 1657–1758. Mostly tombstones laid flat; the earliest inscriptions in Portuguese. A few table tombs. N wall with old brickwork. The later cemetery adjoins to the N and W.

MAJOR BUILDINGS

53 CENTRAL LIBRARY, Bancroft Road. The former Mile End Vestry Hall of 1862–5 by *James Knight*, adapted and extended as a library from 1901 with funds from Carnegie. An ornate, if slightly eccentric, three-bay classical front of two storeys in yellow stone under a heavy cornice with blank frieze. Blocked Tuscan pilasters and paired columns to ground floor and,

above, tripartite round-headed windows with rusticated heads and paired Corinthian pilasters with canted edge. A porch and much rich decoration were removed to harmonize with the plain classicism of the six bay extension to the r. of 1935–7 by *B.J Belsher*, the Borough Surveyor. It has round-arch windows and a little Neo-Grec detail. The first floor lending library was the former Board Room, extended to its present size in the 1930s. Unusually, the decorative ceiling was retained and extended. Coved cornice of shields with the arms and seals of the Vestry and Board of Guardians. At the back, the unexpectedly lavish former Reference Library is part of an extension of 1905–6 by *M.W Jameson*, Borough Engineer. Large room with Composite pilasters and lush Renaissance style ceiling. Arched windows at each end and an octagonal central top light, with coloured glass.

MILE END HOSPITAL, Bancroft Road. Developed from the former workhouse and infirmary of Mile End Old Town, much extended by the LCC in the 1930s and with undistinguished post-war additions. Parts of the workhouse, rebuilt in 1856–8 by *William Dobson*, the District Surveyor, survive. On Bancroft Road, the former offices of the Board of Guardians, in ponderous Tudorbethan, with a two-storey barrack range behind for the casual wards. ALDERNEY BUILDING is a fragment of the workhouse: a truncated T-plan with multi-coloured diapering and brick dressings, dominated by a pair of projecting piers beneath lofty shaped gables, with trefoil heads. The later buildings are of minor interest. BANCROFT BUILDING (day hospital and offices) of 1990, by *Darbourne & Dark*, has a polygonal plan around a courtyard. Curved façade and stepped roof with prominent glazing, and a long range with tall gables.

Former POLICE STATION & MAGISTRATES COURT, East Arbour and Aylward Street. 1920–5, begun by *John Dixon Butler*, completed by *G. Mackenzie Trench*. It replaced the Police Station and Thames Police Courts of 1841. L-shaped, red brick and stone. The three-storey police station faces East Arbour Street with the symmetrical two-storey courthouse set back slightly on Aylward Street; the two parts tied together by a projecting string course. Characteristic Butler canted bays to each façade; the Court has an elaborate arched hood with badge.

MARION RICHARDSON SCHOOL, Senrab Street. A majestic design of 1907 by *T.J. Bailey* in a free Baroque with plenty of flourish. The W front has staircase towers with squat copper turrets, flanking dated triangular stone pediments with the LCC monogram. Stone-banded chimneystacks. The rear elevation is classical symmetry *par excellence*. Built on the site of Heath House, *c.* 1810, home of Thomas Ward, shipowner and merchant.

BEN JONSON PRIMARY, Essian Street; STEPNEY GREEN SCHOOL, Ben Jonson Road (*see* perambulation 4)

GUARDIAN ANGELS SCHOOL (R.C.), Whitman Road. *See* Churches above.

RAGGED SCHOOL MUSEUM, Copperfield Road. Built in 1872 as warehouses on the Regent's Canal, but converted by Dr Barnardo into a ragged school in 1876. He added the triangular pediment on the three-storey façade. It reverted to its original use after 1916 and became a museum in 1990. On the first floor, the 1870s classroom has been recreated.

QUEEN MARY WESTFIELD COLLEGE (LONDON UNIVERSITY)

Mile End Road

Queen Mary Westfield College presents an eclectic sweep of post-war buildings along the N side of Mile End Road either side of the curious People's Palace, from which it originally grew. Established to provide 'intellectual improvement and rational recreation' for the inhabitants of East London, the Palace was the creation of the Beaumont Trust, a group of Unitarian philanthropists. They purchased the site of Bancroft's School and Almshouses from the Drapers' Company in 1884* to fund a worthy successor to the Philosophical Institution founded by J.T. Barber Beaumont in Beaumont Square (*see* Perambulation *4*). *E.R. Robson* was appointed to design the new institution, including technical schools paid for by the Drapers. The Palace was partly inspired by the exotic 'Palace of Delight' described in Walter Besant's *All Sorts and Conditions of Men* (1882) and money was raised quickly at first, provoked by fears of social unrest in the East End during the winter of 1886–7, but soon dwindled. More modest ambitions were enforced by the Drapers who paid to complete the building in 1892. The relationship between the educational and recreational aims of the institution was uneasy and the Drapers gradually loosened their ties with the Palace. The schools, renamed East London Technical College and later East London College, were finally separated shortly before they were recognized as a permanent part of London University in 1915. The partial destruction of the People's Palace by fire in 1931, and the construction of a New People's Palace nearby, gave the college control of Robson's entire building. Queen Mary College received its charter in 1934 but major expansion took place only in 1955–75, with *Playne & Lacey* as the chief architects. A second phase planned by *Feilden & Mawson* after 1984 has brought the campus to its present size and seen the functionalist aesthetic of the earlier post-war buildings superseded by Postmodern eclectic variety. Merger with Westfield College, Hampstead, took place in 1992.†

* New schools were built at Woodford (Redbridge).

† We are grateful to Julian S. Robinson for information on the college's recent buildings.

1. The early buildings

The original People's Palace, now the QUEEN'S BUILDING, forms the focus of the college. Built 1886–92 in stages and set well back from Mile End Road with an isolated clock tower in front. Pevsner described it as 'Grecian gone gaudy. A debased version of what Greek Thomson was doing' but Robson's early designs were, if anything, odder. They included a Crystal Palace and a pseudo-Oriental domed building complete with minarets and cupolas. The executed façade reflects a compromise between the more bizarre elements of the earlier proposals and the sober classicism of Robson's Royal Society of Painters in Watercolours, Piccadilly (1881). Seven-bay centre with colonnade of rusticated Doric piers flanked by pavilions with Corinthian pilasters rising through two floors under broken-pedimented features, crowned by domed minarets. The functional rectangular plan comprised a central concert hall flanked by winter gardens (W), technical schools (E) and an octagonal library at the rear. The block for the Technical Schools forms the dull E flank. Prominent pedimented stone portal with Tuscan column in antis to the entrance. Three-bay centre under a high square parapet with a cut brick panel of the Drapers' Company arms. The anonymous W flank is of 1937–8 by *Sir Aston Webb & Sons*, on the site of the iron-and-glass Winter Gardens.

INTERIOR. Narrow entrance foyer with screen of paired Tuscan columns. This led to the preposterous Queen's Hall, described as 'a drawing room for those to whom high rents forbid the luxury of a drawing room', but really a very extravagant and massive concert hall under a wide barrel vault set with coloured glass and highly decorated plasterwork. Figures of the Queens of England by *Pierre Francois Verhyden* adorned tiers of bow-fronted balconies along its sides, with pride of place given to Queen Victoria. Destroyed 1931, the space is filled by post-war additions including a link block inserted in 1948 by *Wornum & Playne*. Constructed of pre-stressed concrete, an early post-war use in London, and bleakly functional with an unsatisfactory internal courtyard. At the N end of the building, like a pavilion, is Robson's luminous OCTAGON LIBRARY, a deep drum with two tiers of Neo-Grecian iron galleries and eight fancy aedicules under a cross-vaulted roof lit by an octagonal lantern, its base emblazoned with the names of classical authors. Busts of British writers fill niches at the foot of the arches.

THE NEW PEOPLE'S PALACE, lying to the W, was built in 1936–7 by *Campbell Jones & Smithers*. Blockish, stripped classical front, mildly modern in design with reliefs by *Eric Gill*: Drama, Music, Fellowship, Dancing, Sport and Recreation. Although much demanded at the time, the hall was unsuccessful and acquired by the College in 1954; façade altered 1955–6 by *Playne & Lacey* who refaced the base in Portland stone and reoriented the entrance to the side with a cloister

People's Palace (Queen Mary Westfield College), Mile End, Library, 1886–92

link to the Queen's Building. The original interior was designed by the cinema architect *George Coles* but lacks his customary flourish. Shallow hexagonal domed ceiling with coffered band in the main hall. A smaller hall, now lecture theatre, was set across the front of the building at first floor. In the lobby a large memorial stone to J.T. Barber Beaumont, removed from Shandy Park in 1979 (*see* perambulation *4*).

The tour of the rest of the campus is divided between the areas E and W of the Queen's Building and New People's Palace.

2. *East of the centre*

Parallel with the E flank of the Queen's Building is the PHYSICS BUILDING: 1960–2 by *Playne & Lacey & Partners* in consultation with the Professor of Physics, G.O. Jones. Seven-storey teaching block with open top floor of canted balconies and an excellent fibreglass SCULPTURE on the corner by *T. Huxley-*

Jones. 'Scientific' tiled panels to ground floor. Low-rise research wing abuts to the rear with snappy blue uprights between the windows. The site was originally occupied by St Benet's church (*Ewan Christian*, 1872–3; destroyed 1940). In its place the curious gault brick ST BENET'S CHAPLAINCY, 1962–3 by *Playne & Lacey & Partners*. Windowless block abutting a domed circular chapel with hexagonal corona above the roof light. Inside, striking sgraffito murals in a Romanesque style: the Revelations and figures of the Evangelists by *Adam Kossowski*, 1964. Continuing E along MILE END ROAD, the REFECTORY BUILDING of 1991 by *Feilden & Mawson*. Grey blockwork with swooping roofline and glazed ground floor. On the S side of the road, LINDOP HOUSE 1996 by *MacCormac Jamieson & Prichard*, sits bolt upright. Red brick flanks with a taller, projecting centre under prominent eaves. Further along on the N side again, No. 339, the FACULTY OF LAW, converted 1965 from an early C20 Co-operative Wholesale Society clothing factory. Then, the FACULTY OF ARTS by *RMJM*, 1992. Layered façade of red brick over pale brick base, its corner breaking forward to encompass the lecture theatre. Open square plan with projecting rear wings. Inside, specially commissioned artworks including a tapestry by *James More* and paintings by *Howard Hodgkin*, *John Hoyland* and *John Walker*. No. 357 is the ARTS RESEARCH ANNEXE, a square three-storey house, 1820 by *John Gardner*, whose family built the nearby New Globe pub in the same year and developed the pleasure gardens behind.

N along the canal, in WESTFIELD WAY is the STUDENT VILLAGE. Close to the canal are neat, colourful residences of 1991 by *MacCormac Jamieson Prichard*. A nicely varied group around gardens with large blocks to Westfield Way and smaller 'houses' overlooking the canal with projecting centre bays for dining areas. The village has been expanded in 2003–4 by *Fielden Clegg Bradley Architects* for flats for nearly 1,000 students. They have added informal groups of plain four-storey red brick residences with straight façades and windows slightly inset and, close to the canal and railway, two distinguished taller blocks for flats above shops with patterned copper-clad façades and angled balconies to the waterside.

W of the village, a colossal CHEMISTRY BUILDING of 2004 by *Sheppard Robson*: faux industrial with a curved steel roof, prominent chimneys and opaque glazing. This closes one side of the former New Sephardi CEMETERY founded in 1733 by the Spanish and Portuguese Jews congregation; the second of their cemeteries in Mile End (*see* above). Just beyond is the principal public space of the college, LIBRARY SQUARE. The S and E side is closed by the LIBRARY, begun by *Colin St John Wilson & Partners* in 1988, completed to their design by *Fielden & Mawson* in 1992. Solid composition in rough, red brick, with striking angular walls and carefully ordered windows. Sparsely finished interior of exposed concrete frames with block infill. SCULPTURE. Linked Forms II by *Merle Freund*, 1995. White marble, abstract form.

The square's N side has the massive Postmodern MEDICAL SCIENCES BUILDING of 1991 by *Fielden & Mawson*. Yellow brick, red brick dressings and strips of blue metal-framed windows. Stepped back upper floors. Just behind, set into the N boundary wall is an intriguing piece of preservation: three re-set stone reliefs on allegorical themes, by *E. W. Wyon*, salvaged from the courtyard of Drapers Hall in the City in the 1890s.

Behind the Queen's Building is the GEOGRAPHY BUILDING, a messy 1960s remodelling of the remains of the 1930s engineering wing and *Charles Reilly*'s early C20 brick gymnasium (later high-tension laboratories). Facing it across a bleak courtyard is the CHEMISTRY BUILDING, 1963–4 by *Playne & Lacey*. Tower block of nine floors with doubled horizontal bands of exposed concrete.

3. *West of the centre*

W of the Queen's Building along MILE END ROAD, the first important phase of post-war expansion by *Playne & Lacey* was the ENGINEERING BUILDING, 1956–61 bridging Bancroft Road. Portland stone, windows alternating with glass panels with Cubist engineering motifs. The E block, for nuclear engineering, was added 1965–6. Immediately behind, on Bancroft Road, is the distinctive ziggurat-profiled BIOLOGY BUILDING. Begun 1967 by *Playne Vallance Partnership*, completed by *Feilden & Mawson* after 1973. Six storeys linking high over Bancroft Road to an earlier phase which incorporates the STUDENTS' UNION. Remodelled in 1999 by *Hawkins Brown* and reclad in modish style with layered sections of steel and glass and a blue-painted façade making a bold statement amongst its grey neighbours. W of this, the INFORMATICS TEACHING LABORATORY 1990 by *MacCormac Jamieson Prichard* with a rugged fluted-blockwork façade. Wright-inspired glazing and overhanging eaves. Of similar treatment but more unusual is the same firm's COMPUTER SCIENCE STAIR TOWER, an original solution to pressures on space. Angular and bold overhanging upper storey. On the S side, MATHEMATICS BUILDING, 1967 by *Playne & Lacey*. Tower block with a glazed section breaking through the centre.

PERAMBULATIONS

1. *Stepney Green: a circular tour**

STEPNEY GREEN leads S from Mile End Road towards St Dunstan's (*see* above), a route which originally skirted the E boundary of the common land of Mile End Green. In the C17

*This account is substantially informed by Isobel Watson's 'From West Heath to Stepney Green: Building Development in Mile End Old Town, 1660–1820' in *London Topograhical Record* v.27, 1995, pp. 231–56.

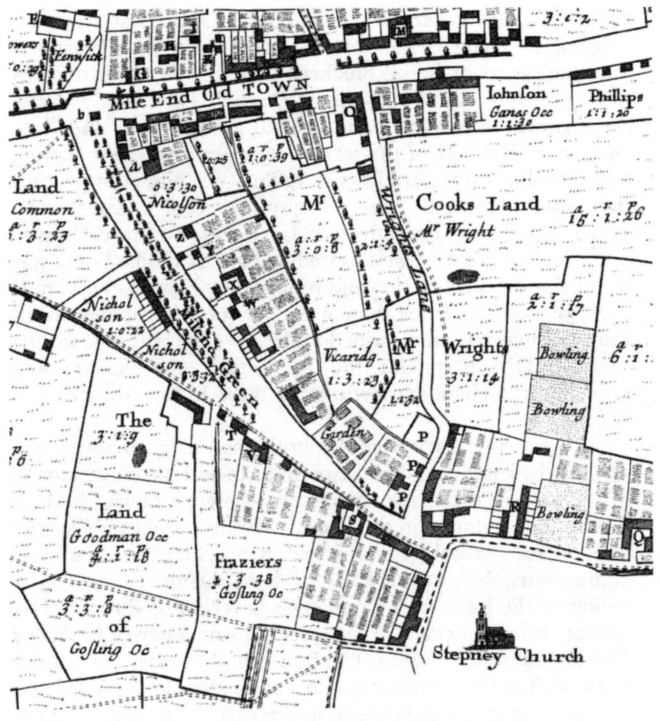

Stepney Green in 1703 from Gascoyne's survey

and C18 this was home to Stepney's wealthier merchants, many of them made wealthy by the river and seaborne trades. Pevsner, writing in 1952, was probably justified in gloomily remarking that '. . . right down to the C19 [Stepney Green] must have been very pretty and peaceful. Now it has lost all its character'. But since then the creation of new green spaces and the restoration of its surviving older houses has done much to recapture the Green's salubrious air.

The best approach to Stepney Green is from Mile End Road, via HAYFIELD PASSAGE, a narrow cobbled alley. This opens S to a broad space separated into two distinct parts by the leafy STEPNEY GREEN GARDENS, created in 1872 by the Metropolitan Gardens Association from one of the last remaining strips of Mile End Green. The ground was originally enclosed and divided into four plots after 1669 when Arnold Browne, a mariner, laid out a gravel pathway along its E side. The present roadway is laid with blue-tinged setts, reputedly brought in as ballast on ships. Of the houses extant in 1684, when the final piece of ground to the S was enclosed, there is no trace. From the N end, Nos. 21–3 are a group of *c.* 1740–50, built by George Newell, a local brewer, in the garden of his own home.

Damaged and substantially but carefully rebuilt post-war, their original character evoked by doorcases with triple keystones and pediments on scroll brackets. Nos. 25–7 are the remains of a terrace of four of 1877–80 by *Davis & Emmanuel*. Narrow proportions with single wide sash to ground floor and deep basement. The rest of the terrace was destroyed by bombing and rebuilt *c.* 1950s in Neo-Georgian style. No. 29 was originally double-fronted: one of a group erected *c.* 1727–31 by *James Mayfield*, a Ratcliffe bricklayer. Good ironwork gates, fine panelled doorcase and fretted fanlight. A similar house was burnt during construction and replaced by Nos. 31–33. Simple brick pilasters and box doorcases. No. 35, with arched flush-frame sashes, has an inscribed tablet over the entrance for the Stepney Dispensary for the Prevention of Consumption, reflecting the changing fortunes of these houses by the early C20.

Sitting further back from the street than its neighbours, No.
23 37 is the best individual house in Stepney and the only example in the area of the many smart brick classical houses built in the London suburbs in the late C17. Built *c.* 1694 for Dormer Sheppherd, a wealthy London merchant with overseas trading connections, but acquired *c.* 1714 by Dame Mary Gayer, widow of the East India Company's governor of Bombay. Her monogram is entwined in the splendid iron gateway by *Robert Bakewell*, a pupil of Tijou. The house is of five bays in reddish brick with rubbed dressings and flat headers to the windows, its S end patched and repaired in the 1950s. Two storeys above basement, with pitched roof and triangular-headed dormers. Handsome but simple domestic classicism: wooden eaves cornice on modillions carved with acanthus leaves, brick platband above the ground floor, and curved outer staircase with iron balustrade rising to a porch under a prominent curved hood with scallop-shell enrichment in plaster, possibly an improvement after 1714. Above, the central window is emphasized by a projecting brick surround. On the S face, narrow, blind windows towards the corners suggest typical late C17 lighting of closets to the principal rooms, while on the garden side, reset windows and irregular brickwork indicate alterations and later extensions, since removed. Inside, the plan is compact and square, two rooms deep with central staircase at the back. In the entrance hall unmoulded panelling but at the rear an elliptical archway with panelled soffits; probably contemporary with the fine staircase, one of several evident changes to the house after 1714. Though the tight well does not permit sufficient display, its quality is worthy of a country house. Walnut and pine, with elegant moulded soffits, shallow carved tread-ends, decorative inlay to the risers (*cf.* Nos. 4–6 Fournier Street), and a variety of twisted and fluted balusters set in the familiar elegant pattern of close-set triplets per step. Fluted newels are repeated as pilasters to the panelling on three sides. The plain upper walls were originally painted with a mural. Of the earlier period, the N rooms on the ground and

1. Havering-atte-Bower, The Green with St John the Evangelist (p. 168)
2. Whitechapel Road, Market with the Royal London Hospital (p. 401)

3. St Dunstan, Stepney, rood, eleventh century (p. 447)
4. St Mary Magdalene, East Ham, twelfth century apse (p. 269)
5. Curfew tower, Barking Abbey, fifteenth century (p. 119)
6. St Helen & St Giles, Rainham, nave interior, twelfth century (p. 185)

3 | 5
4 | 6

ANNE BOLEYN'S PANTRY
OLD DOG BAR

7. The Ancient House, Walthamstow, fifteenth century (p. 755)
8. Pimp Hall, Chingford, dovecote, sixteenth century (p. 721)
9. Spotted Dog, Upton, sixteenth century (p. 249)
10. Queen Elizabeth's Hunting Lodge, Chingford, 1542–3 (p. 719)
11. Eastbury Manor House, Barking, *c.* 1556–73 (p. 129)

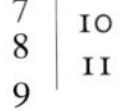

12. St Mary, Woodford. Monument to Rowland Elrington †1595 (p. 364)
13. St Margaret, Barking. Monument to Sir Charles Montague †1625, attributed to Maximilian Colt (p. 123)

14. St Mary, Walthamstow. Monument to Sir Thomas and Lady Mary Merry, 1633 by Nicholas Stone (p. 746)
15. St Margaret, Barking. Monument to Captain John Bennett †1706 (p. 123)

16. Christ Church, Spitalfields, 1714–29 by Nicholas Hawksmoor, west front (p. 388)
17. Christ Church, Spitalfields, 1714–29 by Nicholas Hawksmoor, interior (p. 390)
18. St Anne, Limehouse, 1714–30 by Nicholas Hawksmoor, west front (p. 531)
19. St George-in-the-East, St George's, 1714–29 by Nicholas Hawksmoor, from the south east (p. 479)

16 | 18
17 | 19

20. All Saints, West Ham. Monument to Sir Thomas Foot †1688 attributed to William Stanton (p. 222)
21. All Saints, West Ham. Monument to James Cooper †1743 (p. 223)
22. St Mary, Wanstead. Monument to Sir Josiah Child †1699 (p. 356)

Hic jacet JOSIAS CHILD Baronettus

23. No. 37 Stepney Green, *c.* 1694 (p. 458)
24. Former Raine's School, Raine Street, Wapping, 1719 (p. 512)
25. Fournier Street, Spitalfields, north side, 1720s (p. 416)
26. Directors' House, Black Eagle Brewery, Brick Lane. 1770s, corridor, attributed to Sir Robert Taylor (p. 425)

23 | 25
24 | 26

27. St Matthias, Poplar High Street, 1652–4 (p. 646)
28. St George's Lutheran Church, Alie Street, Whitechapel, 1762–3 by Joel Johnson, pulpit (p. 394)
29. St Mary, Wanstead, 1787–90 by Thomas Hardwick (p. 355)
30. Great Mosque, former Huguenot chapel, Fournier Street, 1743–4 attributed to Thomas Stibbs (p. 396)

27 | 29
28 | 30

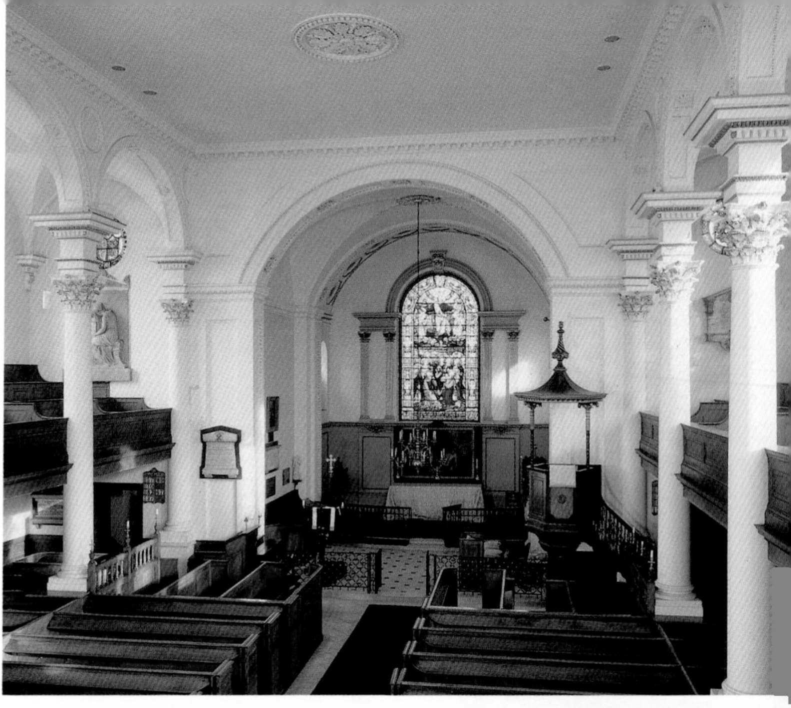

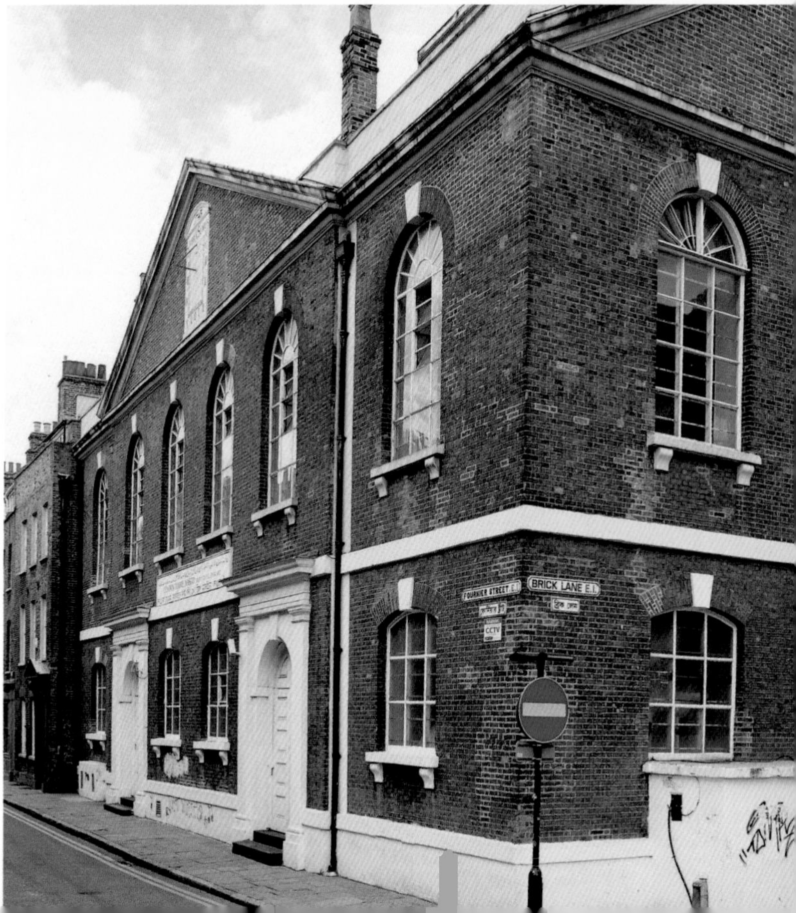

FOURNIER STREET E.1
BRICK LANE E.1
CCTV

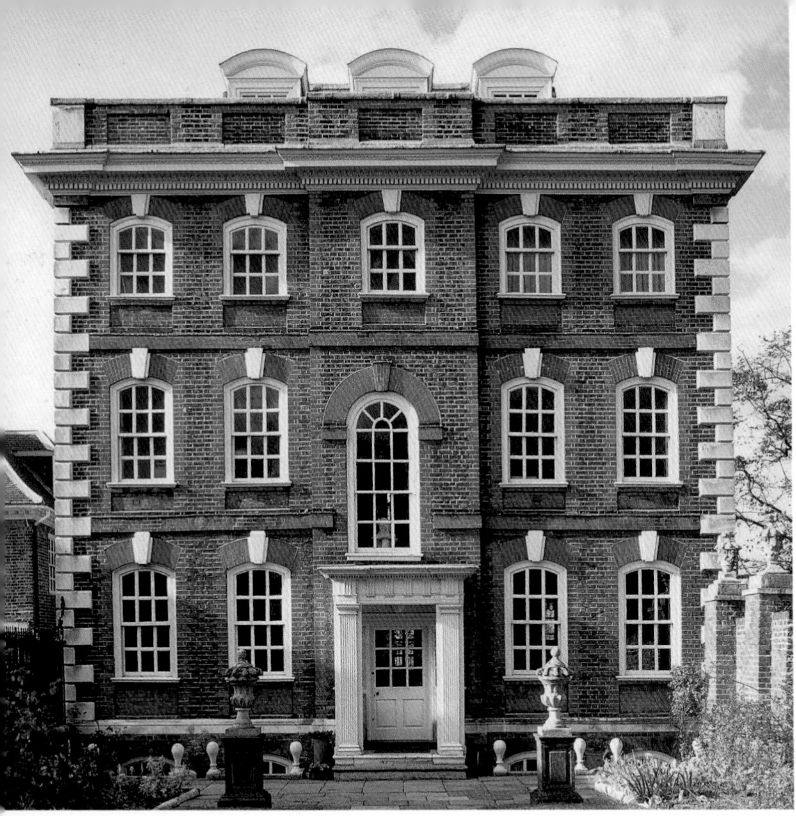

31. Rainham Hall, Rainham, 1729, garden front (p. 187)
32. Bower House, Havering-atte-Bower, 1729 by Henry Flitcroft with later wings, south front (p. 173)
33. Bower House, Havering-atte-Bower, 1729. Stair hall (p. 173)

31
32 | 33

34. Windmill, Upminster, 1802–3 (p. 211)
35. Three Mills, Newham: House Mill (left), Clock Mill (right), eighteenth and early nineteenth centuries (p. 241)
36. Forest School, Walthamstow. 1740s and later (p. 763)
37. Round House, Havering-atte-Bower, *c.* 1792, attributed to John Plaw (p. 171)

34	36
35	37

GURDWARA SIKH SANGAT

38. All Saints, Poplar, 1820–3 by Charles Hollis (p. 639)
39. Gurdwara Sikh Sangat (former chapel), Bow, 1854–5 (p. 610)
40. Unitarian Church, Bethnal Green, 1880 by W.D. Church (p. 557)
41. The Space (former Presbyterian chapel), Isle of Dogs, 1853 by T.E. Knightley (p. 697)

38	40
39	41

42. St John, Bethnal Green, 1826–8 by Sir John Soane, tower (p. 552)
43. St Peter, Bethnal Green, 1840–1 by Lewis Vulliamy (p. 555)
44. St John the Evangelist, Stratford, 1832–4 by Edward Blore (church rooms in foreground by Purcell Miller Tritton, 1998) (p. 223)
45. St Mark, Silvertown (now Brick Lane Music Hall). 1860–2 by S.S. Teulon (p. 315)

42	44
43	45

MUSIC HALL

46. St Peter London Dock, Wapping, begun 1865–6 by F.H. Pownall (p. 500)

47. St Anne R.C., Mile End New Town, by Gilbert Blount, nave 1853–5, east end 1894 (p. 393)

48. No.19 Princelet Street, former synagogue, interior 1869–70 (p. 400)

46 | 47 48

49. Wapping Pier Head, Nos. 1–4, 1811–13 by D. A. Alexander (p. 509)
50. Cyprus Street, Bethnal Green, 1850–1 (p. 575)
51. Tredegar Square, Bow, north side, completed 1833 (p. 616)
52. Albert Gardens, Commercial Road, early nineteenth century (p. 526)

49	51
50	52

53. Former Vestry Hall, later library, Mile End, 1862–5 by James Knight (p. 450)
54. District Board of Works, Poplar, 1869–70 by Hills & Fletcher with A. & C. Harston (p. 646)
55. Former Eastern Dispensary, Whitechapel, 1858–9 by G.H Simmonds (p. 435)
56. Queen Adelaide Dispensary, Bethnal Green, 1865–6 by Lee & Long (p. 593)

53	55
54	56

57. Peabody Buildings, Spitalfields, 1863–4 by H.A. Darbishire (p. 414)
58. Leopold Buildings, Bethnal Green, 1872 by Matthew Allen (p. 590)

59. Merchant Seamen's Orphan Asylum, Wanstead, 1861–71 by George Somers Clarke sen. (p. 358)

60. Albert Cottages, Mile End New Town, 1865 (p. 423)

57 | 59
58 | 60

61. Wilton's Music Hall, St George's, 1858–9 and 1877 (p. 485)
62. Theatre Royal, Stratford, interior, 1884 and 1902 by Frank Matcham (p. 228)
63. Commercial Tavern, Spitalfields, 1865 (p. 415)
64. The Boleyn, East Ham, 1898 by Shoebridge & Rising (p. 281)

61	63
62	64

THE COMMERCIAL TAVERN.

THE BOLEYN
THE BOLEYN

65. West India Quay, warehouses, 1800–3 by George Gwilt & Son, altered by Sir John Rennie, 1827 (p. 670)
66. Trinity House Buoy Wharf, lighthouse, 1864–6 by Sir James Douglass (p. 663)
67. Abbey Mills Pumping Stations, Stratford, 1865–8 by Charles Driver (Sir Joseph Bazalgette, engineer) (p. 229)
68. Bryant & May match factory, Bow, gatehouse, warehouses and offices 1874, factory 1909–11 by Holman & Goodrham (p. 622)

65	67
66	68

69. Bethnal Green Museum, 1868–72 by J.W. Wild with cast-iron structure of 1855–6 from South Kensington (p. 559)

70. Board School, Durward Street, Whitechapel, 1876–7 by E.R. Robson for London School Board (p. 432)

71. Board School, Sandringham Road, East Ham, 1895 by Robert L. Curtis (p. 277)

72. University of East London (West Ham Technical Institute), Stratford, 1895–9, by Gibson & Russell, sculpture by W. Birnie Rhind (p. 231)

69 | 71
70 | 72

73. Town Hall, East Ham, 1901–14 by Cheers & Smith (p. 273)
74. Town Hall, Leyton, 1895–6 by John Johnson (p. 729)
75. Carnegie Library, Manor Park, 1904 by A.H. Campbell (p. 288)

73 | 74
75

SHAKESPEARE
LIBRARY

76. River Police Station, Wapping, 1907–10 by John Dixon Butler (p. 507)

77. Passmore Edwards Sailors Palace, Limehouse, 1901 by Niven & Wigglesworth (p. 541)

78. Boundary Street Estate, Bethnal Green, by the London County Council. Chertsey House and Hurley House, 1893–6 (p. 589)

79. Jewish Soup Kitchen, Brune Street, Spitalfields, 1902–3 by Lewis Solomon (p. 410)

76	78
77	79

SOUP KITCHEN
5662 1902
FOR THE JEWISH POOR

80. Burdett-Coutts fountain, Victoria Park, Bethnal Green, 1862 by Henry Darbishire (p. 566)
81. Mausoleum to Evelina de Rothschild †1866, Jewish Cemetery, West Ham, by Sir Matthew Digby Wyatt (p. 246)
82. Whitechapel Art Gallery, 1898–1901 by Charles Harrison Townsend (p. 398)
83. Toynbee Hall, Whitechapel, decorative roundel, Dining Hall, 1887–8 designed by C.R. Ashbee (p. 397)

80 | 82
81 | 83

84. The Drive, Woodford, *c.* 1900 (p. 366)
85. Leucha Road, Walthamstow, 1895 by John Dunn (p. 761)
86. Barnardo Village, Barkingside, cottages, 1875–6 by Ebenezer Gregg (p. 326)
87. Nos. 36–38 Reed Pond Walk, Gidea Park, Romford, 1911 by M.H. Baillie Scott (p. 207)
88. Jubilee Crescent, Isle of Dogs, 1935 by G.R. Unthank (p. 704)

84 | 87
85 | 88
86

89. Guardian Angels (R.C), Mile End, 1901–2 by F.A. Walters (p. 449)
90. West Ham (Baptist) Central Mission, Plaistow, 1921–2 by William Hayne (p. 252)
91. St Andrew, The Drive, Ilford, stained glass, 1929–30 by Karl Parsons (p. 337)
92. St Andrew, The Drive, Ilford, 1923–4 by Sir Herbert Baker, west end with sculpture by Sir Charles Wheeler (p. 336)
93. Former Fetter Lane Congregational Church, Leytonstone, 1900 by P. Morley Horder (p. 736)

89 | 91 92
90 | 93

EMD CINEMAS
THE VICTORIA
A Warm Welcome
Genuine

94. St Mary, Becontree, 1934–5 by Welch, Cachemaille-Day and Lander (p. 142)

95. Former Granada cinema, Hoe Street, Walthamstow, 1930 by Massey & Komisarjevsky (p. 760)

96. Former Co-operative Wholesale Society offices, Prescot Street, Whitechapel, 1930–3 by L.G. Ekins (p. 436)

94 | 96
95

97. Town Hall, Walthamstow, 1937–41 by P.D. Hepworth (p. 749)
98. Town Hall, Ilford, council chamber, 1931–3 by L.E.J. Reynolds with H.B. Nixon (p. 341)
99. Uphall Nursery School, Ilford, *c.* 1937 by Ilford Borough Architect's Dept. (p. 343)
100. Library, Leytonstone, 1934 by *J. Ambrose Dartnall*, interior (p. 738)

97	99
98	100

101. No. 64 Heath Drive, Gidea Park, Romford, 1934 by Francis Skinner with Tecton (p. 207)

102. Gwynne House, Turner Street, Whitechapel, 1934 by H.V. Kerr (p. 439)

103. Canteen, May & Baker (Aventis), Dagenham, 1943–4 by E.D.Mills (p. 154)

104. Bus Station, Newbury Park, 1937 by Oliver Hill, built 1947–8 (p. 330)

105. Library, Barkingside, 1968 by Frederick Gibberd, Coombes & Partners (p. 324)

101 | 103
102 | 104
| 105

LIBRARY

106. St Matthew, Bethnal Green, 1743–6 by George Dance sen, remodelled 1958–61 by J. Anthony Lewis (p. 554)

107. St Matthew, Bethnal Green, Station of the Cross by Donald Potter, 1958–61 (p. 555)

108. St Paul, Bow Common, interior, 1956–60 by Maguire & Murray, mosaics by Charles Lutyens (p. 607)

109. Our Lady and St George, R.C., Walthamstow, interior, 1995 by Plater, Inkpen, Vale & Downie (p. 748)

106 | 108
107 | 109

110. Hainault Estate, 1947–53 by the London County Council, steel-framed houses in Brocket Way (p. 334)

111. Cranbrook Estate, Bethnal Green, 1961–8 by Skinner, Bailey & Lubetkin for Bethnal Green Borough (p. 576)

112. Balfron Tower, Brownfield Estate, Poplar, 1965–7 by Ernö Goldfinger for the Greater London Council (p. 656)

113. St George's Estate, Tower Hamlets, 1963–70 by the LCC and the GLC (p. 487)

110	112
111	113

114. Mural, Cable Street, St George's, 1979–82 by Dave Binnington, Desmond Rochford, Paul Butler and Ray Walker (p. 486)
115. Storm Water Pumping Station, Isle of Dogs, 1987–8 by John Outram (p. 683)
116. Cascades, Isle of Dogs, 1985–8 by CZWG (p. 687)
117. Prince Regent DLR station, Royal Docks, steel frieze, 1995 by Brian Yale (p. 301)

114 | 116
115 | 117

STRATFORD STATIC
CANARY WHARF
CANARY WHARF STATION
CANARY WHARF

118. Stratford Station, 1995–9 by Wilkinson Eyre Architects (p. 229)
119. Canary Wharf Underground Station, 1991–9 by Foster & Partners (p. 680)
120. University of East London, Royal Docks, 1998–9 by Edward Cullinan Architects (p. 309)
121. Canary Wharf, general view of towers from the north east. No.1 Canada Square 1987–91 (right) and Citigroup 2000–2 (left) by Cesar Pelli & Associates; HSBC 1999–2002 (centre) by Foster & Partners (p. 678)
122. Thames Barrier Park, Newham, 1997–2000 by Groupe Signes (p. 300)

118	121
119	122
120	

123. Blue House, Garner Street, Bethnal Green, 2000 by Fat (p. 598)

124. House, Bacon Street, Bethnal Green, 2000–2 by William Russell (p. 584)

125. The Big Blue, Canada Square, 1998 by Ron Arad (p. 678)

126. Canning Town station, commemorative inscription, 1999 by Richard Kindersley (p. 263)

123	125
124	126

HMS WARRIOR THE WORLDS FIRST
ALL IRON & ARMOUR PLATED BATTLESHIP
WAS LAUNCHED FROM THE YARD IN
DECEMBER 1860. THE PLATES WERE FORGED
BY THE THEN INNOVATIVE NASMYTH STEAM
HAMMER. SHE SERVED IN THE ROYAL NAVY
FROM 1861 TO 1979 & SURVIVES
FULLY PRESERVED AT PORTSMOUTH
OVER 250 LIFEBOATS WERE BUILT AT THE YARD MAINLY FOR RNLI
HMS THUNDERER OF THE
SUPER-DREADNOUGHT ORION CLASS
LAUNCHED IN 1911
WAS THE LAST
MAJOR SHIP BUILT IN
144 WARSHIPS &
287 MERCHANT SHIPS
WERE LAUNCHED FROM
THE YARD. WARSHIPS WERE
BUILT FOR PRACTICALLY
ALL THE GOVERNMENTS OF
EUROPE RUSSIA & JAPAN
TED IN 1843 AND THE SITE
BECAME OPERATIONAL IN 1846
AT ITS PEAK THE YARD

127. Plashet School, East Ham, footbridge, 2000 by Birds Portchmouth Russum, engineers Techniker (p. 278)

128. Container City 2, Trinity House Buoy Wharf, 2002 by Nicholas Lacey & Partners (p. 663)

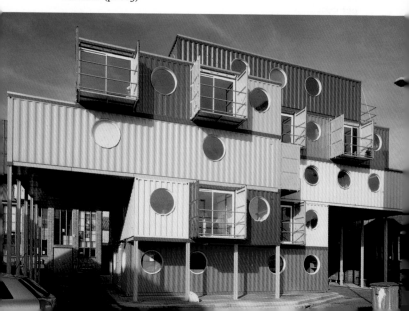

first floors retain their joinery, with typical late C17 bolection-moulded panels, but with early C18 marble fireplaces. The house was subdivided *c.* 1853 and the S rooms much remodelled thereafter although heavy, unmoulded box cornices survive throughout. Between back and front rooms is a back staircase from basement to attic, the upper part original with closed string. Converted for institutional use after 1880 by *Davis & Emmanuel*, first as a Home for Aged Jews, the house returned into private ownership in 1998.

Further S along Stepney Green, C18 speculative building included a continuous terrace of seven houses; erected *c.* 1761–3 by Joseph Bazeley, a sugar refiner from Limehouse, with *John Hockley*, stonemason. Only a single pair, Nos. 61–3, survived post-war clearance but they must have made a handsome group. Fine, restored doorcases with fluted Corinthian pilasters and deep entablature, rubbed brick detail to the windows and cornices. By the early C20 Stepney Green was a largely Jewish enclave; reflected in the number of institutions built to serve their needs. The Jewish Hospital (1918 by *Hall & Hall*) and the splendid C19 Orthodox Synagogue have gone (the latter replaced post-war without distinction) but the former STEPNEY JEWISH PRIMARY AND INFANTS SCHOOL is partially preserved. 1906 by *Joseph & Smithem* in good, deep-red brick. To the fore an attractive School Keeper's House, three storeys under two-bay pediment with terracotta dentilled moulding and badge. Channelled and rusticated brick voussoirs around a carriage arch. The school building is also three storeys but taller, and less appealing, with steep-pitched roof and central dormer. Brick quoins to the end bays. The school closed 1969 and moved to Barkingside (Redbridge). The buildings were converted to artists' studios, an early instance of such a conversion in the East End. STEPNEY GREEN COURT was built in 1895 by *Solomon Joseph* for the Rothschild-funded Four per cent Industrial Dwellings Co. for Jewish Artisans. Two large parallel blocks with single small block to the rear. The suburban situation seems to have encouraged in the architect a greater humanity than his Charlotte de Rothschild dwellings in Spitalfields (1889–92, demolished). Notably well-detailed, with high open staircases in arched recesses under crow-stepped gables, dormers with swan-neck pediments, nice arcaded ironwork screen to the entrance and decorative stucco aprons to the lower windows. Even the ancillary buildings at the S end have charm. The internal planning was also generous and progressive for its date with a club, reading room, communal bathroom and shared boiling-water supply.

Slightly further to the S, set back, is the first large synagogue in the East End, now TEMPLE COURT. 1876–7 by *Davis & Emmanuel*. Its exterior, perhaps deliberately, is unshowy in spite of its size. Pared-down Romanesque with chamfered-arch doorways, two storeyed, the upper level with a rhythm of triplets of arched windows below relieving arches. Bands of purple brick. Its galleried interior, with polychrome arches on tall cast-iron piers was gutted after closure in 1987.* Refurbished in 1997 as flats with the addition of a most inappropriate mansard roof. The former community hall, 1940 (perhaps by *Ernest Joseph*), has also been radically disguised. The E side of the building faces RECTORY SQUARE, laid out in the 1830s but demolished and rebuilt by the *GLC Architects*, *c.* 1982 with groups of two-storey terraces and houses. Nicely landscaped but the dark brick imposes dull qualities.

The walk now returns NW along STEPNEY GREEN, skirting the N side of Stepney Green Park (*see* p. 464). At the corner with Garden Street, hidden in undergrowth is a fragment from Stepney College, for the training of Baptist ministers, erected 1810 on the site of the medieval Worcester House. Ruined doorway of the College Chapel, 1830–1 by *James Savage*.

REDMAN'S ROAD, leading W from Stepney Green, was named after Captain J. Redman (†1760). At the junction is a triangular open space, another fragment of Mile End Green, with a pretty CLOCK TOWER, erected 1913 (originally in Burdett Road, moved here 1934), in memory of Dr Stanley Bean Atkinson †1910 to designs by *M. W. Jameson*, Borough Engineer. Small gabled spire with gilded flame on a solid, square brick shaft inset with allegorical relief carvings of 'Benevolence' and 'Education', by *Gilbert Seale*. Stone cornice enriched with decorative swags and carved lions' heads. Nearby, a featureless red and grey granite FOUNTAIN commemorates the Jewish philanthropist, Leonard Montefiore, 1884 (placed here in 1939; originally at Rutland Street School, Whitechapel). Between Redman's Road and Stepney Green are outliers of the LCC's STIFFORD ESTATE, *c.* 1963 (*see* perambulation *2*). Characterless four-storey maisonettes of reinforced-concrete frame with pale brick infill and angled hoods to the entrances. In Redman's Road is a small, personable group of five staggered houses, in beige brick with weatherboard and angled roofs.

In the angle of Hannibal Road and CRESSY ROAD is the first of two blocks in this area for the East End Dwellings Company by *Davis & Emmanuel*, displaying the advances in philanthropic housing in the wake of the LCC's Boundary Estate (*see* Bethnal Green). CRESSY HOUSES (1894) has a flat corner with a gable and lots of pressed-terracotta detail. Strong brick courses emphasize the long street façades, broken only by the rhythmic projection of balconies to the stairs under dramatic curved gables. Courtyard with balcony access. DUNSTAN HOUSES (1899) face Stepney Green. Two blocks of five storeys in deeply coloured brick with open stair-towers under pyramidal roofs with ball finials and a four-storey dwelling block with bulbous copper dome over an octagonal corner tower. The design provided on each floor four tenements with shared washhouse (instead of a fifth tenement). The cosier domestic

*Tablets of memorial to Jewish dead of the 1914–18 war which surrounded the entrance were taken to Waltham Abbey Jewish Cemetery, Essex.

scale of early C19 STEPNEY GREEN reappears at Nos. 4–10, a terrace of three-storey houses with channelled stucco ground floors and Nos. 12–18, larger houses of *c.* 1815. At the N end, close to Mile End Road, harmonious late C20 infill.

2. *Stepney, from Whitechapel Station to St Dunstan's*

The western part of central Stepney is a mixture of early C19 survivals and post Second World War rebuilding. CAVELL STREET runs S from Whitechapel Road to FORD SQUARE, built on the Hawkins estate, a curious narrow strip of land E of the London Hospital estate (*see* Whitechapel). Only the W side preserves the original early C19 three-storey terraces. Relatively grand for the area: three storeys, arched ground-floor windows and doorways with quarter-fluted columns. Facsimile imitations to the S of this range but the N and S sides have stuccoed terraces of a later date. On the N side pastiche replacement, on the E, sympathetic housing of the 1990s by *Plowman Short Architects* which keeps the scale. At the square's NE corner, ASHFIELD STREET, with a modest early C19 group on the S, Nos. 84–98, restored by *Paul Latham* of *The Regeneration Practice* for the Heritage of London Trust 1996–7. Two-storey houses with arched windows, three-storey ones at each end. They are next to a most unexpected insertion, ELEKTRA HOUSE with a daring, dark windowless facade by *David Adjaye*, 2000; one among a number of individual private commissions for modern houses now appearing in the C21 East End. The interior is generously lit from the S side. SIDNEY SQUARE lies to the E. Here E and W sides remain from the 1820s development; the N side is a 1990s imitation. The square divides the two parts of the SIDNEY STREET ESTATE. This was the Borough of Stepney's first major post-war effort, covering most of the area between Sidney Street and Jubilee Street. Planning began in 1946 but was delayed by the LCC's objections; building work started only *c.* 1950 and continued for the next twenty years.

First the northern part. STEPNEY WAY is the main E–W thoroughfare, but has only an incoherent group of shops and a corner pub: The Artichoke, by *Stewart & Hendry* (now closed), the first post-war pub by Mann's Brewery, modest brick, with later bow windows. Further N at the corner of Sidney Street between Mile End Road and ADELINA GROVE, ANSELL HOUSE, completed 1953, is the grand showpiece. Five to eight storeys, with lower end wings coming forward slightly. A broad, high passage leads through the central block, no longer a main route since the introduction of new fencing in the 1990s. The S side, facing Adelina Grove, now rising behind effectively bold planting, is quite stylish in a Dudokian way, broken up by a generous quantity of private balconies, with curved ones at the stepped-back corners, and strikingly tall, narrow staircase windows. To the E, one of the last parts of the estate, O'LEARY SQUARE (1973–8), another eight-storey slab to the main road; a three-storey block and one-storey row of shops behind; tired, routine detail, brick with concrete floor bands. Opposite, some pre-war survivals: DRON HOUSE, Corporation of London housing of 1925, built for people displaced by Spitalfields Market extensions, four storeys with mansards, frontages in a cramped Neo-Georgian. GROVE DWELLINGS look cosy by comparison: two blocks of tenements at right angles to the road, with the Mercers' badge prominent. Built 1910 by a local builder A.M. Calnan, replacing small factories. The name comes from a grove of trees which until the 1780s stood between Mile End Road and the manor house of Mile End (its site lay near Dron House).

Adelina Grove leads E to JUBILEE STREET, pleasantly broad, with modest, early C19 terraces on both sides, the only surviving part of the Mercers' development in this area. Their property extended E up to Jamaica Street. Nos. 175–93 on the W side is a symmetrical 'palace composition': two storeys with attics, the end houses and two near the centre dignified by parapets and by first-floor windows within arches. Both sides of the street have some pretty Gothic glazing and decorative balconies and fanlights. Back W along LINDLEY ROAD. LINDLEY HOUSE on the N side, 1910, tall and gabled, three storeys over basements, is contemporary with Grove Dwellings in Adelina Grove. Then CALLAHAN COTTAGES, 1963, a plain, low terrace with front gardens. Opposite are taller blocks which were Stepney's preferred building type before the borough adopted the mixture of low- and high-rise pioneered by the LCC. They run N–S (Colverson 1954, Beckett 1953) with the former streets reduced to paths through open areas. The courtyard in front of the dull two-storey brick LIBRARY (1952), is brightened by patterned TILES, 1990–1, designed by children from Redlands Primary School. To the W, Wexford (1959) marks the site of the notorious Siege of Sidney Street of 1911. The siege took place in tenements identical to those at this end of ASHFIELD STREET built in 1900 by Charles Martin, landlord of The Blind Beggar in Whitechapel Road. Originally occupied by Jewish families, they have former workshops behind.

Now back to Sidney Square and the area to its S. On the S side, WOOLLON HOUSE, 1960, a three-storey group with maisonettes above ground-floor flats, and pantiled roofs, a touch of the Festival spirit provided by coloured cladding panels. Between this and the similar DUNDALK, a path leads to the large square of JUBILEE GARDENS. Here the Sidney Street estate adopted for the first time the new principles of mixed development advocated by the LCC. On N and E sides the two-storey VINE and NEWBOLD COTTAGES of 1960 introduce a surprisingly rural note, assisted by burgeoning front gardens and the sizeable central open space. To the S taller blocks (Zion, Kerry, Longford, Athlone, 1956–7) rise to eight storeys. The coarse 1970s coda to the estate is along the

S end of Sidney Street: a terrace of maisonettes (Nos. 9–61) with a curious pattern of exposed staircases under heavy projecting-concrete upper floors (1974), and at the S end the unappealingly massive Siege House, eleven storeys, with adjoining garage podium (1971) at the corner of Commercial Road.

East of Jubilee Street

JUBILEE STREET was named from Jubilee Place, a small alley which commemorated the Golden Jubilee of George III in 1810; the first street to be built N of Commercial Road in this area, and later extended N. On the E side, JUBILEE MANSIONS, 1921, proudly named and dated at the corner of Clark Street; plain three-storey flats built by the Borough of Stepney to replace ten houses on the Mercers' estate destroyed by a bomb in 1918. N of Clark Street a prominent group of Board School and associated buildings of 1882 and 1897–8, built as Dempsey Street School, converted to housing, 2003, with added top floor. Schools were intended to be focal points of post-war neighbourhoods, but the surroundings here show only too clearly the lack of coordinated planning. Along Clark Street is the unwelcoming back of the GLC's EXMOUTH ESTATE, mostly completed 1969–73, displaying the low regard in which the street-front was held at this time. The garage range in Clark Street has a row of flats above, the doorways to the upper walkway with overscaled projecting hoods. The estate makes much use of upper walkways, fashionable at the time for multi-layered pedestrian segregated planning, replacing streets with a confusing series of pedestrian squares surrounded by linked four- and five-storey ranges with glazed staircase ends. They extend S to Commercial Road (*see* p. 526) and E beyond the site of the S end of Jamaica Street.

N of Stepney Way is the CLICHY ESTATE (named after Stepney's twinned French town), bounded to N and W by Jubilee Street and Smithy Street, built by *Riches & Blythin* for Stepney in 1961–4 on land acquired from the Mercers. The layout reflects the new concern to segregate traffic and provide for parking, with low housing around a large but rather bleak paved pedestrian precinct with a single nine-storey tower. Around the perimeter the three- and four-storey blocks are crisply detailed in pale brick with blue panels; a more modern image than Stepney's brick flats of the 1950s. On the N side the blocks zigzag around parking courts, on the S they form a neat terrace along Stepney Way. The E side of JAMAICA STREET, originally with low C19 terraces built by the Mercers, now has uneventful low housing of 2000–1. This replaced the most dramatic post-war composition in the area, the three seventeen-storey towers of the LCC's STIFFORD ESTATE, sited to overlook the new Stepney Green Park. When built in 1958–64 they were the tallest in the East End. They were demolished in 1999–2000, having been declared dangerous in 1994 because of falling windows. Because of the open space a density of 156 p.p.a. was permitted, higher than the 136 prescribed in the county plan.* The original low-rise components of the Stifford Estate remain some way further N between Redman's Road and Stepney Green (*see* above) with two further maisonette blocks N of the Clichy Estate. W between Redman's Road and Smithy Street, two schools: REDLANDS PRIMARY SCHOOL, a late work by *T.J. Bailey*, 1909; his earlier Smith Street School, 1899 rises up behind. In the playground a pleasant caretaker's house with roughcast upper storeys and flat-headed dormers breaking the eaves.

S of Stepney Way is an earlier part of the Clichy Estate built on land initially acquired by the Metropolitan Police from the Mercers in 1938. Three long, staggered blocks (Harriott, Apsley and Pattison), in Stepney's earliest post-war brick style, in an austere setting of drying yards and sheds. S of this, AYLWARD STREET (formerly Charles Street) a fragment remaining from a path which once led NE from Commercial Road to Stepney High Street. It forms the northern boundary of the Arbour Square area (*see* Ratcliffe) and leads toward the ST DUNSTAN'S ESTATE of 1954: three unassuming three-storey LCC blocks with end walls of red brick. Earlier fragments remain here, badly in need of some knitting together: DUNELM STREET with two-storey C19 terraces on both sides, and on the N side of Aylward Street, THE PEACOCK, a simple two-storey pub. Most of this land was developed by the Barnes family of builder developers. SENRAB STREET (a reversal of Barnes), late C19 with a corner shop, terminates at its S end with MARION RICHARDSON SCHOOL, a splendid LCC building of 1907 (*see* above). Back in Stepney Way, SCOUT CENTRE at the corner of Copley Street, a portal-framed shed, built as Stepney Meeting House in 1959, successor to a meeting house founded by Puritans in 1644. On the N side of Stepney Way the former CLARE HALL, a Neo-Georgian Truman's pub of the 1920s by *A.E. Sewell*. Its name refers to Clare College, Cambridge, owners of land to the N of Stepney Way, where streets of good early C19 houses were cleared in the 1970s for STEPNEY GREEN PARK. The semblance of a rural atmosphere is increased by the City Farm on the eastern fringe, close to the extensive churchyard of St Dunstan's.

3. Mile End

3a. The W end of Mile End Road and area to the N: a circular tour

The walk begins at the junction with Cambridge Heath Road and Whitechapel Road, where the Whitechapel Turnpike stood,

*The entrance halls of the towers had murals in mosaic or concrete by *Anthony Hollaway* and the significance of the group was emphasized by a notable bronze SCULPTURE by *Henry Moore*, Reclining Woman, placed on a low mound close to Jamaica Road, one of the most celebrated examples of the post-war LCC's concern to bring art to the people. Now in the Henry Moore Sculpture Park, Yorkshire.

one mile from the City. The buildings on the N side of MILE END ROAD are set well back behind a railed-in remnant of Mile End Waste, originally part of the common land. Planted with trees, 1910–12. Early meetings of William Booth's Salvation Army were held here, commemorated by a pair of MEMORIALS by *George E. Wade*. Of the two, the characterful bronze bust of the General in uniform is best. Erected 1927. Much less good, the crude fibreglass copy of a figure of Booth preaching (cast from the original bronze at the training college, Denmark Hill). Booth's Bible has been stolen and his repaired hands painted silver to unearthly effect. Further along, perched on a pink-granite plinth, is a lifesize bronze bust of Edward VII, dated 1911. Erected 'by the few Freemasons of the Eastern District'.

Behind the Waste, from the corner with Cambridge Heath Road, the WHITE HART was one of many pubs along the road in the C18, but rebuilt *c.* 1900. Quite fancy, taking advantage of its corner site. Good carved relief under cupola, its interior also partly intact with sturdy iron columns with foliate capitals. Adjoining the pub were the stables of the Albion Brewery (*see* Whitechapel), erected in 1885 by *Robert Spence*, heavily damaged in 1941. On the site, CHRONOS BUILDINGS by *Proctor Matthews*, 1999–2000. Long block of flats and shops with a layered façade of terracotta tiles, a late 1990s signature, with a shallow rotunda at the E end: one of the first major private late C20 residential developments in this area. Groups of houses are set behind. Next No. 27a, fanciful Edwardian Baroque of 1905, possibly by *William Bradford & Sons* for the Albion Brewery's engineer. Stepped-back upper floor with corner turret and barber-shop colonette shafts. Mansard roof and central scalloped gable added 1984. Ground floor of three wide gauged arches, the central one originally leading to motor-trolley sheds behind. Built on the site of the Skinners Almshouses (1698, demolished 1894).

Of the clutch of almshouses which were established along the road from the late C17, the only survivors are the charming group at TRINITY GREEN founded under the will of Captain Henry Mudd of Ratcliffe (†1692) and erected in 1695 for the Corporation of Trinity House by *William Ogbourne*, master carpenter. Designed for '28 decayed masters and commanders of ships or the widows of such'. Two rows of brick cottages face each other across a garden, with a compact and pretty chapel closing the view from the street. This has a wide staircase and tall round-arched windows under a wide, dentilled pediment, clock tower and cupola. The cottage rows are splayed and of unequal length but cleverly joined by an elegant stone wall to the street of concave and convex curves. Each range finishes in pretty brick and stone-dressed gable ends with pediments, brick niches and angled rusticated quoins. Atop the copings are fibreglass models of ships, copies of an original pair carved in marble by *Robert Jones*.* The

*The originals are in the Museum of London.

Trinity House Almshouses, Mile End Road, drawn in 1896

garden elevations have heavy, with timber-bracketed eaves and a large central pediment with tympana carved with the Company's arms and decorative maritime motifs of seaweed, anchors and ropes. The cottages have raised entrances coupled under wide timber hoods on delicately carved brackets. Inside, each had a parlour with kitchen below. Flanking the chapel are remnants of C19 almshouses. This remarkable survival is due to *C.R. Ashbee* who led a preservation campaign in 1895, and made the almshouses the subject of the first volume of the *Survey of London*. Restored by the LCC in 1956–62 after war damage. The chapel, reconstructed for community use, has fine early C18 panelling from Bradmore House, Hammersmith. A pair of lead STATUES of Captain Richard Maples and Robert Sandes are now at Trinity House in the City of London.

E of Trinity Green, PARK HOUSE was erected *c.* 1820 by the Barnes family, developers of much of Mile End during the late C18 and early C19. Two bays with Gothic fanlight. Then, the TOWER HAMLETS MISSION founded *c.* 1870 by Frederick N. Charrington, heir to the brewery, who was an evangelical and temperance advocate. The Great Assembly Hall, an elaborate French Renaissance creation of 1885–6 by *Boulnois & Warner,* was bombed and replaced. Further rebuilding in 1985–98 by *Petch & Fermaud* including a new centre, a small group of houses and a chapel. Further along, THE THREE CRANES pub, another old establishment, probably associated in the C18 with the Vintners Almshouses but, in common with the majority of Mile End's inns, rebuilt in the C19. At the corner with Cleveland Way, the former Old Red Cow. Rebuilt 1895 in an unusually striking blue brick with terracotta trim. A short detour off Cleveland Way's E side leads into BELLEVUE PLACE, a neat row of terraces built *c.* 1825–30 on land belonging to Charrington's brewery (*see* below); originally in a U-shape around gardens but later reduced for brewery sheds. At the W end, a later C19 house, also probably for Charrington's.

Along Mile End Road's S side, a pair of early C18 houses stand beside No. 86, a large red brick house of *c.* 1890, with an integral shopfront under carved parapet, richly decorated with cut- and brick rubbed detail. This was the Mile End Distillery, established in the C18, its yard and works still visible behind. A large engraved slate tablet, erected by the GLC in 1971, marks the site of Captain Cook's house, at No. 90, demolished in the 1950s. The house was one of thirty-seven erected by various builders in the decade after 1760 when the last remaining part of Mile End Green was let for building. Most survive, as a long terrace of mangled two-bay houses. Nos. 92–110, patchy and much refaced, still reflect the well-to-do character of Georgian Mile End. No. 102 is particularly well-preserved, a large three-bay house behind a railing with overthrow and traceried fanlight; No. 104 has a pedimented doorcase. In the centre of this range Nos. 112–24, erected after 1766 by *Joseph Rowland*, carpenter, with Assembly Rooms behind. The entire group was known as Assembly Row; Assembly Passage, a cobbled alley through No. 110, was created in the 1790s, when it led to Pleasure Gardens.

Hereafter all the interest is on the N side of the road where the former WICKHAM'S department store is a relic of a period when Mile End Road aspired to be 'the Oxford Street of the East End'. 1925–7 by *T. Jay Evans & Son*, E end heightened (behind the façade) by one storey in 1931–4 by *W.J. Lewis*. Lengthy stone façade, over steel frame, dominated by a screen of giant Bassae Ionic columns rising through three floors and crowned by a bulbous central tower, reduced in scale from the original design. Its pompous aping of West End fashion is comically deflated by the intrusion of a C19 three-storey terraced house, which cuts the design in half. Wickham, unable to buy it, was forced to build around it and thus created what Ian Nairn* called 'one of the best visual jokes in London, a perennial triumph for the little man, the bloke who won't conform'. Then back to a smaller scale with a former London City and Midland BANK, probably by *Whinney, Son and Austen Hall*, *c.* 1928. Pretty temple front with Tuscan columns *in antis*. Banking hall with pilasters and groined vaults to arch windows. Squatting beside it, the compact GENESIS CINEMA of 1939 by *W.R. Glen* for ABC cinemas, replacing *Frank Matcham*'s Paragon Theatre of 1885. Smooth green-mosaic façade with faience panel restored in 1999. It had an Art Deco interior with scalloped coving.

E of this group, Nos. 107–13 is an early example of the uniform London terrace. Built by *Anthony Ireland*, 1717, all in brown brick with red dressings, with flush sashes and hoods on carved brackets. Only No. 113 is entirely authentic, the remainder substantially restored for the Spitalfields Historic

* *Nairn's London.*

Buildings Trust in 1991–5 by *Gus Alexander Architects* who removed later shopfronts. The terrace stood next to the Anchor Brewery, established 1757 by John Charrington. Closed in 1975, the site redeveloped 2001 as a retail park. Only the striking Baroque BREWERY OFFICES remain. 1872 by *Snooke & Stock*. Rounded corners with open upper floor set with single stone column and paired chimneystacks above in Portland stone. Behind this a polite Wrenaissance extension of 1927, probably by *William Bradford & Sons*. Red brick with bracketed projecting stone hoods to first-floor windows and segmental pedimented entrance under central *œil de bœuf* window.

The real showpieces, however, on this side of Mile End Road are Nos. 133–9: an exceptional pair of double-fronted, three-storey and basement houses. Two of an original group of three erected by *Thomas Andrews*, a local developer, in 1741–2. Each of five bays, in good brick with gauged window headers, cut brick cornice and stone platband above first floor. It is hard to remind oneself that the houses would once have had views to the river. The C19 saw separation into four properties and the erection of shopfronts. Nos. 133–5 had an archway driven through its centre by its coachbuilder occupant in 1858 and lost its upper storey *c.* 1941, reinstated in 1999–2000 by *Gus Alexander Architects*. Nos. 137–9 (Malplaquet House) has fared better, in spite of war damage (repaired by *Richard Seifert*, 1952). Henry Charrington extended the house in 1794, adding the fine, arched doorcase with concave reveals (cf. No. 12, Fournier Street, Spitalfields) and remodelling the interior. The staircase, panelling and painted decoration are rare and significant survivals of that date. For buildings further E *see* perambulation *3b*.

The Charringtons' land N of the brewery was developed progressively from the early C19. CEPHAS AVENUE belongs to the 1830s, when higher standards were applied to the design of new houses, well represented at the N end. These have channelled-stucco basements and ground floor, arched windows and stucco parapets. Iron railings. Directly ahead in CEPHAS STREET is the former church of ST PETER of 1838, in pale Suffolk brick (*see* above) with vicarage and schools added by *A.R. Mason*, 1839. Cephas Street leads W, its S side lined with Italianate terraces of the 1840s culminating in the larger and later Gresham Lodge. On the N side, the BANCROFT ESTATE of 1949–54 was amongst Stepney's first major post-war housing schemes and displays its instinctive preference for the low-rise in the tradition of the interwar cottage estates. Cottages and houses are approached along pedestrian streets off COLEBERT AVENUE (*cf.* Limehouse Fields, *see* perambulation *4*). Further W, between Malcolm Road and Wickford Street, are ranks of balcony access flats (opened in 1949), handsomely refurbished in the 1990s.

At the W end of Cephas Street on the S side, the CLEVELAND ESTATE of 1956–63 shows the different attitude of the LCC, with a textbook mixed estate of maisonettes blocks, a few terraced houses (Vawdrey Close) and one eleven-storey slab, Gouldman House. Reinforced concrete frame raised on stilts. An early example in the area; the use of profiled-aluminium cladding was novel at the time. Across Cephas Street, open to CAMBRIDGE HEATH ROAD, is FRANK DOBSON SQUARE, created in the 1980s with a bronze SCULPTURE as its centrepiece: Woman with Fish, of 1963 by *Frank Dobson*, one of several major sculptors commissioned by the LCC to produce work for the new estates and to bring art to the people (as at Avebury Estate, Bethnal Green and Stifford Estate, Stepney). From here Cambridge Heath Road leads S back to the beginning of this walk.

3b. Mile End Road E *of Stepney Green Station: a circular tour*

STEPNEY GREEN STATION was opened in 1902 on the newly-extended District Line, probably by *C.A. Brereton* (cf. Bow Road); low with wide, arched windows along the front. The new line required demolition of three ancient weatherboarded houses along Mile End Road. In their stead, and taking its architectural cue from them, the BLACK BOY INN by *W. Husband*, 1904. Triple-gabled frontage with leaded casements in a quite credible C17 style. It adjoins Mile End's former public baths (now the GLOBE CENTRE for HIV+ and AIDS patients) of 1930–2 by *B.J. Belsher*, Stepney Borough Engineer and Surveyor. Built over the railway line. A likeable, hygienic faience façade, with central recessed bay and loggia at first floor behind a balustrade. Subdued classical detail. Carefully adapted in 1995 by *Colwyn Foukes & Partners* who ingeniously inserted the central curved glass-block wall and lowered the entrance to the pavement. Inside, a double-height, brightly lit atrium with a cantilevered stair.

Opposite the station, S of Mile End Road, in BEAUMONT GROVE are C20 buildings associated with Stepney's ancient Jewish community. First STEPNEY JEWISH COMMUNITY CENTRE, built for the Stepney Jewish Settlement. The earlier part (No. 2), was erected 1938 by *P.V. Burnett & C.J. Eprile*. Unlively, brown brick with projecting concrete hood and cornice band. Extended in 1956 by *Lewis & Hickey*. Functionally composed with recessed entrance and plainly exposed concrete frame infilled with yellow brick and glass. Of the same date and in the same spirit, *Lewis & Hickey*'s ALICE MODEL NURSERY, an abstract composition in brick, neatly fitted onto a corner site. The Settlement, under Alice Model's influence, was the first to establish a nursery to enable women to work during the war. Some older housing in LOUISA STREET: two-storey terraces (S side) of *c.* 1820 with round-arch doorways, fluted lintels and imposts; at the W end, a later row of *c.* 1850 sits slightly back in LOUISA GARDENS. Heavy pointed-arch windows. At the S end of Beaumont Grove, a large house of *c.* 1820 with interlacing tracery to the windows. Then, in

MARIA TERRACE, a picturesque Gothic ensemble with chamfered Tudor-arch doorways, pretty bargeboards and gabled attic dormers with finials.

E of Stepney Green station, Mile End Road is dominated by the buildings of Queen Mary College on the N side (*see* above) and the Ocean Estate (perambulation *4*) to the S. The main building of note is THE HALF MOON pub, a converted former Methodist chapel of 1899–1900 by *Keith Downes Young & Henry Hall*. Triumphal-arch façade with balustraded cornice, open loggia and *œil-de-bœuf* windows over a round-arched central opening with two doors l. and r., to the chapel's galleries, under diocletian windows. Gates with vaguely Art Nouveau ironwork. Octagonal lantern roof on chamfered brackets. Conversion, by *Lawrence Tring Architects* in 1997, incorporated the buildings of the adjoining Half Moon Theatre of 1984–5 by *Florian Beigel* and *Architecture Bureau*. An economical design in brick, concrete and steel set back around a courtyard conceived as a continuation of the 'street' for open-air performance. Overlooking this are phantom 'façades' doubling as galleries. The theatre auditorium, clad in bronzed profiled metal sheeting has been converted to a bar by cutting it open along its side and inserting a glazed curtain wall. Just beyond, almost hidden from view is MILE END PLACE; an unexpectedly secluded group of early C19 workers' cottages with front gardens. The E side is roughcast, the W side brick with two windows to the upper floor. These neat rows draw up short at the wall of the JEWISH CEMETERY, established in 1657 by Spanish and Portuguese Sephardic Jews from the City, who also founded the BETH HOLIM HOSPITAL in 1665 at No. 253 Mile End Road. Later expanded as a home for the elderly and rebuilt 1912–13 by *Manuel Nunes Costello* in an excellent interpretation of a house of the early C18 (now ALBERT STERN HOUSE, a student hostel). Rubbed red brick, stone modillion cornice and iron balcony to first floor. Cosy brick cottages at the rear, originally for married couples, with mullioned windows and leaded panes. E of this, IFOR EVANS PLACE, two parallel blocks of student residences around a small court. Fluted blockwork facings and butterfly-wing roofs. By *MacCormac Jamieson Prichard* for Queen Mary College.

BANCROFT ROAD, N of the University buildings, has the former Vestry Hall and Workhouse of Mile End Old Town (*see* Library and Hospital above). Its W side has terraces of largish houses of the 1860s, which continue into ALDERNEY ROAD. Three storeys with basements and overwrought stucco mouldings to the windows and doors. The S side follows the long wall of the Jewish Cemetery (*see* above) but the N side is open space created by bombing and extended by the LCC as the rather formless Carlton Square Gardens. This area was originally developed *c.* 1848–55 as the Globe Fields Estate of William Pemberton Barnes by his surveyors, *Hammack & Lambert*. CARLTON SQUARE, with two-storey terraces, still has a mid-

C19 flavour. Pubs were integral to the plan, including the Norfolk Arms, at the corner of ARGYLE ROAD, with big solid arched windows. W along MASSINGHAM STREET is a plain late C19 Board school. Flatly unadorned, its entrance enriched by C20 Islamic mosaics.

S now along GLOBE ROAD, which was a meandering trackway between the hamlets of Mile End and Bethnal Green to the N. Houses began to appear *c.* 1813. Nos. 77–81 are the sole remnant of the early C19 ribbon development; a scrappy terrace with stucco heads over narrow doorways. Post-war rebuilding was designed to break up the street-front. On the W side the OSIER ESTATE, 1955–62 typifies the LCC's approach with housing of mixed heights grouped informally around a grassed area. WITHY HOUSE dominates, an eleven-storey slab on stilts, its cross-wall construction revealed on each side as a forceful grid of balconies. On the E side, the GLC's low-rise FRIMLEY ESTATE, *c.* 1967–8 has a parade of shops to the street but arranges its three blocks of maisonettes around an open courtyard with single-storey homes for the elderly. Finally at the corner with Mile End Road, the OLD GLOBE pub, rebuilt 1811. Much altered.

4. *Ocean Estate, between Mile End Road and Ben Jonson Road*

The extensive Ocean Estate, encapsulating every stage of social housing from the 1940s to the early C21, stretches S from Mile End Road to Ben Jonson Road, the heart of 'neighbourhood 3' of the Stepney–Poplar reconstruction area. The area around Ben Jonson Road was built up with small, terrace houses from the early C19 on the estate of J.T. Barber Beaumont, extending N from the village centre around St Dunstan's church. The topically named Trafalgar Square and Ocean Street appear on Horwood's map of 1819. There were plans for slum clearance in the 1930s. A scheme of 1937 by *Wells Coates* for the Beaumont Estate came to nothing because of the war, but a little enclave of new housing, by a housing association, was built in Ocean Street, whose name provided the inspiration for the LCC's post-war estate.*

Planning began in 1946, in the immediate post-war period when LCC housing was under the Valuer's Department, but work was delayed through shortage of building materials. Most of the estate was built from 1948–57, with some later additions around the fringes. In contrast to later LCC work the layout was incoherent, with groups of flats planted between the old streets as sites became available; recent rebuilding at the S end has reacted

*The 1930s flats were demolished in 2000–1. SEARLE HOUSE, Duckett Street by *Mitchell & Bridgwater*, 1937, a symmetrical composition with raised brick bands, and to its W in Ocean Street, FRANCIS GRAY HOUSE, 1932, four storeys, with central arched entrance.

strongly against this, returning to the principle of the terrace with street frontage. The tour starts in Mile End Road and runs roughly anti-clockwise.

Along MILE END ROAD opposite Queen Mary College the fringe of C19 terraces was replaced by a grass sward and a striking array of six-storey blocks (Galveston, Hawke, Genoa, Levant, Magellan, Bantry) of 1953–4, at right angles to the road, with generous spaces between. Two more, Formosa and Biscay, lie parallel. The regular layout, symbolic of the new era in its rejection of the street front, allowed all flats good light and ventilation. It was adopted at the same time for LCC's contemporary Woodberry Down Estate, Hackney. The brisk modern image created by the repeated rhythm of projecting eaves, pale brick walls with projecting concrete balconies and flat roofs was blurred by pitched roofs added in the early 1990s. A few of the blocks have internal staircase access; the others have the more routine (and cheaper) long access balconies.

Now down HARFORD STREET, past ERNEST STREET, where there are more traditional pitched-roof three-storey blocks in red brick (Palliser, Levant 1957). S of Ernest Street an earlier series in the LCC's heavy pre-war style, completed 1950: in red and grey brick, loosely grouped around rather gloomy courtyards. Turning W, SHANDY STREET runs beside Shandy Park, a former graveyard next to the ruin of St Faith's church. Further W along Shandy Street and in DUCKETT STREET terraces of two-storey cottages come as a surprise. A similar type was built at Woodberry Down. They were mostly completed in 1953 and reflect the interest in the Scandinavian tradition current among some LCC architects at the time. Pale-yellow brick, with crisp monopitch roofs with emphatic jutting eaves, small front gardens. They open N off Shandy Street, pleasantly grouped around two greens. To satisfy the prescribed density, taller blocks were needed in compensation: Bengal, on the W side of Duckett Street, taking advantage of views across Shandy Park, is a looming eight-storey reinforced-concrete slab, a daring height for its date, 1949–51. The use of concrete, still a novel material for council housing, was encouraged by shortage of traditional building materials. Pedimented porches and painted trim of the 1990s now adorn the exterior, originally plain except for the three rows of concrete balconies high up which were required for fire escape. To the W, more prosaic blocks in pre-war manner: red and grey brick, with solid balconies and tall parapets concealing pitched roofs: Flores, Riga and Darien, all completed 1950, followed by Caspian, 1956, whose metal balconies provide a lighter touch, and Galway, across White Horse Lane, 1955, five storeys, exposing its concrete floorbands in progressive LCC fashion.

The estate reaches W beyond White Horse Lane into BEAUMONT SQUARE, a C19 square, but all rebuilt. The LCC's dull three-storey blocks of 1952–5 look mean in comparison with SYDNEY HOUSE on the E side, which sports a pediment dated

1953. Erected as a hostel for the elderly by *C.H. James* of *James & Bywaters* in his customary demure Regency manner, marred by obtrusive window replacements of 1999. Extensions also of 1999. On the W side of the square, on the site of the former London Jewish Hospital is the LONDON INDEPENDENT HOSPITAL, 1986, by *Prior Manton Tuke Powell* for an American healthcare company; a sign of the changing East End. A bland rhythm of recessed and projecting bays and chamfered corners.

Back now to WHITE HORSE LANE, which continues S with a remnant of its early C19 domestic character on the W side: a reminder that this is an old road, close to the centre of the village of Stepney. No. 27, early C19, has a doorway with fluted quarter columns; No. 25 has a central doorway and arched ground-floor window. Behind No. 23 a small yard with tactful flats of 1999. A Victorian terrace follows, then the former Rectory in its own grounds: yellow brick, Neo-Tudor with kneelered gables and octagonal chimneystacks.

A little further S is the junction of Stepney High Street and Ben Jonson Road, an area which was devastated in the Second World War. The replacements do not relate well. At the corner, HAILEYBURY GUILD BOYS CLUB, 1954–6 by *YRM*, concrete frame with brick infilling, much altered. The club was founded in 1890 by Canon Hoskyns, Rector of St Dunstan's, an ex-Haileybury pupil. The large precinct of STEPNEY GREEN SCHOOL, 1961–3 by the *LCC Architecture Dept, Schools Division*, has a dominant eight-storey classroom block as its centrepiece, but is set too far back to make an effective contribution to the townscape. Further on along BEN JONSON ROAD, the old shopping street, was re-created, with flats over shops. Some of the first were the plain five-storey blocks flanking the pedestrian close to the S, completed 1950. Above them looms the overbearing ten-storey system-built tower of Allonby, which like the neighbouring towers, Channell and Studland, is a late addition, completed 1966. N of Ben Jonson Road and E of Duckett Street two spreading Y-plan groups of five-storey balcony-access flats, completed 1955, another experimental layout of the 1950s. The only older survival is the tiny early C19 terrace, DURHAM ROW, behind the Haileybury Club.

Nearby, extending E to HARFORD STREET, is a substantial area rebuilt in 1997–9, replacing three 1950s eight-storey slabs similar to Bengal. The low-rise housing has street fronts in C19 Stepney tradition in response to residents' requests; initiated by SHADA (Stepney Housing and Development Agency), designed by *PRP Architects*, and carried out by Laings as a 'design and build' project. The yellow brick terraces of three and four storeys, in a formal layout, are given a little ceremony by front walls which rise in mannered fashion to high parapets. At the S end of HARFORD STREET, HEALTH CENTRE, 1997, more overtly modern, with big projecting eaves and walls of blue plaster and glass bricks. S of Ben Jonson

Road a similar approach has been taken to Stepney's former Limehouse Fields Estate, built from 1932 and continued up to 1951. Demolished 2002–3 except for a sprinkling of post-war cottages around ASTON STREET which fit easily with the spacious new layout. Further E a street runs towards the canal, breaking out in Neoclassical manner into a circle with quadrant blocks topped by Soanian caps, around a paved garden with decorative iron gates. Returning N up CARR STREET and along BEN JONSON ROAD, on the S the low HALLEY PRIMARY SCHOOL, 1990s, with cluster of pitched roofs, faces a long brick wall, all that remains of the GASWORKS of the Commercial Gas Co., opened 1837. The huge site, developed from *c.* 1853, ran alongside the Regent's Canal. The industrial character of the canal area is now recalled only by a group of buildings on its E side, starting with the Ragged School Museum (*see* above), an early effort to bring education to a deprived area.

This tour returns up Harford Street to ESSIAN STREET, where the low BEN JONSON PRIMARY is an undistinguished post-war replacement of one of the very first Board Schools, 1872 by *T. Roger Smith*. It was significant as a pioneer example of the Prussian plan with separate classrooms and assembly halls, considered too extravagant in the 1870s, and not adopted generally for London schools until the 1890s. Schoolkeeper's house, and former Cookery and Laundry Centre added in 1895 remain, with Flemish gable and deep windows framed by pilaster strips, also the triple-gabled School Board's Divisional Offices, 1895 by *Bailey*, altered for the LCC 1914. After a meanly detailed group of courtyard flats of 1949 (Azov, Moray), a change is struck by the GLC additions of the 1970s: EMMOTT CLOSE and SANDALWOOD CLOSE, completed 1975; along carefully landscaped paths are crisply detailed blocks of four and six storeys, their red brick enlivened by projecting balconies. Better than much GLC work of this date. In contrast to this forcefully urban group are the consciously pretty white-boarded, tile-roofed cottagey clusters close to the canal along GRAND WALK, UNION DRIVE and CANAL CLOSE. They were built in 1979–82 (job architect *Norman Bayldon*), some of the very last housing by the GLC, and reflect the reaction at the time against anything that could visibly be identified as 'council housing'.

5. *Mile End Park*

The concept of a 90-acre green space along Regent's Canal, from Victoria Park to the Thames, appeared in the County of London plan of 1943, but made little progress due to lack of funding. By Grove Road, *Rachel Whiteread*'s haunting work, House, 1993, a concrete cast of a whole terrace house, existed for a year before it was demolished as inappropriate for the new park. The area began to be realized as a continuous park only from 1995, through a partnership of the Environment Trust, the Borough of Tower Hamlets and the East London Business Alliance, and was taken up as a £25 million Millennium Lottery project. The brilliant proposal of a Green Bridge providing a link over Mile End Road (with revenue-producing shops beneath), the brainwave of *Piers Gough* of *CZWG*, became part of the masterplan by *Tibbalds Monro*, led by *George Gardiner*. This developed the principle of specific functions for different parts of the park, with an emphasis on community involvement and sustainability. They are connected by a continuous pathway with a network of bicycle routes; tunnels beside the canal avoid road crossings. The bold landscaping by *Hugo Nowell* of the Environment Trust integrates the park with discreet earth-mounded buildings by *Tibbalds Monro*. Currently the park is under Tower Hamlets; a long-term arrangement for adequately resourced management has yet to be resolved.

The northern part of the park was completed by 2002. The park GATES in this area are earlier, erected by Bow Neighbourhood in the 1980s in sympathy with those of Victoria Park. From the N end, first Bow Wharf, modest canal-side buildings converted to restaurants, fitness studio etc. Then a PLAY ARENA (a more ambitious amphitheatre was first proposed). A more visually exciting series of spaces follows, defined by strong swirling curves and given interest by different heights. In the ECOLOGY AREA the path leads over an earth-covered building marked by an undulating line of curved timber posts; below, a glazed wall overlooks a string of small lakes, and a tall wind-turbine circulates the water. The ARTS PARK to its S has more formal landscaping with a viewing mound, and a glass-fronted earth-covered pavilion opening onto a lakeside terrace. Gently rising land leads effortlessly to the GREEN BRIDGE over Mile End Road. The bright yellow bridge, deep enough to take mature trees, is supported by grand curving abutments faced with glazed green tiles, a bold colour scheme typical of *CZWG*. Shops and restaurants are slotted in beneath along Mile End Road and open out towards the pleasant terraced southern slopes. These have drought-resisting plants, providing a 'garden of the senses', overlooking formal water gardens parallel to the canal.

The areas further S are still evolving at time of writing. The SOUTH PARK has a gently mounded walk through meadow grass, leading past sports grounds and older stadium to an entrance in Rhodeswell Road. This area began as KING GEORGE'S FIELDS. Stone gatepiers dated 1936, by *Ansell & Bailey* with crests on cast panels. A new SPORTS CENTRE and swimming pool are intended. Adjacent on the other side of the railway line is a Go-Karting track. Proposals to roof this with a structure forming a 'solar power station' were under discussion in 2004. S of Rhodeswell Road a canal basin and restaurant are planned, along the canal route that continues to Limehouse Basin. S of St Paul's Way a CHILDREN'S PLAY AREA was constructed in 2002, with funding from HSBC.

ST GEORGE'S

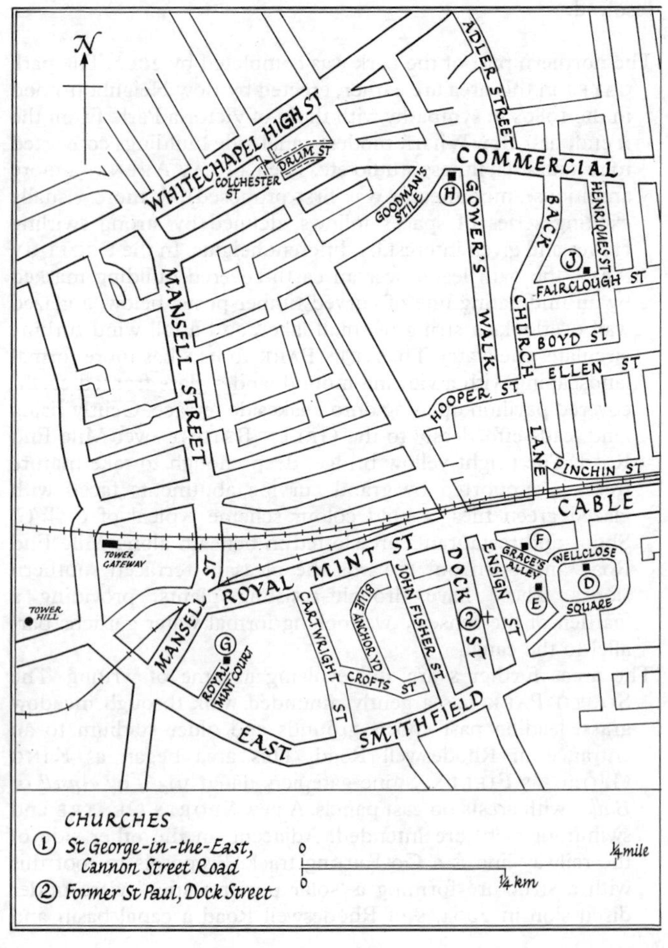

Until the early C19 the land to the N of the old riverside hamlets of Wapping, Shadwell and Ratcliffe remained open and was used for a multitude of activities. The name Cable Street came from the ropeyards in the area, and originally applied only to a short stretch of the W–E road bypassing the riverside settlements. From the later C17 coherent patches of domestic building began to appear, inhabited by skilled artisan and professional families, particularly those with maritime connections. Prince's Square (later Swedenborg Square) and Wellclose Square, known in the C18 as Marine Square, were laid out between Ratcliffe Highway and Cable Street, and further E St George's church was built as part of the early C18 campaign to provide new Anglican churches for the expanding E end. Rocque's map shows that in the mid-C18

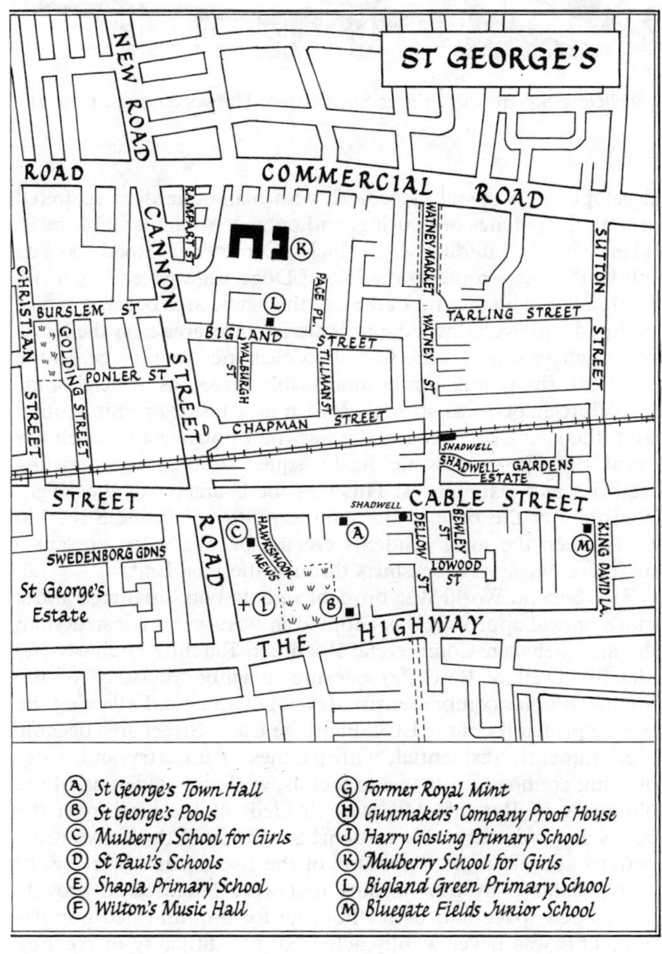

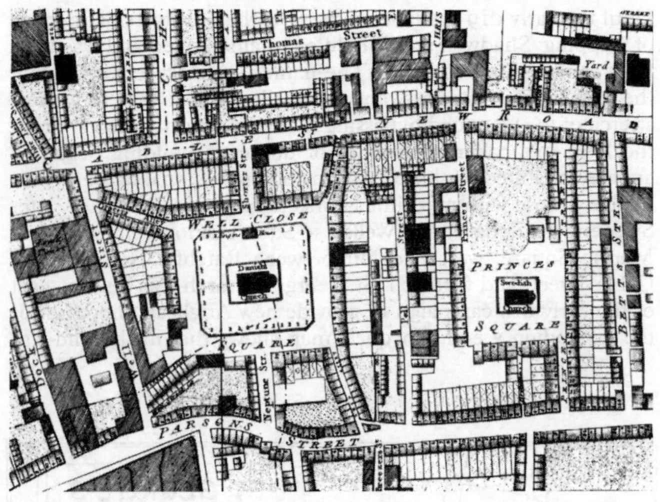

Wellclose Square and Princes Square from Horwood's map, 1819–21

development was still piecemeal, with market gardens scattered among the patches of housing, and open common land to the N. Then with the building of the docks, Commercial Road was laid out in 1803 as a route to the Isle of Dogs; railways and factories followed, and by the end of the C19 the whole area became dense, polluted and overcrowded, particularly in the area near the Royal Mint, where some of the first slum clearance took place. In the early C20 the population around Cable Street, as in neighbouring Whitechapel, was strongly Jewish as a result of immigration from the later C19. Between the wars new housing and amenities began to be provided sporadically, squeezed in between existing factories and warehouses. This was the character of the neighbourhood at the time of the famous 'battle of Cable Street' in 1936, when the local residents erected barricades to prevent a
114 march of Mosley's blackshirts through the East End.

The Second World War brought drastic bomb damage and a more radical approach was adopted in post-war reconstruction; the area between Commercial Road and Ratcliffe Highway (*see also* Shadwell & Ratcliffe) became 'neighbourhood 5' of the Stepney/Poplar comprehensive development area. Following the zoning principles of the LCC Plan, the Cable Street area became predominantly residential, with patches of industry and warehousing confined to its W and E ends, while the widening of the old route of Ratcliffe Highway divided off the area from the docks and older riverside settlements. Much of the dense street pattern as well as the remnants of the two squares were swept away, replaced by new layouts that were intended to provide more open space and better housing for a diminished population. This was never wholly achieved: the difficulty of creating coherent large sites resulted in piecemeal rebuilding; intermittent older buildings survived, and were refurbished after comprehensive clearance fell out of fashion in the 1970s. The result is interestingly varied though visually discrepant: a patchwork of housing estates, some quite distinctive and spacious, but ill-related both to each other and to the old street pattern and remaining clusters of older buildings. The area at the W end between Dock Street and the Royal Mint, where slums were cleared already in the C19, was almost entirely rebuilt in the 1970s–80s. Elsewhere, despite the proximity of the Docklands development area (The Highway marked the N boundary) in the early C21 the area appeared only marginally affected by recent social and economic changes.

RELIGIOUS BUILDINGS

ST GEORGE-IN-THE-EAST, Cannon Street Road. 1714–29 by *Nicholas Hawksmoor*. Built to serve the E part of Wapping and the area to its N; one of the three Hawksmoor churches built in the East End as a result of the New Churches act of 1711. Mainly built by the mason *Edward Strong jun.*, 1714–18. The tower was built in 1720–3, plasterwork in 1723–4, pewing and carving in 1724. It was consecrated in 1729. Pevsner called it 'the most original of Hawksmoor's East End churches, though perhaps not as mighty as Christ Church Spitalfields'. 19

The church was gutted in the Second World War, but the exterior survives intact, now in a more spacious setting than formerly. All the planes are peculiarly sheer and flat, in Portland stone. All the details are idiosyncratic and angular, with window mouldings simply recessed. There is a W tower but no W portico. The arena-like platform in front of the church, now approached by a single wide flight of steps, is a later alteration. Could this have been by *George Dance jun.*, who altered the rectory in 1802–4? Hawksmoor's design had steps approaching the platform on each side, with the door to the vaults straight ahead. The lowest stage has coupled Ionic pilasters and an arched doorway below an oculus. The flanking vestries are linked by big volutes. The three stages above have windows deeply set in sharply cut recesses. Hawksmoor's early drawings show the design of the upper parts evolved gradually and experimentally. A drawing dated 1714 proposed a W tower with classical octagonal turret and domed top, but the final design is an open octagon reminiscent of Perp churches like Fotheringhay or Boston but with buttresses topped by Roman altars, both features that occur in Hawksmoor's unbuilt early designs for St Alfege Greenwich. The combination is typical of Hawksmoor's interest in reconciling classical and Christian architecture. The sides of the church each have two stair turrets providing entrances to galleries, which relates closely to his

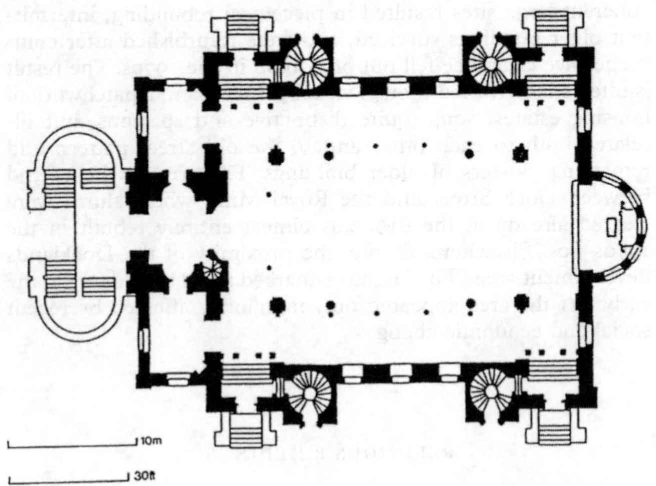

St George-in-the-East, plan as built

unbuilt scheme for Bethnal Green, sketched out *c.* 1711. In an early design these flanked a low central pyramid. In the final design the pyramid was abandoned, and the turrets were heightened from their original squat form, and given octagonal tops and small domes like the first scheme for the W tower. The drama of the cluster of four tall turrets can be compared to Archer's contemporary St John Smith Square, but here they are subservient to the larger W tower. The small doors in the projecting bays next to the turrets have Hawksmoor's typical heavy keystones, on a complicated surround that encloses an *œil-de-bœuf*. The lower nave windows, which sit high above the tall basement, also have oddly shaped and exaggerated lintels and keystones; the upper windows are plainly arched. The E apse continues the cornice line of the sides below the main roof pediment.

The interior originally was a variation on St Anne Limehouse, with groups of piers and columns marking out a rectangle within a rectangle. The lower corner bays suggested a Greek cross plan with the centre emphasized by a shallow plaster cross-vault. Additional E and W bays, as at St Anne Limehouse, separately vaulted, acted as inner lobbies to the side doors.

The post-war reconstruction, by *Ansell & Bailey*, 1960–4, provided for a smaller church within the outer walls, leaving a courtyard within the W end, flanked by flats on the site of the aisles. A hall was created in the vaults. Bailey's W façade is that of a conventional though modern 1960s church, the centre of the W wall glazed with hexagonal panes. Inside, the plain concrete structure has been left exposed, in stark contrast with the C18 apse plasterwork and mosaic panels of 1880. Plain furnishings of 1864, except for the C18 FONT, an octagonal bowl identical to that at St George Bloomsbury (probably by *Strong*) on a baluster stem.

The CHURCHYARD was laid out as a public garden in 1886 (*see* perambulation *1*). GATEPIERS, W one dated 1815, originally very good cast-iron gates as well. – WAR MEMORIAL tall Neo-Grec cross of Portland stone, with 'sword of sacrifice' on the E face. MONUMENTS. Raine monument in memory of Mrs Sarah Raine (†1725), Mrs Elizabeth Raine (†1732) and Henry Raine, brewer (†1738) who founded the school in 1719 in Raine Street (see p. 512). Square pyramid (formerly urn-capped) upon a two-stage base. The pyramid and upper base are of two sorts of marble, veined and statuary. The S face sports an achievement of arms. On the N face relief of a semi-reclining woman, a highly unusual example of an outdoor effigy – Andrew Wilson †1844, near NE gate. Portland stone sarcophagus with draped urn; Doric frieze with triglyphs, rosettes and AW monograms. – NW of the church, unusual and lavish grey marble sarcophagus of *c.* 1740 on claw and ball feet, with acanthus decoration and gadrooning; armorial cartouches on the coved cover. Alexander Wyllie †1741, against S wall, sandstone headstone, probably brought from the N by sea. Other picturesque headstones also placed along the S wall.

ST PAUL, Dock Street. (Converted to a nursery, 2002.) 1846–7 by *Henry Roberts*. Founded as a seamen's chapel, behind their hostel (*see* perambulation *1*), in place of an 'Episcopal Floating Church'. Parochial from 1864. Simple E.E., with W gable onto the street, stock brick with stone dressings; triple lancets with sexfoil window above. NW tower with stone spire and ship weathervane. Five-bay arcades on octagonal piers. *The Ecclesiologist* called the church, rather unfairly, 'a vulgar attempt at First Pointed . . . stale and insipid'. In 1901, the chancel was made by railing off the E bay of the nave, and removing galleries. Some minor STAINED GLASS. The W window with scenes of Christ's miracles is the best, a memorial to Sir John Franklin †1847, one of the founders, though later than his date of death. Minor monuments include a Gothic tabernacle to another founder of the church, Robert James Elliot †1849 (also involved with the Sailors Home and Destitute Sailors Asylum), and a pedimented tablet to Michael Rosenthal †1907, vicar and former Jewish rabbi.

MAJOR BUILDINGS

FORMER ST GEORGE'S VESTRY HALL, Cable Street. 1860 by *G.A. Wilson*, who extended it in 1899 to incorporate a

Coroner's Court. Fairly convincing Barryesque Italianate front, all faced in Portland stone. Originally five bays, enlarged to eight hence the off-centre entrance and inscription in the frieze. Rusticated ground floor and basement with projections carrying engaged Ionic columns at first floor, paired at either end. Between the pilasters, windows with jambs formed into pilasters under round-arched heads, the tympanum decorated with foliage and oak leaves. Above these a dentilled cornice. Portico with banded Doric columns; cast-iron lamps on the balustrade. Inside, the Coroner's Court was accommodated on the ground floor at the rear. An Imperial staircase with decorative iron balustrade leads to first-floor rooms and the council chamber at the front, enlarged in 1899. Classical decorative scheme, the bays defined by Composite pilasters on pedestals, continued as wainscot panelling around the room. The capitals have cherubs' faces. Panelled plaster ceiling with cast-iron ceiling roses bordered by guilloche pattern and egg-and-dart moulding. The public gallery extends intrusively into the space. Former committee room and cloakrooms behind.

ST GEORGE'S POOLS, The Highway. 1965–9 by *R.H. Uren* of *Slater & Uren*. Engineering brick plinth with three storeys of white mosaic and glass bands.

Former ROYAL MINT, East Smithfield. Now only a façade to new offices, with housing behind. The Royal Mint moved from the Tower of London in 1809 to the site of the Cistercian Abbey of St Mary Graces. Designed *c.* 1805 by *James Johnson*, Surveyor to the Mint 1794–1807, and built 1807–12 by Johnson's successor as Surveyor, *Sir Robert Smirke*. The main building looks like a government palace and originally was indeed partly residential, with apartments for the deputy master, the assay master and the provost of the moneyers, as well as bullion stores and the Mint office. A long, rather flat façade of stone: Johnson's Palladian composition was old-fashioned in 1805 (Britton says: 'little that is novel or striking'). Ground floor of channelled rustication, broad central pediment, with the royal arms, carried by six attached Roman Doric columns, end bays marked by four pilasters. The crisp Greek metope frieze must surely be due to Smirke. The whole building is set well back behind railings. Two lodges, set diagonally opposite the Tower, announce it from the street. Elements of Smirke's dignified classical interiors have been reused.

The Mint moved out between 1965 and 1975; the ranges around the courtyard behind, which housed minting machinery installed by *Matthew Boulton* and *John Rennie*, have been replaced and the interior of the main building swept away for open-plan offices, by *Sheppard Robson* and *RMJM*, 1985–9. The latter were masterplanners and executive architects for the whole complex.

The remains of the Cistercian ABBEY OF ST MARY GRACES were excavated (1972 and 1986–8) during the removal of the Mint and the conversion work. They lie under the central court and fragments can be glimpsed. The site was granted by Edward III in 1350 to the Cistercians as a foundation endowment for a new Royal Free Chapel of St Mary Graces on Tower Hill. It became the last Cistercian abbey founded before the Dissolution and was mostly complete by the 1390s. The plan is unusual for a Cistercian church, with a large central tower, no transepts and probably a T-shaped E end with later N and S chapels. The N chapel was a Lady Chapel, added before 1489. The cloisters were detached and the chapter house separated by a small yard from the E end of the church.

Sir Arthur Davey (†1560) pulled the church down and retained the S range, perhaps as a house. In 1560 this was sold to the Crown and became Victualling Yards for the Navy. After 1748, when the Navy moved entirely to Deptford, the buildings became government warehouses, until in 1805 they were demolished for the Royal Mint. On the N part of the site a CEMETERY was found, containing 762 victims of the Black Death.

GUNMAKERS' COMPANY PROOF HOUSE AND HALL, Nos. 46–50 Commercial Road. The Gunmakers' is one of the only City livery companies still to fulfil its original function. Established under its original charter of 1637 to prevent the 'unskilful' manufacture and sale of small arms within the City and its surrounding suburbs. The destructive nature of 'proving' the fitness of guns caused its banishment first to Aldgate in 1657 and then to its present site. This was a wise precaution for in 1757 the proof house and Proof Master's dwelling were 'ruinous' from explosions, and had to be entirely rebuilt. By the early C19 the gunmaking trade had greatly expanded in the area close to the small-arms manufactory at the Tower of London and, in spite of attempts by local residents and the Commercial Road Co. to remove them, the Gunmakers embarked on rebuilding of larger and more secure premises in 1826. The architect was *Robert Turner Cotton*, the Company's Surveyor.* On the l. (No. 50 Commercial Road) the Proof Master's House, a typical late Georgian dwelling in yellow brick with stucco cornice, blocking course, panelled door and fanlight. To its r. is the main entrance to the Receiving Offices, a single-storey block of three bays divided by pilasters with a central entrance with consoled architrave and segmental pediment. Flanking blind windows, originally open but filled in by Cotton to reduce noise. The raised central panel masks the (now disused) copper-lined powder magazine. On the courtyard side, a date plaque of 1757 reset from the previous building.

*By 1813 the Birmingham Proof House had been established to serve the same purpose in England's other major centre for arms manufacture. There the planning is strikingly similar, the buildings rather grander.

Visible along Gower's Walk, behind the Proof Master's House, is the blank brick flank of the PROVING CHAMBER. Here 'black powder' arms (principally smooth-bore barrels prior to finishing by the maker) were tested by firing into sand-banks.* Sound construction is all and walls of double thickness reduced noise and risk. Arched openings are set high up, some blocked, others with iron louvres, which could be shut during testing and reopened afterwards for ventilation. A fire-proof iron roof, capable of containing the explosions, was also a novel feature. Other individual testing chambers for automatic weapons are placed around the internal courtyard, all reconstructed internally in 1994. The basement COURT ROOM, created in 1952 by *Albert Robert Fox* after war damage, contains furniture originally purchased for the adjacent Gunmakers' Hall, sold in 1927 and now commercial premises.

FORMER GUNMAKERS' HALL, to the r. of the Proof House. 1871–2, apparently designed by *John Jacobs*, a builder of Leman Street, after the court refused to employ an architect (although *G.H. Simmonds*, the Company's surveyor in 1869, might have had a hand). Pompous Italianate façade of brick and painted Portland stone with shallow giant pilasters framing the central bay and the Company's arms over the entrance. Two storeys of round-arched and segmental-headed windows under an open stone balustrade. Inside, the former ceremonial hall (now thrown together with adjoining rooms) was top-lit with richly moulded cornice and plasterwork surround, late C17 in style. Neo-Jacobean staircase, inserted 1893 by *W.J. Lambert*.

WILTON'S MUSIC HALL, Grace's Alley. A rare, atmospheric survival, fortunately preserved during the demolition of Wellclose Square (*see* perambulation *1*). A classic public house music hall of the 1850s, with an extravagant interior behind a workmanlike front of four early C19 properties knocked together. The nucleus was the former Prince of Denmark public house (called the Mahogany Bar, on account of its fittings). The first concert room, known as the Albion Saloon, was built immediately to its rear by Matthew Eltham and licensed in 1843. John Wilton, manager of the 'Canterbury Arms' music hall in Lambeth, acquired the Saloon in 1850 and quickly purchased the adjoining properties for the construction, in 1858–9, of a much bigger hall with a capacity for 2,000. Its design was by *Jacob Maggs* of Bath (builder, *Thomas Ennor*). Rebuilt after a fire in 1877, probably by *Wilson, Willcox & Wilson* of Swansea, but with only minor alterations to its appearance. The hall closed in 1880 and was adapted as a Methodist Mission Hall from *c.* 1888. Partly restored 1979–85 by *Kirby, Adair, Newson Partnership* for the London Music Hall Trust. In occasional use from the 1990s, with further restoration planned.

*Although no longer employed in the London Proof House, this method is still used in Birmingham.

The entrance from the street is flanked by pilasters decorated with fruit and flowers; two windows above, under a single pediment. The entrance hall was created in 1858 by enclosing the stone-paved yard of the Prince of Denmark pub. A foundation stone inside records this, with a verse beginning 'to great Apollo God of early Morn/who wakes the song of birds from eastern sky . . .'. A narrow staircase, leading to the warren of former supper rooms above, has two thin iron columns with a small amount of painted-plaster detail; a tantalizing trace of former opulence. Construction must have been hurried and appears to have made use of whatever came to hand: the stone stair treads have risers faced with *papier mâché*, and the massive York stone slabs on the landing rest on light-railway tracks. Larger tracks are used as girders for the floor above. To the r. of the hall is the original 'Mahogany Bar', denuded of decoration but for *papier mâché* on the beams.

The Hall at the back is high, thin and long under an elliptical vaulted ceiling, with an apsed W end and high stage set within a narrow proscenium, modified in 1877. On three sides, a magnificent belly-fronted gallery, with rich Italianate *papier mâché* decoration, supported on barley-sugar iron columns painted gold. Around the gallery walls are paired arched recesses, originally containing mirrors, with wide flat piers and large console brackets. Barrel-vault ceiling with thin ribs between panels delicately decorated with bands of pierced foliage doubling as air vents: a considerable technical innovation, admired by *Building News** which records that *papier mâché* decoration was by *Messrs White & Parlby* and painting and gilding by *Mr Holman*. The hall was lit by a sunlight burner by *Defries & Son* described as a 'solid mass of richly cut glass in prismatic feathers, spangles and spires, brilliantly illuminated by 300 burners'. 61

BLUEGATE FIELDS JUNIOR SCHOOL, Cable Street and King David Lane. 1993 by *GHM Rock Townsend*. Part of the LDDC's legacy, on the fringe of its area of control. A very impressive front to Cable Street, narrow with long sloping eaves to ground floor. Wing-like roofline sweeping up from a long clerestory-lit spine corridor. Classrooms on each side with access to the playground from each and balconies for those at first floor.

For other schools *see* perambulations.

PERAMBULATIONS

1. *From St George-in-the-East to Tower Hill*

The walk starts at St George's, on the E side of Cannon Street Road. E of Hawksmoor's church (*see* above) the CHURCHYARD was enlarged in 1875, taking in the disused burial ground

*4 April 1859.

of St George's Methodist Church and laid out as public gardens in 1886, inspired by the vision of the rector of St George's, Harry Jones.* The area was relandscaped by the LDDC early in the 1990s. In the SE corner, former parish MORTUARY of 1877, inscribed 'Metropolitan Borough of Stepney Nature Study Museum'; opened as a museum in 1904 under the direction of the rector, with living specimens so that East End children could observe nature at first hand. Closed in 1939 and subsequently reduced to a shell.

At the NE end the gardens open to CABLE STREET, beside the former Town Hall of 1860 (*see* above), now the only relic of a group which included St George's Methodist church and a public library (of 1897 by *Maurice Adams*). Facing the library
114 site, on the flank of the Town Hall, a MURAL of the Battle of Cable Street: evidence of the enduring myth of a pre-war anti-fascist East End in which dockers and working-class Jews are shown united in their defiance. 1979–82 by *Dave Binnington*, *Desmond Rochford*, *Paul Butler* and *Ray Walker*, the crowded scene reminiscent of Spencer, but with the vivid activity of Wyndham Lewis. Much research went into providing authentic detail, and it shows. The street is depicted as it was in the 1930s, hemmed in tightly by simple late Georgian terraces on each side. Behind is MULBERRY JUNIOR SCHOOL, the former Cable Street Schools of 1899 by *T.J. Bailey*; three-decker with very attractive terracotta dressings, large brackets and voluted gables.

The N side of Cable Street was replaced with the dull later stages of Stepney's Tarling Estate, originally ultra-plain brick walk-up blocks of the 1950s, refurbished and rendered from the 1990s. On the S side: Nos. 194–244 remain from the early C19, carefully restored by *Anthony Richardson & Partners*, 1978–81, as a mixture of houses and flats for the Newlon Housing Trust. Three storeys, i.e. grander than most in the East End, small houses of two bays, variously detailed: some with elegant doorcases with small pediments, others with plain arches, and one with a Georgian former shopfront. Behind No. 200, Hawksmoor Mews, rebuilt as low housing at a later date. At the W corner with Cannon Street Road the CROWN AND DOLPHIN, a C19 stucco-trimmed pub. Another more fragmentary terrace extends along Cannon Street Road up to the church.

ST GEORGE'S ESTATE begins W of Cannon Street Road, with N–S ranges reflecting the old street pattern: Brockmer House of the 1960s along Cannon Street Road and Betts House, 1937, the only pre-war part of the estate. The main part, begun *c.* 1963 by the LCC and completed 1970 by the GLC, is a mature example of the principle of mixed development first adopted in the 1950s, built just before this type of

* *See* H. Jones, *East and West London*, 1875.

housing went out of favour. The three twenty-eight, storey towers (1968–70) are among the tallest on the County 113
Council's post-war estates. They form part of a confident Brutalist composition with ranges of maisonettes and lower housing, making use of contrasting textures of dark brick, pebbly-faced concrete, and white boarding. Garaging, a novelty of the 1960s, is contrived below raised terraces overlooking a small park which extends S to The Highway. The estate swept away, to the dismay of many, the C18 Prince's Square, whose terraced houses had survived the war. The square once contained a chapel for Swedish merchants, built 1729, demolished *c.* 1920. The scientist and theologian Emanuel Swedenborg was buried there in 1772, and the square was later renamed after him; the name survives in Swedenborg Gardens, a long maisonette range with concrete floors projecting dramatically over balconies.

Across the park is WELLCLOSE SQUARE, its form still just recognizable, although deprived of surrounding buildings. p. 478
This was a square of considerable size, laid out from 1678 and built up piecemeal by Nicholas Barbon and others, with the best houses on the E side. The most prominent feature is ST PAUL'S SCHOOL in the centre of the square, built in 1869–70 by *Reuben Greatorex*, brother of the vicar of St Paul Dock Street. A pretty, quite quirky, Gothic W front in brown brick, with archways and windows enlivened by red brick and white stone. Slim central clock tower with a short steeple flanked by two first-floor gabled schoolrooms, each with a large window with Y-tracery and small panes. At ground level an arcade of six arches, the central two gabled, with Boys' and Girls' entrances labelled. At the back, St Paul's Mission Room and Infant Nursery, 1874, also by Greatorex. The school is on the site of a Danish church established here in 1694 with funds from the King of Denmark; begun by *Thomas Woodstock* and completed by the Danish sculptor and architect *Caius Gabriel Cibber*. It ceased to be used as a church in 1816 and was sold in 1868. Four large Baroque wooden sculptures of saints, two attributed to Cibber himself, are now in the Danish church of St Katharine, Regent's Park.

To the W is the low, unassertive SHAPLA PRIMARY SCHOOL of 1983–5, by *GLC Dept of Architecture and Civic Design* for ILEA (Project Architect: *Ann Webb*). Colourful, profiled-aluminium roofs with bat-like silhouette. Long eaves and exposed timber trusses, yellow brick, timber panels painted yellow and, surprisingly, timber sash windows. Planned around two courtyards, with the emphasis on circulation and away from open-planning.

A peculiarity of Wellclose Square was the little alleys that led diagonally from each corner. Of these, GRACE'S ALLEY to the NW survives, with a C19 stucco-trimmed three-storey terrace along its N side. The reason for its preservation (instead of

Sailors' Home, Ensign Street, St George's, *c.* 1835

building a fourth tower block as originally proposed), is a rare survival, WILTON'S MUSIC HALL (*see* above).

West of Wellclose Square

ENSIGN STREET was originally Well Street, within the Tower of London's Liberty of Wellclose. A series of bollards with the monogram 'RBT' commemorates the Royal Brunswick Theatre (successor to the Royalty Theatre of 1785), erected 1828 by *T.S. Whitwell*. It collapsed shortly after opening. On its site was built the BRUNSWICK MARITIME ESTABLISHMENT, a pioneer example of a sailors' home, promoted by the Rev. George 'Bosun' Smith of the floating seamen's church, who later became the vicar of its replacement, St Paul Dock Street (*see* above). Erected by voluntary subscription, 1830–5 and seemingly designed by *Henry Roberts*.* Now much altered. Three tall storeys and attic with a stuccoed ground floor, but originally with a low Doric arcade and projecting wings at either end. The design was ambitious; there was accommodation for 500 men in each of the wings, in double tiers of cabins; the central block had registry, savings bank, dining hall and reading rooms. The home was the first of its kind to employ agents to encourage sailors to avoid lodgings along the Ratcliffe Highway, notorious for its prostitutes and dens of vice. The S block was demolished for the adjoining Mercantile Marine Office by *Wigg, Oliver & Hudson*, 1893. Asymmetrical, with deep plinth of polished granite. Pilastered bays of pedi-

*An annotated print at the Museum of Docklands attributes the design to *Philip Hardwick*.

mented and Venetian windows to first floor and an upper storey of paired windows between pairs of Ionic half-columns. Converted to flats 1999. Beyond, flats of 2000, in yellow brick with a lively pattern of projecting metal balconies and an inset ground floor behind red columns.

DOCK STREET, parallel to Ensign Street, was laid out for access to the London Docks after 1806 but only became an important route after the opening of Commercial Street in 1843. At the rear of the sailors' home in Ensign Street an extension of 1953–8 by *Brian O'Rorke* and *Colin Murray*, replacing a polychrome Gothic frontage to Dock Street of 1865–7 by *E.L. Bracebridge* and his assistant *T.W. Fletcher*. Only the street range and stair tower were completed instead of the complete rebuilding intended. Brick-faced five-storey slab with its top floor set back. Deep, glazed, lower storeys with balustrades with nautical figure-of-eight ironwork. Next to St Paul's church (*see* above), the VICARAGE, a pretty three-storey house of *c.* 1847 by *Henry Roberts*, with stucco band and architraves to ground-floor sashes. Further on, part of the cartage depot for the Millwall Docks with gabled warehouse of *c.* 1873. Three bays of pairs of slim, round-arched recesses under wide arches. Courtyard gatepiers are surmounted by lions. No. 15 is a double-fronted house of the 1860s. Dock Street ends at EAST SMITHFIELD. The former London Dock's MAIN ENTRANCE stands just W on the S side. Two blocks of simple Neoclassical Customs and Excise offices by *Daniel Asher Alexander*, 1805, each of three pedimented bays by five, with round-headed windows on the ground floor. Extended *c.* 1840 by two single-storey wings and the dock wall brought round to enclose them. For the remains of the Docks, *see* Wapping.

This walk returns N up Dock Street: on the W side S–N: CABLE & WIRELESS, indifferent offices replacing bonded tea warehouses of 1834. Then Nos. 36–8, a pub and workshops of the 1860s. No. 20, a warehouse of 1883 for mustard manufacturers Wallis and Drysdale; segment-headed windows dressed in blue brick. Nos. 12–14 are substantial Italianate offices with prominent bracketed eaves cornice and clumsy moulded windows to upper storeys. Finally, a forceful corner warehouse *c.* 1891 by *Edwin A.B. Crockett* for tobacco manufacturers. Tall iron columns inside.

ROYAL MINT STREET, the W continuation of Cable Street, was formerly called Rosemary Lane, or Rag Fair, from its old clothes market. The area S of Royal Mint Street fell between the governance of the City and the manor of Stepney; giving it a reputation for lawlessness. Mayhew, writing in the 1850s, described it as 'a concentration of all the miseries in the kingdom . . . a large district interlaced with narrow lanes, courts and alleys ramifying into each other in the most intricated and disorderly manner. Houses of the poorest condition seem as if they have tumbled into their spaces at random.' Apart from some street names nothing of this survived clearance after the 1875 Housing Act.

The N side of Royal Mint Street is now a barren space left by the destruction of the 1880s Goods Depot of the London & Blackwall Railway. On the S side only two pubs, first the CITY OF CARLISLE, with a Flemish gable with stamped-terracotta inset, dated 1620 but evidently rebuilt in the 1880s. Then, outstanding in such inauspicious surroundings, the ARTFUL DODGER; converted from an early C19 warehouse. Stuccoed front with giant Ionic pilasters supporting an entablature inscribed 'Wholesale & Retail' and shorter group of the same beneath the parapet inscribed 'Warehouse'. Blithely added to this, a large relief of a Crown and Seven Stars, executed *c.* 1888 by *C.J. Reynolds*, when the pub had that name. The ground-floor entrance is set back behind slender ornamental cast-iron columns supporting the upper floors in an attractively ramshackle way.

In JOHN FISHER STREET nine blocks of the PEABODY ESTATE, 1880–1 by *H.A. Darbishire*, a standardized layout of alphabetical five-storey blocks, facing inwards around a court (originally filled by Block K). Ashen brick, with tight windows deeply set to ensure that they were flush with the interior walls, and with only the very slightest detailing of dentilled brick strings and classicized doorways. Remarkably bleak, even by such austere standards. Block L, added 1909 by *W.E. Wallis*, has the raised attic over the centre bays that distinguishes the Trust's early C20 blocks. Close to its entrance, a simple tablet MEMORIAL to seventy-eight people killed by the bombing of Block K in 1940. Relandscaping and the introduction of a children's playground by *Farrar Huxley Associates*, 1999. The Peabody blocks are the only survivals from the philanthropic tenements put up in the area after the slum clearance enabled by the 1875 Housing Act, and now replaced by more recent housing which preserves some older street names, e.g. Blue Anchor Yard and Swan Passage. These form part of the ROYAL MINT SQUARE ESTATE, by *Andrews, Downie & Kelly* 1978–82, an attractive and civilized mixed scheme of houses and flats arranged in three contiguous staggered blocks around loosely enclosed closes and gardens. Each unit, in dark brick with monopitch slate roofs, is pleasantly varied in height and appearance; indicative of the desire for greater privacy and humanity in public housing of that period.

Along the W side of CARTWRIGHT STREET stood Katharine Buildings, 1883, the first housing experiment by the East End Dwellings Company. On its site, social housing of the late 1980s by *Sheppard Robson* contemporary with their extension of the former Royal Mint (*see* above), whose high arched atrium rises up behind an open court for shops and community centre. Either side, two rows of flats in stock brick, with boldly cantilevered square balconies and upper floors set back under wide eaves. Cartwright Street leads S into East Smithfield (named from a 'smooth field' E of the City, used for fairs), which runs W towards St Katharine Docks (*see* Wapping) and E to Tower Hill.

2. Between Commercial Road and Cable Street, beginning at Aldgate East Station

DRUM STREET, SE of Whitechapel High Street, is the remains of the 1865–70 extension of Commercial Road, linking it to the later Commercial Street N of Whitechapel High Street (*see* p. 427). The fragment of wall with pilasters is a remnant of Gardiner's store (burnt down 1972) whose clock tower was a familiar landmark for 100 years. By the subway one can reach COMMERCIAL ROAD itself, created 1802–6 to provide a direct route between the City and the new docks on the Isle of Dogs. It originally started at Back Church Lane and was laid out across the fields N of the congested Ratcliffe Highway; by 1830 it was almost entirely lined with houses all the way to Limehouse. Its W end remains a hotch-potch of battered domestic terraces overwhelmed by the rag trade, later industry and recent apartment blocks. On the S side, Nos. 32–4, mid-C19; bold lettering proclaims this as the premises of J.J. & S.W. Chalk 'timber merchants and importers, established 1814', operating from Finland Wharf, Limehouse. Archway on panelled brick piers below a dentilled gable on fat stone consoles, flanked by a three-storey house and a two-storey office, each of three bays with matching heavy cornice. No. 42 looks late Georgian (rubbed brick window heads, but much altered); No. 44, THE CASTLE, is a stuccoed mid-C19 pub with rounded end. Then the PROOF HOUSE of the GUNMAKERS' COMPANY (*see* p. 483) whose activities were unacceptable within the City. Opposite on the N side a substantial, irregular four-storey industrial block, built as St George's Brewery (later John Walker & Sons) in 1847 by *Charles Humphreys*. Set at an angle to the road, reflecting the pre-1870 street pattern. The W part has a dentilled cornice above brick pilasters. Interior with cast-iron supports and jack arches. Originally roofed by a large watertank; the present roofline must date from *c.* 1900 when the building was converted for bonded stores. At the corner of Adler Street, No. 35a, MORRISON BUILDINGS, a five-storey C19 Improved Industrial Dwellings Co. tenement block built in 1874, with the usual stucco trim and recessed central bays with iron balconies and stairs. Originally with a pair on the S side of the road. The relentless search for luxury developments close to the City has produced No. 80, SKYLINE PLAZA, an older block crudely enlarged in 1999–2000 into an ungainly twelve-storey cliff of private flats, and opposite, ALDGATE TRIANGLE, three classically informed blocks by *CZWG*. In its shadow, Nos. 41–7, 1964–6 by *C.H. Elsom & Partners*, altered for the London School of Furniture, 1967. Seven storeys faced with white vitreous tiles over a set-back ground floor with exposed columns.

Further on only sporadic C19 survivals remain between the inward-looking post-war neighbourhoods, so this tour now turns S.

S of Commercial Road

On the W side of HENRIQUES STREET, HARRY GOSLING PRIMARY SCHOOL, LCC work of 1910; the main block is plain, but the charmingly detailed Cookery and Laundry building, dated 1903, shows *T.J. Bailey*'s flair for smaller buildings: an orange brick front with stone used for lettered entrance, banded quoins, and tall parapet. Picturesque tower, also banded, with little cupola. Opposite, Basil House, 1934–5 by *Burnet, Tait & Lorne*, Modernist flats for the adjoining former BERNHARD BARON JEWISH SETTLEMENT, founded by Basil Henriques and built 1929–30 by *Hobden & Porri*. Tall, with an imposing arched entrance. Now private flats.

To the E along FAIRCLOUGH STREET. On the S side, the former drug-grinding works of Potter & Clarke, named and dated 1925. Behind, Victoria Mills, incorporating earlier buildings of 1920, extended to the corner with Henriques Street in 1923. Robust brick elevations, four and seven storeys. All by *Wheat and Luker*. Converted to apartments in 1999. Nos. 8–10 are sole survivals here of the earlier C19. A quite stylish two-storey pair: heavy cornice, upper windows within arches, round-headed openings to the ground floor. Original doors with narrow arched panels.

Now into BACK CHURCH LANE (once a route to the church at Whitechapel). The DOG AND TRUCK, three storeyed, with big tiled roof and tall chimneys in Arts and Crafts spirit, was rebuilt 1935 by *William Stewart*, with the start of the adjoining Berner Estate (*see* below). Back Church Lane in the earlier C19 was famous for its vast sugar bakeries, but from the 1890s came to be dominated by the impressive wool warehouses, served by the now demolished goods station to the W, built 1885–6 for the elevated London, Tilbury & Southend railway to the docks. On the N side, from N–S: a three-storey range for Kinloch & Co., wine merchants, by *Hyman Henry Collins*, 1894–5. Converted 1999. Then NEW LOOM HOUSE, a five-storey former wool warehouse for Messrs Browne & Eagle, 1889. Fifteen bays, divided by shallow pilasters into units of three, each with its own entrance. Converted to offices 1998–9; cranes and upper loading doors have been preserved. Opposite, on the E side, No. 74, a long five-storey block: *c.* 1900, probably by *Holland & Hannen*, also for Browne & Eagle. Twenty bays articulated by giant arches enclosing the windows of the three middle floors, with a blind storey above. Loading bays in every fifth bay. A short tower in the centre, and near the N end a doorway with the firm's name boldly engraved on the lintel below a scrolled pediment.

PINCHIN STREET, beside the railway line, completes the warehouse tour: facing up Stutfield Street the premises of Pinchin & Johnson's oil works, 1859, backing on to the railway line. A handsome four-storey building, three main bays with a big cornice; the set-back wing on the l. was part of a sugar refinery. Opposite, MARKAZI MASJID MOSQUE, in a converted early C20 warehouse. Across CHRISTIAN STREET, a former Board School of 1901 with tall gables and big lantern ventilators.

The rest of this tour is largely a story of piecemeal C20 rebuilding, mostly by the LCC. The growth of the BERNER ESTATE over twenty-five years can be followed from SW to NE. The LCC began rebuilding here before the war, with EVERARD HOUSE in Ellen Street, 1934–6, a long five-storey range with just a few private balconies. Access balconies and curved corners give it a streamlined look. Top-floor laundry rooms were remodelled as flats 1958–9. More in similar style followed after the war. S of Ellen Street, HADFIELD (1949) is the centrepiece of a U-shaped composition (greatly transformed in the 1990s). To the E a new approach was introduced by HALLIDAY HOUSE, 1961–2, an eight-storey point block with angled balconies, beside the post-war open space of ROPEWALK GARDENS. E of CHRISTIAN STREET, an extension planned from 1951 demonstrated a more radical approach. N of BURSLEM STREET, a three-storey shopping terrace is the prelude to the grand scale of the eight-storeyed DELAFIELD HOUSE, 1953–4, long and amply balconied, looking out over grass. An angled W end, dictated by an existing street line, contributes a picturesque informality. S of Burslem Street a contrasting low-rise, colourful brick cluster of flats arranged along narrow lanes, with four-storey corner towers. 1987 by *Hunt Thompson Associates* (*Benjamin Derbyshire*; project architect). Further S, long ranges of the 1950s; facing Cannon Street Road the five-storey WELSTEAD, 1954, heavily remodelled in the 1990s.

Cannon Street Road and the area to its E

Both sides of CANNON STREET ROAD N of the railway line were badly affected by war damage, but a few older groups remain on the fringes of the post-war estates. The street is shown built up already on Horwood's map of 1819. On the W side the most interesting is Nos. 121–3, now subdivided and much altered. Inscribed Raine's Boys School, which moved here from Wapping in 1883 and moved out to Arbour Square in 1913 (*see* Shadwell and Ratcliffe). Gothic, three bays with mullioned first-floor windows, on the l. a gabled wing with blue brick diapering. On the r. a three-storey early C19 terrace with shops built out in front. On the E side Nos. 116–22 and 126–30, mostly late C18, still with domestic ground floors. Three storeys above high basements, stuccoed ground floors. The houses are of varying widths and irregular from later alterations, which gives them a battered charm. Not grand, but with a few good doorcases: No. 122 has an open pediment on Doric columns, No. 126 an open pediment on brackets. Further N, behind a rebuilt stretch, the tiny RAMPART STREET, where No. 19, a former pub, *c.* 1890, has attractive terracotta panels on a canted corner.

Further E more of the C20. First, S of Bigland Street, the LCC's BIGLAND ESTATE, 1961–5, squeezing in 268 dwellings at a density of 141.5 p.p.a. A classic example of the LCC's post-war policy of replacing the East End's small streets of low terraced houses with varied 'mixed development' of different heights, with adaptable informal planning to take account of existing buildings. The housing looks inward around plentiful open space, and is in the LCC's severe, clean-cut early 1960s Modernist idiom: dark-grey facing bricks with exposed concrete for floor bands and balconies. Five- and six-storey ranges form an L-shaped backdrop to an open area (a former burial ground). Further E, Miles Court, two-storey housing for old people, built around a courtyard with existing tree; its dour style modified by later roofs and blue paintwork. Beyond are neat rows of four-storey maisonettes with small private gardens, where a lighter touch was provided by coloured panels below the windows (since painted white); to the N is a single twenty-two storey tower. Incorporated rather awkwardly are two pre-war four-storey blocks of private low-rent flats, TURNOUR HOUSE, Walburgh Street and CHAPMAN HOUSE, N of Bigland Street, 1934, built for the Chapman Development Trust by *Joseph Emberton*. Their rendered walls, metal windows and mesh balconies must once have looked ultra-modern amidst the older terraces, but the cramped rear staircases show their limitations.

The neighbourhood was served by an existing Board School in Tilman Street of 1874. Three storeys with a bowed section on the E side and a panel with relief of Knowledge Strangling Ignorance (to a design by *Spencer Stanhope*) sometimes seen on the early Board schools. A new focus for the post-war neighbourhood was provided by a large school site, obliterating the small streets running between Bigland Street and Commercial Road, filled by a three-storey comprehensive school of 1966–7 (now MULBERRY SCHOOL FOR GIRLS), and Bigland Primary, brown brick with monopitch roofs, 1980s.

The land for WATNEY MARKET was sold to the LCC in 1951–3 and 1960, but built up only from 1966–76 by the *GLC Architect's Department*. It occupies part of the site of the Mercers' Company's first development close to Commercial Road, on Little Callis Field, laid out in 1817 with a grid of streets. The early C19 neighbourhood with its street market in Watney Street suffered badly in the war, losing its main landmark, Christ Church, a large brick Neo-Norman building of 1840–1 by *John Shaw jun.*, demolished after the bomb damage. The post-war plan for a pedestrian shopping and market street with low and informal buildings was rejected for a more complicated scheme, a classic exposition of the self-contained, layered precinct of the 1960s, with pedestrians and vehicles segregated. A formal red brick composition of two facing rows of shops across a pedestrian plaza, with car parking below. Flats above open onto raised decks behind, originally flanked by a twenty-five storey tower to E and W, the first parts to be built, 1966–8.

Walkways bridged the pedestrian shopping area as well, a superfluous gesture removed in an iconoclastic refurbishment programme of 1994–7 by *Hunt Thompson Associates*. The western tower was demolished, and its pair WINTERTON HOUSE reclad, after being stripped to its steel skeleton to remove asbestos and the sleek white grp-cladding panels which had been an innovative but unsuccessful feature. Cladding of yellow brick above striped brick arches, capped by an open framework. Pompous landscaped approach and lower doctors' surgery added to the E.

Across the waste areas further E is the TARLING ESTATE, built by the Borough of Stepney immediately after the war. Six ponderous five-storey blocks laid out in parallel pairs, completed 1949. The original design had flat roofs, and – in deference to post-war demands – private balconies in solid striped brickwork, opening off living rooms with shallow bow windows. Gradually transformed from the 1990s by pitched roofs and light metal balconies. To the N FITZGERALD LODGE, a low, dark brick maze of old people's homes, added in 1969, irregularly grouped around courtyards, in studied contrast to the earlier formality. They extend to SUTTON STREET. To their N a former United Dairies depot, dated 1900 with entrance framed by houses of the same date (Nos. 4–14) with the Mercers' Company badge; all that survives from the Mercers' developments in this area.

Sutton Street continues S beneath the railway bridge, with another small C19 survival on the W side: SHADWELL PLACE with the RAILWAY ARMS, a low two-storey pub. The LCC's SHADWELL GARDENS ESTATE, completed 1948, has a formal layout: dignified ranges along the N side of Cable Street in pre-war Georgian style, demurely enlivened with a little brick detail and a few balconies. S of Cable Street down BEWLEY STREET, earlier improved housing. The first part of the LCC's SOLANDER GARDENS was completed 1901; gaunt cliffs of six-storey tenements closely grouped in pairs, slightly enlivened by striped brick and gables, a simplified version of the detailing of the Boundary Street estate, Bethnal Green. To their W an overpowering six-storey range (Nos. 79–157) completed 1969–70, which revels in its intricately chunky urban profile. Inset balconies high up, small back gardens tucked in behind, garaging below. Nearby in Cable Street, Shadwell Station.

WAPPING*

Wapping, though on the fringe of the City of London, was for over 150 years a territory known well only by those who lived and

*The account of Wapping, including the remains of the London Docks, is adapted from *London Docklands* by Elizabeth Williamson, 1998.

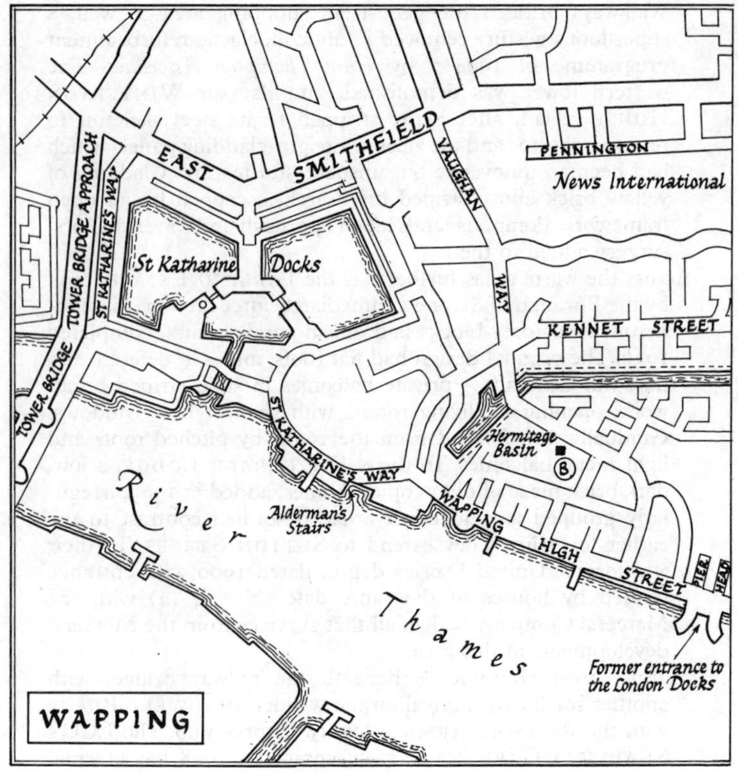

worked there. The London Docks and the St Katharine Docks, developed there in the early C19, covered most of Wapping. They were private territory, well secured from the idly curious, and they cut the riverside settlement off from the City and the rest of the East End, breeding a special 'island' culture and loyalty.

Wapping was originally mainly marshland. Perhaps named after the Saxon Waeppa, its first proper settlement took place after 1327 when part of the marsh was drained and river defences built. From the late C14 wharves were built on Wapping Wall and rapidly spread along the riverside. Much further W, close to the City wall, was the Royal Foundation of St Katharine, founded as a hospital in 1147 by Queen Matilda. In the mid-C15, building began to spread E from the City giving rise to a new hamlet. By 1536 the marsh had been drained by *Cornelius Vanderdelft* and divided to become rich farmland. Building now spread more quickly along the riverside, though the establishment of the City's Legal Quays in 1558 slowed the development of wharves briefly. Stow refers to the new road, now Wapping High Street, laid out *c.* 1570 as a 'filthy straight passage' with 'alleys of small tenements

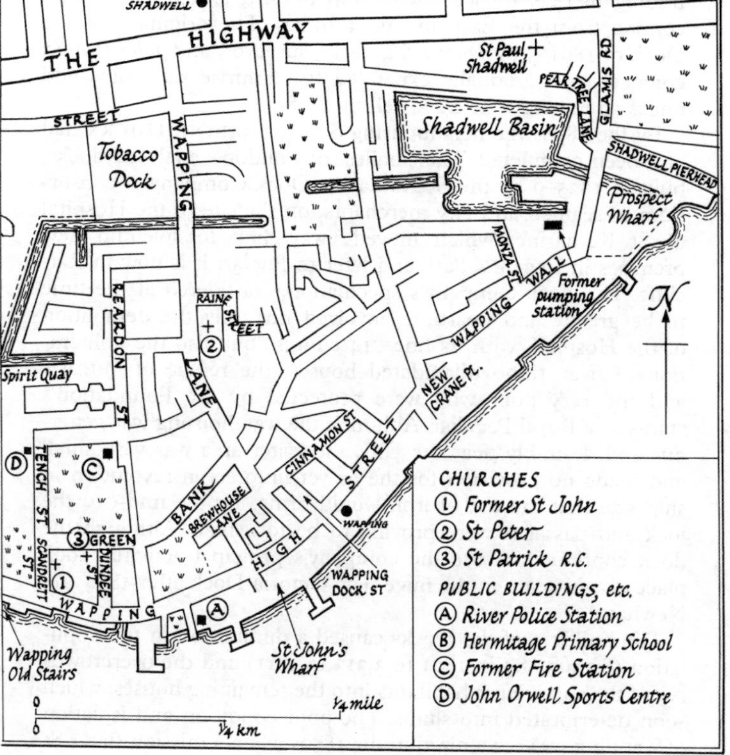

and cottages, inhabited by sailors' victuallers. The whole riverside was increasingly devoted to ships and shipping. In the C18, there were still prosperous houses as well as shipbuilders, wharves and inns, but wealthy householders gradually moved away from the riverfront as it became increasingly industrial and in the C19 houses were replaced by warehouses and wharves for a variety of crafts and trades – biscuit and rope makers, ship builders, engineers, chandlers etc.

In parallel with the development of the riverfront came the establishment and growth of the enclosed, secure and private docks. LONDON DOCK, N of Wapping High Street, was begun in 1801 and opened in 1805. It was the second of London's enclosed docks after the West India Docks (Isle of Dogs), although the site had been intended originally for docks dealing with West India trade. Plans were drawn up in 1794 by *John Powsey* but abandoned in 1799. But the land, so conveniently near the City, was immediately exploited by another consortium of merchants, who formed the London Dock Company. They obtained a twenty-one-year monopoly to deal with all vessels trading in rice, tobacco, wine and brandy, except those ships coming from the East and West Indies. The original London Dock of 1801–5 by *Daniel Alexander*, surveyor, and *John Rennie*, engineer, was gradually expanded to comprise six basins and docks stretching W to Shadwell by 1858.

p. 37 By the 1850s the neighbouring ST KATHARINE DOCKS had also been completed. The smallest of London's enclosed docks, built in 1825–9 by the St Katharine Dock Company, a consortium of seamen and city merchants, on the site of the Hospital of St Katharine, which moved away, first to splendid new premises in Regent's Park and later to Poplar; it is now in Ratcliffe. The dock company's speculation, considered at the time to be greedy and heartless, involved not only the demolition of the Hospital, with its fine C14 church, but also the obliteration of over 1,000 dilapidated houses, the refuge of outcasts and the very poor who were protected by the Foundation's status as a Royal Peculiar. Although the warehousing was generous and desirably near the City, the water area was very small and made no provision for the as yet unforeseen revolution in ship size that the use of iron would bring. By the mid-C19 the lock and passages were proving to be too small. Although the dock continued in use the company's principal activities took place downstream at the huge new Victoria Dock after 1864 (*see* Newham).

The building of the Docks caused a diminution in the population (from 5,889 in 1801 to 3,313 in 1811) and the overcrowding of the surviving inhabitants into the remaining houses, which soon deteriorated into slums. The poor condition and isolation of Wapping was recognized in the 1850s when a mission (later St Peter London Docks) was set up from St George-in-the-East. Very little was done about the condition of the property until between the wars. Then in 1926 all of the housing between the London Docks and Wapping High Street was swept away in a huge clearance scheme by the LCC. A similar scheme replaced the houses alongside St Katharine Docks in the 1930s.

Bombing in the Second World War devastated the E part of the St Katharine Docks, the S side of the Western Dock of the London Docks, and the W end of Wapping High Street. After repairs the remaining dock and riverside warehouses continued in use until the 1960s. The closure of the docks to shipping in 1968 wrought a huge change. The St Katharine Docks were developed commercially immediately from 1971, but the 103 acres of the London Docks were instead crudely infilled. The Borough of Tower Hamlets began redevelopment for housing following a masterplan drawn up in 1977 by *Shepheard Epstein & Hunter*, which envisaged low-rise housing at garden suburb densities (most for rent, some for sale), generous open space, public amenities and wedges of green giving access to the river. Little of this was realized by 1979 when News International acquired a large slice along the N side of the former Western Dock and demolished the North Stack warehouses. The LDDC's strategy of 1983 slightly revised the earlier plan, providing for a majority of houses for sale and creating a new and very distinctive landscape of waterways and broad, well-planted quays within the former docks, but a surfeit of crudely detailed low-rise housing. Though the dock warehouses have gone, most of the extensive and impressive private riverside warehouses have been converted into housing; a process which began in the early 1970s with colonization, in the now familiar way, for artists' studios and since followed by developers on a larger scale. They failed to encourage mixed uses, with the result that after nearly two decades of development and refurbishment Wapping's streets still have a ghostly air, except along the old shopping street, Wapping Lane.

RELIGIOUS BUILDINGS

ST JOHN, Scandrett Street. *see* perambulation *2*.

ST PETER, Wapping Lane. Begun 1865–6 by *F.H. Pownall* for Father Charles Lowder (†1880), and important in the rise of Anglo-Catholicism. It originated as a mission from St George-in-the-East under the auspices of the Society of the Holy Cross in 1856 with a chapel in Calvert (now Watts) Street. This was the first such mission to the poor in the East End and, under Father Lowder, was famous for its advanced ceremonial of the kind that led to notorious riots at St George-in-the-East in 1859. Unfortunately Pownall's church lay unfinished until the 1930s, though the clergy and sisters' houses were built in 1881; architect *Bowes A. Paice*. The W end, with baptistery, mortuary chapel, and tower designed 1884–94 by *Maurice B. Adams*, editor of *Building News*, was not completed until 1939, and then without the top of the tower and the W gallery. The whole church was damaged by bombing the year after (the sisters' house was destroyed) and much reconstructed 1948–50, with new stained glass.

A muscular exterior, originally hemmed in by other buildings and screened from the street by the sisters' house (l., rebuilt 1950 without its gabled top floor) and clergy house (r.) linked by a pair of squat Gothic arches with an image bracket and domestic Gothic window over. Lining the passage to the courtyard, hygienic glazed red and white tiles. The church is in what Father Lowder described as 'later First Pointed Gothic'. Stock brick, black brick patterning and touches of red, except for the later and more genteel red brick W front and stump of SW tower, which can be seen from Raine Street. It has nave, chancel and transepts, all equally high. N and S aisles and S chapel. Bold plate tracery except on the blank N aisle where houses formerly abutted. The E façade almost blank too except for the very elaborate wheel window high up, probably so it could be seen over St George's workhouse and the dock wall beyond, which originally came quite close here. Big quatrefoil S windows, large cinquefoils in the N chancel clerestory, with rows of smaller quatrefoils below.

46 The atmospheric interior is equally muscular in red and black brick, its Ruskinian toughness exaggerated by the huge blocks of uncarved stone where capitals and corbels were left unfinished. Fine carving on the two finished crocketed capitals: one chancel capital includes an angel. Additional polychromy in the nave columns of cold blue Pennant stone and in the red and green of the modest iron chancel screen and rood beam, planned in 1880 in memory of Father Lowder, incomplete until *c.* 1925. Stone wall-shafts carry a crown-post nave roof; painted wagon roof in chancel. Adams's W end includes a BAPTISTERY in the vaulted tower base with FONT and tall FONT COVER with carved figures below crocketed ogee niches; a pelican on the conical top. A stone stair, intended to lead to a W gallery, rises dramatically below ornate ironwork supporting a pulley for the font cover.

Other FURNISHINGS, largely later or imported, create an appropriate High Church ensemble. – PULPITS. One from the ritualist Margaret Street Chapel (Westminster), plain and not used. The main pulpit, on columns but now without its sounding-board, from Blomfield's Anglo-Catholic St Barnabas, Jericho, Oxford. – Undistinguished, sub-Wren High Altar. – REREDOS by *Laurence King*. – In the N aisle (pre-war) REREDOS, Our Lady of Wapping by *Trevor Griffin*, dated 1948. – Many easel PAINTINGS, those in the S chapel fitted into timber panelling, which seems to match the reredos here. Best are Crucifixion, *School of Guido Reni* (High Altar), and Taunting of Christ, Flemish C16 (S aisle). – IRON GATES. Baptistery and Sacred Heart chapel, 1949 by *Romilly Craze*, made by *Fred Sage & Co.* from ironwork salvaged from the church. – STAINED GLASS. S chapel E window. The Good Shepherd to a *Burne-Jones* design; post-war. – By *M.E. Aldrich Rope*: W and S transept windows, strips of grisaille medallions (The Sacraments), 1937–40, from St Augustine, Haggerston; chancel E, in medievalizing reds and blues, 1949; S chapel, with circular illustrations of the work of past vicars, charming and well fitted to the cinquefoil windows within their stumpy arcade, 1950. – NAVE. Ugly Saints signed by *Hardman*. Post-war.

ST PETER'S CENTRE, on the other side of Wapping Lane, W of the green, was the SCHOOL of 1872 by *Rev. W.H. Lowder*, brother of the incumbent and a pupil of Butterfield, with *Bowes A. Paice*. Central gabled bellcote with wrought-iron finial by *Richardson, Slade & Co.* and figure of the Good Shepherd by *Thomas Farmer.* Attractively converted *c.* 1990 by *Architype* for the LDDC.

ST PATRICK (R.C.), Green Bank, Wapping, immediately E of St John. A remarkable, knowingly rustic Italian design by *F.W. Tasker*, 1877–9, perhaps influenced by Cardinal Manning, who was a family friend. Classical and very straightforward, with big shady pediments each end and an overhanging cornice, all of stone. An elegant arcaded narthex was added 1892. Attached to the S the Presbytery, round a charming informal courtyard. Restored externally by *Simon Crosse* and *Roger Jorgenson* of *Feilden & Mawson*, 1987–8.

Grand basilican interior with giant Ionic columns dividing the flat ceiling of the aisle from the coffered-timber wagon roof of the nave; the chancel distinguished by a plaster vault on Corinthian columns. HIGH ALTAR of 1879, framed by the remains of embellishments of the 1890s, partly at the expense of Pugin's patron, Charles Willcock-Dawes of Burton Hill, who also paid for the narthex. Altar Painting (Crucifixion) and paintings on the E wall (Annunciation and St Cecilia) by *P. Greenwood*. LADY CHAPEL to the N, with ALTAR in quattrocento style, the frontal with finely painted grotesques. Said to come from Father Wilfrid Faber's first London Oratory in King William Street. Painting of Virgin and Child, Spanish according to Rottman. Pair of flanking columns without capitals, no doubt from the High Altar furnishings. The building does not provide for further altars, so additional ones and other disparate furnishings are awkwardly distributed around the aisles. They include a large, seated St Peter by *Mayer* of Munich, and a Pietà behind alabaster and iron balustrade, by *Jones & Willis*. Attractive small Arts and Crafts school MEMORIAL, 1900 by *Henry Price*; bronze frame with two boys and mourning women in relief.

MAJOR BUILDINGS

TOWER BRIDGE. 1886–94 (Act of 1885) by *Sir John Wolfe Barry*, engineer, and *Sir Horace Jones*, architect to the City Corporation. A much-loved landmark and the symbolic gateway between the City and the Pool of London and the Docks downstream, Tower Bridge was the lowest bridge on the Thames at that date and the first road vehicle crossing for the expanding districts of East London. Tower Subway, a tunnel opened in 1870 with a small railway, had been a failure. The bridge's position was governed by the demands of the expanding eastern metropolis, its form by navigational requirements – the Pool of London was still intensively used by ships and barge-trains, and a clear passage was stipulated of 200-ft width and 135-ft headroom (as built, slightly larger) to remain unobstructed for two hours at each high tide – and its style ultimately by its historic setting close to the Tower.

The competition launched by the Corporation in 1876 provoked fierce debate within the late Victorian architectural profession between the 'honesty' of clothing functional structures in artistic dress and the appropriateness of brute engineering so close to ancient, medieval fabric. *Sir Joseph Bazalgette* put forward two designs, one for a mighty girder-truss bridge, the other a tall parabolic arch, both set into Gothic stone abutments as a sop to their setting. *Jones*, in the odd position of acting as competitor and judge, produced designs for a chain-operated drawbridge in a medieval style. Ten years would pass before a final decision was made and inevitably, if unregrettably, the Tower Bridge represents a beautiful compromise. In Jones's words these were 'steel skeletons clothed with stone' but the contemporary press was less accommodating, decrying the completed building as 'architectural gimcrack on a large scale'.

Jones's scheme was approved in 1885, but with *Wolfe Barry* employed as engineer the design evolved to its present gatehouse form of a central bascule bridge, flanked by smaller suspension bridges hung from curved lattice girders. The pair of steel-framed towers, clad in a Gothic style with spiky corner turrets in deference to the neighbouring Tower of London, were intended to be of red brick but executed in hard granite. Their purpose was as much functional as aesthetic and they contained passenger lifts serving two high-level footbridges, for use when the bascules were raised. The footbridges were closed in 1910 and the bascules electrified in 1976, but some of the magnificent hydraulic machinery by *Armstrong, Mitchell & Co.* is preserved, including the tandem cross-compound steam pumping engines under the S approach viaduct. Yellow brick boiler chimney and accumulator tower, stern and sentinel-like, alongside. The abutments on the N side included a mortuary, a necessary if grisly space required for bodies retrieved from the river. Visitor Centre by *Michael Squire*, *c.* 1992.

NEWS INTERNATIONAL, No. 1 Pennington Street. The so-called Fortress Wapping forms a frustratingly impenetrable barrier to free passage N–S through Wapping. Monstrous printing works and offices (by Wimpey with *Grove Consultants*) which in 1979 replaced *Daniel Asher Alexander*'s marvellous North Stack warehouses along the N quay of the London Docks (*see* perambulation *2*). Kept but altered and re-roofed were the single-storey Pennington Street sheds built *c.* 1811–13 with 50-ft span iron trusses. Closure of the works was announced in 2004.

TIMES HOUSE (No. 2) on the N side of Pennington Street is linked by a high glass bridge. By *Rick Mather* 1989–92, protectively stepped back with a wall studded with projecting triangular windows, into a courtyard landscaped by *Georgie*

Wolton. The Highway façade makes an exhillarating interlude for the motorist. Big projecting canopy pierced with holes, a 1930s Modernist feature. Below, a skin of narrow bricks gradually peeled back to transform pilotis (E) into full height columns (W). Shooting through the cornice at the centre an angled glass screen.

For other major buildings *see* perambulations.

PERAMBULATIONS

1. St Katharine Docks

The scene at the ST KATHARINE DOCKS is lively but chaotic. Redevelopment for a multiplicity of leisure, residential and office uses following its closure in 1968 (an early example of planned mixed development) has given it new life and preserved its unique enclosed form but, with the exception of one warehouse and the dockmaster's house, has not saved its architecture.

The walk begins at TOWER BRIDGE (*see* above). Along the riverside the hideous TOWER THISTLE HOTEL by *Renton Howard Wood Associates*, 1970–3, a huge overdevelopment of this narrow site. Cruciform plan with brutal, concrete panel clad storeys cascading down from sixteen to nine. Multi-storey foyer, layered with galleries. In front, a pool with a spiralling group of a flying Girl with a Dolphin, by *David Wynne*, 1973. To the E the quay wall of St Katharine's Wharf, 1829, with gritstone cornice and beyond, a functioning TIME PIECE by *Wendy Taylor*, also 1973. Studded stainless-steel ring supported on rigid chains and pierced by a spear-like gnomon.

The ENTRANCE PASSAGE into ST KATHARINE DOCKS is flanked on the E side by the DOCKMASTER'S HOUSE of *c*. 1828, which like the others of its type has a bow facing the river. At the lock original cast-iron BOLLARDS, inscribed 'St Katharine Docks, 1828'. The ENTRANCE LOCK is of 1828, its upper walls now refaced and its mitre gates and sills replaced by flap gates in 1957. Over the S end of the lock a minimalist, lifting FOOTBRIDGE by *Powell-Williams Architects* and engineers *Robert Benaim & Associates*, 1996, and, carrying the road at the N end, a crisp welded-steel LIFTING BRIDGE by *Ove Arup & Partners*, 1973. On the E side, built to serve the burgeoning fraternity of luxury-yacht owners with moorings in the dock, the ST KATHARINE'S YACHT CLUB, 1985 by *Watkins Gray International*; much timber and two belvedere turrets.

From here, the view is of almost the entire docks. Two large BASINS linked by a single entrance basin almost as big, designed by *Thomas Telford*, engineer. The Western Dock opened in 1828, the Eastern in 1829. The quay walls (brick with gritstone copings) in the docks have mooring rings recessed into their face, an unusual feature to reduce congestion on the quay. The basins were originally surrounded by six stacks of five- and six-storey brick warehouses by *Philip Hardwick*, 1826–7. They were unique in the London docks in being placed on the edges of the quays on plain cast-iron Doric colonnades (an arrangement suggested in 1799 by Ralph Dodd for extension to the Legal Quays in the City and used later at Liverpool docks from 1843). Goods could be hoisted straight from ships into the warehouses or sorted for other destinations behind the colonnades. The Blitz of 1940 destroyed the three warehouses round the Eastern Dock, together with the fine offices at the NW corner, but the Western Dock retained its sense of enclosure and unity of scale until the 1970s when the warehouses were progressively demolished and replaced. The view of the Western Dock takes in immediately the battle of styles. INTERNATIONAL HOUSE, designed for the World Trade Centre (now defunct) by *Watkins Gray Woodgate International*, 1977–83, walls in the W side. It replaced the last 1820s warehouse and incorporates the idea of the dockside colonnade with (salvaged) double Doric columns and bays; otherwise, misleadingly semi-historical. On the N side (under construction in 2004) K2: offices by *Richard Rogers Partnership* bringing High Tech to this part of Docklands for the first time. Seven storeys with a full-height atrium and detached service towers. The site is that of the dock company's handsome Greek Revival offices of 1828 by *Hardwick*, demolished after war damage.* To its E, COMMODITY QUAY designed for the London Commodity Exchange, 1984–5, by *Watkins Gray International*. Even more routine than International House. In the foreground, between the Entrance Basin and the Western Dock, the CORONARIUM, begun in 1977 by *Hurden, Gill & Dent* as a chapel (now café) to commemorate the Queen's Silver Jubilee on the supposed site of the church of the Royal Foundation of St Katharine. Eight salvaged Doric columns, ring a lumpen, domed rotunda.

Spanning the W passage is a wooden, Dutch-style LIFTING FOOTBRIDGE by *Ove Arup & Partners*, 1983 leading to THE IVORY HOUSE, so-called, which thrusts forward between the basins. 1856–60 by *George Aitchison sen.*, clerk of works to the St Katharine Dock Co. from 1827. It is the only warehouse still standing, large and T-shaped on a T-shaped spit which effectively divides the docks into their three basins. Only the N front of the W wing stands on the water's edge. It was temporarily converted in 1968 for artists' studios after a campaign by Bridget Riley and Peter Sedgley and subsequently for flats with business facilities and shops in 1972–4 by *Renton Howard Wood Associates*. The original fire-resistant construction has brick jack arches on wrought-iron beams, circular cast-iron columns and brick outer walls, and was perhaps inspired by Fairbairn's then-recent *On the Application of Cast and Wrought*

*Its predecessor on the site, EUROPE HOUSE, of 1962–4, predated the regeneration scheme for the docks.

Iron to Building Purposes (1854, revised edn 1857). Wrought-iron roof trusses. It has a plain S front; the lowest two of the five storeys are embraced within big arches, carried on stanchions and spanned by iron beams: the warehouse was largely open at ground level: bowed shop windows have been inserted beneath the beams. A big, arched passageway leads through to the rear wing with a pedimented three-bay N façade. On the N side of the front block, an Italianate tower springs from the roof. An original mezzanine of York-stone slabs on wrought-iron beams and a similar S canopy have been renewed in reinforced concrete. The upper windows, originally of cast iron and uniform size, have also been altered; re-entrant balconies are cut into some of the openings. All the semicircular openings on the top floor were originally blind. Beneath, the last of the 1828 VAULTS, brick groin-vaults on cast-iron columns.

The DOCK WALL runs along East Smithfield. The N gateway has original vermiculated gatepiers; modern fibreglass elephants. To the E, round the N and E sides of the Eastern Dock an intensely developed wall of yellow brick flats, six-storeys high with taller penthouses and many clichés typical of the date, 1995–7 by *Renton Howard Wood Associates*. In 1975–7 they were responsible for the public housing piled up in the SE corner. Of buff brick with slate-hung boxy upper storeys and multi-level access. They continue the 1930s LCC St Katharine's Estate, which extends to St Katharine's Way. In contrast, along the S quay right on the water's edge, a terrace of silly folksy cottages in weathered brick and weatherboarding by *ATP Partnership*, 1982, apparently built in response to the DICKENS INN, another odd interloper, to which it is connected. The pub's present beguiling, weatherboarded and galleried exterior by *Renton Howard Wood Levin Partnership*, 1974–6, is a fantasy. The internal structure is genuinely old, about one-third of the timber internal frame of a warehouse of *c.* 1793–9 (remodelled by *Hardwick*), bodily moved from its original position and extended post-1978 in imitation. Four storeys and steep-pitched queenpost roof; diagonal struts to the upper floors. Spanning the eastern passage, a RETRACTING FOOTBRIDGE with elegant tubular steelwork. 1994 by *Brian Morton*. Preserved on the quay to the S is its unique double-leaf predecessor of 1829 by *John Lloyd*, one of the earliest moveable iron bridges remaining in Britain. Its cantilevered leaves are of wrought-iron bars in an unbraced construction, springing from cast-iron counterweight boxes which ran on rails. One hand winch of 1829 *in situ*.

TOWER WALK, the crude mongrel-Regency crescent of stucco houses set back behind a piazza SW of the pub, confuses the historical picture further. Built in 1987 (architects *Watkins Gray International*) and inspired, according to the developers, by the terraces of Regent's Park. Responding on its S side, DEVON HOUSE; offices of 1987 by the same architects. U-shaped court to the rear with big Neo-Regency bows to the river.

ST KATHARINE'S WAY starts here and follows the river behind a few restored warehouses, blocks of offices and flats, mostly of the LDDC era; the best is MILLER'S WHARF, the former British and Foreign Wharves 'G' warehouse of *c.* 1860–70, gently converted 1986–7 by *Terry Farrell & Partners;* glazed atrium bursting through the roof.

2. *Wapping: the old centre and London Docks*

The next two perambulations trace what remains of the old centre of Wapping, the warehouses along the river and the fragmentary survivals of the infilled London Docks as transformed by C20 development. Both walks begin at Wapping Underground Station.

2a. *West along Wapping High Street; a circular tour*

WAPPING STATION is of little consequence above ground; a perfunctory pale brick and concrete lid of 1959–60 concealing a richly atmospheric scene below, where the East London Line, originally the East London Railway of 1865–76 by *(Sir) John Hawkshaw*, passes through the earlier, pedestrian, THAMES TUNNEL. This was the first tunnel to be built underwater through soft ground, passing within a few feet of the bed of the Thames. Begun in 1825 by *(Sir) Marc Isambard Brunel*, using a tunnelling shield he had patented in 1818, the first of its kind. Work was interrupted by five major inundations and lack of finances but with government assistance and remarkable perseverance the tunnel was opened in 1843. Spiral ramps for carriages were never built and it remained a foot tunnel until it was converted in 1865–9 for the railway. The 1,200 ft long tunnel has two parallel vaults of horseshoe section 13 ft wide and 16 ft high. Inside, the inner orders of the cross-arches rose from Greek Doric half-columns, while the main vaults had stucco pilaster strips and impost bands; now reproduced in reinforced concrete.

W along WAPPING HIGH STREET, the old flavour of the riverside is maintained by the mighty scale of the warehouses on both sides. First, the high tea and spice warehouses of GUN WHARVES close in on both sides, converted to flats by *Barratt East London* before 1987. The range along the river, *c.* 1920, is in style still C19 but with artificial-stone dressings and reinforced-concrete floors. The thirteen bays to the river are treated as a giant arcade through six storeys, with channelled rustication on the ground-floor piers. The E, F, G and H Warehouses, which line the N side of Wapping High Street and turn the corner into Wapping Lane, were built in the 1930s. Concrete string courses and window mullions, original loading bays but ersatz balconies. Then along the river come warehouses that date from the mid- and later C19: first the tall warehouse of King Henry's Wharf, with pilasters to the loading bays; then a smaller twin-gabled warehouse (No. 112 Phoenix Wharf), once a flour mill, of 1840 by *Sydney Smirke*: its cast-iron columns have unusual tri-branched heads. Converted to flats *c.* 1996. It stands close to Execution Dock, once a sinister spot where pirates were hanged at low-water mark until 1830; Captain Kidd met such an end here in 1701. Then a pair of early C18 houses (Nos. 108–10), each of three storeys and three bays. These, probably chandlers' shops, are representative of riverside buildings before the spread of warehouses. Imaginative re-creation of shopfronts by *Russell Wright c.* 1988. Behind, the former workshop converted into the Captain Kidd pub in 1988–9 by *Goddard Manton Partnership*.

Facing the pub Tower Buildings, one of two blocks built by Alderman Sydney Waterlow's Improved Industrial Dwellings Co., founded 1863. The earlier block facing Brewhouse Lane is the most significant, built in 1864–5, as the company's second major project (the first was Langbourne Buildings, Shoreditch) and, like all subsequent projects, developed by Waterlow's builder *Matthew Allen* from a prototype dwelling exhibited by *Henry Roberts* in the 1850s. Better than most contemporary standard tenements: no courtyard or shared lavatories, better ventilation, and access to individual flats via balconies, in this case with a vaguely Chinese-Chippendale character to their railings. The later block creates a more typical street frontage with a front door in a pre-cast concrete surround (Waterlow was an early proponent of factory-made building components) and balconies at the rear.

Continuing along the river the River Police Station by *John* 76
Dixon Butler, Metropolitan Police architect, 1907–10. Brick and stone; Norman Shawish. Flats for officers along the street. Riverfront more elaborate with tiered oriels in the outer bays and moulded stone gables, cf. Coldharbour Police Station (Isle of Dogs, p. 684). The River Police was founded by Patrick Colquhoun and John Harriot in Wapping in 1798 as the Marine Police Establishment, and funded by the Committee of West India merchants to reduce theft from their ships and wharves. No. 94–6 is the restored Old Aberdeen Wharf; built in 1843–4 as Sun Wharf for the Aberdeen Steam Navigation Co., converted 1998–9. It has a unique monumental-stucco river façade of a plinth with panelled pedestals carrying giant Tuscan columns to the centre five bays and end pilasters. The columns originally carried segmental pediments along the attic. The riverside wall of buildings is interrupted by Waterside Gardens, on both sides of the High Street (transformed from a derelict site by *Cooper Macfarlane* for the LDDC, 1989) with a bandstand, reusing some cruciform cast-iron columns salvaged from Hardwick's St Katharine Docks warehouses of 1828. Then the rude intrusion of the River Police boatyard and

launch maintenance works of 1973 by the *Metropolitan Police Chief Architect*, clad in fibreglass panels boldly moulded in a sculptural relief.

On the land side, between Reardon Path and Dundee Street, is THE SANCTUARY. It incorporates remains of a six-storey granary of *c.* 1880 (No. 79), with white brick window heads and a new, highly sculptural wall-crane in welded steel. Derelict three-storey rear wing with timber stanchions and queenpost roof, in 2004 the only such building on the N bank. No. 78, DUNDEE COURT is an eight-bay, six-storey warehouse of the 1870s, converted to offices and flats. Imposing stucco cornice (renewed) and white brick string courses which arch over the cast-iron-framed windows. Rusticated stone doorway to former office. Wrought-iron lattice-trussed gangways, the last in Wapping, span the street at two levels to the smaller warehouses on the riverside. The plain ORIENT WHARF by *Shepheard Epstein & Hunter*, 1987–9, for the Toynbee Housing Association occupies an unusually prime site. Irregular gabled façades to the river. Next, the most architecturally sophisticated warehouse in the street, OLIVER'S WHARF (No. 64), designed as a tea warehouse in 1869–70 by *F. & H. Francis*. The first warehouse in Wapping to be converted into flats; by *Goddard Manton*, 1970–2. To the river an especially elaborate Venetian Gothic face, six storeys, the attic windows with paired arches in red brick, the four below tied together by giant segment-headed arches. Sandstone dressings. Cast-iron columns and timber beams inside. Finally, up to the Pier Head a survival of the narrow C16 plots. The TOWN OF RAMSGATE pub, perhaps older than it looks and once one of over three-dozen pubs along the street, stands alongside the early and rare survival, WAPPING OLD STAIRS, one of the few remaining passages down to the river.

SCANDRETT STREET turns N off Wapping High Street a few yards E of the Pier Head. Here is clear evidence of the C18 village: the tower of ST JOHN, the former parish church of Wapping, built in 1756 to succeed the first one, established as a chapel in 1615–17 on the S side of Wapping High Street. By *Joel Johnson*, who like so many C18 church designers was trained as a carpenter. The original designs may have owed something to *Boulton Mainwaring*, surveyor to the London Hospital, for whom Johnson worked. Only a fragmentary rectangular shell of the rest of the church survived the Second World War. The tower, restored in 1964 by the LCC, has a handsome continental-looking lead top. In outline above the clock stage, a concave receding stage and then the convexity of the cupola: a somewhat old-fashioned Baroque design. Converted to flats in the 1990s, the new outer walls are brick with quoins. Opposite, the former CHURCHYARD, hemmed in by the former dock wall, was made into a public park in 1951. Portland-stone CHEST TOMBS to the Staple children, *c.* 1730, and to John Robinson, *c.* 1750, are among the few left *in situ*.

As in many of these Thames-side hamlets, the neighbourhood of the church remained residential and still has some attractive though not grand C18 survivors. Adjoining is ST JOHN'S OLD SCHOOL, founded *c.* 1695 and rebuilt, together with the church, after 1756. It is of two-and-a-half storeys plus basement, and five bays. The central bay, very broad and pedimented within the attic, has a double doorcase and, in niches above it, *Coade* stone figures of a boy and a girl. One first-floor room is now lined with the panelling salvaged from the rest of the building when it was restored by *Dransfield Design*, 1994–5, as two houses. Two more were created in its S extension (THE LANTERN HOUSE) of *c.* 1840. Also of five bays. Two doorways with (restored) tablets framed by stone festoons on consoles, rather overscaled and perhaps reset. The attic, pierced with *œils de bœuf*, and square lantern are new, and make the whole composition look more C18.

St Patrick lies immediately behind in Green Bank. On the opposite corner, affixed to the Turk's Head, an interwar Taylor Walker pub, is a tablet inscribed 'Bird Street Erected Anno Dom 1706'. N of here TENCH STREET continues the line of Scandrett Street N, lined on the W side by remains of the E wall of the London Dock and, behind it, the JOHN ORWELL SPORTS CENTRE. An early and very successful venture into the reuse of a London Docks building, by *Shepheard Epstein & Hunter*, 1977–80 for Tower Hamlets Borough Council. The entrance is just a discreet doorway in a stretch of the dock wall. Inside an activities hall converted from a machine-tool workshop, which hugged the curve of the dock wall at the edge of the dock entrance basin; the basin has been infilled for sports pitches. Long and gently curved with full-height arched W windows. At the N end a new sports hall, kept as low and discreet as possible by means of a slate mansard. Round the hall a covered walkway carried on salvaged cast-iron stanchions.

The area of the London Dock

WAPPING PIER HEAD was originally the main entrance from the river into the London Dock. The ENTRANCE LOCK of 1805, in handsome gritstone ashlar still partly visible, was only 40 ft (12 metres) wide and 170 ft (52 metres) long: infilled and first made into a garden in the early 1960s, it is flanked by two handsome terraces of DOCK OFFICIALS' HOUSES of 1811–13 49
by *Daniel Asher Alexander*. Three-storeyed, except for the SW terrace rebuilt as four storeys of offices after the Blitz. Both end S in larger five-bay houses, with broad three-bay bows facing each other and suggesting a gateway to the river. This pair has Doric porches. Tall basements with rusticated heads to the windows and curious keystones linked to the sills above. On the ground floor, doors and windows in arched recesses. The other houses are narrow, of two and three bays. On the E side, No. 6 has a groin-vaulted entrance hall; top-lit stairs at Nos. 5–9. At the end of the E terrace (No. 5), a discreet exten-

sion facing the river, 1982–3 by *Goddard Manton Partnership*. No. 11, facing Wapping High Street, belongs with the group. All the houses of the W terrace were renovated as a single block of flats by a developer in 1971. The lower terraces N of Wapping High Street are reconstructions from 1981 by Tower Hamlets, except the plain Nos. 12–16. They face each other across the infilled lock, now a featureless sunken garden. At the N end, remains of the dock wall with stalactite gatepiers of the type used by *Alexander* throughout the dock; modern continuation across the infilled lock.

The W end of Wapping High Street was damaged in the Blitz. New flats have appeared since 1998 as part of a phased development of Hermitage Wharf by Berkeley Homes. Towards the river three massive blocks by *Andrew Cowan Architects*. Grey panelling and extensive glazing: broad sweeping fronts with balconies angled forward and wide curving eaves; opaque-glass protrusions for the services like the tophampers of a battleship. In a courtyard raised up from the street, VOYAGER by *Wendy Taylor*, a circle of bronze split and twisted to resemble the form of a ship's propellor. A fourth block, HALCYON WHARF, by *Stock Woolstencroft*, *c*. 2003, stands back on the N side of the High Street. In two parts. Grey steel with red-terracotta tiles, almost a cliché of late 1990s design, with a rounded tower of balconies stacked up. The scheme will be completed by a riverside memorial garden to civilians killed in the Blitz; unrealized in 2004.

HERMITAGE BASIN was added to the London Dock by *John Rennie* in 1811–21 to create a second entrance to the dock besides that at Wapping Pier Head. On either side of the entrance lock, two sets of gatepiers with the stalactite rustication that *Daniel Alexander* used throughout the London Dock. The Basin was closed in 1909; by the W gate a former red brick Neo-Georgian IMPOUNDING STATION of 1913–14, the first of a standard PLA-type designed to maintain water levels in the dock basins. The remains of the dock entrance, with fine sandstone ashlar facings, can be seen on the riverside. By the lock, a former hydraulic PUMPING STATION of the London Dock Co., 1856, converted to flats. Italianate tower and small windows with moulded brick voussoirs. The walk continues within the dock walls along the Basin. On the NW side, HERMITAGE WATERSIDE, flats and houses by *Jestico & Whiles* for Barratt, with standard elevations but quite a bold layout. SCULPTURE: reef knot in bronze by *Wendy Taylor*, 1997. At the N end, the INNER ENTRANCE LOCK has fine ashlar walls, with recesses shaped to two leaves of the cast-iron swing bridge, stolen in 1976. In its place the fixed roadway of Vaughan Way, the lock adapted as a subway to pass beneath. Just S, the HERMITAGE PRIMARY SCHOOL by the *ILEA Architect's Department*, 1985–9. The central octagonal lantern tower makes this low-key school a modest landmark. The composition builds up from a single-storey S wing, with veranda to the classrooms, to two storeys at the back where there is street access to both levels. Yellow brick, slate and lead.

Beneath Vaughan Way a pedestrian route runs along the N quay of a narrow CANAL, an imaginative infrastructure designed by *Paddy Jackson Associates*, 1982–5, and excavated from the infilled dock. The original, higher S quay wall, built of yellow stock brick with a limestone rubbing band, has been retained to make a striking contrast, an effect reinforced by the neat and consistently gabled rows of houses down each side. On the lower N quay, three-storey houses raised above a protective embankment of front gardens, 1987–90 by *Boyer Design Group;* on the S quay, now SPIRIT QUAY, houses by *Form Design Group*, pre-1987, on the site of the South Stack warehouses demolished before 1976. Big arched windows form the controlling motif towards the canal. Halfway along, a broad paved piazza fills the former passage to WAPPING ENTRANCE BASIN. The original inner-entrance lock, flanked by massive, curved sandstone walls has been turned into an impressive landscape feature by a grand flight of steps and, on axis, a bronze Neoclassical-style BUST of John Rennie, twice life-size, by *John Ravera*. The canal turns N; on its E side is a Neo-vernacular group of houses that might well have strayed here from rural Essex. By *Ronald Toomey & Partners*, 1983–5. Elevations in rough, ochre brick with much grey slate-hanging and rows of W gables with mock chimney finials. Directly ahead, looms up NEWS INTERNATIONAL'S printing works (*see* above) on the site of the North Stack warehouses of 1805 (dem. 1979).

The canal turns E into the narrow TOBACCO DOCK, first built in 1811–13 by *Rennie* and extended in the 1820s to link the old London Dock with the new Eastern Dock (*see* below). Its S side still has a section of tall brick-and-granite quay wall between granite-walled dock passages, widened *c.* 1912, the date of the steel swing bridge. Before its extension the dock was surrounded on three sides by *Alexander*'s huge NEW TOBACCO WAREHOUSE of 1811–14, a bonded store for tobacco above wine and spirit vaults (later furs and skins replaced tobacco, when the upper floor became known as the Skin Floor), covering an area of 210,000 sq. ft. C19 and C20 demolitions have left only the highly impressive remains on the N side (converted for shops in 1984–9 by *Terry Farrell Partnership* but now deserted). Six parallel halls, covered by 370 ft (112 metres) long, 54 ft (16 metres) span, of queenpost lantern roofs of particular elegance. The structure is as impressive as the scale and belongs to an evolutionary phase in the combination of timber and cast iron for spanning horizontally, before the widespread use of cast-iron arched beams. The roofs are supported on lines of stanchions of an astonishing tree-like form. The stanchions rest on stone bases set 18 ft (5 metres) apart and branch at two levels to carry gutter plates and roof trusses so that there are twice as many roof trusses as stanchions. The struts act compositely with the beams, to form balanced cantilevers.* Before the regrettable introduction of partitions and sheer glass shopfronts in bolted-metal frames, these columns formed a veritable forest. Cruciform cast-iron members except for every sixth column, which is circular and acts as a rainwater downpipe to maintain the high water table which preserves the timber piling of the building. Lateral stability imparted by inverted quadrant braces of cast iron which rise from the floor to the longitudinal fire-break wall.

Farrell tried to create a second Covent Garden Market, opening up parts of the floor into the wine and spirit vaults beneath, and removing the roof trusses above, used to re-create the three eastern roof bays demolished after war damage. Descending to the vaults, unnecessarily massive Postmodern staircases in concrete. Shallow brick groin-vaults on an 18-ft (5 metre) square grid stand on waisted, octagonal stone pillars, with some lines of barrel vaults to give stability. The NE corner of the building is enclosed on two sides by the heightened outer walls of the dock with subtle breaks for entrances, which have Ledoux-inspired elliptical arches on thick Doric columns.

Wapping Lane, originally Old Gravel Lane, one of the causeways which crossed Wapping marsh now crosses the link between Tobacco Dock and the infilled Eastern Dock of 1824–8 by *William Chapman*, consulting engineer, and *Alexander*; part of its wall survives along Raine Street. Here too is the former Raine's Foundation School (now offices).
24 Built in 1719 as a charity school by Henry Raine, who lived in Wapping 1679–1738. Baroque façade of high quality. Two storeys and a basement in yellow brick with rubbed red brick dressings, pilasters and finely carved stone details. Oddly shaped doorcase (rather in Hawksmoor's or Archer's style), linked to a shaped stone plaque forming the apron of the arched window above. Niches at first floor, for figures of charity school children, have stone open pediments on Corinthian pilasters within relieving arches. Two-storey wings: one the schoolmaster's house, the other a replacement *c.* 1985 by the GLC. A bigger boarding school for girls (Raine's Asylum), built to the E in 1736, has gone. The whole school moved to Stepney, first to Cannon Street Road in 1883, then to Arbour Square in 1913 and is now in Bethnal Green. To its E, on the site of the boys' school built in 1820, a tall block of flats converted from the remains of the St George-in-the-East Workhouse. According to the datestone this block is of 1886 by *Wilson, Son & Aldwinckle*, architects, *Charles Cox*, builder.

Slightly S on Wapping Lane, St Peter's (*see* above) was once hemmed in by small houses. These were mostly swept

*The arrangement of raking struts is a three-dimensional refinement of the arch-braces used in *Alexander*'s entirely timber Old Tobacco Warehouse of 1805, destroyed in the Second World War. This had long-span roof trusses in a similar arrangement, and groin-vaults beneath on an exceptionally adventurous 26-ft (8-metre) grid.

away *c.* 1926 for the LCC's WAPPING ESTATE which extends on both sides. An early example of wholesale slum clearance in this area, with characteristic Neo-Georgian blocks, relatively informally grouped around open spaces. A single C19 pub survives, but the Council also provided a small row of shops on the E side of Wapping Lane, something of a rarity. No. 105 (E side), CORBETT'S WHARF (now Gulliver's Wharf), early C19; three storeys with cellars and loading doors. Opposite, with a bowed corner to Brewhouse Lane, No. 78–80, a small later C19 warehouse, converted to a restaurant *c.* 1984. Single storeyed on a semi-basement opened up through a well. Aisled, with cruciform columns carrying king-rod timber trusses on a riveted iron-trussed valley beam. The walk concludes at Wapping Station.

2b. E along the High Street to Wapping Wall and Shadwell Basin

E of Wapping Station the HIGH STREET starts with new development, mostly dreary warehouse-style flats. Making a picturesque coda to the street is the long paved yard of NEW CRANE PLACE, flanked by the warehouses of NEW CRANE WHARF, transformed freely 1989–90 by *Conran Roche* (job architect *Stuart Mosscrop*) into shops and flats with plain grey-metal steps and balconies and small-paned timber windows. The line of four riverside warehouses E–H were first built 1873, burnt out and reinstated in 1885; probably of both periods now. Six storeys, thirteen bays, corbelled brick cornice, white brick window heads. Across the yard's E end a four-storey block (on the site of an ice depot) rebuilt in 1914, probably contemporary with the warehouses on the N side which use more blue brick with concrete lintels. Close to the gates a white-rendered, Neo-Modern section in place of a pub, rubs up against THE THREE SUNS, 1880s Queen Anne for Truman's, with superb cut brick decoration of fluted pilasters and in the centre bay a bucolic rustic lunching beneath a tree.

The best stretch of large C19 riverside warehouses left on the Thames is in WAPPING WALL where the warehouses of New Crane Wharf and its neighbours form a continuous wall between street and river. First GREAT JUBILEE WHARF, a single block of flats by *BUJ Architects*, 1996–7, unifying the façades of three former warehouses. The W half (Nos. 78–80) was previously Lusk's Wharf and Lower Oliver's Wharf, built in 1890 in four storeys and six bays with white brick window heads within giant arcades. Contemporary wrought-iron wall-cranes, with a large one to the river. Curious gablets for former transverse roofs have now been repeated across the E half, and a glass-and-timber attic storey added. The E half, previously Jubilee Wharf (Nos. 76–7) was mid-C19, three-storeyed with a plain stucco entablature, now raised in line with its neighbours. Five bays plus one recessed to the street; loading bays with three forged-iron wall-cranes. Cruciform iron columns retained.

The huge METROPOLITAN WHARF, is utilized as small offices and workshops. The name originally referred to only Nos. 70–4, the largest single block which forms the centre of the range. Warehouse A (No. 70) is perhaps the oldest warehouse along Wapping Wall, built *c.* 1862–3 by *William Cubitt & Co.* Originally four storeys, the top two floors probably added *c.* 1900. A prominent modillion cornice on the street frontage shared by its extension, the twin, six-storey Warehouses B and C (Nos. 72–4) added 1864–5 by *John Whichcord jun.* They have deep, rendered name bands front and rear, a plain pediment with oculi and two magnificent forged-iron wall-cranes. On the riverside the ground floor is open, with cast-iron Doric columns and a riveted girder entablature. Inside, cruciform iron columns with console-shaped flanges to their caps and 'shoe' heads housing the timber beams. It encroached 40 ft (12 metres) into the river, plus a C20 jetty. Warehouse D (No. 75) of 1898–9, was built by *Holland & Hannen.* Only three bays but seven storeys with giant, arched niches and an oculus in the gable. Warehouses N and O (Nos. 65–9) of 1898–1900, seven storeys and ten bays, modern-looking with their rolled-steel lintels though still with cast-iron windows.

Further along on the S side, PELICAN WHARF at Nos. 58–60 makes a great contrast with its massive riverside neighbours. By *Shepheard Epstein & Hunter*, 1986–7. The yellow brick façade is split, deeply recessed and filled with semicircular green metal balconies, like a half-open atrium. Simpler river façade. There is no river access here except for the narrow Pelican Stairs. Its neighbour is the famous inn, THE PROSPECT OF WHITBY, which may date from *c.* 1520, said to be named after a ship that moored here in the C18. It is still the narrow width of the C16 riverfront plots. C19 façade with very small-scale classical features – pedimented first-floor windows, tall attic with the name in bold letters and lion masks; informal and rambling at the back. The oldest obvious feature is some C18 panelling, probably not *in situ*.

Opposite, the WAPPING HYDRAULIC PUMPING STATION (now The Wapping Project gallery) of 1889–93 marks the junction with Glamis Road. By *E.B. Ellington*, engineer to the Hydraulic Engineering Company of Chester who supplied machinery it was originally steam powered. Tall, single-storey red brick buildings, the rear boiler house has a clerestory of 1923–5 under cast-iron water tanks; the S extension to the engine house in front is also of the 1920s. Tall accumulator tower with miniature temple-fronts rising above the parapet. Engineers' house adjoining. This was the last working station of the five built by the London Hydraulic Power Company to provide power for cranes, lifting bridges etc. throughout inner London, and is the best surviving. Closed in 1977, it was finally converted in 2000 by *Shed 54 Limited.* The rough, tough industrial aesthetic has been preserved, a smaller but grittier version of the contemporary Tate Modern. The minimalist bar and restaurant shares space with the engines under a timber-

and-iron Polonceau-truss roof and the gutted boiler house provides a lofty, no-frills exhibition space.

N of the pumping station is SHADWELL BASIN, the final extension of the London Docks E of the Eastern Dock. The Old Shadwell Basin of 1828–32 by *J.R. Palmer* is now amalgamated with the New Shadwell Basin to the N of 1854–8 by *J.M. Rendel*, its quay walls constructed with mass concrete piers and brick relieving vaults. Glamis Road crosses the basin on a steel LIFTING BRIDGE of Scherzer rolling-bascule type. 1930s by the PLA, restored by the LDDC as a fixed bridge pre–1987. There is another such bridge at the W end of the basin over the 60-ft (18 metres) wide and 350-ft (107 metres) long Inner Entrance Lock, of 1858. The HOUSING round three sides of the basin, scaled to its quite modest size, is a design-and-build scheme by *MacCormac, Jamieson, Prichard & Wright*, 1985–7 and acknowledges, though not slavishly, the forms of C19 dock buildings, for instance in the quayside colonnades. The terraces of flats are clearly articulated into portal-like sections rising from Venetian openings of an arch flanked by two narrower sections on the ground floor to split gables at the top. Smaller, similar houses at the NE corner.

In the centre of the N side, a broad gravelled terrace, created by the LDDC to reveal the dock wall and a gateway to the churchyard of Shadwell parish church (*see* Shadwell) high above the level of the basin. E of the basin less ambitious housing in PEARTREE LANE stands beneath the high dock wall that runs S of The Highway and down Glamis Road. In the NW corner, below the retaining wall of the churchyard, Nos. 1–3 ST PAUL'S TERRACE, a row of tiny, one-bay artisan cottages of *c.* 1820, originally accessible only via an alley from the dockside. E of Glamis Road is the pier head of the New Shadwell Basin. On the N side of the pier head, the SHADWELL PROJECT, a community sailing centre by *Bowerbank Brett & Lacy*, 1980s for LDDC; brick with a little leaded lookout. On the S side Thames Path turns into a big circular deck projecting for a prospect of the river and has PROSPECT WHARF as its background, a huge development of flats by *Shepheard Epstein & Hunter*, 1985–7, with a big hollow landscaped court and a concave riverfront with brick walls rising sheer to a skyline of irregular gables. The walk returns to Wapping Station; here and there one may walk along the riverside.

SHADWELL AND RATCLIFFE*

Stepney's riverside hamlets of Shadwell and Ratcliffe have ceased to exist in all but name. Both were gradually obliterated in the

*The account of Shadwell and Ratcliffe is adapted from *London Docklands* by Elizabeth Williamson, 1998.

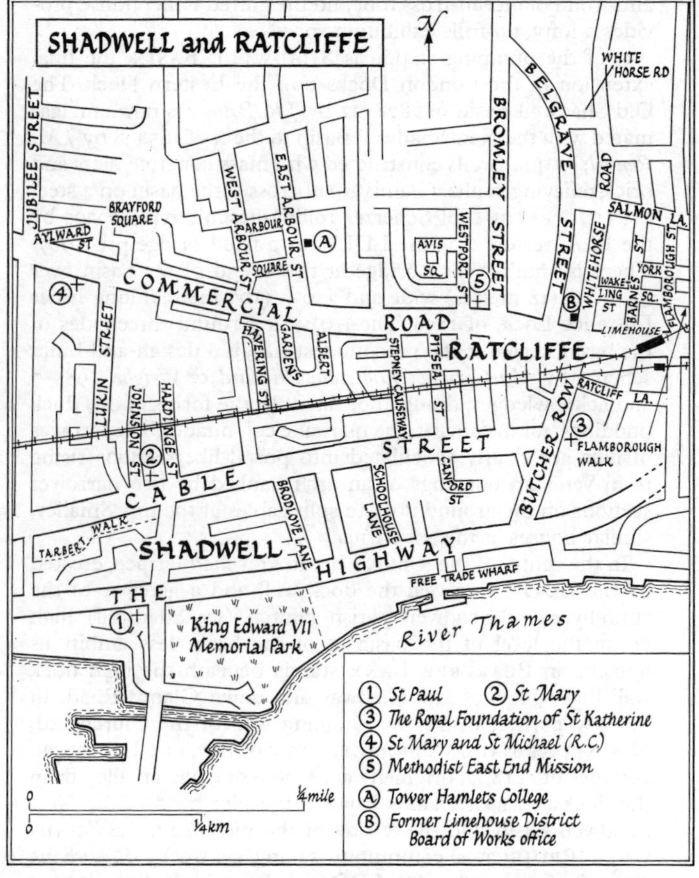

C19 by the creation of Commercial Road, the encroachment of the London Docks and in the C20 by the road developments for the Rotherhithe Tunnel and Limehouse Link.

RATCLIFFE was the first landfall downriver with a good straight road to London. A wharf existed here in 1348, the first known exploitation of the riverside E of the City, and by the C16 many famous voyages of discovery were setting off from here. The hamlet, originally restricted to the riverside, expanded in the C15 N towards Butcher Row, the main route to Stepney and Hackney. In the early C17 it was the most populous of Stepney's riverside hamlets (about 3,500 inhabitants). Its main street, later known as the Ratcliffe Highway (now The Highway), was lined with wharves, warehouses and shipbuilders' yards, and became a centre for glassmaking. But in 1794 a fire, which spread fiercely from an ignited barge of saltpetre at the East India Company's warehouses (*see* Free Trade Wharf, below), wiped out half of Butcher Row and necessitated much rebuilding. Soon after this, as the docks were established downstream, Ratcliffe's character changed dramatically as its population expanded from about 5,000 in 1801 to 17,000 in 1861 (it became a parish distinct from Limehouse in 1838) and prosperous wharfingers and tradesmen gave way to seamen and dockworkers. The building of Commercial Road in 1806–10 divided C19 Ratcliffe in two. The southern part towards the river became teeming slums around Ratcliffe Highway, made notorious by a series of murders in 1811. But a more respectable enclave survived to the N towards St Dunstan's church, where land, originally the estate of Dean Colet, was developed by the Mercers' Company under the direction of their surveyor, *George Smith,* from 1819. The Mercers favoured 'respectable' working-class tenants and maintained their property more carefully than some other East End landowners, so early post-war plans for total rebuilding here were abandoned. Fortunately by the time the property was acquired by the GLC in 1969, the tide had turned in favour of rehabilitation.

SHADWELL was virtually unknown before 1600 (although significant Roman burials and remains of baths have been found in the area). It grew rapidly between 1630 and 1650, with the establishment of numerous industries. A chapel was built by its inhabitants in 1656 and altered after 1664 when the progressive speculator Thomas Neale (*see* Seven Dials, Covent Garden) inherited an interest in Shadwell. By the time Shadwell became a separate parish in 1669, about 8,000 lived there, many of them mariners. Shadwell market house (also built by *Neale,* 1681–2) lay just E of the church, rebuilt in 1821, which still stands on The Highway. Shadwell and Ratcliffe's slums became the object of philanthropic endeavours as early as the 1840s when baths and a washhouse were opened in a converted building in Glasshouse Fields (amongst the earliest in London).* Much of Shadwell riverside vanished with the expansion of the London Docks in the 1850s. Attempts at slum clearance began in the 1860s but it was only fully achieved with the post-war reconstruction of Stepney, to mixed effect and with little focus.

RELIGIOUS BUILDINGS

ST MARY, Johnson Street. 1848–50, an early work by *Frederick J. Francis.* A mission church in a very poor area, founded by

*The experiment led to the founding of purpose-built baths in Old Castle Street, Whitechapel, *see* p. 411.

William Quekett, vicar of Christ Church Watney Street, and paid for by Lord Haddo, son of the Earl of Aberdeen. On a tight site at the corner with Cable Street. Faced in coursed ragstone; the Gothic detail simpler than in later churches by this firm, but given character by a tower rising above the S chancel aisle, with octagonal pinnacles and thin spire with lucarnes. It was added at Haddo's suggestion. Plain but attractive cream-plastered interior: aisles with circular columns and moulded capitals, tall clerestory, steep open roof. Side windows with plate tracery; Dec E and W windows. In the short sanctuary, High Altar with tester of the 1950s; nave altar added in a reordering of the 1980s. Below the W gallery, iron grille (1988–9) allowing views into the church. High Church practices were established in the later C19, but furnishings now are simple. LECTERN. Made up from late C17 woodwork, the main piece a finely carved angel holding an anchor. COMMUNION RAILS, S aisle. Also made up from older pieces; openwork foliage with angels, perhaps C17 continental. STAINED GLASS. Several N aisle windows of the 1930s, traditional in style, by *C.C. Powell.* MEMORIAL BOARDS. Unusual; nine panels with names, including donors, from 1864–1956.

CHURCH HALL to the N, three storeys, with quite arresting exterior of brick and glass; 1991 by *Tom Hornsby* of *Keith Harrison & Associates.*

ST PAUL, The Highway. 1817–21. Plaques read: '*J. Walters*, Architect: rebuilt 1820; *R. Streather*, Builder'. It replaced Shadwell's chapel of 1656. 'Cheaply built and designed without fire' was Pevsner's verdict, perhaps too harsh on a building whose spire makes such a handsome landmark. The stone steeple evokes Wren's St Mary-le-Bow via Dance's St Leonard Shoreditch. The base, with plinth and cornice broken out in response to paired Corinthian angle columns, looks particularly Baroque. Corinthian columns also form a circular tempietto above. An obelisk top-stage rises above a ring of volutes. The rest is simple: yellow brick with stuccoed pilasters on a plain Greek Revival W front. Blind niches flank a big W door, inscription tablets above. Two-storey side elevations with rectangular windows and bold stone string course below the parapet. Chancel with angle pilasters as on the W front.

The plan was for a square nave with saucer dome, originally with four galleries, a W projection for gallery stairs and an E one for shallow vaulted chancel flanked by vestries. The centralized effect was diminished in 1848 when *Butterfield* took out the E gallery and added a tripartite E window. His chancel arch and vault were removed by *W.C. Waymouth* in 1931. Dark wooden W, N and S galleries on squat Tuscan columns. COMMUNION TABLE, C17, walnut, and RAILS, *c.* 1820. PULPIT, of bombé form, oak, *c.* 1700. – ORGAN. Early C19, formerly on the E gallery. A large part dates from 1714, one of the few surviving works by *Abraham Jordan.* – STAINED GLASS. Post-war E window by *John Hayward*, 1964.

Brick CRYPT, with burial vaults; converted into a community centre by the LDDC, 1983–4, when the church was restored and the CHURCHYARD and terraces were landscaped. Good early C19 iron railings and lamp brackets. On the S side the dock wall, with doorway to Shadwell Basin.

ST MARY AND ST MICHAEL (R.C.), Commercial Road. 1856 by Pugin's pupil *W.W. Wardell*, repaired by *A.V. Sterrett* after war damage. One of the first major C19 R.C. churches in the East End, and the largest, successor to an C18 R.C. chapel in Virginia Street, Wapping. An ambitious stone-faced building, oriented N–S, with high, rather bleak clerestoried nave of eleven bays. The intended W tower was begun but never completed. Three-bay chancel, distinguished by clustered piers and a large seven light window, its tracery simplified in the post-war rebuilding. Chapels on each side. FONT, octagonal with marble band; mosaic of Baptism behind. ALTAR RAILS, alabaster, finely detailed, with angels and pierced quatrefoil tracery. Probably part of a sanctuary reordering of 1909 by *Robert L. Curtis*. Post-war furnishings include, in the chapel of Stepney Martyrs, painted ALTARPIECE with two scenes in relief, with STAINED GLASS of martyrs above. E, W and N chapel windows also with post-war glass.

METHODIST CENTRAL HALL (East End Mission), Commercial Road. 1907 by *James Weir*. Tall, busy street front with offices and flats. The church is at an upper level at the back, refurbished post-war with timber cladding and shallow arched ceiling.

ROYAL FOUNDATION OF ST KATHARINE

No. 2 Butcher Row

The Foundation is a remarkable survival: established by Queen Matilda in 1147 as a religious community next to the Tower of London and refounded by Queen Eleanor in the later C13, it survived the Reformation as a Royal Peculiar. Its largely C14 and C15 buildings, partly rebuilt by one of the lay masters, Sir Julius Caesar (†1636), were demolished in 1825 for St Katharine Docks, but some of the fittings from the chapel were preserved. They were taken to the Foundation's new home in Regent's Park designed by *Ambrose Poynter*. This began as an almshouse but was reorganized in 1878 with clerical master, three sisters, ten bedesmen and ten bedeswomen. It was re-established in the East End in 1914, at Bromley Hall, Poplar (the Regent's Park buildings becoming the Danish church), and after the Second World War, under the Rev. St John Groser, moved to Butcher Row to the site of the bombed St James Ratcliffe (1837–8 by *Edward Lapidge*). The old furnishings were transferred to a new chapel by *R.E. Enthoven*, 1950–2, built, with adjoining buildings, in time for the Festival of Britain. In 2003–4 the chapel was refurbished, with extra accommodation and conference facilities by *PRP Architects*.

The centrepiece, facing W to Butcher Row, is the MASTER'S HOUSE, built in 1795–6 for Matthew Whiting, sugar refiner and director of the Phoenix Assurance Company, which had been used in the C19 as Vicarage for St James Ratcliffe. A plain, square three-bay, two-and-a-half storey Georgian house with slightly advanced centre, restored four-column Ionic porch, and parapet with balustrading above the windows. Possibly by *Thomas Leverton*, who was surveyor to the Phoenix Company, and who worked with Whiting after the Ratcliffe fire of 1794 which had destroyed Whiting's previous house on this site. The remarkable internal features of the Master's House are the large MURAL PAINTINGS in the ground-floor rooms facing the garden, unusual survivals dating from the late C18 or early C19. In the Drawing Room a classical landscape and seascape, based on Claude's Arch of Titus and Landing of Aeneas, both engraved in 1772. In the Dining Room, which has an added bow window, two panels remain, one based on a seascape by Vernetone showing coastal fortifications against Napoleon, and one of a painting of Italian subjects by Richard Wilson, both engraved in the early C19.

The post-war additions are in stock brick, a two-storey residential N wing extending E, simply detailed in a self-effacing Modern style with Arts and Crafts touches; shallow pantiled roofs. The early C21 extensions are sympathetic in scale, plainly detailed but slightly more flamboyant in effect, with a new N entrance and a bowed conference room in an E wing facing the garden. A covered cloister of 1951 on the S side provides a route from the house to the chapel and a home for some of the monuments moved from Regent's Park.

The CHAPEL of 1951, a simple brick-faced portal frame, was transformed in 2003–4 by enlarged windows with thick metal mullion-and-transom grids under faintly Perp arched heads with tiny dripstones. By the entrance, relief of St Katharine, moved from the E wall to make way for a new circular window. The chapel FURNISHINGS have two claims to fame. As first conceived, the plain plastered interior both acted as a foil to the exceptional fittings preserved from the medieval site, mostly placed at the W end, and was the envelope for controversially radical furnishings of 1954, designed by *Keith Murray*, with a freestanding altar placed well forward on a platform to allow the priest to face the congregation.* In the more balanced but less intense reordering of 2003–4 by *Jonathan Dinnewell* of *Christopher Smallwood Architects*, old and new are decorously integrated in a brighter and lighter interior. REREDOS. Timber Neo-Gothic frame of 2004, around a remarkable marble relief panel of the Adoration of the Magi with much delicate low-relief detail in the background; the two sides of the foreground differ in style. Thought to be Italian. The iconography is identical to a painting in the National

*Above it was a spare star-shaped wrought-iron Corona, also by *Murray*, partly covered in fabric, and hanging pyx, with delicate leaf decoration in silver.

Gallery, Washington, by Benvenuto di Giovanni, dated to *c.* 1470–5. Which copied which, and whether the sculpture might even be C19, is a matter of debate. ALTAR composed of dark-grey slabs, and carved with inscription and symbols from the Roman catacombs, by *Ralph Beyer*, 1954, who went on to work at Coventry Cathedral and at St Paul Bow Common. – SCULPTURE. Crucifixion, in teak, *c.* 1952, a majestic, stylized figure, by *Michael Groser*, son of the first post-war Master. Now on the W wall. It was designed to hang above a small Sacrament Altar against the E wall.

The richly carved CHOIRSTALLS from the medieval chapel are outstanding on a national level, the only example in London to demonstrate the high standard of C14 wood carving under royal patronage. They are only a fragment of what still existed in the C18: A.C. Ducarel's book of 1780 shows twenty-four canopied stalls, fifteen of them with misericords. Two groups now at the E end, much restored in the C19, have gabled canopies, along the lines of a single original traceried canopy preserved in the V & A. Tall canopied stalls were a C14 fashion. The design is simpler than similar ones at Lincoln of *c.* 1370, supporting a date in the 1360s, when St Katharine's was being remodelled after new ordinances from Queen Philippa. These groups have lost their misericords; their stall fronts now have an assortment of later carving: eight classical panels with busts in medallions surrounded by Renaissance grotesques; four standing figures with exuberant draperies, including Charity and Faith(?), later C16 or C17. Against the western wall are two further groups with vaulted canopies (probably early C19) over two sets of four seats, each with a return of two further seats. All have misericords, a total of twelve. Busts of Queen Philippa and Edward III appear at N and S corners, and there is a stray misericord on a made-up chair. The details are a delight, lively figures with the stylized curling hair of the C14, often heavily undercut; they include an unusual profile head, an angel with bagpipes and an elephant with castle and rider. The single misericord has the devil gripping two chattering women. The main subjects are flanked by vigorously carved supporters, the elbow rests made knobbly by animals and foliage A closer look shows that the relief carvings have all been cut out carefully and set into new seats; two of them (green man and foliage) do not correspond with Ducarel. The W DOORS, with Gothic tracery and coloured marginal glazing, appear to come from *Ambrose Poynter*'s chapel of 1828 in Regent's Park. Above them three later C17 carved panels with putti, the side ones making music and singing; they were set below the organ at Regent's Park. The evidence suggest that in the 1820s much effort was made to provide a sympathetic setting for what could be rescued from the woodwork which had been accumulated over the centuries. – PULPIT. A fine and unusual piece (now without its base and sounding board). Hexagonal, with marquetry panels of architectural scenes, several with domed or spired churches. Inscription below from Nehemiah: 'Ezra the priest stood upon a pulpit of wood which he had made for the preaching'. Supposedly given by Sir Julius Caesar, but recent study of the mouldings suggests this is an unusual piece of early C18 antiquarianism. – STAINED GLASS. E and W windows by *Alan Younger*, 2004.

In the entrance lobby. – FONT, given by Queen Victoria, marble bowl in wooden surround made up from linenfold panelling, on a late C17 column. – PASCHAL CANDLESTICK. Barley-sugar column; base with St Blaise and St Catherine, later C17. Other older pieces include: small relief WOODCARVING of angels, late medieval. – Small hexagonal CANDELABRA, said to come from the chantry chapel of John Holand (the tomb is now in St Peter ad Vincula in the Tower); the delicate structure with leafy spandrels C15 Gothic, with later classical busts slotted into spaces for upper candleholders. – CLOCK by *Vulliamy*, London 1828, incorporating some C14 foliage work in the spandrels. Masters' coats of arms from the C15–1889. Outside the W door, stiff standing figures of King Edward III and Queen Philippa, C19.

MONUMENTS. In the chapel. – William Cuttinge †1599, benefactor. Brass with two kneeling figures at prayer desk, set in a Purbeck-marble frame incorporating an enamelled brass coat of arms in the pediment. – Frederick Becker of Holland †1663, who drowned in the Thames. Inscription in Latin, in bolection-moulded frame with armorial above. – Lady Ann Poyntz †1729, a descendant of Sir Julius Caesar. Plain classical surround. In the CLOISTER. (E–W). George Montacute †1681. Large classical surround with broken pediment. – Small tablets to sisters of St Katharine: Emily Wynyard †1832, Lucy Northey †1874, also George Baxter †1811, Rev. R.W. Baxter †1850. – Andrew Coltee Ducarel †1785. Simple oval with coat of arms. – William Waterson †1710. Inscription and coat of arms, surround lost. – Mrs Elizabeth Grigg †1760, erected 1792 signed by *Nollekens*. Large. Grieving putti on a rock with reversed torch, against grey-slate obelisk. – Mrs Pierce †1777. Inscription on feigned drapery held by large, rather clumsy putto. Armorial below. – Lt. Gen. Sir Herbert Taylor †1839. Gothic frame, military trophies below, armorial on base. Signed by *P. Rouw*. – Mary Louise Taylor †1845, scroll with dove. – In the vestibule. Joanna Caesar †1694, wife of John Rampayne. In an oval with flowers.

In the garden, Genesis, by *Naomi Blake* an abstract mother and child, fibreglass.

PERAMBULATIONS

1. Riverside

S of The Highway, the old centre of Shadwell around the church of St Paul (*see* above) was obliterated by the building of the

New Basin of the London Docks (*see* Wapping), reducing the population from 12,000 (1851) to about 9,000. The rest was cleared by the LCC for the EDWARD VII MEMORIAL PARK. Planned 1910, opened 1922 when it was the only park in Stepney. Landscape restored and improved by *Cooper Partnership* for the LDDC. – FOUNTAIN by *Sir Bertram McKennal.* On axis, a plain stone CENOTAPH (N) and a roofless, classical brick ROTUNDA, the air shaft of the Rotherhithe Tunnel (*see* Limehouse). Of 1904–8, it predates the park. In front of it, a roughly hewn MEMORIAL stone to 'Sir Hugh Willoughby . . . and other navigators who in the latter half of the sixteenth century set sail from this reach of the River Thames near Ratcliffe Cross'. Erected by the LCC, 1922. Porcelain plaque painted with galleons. – From the embankment, a magnificent view up and down river.

Just E along THE HIGHWAY, on the N side, the former NICHOLAS GIBSON SCHOOL of 1898, one of the oft-repeated three-deckers with Neo-Grec pediments. Gibson, a member of the Grocers' Company, founded *c.* 1536 the first Free School in Ratcliffe on the opposite side of Schoolhouse Lane. Later the Coopers' Company school (*see also* Bow, Upminster and Havering).

On the S side of The Highway the entrance to FREE TRADE WHARF, the only remnant by the river of the hamlet of Ratcliffe, is announced by a handsome gateway of 1846 (rebuilt 1934). It bears lions and the coat of arms of the East India Company, the original owners of the wharf, renamed after the Company closed in the 1830s. The Company housed saltpetre here, away from their main warehouses in Cutler Street (*see London 1: The City*). An explosion at the warehouses caused the disastrous Ratcliffe fire of 1794. The present elegant warehouses, facing each other across a long paved court, were built in 1795–6, probably by *Richard Jupp*, Company Surveyor. Enlarged in 1801 and 1828, much renewed inside since. Yellow brick, nine bays, with a tenth bay expressed as a pedimented two-storey pavilion to The Highway. The two lower floors embraced by an arcade, the first floor glazed in. Upper floor altered in the 1930s. Converted in 1985–7 to flats over offices by *Holder Mathias Alcock.* To the W lies the modern part of the scheme by the same architects, a huge development replacing other warehouses along the rest of Free Trade Wharf. Prominent piled-up red brick flats with layers of balconies facing the Thames.

2. *N and S of Commercial Road*

The walk begins at Limehouse Station and begins with exploration of the streets N of Commercial Road. Off FLAMBOROUGH STREET an extraordinary survival: FLAMBOROUGH WALK, a little row of stuccoed villas in a triangle of land by the railway line. Individually developed by the lessees of the plots from 1819–41 and, unlike neighbouring houses, set back from Commercial Road behind a meadow. Among them, Devonshire Cottage, of 1834, is dignified by giant Ionic pilasters. YORK SQUARE is the centre of the Mercers' development of *c.* 1825 by *George Smith*, tiny but complete with its surrounding streets of two-storey two-bay terraced houses with simple arched doorways. Acquired by the GLC in 1973, and among the first of such terraces to be renovated. They now present a very different image from the dingy, overcrowded scenes of the East End that prompted so much ruthless redevelopment. The boundary between Limehouse and Ratcliffe runs down Barnes Street, see the parish markers.

WHITE HORSE ROAD, reached via Wakeling Street, was the medieval route from Ratcliffe to St Dunstan's Church and known from the C14–C16 as Cliff Street. It was lined with houses by the early C17 when its name changed to White Hart Street. The W side begins with the former LIMEHOUSE DISTRICT BOARD OF WORKS OFFICES, 1862–4 by *C.R. Dunch*, Limehouse District Surveyor. Converted for Half Moon Youth Theatre in 1994 by *Wallbank & Morgan*. Heavy white-stucco five-bay front, of two storeys over deep basement, with a grossly decorated round-arched entrance beneath a portico on massive festooned brackets. Shallow loggia to first floor, behind slender Corinthian columns, with three segmental-arch windows with 'LDB' emblem. Pedimented windows to end bays framed by vertical bands of plain rustication, vermiculated at ground floor. The roofline was originally made lively by urns set on plinths. Separately constructed Board Room to the rear, its interior much damaged. Just beyond, the former HAMLET OF RATCLIFFE C.E. SCHOOL founded in 1710. Neo-Tudor of 1853–4, replacing a schoolhouse erected in 1719–20. Two storeys in brick with mullioned windows beneath hoodmoulds. Canted bay window over the entrance, into the sides of which are set two canopied niches, designed to hold charity figures of a boy and girl, now at Stepney Greencoat Primary (*see* Limehouse). Opposite, miscellaneous small houses and the White Horse pub. To the N, larger three-storey houses with stucco trim and entrances between fluted Ionic pilasters, then a curious Gothic set of flats. At the corner with Salmon Lane, the Vicarage built in 1882 for St Matthew's, Commercial Road (destroyed 1941, *see* London City Mission, Limehouse). Previously on the site was a house provided on Dean Colet's estate for the headmaster of St Paul's School.

SALMON LANE, an ancient way to Limehouse, has later Mercers' housing of *c.* 1845. At the N corner with White Horse Road is a tiny Nonconformist CEMETERY purchased in 1779 and vested in the Stepney Meeting House by the will of a local mariner Captain Truelove (†1691). Some good Georgian headstones and a single sarcophagus monument. It was originally attached to a set of almshouses. At White Horse Road's N end, facing the S side of St Dunstans' churchyard, are Mercers' Cottages of 1854–5 by *George Smith*, succeeding almshouses built in 1691 under the gift of Dame Jane Mico. Two storeys in a pale brick with projecting brick porches under stucco pediments.

To the E are a pair of former rope walks: BELGRAVE STREET retains terraces with stuccoed lower storeys on the W side; BROMLEY STREET, built up 1829–43 by *Daniel Goody*, has similar terraces on both sides. Between the two streets, a large 1990s development keeping to C19 scale. W of Bromley Street to the LCC's MONTMORRES ESTATE of 1957–63. This was a rebuilding of the badly-bombed area around AVIS SQUARE. Quiet, uneventful layout respecting traditional street patterns: the square itself was re-created, with cottagey two-storey pitched-roof terraces on three sides, surrounded by an outer square of four-storey maisonettes. A seventeen storey tower was included to bring the density to the required level. At the S end of Westport Street, at the corner with Commercial Road, the METHODIST CENTRAL HALL (*see* above), which grew out of the Wesleyan Seamen's Mission.

On the S side of COMMERCIAL ROAD, the former TROXY cinema, 1931–3 by *George Coles* and *Arthur Roberts*, tripartite front in pale faience with strong horizontal patterning. Unusually lavish auditorium, designed for 3,000, in French Art Deco style. Richly patterned ceiling with octagonal three-tier light fitting suspended from quasi-Egyptian feathers. Two large panels of cascading fountains flank the proscenium, panels at the rear are inset with dancing figures and between them smaller fountains in bowl light fittings. Well preserved despite conversions. Next door, the BREWER'S TAP, C19 stucco upper floors with emphatically pedimented windows.

W of the Troxy is the PITSEA ESTATE, where a dramatic composition by *Noel Moffett & Associates* builds up, with the glazed-staircase prow of a tall slab, Corringham House, thrusting above the ribbed concrete balconies and dark brick sawtooth frontage of Chalkwell House. The completion date of this is 1966, the time when the Brutalist aesthetic was gaining ground. Quieter low-rise parts of Pitsea estate S of the viaduct (*see* Cable Street, below). Tucked in next on Commercial Road, the ROYAL DUKE, 1879 by *W.E. Williams*, stucco-trimmed but down at heel, faces the homely post-war ROYAL DUCHESS opposite.

More Mercers' housing at Nos. 495–517, and slightly grander, Nos. 519–29; the arched doorways with quarter-fluted columns. The narrow oblong of land behind was laid out with ARBOUR SQUARE in the centre, and East and West Arbour Street running N to Aylward Street. In the square, terraces remain on S and W sides. The Mercers briefly considered rebuilding St Paul's School here, instead on the E side is the former Raine's Foundation School, now TOWER HAMLETS COLLEGE. 1913 by *Herbert O. Ellis*. Its older buildings survive in Wapping and Cannon Street Road. The school is now in Bethnal Green. A large building on a tight site, its height emphasized by rising directly from the pavement. A consciously ornate seven-bay front in brick and stone, mixing Wrenaissance, Baroque and Palladian detail. Assembly hall on the first floor with classrooms and workshops above, and an attic shooting gallery. The N side of the square was acquired in 1921 by the Borough of Stepney who proposed to build a grand town hall (design won in competition in 1909 by *Briggs Wolstenhome and Thornely*). Instead, the site was developed with flats: Arbour House, by *B.J. Belsher*, the Borough Surveyor, 1937 in a Modernistic style with curved balconies and stair towers. More C19 terraces remain further N in East and West Arbour Street. Between them was the church of St Thomas (demolished 1955) by *George Smith* and *William Barnes*, 1838, replaced by flats.

52 ALBERT GARDENS (formerly Albert Square), opening up to the S of Commercial Road, was another development responding to the creation of the new road. Three appealing terraces of simple three-storey houses with arched doorways and ground-floor windows face each other across a railed garden. In the gardens, iron plinth with DRINKING FOUNTAIN (initials D.F.F.) surmounted by an Arcadian figure of reaper with sheaf and sickle. Dated 1903 by 'Fonderies d'art du Val D'Orne . . . Paris'. To the E, Nos. 440–50, a four-storey group along Commercial Road. Two-storey terraces also remain on both sides of HAVERING STREET (W, concealed from Commercial Road by Sims House) which is brought up short by the railway: a classic vision of the C19 East End.

W of Arbour Square along Commercial Road, Rochelle Court (Nos. 485–9), 1938, described as 'the first of its kind for people in good circumstances residing in Stepney'.* A small group of flats over shops, then almost opposite, a long frontage including STEEL'S LANE HEALTH CENTRE (Nos. 384–96). This began in 1889 as the East End Mothers Home at No. 394, extending into neighbouring houses in 1908 and, later, the adjacent premises built as the Church Training College for Lay Workers, by *Young & Hall*, 1898 (altered 1925). This has windows with terracotta mullions and canted bays at either end. A chapel with trefoil-headed windows survives at the rear. Some good early C19 details on the remaining houses. No. 368, stuccoed, was a bank, now surgery.

Further W the main landmarks are a dignified Telephone Exchange on the N side, 1934–5 by the *Office of Works*, demonstrating how Georgian proportions and detail could be employed to good effect for such a building: a low ground floor with rusticated entrance, central window in an arched niche, and stone floor bands. W extension of the 1970s. The surrounding land to the N was acquired gradually in the 1950s for the GLC's EXMOUTH ESTATE (*see* also p. 463). From 1969 the C19 street pattern was replaced by an extensive grid of linked four- and five-storey slabs of flats and maisonettes, set among lawns, stretching N to Clark Street and abolishing most

*H. Clunn, *The Face of London*, 1951.

of Aylward Street, which followed the diagonal line of an old path to Stepney High Street. BRAYFORD SQUARE, a small pedestrian shopping area, is an addition of 1978 replacing C19 buildings along Commercial Road. Shops are tucked away among a low cluster of brown brick buildings with community facilities. Further W, the mid-C19 GEORGE TAVERN is set prominently at the corner of Jubilee Street, a handsome three-bay stucco face to its two fronts: arches to the ground floor, a central pediment at first floor, dentilled cornice, and bevelled corners with channelled quoins in French taste. Probably by *James Harrison*, 1862 with alterations by *R.A. Lewcock*, 1891.

South of Commercial Road

Opposite, the R.C. church and school of St Mary and St Michael (*see* above) the first of a group of Catholic foundations built to serve the Irish population of southern Stepney in the C19. In LUKIN STREET, the BISHOP CHALLONER SCHOOL has a long history in this district. Mostly 1980s, in yellow brick with dark trimming around the arched windows and big rooflights. Intriguingly extensive use of prefabricated classroom blocks to the S, like stacks of bright red building blocks.

S of the railway in JOHNSON STREET is the school's C19 predecessor, now MASTER'S LODGE, converted for flats in 1985–6 by *George Watt Partnership*. The earlier, vaguely Gothic, part of *c.* 1854 comprised a church and schools. Partially rebuilt and extended in 1905 to three and five storeys with a roof playground. The schools were associated with the Virginia Street chapel, Wapping (an early R.C. centre in the East End, rebuilt after destruction in the Gordon riots) and the buildings may have been used as a chapel of ease while St Mary and St Michael Commercial Road was under construction. The other buildings in Johnson Street are mostly associated with the social and educational provision of the Anglican church of St Mary, Cable Street (*see* above). On the W side: ALL SAINTS COURT and ST MARY'S CLERGY HOUSE, a symmetrical group with gabled wings and cut-away corner balconies. 1990s, built on the site of the C19 National Schools for St Mary's and Christ Church, *c.* 1840 by *George Smith*, surveyor to the Mercers' Company, whose badge is prominent on the other buildings in the street.

On the E side of the street, N of the Church Hall, St Mary's Mission Hall, later acquired by the Catholic church as a memorial to Cardinal Vaughan and renamed 'Our Lady's Hall'. The figure of the Virgin in a canopied niche may date from this time. Painted brick, with ground-floor arches, originally open for a playground, and central turret. 1906–7, probably by *R.L. Curtis* for local builder developer *A.M. Calnan*, who also erected Nos. 61–7, two-storeyed houses with Mercers' badge. In HARDINGE STREET to the E, *R.L. Curtis* was architect for the CONVENT OF MERCY, 1905–6; which provided teachers for the school in Johnson Street. Brick front with statue on a corbel against a projecting bay. Extended 1952 by *Roff Marsh*, with large window of obliquely set panels of glazing. Contemporary with the convent, *Curtis* also designed COBURG DWELLINGS, four-storey tenements.* At the corner with Cable Street THE SHIP, an attractive stucco-trimmed two-storey pub.

S of CABLE STREET is the GLAMIS ESTATE. The earliest part is at the S end towards The Highway and W of Glamis Road: Gordon House, a twenty-two storey tower block of 1963–5. Between this and Cable Street more innovative housing of 1976–7, one of the last major estates by the GLC, demonstrating the new concern for greater privacy and a more humane scale. Along Cable Street a low terrace in pale brick, with a strong rhythm of projecting glazed staircases to the upper flats. This apparent simplicity is misleading, for the quite steep slope behind is exploited by intricate three-dimensional planning, creating a dense multi-layered layout, the type of design experimented with after towers had fallen out of favour. On either side of the narrow TARBERT WALK flats are grouped around small enclosed green spaces, with garages below.

In GLAMIS ROAD (E side), the EVA ARMSBY FAMILY CENTRE, a friendly, transparent building in orange brick with much glazing. Built on the site of the East London Children's Hospital by *Robson Kelly Architects* for Tower Hamlets and the LDDC, 1994. From the foyer steps lead down to a long wing at a lower level. In CABLE STREET Nos. 432–46 on the S side, a humble terrace of early C19 dockers' houses with simple arched doorways was allowed to remain amongst a further stretch of the Glamis Estate, ending in the seven-storey Roslin House in BRODLOVE LANE. Further S, a Peabody estate of 1866, designed by *H.A. Darbishire*; the third of his estates for the Trust and following the pattern of four, six-storey blocks grouped around a courtyard which he pioneered at Islington (*see London 4: North*). N of Cable Street and extending beyond the railway viaduct, BARNARDO GARDENS ESTATE: a three-storey block of 1957, the rest completed 1969–71. Three to six storeys, buff brick with exposed concrete floors, with private gardens opening onto small walled communal spaces. Dr Barnardo founded his first boys' home in Stepney Causeway in 1870.

At the corner of STEPNEY CAUSEWAY, the KING'S ARMS, 1931 by *William Stewart* in pseudo-Dutch, is followed by late additions to the GLC's PITSEA ESTATE (*see* above) of 1978–9, and EDWARD MANN CLOSE, two interwar blocks, much refurbished with blue trimmings. Luxury flats have also appeared, a pertinent reminder of social change in the C21 East End. S of Cable Street in a largely industrial landscape, Cranford Cottages in CRANFORD STREET date from a modest slum clearance scheme by the *Housing of the Working Classes*

*Information on these buildings gratefully received from Mr D.P. Rigg.

Branch of the LCC Architects, 1898 (i.e. contemporary with Bethnal Green's Boundary Street estate). Two rows, each of two storeys, one-bay wide cottages with entrances paired within arched recesses. The cottages are hidden behind THAMES HOUSE, at the corner of Cable Street and BUTCHER ROW. 1919–22 by *E.J. Gosling* for Batger & Co., confectioners and cracker manufacturers. Baroque with corner dome and arched entrance to a long courtyard. Converted to galleries and studios after 1998. Almost opposite its entrance, the forlorn relic of the Ratcliffe Baths of 1900, with mullioned windows to a red brick gabled block.

Across Butcher Row lies the sole significant reminder of the hamlet of Ratcliffe as it was in the C18, the Royal Foundation of St Katharine (*see* above). N, close to the Limehouse DLR Station, JOHN SCURR HOUSE in Ratcliffe Lane; originally one of a pair, part of a small slum clearance scheme. Modernistic style of 1936–7 by *Adshead & Ramsey* for Stepney Borough Council. A six-storey U-plan. Central stair tower with glass brick inset and access balconies but also, unusual for the date, lifts to each floor. Refurbished in 1997 by *Architype* with funding from the LDDC, a showpiece embellishment of social housing with metal balustrades, render, black tiled walls and a subtly pitched roof.

LIMEHOUSE*

Limehouse gained its name from the lime kilns around Limekiln Dock, established in the C14 when chalk was brought from Kent to serve the London building industry. Stow in the C16 knew the hamlet as Lime Hurst. It then lay out in the country and housed a busy seafaring community. Late in the same century it specialized in shipbuilding and provisioning, with ropewalks out in the fields to the N of Fore Street (now the E end of Narrow Street).

The hamlet more than tripled in size within a hundred years (2,000 in 1610; 7,000 in 1710) and spread N. The surviving late C17–C18 houses in Narrow Street and the magnificent St Anne show the wealth and sophistication of at least some members of the burgeoning population. By the early C18 London had spread so far that Limehouse was now its easternmost suburb. In 1767–70 the Limehouse Cut was created by *Thomas Yeoman*, upon the recommendations of *John Smeaton*, to link the Thames to the Lea at Bromley-by-Bow. Industry followed along its banks. Then in 1820 the Regent's Canal Dock (Limehouse Basin) opened at the entrance to the Regent's Canal to handle huge amounts of coal and timber. New routes to the Docks – Commercial Road,

*The account of Limehouse is adapted from *London Docklands* by Elizabeth Williamson, 1998.

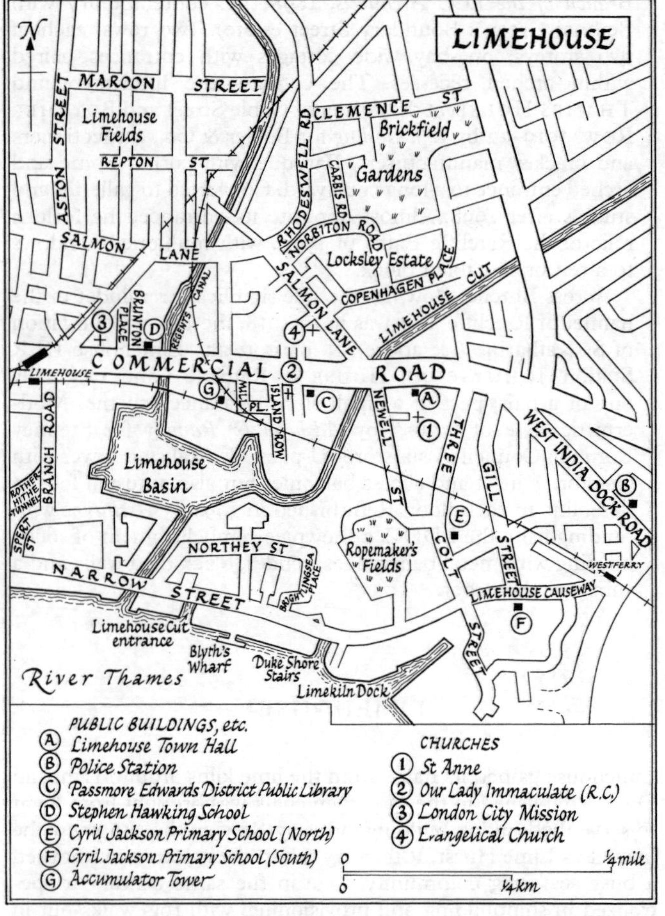

West India Dock Road and the London and Blackwall Railway – encouraged further industry and, associated with the river, large missions and hostels for sailors, the best of which survive. By 1880 the riverside had been built up with small warehouses and industrial buildings including the large Barley Mow Brewery and Stepney Power Station (all demolished). Limehouse also became notable for Chinatown, centred before the war on Limehouse Causeway, but this aspect of its cultural life waned with the closure of the staple riverside industries and the river-borne trades. Further change was already under way with the pioneering gentrification of Narrow Street's C17 and C18 houses from the late 1950s, followed in the 1970s by the conversion of decaying warehouses. Though a few factories remained into the

1980s, the decision to free Commercial Road of traffic by building the Limehouse Link (projected since the 1930s) relief road and to hide it beneath Limehouse Basin in a tunnel, has led to the riverside part of Limehouse becoming distinctly exclusive and residential. Speculative houses and flats have joined those in converted warehouses and in refurbished council blocks, a process of regeneration extended to the inland council estates N of Commercial Road in the 1990s, most notably at Stepney's Limehouse Fields Estate, where low-rise housing and varied planning hails a return to the scale of the C19 East End.

RELIGIOUS BUILDINGS

ST ANNE, Commercial Road. One of *Hawksmoor*'s three great East End churches. Like St George-in-the-East and Christ Church Spitalfields, begun in 1714. The steeple was built in 1718–19, the church furnished 1723–5 but not consecrated until 1730. The master mason was *Edward Strong Jun*. The composition is as original as that of St George, but the vocabulary is more conventional and elaborate, the mouldings all exquisitely carved and enriched. The W tower is a spectacular sight from a distance. It has nothing of the routine character or skimpiness which so often spoil the appearance of later Georgian towers. The tower is neither embraced by the body of the church, as at Christ Church Spitalfields, nor projects from it, as at St George. Instead it is incorporated in a 'westwork' of vestibules, with attics pedimented to N and S and, below these, strongly rusticated quoins. The front has no portico, but instead an apsidal projection, the expression of a circular vestibule within the tower base. (Colvin suggests the portico might have been inspired by one of Montana's published versions of ancient temples.) The upper part of the tower is like St George's in shape, rectangular and appearing from the W wider than it really is, by means of buttresses grouped with the tower's angle pilasters and far projecting to the N and S. A bell-opening, its arch rising above the main entablature, echoes the dome of the vestibule below. The octagonal top is the equivalent perhaps of a medieval lantern, very Baroque in its changes of direction but with no sinuous flourishes at all. Groups of square piers as buttesses. Even the finials and urns have a consistent angularity. The order applied to all stages is a dignified Doric. The sides of the church, also stone-faced, 18 are very restrained in adornment, as always with Hawksmoor. Tall arched gallery windows over squarish ones, below which are windows to the high crypt, perhaps intended for use as a school, now a clubroom. E and W bays are slightly recessed, expressing the internal arrangement. Cockerell's drawings show three recesses over the centre of the sides which are no longer there. The E wall has a triumphal-arch motif, repeating the Doric order of the front. The flanking E vestries have rusticated angle quoins to match the 'westwork' and curiously brutal rectangular angle towers; their interlaced ornament seems to follow no historical precedent. An early drawing shows them capped by pyramidal or domed tops, and in between, a statue of Queen Anne within an aedicule (rejected by the Commission on grounds of cost).

The interior was gutted by fire in 1850, and reconstructed by *Philip Hardwick* and the local *John Morris*, 1850–1. Restoration (surprisingly faithful to the original) resumed under *P.C. Hardwick* in 1856–7, with reseating and pulpit by Hardwick's pupil, the young *Arthur Blomfield*. In 1891, as *Sir A. Blomfield*, he remodelled the chancel. Restoration 1983–93 by *Julian Harrap*, when tubular-steel trusses by *Hockley & Dawson*, consulting engineers, were added to support the C19 roof. This, with its wrought-iron hanger rods, closely resembles those used by the Hardwicks in the Great Hall of Euston Station in 1846 and conforms to a pattern favoured by the builder of the church, *William Cubitt*.

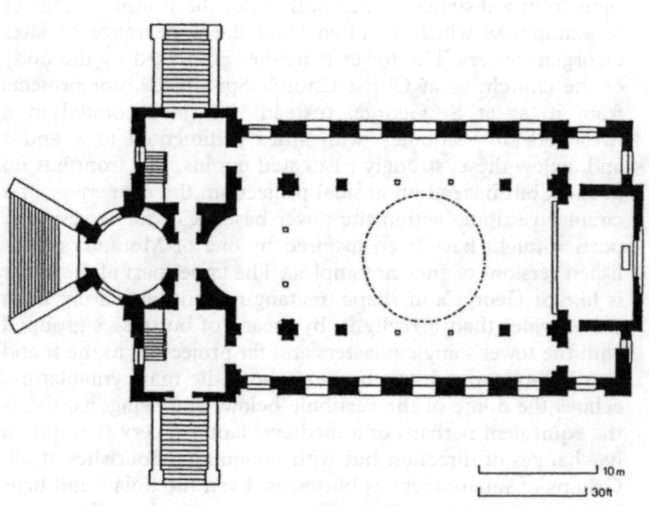

St Anne, Limehouse, plan

The circular vestibule is domed, stone-lined and lit with a clear even light from big arched upper windows. From it, a disappointing entrance to the church, oppressed by *Hardwick*'s organ gallery. The interior, as was the case at St George, is less inventive than the exterior. It is developed from the cross-in-square plan of, e.g. Wren's St Anne and St Agnes. To E and W an additional bay. The E bay is the prelude to the broad, rectangular and tunnel-vaulted chancel, flanked by vestries; in the chancel walls, quartets of arched windows, pierced by *Blomfield*, 1891. His chancel seating has gone. The W bay emphasizes the longitudinal direction and hints at a narthex, perhaps a reference to the arrangements of Early Christian churches, in which Hawksmoor and contemporary theologians were interested. The Corinthian order is used throughout. The main columns and entablature are of stone, timber columns support the galleries. *Hardwick*'s intervention is most obvious in the heaviness of the plasterwork and W gallery (screen beneath) carrying an ORGAN by *Gray & Davison*, which won a prize at the Great Exhibition of 1851 and was installed soon after. Fortunately unaltered. – FONT by *Hardwick* and *Morris*, 1853. Discordant Neo-Medieval stone bowl carved with big lilies. Neo-C17 font cover, post-1894. – PULPIT. By *Blomfield*, 1856, carved by *William Gibbs Rogers*. Faithful C18 style, unusual at this date. It originally stood further E and was reached from the chancel by a long flight of stairs. – COMMUNION TABLE. C18, small, oak. – STAINED GLASS in the E window: large and richly coloured scene of the Crucifixion, painted in enamels by *Charles Clutterbuck*, 1853. – MONUMENT. In the porch, high up in a niche, monument to Maria Charlesworth, apparently C19. Hope with her anchor. The CRYPT has beautifully constructed groin-vaults in red brick.

The approach to the W front is via Newell Street, through a passage between houses. In the CHURCHYARD, the most interesting monument is a remarkable PYRAMID, NW of the church. Panelled in stone and inscribed with 'The Wisdom of Solomon' in English and Hebrew with a weathered armorial shield below. A mid-C19 print shows that it formerly stood on a square plinth, *cf.* the Raine monument at St George-in-the-East. – WAR MEMORIAL. Blessing Christ in bronze on a tall pedestal with a harrowing relief of a corpse-filled no-man's-land. By *Arthur G. Walker*, unveiled 1921. – Dozens of half-buried ledger slabs line the perimeter wall, taken from demolished tomb chests, an indication of the C18 affluence of this parish. – RAILINGS. Reproduced to original design in the 1980s.

OUR LADY IMMACULATE with St Frederick (R.C.), Commercial Road. Designed 1925 by *A.J. Sparrow*, completed 1934, replacing a temporary church of 1881 by *H.J. Hanson*. Austere exterior of dark red brick over a black brick plinth, with windowless apse towards the road, small arched side windows, and NW campanile with copper pyramid roof. Surmounting the end of the nave, raised up on a plinth, a chunky oak statue of Christ the Steersman, designed to be seen from the river. In front of the church, bronze SCULPTURE: Christ Crucified, with low relief panels on both front and back. 1997 by *Sean Henry*, made by *Bronze Age*, a local foundry. On the apse, memorial to Father Higley (†1934), builder of the church.

The elegant classical interior with its play of curves is a surprise; plastered walls, barrel ceiling pierced by ample clerestory windows. Round-arched arcades on square piers and apse, above them an emphatic horizontal cornice, continuing around the apse. W gallery, bowing forward (side galleries were planned but rejected). Contemporary FURNISHINGS in yellow Sicilian marble: High Altar, Pulpit, octagonal Font. SCULPTURE: Our Lady of Grace, French C19, finely carved white marble, from Sisters of Charity convent, Mill Hill, now effectively set against a silkscreen print with red oval on blue, by *Pauline Corfield*, *c.* 2000. Small carved wooden figure of St John Roche, shown as a boatman. PAINTINGS. Crucifixion, by *Armando Seijo*, *c.* 1999. STATIONS OF THE CROSS, on canvas over copper. Flemish late-Gothic style, by *Louis Beyaert-Carier* of Belgium (b.1876), erected 1935. STAINED GLASS. Several saints; by the stairs to the gallery, a good circular window (St Joseph).

Below the church a HALL, and to the S, PRESBYTERY, 1934; an adjoining convent was intended.

LONDON CITY MISSION. Built as DANISH SEAMEN'S CHURCH, Commercial Road and Yorkshire Road. 1958–9 by the Danish architect *Holger Jensen* in association with *Armstrong & MacManus*. The church forms one corner of a compact block with social rooms and minister's accommodation. Dark brick, given character by asymmetrical copper monopitch roofs, which intersect to provide clerestory lighting for the church. Inside, the church is a small space with plain brick walls and a gallery. Good STAINED GLASS by *Palle Bruun*. Sliding doors connect the church to the main room which has a big fireplace and two lancets with C19 glass (SS Michael and Uriel) from a previous church.

SALMON LANE EVANGELICAL CHURCH, Salmon Lane. 1970s. Dark brick, entrance in the three-storey end, the church to its r. with large hexagonal clerestory windows below a zigzagging roof. Hall in basement.

MAJOR BUILDINGS

Former LIMEHOUSE TOWN HALL, Commercial Road. 1879–81 by *A. & C. Harston*. A white brick palazzo with stone dressings. Arched moulded windows, channelled angle piers, central pediment and strong projecting cornice; chimneys rising from stone aprons on the face of the building. Projecting doorcase with polished granite columns.

LIMEHOUSE POLICE STATION, West India Dock Road. Of c. 1940 by *G. Mackenzie Trench*, Metropolitan Police Architect. Large, handsome and well planned. Brick and streamlined in a pre-war Dutch way, but with up-to-date touches, see the bold angle tower with snapped headers to Birchfield Street. Courtyard with large section house behind.

PASSMORE EDWARDS DISTRICT PUBLIC LIBRARY, Commercial Road. 1900–1 by *J. & S.F. Clarkson*. Stone except for the yellow brick upper-outer bays with shaped gables. Two storey with attics in gables. Behind, the main library looks post-1945. – Large MURAL of Limehouse Reach by *Claire Smith*, 1986. An androgynous angel broods over a Turneresque river with unpleasant flotsam. – In front, Clement Attlee, Prime Minister 1945–51 and Member for Limehouse 1922–50. A touchingly prosaic portrait in bronze, 1988, by *Frank Forster*, who won a GLC competition in 1986.

CYRIL JACKSON SCHOOL. In two parts; the earlier building in Three Colt Street, completed c. 1973 for ILEA by the *GLC Architect's Department*. Hipped-roof brick building, an early example of the softer, more vernacular approach adopted for some schools in the 1970s. The later part is in Limehouse Causeway, of 1991–5 by *Robert Byron Architects*. A wilful composition, with walls at different angles and a profiled metal roof like folded paper.

STEPHEN HAWKING SCHOOL, Brunton Street. 1997 by *Haverstock Associates*. A special needs school. Single storey, on a T-shaped plan, with steel superstructure and external walls in stock brick. Its profile is defined by an elegant butterfly-pitch roof along the spine. Monopitch roofs abut it on both sides to form glass clerestories providing light for the internal corridors and communal spaces. These are flanked by long classrooms, each opening to outdoor play spaces. Secure looking but not severe or forbiddingly institutional.

PERAMBULATIONS

1. Limehouse Riverside: Limehouse DLR to St Anne's Church

The walk begins at LIMEHOUSE DLR STATION, first built as Stepney Station on the London & Blackwall Railway (opened in 1839–40, *see* below). Crossing COMMERCIAL ROAD is the extension originally built in 1847–9 to link up with the Great Eastern Railway at Bow but later rebuilt by the London & Tilbury railway. In two parts: the short bridge over Bekesbourne Street is by *Joseph Westwood*, engineers, 1889, the main viaduct of 1874–6 by *Langley*. Beneath the bridge are blocked entrances to the station with bold voussoirs. Then pinched into the angle of the bridge and the DLR is BRUNSWICK TERRACE (Nos. 583–8), a handsome group of four (originally six) houses of c. 1820–30; some of the grandest to survive in Commercial Road. In their setting they seem worthy of a scene by Doré or Dickens and determined to keep up appearances. Three storeyed, with honeysuckle balconies, doorways with fanlights and Greek Doric columns. Opposite, the London City Mission, then Stephen Hawking School (*see* above). Parallel with the S side of Commercial Road is the VIADUCT of the London & Blackwall railway (refurbished in 1984–7 for the DLR) crossing the Limehouse Basin (*see* below). By *George & Robert Stephenson* and *G.P. Bidder*, 1839–40. Three magnificent segmental brick arches, each spanning 85 ft (26 metres). Original cast-iron railings.

BRANCH ROAD leads towards the Rotherhithe Tunnel. Close to its entrance is a low single-storey Neo-Georgian building of 1912 built 'to commemorate the 30th Anniversary of the inauguration of the Finnish Seamen's mission in London'. Cut brick voussoirs and dressings, refurbished with a copper-clad mansard roof.

ROTHERHITHE TUNNEL by *Sir Maurice Fitzmaurice* 1904–8, renovated 1979–81, is 4,680 ft long with a 27 ft internal diameter. Imaginatively re-erected over the entrance is one of the flanged-and-bolted cutting edges of the tunnelling shields (its pair frames the entrance of the Rotherhithe side). Polished pink-granite piers to the portal. Crossing the tunnel entrance is a graceful cable-stayed footbridge, which links gardens on each side and provides a route to the Foundation of St Katharine at Ratcliffe (*see* p. 519) The gardens on this side were built over the LIMEHOUSE LINK TUNNEL of 1989–93 (engineers *Sir Alexander Gibb & Partners*) whose immense, stripy pink and buff stone PORTAL designed by *Rooney O'Carroll* with *Anthony Meats* houses the services and make a dramatic Postmodern statement in its surroundings. Powerful and muscular close-up with strongly sculptural steps to the gardens. Above the tunnel entrance on the W side, a SCULPTURE, Restless Dream, by *Zadok Ben-David*, huge but lightly done in painted aluminium. A silhouetted sleeping figure dreams of dozens of tiny active figures whirling in a circle above.* The tunnel was built to link The Highway with new roads on the Isle of Dogs instead of an overground relief road which would have destroyed Limehouse. A worthwhile but exceptionally expensive endeavour, requiring the construction of an open cofferdam behind Limehouse Basin and the rehousing of 556 households.

S of here NARROW STREET follows the river for nearly half a mile. On the S side former riverside warehouses, of various dates, are quite small, up to five storeys and only a few bays wide. Nos. 22–8 were among the first to be converted for

*The EAST SERVICE BUILDING, over the sliproads to Westferry Road, has On Strange and Distant Lands by *Michael Kenny*. Impressive geometric monoliths of Kilkenny limestone. On the NORTH QUAY PORTAL in Aspen Way, an untitled abstract of interlinked Cor-Ten steel bars by *Nigel Hall*.

residential use in Docklands, a thoughtful work by the designer *Rae Hoffenberg* (with architects *Berman & Guedes*) in a phased development from 1976. Industrial zoning had to be overturned here to permit change of use (cf. Oliver's Wharf, Wapping). COMMERCIAL WHARF (No. 24) was the earliest conversion, completed 1980. Internal timber and ironwork retained. No. 28 was also industrial, with its roof timbers retained in the rebuilt upper floor; see the interesting details in blue bull-nosed brick. SUN WHARF (No. 30) is a lavish and unusual scheme by *Scott, Brownrigg & Turner*, 1983–5, for the film-maker Sir David Lean, which shares the romantic approach to derelict industrial areas then popular amongst landscape designers and architects in continental Europe. A house and garden created from four C19 warehouses, two of them left as burnt-out shells. After that a long stretch of Narrow Street has been spoilt by ostentatious speculative flats packed on to restricted sites.

LIMEHOUSE BASIN, the former Regent's Canal Dock, opens up on the N side. Now a marina surrounded by largely indifferent housing of the 1980s and later, the dock was created 1812–20 by the Regent's Canal Company as a barge basin at the mouth of the Regent's Canal. At first it linked the Grand Junction at Paddington with the Thames but later became the gateway into the whole of Britain's canal system. Enlarged in 1819 to receive ships, and again in 1852–3 to compete with Poplar Dock (*see* Isle of Dogs). Hydraulic power for cranes was installed then, possibly the first use of this technology in the docks. Coal jetties and, later, low-rise warehouses stood all round it but these have gone and the wonderful site wasted in the later development. The housing in GOODHART PLACE, by *Richard Seifert & Partners* 1985–6, is gimmicky and matched by a ludicrous timber and brick pagoda for the HARBOURMASTER'S STATION of 1989 by *Peter White* and *Jayne Holland* of the British Waterways Board. On the N side are four prominent but banal blocks (Marina Heights). The better housing, on the W and E sides by *RMA Architects*, has been added since the late 1990s. Decent groups of appropriate scale with speckled brick patterning and balconies on I-beams, and two landmark white-walled blocks including The Pinnacle with sail-like section, designed as a baffle to the railway along the N side. On the E side, facing Island Row, are straightforward terraced houses with balconies to the waterside and a taller block.

Now along the part of NARROW STREET E of the Limehouse Basin. By the S entrance lock is the former Dockmaster's House *c.* 1905–10, now the NARROW STREET PUB. Queen Anne style, red brick. Across the dock entrance a SWING BRIDGE of steel box-girder construction, by *Husband & Company*, 1962. Further down NARROW STREET, No. 48, a late C18 house by the disused bell-mouthed entrance to the tidal entrance lock of the LIMEHOUSE CUT, created in 1770 to connect the Thames with the River Lea at Bromley-by-Bow.

Diverted through the Regent's Canal Dock in 1853–64; the Cut's opening is crossed by a wrought-iron girder bridge of 1865. Part of the lock is also preserved on the N side as a shallow water feature, lined by a late C19 row of former LOCK-KEEPERS' COTTAGES. Preserved parapets of another bridge, *c.* 1865, carry Northey Street across the N end of the lock.

Several riverside wharfs are partly preserved along the S side of Narrow Street but there is nothing of interest before BLYTH'S WHARF, idiosyncratic houses of 1985–6 by *Heber-Percy & Parker Architects*, set back behind a wall and trees. Slight bow over the passage to the former coaling wharf which projects into the river, built in 1923 for colliers delivering to Stepney Power Station. On the riverfront, a gabled, bowed and weatherboarded top floor echoes the character of houses seen in views of the C18 riverside.

Facing on the N side is THE WATERGARDEN (formerly ROY SQUARE), built on the site of the Power Station, a more rigorous interpretation of Georgian urban housing by *Ian Ritchie Architects*, 1986–8. Long, introverted courtyard of flats, raised on a tall car park podium, screened by gridded bay windows of studios and workshops. The entrance is via a narrow entrance slot of steps, edged with rills, which lead up to the lush courtyard garden, bisected by a canal and enclosed by crisp pavilions of flats and maisonettes and lower, glass-walled stair links. To its E BRIGHTLINGSEA PLACE, with a refurbished tenement, Faraday House, built by *B.J. Belsher* of Stepney Borough Council in 1931. Modernistic with curved stair tower.

Narrow Street now opens out into a charming wedge of open space, laid out by the LDDC, 1994 with Indian bean trees and seats; screaming copper HERRING GULL on a coil of rope by *Jane Ackroyd*, 1994. Prominent on the N side, a well-designed stock brick terrace of four houses by *Proctor Matthews Architects*, 1992–6. Four houses paired by two-storey window units and balconies in layers. Rooftop terraces and plain rear elevations with long windows. It takes its cue from THE HOUSE THEY LEFT BEHIND, the plain, late Georgian-style pub that remains from a previous mid-C19 terrace. Beyond, ROPEMAKER'S FIELDS is open space named after the several ropewalks that lay N of Narrow Street before the C19. Landscaped by the *LDDC* and *Churchman Associates.* Sturdy rope-moulded railings and a bandstand which incorporates cast-iron columns saved from one of the former warehouses at St Katharine Docks.

THE GRAPES introduces the long run of C17 to early C18 houses (Nos. 78–94) on the S side of Narrow Street, with a slightly later two-bay stock brick façade. This row is one of the most picturesque in Docklands. The houses are remarkable as rare survivals of this type of riverside dwelling in the area. Well-preserved façades, the shuttered lower floors formerly shops or stores. The backs, looking on to riverside gardens, have been much altered.

First (Nos. 78–86), a ten-bay, slightly cranked row of four early C18 houses, apparently built *c.* 1718 by Thomas Wakelin of Ratcliffe. Stock brick, with red brick dressings including the strings. Flush segment-headed sashes on two storeys in pairs. In the attic, similar smaller windows centred over each pair and narrow blind panels between them. No. 80 has a rusticated ground floor with arched door and window, perhaps early C19.

No. 88 has a painted two-bay front, apparently a C19 recasting with moulded window surrounds and cornices on consoles poised over them: early C19 shopfront. No. 90 is plain, also early C19, and two bay. No. 92 (BOOTY'S BAR), the least altered of these early houses, still has much original fabric (probably late C17), including the roof. The segment-headed sash windows have rubbed brick voussoirs and keystones topped by a narrow moulding. One smaller window below a small central gable. Another plain gable to the rear, shown as a shaped gable in a late C19 photo, though perhaps not as original. The plan seems late C17 too, with one-and-half flights of the original stairs flanking the central chimney. Original cupboards in the alcoves formed by the chimney.

Continuing the row of houses, an early C19 barge-building works (No. 94), where barges were repaired until the early 1950s. Dwelling over the double-height ground floor with a big archway through it. A timber-mould loft used to straddle the yard on the riverside. DUKE SHORE STAIRS was the lowest point on this side of the river for passenger embarkation. Pepys came here in 1660 to be ferried upriver to the Tower of London. No. 98 has a sturdy early C20 shopfront and C19 No. 100 still has its original cast-iron windows and loading doors (with wall-crane) on the ground and first floors. At No. 102 a four-storey early to mid-C18 house, heavily restored, and at DUKE SHORE WHARF flats by *Barnard Urquhart Jarvis*, 1985–8, that pick up the arch motif from No. 94. At the back a big drum of flats with good and contrasting views that can be shared by pedestrians on the riverfront here.

Further E, Nos. 136–40, the well-converted DUNBAR WHARF, a two- to three-storey mixture, with cast-iron and sash windows, loading doors, wall-cranes and sail loft; the rear boarded at No. 136. These small early C19 warehouses formerly belonged to Duncan Dunbar & Sons which ran a famous fleet of fast sailing ships to India, Australia and North America. They back on to the tidal inlet LIMEKILN DOCK. Continuing along Narrow Street, ST DUNSTAN'S WHARF of 1878 at No. 142, has just the gable front with decorative moulded brick plaque; the rest has been rebuilt. Nearer the head of the inlet, LIMEHOUSE WHARF (Nos. 148–50) still conveys atmosphere. It is mid-C19, of three storeys and five bays, with original loading doors and cast-iron windows. Last on this side at the corner of Three Colt Street, a former pub of *c.* 1850 (No. 154), still with its pilastered front and Corinthian aedicules round the upper windows. At the corner a curious half-figure of a cherub holds a pyramid in its hand. THREE COLT STREET is also one of the original streets of Limehouse at its S end was the Lime House (for this and other buildings between here and the river *see* Isle of Dogs, perambulation 2).

The W end of LIMEHOUSE CAUSEWAY was realigned and widened in 1904. On the S side, the contemporary POTTER DWELLINGS, early Stepney Borough Council housing, an L-shaped three-storey block in yellow and red brick, glazed brick stairs to access balconies at the rear. To the N Stepney's ROCHE ESTATE, built from the 1930–50s, offers the same recipe, but on five storeys. Prominent just W of Three Colt Street is the BARLEYMOW ESTATE built after 1960 on the site of Taylor Walker's Barley Mow Brewery, founded in 1730. When built, the estate was one of the few examples in Tower Hamlets of the GLC's flirtation with industrialized building. Now the towers and lower blocks are crisply white-clad, the result of an energy-efficient refurbishment by *ECD Architects* for the LDDC and Tower Hamlets, 1989–93. The blocks of various heights edge Three Colt Street, as it continues N of Limehouse Causeway. Close by is the older part of CYRIL JACKSON SCHOOL (*see* above). Finally, tucked in N of the railway, the former LIMEHOUSE CHURCH INSTITUTE, 1903–4 by *W.H. White*, a Free Baroque front in pale terracotta, boldly lettered. Now converted to flats. Its neighbour, the FIVE BELLS AND BLADE BONE, has an unaffected C19 pub exterior.

2. *Around St Anne's Church and N of Commercial Road, ending at Limehouse Station*

To the W of St Anne (*see* above), ST ANNE'S PASSAGE leads to NEWELL STREET, the remains of the smart C18 quarter around the church. No. 11, at the corner, is the largest house; open-pedimented doorcase with delicate brackets to the side; a bow to the front. Nos. 13–23 are all two-storey and three-bay; No. 21 is stuccoed. On the W side, overlooking Limehouse Cut, an early detached villa at Nos. 2–4, converted *c.* 1850 for use as a training establishment for boys. The E façade still has a tin plaque reading British and Foreign Sailors' Society. Off-centre entrance through a low forebuilding articulated to the street with a row of blind arches. Later C19 extension with paired arched first-floor windows (for a chapel?). Built into the S boundary odd little later C20 houses (Nos. 6a–b) roofed in big pantiles and with an Italianate tower.

COMMERCIAL ROAD sliced off the N corner of the churchyard. The road attracted the principal public buildings and new amenities for the old hamlet. E of Three Colt Street, a former London Joint Stock Bank (No. 660), tall and classical; angled entrance at the corner with Gill Street. Rusticated ground floor, upper floors with giant Corinthian columns of polished granite. Then housing of 2000, by *Baily Garner*; shallow curved roof. Next door is the former PASSMORE EDWARDS SAILORS

PALACE (No. 680), HQ of the British and Foreign Sailors Society, an unusually pretty building of 1901 by *Niven &* 77
Wigglesworth, two architects always worth watching for. The façade's chief motif is a very Arts and Crafts 'gatehouse', as at Townsend's Bishopsgate Institute and Whitechapel Art Gallery. Octagonal flanking turrets, a flat three-storey rectangular oriel and lavish carving on a nautical theme, including a regal figurehead keystone (presumably Britannia) grasping two galleons, flanked by the names of the winds, finely lettered. A rope moulding twisted around the names of the continents, and delicate reliefs of seagulls touching down lightly on the waves as label stops. Anchors, dolphins, shields etc., embossed on the metal panels here and on the side to Beccles Street, which is articulated by flattened bays projecting slightly over a segmental arcade of windows. W wing rebuilt *c.* 1960. Converted into flats 1983–4 by *Shankland Cox* for Rodinglea Housing Association. Next door in Beccles Street, plain early C19 houses, which look like a pair but have only one doorway. At the start of WEST INDIA DOCK ROAD, No. 14, the former German Sailors' Home of 1910, by *George and W. Charles Waymouth* for Sir J.H.W. Schroder; red brick and stuccoed, some relief garlands in the gabled bays, and a tiny oriel within the entrance arch. Accommodation for fifty men in rooms partitioned by reinforced-concrete walls. On the E side, No. 11, THE SAILMAKER BUILDING, erected 1860, as a sailmakers and shipchandlers, according to the lettering on the string course. Three-bay pedimented façade like a tall Nonconformist chapel. Interior altered, with new floor levels.

Now from E–W along the N side of COMMERCIAL ROAD; its C19 character especially complete here, compared with the stretches further E. First Nos. 815–21, an early C19 terrace with the common motif of first floor windows within arches. Then a more varied group: No. 811 is a tiny two-storey building, with shopfront elaborately lettered for a funeral director. The dominant centrepiece is the colourfully detailed later C19 front of the STAR OF THE EAST pub. Its first floor has Gothic arches in groups of three and two, with voussoirs of red and white stone against terracotta diapering. In the centre a second floor with smaller five-arched arcade. Carved heads in all the tympana. Adjacent to the W, No. 803, only two bays, but elaborately stuccoed, with garlands above the top windows.

Further W, hugging the curve around St Anne's churchyard, and backing on to the Limehouse Cut, a group of red brick industrial buildings (Nos. 777–85), the former offices and engineering workshops of Caird & Rayner, a firm established 1889, which specialized in evaporators and condensers for distilling seawater.* No. 785 dates largely from 1902–3, by *Marshall & Bradley*. Then Nos. 779–83, 1896–7 by the same firm; three-storey offices to the road, with central archway leading into a

*We owe the following details to Tom Ridge.

rare survival, a large steel-framed, galleried engineering workshop with integral travelling crane gantry. The galleries are top lit with pitched glazed roofs. No. 777 has an office building of 1893–4 in front of a workshop converted in 1889 from a sailmaker's and shipchandler's warehouse and sail loft of 1869. Original timber upper floor on strutted timber posts; queen-rod roof trusses. Loading door at first-floor level.

W of Limehouse Cut at the corner of Salmon Lane, THE MISSION, the former Empire Memorial Sailors' Hostel, by *Thomas Brammall Daniel & Horace W. Parnacott*, 1923–4; Salmon Lane wing 1932 by *George Baines & Son*. A stripped Perp exterior on a cathedral-like scale. The inspiration must have been the Sailors' Palace down the road. The stone-clad façades, with vertical strips of window and seaweedy foliage carving, masked completely plain interiors round a courtyard; subdivided as flats in 1989. From here one can take in the principal public buildings of Limehouse on the S side of Commercial Road, the Town Hall and further on, the Library and R.C. church.

North of Commercial Road

SALMON LANE, an old route leading towards the centre of Stepney, was named after Robert Salmon, local landowner and Master of Trinity House. It became a shopping street for the small district of houses built up in the C19. NE, filling the area between the Limehouse Cut and the Regent's Canal is the LOCKSLEY ESTATE, begun in the 1950s by the LCC immediately following their work at Lansbury (*see* p. 651), with housing for over 3000. *Walter Bor* was architect-planner in charge, *E. Humphrey* the architect-in-charge. As at Lansbury, the intention was to create a neighbourhood which excluded through-traffic and where amenities and housing were provided in buildings of mixed sizes. Starting from Salmon Lane, and continuing around COPENHAGEN PLACE one sees first hefty maisonette blocks, added in the 1970s and typical of the GLC era; red brick with exposed-concrete floors and linking upper walkways. This late addition replaced industrial buildings along Limehouse Cut. Further up Salmon Lane are low blocks of flats with balconies extending over shops neatly framed by black tiles, 1957–8.

NORBITON ROAD leads E with pleasantly detailed three-storey blocks, also of 1957–8, pale brick panels, glazed private balconies, shallow-pitched roofs; Midhurst House curves to the street line, and there is further variety provided by two-storey cottage terraces in CARBIS ROAD, a badly bomb-damaged area. Simple PRIMARY SCHOOL (Stepney Greencoat C.E.) of one and two storeys. 1970, successor to the Hamlet of Ratcliffe charity school. BRICKFIELDS GARDENS, the heart of the estate, is a figure-of-eight green, designed to provide a continuous link to the grander open space to the N which was to be realized when St George's Fields was linked to Mile End Park. Two big eight-storey blocks of 1954–6, REDBOURN HOUSE (S) and GATWICK HOUSE further N, have on their access sides a strong abstract pattern created by the solid and railed balconies; crowned by two curved lift towers on the roof. Quieter on the other side, which has recessed private balconies and generous living-room windows. In the garden in front of Gatwick, the novelty of a concrete play sculpture in Festival of Britain spirit: GULLIVER, a stylized figure by *Trevor Tennant*, now sadly battered. CLEMENCE STREET remains to show the modest mid-C19 character of the original streets; small stucco-trimmed terraces, two storeys over basements, with the more elaborate Prince Alfred pub. Returning along RHODESWELL ROAD, the five-storey DORA HOUSE of 1939 is a solitary example of the LCC's pre-war Neo-Georgian manner. Opposite is a forbidding six-storey range of GLC maisonnettes, completed 1976, but pleasantly landscaped on the side to the canal.

REGENT'S CANAL can be reached close to the railway bridge over Rhodeswell Road, built *c.* 1876 for the London, Tilbury & Southend line, and the walk can continue S along the tow path to Limehouse Basin. Just N of the bridge is a tall brick sewer vent built *c.* 1906 by the LCC. S is Salmon Lane Lock with a lock and pump house of 1864. Bridging this a footbridge of the 1990s with two bowstring sections. Further on, a small two-arched BRIDGE of 1820 carries Commercial Road across the canal, followed by twin LOCKS beneath the splendid viaduct of the former London and Blackwall railway. A 1990s FOOTBRIDGE now spans the canal at the entrance to Limehouse Basin making it possible to walk back to the DLR station. (For the buildings around the basin, see perambulation 1.)

Alternatively a short detour can be taken E to MILL PLACE, where tucked in hard against the viaduct is the ACCUMULATOR TOWER associated with a hydraulic pumping station built in 1868–9 to serve the ship lock at the Basin. A most impressive survival and, as renovated by *Dransfield Design* 1994–5, accessible to the public. Octagonal tower, with slit windows, and an octagonal N chimneystack. It has a huge riveted wrought-iron weight-case, 24 ft (7.25 metres) high, which held some 80 tons of gravel. This weight-case, which was driven up the tower to maintain the hydraulic pressure by steam engines under the viaduct, has been fitted with a helical iron staircase to an exhibition area and, at the top, a viewing platform. The last part of the walk can return to Limehouse Station along Commercial Road under the wrought-iron trussed BRIDGE, built on the Limehouse Curve in 1880 as an additional link between the London and Blackwall Railway and its extension to Bow. In its shadow are several good terraces of early C19 houses, contemporary with the original development of Commercial Road.

BETHNAL GREEN

Bethnal Green, thought to derive from the Anglo-Saxon Blithehale, was a hamlet of the manor of Stepney until 1743. There was settlement in the C13 and a chapel of ease was already established in 1512. Like Mile End, the hamlet became the haunt of wealthy merchants and courtiers in the Middle Ages and the Tudor and Stuart period. They erected mansions around the common land of the Green itself, which lay on either side of the road between Mile End and Hackney (now Cambridge Heath Road). Only Netteswell House survives in part, begun originally for Sir Ralph Warren in the 1540s, but early country houses included not only the manor house belonging to the Bishops of London (slightly NE of the Green, known for much of its history as Bonner Hall, dem. 1848) but also Aldgate House which belonged to Lord Wentworth, Lord of the Manor from the C16,

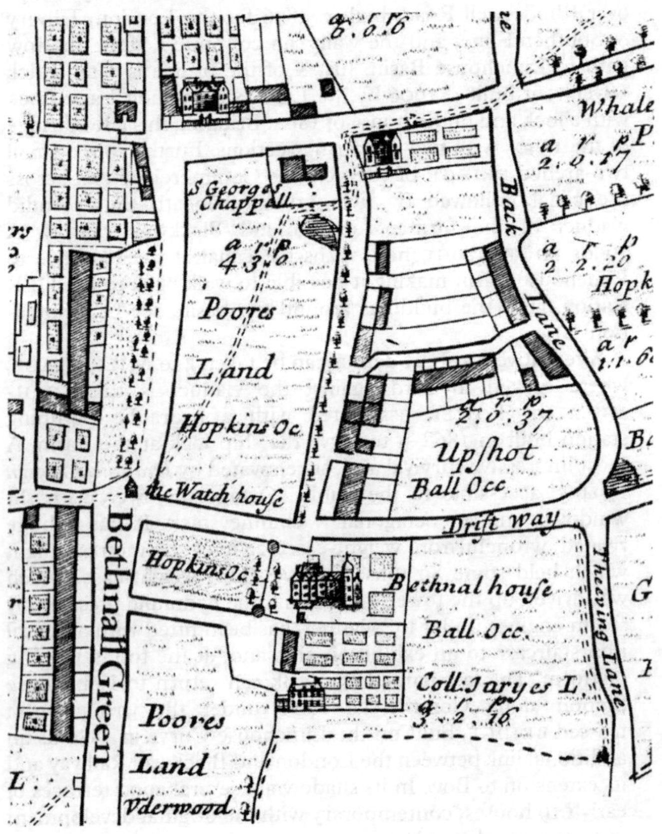

Bethnal Green in the early C18 (Gascoyne's survey 1703)

and Bethnal House, known as Sir John Kirby's Castle, where Pepys moved his possessions while the Fire of London raged. This mansion was also associated with the legendary Blind Beggar, subject of an obscure ballad so popularized during the C16 that its character had become an emblem of the beadle's staff by 1690.

To Stow in 1598 and even to Strype in 1720 most of Bethnal Green was still fields and pasture grounds but from about 1700 London began to encroach. The population which came was an overflow from Spitalfields and Shoreditch to the SW as the silk-weaving and furniture industries expanded. Here by Brick Lane and Cheshire Street and Crabtree Row close to Shoreditch, a map of 1703 already shows proper streets. Otherwise there is only a cluster of houses at the junction of St Matthew's Row and Bethnal Green Road, where the first Bethnal Green parish church was built in 1743–6, and a ribbon reaching up from Mile End Road known as Dog Row (now Cambridge Heath Road). Acting out of laudable self-interest and welcome foresight, Thomas Ryder of Bethnal House and his comfortable, countrified neighbours had already assisted in the purchase and enclosure of the Green in 1678 to prevent its development by placing it in trust as the Poors' Lands. Horwood's map (1819) shows the parish was built up along Bethnal Green Road as far E as the Green and beyond it, where around Globe Road a suburb of small well-to-do houses was built speculatively as Globe Town in the 1820s. A more ambitious attempt to create a middle-class district was made around the edges of Victoria Park, laid out in 1845 as an expansive 'green lung' for East London. Any pretensions to gentility were, however, short-lived and by 1851 the total population was 82,000 mostly housed in tiny cottages or worse.

The Eastern Counties Railway to Shoreditch was driven through the parish in 1840 but no station was built at Bethnal Green until the 1870s. In the intervening decades Bethnal Green earned its reputation as London's slum area *par excellence*, worse even than Whitechapel, and loomed large in the reports of early reformers such as Chadwick and Southwood Smith in the 1840s. The health reformer Hector Gavin's *Sanitary Ramblings* (1848) described 'the enormous number of dwellings which have been constructed in defiance of every law and principle on which the health and lives of occupants depend' and illustrated this with a map delineating the progress of the 'Disease Mist' across the parish. Water was supplied 'only thrice weekly and for two hours at a time and at low pressure' but it was enough to transmit cholera rapidly round the parish in the successive outbreaks that affected the East End until the 1860s.

The insanitary conditions provoked activity by philanthropists from the 1850s, initially with dispensaries and soup kitchens but more importantly for housing. First, and foremost among these was Baroness Burdett-Coutts, who was encouraged by Dickens to purchase land around the dust heap of Nova Scotia Gardens, in the NW of the parish. A 'huge mountain of refuse' was cleared for one of the most extraordinary philanthropic endeavours in

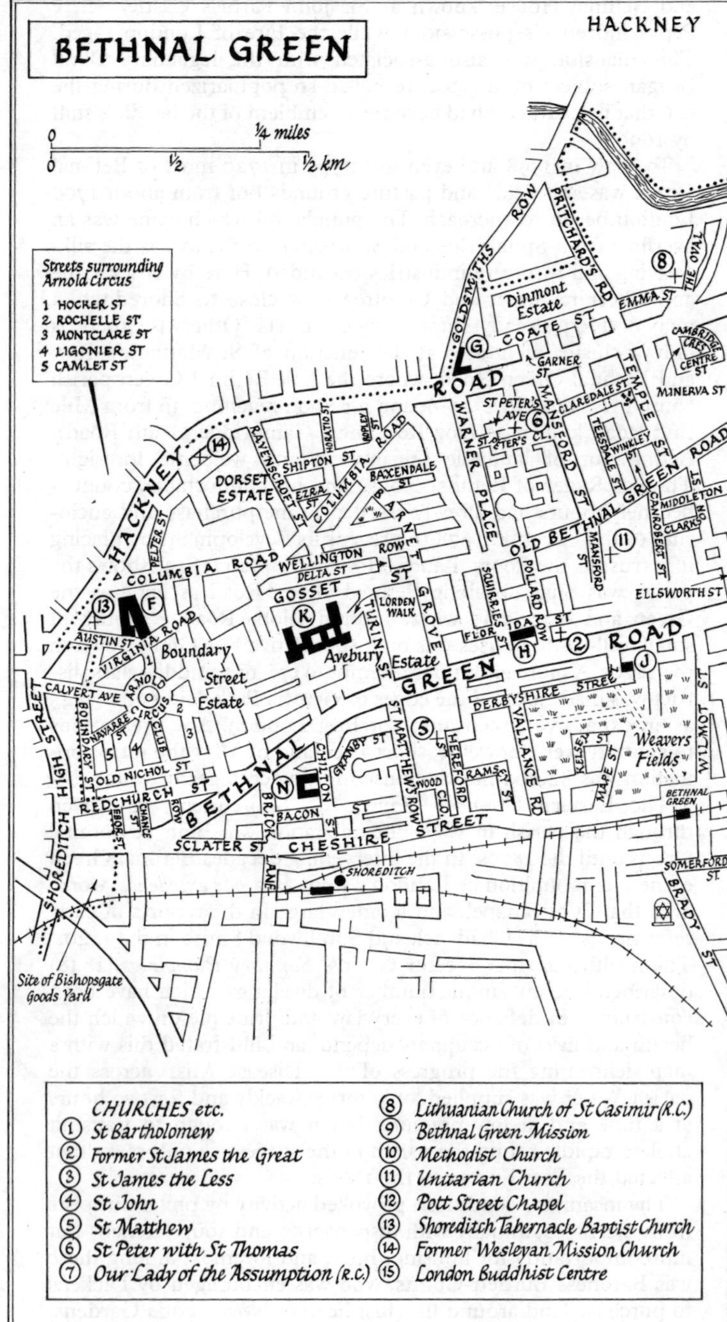
BETHNAL GREEN
HACKNEY
0 ¼ miles
0 ½ ½ km
Streets surrounding Arnold Circus
1 HOCKER ST
2 ROCHELLE ST
3 MONTCLARE ST
4 LIGONIER ST
5 CAMLET ST
Dinmont Estate
DORSET ESTATE
Boundary Street Estate
Avebury Estate
Weavers Fields
Site of Bishopsgate Goods Yard
HACKNEY ROAD
GOLDSMITHS ROW
PRITCHARD'S RD
THE OVAL
EMMA ST
COATE ST
GARNER ST
CAMBRIDGE CRES
CENTRE ST
MINERVA ST
TEMPLE ST
CLAREDALE ST
MANSFORD ST
WARNER PLACE
ST PETER'S AVE
ST PETER'S CL
TEESDALE ST
WINKLEY ST
OLD BETHNAL GREEN ROAD
MIDDLETON ST
CANROBERT ST
CLARKSON ST
ELLSWORTH ST
RAVENSCROFT ST
SHIPTON ST
HORATIO ST
ROPLEY ST
COLUMBIA ROAD
BAXENDALE ST
EZRA ST
BARNET GROVE
ROWE ST
WELLINGTON ROW
DELTA ST
GOSSET ST
LORDEN WALK
TURIN ST
SQUIRRIES ST
POLLARD ROW
FLORIDA ST
PELTER ST
AUSTIN ST
VIRGINIA ROAD
CALVERT AVE
ARNOLD CIRCUS
BOUNDARY ST
NAVARRE ST
CLUB ROW
OLD NICHOL ST
REDCHURCH ST
EBOR ST
CHANCE ST
BETHNAL GREEN ROAD
SHOREDITCH HIGH STREET
CHILTON ST
GRANBY ST
ST MATTHEW'S ROW
HEREFORD ST
WOOD CLO.
RAMSEY ST
DERBYSHIRE STREET
VALLANCE RD
KELSEY ST
MAPE ST
WILMOT ST
BRICK LANE
BACON ST
SCLATER ST
CHESHIRE STREET
SHOREDITCH
BETHNAL GREEN
SOMERFORD ST
BRADY ST
CHURCHES etc.
1 St Bartholomew
2 Former St James the Great
3 St James the Less
4 St John
5 St Matthew
6 St Peter with St Thomas
7 Our Lady of the Assumption (R.C.)
8 Lithuanian Church of St Casimir (R.C.)
9 Bethnal Green Mission
10 Methodist Church
11 Unitarian Church
12 Pott Street Chapel
13 Shoreditch Tabernacle Baptist Church
14 Former Wesleyan Mission Church
15 London Buddhist Centre

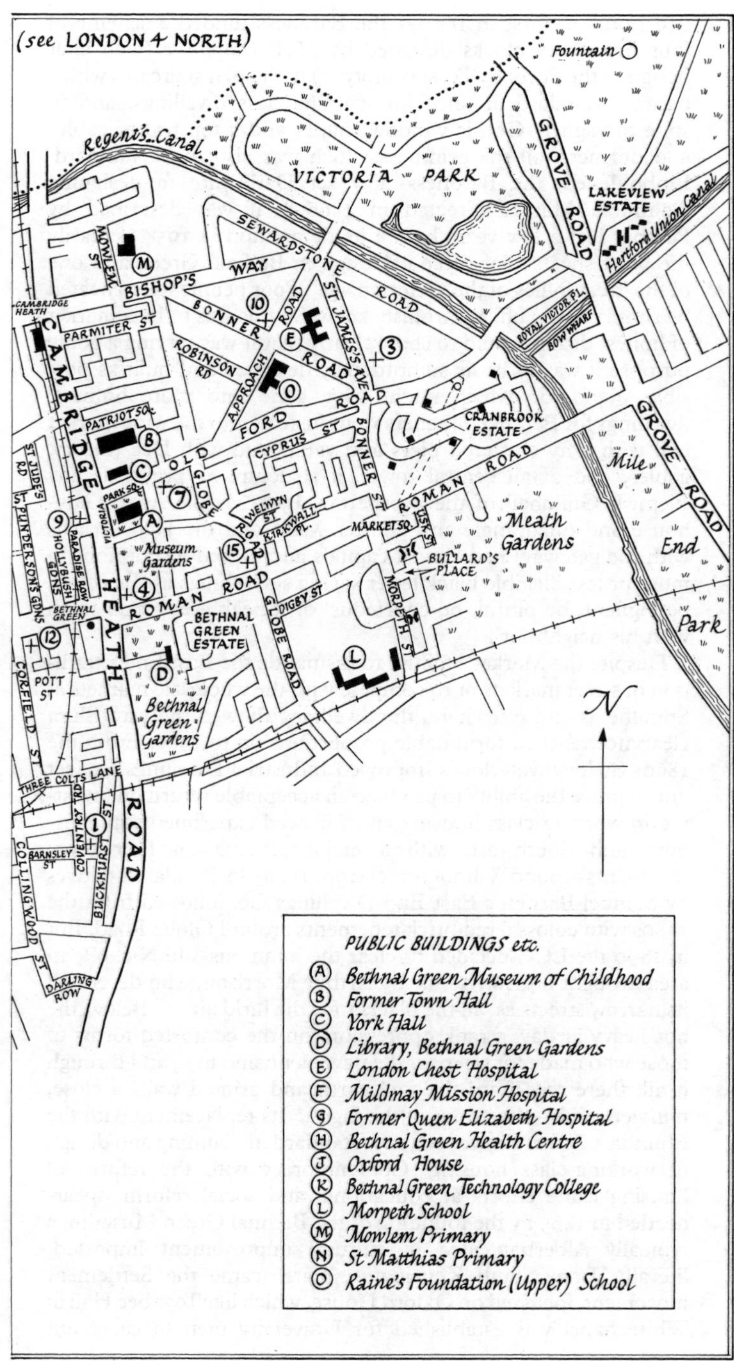
(see LONDON 4: NORTH)
Fountain
Regent's Canal
VICTORIA PARK
GROVE ROAD
LAKEVIEW ESTATE
Hertford Union Canal
SEWARDSTONE
WAY
ROAD
MOWLEM ST
BISHOP'S
CAMBRIDGE HEATH
PARMITER ST
BONNER
ROAD
ST JAMES'S AVE
ROBINSON RD
APPROACH
ROYAL VICTOR PL
BOW WHARF
CRANBROOK ESTATE
PATRIOT SQ
OLD
FORD
CYPRUS ST
BONNER ST
GLOBE
ROMAN ROAD
Mile End Park
ST JUDE'S RD
ST
PLUNDER SON'S GDNS
VICTORIA PARK SQ
HOLLYBUSH GDNS
PARADISE ROW
WELWYN ST
KIRKWALL PL
MARKET SQ
USK ST
Meath Gardens
Museum Gardens
BULLARD'S PLACE
CAMBRIDGE HEATH ROAD
BETHNAL GREEN
BETHNAL GREEN ESTATE
DIGBY ST
MORPETH ST
GLOBE ROAD
CORFIELD ST
POTT ST
Bethnal Green Gardens
N
THREE COLTS LANE
COVENTRY RD
BUCKHURST ST
BARNSLEY ST
COLLINGWOOD ST
DARLING ROW
PUBLIC BUILDINGS etc.
A Bethnal Green Museum of Childhood
B Former Town Hall
C York Hall
D Library, Bethnal Green Gardens
E London Chest Hospital
F Mildmay Mission Hospital
G Former Queen Elizabeth Hospital
H Bethnal Green Health Centre
J Oxford House
K Bethnal Green Technology College
L Morpeth School
M Mowlem Primary
N St Matthias Primary
O Raine's Foundation (Upper) School

C19 London. First in 1860–2 the Baroness funded a scheme of four five-storey blocks designed by *H.A. Darbishire* (who later designed the Peabody Trust prototype) with open staircases which became standard at once for working-class dwellings, and in spite of vaguely Gothic window shapes and a top frill of gables and dormers, all the grimness which was also to be standard. Emboldened, the Baroness now set Darbishire to designing Columbia Market. Erected in 1866–8, it was described by Pevsner just a few years before its demolition in 1958 as 'easily the most spectacular piece of design in Bethnal Green and one p. 80 of the great follies of the Victorian age'. Poor people were cheated by shopkeepers; philanthropists knew. So this was to be a market of honest dealings, and to show clearly that it was serving a godly purpose it was to be as sumptuously designed and built as possible. £200,000 which might have gone into more humane dwellings for Bethnal Greeners went instead into the wide market hall with lofty clustered piers and vaults and with Dec tracery, gables, and a tall central tower, a structure as proud as any Flemish Guildhall of the prosperous Late Middle Ages. Gatehouse and quadrangle and cloister walks and the Hall (in axis with the gateway) had carved capitals and carved inscriptions in more or less illegible black letter saying such things as 'Be sober, be vigilant, be pitiful, be courteous' or 'Speak every man truth with his neighbour'.

Despite the Market's failure to dismantle the East End's tradition of street markets or to compete with the wholesale markets at Spitalfields and elsewhere, the dwellings showed the way. Slum clearance reached formidable proportions up to 1900. From the 1860s Sydney Waterlow's Improved Industrial Dwellings Co. set out to prove the ability to produce an acceptable return on investing in working-class housing and followed experiments in Finsbury and Southwark with a major scheme for four-storey tenements around Wilmot Street from 1868–80. Similar initiatives by Samuel Barnett's East End Dwellings Co. followed from the 1880s with colossal red brick tenements around Globe Road. But in 1890 the LCC decided to clear the infamous 'old Nichol', an area brought horribly to life by Arthur Morrison, who described its narrow streets as 'all the blacker for the lurid air . . . Below, the hot heavy air lay, a rank oppression, on the contorted forms of those who made for sleep on the pavement; and in it, and through p. 587 it all, there rose from the foul earth and grimed walls a close, mingled stink – the odour of the Jago'.* Its replacement with the Boundary Street Estate set a new standard in planning and design of working-class housing. Contemporary with the reform of housing came efforts at educational and social reform, spearheaded in 1865 by the founding of the Bethnal Green Museum, a typically Albertian idea of cultural improvement imported, literally, from South Kensington. Later came the Settlement movement, focussed on Oxford House, which like Toynbee Hall in Whitechapel was established for University men to carry out

* *The Child of the Jago* (1896).

residential social and educational work. Numerous smaller settlements and missions, mostly set up by the University colleges and public schools, flourished in the last decades of the C19.

Bethnal Green's population reached a peak of 130,000 in 1901, increased steadily by immigration, although most of its inhabitants were still the descendants of rural workers from the eastern counties. Jews, though resident in Bethnal Green from at least the C17, made up the majority of foreign arrivals after 1860, engaged in the textile and bootmaking industries and settling primarily in the streets closest to the Jewish areas of Spitalfields and Whitechapel but also creating small enclaves around Old Bethnal Green Road.

Bethnal Green became a metropolitan borough in 1900, its civic identity sealed in 1909 with the erection of a new Town Hall. It proved itself able in the provision of public buildings including libraries and washhouses. The council's attitude to housing was fairly relaxed, confining itself to limited schemes of slum clearance after 1918, for which *E.C.P. Monson* was employed as architect. Its left-wing members gained some notoriety in the late 1920s for naming one of the estates after Lenin. But it was the LCC who took the initiative with large schemes of slum clearance throughout the borough, even as late as the 1930s laying waste to C17 and C18 timber and weatherboarded houses.

Although war damage was less severe than in the vulnerable East End districts close to the river and docks, Bethnal Green's population had declined to 58,000 in 1951 partly caused by a policy of reducing density and encouraging dispersal to the suburbs of outer East London. That there was need for reconstruction was not in doubt, even in 1934 the MARS group had presented Bethnal Green as a case study for rebuilding and separation of the old pattern of housing and industry living cheek-by-jowl. Forshaw & Abercrombie's *County of London Plan* (1943) also identified large parts of the borough as a priority for clearance and the LCC's first post-war estate opened here in 1947. The social consequences were only gradually made clear however in Wilmott and Young's *Family and Kinship in East London* (1950), which mapped the unravelling of a tight web of close familial ties, even within individual streets, as people moved away. This prompted Alderman Peter Benenson in 1951 to encourage higher-density housing which would alleviate the need for dispersal and revive the close communality of pre-war Bethnal Green. To achieve this he established a panel of approved architects, many of them young and all of them radical. Many had associations with the avant-garde MARS and Tecton groups:
not only *Skinner, Bailey & Lubetkin* who had carried out innova- 111
tive work in pre-war Finsbury, but also *Yorke Rosenberg &*
Mardall and *Denys Lasdun*, whose 'cluster blocks' at Usk Street p. 595
and Claredale Street became an emblem of the new East End. Each competed for the housing schemes and the results were impressive, if varied, and set Bethnal Green's reputation ahead even of the LCC who ploughed on with less imagination during this period in this area. The coherence of these individual

schemes, however, within the context of an area in which piecemeal rebuilding got under way almost immediately after 1945 means the landscape for post-war Bethnal Green is frustratingly unfocussed, increasingly so in the years after 1965 under the new borough of Tower Hamlets.

The endless streets of two-storeyed cottages noted by Pevsner as the characteristic feature of domestic Bethnal Green were becoming a distant memory by the mid-1970s, but at the same time the turn of the tide towards conservation was beginning in those areas where pockets of good mid-C19 terraces survived. This gained momentum in the 1980s, particularly around Columbia
50 Road, where the weekly flower market provided an additional draw for new residents. Houses became gentrified while in former industrial districts around the fringes of Shoreditch and Brick Lane artists leased and colonized cheap warehouse property. By the beginning of the C21 this had sparked a visible transformation of those areas and even heralded the advent of individual new houses by architects either for themselves or artist clients.

RELIGIOUS BUILDINGS

Bethnal Green lay within the medieval parish of Stepney. The need for a new church for the fast expanding suburb N of Brick Lane was apparent by the early C18, when Hawksmoor drew up a plan for a 'basilica after the Primitive Christians,' a revealing indication of his interests, immediately after the Act of 1711 for new churches. But nothing came of this and the first new parish church was the mid-C18 St Matthew, supplemented by St John in the early C19. By 1850 the number of Anglican churches had risen to twelve (each dedicated to one of the apostles), largely paid for by Bishop Blomfield's special fund for Bethnal Green churches, an offshoot of his Metropolis Church Fund. But even in the later C19 they were not filled, and by the 1950s many of the Victorian churches had been demolished. Of fourteen Anglican establishments in existence in 1903, five remain in use; two have been converted to housing, the rest have disappeared.* The vigorous tradition of Nonconformity (in 1851 their total numbers were stronger than the Anglicans) has likewise left little to see, and the same is true of C19 Judaism.

ST BARNABAS, Grove Road and Roman Road (*see* Bow and Bromley).

Former ST BARTHOLOMEW, Coventry Road. 1843–4 by *William Railton*. Lancet style. Aisled nave, shallow transepts, an incomplete SW tower with pyramidal slate cap. Brick with stone dressings. Gutted in the war and restored; converted to flats in the 1990s, quite tactfully.

Former ST JAMES THE GREAT, Bethnal Green Road. 1842–3 by *Edward Blore*; made redundant *c.* 1983, converted to flats *c.* 1990, together with the vicarage to the E. The prominent red brick shell still makes a picturesque composition to the street, with a thin spirelet to the W of the big gabled S transept. But the once impressively tall lancets have been obtrusively subdivided into latticed windows, and the roofs peppered with skylights. The interior had tall octagonal columns and an open roof. The former VICARAGE to the E has a gable above an attractive variety of Gothic windows.

ST JAMES THE LESS, St James Avenue. 1842 by *Lewis Vulliamy*, reconstructed by *J. Anthony Lewis* after war damage, 1960–1 (his third remodelling in Bethnal Green). As at St Peter, Vulliamy adopted a Norman style, although here using only plain grey brick. The prominent SW tower with short steeple has doorways on both N and S sides, the N one with carved tympanum. The church retains Vulliamy's outer walls with their small round-headed windows between buttresses, but the W wall is entirely new, with a big angular W window following the shape of the broad pantiled roof. Excellent STAINED GLASS by *Keith New*: a grid of deeply coloured glass in abstract shapes, mostly blue, the verticals crossed by bands of hexagons. Plain, frosted panels in between, giving plenty of light to the broad interior. Inside, the grid pattern is echoed by the roof with its strong lines of plain purlins and trusses curving down the walls. In contrast the shallow E sanctuary is framed by Vulliamy's big Norman moulded arch in three orders.

*Demolished: St Andrew, Viaduct St, 1841 by *Wyatt & Brandon*; St Jude, Old Bethnal Green Rd, 1842–6 by *H. Clutton*; St Matthias, Cheshire St, 1846–8 by *Wyatt & Brandon*; St Paul, Virginia Road, 1863–4 by *W. Wigginton*; St Philip, Swanfield St, 1841–2 by *T.R.L. Walker*; St Simon Zelotes, Morpeth St, 1840–7 by *B. Ferey*; St Thomas Baroness Road, 1848–50 by *Lewis Vulliamy*.

Canted apse with three windows, their glass with motifs of bread and wine disappointingly weak compared with the W window. Simple well-crafted furnishings of 1961, low pulpit and reading desk treated as a matching pair. Liturgically traditional in comparison with St Paul's Bow Common, but here too the interior reflects the harder aesthetic that was taking hold at this time. Older FONT, octagonal, of coloured alabaster; C19 glass reused in the tower lobby.

To the N, VICARAGE, vaguely Norman, with three storeys of round-arched windows under a steep gable, and linked chimneystacks. Behind, the much altered former CHURCH SCHOOLS and HALL (now Gatehouse School); 1890 by *Elijah Hoole*, extended 1901; symmetrical centre to Sewardstone Road with angular doorheads either end and bold tracery within rectangular windows.

42 ST JOHN, Cambridge Heath Road. 1826–8 by *Sir John Soane*, his third church for the Commissioners, and much more perverse and unconventional than his churches in St Marylebone and Walworth. The exterior of stock brick is unmistakeably Soane, except for the unfortunately crude window tracery of 1871, which now fills the round-headed arches on N and S sides.* The W front is the least altered part. Like the N and S walls, it is divided into bays by pilasters with minimal fluted capitals. Wide central bay, with tall panelled door below a pediment on elongated consoles, flanked by an obstinately original placing of lower entrances in narrow recesses. The centre continues upwards in an attic providing a solid support for the square stage of the tower (the absence of a portal avoiding the dilemma of how to combine a tower with a classical W façade). The tower is of a design which only Soane could conceive, with pairs of detached pillars at the angles. The circular cupola on top is, after all this precise regularity, an anticlimax. The original design proved too expensive and an intermediate storey was omitted. The receding composition of W block, attic and tower was stressed by eight of Soane's favourite blocky curved finials. Only the ones on the tower remain.† At the E end a tactful two-bay chancel by *Bodley*, 1888, externally matching Soane, and preserving Soane's low vestry and robing room on each side. Originally these were approached by a central double-curved stair against the E wall. The aisle roofs were restored to Soane's original shallow profile by *Brady & Mallalieu*, 2004, as the first phase of a larger repair programme.

The three W doors lead into a centre vestibule, with tall round-headed arches opening into end staircase bays. Stone stairs with Soane's iron balusters. The rest of the interior was, alas, remodelled in 1871 by *William Mundy* after a fire, retaining the six bays of stone Greek Doric columns at ground

*The drawings in the Soane Museum show that within each round-headed arch were two windows, divided by a projecting stone band, the lower windows smaller and rectangular.

†The *Gentleman's Magazine* in 1831 called them 'nondescript blocks of stone with handles' and found the tower a 'monstrous excrescence'.

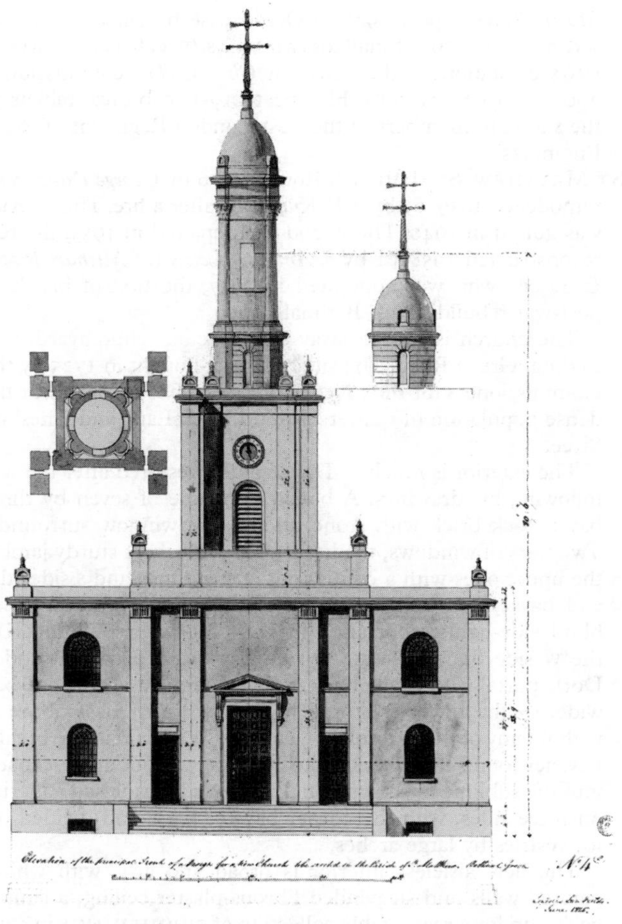

St John, Bethnal Green. Early design for tower, 1826–8

level but rebuilding the upper parts. Soane's flat nave ceiling and his upper octagonal piers (timber around an iron core) carrying plain round-headed gallery arches, were replaced by a gaunt hammerbeam roof and timber gallery arcade, both with openwork spandrels in metal. A stilted chancel arch was inserted between fifth and sixth bay. The sixth bay, distinguished by paired columns, was the site of Soane's identical hexagonal pulpit and reading desk.

The present PULPIT, no doubt by *Mundy*, is eclectic Gothic, timber arcading below a huge cove with bold timber and iron stair. Bodley's chancel is dominated by an overpowering REREDOS by *C.G. Hare*, made by *Farmer & Brindley*, 1913, with standing statue of Christ (a copy after Thorwaldsen) framed in a marble aedicule. – N chapel with AUMBRY by

Martin Travers, post 1947. – Organ case by *Travers*. – S aisle screen, post 1929. – Small ROYAL ARMS (W gallery). – (PAINTINGS of Stations of the Cross, by *Chris Gollon*, commissioned 2002). – MONUMENTS. Five neat C19–C20 bronze tablets in the S aisle to members of the East London Regiment of Royal Engineers.

ST MATTHEW, St Matthew's Row. 1743–6 by *George Dance sen.*; remodelled 1859–61 by *T.E. Knightley*, after a fire. The interior was gutted in 1940. The W end was repaired in 1955, the rest reconstructed 1958–61 by *J. Anthony Lewis* (of *Michael Tapper & Lewis*) who was appointed in 1957, the first of his three post-war rebuildings in Bethnal Green.

The church is tucked away in a spacious churchyard, S of Bethnal Green Road. The site had been bought in 1725 by the Commissioners for Fifty New Churches, chosen to be near the dense population of weavers around Brick Lane and Cheshire Street.

The exterior is much as Dance left it, restored after the war following his drawings. A blocky rectangle of seven by three bays; stock brick with stone quoins and window surrounds. Two tiers of windows, the lower ones with short sturdy jambs, the upper ones with a continuous string. On N and S sides the end bays project slightly. E end with Venetian window with blind side-lights, shortened in the post-war rebuilding. On the W side the projecting central bay has a pediment and a Doric portal with triglyph frieze. The pediment is only one bay wide, so the tower (restored to its C18 form) rises above it without any of the painful illogicality of St Martin in the Fields. Pevsner found the exterior 'businesslike without any escapade into the sublime or the operatic'. Dance's interior had galleries on three sides, with the corner bays of the E end divided off for vestries by large arches.

106 The new aisleless interior is broad and airy, with white-painted walls and suspended fibrous-plaster ceiling, a simple backdrop for a remarkable collection of FURNISHINGS in contemporary style, incorporated into the structure, exceptional among post-war E London churches. They follow the parish's Anglo-Catholic tradition established in the later C19 by the Rev. Septimus Hansard and his curate Stewart Headlam. Little altered since, apart from removal of pulpit and altar rails. Freestanding altar, emphasized by a tester, an early example of a nave altar, standing on a raised floor of black terrazzo. (The original sanctuary space is used for vestries). Behind and above it an E gallery, intended for the organ, of concrete on piers, reached by a prominent S staircase. The gallery has a folding timber SCREEN with hieratic figures of apostles by *Peter Snow*, ingeniously forming a kind of elevated reredos or iconostasis behind the main altar, to powerful effect. Behind is an upper Lady Chapel. In contrast, the W gallery shows its 1950s date, a cantilevered steel structure, with concave front and light metal railings. Furnishings are by a variety of young artists commissioned by Lewis. – Altar with SCULPTURED PANELS

by *Robert Dawson*, S staircase reliefs (St Michael and Lucifer) by *Kim James*, both in a strong, clumpy semi-abstract style. – TESTER above the altar (intended for a hanging pyx) designed by *Lewis*, painted by *Dorothy Rendel*. – STATIONS OF THE CROSS. Sensitive, delicately drawn ceramic relief panels in 107
irregular shapes, by *Donald Potter*. – WALL PAINTINGS in the Lady Chapel by *Barry Robinson*. – Sandblasted GLASS DOORS to the Lady Chapel with Christian symbols by *Heather Child*. – Among the freestanding STATUES, behind the altar, a well-carved St Matthew holding a model of the church, a Crucifixion; good Virgin and Child at the foot of the S stair. – Elegant vesica-shaped marble FONT by *Lewis*, COVER by *Brian Wood*. – STAINED GLASS, St Philip's chapel (SW) by *Laurence Lee*, 1955, the SW window ingeniously made up from C19 glass from St Philip Swanfield St, the W window with symbols of lost Bethnal Green churches.

The CHURCHYARD has C18 railings. Few tombs remain. To the SW is the little WATCHHOUSE of 1754, built to prevent grave robbing; extended 1826 to house a fire engine. Openings within blind arches with Gibbs surrounds; vermiculated quoins. For SCHOOL and VICARAGE *see* perambulation 2a.

ST PETER with St Thomas, St Peter's Close. 1840–1 by *Lewis* 43
Vulliamy. The first of Bishop Blomfield's churches in Bethnal Green. Knapped flint and stock brick with stucco and terracotta trim. In Norman style, as was briefly popular at the time, with a minimum of decoration. A curious though attractive design. The W front has the pitch of the roof exposed, and a starved W tower placed in front with a W portal of four orders, and high up, a roundel with shield-bearing angel. The top stage and spire are octagonal. The W windows step up towards the tower. Tall, thin side windows edged in brick, between brick pilasters. The nave is dominated by an elaborate open roof with elementary tracery in the spandrels. Originally there were galleries. A large Norman arch frames the sanctuary (cf. St James the Less) whose E wall has arches formerly with figure painting, painted out in 1950s, but now effectively filled with icons of saints in Greek Orthodox style by *Gregory Papagiourgiou*, 2000.

Much refurbishing from 1905 under the Rev. W.H. Maynard: vestry added, galleries removed, organ moved to the E end. From this time the Gothic SCREEN of 1911 (its ironwork added 1921), PULPIT, marble FONT and STAINED GLASS (N and S sides) by *Heaton Butler & Bayne*. E window 1909, with vigorous kneeling angels flanking a figure of Christ.

Originally the church was in the centre of a square with terraced houses, now all replaced by flats apart from the VICARAGE E of the church, by *Vulliamy*, originally very mean and small, enlarged 1908. Close by is the former SCHOOL with attached schoolmaster's house, also of the 1840s, incorporating an earlier building, enlarged since. Now Noel Mander organ works. CHURCH HALL across the road to the W, 1912, nicely detailed street front of red brick in Flemish bond, Tudor detail, with oriel over the entrance. Remodelled 1991–4, with the addition of the PEBBLE CENTRE to the S providing sheltered housing and community rooms.

OUR LADY OF THE ASSUMPTION (R.C.), Victoria Park Square. 1911–12 by *Edward Goldie*. The site was given by Florence Cottrell-Dormer. A good urban church, stock brick, soaring up from the pavement. W end with a big seven-light Dec window over a gabled porch; impressive N wall with five tall windows with reticulated tracery between coped buttresses rising above eaves level. The lower wall projects out to allow for internal recesses. Two-bay chancel with shallow apse, very hemmed in. Bellcote on the nave E end, no tower. Fine lofty interior, well lit by the upper windows, still with its early C20 fittings. HIGH ALTAR by *Earp & Hobbs* with gilded relief of the Last Supper and elaborate wooden Gothic pinnacled REREDOS with central monstrance and two standing figures. – Wrought-iron ALTAR RAILS by *Hardman*. – Flanking the tall chancel arch, SIDE ALTARS, also by *Earp & Hobbs*, with similar pinnacled structures. – STAINED GLASS. E window and first N and first S; by *Hardman*, 1913.

Adjacent to the S, PRIORY of the Assumptionist Fathers, tall, institutional Jacobean.

LITHUANIAN CHURCH OF ST CASIMIR (R.C.), The Oval. First established 1899 in Cable Street. 1912 by *Fr. Benedict Williamson*. An odd but functional plan: four-storey presbytery to the l., church to the r., with church rooms above it. The brick frontage facing E to the street is strangely dominated by large circular windows over the entrances. These are used also for the clerestory of the aisled church. Round-headed arcades; capitals painted in pale green and cream with Lithuanian folk patterns, which appear also in stencilled friezes on the aisle walls. The fittings reflect the lively Lithuanian tradition of Catholic Baroque art. In the sanctuary (at the W end) within a large arch on columns, a remarkable painted ALTARPIECE given to the church in 1912 and said to be Tyrolean work. Its subject is the Coronation of the Virgin, the figures of carved wood in three dimensions against Rococo-style clouds in relief. Repainted *c.* 1990. On the S wall a large well-carved painted CRUCIFIXION, possibly brought from the previous church. Many other statues. Wooden Lithuanian CANDELABRA.

BETHNAL GREEN MISSION, Bethnal Green. Rebuilt in 1955 by *E.F. Starling*, formerly Bethnal Green Medical Mission. Not churchy: an asymmetrical brick front, with recessed entrance, curved on the left to allow for a stair in the foyer. Plain roof-lit hall.

METHODIST CHURCH, Approach Road and Bonner Road. 1959 by *J.C. Prestwich & Sons*. A modest L-shaped group on the site of a classical building of 1868 which was the largest Methodist church in Bethnal Green. The post-war church is of brick with rectangular windows set in frames. Simple, light interior; in the E window STAINED GLASS.

Attached halls and manse to the N.

UNITARIAN CHURCH, Mansfield Street. The only Unitarian 40
church in the East End, but not typical, for it was built for Congregationalists. 1880 by *William D. Church*, sold to the Unitarians in 1889. A broad, festive Italian Romanesque front with wheel window; arches with red and white brick voussoirs. Three bays divided by pilasters with crisp foliage caps; a big pediment over the whole. Tall basement; the church entered up steps through paired doorways below gables. The church clearly flourished in the early C20, but the building is now subdivided for multi-purpose use.

Interior altered 1986–7 by *Stephen J. Muller* of *Form Design Europe*. A small worship space was made within the area of the W gallery, lit by the wheel window. The balustrade with iron openwork remains, overlooking the main church, now bare below a coved ceiling. Plain tablet to Charles Loftus Cochran †1901. A fine large MOSAIC TILE PANEL of *opus sectile* in Pre-Raphaelite style, showing acts of charity, to Elizabeth Jacqueline Garrett. Probably pre-1890 by *Henry Holiday*, made by *James Powell & Sons* (*Peter Cormack*). Early C20 refurbishment by *Ronald Potter Jones*, who gave the panelling now in the upper room (moved from the church). More panelling in the basement (its main hall now divided up). Adjoining to the S, the former MANSE, 1891, with starved brick trim; single-storey church parlour behind, with panelled interior. E of the church, facing Blythe Street, *R.P. Jones* added a set of club rooms on three floors; 1905. They have an elegant Neo-Georgian red brick front: classical doorcase and window aprons with scrolly detail.

POTT STREET CHAPEL. Chapel and schools were built by *John Tarring*, 1849, for Calvinistic Independents, Congregationalists in Bethnal Green since 1669. The dismal remains consist of a ragstone tower to the N of a two-storeyed range, with school below and meeting room above. Much damaged by bombing; upper windows now straight headed. Ground floor adapted for worship *c.* 1985 for Praxis, a United Reformed church; with new flats and offices adjoining.

SHOREDITCH TABERNACLE BAPTIST CHURCH, Hackney Road. The grand classical chapel of 1879 by *T. Lewis Banks*, a major late Victorian landmark, was demolished after war damage. It had a polygonal interior which seated 2,000. Plans were made in 2003 for a new church by *Matthew Lloyd Architects*, to replace its austere successor, a brick-clad portal-frame with continuous clerestory, 1960–3 by *Goddard & Phillips*. The ingenious SUNDAY SCHOOL HALL by *George Baines*, 1890–1, survives at the back of the site, built, like the C19 church, during the energetic ministry of William Cuff. No exterior of note, as it was surrounded by buildings, but a light and spacious interior, with a continuous band of clerestory windows to the horseshoe-shaped hall, and deep roof-lit galleries on columns around three sides. It was planned as a central schoolroom surrounded by ten classrooms on two levels, divided by panelled partitions. Revolving wooden shut-

Shoreditch Tabernacle Sunday Schools,
Hackney Road, Bethnal Green, 1890

ters allowed the ground-floor space to be opened up. Shallow-pitched open roof with tie-beams reinforced by steel rods.

Former WESLEYAN MISSION CHURCH, No. 162a Hackney Road. 1841. Now flats. Unusual W front with entrance and geometric-tracery window above, within a recessed giant arch under a steep gable. Flanked by low pinnacled towers, like a reduced version of Peterborough cathedral.

Former BETHNAL GREEN GREAT SYNAGOGUE, Bethnal Green Road. *See* perambulation 2a.

LONDON BUDDHIST CENTRE, Globe Road. Former Fire Station of 1888–9 by *Robert Pearsall* for the Metropolitan

Board of Works, enlarged 1911. Converted in 1978. Typically lively free Arts and Crafts Gothic in red and blue brick with stone dressings and stamped-terracotta decoration. Symmetrical front, tall with two rows of gabled dormers, the lower rank gabled with decorative flame keystones. Former vehicle entrances with segmental brick arches between heavy buttresses. The former hose tower was originally topped by a tall, hexagonal turret. After conversion a new entrance was made, through a gateway with decorative wrought-iron overthrow inset with coloured stones depicting the crest of Nalanda, the ancient Indian monastic university. By *Arya Daka*. The interior, remodelled by *M.F. Wharton* with *Windhorse Design* (*Desmond Crowe*), has murals of natural landscapes by *Chintamani*. Two shrine rooms, partly occupying the former engine room, with figures of Buddha, also by *Chintamani*. Residential rooms and offices on the upper floors; associated shops including arts centre etc., have spread along Globe Road.

JEWISH CEMETERY, Brady Street. A large walled enclosure, founded in 1795 by the Ashkenazi community. Crowded with mainly later Victorian monuments, some of considerable lavishness (e.g. that of Hannah Levy, *c.* 1850), and with several to members of the Rothschild family, including Nathan Meyer Rothschild †1836. Changes in ground level reflect the requirements of rabbinical law and layers of burial.

MAJOR BUILDINGS

BETHNAL GREEN MUSEUM OF CHILDHOOD, Cambridge Heath Road. 1868–72 by *James Wild*, incorporating the iron structure of the first, temporary, museum erected at South Kensington in 1855–6 with the proceeds of The Great Exhibition.

When first erected at South Kensington, the tripartite structure, of prefabricated corrugated–iron-clad 'sheds' with vaulted roofs, was dubbed the 'Brompton boilers' despite efforts by an embarrassed Prince Consort to soften its utilitarian appearance by painting the exterior and adding a porte-cochère. In 1865 (as work was beginning on the permanent museum at South Kensington) the government offered the building to any London district capable of, or interested in, taking it. The hope was to separate each of the sections and establish museums in London's N, E and S suburbs. Instead, a single application was made to re-erect the entire structure in Bethnal Green. Sir Antonio Brady, and other prominent local philanthropists, purchased the N close of the Green (Poors' Lands) from its Trustees for £2,000 and transferred it to the government who guaranteed to maintain the remaining open ground as public gardens. Pevsner observed in 1952 that, 'it represents the one solitary (and alas not really successful)

Bethnal Green Museum, as planned, 1871

attempt at bringing some of the art of the national collections to a population not likely to visit the West End'. At its opening, the museum was loaned Sir Richard Wallace's collection, later moved to Hertford House, Manchester Square (*see London 3: North-West*) but attempts to distinguish itself from South Kensington were made with exhibits appropriate to the trades and industries of East London. It became the Museum of Childhood in 1974. Plans in 2004 by *Caruso St John* for a new entrance.

Of the original structure, only two-thirds were removed to Bethnal Green* to be re-erected and reclad by *James Wild*, Assistant Director of New Buildings at South Kensington. His drawings of 1871 show ambitious but unexecuted proposals to establish the museum at the heart of an educational institution, which included library, art schools and refreshment rooms linked by cloistered arcades to the main building. Only the latter's EXTERIOR was executed to the published design, but with only a perfunctory entrance. Denied its intended sculptural enrichment the museum wears an unintentionally sober face. Red brick, in a restrained and well-detailed version of the South Kensington round-arched style. Across the front and back are three wide pointed gables with big thermal windows. The long flanks are divided into bays by large flat pilasters, with windows set low in each and mosaic panels high up, representing the works of man in the arts, sciences, industry and agriculture. By *F.W. Moody*, an important figure at South Kensington, and executed by his students at the National Art Training Schools in association with *Minton, Hollins and Co.* Almost monochrome except for an appropri-

*The remaining part was demolished during *Aston Webb*'s rebuilding at Brompton Road in 1906.

ate burst of colour in the panel depicting 'Spectral Analysis'.

INTERIOR. The iron structure, one of the most important surviving examples of its type, is fully revealed inside. Constructed by *C.D. Young & Co.* (perhaps from designs by civil engineer, *William Dredge*). Each of the three 'naves' is top-lit by a spine of glazing running the length of roofs carried on light, bow-shaped wrought-iron trusses. The internal space is arranged exactly as it had been at South Kensington. Galleries with X-pattern balustrades at first floor supported by simple brackets on slim cast-iron columns. In the central nave is a court, originally designed to display sculpture, with a fish-scale-pattern floor of black and white mosaic laid by female convicts from Woking Gaol. Surrounding on three sides, raised platforms introduced originally for display of anthropological and entomological exhibits.

In the museum's gardens, a SCULPTURE: The Eagle Slayer by *John Bell*, brought here in 1927 and now much damaged. It may be the version cast in iron by the Coalbrookdale Company in 1851 and shown at the Great Exhibition at the centre of a fantastic cast-iron structure, referred to as a 'rustic summerhouse', carrying the eagle.

Former TOWN HALL, Cambridge Heath Road. 1909–10 by *Percy Robinson & W. Alban Jones* in pompous Edwardian Baroque. Austere E extension to Patriot Square by *E.C.P. Monson*, 1937–9 for council chambers and electricity board offices. The principal front is set too close to the road to make much display. Portland stone with a central pedimented arch and an octagonal domed tower. Deep, arched recess over the entrance containing a sculptural group by *Henry Poole* of a female figure and cherubs representing the Municipality protecting the industries of the Borough, the fruits of which pour forth from cornucopias. On the northern elevation a *bas-relief* figure of Justice. The 1930s extension eschews Edwardian grandeur for stripped classicism with panels of stylized foliage and a relief of the Blind Beggar over the entrance. The interiors show greater flair and diversity. The earlier part has a central staircase hall lined and floored in green and grey marble and the heavy, ornate staircase lined with green and white marble panels. On the upper floor, veined marble Ionic columns and pilasters with bronzed capitals. Oak-panelled offices and committee rooms. Council chamber with heraldic glass including the arms of Middlesex, Gresham, the City of London and De Bathonia (from which the Borough's name was thought to derive). Pilasters bear plaster reliefs of Truth and Happiness, Industry and Temperance, also by *Poole*. Subtle but expensive Deco style for the 1930s wing with black and white geometric-pattern marbling to the entrance hall staircase. On the first floor, elegant suites of chambers lined with Austrian walnut in streamlined style. Windows enriched with heraldic glass.

YORK HALL & BATHS, Old Ford Road. 1929 by *A.E. Darby*,

Bethnal Green Borough Surveyor and Engineer. Rather ordinary Neo-Georgian but respectful to its setting close to the Green. Reinforced concrete, clad in red brick with Portland stone dressings, deep cornice and stone balustrade with attic behind and a solid cupola. Arcaded entrance to the public hall, the former laundry and wash house (l.) and Turkish baths (r.). Well-preserved interior, with original wooden ticket booths. Top-lit staircase hall with a dome supported on square columns and pilasters and inset with decorative glass. The hall, which originally doubled as the main swimming baths, has a cantilevered balcony on three sides and stage at the N end. Proscenium arch crested by the Borough badge. Undistinguished addition for new swimming pool, 1967 by *Wakeford, Jeram & Harris*.

PUBLIC LIBRARY, Bethnal Green Gardens. 1896, probably by *James Tolley jun.*, built as the male wing of Bethnal House Lunatic Asylum; adapted as a library in 1922 by *A.E. Darby*, Borough Surveyor and Engineer. Two-storey, red brick Queen Anne with segmental pediment and good rubbed brick detail. Fifteen bays with Ionic pilasters to the upper floor, paired under triangular pediments on the N and S projecting end bays. The centre bay has a segmental pediment. The entrance was sensitively remodelled in the 1920s, with flanking pairs of engaged square Ionic terracotta columns and a nicely lettered inscription above. Also of this date, discreetly set back at the S end, is the service wing.

Neo-Georgian interior of 1922 with a sober, panelled entrance hall. Pedimented doorcases to the reading rooms, which have Adamesque ceilings of plaster roundels with scallop edges bordered by husk garlands and ribbons. At the rear of the hall is the lending library, with an original curved and glazed entrance screen ornamented with Ionic pilasters. This room, added in 1922, is top-lit through a shallow vault, with decorative glass lights. On the E wall, four unusual oval plaster reliefs of Darwin, Marx, Morris and Wagner, apparently by a local artist, *Karl Roberts,* and perhaps reflecting the interests of the Labour/Communist alliance which governed Bethnal Green at this date. WAR MEMORIAL, on first floor, unveiled 1923. Stained glass of 'Peace', flanked by the figures of 'Manhood' and 'Motherhood', set within a Venetian-window surround. Bethnal Green's War Memorial Committee had intended to pay for the Children's lending library and Reading Room as a permanent memorial, but only raised £282, so the window was all they could afford.

LONDON CHEST HOSPITAL, Bonner's Road. Founded 1848 by philanthropic City bankers and merchants; built 1851–5 by *F.W. Ordish* on a spacious and leafy site originally occupied by the Stepney manor house (demolished 1848).* One of

*A scheme was promoted in 1851 for a 'crystal sanatarium' by *Joseph Paxton*, a modified version of his hothouse at Chatsworth, and intended as an air-conditioned exercise pavilion of a type that Paxton had been promoting for all hospitals in large towns.

the first consumption hospitals in London after *Francis*'s Brompton Hospital, Kensington. Symmetrical main block of three storeys – ostensibly late Baroque style in red brick with quoins and squat central clock tower. Some curious stucco detailing including medievalized twisted mouldings to the window mullions and, over the door, staggered scroll brackets supporting figures, possibly Samaritans, and a later figure of a woman carrying flowers. Keystone to the central second-floor window with a figure of Christ. Inside, the entrance hall has vaults of hollow-pot construction and chamfered arches with mask keystones and decorative capitals, e.g. pelican in its piety. The original layout of wards was, as at Brompton, on a corridor plan and ventilated by a revolutionary system of regulating cold and hot air devised by *W. Jeakes*.

Extensions were quickly required, first the S wing of 1863–5 by *William Beck* in a manner sympathetic to the main façade. The N wing of 1871–81 by *Beck & Lee* was rebuilt 1983. Octagonal N tower 1890–92 was part of the improved sanitary arrangements; a similar S tower was not built. Open, cast-iron sun balconies added to SE corner in 1900 have been enclosed. Prominently linked to the S wing, the Outpatients Department of 1972 by *Charles Tarling* of *Adams Holden and Pearson*. Octagonal, concrete-framed three-storey tower for day rooms and single-storey treatment wing. At the rear of the site a long, two-storey NURSES' HOME of 1905. Neo-Georgian, much extended and rebuilt. The chapel by *E.B. Lamb*, 1858–60 was destroyed in 1941.

MILDMAY MISSION HOSPITAL, Hackney Road and Austin Street. Now an HIV/AIDS care unit. 1890–2 by the hospital specialist *R.H. Hill* with later additions, due for redevelopment in 2004 by *Feilden Clegg Bradley*. Successor to a free dispensary, established by Rev. William Pennefather, an evangelical of Mildmay Park, Islington, following the cholera epidemic of 1866. Moved here when the surrounding Boundary Street area (*see* p. 586) was rebuilt. The older part faces Austin Street. Plain red brick with stone dressings under a steep slate roof with cupola. Originally U-plan with a central block and splayed projecting wings, much altered. The undistinguished extension facing Hackney Road of 1964–5 is due to be replaced, but the friendly, yellow brick CLINIC by *Powell Moya Partnership*, 1994, will be retained. This contains bedrooms on the upper floors with balconies overlooking Hackney Road.

Former QUEEN ELIZABETH HOSPITAL FOR SICK CHILDREN, Hackney Road and Goldsmith's Row. Founded by Quakers. Begun 1867 by *William Ward Lee*, extended 1902–4 by *W.C. Marshall*. The later part faces Hackney Road, a solid Italianate frontage of four storeys with basement and attic faced in white brick with stone dressings. Projecting four-bay centre originally flanked by cast-iron balconies for the patients (now enclosed). Arched entrance with deeply carved surround of foliage and the badge of Lord Amherst of Hackney. In Goldsmith's Row, the earlier hospital, red brick Queen Anne with bands of terracotta detail and stair tower with staggered windows. It contained the Outpatients Department on the ground floor with offices and consulting rooms to l. and r. and wards above. Adjacent, laboratories of 1969–72 by *Lyons, Israel & Ellis* to design by *Mercer & Miller*. Typically brutal, five-storey tower with chamfered corners, aggregate-faced floorbands and continious bands of glazing. Exposed staircase on a glazed plinth.

HEALTH CENTRE, Florida Street. A large but engaging design of 1988 by *Avanti Architects*. Formidable symmetrical façade, with the lower storey in mellow brick with raked joints, broken by an angular projecting entrance penetrating into the centre of the plan. Upper floors built up in tiers with roof terraces backed by large parapet walls pierced by circular openings.

OXFORD HOUSE, Derbyshire Street. 1890–2 by *Sir Arthur Blomfield*, extended 1894. Refurbished 1999–2002 by *All Clear Designs Limited*.

Oxford House was established in temporary premises in 1884 by staff and students of Keble College and New College as a rival to the Universities Settlement at Toynbee Hall, Whitechapel, which was considered too secular in its character. In 1886, the mission founded the apolitical Federation of Working Men's Clubs and helped to foster numerous recreational and educational clubs within the East End. Rev. Winnington-Ingram, later Bishop of London, commissioned Blomfield to design 'a house to hold twenty residents . . . along with a lecture room, classrooms and club premises'.

As at Toynbee Hall, the building is inspired by C16 and C17 domestic architecture and when originally surrounded by streets of small weavers' cottages must have strongly evoked the character of a manor house in an urban setting. Red brick, symmetrical four-storey S façade of seven bays, shallow two-bay wings under kneelered gables with stone copings and hexagonal ball finials. Two ranks of dormers in the pitched roof and a cupola. Two-bay hipped roof E extension for the Oxford House Club of 1894 in similar style. To its r. small C21 extension in red tiles and render.

The symmetrical façade to Derbyshire Street is three bays with a taller centre under a gable and a broad arched entrance with headstops. Perp windows with moulded surrounds light the staircase to the l. The present entrance, created in 2002, is to the l. into a discreet top-lit hall along the back of the building with ramps descending to a basement THEATRE. The café occupies the former dining room. The rest of the interior has been much altered except for the attic CHAPEL (refurbished as a performance space) which has a timber barrel-vaulted roof lit by three N dormers. At the W end, a Neo-Jacobean oak screen surmounted by strapwork carving, obelisk finials and central crucifix. Four-bay N arcade to a narrow 'aisle' with low Tudor arches carried on octagonal piers. Some original FURNISHINGS, including an altar with triptych altarpiece. Painted panels of Old Testament subjects and the emblems of the Four Evangelists flank a gruesome Crucifixion, 1914.

Schools

Bethnal Green has an exceptional collection of BOARD SCHOOLS, indicative of the pressing needs of this part of the East End after 1870. Most are detailed in the perambulations.

BETHNAL GREEN TECHNOLOGY COLLEGE, Gosset Street. The former Daniel Street School by *T.J. Bailey*, 1900. Assured Wrenaissance of red brick with terracotta trimmings: an off-the-peg design also used at Gordon Primary School, Greenwich. Central block of three floors with full-height hall and classrooms adjoining flanked by tall stair towers linking to pedimented pavilions. Two-storey science and craft block by *Armstrong & Macmanus*, 1959 in humane style arranged around a central pond. Later, butterfly-roofed extensions. Yellow brick Sports Hall, 1998 by *Stefan Zins Associates*.

MORPETH SCHOOL, Morpeth Street/Portman Place. Several phases, mostly distinguished, including the former Portman Street School of 1896 by *T.J. Bailey*, displaying his repertoire of shaped gables and a tall, pyramidal roof to the stair tower at the S. On Morpeth Street, the former Morpeth Central School of 1910, also by *Bailey*, with outstanding detail. Shaped gable, red-tiled roof, roughcast rendering and chequer-pattern tiles. Cupola with a weathervane of swallows in flight. It follows the pattern for central schools of a hall flanked by gabled pavilion wings and single-storey rear classroom block. Entrances with Art Nouveau detailing. Inside, a pair of excellent staircases with glazed brick dados and bow-fronted balustrades pierced by Voysey-esque heart-shaped motifs. To Portman Place, extension of 1997 by *Norman & Dawbarn*. L-shaped plan of five bays to the front with barrel-vault roofs carried forward as a canopy. Off-centre entrance hall; triple-height atrium with circulation galleries at first and second floor. By the same firm, the library completed *c.* 2001. Big oversailing roof and glazed façade.

MOWLEM PRIMARY, Mowlem Street. 1997 by *Paul Irons*. A cheerful note in the centre of the dreary Wellington Estate. Single storey, admirably scaled under a long sloping pitch roof with broad overhanging eaves supported on columns. Free-standing glazed canopy to the entrance. Classrooms open to the playground through brightly painted doors with porthole windows.

ST MATTHIAS (C.E.) PRIMARY SCHOOL, Granby Street. 1874 by *Joseph Clarke*. Former National School with modest Gothic detailing. Stock brick facings dressed in red brick and Bath stone. The deprived character of the district meant that the building originally had zinc gutters (rather than more valuable lead) and, as today, heavily wired windows. 1980s S extension.

RAINE'S FOUNDATION SCHOOL, Approach Road. 1887 by *T. Chatfeild Clarke*. Built as the Parmiter's Foundation School, established by Thomas Parmiter, a silk merchant, in 1686. Red brick Gothic with picturesque silhouette of pointed gables and a stair tower with spire on half-timbered base. At the E end, a double-height bay window of small panes of coloured glass. This lights a lofty, galleried Hall with timber hammer-beam roof. Contemporary iron electroliers. Less distinguished later additions including unassuming science block, 1962 by *Sidney Lowett*. Brick with horizontal casement windows with concrete dressings. Extension of *c.* 1985 for the Raine's Foundation School, previously in Arbour Square (*see* Shadwell and Ratcliffe). Set into alcoves are figures of charity children, copies of an original pair taken from the first school in Wapping. Further extensions behind, in dark brick and raised on arches. 1995 by *Michael Madgwick*.

VICTORIA PARK. The first and largest of London's C19 parks. It belongs to the general movement to bring amenities to the labouring classes of the East End and was created after a petition was presented to the Queen in 1840, instigated by George Young, M.P. An Act was passed in 1841, and money was found from the sale of York House, St James. The park was designed by *James Pennethorne* of the Office of Works, and opened in 1845. The 290-acre site called Bishop Bonner's fields, previously used for market gardens, was bounded on the S by the Regent's Canal, and on the SE side by Sir George Duckett's (Hertford Union) canal of 1830 linking Regent's Canal with the Lea Navigation. Grove Road divides the park into two parts, landscaped with perimeter drives and clumps of trees. The smaller W part was given the more elaborate treatment, embellished in 1849 by a large lake, with waterfall islands, made in former gravel workings. Smaller lakes were provided in the E part. In the 1980s the park was one of the first to benefit from government funding to encourage revival of interest in open spaces. New railings, lamp standards and entrance gates were provided, also a new café by the main lake and other improvements.

The park is now much simpler than it was in the later C19, when its numerous attractions were much appreciated. Planting by *John Gibson* introduced sub-tropical vegetation, there were celebrated bedding displays and several ornamental buildings, including a pagoda on an island in the main lake (acquired in 1847 from a Chinese exhibition in Knightsbridge), and a Hispano-Moorish arcaded shelter, designed by *Pennethorne*. These were damaged in the Second World War and demolished, as was Pennethorne's elaborate Tudor Lodge at Bonner Gate, the main S entrance. A bandstand was added in 1865, a greenhouse in 1892. Both have gone, as has the Lido of 1936, which replaced earlier swimming pools. So too has the bronze fountain in the flower garden, by *Bainbridge Copnall*, of 1950, which was moved to Golders Hill Park.

The chief survivals are BONNER GATE itself, with Pennethorne's chunky Jacobethan gatepiers in brick and stone,
80 and the oddly palatial DRINKING FOUNTAIN in the eastern part, given by Baroness Burdett-Coutts in 1862, an elephan-

tine polygonal structure with oversized putti and dolphin in niches, the whole in a Gothic-cum-Moorish style. It was designed by *Henry Darbishire*, also the architect of Baroness Burdett-Coutts's even more impractical and ambitious (and now demolished) Columbia Market in Bethnal Green. Near the E end of the park, two SHELTERS were erected in 1860, stone alcoves, which came from *Taylor* and *Dance*'s remodelling of London Bridge in 1758–62. At St Mark's Gate a small patterned brick LODGE.

The intention was to surround the park with respectable terraces and villas, and provide a formal double avenue from the S. Little of this came to pass, although in 1862 Burdett Road was laid out to link Grove Road to East India Dock Road. In the later C20 the park became a major element in the vision of a more extensive green landscape, as Mile End Park took shape immediately to the S (*see* Mile End) and the Lea Valley Regional Park continued the pattern of open spaces to the NE.

PERAMBULATIONS

1. East Bethnal Green

1a. The Green and Cambridge Heath Road

The preservation of the medieval Green or Poors' Lands on either side of CAMBRIDGE HEATH ROAD is a remarkable asset to this part of Bethnal Green. The land is still divided into its three closes on the road's E side: the part S of Roman Road was preserved as BETHNAL GREEN GARDENS and recreation ground by the LCC in 1895. The Underground station (1939 by *Holden & Heaps*; opened 1946) was built beneath the gardens and at their NW entrance are classical gatepiers designed to disguise vents. In the NE corner of the gardens, performing the same function, is a PUBLIC SHELTER and kiosk, erected in the late 1940s. The style is elegantly Modernist, wholeheartedly in the manner of Holden's stations with rounded ends and a thin, projecting concrete roof. The N close of the green is now MUSEUM GARDENS, preserved by the government upon purchase of the land for Bethnal Green Museum in 1868 (*see* above) and opened in 1875. They are still, as the Act for its purchase required, 'laid out and for ever maintained . . . as an ornamental garden': the original layout was designed by *A. McIntyre*, the superintendent of Victoria Park. Drinking fountain of 1903.

The tour of the surrounding buildings begins close to the Museum's NE corner at the junction of Victoria Park Square and OLD FORD ROAD, with a small group of buildings associated with early developments in this area and with their fronts originally to the open space. First, at the corner with Victoria Park Square, is NETTESWELL HOUSE, the oldest surviving house in Bethnal Green. Over its S door is an inscription: 'AD1553 – restored 1705 and 1862'. The earlier date corresponds to the death of Sir Ralph Warren, former Lord Mayor of London, to whom a cottage and adjacent St George's chapel were leased in 1547 by Bishop Bonner. There is evidence that he had rebuilt the house but its present appearance, of two storeys and attics in Flemish bond, must be *c.* 1646, when Warren's lease expired. Of that date at least the two curved gables with their pediments are characteristic (cf. the Dutch House, Kew, 1631). The rubbed brick window dressings are surely 1705, while the blocked centre bay and rusticated stone doorcase reflect the Victorian changes. The interior is no less of a palimpsest and the plan of the C17 house has been obscured by Victorian remodelling: only the reused balustrades to the attic and cellar stairs look earlier, perhaps 1705. Discreet glass, brick and timber extension for a new entrance from Old Ford Road, by *Macdonald & Berridge* 1997–8. The house was originally attached on its W side to the chapel of ease erected for the Green's inhabitants *c.* 1512 but this seems to have fallen out of use and been replaced *c.* 1720 by two houses. These were replaced by the present group of four (Nos. 1–4 Old Ford Road) in 1787–91 by *Ruby*, a carpenter, for Anthony Natt jun., Rector of Netteswell, Essex. They face the Museum, forming a handsome terrace with Bedford Square-type *Coade* stone door surrounds.

Opposite, in OLD FORD ROAD, alongside the YORK HALL (*see* above), Nos. 17–21 are also C18 but of the previous generation; erected 1753 by Anthony Natt sen. of Netteswell House, who subsequently resided at No. 19. Symmetrical, the original window pattern was probably 3:2:3:2:3, originally red brick with hipped roofs, No. 21 now stuccoed. They have good panelled rooms and staircases: No. 17, with both straight-headed and shallow segmental sashes, was restored 1972–5 by *Thomas Saunders* who also built the purple brick offices (No. 15) at the rear for his practice. The history of No. 21 is indicative of the social decline of the Green in the C19. By 1815 it was a girls' school for the London Society for Promoting Christianity among the Jews; by 1873 it was in use as an asylum for 'fallen women'. Of this date, the two-bay E extension. Since 1900 it has been occupied by ST MARGARET'S HOUSE, which began as a women's settlement associated with Oxford House (*see* above). The pedimented doorcase is a restoration of 1960, modelled on the original at No. 19. Behind is a wing for the settlement's workers, *c.* 1903, with bolection panelled overmantels and Delft-tiled fireplaces in the former bedrooms. Tiny brick chapel of 1904 by *Paul Waterhouse*, with a della Robbia-style memorial tablet of The Annunciation. Inside it has a sanctuary behind a rood screen of four octagonal Ionic columns supporting an entablature swept up over a semicircular central arch. Stained glass in the N wall: W, SS Mildred, Margaret and Cecilia by *Heaton, Butler & Bayne*; E, St Mary by *Powells*.

VICTORIA PARK SQUARE skirts the E side of the Green. It begins with the CHURCH AND PRIORY OF THE ASSUMPTIONISTS (*see* above) which stands on the site of Aldgate House built by the Greshams in the C16 and adapted in 1760 by the antiquary Ebenezer Mussell to incorporate within its walls part of the City's medieval Aldgate. At that time, the Green must have been as lovely as Highgate village but from the late C19 there was need for slum clearance and large blocks of improved dwellings began to encroach. MULBERRY HOUSE, S, by *Arthur Kenyon*, 1934–6 was one of the last schemes for Samuel Barnett's East End Dwellings Co. Neo-Georgian with three-storey canted bay windows either side of a central opening to a garden. Set back alongside is MONTFORT HOUSE, an earlier work for the company by its principal architects *Davis & Emmanuel*, 1901, part of a larger scheme towards Globe Road (*see* perambulation *1c*). Pink- and yellow brick façade with a high-stepped gable and hooded porch to the door. The internal provision was of a better class than usual with enclosed stairs and self-contained flats rather than single rooms.

S of Sugar Loaf Walk are much older survivors, Nos. 17 and 18, dating from the period when large mansions around the Green gave way to the middling sort of suburban house. Built as a pair, *c.* 1683–90. Five bays, two storeys with brick band to first floor and wooden modillion eaves cornice, the door of No. 17 central but that of No. 18 eccentric. Flat hoods with panelled soffits supported on carved and scrolled brackets are original but shaped wooden dormers are probably later. Both houses have well-preserved interiors with a mixture of plain- and bolection-moulded panelling, some original fireplaces (No. 18) and staircases rising from hall to attic with bracketed strings, paired corkscrew balusters and a heavily moulded handrail with square newels and ball terminals: their style advanced for their date. The staircase of No. 17 (Institute of Community Studies)* incorporates a dog-gate. Its gateway was brought from Hythe Church, Kent, by Sir Wyndham Deedes, principal of the University House Settlement, a working-class club established here in 1886. The settlement, associated with Oxford House, built No. 16 *c.* 1888 in sympathetic style and later added the prow-like Gothic chapel to the front. Distinctly less grand, Nos. 13–15 form a quiet terrace of various dates, alongside the lamentable Neo-Georgian POLICE STATION of 1997 and rugged Brutalist flats for the adjoining FIRE STATION of 1967–8 by *GLC Architect's Department*, a tough composition, finely executed in dark brick and concrete with exposed aggregate bands.

ROMAN ROAD divides the N and S closes of the Green. It is shown on Gascoyne's map of 1703 as a driftway but as Green Street by 1883 when a small area of slum housing was cleared

*Founded by the sociologist Michael Young, co-author of *Family and Kinship in East London*.

on its N side by the Metropolitan Board of Works. It was replaced by MUSEUM HOUSE, 1888 (Nos. 19–35), E of the Fire Station, the earliest surviving tenement by *Davis & Emmanuel* for the East End Dwellings Co. Three storeys above shops on Roman Road, it contained 'associated' flats (i.e., with shared WCs) for 166 and follows the no-frills-or-finishes standard set by Peabody. A further-reaching effort at rehousing was made S of Roman Road in 1922–4 with BETHNAL GREEN ESTATE, the borough's first effort at mass housing; like Poplar's Chapel House Estate of 1919, it was designed and built by the *Office of Works* (Chief Architect: *Frank Baines*) but here using plain four-storey brick Neo-Georgian blocks of flats arranged around a long inner courtyard (recently relandscaped). The estate was built on the site of the Bethnal House Asylum, a private institution originally established in the largest house on the Green, Sir John Kirby's Castle of *c.* 1570, and much rebuilt thereafter. Only two buildings were retained: a ward block, now the Public Library (*see* above) and, in the SE corner of the Estate, a pretty Arts and Crafts cottage with pointed gable over the porch set against the asylum's boundary wall. Immediately E, N off Cornwall Gardens are SUTTON DWELLINGS, three heavy blocks with large, shaped gables. 1909 – erected 'under charitable trusts' of William Richard Sutton, carrier of Golden Lane.

W of the Green, CAMBRIDGE HEATH ROAD runs between Whitechapel (S) and Hackney (N). Its character is mixed and dominated on the W side by the massive former Electricity Showrooms and Offices of 1959 by *Watson & Coates*; a striking effort at reintroducing large public buildings to the heart of the borough.* Rugged chequerboard panels of concrete and nascent curtain walling to the main block, and S wing in yellow brick channelled with courses of engineering brick. The rest of the street is a ragged two- and three-storey range punctuated to the N by the former GREEN MAN, with an attractive ironwork front probably by *Edward Brown* 1885, and the SALMON & BALL, a big mid-C19 corner pub.

N of Bethnal Green Road, the civilized character of the late C18 and early C19 suddenly re-emerges in PARADISE ROW which stands slightly back from the road behind a wedge of open land, part of the original green. The houses are shown on Horwood's map of the early C19. Nos. 5–11 were added 1807–20, though only Nos. 7–11 retain their good, plain yellow brick fronts with recessed arched doorways and straight-headed windows. The rest of this side of Cambridge Heath Road, including the Bethnal Green Mission (*see* above), is exceptionally drab and blighted by the railway viaduct which passes behind rows of forlorn shops. On the E side MAYFIELD HOUSE, an unremarkable but prominent slab of flats by Bethnal Green, 1962–4, in Portland stone with windows in a grid. At its S end, a curious section with a curved roof and large

*There are plans in 2004 to build a new Town Hall for Tower Hamlets on this site.

window overlooking the Green, designed as the borough's music library.

Alongside, in a surprisingly unprominent position, stands the Edwardian former TOWN HALL (*see* above). It is placed too close to the road to have the impact that its exuberant façade demands and its 1939 extension along Patriot Square is too plain. A plan of 1885 to build the town hall in Paradise Row* with an infirmary on the S close of the Green was thwarted so both were erected here. The former Infirmary, further N, is only part preserved. By *Giles, Gough & Trollope*, 1900, refurbished as flats. Asymmetrical front, in yellow brick with stone dressings. Large keyed arches to ground floor entrances and windows, broken and swan-necked pediments to first floor and paired round arches above. Projecting central oriel; lion's head corbels under the cornice. Pavilion wards to the rear were replaced by low-rise housing by *Baily Garner*, 1990–3. Then, to the corner with Parmiter Street, is the former Cambridge Heath Estate by *E.C.P. Monson*, 1926–7 for Bethnal Green; the estate became the object of outrage when the Communist-Socialist council named it the Lenin Estate. Yellow brick with hipped roofs and small sashes, and cranked gables with Venetian windows. On the N corner, an attractive large brick warehouse, its ground floor bays divided by glazed brick pilasters with ornate caps of foliage and masks. Three storeys of big windows above. On the W side of the road, CAMBRIDGE HEATH STATION, opened in 1870, is much remodelled. Its original part, on the W side of the line facing Clare Street, has blind windows and curved gables.

1b. SW of Victoria Park

The farmland NE of the Green surrounded the manor house, Bonner Hall, but was sold off to the Crown in 1841 for the laying out of Victoria Park (*see* p. 566) and the creation of a suitably impressive approach to its main SW gates. Here *Sir James Pennethorne* devised an axial set of streets, broadly tracing the older field divisions, with three radial avenues joining at the gates to provide good access from the City and the West End. The streets were to be lined with superior villas, as at Regent's Park where Pennethorne had worked on the Park Villages from 1841. Investors for such a proposition were hard to find and ultimately development was carried out by local builders who erected modest Italianate terraces instead.

The principal street is APPROACH ROAD, lined on each side by mature plane trees. Its proportions are commensurate with a formal grand avenue but it begins oddly, off the minor Old Ford Road at the NE edge of the Green. This was unintended: Pennethorne had hoped to drive it through the open space of

*Design won in competition by *Isaac & Lawrence*.

the Green to provide a continuous street from Bethnal Green Road; even in 1874 efforts were still being made to achieve this by the MBW. In spite of later rebuilding much of the avenue retains its 1860s terraces, evidently the work of several hands. On the SE side, Nos. 2–24, stock brick with restrained stucco detail: windows with moulded architraves, doorways with tented tops, vermiculated spandrels and keystones. Nos. 27–45, opposite, are similar but with round-arched first-floor windows. THE APPROACH TAVERN (now also a gallery) by *Hammack & Lambert*, 1860, was in matching style but was reconstructed above first floor, after bombing, in Neo-Georgian dark brown brick. The major event is the turreted group of RAINE'S FOUNDATION SCHOOL on the SE side (*see* p. 565), one of several institutions drawn to the area near the park in the late C19, including a large Methodist Church (rebuilt 1959, *see* above) on the corner with Bonner Road, diagonally opposite.

The smaller crossing streets have cheaper terraces and fewer pretensions, e.g. Nos. 2–14 ROBINSON ROAD developed by small local speculators with simple terraces. In the parallel, slightly grander, BONNER ROAD, Nos. 46–72 were built as Princes Terrace. Skinny houses in a pretentious Italianate with entrances raised sharply and steeply off the street. They back on to a former Brush Manufactory (now artists' studios), an indicator of the area's quickly declining character. Bonner Road's SE end has larger terraces of the 1860s facing the large triangular site occupied by the London Chest Hospital (*see* above), built on the site of the manor house, where Pennethorne had originally planned ornamental gardens.

The junction at the top of Approach Road where it enters the park was ravaged by bombing (including the destruction of Bonner's Lodge) and much rebuilt post-war, diminishing the strong axial layout of the original plans. In the angle of Approach Road and BISHOP'S WAY is REYNOLDS HOUSE of 1951–3 by *Donald Hamilton, Wakeford & Partners*. Built as the Borough's contribution to the Festival of Britain and done with its spirit, though ploddingly so. Six-storey right-angled block with end stair-towers, balcony access and flat roofs, brightened by some blue and yellow tile panels. The adjoining primary schools of St Elizabeth (1955) and St John the Baptist (1968) are equally dull. Facing are some attractive larger houses of the 1840s (Nos. 89–127) with broad windows and remains of a bold cornice. But Bishop's Way is no longer the grand thoroughfare to Hackney Road, with much of its street frontage lost to inward-facing post-war housing, notably the LCC's grave WELLINGTON ESTATE, built from the late 1930s on the site of the Waterloo Workhouse (1841) and continued after the war.

SEWARDSTONE ROAD, laid out with smaller houses along the Regent's Canal on each side of the park gates, is more charming. Its NW end still has 1850s terraces on both sides with small front gardens but the superior S side has good stucco detail and pilastered doorways. Nos. 65 and 67 are double-fronted. The simpler N side, backing on to the canal, has pairs of deeply recessed round-arched doors and stucco architraves. Close to the park gates, a Health Centre and Sheltered Housing of the early 1990s by *D.Y. Davies* in a mottled yellow brick under low sloping roofs. Sewardstone Road's SE end is quite different. It leads through the LCC's PARK VIEW ESTATE, of 1950–3 by *de Metz & Birks*, who retained the C19 street pattern but placed the blocks of flats to achieve some pleasant effects; most notably the four blocks obliquely set to give views along the canal and over the park, their stair-towers punctuating the vista along the street. Cantilevered balconies and entrances under flat sloping concrete canopies carried on V-shaped tubular supports. In the centre of the scheme, on the S side, stands Rosebery House, a long four-storey block in brick, staggered in plan to allow views to E and W. The overwhelming inspiration is Swedish, emphasized by the good landscaping of open spaces with mature birch trees softening the edges. The SE half of the estate, laid out E of the Church and School of St James the Less (*see* above) and up to Old Ford Road includes the larger and gloomier Pomeroy House, a single block of flats over shops, and two L-shaped six-storey blocks, Mark and Sidney Houses. In their midst is a splendid little Community Centre and Laundry with a top storey sloping outwards under a rippling concrete roof.

OLD FORD ROAD continues NE skirting the S boundary of the park. (For its W end and streets to the S, *see* perambulation *1c*.) At BRIDGE WHARF, close to the canal, is a nurses' home for the London Chest Hospital by *Pentarch*, 1998. Given presence by striped brick balconies describing a sinuous four-storey curve, and two plain stair-towers, one brick the other steel. At the canal bridge, THE CRICKETERS of *c.* 1850. Here the ancient shape of the road combines with views along the canal and into the park in an unexpectedly attractive manner. Facing the park, a long terrace on OLD FORD ROAD of big Italianate houses of *c.* 1865 with paired doorways in flat arches on stubby, composite, engaged columns. In the centre, some sympathetic modern infill built in 1987 on the site of the Royal Victoria Music Hall (demolished 1983). The terrace terminates at Grove Road with the ornate curved front of THE CROWN, one of the typical large 'hotels' which sprang up around the entrances to the park in the 1860s.

At the W end of this range, slightly S, is the cast-iron stop-lock BRIDGE, designed to carry the towpath of the Regent's Canal S across the mouth of the HERTFORD UNION CANAL. This was opened in 1830 to provide a link with the Lea Navigation at Hackney Wick. On the N side of the Union Canal is ROYAL VICTOR PLACE, houses of the 1980s with studio windows and balconies. They face a group of former industrial buildings on the canal's S side, originally Victoria Park Wharf, now BOW WHARF. They comprise a three-storey warehouse of 1901 (now Jongleurs) and the former Victoria Veneer Mills which has buildings of 1896–1912 (now restaurant and fitness centre).

At the E of Royal Victor Place a bridge carries GROVE ROAD, the main S approach to Victoria Park laid out in 1861 to provide a continuous route between Limehouse and Hackney. Where it enters the park are the Crown Gates, with regal lanterns on ironwork piers, and the picturesque Neo-Tudor Llanover Lodge. Diagonally opposite, E of Grove Road, is the compact LAKEVIEW ESTATE of 1956–8 by *Skinner, Bailey & Lubetkin:* the second of the firm's three estates for Bethnal Green. It is squeezed on to a narrow single-acre strip by the canal: the proximity of open space allowed for a higher than usual density of 160 persons per acre, the majority housed in an eleven-storey tower block. To avoid a single N façade, this is conceived as a staggered H-plan, allowing principal views E–W, with access balconies on the inward façades and a linking central tower for stairs and lifts. The blocks' façade demonstrate Lubetkin's undying interest in pattern-making with geometrical grids of exposed-concrete vertical piers and panelled facings. Flanking the tower's base are four two-storey old people's 'cottages', each containing four flats with through rooms for views to park and canal. They carry an unexpected echo of Regency villas with the exposed-concrete frame slightly advanced at the centre like a portico.

1c. *Globe Town: a circular tour* N *and* S *of Roman Road*

The walk begins in ROMAN ROAD at the junction with Globe Road, formerly a trackway between Bethnal Green and the Globe pub at Mile End. The burgeoning district was known as Globe Town in the early C19, the name revived in the 1980s as one of the borough's neighbourhoods. Dating from this time is the cumbersome brick arch holding a metal sphere placed close to the junction. On the N side of Roman Road, facing down Globe Road is the landmark of the former fire station (now London Buddhist Centre, *see* above). Its foil, opposite, is BACTON TOWER of 1965–6 by *Yorke Rosenberg & Mardall.* The first fully industrialized (i.e. system built) tower in the new Borough of Tower Hamlets, of pre-cast reinforced concrete clad with YRM's trademark white tiles. Since 1990 it has worn a pitched roof and flimsy porch. The adjoining two-storey block (council offices) was built as part of the scheme for shops and an old people's café. Refurbished with a profiled-metal roof and yellow uprights. Roman Road's N side here still has a recognizable mix of C18 and C19 houses with later shopfronts, including the sea-green tiling of the former Black Horse pub of 1883 (No. 67) by *Hammack & Lambert.*

N of Roman Road, GLOBE ROAD traces a curvy line to Old Ford Road, echoing its origins as Back Lane, a rural trackway at the E boundary of Bethnal Green village. The old scale of two- and three-storey terraces remains at the S end, replaced further N by a large Board School and late C19 mass housing for the East End Dwellings Co. by *Davis & Emmanuel.* Along the E side to Kirkwall Place and Welwyn Street: MENDIP HOUSE, 1900, with square corner towers, open staircases and shaped gables, and the stark SHEPTON HOUSE of the same year. They make a good group with the Board School to the NW, whose cliff-like façade towers over THE CAMEL pub, faced in vaguely Art Nouveau tiles. Just beyond in Globe Road, the massive scale continues with the EEDC's VICTORIA PARK ESTATE of large five-storey tenements, all also by *Davis & Emmanuel*, 1901–6. First MERCERON HOUSES (1901); octagonal corner tower and broad curve-topped gables, continuing as a single range with GRETTON HOUSES, originally two blocks with wide carriage arch between, now blocked. Rear blocks rebuilt after bomb damage by *Henry C. Smart & Partners*, 1947–9. Barrack tenements were not all that the Company provided and on the E side of Globe Road is an attractive group of cottages (1906) in hard red brick with rendered arched panels over pairs of doors. They replaced weavers' cottages of the 1850s. Finally, EVESHAM HOUSE on the W side, with its front to Old Ford Road.

OLD FORD ROAD is predominantly of the 1850s and 1860s, mostly erected in the aftermath of the creation of Victoria Park (*see* above): two-storey terraces with paired doorways in wide round-headed stucco architraves. On the S side, further E, No. 92 is the only double-fronted house, with rusticated ground floor, vermiculated quoins and mask keystones to the ground-floor windows. Nos. 94–6 are earlier, probably survivors from the first developments in Globe Town *c.* 1820: round-arched windows with interlaced Gothic tracery. Slightly further on, Cyprus Place leads S into CYPRUS STREET, one 50
of the most pleasing streets in the area. Built as Wellington Street in 1850–1. Mostly even two-storey terraces in plain yellow brick with lugged architraves to upper storeys, panelled doors and single-arched ground-floor windows with shutters. Set flat against the S side, facing Cyprus Place, is a WAR MEMORIAL. Simple grey marble tablet, with smaller shield below, erected by the Duke of Wellington's Discharged and Demobolised [sic] Soldiers and Sailors Benevolent Club in 1920. Such memorials were common in this part of East London after 1916, often beginning as temporary wooden shrines. Bethnal Green had the highest number of volunteers of any London borough, which accounts for the disproportionate number of names inscribed for a single street. The setting is strangely dramatic and moving. W is the DUKE OF WELLINGTON pub, its ground floor divided by tall pilasters and half-columns. Coeval shopfronts to the adjoining houses.

At Cyprus Street's E end BONNER STREET leads S to Roman Road. At the SE corner is an early Board School by *E.R. Robson* and *J.J. Stevenson*. Built 1876, at a time when pressure was immense for new schools in the dense East End parishes. It bears the relief of Knowledge Strangling Ignorance by *Spencer*

Stanhope that appeared on some of the earlier Robson schools, along with Flemish gables which must once have towered above the surrounding streets of low, two-storey weavers' cottages. These were swept away in the 1960s. A poignant memento of their inhabitants is the War Memorial set into the school's N wall on HARTLEY STREET which has a stone tablet beneath a della Robbia-style wreathed roundel of infant in swaddling bands. Erected in 1936, in place of a temporary wooden shrine of 1916, to commemorate the dead of Mace and Tagg Streets.

Post-war clearance of fifteen acres of C19 terraces E of Bonner Street was designed to reduce the population density to 136 persons per acre. 600 families were to be housed in the CRANBROOK ESTATE, a mixed development completed in 1961–8. This was the last, and largest, of the three estates designed for Bethnal Green by *Skinner Bailey & Lubetkin*, formerly members of Tecton, the firm responsible for radical post-war planning in the borough of Finsbury. The planning was typically novel, laid out as an 'X'* of wide pedestrian avenues designed to echo the surviving pattern of C19 streets to the N. Playing with scale and perspective informs much of the design. This builds up progressively from the perimeter with one- and two-storey houses and flats giving way to four-storey angled blocks of maisonettes and six square towers increasing in height towards the main axis, on tapering bases and with flying cornices. They are set at different angles, with the intention of creating 'movement', but the effect is bulky. Brick was specified, in preference to the concrete facings of the Dorset and Lakeview Estates, but projecting panels (now painted green) provide the firm's characteristic exterior patterning. Typically for Lubetkin, the greatest flourish is reserved for a dazzling series of staircases within the towers (cf. Dorset Estate). A more public amusement is at the NE corner of the estate, where the SW–NE avenue is concluded by a joky *trompe l'œil* 'sculpture' of a tapering path flanked by stone benches of diminishing scale beneath iron arches. On the S side of the estate are single-storey houses for the elderly grouped behind an open
111 green towards Roman Road. In the centre of the green, on an elevated fountain of overlapping stone sections is a SCULPTURE of the Blind Beggar and his dog by *Elisabeth Frink*. Commissioned by Bethnal Green Council in 1957 especially for the estate, and installed in 1963. The tense composition renders the much-loved mythical subject in a rough, battered form that is both appealingly vulnerable and serious. A community centre, by *Pentarch*, 1993, carries echoes of Lubetkin in its Y-plan and splayed entrance. Stripy brick. The same firm designed the conspicuous building at the NE edge of the estate (*see* perambulation *1b*). Closing the E end of the estate, the high-gabled profile of the late C19 former Cranbrook Board School (now flats).

* Relandscaping has made this into a figure-of-eight.

The S side of ROMAN ROAD was redeveloped post-war in several phases on small sites cleared by bombing. They are now drawn together without any sense of unity as the GREENWAYS ESTATE. The earlier parts of 1949–51 by *Donald Hamilton, Wakeford & Partners* are standard five-storey balcony-access flats of the pre-war type with blocks containing shops along the main road. Much refurbished and enhanced by *Levitt Bernstein* in the 1990s (project architect *Patricia Pearson*) with new roofs and remodelled stair towers. The next phase, W of Usk Street, was built 1956–9 by *Yorke Rosenberg & Mardall* (architect in charge, *J.S.P. Vulliamy*), one of several young practices patronized by the borough after 1951. It typifies more advanced attitudes to post-war urban planning with the creation of a new market square to supersede Roman Road's traditional street market: its character has been far better preserved than the similar square at Lansbury in Poplar. Surrounding the square are five-storey blocks of flats above shops constructed of reinforced concrete with brick flanks and infill of pre-cast concrete panels dotted with stone chippings. Barrow stores are placed discreetly at the rear.

SULKIN HOUSE makes a powerful contrast in the gap on the SE side of the square, one of two signature cluster blocks designed by *Denys Lasdun* of *Fry Drew Drake & Lasdun*, 1955–8. Its twin, TREVELYAN HOUSE, stands further S. Each has eight storeys with maisonettes accommodated in two angled blocks linked, in a butterfly pattern, to a slender, rounded central service tower.* The innovative design, repeated on a less intimate scale in Claredale Street (*see* perambulation *3a*), had the practical virtue of allowing high-density housing which respected the existing street pattern and required little demolition in advance. The adjoining four-storey blocks, also by Lasdun, are unimpressive in spite of sculptural external staircases, and the awkward site militates against a sense of unity between the flats and the older fabric with which they are interspersed. In BULLARDS PLACE, W, is St Simon Zelotes' Vicarage, Tudor Gothic by *A.R. Mason*, 1849, and the square brick Institute by *Walter B. Medlicott*, 1906–7, retained as a community centre. At the E end of Bullards Place is a Gothic arch with plain initials 'VPC' and date 1845. This was the former entrance to Victoria Park Cemetery, opened in 1845 but closed due to overcrowding in 1874 and reopened by the Metropolitan Gardens Association in 1893 as MEATH GARDENS. The arch may be by *Thomas Ashpitel*, who designed a mortuary and chapel (demolished).

W of the Market Square, along DIGBY STREET are pre-war council blocks of the DIGBY ESTATE, 1935–6 by *E.C.P. Monson*, and BUTLER HOUSE also by *Monson*, 1934, with the same hipped roofs, wide eaves and stripy brick. Regeneration of the estate in 1998 by *Levitt Bernstein* saw the conversion of a former LCC tram-shed of *c.* 1900, with a distinctive row of

*The commission was originally given to *Powell & Moya*.

circular windows, as a community centre. Behind, on the S side, TUSCAN HOUSE, a twelve-storey system-built tower by Tower Hamlets Council *c.* 1965.

1d. Bethnal Green Road and neighbourhood, a circular tour

BETHNAL GREEN ROAD linked the Green with the E edge of the City W end as housing spread E from Spitalfields and Shoreditch in the late C17. The walk can begin at the Underground Station. At the SW exits PUBLIC ART: pavement-set lights in glazed segmental-curved trenches with embossed images of 'child-friendly' objects, by *A.J. Bernasconi*, 2004. Across the E end of the road, the Great Eastern Railway BRIDGE of 1893 (by *Horseley & Co.*, Staffordshire) cuts across brutishly, spoiling the visual impact which Soane's St John was clearly intended to make on travellers approaching from the City. But by the late C19 Bethnal Green was a slum and its landmarks held in low estimation. It is an inauspicious start to the long, uneventful road whose sole architectural landmark is the tiny spire of St James the Great amongst a drab succession of fronts which combine warehouses, pubs, shops and flats in an unrewarding mix. The streets to N and S, e.g., Gale's Gardens, Hollybush Gardens and Punderson's Gardens were laid out with market gardens in the C18 but later formalized as streets when even garden sheds were adopted as dwellings. They were squalid by the 1840s when Gavin was investigating the district and were cleared progressively from the late C19.

Beginning on the S side, No. 488, at the E corner with Gale's Gardens has a modest shopfront with rusticated pilasters. Built for the SunLife Insurance Company in 1882 by *A. & C. Harston* who carried out slum clearance here for the Bethnal Green House Property Association. Further W clearance was undertaken by the LCC in the 1930s with large blocks for the HORWOOD ESTATE around Pott Street, retaining only the former Congregational Church. Then a neat group of three, LUPIN HOUSE (La Forchetta) a late C19 former clothing warehouse with an arcaded-shopfront and bands of stamped-terracotta tiles beneath the windows of the upper floors. Tucked in next to it, THE SHAKESPEARE, an 1890s refronting of an older pub in glazed green faience with fluted Ionic pilasters, and the former POLICE STATION (now Providence Row Housing Association) with a rather severe domestic front of two bow windows, stone faced on the ground floor. 1917 by *John Dixon Butler*, who refronted and enlarged an existing station, erected by his father *John Butler* in 1892. In the back yard are two-storey married quarters and an imposing four-storey section house in yellow brick with three short pointed gables (now flats). Next, THE CAMDEN'S HEAD, formerly the Lord Camden, established *c.* 1766 but rebuilt, probably in 1864 by *Edward Brown*. Painted front with pedimented stucco window surrounds and a later projecting ground floor with polished-granite piers.

A detour S between these buildings along AINSLEY STREET leads into an area cleared of its C18 fabric in 1868–*c.*1880 for a singularly ambitious rebuilding by Sydney Waterlow's Improved Industrial Dwellings Co. of large blocks of dwellings along CORFIELD STREET and WILMOT STREET. This extraordinary group was the company's first attempt at such a scale of provision. Up to that date it had produced small schemes of repetitive tenement blocks with open staircases entered from the street (e.g. Columbia Road) but here 1,025 families were to be housed in tall five-storey blocks laid out in linear fashion on both sides of the street. This created an overwhelming canyon-like scale, still partly preserved despite selective demolition and refurbishment (including tile-hung upper storeys) by *Stefan Zins Associates c.* 1985. The detailing is typically modest, in the company's trademark Jacobean-Italianate, but with the novelty of canted bay windows and, in contrast to the company's previous dwellings, semi-enclosed staircases. The dwellings on the W side of Wilmot Street are grandest, possibly designed for better-off artisans, with half-basements and stucco quoins, and Nos. 31–90 which are set slightly back. Space was left for HAGUE PRIMARY SCHOOL, now a 1930s replacement for one of the area's earliest Board Schools, built in 1873 by *John Giles & Gough* in the Gothic style favoured at that date. The school-keeper's house remains at the NW corner. The success of the development was enhanced by the opening of BETHNAL GREEN STATION on the GER in 1872 on THREE COLTS LANE. Facing the station is the self-advertising Waterlow Buildings, a small block including ground-floor shops: an uncommon feature only repeated in the Company's contemporary buildings at Ebury Street, Westminster.

E along Three Colts Lane, hard up against the back of the tenements along Corfield Street is a surprising industrial survival of C19 Bethnal Green, the former works of Allen & Hanbury, druggists (GREENHEATH BUSINESS CENTRE), established in 1874. Only the 1918 warehouse survives, its high elevations divided by brick and concrete piers and with a tall Italianate hydraulic tower corbelled out at the top for its water tank. Returning W along Three Colts Lane, the GOOD SHEPHERD MISSION, founded in 1855, rebuilt in 1871 after its first buildings were cleared for the railway. Simple gable front with five lancet windows to the school with voussoirs and arches of red and blue brick. Taller elevation alongside for the mission, with three slim lights and pointed-arch doorway.

From here, the walk can return to Bethnal Green Road across WEAVERS FIELDS, attractively planted and landscaped open ground created in the 1970s by the complete destruction of a densely packed area of early C19 two-storey weavers' cottages. A sculpture (N side), WEAVING IDENTITIES by *Peter Dunn,* has stainless-steel figures on a mast (carrying security cameras!)

rising from a base of bricks laid in a warping woven pattern. Of the vanished district only two buildings now survive, their scale a forcible reminder of the tight plots available by the late C19: the lonely but striking mass to the SW is the former WEAVERS FIELD SCHOOL of 1883 by *E.R. Robson.* Three storeys, with crenellated stone parapets and a canted stair-tower with steep pavilion roof; OXFORD HOUSE (*see* above), close to the gates on N side of the park in DERBYSHIRE STREET, is of matching height and must have once towered amongst its neighbours.

Back now N to Bethnal Green Road and turning W along the S side. The highlights are meagre, but worth making the journey for No. 332, E. PELLICI, an Italian café, established 1900 and still owned by the founding family. It is tiny but has a strikingly intact fascia of enamelled glass and chrome lettering, probably contemporary with the cosy interior which has beautifully crafted marquetry panelling done in a Deco style *c.* 1950 by the present owner's grandfather, *Achille Capucci.* Serving hatch at the rear with decorative glass panel below. Further on, the MARQUIS OF CORNWALLIS, a large pub of *c.* 1850, plain stucco with curved corner.

W of Vallance Road, the scene is even patchier. Only Nos. 281–5 (N side) stands out for its concave front and vertical tower, part of a remodelling of 1934 by *George Coles* for Smarts Picture Palace, a pre-1914 picture house (now warehouse). The walk returns E along the N side, past the landmark of the 'red church', *Blore*'s St James the Great (now flats, *see* above). Further E, the PLEASURE UNIT (No. 359), is a typical C19 drinking palace with big arch windows to the top floor and panels of sunk rosettes; the simpler type of pub is found at the stucco-trimmed and balustraded OLD GEORGE (No. 379), one of the oldest surviving pubs in Bethnal Green, rebuilt 1880 by *Edward Brown.* Small parts of the road's early C19 ribbon development survive beyond but the side streets are cut short by the extensive rebuildings of the backlands in the post-war era. ELLSWORTH STREET begins with dull blocks (Stapleton House) on its W side by *Howes & Jackman* for the LCC, completed 1948–9 with flat roofs and chunky balconies. The same firm extended the estate N *c.* 1957–62 with flats around a new square. Mixed development of two-storey homes and bedsits for the elderly, facing four- and six-storey maisonettes and an eleven-storey tower, Stockton House. The combination is surprisingly successful, retaining a C19 pub, the former Duke's Head, in one corner. A short alley off the square's NE corner leads into PUNDERSON'S GARDENS, a foul slum in the mid-C19 described by Southwood Smith (1838) as 'a long narrow street, in the centre of which is an open rush-gutter, in which filth of every kind is allowed to accumulate and putrefy . . . sometimes, and especially in wet weather, the gutter overflows; its contents are then poured into the neighbouring houses, and the street is rendered nearly impassable. As if to concentrate the evil still further, there are large cow-sheds and pig-styes close by, from which very nauseous odours were given off.' Several times rebuilt, its S end emerges into BETHNAL GREEN ROAD between a factory and one large former warehouse (CITY VIEW HOUSE). Red brick with uneven curved cornice, flat brick pilaster verticals and ranks of windows under concrete lintels. Finally HSBC, built as the London City & Midland Bank by *T.B. Whinney*, 1905. Corner site for conspicuousness with big segmental arch over the entrance and upper floors with Italianate detail.

1e. *The Collingwood Estate*

The COLLINGWOOD ESTATE, W of Cambridge Heath Road, was one of the first major interwar slum clearances in the East End by the LCC under its Chief Architect, *G. Topham Forrest*, and set a pattern of planning and design which would continue until 1939. The first block opened in 1923 and the estate was mostly complete by 1930 but expansion continued into the 1970s. A handful of older buildings including church, schools and a small number of earlier working-class dwellings were retained.

A tour of the estate begins with DARLING ROW off Cambridge Heath Road. It follows the line of a track to one of the farms that occupied the land in the C18. On its N side, Collingwood and Grindall Houses of 1949 are utilitarian in character, of five storeys in pale brick, angled slightly to follow the line of the street. These were late additions to the core of the estate which lies W between Collingwood Street and MERCERON STREET with six Neo-Georgian blocks, nicely detailed with round-arched windows and parapets carrying pineapple finials. They group around an open space and have the customary balcony-access plan but each block is of four storeys plus attics to allow for an additional floor without adding to the bulk, a deliberate ploy. In BRADY STREET to the W, earlier provision of improved housing is exemplified by MOCATTA HOUSE, a small tenement block by *Joseph & Smithem* for the Four Per Cent Industrial Dwellings Co., 1905. Tall and narrow, four storeys and attics, the height emphasized by a pair of high pointed gables breaking the eaves. The entrance has boldly articulated tapered-stone buttresses with domed finials, a Secessionist motif, and Art Nouveau ironwork. Built on the site of Jewish almshouses; immediately behind lies the JEWISH BURIAL GROUND (*see* above). Further N in SOMERFORD STREET, the LCC also retained the existing BOARD SCHOOL of 1881 with few frills; it makes maximum use of the tight site by means of a roof playground with characterful iron railings.

A more original approach to housing is made at ASHINGTON HOUSE by *Noel Moffett Associates*, 1970–4 for the GLC, which attempted to reconcile the needs for high-density housing within a compact plan that also recognized tenants' desire for character within a large block. This is conceived as an L-plan with two blocks hinged around a rather weak glass stair-tower but the main elevations, faced in brown brick, are strongly modelled with chunky projecting bays between recessed balconies and tough aggregate-faced floor bands and end walls. Harshness is countered, however, by the staggering of the flats to provide an unusually high degree of privacy and a generous provision of roof gardens. Nos. 46–8 Somerford Street were built as flat-roofed houses for disabled tenants, a series of hexagonal units whose wide angles allow for increased mobility. This hexagonal form was a feature of Moffett's earlier housing at Kilburn Priory Estate and White City; an idea which seems to derive from *Neumann, Hecker, and Sharon*'s apartment block at Ramat Gan, Israel of 1960–5. The design was an understandable reaction to earlier developments to the E built by the *GLC Architects* between 1964–70, typified by ORION HOUSE, a ten-storey maisonette slab on piloti, presiding over a nasty car park. At the E end of BARNSLEY STREET is the former St Bartholomew's Church (*see* above) of 1843–4 by *William Railton*, now flats (Steeple Court). The vicarage, at the corner with Buckhurst Street, has also been converted, while the churchyard, now St Bartholomew's Gardens, retains a single obelisk. E of the church, extensions to the estate of 1968–70 stretch as far as Cambridge Heath Road.

2. *West Bethnal Green*

2a. *St Matthew's Church to Bethnal Green Road*

The tour starts by St Matthew's Church in ST MATTHEW'S ROW, built in 1743 (*see* above) to serve the new parish. Facing the street on the churchyard's N side are the former St Matthew's National Schools of 1820. The bays to the street have Gothic windows, repeated along the flanks with iron frames and interlacing tracery. The schools were built over vaults to ease pressure on the burial ground (closed 1853); Hector Gavin claimed to note the stench of rotting corpses. Infants' schools (demolished) were added in 1862 by *Caesar A. Long*. Converted for flats 1998–9 with attic storey under a curved roof. Almost opposite the church gates in St Matthew's Row once stood the parish's first Town Hall, an early example for East London, built of Caen stone in a Neo-Tudor style in 1851 by *G.H. Simmonds*. Demolished in the early 1970s for housing. SE of the church in HEREFORD STREET stands its handsome RECTORY of 1905. Attractive William and Mary style with hipped roof, bracketed eaves and dormers. Regular S front of five bays with two bay windows. S of this a plain parish hall of 1904.

S of RAMSEY STREET, off Hereford Street to the E, is a tight group of C19 buildings, now converted to flats, including the former ABBEY STREET BRITISH SCHOOLS. Erected 1839, probably by *William Wallen*. Its low, unadorned W range (now largely obscured by a wall), faced a narrow alley with entrances between pilasters at either end. A central block for washrooms and rooms for master and visitors (heightened in 1872) was flanked by two large classrooms. The original cast-iron windows, iron truss roof and original joinery to the boys' classroom were removed on conversion. The infants' school, probably added *c.* 1841, lies behind at right angles. Two storeys with pitched roof and utilitarian arched window recesses along the sides. Parallel to the S, facing CHESHIRE STREET, are the former public baths and washhouse of 1898–1900 by *R. Stephen Ayling*, converted for flats 1999–2000 by *Yeates Design & Architecture*. The first baths built in Bethnal Green under the 1897 Public Baths and Washhouses Act. Two-storey red brick block in a domestic Flemish style with excellent relief carvings of cherubs over the male and female entrances. Stripy stone-banded second storey and curved gable ends with oriel window supported on carved, winged female terms (badly restored), over the E entrance to the Board Room and Superintendent's flat. The iron and glass bathhouse to the N was demolished for a discreet, uninspired new wing but the utilitarian single-storey former washhouse survives, W, with its iron and glass lantern roof. Its provision of space for prams 'in which the washers usually bring their linen' was a noted improvement.

We return W along CHESHIRE STREET, known as Hare Street in the C18 when Harefields lay along its S side. The open ground was taken in 1839 for the Eastern Counties Railway. Its successor, the Great Eastern, built REFLECTION WORKS, a large 1860s goods depot, along the street's S side. It has a single-storey gabled range of five bays in red, yellow and blue bricks with a taller two-storey W range adjoining designed as multi-storey stables. Facing on the N side is the little enclave around WOOD CLOSE, recorded in 1643 as a field 'new dug for brick' but built up with houses on both sides by the late C18 including the parish watch house (rebuilt 1826, *see* St Matthew's above). The square is now filled by a towering Board School (William Davis Primary School) of 1900–1 by *T.J. Bailey*, built in spite of resistance from the local church schools and serving a largely Jewish population. Tall and narrow even by the standards of the East End, a classic three-decker with Baroque dressings of buff terracotta and an unusual, red brick and terracotta external covered stair on the N side.

E of Wood Close in Cheshire Street new developments have crept in since the late 1980s, e.g. the Postmodern CITY PAVILION, by *Spiromega*, *c.* 1989 for flats, offices and workshops within a very tall, symmetrical composition around a gated courtyard. Red and yellow brick with a central entrance under a broad gable and angled corner towers. Within the inner precinct, four storeys with balconies. Built on the site of St Matthias, a Commissioners' church of 1846–7 by *Wyatt & Brandon* (demolished 1951). In CHILTON STREET, No. 52 was the church Mission House and Hall, 1887–9 by *William Reddall*

& Son; Neo-Tudor with ground-floor windows with Gothic lights, plentiful hoodmoulds and off-centre gable.

The S side of CHESHIRE STREET was built up with continuous frontages of two-storey cottages in the early C19. They have gone but a few surprising survivals remain e.g., No. 46, C18, with a later, glazed and shuttered shopfront. Tripartite weaver's windows to first and second floors – a rare sight now but once ubiquitous in Bethnal Green. The much larger No. 44 was a pub, *c.* 1860, and retains its arcaded and shuttered front. Round-arched windows between broad pilasters. Then a very complete late C19 terrace (Nos. 8–38) with integral shopfronts, built *c.* 1870–2 by *Reddall & Cumber*. Brick with first-floor windows framed by segmental arches, and moulded brick cornice, the regular design brought out by the refurbishment in 1991 by *Building Design Prospect*. The N side here is less interesting, modest flats by *Michael Sierens Architects*, *c.* 1998–2002 on the site of the Wlodowa Synagogue, a working-men's synagogue for Polish Jews, mostly cabinet-makers, who created its panelled interior and fittings (now destroyed). It was here too that *Hawksmoor* surveyed land for the Church Commissioners in 1711 (later turned down in favour of the site of Christ Church, Spitalfields) and produced his plan for a 'Basilica after the Primitive Christians' set within a precinct* and with its entrance on Brick Lane to the W.

Cheshire Street emerges onto the N end of BRICK LANE. This is cut in two, just S of here, by the railway which marked the boundary between the parishes of Bethnal Green and Spitalfields. Built 1840 by the Eastern Counties Railway to serve the Bishopsgate Goods Station on Commercial Street (partly demolished 2003, including most of the dramatic vaulted viaduct by *Braithwaite*). N of this line, something of the character of C18 Brick Lane still persists. Nos. 125 and 127 at the N corner with SCLATER STREET began as one large house, rebuilt in 1778 as two houses with one-room-deep weavers' workshops in the upper floors (restored 2001; it was originally four storeys tall with a long garret window). On the S wall is a fine sculpted plaque, set within a classical frame and inscribed 'THIS IS SCLATER Street, 1778'; a late date for its Rococo style. Sclater Street, the centre of the live-bird markets in the C19 and C20 had tall rows of weavers' tenements on both sides. Only the pantiled roofed Nos. 70–74 survive (derelict in 2004). A plaque dated 1723 was also recorded in 1871 by *The Builder*† in BACON STREET. Here on the N side, E part, is a notable example of the new character being established in this part of the East End by artists and architects at the beginning
124 of the C21. A four-storey house of 2000–2 by *William Russell* for himself in rough concrete, clad in galvanized steel at the base and giving way in the upper floors to partly opaque glazing and a sliding screen to a double-height space inside.

* An idea partly realized at St George-in-the-East (*see* p. 479).

† 28 January 1871.

Continuing up BRICK LANE, Nos. 149 and 161 (W side) are indicative of the early C18 single-room tenements specifically erected for weavers, poor relatives indeed of the smart houses in Spitalfields.*

Brick Lane joins BETHNAL GREEN ROAD. E of the junction, Nos. 120–60 (S side) are a partly surviving range of early C18 houses, while the N side is mid-C19 Italianate, including No. 143, the stuccoed three-bay front of the former Well & Bucket pub, rebuilt in 1873.† W of Brick Lane, the road was re-aligned by the Metropolitan Board of Works in 1878–9 to create a broad thoroughfare to Shoreditch High Street. Nos. 113 and 115, now set back on the N side from the new line of the road, are three-storey weavers' houses of 1735, much altered but their garrets still visible. One-room-deep, they originally had front, winder staircases making space for large workshop windows in the timber-framed rear walls. The realigned N side was entirely rebuilt after 1879, mainly with warehouses and factories but also with large pubs, e.g. No. 25, at the corner with Club Row, the former KNAVE OF CLUBS (now Les Trois Garçons) built in 1880 by *E. Dunch*. The bar and three exceedingly fine engraved-glass mirrors (one of which is modern) were retained in the conversion by *Michael G. Humphries*, 1996. Alongside, W, a former boot manufactory of *c.* 1884, three storeys with half-columns and pilasters to the ground floor, broad windows with column mullions and iron-beam lintels. To the corner with Chance Street, the former Bethnal Green Synagogue, established in 1906 but rebuilt after bombing in 1958. A grey brick box. Now the studio of the sculptor, *Rachel Whiteread*, who has cast its interior for several works since 1999. Decorative coloured glass has been removed from the windows. At the corner with Ebor Street, another former pub of 1880, THE SWAN, originally brick and terracotta with large relief panel of a swan over the corner elevation. Finally, a large complex of warehouses occupying an entire block between here and Shoreditch High Street. Nos. 5–11, *c.* 1879–81, were originally for timber merchants. Five storeys, twelve-bays wide with a projecting stone cornice and windows in the (rebuilt?) upper floors grouped in arched pairs. Rear rebuilt behind after 1923 by *J.H. Storrar* for Pearks Dairies, part of Lipton's, who also built the vast eight-storey warehouse, now THE TEA BUILDING, at the corner with Shoreditch High Street in 1931–2. Steel-framed, the verticals faced in patterned brick. Deep concrete floor panels and steel-framed windows. Converted to live–work space by *Alford Hall Monaghan Morris*, 2003. Lipton's also erected the block in EBOR STREET, 1933 by *Hal Williams & Co.*, reinforced concrete with hard classical detailing of fluted brackets in the top storey but one.

*Information on the C18 development is indebted to Peter Guillery of English Heritage.

†It had an excellent interior of tiled panels by *Wm. B. Simpson & Son*, including one which depicted 'Club Row in ye Olden Times', showing the local markets and trades.

REDCHURCH STREET, parallel to Bethnal Green Road to the N, was originally Church Street, the old road from Shoreditch to Bethnal Green. Its narrow proportions are a good reminder of the cramped confines of this district in the C19 and it still has a ragged appearance with houses, pubs, small factories and warehouses jostling together. No. 34, the OWL & THE PUSSYCAT (formerly The Crown) may have a late C17 origin but is primarily an 1890s refronting of a mid-C18 pub. Unexpectedly grand, with a classically detailed five-bay stucco façade, and inside good 1760s panelling, furniture and staircase. In CHANCE STREET (r.) DIRTY HOUSE of 2002 by *David Adjaye* for the artists Tim Noble and Sue Webster, is a converted warehouse covered in a thickly impastoed texture of black anti-graffiti paint, with strange smoked-glass flush windows to the ground floor, rectangular windows above and the roof raised to float above a terrace. Marking the gradual encroachment of distinguished new-build in this area is No. 16 CLUB ROW (N) by *Howard Carter* and *Sarah Cheeseman* (a.k.a *Thinking Space*), 2001. A tiny and ingenious piece of infill with a fully glazed façade, rubbing up against a formidable late C19 warehouse. N along Club Row lies the Boundary Street Estate (*see* Perambulation 2b).

2b. The Boundary Street Estate

BOUNDARY STREET marked the division between the parishes of Shoreditch and Bethnal Green. By the end of the C19 it also marked the gap between 'respectable' East London and the 'criminal' district of 'The Nichol'. Here was one of the worst slum areas, made notorious by Morrison's novel, *The Child of the Jago* (1896), and condemned by health officers as early as 1883. One in every four born here died in childhood. Its poverty and desperation drew philanthropists from as early as the late C18 and individual reformers and building companies attempted to improve both health and housing in the following century. But it was only in the 1890s, and no doubt under the influence of Morris and early Socialism, that planners began to regard the working class in their demand for decent living conditions as human beings not essentially different from themselves.

The LCC was more than any other body instrumental in bringing about a change, and the BOUNDARY STREET ESTATE* is a milestone. The 1890 Housing of the Working Classes Act enabled the comprehensive plan for The Nichol's clearance and redevelopment and the LCC planned for the rehousing of 5,300 people. The first PLAN, for a grid of 40-ft wide streets lined by parallel blocks, was replaced in 1893 after the *Housing of the Working Classes Branch of the Architect's Department* had been

*The fullest account of the estate's planning, design and the contribution of individual architects is given in Susan Beattie, *Revolution in London Housing. LCC Architects and their work 1890–1914*, 1980.

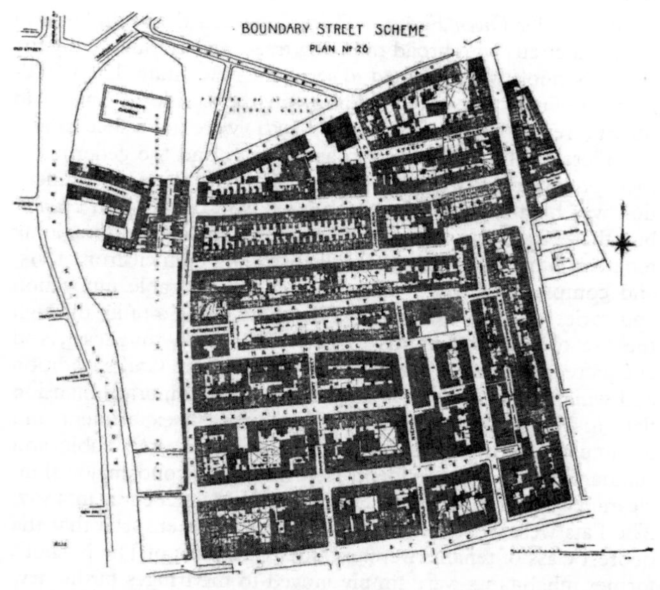

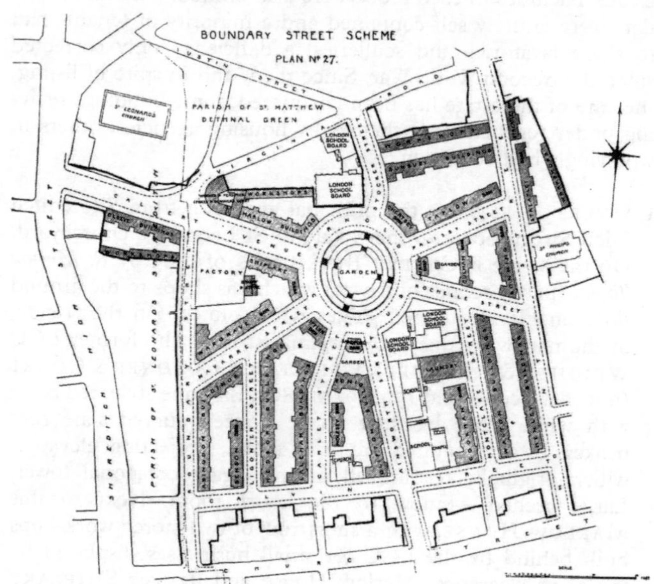

Boundary Street Estate, Bethnal Green
Plan of the area before 1890 and as replanned in 1893

formed under *Owen Fleming*. They replanned the estate around a central circus with broad radiating tree-lined avenues. Only the Board Schools were retained to serve the new estate. The LCC's first dwellings, Streatley Buildings on the E side of Swanfield Street (erected 1893–4; demolished 1971) were not a success and considered both too spartan in appearance and too generous in their provision of two self-contained flats per floor. A competition was held for the next two blocks, won by *Rowland Plumbe* but these too were a costly disappointment so the remaining nineteen buildings were undertaken by the council from 1895, and completed in 1900. They showed considerable innovation and variety in their treatment while maintaining a unity through the use of common motifs of patterned brick, roughcast, and chequered decoration that is in the best Arts and Crafts tradition and which looks at least as attractive as contemporary mansion flats in Kensington. Boundary Street was an experiment and in time the LCC's flats would become more predictable and standardized: a trend evident even in their second major slum clearance for the Millbank Estate, Westminster begun in 1897. The flats were generously sized but high rents ensured that the poorest class of tenants were excluded and most of The Nichol's former inhabitants were simply moved to the fringes of the new estate. Facilities in each block were also limited: only half of the flats were entirely self-contained and a minority of tenants had to share lavatories and sculleries, a deficiency only corrected since the Second World War. Since then, and in spite of listing, the care of the estate has been chequered, some buildings reviving under regeneration schemes by housing agencies, others in worryingly bad condition.

CALVERT AVENUE is the principal approach from Shoreditch High Street, open on the N side to St Leonard's churchyard. On the S side is CLEEVE BUILDINGS of 1895 by *R. Minton Taylor* (partly rebuilt post-war) which has shops to the ground floor and large stepped gables with volutes. On the N side, in the narrow wedge with Virginia Road, is the former LCC WEIGHTS & MEASURES OFFICE and CORONER'S COURT (now flats, converted 1998–9) of 1898. Baroque style, red brick with white stone banding under a steep curved slate roof broken by the pointed gable of a flat, projecting elevation which originally terminated in an elegant octagonal tower. Large arched window to the court room. Next to this MARLOW HOUSE, with a short row of two-storey workshops built behind by the LCC for small businesses displaced by the slum clearance. Marlow House and its pair SHIPLAKE HOUSE flank the opening to ARNOLD CIRCUS, the focus of the estate. At its centre is a high terraced garden crowned by a BANDSTAND, a pretty timber construction with sweeping tiled ogee roof much in need of repair. The buildings around the circus set the tone for the estate, with red and yellow stripy brickwork, round-arched doors with chequerboard patterning, salt-glazed brick for the ground floors and high slate roofs. Five blocks, mostly by *R. Minton Taylor*, 1895–6, but each deliberately varied in scale and form. The best is Chertsey House 78 (NE quadrant), which has a wide gable over a pair of oriels and upper floors with deepening bands of red and pink brick and stripy chimneys, diagonally set at the centre, breaking through the hipped and mansarded roof. The smaller Hurley House (E) and Sandford House (S) are charming, with three-bay fronts, wider bands of pink and orange brick and windows framed by projecting vertical strips. Between them stands the former Rochelle Primary School of 1879 by *E.R. Robson*, one of two Board Schools built to serve The Nichol and retained in the rebuilding. The jollier caretaker's house at its W end, a half-octagon with a chimney, dated 1899, was added by *T.J. Bailey* who also erected the plain Infant's School along Club Row, S, which has a covered playground on the upper floor. The other school stands in the NW quadrant of the circus, Virginia Primary, Virginia Road, of 1875 (with later alterations): a classic *Robson* three-decker, for once satisfactorily in proportion to its neighbours.

Of the other buildings, the following should be mentioned. On the SW quadrant, the classically detailed Iffley House, 1896–8 by *A.M. Phillips*, has its entrance at the rear, leaving the N façade free for a pair of broad Diocletian windows to the ground floor of glazed brown brick, beneath three-storey canted oriels and curved and pointed dormers. In Navarre Street immediately W: Wargrave House, 1897 by *William Hynam*, with wide projecting eaves over brown brick, and small gables over strange shallow bay windows to the upper floors; Hedsor House, one of four excellent designs by *C.C. Winmill* (*see* below), 1898; Abingdon House, 1896–8 by *A.M. Phillips*, five storeys with swept double gables and a monumental conical tiled roof above the canted corner with Boundary Street. In Camlet Street, a group of three by Winmill: Laleham House (1898), Molesey House (1896), and Clifton House (1897).

In Club Row, St Hilda's East community centre (1994 by *Mackenzie Wheeler*) adopts the estate's motifs including a canted stair-turret with ogee roof, banded brickwork and rendering. It began as a ragged school established in the C18 by Nicholas Duthoit, a Spitalfields silk merchant, rebuilt in 1879. The C19 building survives to the l. of the main entrance. The earliest surviving residential blocks, by *Plumbe*, 1894, are to the E between Montclare Street and Swanfield Street. Two long blocks with courtyard between and resolutely flat façades with ranks of narrow windows under Dutch gables; a treatment scarcely showing much advance upon earlier philanthropic housing. The contrast between these and the mature style of Cookham House, on the W side of Montclare Street, is instructive. 1897 by *R. Minton Taylor*, who broke up the wall plane with tall, projecting bays and huge two-storey gables. Taylor repeated this device at the Millbank Estate Westminster, begun in the same year. The absence of washing facilities within the blocks required a communal LAUNDRY, N of Cookham House, but no bath-house was provided. 1894–6 by *William Hynam* in mid-C17 domestic style. Two storeys with a hipped roof on deep eaves, modillion cornice and dormers. Paired arched chimneys. Mullioned windows and Tudor-arched doorway. The blocks N of ROCHELLE STREET, SONNING, CULHAM, TAPLOW and SUNBURY are of 1894–6 by *C.C. Winmill* and of an altogether superior quality with good textural variety. Sunbury Workshops are two-storey in eight units, of four workshops each, with central recessed entrance, loading door and hoist jib, very large cast-iron windows, and a north-light roof.

2c. Columbia Road, the Jesus Hospital Estate and Avebury Estate

The expansion of Shoreditch's E fringe across Hackney Road began in the C18 along COLUMBIA ROAD (known as Crabtree Row at that date) a small lane leading to the Nag's Head pub on Hackney Road. Its W end was already crammed with houses and furniture workshops by the mid-C19 when the district first began to draw the attention of philanthropic
58 building companies. Its S side here is dominated by LEOPOLD BUILDINGS of 1872 for Sydney Waterlow's Improved Industrial Dwellings Co., extending the possibilities of the flat prototype developed by Waterlow's builder, *Matthew Allen*, in the 1860s. To the r. is a short range of three and four storeys with shops, but most of the flats are contained within the large symmetrical terrace with open stairs and access balconies behind curly iron balustrades and with the company's usual coarse hybrid of Jacobean/Italianate decoration. Refurbished in 1996 by *Floyd Slaski Partnership* who maintained the integrity of the façade but added new stair-towers at the rear. Facing is a tall point block, CUFF POINT by the *GLC Architects*, 1972 on land earlier cleared of industry. Fourteen storeys, in dark brick with exposed aggregate-faced floor bands and a concrete parapet with a horizontal slot. Contemporary maisonette blocks along PELTER STREET and a neat MEDICAL CENTRE of 1993 by *Stock Woolstencroft*, in stripy brick with a projecting glazed upper floor over the entrance in the friendly style of Lubetkin's pre-war Finsbury Heath Centre.

Continuing E along COLUMBIA ROAD, the NURSERY SCHOOL on the N side has Gothic railings and gatepiers, the sole remnants of the extraordinary Columbia Market (*see* Introduction, above), regrettably demolished in 1958. Its site is occupied by lamentable slabs of flats (completed 1963–4 by the LCC) which turn inward to face OLD MARKET SQUARE, a cheerless space crossed by elevated ramps and pedestrian walks. Adjoining this to the E were Columbia Dwellings, early improved flats by *H.A. Darbishire* commissioned by Baroness Burdett-Coutts to replace Nova Scotia Gardens, one of the famous and foul heaps of rubbish from the City. St Thomas'

Church lay immediately behind, 1848–50 by Vulliamy (demolished). The formal arrangement of buildings and C19 streets was wiped away from the 1950s. On the site of the dwellings stands SIVILL HOUSE, a strikingly high brick tower by *Skinner & Bailey*, 1964–6, actually two blocks with angled plans and flying roof-grids linked by a circular service tower concealing a dramatic internal spiral staircase; evidence of the hand of their former partner *Lubetkin*, who also designed the characteristic patterning of the principal elevations with their applied concrete panels. The tower was a late addition to *Skinner, Bailey & Lubetkin*'s DORSET ESTATE of 1955–7, which lies immediately N towards Hackney Road. It comprises eight blocks, each named after one of the Tolpuddle Martyrs, with most of the flats contained in a pair of massive eleven-storey Y-shaped blocks* with patterned façades of reinforced concrete faced in Kentish-ragstone aggregate. In line with their S axes are smaller blocks of four storeys and in the centre of the estate, diminutive between the high blocks, is a circular brick-and-concrete LIBRARY. Its upper storey, for a community room, originally overhung the ground floor. The firm also designed the ROYAL VICTORIA pub on the E side of the estate, in matching style. In spite of the underlying geometry of the plan, the executed arrangement is awkward and there is little of the engagement with the urban pattern that made a success of Holford Square, Finsbury. No doubt the large blocks seemed less insensitive during the brief period when Columbia Market acted as a foil.

The E part of COLUMBIA ROAD, known as Birdcage Walk after 1760, crossed the estate of the Jesus Hospital, founded in Barnet by James Ravenscroft in 1670. In the first period of its development, after 1830, houses were built along the N side but these were mostly replaced from the 1880s with a Board School and small industrial workshops and factories. The S side has plain 1860s terraces with shops, contemporary with development of the streets behind (*see* below). Nearly all the shopfronts survive and these have been elegantly restored to capitalize on the weekly draw of the long-established Sunday flower market, which was one of the largest in London by 1900 and remains a remarkable sight in such a narrow street. Halfway along on the N side, the ROYAL OAK public house is a typically good design of 1925 by Truman's architect *A.E. Sewell*, in a variation of his Anglo-Dutch style with curved faience-clad gables. Inside, an unusual glass ceiling. EZRA STREET lies behind, a remarkably intact and atmospheric L-shaped Victorian alley with workshops, a former dairy, and a large warehouse (No. 1) by *W.A. Finch*, 1894, converted and reconstructed for industrial units and residential studios in 1991 by *Hunt Thompson Associates*. Immediately N of it, they also designed Nos. 51–61 RAVENSCROFT STREET, four

*A third was planned towards Hackney Road.

terraced houses and a Postmodern block of flats in stripy brick with a pedimental gable with a lunette.

To the N, turning E, SHIPTON STREET has housing of various dates. The S side begins with Nos. 2–14, Neo-Georgian cottage flats of 1939 by *Ian B. Hamilton* with large sashes and bracketed hoods to the doors, next to a short terrace of Victorian workers' cottages with wide arched ground-floor windows. WILLIAM FENN HOUSE is a terrace by *Skinner, Bailey & Lubetkin* in the brick and concrete livery of the Dorset Estate. The N side was cleared of its housing in 1933 for the NAG'S HEAD FIELDS ESTATE, a joint venture between the LCC and the Nag's Head Housing Society for eight blocks of flats, designed in *Ian Hamilton*'s usual Moderne Neo-Georgian. Mostly completed by 1937 with some post-war additions by the LCC. Horatio House of 1936 in Horatio Street has square concrete balconies stacked up on iron columns, while the other four blocks enclose a courtyard, each block with arched through ways and dated rainwater hoppers decorated with horse heads. The inner elevations are of different heights and variously treated. At the corner with Ropley Street and Columbia Road, the estate included THE GLOBE pub with high pointed gable, rendered in a Deco style. Almost opposite, on Columbia Road, a single surviving block of the Guinness Trust's only venture in East London. 1890–2 by *F.L. Pilkington*. Featureless with a quadrant end. Two similar blocks have been replaced by the Peabody Trust. S of Columbia Road, the Jesus Hospital's estate was fully laid out by *Henry Robert Abraham* c. 1862–8 with streets of two-storey terraces, mostly of two bays with arched windows and stucco sill bands. Its excellently preserved character is indebted to the GLC who compulsorily purchased the estate in 1979, and cleared part of the housing to create the triangular JESUS GREEN. The housing was sold to private developers in 1986 for refurbishment, controversially heralding the triumph of gentrification over renovation for council housing. In BAXENDALE STREET, E, the older housing is book-ended by colourful housing for the elderly by *Hunt Thompson Associates*, 1986 for Circle 33 Housing Trust, with crowstepped gables and lunette windows, cf. Ezra Street, above. BARNET GROVE runs S. At the junction with WELLINGTON ROW is a pair of corner pubs, now converted to flats. The former Prince of Wales faces the former Queen Victoria, E, which has a large coat of arms on its parapet.

The streets to the S between Wellington Row and Bethnal Green Road, far less salubrious, were the object of small-scale slum clearance by Bethnal Green before 1939. In DELTA STREET is DELTA HOUSE, walk-up flats of 1936–7 by *E.C.P. Monson*, enlivened by jazzy Expressionist detail of projecting, faceted stairlights and flat, curved-concrete canopies. Refurbished as private housing in 2000–2 by *Pollard Thomas Edwards*, who added a penthouse and created ground-floor gardens. At the S end, GOSSET STREET was scheduled for clearance by the LCC before 1939 but this was carried out only after 1945. The result was the Avebury Estate. *T.P. Bennett & Son* designed the earlier blocks laid out 1948–50 on the s side of the street. They form a core of dull, rectangular five-storey flats set around a courtyard. Identical blocks were added as late as the 1960s but in 1955–7 the youthful team at the *LCC Architect's Department* adopted a more innovative and humane approach for a mixed development on the adjoining site to the w, either side of Gosset Street. The part standing along the n side is rather commonplace, with five-storey balcony-access flats behind green spaces with mature trees. Real ingenuity was achieved opposite with the picturesque grouping of Eversley House, a five-storey point block, and a staggered terrace of six two-storey pitched roof houses along Lorden Walk. These serve as the backdrop for The Lesson, a bronze sculpture of a mother teaching her child to walk, by *Franta Belsky*, 1958: a characteristic effort by the LCC to humanize the new estates with specially commissioned artwork. Further w on Gosset Street, the existing Board School (now Bethnal Green Technology College, *see* above) was expanded to serve the reconstructed district. Gosset Street returns n to rejoin Columbia Road, close to the start of this tour.

3. North Bethnal Green

3a. Old Bethnal Green Road and Neighbourhood

A tour can begin from St Peter's Church, just s of Hackney Road, set in a little square with its vicarage and the former schools (*see* above), but with the unwelcome surrounding of St Peter's Estate, interlinked slab blocks by Tower Hamlets Council, 1965–7. Infinitely more sensitive to the church precincts are the low, asymmetrical clusters of brick houses, maisonettes and flats to the s, erected up to *c.* 1976 by the GLC, which extend s and se down to Old Bethnal Green Road (despite its name, never the main route to the Green). Rocque's map of 1747 shows it as Coats's Lane, a track skirting the w and n boundary of Coats' Farm. The n–s part to Bethnal Green Road, parallel to the s, was renamed Pollard Row; a detour here takes in the former Queen 56
Adelaide Dispensary (converted and extended for housing 1990 by *Cazenove Architects Co-operative*). Founded 1849 in the wake of the cholera epidemic. Rebuilt on this site in a superbly lavish Renaissance style by *Lee & Long*, 1865–6. Red brick abundantly decorated with carved-stone ornament of fruit and flowers. On the main front, a bust of Queen Adelaide is set into a broken pediment beneath an elaborate clock tower (restored in 1990) with an open cupola. Almost opposite, Working Men's Club (No. 44) built in the 1890s as the Bethnal Green Radical and Liberal Club. Three bays, its

central entrance flanked by engaged Ionic columns. Dentilled cornice beneath a row of large segmental pedimental hoods breaking through the roofline. Across the open space to the S stands the HEALTH CENTRE in Florida Street (*see* p. 564).

E along OLD BETHNAL GREEN ROAD. At the junction with MANSFORD STREET is a handful of older survivals from the dense pattern of streets built up towards the end of the C19 when this area had a strongly Jewish population, mostly engaged in tailoring: Blythe Street and Teesdale Street (mostly demolished in the 1960s) were referred to by Booth in the 1880s as a 'Jewish island'. Mansford Street's S end was newly laid out by 1880 to a more generous width than its early C19 neighbours and lined with new institutions including the former LAWDALE SCHOOL (SW of the crossing) of 1882, by *E.R. Robson*, with a straight, sheer façade with short pilaster buttresses and characteristic tall windows, variously treated. To its S, since replaced, were improved dwellings and even baths. On the opposite side, E, Congregationalists built their handsome Romanesque church (later Unitarian, *see* p. 557). Slightly later and N of Bethnal Green Road, the School Board erected Mansford Street Central School (now OAKLANDS SCHOOL), an early attempt, though not officially sanctioned, to provide technical training in an industrial district. 1896 by *T.J. Bailey*. Symmetrical, with a central block containing a single-storey hall and classroom with linked pavilion wings for workshops. Linked by a bridge across Bethnal Green Road, Arts Building by *Edwin Brear Associates*, 1994.

Next to the E is a fascinating and unusual example of mixed speculative development of the late C19 undertaken 1899–1904 by *Charles Winckley*, a Hackney builder. He replaced four existing streets with a carefully planned arrangement of shops, houses, warehouses and workshops. Facing OLD BETHNAL GREEN ROAD and TEMPLE STREET (E) are four-storey dwellings of the type erected by philanthropic companies with open staircases, cast-iron balustrades and two self-contained dwellings per unit, but opening onto TEESDALE STREET (W) are shops and flats with archways through to rows of workshops for bootmakers laid out in parallel behind. Three-storey houses line the inner cross-streets of CANROBERT STREET and WINCKLEY STREET with high fronts and a minimum of detail save for chamfered lintels. The variety of provision and the considered nature of its conception are wholly remarkable.

Rising assertively above this in CLAREDALE STREET, N, KEELING HOUSE belongs to the post-war age. The contrast between the two is one that excited or alarmed in equal measure the recorders of the changing face of the post-Blitz East End. There are only a handful of one-off tower blocks in the East End but Keeling House has been loved and loathed more than most.

Of 1955–9 by *Denys Lasdun* of *Fry, Drew, Drake & Lasdun*, the tower is a sixteen-storey 'cluster' block, designed as a much larger version of the prototypes developed in Usk Street (*see* perambulation *1c*) in the early 1950s. Two-storey maisonettes are contained in four stacks linked at angles by bridges to a service core, the planning designed to increase light and privacy for the tenants. The detailing is as good as one would expect of this architect, with L-shaped concrete hoods over the doorways and the individual units expressed externally by a concrete cross-frame with pre-cast balcony fronts creating a rhythmic pattern of horizontals. These are interrupted lower down by a floor of single-storey flats, designed to reflect the height of its C19 neighbours. The blank outer walls of each stack have pre-cast concrete cladding (now painted) which finishes at the base in a downward-pointing 'V'. The virtue of building so high, still a novelty at this date, was seen to be the ability to preserve the existing street pattern and minimize the need for extensive demolition during reconstruction. In Lasdun's opinion, the 'cluster' would also preserve some semblance of the established traditions and modes of East End life, then widely perceived to be disappearing, by creating a 'street in the air' with the communal areas around the service core designed as modern successors to the traditional backyard. It inescapably seems optimistic now and by 1993 Tower Hamlets had evacuated the block, partly for structural reasons. It was rescued by refurbishment for private owners in 1999–2001 by *Munkenbeck & Marshall*, with Lasdun as consultant, who added a penthouse and flashy glass entrance with a little bridge over a pond and stream. Two maisonette blocks by *Denys Lasdun & Partners*, with deeply recessed balconies and ugly flanks of purple tile facings were built slightly later, in the tower's shadow immediately W, after a second cluster block, planned to replace the C19 housing around Teesdale Street, was unrealized. One demolished *c.* 2002, the other scheduled for

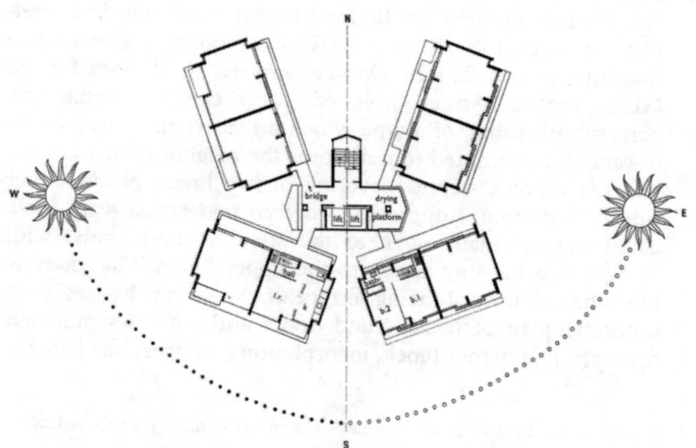

Keeling House, Claredale Street, Bethnal Green, 1955–9, plan

demolition in 2004. A more traditional approach to council housing, facing Keeling House to the N, is CLAREDALE HOUSE by *E.C.P. Monson*, 1931–2. Large arch gateway under central projecting bays in good red brick and curiously textured render to the rest.

Return S to OLD BETHNAL GREEN ROAD which was cleared on both sides after the war. The most urgent local priority was MINERVA ESTATE (1946–8) on the N side. This was the LCC's first large development after the war, of 253 dwellings in long, three- and four-storey blocks, named after Greek heroes and arranged in parallel pairs. Built by the Valuer's Department under *Cyril H. Walker*, based on plans by *J.H. Forshaw*,* using a rapid construction technique of monolithic concrete slabs laid over load-bearing concrete walls, serving to prove the economy of materials and labour in austere times.† There was no external embellishment. Roof playgrounds to the lower blocks were a novelty, but all the blocks were extensively refurbished up to 2003 with pitched roofs and lift towers.

The S side of Bethnal Green Road is an incoherent mess of piecemeal rebuilding which continued into the 1970s. E of a small area of open space is RAINE'S FOUNDATION SCHOOL in a light Festival style, with recent additions in blockwork faced with square windows of different sizes, randomly arranged. Just to the E in ST JUDE'S ROAD, BEATRICE TATE SCHOOL for disabled children of 1967 by *John D. Hume*, Tower Hamlets Borough Architect. Single storey with parabaloid timber shell-dome over the hall. Jolly, coloured tilework on the theme of 'the Silk Road' by *Freeform Arts Trust* 1997. Also in St Jude's Road, QUEEN MARGARET'S FLATS; four-storey flats for the Bethnal Green and East London Housing Association by *Ian B.M. Hamilton*, 1929, in his customary friendly Neo-Georgian.

In MIDDLETON STREET just to the W, JAMES MIDDLETON HOUSE, 1952–3 by the always dull *Donald Hamilton, Wakeford & Partners* for Bethnal Green looks positively welcoming against KEDLESTON WALK, opposite, seventy-two maisonettes and flats by *Douglas Stephens & Partners* for the GLC, 1970–2. An example of (over) clever, medium-rise compact planning, of a type which provided an alternative to towers and attempted to rediscover the neighbourliness of the street. Complex stepped layering of two linear blocks either side of a dark and oppressive covered pedestrian walk (now gated but originally open to the street at both ends) with bridges and balcony access to the upper floors. The lower W block has an inward-facing terrace of two-storey 'houses' with unforgiving brick façades and doors and windows punched through. The higher block, incorporating garages, has flats for

*This was a priority area under Forshaw's County of London plan for reduction of density.

†Contemporary claims that Portland stone salvaged from blitzed buildings was used as aggregate are baseless.

the elderly on the first floor and maisonettes above which open onto roof gardens bridging the inner walkway.

3b. Hackney Road and North

HACKNEY ROAD appears at least in part to have been pre-Roman, but in spite of its age was scarcely built upon until the late C18 when ribbon development began to spread eastwards from Shoreditch. For a time it may have had claim to homes of some quality but now, E from St Leonard's Shoreditch to Cambridge Heath Road, the highlights are meagre. At the W end, there is scarcely anything of interest until Goldsmith's Row and the former Queen Elizabeth Hospital for Children (*see* above). Diagonally opposite (SW), No. 324a was the NAG'S HEAD pub, an old inn, remodelled by *Arthur W. Saville* in 1888. Single-storey pub front with elliptical arch mouldings, an iron crest of trefoils and an excellent integral painted stucco horse-head. Thereafter the N side has good, if usual, early C19 middle-class brick three-storey terraces, e.g. Nos. 337–53, which still have their front gardens. Of similar date, but more modest are Nos. 359–61, with round-arch windows and tented iron porch, and a string of paired two-storeyed villas linked by doorways (Nos. 363–65 are dated 1820).

Facing on the S side, the stripy brick HADRIAN ESTATE of 1990 by *Levitt Bernstein Associates* for the Samuel Lewis Housing Trust to replace pre-war flats by *E.C.P. Monson*. Two rows of flats to the street, with porches inset under curved gables and small square windows, form a gatehouse to a courtyard development. E of Mansford Street, WHITE LION WORKS (now flats) and more early C19 ribbon development. Nos. 499–505 on the N side are later, in red brick with much cut and rubbed decorative detail of garlands and swags in brick, thin pilasters and aprons of cornucopias. Iron balustrade over integrated shopfronts. Furthest E on the S side, in MINERVA STREET, crammed into a wedge of land between Cambridge Crescent and Centre Street is a PEABODY ESTATE of eight blocks, inward facing to a courtyard (now playground). Opened 1910, reputedly the first by Peabody to have large numbers of self-contained flats in its dwellings but even at this late date still following the simple elevations developed by *Darbishire* in the Trust's buildings of the 1860s, albeit in a smart red brick lined in yellow bands. The stair towers project as square attics above the roofline with ironwork cresting. A small extension to Minerva Street heralds the next generation of the Trust's design, by *Victor Wilkins*, 1915–16, in stripy brick and stone under a wide stone cornice and attic behind cranked gables. Estate office added in sympathetic style, *c.* 1998.

The area to the N of Hackney Road towards the canal still has a strongly industrial character, though it began as a residential district of some pretension, hopelessly compromised after the Regent's Canal opened in 1820. THE OVAL is indicative of the area's decline, conceived as a double crescent of modest houses but now entirely composed of works and warehouses. At its S end, stubbornly holding on, is ST CASIMIR'S (R.C.) CHURCH. NW of this, on the E side of PRITCHARDS ROAD the arrival of the Imperial Gas Company's gasholder station in 1853 (an outpost of their Shoreditch gasworks) must have confirmed the triumph of industry. The oldest gasholder now is of 1865–6 by *Joseph Clark*, the company's engineer. The ironwork was cast by the *Staveley Co.* of Derbyshire. Two tiers of girders with guilloche bands and 16 cast-iron columns of two superimposed orders (the earliest surviving example of this form, developed here in 1858), the lower Doric, the upper Corinthian but divested of its foliage. Its much taller neighbour is of 1888–9 by *George Trewby*, the Gas Light & Coke Company's engineer, in lattice steelwork.

Land W of Pritchards Road was cleared for the LCC's DINMONT ESTATE, 1935–6 by *G. Topham Forrest*. Four blocks of the usual Neo-Georgian type but strongly modelled and rather sympathetically arranged, each forming a C-plan turning inward to form courtyards off a central roadway which is landscaped with rond-points. Later blocks (Beechwood and Sebright) to the W of 1948 are dull. Nearby in GOLDSMITH'S ROW (within the borough of Hackney), Nos. 66–74 are a one-off series of cottages designed by the *LCC Architect's Department* c. 1900 to absorb tenants displaced from Boundary Street (*see* perambulation 2b). S of the Dinmont Estate, just S of COATE STREET, the walk ends on a comic note with THE
123 BLUE HOUSE (Nos. 2a–c GARNER STREET), by *Fat*, 2000 with a communicative cut-out façade in the tradition of Robert Venturi: a flat cartoon of a house with blue clapboard facing and gabled roof in front of an office block, with regularly spaced but much smaller windows, expressive of the building's dual purpose. To complete this trick effect there's even the outline of a tree top appearing above the fence – its cut-out form is taken up as a void on the other side of the garden door. To its N in Coate Street, No. 2 (with door in Garner Street) ADELPHI CHAPEL SCHOOL, big Italianate block with pedimental gable dated '1853, enlarged 1868'.

BOW and BROMLEY-BY-BOW

Bow and Bromley-by-Bow grew up as settlements along the W side of the River Lea, close to the ancient fords across the river, which were improved during the Roman occupation to carry the London–Colchester Road. Herringbone masonry was discovered on the bed of the river in the C19 and there is also evidence of Roman burials in the area near the crossing later known as 'Old Ford', when it was superseded by the 'Strat ford' to the S, where the bridge crossing at Bow remains today. It was the 'bow' shape of the arches of the first stone bridges built in the C12, apparently at the instigation of Queen Matilda to ease access to royal lands in Essex, which traditionally gave the settlement its name of Stratford-le-Bow. Just S was Bromley, an ancient parish which grew around the Benedictine nunnery of St Leonard, in existence by 1122 and perhaps a pre-Conquest foundation. Although Bromley continued to expand in the medieval period its status was increasingly secondary to Bow, which by 1311 had its own chapel and was one of the largest of East London's hamlets. The Lea served its staple industries of textile dyeing and fulling but also provided supplies of malt and grain from Hertfordshire for Bow's mills and bakeries – the bakers' Guild of St Clement was attached to the chapel. Bow became a separate parish in 1730, by which date most of the open land was used for market gardening and farming.

In the C17 Bromley and Bow enjoyed favour as a rural retreat. The nunnery buildings at Bromley were adapted to domestic use, and there were a number of mansions in spacious grounds, notably Grove Hall and King John's Palace, both N of Bow Road, the Old Palace at Bromley and further S, Bromley Hall overlooking the then unspoilt river. By the C18 the area was still rural enough to tempt travellers from London – the May Fair was moved from the West End to Bow in 1764 – but suburbanization began in the 1820s, at first to a superior standard along Bow Road and the area to its N around Tredegar Square (historically in the parish of Stepney) and the neighbouring Coborn Charity estate. But the impact of creeping industry and the arrival of the railways discouraged similar efforts thereafter. The Limehouse Cut, made in 1770 to connect the Lea with the Thames, severed South Bromley (*see* Poplar) from the old village. Horwood's map of the early C19 shows farmland with a scatter of ropewalks and other industries, traversed by the winding route of Bow Common Lane, which led to Bow Common, on the edge of the parishes of Bow, Bromley and Stepney. In the early C19 there was already a distillery, and from 1799 Foster's calico-printing works were attached to the manor house of Bromley Hall. Noxious industries and services developed along the Cut and the Lea valley and over Old Ford Marsh in the NE of the parish as dyeworks, chemical works, print works and manufactories of every sort colonized the river's wharfs, giving rise to a peculiar (partly preserved) enclave in the NE of the parish known simply as 'the Island', later Fish Island, where workers' housing, multi-storey factories, pubs and schools were created cheek-by-jowl. Countless numbers of Bow's inhabitants were engaged in piecework in the home making matches for Bow's many small manufacturers. Bryant and May (established 1860) was exceptional in establishing its own large factory and became the object of the celebrated strike by female workers led by Annie Besant in the 1880s. In the C19 a tangle of railway lines carved the parishes of Bow and Bromley into ever more disparate parts: the Eastern Counties railway (1839), N and parallel to Bow Road; the Blackwall Extension Railway (1849, later LTS), N and parallel to the Limehouse Cut;

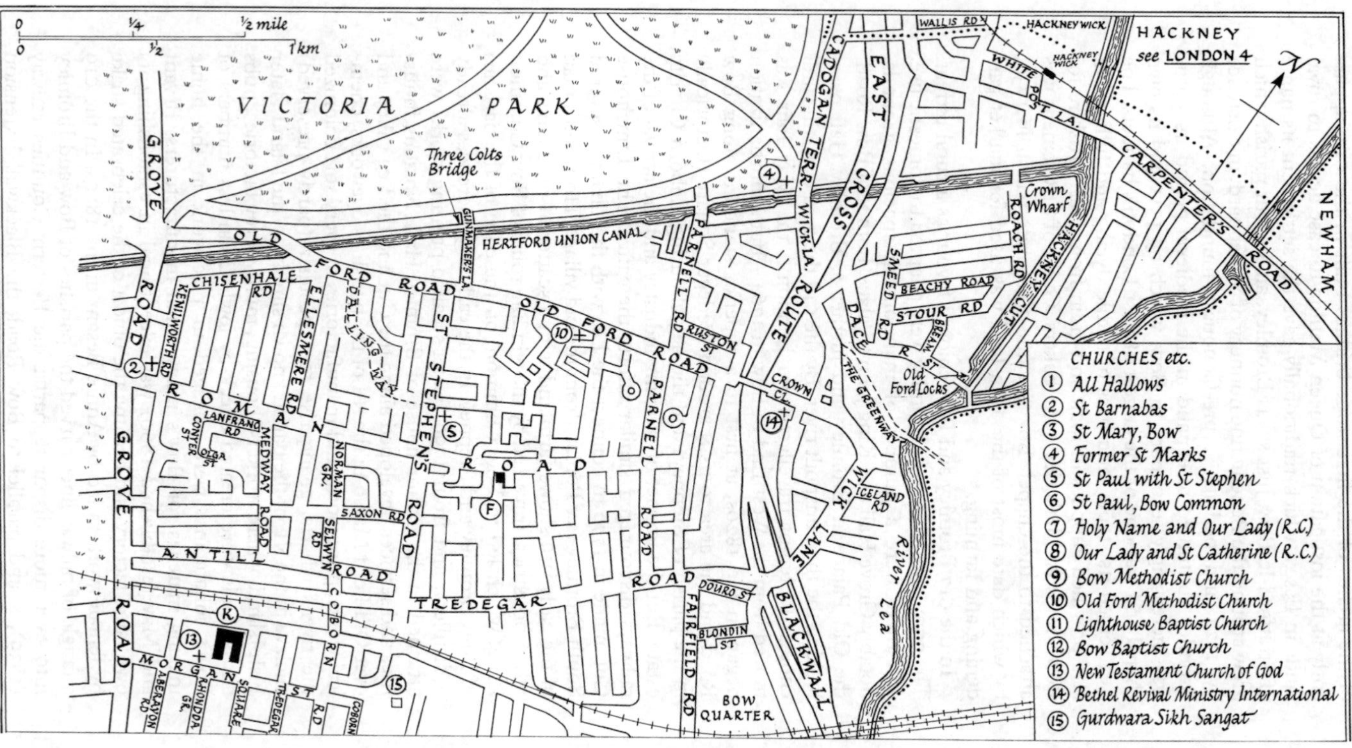

0 1/4 1/2 mile
0 1/2 1km
VICTORIA PARK
HACKNEY
see LONDON 4
N
NEWHAM
HACKNEY WICK
HACKNEY WICK
WALLIS RD
WHITE POST LA.
CARPENTER'S ROAD
Crown Wharf
HACKNEY CUT
ROACH RD
BEACHY ROAD
STOUR RD
SMEED RD
BREAM ST
R. ST
DACE
Old Ford Locks
THE GREENWAY
River Lea
ICELAND RD
WICK LANE
BLACKWALL
EAST CROSS ROUTE
CADOGAN TERR.
WICK LA.
CROWN CL.
DOURO ST
BLONDIN ST
BOW QUARTER
FAIRFIELD RD
Three Colts Bridge
GUNMAKER'S LA.
HERTFORD UNION CANAL
OLD FORD ROAD
OLD FORD ROAD
PARNELL RD
RUSTON ST
PARNELL ROAD
CHISENHALE RD
KENILWORTH RD
ELLESMERE RD
DALLING WAY
ST STEPHEN'S ROAD
ROMAN ROAD
LANFRANC RD
CONYER ST
OLGA ST
MEDWAY ROAD
NORMAN GR.
SAXON RD
SELWYN RD
ANTILL ROAD
TREDEGAR ROAD
COBORN
GROVE ROAD
GROVE ROAD
MORGAN ST
ABERAVON RD
RHONDDA GR.
SQUARE
TREDEGAR
COBORN RD
F
K
CHURCHES etc.
1 All Hallows
2 St Barnabas
3 St Mary, Bow
4 Former St Marks
5 St Paul with St Stephen
6 St Paul, Bow Common
7 Holy Name and Our Lady (R.C.)
8 Our Lady and St Catherine (R.C.)
9 Bow Methodist Church
10 Old Ford Methodist Church
11 Lighthouse Baptist Church
12 Bow Baptist Church
13 New Testament Church of God
14 Bethel Revival Ministry International
15 Gurdwara Sikh Sangat

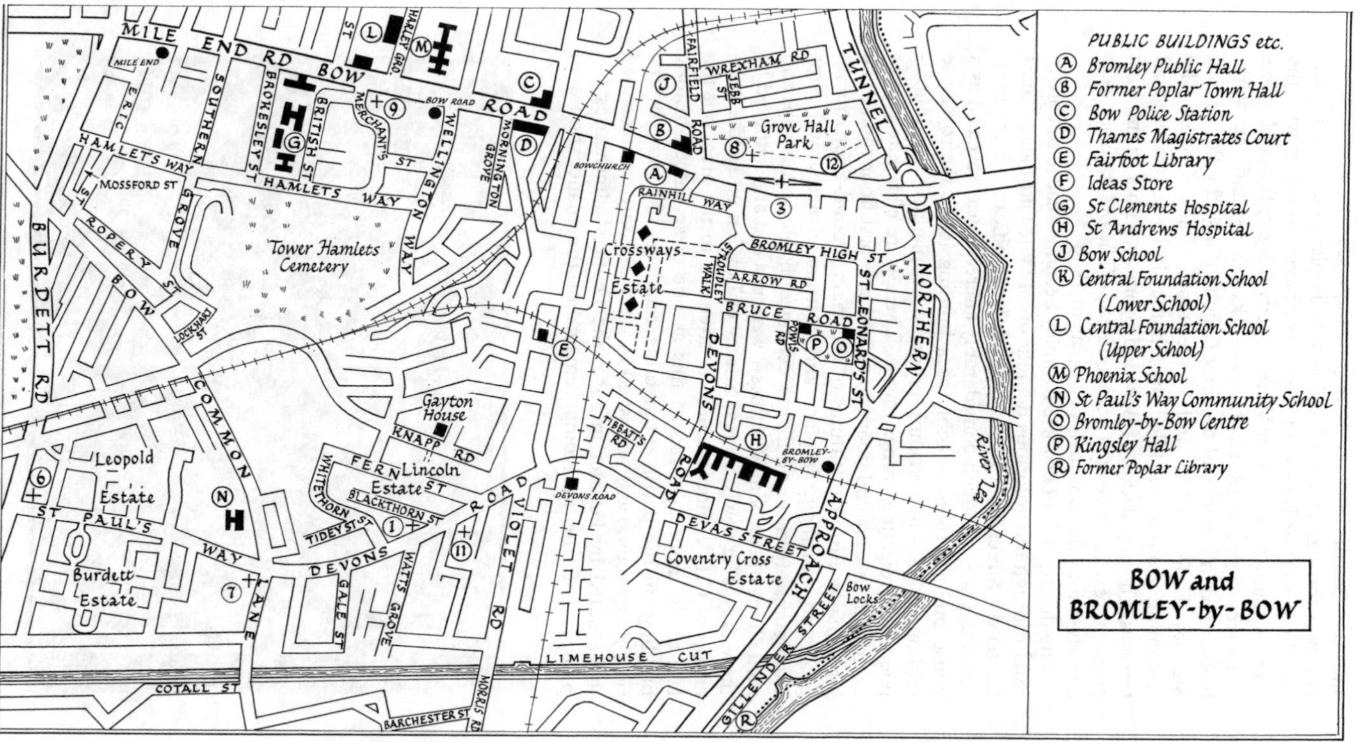
PUBLIC BUILDINGS etc.
A Bromley Public Hall
B Former Poplar Town Hall
C Bow Police Station
D Thames Magistrates Court
E Fairfoot Library
F Ideas Store
G St Clements Hospital
H St Andrews Hospital
J Bow School
K Central Foundation School (Lower School)
L Central Foundation School (Upper School)
M Phoenix School
N St Paul's Way Community School
O Bromley-by-Bow Centre
P Kingsley Hall
R Former Poplar Library
BOW and BROMLEY-by-BOW
MILE END RD
MILE END
BOW ROAD
HARLEY GRO.
ST
ERIC ST
SOUTHERN GROVE
BROKESLEY ST
BRITISH ST
MERCHANT'S ST
BOW ROAD
WELLINGTON WAY
MORNINGTON GROVE
HAMLETS WAY
MOSSFORD ST
ROPERY ST
BOW
LOCKHART ST
Tower Hamlets Cemetery
BURDETT RD
FAIRFIELD ROAD
WREXHAM RD
JEBB ST
Grove Hall Park
TUNNEL
BOWCHURCH
RAINHILL WAY
Crossways Estate
STROUDLEY WALK
BROMLEY HIGH ST
ARROW RD
BRUCE ROAD
POWIS RD
ST LEONARD'S ST
NORTHERN
DEVONS ROAD
TIBBATT'S RD
BROMLEY-BY-BOW
River Lea
APPROACH
DEVAS STREET
Coventry Cross Estate
Bow Locks
GILLENDER STREET
COMMON
Gayton House
KNAPP RD
FERN ST
Lincoln Estate
WHITETHORN ST
BLACKTHORN ST
TIDEY ST
ROAD
DEVONS ROAD
VIOLET RD
Leopold Estate
ST PAUL'S WAY
Burdett Estate
LANE
DEVONS
GALE ST
WATTS GROVE
LIMEHOUSE CUT
COTALL ST
BARCHESTER ST
MORRIS RD

and the North London Railway (1846–52) running S from Hackney through Old Ford and Bow to Poplar Dock. During the C19 the land N of Bow Common Lane began to fill up with the utilities characteristic of the Victorian city fringes: Tower Hamlets Cemetery (opened 1841), the gasworks (1850), and the workhouses and infirmaries of the City Union (1849), the Poplar and Stepney Union (1871) and Whitechapel Union (1872). The remaining ground was filled up relentlessly by streets of small terraces. The population of Bow and Bromley, with a strong Irish element, reached a peak of 70,000 in 1891. The old parishes were absorbed into the Borough of Poplar in 1899.

The destruction of historic Bromley became a cause célèbre in 1894 through the notorious demolition of 'The Old Palace' in St Leonard's Street for a Board School. Its significance was recognized too late: although considerably altered it was revealed as a house built in 1606, possibly as a hunting lodge for royal use (although this is not certain), progressively planned as a double-pile with projecting corner towers. There were elaborate plaster ceilings in two ground floor rooms and one first floor room. The high quality early C17 fittings of the main ground-floor room – pilastered panelling, fireplace and overmantel with royal arms and figures of Peace and Plenty, ceiling with intersecting ribs and medallions of the Nine Worthies – were rescued and acquired by the V & A. The newly formed Survey of London under the leadership of C.R. Ashbee turned its attention to the area, but too late to do more than record this as one of seventeen historic buildings in the parish. Four other buildings had gone by the time their volume was published in 1900 and only two remained to be noted by Pevsner in 1952: the Drapers' almshouses (*see* p. 633) and the intriguing remains of the manor house of

Old Palace Bromley, early C17 ceiling, measured drawing

Bromley Hall (*see* p. 634). The Royal Commission in 1930 recorded several important houses and at least one with good Jacobean plasterwork but most were cleared for the LCC's Bow Bridge Estate soon after.

After 1945, the architectural significance of the surviving early C19 terraces around Tredegar Square ensured their exclusion from the Stepney–Poplar Reconstruction Area which halted at Bow Road. The haphazard C19 development elsewhere created a difficult legacy for the three post-war neighbourhoods devised here: No. 6, which wraps around the N and W sides of Tower Hamlets Cemetery; No. 7, between the Limehouse Cut and the railway line to its NW, and No 8, which consists of part of the old parish of Bromley to the E of the DLR railway line. The most innovative of the post-war areas is the Lincoln Estate in part of Neighbourhood 7, developed by the LCC from the 1950s following their new mixed development principles. The creation of the Blackwall Tunnel approach road from 1959 and its N extension for the East Cross Route in 1973 blighted Bromley, isolating its eastern part towards the Lea. Rescue from dereliction began in the early C21. Further N at Old Ford a separate industrial zone along the river still persists in 2004 in spite of extensive plans for regeneration and replacement allied to the wider plans for the 2012 Olympic village. p. 89

RELIGIOUS BUILDINGS

ALL HALLOWS, Devons Road. The original church was by *Ewan Christian*, 1873–4, funded through the Grocers' Company from sale of the City church of All Hallows Staining. Rebuilt 1954–5 by *A.P. Robinson* of *Caröe & Partners*, ingeniously reusing the core of the war-damaged older church to create a free composition of Early Christian inspiration, pantile-roofed, with a

NE belltower over the former organ chamber. The shape of Christian's big brick apse is preserved, towering above the street behind the red brick outer wall of his eastern vestries. The apse now has small lancets with 1930s-style curved heads, within plain pointed arches of stock brick. Christian's overpowering interior had a long, broad nave in the low-church tradition, with mighty brick arcades on stout columns. The post-war transformation created a calm, light space with flat ceiling and white walls, lit by tall windows on the S side in place of the S aisle, and with a N aisle and chapel divided by low, unmoulded round-headed arches. Reordering in 2001 by *Tom Hornsby* of *Keith Harrison Architects* divided off the N aisle and provided a multi-functional hall in the nave, separated by a low timber and glass screen from a raised worship area extending from the sanctuary. Seating arranged in an intimate semicircle, with the excellent 1950s FURNISHINGS rearranged less formally. Pulpit, reading desk, clergy chairs, with subdued eclectic classical detail in the Caröe tradition. FONT with carved cover with dove, moved from the W end. Apse glass of *c.* 1955 by *F.W. Cole* of *William Morris & Co.*

To the S is the former VICARAGE of the 1870s, with Gothic doorway and gables. To its W clumsily detailed apartments created 2001–2 from the church hall of 1940. WAR MEMORIAL tablet, on the E wall of the former vestries, commemorating 'the great war for freedom'.

HOLY TRINITY, Morgan Road *see* below, New Testament Church of God.

ST MARY, Bow Road. Built as a chapel of ease to Stepney (licence of 1311), and apart from St Dunstan, the only medieval church to survive in Tower Hamlets. A parish church from 1719. On an island site, with traffic sweeping past on either side; but set in a small, trim CHURCHYARD, enlarged to the E in 1824. The whole is enclosed by pretty Gothic railings (reinstated 1984). Sturdy late C15 W tower with SE turret, of ashlar masonry above a bold plinth, the brick upper part with timber clock turret rebuilt after war damage (replacing a rebuilding of 1829). Perp W door with square label, Perp window above, the detail badly eroded. The rubble-stone N aisle wall is the oldest part, and may date from the C14. Aisles, clerestory and chancel have straight-headed late Perp windows with elaborate cusping, renewed in the C19. The S aisle was refaced in 1794, and a small Tuscan portico added to the S door in the C20. On the N side, brick vestries, early C18 and 1900.

All this survives only because successive proposals for complete rebuilding and enlargement (early C18, 1829, 1882, 1895) came to nothing for lack of funds. Collapse of the chancel roof in 1896 brought matters to a head and spurred the SPAB and fledgling Survey of London committee under *C.R. Ashbee* to insist on a more conservative approach. Pioneering conservation work designed to retain old fabric of all periods was undertaken by *Osborn C. Hills* of the local firm *Hills & Son*, supervised by a committee including SPAB members.* Ashbee's *Guild of Handicraft* provided the metalwork (see the curly rainwater heads of 1899 on the S wall). The committee designed the new N vestry – in brick, to match the older one, rather than in Hills' preferred ragstone – and insisted on the rebuilding of the incongruous red brick gable over the chancel instead of reverting to the lower, late medieval roofline.

Inside, tall Perp tower arch with moulded caps on rounded shafts, and six irregular bays of low octagonal columns with moulded capitals, carrying double-chamfered arches. The arcades may be pre-C15, but regularized later (a drawing of 1820 shows half-arches and bulkier piers at the E end). Of 1900 the wall panelling and double glazing with small-paned leaded windows, sensitively done, giving the interior a homely feel. Coupled-rafter roof without purlins. Chancel of two bays with low-pitched late medieval chancel roof, with moulded tie-beams and carved bosses, the panels renewed in 1900. Sanctuary floor, raised 1881 during repairs by *A. W. Blomfield*, paved with TILES based on two authentic medieval types, green-glazed relief patterns and red and white slip, some perhaps original.

Designs for repairing Second World War damage were made by *H.S. Goodhart Rendel*, with a new E window by his partner *H. Lewis Curtis*. The striking STAINED GLASS in the E window appears to be cut down from something larger: a most unusual series of golden classical aedicules each wittily embellished with a small animal or bird. Post-war CHAPEL, W end of N aisle, with memorials of the Tower Hamlets Rifles Regiment, from St Stephen's church.†

FONTS. Octagonal, with Perp tracery. PANELLING in the chancel, C18. COMMUNION TABLES, one *c.* 1630 with four Tuscan columns as legs and an arcade on smaller Tuscan columns to support the centre. The other early C18 with grouped twisted balusters as legs. PULPIT 1887.

MONUMENTS. Grace Amcottes †1551, shields under concave crocketed gables, still completely Gothic (S aisle). In the nave two very grand wall monuments: to the local benefactor Alice Coborn †1689, with bust and scrolly pediment, and to Prisca Coborn †1701, a long inscription in Latin, Greek and Hebrew framed by Corinthian pilasters. James Walker †1712 and Dorothy †1706. Inscription under draped canopy held open by two putti, to the l. and r. busts on brackets (chancel S).

In the CHURCHYARD, Joseph Dawson †1834; draped urn on a tall stele with acroteria. Portrait head in relief. Some C19 railed chest tombs in the E part.

*The church was the subject of the second Survey of London monograph, by Osborn C. Hills, 1902.

†St Stephen Tredegar Road, 1856–8 by *S.J. Nicholl*, was demolished after war damage.

Former ST MARK, St Mark's Gate *see* p. 630.

ST PAUL WITH ST STEPHEN, St Stephen's Road, Old Ford. By *Newman & Billing*, 1873–8. Foundation stone laid by J.D. Allcroft, chairman of the building committee (and patron of the eccentric St Martin Gospel Oak, Camden). Economically detailed, but an urban church on the grandest scale. 'Ugly, self-confident and very likeable' wrote Basil Clarke in his notes, apt comments. Disused for ten years until funds became available in 2003 for a radical conversion to mixed uses by *Matthew Lloyd Architects*.

Stock brick with red brick trim, details in an eclectic transitional Gothic. Impressive from the N, with low slated roofs to lean-to passage aisles, big buttresses and a dramatic row of gables above tall clerestory windows with coarse plate tracery of varying design. The wide W front has a window of seven lights above a small Baptistery apse, and a round NW corner turret now without its spire. The plan follows the low church tradition, with single space for the congregation and shallow open sanctuary. A broad and light interior, dominated by huge upper windows above passage aisles squeezed to the narrowest space, with a flat panelled ceiling rising from coved sides. This is now partly obscured by the insertion of a timber-clad mezzanine, a pod supported on four sturdy angled stilts. The generous apse lit by seven lancets, with ribbed ceiling, and remains of painted decoration, remains as the worship area, together with the E bays of the nave, entered from a new N door. A little bit of carving in apse and Baptistery, red brick walls with minimal tile bands. Ample stairs with views through to the church lead to the plain white-walled mezzanine. A gym specializing in the disabled is tucked between ceiling and roof, accessed by a lift.

FURNISHINGS. ORGAN, busily notched CHOIR STALLS curved to fit the apse, some cut down PEWS, stone FONT with marble columns. Weak GLASS of 1954 in the central E lancet.

VICARAGE to the S, tall and imposing, with some Gothic windows with brick and tile tympana.

ST PAUL, St Paul's Way, Bow Common. 1956–60 by *Robert Maguire and Keith Murray*, replacing a bombed church of 1856. Their first church, and the first major expression in England of the principles of the liturgical movement (developed further in their later churches at Crewe and Perry Beeches, Birmingham), which aimed to bring priest and sanctuary close to the congregation. German churches had experimented with central plans before the war, but in England this was still daringly innovative in the late 1950s, and so was an aesthetic of geometric cubic forms which deliberately revelled in inexpensive, industrial materials and romantically rough textures. It shocked many ('looks like a rather seedy stable-yard' was the comment in Basil Clarke's notebook). The plan is a square within a three-by-four-bay rectangle. Externally the austere, windowless red brick walls are relieved only by the

zigzagging concrete-slab roofs of the aisles; above and behind them a plain brick square is crowned by the large glazed gables of the pyramid-topped lantern. Although quite low, this forms a decisive landmark from afar. Octagonal porch with intense, bold lettering by *Ralph Beyer*: 'This is the house of God, this is the gate of heaven.' Inside, the entrance area, with the font, 108
is a low, dark prelude to the light and space in the centre of the three eastern bays, which is lit from above and defined by the slender white columns dividing it from the surrounding triangular-vaulted aisles. The altar is raised on steps, emphasized by the hanging steel CORONA and BALDACCHINO. The sanctuary is indicated only by different paving; no altar rails. Seating on three sides, on portable benches, an arrangement which can extend into the aisles if required. Two small chapels, on N and E sides. Tough LIGHT FITTINGS, matching the geometric austerity of the baldachin. Hemispherical FONT, an industrial stoneware vat set on an octagonal concrete block. MOSAICS by *Charles Lutyens*, 1964–9, but part of the original conception (funded by war-damage money allocated for stained glass). Half figures of angels in the arcade spandrels, the Four Elements in the corners; subtle colours.

Adjoining VICARAGE to the E.

Former ST MICHAEL AND ALL ANGELS, Teviot Street, *see* p. 657.

HOLY NAME AND OUR LADY (R.C.), Bow Common Lane and St Paul's Way. (Vietnamese chaplaincy). 1893–4 by *F.A. Walters*, replacing a mission church founded by Cardinal Manning. Burnt out 1944; restored by *David Stokes*, 1957–8. Thinly detailed but a good landmark; dark red brick, with windowless canted apse, tall clerestory windows framed by arches linking the buttresses, and a tower porch with curved W stair turret and octagonal belfry. The skimpy aluminium spire and shallow-pitched nave roof date from 1957. Inside, the flat postwar ceiling is dispiriting, but Walters' passage aisles remain: simple Gothic arcades without capitals, as do his angled arches linking nave to chancel, with four statues in niches above. A broad arch carries a W gallery; W Baptistery with carved C19 FONT. BALDACCHINO of aluminium, replacing a C19 one, delightful in its light-hearted 1950s detail. Lavish furnishings were lost in the war; sole survivor is a C19 metal TABERNACLE, rescued from the ruins and restored, drum shaped, with enamel work. STAINED GLASS by Kingston Polytechnic students, 1970s, S aisle, simple figures of English Martyrs, in glowing colours. W windows with history of Catholicism in England. Well-carved STATUE of St Anthony by *Anton Dapre*. CROSS, in Baptistery, a forceful composition of stainless-steel bars, later C20, from Sisters of Sion convent, Notting Hill; also from there the nave ALTAR in similar style, and an enamelled XR symbol. MONUMENTS, SW chapel. Marble tablets to the founders, William (†1900) and Susan Lyall, and to Father Gordon Thompson †1905. To the S nicely panelled church room and adjoining presbytery, 1958.

OUR LADY AND ST CATHERINE (R.C.), Bow Road, adjoining the former St Catherine's convent for Dominican nuns. 1869–70 by *Gilbert Blount*. Kentish rag with Portland-stone dressings. Plain aisleless nave (rebuilt after war damage), gable to the street with big W wheel window flanked by niches, entrance porch to the side. Arch-braced timber roof and W organ gallery (organ from Holloway Prison). The chancel is more ornate, with a large Dec E window, sexpartite wooden rib vault and shafts on angel corbels. Enlarged 1882 by *A.E. Purdie*, with a (ritual) S transept, formerly the nuns' choir, divided from the chancel by a clustered polished-granite pier with bold foliage capitals. Another chapel opposite with a pair of columns. E window with STAINED GLASS; elaborate REREDOS, designed by *Blount* and made by *Farmer & Brindley*: figures within Gothic niches, flanking a pinnacled Monstrance throne. High Altar with relief of the Miracle of Loaves and Fishes. Sacred Heart Altar, painted wood, with carved statue by *Mayer*.

NEW TESTAMENT CHURCH OF GOD, formerly HOLY TRINITY, Morgan Street. 1834–9 by *Daniel* and *James Austin*, local surveyors. On a large site, with its own burial ground. The NTCG took over the church in 1996 after a sad period of redundancy and vandalism. At time of writing it occupies the plain Church Hall of 1901 facing Lichfield Street, which was given a new space-frame roof and two gaily coloured W windows. The substantial C19 building awaits adaptation following repair in 2001–2. It was designed as a proprietary chapel, initially funded by a lawyer, E.A. Dickenson, who had hoped to make his son the clergyman. The site was given by the landowner and developer of Tredegar Square, Sir Charles Morgan. By 1836 Dickenson's money had run out; the church was completed by the Metropolis Churches Fund in 1839 and given its own district in 1841. The 'W end' of the church faces S to take advantage of the view down Rhondda Grove. Gabled front in Perp style with octagonal buttresses, originally with pinnacles. Stone-faced centre, the rest yellow brick with stone dressings. Some eccentric detail, as often found in 1830s Gothic, for example the semicircular gables of the aisles connected to the nave by ogee curves. The aisles have large two-light windows with cusped tracery and transoms. Below is a burial crypt, its circular ventilators with cast-iron tracery. An impressive, well-lit interior, the arcades with very tall, slim Perp piers, with high bases intended to be concealed by box pews; no clerestory. Flat ribbed ceilings to the aisles, canted ceiling with simple hammer beam braces to the nave. Originally of five bays; two chancel bays in identical style, flanked by chapel and organ chamber, were added 1910–14 by *Edwin C. Stimson*, replacing the original shallow sanctuary. At the same time galleries were removed, and the gallery stairs replaced by W vestries.

Stone REREDOS with Perp tracery, the central part moved to the N chapel and the side parts reused in the new chancel.

The chancel is surrounded by a cage-like ironwork SCREEN of *c.* 1910, a lively design (could it be by *Ashbee*'s Guild of Handicraft? Ashbee designed an unexecuted church hall and vestry extension for the W end *c.* 1900). N chapel redecorated 1949. On the aisle walls a neat array of minor MONUMENTS; contrasting styles of the 1840s are demonstrated by a scroll with arms, to Thomas Brown of Trinity House, †1841, a stele with urn, laurel wreath and inverted torch, to William Bridges †1843, and a Gothic niche with ogee head and angels, to William Simons †1844, all by *M.W. Johnson*, New Road. The grander tombs of the churchyard (closed 1853) include a broken column on the N side and on the S, a draped urn, to Eleanor Souttar †1839.

NEW BETHEL REVIVAL MINISTRY INTERNATIONAL, Crown Close (E of East Cross Route, Wick Lane). 1890 by *W.A. Hills & Son*. Simple, nicely detailed Gothic front in stone; plate-tracery windows flanking the porch, a triplet of lancets above.

LIGHTHOUSE BAPTIST CHURCH, Devons Road and Brock Place. 1895 by *E. Holman*. An austere stock brick building; tripartite W window below a shallow gable, to the r. an unfinished tower intended to command its corner site.

BOW BAPTIST CHURCH, Bow Road. Close to the flyover. Small brick building by *H. & H.M. Lidbetter*, 1956–7. Reused stock brick, shallow-pitched roof, the centre entrance recessed, with cantilevered porch.

BROMLEY-BY-BOW CENTRE *see* p. 631.

METHODIST CHURCH, Bow Road and Merchant Street. Now shared with Holy Trinity C. of E. 1951 by *Alick Gavin* of *Paul Mauger & Partners*, on the foundations of a church of 1865 by *W.W. Pocock*, destroyed in 1940. The first bombed Methodist church to be rebuilt. Brick; central triple entrance, in a frame enclosing a balconied window above, but with a Modernist asymmetrical grouping of side windows; a corner tower to the r. Tall rectangular windows along the flank; set back upper floor, originally planned as a youth centre.

Aisled interior with slim fluted columns, alas now subdivided; aisles clumsily partitioned off, the main space divided into two rooms, worship area and hall with raised stage.

To the S, chapel-keeper's house of 1865, then Wesley Hall, former Maulay Memorial Schools, 1891 by *B.J. Capell* of Whitechapel. A broad, florid stucco-trimmed front with wreathed Ionic pilasters to door and round-headed upper windows. This is now a doctors' surgery with entrance in the blank side, which is covered by a large MURAL of people at work and play, signed by *Ray Walker*, restored by *David Bratby* 1986.

OLD FORD METHODIST CHURCH, Armagh Road. 1950s church with entrance in a square recess, attached to a plain brick Congregational hall dated 1883.

BOW MUSLIM COMMUNITY CENTRE, Nos. 515B–517 Roman Road. Established 2000 in a new building.

GURDWARA SIKH SANGAT, Harley Grove. A handsome

stuccoed former chapel of 1854–5, in the grand classical spirit of nearby Tredegar Square. Converted to Mile End and Bow
39 Great Synagogue 1927, reopened as a Sikh temple 1979. Two giant Ionic columns in antis, under a central pediment, end bays with lower and upper windows recessed within round-headed arches, chanelled corner quoins. Within the portico a large double entrance and side doors to the gallery stairs. (Gallery, on slim iron columns, rebuilt as a ladies' gallery in 1927, with elaborate curved iron balustrade and grille, and named and numbered seats. An aedicule for the Ark remains at the W end. At the back, large galleried hall, enlarged 1876–7 as a Sunday school, later a Talmud Torah.)

TOWER HAMLETS CEMETERY, Southern Grove. Now a nature reserve created by a century of neglect. Most of the 33 acres are thickly wooded; deep among the trees and glades only glimpses of a few looming tower blocks are reminders of London. The cemetery was established 1841, the last of the ring of seven private cemeteries opened on the fringes of Victorian London, which began with Kensal Green in 1833. Laid out with winding paths by *Thomas Wyatt and David Brandon.* Nothing remains of their lodge and two chapels of 1849. The Dec Gothic Anglican chapel was in the centre approached by a path leading SE from the main entrance, an octagonal Dissenter's chapel in a vaguely Byzantine style lay further N.

Burial figures demonstrate the growth of the East End: 5,000 in the first ten years, *c.* 250,000 by 1889. Up to 80 per cent of the burials were common interments, and there are few grand memorials, but there is no shortage of densely packed tombstones receding into the rampant undergrowth, poignant records of families and individuals. Burials continued until 1966. The neglected and war-damaged cemetery was acquired by the GLC in 1965, and the two chapels demolished in 1972. Close to the main gates is the box-like SOANES CENTRE for environmental studies, of 1993, with forbidding vandal-proof shutters, practical rather than picturesque. Named after the family which owned a ropewalk S of the cemetery, whose monuments are close by.

MONUMENTS. Close to the entrance, WAR MEMORIAL, moved here in 1999, from near the site of the Anglican chapel. A stark demi-polygon of polished grey granite walls inscribed with names, numbered in military fashion, rising to a central gable pierced with a cross. The most prominent group of monuments are the early ones in the NW corner. Thomas Lee of Mare Street †1852 has a handsome tapered sarcophagus placed above the chest tomb of George Morris †1843. William Henry Hope, Master of the Ratcliffe workhouse †1860 has one of the few Gothic structures. Close by, a semicircle of monuments, mostly draped urns on tall bases. Among them an ornately Grecian one to the Llewellyn family of doctors (†1854 onwards), with reversed torches on the base. Further S, near the W boundary, and not to be missed, is an eerily overgrown collection of twenty close-set headstones to the brothers of the

Charterhouse, all to an identical gabled design, dating from the 1870s–90s. Along the main path leading SE, a later cluster shows how grandiose memorials could be by the early C20: two in the form of Celtic crosses with angels, two with angels alone. The second cross is to Esther Brown, †1896, wife of the celebrated Charlie Brown, 'uncrowned king of Poplar', publican and antique collector. Elsewhere among the countless tombstones there are occasional red granite obelisks, and one ambitious Gothic openwork structure with spire above crocketed arches formerly sheltering a figure: to the family of Joseph Westwood of Tredegar House, Bow, †1883, a founder of the ship- and bridge-building firm of Westwood, Baillie. Further E, an unusually substantial monument to Ann Francis †1859, wife of Charles Francis, corn merchant, one of the founders of the cemetery, with iron door in the base. Just a few tombs have some sculptural detail: near the site of the Dissenters' chapel in the NE part, the strikingly large pedimented monument to the family of Henry Bear, tobacco and sugar merchant, 1855 onwards, recording the early deaths of three sons; along the plinth a bold relief of wheat, with explanatory quotation 'except a corn of wheat fall into the ground and die, it abideth alone . . . but if it die it bringeth forth much fruit'. Near the E boundary Elizabeth Louisa Gill †1867 'who died suddenly aged 25', has a headstone with relief of a shipwreck: 'such is life'. Also close to the E boundary, tombstone to Harry Orbell †1914, a leader of the Dock strike of 1889, a rough hunk of red granite; adjoining is the tomb of Will Crooks, first Labour mayor of Poplar, †1921, with marble headstone recarved by *Chris Brown* in the 1990s. Nearby, small curved brick wall, sole remnant of a memorial garden created in 1952 to the 747 Poplar victims of the Blitz. SW from here, buried in undergrowth, are tiny memorials of the 1940s–50s, a telling contrast to the aspirations of a century earlier.

MAJOR BUILDINGS

BROMLEY PUBLIC HALL, Bow Road. 1879–80 by *A. & C. Harston*. The former Vestry Hall for St Leonard's parish. Typical Barry Italianate. Stone faced with a balustraded parapet. Short, set-back brick wings, added 1904 by *R.F. Atkinson*. Two storeys of round-arched windows with Corinthian and composite pilasters, the centre bays slightly advanced above a projecting arched porch. Inside, a slim entrance hall with offices to l. and r., and an attractive staircase with iron balustrade. Marbled and gilded pilasters with scroll brackets. The first-floor Board Room has plain pilasters and two large sun-lighters.

Former POPLAR TOWN HALL, Bow Road and Fairfield Road. Now offices. 1937–8 and early work by *Clifford Culpin (E.G.*

Culpin & Son),* replacing Bow Vestry Hall. Tall and large with long superimposed window strips, rounded corner and square tower above it. Floors faced in Portland stone, the upper floor set back. The corner site allows for display but the result is disappointing, lacking the originality of composition that Culpin later realized at Greenwich Town Hall. On the corner are five relief panels with socialist realist depictions of the workers involved in the building's design and construction: welder, carpenter, architect, labourer and stone mason. By *David Evans*, who also designed the mosaic on the canopy above the former Councillors' Entrance in Bow Road. On the underside are shown the Docks and industries, with figures of Art, Science, Music and Literature on the fascia.

The plan is trapezoidal with three blocks grouped around an open court. The main block contained offices and committee rooms with Council Chamber at the rear. This linked to a public hall† in Fairfield Road (demolished 2000 and replaced by indifferent flats). The muted Art Deco INTERIOR is well preserved if unexciting. In the lobby to the Council Chamber is a prayer of dedication by a Socialist Sunday School pupil, originally in Bow Vestry Hall. Double height COUNCIL CHAMBER with deep-recessed circular opening in the ceiling.

POLICE STATION, 111 Bow Road. By *John Dixon Butler*, 1903 and amongst his finest in East London. Neo-Baroque, in good red brick with plenty of ebullient stone detail. Five bays to the street. The ground-floor windows have shaped aprons and lugged architraves with broken-segmental pediments linked by their keystones to the aprons of the windows above. Balustraded parapet, tall pedimented dormers and big, round-arched gable ends with volutes under banded chimneystacks.

To the rear of the yard in Addington Road are STABLES and married quarters in a surprisingly pure Modern of 1937–8 by *Gilbert Mackenzie Trench*, Metropolitan Police Architect. White, roughcast concrete, tubular railings and metal casements give it the character of a seaside villa rather than urban housing. The flats form a gatehouse to the stable yard, which has a working forge and stables for twenty horses.

THAMES MAGISTRATES COURT & JUVENILE COURT, Bow Road. 1990 by *Phillip Arrand*, Architect to the Metropolitan Police. On the site of *Charles Reeves*' Italianate courthouse of 1860. A flashy attempt to move away from the dour style of later C20 courthouse design. Lengthy and fortress-like elevations of yellow brick and caramel marble cladding rising from a sloping plinth. Strips of metal-framed windows, a double-height entrance, glazed corner section and discreet side entrance for the Juvenile Court. A secure brick core contains

*The design was originally assigned to *Culpin & Bowers*, a firm with solid socialist credentials, but the partnership split before work could begin and Culpin went into practice with his son.

†It contained a splendid series of etched glass panels by *Suddaby and Fryer* depicting Father Thames and the parishes of Poplar.

the courts at first floor, with high clerestory windows lighting the plainly detailed public and private spaces on either side.

FAIRFOOT LIBRARY, Campbell Road. By *Harley Heckford*, 1931, contemporary with his Poplar Baths but without any of the novelty displayed there. An eccentric two-storey façade of brick, over a deep basement, in a blockish Neo-Georgian taste with a dominant projecting entrance bay adorned by the borough arms.

IDEAS STORE, Roman Road and Gladstone Place. The former Passmore Edwards Public Library of 1900–1 by *S.B. Russell*. A pretty specimen of its date, assisted by its corner site, in red brick and stone with a wildly Baroque commemorative plaque with heads of winged cherubs. The façade to the street reads like a three-bay house, with stone modillion cornice, steep slate roof and dormers, but with a solid stone base, pierced by openings with short Ionic columns. Side entrance set within a Gibbsian surround. Elaborate carved overdoor of medieval figures, doubtless by *H.C. Fehr*, Russell's favoured sculptor. A rounded tower was originally intended to tie the main library to the lower S range of newspaper and magazine rooms lit by a neat row of lunettes. Crisply stylish internal refurbishment by *Bissett Adams*, 2002 as the first of Tower Hamlets' new style library-cum-educational centres sited in shopping areas (*see* also Poplar, p. 649, Whitechapel p. 400).

ST CLEMENT'S HOSPITAL, Bow Road. 1849 by *Richard Tress*. Opened as the City of London Union Workhouse, it became an Infirmary in 1874 and was expanded as a hospital by the LCC from 1932. The earlier buildings facing Bow Road form an especially graceful and attractive group behind a wall. Venetian style with high campanile tower over a two-storey block, which incorporated offices and a Board Room. Flanking this on either side lower ranges for receiving wards, remodelled, probably after 1874. Central lodge with pedimented doorway in the boundary wall added 1896 by *Francis Hammond*, Architect to the City of London Guardians. To the rear are the remains of the main ward block, a fragment of the original pavilion arrangement. The W pavilion and chapel were destroyed by bombing. Behind this, a Nurses' Home of 1937 by the *LCC Architects* in a Moderne style with flat roof and curved ends. In the SE corner of the site is the original workhouse Infirmary. Unrelentingly brutal appearance in yellow stock brick with octagonal sanitation towers added to the S façade.

ST ANDREW'S HOSPITAL, Devons Road. The grim remains of the former Poplar & Stepney Sick Asylum, associated with the workhouse that stood to the N of the railway. 1868–71 by *A. & C. Harston*. One of the first and largest workhouse infirmaries built under the Metropolitan Poor Act of 1867. Its pavilion plan was still a novelty in public hospitals (e.g. St Thomas' Hospital, 1868–71) and became a model for workhouse infirmaries. The style is heavy Italianate, especially the chunky water tower in the centre. The later C19 blocks at the E end were originally independent. The sick asylum became St Andrew's Hospital in 1925. At the SW end of the site NURSES HOME. Five-storey block, with three-storey wings added 1928 by *Harley Heckford*. Dismal later additions.

BOW SCHOOL, Paton Close/Hartfield Terrace. 1913 by *LCC Architects Dept*, replacing a school of 1876. Large but attractive with rendered upper floors, exposed brick quoins, Dutch-style hipped roofs with kneelered gable ends and dormers. Similar schoolkeeper's house on Paton Close. The Performing Arts Centre, 1995 by *Robert Byron Architects*, is expressive, but the earlier annexe on Bow Road is a dull affair.

CENTRAL FOUNDATION SCHOOL FOR GIRLS (UPPER SCHOOL), Morgan Street and College Terrace. 1909 by *Figgis & Munby*. Large, impressive buildings in a red and white Neo-Wren style. Built as the Coopers' Company's Boys School on the site of the Stepney Grammar School of *c.* 1878, inherited by the Company when they amalgamated in 1891 with the Coborn Girls School (*see* Lower School, below) as the Stepney & Bow Foundation. Symmetrical composition of central range of three bays; eight windows in two tiers to classrooms with a hall behind. Steeply pitched roof surmounted by cupola. Attractive stair towers, with turret cupolas and *œil-de-bœuf* windows under small broken pediments, in the angle of a pair of long projecting wings which have full-height rusticated stone arches to their ends. Linking the wings is a curved Doric colonnaded screen with an arched centre. The W wing has been altered. The façade to College Terrace has a floridly carved frieze by *E. Whitney Smith*. Inside, a small entrance hall, panelled with a plaster ceiling in C17 style, opens to a large hall (87 ft by 47 ft) with a gallery on elongated consoles and a cross-vaulted ceiling pierced by deep lunette windows. Diocletian windows at each end. The stair towers have stained glass of the Coopers' Company arms.

CENTRAL FOUNDATION SCHOOL FOR GIRLS (LOWER SCHOOL). Bow Road and Harley Grove. The earlier part (Nos. 31–3 Bow Road) of 1897–8 by *George Elkington jun.*, was built as the Coborn Girls School for the Stepney & Bow Foundation (*see* Upper School, above). The Central Foundation School moved here in 1975 from Spital Square, Spitalfields, when the Coopers' & Coborn Schools moved to Upminster (*see* p. 210). Lively and striking Neo-Jacobean. Asymmetrical red brick and Portland stone façade dominated by a central block with staggered quoins rising to paired pilasters and crested by a high shaped gable. Central three-storey bay window with small arcaded upper lights and attached Ionic columns to second floor. High stair tower stands to the l. and slightly back. Handsome upper storey with rounded corners and gabled cupola. Behind is a top-lit galleried hall with an open timber roof and classrooms wrapping round. Gymnasium, added 1931 by *George Elkington & Son*, fastidious Neo-Georgian in red brick. Laboratory of 1957. In Harley Grove, main building of

1997 by *Tower Hamlets Building Services* in patchy pale brick. Linear plan with a curved two-storey centre expressing the circular atrium inside. Long classroom wings on either side divided by full-height corridors with galleries.

PHOENIX SCHOOL, Bow Road. 1951–2 by *Farquharson & McMorran* as an LCC open-air school, now for special needs children. An exemplar of the optimistic and caring aspect of good post-war design, with one- and two-storey, copper-roofed brick buildings set in peaceful, green surroundings. The blocks are arranged as pavilions linked by covered walkways, which were originally open to the tree-lined courts. The pastoral theme is set on the entrance side by playful reliefs of the Four Seasons by *Steven Sykes*. At the back, the fully-glazed assembly hall was designed to open to a small garden, which has an Italian well-head of Istrian stone. Around the other sides of the garden are sensitive additions of 1996 by *Lister, Grillet and Harding* for a primary school.

BROMLEY-BY-BOW CENTRE, St Leonard's Street. *See* p. 631.

KINGSLEY HALL, Powis Road. *See* p. 632.

PERAMBULATIONS

1. Bow

The first two perambulations cover areas which were formerly in the parish, later borough, of Stepney. The others cover the historic centre of Bow.

1a. Tredegar Square and Neighbourhood

The development of the W end of Bow was begun in the early C19. N of Mile End Road, and its continuation Bow Road, fields and market gardens were exploited for the building of superior middle-class housing. The estates of the Coborn Charity were built up from 1817 under the supervision of *George Smith*, surveyor to the Coopers' Company. The neighbouring land, owned by Sir Charles Morgan of Tredegar, Monmouthshire, was let to local surveyor *Daniel Austin* in 1822 but seemingly laid out by local architect and surveyor *William King*. The showpiece, Tredegar Square, was complete by the 1830s but the Eastern Counties Railway was driven through the northern part of the estate in 1839, prompting a second phase of less exclusive development in the 1850s under *George Hammack*.

The tour begins at Mile End Station in MILE END ROAD (historically within Stepney). Open land for the building of large institutions in the mid and later C19 attracted several workhouses. In Southern Grove, just E of the station is the former Whitechapel Union Workhouse (now council offices), built *c.* 1872. Low ward wings either side of an entrance block with stone-capped gables and an octagonal domed cupola. Much more impressive to the E is St Clement's Hospital, the former City of London Union Workhouse (*see* above).

Along the N side of the road the smart survivors of the early C19 suburb are set well back behind gardens, beginning with three terraces erected on the Morgan and Coborn estates in 1822–4 by the Ratcliffe builder, *William Marshall*. Nos. 417–35 and Nos. 441–56 Mile End Road (Rodney Terrace) are three storeys with arched surrounds to the first floor windows and doorcases with fluted columns; Coborn Terrace (Nos. 3–23 Bow Road) is identical. The former Coborn Girls School (Central Foundation School, *see* above) at No. 30 was the late C19 successor to a charity school founded at Bow in the will of Prisca Coborn (†1701).

N along COBORN STREET, completed by 1827, are attractive two-storey paired villas (Nos. 24–35) with Gothic cast-iron balconies and ground-floor arched windows in recesses. Originally detached with entrances at the sides but later extended with single-storey entrances facing the street. Similar villas on the E side were demolished in the C20 for the Malmesbury Primary Schools (1885) and a Postal Sorting Office of 1912 by the *Office of Works* in blockish Neo-Georgian.

COBORN ROAD, parallel to the W, was known as Cut Throat Lane before 1800 and marked the division between the Coborn and Morgan estates: it later delineated the parish and borough boundaries. Its W side has particularly charming pairs of small houses with linked entrances forming a continuous terrace, and a few timber and iron porches, including Nos. 17 and 19 with cobwebby patterns. On the E side, more cottages paired under single pediments and THE COBORN pub. Further N at the corner with Morgan Street is the MORGAN ARMS, rebuilt by *Hammack & Lambert* in 1891: the red brick and stamped-terracotta detail is characteristic of its date. Nos. 49–51 are by the same firm and the character of the street, as far as the railway bridge (Coborn Road station opened 1865; closed), belongs predominantly to the later C19, including Holy Trinity Vicarage.

TREDEGAR SQUARE formed the showpiece of the Morgan estate's development and remains the most sophisticated piece of late Georgian planning in the East End. Completed 1828–9, the square puts the rest of the surrounding streets to shame with tall, three-storey terraces on the E, W, and S sides, of stock brick with good doorcases, fanlights and stucco dressings. The eight-bay centres are emphasized by incised-stucco pilaster strips and the penultimate bays given pediments. The N side was refronted in stucco in the 1830s, contemporary with the building of Holy Trinity Church (*see* above). Its grand design is properly architectural in the Nash manner with two main motifs of giant recessed columns. Twenty-eight bays wide with windows symmetrically placed in a pattern of 7:2:10:2:7. The outer blocks have five-bay projecting centres with the centre three set well forward between giant pilasters. No. 26 was fitted out in 1836–7 and remains the grandest house. (One room has original painted decorative wallpapers arranged as panels with roundels of putti at the centre representing the arts and sciences.) By the end of the C19, in spite of the general decline of Stepney, the houses of Tredegar Square and its surrounding streets were still the domain of clerks and officials, predominantly connected with the Docks. The square's garden was relandscaped in 1951 and the terraces much restored since the 1970s. The SW corner is a replica rebuild of the 1990s.

W of the Square, in MORGAN STREET is the CENTRAL FOUNDATION GIRLS SCHOOL, built as the Coopers' Company Boys School and, next door, HOLY TRINITY CHURCH (*see* above). The church faces down RHONDDA GROVE, which has, on both sides, large and distinguished groups of paired villas with broad overhanging eaves on coupled brackets, and doorways set back at the sides, some with Doric columns and fanlights. Good infill at Nos. 12–13 by *MacDonald & Berridge*, of equal height with its neighbours but with a steeply sloping monopitch at the rear. Unadorned façade of yellow brick with porthole windows in the upper floor and inset doorways.

ABERAVON ROAD was laid out as Frederick Place and developed from 1824 with a two-storey terrace, built in stages, with projecting centre on the W side. Cast-iron basket balconies and windows in arched recesses. Facing, EATON TERRACE by *CZWG* for Kentish Homes, 1983–5; it emulates the Georgian scale but with this firm's usual jokiness and introducing unlikely elements, such as double-height entrance lobbies lit by exaggerated fanlights, small windows tucked into the eaves and doorways flanked by huge curving pedestals with ball finials, designed to disguise rubbish bins. ONYX HOUSE, an office block facing MILE END ROAD, is part of the same development but less inspiring. The key element is the coved cornice breaking free of the parapet and swooping in a deep inverted curve through the brick façade to reveal glass curtain walling. The office was built on the site of *Andrew Mather*'s Odeon in 1938, which replaced Essex House, the C18 mansion where C.R. Ashbee ran his Guild of Handicraft from 1891–1905, before moving to the Cotswolds.

1b. *S of Bow Road, from Mile End Station to Bow Road Station*

Just W of Mile End Station is BURDETT ROAD. It was opened in 1862, and became an important N–S artery; a little indifferent building of that date remains on the E side, together with the East London Tabernacle, a post-war rebuilding of its war-damaged predecessor (*see* p. 449). To its E, the WENTWORTH ARMS at the corner of Wentworth Mews, a decent Victorian stucco-trimmed corner pub. Nearby in ERIC STREET, an interwar TELEPHONE EXCHANGE by the *Office of Works*, tall, with brusquely Hawksmorean classical keystones. Redevelopment here took off slowly. Around HAMLETS WAY, the LCC's TREBY ESTATE keeps to the original street pattern with low-key 1950s medium-rise red brick parts and one nine-storey slab. The grander scale of the ERIC ESTATE further E, extending to Southern Grove, reflects the ambitions of the newly formed borough of Tower Hamlets twenty years later. Forceful but ungainly blocks of maisonettes on three sides of grassed areas. Coniston House, 1968, is on tapering piers, the six-storey Derwent House (1973) has a dramatic exposed concrete grid. A nineteen-storey tower, Ennerdale House (1970–4), composes badly with its older dumpier neighbour of eleven storeys, the Treby Estate's Beckley House of 1961. But by the 1970s total rebuilding was going out of fashion, and further S along Eric Road and to the W in MOSSFORD STREET quite stylish terraces of *c.* 1870 remain, with two-storeyed bay windows and lavish stucco trim. Towering above them is SOUTH GROVE SCHOOL of 1904, by *T.J. Bailey*, a stately three-decker with terracotta-trimmed ogee gables and fancy parapets with little Jacobean finials against the buttresses. The adjacent, two-storey block with pointed arches is the earlier school, of 1874 by *Robson*. More terraces with simpler details, in ROPERY STREET, around the S edge of the cemetery, and LOCKHART STREET which leads into BOW COMMON LANE, the S boundary of this area of older buildings. Further S, the triangular area up to the railway line is all post-war: Stepney and Tower Hamlets' BEDE ESTATE, mixed development built 1967–72. Four-storey maisonettes, in a grid at an awkward angle to Bow Common Road, and one twenty-four-storey tower, Lewey House, planned 1964. Its profile with five insets is a paler reflection of the more forceful LCC towers of the early 1960s.

From Ropery Street SOUTHERN GROVE leads N to the entrance to TOWER HAMLETS CEMETERY (*see* above). Along a path by the northern perimeter first BROKESLEY STEEET, which has a complete 1860s terrace on the W side, much shaved although some cornices and pedimented doorcases remain, then the start of BRITISH ESTATE, which extends to Wellington Way. This is named from the street it replaced: an unfortunately representative-sounding title, for it is memorable for the drabness of its repetitive system-built blocks of 1970–6. Later roofs slightly soften the grim four-storey maisonettes of grey- ribbed squares of concrete, arranged in a semi-pedestrian layout with vehicle cul-de-sacs. Two towers of 1969–70 at the E end.

WELLINGTON WAY has remnants of a respectable Victorian neighbourhood. On the E side a small, symmetrically composed group of picturesque mid-C19 Gothic gabled houses with mullioned windows and angled chimneystacks; No. 3 has two gables, Fife Cottage a gable on the l., No. 5 a gable on the r. They survived in use as a Tuberculosis Dispensary, until the Neo-Georgian CHEST CLINIC, 1927 by *Harley Heckford*,

Borough Surveyor, was adapted in the 1980s from its original use as a Maternity Centre. Nearby, WELLINGTON PRIMARY SCHOOL, 1928 by the LCC, a fine example of an open-air school; shallow V-shaped plan with long two-storey open-air classroom wings facing S, the W wing with balcony and glazed screens. To the rear a hall and modest schoolkeeper's house. Further S a pair of mid-C19 villas, and some 1990s housing, squeezed on to land close to the railway line.

At the N end, close to Bow Road, WELLINGTON BUILDINGS, two blocks of tenements with projecting bays for staircases, originally open, under pointed gables. Glazed plinth and some patterned brickwork diapering. A low range on the S side of the courtyard was originally for a laundry and bathhouse. Built 1900–1, by *C.A. Brereton*, Engineer to the Whitechapel and Bow Railway, to house residents displaced by the building of the railway line and BOW ROAD STATION (opened 1902). Just E of the station, parallel to Wellington Way, MORNINGTON GROVE. On the W side tall pairs of houses of *c.* 1860; they seem unusually grand for the area. Three storeys, eclectic detail: bracketed eaves and tripartite windows which are pedimented on the ground floor, arched on the first floor.

This part of BOW ROAD, between the old centres of Bow and Mile End, has some miscellaneous but quite dignified buildings. Almost opposite the station, Nos. 41–7 (Council Offices) were built 1938–9 for Spratt's biscuit manufacturers (*see also* p. 636) probably by *Andrews & Gale*, a local firm. Classically detailed three-storey front block in brick, the middle bays slightly advanced and dressed in faience. On the corner with Alfred Street, ELECTRIC HOUSE of 1925–6 by *Harley Heckford*, Poplar Borough Surveyor and Engineer, contained the borough's electricity showrooms, and flats above for 100 families. Poplar, unlike the LCC, introduced electricity into its interwar housing schemes as standard. Five storeys, consciously grand Neo-Georgian, with stone pediments over first-floor windows. Then to the E, Nos. 69–95, erected as Tredegar Terrace in 1826; tall, three storeys with doors in concave surrounds and round-arched first-floor windows. The houses at the W end are slightly advanced. The terrace originally incorporated an older mansion subsequently called Tredegar House. Joseph Westwood, iron shipbuilder, occupied the house during the 1860s and 70s, but it was rebuilt in 1911 by *Rowland Plumbe* as a Nurses' Training Centre for the London Hospital. Tall, with a fine centrepiece in stone incorporating the ground-floor windows and entrance beneath a curved pediment and balcony. The E end of the terrace is curtailed by the Police Station, which faces the Thames Magistrates Court (*see* above). Crossing the street is the viaduct of the (disused) Blackwall extension to link traffic from the docks with the Great Eastern Railway. The former station (WILLIAM HILL) survives; by *E.H. Horner c.* 1869. Next door, the fancy LITTLE DRIVER pub of similar date. For Bow Road further E *see* 1c below.

1c. Bow Church and neighbourhood

The historic centre of Bow was grouped around the parish church in BOW ROAD. A tour can begin at BOW CHURCH DLR, opened in 1987 on the revived line of the North London Railway. The tremendous North London Railway Station of 1870, described by Pevsner 'with a front of nine bays, stock brick with giant pilasters, a kind of roundheaded Tuscan Trecento style' stood on the N side of Bow Road until 1975. In front was an elaborate Gothic fountain, erected in 1872 by Bryant & May to commemorate the repeal of the Match Tax. It held a seated figure of Justice. Demolished in 1953 for road widening.

This end of Bow Road also provided the centre of local government for Bow and Bromley-by-Bow. On the N side, on the site of the Bow Vestry Hall, is the former Poplar Town Hall (*see* above) of the 1930s, but on the S side are some older survivals. First, the BOW BELLS pub of the 1860s: Gothic Italianate with triplets of pointed windows in the first floor, then BROMLEY PUBLIC HALL (*see* above). Further E on this side, No. 116 is a fine example of an early police station. 1859 by *Charles Reeves*, Surveyor to the Metropolitan Police. Lofty three-storey Italianate façade in yellow brick with a neat dentilled brick cornice and round-arch sash windows with lugged architraves. Brick quoins and rusticated surround to the entrance.

In the centre of Bow Road is the landmark of the parish church of St Mary (*see* p. 604). It was originally surrounded by houses but now stands alone on a traffic island. Set in front on a granite plinth is a powerful bronze STATUE of W.E. Gladstone in oratorical pose. 1881 by *Albert Bruce Joy*, commissioned by Theodore Bryant, match manufacturer, who it was widely (but falsely) claimed docked one shilling from each of his workers to pay for it. Since 1900 Gladstone has had to preside over the public lavatories.

Of the old houses in Bow Road listed by the Royal Commission in 1930 nearly all have gone: the few survivors on the N side close to the church are small beer. From E–W, first No. 223, which has first-floor canted bays (typical of the late C17) over a C19 shopfront. No. 215–17 is an interwar garage, built *c.* 1930 on the site of a C16 house with excellent Jacobean strapwork ceilings, recorded by the Royal Commission in the year of its demolition. No. 199 is of three storeys with an early C18 brick front with a brick band at first floor, but with its windows altered and a Neo-Georgian shopfront. No. 195; big late Victorian works with wide piers faced in glazed brick dividing six bays under gabled dormers. No. 181 was the Clergy House attached to the Church of Our Lady and St Catherine of Siena (*see* above); behind, rather awkwardly facing a narrow alley is the former Convent, from 1996 the Nunnery studios and gallery, in red brick with four crow-stepped gables. Part of the Bow Arts Trust, together with the factory opposite. Further on, The KINGS ARMS, a nice reminder of the C18 village with gabled mansard roof and a C19 pub front, stands next to COSTCUTTER, built for the Stratford Co-op in 1919 by their Surveyor, *H.E. Tufton*; the large round gable bears the usual relief of a beehive. Finally on this side, NATWEST, *c.* 1900 Baroque.

FAIRFIELD ROAD leads N from Bow Road. No. 2a was the Rectory, by *W.A. Hills & Son*, 1898 in a vivid red brick with large egg-and-dart cornice, mullioned windows in stone and recessed arched entrance. Then a terrace of the 1820s, with decorative laurel wreaths to the flat-headed paired entrances, part of the suburbanization of Bow which brought an end to the annual May Fair, held here after its removal from the West End in 1764. The Fair Field was built up with houses by 1862, a few of which survive on the W side of the road, the field itself taken for Bow School (*see* above) from 1876. Further N on Fairfield Road's E side is the BUS GARAGE, built as the LCC's tram depot in 1907–8; extended on either side 1910–11. Symmetrical brick façade with gables at either end. Tall round-arched entrances and windows with big key blocks. The garage was built on the land of the largest mansion in Bow, the late C17 Grove Hall (extended as a lunatic asylum in the C19 and demolished 1909), the rest of whose grounds were soon built up with houses. Off Jebb Street, S of Wrexham Road, a small part of the gardens were preserved as GROVE HALL PARK. In the southern part are memorial gardens paid for by Bryant & May as a setting for the company's WAR MEMORIAL: a simple white stone cross, lightly carved with Gothic tracery. On the park's S side is a passage leading back to the church.

1d. Bow Quarter – the former Bryant & May Match Factory

The former Bryant & May Match Factory in Fairfield Road was founded in 1860 by Quaker merchants. Its scale is unusual for East London industry outside the docks and riverside and forms a great brooding mass, more redolent of Blackburn than Bow. Closed in 1979 and redeveloped from 1987 as Bow Quarter, an 'inward-looking' private housing development of a type at that time without parallel in East London outside Docklands.

Bryant & May began to import Swedish safety matches in the 1850s from Johan Lundström's factory in Jönköping before adapting an existing works on the present site with advice from Lundström and his engineers: the factory was run on the Swedish model of semi-mechanized production and relatively healthy working conditions. Raw supplies of timber and chemicals were transported down the River Lea; by 1862 the firm was producing nearly two million matches, an unparalleled scale of production at a time when most of Bow's match industry was undertaken in the home as piece-work by cheap labour. The works were extended in 1874 for warehousing and offices. Although conditions at the factory were unusually good, including provision of a doctor and dentist to monitor cases of 'phossy jaw', a strike by female workers in 1888 led by Annie Besant gave the company a notorious reputation which led to further improvements in pay and amenities. The introduction of continuous matchmaking machines required construction of a massive new factory in 1909–11, designed by *Holman and Goodrham*, capable of producing 10,000 million matches a year.

The masterplan for Bow Quarter was produced by *ORMS Architects* in 1987 but not completed to their design. The approach, as in parts of Docklands, was based on the model of reuse of industrial buildings in the United States and several architects were employed by the developers to introduce the 'loft-style' living popularized in Manhattan. This mid-Atlantic styling, visible throughout the development, now looks very dated and inappropriate for buildings that need little set-dressing.

The works are closed behind a splendid red brick Gothic wall with pointed-arch recesses created in 1874. Close to the gates are a series of COTTAGES (Moreland Cottages) for company employees, also Gothic with slate roofs creating a highly effective street frontage. The earliest is No. 2, with a private gate to the street beneath a crow-stepped gable, erected in 1867 as offices for the Directors. Red brick with blue brick strings, and white brick courses under the eaves. It has a carved roundel of a lighthouse guiding a ship, one of the company's several emblems. No. 1, a substantial house with a steep pyramidal-roofed stair tower and raised entrance, is of 1874. Also of this date, the two-storey GATEHOUSE which has a carved emblem of Noah's Ark and the inscription, 'Security'. Over the bay window on the S side, terracotta panels of beasts and a panel with a flaming torch and the inscription '*Luce Ex Lucellum*'.
68 Attached to the gatehouse, Nos. 3 and 4 Moreland Cottages have a spooky witch's-hat roof over the curved N end, while Nos. 5 and 6 have a delightful date panel modelled in terracotta tiles and fine projecting porches with sandstone columns.

Ranged across the entrance forecourt is the three-storey ARLINGTON BUILDING, designed in 1874 as warehouses and offices. Originally symmetrical, but partly demolished. Over the elliptical arcaded throughway, carried on polished-granite columns with cast-iron columns behind, is a showy carved-stone panel with a clock and the firm's emblems and monogram. Window bays to l. and r. are set within their original pointed relieving arches, remodelled with larger windows in the outer bays, possibly *c.* 1920 when the building was extended N. Attic floor added in 1989 by *Forum Architects*. The N extension (1961) was built on the site of the staff canteen, one of the concessions won by the strikers in 1888.

Attached to the S end of the Arlington Building and stretching out E is the awesome former factory, erected in 1909–11 by *Holman & Goodrham*. Built in two sections, now the MANHATTAN BUILDING: converted 1992–3 by *ORMS Architects* and LEXINGTON BUILDING: converted 1988–9 by *Forum Architects*. Atriums were cut into the face of each part for lift shafts. F-plan of two wings set at right angles to the S spine. Five tall deep storeys and basement in ruddy-coloured brick, with projecting piers and buttressing between the window bays and, in the inner angles with the wings, massive 136-ft high Italianate stair towers capped by corbelled-out water tanks for the sprinkler system. At the base of each are reset foundation stones from earlier buildings of 1868 and 1870. The factory contained the entire production process: timber was taken into the saw mill on the ground floor of the W wing and reduced to match splints on the upper floors before dipping and boxing in the fourth-floor match rooms which were ventilated and lit by lantern roofs. Boxing and packing was conducted in the E wing before the matchboxes were delivered via a platform into the railway sidings on the S side.

N of the Manhattan Building is a lofty free-standing brick chimney, once connected to the power house which was replaced by a leisure club with roof gardens, contemporary with the first phase of conversion in 1988. In front of the Lexington Building, hard landscaping of reset granite setts around a fountain and pond. Beside the latter, a SCULPTURE by *Maurice Agis*, 1990. Smooth blocks of Provençal stone with a dark, curved seam of lead, apparently commissioned to commemorate the match girls' strike. Immediately N of the factory stand CENTRAL PARK BUILDINGS; three six-storey apartment blocks of 1993–5 by *CZWG*, for Ballymore Properties, but with little of the memorable style of their earlier Docklands work. Closing the N side of the site, BLONDIN TERRACE of 1989, a group of terraced houses on either side of a gated opening, planned in the original scheme by *ORMS* as the principal entrance to the site but not executed to their design. Further along some small C19 workers' houses.

2. *Old Ford*

2a. *Roman Road and Neighbourhood*

The tour begins at the junction of Grove Road and ROMAN ROAD, Old Ford's principal shopping street, so-named since the 1860s when Roman remains were first discovered at its E end close to the site of the 'old ford' across the River Lea. Its character is still principally mid-C19 when the first development of the area was prompted by the opening of Victoria Park to the N. Roman Road's N side is almost all of a piece, roughly contemporary with streets behind which were progressively laid out with houses after 1857 as the Victoria Park Estate of the London and Suburban Freehold Land & Building Society. Their surveyors were *Hammack & Lambert*, who also carried out the later phases of development on the Morgan estates to the S (*see* perambulation *1a*). Most are two storeys, a number are dated and named with plaques set just under the eaves, e.g. Charles Cottage and Eliza Cottage in KENILWORTH ROAD of 1857–60. CHISENHALE ROAD backs onto the Hertford Union Canal (opened 1830) and already had factories in the 1850s: it is still dominated by the former CHISENHALE WORKS (now Chisenhale Gallery), established by Morris Cohen for the manufacture of veneers and rebuilt in 1942 to supply veneers for fighters and bombers. Facing, CHISENHALE PRIMARY SCHOOL of 1893 by *T.J. Bailey*, remodelled 1902. Lofty four-decker with classrooms grouped around a hall. Some Neo-Grec detail but also, crowning the staircase towers, a witty cupola with mini-dormers and delicate weathervane and ogee dome. Further E, some taller houses of three storeys including No. 8 called 'Uncle Tom's Cabin 1858'.

In the streets S of Roman Road are more terraces in MEDWAY ROAD. On its W side, the secluded OLGA PRIMARY SCHOOL of 1979–82 by *Ann Webb* of the *GLC/ILEA Architects*; a semi-open plan in brown brick with mono-pitch roofs on open timber trusses. To the S are earlier school buildings converted to housing in SCHOOLBELL MEWS. The Olga Street Board School is of 1874, done before E.R. Robson had been given authority over all designs. By local surveyors *Hammack & Lambert* with Gothic detail of paired gables and quatrefoil windows to the N range. S range by *Robson*, 1881. Infants school added 1900 by *T.J. Bailey*; particularly attractive with roughcast gables, tall chimneys, terracotta dressings and tiled roofs like a pretty row of Arts and Crafts cottages. Conversion by *ATP Group Partnership*, 1984.

Most of the surrounding area is covered by modest terraces built up from the mid-1860s after the Great Eastern Railway station opened at Coborn Road (closed 1948). In ANTILL ROAD, at the S end of Medway Road close to the railway, No. 129 was built *c.* 1869 as the Duke of York pub, for the Smith, Garrett & Co. brewery of Bromley-by-Bow. Good tiled signage, mostly retained in conversion to housing. N from the pub along SELWYN ROAD, the rigid pattern of streets was broken up as part of post-war reconstruction to create an informal centre around Selwyn Green. N of the Green, NORMAN GROVE has a mixture of mid-C19 cottages. At the rear of No. 43a, workshops were converted into a house by *Piers Gough* for himself, *c.* 1977. W along SAXON ROAD are the former St Stephen's National Schools, by *James Tolley*, 1859. Attractive Neo-Tudor with diaper brickwork, mullion windows and gables, but a bludgeoning hall extension of 1893–4 by *G.E. Holman*. These face the ROSEBANK ESTATE, a small, rather grim, low-rise development completed in 1974 by Tower Hamlets.

The walk now returns along St Stephen's Road, dominated by the large and boring ST STEPHEN'S ESTATE of 1966–9 by *Norman & Dawbarn* for Tower Hamlets, to the W end of ROMAN ROAD. There is little of intrinsic architectural value here except the former library (now Ideas Store, *see* above) and perhaps Kelly's Eel and Pie shop at No. 660 with an original 1930s tiled interior. Nevertheless the narrow road has a vibrant atmosphere brought to it by the long-established street market.

Closing the market street at either end are archways erected in 1986 which bear pompous Latin inscriptions alluding to the street's purportedly Roman past.

Continuing N along ST STEPHEN'S ROAD past the Church of St Paul with St Stephen (*see* above), the area was thoroughly cleared of its C19 housing and industry from the 1960s, principally by the LCC and GLC, frustrated by the slow progress of Poplar Borough's own rehousing programme. On both sides of St Stephen's Road is the RANWELL ESTATE, laid out in two phases around a pre-war LCC scheme. The W part, opened in 1969, is dominated by three twenty-two-storey towers, the rest consists of unadventurous and dour four-storey flats and maisonettes added in 1972–5.

OLD FORD ROAD crosses the N end of St Stephen's Road. Along its N side, after the opening of the Hertford Union Canal in 1830, the land was taken for wharves, warehouses and timber saw mills which have now made way for residential conversions and developments drawn by the picturesque setting of the de-industrialized waterway. Close to the junction on the N side of the road is CONNAUGHT WORKS, a long three-storey range with steel windows and central carriage arch, dated 1918 for the London Small Arms Co. (*see* below). Just behind, a converted five-storey warehouse survives from the adjoining Albany Works. GUNMAKERS LANE is a narrow passage alongside these works to the canal and originally led to the works of the London Small Arms Company who occupied the canal wharf from 1867–1919. During the First World War they produced up to 2,000 rifles a week. The canal also provided an essential link to the Lea Navigation and the Royal Small Arms Factory at Enfield where components produced at Old Ford could be assembled and tested. The site has been completely redeveloped for smart flats in yellow brick with transparent glazed stairs, by *PTE Architects*, 1999–2001, part of a much wider programme to replace the Monteith Estate's system-built flats (with the exception of a single tower). Low-rise housing behind by *AFH Shaw Sprunt*. The walk can now continue along the N towpath of the HERTFORD UNION CANAL, opened in 1830 to link the Regent's Canal with the Lea Navigation at Hackney. The contemporary THREE COLTS BRIDGE which crosses into Victoria Park is of cast iron, slightly bowed and carried on brick abutments which still bear the grooves of tow-ropes. Further E is a second footbridge (Homerton Footbridge) in matching style. This crosses above a set of locks, overseen by the original lock-keeper's cottage (No. 1) of 1830, two storeys with low, hipped roof, and later neighbours set back on either side.

The footbridge leads into PARNELL ROAD which runs back to Old Ford Road. On the W side, the towers of the LCC's LOCTON ESTATE of *c.* 1959–65, are countered opposite by a novel mixed-use scheme by *Peter Barber Architects* begun in 2003 for Circle 33 Housing Association which returns to traditional terraced street patterns and house forms with novel two-storey dwellings of stacked form, each with private open space.

OLD FORD ROAD has at its E end a few curious fragments of the C19 parish including a former WESLEYAN CHAPEL of 1880–1 by *S.J. Newman* (Old Ford Catering Equipment) with a showy front in South Kensington round-arched style: under a broad gable a giant arch in moulded terracotta enclosing three former entrances, with roundel above. At the sides, set back, curved stair turrets. The flanks have large upper windows with geometric leaded glass (in a bad way). Interior subdivided. Just beyond a few houses and the former WHITE HART pub remind one of the scale of the area before the War. Just behind, in RUSTON STREET, is a HEALTH CENTRE, built as a maternity and child welfare clinic in 1937–8 by *Rees J. Williams*, Poplar Borough Surveyor & Engineer, with *Douglas K. Dick*, Assistant Architect. In the up-to-date modern style one associates with Poplar at this date, with a functional two-storey part containing the waiting hall and treatment rooms and a lower wing to the street, designed for pram storage, lit by porthole windows. The street frontage is clad in small aggregate-faced tiles.

The tour can conclude here or continue E into Old Ford's industrial fringe.

*2b. The Lea riverside and Fish Island**

Until the 1960s Old Ford Road continued, as it had done from earliest times, as far as the 'old ford' across the Lea where Roman herringbone masonry was discovered in the late C19. Close to the road in the medieval period stood one large house, latterly known as King John's Palace (demolished 1863), but most of the surrounding area was marshland. This was first cut through by the Hackney Cut and the Hertford Union Canal in the C18 and C19 and from the 1850s by the North London Railway, who established a coal and goods depot with a station on Old Ford Road. The sale by the railway of surplus land fostered the development of a tight industrial district to its E, building further on the established industries of dyeing, printing inks and cloth fulling along the river. In 1865 the Imperial Gas Light & Coke Co. purchased 30 acres for their new gas works but subsequently developed them on the E bank of the Lea nearer Bromley (*see* p. 231). The land passed to the separate Gas Light & Coke Co. who laid out the land for small houses and multi-storey factories in streets whose names have given the district its present name of Fish Island. In spite of encroaching development for housing and promised regeneration, the 'Island' still retains its C19 character and atmosphere: a survival unique in the C21 East End.

*The research for this area was undertaken by Tom Ridge.

The construction of the EAST CROSS ROUTE in 1959 replaced the North London Railway's goods yard and severed Old Ford Road in two. On its W side, Tower Hamlets built the fearful looming slabs of the LEFEVRE WALK ESTATE in 1969–70, the no-man's-land between this and the road now being redeveloped with traditional patterns of low-rise housing, the terrace nearest the road presenting a solid sheer, curving flank. In the distance further S are the picturesque Italianate towers of Bryant & May's match factory (*see* perambulation *1d*). Old Ford Road's E end was partly renamed CROWN CLOSE. This is reached via a FOOTBRIDGE, remodelled in 2003 with a skeletal superstructure resembling the silhouette of a fish, a punning reference to the area's new identity. First on the S side, a curious late C19 survivor, the former Christ Church Mission of 1890 (now New Bethel Revival Ministry International, *see* above). It adjoins the site of the medieval 'King's John Palace', demolished in the 1860s and replaced by a match works. The Palace's Gothic 'Ivy Gate' survived into the 1890s as a folly. Old Ford Road (now WICK LANE) led E down to the old ford. Close to its site is RIVERSIDE WORKS (No. 419),* a former printing-ink and varnish works, partly on the site of an early C18 scarlet dyehouse. The blocks extend E and are of various dates, mostly of stock brick with blue brick dressings. Two-storey N range of 1897, extended 1914 (E) and 1936 (W) by *Holman & Goodrham*, the latter bearing a Second World War memorial to its workers: an oval plaque with good lettering. Lower parallel S range for grinding mills, of 1897–8 and *c.* 1890 with E extension and boiler house by *Eugene C. Beaumont*, 1914–15. Nearby, on Iceland Road, THE ICELAND, a typical workers' pub.

Returning N, beyond Crown Close, stands a landmark chimney which belonged to the Crown wallpaper factory. Just beyond is the entrance to THE GREENWAY, a footpath created in the 1980s to link Old Ford with Beckton along the embankment of *Bazalgette*'s Northern Outfall Sewer of 1860–4 which crosses the River Lea to the E in four huge pipes supported by plate girders beneath a bridge. At the bridge, traces of Second World War defences including tank-traps and pill box in rough concrete. Descending to the river, one may follow now along the E towpath. On the bridge's N side, a high wall skirts the boundary of the former East London Waterworks' Old Ford pumping station of 1902–3. Only the foreman's house, by *Frederick Meeson*, survives, in red brick with half-timbered gables. On the W side of the river is a decrepit former engineering workshop and forge of 1904, with gable to the river and four short, square chimneystacks on its S side for the forges.

From this point the Lea meanders E, but a more direct and navigable bypass route N was made in 1768–9 with the HACKNEY CUT, part of the Lea Navigation which is joined

*Under threat in 2004.

by the Hertford Union Canal from Bow. OLD FORD LOCKS are of *c.* 1856. The W banks of the cut were built up at this time in ragstone blocks to support wharfs for the industrial district on this side.

A footbridge on the W side of the locks leads into DACE ROAD. At the entrance, bronze gates and gatepiers by *Jan Rosser* and *Penny Sadubin*, 2002, designed with local schoolchildren. Dace Road is the first of the piscatorially-named streets laid out by the Gas Light & Coke Company in the 1870s on a roughly triangular site between the sewer and the canals. Its separate and self-contained character, still resonant in 2004, meant its residents and workers always knew it as 'the Island'. The first block on the S side was built as a multi-storey stables for cartage contractor Henry Crane in 1906–12. Plain front with rows of small openings (now blocked) with bull-nosed blue brick dressings. Access to the upper floors was at the rear via external ramps (demolished). Crown Wharf behind is being developed in 2004 by *PTE Architects* for live–work units. Next, BRITANNIA WORKS, originally built 1898–9 for the Britannia Folding Box Company Ltd but much reconstructed after war damage. The earlier surviving parts are the angled eastern end, of 1907 with concrete upper floors on partly exposed steel girders and cruciform stanchions and the matching bays to the r., of 1898, which have rolled steel lintels on cast-iron mullions and blue brick sills. The post-war W end has classically derived features of the type which one usually associates with the 1930s. Separate from the main works at the W end is the former 1890s gatehouse, with a rendered façade and straight gable to the street; extended to the r. in matching style, 1902, 1907 and 1910.

The N side of DACE ROAD is taken up by a group of multi-storey factories and warehouses, originally erected as rubber works for Bernard Birnbaum, a rubber-clothing manufacturer from Spitalfields. The blocks stand either side of Smeed Road. On the W side, a four-storey former waterproof clothing department of 1882 (now BLUTEX) with three bays of stilted red brick arches under triangular gables with (blocked) oculi. The original stucco name panel survives on the W end, painted over. Corresponding on the E side of Smeed Road is another four-storey block for waterproof clothing, this one of 1889 by *Maxwell & Tuke* of Manchester (designers of Blackpool Tower in 1891), now artists' studios. Adjoining is a narrow, two storey 'farina' house of 1887 with a blind-arcaded front and lantern roof, and boiler house of 1889. The main entrance to the works (now PERCY DALTON'S) is in SMEED ROAD, through a two-storey office range with impressive carriage arch. This is flanked by square brick piers with pedimented capitals supporting piers with large ball finials framing a raised parapet. The Birnbaum works closed in 1906 and the eastern part was taken over in 1907 by the printers, Waterlow and Sons of Shoreditch, who erected ALGHA WORKS, a former print works by *Henry C. Smart*, at the corner with Stour Road. The design is rather striking; four-storeys in yellow brick above a deep semi-basement in blue brick which has multi-paned windows which slope inwards at the top. Unusually, the floor levels (indicated by the loading bays on the r.) do not correspond with the lintels of the tall windows. Instead, each is cut back to allow the window to continue higher up so as to provide maximum illumination for the printing machines inside.

STOUR ROAD contained the main part of the Broadwood piano factory in the C20 but this was cleared for an anonymous business park. Off its S side, between BREAM STREET and the canal, are relics of the former London Carbonic Acid Gas Works. These are: a three-storey block of *c.* 1898 designed for gas purification, a two-storey block of *c.* 1933 for production of gas from magnesite and closest to the canal, a single-storey works for production of ebonite screw stoppers, *c.* 1924.

STOUR ROAD leads into the parallel BEACHY ROAD, on the l. is a small 1902 group associated with the large Broadwood piano factory, which includes a boiler house with square tapering CHIMNEY SHAFT with a blue brick ornamental cap. From 1903 a tramway ran between the factory and its timber wharf on the canal at the E end of Beachy Road. On the S side at this end is the former gatehouse (now Nichols and Nichols, woodturners). N of this, along ROACH ROAD is ROACH WORKS and CROWN WHARF, undergoing major redevelopment in 2004 for flats and live–work units by *DWA Architects*, of a type now familiar in the East End but the first of their kind on the Island. Only a circular, red brick CHIMNEYSHAFT of 1900 with a blue brick cornice has been retained as a landmark from the former yard of J. Chessum and Sons, builders. The new buildings (partly complete in 2004), occupy a site bounded on two sides by the Hackney Cut and the Hertford Union Canal. Main elevations facing the waterways are in a haphazard mix of glass and coloured render but behind is a stylish open-ended inner courtyard overlooked on three sides by steel-and-timber access balconies. As part of the scheme a new FOOTBRIDGE by *Alan Baxter & Associates* is being erected across the Hertford Union Canal to provide a continuous walk along the towpath to the bridge over the Lea at CARPENTER'S ROAD. (In 2004 this can only be reached by retracing one's steps to Old Ford Locks and walking N along the E towpath.)

E of the canal in CARPENTER'S ROAD on the N side, is KING'S YARD, a former confectionery and jam factory of 1903–12 built for their own use by Clarke, Nickolls and Coombs Ltd. Two three-storey blocks, two-storey ranges; and a single storey range with their original Belfast-truss roofs. On the E boundary, a single-storey former stable block with some its original high-level windows, next to two-storey former the company fire station house. The same firm erected the six-storey building in QUEENS YARD, W of the canal, on WHITE POST LANE, as a chocolate factory. Base and piers of blue brick. Facing, opposite, the similarly treated No. 92, erected in 1904–5 as a dyeing and dry-cleaning works for Achille Serre

Ltd, extended behind *c.* 1923–4. Abutting this, the smaller scale of THE LEA TAVERN, a Truman's pub of 1897 with cut brick gables. White Post Lane bends N; its E side was occupied by Achille Serre from the 1870s, who set up possibly the first dry-cleaning works in England. It stood in the corner of an existing tar and chemical works, one of several established here from the late 1850s, which Serre partly absorbed as the business expanded. They built their offices at the N end of White Post Lane in 1911, with a prominent porch and the firm's name in mosaic to the parapet, still partly visible. Earlier wings of *c.* 1897–8 adjoining. White Post Lane leads towards HACKNEY WICK STATION. N of the railway (within Hackney borough) the C19 scale of modest terraced houses intermingled with multi-storey factories and warehouses still exists. This tour continues, however, W along WALLIS ROAD and the FOOTBRIDGE (identical to that at Crown Close, above) over the East Cross Route to CADOGAN PLACE, a short street which slopes upwards to Victoria Park and CADOGAN TERRACE, a fine row of smart terraced houses making a staggering contrast to the buildings just seen. At the corner is a former Truman's pub, The Morpeth Castle, 1926 by *A.E. Sewell*, in an appropriate but unorthodox crenellated style with a canted ground floor and Neo-Tudor windows with rounded heads. Hoodmoulds to the upper-floor windows with small masks. Adjoining to the r. a well-preserved shopfront for a former Post and Telegraph office. The rest of the terrace, developed in the 1860s to take advantage of the park-side setting, is shabby genteel, in brick trimmed with stucco and by various hands, so without any sense of uniformity but with common motifs of heavy porches on Doric columns. Only a few strike out more ambitiously. The terrace, and this tour, concludes at St Mark's Gate, where the brick Gothic MORPETH LODGE marks the entrance to Victoria Park. By the gate, the former ST MARK'S CHURCH, now a nursery, a small defensive-looking building of dark brick, with slit windows and canted corners, built for the Rev. H.E. Roberts as a 'church centre and communal lounge', 1973–6. Flexibly planned with hall opening up to the church (cf. the contemporary church centres in Newham by APEC). With the adjacent housing, it replaced a big Gothic church by *A.W. Blomfield* of 1872–3. For Victoria Park *see* p. 566.

3. *Bromley-by-Bow and Bow Common*

3a. *From Bow Church DLR to Devons Road DLR*

The first tour starts just E of Bow Church DLR. On the S side of Bow Road is BROMLEY PUBLIC HALL (*see* p. 611), testimony of the independence of the parish of Bromley until it became part of the borough of Poplar in 1899.

BROMLEY HIGH STREET leads S from Bow Road, then curves E. A little remains from the C19 at the W corner, around the

ROSE AND CROWN, three bays, with stucco-trimmed central window, but elsewhere the scene is dominated by the LCC's BOW BRIDGE ESTATE, opened 1933 and nearly doubled in size after the war. On the N side are stolid blocks of the usual walk-up pre-war flats; opposite, four dumpy eleven-storey towers of the 1960s unconvincingly represent post-war ideals. To their W is STROUDLEY WALK, a 1970s pedestrian shopping precinct by the GLC, curiously formal, with two opposing lines of plain round-arched arcades, like a surreal painting by de Chirico. Behind the arcades, upper flats step back, in multi-level ziggurat fashion, an echo of Watney Market (*see* p. 494).

Along the nondescript Bromley High Street only a few pre-war buildings remain as evidence of the old village; at the E end the former SEVEN STARS, 1895, with Gothic arcading on the first floor, is an uninspired replacement of its picturesque timber-framed predecessor. This bleak junction with St Leonard's Street was once the centre of the village. To the E are the derelict remnants of the CHURCHYARD of St Leonard's, entered through a stone archway of 1894. Most of the site, with its early Huguenot tombstones, together with the war-damaged parish church was swept away in 1959 for the Blackwall Tunnel Approach Road. The church dated from 1842, a replacement of a building of C12 origin surviving from the medieval nunnery, later adapted for parish use. The house built immediately S, on the site of the priory buildings, had disappeared already in the early C19.

Along St Leonard's Street is the site of the Board School which replaced the Old Palace (*see* Introduction, above). The school of 1894 was destroyed in the war. Its replacement is OLD PALACE PRIMARY, 1952 by *Cecil C. Handisyde* (architect of the Congregational church at Lansbury). Light curtain-walled buildings in the Festival tradition, fresh and cheerful. One- to three-storey ranges around a playground, the tallest for the juniors, with open ground floor. The construction combined pre-stressed and *in situ* concrete units, a system much used for later schools. In the playground a contemporary SCULPTURE: 'No': bronze figure of boy wrestling a cat, by *Bainbridge Copnall*. 1990s additions to the S.

BROMLEY-BY-BOW CENTRE, at the SW corner of St Leonard's Street and Bruce Road, provides welcome evidence of new energy. An enterprising and innovative social centre, unusually combining a healthy-living centre with teaching, training and other activities to encourage local economic regeneration. It developed gradually around a modest CONGREGATIONAL CHURCH, damaged in the war, which was rebuilt in 1958 by *John S. Broadbent*. Simple brick-gabled end to St Leonard's Street with tall triangular-headed glazed window. Adjoining in Bruce Road is an older church hall. Between them a tiny planted courtyard was created as part of the imaginative conversion for multi-purpose use by *Gordon MacLaren* of *Wyatt MacLaren*, planned from 1985. The church interior was remodelled in 1991–2 to provide a central worship area defined by a fabric sail-like canopy, with space for other activities around the perimeter. The church hall was subdivided, with classrooms on the upper floor.

Other buildings by *Wyatt MacLaren* have followed. To the W, opening up to the park behind, is a café, PIE IN THE SKY, 2002: glazed ground floor, timber-faced upper wall and elegant interior. Coloured brickwork on the side to the park. Round the corner in St Leonard's Street is the surprise of a grand stone ARCHWAY erected here in 1998. This arresting C18 Palladian piece, with heavily vermiculated rustication, carved keystone head and (renewed) top balustrade, came from an entrance from the riverside to Northumberland House in the Strand. It possibly dates from when *Daniel Garrett* was working on the house in 1748–50. When the building was demolished in 1874, the arch was bought by G.G. Rutty, owner of the nearby 'Tudor House', to embellish his garden. It now forms the entrance to the HEALTHY LIVING CENTRE, an informal curved building in vivid orange brick, by *Wyatt MacLaren*, 1997, which houses a doctors' practice and other services. Friendly glazed foyer with attractive timber-clad ceiling. A loggia forms a covered link to the church, beside a small landscaped courtyard with a SCULPTURE: the Passenger, by *Paula Haughney*, artist-in-residence.

To the S a gateway leads into the GARDENS, made from the grounds of Tudor House, laid out as a recreation ground by the LCC in 1900 (the house was later demolished). By the entrance, WAR MEMORIAL, obelisk with wreath, resited here as part of the relandscaping of the gardens undertaken by the Centre from 1999. This has contributed many intriguing features on an intricate scale: curving paths of yellow-mosaic brickwork, a herb garden, and play and seat sculptures.

KINGSLEY HALL, W of the gardens in Powis Road, has a longer history of social work in Bromley-by-Bow. 1926–8 by *C. Cowles-Voysey*, restored 1982–5. Established as a Christian fellowship in 1915 by Doris and Muriel Lester, for whom Cowles Voysey designed the Children's House Nursery in Bruce Road (*see* below). Neo-Regency with an Egyptian-style cornice. Slightly asymmetrical four-storey façade with a stair tower set back to the l. Tall arched windows and iron balcony to the first floor and square windows to the upper floor, originally open to a roof-top loggia. Inside, a ground-floor hall, rather like a chapel with panelled dados and raised dais at E end in a shallow apse set with single round-arch window. Low ceiling and awkward window vaults. Recreation rooms above and a roof garden with a small fountain designed to hold a sculpture by *Gilbert Bayes*, donated by A.A. Milne (removed). In the centre of the roof is a small block of rooms designed for male and female residential workers. Responsibilities, housework and income were shared on the model of an ashram, prompted by Muriel Lester's visit to Gandhi at Ahmedabad. Gandhi was a guest here during the Round Table Conference in 1931 and his room is kept as a memorial. The adjoining Peace Garden, opened *c.* 1985, has a twisted abstract metal SCULPTURE and decorative railings. A sister settlement was established in the 1930s on the Becontree Estate (*see* Barking and Dagenham) by former residents.

Along BRUCE ROAD something of the character of C19 Bromley remains: a set of demure small villas: Jesse's Cottages 1865, Isaiah Cottages 1866, Glenifer House 1870, also a neat terrace of houses built by the Bromley-by-Bow Centre *c.* 1992. ARROW ROAD, parallel to the N, has a remnant of a mid-C19 stucco-trimmed terrace and on the S side, a 1990s version of the same, also two storeyed, but the frontages more generous and the detail cruder, all in explicit contrast to the tall towers of the Crossways Estate visible to the W.

THE CHILDREN'S HOUSE, Bruce Road, E of the shopping centre was built as a nursery school, 1923–4 by *C. Cowles-Voysey* for Muriel Lester. An attractive building, homely but dignified, in an original version of Regency style, with thin projecting cornice and deep bracketed eaves over the attic. Tall sashed windows with moulded surrounds to the ground-floor nursery school. First and attic floors with smaller windows, providing accommodation for staff and settlement workers. Overdoor with a coloured ceramic Virgin and Child by *Gilbert Bayes.* The interior has a MURAL by *Eve Garnett*, 1935, showing children walking out of the East End to the countryside. Six large paintings donated by C.F.A. Voysey have gone.

To the W is the GLC's CROSSWAYS ESTATE, the most dramatic and daring of the estates in this area. It was built on the difficult site of the Bow locomotive works; the three twenty-five-storey towers were constructed in 1968–70 while the tracks were still in use. They stand in austere and grim isolation against the skyline, visible from afar and approached by walkways which now sail over rough sunken parkland, a different world from the low-rise housing along the higher ground to E and W. N of the eastern terrace is a little cul-de-sac with the DRAPERS' ALMSHOUSES of 1706, a surprising survival. A brick group, facing N, of four tenements with central raised and pedimented chapel. Nice carved brackets l. and r. of a centre door with swan-neck pediment. Restored 1982. Originally part of a larger group founded by Sir John Jolles in 1617. The present range was erected from the benefaction of John Edmanson.

The tour can end here, returning to Bow Road. For the intrepid who venture S to Devons Road station, the rewards are sadly few. This was the post-war reconstruction area's 'neighbourhood 8' but there is little evidence of new thinking in its planning. DEVONS ROAD, running S from the Stroudley Walk shopping centre, is the main artery of the sprawling DEVONS ESTATE with a total of 442 flats. Opened 1949, but entirely in the LCC's pre-war manner, but with all the drabness of post-war austerity. N of Devas Street is ST ANDREW'S HOSPITAL, a workhouse infirmary of 1871 (*see* above). Opposite is

COVENTRY CROSS ESTATE, opened 1935 with 178 pre-war flats. The street front shows the LCC in unusually pompous Baroque mode. On either side of a school is a tall stone entrance archway with Gibbsian surrounds, leading to a formal layout of four- and six-storey blocks (refurbished 1999). After these huge and monotonous stretches, a refreshing finale is in TIBBATTS ROAD just N of Devons Road station: an intimate cluster of low housing of the 1990s in pale brick around a smartened-up mid-C19 pub, the DUKE OF CAMBRIDGE. In front, a landscaped play area of 1994, a sadly rare case of the penetration of LDDC funding into this area. Close to the station, on former railway land, ST ANDREW'S HOUSE, London Ambulance Service, *c.* 1998, a crisp L-shaped composition with curved tower; three metal-clad floors above a tall grey brick service basement. On the other side of the line, THE WIDOW'S SON or BUN HOUSE, five-bay front with stucco trimmings and boarded parapet; Victorianized interior of the 1990s.

3b. Bromley-by-Bow Station to Devons Road DLR

This tour takes in an unpromising site, callously isolated in the 1960s by the Blackwall Tunnel Approach Road, where a small but interesting group became the spearhead of the Leaside regeneration programme in 2003–4. From outside the station, raised up on a bridge, first a bleak introductory panorama: flats and hospital to the W, industry and cleared land around the Lea, the filigree outlines of gasholders, and the looming curve of the Dome to the S. Accessible via a subway, and hard by the deafening traffic, is GILLENDER STREET, a fragment of the former Brunswick Road, with some relics of its former existence as part of Bromley-by Bow. First a lone remnant, the C19 QUEEN VICTORIA pub, two storeyed with stucco trim and curved corners. It was previously surrounded by the post-war part of the Coventry Cross Estate, now demolished. S of the Limehouse Cut (*see* below), a fine group of late C19 WAREHOUSES remains ('Aplins Spirit and Liqueur'); a four-storey range with windows below giant arches, and a lower two-storey part of 4+1 bays, interrupted by a later opening. Both parts with strongly modelled cornices. A C20 warehouse follows, sleekly curved to follow the road, alternating floors clad in red and yellow brick. Then a former LCC FIRE STATION (now studios), 1909–11, built for both horse and motor engines. Five storeys, with three white corbelled-out bay windows providing a domestic touch. Glazed brown brick ground floor.

No. 43, BROMLEY HALL, for long was a pathetic survival, patched up after serious damage in the Second World War. Recent rescue work in 2003–4 rediscovered its remarkable history. At first sight it is a two-storey, four-bay house of *c.* 1700, with coved eaves and hipped roof, and a doorway in the l. bay with small pediment on brackets. On a closer look it is clearly a remodelling of something much older. Polygonal brick corner turrets, a staircase turret projecting to the N and extending through three floors (with Tudor window openings visible inside), and recent tree-ring dating of timbers to *c.* 1490, suggest that this building was part of the early Tudor manor house of South Bromley, all that survives from a larger group shown on Rocque's map. Bromley Hall was leased in the early C16 to John Blount; later occupiers included William Cecil (later Lord Burghley); from the early C18 the site, close to the river Lea, was developed for calico production.

The original form of the present building is uncertain. It appears to have had four rooms on each floor, but may have extended further S, and could have been a gatehouse range. The S wall, now within the present low S extension, built in the 1920s as part of a training hospital, has Tudor limewashed brick on the ground floor and is plastered on the first floor, possibly suggesting a carriageway with a room above. Inside, the principal SW ground-floor room has its original ceiling with moulded beams (the central roll trimmed off for a later ceiling inserted below), and traces of wall painting on the S wall (outline panels). In its E wall was discovered a tall, well-preserved Tudor doorway of timber, with carved spandrels on its E face depicting a hound and hind. There was later remodelling, both *c.* 1700 and in the Regency period. From the latter is the elegantly curving staircase with stick balusters, from the former, a fragment of the upper flight with closed string and spiral balusters. On the first floor are remains of another timber Tudor doorway, also stone quoins in the S wall, possibly of a doorway to a lost extension. The story of the house is complicated by much reuse of earlier timbers and by tactful reconstruction at various dates: the SW polygonal corner and the very thick W wall appear to have been rebuilt in the C18; the sash windows and the whole of the E wall are post-war replacements. Puzzles remain: for example the lack of evidence for any Tudor fireplaces, and the two stone walls at cellar level (remains of something earlier?). They run E-W beneath the SW room and carry a wide Tudor brick arch.

Set back, SE of Bromley Hall, is a pile of bright red containers adapted as temporary offices, with porthole windows. By *Containerspace Ltd* (*Nicholas Lacey & Partners*), 2004 (for their prototypes *see* p. 663). This site is Poplar Riverside Phase One, the start of Tower Hamlets and Leaside Regeneration's effort to transform this part of the Lea Valley.

No. 45 Gillender Street was built for the Borough of Poplar as BROMLEY LIBRARY, 1904–6 by *Squire, Myers & Petch.* The first of the group to be rescued from long neglect, sensitively converted to offices and live–work units in 2002–3 by *The Regeneration Practice* for the Heritage of London Trust. A handsome stone front with a short return; deep rusticated basement, two storeys and attic with balustrade. The Baroque composition has four slightly recessed centre bays, divided by giant engaged Ionic columns; good carving by *Gilbert Seale.*

Arched windows to ground floor, triple windows divided by Doric colonnettes above. Entrance with steep pediment on heavily blocked Doric columns. Mosaic entrance floor; the former library space is divided by iron columns painted in the original rather surprising colours of blue and orange, with yellow walls. The ground-floor projects at the back with lantern roofs over the former reading rooms; the librarian's flat high above has the nice touch of two E-facing canted bay windows. New E range with apartments and workshops.

Around the LIMEHOUSE CUT made in 1770 to link the Lea to Limehouse Basin, a swathe of industry grew up, its buildings not yet entirely displaced. From BOW LOCKS just E of the Northern Approach Road, the tow path leads NE to Three Mills in Newham and SW through South Bromley past the rebuilt fringes of the Teviot estate (*see* p. 657). By MORRIS ROAD is the major landmark of SPRATTS BISCUIT FACTORY, now flats, a stately group of four- and five-storey buildings, orange brick with stone cornices, and a little early C20 free classical detail. Nos. 45 and 48 have curly volutes to their gable ends. Further W extensive new housing of two to four storeys in bland pale brick, *c.* 2002, developed by Countryside Properties and several housing associations. The BRIDGE over the Limehouse Cut was provided in 1890 by Poplar Board of Works; from it VIOLET ROAD leads N to Devons Road DLR station.

3c. Bow Common: from Devons Road DLR to St Paul's Way

This area was designated as the post-war 'neighbourhood 7', its boundaries defined by the railway lines and the Limehouse Cut. Later C19 housing grew up around gasworks, railway lines and canal, a fragmented society, as was revealed by a social survey carried out before redevelopment.

The nearest approach to the centre is at the junction of DEVONS ROAD, Watts Grove and Blackthorn Street, with All Hallows Church and its attendant buildings (*see* above). Here are still some humble buildings of the C19: the Lighthouse, a plain Baptist church (*see* above) and the TENTERDEN ARMS, simple mid-Victorian Italianate. To the N, DEVONS ROAD SCHOOL, 1905, a formal three-decker front with striped-stone pilasters and roof-top playground facing Knapp Road.

The LINCOLN ESTATE, N of Devons Road, is the LCC's most ambitious post-war effort here, involving the reconstruction of 1,495 acres, an unprepossessing site, dominated on the W side by gasworks. Planned from 1956 (architect-in-charge *A.J.M. Tolhurst*). Rebuilding around TIDEY STREET began in 1958, with over 805 dwellings by the 1970s. Almost every trace of the surrounding terrace housing was swept away, replaced by a scheme of mixed development, with two nineteen-storey towers of maisonettes, at the time the tallest in East London, included to bring the housing up to the required density. Refurbished in 1999–2000, they stand in an appealingly green setting at the S end of a new park; previously there was no open space here. A glimpse of the earlier character of the area is provided by the response to objections in 1956 to the first Tidey Street tower; it was argued in its favour that the upper half would be 'above the smoke, grime and fog'. The towers were designed with concrete cross walls and the novelty of a crossover plan with central access corridor, so that all living rooms could face S away from the gasworks. The low two-storey terrace houses around WHITETHORN STREET are attractively detailed, but overwhelmed by the looming gasholders. Much other housing, in four-storey maisonette blocks, now dressed up with roofs of the 1990s.

At the junction with TIDEY STREET, a 'model dairy' of 1890 has survived, now part of OPEN HOUSE, a MIND centre. Behind, a pretty group added in 1993–5 by *Wyatt MacLaren*, patterned brick buildings and a consciously picturesque little tower around a landscaped courtyard. Opposite, QUEEN MARY'S CHILDREN'S CENTRE, 1937 by *S.P. Dales*, founded as part of a Methodist mission; in a dour 'good-works' spirit; with carved brick relief of a figure with two children high up. On FERN STREET No. 70, the LINC CENTRE, a low, informal advice centre of the 1990s, in pale brick with angled roofs. Further E, the estate was extended N by the GLC, in and around CAMPBELL ROAD, where brown brick groups of terrace houses of *c.* 1973 were added among older housing; such infilling may seem dull now, but at the time was hailed as a breakthrough, a reaction against the total redevelopment of previous decades. Among them a focus is provided by the pre-war FAIRFOOT LIBRARY (*see* p. 613).

Along VIOLET ROAD a long, proud range of Poplar Borough Council housing of 1929, Neo-Georgian detail in front, utilitarian at the back. On the S side of DEVONS ROAD the PERRING ESTATE, the pre- and post-war LCC work easily distinguishable. Reticent pre-war walk-up blocks with Neo-Georgian frontages enclosing courtyards on three sides; later parts between Gale Street and Watts Grove of white-painted concrete with hefty walkways on two levels.

At the junction with Bow Common Lane the spire of Holy Name and Our Lady (*see* above) forms a much needed landmark. ST PAUL'S WAY continues W with a straggle of shops and a low pantiled Health Centre, but like many post-war shopping streets, lacks any urban coherence. ST PAUL'S COMMUNITY SCHOOL, a big post-war secondary, lies to the N.

S of St Paul's Way, the BURDETT ESTATE hits the eye: early post-war LCC blocks of four and six storeys, transformed by pitched roofs and other trimmings in 1998–2000 provided through estate renewal challenge funding, by *SW Thames Housing Group*. To the N is the more forceful LEOPOLD ESTATE, 1965–7 by the GLC. The main element is a mighty seven-storey range of maisonettes in dark red brick. The street side is dull but the S-facing side is of surprising grandeur with projecting balconies overlooking a green lawn toward St Paul's Way. The western apex of the estate is Elmslie Point on Burdett Road, a tower with forceful pebbly concrete surfaces (tamed by painting in 1999) looking out across Mile End Park. Close by, ST PAUL'S PRIMARY SCHOOL, 1972 by *Maguire & Murray*, with broad sweeping roof over an (originally) open-plan layout, and St Paul's church by the same firm (*see* above), not tall, but distinctive in its blocky outline.

POPLAR, BLACKWALL AND LEAMOUTH*

Poplar took its name from the hamlet which developed N of the marsh levels of the Isle of Dogs, along the gravel ridge between Limehouse and Blackwall. The East India Company, founded in 1600, which established its shipyard E of the Isle of Dogs at Blackwall, soon came to dominate the hamlet, supporting the local chapel and providing its own almshouses. In the mid-C17 there was just a double row of houses along the High Street, with a population of about a thousand. Though respectable in the C17 and C18, Poplar was never rich, for merchants and shipbuilders preferred to live further N or to retreat to more rural parts. After the opening of the West and East India Docks the population rose sharply, from 4,493 in 1801 to 7,708 in 1811. In 1820–3 a parish church, All Saints, was built close to the newly created East India Dock Road further N, and quite a smart residential quarter was laid out around it. The population mushroomed in the mid-C19 (28,432 in 1851; 43,529 in 1861), Poplar Chapel was recast as the church of St Matthias and public buildings were erected, but prosperity declined after 1880 as the down-river docks grew in importance. The High Street ceased to be a civic centre after the Metropolitan Borough of Poplar, formed in 1899, took in the separate parishes of Bow and Bromley to the N and built a new Town Hall in Bow Road. The High Street lost its shops and the alleys degenerated into slums.

New council housing following clearances in the 1930s, and post-war rebuilding after extensive Second World War bomb damage transformed much of the High Street and its hinterland, 'neighbourhood 11' of the Stepney/Poplar reconstruction plan.
p. 89 The remarkable St Matthias remains as a community centre, together with a miscellany of institutional buildings. C19 housing survives best around All Saints. This remains the principal older landmark on East India Dock Road. Here there was much destruction in the Second World War, but a sequence of former

*The parish of Poplar and the Docklands areas were respectively covered by the Survey of London Vols XLIII, XLIV and by Elizabeth Williamson's account in *London Docklands* (1998). This account is much indebted to both.

seamen's missions recalls Poplar's maritime connections, the earliest built by George Green of Blackwall Yard.

Much of the mid-C19 growth had taken place N of East India Dock Road, where Poplar New Town was built up with modest terrace housing from the 1830s–60s. This area was almost entirely replaced by the post-war 'neighbourhood 9', named after George Lansbury, the local M.P. The first phase of Lansbury was displayed as part of the Festival of Britain of 1951, as an example of the type of integrated rebuilding which was the aim of the reconstruction area.

The historic link with Blackwall was callously severed by the Tunnel Approach Road in the 1960s. Outer walls alone remain from the great enclosed docks of the East India Company, closed in 1965, filled in and covered by commercial buildings from the late 1980s. Only the isolated Trinity House Buoy Wharf on the tiny peninsula at Leamouth retains some vestiges of its historic maritime character.

RELIGIOUS BUILDINGS

The C17 Poplar Chapel which served the East India Company's workers remarkably survives as a community centre, its exterior disguised by C19 cladding after it became the parish church of St Matthias (*see* p. 645). By 1903 there were another eight Anglican churches, as well as R.C. and Nonconformist places of worship. Many disappeared in the Second World War.

ALL SAINTS, East India Dock Road. 1820–3 by *Charles Hollis*. A competent design by an architect with few other buildings to his name. In Portland stone on a granite plinth, the latter a new material for London at this time although used in the docks from *c.* 1800. The W steeple is still composed in the Wren-Gibbs tradition of at least a hundred years earlier, but with a Grecian Ionic portico with four fluted columns, based on the Athenian Temple on the Ilissus. The W front turns the corners with two pilasters which make the transition to side porticos *in antis* (cf. Gibbs's St Martin in the Fields), which gave access to the large staircase lobbies (now social centre and vestry). Otherwise, the sides have two tiers of windows, the upper ones arched. Coupled pilasters at the E corners too,

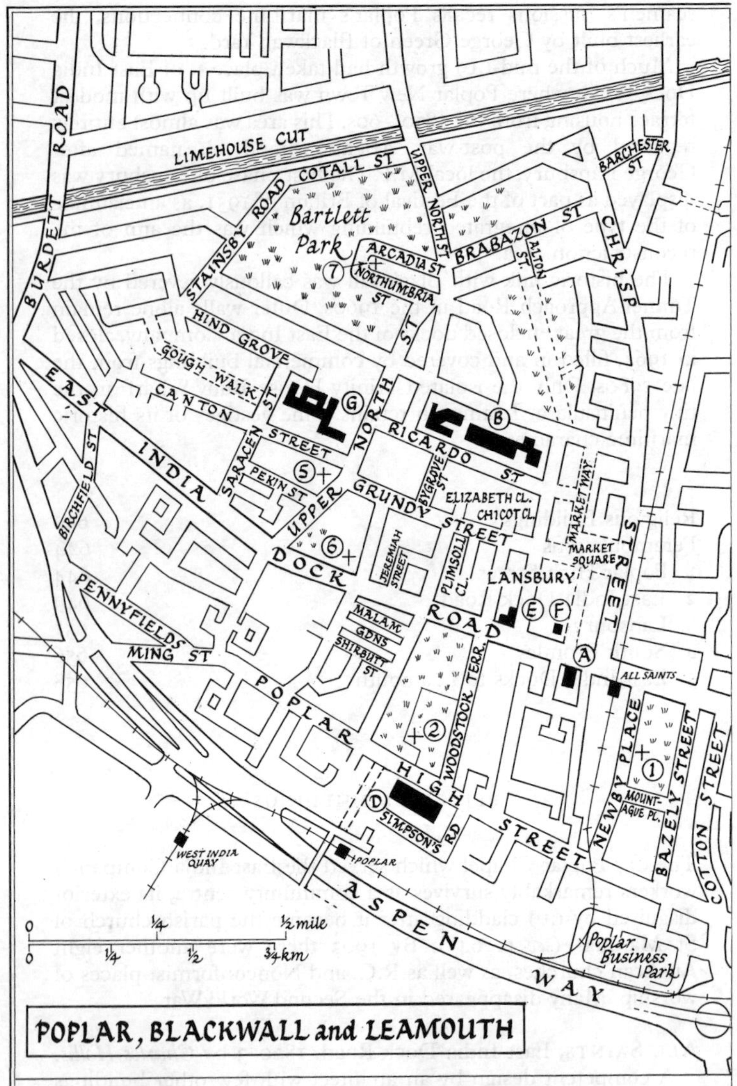

POPLAR, BLACKWALL and LEAMOUTH

CHURCHES	PUBLIC BUILDINGS
① All Saints	Ⓐ Former Poplar Baths
② Former St Matthias	Ⓑ Susan Lawrence Primary School and Elizabeth Lansbury Nursery School
③ Former St Michael and All Angels	Ⓒ Woolmore Primary School
④ St Nicholas and All Hallows	Ⓓ Tower Hamlets College
⑤ St Mary and St Joseph (R.C.)	Ⓔ George Green Schools (Tower Hamlets College)
⑥ Trinity Methodist Mission	Ⓕ Ideas Store
⑦ Celestial Church of Christ	Ⓖ Blessed John Roche R.C. Secondary Sch.
⑧ Poplar and Berger Baptist Church	

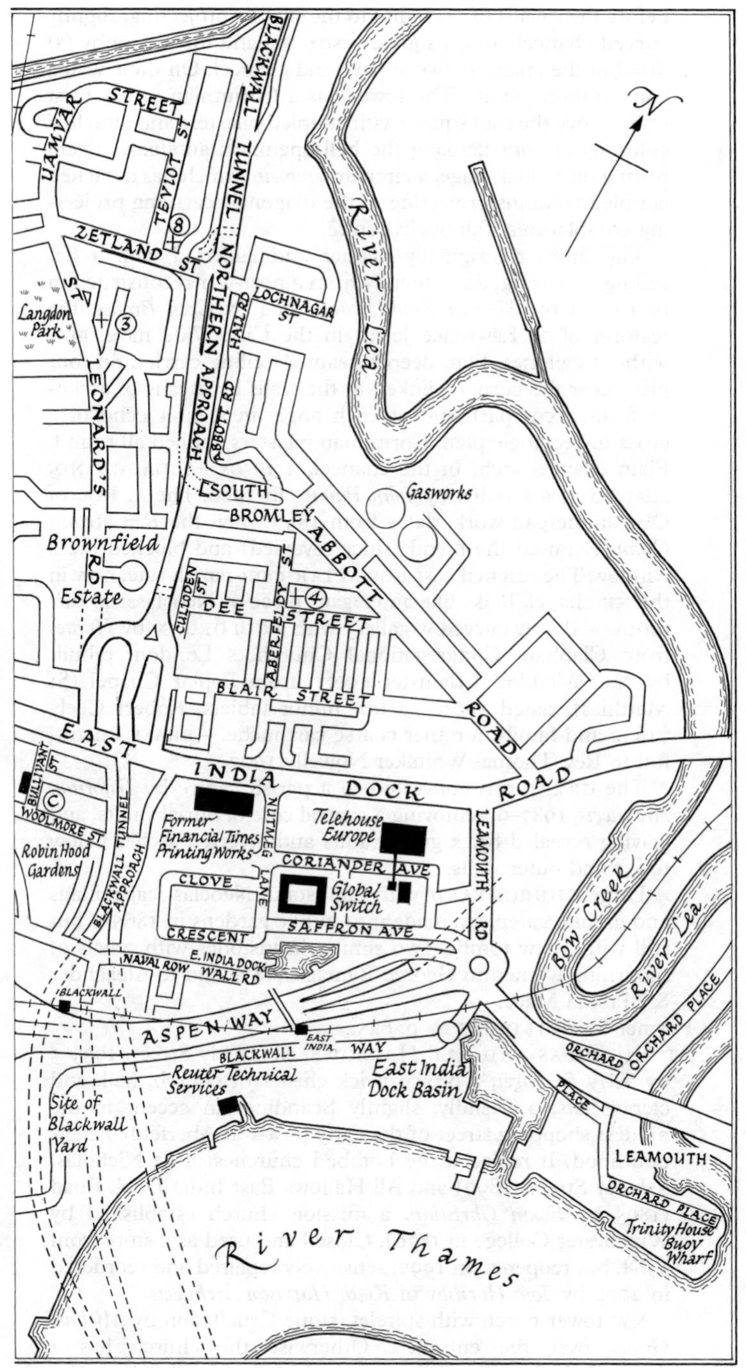
N
River Lea
BLACKWALL TUNNEL NORTHERN APPROACH
UAMVAR STREET
TEVIOT ST
ZETLAND ST
LOCHNAGAR ST
HALL RD
Langdon Park
ST LEONARD'S RD
ABBOTT RD
SOUTH BROMLEY
ABBOTT ROAD
Gasworks
Brownfield Estate
CULLODEN ST
DEE STREET
ABERFELDY ST
BLAIR STREET
EAST INDIA DOCK ROAD
BULLIVANT ST
WOOLMORE ST
Robin Hood Gardens
BLACKWALL TUNNEL APPROACH
Former Financial Times Printing Works
NUTMEG LANE
Telehouse Europe
LEAMOUTH RD
CORIANDER AVE
CLOVE CRESCENT
Global Switch
SAFFRON AVE
E. INDIA DOCK WALL RD
NAVAL ROW
BLACKWALL
ASPEN WAY
EAST INDIA
BLACKWALL WAY
Bow Creek
River Lea
ORCHARD PLACE
ORCHARD
PLACE
East India Dock Basin
Reuter Technical Services
Site of Blackwall Yard
LEAMOUTH
ORCHARD PLACE
Trinity House Buoy Wharf
River Thames

before the E wall curves round to the slightly projecting, slightly curved chancel; lower, square vestry (N) and former lobby (S) fitted in the angles between nave and chancel. On the E wall a consecration plaque. The tower has a Corinthian order. First stage above the roof square with coupled pilasters and attached columns *in antis* flanking the bell-openings: antefixae. Then, resting on a clock stage, a circular *tempietto* which has detached coupled columns projecting in the diagonals carrying projecting entablatures. Tall obelisk spire.

The interior, originally plainer and galleried with a flat ceiling on coving, dates mainly from a post-war reconstruction of 1951–3 by *Wontner Smith*, succeeded by *Cecil Brown*, the restorer of St Lawrence Jewry in the City. Wide nave, now without galleries. Flat, deeply beamed ceiling carried on four piers near the corners, linked to the walls by means of arches to form a compartment at each angle in a faint echo of a cross-in-rectangle plan. Corinthian pilasters applied all round. Plain chancel arch. In the chancel, a 1950s BALDACCHINO, adapted as a reredos by *John Phillips* in 1986. The ALTAR, of Oberammergau work, dates from 1897 when the *Rev. Arthur Chandler* raised the E end (since reversed) and blocked the E window. The original cast-iron ALTAR-cum-parish safe, now in the NE chapel, looks like an elegant piece of Neoclassical furniture. – Boldly curved W gallery with a C19 ORGAN by *Hunter* from Clapham Congregational Church, S London, rebuilt by *Noel Mander*. – Baluster FONT, from Poplar Chapel (St Matthias), dated 166? – a few minor tablets: Robert Ceely †1842 and family, a rather coarse cartouche. – BRASS quatrefoil to Rev. Thomas Whitaker Nowell †1902.

The CRYPT was converted to a parish centre by *Triforium Architects*, 1987–9, removing a central core of burial vaults, and leaving revealed brick groin-vaults and inverted arches below tower and outer walls.

Large CHURCHYARD with handsome Neoclassical railings and granite gatepiers; made into public gardens in 1865–6 but still with a few tombs. Two similar headstones with reliefs of mourning women to George Ramage †1838 and to Alexander & Matilda Mace.

Former ST MATTHIAS *see* p. 645.

ST NICHOLAS AND ALL HALLOWS, Aberfeldy Street. 1953–5 by *Seely & Paget*, a brown brick cluster of church, hall, and clergy flats, a friendly, slightly Scandinavian accent in the modest shopping street of the early post-war Aberfeldy neighbourhood. It replaced the bombed churches of St Nicholas, Yabsley Street (1899) and All Hallows East India Dock Road (1895 by *Ewan Christian*, a mission church established by Winchester College in 1876). Closed and used as a store from 1968, but reopened in 1997; sensitively repaired and reordered in 2002 by *Tom Hornsby* of *Keith Harrison Architects*.

NW tower-porch with spirelet, stone Crucifixion by *Michael Groser* over the entrance. Otherwise the church has a domestic look, with shallow-pitched roof and tall rectangular windows along the S side. Simple, dignified interior; a plain rectangle with side walls of exposed brick above panelling of 2001, E wall plastered, with a shallow top-lit recess framed by thin pilaster strips. The remarkable feature is the PAINTED CEILING by *Brian Thomas*: twenty panels on canvas depicting a visionary land towards the E, and a lively angelic host over the nave, painted with brio. In need of repair. The ceiling was first used temporarily to conceal repair work at Lambeth Palace (Seely & Paget were the architects) during the conference of 1948. Pre-war wooden ALTAR and CRUCIFIXION retrieved after dispersal in 1968. The projecting curved step to the sanctuary dates from 2002, as does the tall cylindrical stone FONT by *Tom Hornsby*. STATUE of St Nicholas by *Michael Groser*, formerly outside. Three ICONS by *Michael Coles*, to be installed 2003–4.

The HALL adjoins to the N, divided by a space (now partly a children's room) originally with moveable partitions. Austere interior, but generous stage and facilities built for the Poplar Theatre Workshop.

ST MARY AND ST JOSEPH R.C. CHURCH, Upper North Street. By *Adrian Gilbert Scott*, planned 1950, but not completed until 1954. A replacement for a fine cruciform church by *W. Wardell*, 1856, destroyed in the Second World War. A monumental design, its blocky forms in light-brown brick, with tiled roofs and stumpy central spire, are a landmark from afar. The mannered modernistic Gothic detail is totally at odds with the character of the surroundings, the low-key Lansbury estate of the time of the Festival of Britain (*see* p. 651). Impressive, well-crafted interior on a Greek Cross plan, narthex and porch to the E; the seating (for 800) spreads across the arms of the cross to provide a clear view of the altar under its elaborate baldacchino at the W end. The crossing rises to an open lantern (as did the previous church). Lower walls are faced with blue Hornton stone, with reliefs of the Stations of the Cross by *Peter Watts*. FONT and PULPIT also of Hornton stone. STAINED GLASS by *William Wilson* of Edinburgh. CLERGY HOUSE in Pekin Street also by *Scott*, in the same materials as the church.

TRINITY METHODIST MISSION, East India Dock Road. By *Cecil C. Handisyde* and *D. Rogers Stark*, 1949–51. A replacement for the Congregational church of 1841 by William Hosking, paid for by George Green, destroyed in the war. Built in time for the Festival of Britain's demonstration of post-war building at Lansbury. An ingenious and original design, the exterior dominated by the angular structure of the portal frame from which the roof is suspended. Delicate bell-tower with open skeletal top at the W end. The church wanted a space for a small congregation which could expand to seat 400. The additional seating was provided in galleries built out over an open cloister around the church. The interior is cleverly lit by circular roof lights and windows high up. Adjoining memorial hall and club room, the upper part of the latter later converted to flats. Refurbished by *E.D. Mills*, after the Methodists took over the building in 1976. Some furnishings including a STAINED GLASS window by *Frank O. Salisbury*, 1933, were brought from their previous building.

POPLAR AND BERGER BAPTIST CHURCH, Zetland Street, 1950–1. Small portal-framed building with nicely lettered name over the entrance. Furnishings of mahogany. CHURCH HALL of 1957–8.

CELESTIAL CHURCH OF CHRIST, Northumbria Street. 1873–4 by *F.J. & H. Francis*. The centre of a little enclave in Bartlett Park on the N fringe of Lansbury, originally with a school as well as the former clergy house to the N. Built as the Anglican St Saviour, made redundant 1976, given to the West African sect in 1984. A large, lofty aisled church of polychrome brickwork, with E bellcote, gabled S chapel, N sacristies and W narthex. Dec tracery; the clerestory with quatrefoil windows. Inside, the upper parts are now hidden by a clumsy suspended ceiling of the 1990s, cutting across the nave arcades. These are also of coloured brick, on columns with plain moulded capitals. The chancel capitals have the emphatic foliage carving often favoured by the architects. Fine E window by *Heaton Butler & Bayne c.* 1880, figures in pre-Raphaelite style.

POPLAR MOSQUE, 253 East India Road. A steel-framed building of 1938–9, built for clothiers; later a snooker club. A mosque since 1997. Two large prayer rooms on the upper floors, the front given windows with coloured glass in 2002.

PERAMBULATIONS

1. Poplar High Street

POPLAR DLR STATION straddles the no-man's-land between the old centre of Poplar and the high-rise world of Docklands to the S. One of *ABK*'s elegant stations on the Beckton line, 1992–4, flying high above a concrete substructure, with a dramatic suspended tubular link over Aspen Way to West India Quay station.

From the station a path leads N to POPLAR HIGH STREET, now a backwater, entirely detached in spirit from its backdrop of sleek, gigantic commercial towers. The change in level is clearly visible up to the High Street on its gravel terrace. Fitted onto an awkward site by the footpath is the WORKHOUSE, a neat monopitch-roofed leisure centre with timber-boarded wall, by *Proctor Matthews*, 1999. Cramped sunken courtyard with tiled wall of children's artwork. The name commemorates the sprawling Poplar workhouse of 1817, rebuilt 1866, some of whose buildings survived on this site until 1960. On the W side of the footpath, part of TOWER HAMLETS COLLEGE, a range of 2004 by *Gibberd Limited, Architects*, ending in an angular corner tower with an awkward tapered glazed area. The main building faces the High Street, built as the School of Marine

Engineering and Navigation by the *LCC Architect's Department*, 1902–6: *Percy Ginham* may have been the dominant designer. Portland stone-clad front, Mannerist and asymmetrical. Paired columns and arched windows mark the first-floor class and lecture-rooms, contrasting with bold functional drawing-office and labs' windows in the mansard above. Main doorcase carved with cherubs and sea-creatures by *Bertram Pegram*. Extended 1929–31, in 1951–5 by *Pite, Son & Fairweather*, and with a large, clumsy W extension by *John R. Harris Partnership*, opened 1991, with prefabricated bays and yellow brick walls oddly combined; the top storey opens as a balcony. To the E, incorporated in 1957 as part of the college, the former POPLAR CENTRAL LIBRARY (No. 126) 1893–4 by *John Clarkson* (District Surveyor) of *J. & S.F. Clarkson*. Tall central block of yellow brick unified by an arched centrepiece and unrelated low wings with wavy parapets, a clumsy composition explained by the fact that the centre was designed for a narrow site on East India Dock Road and adapted for this one.

Across the road on the N side is the large piece of land which was acquired by the East India Company in 1628. Their almshouses have gone, apart from the former CHAPLAIN'S HOUSE, No. 115. This was the centrepiece of an almshouse composition of 1801–2, by the company surveyor *Henry Holland*, which opened to the N, facing the chapel (later St Matthias) which the EIC had maintained from 1659. (Holland's buildings replaced an adapted house which had been given a new street front by *Edward Carter* in 1628.) The chaplain's house has a simple three-bay S front with small upper windows and the company's arms on the tiny stone pediment. Big doorway on skinny columns, by *Cecil Brown*, 1964, replacing a porch of 1826. Bay window of 1878. On the N side Gothic extensions of 1868 by *H.J. Tollit*, when the house became the vicarage of St Matthias. To the W, POPLAR PLAY CENTRE, a neat little monopitched building with covered loggia, extended with two colourful pitched-roof ranges, by *Proctor Matthews Architects*, 1992–3.

ST MATTHIAS OLD CHURCH, now a community centre, lies to the N. The chapel, built from bequests by local residents, was laid out in 1639 but not built until 1652–4, i.e. after the Civil War. It was closely based on the just-completed Broadway Chapel, Westminster (1635–8), then a rare model of Protestant church building. Externally this is not apparent, for after the chapel became a parish church in 1866 it was remodelled and clad in Kentish rag by *William Milford Teulon*, 1870–6, with an uncompromising eccentricity more usually associated with his older brother Samuel Sanders Teulon. It was given a bell-turret of unprecedented Victorian shape, bold pastry-cutter tracery, N and S porches and a chancel. But all this is only a superficial skin enclosing the handsome red brick C17 Chapel, the only Interregnum church still standing in London. Like the Broadway Chapel, it had a predominantly Gothic exterior with some classical features. Teulon's reseating in 1867–8 (now removed) involved the removal of N and S galleries, cutting back the W one, and the addition of a conventional chancel in 1875–6, supervised by Teulon's partner *Edwyn Evans Cronk*. Closed 1976 and derelict for many years; restored with LDDC funding in 1990–1 by *Peter Codling* (*Roger Taigel*, job architect).

The rectangular body of the church consists of a symmetrical Latin cross of nave and transepts, with aisles to complete the rectangle. The parts are clearly differentiated outside by separate roofs, very early examples of a continental type of kingpost roof introduced to England in the C17, perhaps by Inigo Jones: especially complicated and experimental over the
27 crossing. Inside, the nave and transept have elliptical vaults which meet in a depressed cross-vault, with the arms of the East India Company in plaster at the centre. The vaults are carried on columns (all timber except one of stone) of an incorrect Tuscan order and by entablatures which, because continuous from W to E, stress the longitudinal axis. There is no other eastward emphasis and no evidence of how the furnishings were laid out. Unpretentious moveable screens of 1990–1 now divide the interior according to function. SCREEN to former choir vestry, N aisle, by *W. Charles Wheeler*, 1927. Tudor-style panelling. Most of the windows now with clear glass or geometric patterns; a little figural STAINED GLASS remains: in the E window evangelists from a Crucifixion window of 1875 by *N.H.J. Westlake* for *Lavers & Barraud*; a scene of Christ and the doctors (SW); four virtues, a war memorial window by *Cakebread, Robey & Co.* (N transept). MOSAIC: Evangelist symbols below E window, 1903. Many evocative minor MONUMENTS with East India Company connections.

Large CHURCHYARD. Among the C18 and early C19 tomb chests, Captain Samuel Jones †1734. Pedestal with relief of a 'man o' war' and a naval trophy upon a tall base, erected to a naval officer who distinguished himself against the French in 1706–7. Much restored in the late C19. John Smart †1777, distiller of Limehouse. Elegant Neoclassical sarcophagus with reliefs of vases on pilasters. – Hugh McIintosh †1840, dock contractor. Heavy Egyptian sarcophagus of granite. The RECREATION GROUND to the N was created by the Poplar Board of Works in 1866 on the site of a group of EIC almshouses of 1798–9 by *Richard Jebb*.

54 At the corner of Woodstock Terrace, former POPLAR BOARD OF WORKS, 1869–70 by *Hills & Fletcher* with *A. & C. Harston*. Italian Gothic in stock brick, subtle polychrome with tile decoration and richly carved Portland-stone trimmings. Eye-catching octagonal corner tower with spired dome, standing almost detached. The elaborate E wing has granite columns; they mark the first-floor boardroom (subdivided 1987 by *Peter Eley*). Running N is WOODSTOCK TERRACE, lined with two- and three-storey terrace houses of the 1850s, grand enough to have basements with railed areas.

On the S side of the High Street, No. 130 (Vietnamese Pastoral centre), built as a youth club for the now vanished R.C. Settlement of the Holy Child. 1955–6 by *Adrian Gilbert Scott* (architect of the R.C. church in Lansbury), minimal Neo-Georgian, with a recessed arch in the end wall, and large pantiles.

The flats which follow demonstrate the piecemeal transformation of Poplar housing that took place from the 1930s. Tucked into a small site between High Street and railway in SIMPSON'S ROAD, a group of flats for the Presbyterian Housing Scheme: GOODSPEED HOUSE, 1926–9, austere, GOODWILL HOUSE, 1932, more playfully Italianate, both by *T. Phillips Figgis*. Building continued after the war with the American-financed WINANT HOUSE, 1951 (speeded by being made an outlier of the Festival of Britain exhibition at Lansbury) and GOODFAITH and GOODHOPE houses, 1955, all by *Harry Moncrieff* and *Edna M.I. Mills* of *Co-Operative Planning Ltd.* The influence of Lansbury shows in their cul-de-sac grouping and brick detailing.

Back on the N side of the High Street CORONER'S COURT and MORTUARY, 1910–11 by the LCC, like a sweet little Arts and Crafts house in red brick with stone mullioned windows, gables and moulded chimneystack.

On the S side, NORWOOD HOUSE, 1965–72 by *Trevor Dannatt*, the last addition to a small LCC clearance site. Handsome sculpted red brick and shuttered concrete, expressing the maisonettes within. CONSTANT HOUSE and HOLMSDALE HOUSE, 1936–8 by *Rees J. Williams*, Poplar Borough Architect, are typical examples of Poplar's pre-war streamlined blocks, red brick with long concrete access balconies and quite flamboyant staircase towers. Two more across the road, COLLINS and COMMODORE HOUSES, 1935–6, replacing courts criticized as unfit housing already in 1919. They were some of the first to adopt metal windows (since replaced) as part of the borough's modernistic image. By the railway bridge No. 212, former goods manager's office for the North London Railway Co. 1876–7. Further on Nos. 255–6, the sole surviving C19 houses, *c.* 1812, much rebuilt and converted to flats 1984–5. Then, set back, neat grey-clad one- and two-storey units of POPLAR BUSINESS PARK, 1987–8 by *YRM* for the LDDC. In front, No. 260–8 was the former South Poplar Health centre, 1978–9 by *Derek Stow*. A steel-framed, steel-clad box composed of separate modules, designed as a prototype for transportable hospital units. Now a training centre. On the N side BAZELEY STREET leads N to the pleasant area around All Saints (*see* below), but to experience a grimmer face of Poplar one should press on E.

Across Cotton Street is ROBIN HOOD GARDENS, next to the Blackwall Tunnel approach. Of 1966–72 by *Alison & Peter Smithson* with *Christopher Woodward* and *Ken Baker*, for the GLC, the apotheosis of public housing in the borough and an icon for the Smithsons' admirers. It is a late expression of the Smithsons' early 1950s ideas about 'the building as street' (cf. their unbuilt designs for Golden Lane housing and the first built expression of those ideas by the Sheffield City Architect at Park Hill, Sheffield, in 1956–61). Over 600 people live (at a density of 141.8 per acre, more than the GLC's then-average of 136) on this horrible site flanked by two trunk roads full of thundering traffic. The two long, high walls of stark grey-concrete flats bend to follow the curve of the roads. Their finish is rough and tough shuttered concrete precast in big pieces on the Swedish SUNDH system. The Cotton Street section was cast *in situ*, because there was no access for large cranes. Though impressively monumental, the scheme is ill-planned to the point of being inhumane. The 'streets' are only decks cantilevered off the cross-walls of the reinforced concrete box-frame, much narrower than those at Park Hill and with a grim aspect towards the traffic. They buffer the living rooms which open off them. Bedrooms and kitchens face inward to a sculpted open space, but on this more peaceful side the tiny balconies are too small to enjoy and can be used only as fire escapes. Below in a dry moat is parking and storage.

To the N of this open space WOOLMORE PRIMARY SCHOOL, 1912–16 by the LCC, Neo-Georgian, with a severe row of tall chimneys and elegantly bracketed eaves. Round the corner in Bullivant Street, LCC manual training centre (St Matthias Centre), single storey with shaped gables. Three rows of yellow brick terraces with sharp monopitch roofs, *c.* 2002–3, sheltering behind a high wall, fill the gap next to the bleak road junction where the Blackwall Tunnel approach cuts across the East India Road, just in front of the site of the Dock entrance.

EAST INDIA DOCK ROAD was built in 1806–12 as a route to the East India Docks, an E extension of Commercial Road. Among remnants of C19 terraces on the N side, the POPLAR CENTRAL MOSQUE at No. 253 (*see* above).

To the W is the large CHURCHYARD of All Saints (*see* above), good (reinstated) railings and granite gateposts. Fragments of its respectable early C19 neighbourhood remain. In BAZELEY STREET on the E side Nos. 45–51, of the 1830s, three storeys, balconies with Gothic detail; opposite is the GREENWICH PENSIONER, a trim three-bay front of 1827, the upper windows within arches. The Greek Doric porch to the l. belongs to No. 12 Mountague Place. Nos. 5–12 MOUNTAGUE PLACE, S of the churchyard, survive from a row of three-storey houses built up piecemeal from 1822 by *James Mountague*, a City District Surveyor. Original door to No. 6, with Gothic panels. On the W side, NEWBY PLACE, with the RECTORY opposite the church. A dignified Neoclassical design by *Charles Hollis*, 1822–3 in yellow brick with bold and precise stone cornices. Recessed centre with pilastered porch, delicate balcony above, between outer bays with two-storey segmental bow windows. In the centre of the house a plaster cross-vault between entrance hall and staircase. Two pairs of fine granite gatepiers, opposite those to the churchyard. Red-granite OBELISK of 1854. At the NW corner, NEWBY PLACE HEALTH CENTRE, 1993–5, a design-and-build scheme with architects *Janka & Tony Mobbs*, a clumsy imitation of the Neoclassical style of the rectory.

2. East India Dock Road, ending at Poplar DLR

In EAST INDIA DOCK ROAD, opposite All Saints DLR Station, a disturbingly large intruder, a tower of private flats, clad in red tile, 2003–4. Further W, on the wider pavement in front of Poplar Baths, a bronze STATUE of Richard Green †1863, shipbuilder, of the Blackwall Yard, with his dog. By *Edward W. Wyon*, 1865–6. On the plinth atmospheric reliefs of the Yard and a Green-built ship.

POPLAR BATHS, East India Dock Road (disused). 1931–4 by *Harley Heckford*, Poplar Borough Engineer and Surveyor, the design probably by *D.L. Dick* with the engineer *R.W. Stanton*. Not immediately recognizable as baths. Its grey brick front looks like a cinema or arterial-road factory. The towered centrepiece, with Art Deco overtones, screens the first-class swimming bath. To the l. a more functional coda (mainly slipper and second-class baths) and an E projection, with vertical windows strips, designed to house lettable offices. Familiar layout for baths of the period, but more luxurious, streamlined finishes than usual, especially in the foyer, faced hygienically in vitrolite. On the ceiling since 1985, three PAINTED SCENES of the history of the baths by *David Bratby*. Though the rest is steel-framed and brick-clad, the large bath is spanned by dramatic elliptical concrete arches supporting stepped clerestories, a formula taken from Easton and Robertson's Royal Horticultural Hall of 1927–8, an early appearance of such a structure over an English swimming bath.

The IDEAS STORE, on the N side of East India Dock Road, 2003–4 by *Adjaye Associates*, now dominates the once low-key approach to Lansbury market square (*see* below). This is the second of the borough's new combined library and learning centres deliberately sited in busy shopping areas (for two others see pp. 400, 649). A steel-framed structure built on a former rooftop playground above shops, extended S for a foyer with bold metal staircase and escalator. Full height glazing in arresting stripes of blue and green, alternating with clear glass, provides pleasantly modulated light to the long upper floor library, a gently tapering space with low curving bookcases; classrooms open off at the side. The FOUNTAIN of steel pipes is of 1989, provided by the LDDC.

Further on, GEORGE GREEN SCHOOLS, now part of Tower Hamlets College. 1883–4. Designed for the endowed school founded 1828 by George Green, †1849, prominent local shipbuilder and Nonconformist philanthropist. He also paid for a seamen's mission (*see* below), the Trinity Congregational

Chapel nearby, destroyed in the war, and almshouses (*see* Lansbury p. 654). The schools, by *(Sir) John Sulman*, 1883–4, have a Northern European picturesqueness and, despite the bold High Victorian stripes of brick and stone, Arts and Crafts feeling in the asymmetrical fenestration and areas of blank walling. An E tower with a Rhenish roof forms the girls' entrance and screens the NE classroom block. The boys' entrance tower is central with a gabled timber lantern. To its E and rising behind, the galleried Hall. To the W a thin decapitated gallery stair-tower with projecting clock of 1928. NE lab block by *William Clarkson*, 1902.

Further W No. 153, a lone villa of 1834 with canopied veranda and Doric porch, converted to a hostel by *Anthony Richardson & Partners*, 1983–4. Opposite, on the S side is the Recreation Ground that goes through to Poplar High Street on the East India Company almshouses site (*see* above). At this end, a FIRST WORLD WAR AIR RAID MEMORIAL to eighteen children killed by a bomb which fell on the Upper North Street LCC school in 1917. Memorial plinth crowned by the sort of angel familiar from C19 cemeteries. Signed *A.R. Adams*, a local undertaker.

POPE JOHN HOUSE (No. 154) wraps round the corner of Hale Street. It was built as the Anglican Missions to Seamen Institute by *Sir Arthur Blomfield*, 1892–4. Jacobean domestic-style in red brick. At the end, a plain chapel, also by Blomfield, and a more relaxed vernacular chaplain's house, 1898. In Shirbutt Street further W, Trinity House for lady workers, rebuilt 1934. In the 1930s the Mission moved to the Royal Docks (q.v.) and this building became the Commercial Gas Company's Co-partnership Institute. The modest houses built to the W for their employees, 1934–6 by *Victor Wilkins*, back on to the main road from MALAM GARDENS: three rows of cottages along three private lanes. Originally completely gas-powered: still-working gas lamps in the lanes.

On the N side No. 133 appears to be a stuccoed late Georgian terrace, but began as a seamen's home, an early example, built by George Green of the Blackwall Yard in 1839–41. It originally had a Doric colonnade and balcony filling the recessed five-bay centre. Well converted to social housing *c.* 1983 by *Anthony Richardson & Partners*. Another seamen's home, the QUEEN VICTORIA SEAMEN'S REST (Seamen's Mission of the Methodist Church) fronts the road from Nos. 121–31 with a long block of 1951–3, which builds up in the centre in a 1930s way. Chapel plain except for stained glass by *Goddard & Gibbs*. Facing E to Jeremiah Street, the earliest part of 1901–2, free C17 style, originally with a cupola on the entrance tower. All by *Gordon & Gunton*.

A long way further W on the S side, URBAN LEARNING FOUNDATION (No. 56), a courtyard of flats and teaching rooms by *Paul Hyett & Partners*, opened 1992. Four storeys of smooth red brick, discreetly and lovingly detailed. Glazed green-tile strings link simple steel-lintelled windows. Set into the brick, lead roundels with symbols and tools of learning (letters, numbers, notes of music). Continuous row of windows under the upswept eaves. Sturdy gate with good lettering within the gateway into the courtyard, which has simple elevations except for a glass-roofed gallery. Its neighbour at the corner of BIRCHFIELD STREET is a former branch of the London and County Bank (No. 52), 1885 by *Zephaniah King*, very old-fashioned but dignified (converted for housing 2003). Attached Greek Doric columns round the ground floor and for the corner porches. A terrace (Nos. 2–50) of 1850–60 continues to the junction with West India Dock Road.

Before reaching West India Dock Road one can turn down Birchfield Street to PENNYFIELDS, part of the old route from Limehouse. It became the home of the Chinese community shifted from Limehouse Causeway in slum clearances of the 1930s. Apart from a sprinkling of shops, almost entirely rebuilt with C20 council housing, mostly post 1945. Further E on the N side, the LCC's BIRCHFIELD ESTATE, mixed development of four-storey flats, 1955–64 and one forceful slab block, THORNFIELD HOUSE, 1960–2, with balconies set behind its steel uprights and a full-height abstract concrete relief. The start of POPLAR HIGH STREET is signalled by a white horse of painted lead on a post, all that remains from a pub which was on this site from the C17 and was last rebuilt in 1927–8 by *A.E. Sewell*. Then on both sides the LCC's large and amorphous WILL CROOKS ESTATE named after the radical local Labour leader (†1921) who was Poplar mayor and M.P. Built following one of Poplar's largest slum clearance schemes, declared 1934. On the N side five blocks of five-storey LCC flats of the usual Neo-Georgian kind, 1936–9. Extended S by DINGLE GARDENS, 1955–7, and in 1973–5 by town houses further W round Saltwell Street.

3. *Lansbury*

Lansbury, named from the local M.P. George Lansbury, is the best known part of the post-war Stepney/Poplar reconstruction area. The area stretching from East India Dock Road to the Limehouse Cut, known as Poplar New Town, developed from the 1840s–70s, densely built up, mostly with streets of two-storey terraces, sprinkled with a handful of churches and schools. It suffered badly in the Second World War, and was designated as 'neighbourhood 9' in the post-war plans. Lansbury owes its special cachet to the fact that part of the area was selected as the Live Architecture exhibit at the Festival of Britain in 1951. In addition to a temporary exhibition, the buildings that were planned and completed for this event were intended as show-pieces to demonstrate the possibilities of post-war planning and rebuilding. The planning was by the LCC, but variety was sought by also involving private architectural firms (thus avoiding the dominance of the LCC's Valuers' Department responsible for housing in the immediate post-war years), and exceptionally, efforts were made to cut through bureaucratic delays and provide amenities at the same time – shops, new schools, and new churches to replace those lost in the war. The clock tower was provided by the Poplar Borough Council, which otherwise had little to do with the early development.

The planning was intended to demonstrate the precepts of the Forshaw & Abercrombie, *County of London Plan* of 1943: the separation of industry, plentiful open space, a reduced population grouped in neighbourhoods sited away from main roads and based on primary school catchment areas. These were the ideals shared by the contemporary new towns built for the surplus London population, and the early parts of Lansbury have a distinct new-town feel about them. In contrast with the novel planning London stock brick and slate were recommended as materials, to be in keeping with local tradition.

Only a small part of 'neighbourhood 9' formed the 1951 exhibit. The difficulties of acquiring land explain the patchy pattern of development, and not all the planning objectives were completed in time for the Festival. Streets were reduced in number, and the novelty of a pedestrian market square was introduced – the first to be built in England (though Coventry had been planned earlier). The new market and its shops were intended to serve as a district shopping centre for several of the new neighbourhoods. But through routes were not diverted as intended, and the main open space to the N, Bartlett Park, was p. 91 completed only in the 1980s. By that time the core of low-key houses and flats, mostly of two to four storeys, which gave the first phase a relaxed, somewhat garden-suburb character, had been enveloped by later work on a larger scale, which expressed the grander ambitions of the *LCC Architect's Department* formed in 1950. The additions of the 1950s–60s to the N of the exhibition site followed the LCC 'mixed development' pioneered at Roehampton, with point blocks to satisfy the 136 people per acre density requirements, which had largely been ignored in the first phase. The 1970s brought the more intricately planned medium-rise groups of Gough Walk at the W end; then from the later 1970s, as the merits of low-rise were rediscovered, a return to more modest infilling of empty sites. In the older parts the sadly shabby buildings around the lively market now contrast with trim individual 'right-to-buy' transformations in many of the early housing areas.

The tour starts with the market, traverses the early parts of the estate from E–W, returning through Bartlett Park and the later northern areas. Schools follow at the end.

The approach to MARKET SQUARE from East India Dock Road, opposite Poplar Baths, is through the least appealing of the later additions, the ungainly GLC extensions of 1968–70, with flats and maisonettes raised upon a concrete podium with shops. Now transformed by the IDEAS STORE built on the podium in 2003–4 (*see* above). When the square was laid out older buildings still remained on the S side, so only the N and W sides were new. The E side remained open to Chrisp Street, the original site of the street market. The square is now dominated by aggressively large canopies on steel posts, set diagonally, installed in the 1990s to replace most of the original covered meat and fish stalls. The CLOCK TOWER at the E end, completed 1952, has an open scissor-plan double stair, intended to provide access to and from a public viewing point. Dwarfed by the canopies, and even more so by the Canary Wharf towers on the horizon, it stands wired off and forlorn, a monument to the lost innocence of the 1950s. The clock tower, and the three-storey shopping terraces on the N and W sides and along MARKET WAY to the N, were designed by *Frederick Gibberd*, who had suggested the idea of the live architecture exhibition adopted by the Festival. His buildings are in a gentle Modern style with slight Regency allusions – see the bowed upper windows, with touches of colour provided by tiles between the shop windows and blue mosaic cladding (now gone) to the concrete columns in front of the shop at the curved NW corner. The accents are picturesque and asymmetrical, with the blue-painted Festival Pub at the W entrance to the square, and a larger corner building (now Poplar Housing Office) to mark the start of Market Way, also pedestrian. This is kept narrow and intimate as a contrast to the square, an effect that Gibberd also had wanted in his contemporary designs for the centre of Harlow New Town. The buildings at the N end of Market Way were completed only in 1962–3 (*see* below).

A passage to the W leads to RICARDO STREET, where a long four-storey terrace of maisonettes of pale brick runs W in three stepped sections, part of a diverse collection of housing types by *Geoffrey Jellicoe*. This is the most urban looking of his groups: lack of period detail, intermittent access balconies neatly inset, and sturdy projecting concrete door frames (a Jellicoe signature) mark it out as different from pre-war LCC flats. It faces the playground of Lansbury Lawrence School (*see* above), which has an undulating wall to accommodate trees. Parallel and to the S is GRUNDY STREET, with CHILCOT CLOSE and ELIZABETH CLOSE opening off, also by *Jellicoe*, pleasantly simple three-storey terraces with pitched roofs and small balconies. Entrances in side passages allow for large front rooms. Between them, HECKFORD HOUSE, Poplar pre-war housing of 1920, yellow and red brick with mansard roof, in a vaguely Queen Anne style, named after the Borough Surveyor *Harley Heckford*. The yellow brick low-rise housing to the S around PLIMSOLL CLOSE is a late addition of 1982, sympathetic in scale to the older groups, but more tightly planned; a back-to-front arrangement with front doors facing footpaths, and car parking in the Close arranged around trees. At the corner of Duff Street the AFRICAN QUEEN, a bold corner pub, a solitary C19 survival. More by *Jellicoe* further along Grundy Street and in BYGROVE STREET, which is different again, a three-storey terrace with front doors to ground-floor flats and the upper dwellings (with roof gardens) reached by side entrances.

The unmissable *point-de-vue* down Grundy Street is the cuckoo in the nest, the monumental Catholic Church in a jazzed-up Gothic style (*see* above), not yet built at the time of the 1951 exhibition, and greeted with dismay by the progressive architects as it rose to tower over their modest housing groups. It faces an Old People's Home, SHAFTESBURY LODGE, a 1990s replacement for Lansbury Lodge of 1951 by *Booth & Ledeboer*, demolished after a fire.

Further S in UPPER NORTH STREET some more survivors, the MAYFLOWER SCHOOL of 1928, replacing the school bombed in 1917, which had its origins in Trinity chapel day-schools founded by George Green in 1843, and the GEORGE GREEN ALMSHOUSES, 1849, for twenty-one poor women, the latter a severe but handsome three-storey C19 terrace, identically sized windows on each floor, providing for a flat on each floor.

TRINITY GREEN beyond has a vista of the second post-war church (now Trinity Methodist Mission, *see* above), its skeletal tower top rising above trees. The green had at first a small lake, now filled in; a fibreglass and concrete sculpture was added in 1962, The Dockers by *Sydney Harpley*, of which only a fragment is left. This miniature picturesque landscape was a showpiece adjacent to the 1951 temporary exhibition site on the other side of Upper North Street, built over afterwards with flats by *Bridgwater & Shepheard*. The same firm was responsible for the area to its N around PEKIN STREET. PEKIN CLOSE had small houses, now so altered that their early character is hard to discern (although the ornamental street bollards are original). To their N are a small group of semi-detached houses, a rarity at Lansbury, and a terrace on Canton Street. Across SARACEN STREET is a scatter of flats by the LCC, a group of three with projecting balconies formally arranged, facing East India Road across a generous lawn. Others more loosely grouped further N. Their hallmark is the striking balcony design with a chequer of glass bricks. The six-storey blocks were the tallest in the first phase of Lansbury, the start of an acknowledgement of the reality of the 136 p.p.a. density requirement. On the E side of Saracen Street, a terrace of houses with flats above, by *Norman & Dawbarn*, given a little panache by modish balconies. It ends with The Chimes, a typically unassuming post-war pub by *Stewart & Hendry*.

Lansbury after 1951

The expansion of Lansbury in the 1950–60s was at first entirely by LCC architects, but in 1970 *Shepheard, Epstein and Hunter* were brought in by the GLC to design an extension to the W known as the GOUGH GROVE scheme. This was an exploration of how 136 p.p.a. density could be achieved through a tight arrangement of ingeniously planned three- and four-storey buildings. This type of medium-rise planning (cf. Lillington Gardens Westminster, Marquis Estate Islington) developed in reaction to the tall towers and open planning of the previous decade and also attempted to tackle the car parking problem. Two long four-storey spines of maisonettes over sunken garages run E–W, from these three-storey wings with one- and two-bedroom flats project S to form sheltered and intimate grass courts. From 1977 the housing was continued W of Stainsby Road, at an angle reflecting the different road pattern, creating some interesting if rather overpowering grouping of blocky forms at the junction. The area was made largely pedestrian, with the multi-layered access with linking upper walkways so fashionable at the time, but also with much attention given to landscaping and the creation of intimate spaces. Details are kept simple: brown brick, pitched roofs. The extension includes a small group of shops and the low HIND GROVE COMMUNITY CENTRE.

Further N BARTLETT PARK was provided as a new open space. In the heyday of the tower block the open expanse inevitably attracted tall buildings on its fringe, built as part of neighbouring LCC estates. At the SW corner ANGLESEY HOUSE, a ten-storey tower of 1959–61, dressed up some thirty years later with curved roof, glass balconies and colour. Along the NW edge by COTALL STREET a long six-storey range of maisonettes, 1961, in a more austere Corbusian spirit, with a powerful concrete exposed grid dividing the individual units. The park itself was left as an almost featureless sea of grass around a strangely fortress-like cluster. Its centrepiece is St Saviour's church, Northumbria Street (*see* p. 644), surrounded by Arcadian self-build housing of 1987–9, designed by the *Beavan Sutters Partnership*. The enterprise was planned from 1983 and inspired by the Great Eastern self-build housing on the Isle of Dogs (p. 693). A wide variety of house types and sizes, nicely grouped, especially on the entrance side. Conventional neo-vernacular detail.

UPPER NORTH STREET runs E of this group, empty except for a solitary former pub towards a crossing over the Limehouse Cut. To its E is a large expanse of LCC housing of 1955–9 (Barchester Street) and 1958–61 (Alton Street) by the LCC. This post-Festival expansion of Lansbury demonstrates the new confidence of the *LCC Architect's Department* in reaction to the cosy villagey character of the Festival area. This is mixed development on a grand scale, with terraces interspersed with eight eleven-storey point blocks (cf. Alton East Estate Roehampton), with some later low-rise infilling in the middle (Brabazon Street, 1976–7 by the GLC). The overall effect of the informal grouping is best appreciated from the broad grass swathe with footpath running diagonally N from Cordelia Street, where the taller maisonette blocks alternate with the towers. Lower terraces of houses lie beyond on each side, some of them stepped to achieve the best lighting while following the older street lines. The residents have challenged any monotony with characterful gardens. The S end of the path faces the N end of Market Way, completed with a group of maisonettes and the Young Prince pub, by *Norman & Dawbarn* 1962–3.

LANSBURY LAWRENCE PRIMARY SCHOOL, Ricardo Street. By *Yorke, Rosenberg & Mardall*, 1950–2, the first post-war building in Lansbury, on the site of a bomb-damaged Board School. Long two-storey classroom range, for juniors above infants, steel framework with concrete panels, using *Hills* prefabricated system, with large windows to the playground to the S and brick cladding to other walls. The unusual feature is the light-well along the centre, crossed by bridges to the upper class-rooms, allowing for crosslighting and ventilation. At the E end a spacious foyer with cheerful yellow patterned wall tiles by *Peggy Angus*, leads to the halls, with flying stair to the Junior hall on the first floor. At the W end is the single-storey ELIZABETH LANSBURY NURSERY SCHOOL, by the same architects, 1952, with two large S-facing playrooms linked by an entrance wing approached from the W.

BLESSED JOHN ROCHE R.C. SECONDARY SCHOOL, Upper North Street. 1950–2 by *David Stokes*. Enlargements to the N of *c.* 1970–3. On the site of the bombed R.C. church (of which some ruins remain in the landscaped area S of the school). Two-storey S-facing classroom range with reinforced-concrete frame and brick infilling, from which the practical wings project N, and the Assembly Hall S. A further wing at an angle to the E has the Dining Hall, a trim structure with exposed columns to the ground floor.

4. South Bromley. A circular tour starting from All Saints DLR

The main local route through this part of the old borough of Poplar is ST LEONARD'S ROAD, the old route to St Leonard's church, Bromley (*see* p. 631). It runs parallel to the Blackwall Tunnel Northern Approach Road which was carved out in the 1960s. Almost nothing remains of the dense terrace housing that covered the area by the end of the C19. N of East India Dock Road St Leonard's Road starts as a pedestrian route. To its E, on a difficult site close to the Northern Approach Road,
112 BALFRON TOWER, part of the BROWNFIELD ESTATE by *Ernö Goldfinger* for the GLC, 1965–7. Its superior quality is at once apparent. The twenty-six-storey block is immediately arresting, with its slender semi-detached tower containing lift, services, and chunky oversailing boiler house. It was Goldfinger's first public housing, a precursor of his similarly arranged and better known Trellick Tower, N Kensington. The lifts serve every third floor, and the flats vary in size. The rugged concrete surfaces have worn well, and contrast effectively with the floor-to-ceiling glazing. Equally impressive is the way in which this and the neighbouring CARRADALE HOUSE,

1967–9, are integrated within the surrounding spaces by well-detailed hard landscaping. Carradale House is a slab block of eleven storeys, with lift block in the centre, and some variety created by intermediate balconies. W of St Leonard's Road the fifteen-storey GLENKERRY has more streamlined concrete balconies, curved at the ends. Banded concrete details, alternating with pale brick, are continued by two lower blocks along the planted walk to the W. The promising start gives way to an indifferent grid of the usual LCC/GLC mix of slabs of flats and lower terraces.

Further N St Leonard's Road becomes uneventfully suburban, with the occasional C19 pub among low post-war housing. LANGDON PARK was created as a new open space, but is sadly uninspired. LANGDON PARK SECONDARY SCHOOL, close by, is an accretive complex around a big three-decker of 1907 with curvaceous copper-domed turrets; science building 1957, classroom block 1964 by *Katz Vaughan & Partners*, sports hall and sixth-form blocks 1977–80, clad in rolled steel.

More rewarding is the recognizably Victorian centre surviving around the former ST MICHAEL AND ALL ANGELS, St Leonard's Road, built 1864–5 by *R.W. Morris* to replace a mission chapel of 1861. Now flats, but still a substantial focus, with its sturdy and idiosyncratic SE tower with gabled slate pyramid roof incorporating a clock. Ambitiously planned with aisles and transepts, of coloured brickwork with early Gothic detail, the triplet of E lancets distinguished by stone hood-moulds. On the W side, a low mid-C19 terrace faces the attractive former VICARAGE, twin-gabled, with some Gothic detail. In front is an unusual WAR MEMORIAL of white marble, 1920 by *A.R. Adams*: a standing figure of Christ places a wreath on a kneeling soldier in medieval dress. Large church hall to the N.

Further N, TEVIOT and RADFORD HOUSE, three-storey Poplar Borough housing of 1921, red and yellow brick, built with flat roofs for clothes drying, stand out among the blander low-rise parts of Poplar's post-war TEVIOT ESTATE, grouped around a primary school and small green. Toward the N end along Uamvar Road the estate ended with a loose group of nine-storey slabs, 1954–6, largely demolished in 2003. Refurbishment and new building with 145 extra dwellings, to a master plan by *Baily Garner*, in progress 2004, will include an undulating terrace along the Limehouse Cut. Close to the Northern Approach Road's bridge over the Cut, TWEED HOUSE, an austerely Brutalist ten-storey block of 1961 by the LCC. Its Civic Trust award of 1964 indicates the 1960s admiration for tough architecture on challenging sites. To its S a tight grid of courtyards surrounded by three- and four-storey blocks in red brick, 1976–7.

A subway below the Northern Approach Road, reached via ZETLAND STREET, by Poplar Baptist Church, leads to a triangle of land between the road and the River Lea. (For the northern part of this area *see* p. 634.) S of the subway, BROMLEY HALL SCHOOL, Bromley Hall Road, built for physically disabled children, 1967–8 by GLC/ILEA (Project Architect: *Bob Giles*). An inward-facing design that was intended to shield the single-storey school from the depressing surrounds of light industry and the deafening road. The aggressiveness of its brown brick and slate exterior is mitigated by the silhouette of sweeping 'oasthouse' roofs which provide a well-lit interior. Communal facilities in the centre, enclosed by a circulation corridor, leading to classrooms around the perimeter, each with a secluded paved courtyard.

To the S is the ABERFELDY ESTATE of the 1970s, three- and four-storey ranges enclosing small pedestrian courtyards. The area was originally developed with small terrace houses from 1864–85, first by David McIntosh (hence the Scottish street names), and from 1873 by the chemist turned developer John Abbott, whose works were at Iceland Wharf, Old Ford. ABBOTT ROAD skirts the POPLAR GASWORKS built by the Commercial Gas Co. from 1876 and runs SE. No. 1 Gasholder of 1877 by *Harry Jones*, engineer, has an early wrought-iron lattice guide frame with daintily tapered members, dwarfed by the adjacent one of 1929. It starts with a Victorian terrace, but the rest is all Poplar's sprawling ABBOTT ESTATE, low-rise housing begun in 1947, now largely rebuilt. Unusually ambitious for its date is the extensive six-storey range along Abbott Road, BRAITHWAITE HOUSE, with 105 dwellings, completed 1950, and built with an experimental steel frame (reclad since). Three angled wings to the W, articulated by vertical features with pairs of private balconies, and by lift-towers with curved tops. ABERFELDY STREET was rebuilt from 1948 as the main local shopping street: modest three-storey blocks of flats over shops, opposite St Nicholas and All Hallows (*see* p. 642), more recent amenities are ABERFELDY NEIGHBOURHOOD CENTRE, 2003, low, with shallow-pitched roofs and thick fascia boards, and in Dee Street, CULLODEN PRIMARY SCHOOL, 2000, pale brick, with two long angled ranges with covered walkways facing the playground. The solitary chimney SW of the school is a relic of Poplar Hospital, destroyed in the Second World War. From Dee Street an UNDERPASS with cheerful coloured tiles leads back beneath the A12 to St Leonard's Road.

5. *The East India Docks, Blackwall and Leamouth: a circular walk starting from East India DLR*

This stretch of the riverside has a venerable history as a victualling point and a place where passengers disembarked for the overland route into London; ship repairing began probably in the late C15. During the period 1614–52 the newly founded East India Company, whose ships berthed in this part of the Thames, established the Blackwall Yard, which expanded hugely in the C17

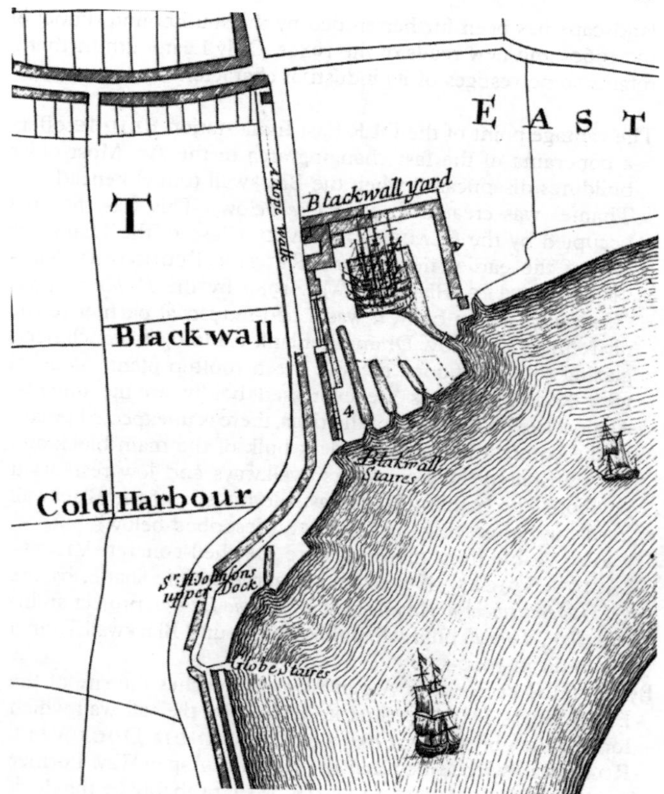

Blackwall Yard, Blackwall in 1703 from Gascoyne's survey of Stepney

and C18. A small wet-dock was added in 1661, and further E the 8-acre Brunswick Dock in 1789–90. This became the Export Dock of the East India Docks, a secure, walled enclosure constructed in 1803–6 by the engineers *John Rennie* and *Ralph Walker* in imitation of the West India Docks (Isle of Dogs), but about half their size. An Import dock was built to the N, and both docks were connected to an entrance basin E of the export dock. Little remains: the export dock was bombed in the Second World War and the whole complex finally closed in 1967; most of the docks were filled in, and the area was redeveloped from the 1980s as part of the LDDC's Enterprise Zone. Blackwall Yard survived longer, although the N part was sold after being cut off by the London & Blackwall Railway in the 1830s. The W part became a Midland railway collier dock in 1877 but the E part was worked, until it closed in 1987, by R. & H. Green, at first alone and then as part of larger companies. Much of the surrounding area was cleared in the 1890s for the Blackwall Tunnel, and the older landscape has been further eroded by the southbound tunnel of the 1960s and new roads of the 1980s. Only Leamouth further E retains some vestiges of its industrial character.

The vantage point of the DLR East India station BRIDGE offers a panorama of the fast changing area to the SW. Most older buildings disappeared when the Blackwall tunnel beneath the Thames was created in 1893 (*see* below). This was the area occupied by the BLACKWALL YARD. Close to the Thames is one of the earlier newcomers, REUTER TECHNICAL SERVICES CENTRE, Blackwall Way. 1989 by the *Richard Rogers Partnership.* When built, it was a neo-industrial partner to the oil refinery close by. Dramatic blank cladding to machinery, glazing to office floors, massive green rooftop plant. As usual with Rogers, services are expressed boldly on the outside. Against the background of the river, there is unexpected poetry in the contrast between the dark bulk of the main block and the transparent service towers, walkways and low restaurant pavilion. The building stands astride the site of the Blackwall Yard's upper graving dock of 1878 (described below).

Also visible from the bridge are the shell-concrete VENTILATION STACKS, of eyecatching aerodynamic shape, by the *GLC Department of Architecture and Civic Design*, project architect *Terry Farrell*, built when the southbound Blackwall Tunnel was built in 1960–7.

By the DLR bridge over Aspen Way one reaches the site of the EAST INDIA IMPORT DOCK, defined by the tall wall which formed the S boundary. First, along EAST INDIA DOCK WALL ROAD, sandwiched between the wall and Aspen Way. Former HYDRAULIC PUMPING STATION, 1857, probably by the dock company engineer *Henry Martin*. Italianate in style and unusually architectural: handsome three-bay N front with shallow central gable, and three large round-headed arches with projecting brick voussoirs and keystones. The accumulator tower has blind arcading, oculi and a pyramidal cap. Extended 1877–8 to power new lock gates, probably by *A. Manning*, then engineer, with a W engine room in matching style. Machinery (by *William Armstrong & Co.*) replaced by electrically powered machinery 1925. NAVAL ROW continues W beside the dock wall with a surprising little group of survivors. No. 36, 1928–9, a four-storey, U-shaped block of flats by *Harley Heckford*, Poplar Borough Surveyor. No. 26 is a group of workshops, their later street front with elegantly curving parapet, 1910 by *Alfred Roberts*. The STEAMSHIP, 1885 by *Edward Brown*, has a spreading one-storey pub extension attached to a three-storey house which once stood in line with the backs of a now demolished C18 terrace.

The SOUTH WALL of the EAST INDIA IMPORT DOCK dates from a rebuilding in 1833–4 by *James Walker*, when it was set back to allow for a new road to Brunswick Wharf. Unlike the West India Docks, the wall was the only protection; goods were originally not stored on the dockside, but taken to the company's warehouses in Cutler Steet on the edge of the City. The DOCK WALL curves around the SW corner. On the W side a walk leads along a remnant of Tunnel Gardens, a playground and raised terrace made in 1902 by the LCC. Most of this disappeared in the 1960s, together with the main dock gate at the NW corner, when the Blackwall Tunnel was doubled and East India Dock Road widened. A replica of the inscription on the gate is at the entrance to the tunnel (*see* below).

Now to explore what lies behind the dock wall. Very little is older than the 1980s. The Import Dock was pumped dry in 1943 for the building of wartime Mulberry Harbours, but was not filled in until after the docks closed in 1967. Around a series of water features is the NCC BUILDING, Nutmeg Lane, partly used as Tower Hamlets Town Hall. A Swedish commercial development designed by a Swede, *Sten Samuelson*, with *Beaton Thomas Partnership*, 1989–92. Pompous Postmodern, with expensive cladding materials, much reflective glass, and landscaped atria. The main axis is a deep court with a canal, trees and footbridges, flanked by arcades. The canal turns N between further blocks of up to ten storeys. Within the bleak courts, lavish use of SCULPTURE. – Renaissance by *Maurice Blik*, symbolizing the building and regeneration of the docks. Expressionist bronze figures, the strong male reaching up to capture an elusive female form. – Meridian Metaphor by *David Jacobson*. A landscape assemblage, which uses granite blocks salvaged from the East India Dock pier to create a meeting place with ritualistic overtones. – Shadow Play by *David King*, a strong piece in painted steel: cut-outs of dockers at work help to compose a form evoking the original dock entrance arch; a cut-out tree grows from it and a bronze figure dances on top. – Domino Players in bronze by *Kim Bennett*; very literal. – The series of bronze PLAQUES on different local themes were produced by children from six local schools.

To the N is the back of EAST INDIA DOCK HOUSE, built as the FINANCIAL TIMES PRINTING WORKS (No. 240 East India Dock Road), 1988 by *Nicholas Grimshaw & Partners*; sadly abandoned by the FT in 1995 in favour of the aesthetically inferior West Ferry Printers (*see* p. 692). An innovative high-tech box which added drama to its surroundings at night, when the N façade lit up from within to show the printing process, in the manner of Sir Owen Williams's works of the 1930s for the *Daily Express* in London, Manchester and Glasgow. The S façade is a mirror image except for the bold aluminium-clad staircase-towers that serve the three floors of offices on this side; planned with print shop and offices divided by a spine of plant. Metal fins project along each wall and support the network of steel braces on to which the glazing is bolted, so that inside, the glass walls are absolutely flush.

To the E GLOBAL SWITCH faces W, warehousing for storing Internet service providers, with a large atrium flanked by silver stair-towers. By *Webb Gray*, 2001. Beyond is TELEHOUSE EUROPE, Coriander Avenue, designed by *YRM*, 1988–90, intended as a disaster-recovery centre for the financial world, then adapted for Global Switch. Silvery-grey boxes suspended from a taller, slimmer, darker-grey service core. A grid of cladding and narrow horizontal window strips, co-ordinated with a decorative maintenance grid-cum-brise-soleil hung from trusses projecting from the core. Now linked by a bridge to a massive, less distinguished block to the S. Also clad in grey, with glass brick stair-turrets against black end walls and a formal glazed W entrance.

Along LEAMOUTH ROAD are stretches of the original WALL on the E side of the Import Dock, 20-ft (6 metres) high with battered buttresses, and one of the three simple arched openings flanked by niches. Across the road but rebuilt in 1993 by the LDDC on a slightly different site, is the former entrance GATEWAY to the East India Company's group of Pepper Warehouses, sited just outside the secure area because designed for bulky goods of small value not worth importing to Cutler Street. The gateway is of 1807–21 by *S.P. Cockerell*, early Egyptian revival; Portland-stone pylons with *caducei*, originally in *Coade* stone but now carved in Portland. Timber gates and, above, a timber 'portcullis' to strengthen them when lowered (reconstruction of 1993). The warehouses were bombed in the Second World War and the site cleared 1983. Leamouth Road ends in a roundabout with a SCULPTURE: huge silhouetted, painted-metal figures of Aerobic, by *Allen Jones*, 1993. Designs for a pedestrian and cycle BRIDGE, close to the road crossing, linking Leamouth to Canning Town, were won in competition by *Whitbybird* in 2004. An ingenious blend of a lifting and swing bridge, which moves in a tilt-and-pivot motion; Y-shaped, with 45-metre mast, and cables to support the bridge.

The Leamouth Peninsula

A footpath starts off the Leamouth Road junction and runs along BOW CREEK, a loop of the River Lea, to Orchard Place. The Leamouth peninsula, remote and isolated before the building of the lower Lea crossing, was the site of much C19 industry. From 1835–74 the major works at the N end were the Thames Plate Glass Works followed by the Blackwall Galvanised Iron Company. The view in 2004 was still dominated by their successor, a huge vegetable-oil processing works; the final example in this area of a working factory on this scale.* In total contrast the opposite bank is an empty strip of land, transformed by the LDDC into an Ecological Park in 1996.

S of Orchard Place the EAST INDIA DOCKS ENTRANCE BASIN is now a nature reserve, the irregular W side reflecting the entrances to the two vanished docks. An entrance is filled by the austere and architectural SALOME GATES by *Sir Anthony Caro*, 1996. The ENTRANCE BASIN LOCK is of 1897, a new

* The site was sold in 2004 to a developer and a housing scheme by *Llewelyn-Davies* proposed.

cut s of the existing passage made by *H.E. & F.A. James*; gates by *Thames Iron Works Co.*, gate machinery by *Sir W.G. Armstrong Whitworth & Co.*

The southern part of the odd L-shaped peninsula of Leamouth was, through the C19, occupied by a variety of industrial and shipping concerns. On the Thames side, by Orchard House stairs, they included a yard with a dry dock of the 1840s for the ship builders R. & H. Green (filled in the 1970s but retaining its iron caisson of 1860). At the SE point is TRINITY HOUSE BUOY WHARF. This is one of the few riverside sites where enough remains to convey some pre-1980s character. The buildings are now occupied as studios or offices (the area was leased by Urban Space Holdings in 1998 and is intended to be a place for 'cultural enterprises'). So far there is none of the glitz of smart Docklands developments, only the rather endearingly incongruous FATBOY DINER, all streamlined chrome, built 1941 in Elizabeth, New Jersey and brought here in 2002.

Trinity House, the coastal lighthouse authority established by the early C16, had a buoy store here from the 1760s. In 1803 the corporation began to acquire land and built a timber river wall to make a wharf along the Lea; the existing wall is its brick replacement of 1822, which was continued in stone along the Thames in 1851–2. At the end of the quay is the CHAIN AND
BUOY STORE and EXPERIMENTAL LIGHTHOUSE of 1864–6 66
by *(Sir) James Douglass*, Engineer-in-Chief. The store is a brick shed. A railway track for moving buoys originally ran right through it. Rising against its E wall is the short polygonal brick lighthouse-tower, by engineers *Campbell, Johnstone & Co.*; above the stone cornice a railed walk around the glazed lantern; thick diamond panes by *Chance Bros.* It superseded the original experimental lantern (put up in 1854 on a storehouse but moved to the W gable of the buoy store where it stood until the 1920s). Faraday, the Company's scientific adviser, used it for lighting trials which led to the first installation in 1858 of electric lighting in an operational lighthouse (the South Foreland, Dover). Faraday's experimental chamber within the store has gone, as have other buildings of the earlier C19.

The miscellany of survivals includes part of the PROVING HOUSE of 1875, a long one-storey shed against the W boundary, built after Trinity House took on the testing of cables, chains and anchors. Further STORES (later packing sheds) were added, and other buildings were put up in the early 1950s after bomb damage, including the BOILERMAKERS SHOP (converted to a performance space by *Buschow Henley*) in front of the Proving House, and the neatly designed two-storey brick FITTING SHOP to its N, 1952, which has a more adventurous concrete-shell roof, with a travelling crane. In the space
between is CONTAINER CITY 2, 2002, an irregular five-storey 128
pile of corrugated steel shipping containers adapted to provide low-cost workspace. Cheerful colours with eyecatching

portholes alternating with larger windows and balconies, the effect not unlike an Archigram sketch. Smaller and simpler prototype, CONTAINER CITY, 1 behind, 2001. Both by *Nicholas Lacey & Partners* for *Trinity Buoy Space Management*.

The return to East India DLR by BLACKWALL WAY is past extensive Barratt housing on the site of the East India Company export dock which had been filled by the huge Brunswick Power Station (1947–56, architects *Farmer & Dark*). This was demolished 1988–9 apart from the low red brick SWITCHGEAR HOUSE, which was extended upwards in 2003 as a ten-storey apartment block. Further on in Blackwall Way, flats by *Michael Squire & Partners*. A diversion S can be made to Reuters (*see* above) and the remains of the BLACKWALL GRAVING DOCK. Reuters straddles the site of the upper dock of 1878. The earlier dock was refurbished 1991–2 and cut back to its original length. It was the yard's fourth dry dock, probably built between 1779 and 1799, i.e. one of the earliest remaining on the Thames. The stepped bottom faced with ashlar-granite blocks dates from a rebuilding and lengthening before 1850.

BLACKWALL TUNNEL. The NORTHBOUND TUNNEL was built by (*Sir*) *Alexander Binnie* of the LCC, 1891–7, 4,410-ft (1,344 metres) long excluding the approach cuttings. 3,115 ft (949.5 metres) were driven through mixed water-bearing strata using a Greathead shield and compressed air; it was the first time that these techniques had been combined, representing a major advance in sub-aqueous soft-ground tunnelling. A temporary sealing layer of clay was laid on the riverbed. The lining, of cast-iron segments filled with concrete, is faced with white-glazed bricks. The pattern was followed for the LCC's other tunnels at Greenwich, Rotherhithe, and Woolwich. The internal diameter is 24 ft, with a carriageway only 16-ft wide, and sharp bends. The SOUTHBOUND TUNNEL (1960–7) is by the *GLC Directorate of Highways and Transportation*, the 2,870-ft bored section by *Mott, Hay & Anderson*. Internal diameter 27 ft: driven under compressed air with the ground consolidated by grouting from two pilot tunnels. Erected near the N entrance is a replica of the giant inscription plaque which stood at the main entrance to the East India Docks. Re-erected on the E side of the cutting, a delightful bronze plaque by *Alfred Drury*, *c.* 1897: two allegorical women and the head of Father Thames, diagram of the tunnel construction below.

ISLE OF DOGS

Until 1800 the Isle of Dogs was a lonely windswept peninsula S of the hamlet of Poplar, lying below high tide level. The name appears from the 1520s, and was reputedly derived from dogs kept for royal hunting at Greenwich Park. In the Middle Ages it was known as Stepney Marsh, and was part of the large parish

of Stepney. After earlier intermittent efforts the marsh was finally drained in the C17 but the Isle kept a melancholy reputation. Windmills were built along the W flood bank, known from the late C18 as Mill Wall (there were twelve by the 1740s) but apart from a single farmhouse there were few other buildings. On the
E side, at Blackwall, near the mouth of the Lea, the East India p. 660
Company had a small dock already in the C17, and in the later C18 a scatter of industries began to develop along the river. From 1800 all began to change as the N of the peninsula was transformed by the building of the great enclosed docks.

The campaign to build secure docks specially devoted to the West India trade, with its exceptionally valuable cargoes and large ships, began when a committee of merchants was formed in 1793, led by William Vaughan, a naval architect, and Robert Milligan a planter. Several rival schemes were put forward for different sites, but in 1799 royal assent was granted for a scheme on the Isle of Dogs, financed by West India merchants and planters. The plan drawn up in 1797 and carried out by the newly formed West India Dock Company was by *George Dance jun.*, Clerk of the City Works, and his assistant *John Foulds*, with *Ralph Walker* as resident engineer. The more experienced *William Jessop*, employed as consultant engineer, was the principal designer and superviser up to 1804. The Board of Excise insisted on two docks, for import and export, each with access to the Thames, surrounded by a secure wall and ditch. The Import Dock, together with a shared entrance lock and basin (the Blackwall Basin), was opened in 1802, the Export Dock to its S in 1806. Although the surroundings have been transformed, the sheets of water remain (the Export Dock partly filled and built over), with some of Jessop's quay walls visible. Along the N side of the Import Dock a string of huge warehouses half a mile long was built by *George Gwilt &*
Son in 1800–3. A fragment remains, the most substantial of the 65
structures to survive from this period of the docks, together with dock offices, traces of the dock wall and some ancillary buildings (*see* perambulation *1a*). Nothing remains of the warehouses and sheds on the S side of the Import Dock, built for Rum and Mahogany. These were first built in 1804–8 and largely reconstructed in 1817–18 by *Rennie*.

To the S of the West India Docks a canal was constructed by the City of London in 1802–5 to provide a direct route through the Island to the Port of London. This proved a failure; it was bought by the Dock company in 1829, and renamed South Dock; *(Sir) John Rennie* (who had followed his father as engineer to the company), added a timber pond in 1832–3; the two were united in 1866–70 by *Sir John Hawkshaw*, when the surviving entrance lock on the E side was built, and the whole complex was remodelled again in the 1920s. Other survivals are some of the buildings provided by the Rennies: a cooperage close to the Import Dock, and some handsome houses for the dockmasters.

Yet further S is the vast L-shaped expanse of water of the Millwall Docks, created in 1863–9, with a SW entrance lock to the Thames, to provide non-tidal wharves for general industry, shipbuilding and repair. Several graving docks were planned, but only one built. By the 1880s the Millwall Docks had become the centre of the European grain trade, with huge granaries (now vanished), and travelling cranes, introduced from 1873. The timber trade was also important, with timber stacks occupying the land to the S.

The creation of East Ferry and West Ferry roads in 1812–15 as routes to the Greenwich ferry encouraged development over the rest of the island. Shipyards and industry developed on the large SW sites along the river, the most celebrated being Sir William Fairbairn's Millwall Ironworks (later Burrell's Wharf) laid out from 1836, and the shipyard nearby where Brunel's Great Eastern was launched in 1859. The SE side was developed from 1842 by *William Cubitt*, who embanked the river, leased wharves, laid out roads and encouraged speculative builders to create the area which became known as Cubitt Town. Further N at Blackwall, Poplar Dock was created in 1850–1, for coal and exports, the first to be linked to a railway, and enlarged in 1875–7.

By 1901 the population of the Isle of Dogs was *c.* 21,000 (compared with *c.* 5,000 fifty years earlier) but even this supplied insufficient workers for the docks and the vast range of industries, which by this time ranged from milling flour and oilseed to ironworks and maritime trades, chemicals and engineering. The first council housing in the area was built in the 1920s at Chapel House, the last greenfield site. By 1970 almost all Isle of Dogs housing was council-owned, the result of clearances in the 1930s and post-war rebuilding after massive war-time destruction by the planes which targeted the docks. Reconstruction continued up to *c.* 1970 by both Poplar Borough and its successor Tower Hamlets, and by the LCC/GLC, replacing almost all of Cubitt Town and scattering towers of flats on other inland sites.

During the C20, many of the industries moved away to sites more conveniently located for road transport, leaving a rump of warehouses, depots and scrapyards. As for the docks, it had for long been clear that because of the increased size of ships the future for shipping lay further downstream. The docks on the Isle of Dogs, in decline for some time, finally accepted their fate, and closed in 1980.* To encourage alternative development, the London Docklands Development Corporation was set up in 1981, covering the riverside areas both N and S of the Thames, and in 1982 the government created an Enterprise Zone around the Docks in the Isle of Dogs, in which tax and planning concessions were granted. After a slow start a rush of activity began in 1985 when planning began on what became known as the Canary Wharf Estate. Building began in 1987, proceeding rapidly until the slump of 1991 and more slowly thereafter, to a master plan by *Skidmore Owings & Merrill*, for the Canadian developers Olympia & York who took over after the first developer failed to

*A last-ditch effort to promote trade was made by the Fred Olsen line for which sophisticated warehouses were built, with a glamorous passenger terminal at Millwall docks by *Foster & Partners*, 1966–70.

raise the capital. The buildings of the Canary Wharf Estate now 121
dominate the Isle, and indeed the skyline of the whole of London, with a Manhattan waterscape of commercial offices towering over the sparse relics of the old docks. Elsewhere, developments have been more piecemeal, with a mixture of commercial and residential buildings fringing the Millwall and South Docks, and private housing further S on the site of the riverside wharves, all quite separate from the old working class communities.

The LDDC, until it handed over its powers to Tower Hamlets in 1998, was responsible for creating the infrastructure, not only in the form of new transport links, but for the top dressing aimed to attract the new clientèle. The former LDDC area, and especially Canary Wharf with its formal landscaped centrepieces, is notable for its elegant footbridges and lighting schemes, and the largest quantity of contemporary public art in London.

PERAMBULATIONS

1. West India and Canary Wharf

1a. The Import Dock and its buildings. From West India Quay DLR to West Ferry DLR

From the elevated DLR West India Quay Station all the 65
stages of Dockland development are visible. The railway spans the centre of the long stretch of water that formed the West India Import Dock. Alongside the N quay there were originally nine sugar and coffee warehouses of 1800–3, designed by *George Gwilt & Son,* an immense wall of brick building that stretched for over half a mile, forming a massive perimeter wall between the docks and their outer defences. All except Nos. 1 and 2 at the W end were destroyed by bombing. The survivors, once so impressive when they stood alone, now look puny in comparison with the commercial giants all around.

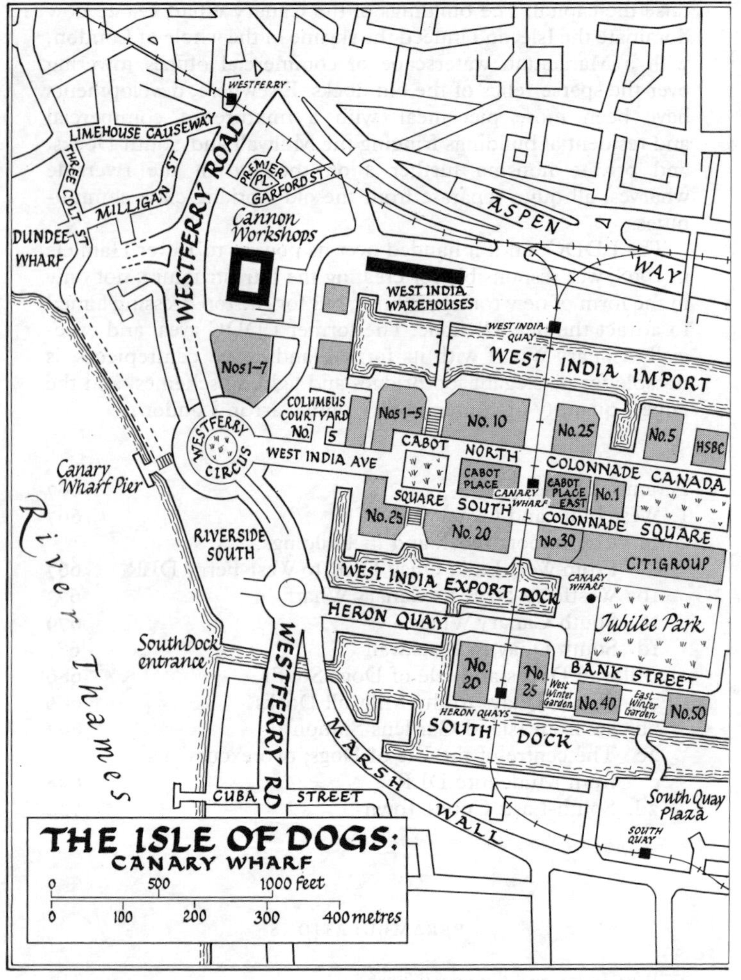

To the E of the railway line, beyond the still empty spaces is one of the first results of redevelopment after the docks closed in 1980, the NEW BILLINGSGATE MARKET, 1980–2 by *Newman Levinson & Partners*, now looking very unsophisticated in its slicker surroundings. It is merely a conversion of one of the concrete-framed transit sheds built on the *Hennebique* system by the PLA from 1912: Shed E, completed 1917, closed 1971. Extended N with a steel-clad pavilion, whose prominent feature is the bright yellow cluster of tubular-steel masts projecting high above the roof to support a spaceframe.

A masterplan for the West India Docks by *Michael Squire & Partners*, conserving the old warehouses as the centrepiece among

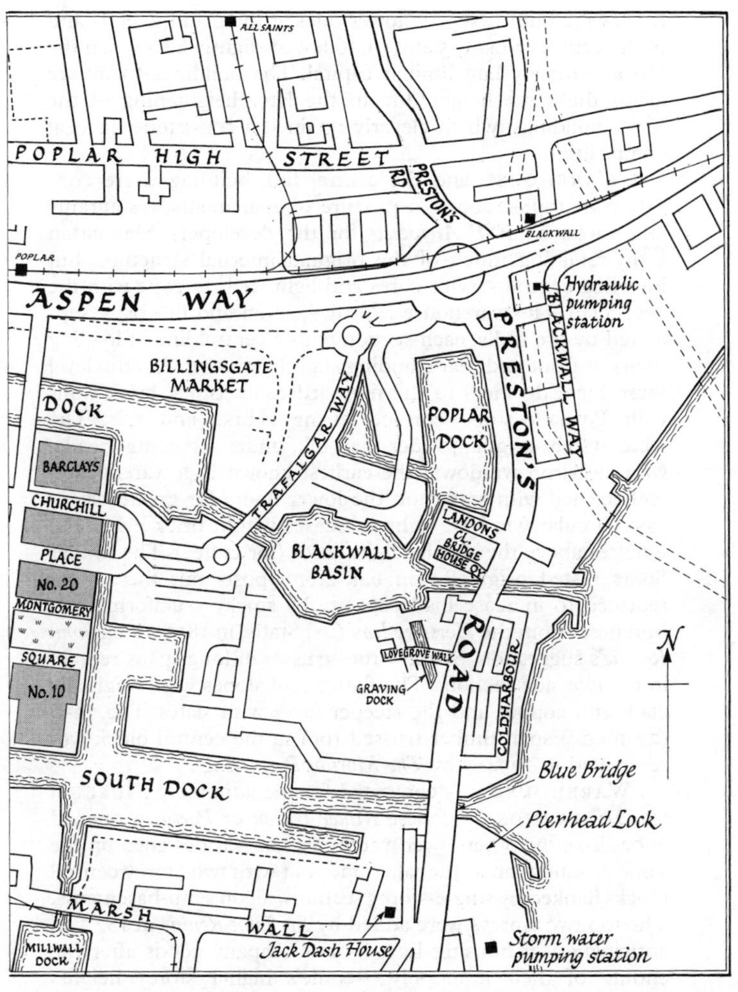

new buildings, was agreed in 1997. Descending to the W of the railway, first comes No. 1 WEST INDIA QUAY, hotel and apartments by *HOK*, completed 2003. A thirty-three-storey, sleekly glazed curved-S frontage, with a lower N wing clad in red terracotta. Set back forming the N side of a new square, is *Michael Squires & Partners'* twelve storey apartment block with adjoining cinema, car park and leisure facilities tucked in beside the railway line, 2000–2.

Now for the remaining WAREHOUSES. These consisted originally of six tall and three lower warehouses, each 223-ft (68 metres) long, divided by one-storey link buildings. The taller ones, five storeys and attic to the quay, with a semi-basement below quay level, were built first. The lower ones at the E and W ends and in the centre (Nos. 1, 5 and 9), followed slightly later when the Dock company had limited capital. The buildings today are all of the same height due to the later heightening of the lower buildings, which cleverly retained a consistent classical composition.

65 No. 2 WAREHOUSE and the central link buildings were converted in 1998–2000 to a mixture of apartments, restaurants and shops by *FSP Architects* for the developers Manhattan Loft, retaining much of the original internal structure, but inserting central service cores and light wells to cope with the deep plan. The warehouse is of five, seven and five bays, separated by fire walls, each section with a central line of loading doors at front and rear standing slightly forward. At attic level these form dormers to the mansard roofs. Stock brick walls with Portland-stone cornice, string course and sills. The windows are original, wider than tall, under segmental heads, with cast-iron windows (the earliest known in a warehouse), embellished with spikes on the lower floors for greater security. Circular windows light staircases within brick cylinders; lunettes above the cornice light attics (for coffee). The timber floors rested originally on oak storey-posts but these were replaced to increase load capacity by stocky cruciform cast-iron posts from the *Horseley Iron Co.*, Staffs, in 1813–18 on *John Rennie*'s suggestion. Shallow roof trusses of long spans remain in the two side sections. The flatter roof slopes were originally clad with copper and the steeper faces with slates. The 72-ft (22 metre) span timber-trussed roof in the central block was re-created in 1994–5 by *The Morton Partnership*.

No. 1 WAREHOUSE was converted for the admirable MUSEUM IN DOCKLANDS, by *Purcell Miller Tritton & Partners*, opened 2002. Like the other lower warehouses, it was designed on the same ground plan as the taller ones but with two-storey central blocks flanked by single-storey sections, all on semi-basements. The top two storeys were added by *Sir John Rennie* in 1827, in anticipation of housing East India Company goods after the ending of their monopoly. Rennie's higher storey heights allowed the cornice to line up with that of No. 2. Its loopholes do not rise into the roof. The interior was severely damaged by fire in 1901, but replaced almost as original.

The four-storey blocks without attic storeys, between Nos. 1 and 2 and at the W end, are the heightened LINK BLOCKS, originally one-storey-and-basement sheds, raised to three storeys in 1827. Their cornices also line through. Five-bays wide with central loopholes and round-headed windows to the quay. The W link, a baggage warehouse, has blocked W windows and a more generous staircase. Attached to the W is the *Gwilts*'s single-storey Dock Office of 1803–4, remodelled as a ledger office by *Sir John Rennie*, 1827. Symmetrical façade with round-headed windows within relieving arches and rectangular panels over; timber Doric four-column portico, probably a later addition. General office to the E, its strong-room, 1889,

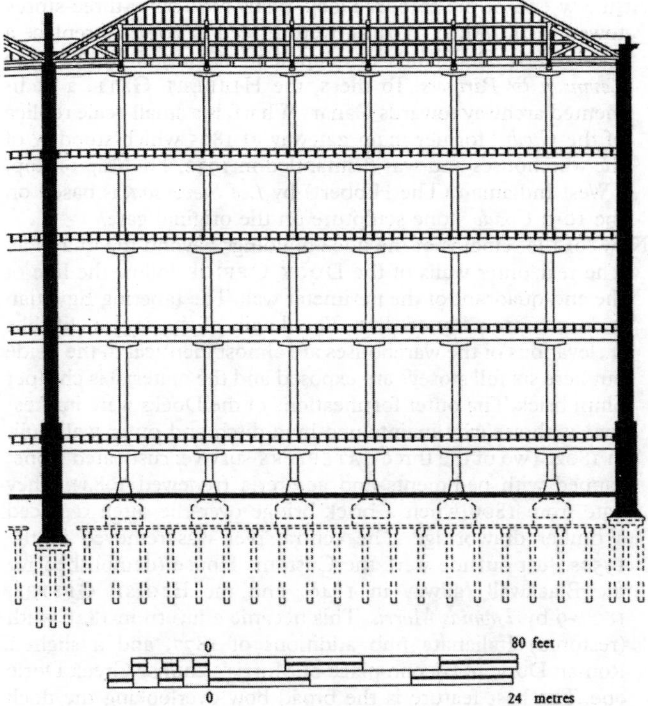

No. 1 Warehouse, West India Quay, Isle of Dogs. Section

projecting into No. 1 Warehouse. The W annexe was a fire station, remodelled 1812 as a police office; top storey perhaps 1875.

On the quayside, the bronze figure of Sir Robert Milligan (†1809), the merchant who proposed the docks, and was later chairman of the West India Company. 1810–12 by *Sir Richard Westmacott*. Bluff, in everyday clothes and quite unusual for Westmacott, who preferred the dignity of classical dress.

The DOCK WALLS exposed on the N side of the IMPORT DOCK are *Jessop*'s, of concave section to fit the ships' hulls; 2 metres thick, with counterforts, i.e. buttresses behind bound to the walling by hoop iron, the extant example of such reinforced brickwork. Jessop had used such construction before at the Ringsend Docks in Dublin (1791–6) and at Bristol.

The S quayside of the 1980s (*see* p. 675) is reached via the delicately poised deck of *Future Systems*' FLOATING FOOTBRIDGE, engineers *Anthony Hunt Associates*, 1994–6. As much a work of art as a practical structure that respects the dock walls. Lime-yellow tubular cross-braces straddle between pairs of pontoons like rubber shoes. The central section can be lifted hydraulically to let boats through.

At the W end of the Import Dock, plans for a sixty-three-storey tower, COLUMBUS HOUSE were agreed in 2004, to replace a feeble early Docklands development of 1987–8 by *Newman Levinson & Partners*. To the S, the HIBBERT GATE, a pedimented archway towards Canary Wharf, is a small-scale replica of the *Gwilts*' former main gateway of 1805 which stood W of the warehouses and was dismantled in 1932. The ship on top, a West Indiaman (The Hibbert) by *Leo Stevenson*, is based on the 10-ft *Coade* stone sculpture on the original gate.

Now for the remains of the dock buildings beyond the quayside. The rear outer walls of the DOCK OFFICE follow the line of the end quadrant of the perimeter wall. The tapering Egyptian N door is probably of 1827. The details of the severe cliff-like N elevations of the warehouses are almost identical to the S side but here six full storeys are exposed and the material is cheaper plum brick. The outer fortifications of the Docks were impressive, with security maintained by a ditch and outer wall built in 1802. Two of the three GATEPIERS survive: rusticated stone, capped with pediments and acroteria (renewed 1984). They date from 1809 when a brick bridge over the ditch replaced a timber drawbridge. The central pier was removed in the 1950s. Just outside were the Customs House (demolished for the Blackwall railway in 1846) and the EXCISE OFFICE, 1807–9 by *Thomas Morris*. This became a tavern in 1846, with (restored) Italianate pub additions of 1877, and a slighter Roman Doric portico in place of Morris's clumsy Greek Doric one. The best feature is the broad bow overlooking the dock entrance (cf. the dock officials' houses in Blackwall). The garden boundary is a restored section of the OUTER DOCK WALL, mostly dismantled in 1928–9; the ditch, mainly covered in 1892, is represented by the drop to the garden.

Within the dock precinct, the former PLA POLICE OFFICES, 1914 by *C.R.S. Kirkpatrick*, Chief Engineer, red brick with a tetra-style Doric portico. Then a large open space, formerly the works yard. The small, circular, domed GUARD HOUSE, 1804–5 by the *Gwilts*, was one of two: this one was an armoury for the Military Guard and the dock's own regiment; the S one (dem. 1922–3) was a lock-up. They flanked the main gateway through the inner wall, dismantled 1932. In line with this is the approach to the stores, workshops and cooperage of 1824–5 by *Rennie*, a quadrangle entered through a large triumphal arch of Portland stone. Now CANNON WORKSHOPS, small business units created by *Charles Lawrence* and *David Wrightson*, 1980–1, in one of the PLA's early attempts to introduce new industry after the docks closed in 1980. Single-storeyed buildings with broad-eaved roofs. Brick-built E and S ranges: the offices (SE) were entered from within the arch. Stores (NE) continued round the N and W ranges: here wooden slats, later replaced by weatherboarding, originally concealed the slim cast-iron columns, but aluminium cladding has been set back behind some to form loggias. Centre S, the former carpenters' shop, well lit by continuous S glazing: doubled by an inner block, 1980–1. In the quadrangle, the cooperage, U-shaped, its courtyard now roofed over. Near the arch the C19 cannon, after which the group is called, and the cast-iron benchmark for the docks inscribed TRINITY H.W. 1800. It represents the mean high-water level of spring tides: the ground level is lower.

Outside the dock gates to the W is GARFORD STREET, created in 1807 just after the docks opened. On the S side a row of DOCK CONSTABLES' COTTAGES (Nos. 10–18). The Dock Police Force was formed in 1802. Designed by *John Rennie*, 1819, two pairs and one detached for the sergeant, behind small front gardens. Lower windows set in segmental-arched recesses. They are echoed in scale (but not in detail) by late C20 houses along the N side. Also on the S side, tucked in by the dock, two Salvation Army hostels, originally the Scandinavian Seamen's Temperance Home. RIVERSIDE HOUSE, 1887–8, by *Richard Harris Hill*, a specialist in such institutions, very plain. GRIEG HOUSE, for officers, 1902–3 by *Niven & Wigglesworth*, free and festive despite its awkward site. Queen Anne with Scandinavian overtones, in yellow and bright-red rubbed brick and terracotta. The end bays are blank except for arched doors and read like broad pilasters, framed with angle pilasters linked by festoons. Hipped roof with central cupola. Linked to lower C20 offices on Garford Street.

Garford Street continues to West Ferry, past a mixture of C20 housing. On the site of St Peter's church (*Ewan Christian*, 1882–4), the pre-LDDC MARY JONES HOUSE, social housing for the single by *Christopher Beaver Associates*, succeeded by *Prior Manton Tuke Partnership*, 1978–9. Collegiate in style with a Kahn-inspired red brick perimeter heavily modelled with staircases; generous bay windows to the courtyard garden. Also bold but more conventional the intensely coloured PREMIER PLACE by *Chassay Architects*, 1995–8, speculative flats with rendered walls and bright blue attic storeys.

1b. Westferry DLR to Canary Wharf

We begin at WESTFERRY DLR STATION, close to the boundary between Poplar and Limehouse and visibly at the fringe of the Docklands development on the Isle of Dogs. At the corner with WESTFERRY ROAD is the powerful landmark of *CZWG*'s 'live work' building of 1999 for the Peabody Trust, the name West Ferry incorporated in giant lettering in grey brick on the yellow brick wedge facing the station (an idea reminiscent of Erskine's Byker wall at Newcastle). U-shaped rear, for workshops, with a consciously industrial image created by austere metal and mesh balconies. Smaller blocks of flats behind. At the corner with MILLIGAN STREET: the LIMEHOUSE CLUB, a simple youth club and community hall, makes quite a bold statement on this prominent corner. 1994–5 by *Michael Squire Associates*. Clerestory-lit hall flanked by lower vaulted rooms. Smaller hall over the entrance foyer and office. Glass bricks in the curved stair-tower, which lights up as a welcoming beacon after dark. From here Milligan Street curves S towards the river, lined on each side by traditional groups of late C20 houses, but at its E end, where it joins THREE COLT STREET, is a diverting group associated with the Limehouse riverside. To the r., in the boundary wall of LIMEKILN WHARF is a round-headed timber doorcase, with narrow neck supporting a miniature pediment, a replica of the doorway* from the famous LIME HOUSE, which was built in 1705 and demolished in 1935 (with the adjacent last remaining lime kiln). S is the late C19 classical office building, in red and yellow brick, of the original Dundee, Perth, and London Shipping Co. Galleon in the pediment and a cupola on the roof. Extended behind with a sheet-steel clad box on stilts.

DUNDEE WHARF stands between here and the river: best seen from the riverside are flats, part of a large group of housing by *CZWG* (1995–7) which make a massive landmark to answer the same architects' Cascades further downriver (*see* perambulation *2a*). Though less original, this block is nearly as theatrical. The vocabulary of quayside engineering is dramatically expressed; giant 'hoppers' top the service towers towards the horseshoe-shaped rear court, enclosed with lower blocks of flats and houses and a drum of leisure facilities. Sinister crane-like attachments support balconies along the sheer river façades and form an eleven-storey free-standing tower at the angle. From here a wonderful FOOTBRIDGE by *YRM/Anthony Hunt Associates* for the LDDC, 1996, takes the Thames path in a sinuous curve across the mouth of Limekiln Dock and is stayed by a single mast.

At this point the full drama of the riverside setting takes hold with the promenade of the Thames Path at CANARY WHARF RIVERSIDE commanding an impressive panorama from Limehouse to Millwall on the N bank and Rotherhithe to the S. The advantages of this position have been fully exploited by the developers: including the distinguished FOUR SEASONS HOTEL, a highly individual design by *Philippe Starck*, 1998, with the main hotel set at the higher level of the deck on which Canary Wharf sits. Massive Egyptian-style roof of green aluminium. Cream walls with a tight grid of square, projecting windows and tall temple-like doors in polished wood. Lower down to the riverside, separated by gardens, is a glazed swimming pool and a lantern-topped block with splayed sides clad in dark-metal scales. Flanking this, and clustered around garden squares, are tall, run-of-the-mill flats in yellow brick by the firm of *Koetter Kim & Associates*, who as one of the principal masterplanners at Canary Wharf envisaged a balancing group of towers at Riverside South. Instead in 2004, *Richard Rogers Partnership* plans two glass towers. Also designed for this site, *Ron Arad*'s Windwand, a 50-m high carbon-fibre needle.

*The original was donated to the Ragged School Museum, Copperfield Road, in 1988.

From the riverside one ascends to the level of the raised deck on which the whole of the Canary Wharf development floats above the level of the old docks. WESTFERRY CIRCUS, created in 1987–91, provides the formal W entrance to West India Avenue on the main E–W axis of the Wharf and from here we catch our first view of *Cesar Pelli*'s celebrated tower at Canada Square (*see* below). In one view, one can instantly appreciate the strongly formal Beaux-Arts planning and landscaping of the original masterplan which complemented the transatlantic scale of the buildings and set the Wharf apart from contemporary British developments. In the centre of the circus is a circular garden with free-spirited leafy entrance gates and railings by *Giuseppe Lund* enclosing a circle of fairly informal planting and lawn. The circus's NE quadrant is filled by No. 1–7 by *SOM* and No. 5 WEST INDIA AVENUE by *Fred Koetter* of *Koetter Kim & Associates*, with *Perkins & Will*. These form eight- to ten-storey interlocking buildings, designed as a single scheme and in the same vein. Massive, dull and limestone-clad; built 1991–3. At the back, the blocks face COLUMBUS COURTYARD, a piazza designed by *Igor Mitoraj* as a formal setting for his sculpture Centurione I, a 3-m high Neoclassical bronze mask. The N and E sides are closed by late 1990s blocks. On the courtyard's N side is a cut-steel screen by *Wendy Ramshaw* on the theme of sea navigation with a jewelled eye in the centre.

WEST INDIA AVENUE is planted with shady trees, a central double row of limes with a carpet of periwinkles beneath. The handsome aluminium lamp standards by *SOM*, used throughout Canary Wharf, are especially prominent here. In the centre of the avenue MAN WITH OPEN ARMS by *Giles Penny*, 1995, roughly textured bronze.

After the broad avenue, the tight enclosed space of CABOT SQUARE comes as a surprise. This was the heart of the Wharf's first developments in 1988–91 and represents the importance placed from the outset on high quality, strongly formal green spaces and the use of public art in attractive settings. The square is small, hemmed in at all four corners by buildings alike in height but intentionally different in style, each paying homage to different periods of North American and British architecture. The central GARDEN is turned into an island by the roadway that rings it and at each end, steps lead up between over-prominent pavilions (car park access) to the paved central piazza with stepped seating. Central fountain, a shallow basin with rhythmical play of jets by *Richard Chaix*. Bronze planters by *Philip Jackson*, and at each angle four small circular vents enclosed by translucent glass panels by *Jeff Bell* that light up at night. Couple on Seat of 1984 by *Lynn Chadwick* in his characteristically geometric style, face WREN'S LANDING, down to the Import Dock (*see* p. 671); its steps have scribbly metal railings by *Bruce McLean*. On the S views towards Canary Wharf South and Heron Quays (*see* below).

At the NW corner with West India Avenue, No. 1–5 CABOT SQUARE is by *Pei Cobb Freed & Partners* for Crédit Suisse First Boston and extended for them in 1998. Silver-limestone cladding, striped with darker grey granite beneath the sills. Regular windows slightly canted within the openings. The tallest part is over eighteen storeys, with lower wings. The extension to West India Avenue, designed to contain two massive 7,500 square metres trading floors, bridges Willoughby Passage, which is closed by an engaging set of GATES by *Kate Hackney*, with coloured lights set jewel-like into bronzed serpentine ironwork.

No. 25, SW, designed as the HQ of Morgan Stanley, answers No. 5 as the frame to West India Avenue. By *SOM* (*Chicago*) and inspired by Chicago's late C19 steel-framed buildings. Polished ox-blood granite and cream cast-stone. Like No. 5 it has a stubby tower with an open top stage detaching itself from the main block, which steps S from this in flat-topped stages down to the quay. Regular mullioned and transomed windows in the Chicago tradition.

No. 10, diagonally opposite (NE), was also designed by *SOM* but here the Chicago classicism is infused with what the architects perceived to be 'the spirit, human scale and texture of the traditional buildings of London'. Hence the medley of classical details deployed in the profligate manner of the Edwardian Baroque. The composition is crude, on a large scale to be read from afar. Ground-floor arcades with teak shopfronts and hanging lanterns inspired by the covered arcades off Piccadilly, and yellow brick cladding. All very close in style to their Broadgate Exchange at Bishopsgate (1987–91). SW corner-drum with an entrance porch in its base, domed with bronze gallery. Elaborately stone-panelled foyers and an opulent nine-storey central atrium: three tiers of balconies ornamented by bronze grilles and a *faux* oval lantern dispensing artificial light.

In the SE corner No. 20 CABOT SQUARE and No. 30 THE SOUTH COLONNADE by *Kohn Pedersen Fox*, with *EPR Partnership*, draw knowingly on the commercial styles of 1920s and 30s America. Composed as a single group along the Export Dock but split into two by the track of the DLR: where it splits, girders project as if the two halves have been forced apart. Each block ends in a slow curve to the quayside, divided into bold horizontal divisions, in the style of an American Beaux-Arts classical office block. Light-reflecting, silvery cladding and coarsely detailed with 'clip-on' details of projecting metal fins flanking the window strips, all typical of KPF.

CABOT PLACE, at the W end of the square, is the solid anchor to Pelli's soaring tower (*see* below) and the result is a slightly uncomfortable combination of monumentality and delicacy. This part of the scheme was executed by *Pelli* with *Adamson Associates* and *Frederick Gibberd Coombes & Partners*. Distinctly Postmodern façades subtly striped in red and cream sandstone and greenstone which continue with polished luxury into the magnificently spacious foyer at the base of the tower. Inside, three levels of shopping mall (*Building Design Partnership*), mostly top-lit but uninspiring. Cabot Place East has a glazed rotunda with above-ground shopping and restaurants on three levels.

Between Cabot Place and the tower is the dramatic red-painted steel and glass canopy with high parabolic arches above CANARY WHARF DLR STATION, by *Pelli* with *ASFA Ltd.* This reinterpretation of the C19 station shed makes a most exciting gateway into the centre of the development. Masking the underside of the track as it passes over the North Colonnade are translucent panels by *Martin Richman*, which illuminate at night.

Canada Square

An account of Canada Square must start with an appreciation of the first building to be completed, No. 1, CANARY WHARF's first tower, the showpiece of Phase 1 and the hub and landmark of the whole development.* By *Cesar Pelli & Associates.* Pelli claimed this to be England's first skyscraper. To celebrate that fact he designed the simplest form possible, square in plan, pyramid topped and sheer, with a taut skin of stainless steel to reflect the English sky – a simple gleaming prism that, as Pelli sees it, has an elemental quality and responds to changes of light on the water and in the sky and to the misty English weather. Stepped recession at the angles and at the top to make the forty-six storeys seem more slender (the slight squatness results from a conflict between a height restriction imposed by flight paths from the City airport and the developers' demand for maximum floor space). When finished in 1991 the building surpassed in height all British and all but one European rivals, at over 800-ft (244 metres) high compared with the City's 618 ft (188 metres) NatWest tower, completed 1979, and Helmut Jahn's Messerturm, Frankfurt, of 1985–91 (251 metres). The tower seems to touch ground lightly, with no modulation in the even, steel walling except a band of triangular patterning above the two-storey-high flush glazing round the base. At ground level along the N and S sides, projecting steel posts make schematic colonnades. For those accustomed to the work of Foster, Rogers and Grimshaw, the use of stainless steel seems unexceptional, but in 1987 it had never been used for cladding an American skyscraper. Pelli's choice of material was an open acknowledgement of the pervasive influence of the English High-Tech style. The panels are technically a rain screen attached by aluminium framing to a curtain wall; the pyramid is a perforated cap to the cooling towers. The ground floor of No. 1 forms a grand public thoroughfare. In the centre eight marble-faced banks of lifts provide access to the offices above. On the outer walls, four

*The account of No. 1 is from *London Docklands*, 1998, by Elizabeth Williamson.

large discs carved with names of C20 luminaries, by *Keith Milow*, 1998. Also four ceramics by *Lawson Oyekon*, 1998.

121 The rest of CANADA SQUARE is in a very different spirit from the buildings around Cabot Square to the W; more coherent in overall appearance, and less bombastic. Its curtain-walled offices frame a calm and dignified forecourt to the formal entrance of No. 1. The square in front, landscaped by *Olin & Partners*, with hard landscaping by *Koetter Kim & Associates*, is
125 a grass lawn. In the centre The Big Blue, an exquisite blue flying saucer of fibreglass, by *Ron Arad*, 1998, poised at an angle over a glass ring forming a roof light to the underground shopping mall. In front of Citigroup, the bone-shaped It Takes Two, by *Bob Allen*, 2002.

The overall scheme, with two tall towers grouping with No. 1, goes back to the 1980s, although heights and details evolved later. The glass envelope, exploited in new ways, is the unifying motif of Canada Square. Clockwise from the NW the earliest is No. 25 North Colonnade, by *Troughton McAslan* with *Adamson Associates*, 1998. The elegant Minimalist design (the first on the estate by a British firm) replaced an earlier scheme by *KPF* intended to match their stone-faced building in Cabot Square. Ingeniously planned: two blocks with a sleek external skin of flush windows and floorbands, linked by a space-frame porch, the second block wedge-shaped and breaking the street line. To its E, ADAMS PLACE, a waterside passage below tensile fabric roofs, leads to the quayside of the Import Dock. Here there is a sculpture of twisted wooden planks of Douglas Fir: Original Form, by *Keith Reid*, 1999.

No. 5 Canada Square is a less interesting speculative block by *SOM*, with three big trading floors, 2000–3, partly occupied by Bank of America. Curtain-walled, with a set-back centre and inverted truss floating above the roof. Then the forty-four-storey No. 8, HSBC, 1999–2002 by *Foster & Partners*, architects of the Bank's highly original 1980s offices in Hong Kong. Built as headquarters for the 8,000-strong UK staff. While the Hong Kong building displayed its structure, here all is concealed behind impeccable curtain walling. The technical innovation is the use of curved double-glazed panels at the corners, prefabricated in groups of four. At the top is an opaque band with flagrantly large lettering. From a distance the tower clusters clumsily with the slightly taller No. 1, from the square it appears reticently dignified. Within the vast entrance hall is the 'History Wall' by *Thomas Heatherwick Studio*, 2002, an ingenious and delightful shimmering composition of 3,743 archive images, arranged at an angle so as to provide a ghostly projecting HSBC logo. Three double-height open-plan trading floors, three levels of underground car parking, with the dock wall preserved beneath. The bronze lions at the entrance are replicas of those outside the Hong Kong office.

Beyond the NE corner, CHURCHILL PLACE, with BARCLAYS, by *HOK*, 2001–3. The rather bulky thirty-three-storey glass tower follows the aesthetic of Canada Square, its glazing disguising a structure which was redesigned after the September

11 disaster to provide extra security through features such as additional concrete escape stairs.* More blocks are to to rise in front of the water linking the Import and Export Docks. From here the symmetrical pattern of the three tall towers of Canada Square becomes clear, rising around the foothill of the lower building between Canada Square and Churchill Place, 2002–3. This houses sports centre, swimming pool and restaurant, with supermarket and shop below. Much effort had been expended to give the rather dumpy form an interesting exterior. The building is by *Chapman Taylor* with *Arup* as structural engineers. The glass envelope is by *Zeidler Grinnel Partnership*, with engineering by *Whitbybird*. The 24-metre high transparent façade to Canada Square makes a show of its complex bracing, with pre-stressed cables restrained by horizontal trusses, in front of an atrium which neatly links the shop to the malls below. Along the sides the walls have delicately fritted panels of opaque-green glass, enlivened by subtly undulating transparent glass fins. From certain angles, changing light gives the building a surprising ethereal quality. The cone-shaped E projection, with curved-glass panels, shelters an unloading bay.

Continuing around Canada Square, No. 20 on the SE corner is a clumsy curtain-walled block with curved corner features, by *SOM*. The third of the tall towers is CITIGROUP, on the S side, matching HSBC in height and building period but not in detail. The tower, with main entrance and a finicky curtain-walled elevation, is by *Cesar Pelli & Associates*, with *Adamson Associates*, 2000–2. The difference between it and HSBC is most apparent at the top, especially when lit up at night: instead of a lightbox, Citigroup has transparent receding storeys. The earlier western part of Citigroup, bolder and more individual, is by *Foster & Partners* 1998–2000. Very large, immaculately neat triple-glazed panels curve round the corner, a more expensive and complicated version of the later HSBC glazing. This contrasts with a sturdily cross-braced atrium on the l., in Foster's more overtly industrial High-Tech tradition, which links to the later tower. In the atrium artwork by *Alexander Beleschenko*.

From the calm of Canada Square and the marble-faced splendours of the ground floor of No. 1, one can descend to the busy and extensive SHOPPING MALLS which continue from Cabot Place, and link up with those below Jubilee Park (*see* below). They are more attractive than the earlier ones, with subtler lighting and some off-centre touches to avoid monotony. The passage to Citigroup is cheered by white-glass walls with abstract splashes of colour, by *Alexander Beleschenko*.

1c. *South Canary Wharf*

On the S side of Canada Square, NASH COURT descends to South Canary Wharf, the latest phase of development since

* Claimed to be the first terrorist-proof tall building in Britain.

1999. It has become the principal public space, confirmed by
119 the position of *Foster & Partners'* UNDERGROUND STATION, which is sunk into part of the former Export Dock and covered by gardens. The most prestigious (if not the most dazzling) among a string of glamorous stations opened in 1999 on the Jubilee Line extension to Stratford. Nevertheless it is a low-key solution that interferes little in the overall townscape and reserves its drama for subterranea. Above ground, entrances through two truncated oval glass bubbles are embanked in the grass slopes of Jubilee Park (cf. Foster's Hangar at the Duxford Aerodrome, Cambridgeshire). A lesser glazed escalator entrance lies E in Montgomery Square, a favoured Foster motif used earlier at Bilbao. Below ground, in keeping with the
p. 109 dominant aesthetic of the Jubilee Line stations, steel and concrete combine to sublime effect. The rectangular envelope, a box created within cofferdams, allows one to descend straight to the concourse level, a broad, long and airy thoroughfare from which immense and widely-spaced elliptical columns soar upwards to bear the swooping *in-situ* concrete roof vaults. Outside the W entrance of the station a sculpture: Tessa Addormenta, a sleeping Neoclassical bronze head by *Igor Mitoraj*, 1983.

JUBILEE PARK, covering the station, is the most inviting and successful of all of Canary Wharf's landscaped public spaces. Designed by the Belgian landscape architects, *Jacques and Pieter Wirtz* in 2000–2, it eschews the formal Beaux-Arts style of the earlier green spaces in favour of an organic layout of mature sequoia trees and two informal raised beds in rough grey-granite blocks with cascading water courses along their tops. These frame a serpentine, undulating lawn and pathway.

Now along BANK STREET, on the park's S side, which is lined by colossal offices completed 2000–3 for law firms, which followed the financial and media institutions drawn to Canary Wharf in the early years. The masterplan for this phase, by *Cesar Pelli Associates*, required building out of the quayside over the old South Dock (*see* perambulation *1d*). Architecturally the fascination lies in seeing the firms who produced the key buildings of the first phase around Cabot Place (*see* above) now moving from historicism and Postmodern-styling to homage to the International Style of the mid-C20.

Beginning from the E end No. 10 UPPER BANK STREET (Clifford Chance) by *Kohn Pedersen Fox* with *Adamson Associates*. Thirty storeys high with a ten-storey pedestal block and linking glazed atrium. Glass with narrowly set vertically extruded steel fins. The tower overlooks MONTGOMERY SQUARE, planted with elm trees, which opens the view E across the water to Greenwich. SCULPTURE of a Centaur. Then W along BANK STREET, a group of three towers by *Cesar Pelli & Associates* with *Adamson Associates*: No. 50 (Northern Trust) a grid of highly polished brown granite clasping and overlaying a taller glazed tower; No. 40 (Allen & Overy) is a taller version of the same and linked to its neighbours by WINTER

GARDENS. The eastern one has a vaulted roof, similar to the Winter Gardens in Manhattan's Battery Park but as English as Paxton. W is a simpler flat-roofed glass box, with a richly inlaid floor of black and white geometric patterns. The last of Pelli's trio, No. 25 (Lehmann Bros.), is a thirty-storey tower with a light steel outer skin of vertical mullions criss-crossed at floor level by horizontal bands increasing in density at the summit. Finally *SOM*'s No. 20: a polished red-granite casing for a glass box with a deep recessed section on the S side for an atrium. Between this and No. 25 is a smaller curtain-walled link block which straddles the DLR with angled tapered legs. Tucked underneath, in a thoroughly cocky manner, is one of the most individual contributions to the Wharf's architecture: HERON QUAYS DLR STATION, a characteristically unorthodox remodelling of the existing station by *Will Alsop*, 2003 and the first on the line to depart from a uniform palette. Encasing the line is a mighty concrete hull, clad in metal scales, which hangs from angled steel columns only just above the ground-floor concourse. Its purpose is practical, to muffle the noise of the trains as they pass through this space, as well as aesthetic. Either side of this stairs and escalators ascend to the platform level, where light-boxes pulsate overhead in ever-changing combinations. On the S side of this group, overlooking South Dock, new landscaping and solid quay walls with obelisk shaped lanterns. From here one may cross S to South Quay (*see* perambulation *1d*) or continue W to Heron Quays (perambulation *2a*).

Beneath South Canary Wharf lies an underground shopping mall, JUBILEE PLACE, by *Building Design Partnership*, with a public entrance through an angular glass opening and underground links to each of the towers. On two levels; on a scale worthy of a small town and providing precisely the commercial infrastructure that the earlier phases of development so visibly lacked. Inset into the floors, square pictorial mosaics depicting dock life and trades.

1d. South Quay to Blackwall

The South Quay of the old South Dock lies outside Canary Wharf but within the area designated as the Enterprise Zone in 1982. In 1996 an IRA bomb-blast caused extensive damage to buildings completed here in the first phase of development but improvements quickly followed. The original dominance of offices gave way to residential blocks in the C21. The area S of Marsh Wall is scheduled for redevelopment as the residential MILLENNIUM QUARTER (masterplan by *EDAW* for Tower Hamlets). In 2004 only isolated elements are under way. The walk ends on the E side of the island at Poplar Dock.

South Quay is best approached on foot from Canary Wharf across the thrilling, magnificent sculptural steel 'S' of a cable-stayed FOOTBRIDGE by *Chris Wilkinson Architects* with *Jan Bobrowski*, engineer, 1994–7. The bridge originally spanned from here to Heron Quays, and was composed of a fixed-half and a movable part, each with its own dramatically inclined mast and cables. The intention was eventually to separate these, once the dock's width had been reduced by the development at South Canary Wharf, and relocate them where each could bridge the water in a single span. To date only one section has been re-used.

From the bridge, the architecture of South Quay appears as a poor cousin to its richer neighbour, with small-scale developments of the mid-1980s Enterprise Zone nudging uncertainly against the high-rise flats of the early C21. Along the quay low, domestic-style office apartments by *Richard Hemingway*, 1985–6, to its r. the medium-rise speculative BEAUFORT COURT and QUAY HOUSE, 1987–8 by *Newman Levinson & Partners*. To the l. DISCOVERY DOCK, two blocks of apartments of 2003–4. The larger Discovery Dock West is a recladding by *EPR* of the former EURO TRADE CENTRE, built in 1988–92. The more pedestrian Discovery Dock East is new-build by *Chantrey Davis Architects*. Two further residential blocks are planned either side of Marsh Wall: No. 1 Millharbour (S) and Arrowhead Quay (N), both by *SOM* and firmly within the International Modern tradition of glazed slabs on pilotis. Buildings more characteristic of 1980s Docklands are E of Discovery Dock. SOUTH QUAY PLAZA, a particularly glum concrete-framed, blue glass-clad block with pedimental gables, originally one of three designed by *Richard Seifert & Partners*, 1986–9, badly damaged in 1996. *Swanke Hayden Connell* refitted the entrance and all common areas while the tallest block was reclad with a lighter touch by *Rolfe Judd*. The third block, a low group of shops with a central covered arcade, is by *Whinney Mackay-Lewis*.

Continuing E of the passage between the West India and the Millwall Docks, THAMES QUAY is perhaps the best building of the 1980s in this part. Designed in 1985 by *YRM* as a company headquarters, something rare at that date in the Enterprise Zone, but finally built speculatively in 1987–9. Crisply anonymous and, despite being specially tailored for its site, somewhat cavalier about the charms of the waterside setting. Three grey-clad blocks, linked in a generous L-shape, step down towards the dock in broad terraces allowing maximum daylight within; between them glass slopes, roofing light wells. Service towers break up the horizontality. But a decent building is let down by its neighbours: THE MANSION (No. 197 Marsh Wall), a pretentious Postmodern block by *Richard Seifert Ltd*, 1988–9, and MERIDIAN GATE, 1987–90 by *SSC Consultants*. Continuing behind is a much better building, the INNOVATION CENTRE (No. 225), 1989–92 by *Feilden & Mawson*, its silvery metal cladding of high quality, its details restrained and thoughtful. Just S on Limeharbour, SKYLINES office village, 1984–6. Planned when the huge spreading dock sheds of the Fred Olsen Line lay to the W and N, it asserted itself by the angular sail-like prisms of the individual blocks and the bright colours. By *Hutchinson Partners, Libby & Co.*, extended in a similar way by *Sidney Kaye Firmin*, 1988–9.

Near the E end of the dockside one can turn S down LAWN HOUSE CLOSE to take in JACK DASH HOUSE, the neighbourhood centre at the corner of Marsh Wall, 1988–91 by *Chassay Architects* (*Tchaik Chassay and Malcolm Last*), one of the few public buildings to be built at this time in Docklands. Though modest in size, it has great presence on its prominent corner site. Commissioned by the LDDC for the Isle of Dogs Neighbourhood Council, one of the several neighbourhood councils into which the administration of Tower Hamlets was devolved until 1994. Local democracy – in the form of the drum-like council chamber – is symbolically separated from the five-storey administrative offices and community hall. There is a clear articulation of smooth and simple geometrical forms that recalls North Italian Postmodernists. The offices have a sinuous roof, glazed attic, and pilotis. On the ground floor of the drum is an exhibition space; the office foyer is screened only by a long curving blue brick wall. The U-shaped group encloses a courtyard, intended to be public; on this side the brick drum is wrapped by a spiralling exterior stair with a contrasting rendered surface.

Close to the junction with PRESTON'S ROAD is the QUEEN OF THE ISLE pub, in the angle between Manchester Road and East Ferry Road, of 1855–6, extended 1875. Neat one-storey pilastered front projecting in a wedge from the three storeys of the rest.

Now across PRESTON'S ROAD and towards the riverside to one of the most spectacular newcomers of the 1980s.

STORM WATER PUMPING STATION, Stewart Street. By *John* 115
Outram, 1987–8. A primitive classical temple, Postmodern in its symbolism, classicism and vivid colour, inside and out, but in no way routine. It is a utilitarian building imbued by the architect with layers of meaning: according to him, it is 'a temple to summer storms' in which the walls represent a blue brick river flowing between tree trunks, and the round hole of the fan which splits the gable is the cave between mountain peaks through which the river issues, falling as blue bricks down the wall. In the paving of the river terrace, columns are represented by discs of red brick; between them the river of paving swirls in waves of dark and light blocks. Practically, the brick chamber conceals a subterranean concrete pumping chamber, tank and control room. The columns carry ducts, and the axial fan in the metal-panelled gables prevents build-up of methane. Gates painted like an Egyptian eye in a battered and curved engineering brick wall.

To the N PIERHEAD LOCK, 1997 by *Goddard Manton Partnership*, a large group of flats whose white surfaces, sleek curves and nautical railings pay homage to the Modernism of the 1930s, but on the scale of the millennium. The stepped-back crescent surrounds a former graving dock. It builds up in height towards a fifteen-storey tower at the S end, echoed by a detached tower to the N.

At this point the riverside walk is interrupted by the entrance to the Dock Basin leading to the South Docks. On the S pierhead, DOCKMASTER'S OFFICES (now British Waterways), single-storey Neo-Georgian, the centre with big hipped roof and pedimented entrance, built 1927–9 when the South Dock entrance was remodelled. Adjacent office of the 1990s, echoing the massing but opening it up rather oddly with balcony and glazed roof apex.

The E ENTRANCE to the SOUTH DOCK is the only remaining working lock in the West India and Millwall Docks. The lock was rebuilt in 1926–9 to serve the whole West India and Millwall system, engineer *Sir Frederick Palmer*, when the South Dock and South Dock entrance basin were united. The lock is vast, the same size as that of the Royal Albert Dock 995 ft (303.24 metres) overall; and 35-ft (10.66 metres) deep. The lock walls and invert are in mass concrete, dressings originally of granite and granite concrete. Repaired 1959–60. Waterborne steel gates. Across it, BLUE BRIDGE (Manchester Road Lift Bridge), a single-span steel drawbridge, 1967–9 by the PLA, the fifth bridge on the site. Along the N quay, three cranes. The area beyond remains largely undeveloped in 2004 apart from a number of technical service buildings.

N of Blue Bridge COLDHARBOUR runs northward close to the riverside, forming a narrow backwater parallel with the E side of Preston's Road. This is the one place on the Isle of Dogs that still has a close-packed riverside character. It is a continuation of the causeway from Blackwall, probably developed from the pathway along the top of the 'Blackwall' protecting the marshes from the Thames. The name goes back to the C14. The hamlet of Blackwall developed around the C17 and C18 shipbuilding concerns clustered round Blackwall Stairs just beyond the bend of the river E of the Isle of Dogs. Apart from Coldharbour, the houses were all swept away when the Blackwall Tunnel was built in 1893 (*see* p. 664).

There were buildings in Coldharbour by the second decade of the C17, but no houses now date from before the early C19. Nos. 29–51, 1889–90, stand on the E end of the South Dock Pierhead. THE GUN (No. 27) may incorporate old fabric (there has been a pub here since the 1710s). Oldest part the N end, single-storey to street, extended by a stucco-trimmed two-storey part, 1875 by *F. Frederick Holsworth*. No. 19–19a is the former BLACKWALL RIVER POLICE STATION of 1893–4 by *John Butler*, Metropolitan Police Architect. Very similar to the Wapping station but simpler. Barge entrance below a banded brick and stone façade with a single gable and two small triangular oriels. Converted to flats with two houses in the yard by *Rothermel Cooke*, 1981–2. No. 15, 1843–5, tall and plain, built by Benjamin Granger Bluett, block and mastmaker. Three residential storeys above a ground-floor workshop (later subdivided) which was the full width of the house and opened to the river. The interior is largely preserved, with good joinery, doors and fireplaces with reeded surrounds on the upper floor. Then Nos. 9–13, CROWN WHARF, in 1971 an isolated effort by *Bernard Lamb* to upgrade the neighbourhood. A tall white-boarded terrace, ground floors open as carports, rooftop terraces with belvedere penthouses and severe river fronts that fit well with the early C19 neighbours. Nos. 5–7, perhaps 1820s, four storeys, minimal. No. 3, NELSON HOUSE, very narrow, is an amalgamation *c.* 1820 of two houses by Samuel Granger, coal merchant and lighterman, who added tall arches round the windows, and two (timber-framed) bows to the river above a veranda. The front doorcase (restored) has part-fluted Doric columns *in antis*. At the N end, ISLE HOUSE (No. 1), a dock-master's residence of 1825–6 by (*Sir*) *John Rennie*. Similar to Bridge House (*see* below) but simpler, and with an unusual plan presumably to command dock entrance and river. The raised ground floor has three rooms along the river-front with bows to the N and the centre room. The entrance hall runs parallel with the street, staircase at the E end. Restored by *Carole A. Gannon* of the *Welling Partnership*, 1995–6.

BRIDGE HOUSE QUAY was the entrance to the BLACKWALL BASIN. The ENTRANCE LOCK, rebuilt to a larger size 1893–4, was dammed under a new bridge as part of the LDDC's improvements to Preston's Road in the 1980s, the middle one of the nearly 40-ft (12 metres) high steel and wrought-iron gates was removed. It was the first to use direct-acting hydraulic rams to the gates: original equipment derelict. As originally built in 1800–1, the BLACKWALL BASIN was a shared entrance basin, oval in shape to facilitate the towing in of ships, with passages to both the West India Import and Export Docks (the passage to the latter filled in 1926–8). It was the first impounded, i.e. non-tidal, entrance dock ever built, with a water-level to match that of the docks, originally with banked not walled sides.

On the N side of the entrance lock, the very handsome BRIDGE HOUSE, 1819–20 by *John Rennie* for the West India Dock Company's Principal Dockmaster or Superintendent. Like a Thames-side villa, its pyramidal roof with flues gathered into an arched, almost Baroque chimneystack. Ground floor raised over a basement with originally blind windows. Bows each end face docks and river; Greek Doric distyle *in antis* portico. C19 external alterations reversed by *Whittam, Cox, Ellis & Clayton*, who radically changed the interior for flats, 1987.

LOVEGROVE WALK crosses what was the Blackwall Basin Graving Dock of 1875–6; it projects SE from the Basin. Now surrounded by unexceptional Wates housing begun 1982 by *Whittam, Cox, Ellis & Clayton*. In the graving dock, LEAP, *c.* 1982, by *Franta Belsky*, a sculptor whose work was popular in the post-war New Towns: eight stylized dolphins spouting water. Just N at Landon's Place, the simple pyramid-roofed shell of a remote ACCUMULATOR TOWER, built in 1877–8 when the 1850–1 hydraulic system was extended (there is another due W inside the curtilage of Billingsgate Market).

POPLAR DOCK, W of the N end of Preston's Road, is protected by a wall of 1828–9, raised 1850. The wall dates from the reservoirs developed by the West India Dock Co., which were converted to a timber pond in 1844. The pond was developed into London's first railway dock, built for coal and goods export traffic in 1850–1 by the Birmingham Junction (later North London) Railway Co. A second, W basin (partly infilled 1988–9) was added in 1875–7 to provide depots for other railway companies.

The dock still has its timber WHARF WALLING, very old-fashioned for its date. On the W quay two *Stothert & Pitt* travelling CRANES in front of apartments of *c.* 2002 by *RMA Architects*, cul-de-sacs of mixed heights, four to seven storeys, differentiated from offices by an enterprising mixture of textures: cladding of timber, red and yellow brick and coloured render. At the dock's NE corner, pierced-metal FIGUREHEAD by *Anna Bissett*, 1997. On Cartier Circle, VOLTE FACE by *Alex MacGregor & Richard Clark*, 1994.

Nothing remains of the railway works. On the E side of Preston's Road a former HYDRAULIC PUMPING STATION squeezed between Duthie Street and Blackwall Way, almost the only relic of the area redeveloped in the 1880s by the Midland Railway Company with branch lines to serve a new coal dock at Blackwall Yard. Of 1881–2 by *John Underwood*, Midland Railway engineer, in the characteristic house style, see the brick corbelling and cast-iron tracery of the squat accumulator tower. Amongst the confusions of the road engineering to the N, created to provide traffic access to Canary Wharf, a pedestrian route leads to Blackwall DLR.

2. *Millwall Docks and Isle of Dogs South*

2a. *Heron Quays to the Millwall Docks*

This perambulation looks at the northern part of Millwall, the residential developments along the riverside, public housing and development around the Millwall Docks.

HERON QUAYS, W of Heron Quays station at the W end of the South Dock, is the most imaginative piece of architecture from the first phase of the LDDC. By *Nicholas Lacey, Jobst & Hyett*, 1981–9. Mixed development of deep-red and purple units, of up to three storeys and with a variety of roof pitches and angles, composed like a waterside village round leafy courts and projecting over the dock wall on to steel piers. (A single block over the Export Dock has been demolished.) A further five stages were originally planned for the area now occupied by the looming towers of South Canary Wharf (*see* above). The building out of the deck for the new blocks has spoiled the opportunity for long views E along South Dock but instead created a separate pool for Heron Quays. Rising from the water, a steel SCULPTURE (Spirit of Enterprise) by *Wendy Taylor*. Interlinked shapes based on the outline of the Isle of Dogs.

On the roundabout at the entrance from WESTFERRY ROAD, TRAFFIC LIGHT TREE, 1997, by *Pierre Vivant*. Immediately S, in the angle between Westferry Road and Marsh Wall, a red brick former IMPOUNDING STATION, built by the PLA in 1926–8 when they dammed the South Dock's W entrance. From here one can walk to the river and continue along the Thames Walk, crossing the former entrance passage to the dock. Part of the original LOCK CHAMBER survives. By *William Jessop* 1803–5, when this was the W entrance to the City Canal: three-centred brick invert, and sides faced with stone ashlar.

On its S side, CASCADES, another of early Docklands' most memorable landmarks, by *CZWG* for Kentish Homes, 1985–8. A surprising use of residential high-rise in a period that generally eschewed it and shocking when first completed. Cascades conveyed a sense of fun then lacking in Docklands except in this firm's work. Its dramatic silhouette and delightful details wear well. A narrow twenty-storey slab of concertina form, banded in yellow and blue brick. To the S the cascade of terraces and conservatories, bisected by a glazed slope of fire escape, that gives the block its name. Lots of entertaining nautical references culminating in the N prows with their clever little crow's-nest balconies, sculptural in the upward view. Alongside the entrance from Westferry Road, a restrained six-storey block including shops. Next ANCHORAGE POINT by *Michael Squire Associates*, 1988–90; it has none of Cascades' daring. Ten-storey crisply articulated block by the water, white rendered behind an outer skin of yellow brick, forming balconies, and emerging at the top in a series of barrel-vaulted penthouses. At ground level a double-height arcade and bold blue post-and-lintel portals. 116

In the shadow of these major developments are a few old fragments of northern Millwall, strongly evoked in the street names, Cuba, Tobago, Manilla. These were the first streets to be developed in 1807, just after the West India Dock had opened. Millwall's principal industry is remembered in the tired BLACKSMITH'S ARMS on Westferry Road. S, at the corner with CUBA STREET, THE ANCHOR AND HOPE, early C19 with later green-tiled facing. Further down the street, beyond industrial relics, No. 1, built in 1900–1 as the short-lived Millwall Working Men's Club and Institute; a plain brick building, by *William Bradford* for Stansfeld & Co. of the Swan brewery, Fulham. The upper floor had a concert hall to seat 500. In use as a warehouse by 1906. Perhaps the most surprising survival is Nos. 15–19, a short terrace of mid-C19 workers' houses.

Back now to the W side of WESTFERRY ROAD which was laid

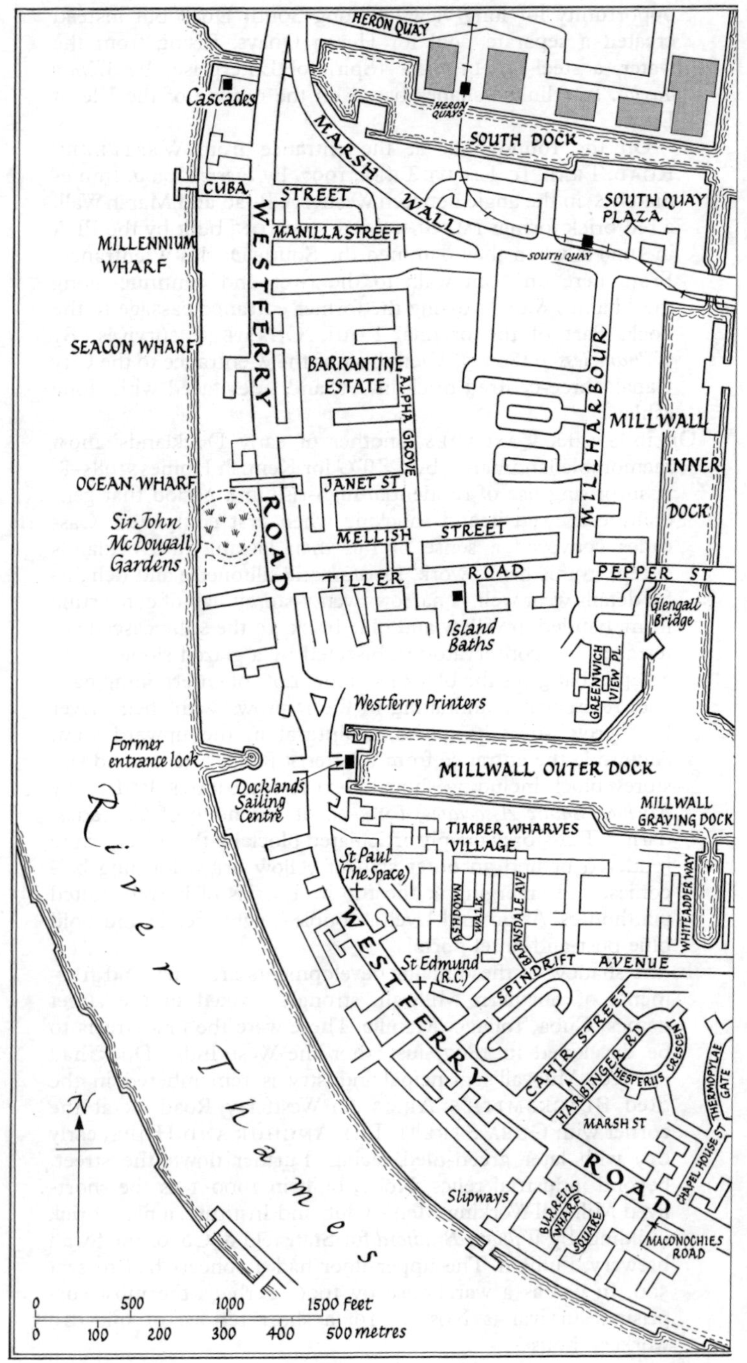
HERON QUAY
HERON QUAYS
Cascades
MARSH WALL
SOUTH DOCK
CUBA
STREET
SOUTH QUAY PLAZA
MILLENNIUM WHARF
MANILLA STREET
SOUTH QUAY
WESTFERRY ROAD
SEACON WHARF
BARKANTINE ESTATE
ALPHA GROVE
MILLHARBOUR
MILLWALL INNER DOCK
OCEAN WHARF
JANET ST
Sir John McDougall Gardens
MELLISH STREET
TILLER ROAD
PEPPER ST
Glengall Bridge
Island Baths
GREENWICH VIEW PL.
Westferry Printers
Former entrance lock
MILLWALL OUTER DOCK
Docklands Sailing Centre
MILLWALL GRAVING DOCK
TIMBER WHARVES VILLAGE
St Paul (The Space)
ASHDOWN WALK
BARNSDALE AVE
WHITEADDER WAY
St Edmund (R.C.)
SPINDRIFT AVENUE
River Thames
WESTFERRY ROAD
CAHIR STREET
HARBINGER RD
HESPERUS CRESCENT
THERMOPYLAE GATE
MARSH ST
CHAPEL HOUSE ST
Slipways
BURRELLS WHARF SQUARE
MACONOCHIES ROAD
N
0 500 1000 1500 Feet
0 100 200 300 400 500 metres

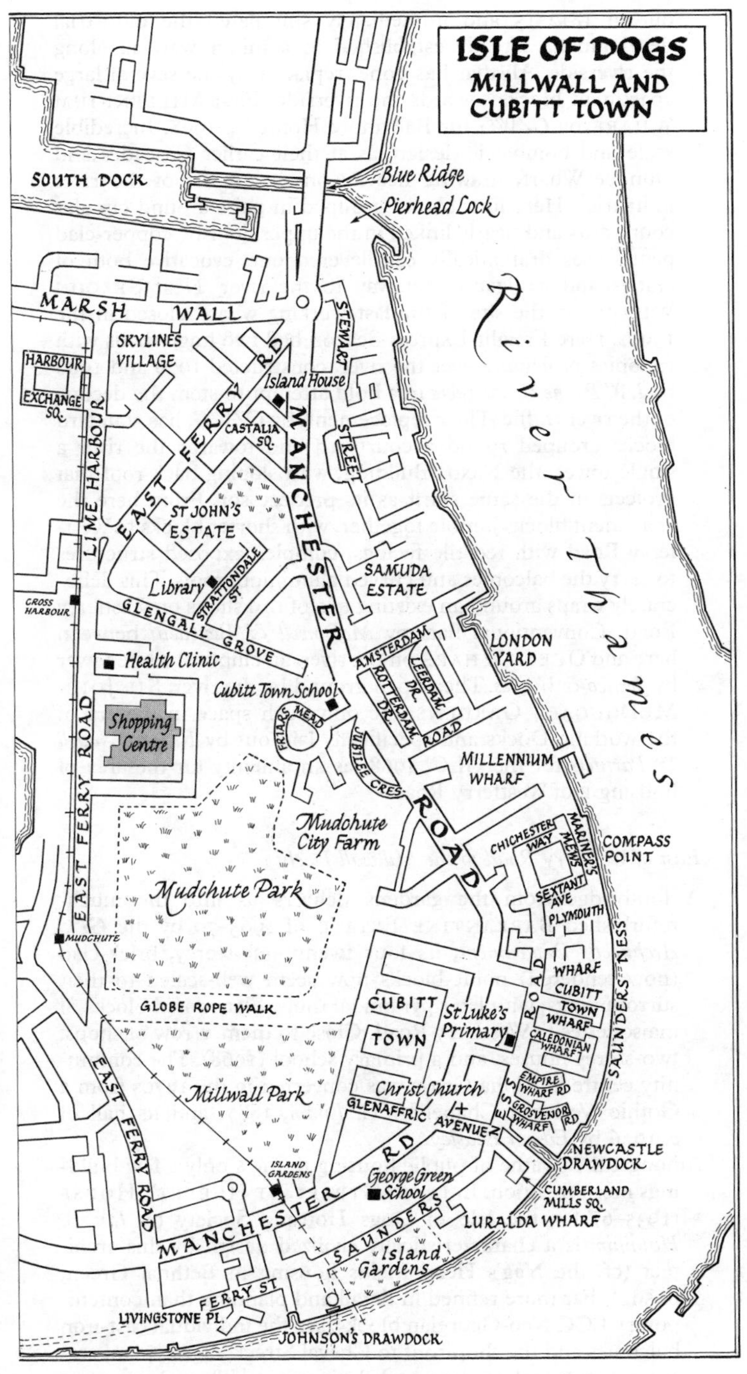
ISLE OF DOGS
MILLWALL AND CUBITT TOWN
SOUTH DOCK
Blue Ridge
Pierhead Lock
River Thames
MARSH WALL
SKYLINES VILLAGE
HARBOUR EXCHANGE SQ.
EAST FERRY RD
Island House
STEWART STREET
CASTALIA SQ.
MANCHESTER ROAD
LIME HARBOUR
ST JOHN'S ESTATE
SAMUDA ESTATE
Library
STRATTONDALE ST
CROSS HARBOUR
GLENGALL GROVE
LONDON YARD
Health Clinic
AMSTERDAM ROAD
LEERDAM DR.
ROTTERDAM DR.
Cubitt Town School
FRIARS MEAD
JUBILEE CRES
Shopping Centre
MILLENNIUM WHARF
EAST FERRY ROAD
Mudchute City Farm
CHICHESTER WAY
MARINER'S MEWS
COMPASS POINT
Mudchute Park
SEXTANT AVE
PLYMOUTH WHARF
MUDCHUTE
CUBITT TOWN WHARF
SAUNDERS NESS ROAD
GLOBE ROPE WALK
CUBITT TOWN
St Luke's Primary
CALEDONIAN WHARF
EMPIRE WHARF RD
Millwall Park
Christ Church
GLENAFFRIC AVENUE
GROSVENOR WHARF RD
NEWCASTLE DRAWDOCK
ISLAND GARDENS
George Green School
CUMBERLAND MILLS SQ.
LURALDA WHARF
MANCHESTER RD
SAUNDERS NESS RD
Island Gardens
FERRY ST
LIVINGSTONE PL.
JOHNSON'S DRAWDOCK

out in 1812–15 and immediately stimulated the industrial development, already established in a minor way, all along the riverside. All that has gone, replaced by the several large apartment blocks towards the riverside. First MILLENNIUM WHARF by *CZWG* for Ballymore Homes *c.* 1998. Incredible scale and bombastic design, as at their earlier Cascades and Dundee Wharf, drawing heavily on the motifs of the river industries. Here four blocks grouped in pairs around circular courtyards and nearly linked in the upper floor by copper-clad penthouses dramatically cantilevered out, evocative both of cranes and a gigantic gateway to the river. Next SEACON WHARF, on the site of the last working wharf, closed in the 1990s. Here Freight-Express-Seacon had two huge sheds with canopies projecting over the river, constructed 1976 and 1986 by *I. W. Payne & Partners* in a bold attempt to stem the decline of the river traffic. Their replacement, by *CZWG*, has standard blocks grouped round a courtyard and towards the river a single tower, the Naxos Building, with sloping back roof that projects in the same spirit as its predecessor. From here the apartment blocks jumble together, with shorter blocks to Westferry Road with red tile facings, complex exposed structures to carry the balconies and curved aluminium roofs. This deliberately wraps around an existing trio of C19 shops on Westferry Road. Conventional flats by *McDowell & Benedetti* between here and OCEAN WHARF on the river, an elliptical white tower by *Jestico & Whiles*. Then open ground by the river, SIR JOHN MCDOUGALL GARDENS, the only such space in the era of the working Docks and specifically laid out by *Richard Sudell & Partners* for the GLC, 1968, as an amenity for the area of housing E of Westferry Road.

East of Westferry Road to the Millwall Docks

A footbridge from the gardens delivers us into the much-refurbished BARKANTINE ESTATE of 1965–70 by the *GLC Architect's Department*; its four twenty-one-storey, brick-clad (now rendered) point blocks now seem well-scaled to their surroundings, with later pyramidal roofs. Flat-roofed blocks of maisonettes to Westferry Road. Close to them, a row of shops, two-storey houses, and a primary school (1968). The community centre in Alpha Grove was converted in the 1970s from a Gothic Wesleyan Chapel by *G. Limm*, 1887, and its hall of *c.* 1926 by *Edwin Beasley*.

Amongst the swathe of public housing to the S only a few buildings merit mention. In JANET STREET, ST HUBERT'S HOUSE (1935–6) for the Isle of Dogs Housing Society by *Ian B. Hamilton* is a characteristically civilized design by this architect (cf. the Nag's Head Fields housing in Bethnal Green, p. 592). Far more refined in detail and planning than contemporary LCC Neo-Georgian blocks: see the individual cast-iron balconies and the shopfront to Cheval Street. Zigzag plan, creating communal gardens and drying areas. These have posts with St Hubert's stags, probably in Doulton's Polychrome Stoneware by *Gilbert Bayes* (cf. St Pancras Housing Society estates where Hamilton also worked). Mid- to late 1970s modernization by *Max Lock & Co.* has rather spoilt Hamilton's composition. S of the W end of MELLISH STREET are beautifully planted MEMORIAL GARDENS, opened 2001. Two sunken circular lawns with surrounding pergola walks.

In TILLER ROAD to the S: cottage-style Poplar Borough Council housing next to taller Neo-Georgian flats of 1926–7. By *Harley Heckford*, Borough Architect. Next door, Nos. 23–5 set at right angles to the street, are the last remaining of many Orlit houses built in Millwall by the *Ministry of Works* in 1945–6, using a prefabricated system of concrete pier-and-panel construction. Further E, on the S side, ISLAND BATHS of 1963–6 by *Adams, Holden & Pearson*, who designed some of the Isle of Dogs' council housing. Brown brick walls, copper roof. Foyer whale MURAL by *Will Adams*, 1991. On the N side, at the far end of the street HAMMOND HOUSE, 1937–8 by *Rees J. Williams*, one of the best examples of the Borough Council's late 1930s streamlined housing.

At the E end of Tiller Road a narrow gateway leads into Millharbour and continues along PEPPER STREET towards Glengall Bridge, conceived as a narrow pedestrian bridge across Millwall Inner Dock lined with shops, flats and offices. The architecture, by *Richard Seifert & Partners*, 1987–91 is dismal. Brownish-red brick elevations with green-tinted windows throughout. Oversized office blocks round gloomy, uninviting courts with underground parking, an arcaded quadrant of offices and rows of shops sheltering behind concrete arcades. Spanning the dock, a Dutch-style double drawbridge built out on jetties flanked by asymmetrical groups of small apartments.

The L-shaped MILLWALL DOCKS were opened in 1863–9. The contractors were *John Kelk* (builder of the 1862 Exhibition and the Albert Memorial) and *John Aird & Son. William Wilson*'s original plan, refined by *(Sir) John Fowler*, was reduced in execution from an inverted 'T': never very successful financially, it was linked at its N end to the West India Docks in 1924. The view N from the bridge shows the area around Millwall Inner Dock is in transition in 2004. On the W side, backing to MILLHARBOUR, high-rise flats keen to colonize the waterfront, e.g. No. 42 by *Chantrey Davis Architects*, are replacing small-scale business parks associated with the 1980s Enterprise Zone. Similar plans were envisaged in 2004 for the E side, replacing the LONDON ARENA. This had been converted in 1985–9 by *Stewart K. Riddick & Partners* from a former dock building, Fred Olsen's shed No. 2 of 1969, designed by PLA architects. N of this a row of *Stothert & Pitt* cranes is barred from the water by Harbour Island, an ill-conceived moored paddle-steamer of a building resting on piles over the dock. By *Haverstock Associates*, conceived as part of the HARBOUR EXCHANGE development of 1986–90, which commandeers the NE corner of the Inner Dock.* Mostly by *Frederick Gibberd Coombes & Partners*, facing inwards towards the well-landscaped Exchange Square. Nos. 3–5 Limeharbour, by *Sheppard Robson*, has a curved multi-storey wall of blue reflective glass following the line of the DLR.

E of the Dock, the walk concludes at CROSSHARBOUR DLR but a detour S from Glengall Bridge can take in the Millwall Outer Dock. The view S as far as the low-rise housing all along the S side is dispiriting. Along the W side, S of the bridge, salvaged *Stothert & Pitt* cranes stand in front of GREENWICH VIEW of 1985–8 by *Richard Seifert & Partners*. Mirror-glazed with sliced-off round towers. Then the desperately overweening City Reach (1988–9), two tall tinted-glass office slabs linked by a lower gabled atrium at the angle of the dock, and Pointe North (1988–90) projecting into the water on a platform. Equally awful, the CITY HARBOUR development, by *BDP* and *Holford Associates*, 1987–90, on the Dock's E side. In two parts: one part yellow brick, the other parts clad in grey panels. Along the N side of the Outer Dock is WEST FERRY PRINTERS, designed as the *Daily Telegraph* printing works by *Watkins Gray Wilkinson Associates*, 1984–6. Extension 1988–9 for printing *Express* newspapers and from 1995 also the *Financial Times*, in retreat from their far superior building in Blackwall (*see* above). In form a massive press hall, spanned by huge trussed-steel girders, surrounded by multi-storey offices. A glass-roofed 'street' links a smaller, lower section. At the far end of the Dock, making an effective *point-de-vue*, is the DOCKLANDS SAILING CENTRE, 1987–9 by *Kit Allsopp Architects*, who won a limited LDDC competition. The roof is the governing feature, shallow-pitched and extending far on the l. to cover the entrance in a way characteristic of this architect. It is carried on exposed trusses set on concrete columns, the glazed front wall being set back; the effect is of a kind of rustic Tuscan portico. Beyond, W of Westferry Road, the ENTRANCE LOCK was filled in by the LDDC in 1990 as far as the outer gate recesses, leaving a slipway to the river. S pier head landscaped, with housing by *Jestico & Whiles*, and a hydraulic jigger of *c.* 1875 which worked the gates now mounted on display. Some early BOLLARDS survive here too. From here one can retrace one's steps N along Westferry Road.

2b. South West from Island Gardens Station

ISLAND GARDENS STATION, by *W.S. Atkins Consultants*, 2000, rebuilt when the DLR was extended S of the river, presents a

*It replaced the rest of Fred Olsen's No. 2 shed and the famous Fred Olsen Centre, 1966–9, which contributed to establishing the reputation of *Norman Foster* as a master of High-Tech. His intervention at Olsen's was especially important for its early use of mirror glass, specially made in Pittsburgh, for the walling of the office and amenity block slotted between two of the transit sheds.

symmetrical front to the S; an open foyer spanned by a big blue bowed roof; two ventilation towers for the tunnel rise above, with curved tops, and platform canopies form an inverted bow beyond. From the station, FERRY STREET leads S to JOHNSON'S DRAWDOCK, a well-designed slipway for small craft that opens a window on to Greenwich opposite. By *LDC Ltd* for the LDDC, 1989. Alongside it at Nos. 50–6 Ferry Street, DR BARRACLOUGH'S HOUSES, a highly individual group, the result of a special commission, unusual in Docklands, given in 1975 to *Stout & Litchfield* by a local doctor, Michael Barraclough. An emphasis on natural materials (white brick, Westmorland-slate roofs, grey-stained casements, lead details) and Expressionist forms (a series of peaked roofs, random elevations, upper storeys cantilevered out in sections). The fronts, which command a view of Greenwich Hospital, cannot be seen from anywhere but the river. The rear is hidden by a C19 wall and long gardens along Ferry Street; at the W corner a C19 building is incorporated, a survivor from a paint factory formerly on the site. Timber salvaged from the demolished North Stacks of London Docks predominates in the multi-level interior of Dr Barraclough's own house (N). To the W facing a riverside walk, MIDLAND PLACE and LIVINGSTONE PLACE: simple and nicely consistent housing by *Levitt Bernstein* for Circle 33 Housing Association, 1979–83, i.e. pre-LDDC. A restricted palette of buff brick, blue brick strings and pale-green profiled metal roofs. V-shaped layout: two-storey rows by the river walk, rising to three-storey houses with flats at each end behind. Bay windows, also set on the diagonal, under far-projecting roofs, open on to tiny individual gardens. After this, unexceptional housing continues along the riverside and along Ferry Street. Here the irregular two-storey stuccoed FERRY HOUSE pub looks late C19 but may partly date back to 1748–9, when a Ferry House stood alone on this shore by the Greenwich ferry. To the N, where EAST and WESTFERRY ROADS join, another pub, the LORD NELSON, 1855, a more urban type, three storeys with curved corner, a western outlier of Cubitt Town (*see* below). Opposite to the W, an LCC FIRE STATION, 1904–5. Queen Anne style, with big chimneys, central swan-neck pediment and pedimented dormers. Firemen's cottages N of the courtyard.

MACONOCHIE'S WHARF, off Westferry Road at Maconochie's Road, is rare in Docklands as a self-build scheme for local people, initiated by Jill Palios and Dr Michael Barraclough, and as for Dr Barraclough's own house, by *Stout & Litchfield*. Built in three phases, 1985–90, continuing the cottage tradition of early garden suburbs. Picturesque but forceful. Many of the early self-builders, who formed the Great Eastern Self-Build Housing Association, were involved in the building trade so the construction is traditional. Simple terraces step from two to three storeys under catslides and gables, each house slightly varied. Bay windows with slated roofs or sturdy cross-braced timber balconies. Taller houses to the river. The first houses (E) are of white calcium-silicate brick, the later ones (W, 1987–90) of yellow brick. Good landscaping by *Livingston McIntosh Associates*, continuing along the riverside promenade.

BURRELL'S WHARF has considerable remains of INDUSTRIAL BUILDINGS of great historical interest*, incorporated as part of a housing development begun in 1987. This started as one of Kentish Homes' imaginative projects (cf. Cascades), but was completed after they went bankrupt in 1989 by other developers. Approaching from the riverside walk one first sees the new blocks of flats, designed with an industrial toughness by *Jestico & Whiles*. Their monumental CHART HOUSE and DECK HOUSE respectfully frame the C19 PLATE HOUSE, leaving it with a view of the river across BURRELLS WHARF SQUARE, a space formerly occupied by yard and slipways. The new flats are concrete-panel clad with an ochre tint, with massive details such as the broad torus round the base. The roof line builds up from six to nine storeys plus a penthouse.

This part of the site was first laid out in 1836–7 and occupied by *(Sir) William Fairbairn*'s Millwall Ironworks, one of the country's first large iron ship-building yards. In 1853 John Scott Russell & Co. leased the adjoining Napier Yard to the W for the building and sideways launching of the *Great Eastern*, *I.K. Brunel*'s gigantic steamship built in 1854–9 to carry 4,000 passengers on the busy India route. The venture bankrupted Scott Russell and from *c.* 1859, C.J. Mare & Co. occupied the works, which included land N of Westferry Road, until 1862. Iron shipbuilding at the Millwall Ironworks more or less ceased in 1866 after the difficult and expensive launch of HMS *Northumberland* closed the works and started the decline in Thames-side ship building, which finally ended in 1912. Burrell & Co., colour, paint, and varnish manufacturers, bought the original part of the site *c.* 1888.

The truncated octagonal CHIMNEY SHAFT, with arcaded octagonal base, dates from Fairbairn's time, and drew smoke through underground ducts from all the furnaces and forges. At the centre is Scott Russell's PLATE HOUSE, built 1853–4 by *W. Cubitt & Co.*, now converted to flats with ground-floor car park and swimming pool. So-called because it was thought to have been the place where the iron plates for the *Great Eastern* were prepared, but its exceptional size and surviving internal features suggest it was specially built, with overhead travelling cranes, for assembling the *Great Eastern*'s 40-ft high paddle engines, the largest ever built. It is London's only surviving former marine engine works, and retains its large engineering workshop windows. S tower with tall round-arched windows within keyed giant arches, a line of circular windows above. The tower probably had offices for the mechanical engineers; the adjacent stair-tower, topped by a rebuilt campanile, provided access.

*We are grateful to Tom Ridge for details on these.

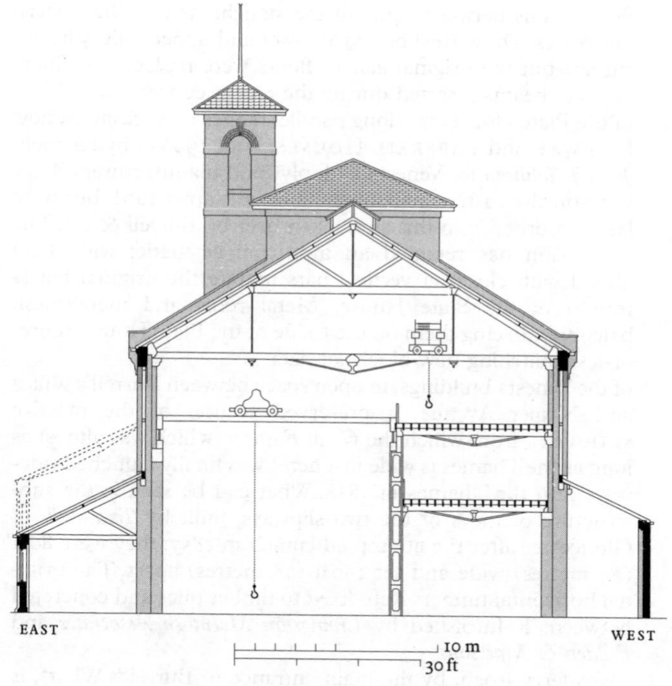

Plate House, Burrells Wharf, Isle of Dogs. Section, showing original form of galleried workshop

The 60-ft-high former Hall now contains flats between the original roof trusses and on inserted floors spanning the full width of the building. This still contains its line of seven stepped cast-iron gantry/gallery stanchions and internal brick buttresses with padstones and corbels. The western buttresses and the western sides of the stanchions carried galleries for machine shops whilst the padstone-capped lower stages of the eastern buttresses carries a 130-ft-long gantry beam, and the eastern 'steps' on the stanchions carried a similar beam. Spanning between and running on rails on the beams were one or more overhead travellers for craning marine engine components into position. Components were machined in the AISLES with lean-to roofs and on the galleries. To crane components from the galleries to the main assembly floor there may well have been a number of overhead travellers running across the width of the building, on rails on the roof truss tie beams. The seven unusual double-timber-beamed roof trusses (with cast-iron fittings and wrought-iron rods) survive. An attic floor on the upper faces of the tie-beams was probably inserted by Burrells at the same time that they removed the overhead travellers and 130 ft long gantry beams. By 1927 Burrells had inserted steel floor beams between some of the stanchions and the eastern buttresses. These steel beams at lower and upper gallery height survive but the original gallery floors were replaced by floors on steel beams inserted during the recent conversion.

W of the Plate House, two long parallel ranges of workshops, now SLIPWAY and TAFFRAIL HOUSES, built 1906–7 by engineer *John J. Johnson* for Venesta Ltd, plywood manufacturers. They were on the eastern part of the former Napier Yard, but were later absorbed into this site, taken over by Burrell & Co. The conversion has retained an industrial aesthetic: wide bays glazed with close-set vertical bars imitate the original fenestration of the Plate House. Metal roofs and metal-mesh balconies. Facing them on the E side of the Plate House, more-or-less matching new blocks of flats.

W of the Venesta buildings, in open space between Burrell's Wharf and Napier Avenue, a preserved section of the massive SLIPWAYS from which the *Great Eastern* (which was almost as long as the Thames is wide just here) was finally launched sideways into the Thames in 1858. What can be seen is the substructure of the S of the two slipways, built by *Treadwells* of Gloucester after the attempted launch in 1857: they were 80 ft (24 metres) wide and set 160 ft (48 metres) apart. The original horizontal timbers were fixed to timber piles and concreted between. Refurbished by *Livingston McIntosh Associates* and *Feilden & Mawson*.

On Westferry Road, by the main entrance to Burrell's Wharf, is the 1854 former COUNTING HOUSE (Nos. 264–6), with its original Scott Russell & Co. stucco name panel, and an adjoining house (No. 268) of the 1850s. Opposite, but further W, is another rare survival, C.J. Mare & Co.'s 1860 single-storey twin-roofed former FORGE; six recessed panels under keyed round arches, cast-iron date and name plate. The steam-hammer forge was probably designed by *William Henry Dorman* and Mare's resident ironmaster *John Hughes*. The valley roof is carried on a central colonnade of cast-iron columns and cast-iron beams with integral gutters. The rain-water thus collected was probably used for a boiler serving a steam blowing engine providing high pressure air for the furnaces. The six steam-hammers forged parts for the armour-plated warship HMS *Northumberland*, launched 1866. Later the building was used by Westwoods for girder manufacture: two travelling-crane gantries were inserted; the eastern one of the early 1890s has an overhead travelling gantry with early C20 electric overhead traveller; in the western hall is an early C20 suspended gantry. The building is London's only surviving example of a former iron ship builder's forge and former girder fabrication workshop.

Off Westferry Road there are still a couple of streets which were squeezed between industrial sites to accommodate local workers. HARBINGER ROAD and CAHIR STREET have straight rows of yellow and red brick flat-fronted artisan cottages of 1902–4, their front doors opening straight onto the street. HARBINGER PRIMARY SCHOOL, 1872–3, is a rare early Board School design by *R. Phené Spiers*, Master of Architecture at the Royal Academy schools, who won a limited competition at a time when Board School design was still evolving. A three-decker, with Gothic details to the top floor. The main front facing Marsh Street has an attractive plaque in coloured tiles. The building followed Robson's principles in segregating girls, boys and infants, but had an unusual plan, with entrances and staircases in a wing projecting S; demolished when the school was remodelled in 1906–8. Schoolkeeper's house 1909.

This tour turns inland up Harbinger Street but first a detour can be made up WESTFERRY ROAD, which continues towards the entrance to the Millwall Dock (*see* above) to see two churches.

ST EDMUND (R.C.), close to the edge of the C20 Timber Wharves village (*see* below). 1999–2000 by *David Aitken*, replacing a church of 1873–4 by *F.W. Tasker*. Undistinguished but on a friendly scale. Yellow and red brick exterior with pitched roofs, narrow windows with opaque glass in patterned leading. Inside, the walls of the church are banded in black brick. The triangular sanctuary is echoed by an angular weekday chapel opening off the entrance foyer. A large hall with glazed screen can be opened up to the church. Main altar and weekday altar are made from the marble altar of the old church. Font, sculptures and hanging crucifixion (on a new cross) from the same source. The best features are the STATIONS OF THE CROSS, in the manner of Eric Gill, small, richly coloured paintings on cork, 1956 by *Sister W.W.* of Stanbrook Abbey.

R.C. SCHOOLS nearby, a tall red brick three-decker of 1908–9 by *Robert L. Curtis*, extended 1928–9 and a low later C20 addition.

THE SPACE, built as ST PAUL PRESBYTERIAN CHURCH IN 41
ENGLAND. 1859 by *T.E. Knightley*. Saved from dereliction and fitted-out discreetly as a performance space cum film theatre 1993–6 by *Janet Collings* and *Bevis Claxton* of *Claxton d'Auvergne Collings*. Italian Romanesque front, a miniature, polychrome interpretation of the W front of Pisa Cathedral, with three tiers of stone arcading and red, yellow and dark-blue brick. The clerestory is clad with fishscale slates. Big SE door left over from a former use in a crane-maintenance shop. Vestry and classrooms (now bar etc.) behind, with Venetian window: 1906 by *T. Phillips Figgis*. Art Nouveau-style railings and overthrow, 1993–6.

The plan is not basilican, as it appears outside, but a single clerestory-lit space with small sanctuary of 1906. Open timber roof with three semicircular ribs of laminated timber below the clerestory carrying an upper truss. Known as a monitor roof and unusual in church building at this date; laminated ribs were more commonly used then for large spans in textile mills and public buildings (e.g. Leeds Town Hall, 1853–8). Later wrought-iron tie-rods. Windows with cast-iron tracery and Art Nouveau-inspired GLASS engraved with the building history.

(For the successor to this church see Island House, Castalia Square, p. 705). The church stood close to a pocket of cottages built in the mid-C19 for shipworkers, including Scots who had flocked to work on the *Great Eastern*.

Turning N up HARBINGER ROAD the route takes in two groups of council housing built on land which remained undeveloped until the C20. Here the Poplar Borough Council's work is in marked contrast to the neighbouring terraces. HESPERUS CRESCENT, together with the N end of Harbinger Road, describes a circle of cottages and cottage flats with tight cul-de-sacs opening from it; 1929–30 by *Harley Heckford*, Borough Engineer. Simple cottage vocabulary in long terraces behind front gardens, whose walls of ceramic waste and brick rubble contribute a certain rusticity. Linked by footpath to the E is the CHAPEL HOUSE ESTATE. The name comes from a long-vanished house and chapel of medieval origin, which stood near Millwall Docks. The estate dates from 1919–21, the first public housing promoted by the borough as part of the government's post-war drive to provide 'Homes for Heroes'. This more sophisticated garden-suburb essay was also laid out by *Harley Heckford*, with houses built by *H.M. Office of Works* to designs by their Chief Architect, *Sir Frank Baines*. The whole has the variety seen at Baines's pioneering Eltham Well Hall Estate, but adopts not a vernacular style, but the manner of early C19 London houses (cf. the contemporary Duchy of Cornwall estate, Kennington). Stock brick terraces and four-in-block cottage flats. THERMOPYLAE GATE (named liked Macquarie Way after clippers on the Australian route) has blocks of three-storey flats with mansards, round a square, unusual for such a scheme. The corner terraces of four houses set at an angle have straight parapets with sunk panels. Other houses have single round windows in the upper storey over bracketed hoods, or shell tympana over groups of three windows. The subtleties and fine proportions deserve protection from creeping 'improvement'; fortunately, the estate is now a conservation area. The N end of Thermopylae Gate leads to Mudchute Station.

2c. *The centre of the Isle of Dogs; two excursions from Mudchute DLR*

MUDCHUTE DLR station, 2000 by *W.S. Atkins Consultants,* is minimal as befits its semi-rustic setting, submerged into the landscape. Each platform has a pair of curved shelters on raking struts.

The area S of Millwall Dock was developed for housing from the 1980s. NW from Mudchute station is CLIPPERS QUAY, built round the former MILLWALL GRAVING DOCK, flooded as a barge berth in 1968. It was one of the largest dry docks on the Thames when made in 1865–8, founded on a series of inverted brick arches resting on concrete. The nine 'altars' or steps for the wooden supports for steadying a ship are now covered by walkways to moorings, and a high-arched, laminated-timber bridge spans the dock entrance. This long, narrow slot of water makes an attractive setting for dull two- to three-storey houses of 1984–8 by *Robert Martin & Associates*. White-rendered blocks with pyramidal roofs emphasize the dock entrance. From here, a broad quayside walk leads N along the Millwall Dock to a grassed amphitheatre which terminates the E end of the dock and links it with parkland E of East Ferry Road. By *LDC Ltd* for the LDDC, 1992. As a landmark here, a lone tall CHIMNEY, the romantic relic of the unromantic refuse incinerator built here in 1952 by *Heenan and Froude*, engineers. Also, an *objet-trouvé* sculpture, a PUMP of 1924 salvaged from pneumatic grain-handling equipment in front of the flour mills at the Royal Victoria Dock. From here the view down the dock is stopped effectively at the W end by the spreading roof of the Docklands Sailing Centre (*see* perambulation *2a*).

W of the graving dock is the much larger housing area of TIMBER WHARVES VILLAGE, 1987–92, built over the many acres previously used for the stacking of timber. One of the most extensive housing schemes in Docklands, built speculatively and acquired by the LDDC primarily to rehouse those displaced by the building of the Limehouse Link (*see* Limehouse). Its main feature is ASHDOWN WALK, on axis with Millwall Dock, which ends with a six- to seven-storey curved S block with punched-out windows and tall central arch, the sort of monumental gesture beloved by the Italian Rationalists and their post-war imitators. The rest consists of nearly five hundred houses and flats on a relentless urban grid of streets and N–S walks without shops or landmarks. Crisp but rather forbidding small-windowed blocks by *Barnard Urquhart Jarvis*. In Barnsdale Avenue at the corner of SPINDRIFT AVENUE, DOCKLANDS MEDICAL CENTRE by *Jefferson Sheard*, 1990–2, a white-rendered front with bowed centrepiece. Spindrift Avenue, skirting the new housing to its N, takes one back to Mudchute.

Mudchute to Island Gardens DLR

The excursion E from Mudchute station is the closest one gets to a rural walk in the Isle of Dogs. From 1875–1910 part of the area was used for dumping mud dredged from the Millwall Docks through a pneumatic pipe, creating a notoriously messy and uneven surface. Nearby, the Millwall Football Club had their grounds from 1889, until they moved to New Cross in 1910. The present broad expanse of MUDCHUTE PARK was mainly created post-war from derelict land, and relandscaped by the LDDC post-1981. Through it, the GLOBE ROPEWALK, on the site of a late C19 rope works, forms an important formal link between the docks, housing, shopping centre near Crossharbour of 1981–3 and the park with Mudchute City Farm.

MUDCHUTE CITY FARM, N of the Ropewalk, was created in 1977 on a landscape of low mounds used as gun emplacements in the Second World War. The pillboxes have been adapted for livestock. FARMHOUSE on Pier Street by *Kate Heron*. STABLES by *Kit Allsopp Architects*. Landscaping and trellised entrances by the LDDC, 1985–6.

MILLWALL PARK, S of Mudchute Park close to Island Gardens Station, was designed as an LCC recreation ground in 1919. On its E edge, the ONE O'CLOCK CLUB (recreation centre). A crisp Neo-Modern Movement design by *Avanti Architects*, 1991–2, commissioned by the LDDC. N entrance under a glazed canopy that divides the simple wing of changing rooms from the main hall with its serpentine glass brick wall screening a cloakroom area. Rendered walls, warm-coloured on the N and E, cool to the S and W facing a generous garden.

2d. *South-East: Cubitt Town*

Cubitt Town, at the SE corner of the Isle of Dogs, was a development by *William Cubitt*, brother of the famous builder Thomas Cubitt. The ground landlord, the Countess of Glengall, hoped it would encourage house building on the rest of her estate in Millwall (where Millwall Docks was later to be created). From 1842 Cubitt established timber wharves, sawmills, cement factories and brickfields, laid out roads, built a church and terraces of houses, and developed wharves along the river, leasing them to a variety of industrial concerns. Nearly all his plain terraces, built slowly up to the 1880s, were destroyed as a consequence of the Second World War. Now almost everything except Christ Church and a few pubs is post-war. The other Anglican church (St John Roserton Street by *A. W. Blomfield*, 1871–2) has gone. In place of Cubitt's houses there are council estates and, along the once industrial riverside, the housing begun from the late 1970s, incorporating a few remnants of older buildings.

The walk starts from Island Gardens station (*see* above). It is named from ISLAND GARDENS just to its SE, which has a breathtaking view across the river, the best view of Greenwich Hospital according to Wren. The land was part of that acquired from Cubitt by the Hospital Commissioners in 1850 expressly to preserve this view free from industry. The small park was designed 1895 by *John J. Sexby* of the LCC Parks Sub-Department. Railings of 1985. To the W, the red brick ENTRANCE ROTUNDA to the GREENWICH FOOT TUNNEL, 1896–1902, to plans by *(Sir) Alexander Binnie* (LCC Engineer). The rotunda has a glass and steel dome. Staircase and lifts in the steel entrance shaft. The tunnel beneath the river, 12 ft 9 ins in external diameter, 11 ft internal, is of cast-iron rings lined with concrete and white-glazed tiles.

SAUNDERS NESS ROAD runs eastward. *Philip Hardwick*, architect to Greenwich Hospital, advised on its laying out in 1856, with detached villas in a garden by the river (two were built but were short-lived) and terraced houses between Saunders Ness Road and Manchester Road on the site now occupied by George Green School.

GEORGE GREEN SCHOOL 1972–7 by (*Sir*) *Roger Walters, GLC Department of Architecture and Civic Design*, job architect *R.A. Dark*, was built as successor to the C19 George Green School, East India Dock Road, Poplar. It responds to the sensitive site by following the curve of Manchester Road with four storeys of concrete blocks stepping back gently, the steps broken into for entrances to the main school, day centre and social services, and a thrusting wing of sports facilities. Concrete decks and staircases step down casually towards the river in a series of broad terraces. Informal teaching spaces inside, as in most 1970s GLC secondary schools. Crisp SW wing of 1996.

Along the riverside, late C20 housing developments which replaced heterogeneous industry. First LURALDA WHARF, five storey gabled groups in a docklands warehouse idiom, then the more complex CUMBERLAND MILLS SQUARE. 1987–9 by *Alan Turner & Associates*. Sombre brown brick cluster blocks with layers of balconies rise to nine and ten storeys around a courtyard (now gated), the intricacy and tough style reminiscent of GLC flats at Odham's Walk, Covent Garden (*Donald Ball* worked on both schemes). A masterly interlocking spiral plan gives most flats a river view. The NE block overlooks the former NEWCASTLE DRAWDOCK of the 1840s, brick-walled with wooden fenders. Built into a wall are some fragments from a chapel destroyed in the Second World War, including a small relief of a kneeling woman.

The turning W past George Green School leads to GLENAFFRIC AVENUE which has the only coherent group remaining from Cubitt's new town, an important visual focus for the rebuilt neighbourhood.

CHRIST CHURCH AND ST JOHN. 1852–4 by *Frederick Johnstone*, built and paid for by *William Cubitt*. E.E. in stock brick, with Portland stone dressings. Cruciform and aisleless, with a tower in the angle of nave and S transept; the heavy broach spire a prominent landmark. Thoroughly repaired and given a larger vestry (N) in 1906–7 by *J.E.K. & J.P. Cutts*. W end subdivided 1982–3 by *Levitt Bernstein Associates*, but plans of 2003 by *Robin Mallalieu* propose a reordering with W end and S transept opened up for use by the Trinity College of Music.

The nave and chancel and the broader transept arms are all embraced by a prominent timber crown-post roof with arched braces intersecting at the crossing. Gold decoration in the E arm. Long chancel with chancel arch. The S transept was screened off as a S chapel, with an upper room behind the elaborate organ loft, presumably in the early C20. The timber roof inside the tower is painted green and red with gold brattishing, remains of a 1909 baptistery created within the tower base by *Bodley & Hare*.

The High Church FURNISHINGS are more interesting than

the architecture. Some of them come from the grander St John, Roserton Street, by (*Sir*) *A. W. Blomfield*, 1871–2, demolished in the 1950s, which had been much embellished with ritualistic furnishings from the late 1880s. A few other items come from St Luke (demolished 1960). – MURAL PAINTING. Over the chancel arch, The Company of Heaven, by *F.A. Jackson* of Ealing to designs by *J.R. Spencer Stanhope*, 1907–14. – chancel redecoration, 1954–5 devised by *Alan Lindsay*, architect *J. Morris*. Handsome red-and-white 'contemporary' wallpaper by *Coles*; black-line figures in three blocked E lancets after sketches by Lindsay. – PULPIT painted with Pre-Raphaelite-style panels of the Annunciation, given and painted by *Gertrude Spencer Stanhope c.* 1914, a memorial to her brother Edward Collingwood †1906. – ALTARS. Chancel altar with neo-Quattrocento paintings. Plainer High Altar, and the altar and reredos, N transept, with Italian Primitive-style painting, both from St John. – STATIONS OF THE CROSS, *c.* 1938. Well-drawn figures on gold backgrounds by *Ian Howgate*, from St John. – ORGAN, 1911, possibly containing C17 pipework; rebuilt 1950s by *Noel Mander*. Along the organ loft, angel CANDLEHOLDERS, *ex situ*. – SCULPTURE. Lamb by *Paula Haughney*, 2001. – STAINED GLASS. N transept S. Fragment of 1902 glass from the demolished girls' institute, St Mildred's House, Westferry Road (founded 1897), moved here 1991. – SW lancet, Edward the Confessor by *A.K. Nicholson*, *c.* 1920. – MEMORIAL, S porch. Frances, wife of Thos. Murray Gladstone †1863. Cast-iron tablet with good heraldry.

VICARAGE to N. 1858, also built by *Cubitt*. Plain gabled brick.

Opposite Christ Church, at the corner, the stucco-trimmed WATERMAN'S ARMS, 1853, probably also built by *Cubitt & Co.* Cavernous Neo-Victorian interior of 1972 by *Roderick Gradidge*. Alongside it, neat and unaffected housing association flats and houses, banded in dark and yellow brick, by *Levitt Bernstein Associates*, 1993–4.

Now along SAUNDERS NESS ROAD. Towards the river, GROSVENOR WHARF ROAD and Empire Wharf Road, a pre-LDDC, council-built housing group, laid out to give as many homes as possible a view of the river. Staggered terraces round courtyards of 1978–81 by Tower Hamlets Borough Council (project architect *Martin O'Shea*). To the W, the small house at the corner of Glenworth Avenue, 1909, was built as a Manual Training Centre, the oldest surviving part of the local school, now ST LUKE'S PRIMARY, rebuilt by *Howard V. Lobb*, after bombing in 1940, completed 1952, incorporating 1930s parts of the former Board School. A bit Swedish. Yellow with red brick pilaster strips to the three-storey part. MURAL by *W. Kempster & B. Evans*: the docks and Greenwich Observatory.

Up to the riverside at CALEDONIAN WHARF, 1984–7 by *Alan Turner & Associates*, which lies around the site of Cubitt Town Dry Dock. The dock was built in 1877 by ship-repairer Thomas Rugg on the site of Cubitt's cement factory. Distinctive barrel-vaulted canopies over the balcony bays of the flats overlooking the river; similar porches on the houses behind. Close to the river, on Saunders Ness, a big industrial building remains at CUBITT TOWN WHARF, converted to apartments *c.* 2000. Rebuilt in 1927 after a fire, but on the lines of its C19 predecessor. Five storeys above basement, with brick pilasters and a little brick ornament below the parapets. Remnants of other buildings remain as car park walls. PLYMOUTH WHARF beyond has speculative housing by *Lindsay Associates*, completed 1986.

COMPASS POINT, 1985–8, closes the N end of Saunders Ness Road. Here *Jeremy Dixon* has created a small world of its own, inspired not by the industrial past but by early to mid-C19 London suburbs. With its paired villas and terraces, mews and mixture of styles (from Late Georgian to Italianate and Dutch-cum-Jacobean), it has more in common with parts of Camden and Kensington than with any C19 development on the Isle of Dogs. The English picturesque layout exploits every advantage of the site, formerly Dudgeon's Wharf. Some of the house designs are reworkings of Dixon's previous interpretations of the London house in NW London. All in purple-brown brick and thin off-white stucco, laid on like icing. Inventive details throughout, though perhaps because the scheme was carried out under a design-and-build contract (architects, *Jeremy Dixon/BDP*; builders, Costain Homes), the execution frequently does not match the ambition. SEXTANT AVENUE, the main street with the largest semi-detached villas, ends W in THE CRESCENT, a curved neo-Nash terrace with an open central slot for access to Manchester Road. At the E end, a view of the river is framed by tall blocks that repeat the emphatic uprights of silos on the far bank of the river. On the river wall, two white obelisks, and a tablet commemorating those killed in an explosion here in 1969. To the S, a slightly rustic boathouse-like block. To the N the river walk passes below pergolas, in front of a terrace of three-storey houses, set back behind stepped gables and bows, each topped by a balcony and glass canopy. Shaped gables to the separate blocks at each end. The houses are entered from MARINERS MEWS, through stuccoed porches alongside garages. Down CHICHESTER WAY, single-gable pairs face a terrace with full-height projecting triangles of windows. The vista back to the river ends in two gabled riverside blocks. A green alley runs between the gardens here and those in Sextant Avenue. BLYTH CLOSE and FRANCIS CLOSE are mews courts opening to Manchester Road, where the old wharf wall is pierced by stuccoed gateways.

Now back to the river and past MILLENNIUM WHARF, with plain housing of 2000, incorporating MILLWALL WHARF. Single-storey, twin-gabled warehouse units built 1901–2 by *Edwin A.B. Crockett*, Surveyor to the London Wharf and Warehouse Committee, for the storage of sugar and fibre by Cook & Co. Some of them may incorporate the remains of early C19 sheds. Also a plain brick warehouse dating from 1907–8, converted to apartments *c.* 1998. Further N, LONDON YARD, redeveloped in 1984–8 by Dutch developers VOM and Dutch architects *ED* (see the street names); scheme executed by *BDP*. Gabled flats and houses in brick with pantiles, conventional but quite well done and with a landscaped drainage lake at the centre. Unusually for such developments, there is one short street of small shops.

Here one can leave the riverside and continue along MANCHESTER ROAD, all rebuilt since Cubitt's time apart from a couple of pubs, the PIER TAVERN further back on the W side, and the CUBITT ARMS on the E. Opposite the latter, the
88 cheerful JUBILEE CRESCENT, set back behind its own garden. Flats for workers retired from the local ship-repairing firm R. & H. Green & Silley Weir Ltd (who had built a similar scheme at Falmouth, Cornwall). 1935 by *G.R. Unthank*. Five blocks, each of six two room flats, that look like interwar houses linked at the first floor by a continuous concrete balcony. Otherwise brick-and-render with modest patterns of terracotta diamonds and rectangles. On the balcony relief portraits of King George V and Queen Mary. A diversion just to the N can take in FRIARS MEAD, E of Manchester Road, 1983–6 by *Ronald Quin Associates*, who with Comben Homes won an early limited LDDC design competition. A secluded, luxuriantly planted loop of semi-detached houses and four-in-a-block flats forming an island amid the would-be countryside of Mudchute City Farm. The inspiration is garden suburb, the low blocks of flats set diagonally, the houses cottage-style with overhanging pantiled roofs and dovecote-style ventilators. At the centre of each block of flats a staircase sheltered by a cascade of glass roofs. The smaller and simpler Nos. 105 and 107 belong to the adjacent Glengall self-build scheme, 1985–7.

CUBITT TOWN SCHOOL follows: a much altered early Board School, three phases by *E.R. Robson*, 1874–6, 1878, 1884–5. Further addition 1935–9, by *Albert Monk*. Reorganized as a primary school, 1970–1. Two to three storeys with pantile-roofed towers.

The rest of this tour is mostly concerned with public housing. Between Manchester Road and the river the crisply detailed but austere SAMUDA ESTATE by *Burnet, Tait & Partners*, for the GLC, 1965–7, a fortress-like plinth of covered car parking with six-storey blocks grouped around a bleak pedestrian plaza, and a twenty-five-storey slab, heavily glazed, with narrow floor bands and a slightly separated service tower. Scissor-plan maisonettes, the complicated type introduced in the LCC's Pepys estate, Deptford, which allowed the dwellings to be dual aspect with internal access corridors on alternate floors.

While the GLC demonstrated its radical approach in the area E of Manchester Road, Poplar Borough Council was responsible for the gradual reconstruction of the badly bombed streets between Manchester and East Ferry Roads as ST JOHN'S ESTATE, 1952–81. First through ST JOHN'S PARK, created

1966, with some decorative metalwork from a relandscaping of 1989. The estate was one of Poplar's largest post-war efforts, approved 1949, with the aim of creating a neighbourhood similar to the LCC's Lansbury. The first houses indeed had that Lansbury lightness of touch, but later phases, though still of brick, and almost all low-rise, are more brutal and tightly planned and there is no overall coherence. The original vision can best be glimpsed around CASTALIA SQUARE, N of the park, informal and partly pedestrian. Here Nos. 1–17 is a simple three-storey terrace with a row of shops, 1956, given a dramatic projecting monopitch roof in a refurbishment of 1992. The square also has a low health centre and the tough but not unfriendly community centre-cum-church, ISLAND HOUSE, now United Reformed, built by the Presbyterian Church to replace St Paul's (*see* perambulation *2b*), 1971–2 by *Philip Pank*. It has an industrial flavour, dark brick inside and out, painted stanchions along the upper wall and an exterior staircase.

East Ferry Road leads S to COLDHARBOUR STATION. In this area a few buildings from the area's older history. The GEORGE, at the corner with Glengall Grove, was rebuilt in 1932 in domestic Neo-Georgian. The best is the CARNEGIE LIBRARY, off Glengall Grove in Strattondale Street. 1904–5 by *C. Harrold Norton*. A long Bath-stone front of odd proportions, with the air of a French railway station. Heavy stone cornice below the attic, panelled piers marking the bay. Centrepiece with an *œil de bœuf* above the doorcase and a crowning cupola. The interior, though opened up and with an early 1960s E addition by *Welch & Lander*, still has some 1904 character.

Immediately S of Glengall Grove is the big retail centre of 1981–3, the first of its kind on the Isle of Dogs, with supermarket and shops next to a vast car park. Near the entrance, the white-walled and glass brick ISLAND HEALTH CLINIC, 1991 by *John Duane Architects*. Double-height waiting room with glazed lantern and a bow window to the N.

WALTHAM FOREST

The borough takes its name from the area of Epping Forest owned by the medieval Waltham Abbey, whose site lies further N in Essex. It comprises the three older boroughs of Chingford, Walthamstow and Leyton, which developed from three medieval parishes beside the River Lea, stretching E from the river marshes toward the Forest. In the later C19 Leyton and Walthamstow changed rapidly from rural retreats for the wealthy to dormitory suburbs expanding around their stations. The introduction of workmen's trains from the 1870s made the area accessible and encouraged the building of streets of modest houses that still characterize much of the area. Highams Park, on the borders of Chingford and Walthamstow, and the more remote Chingford developed as superior suburbs from the early C20. The three boroughs all developed from villages rather than towns and no truly urban centres resulted, although in the 1890s and the 1930s respectively both Leyton and Walthamstow built ambitious town halls, in tellingly contrasting styles. Amidst the ubiquitous streets there are plenty of discoveries to be made. Chingford still has a village green and the exceptional treasure of a C16 royal hunting lodge; Walthamstow can offer both a quiet backwater around the medieval church and a bustling High Street market, while Leytonstone, once a hamlet of Leyton on the Forest fringe with its own church by the 1830s, retains some echoes of the time when it was an attractive village frequented by the local gentry. Although so many of the larger houses have vanished, Walthamstow still has some excellent examples of the elegant if unadventurous red brick Georgian buildings that were once scattered over the countryside, and their owners are recalled by some fine memorials in the churches. Among individual houses, the late C18 Highams (Woodford County School) is the most distinguished. The suburbs themselves have their own interest, not least in the diversity of styles and denominations of places of worship built by energetic new communities. In 1998 the population of Waltham Forest was 221,400, making it the most densely built up of the outer London boroughs. Yet it is also memorable for its water and woodland. On the W border are the broad expanses of the Lea Valley reservoirs, opened up as part of the linear Lea Valley Park, and along the northern and eastern fringes are extensive remnants of Epping Forest, preserved from development by the Act of 1878.

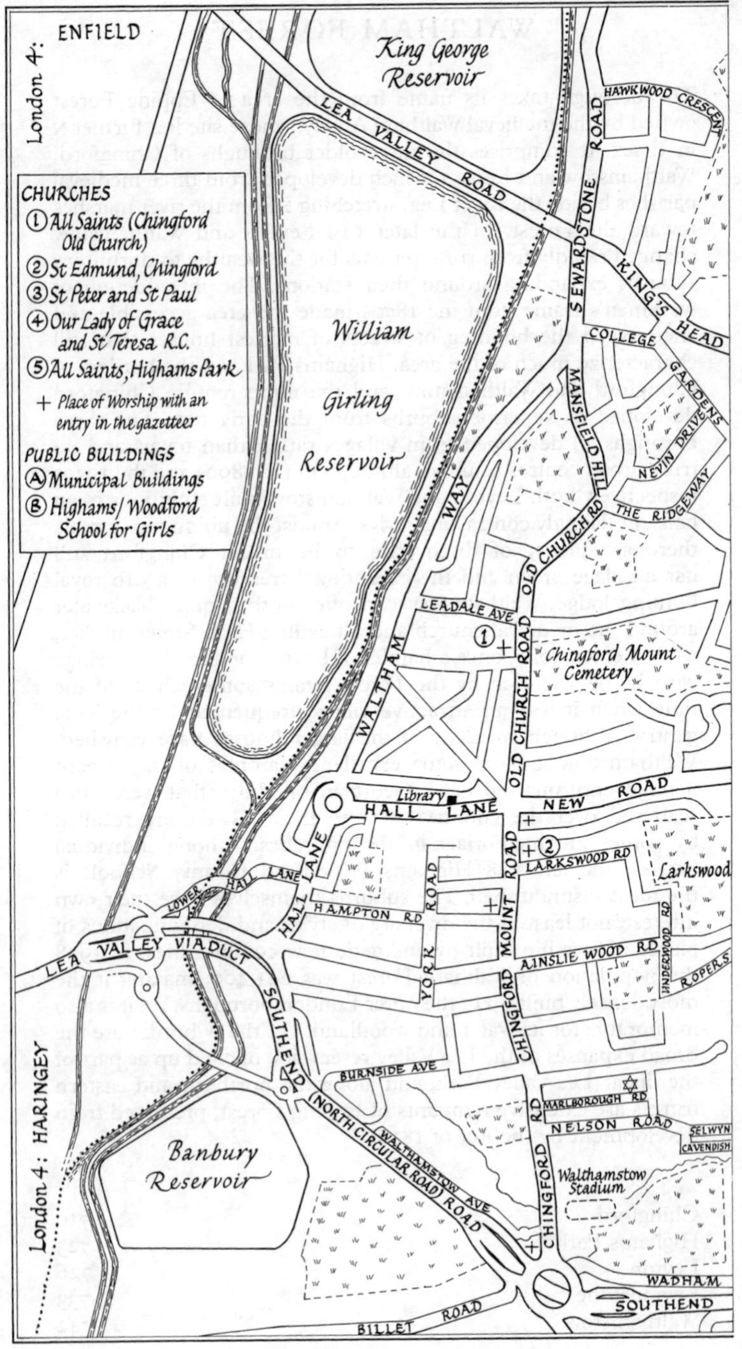

London 4: ENFIELD
King George Reservoir
LEA VALLEY ROAD
HAWKWOOD CRESCENT
SEWARDSTONE ROAD
KING'S HEAD
COLLEGE GARDENS
CHURCHES
1 All Saints (Chingford Old Church)
2 St Edmund, Chingford
3 St Peter and St Paul
4 Our Lady of Grace and St Teresa R.C.
5 All Saints, Highams Park
+ Place of Worship with an entry in the gazetteer
PUBLIC BUILDINGS
A Municipal Buildings
B Highams/Woodford School for Girls
William Girling Reservoir
MANSFIELD HILL
NEVIN DRIVE
THE RIDGEWAY
OLD CHURCH RD
WAY
LEADALE AVE
WALTHAM
Chingford Mount Cemetery
OLD CHURCH ROAD
Library
HALL LANE
NEW ROAD
LARKSWOOD RD
Larkswood
LOWER HALL LANE
HALL LANE
HAMPTON RD
YORK ROAD
CHINGFORD MOUNT ROAD
UNDERWOOD RD
AINSLIE WOOD RD
ROPERS
LEA VALLEY VIADUCT
SOUTHEND
BURNSIDE AVE
MARLBOROUGH RD
NELSON ROAD
SELWYN
CAVENDISH
(NORTH CIRCULAR ROAD) ROAD
(WALTHAMSTOW AVE
CHINGFORD RD
Walthamstow Stadium
London 4: HARINGEY
Banbury Reservoir
WADHAM
SOUTHEND
BILLET ROAD

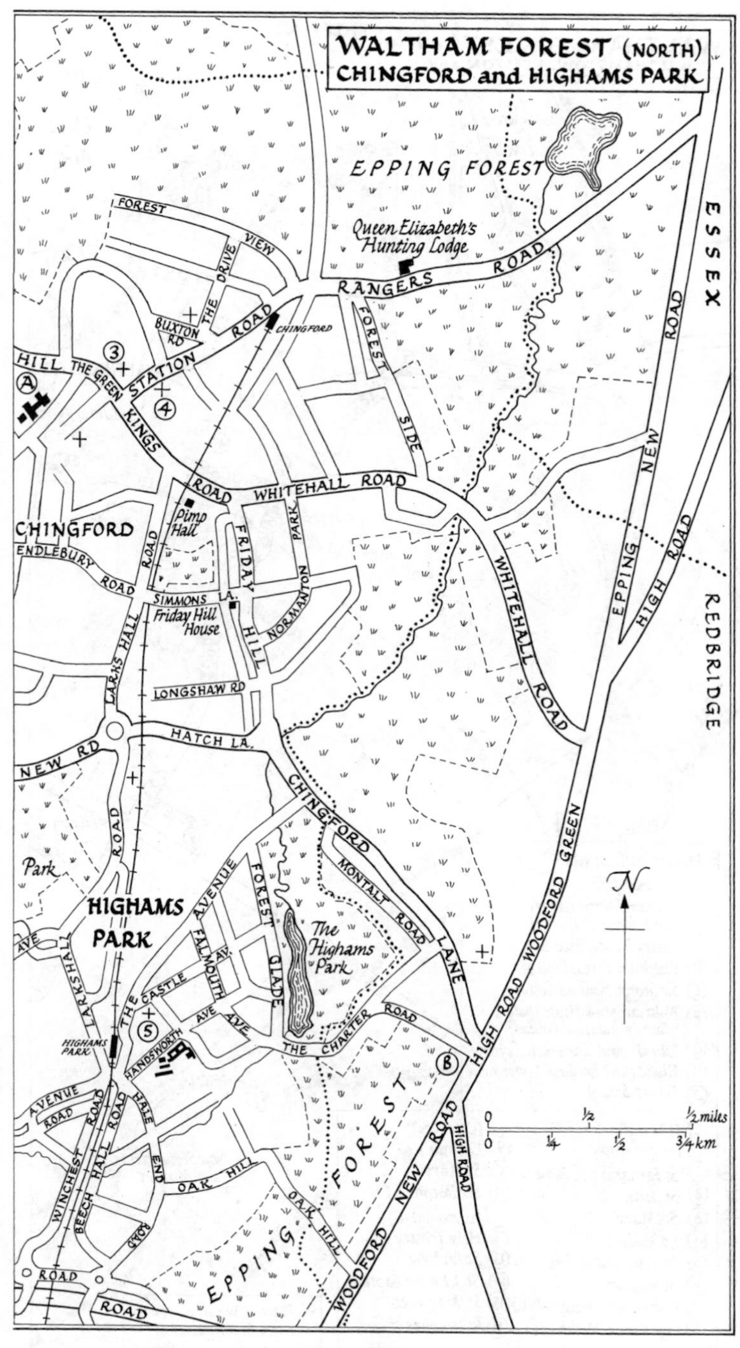
WALTHAM FOREST (NORTH)
CHINGFORD and HIGHAMS PARK
EPPING FOREST
Queen Elizabeth's Hunting Lodge
RANGERS ROAD
ESSEX
REDBRIDGE
FOREST VIEW
THE DRIVE
BUXTON RD
STATION ROAD
CHINGFORD
HILL
THE GREEN
KINGS ROAD
FOREST SIDE
WHITEHALL ROAD
NEW ROAD
EPPING NEW ROAD
Pimp Hall
CHINGFORD
ENDLEBURY ROAD
FRIDAY HILL
PARK
NORMANTON
SIMMONS LA.
Friday Hill House
LARKS HALL ROAD
LONGSHAW RD
HATCH LA.
NEW RD
CHINGFORD LANE
MONTALT ROAD
Park
HIGHAMS PARK
AVENUE
FOREST GLADE
FALMOUTH AV.
The Highams Park
THE CASTLE AVE
HANDSWORTH AVE
THE CHARTER ROAD
HIGH ROAD WOODFORD GREEN
HIGHAMS PARK
LARKSHALL
AVE
AVENUE ROAD
HALE END ROAD
HALL ROAD
WINCHEST
BEECH HALL ROAD
OAK HILL
ROAD
EPPING FOREST
WOODFORD NEW ROAD
HIGH ROAD
N
1/2 miles
1/4 1/2 3/4 km

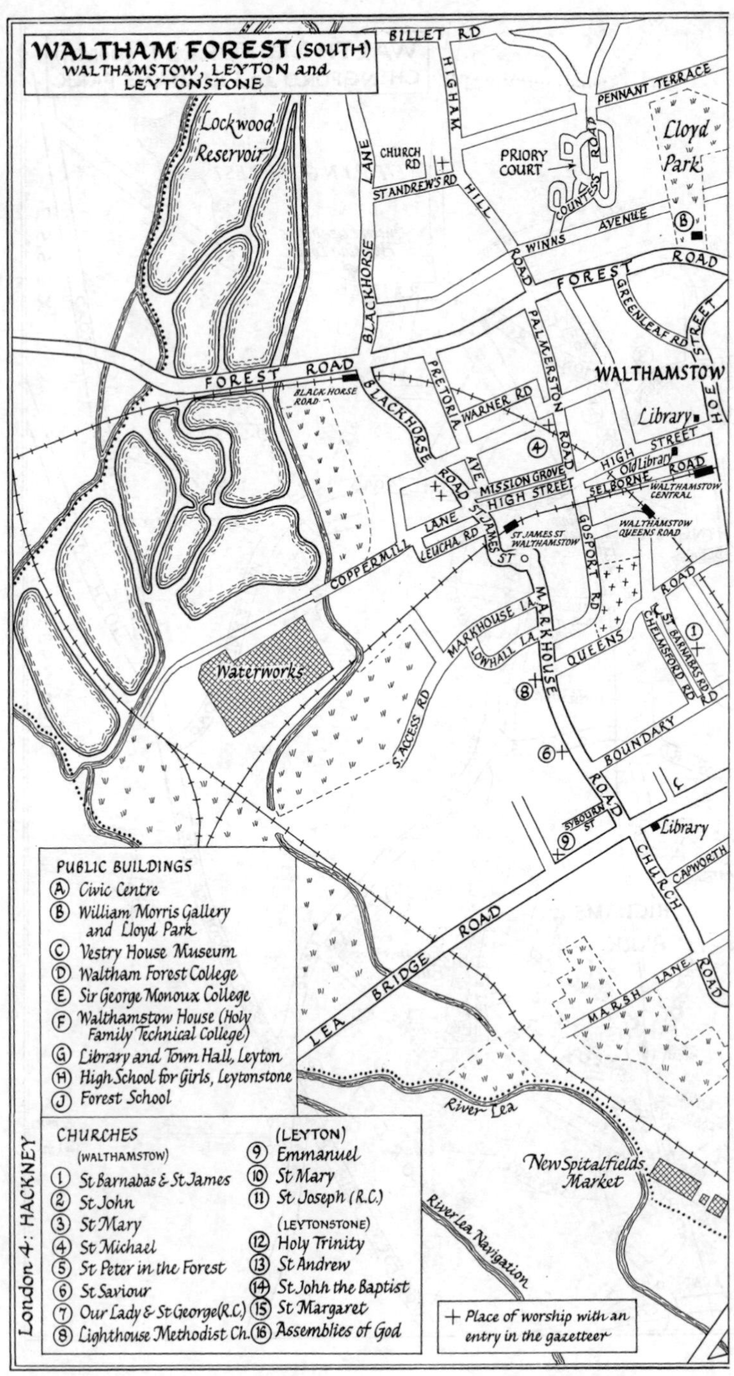
WALTHAM FOREST (SOUTH)
WALTHAMSTOW, LEYTON and LEYTONSTONE
Lockwood Reservoir
Waterworks
WALTHAMSTOW
Lloyd Park
Library
Old Library
WALTHAMSTOW CENTRAL
WALTHAMSTOW QUEENS ROAD
ST JAMES ST WALTHAMSTOW
River Lea
River Lea Navigation
New Spitalfields Market
London 4: HACKNEY
PUBLIC BUILDINGS
Ⓐ Civic Centre
Ⓑ William Morris Gallery and Lloyd Park
Ⓒ Vestry House Museum
Ⓓ Waltham Forest College
Ⓔ Sir George Monoux College
Ⓕ Walthamstow House (Holy Family Technical College)
Ⓖ Library and Town Hall, Leyton
Ⓗ High School for Girls, Leytonstone
Ⓙ Forest School
CHURCHES
(WALTHAMSTOW)
① St Barnabas & St James
② St John
③ St Mary
④ St Michael
⑤ St Peter in the Forest
⑥ St Saviour
⑦ Our Lady & St George (R.C.)
⑧ Lighthouse Methodist Ch.
(LEYTON)
⑨ Emmanuel
⑩ St Mary
⑪ St Joseph (R.C.)
(LEYTONSTONE)
⑫ Holy Trinity
⑬ St Andrew
⑭ St John the Baptist
⑮ St Margaret
⑯ Assemblies of God
+ Place of worship with an entry in the gazetteer

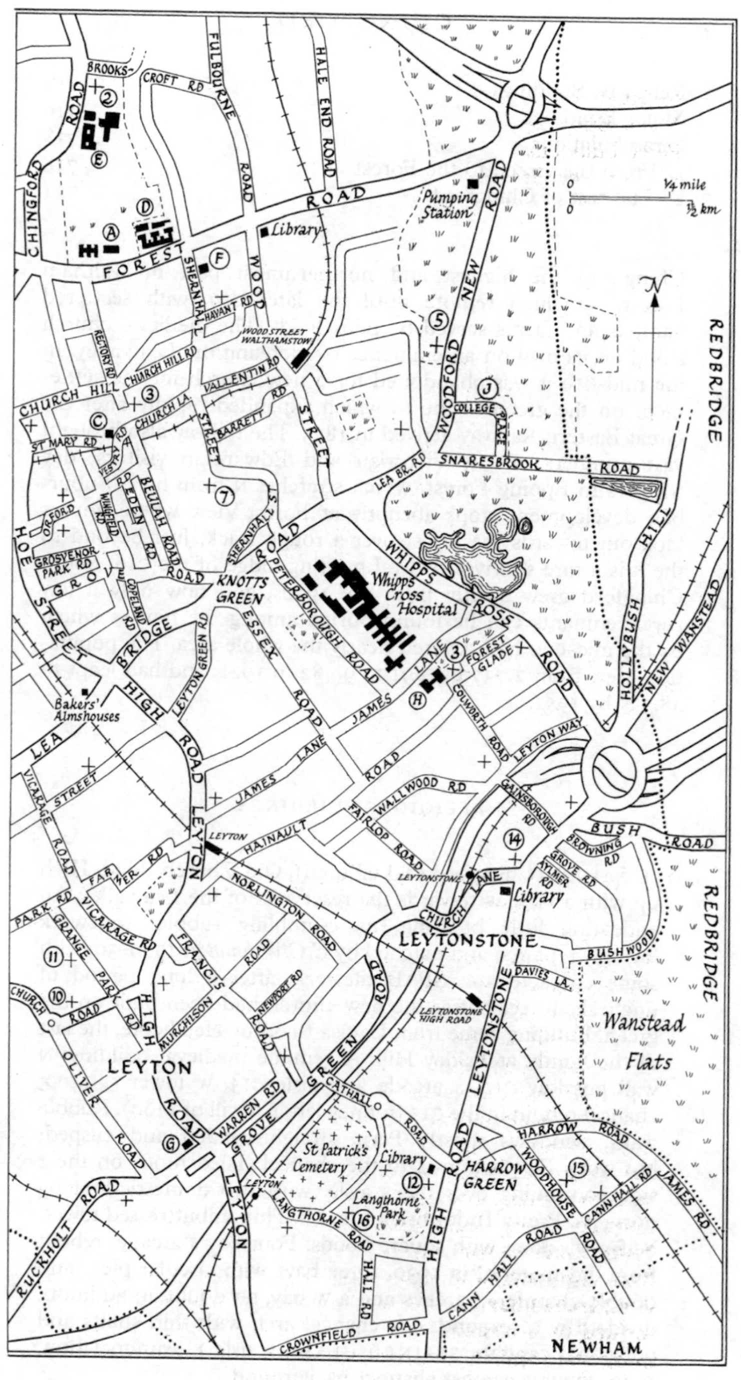

BROOKSCROFT RD
CHINGFORD ROAD
FOREST ROAD
FULBOURNE ROAD
HALE END ROAD
Pumping Station
NEW ROAD
WOODFORD NEW ROAD
Library
WOOD STREET
WOOD STREET WALTHAMSTOW
SHERNHALL ST
HAVANT RD
RECTORY RD
CHURCH HILL RD
CHURCH HILL
CHURCH LA
VALLENTIN RD
BARRETT RD
COLLEGE PLACE
SNARESBROOK ROAD
LEA BR. RD
ST MARY RD
VESTRY RD
HOE STREET
ORFORD RD
WINGFIELD RD
EDEN RD
BEULAH RD
GROSVENOR PARK RD
GROVE RD
COPELAND RD
KNOTTS GREEN
PETERBOROUGH ROAD
ESSEX ROAD
WHIPPS CROSS ROAD
Whipps Cross Hospital
HOLLYBUSH HILL
NEW WANSTEAD
REDBRIDGE
FOREST GLADE
LEYTON GREEN RD
BRIDGE ROAD
HIGH ROAD LEYTON
Bakers' Almshouses
LEA BRIDGE
JAMES LANE
COLWORTH ROAD
LEYTON WAY
VICARAGE ROAD
LEA STREET
WALLWOOD RD
GAINSBOROUGH RD
BUSH ROAD
LEYTON
HAINAULT ROAD
FAIRLOP ROAD
BROWNING RD
GROVE RD
AYLMER RD
FARMER RD
NORLINGTON ROAD
LEYTONSTONE
CHURCH LANE
Library
PARK RD
VICARAGE RD
GRANGE PARK RD
FRANCIS ROAD
LEYTONSTONE
BUSHWOOD
DAVIES LA.
CHURCH ROAD
NEWPORT RD
LEYTONSTONE HIGH ROAD
Wanstead Flats
MURCHISON ROAD
HIGH ROAD
LEYTON
OLIVER ROAD
GREEN ROAD
CATHALL ROAD
WARREN RD
GROVE GREEN ROAD
HARROW ROAD
St Patrick's Cemetery
Library
HARROW GREEN
WOODHOUSE ROAD
CANN HALL RD
JAMES RD
RUCKHOLT ROAD
LEYTON
LANGTHORNE ROAD
Langthorne Park
HIGH ROAD LEYTON
HIGH ROAD LEYTONSTONE
HALL RD
CANN HALL ROAD
CROWNFIELD ROAD
NEWHAM
0 ¼ mile
0 ½ km
N

CHINGFORD

Chingford, the highest and northernmost part of Waltham Forest, remained remote until the later C19, with scattered hamlets and farms served by poor roads. The medieval church stood on its own on an eminence overlooking the Lea Valley. In the mid-C19 it was abandoned for a new church for the settlement on the green to the N, which expanded rapidly after the Great Eastern Railway arrived in 1873. The railway also brought vast numbers of late Victorian and Edwardian visitors, day trippers to Epping Forest, which stretches N from here. Suburban development stops abruptly at Forest View where houses look out towards the forest over a rough track. Just beyond to the E is a rare survival, a royal hunting lodge of the C16. South Chingford grew swiftly from the 1930s, and now only a few rural remnants can be found buried among the houses which by the mid-C20 had covered nearly the whole area. The population grew from 2,737 in 1891 to 9,482 in 1921, and had leapt to 48,355 by 1951.

RELIGIOUS BUILDINGS

ALL SAINTS (Chingford Old Church), Old Church Road. High up with a view W towards the reservoirs of the Lea valley. An endearing little building, its crumbling rubble stonework lovingly repaired and patched by *C. C. Winmill* in 1929–30, with some characteristic SPAB tilework, after a long period of unchecked decay after the new church had been built on the green. Funding came from Louisa Boothby Heathcote, the last of the family at Friday Hill. A genuine medieval building: N wall possibly C12, S arcade and aisle C13, W tower *c.* 1400; chancel rebuilt in the C15 (money left in a will of 1460). Rubble walls, windows mostly Perp, straight-headed and cusped, but worn Dec windows to the chancel. Tiled roofs, on the S side continuing over the S aisle, with two domestic-looking dormers. Pretty Tudor brick S porch. Thin unbuttressed tower, belfry windows with square hoods. Four-bay S arcade, rebuilt from old material in 1930, three bays with circular piers and double-chamfered arches and a W bay, no doubt an addition, divided by a respond. C15 chancel arch with thin shafts and polygonal capitals. STAINED GLASS, S aisle E, Annunciation, 1963. Figures against abstract background.

MONUMENTS. Indent of brass to Robert †1585 and Margaret Rampston, from a chest tomb. – Mary Leigh, small tablet with reclining woman and baby behind her, in relief; frame with arabesques. – Her husband, Sir Robert Leigh †1612, and Margaret Leigh †1624, both have kneeling figures, in frames with obelisks. – Thomas Boothby †1669. Two putti holding up drapery. – John Heathcote †1795, tablet with mourning woman. – Lydia Heathcote †1822, with urn.

A nice CHURCHYARD, quite small, with several chest tombs. The Boothby and Heathcote families (Robert Boothby of Friday Hill †1733) have a tapered chest with curved ends. – Harriet Colville †1830 is commemorated by a curious Soanian construction, a sarcophagus on feet bisected by a cubic pedestal carrying a shallow urn.

W of the church, buried among C20 suburbia, the C18 former RECTORY, rebuilt 1829, much altered and converted to flats; three bays, with addition of *c.* 1880.

ST ANNE, Larkshall Road. 1953 by *Tooley & Foster*. Red brick, very plain. W tower with a little brick patterning. Matching parsonage at rear.

ST EDMUND, Larkswood Road. 1938–9, conservative work by *N.F. Cachemaille-Day*. Hard-edged church of dark brick and flint flushwork, with straight-headed windows with brick mullions. Aisled, with steep roofs and low squat crossing-tower over the chancel; an original combination of Norman massing and detail derived from East Anglian Perp. Inside, plastered walls, pointed transverse arches, thin chamfered nave arcades without capitals. No clerestory, but well lit by the open tower above the chancel, a favourite *Cachemaille-Day* arrangement. The tower has a balcony, said to have been intended for the organ (which is now in a transept gallery proposed for children). Simple, solid FURNISHINGS: pulpit, stalls, lectern with fluted stem; elegant light fittings with hanging bulbs. STAINED GLASS, E window by *Geoffrey Webb*, Christ and two angels. SE window †1948, Crucifixion. Transept, behind the organ: roundel with Evangelist symbols, by *Laurence Lee*, richly coloured. S side 2nd from E, maritime themes by *Clayton & Bell* from the chapel of the Merchant Seamen's Orphanage, Wanstead (*see* p. 359).

HALLS to the W: 1908, with slightly Arts and Crafts tapering buttresses, 1927.

ST FRANCIS, Hawkwood Crescent, 1951. Small and pantiled.

ST PETER AND ST PAUL. The Green. 1844 and 1903. The earlier W part, by *Lewis Vulliamy*, was intended as a replacement for the old church further down the hill, and paid for by the rector and Lord of the Manor, Robert Boothby Heathcote, of Friday Hill (*see* below). W tower with lancets, spire and corner pinnacles. White brick with much flint chequerwork and flushwork. The E parts, of flint with brick banding, and wide windows in a Perp spirit, are uncommonly bold additions of 1903 by *Sir Arthur Blomfield & Son*; S chapel in similar style completed 1936 by *N.F. Cachemaille-Day*. Vulliamy's nave is a broad unaisled space with a W gallery with turned balusters, supported on iron columns. The heavy low-pitched queenpost roof is curiously elaborated by pierced circles and vertical timbers. Blomfield's more elegant chancel has three aisled bays, viewed from the nave through three arches: circular piers, clerestory, and a graceful roof with arched purlins as well as triple-arched principals. From the old church: C12 Purbeck-marble FONT, square with five shallow arches to each side of the bowl, top renewed. Good early C18 PULPIT; C17 CHEST. STAINED GLASS. E window, 1913 by *Clayton & Bell*, Christ in Majesty. S chapel GLASS by *Christopher Webb*, 1937. Inner W DOOR with engraved glass figures of SS Peter and Paul by *Sally Scott*, 1990, part of a reordering of the W end. – MONUMENTS. Two tablets in Gothic frames: to the Rev. Robert Boothby Heathcote †1865 and his family, and a pretty *opus sectile* tile panel commemorating the addition of the E end in his memory, 1903, each nicely demonstrating the taste of its time.

CHRIST THE KING (R.C.), Chingford Road. 1996 by *Scott Tallon Walker*, replacing a church of 1932. A landmark at the North Circular Road roundabout. Brown brick. A stark triangular bell-tower beside a semicircular church with small windows high up. Austere, quiet interior with concrete-block walls and big radial roof beams fanning out from the top-lit white-plastered sanctuary. Furnishings by *Herbert Read* of St Sidwell's Artworks, Tiverton. Opening off the glazed foyer is a small triangular Blessed Sacrament chapel, with engraved metal TABERNACLE, and abstract STAINED GLASS by *Sarianne Durie*, 1998.

OUR LADY OF GRACE and ST TERESA of AVILA (R.C.), Kings Road. A hall was built in 1919. The nave of the church was built 1930–1, transepts and sanctuary completed 1939, SW tower 1956. The new church was a thank offering, designed and built at cost by *G. W. Martyn*, a Catholic convert. Carefully designed Gothic, with unusually good details in an Arts and Crafts tradition. Brick, with Perp aisle windows; half-timbered porch with carving by *Donald Potter*, a Chingford resident who was a pupil of Eric Gill. A fine interior with lofty arch-braced roof with crown-posts, lit by little dormers. Stone octagonal columns to the arcades. Plasterwork band, carved foliage corbels, angels flanking the chancel arch, panels with symbols of the Passion. W gallery with carved newel posts to the stair. Furnishings of an equally high standard. Stone REREDOS and limed-and-gilded panelling, now behind the organ. STATIONS OF THE CROSS, low relief panels, by *Kathleen Nicholas*. STAINED GLASS. A fine, colourful E rose window and a subtle Lady Chapel N window by *Veronica Whall*, 1939, the latter with delicate figure of Virgin and Child, largely white against a band of blue, intricately leaded. A sympathetic reordering, 2002 by *Richard Hurley & Associates* of Dublin, introduced good new paving and restrained stone furnishings with a little incised carving, by *Angela Godfrey*: square ALTAR, READING DESK, hexagonal FONT and TABERNACLE STAND. The TABERNACLE has a striking black-and-silver pattern, with a red-and-gold panel set behind.

NORTH CHINGFORD METHODIST CHURCH, Station Road. By *George Baines*, 1927. A late version of the firm's free Perp. Cruciform, with a canted-out porch. Flèche over the nave. A good unaltered interior; a single space with a curved sweep of pews, echoed by a curved communion rail. Organ and panelled seats in the lower polygonal space behind, framed by a sharply angled stone arch. Large, light windows, the patterned leading sparely decorated with jewel-like diamonds.

UNITED REFORMED CHURCH, Buxton Road. An imposing Congregationalist group in superior turn-of-the-century suburbia. Facing the road junction, SPICER HALL, 1890 by *Rowland Plumbe*, built as the first church. Converted to flats 2003–4. Orange brick with stone dressings, the gable with handsome geometric–Gothic window fronting The Drive, and a playful timber-topped tower next to the adjoining two-storey Sunday schools. The adjacent church, 1910 by *J.D. & S.T. Mould*, faces W to Buxton Road. Of duller red brick with stone banding. Elaborate triple entrance of stone, with some carved decoration below a free Perp window with Art Nouveau leading, a tower on the r. with stumpy pinnacles and copper-clad steeple. The plan is a smaller version of the central type adopted by some major late C19 Congregationalist churches. A foyer (with gallery above) leads to a square nave, made octagonal by pointed stone arches across the corners; rafters rise to the centre of the octagon. Across several of the arches large carved beams with boldly lettered texts. Windows on two levels. A larger arch and low stone screen divide off the polygonal sanctuary. This has panelling and later STAINED GLASS window on the theme of mission, in memory of the influential Congregationalist and donor, James Spicer of Woodford, paper manufacturer, †1932. Alterations of 2003–4 (floor levelled, pews removed and a link made to the church hall of 1923).

CONGREGATIONAL CHURCH, Hampton Road. 1952–3 by *Trevor Blake*. Clean-cut building of buff brick. Tower-porch with tiled round-arched entrance; flanking extensions of 2001. Plain barrel-vaulted interior.

SOUTH CHINGFORD METHODIST CHURCH, New Road, 1935. Elegantly restrained, faintly Georgian round-headed windows to clerestory and W gable. HALL of 1931 a little more classical: arched window with keystone, between broad corner pilasters.

CHRISTIAN SCIENCE CHURCH, Woodland Road, 1937. Low and pebbledashed. Given a little style by a pair of recessed, canopied entrances to roof-lit reading room and taller church.

SYNAGOGUE, Marlborough Road. 1937 by *Israel Schutz*. Plain Modernist exterior; low foyer with rounded corners in speckled buff brick, with faience-tiled entrance. Extended in matching style with HALL of 1968.

CHINGFORD MOUNT CEMETERY, Old Church Road. 1884, on the site of Caroline Mount House, developed by the Abney

Park Cemetery Co. and used for reburial of remains from the grounds of Whitefields Tabernacle, Tottenham Court Road (1898), and Ram's Chapel Homerton (1933). The original buildings have gone. The best feature is a fine avenue of plane trees approached through the S entrance, which has a semicircle of brick piers. Discreet offices of the later C20. Among many small crowded tombstones a few granite monuments of the late C19 to early C20.

MAJOR BUILDINGS

MUNICIPAL BUILDINGS, The Ridgeway. Built as Chingford Town Hall, 1929 by *Frederick Nash* and *H. T. Bonner*. Red brick with stone dressings, three bays with lower wings; the free-Baroque pedimented centrepiece with cartouche still in an Edwardian spirit. Reticent modern extension to the l., 1959 by *Tooley & Foster*, brick-faced, with recessed ground floor and ranges round a rear quadrangle with fountain.

CHINGFORD ASSEMBLY HALL and LIBRARY, Station Road. Also by *Tooley & Foster*, 1959. Plain two-storey block with stone-faced ground floor. Mosaic mural, roundels with local allusions, by *Wallscapes*, 2000.

TELEPHONE EXCHANGE, The Ridgeway. Nicely proportioned three-storey building with sandstone dressings, in *Office of Works* between-the-wars Neo-Georgian.

SOUTH CHINGFORD LIBRARY, Hall Lane. By Essex County Council 1935, their first library. A single one-storey room. Brick, with tall, narrow windows; given a little character by a mannered elliptical-arched entrance.

LARKS WOOD LEISURE CENTRE, New Road, with swimming pool, 1994 by *Hazel, McCormack & Young*. The pool has a monopitch roof and horizontal timber cladding, making an effort to respect the *genius loci* on the edge of Larks Wood, but is swamped by its neighbours unimaginatively grouped around a car park. They include indifferent refreshment places, a square pavilion housing a nursery, and a large Health and Fitness Centre of routine kind, yellow brick with glazed foyer and top-lit central mall.

WAR MEMORIAL RECREATION GROUND, S of Larkswood Road, opened 1930. Chingford's first municipal park, laid out around an existing Garden of Remembrance. Near the pond a SCULPTURE by *Jack Gardner*, Tao Column 92.

RIDGEWAY PARK, The Ridgeway, laid out *c.* 1938, with boating lakes, model railway etc.

WATERWORKS. The string of East London Waterworks reservoirs up the Lea valley starts in Walthamstow (*see* p. 752). The William Girling Reservoir, taking in the course of the river and the site of Chingford's First World War aerodrome, was built from 1935–51. The King George Reservoir beyond (since the 1990s in Enfield) dates from 1913.

CHINGFORD MILL PUMPING STATION, Lower Hall Lane. A handsome group by *W.B. Bryan* of the East London Waterworks. Engine House over the well; dated 1895. Brick, with half-timbered gable, and a tall tower in Bryan's characteristic Germanic style; low half-timbered Turbine House, 1891, astride a former mill stream. Both derelict.

GREAVES PUMPING STATION, North Circular Road. Also by *W.B. Bryan*, 1902–3. Red brick with Portland-stone dressings, the waterworks' first use of the Baroque style, with giant rusticated aedicules framing the windows. Formerly with a prominent chimney.

Schools

CHINGFORD (C.E.) INFANTS, Kings Road, still shows its origins as a village school of 1865, built by the parish surveyor *Walter Stair*. Originally a single room with doorway in the centre, enlarged by a gabled wing to the N in 1887, by another to the S in 1911, the first with bargeboards, the second with brick dentilled mouldings. Behind are a teacher's house and further extensions of 1938.

CHINGFORD HALL COMMUNITY SCHOOL, Burnside Avenue. Two 1970s system-built schools remodelled by *Cullinan & Buck Architects*, 2004, with shared outdoor play centre. The former semi-open-plan Infant School, now a Learning Support Centre, is subdivided by a bold cork wall. A typical early C21 transformation, responding to falling school rolls and the need for special teaching.

LARKSWOOD PRIMARY, New Road. 1904–13 by *Frank Whitmore*, Essex County Architect. A large, low group, the range to the street has a jolly corner with octagonal turret and pedimented windows. Other windows with hipped dormers. Behind, a more sober range with dentilled gables, and a separate Manual Instruction Centre. Future uncertain.

LONGSHAW PRIMARY, on the Friday Hill Estate. 1947–9. Long, light, unadorned classroom ranges, of the post-war finger-plan type, with corridor access to S-facing classrooms and an assembly hall at each end. A well-preserved example of the new type of primary developed by Essex County Council for the fast growing LCC estates. Made up of a series of standard units; intended to be steel-framed, but shortage of materials dictated the use of pre-cast reinforced concrete.

WHITEHALL PRIMARY, Normanton Park. Forceful forms of the 1980s. Big sloping roofs with roof lights, and a roof-lit triangular lantern.

AINSLIE WOOD PRIMARY, Ainslie Wood Road. *c.* 1990. A return to a vernacular tradition: brick with pantiled roofs.

COUNTY HIGH SCHOOL, Nevin Drive. 1939–41 by Essex County Council.

HEATHCOTE SECONDARY SCHOOL, Normanton Park. By *H. Conolly*, Essex County Architect, 1950, good of its date. Long two-storey classrooms ranges, well proportioned. Steel-framed, clad in brick with long bands of glazing, a small brick tower with circular windows.

PERAMBULATIONS

A walk around the Green and its surroundings and then E towards the hunting lodge can be recommended, but other points of interest are more isolated. They are described roughly clockwise.

1. From the Green to the Forest

The GREEN is a breezy hilltop with the church in the centre. Opposite the junction of Kings Road and Station Road the former BULL AND CROWN, 1899, with lots of terracotta and a flurry of gables in Chambord style, rebuilt by Taylor Walker to cater for Forest visitors. Nearby is KILGREANA and THE LODGE, survivors from Mellish's Staghound Kennels, 1798. At the crown of the hill is the KING'S HEAD, still with simple two-storey stuccoed pub front (but much enlarged behind). Opposite, Nos. 3–7 King's Head Hill, part-weatherboarded cottages, early C19. They frame a spectacular view of the reservoirs. At the corner with the Ridgeway, WAR MEMORIAL, a tall, plain Celtic cross. Behind, sheltered housing by the borough, 1978–81, ingenious monopitch-roofed clusters of dark-red brick with white walls, private roof terraces and self-consciously vernacular detail. Further along the Ridgeway is the former Town Hall.

High up to the N, granite OBELISK on Pole Hill. Put up in 1824 as a N mark from Greenwich Observatory.

On the E side of the green, not far from the church, the once rural hamlet is recalled by CARBIS COTTAGE, facing the green, a sweet white-painted weatherboarded and tile-roofed cottage with central entrance and end stack. A larger weatherboarded house, two full storeys, to its l. STATION ROAD continues E past assembly hall and library (q.v.) as the main shopping street. To its N BUXTON ROAD and THE DRIVE, begun *c.* 1890, are the start of the superior suburb of Chingford Rise, laid out on the edge of the Forest by *Edmond Egan* of Loughton for Jabez Balfour's Liberator Building Society; building work ceased when this collapsed in 1892. Ample villas in an Old English mode: half-timbered upper floors, steep tile roofs and clustered stacks, with a Congregational church (*see* above) as a focus.

At the N end of Station Road, a low MASONIC HALL, 1930 by *Stanley Miller*, carefully detailed; round-headed windows with fancy tracery, somewhere between Gothic and Art Deco. The

STATION of 1878 (Great Eastern Railway) is two-storeyed, domestic-looking. Red brick with coved eaves and hipped slate roofs. Further on in RANGERS ROAD is the huge ROYAL FOREST HOTEL. Originally of 1881 by *Edmond Egan*, but much rebuilt after a fire in 1925. Close to the royal hunting lodge (also repaired by *Egan*, *see* below), and a telling contrast; fake Tudor on the grandest scale, its size indicative of the popularity of Epping Forest as an excursion. Remains of former STABLES to the r. (now Forest offices): a formal frontage to two brick ranges.

S of Rangers Road CRESCENT ROAD and FOREST SIDE were part of Balfour's development. They have an assortment of grand villas and another large gabled pub by *Egan*, the QUEEN ELIZABETH, which sports exotic monsters on its roof cresting, and Art Nouveau lettering.

QUEEN ELIZABETH'S HUNTING LODGE, Rangers Road. A remarkable survival on the fringe of Epping Forest. It was commissioned by Henry VIII in 1542–3, as part of his plans, never executed, for a royal house at Waltham Abbey with adjacent hunting parks. The best preserved example of a timber-framed building built as a royal standing for hunting.* Deceptively unassuming, with pale limewashed exterior, the result of *Purcell Miller Tritton*'s restoration of 1989–93, especially when compared with its more ornate later C19 appearance. The L-shaped building is of three storeys, with tiled roof on a structure of massive oak timbers. A main room on each floor facing N, with rear stair wing. The brick fireplace on the S wall was added 1589. Kitchen and service area are on the ground floor. A separate door (its position unclear) probably led to the stairs, which are on a generous scale with shallow steps of triangular oak beams, possibly planned for easy access by the ailing king. They rise around a hollow-square core. The window openings of both the upper floors were originally unglazed. The low first floor was a shooting gallery, from which crossbows could be aimed at the hunt's quarry. It has two big moulded ceiling beams. The grander top floor for spectators has a splendid three-bay open roof. This is of traditional form, with arch-braced trusses, S-shaped struts above, and two tiers of purlins with curved windbraces, but the arch-braces have ovolo mouldings, very progressive for this date. Other innovative constructional details (including a 'double diminished haunch tenon joint') demonstrate the ingenuity of the royal carpenters. Tree-ring dating shows that the timbers were cut in 1542.

The later history of the building and changing approaches to its repair have their own interest. From the C17 the building was a keeper's lodge, and the openings were filled in or glazed. The top floor was used as a Courtroom from 1608–1851. William Morris visited as a boy, and recalled 'a room hung with faded greenery . . . and the impression of romance that it made

*Another, encased in later building, survives at Loughton, Essex.

Queen Elizabeth's Hunting Lodge, Chingford

upon me'. It later became a tearoom for visitors to the Forest. After the Corporation of London acquired the building in 1878 together with Epping Forest, repairs by *Edmond Egan* followed in 1881, and further work in 1897–1903 by *J. Oldrid Scott*. At this time the building was thought to be C15, and efforts were made to reinforce this impression: plaster was removed, leaded windows added, and timbers applied to resemble close studding. In 1897–9, Scott replaced Egan's bargeboards, removed internal partitions and rebuilt much of the walls of the stair-tower. Work of 1989–93, prompted by death watch beetle and based on very detailed examination, repaired the building with traditional materials and techniques but did not seek to return it to its 1543 condition. The present appearance is a judicious compromise. The later windows were retained, and so were Scott's pretty bargeboards. The expanded-mesh wall panels of 1881 were replaced with traditional wattle and daub infill, and the exterior was limewashed, but not coloured.

Just beyond the hunting lodge, BUTLER'S RETREAT, a weatherboarded barn used from 1890 for serving refreshments to visitors, one of a number of teetotal establishments that once existed in the Forest to cater for large numbers.

2. *The rest of Chingford*

PIMP HALL DOVECOTE. S off Kings Road, now within a small nature park. All that remains from a cluster of timber-framed buildings, bought by the District Council in 1934. Attractive square building, of the C16, timber-framed with curved braces, on a brick base. Gablet opening above a tiled roof. Inside, five tiers of nesting holes. The farmhouse was demolished in 1939, the barn destroyed in a gale of 1990.

FRIDAY HILL HOUSE, Simmons Lane. Now an adult education centre within the former LCC estate. A small early Victorian country house of white brick in a mixed Elizabethan style by *Lewis Vulliamy*, 1839–47, for R.B. Heathcote, lord of the manor and rector (*see* St Peter and St Paul above). It replaced an earlier Heathcote manor house. The present U-shaped entrance front is a clumsy composition facing N, with big staircase window in the centre. The S front looks as if it was intended to be the polite approach, but is hardly more satisfactory, neither harmoniously balanced, nor sufficiently asymmetrical to be picturesque. Perhaps the planning was conditioned by the footprint of an older building. The S side has a two-storey centre with three tall timber mullion-and-transom windows linked by continuous Tudor hoodmoulds. To the l. a four-centred doorway with lozenge-patterned fanlight, the lozenge motif repeated on the door. The W wing on the l. has a big canted bay on two floors. A small domed stair-turret marks the division between the polite rooms and a three-storey service range further E, which incorporates a tower. Much altered and battered inside, but remnants of sumptuous interiors. The centre room facing S has an elaborate cornice and marble fireplace. In the W wing the NW room has two walls with *trompe l'œil* panels, prettily painted with flowers and birds on a green background, each one different. Attributed to *Thomas Kershaw*. The stairhall has Jacobean-style overmantel and panelling, partly made up of old pieces, and a sloping roof with exposed beams. Stair of debased C18 type, with fat C19 turned newel. Smaller overmantel in the back entrance hall, with the date 1668. Is the entrance from the N via the large stair hall a later adaptation, or is this a precocious example of the large living-room-cum-stair hall that became popular in the later C19?

The estate was sold to the LCC just before the Second World War. The large low-rise FRIDAY HILL ESTATE, begun in the 1940s, was one of several built by the LCC outside its area (*see also* Harold Hill and Hainault pp. 164, 333). It spreads down the hill, spaciously laid out with conventional brick houses, but undistinguished in its details. In HATCH LANE is a shopping parade of 1949, bleakly detailed apart from a central panel with vase of flowers.

The addict of C20 suburbs may sample some other areas. Set back from LARKSHALL ROAD is the LARKS HALL, a pub converted from a farmhouse. C16–C17 timber-framed

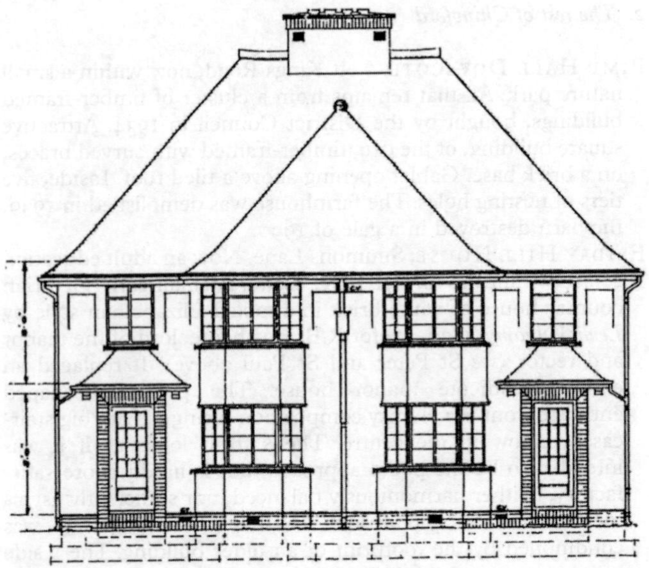

Ropers Avenue, Chingford, 1945

lobby-entrance plan with central chimney; genteel S wing with new entrance, added 1890 by *Arthur Crow*, who had married into the Young family, the landowners. Refurbished 1982. The older part now with first-floor ceiling opened up. The land to S and W was laid out as the LARKS HALL CRESCENT ESTATE, also by *Crow*, 1933–6, with terraces and semi-detached houses for owner-occupiers of modest means.

In and around ROPERS AVENUE, off Larkshall Road, some borough housing from immediately after the Second World War, when standards were high and before economies prevailed. Designed in 1945 by *Reginald W. Lone* with the borough engineer and surveyor *S.J. Hellier*. Generously laid out semi-detached houses in the garden-suburb tradition, with elegantly detailed pantile roofs and (originally) Crittall windows. Their distinctive feature is a pair of canted full-height bays, crowned alternately by a single large half-hip or a single plastered gable.

CHINGFORD MOUNT ROAD. No. 215, Beech House, decent Neo-Georgian, was built as a 'Home of Rest' for women, 1935 by *Arthur R. Mayston*. At the junction with Hall Lane, ALBERT CRESCENT, later 1930s shopping parade with central tower and Art Deco detail.

On WALTHAMSTOW AVENUE,* overlooking the North Circular Road, Holiday Inn Express. The front was built as headquarters for Hitchman's Dairy, *c.* 1930. Symmetrical, with

* Historically, in Walthamstow rather than Chingford.

green-glazed surrounds to the end pavilions and centre, all with hipped roofs of green pantiles.

HIGHAMS PARK

Highams Park is a suburb on the N borders of Walthamstow. It grew around a railway station of 1873 on the Chingford line, renamed in 1894 to draw attention to the new developments around the parkland to its E which originally formed the grounds of the mansion of Highams. The house, facing Woodford Green, survives as Woodford County High School (*see* below).

ALL SAINTS, Castle Avenue. Mission church 1897–8 by *J. Lee & Sons*. A long Perp building, red brick with Bath-stone dressings. NW porch 1911 by *S. Armstrong*.

BAPTIST CHURCH, Cavendish Road. Simple red brick front of 1931, an extension to a church that originated *c.* 1917. Perp central window, chequer brickwork over the entrances. Low adjoining Hall to the r.

METHODIST CHURCH, Winchester Road. A pretty and playful late Gothic frontage by *G. & R.P. Baines*, 1903, typical of their lively turn-of-the-century work. Brick with stone dressings. Corner buttresses flank a broad gable with perky twists and flourishes, above a generous seven-light Perp window. Projecting central entrance with flattened-ogee arch rising to a finial above the parapet. At the sides low, straight-headed windows with cusped tracery. Broad interior without galleries, with extra lighting from dormers in the roof.

Adjoining to the N, restrained brick additions by *Paul Mauger*: Church Rooms, 1955, two storeyed, with bowed front to the road; and HALL, 1959, entered from an airy glazed lobby in Wickham Road.

SCHOOLS, Selwyn Avenue, 1904 by *H. Prosser*, architect to Walthamstow Education committee. A handsome group, all very similar, spaciously set out. Infants and Juniors face Selwyn Avenue, with another Juniors block in between, facing Cavendish Road. Each has a tall main range with curly Jacobean gables and bellcote on a hipped roof, flanked by gabled wings, with lower classroom ranges behind.

HIGHAMS PARK SCHOOL, Handsworth Avenue. Large, plain Essex County Council Secondary, the usual composition of between-the-wars; two-storey centre with lower wings.

PERAMBULATION

The STATION of 1900 is pleasant domestic revival by *W. Ashbee*. Around it a typical suburban centre with the COUNTY ARMS and PARADE, both in Arts and Crafts style, and opposite, the former REGAL cinema, a plain brick front of 1935 to the Electric Cinema of 1911. Across the level crossing to the W, churches and schools (*see* above) are the main interest in the long streets of late Victorian terraces. To the S HALE END ROAD winds downhill to the ROYAL OAK, a jolly pub of *c.* 1900. On the higher ground to the E there are superior houses of slightly later date. THE AVENUE leads NE to All Saints church in Castle Avenue (*see* above). Opposite, CASTLEBAR, 1904, an attractive single Arts and Crafts house, rendered above a brick base, steep roofs, simple casement windows. Further along CHURCH AVENUE a row of semi-detached interwar houses with a few streamlined Deco touches, but much altered. From the top of Castle Avenue, FALMOUTH AVENUE runs E, down to a crossing over the River Ching. Here something remains of *Repton*'s landscaped PARK created from 1794 for John Harman of Highams, with a lake and island made by damming the river Ching. The main lake, with large boulders on the banks, was planned as the principal view from the house. Permission had been given for this extension into Epping Forest, provided that deer were allowed access to the lake. Some of the planting may be Repton's but much of the present woodland developed after the land was acquired in 1890 by the Corporation of London as an extension to their parts of Epping Forest, to save it from development. E of the main lake THE HIGHAMS PARK was made by Walthamstow on land bought from the Warner estate in 1934–7.

The grounds of Highams, seat of the Warner family until 1904, began to be built up from the 1890s. Warner developments in this area aimed at a higher class of occupants than on their Walthamstow estates. MONTALT ROAD, to the E of The Highams Park, begun 1898, has a series of very grand semi-detached 'lodges' by *John Dunn*; THE CHARTER ROAD has typical houses of the 1920s with bow-fronted bay windows, by *William* and *Edward Hunt* for Warner's Law Land Building Company.

WOODFORD COUNTY HIGH SCHOOL FOR GIRLS, Woodford New Road. The core of this large group of buildings facing E across Woodford Green is the house known as HIGHAMS, built by *William Newton* for Anthony Bacon M.P., who acquired the estate in 1764. It was enlarged by an upper storey in the later C18, probably for William Hornby, a former governor of Bombay, who owned the house from 1788. The next owner, John Harman, banker, commissioned *Humphry Repton* in 1793 to make further improvements and landscape the grounds. From 1849–1904 the estate belonged to the Warner family, developers of much of Walthamstow. The house was used as a hospital in the First World War, and a school from 1919. Additional buildings were added in the 1920s after it was acquired by Essex County Council.

Newton's house is still recognizable, a smart Neoclassical villa, with ground floor raised above a basement, and at first with only one floor above. The centre is distinguished by giant pilasters whose Ionic capitals are ornamented with ramsheads. The front door was originally approached up steps, replaced by a clumsy porch in the C19.

Inside, a flight of steps from the porch was cut into the entrance hall in the C19, and another flight, very oddly, was made down to the basement. Otherwise the hall is of the C18, a spacious marble-paved room with three arches on square pillars dividing it from the entrance passage, and three more opening to the spine corridor behind. On the r. this corridor broadens to a handsome stairhall, the stone steps with moulded soffits and iron balustrading, the landing lit by a Venetian window in the N wall. Good cornices; the one in the entrance passage with Doric guttae. A square room to the r. of the entrance passage, also with nice cornice; plainer rooms along the W front. To the S, a broad bow-fronted room, added in the later C18. At the same time the extra floor was added; through it a tiny staircase climbs to a prospect lantern on the roof, a favourite C18 feature in this area of countryside.

Repton in his Red Book for the house (1794), was dismissive of the interest in distant prospects and was concerned to integrate the house in the immediate landscape. To this end he added a simple iron-railed veranda raised on arches against the W side, formerly with a roof. He also made alterations to provide an uncluttered lawn to the W, framed by trees which concealed the farm buildings, but today the vista is only of tennis courts, and the lake (*see* above) is no longer visible from the house. The school buildings of the 1920s to N and S are discreetly classical.

THE WHITE HOUSE. Down a lane off Woodford New Road, idyllically sited within MALLINSON PARK WOODS, originally part of the grounds of Highams. Built in 1906 for Lady Henry Somerset (who had earlier lived at Highams), based on a design by *C.F.A. Voysey*. Converted in 2003 to a children's hospice by *Praxis*. Although Voysey's design was modified in execution and there have been later alterations, especially since a fire in 1983, his stamp is still recognizable in the white-washed, roughcast walls with tapering buttress, pegged-timber casements with leaded lights, and long sloping tiled roof ending in a half hip. The house is of two storeys, L-shaped, with an entrance hall projecting out under a catslide roof, entered by an unassuming door. A string course arches over it. Adjoining the hall a small former chapel with a row of five tiny pointed windows. Inside, a couple of doors with Voysey's typical heart-motif hinges survived the fire; the rest is much altered. E of the house a roughcast garden wall also has a Voysey character.

The estate was acquired by the Mallinsons, wealthy timber merchants. Sir Stuart Mallinson, who lived there from

1925–81, used the house for political entertaining, and created gardens in the enlarged grounds. In front of the house an arboretum, planted with 128 trees by famous people, 1953–81. In Woodford New Road, near the boundary with Redbridge, ST MARGARETS, a mixture of dates, early C19 bargeboarded gables and a l. part with Georgian parapet.

LEYTON

Leyton was a large parish, originally including Leytonstone (*see* below). Until the later C19 it was a straggling village on the higher land E of the Lea marshes, with gentry houses and merchants' villas in fine grounds, and surrounding land used for market gardens. Stations were opened on the line to Loughton in 1856 but transformation to an artisan and working-class suburb came later, as development spread N from Stratford, especially after 1870, when workmen's fares were introduced on the Great Eastern Railway. The population rose from 10,394 in 1871 to 23,016 in 1881 and had doubled again ten years later. By 1911 (including some parts of Walthamstow and Wanstead) it had risen to 124,735. In the 1890s civic aspirations were expressed by a grand town hall near the station, a mile to the S of the old village, but this area never became a real town centre. The main shopping centre (much rebuilt after war damage) developed at the N end of the High Road, between Leyton Green and the junction with Lea Bridge Road, where the most distinguished buildings are the amply laid out Bakers' almshouses. A few remnants of pre-suburban Leyton are to be found along the High Road and in the neighbourhood of St Mary's church, where a fine collection of monuments hints at the older history of the area.

RELIGIOUS BUILDINGS

ALL SAINTS, Capworth Street 1973 by *Laurence King & Partners*, replacing a church of 1865 by *W. Wigginton*. Triangular in section, a forceful intrusion in an uneventful street. Plain yellow brick W wall. Restful interior with E lights, incorporating stained glass from the old church.

CHRIST CHURCH. Francis Road. 1902 by *Sir Arthur Blomfield & Son.* Buff brick with red brick and stone dressings. Only nave and S aisle built. Completed 1959 by an E wall by *Humphrys & Hurst.*

EMMANUEL, Lea Bridge Road and Hitcham Road. Built for the Warner Estate suburb that sprang up in the area from the 1890s. The CHURCH HALL in Hitcham Road was the first church, 1906 by *E.C. Frere*. Gabled front with lunette, clerestory below dentilled eaves, elegantly done. Adjacent is the neat group of VICARAGE, in chequered brick, and slim CHURCH in red brick, with matching chamfered corners; by *Martin Travers* and *T.F.W. Grant*, 1933–5. (Sir T.C. Warner, by then Lord Lieutenant of Suffolk, laid the foundation stone with 'masonic ceremonial'.) The church has W and N entrances boldly enriched by cast stone with flat decoration. No tower, a cupola was planned but not built. The S aisle has blind buttressed walls to the busy main road, but the N aisle windows are tall, with cusped lights. The simpler clerestory windows, roughly rendered interior, and shallow arcade arches on chamfered piers without capitals provide a vernacular Gothic setting for Travers' hallmark, a painted outline of a steep Baroque arch behind the altar (the colours not original). The same motif is found on the PULPIT and in the STAINED GLASS in the N aisle, a Baroque St George and heraldry against clear glass. S aisle E, St Andrew, post-war.

ST LUKE, Ruckholt Road. Now Greek Orthodox. 1914 by *E.D. Hoyland*. An unusual low barn-like building with incomplete NW tower, similar to the architect's St Michael, East Ham (*see* p. 272). Canted apse and E vestries. Grey terracotta blocks on a steel frame, with Arts and Crafts detailing. Timber arcades inside, carrying an elaborate timber roof.

ST MARY WITH ST EDWARD AND ST LUKE, Church Road. The old parish church, much altered, set in an atmospheric churchyard. The parish was large, originally including Leytonstone. John Strype, the antiquarian, was rector in the early C18. There was a church here from the C11, but the oldest surviving part is the red brick W tower with diagonal buttresses, of 1658, with an C18 clock cupola brought from Leyton Great House in 1806. The N aisle wall and part of the chancel may also date from a C17 rebuilding. The present exterior reflects later alterations: repairs by *Jesse Gibson* in 1794, a new S aisle of brick with Y-tracery windows, 1822 by *John Shaw*; extended by a SW baptistery in 1884. Extensive restoration took place in 1929–32 by *J. Andrew Minty*, when the chancel was lengthened. Inside, the arcades with round-headed arches on slim octagonal piers date from 1932 (casing iron columns of 1822), as does the chancel arch of concrete. W gallery of 1711. E window with reset curvilinear tracery of 1853, enlarged 1932. The former chancel SCREEN, 1920 by *Minty*, now glazed, divides off a crèche at the W end. This was made after a fire in 1995, part of alterations by *Kay Pilsbury Architects* which included the creation of a chapel under the tower, and clever remodelling of the S entrance and baptistery area. – FONT, C15, on later pedestal. – REREDOS, 1920 by *Minty*. – HOURGLASS, 1693, four-in-one, from the Augustinian church, Munich. – Carved POOR BOX, 1826.

MONUMENTS. Ursula Gasper †1493, small brass. – Sir Robert Beechcroft †1721, cartouche attributed to *T. Stayner* (GF). – Sir Michael Hicks †1612 and wife, two semi-reclining effigies, propped up on their elbows, lying in opposite directions, probably not in original state. Attributed by Adam White to *Atye & James*. – Sir William Hicks †1680 and his son Sir William †1702 and daughter-in-law, large wall monuments with standing figures of man and woman in Roman dress, between them the father, semi-reclining. The Hicks monuments, now in the tower, were moved from the chancel in 1853.* – Newdigate Owsley †1714, small tablet signed by *S. Tufnell*. – John Storey by *J. Hickey*, 1787. Good standing figure of Fame against large grey obelisk. – Hillesden children, 1807 by *John Flaxman*. Woman seated on the ground, reading. – William Bosanquet †1813, fine relief of the Good Samaritan, also by *Flaxman*. – E. Brewster †1898, signed by *Gaffin* of Regent Street. Woman mourning over an urn, just like a hundred years before.

The CHURCHYARD has an enjoyable variety of weighty tombs from the time when Leyton was an attractive retreat for gentry and City men. Much has become a wildlife area, but a fine row of chest tombs is visible along the path to the N. Some of the more individual structures have been restored: Benjamin Moyer †1759, unusual hexagonal monument with cupola. – E. Bertie †1757, square, of two stages. – Near the road, Tench family of Leyton Great House, C18, square, the upper part with corner scrolls supporting an obelisk. – Sparks family, 1820s etc. Austerely Neo-Grec. The tomb to Samuel Bosanquet, 1806 by *Sir John Soane*, is no longer visible.

ST JOSEPH (R.C.), Grange Park Road. Built as a First World War memorial, 1924 by *Ernest Bower Norris* of *Sandy & Norris*, replacing a temporary church of 1904. A large church on a tight site, given presence by a substantial blocky westwork with a Lutyens-like taper. Eclectically classical: giant corner pilasters with patterned brickwork and a stepped parapet with niche over a tall round-arched window. Economical plaster barrel-vaulted interior (concealing a steel frame) in plain round arched style with passage-aisles and clerestory. Roundels with plaster reliefs of angels remain on the nave walls, but the original marble furnishings were removed in a reordering of 1978 by *John Newton* of *Burles Newton*, when the tabernacle was placed centrally and remains of the high altar set against the rear wall. Later paintings, copies of famous originals, have been added: altarpiece Crucifixion after Cimabue, and on the walls and ceiling, rather lost in their plain surroundings, Trans-

*Described by the antiquarian John Strype, in his appendix to Stow's *Survey of London* (1720). He mentions 17 monuments in the church, most of them now gone.

figuration after Raphael, by *Leo Stevenson*, 1995, Creation of Man after Michelangelo by *Stevenson* and *Fleur Kelly*, 2003.

TRINITY METHODIST CHURCH, Leyton High Road. Tough and inward-looking, of the 1970s. Reused stock brick, shallow asymmetrical roof with lantern, l. a band of small windows below the eaves.

YOUNG PEOPLE'S HALL, Lindley Road. Salvation Army. By *F.J. Coxhead*, 1931. Battlemented.

BARCLAY HALL MISSION, High Road, 1907 by *E.C. Frere*. Simple yellow brick, with four full-height windows to the road, but much altered.*

MOSQUE, Lea Bridge Road, Rochdale Road (No. 439–57). A former carpet factory converted and refronted in the 1990s. A well-balanced frontage in glazed brick of two colours. Tall pointed arches, a small minaret at either end.

MAJOR BUILDINGS

The LIBRARY, High Road and Ruckholt Road, 1882–3 by *J.M. Knight*, was built as offices of the Local Board, but was soon inadequate and was converted to library use in 1896–7 by the Council Surveyor, *W. Dawson*. Pale gault brick and stone, with iron cresting to the roof and a pinched angled entrance tower at the corner with French pavilion roof. Next door, the much grander TOWN HALL, with technical institute attached, 74
1895–6 by *John Johnson*. Fussy but enjoyable, in an eclectic and enriched Italianate style. High Road frontage of striped brick and stone with pedimented entrance, three large arches on the first floor enclosing blind niches, and a raised central attic flanked by thin corner turrets. The N flank along Adelaide Road contains the first-floor assembly hall, with pretty ventilating turrets on the roof. The design repeats the arches of the High Road, but here they have large windows and carved heads in the spandrels. Grand entrance, further on a more modest one (now blocked) to the technical institute with relief above showing workmen studying and at work. To the S in Ruckholt Road, a wing with the Council Chamber, a later addition (shown on map of 1916). An interesting contrast: a mannered rather Hawksmorean composition of brick and stone, with central giant arch breaking through the cornice and no windows at first-floor level. Behind the parapet, hipped roof with cupola. Inside, the council chamber has four Ionic columns supporting a dome on pendentives with central lantern, and some original panelling and furnishings. It is approached by a small but imposing marble stair. The assembly hall (now offices) has a stage and is embellished with coved ceiling and pilasters between the windows.

*Founded by J.G. Barclay of Knotts Green in a hall attached to the Gardener's Lodge of the Barclay estate.

CARNEGIE LIBRARY, Lea Bridge Road. 1905 by *W. Jacques*. Five bays to the street with off-centre door and a small central turret; one-storey rear wing. Pleasant free Baroque with chunky stone detail: banding to the ground floor, blocked window surrounds above, and Ionic columns used for mullions. Each gable end has a Venetian window. The interior is now a single space, divided by two rows of Ionic columns.

FIRE STATION, Church Road, 1992 by *Rock Townsend*. Main block with crisp yellow brick walls, deep projecting eaves, and quirkily placed windows. The fire engines gleam within a glazed, barrel-vaulted shed. Drill tower behind with odd floating pitched roof, apparently a contextual demand from the planners but looking more like an homage to Canary Wharf.

NEW SPITALFIELDS MARKET, Ruckholt Road and Sherrin Road, by Hackney Marshes. By *EPR*, 1987–91, an early example of the reuse of the railway lands in this area. Vast, steel-framed market hall with internal roadways, for the fruit and vegetable markets removed from Spitalfields. The gable ends have a spiky profile of three big peaked roofs over the three roadways and smaller peaks in between over the roof lit corridors. Far projecting eaves project over the loading bays on each side. In contrast to the hall's strident yellow frame and blue cladding, the four symmetrically disposed cafés around the perimeter are demure cubes of striped grey concrete.

PORTERS FIELD RIDING SCHOOL, Lea Bridge Road. By *J.M.V. Bishop* and *M.G. Quintin* of the Lea Valley Regional Park Authority, *c.* 1982. Walled enclosure with brick-and-flint stables and low-maintenance indoor riding school, clad in translucent glass-fibre panels.

LEA VALLEY ICE RINK, Lea Bridge Road. Another facility at the S end of the Lea Valley Park, *c.* 1982 by the *Building Design Partnership*. Big, curved, lightweight steel roof. Space for 1,000 spectators.

WATERWORKS, Lea Bridge Road. Metropolitan Board of Works. Sluice House 1885. Engineers Office 1890–2 by *G.E. Dolman*. Red brick with tilehanging and timberwork. Musgrave Engine and Boiler House, 1922–4.

Schools

Some of the numerous schools built between 1877 and 1910 for the rapidly growing population survive;* a sample are included in the perambulation. The School Board architect, as at West Ham, was *J.T. Newman* (†1896), succeeded by his partner *W. Jacques*. The Council took over from the board in 1911.

* Church Road 1877, Newport Road 1887, Downsell Road 1887, Capworth Street 1896 and 1909 (by *Frere*), Farmer Road 1903, Barclay Estate 1910, Sybourn Street 1910.

PERAMBULATIONS

1. High Road and Church Road, S–N *from the Station*

The civic buildings near the present station at the S end of the High Road (*see* above) stand alone, looking incongruously grand compared with the few minor shops opposite. The bank at No. 267 built by J.H. Bethell, 1896, is the only more urban effort. Much of the area W of this part of the High Road was built up only in the early C20. The road winds N past the neat CORONATION GARDENS (laid out *c.* 1902, enlarged later) with bandstand. The three-tier fountain with cherubs, stamped *A. Durenne* was added in 2000. The old village centre lay near the junction with Grange Park Road. Here is the former CO-OP, 1909 with beehive motifs, probably by *W.H. Cockcroft*, as at Hoe Street Walthamstow, and on the E side, set back, a badly mauled big villa (now a club), GROVE HOUSE, 1806.

To the W down CHURCH ROAD is the parish church of St Mary (*see* above). By the churchyard, single-storey flint-faced ALMSHOUSES in Tudor style, founded 1656, rebuilt 1886 by *Richard Creed.* Nearby is a scatter of smaller pre-suburban housing. Church Road turns N towards Lea Bridge Road past the Fire Station and council housing. The only older building of note here is ETLOE HOUSE, set back on the W side. The trim early C19 stucco-Gothic front, a three-bay, three-storey centre with lower wings, was a remodelling of a house built *c.* 1760 on an older site by Edward Mores. From 1856 it was the country retreat of Cardinal Wiseman. Mullioned windows with dripstones, embattled parapet with corner pinnacles, and an open porch with Gothic arches. At the back two full-height canted bays. Converted to flats and now surrounded by two-storey terraces. Off MARSH LANE, in the former grounds of Etloe House, now within ST JOSEPH'S SCHOOL, an ICE HOUSE, late C18 or early C19 with domed brick chamber and tunnel entrance set in a stone wall.

The lane ends in the LAMMAS LANDS by the Lea, preserved as open space as a result of a local campaign in 1892, as one learns from a tablet erected on 'the Cottage'. Back in Church Road, Leyton's first BOARD SCHOOL, 1877, a long gabled building, still rural in character, with attached teacher's house at the N end. Rustic porches and pretty tiled lettering. Enlarged to the rear in 1891; two-storey Neo-Georgian buildings to the S, 1913.

*2. Lea Bridge Road (*W–E*)*

By Church Road, the former SAVOY CINEMA (now Classic) 1928–9 by *George Coles.* To its E the Public Library (*see* above). Then not much to dwell on. On the S side Woolworths is a cream faience-clad store of the 1930s with Art Deco verticals. On the N side, a villa with triplets of arched windows, now THE

DRUM public house. The high point is the LONDON MASTER BAKERS' BENEVOLENT INSTITUTION, by *T.E. Knightley*, 1857–66, a splendid display, buildings on three sides of a large railed court open to the street and extending along Lea Bridge Road to E and W. Yellow brick with stucco. The style is a debased rustic Italianate crammed full of quirky detail. Numerous chalet gables and two towers in the re-entrant angles. The terraces are of two storeys, with raised end gables. The houses facing the street are more elaborate than the rest, with projecting bays below upper windows with their own bracketed little gables. The main range has a centrepiece with informative plaques and a pretty tablet above with a harvesting putto. Reliefs of ploughing and breadmaking on the side ranges.

The junction with the High Road is architecturally feeble. The BAKERS' ARMS, familiar as a bus destination, is a two-storey pub, tarted up with granite pilasters, and with a row of pineapples on the parapet.

3. High Road N–S from the Bakers' Arms

A scrappy sequence. First the WILLIAM IV pub, by *Shoebridge & Rising* 1897. At the corner of Belmont Park Road the former King's Cinema, a symmetrical white Art Deco front with vertical fins. LEYTON GREEN is a mess, dominated by bus garages on the E side. The N corner has a curved range of shops and a tower of flats behind, *c.* 1963. On the W side the brash and busy LEYTON LEISURE LAGOON of the early 1990s by the *Waltham Forest Borough Architect's Department*. This has canted glass bays and exposed services in High Tech fashion; top-lit interior with branching supports for the roof. It replaced earlier baths of 1934 (their site now occupied by Tesco). On the S side is the Barclay Hall Mission (*see* above).

S of the green the road becomes residential with a scatter of small shops. No. 500, WALNUT TREE HOUSE (Conservative Club) at the corner of Jesse Road, is a rare survival, the oldest house in Leyton. A substantial two-storeyed timber-framed house with jetty, its early character disguised by render, later sashes and a Doric porch. It appears to have started as a later C15 building, with wing on the l. added *c.* 1600 and to the r. a SE wing probably of the mid-C17. Much altered inside, but several Tudor stone fireplaces remain, one with an arabesque frieze (and a painting of *c.* 1500 on an upstairs corridor wall). Rear stair projection with good early C18 staircase with twisted balusters.

Opposite is the cricket ground established here in 1885 for the Essex County Cricket Club, with a magnificent PAVILION by *Richard Creed*, 1886. Timber on a brick base. Flamboyant roof with half-timbering, dormers and domed cupola. Separate side pavilions, linked in 1935.

Further on, No. 669. A charming C18 Georgian Gothic

frontage with ogee windows and pedimented porch, the ground floor restored to its original form, but alas, the building is only a façade to vast and ungainly Post Office premises behind.

KNOTTS GREEN is reached from Leyton Green by Leyton Green Road. Nothing to see now. There was an C18 mansion with excellent grounds, in the C19 the home of the Barclays (a branch of the banking family). The streets to the NE began to be laid out after the death of Joseph Gurney Barclay in 1898. The house became Livingstone College, a training college for missionaries; it was replaced in 1961 by a block of flats, since demolished.

LEYTONSTONE

The hamlet of Leytonstone, named from a reputedly Roman milestone (now below an obelisk at the start of New Wanstead), developed on the edge of Epping Forest at the eastern end of the parish of Leyton. Its character as an attractive pre-suburban centre with an early C19 church is still just recognizable. The fringes of Epping Forest attracted wealthy and influential landowners to the neighbourhood up to the later C19, but now the only survivor among their houses is Leytonstone House, at the N end of the hamlet. In the C19 it was the home of Thomas Fowell Buxton the younger, of the brewing company.* To its W was Wallwood House, bought in 1817 by William Cotton (1786–1866), cordage manufacturer and later governor of the Bank of England. He was a founder of the National Society, treasurer of the Metropolis Churches Fund and paid for three East End churches,† as well as contributing to the new St John, Leytonstone. His family gave the site of St Andrew's church when the Wallwood estate was developed in the late C19. Whipps Cross Hospital, further N, occupies the grounds of Forest House (demolished 1964), which was built in 1683 by the Huguenot banker Sir James Houblon, sold 1703 to Sir Gilbert Heathcote, and from 1730–1831 was home of the Bosanquet family (for whom *Sir John Soane* made alterations in 1786–7).

The Eastern Counties Railway arrived in 1856, the first of two lines to cross the area, and prompted some suburban development. The Forest fringes remained superior, the humbler southern suburbs followed tramway development in the 1880s, swallowing up the old hamlet of Harrow Green and merging with working-class Stratford, where the vast railway works were a major employer.

* For well-to-do life in Leytonstone in the mid-C19 *see* the childhood diaries and sketch books of his daughter, Ellen Buxton, ed. E. Creighton, 1967.

† St Peter Stepney, St Thomas Bethnal Geen, St Paul Bow Common.

RELIGIOUS BUILDINGS

HOLY TRINITY AND ST AUGUSTINE, Holloway Road, Harrow Green. 1973 by *Gerard Goalen*, replacing a church of 1878. Built among grim new council housing, replaced since by a friendlier environment. That helps to explain its defensive, windowless exterior of dour brown brick. It is relieved only by a small bellcote and the lintel of the W door: cast concrete with Trinity and other scenes. (A more welcoming porch by *Ronald Wylde Associates* was planned in 2004.) But the interior is pleasing: intimate but geometrically precise spaces within pale brick walls. The cross-in-square nave is defined by concrete corner posts, with low timber ceiling, surrounded by taller aisles, which in a rather Soanian way are lit from an inward-facing clerestory. Square corners act as recesses for statues. On one side there is a broader space for a Baptistry, with circular rooflight over the font, and a Morning Chapel with glazed walls, below an organ loft. Sanctuary with altar on a platform of two steps, blind E wall. In the Chapel four lights with figures of saints, good quality Victorian glass, said to come from St Augustine Haggerston. Adjoining hall to the W.

ST ANDREW, St Andrew's Road and Colworth Road. 1887–92 by *Sir Arthur Blomfield*. The site was given by the Cotton family in memory of the energetic philanthropist and church builder William Cotton (†1866) of Wallwood House, whose estate was developed as a superior suburb from 1875. Large and impressive, knapped flint with stone dressings. W gable with corner pinnacles flanking a group of four lancets, the centre two under an arch with a roundel. Slim flèche over the crossing, pinnacles also at the E end.

Plain interior, poorly converted in 1977 after threatened redundancy, with the western bays divided off as a hall. The chancel, paid for by the Cottons, is a little richer than the rest, ashlar-faced, with some stiff-leaf carving on the chancel-arch corbels, and the E wall lancets, with glass of 1892, enriched by Purbeck shafts. ALTAR FRONT with lamb and painted angels. The only remarkable fittings are the STAINED GLASS windows in the aisles by *Margaret I. Chilton*, a pupil of Christopher Whall, her most important commission in England. Several were designed as First World War memorials. Large, strongly leaded figures in bold colours, less sentimental than many of this time. The early windows are delicately detailed, the later ones more Expressionist. Three lancets in the N aisle; two in the S aisle of *c.* 1917. In the present hall two more war memorial windows in the S aisle, and a later W triplet (†1946). In the N aisle in the hall two of 1938 and a W triplet (†1940).

At the E end of the N aisle, lit artificially, a triplet of *c.* 1955. In the vestry lobby, window of 2002 by *Hilary Davies*; priest with a chalice; the glass with bubble roundels.

CHURCH ROOM, 1904 by *H.C. Smart.* A nice Arts and Crafts doorway, the rest burnt out.

ELIM PENTECOSTAL CHURCH (from 1997), Hainault Road. Built as St Catherine (C.E.), 1893 by *Richard Creed.* Stock brick, Perp, in the tradition of Bodley. An elaborate S porch with stone dressings, otherwise very plain. Amply lit: the very wide nave has a seven-light window in the tall gable, and two clerestory windows to each bay. Four-bay arcades of moulded stone on clustered piers. Three-bay raised chancel, now painted white and used as a music stage with the E end divided off as an office.

ST JOHN THE BAPTIST, Church Lane. Set on raised ground within a spacious, attractively railed churchyard in the centre of Leytonstone. The church of 1832–3 by *Edward Blore* replaced an older chapel of ease; it was partly funded by William Cotton of Wallwood House. From the S the view is of the livelier aisle added by *Caröe & Passmore* in 1909–10. It has alternate windows taller and gabled, and is prefaced by a very prominent dog-leg ramp of brick and stone to the SE entrance, by *Kay Pilsbury Architects*, 2002–3, part of a ten-year improvement scheme. Also by Caröe are the attractive steps leading up to *Blore*'s SW tower-porch; this has diagonal buttresses and a plaster vault. The character of the rest of Blore's church is now best seen from W and N: grey brick with E.E. detail, N wall with lancets between thin buttresses, W wall with two tall two-light windows with plate tracery. The chancel was added in 1893 by *Adams & Mann.* The E vestry, also by *Caröe & Passmore*, wraps round the chancel; a typical Caröe doorway: shallow niche and canted sides.

Broad interior, curiously lopsided, opened up on the S by *Caröe*'s arcade on quatrefoil piers, set within the original nave. The eastern bay canting in towards the chancel arch gives some character to what must originally have been a bleak barn-like space below heavy tie-beams. Deep W gallery of 1893, when the church was refurnished with low iron SCREEN, octagonal FONT with carved quatrefoils, new pews, and good patterned TILES in the new chancel. Pulpit and chancel panelling of the 1930s. STAINED GLASS. E window, a powerful Christ in Majesty by *Clayton & Bell*, 1935. N and S chancel windows 1898 by *Powell*; S chapel with two E lancets by *Kempe & Co.*, 1928. In the tower some good BELLRINGERS' BOARDS and a turret clock of 1898.

ST MARGARET, Woodhouse Road, Harrow Green. 1892–3 by *J.T. Newman* and *W. Jacques*, for the working-class district near Wanstead Flats. A mighty basilica, with furnishings in the High

Anglican tradition, little altered. It stands prominently on a corner site, though without its intended NW tower. Stock brick with red brick dressings. Three tall lancets under an arch in E and W gables, the tall clerestory windows similar, under continuous eaves (not gabled like Newman's earlier St Paul, Bow). N transeptal organ chamber, with very thin lancets and a corner turret.

An impressive interior, with tall arcades and clerestory, and high, boarded barrel ceiling canted out on brackets like a hammer beam roof. The narrower chancel has an even loftier arch-braced roof. Between the two, adding to the drama, a painted and cambered beam with carved ROOD by *Sir Charles Nicholson*, 1921, above a low wall with painted figures. In the chancel elaborate Dec SEDILIA with crocketed canopies, but the nave details are odd and finicky for such a grand scale: brick lozenge piers with recessed mouldings, very thin upper corbels and shafts. The walls are of polychrome brick, alas now whitened. A rather mean projecting Baptistery at the W end.

HIGH ALTAR 1893, a memorial to the first Bishop of St Albans, designed by *Louth*, with elaborate carving by *Sebastian Zwinck* of Oberammergau, gilded later. Lady Chapel added 1912 by *Cutts, Johnson & Boddy*; in a more Arts and Crafts spirit, with small Dec windows, green terrazzo floor, and painted altar frontal. Baroque PAINTINGS, including the Virgin (school of *Murillo*) originally in the Lady Chapel, now above the High Altar, another of Christ (school of *Guido Reni*). STATIONS OF THE CROSS: paintings in a historicist style: one signed by *A. Fellowes Prynne* (Jesus meets his mother); others by his pupils (cf. a similar set at St Mary Ilford). STATUES of Virgin and Child, and St Margaret by *Nicholson*. STAINED GLASS. Lady Chapel E by *Terence Randall*. Nave S, two by *G. Beningfield*, 1965 (St Joseph and St John Baptist), good bold figures.

Church INSTITUTE, 1910 by *T.E. Lidiord James*, of striped red brick, with rather odd Perp window with brick-and-stone striped mullions. First-floor hall with arch-braced roof and stage.

ST PATRICK'S R.C. CEMETERY, Langthorne Road. Crowded with white-marble monuments, among which an angular memorial to Lucia Ferrari †1965 makes an odd exception. Lodge and Chapel with wheel window, 1861–2 by *S.J. Nicholl*.

93 NEW TESTAMENT ASSEMBLY, formerly FETTER LANE CHURCH, Langthorne Road. 1900 by *P. Morley Horder* for Congregationalists who traced their origin to the Fetter Lane chapel in the City. Outstandingly original. In a reticent Arts and Crafts domestic style with a Scottish flavour. Harled walls, three tall storeys with small mullioned windows; the prominent N flank wall articulated by a subtle rhythm of major and minor tapering buttresses. In the W gable a small Venetian window high up with a little terracotta ornament. This lights the two-storey church, raised above a ground-floor hall. Interior with

flattened barrel vault and galleries on iron columns around two-and-a-half sides: panelled gallery fronts. PULPIT in the centre of the E end within a Venetian arch, with Ionic capitals to the square piers, and a lunette window at the back. Interior now all painted white.

BAPTIST CHURCH, Cann Hall Road. 1886–7, an early work by *George Baines*. Dark brick with painted-stone dressings, in a round-arched style. Paired entrances. At the back SCHOOLS of 1880 by *J. Randall Vinning*, brick with red brick pilasters. The oldest survival from a number of Baptist churches active in the area from the 1870s.

WESLEYAN CHRISTIAN CENTRE, Harrow Green, by *J. Reeve Young*, 1959. Replacing a bombed church. Simple, with tall rectangular windows and small square tower.

BAPTIST CHURCH, Hainault Road, 1926. Built for Strict Baptists. Very modest. Red brick gable with round-headed arch.

UNITED FREE CHURCH, Fairlop Road (Baptists and United Reformed). 1991 by *Ian Morton Wright*, on the site of the Baptist Fillebrook church founded 1874. Ingenious T-shaped plan of church and hall, with strong, strikingly angled roofs. Thin, full-height windows to the church, which faces towards the corner with Wallwood Road, the apex flanked by windows with coloured glass. Complex folded-timber ceiling.

CANN HALL METHODIST CHURCH, Cann Hall Road. 1992 by *Higgins Group plc. Design & Build*, replacing a church founded 1887. Monopitch gable to the road with three circular windows with stained glass, irregularly placed. Recessed entrance on the l.

INTERNATIONAL PENTECOSTAL CITY MISSION, Colworth Road and Wallwood Road, 1901–2 by *Clark Hallam*, minister of Stepney Green Tabernacle, for Primitive Methodists. Tall, the church raised over a ground floor. A proud front in eclectic mixed Renaissance with much terracotta ornament (repaired in concrete after war damage); shallow scrolled pedimental gable, and a pompous porch with squat corner turrets.

MOREIA WELSH CHURCH, High Road. 1958 by *T. & H. Llewelyn Daniel*. For a Calvinistic Methodist congregation founded in Walthamstow in 1901. A restrained, carefully detailed building, set back from the road, with Church Hall adjoining to the N. Brick, tower-like raised central gable with raised bricks forming a cross. Windows with angled heads, framed in slate, below a stylish continuous moulded stone string course. Foyer below W gallery. The interior is a broad single space; slightly raked floor below a shallow curved roof. Raised dais; in the apse four pointed windows with vivid STAINED GLASS by *Howard Martin* of *Celtic Studios*, showing Welsh missionaries and preachers. Original, simple wooden furnishings.

LEYTONSTONE MOSQUE, Dacre Road, former church hall, refaced after 1992 with entrance below. Islamic arch; circular minaret and gilded dome.

HINDU TEMPLE, Whipps Cross Road. Built as First Church of Christ Scientist. 1937 by *T.E. Davidson, Son & Sherwood.* Georgian style with semicircular columned porch.

MAJOR BUILDINGS

100 LIBRARY, Church Lane. 1934 by *J. Ambrose Dartnall.* Within a Neo-Georgian commercial frontage of ten bays which incorporated the municipal electricity showrooms; red brick with pantiled roof behind a parapet. The library is distinguished by a serious classical frontispiece in stone; grouped Ionic columns over fluted Doric columns flanking a coffered porch. The interior is a surprise, a coherent Art Deco period piece. Octagonal lobby from which stairs divide to lead up to an elongated octagonal top-lit hall providing access to the library. Doorways with emphatic angled corners and chamfered mouldings outlined in black against shiny cream surfaces, brass handrails and a display cabinet in the centre, of the same shape as the hall. The separate library rooms are now united.

HARROW GREEN BRANCH LIBRARY, Cathall Road. By *John H. Jacques.* Begun 1938 but completed only in 1959. A pale imitation of the main library, the flanking wings depressingly skimped. Awkward classical detail to the stone-faced centre: engaged half-octagonal columns on a high rusticated base. Pleasant, well-lit library rooms on the upper floors at the back.

CATHALL ROAD RECREATION and COMMUNITY CENTRES *see* perambulation.

LANGTHORNE HOSPITAL, THE CLICK and LANGTHORNE PARK *see* perambulation.

WHIPPS CROSS HOSPITAL, Whipps Cross Road. 1900–3 by *Francis J. Sturdy*, built as an infirmary for the West Ham Board of Guardians, in the grounds of the Forest House estate, acquired in 1889. Now a confusing warren, but the original plan is still evident, a vast group of buildings designed for 762 patients laid out on a pavilion plan, with striking roofline. Central administrative block in Northern Renaissance style, with board room and Perp chapel on first floor (fireplace from the demolished Forest House on the ground floor). Ground-floor corridors and bridges on brick arches link the central block and the four ward blocks, which have verandas. Additions 1936–7 by *W. Lionel Jenkins*, Borough engineer, to house a further 500 patients.

HIGH SCHOOL FOR GIRLS, Forest Road and Colworth Road. Begun as a private school in 1884. 1911 by *W. Jacques.* Very pretty red brick building with two asymmetrical projecting wings and one asymmetrical turret in one of two re-entrant angles. Several gables with black and white chequer pattern. Extensions of 1932 and 1957.

CORPUS CHRISTI HIGH SCHOOL, Elmore Road. Late C19, Queen Anne style. Eighteen bays in three groups.

SENIOR GIRLS' SCHOOL, Connaught Road 1932, extensions 1960–1, 1964.

Other schools are described within the perambulations.

PERAMBULATIONS

1. Leytonstone High Road, N of the Central Line Station

From the 1940s Central Line station (no trace of the 1856 station remains) CHURCH LANE leads toward the High Road. On the corner of KIRKDALE ROAD, on a triangular site, INDEPENDENT BUILDINGS, newspaper offices and commercial premises of 1934; central entrance and clock tower. Past the Library and St John (*see* above) to the HIGH ROAD. On its E side the RED LION (now Zulus), 1890 by *W.D. Church*, makes an urban show with curly strapwork decoration, stucco foliage panels above the windows and a lead corner turret. A terrace in the same style continues N. But squeezed behind High Road shops comes a surprise, AYLMER ROAD, a row of smart late C18 three-storey houses, the first two with channelled stucco and later big Doric porches. Behind, London City Mission rooms of 1885, later a clothing factory, suggests a decline in the social status of the area. Further N, GROVE ROAD has been perked up by a SCULPTURE of a leaf-covered figure, by *Stephen Duncan*, 'Leaf Memory', 2001.

BROWNING ROAD, the next road E, leads to a now-cherished enclave of two-storey cottages, irregularly sited, with long front gardens. They were built *c.* 1840 on the 'back lane' to Epping Forest. The NORTH STAR pub was converted from two cottages in 1858 (its terracotta window surrounds perhaps later additions). Reprieved from redevelopment, unlike the area beyond which was partly rebuilt after the Second World War and has since been redeveloped. The N end of the High Road dissolves dismally into road engineering. The GREEN MAN pub existed from the C17; the present building, with Ipswich windows along a spreading convex front, is of 1927.

On the W side of the High Road, LEYTONSTONE HOUSE. Built *c.* 1800. Five bays, two-and-a-half storeys with Doric porch; lower wings l. and r., set back, with windows in arched recesses. These have canted bay windows at the rear. More unusual is the projecting staircase bow in the centre of the rear elevation, with curved Venetian window at first-floor level. Ground-floor room on the l. of the front door with pretty plasterwork ceiling. In the C19 the home of Sir Thomas Fowell Buxton of the brewing family (†1858). From 1868–1937 used for Bethnal Green Industrial Schools, then Leytonstone House hospital. Restored as offices 2002. Facing the road an Italianate C19 range, now offices; behind, three-storey gabled school buildings in stock brick by *A. & C. Harston*, 1881–9, sympathetically converted to terrace housing. They consisted originally of six 'homes', each with four twelve-bed dormitories and dayroom.

The grounds to the S are covered by a large Tesco supermarket; a cedar tree remains in the car park. The imposing HALL of the industrial schools, with good timber roof, is now the chemist's shop.

2. *Whipps Cross Road and the Wallwood Estate*

For the pedestrian, most easily approached from the centre of Leytonstone by a footbridge over the A12 from Gainsborough Road. The suburb was built up with middle-class housing after the sale of the Cotton family's Wallwood Estate in 1873; building began in 1890, Wallwood House survived until the 1920s. Past the grand Primitive Methodist church down Colworth Road to the main interest: St Andrew's church (the site given by the Cottons), and the pretty Girls' School (for all these *see* above). N of the church FOREST GLADE leads past a fragment of Epping Forest to the busy WHIPPS CROSS ROAD. At the corner a Hindu temple (*see* above). To the E, ASSEMBLY ROW: six altered houses remain from twelve two- and three-storey houses built 1767: Nos. 133–5, 143 (with Doric doorcase), and 153–7. There was formerly an Assembly House at one end, said to have been used by London merchants during the plague of 1665.

3. *Leytonstone High Road, N–S*

Just to the N of Leytonstone High Road Station, DAVIES LANE. At the corner, LINCOLNS, a plain three-storey pub of *c.* 1870, five bays with big projecting eaves. On the S side, YOUTH CENTRE, 1990s, unappealing dark brick, with arched openings, a harsh intrusion in the grounds of The Pastures, a house of *c.* 1676–7, remodelled in the C18 and demolished in the 1960s. In 1879, Agnes Cotton, a daughter of William Cotton, and owner of the estate in the later C19, built a girls' industrial home with chapel and laundry, known as the HOME OF THE GOOD SHEPHERD, by *Milner Hall*. From this a three-storey building remains close to the road. Austerely detailed toward the road, but with a S front in a picturesque asymmetrical Old English style, with a mixture of rendered and tile-hung walls. The primary school further E was built as DAVIES LANE BOARD SCHOOL, 1901. A proud three-decker; 1-4-1 gables, a balanced composition with end bays projecting, stairs by the second and fifth bays. Plain except for pretty tiled name plaques and a terracotta panel at the side. It is a surprise to find WANSTEAD FLATS beyond: open land preserved despite repeated threats as part of Epping Forest. By the entrance path a small red granite drinking fountain.

Further S along the High Road on the E side, POLICE STATION (No. 470), 1908 by *John Dixon Butler*, in his domestic Jacobean style, all brick, including the window mullions.

THE BELL, a hipped-roof 1930s pub, is followed by a jolly FIRE STATION of 1914 with striped stone-and-brick quoins, the tower with clock and parapet, built as headquarters of the Leyton Fire Brigade. On the W side, MAYVILLE INFANTS SCHOOL. One building survives from the Board School of 1889; red brick pilasters and three shallow gables; low additions in front. Given presence by greatly enlarged grounds.

HARROW GREEN is the site of an old hamlet, marked by a triangular patch of grass with War Memorial, a simple granite obelisk. Much war damage and later replacement here, including the Wesleyan Church. On the W side a survivor, the PLOUGH AND HARROW, a big half-timbered pub.

CATHALL ROAD to the W starts with a branch library (*see* above). The area has seen much rebuilding. Crowded C19 housing to the S was cleared in the 1960s for a large and unappealing council housing development of slabs and towers, 1963–75, swept away in the late 1990s and replaced by friendlier streets and cul-de-sacs of terrace houses in traditional materials, with square tile-hung oriel windows as a novel feature. In Cathall Road, The EPICENTRE, community buildings in an elementary neo-vernacular style, L-shaped, with big roofs and an angular lantern at the junction. Nicely paved entrance courtyard leading to a broad foyer, with meeting hall at r. angles. Beyond, a LEISURE CENTRE of 1974–7 (*N.P. Astins*, Borough Architect). In front is preserved the pump and motor of an artesian well which pumped water to the baths on this site from 1899–1972. In Holloway Road, Holy Trinity Church (*see* above), a 1970s replacement of two older churches.

Further S another radical transformation has overtaken the large area occupied by the former Langthorne Hospital. On the High Road it is heralded by THE CLICK, an internet café in a crisp oval building, unapologetically modern. By *Van Heyningen & Haward*, 2001. Three storeys, unframed glass panels to the ground floor with horizontal bands of sunshading. White render above with punched-out square windows. In front, a bus stop in matching idiom. Paving echoing the curve of the building, and pierced-metal screens with plant forms by *Dee Honeybourne*, invite one to the park behind, announced by a mosaic sign by *Stewart Hale*. Alongside, some distinctive housing of 2001, slate hung with upper bay windows.

LANGTHORNE PARK consists of 4½ acres laid out 2000–1 on part of the hospital site. Imaginatively landscaped by *Arnold Stroud,* landscape architect to the Borough, with miniature mounded hills, creating 'zones' of different character. Small lake with fountain and boulders in the ecology zone, with seating by *Tim Norris*. Nearby an Amphitheatre and play areas. Further N, picnic zone with Totem figures by *Robert Koenig*.

S of the park, facing Langthorne Road, are the older buildings remaining from the hospital, converted for housing and other uses in 2001. The hospital, used from 1948 for care of the elderly, originated as West Ham Union Workhouse, laid out on the then rural site of Holloway Down in 1839–42 by *A.R. Mason*. In the centre is the former chapel of 1840, in plain round-arched style. The two flanking houses, elaborately Italianate with ample stone dressings, are a rebuilding possibly by *Lewis Angell*, architect to the Guardians from 1873. South Forest Lodge on the l. contained the Board Room (the interior remodelled by *J. W. Dunford*, 1905). The simpler Red Oak Lodge on the r. was the stores building. Former doctor's house to the r. and small one-storey Lodge further S. Behind is the original main workhouse range, a long, plain classical composition of nineteen bays and three storeys, the centre canted forward with pilasters and pediment. A clock on top of a flat stuccoed frontispiece. Pediments also at the ends. At the back are projecting wings with courtyards in between.

To the W Langthorne Road continues past St Patrick's Cemetery and a noteworthy former Congregational Church (*see* above) to Leyton underground station.

E of the High Road is the CANN HALL district (formerly partly in Wanstead); where the late C19 housing is still largely complete, the other buildings a mixture of old and new. CANN HALL ROAD, the main thoroughfare, has Baptist (C19) and Methodist (C20) churches and several SCHOOLS: JENNY HAMMOND, Worsley Road, is a two-storey simply detailed Board School of 1882 on a half-H plan (built by Wanstead School Board); further N, CANN HALL PRIMARY, on the site of St Margaret's vicarage, is one of Waltham Forest's late C20 primaries, a group of low polygons with sloping metal roofs and glazed lanterns, next to a small new PARK. St Margaret's church (*see* above), contemporary with the surrounding housing, occupies a commanding corner position in Woodhouse Road. To its N in Newcomen Road a quite stylish 1990s terrace of linked gabled villas in a vaguely Regency manner.

WALTHAMSTOW

Walthamstow has much variety even though it is no longer the countryside of William Morris's boyhood, 'all flat pasture, except for a few gardens . . . the wide green sea of the Essex marshland, with the great domed line of the sky and the sun shining down in one peaceful light over the long distance'. This sense of openness remains now only on the western fringe, originally marshes bordering the River Lea, transformed by the great sweeps of water of the later C19 and early C20 reservoirs, and now interspersed with recreational areas and nature reserves forming part of the Lea Valley Park. White's *Directory* in 1848 called Walthamstow 'one of the largest and handsomest suburban villages near the metropolis . . . with many large and handsome villas'. Something of this character is still evident for despite some grievous losses Walthamstow has more of its C18 houses remaining than any of its neighbours. Several lie along Forest Road and others on the eastern fringe, some way from the surprisingly secluded and still village-like area around the parish church, with its almshouses and former C18 workhouse. The main commercial centre, much rebuilt after Second World War damage, lies further W around Hoe Street and the High Street. The civic centre, created after Walthamstow became a borough in 1929, lies apart, built to the N of Forest Road, when there was still open land.

Suburban development began in the mid-C19 with middle-class villas S and E of the church, from where coaches ran to Lea Bridge Station, opened 1840. The turning point came with the Great Eastern Railway's introduction of workmen's trains which conditioned the social character of the new suburbs. From the 1870s Walthamstow was well served by stations. Central Station (formerly Hoe Street, on a branch line from Lea Bridge), opened in 1870. St James's Street opened the same year, followed by Wood Street in 1873. The UDC's tramways, established 1905, encouraged development N of Forest Road. The underground reached Walthamstow with the Victoria Line in 1968.

The appearance of Walthamstow's suburbs owed much to one of the chief local landowners, Sir Thomas Courtenay Warner. He began by laying out streets in the 1880s around the former family home near the High Street. His building company, formed in 1891, which gained a high reputation for quality, went on to develop large areas of both Walthamstow and Leyton, moving on in the early C20 to provide more affluent housing in areas bordering Woodford and Chingford. But development was limited by the 1878 Act preserving Epping Forest, and here suburbia merges into the semi-rural wooded areas reclaimed as part of the Forest.

The pace of growth in the later C19 was colossal: from a modest figure of 4,258 in 1831 the population had grown by 1891 to 46,346; in 1901 it had reached 95,131. By 1932 it was the most densely populated non-county borough in the country. Between the wars a variety of small-scale industries flourished along the Lea Valley and N of Forest Road, particularly furniture making and electrical trades. In the 1950s–60s Walthamstow was still predominantly a working-class suburb, though in the later C20 its character became more mixed. The architectural character remains predominantly late C19 to early C20, sufficiently well built to have avoided extensive reconstruction, apart from war-damaged areas. The largest area of earlier–mid-C20 social housing is Higham Hill N of Forest Road. The new Borough of Waltham Forest built mostly low-rise housing, and only a few towers of flats, and added new schools, including nursery schools, to complement the sturdy educational buildings of the Edwardian era.

RELIGIOUS BUILDINGS

ST ANDREW'S CHRISTIAN CENTRE, Church Road, Higham Hill. Shallow-pitched-roof cluster, by *APEC*, 1988, for C. of E. and Baptists, with worship centre and ancillary rooms around a hall of 1962.

ST BARNABAS and ST JAMES, St Barnabas Road. 1902–3 by *W.D. Caröe*, for the new Warner Estate suburb. The whole cost was met by Richard Foster (*see also* St Saviour). Arts and Crafts free Gothic, an interesting contrast to St Michael of twenty years earlier (*see* below). The exterior is of red brick (stone was intended but proved too expensive), relatively conventional, with early Perp tracery in the lean-to aisles. Some lozenge decoration and a thin NW turret with Caröe's favourite segmental arches as the only fanciful motifs. The W windows are divided by thick brick buttresses. The interior is more original and full of intriguing detail. Wide, six-bay nave with quite a complex elevation. The thin diamond-shaped piers with large crenellated caps carry delicately moulded arches of brick and stone; the clerestory windows are set back behind stone shafts, their upper parts fluted, set against brick walls. The vertical emphasis is countered by a band of brick quatrefoils. The aisle roofs are supported on dramatic arched buttresses, springing from moulded corbels high up on the arcade walls but descending low on the outer walls. The nave cants in towards the tall chancel, which is lit by a grand seven-light E window with an ingenious mixture of Dec and Perp motifs. Foundation stone behind the altar, by *Eric Gill*, then a pupil of Caröe.

Unusually many high quality FITTINGS, carefully preserved, and others brought in later.* The variety of excellent wrought-iron door furniture is worth study. Carved oak ALTAR by *Dart & Francis*, with altar frontals designed by *Caröe*; a tall stone reredos was intended behind, instead panelling was added by by *Alban Caröe* in 1937. Fine METALWORK, made for the demolished church of St James by *Ashbee*'s *Guild of Handicraft* c. 1905 (alms dish, altar cross and candlesticks, hanging lamp, font ewer) and by *Edward Spencer* of the *Artificers' Guild* (processional cross and torches, 1933). STATUE of St Michael and

*Both details of the fittings, and their conservation, owes much to Julian Litten.

two angels on the reredos carved by *Alec Miller* of the Guild of Handicraft, *c.* 1904–6. In the chancel, organ case by *Caröe*, the corbels below it carved in 2000 by *Charles Gurrey*. WOODWORK designed by *Caröe* includes a trumpet-shaped PULPIT and oak LECTERN. FONT of Purbeck marble in a shallow-arched W recess. HANGING ROOD designed by *Caröe* as war memorial in 1921, made by *Nathaniel Hitch*. STAINED GLASS by *Clayton & Bell*: E window *c.* 1903, W windows *c.* 1917.

In the S aisle, W end, fittings brought from St James, also a REREDOS designed by *Julian Litten*, incorporating paintings of *c.* 1860 from J.S. Crowther's St Alban Manchester. In the Lady Chapel on the N side, fittings brought from other churches, including a reredos, by *Christopher Webb*, 1925, from St John Holborn. Lady Chapel windows also by *Clayton & Bell*: E *c.* 1918, N 1920s.

To the S, *Caröe*'s Vicarage, of 1903–4, gabled, with tile-hung mansard, and neat tilework above the windows. Behind is his Parish Hall, designed 1909, built 1912, with main entrance from Wellesley Road, forming an attractive group with the church. Open arch-braced roof.

Down St Barnabas Road, Stafford Hall is the original temporary iron church of 1900.

ST GABRIEL, Havant Road. 1884–5 by *J.T. Bressey*. Built as Sunday school and mission room. A long brick shed with five dormers in the roof, a little cupola at the E end, and some terracotta decoration. A good example of the simplest type of chapel, so often replaced later. Church hall 1980.

ST LUKE, Greenleaf Road, 1901–2 by *Bottle & Olley* of Yarmouth. Mission room and church; stock brick with wooden-tracery windows. Chancel widened and refurnished 1923.

ST JOHN, Chingford Road and Brookscroft Road. 1924–6 by *H.P. Burke-Downing*, replacing a chapel of ease of 1829 by *Vulliamy*. Decent reticent Gothic in the Bodley tradition; brown brick, three bays of aisle windows with Dec tracery below gables. Completed 1960–1 by *John Phillips* with a simpler W bay with rose window and five lancets under a deep arch. Drastically altered 1996 by *John Goldsmith* when a worship area was made above an inserted floor in the nave. Here the upper parts of the arcades are visible, with C14-style dying arches and a ceiled open roof. The chancel, stripped and divided off at the same time, retains an elaborate Dec window, carved hood-moulds and plaster ceiling with angels. S Lady Chapel; N organ chamber and vestry with octagonal turret. Church hall 1916 by *G.D. Hamilton*.

ST MARY, Church Lane. In the centre of the old village, now a pleasing backwater. Rectangular, with aisles and E chapels, S porch and W tower. The tower is of the usual late medieval Thames Valley type, with diagonal buttresses and SE turret. On the N side an unusual C15 carved roundel with lamb and flag. Outside, the early history of the rest is obscured by a thick coat of rendering and by yellow brick refacing from repairs of

1817–18 by *Charles Bacon*. Inside, extensive restorations have replaced much of the older fabric, but arcades formerly with circular columns (see the bases on the N side) suggest the church was already substantial by the C13. The present octagonal columns date from a restoration of 1876, when Georgian box pews and ceilings were removed and tracery added to the windows. C16 E chapels, built by two Lord Mayors, Sir George Monoux (N chapel) and Robert Thorne (†1532), heightened in 1818. The chancel extension and E vestry date from 1938. FONT, fluted marble bowl on a baluster, given 1714.

The fine collection of MONUMENTS is the chief interest. The earliest are BRASSES. Sir George Monoux, †1543 and wife, brass with two small kneeling figures, scrolls and shields, originally a Trinity above, from a chest tomb formerly between chancel and N chapel. – Thomas Hale †1588 and wife, originally two figures and children (upper part of her effigy and children missing). Inscriptions of 1585 and 1596 (William Rowe, with achievement). The stone monuments start with Lady Lucy Stanley *c.* 1615, kneeling figure under an arch. Originally it stood away from the wall. Described by Strype as 'a very fair monument'; attributed to *William Cure the younger* by
14 Adam White.* – Sir Thomas and Lady Mary Merry, 1633 by *Nicholas Stone*, half figures in oval niches and four busts of children in flat relief below, open pediment above. Of very fine sculptural quality, especially the modelling of the hands. – Sigismund Trafford †1723 and wife, ambitious wall-monument with standing figures, the husband in Roman dress, the daughter kneeling between. The artistic quality not as high as for example at C18 Wanstead. – Many lesser monuments: Henry Maynard †1646, two standing cherubs. – Henry Birchenhead †1656, Tristram Conyers †1694, both decorated with cherubs. – Bonnell family *c.* 1690, big garlanded sarcophagus (part of a larger monument). Thomas Clarke †1746 tablet with draped urn, very similar to a design by *Sir Robert Taylor* (GF). – Elizabeth Morley †1837 by *W.G. Nicholl*.

Railed CHURCHYARD, picturesquely crowded. Among the most prominent monuments: Edward Solly †1776, a raised *Coade* stone sarcophagus on feet, and Jesse Russell †1820, Grecian white-marble sarcophagus.

ST MICHAEL, Palmerston Road. 1884–5, built for the first incumbent, Father William Ibbotson, by *J.M. Bignall*, who was a pupil of Sir Gilbert Scott and died young in 1885. Richard Foster contributed to the cost (*see also* St Saviour and St Barnabas). A mighty church in the ecclesiological tradition, though lacking its intended NE tower and spire, awkward but memorable. Stock brick with red brick bands, with a lively roofline of gabled clerestory windows. NW entrance, completed 1890. Heavily buttressed W end, containing a Baptistery, N and S porches, chancel with raised sanctuary and NE chapel. Inside, a dim and lofty space with busy detail and lavish High Church

*Walpole Society Vol. LXI, 1999.

furnishings. Six-bay nave arcade with compound piers with stone stripes and stone capitals, arches with intersecting hood-moulds. The unusual clerestory has two pairs of large windows each side with a central roundel breaking through the cove of a complex cross-braced roof, which has tie-beams linked by flying purlins. The great E window, with STAINED GLASS of 1915 by *Hardman* showing St Michael triumphant over Satan, rises high into the E gable, flanked by niches with statues. Below it a spiky pinnacled REREDOS with painted saints on gold ground, 1889–92, by *J. T. Wilson* and *Hardman*, with carved figures by *Sebastian Zwinck* of Oberammergau, and painted ALTAR FRONTAL by *Ernest Geldart*. The interior remained incomplete (a W narthex, NE Lady Chapel, mosaics at clerestory level and chancel screen with hanging rood were intended) but other rich contemporary fittings were provided. – PULPIT with openwork tracery, and LECTERN, of 1886. – Stone FONT on a mosaic floor with fishes. – STATIONS OF THE CROSS, from St Michael Shoreditch, late C19. The STAINED GLASS in the aisle windows, with a variety of angels, planned by *Ibbotson*, but completed only gradually, are by *Hardman*. The E bay of the N arcade, with a stained-glass lancet of 1896 and oak figures added 1895, forms the entrance to the N CHAPEL, richly furnished in 1893 with altar, reredos and windows by *Hardman:* six tiny lancets with silver-stain glass. Copper aumbry built into the wall. – Opus sectile PANEL, kneeling angel (S arcade pier) by *Whipples*.

VICARAGE to the SE, 1888–9, gabled with brick stripes. SUNDAY SCHOOLS of 1885, both by *Bignall*.

ST PETER IN THE FOREST, Woodford New Road. By *John Shaw jun.*, 1840, to serve the scattered population on the fringes of the Forest; used by Forest School until it had its own chapel. Lombard Romanesque in yellow brick. Originally a compact design, square, with canted E apse, NE vestry and SW tower. Altered 1854 by *Charles Ainslie*, extended W in 1887 by *J.C. Lewis*. Damaged in the Second World War and in a fire of 1975. The interior is now a barn-like space with round-headed arch to the sanctuary. The large W gallery formerly extended along the sides. N wall rebuilt 1951 with windows lengthened. Apse with mural paintings of 1901–5.

ST SAVIOUR, Markhouse Road. 1873–4 by *Francis T. Dolman*. The first church in the area funded by the merchant banker Richard Foster, a keen high churchman who had earlier been involved in promoting new churches in Haggerston, Shoreditch (*see also* St Barnabas and St Michael). The site was on land which Foster inherited from his uncle; a clergy house to the N and nunnery to the S were also provided, the latter now replaced by housing. The foundation stone was laid by his business partner, John Knowles. The best feature is the massive broached spire on the NW tower-porch, visible from afar, though from close up disappointingly tucked away at the back of a dull ragstone exterior, with canted apse facing the road. Tall clerestory with plate tracery, aisles with alternating single and two light windows. Interior on an impressive scale, but deprived of its lofty open roof. This was replaced by a canted ceiling after a fire in 1945, when the fittings of the E end were also lost. Five bay nave arcades with quatrefoil piers of Tisbury stone, the details rather hard and mechanical. Uncarved capitals, but some foliage carving on the chancel arch responds. The arch itself, and the circular W window above the W lancets, were removed after the fire. Lady Chapel of 1926 with screen of 1934. Fine *Willis* ORGAN of 1872, brought from Bacup. Small FONT from St James Chignall, Essex. E end reordered and W end glazed off as a foyer, with low barrel ceiling on timber columns, by *John Burton*, 1987–8. Much STAINED GLASS remains in the nave, the better windows on the S side: First from E, St Mary, 1878, second from E, Annunciation, by *Heaton Butler & Bayne*, 1900. W window given by Dolman, 1877; three lancets with Christ, Moses and Aaron, small scenes below, busy and colourful.

The substantial former CLERGY HOUSE, plain, with half-hipped roofs, is now offices for the Bishop of Barking.

ST STEPHEN, Copeland Road. 1994 by *APEC*, a small church and housing for young people. There was a church on the site from 1877.

CHRIST THE KING (R.C.), Chingford Road, *see* Chingford.

OUR LADY OF THE ROSARY AND ST PATRICK (R.C.), Blackhorse Road and Tenby Road. 1908 by *Benedict Williamson* (supervising architect *J.H. Beart Foss*). Spare version of Early Christian: plain stock brick with round-arched windows, apse with a semi-dome. Tympanum with mosaic. Sanctuary reordered by *Gerald Murphy* of *Burles Newton & Partners*, 1990s, with curved screen wall inserted within the apse.

109 OUR LADY AND ST GEORGE (R.C.), Shernhall Street. 1995 by *Plater, Inkpen, Vale & Downie*. The third church on the site, replacing one destroyed by fire in 1993. Impressive and unusual. The plan is an oval with an apse, balanced by a curved entrance with drum tower with a short spire. Curved, windowless aisle walls of pale brick, broken by a little bubble chapel by the entrance. The massing is awkward, although pulled together by white-glazed cornices. But the interior is a delight. Curved rows of seats echoing the curve of the aisle walls. Plain white columns. The nave is flooded with light from large circular clerestory windows and roof lights which tunnel into the complex lattice-ribbed ceiling, an effective contrast to the quieter brick-faced aisles. The apse is also lit by upper windows. Simple furnishings, the seating by *Hays & Finch*. STAINED GLASS by *Ray Bradley*, bronze STATUE of the Virgin by *Bernard Merry*, painted STATIONS OF THE CROSS by *Dennis Allaway*. Prominent immersion FONT enclosed by a curving wall, below the W tower. Large entrance foyer with sacristy beyond, and small circular weekday chapel at the opposite end of the church.

Nonconformity was strong in Walthamstow. The following is a

sample of buildings of different dates from the large number of other places of worship.

THE LIGHTHOUSE METHODIST CHURCH, Markhouse Road. 1893. An eccentric landmark in a dull area, paid for by Captain King of the Bullard Line of steamers. The 'lighthouse' is a sturdy circular turret-stair with steep slated spire topped by a lantern. Broad two-storey front with red-terracotta trim in Queen Anne style. Subdivided inside.

LIVING FLAMES BAPTIST CHURCH, Fulbourne Road, 1910. Humble red brick front, a triplet of lancets in the gable with leafy capitals on square piers, pairs of lancets flanking the entrance.

CENTRAL BAPTIST CHURCH, Orford Road. 1913–14 by *W.D. Church & Son*. Handsomely sited for a view from Hoe Street. Free Gothic with elaborate Dec windows, stumpy right-hand tower and chequerwork gable.

BAPTIST CHURCH, Blackhorse Road and Southcote Road. 1932 by *K. Francis Clarke*. A spreading front given a coy vernacular touch by half-timbering to the gable and to the two little porches flanking the projecting brick centre

CHURCH OF JESUS CHRIST OF LATTER DAY SAINTS, Hoe Street. Simple low white building in New England style, *c.* 2000, with red-tiled roof and central glazed gable. Slim central flèche.

MASJID-E-OMER, Chelmsford Road. 2003–4 by *G. Potter & Associates*. Yellow brick, with dome and minaret.

QUEEN'S ROAD CEMETERY. 1872. Lodges, gates and railings; two small Dec Gothic chapels in one composition, flanking a central arch with cupola and spire, by *R.C. Sutton*.

MAJOR BUILDINGS

CIVIC CENTRE, Forest Road. An impressive group of Town Hall, Assembly Hall (1937–43) and Courts (1972–3). A competition for an ambitious civic centre for the new borough created in 1929 was won in 1932 by *P.D. Hepworth*, an architect known chiefly for his elegant private houses. But the timing was unfortunate. By the time work started in 1937 the scheme had been much simplified; only two of the three intended buildings were begun, and their fitting out was limited by wartime restrictions. The ample, well-landscaped setting (the site of Chestnuts or Clay Farm) slopes downward from Forest Road. The Town Hall benefits by being set far back, beyond a formal forecourt with large circular basin and fountain (renewed 1999).

The TOWN HALL has an austere but dignified exterior of 97
stone, with copper clock turret and three-storey-high portico with square piers, rather different from Hepworth's more

conventional competition scheme, which had a traditional central pediment on columns. Sweden was the source of this type of reduced classicism combined with refined and original decorative detail, which had been popularized through a Swedish exhibition held in London in 1931 and which appealed, as Pevsner remarked in 1954 'to those who were not satisfied to be imitatively Neo-Georgian nor wanted to go Modern in earnest'. The use of Portland-stone cladding rather than brick for the whole building was apparently at the council's request. Countering this extra expense was the simplified plan: an E-plan with council chamber projecting at the back, in place of the double courtyard proposed in the competition entry, and instead of the traditional ceremonial stair, four equal but lesser staircases. On the main front decoration is confined to a little rustication and first-floor windows with minimal mouldings and tapering iron balconies, their playfulness another Swedish trait. A little sculpture is included: the sides of the portico piers have small square panels in flat relief, showing crafts and industries. The exterior of the council chamber has five bolder figures in an angular style: Fellowship, modelled on William Morris, with Motherhood, Work, Recreation and Education. They are by *John F. Kavanagh*.

Economical but elegant interior detail: entrance hall with two octagonal marble-faced columns, good light fittings, plasterwork with Greek key and star motifs, the latter repeated for the brackets of the twisted stair balustrades (of iron instead of the intended bronze). In the committee rooms effective use is made of inexpensive, locally made plywood panelling with chevron-decorated pilasters, though for the council chamber war-time economy enforced the reuse of furnishings from the old building in Orford Road. All this was achieved despite use as an ARP centre during the war. The extra-fortified basement had a later role as a Cold War shelter.

ASSEMBLY HALL, completed 1943. Very restrained, the classical detail limited to a plain cornice and subdued mouldings. Entrance from the W through an inset portico with five full-height openings between square piers. Full-height foyer with star-shaped window high up. The hall has nine bays of generously large windows along the sides, a stage, and a ceiling with shallow domed recesses. WAR MEMORIAL in front of the S side, mourning figure in granite standing beside an aedicule.

COURT HOUSE, 1972–3 by the *GLC Special Works Department* under *Geoffrey F. Horsfall*. To the l. of the Town Hall, and forming part of the group of public buildings, but firmly of its own time, a tough nephew beside a maiden aunt. Strongly horizontal, of reinforced concrete faced with Portland stone, the heavy massing rebutting the delicacy of the Town Hall. The planning is skilful: the first scheme to carry out recommendations of 1969 for new Magistrates Courts in London. Five informal, flexibly planned courts on the first floor, all with natural lighting through the roof, which brings some interest to the skyline. Juvenile court on the ground floor, public access on the S side, the various court entrances and car parks discreetly tucked away on the W side instead of facing the main forecourt, as Hepworth had envisaged.

WILLIAM MORRIS GALLERY, Forest Road. A large house in its own grounds, now LLOYD PARK, on the N side of Forest Road. The previous name, Water House, comes from the square moat in the grounds, sign of an ancient site.* The attractive front looks later C18, but the red brick rear shows that this is a mid-C18 house remodelled. So first the rear elevation: very plain, six irregular bays, three tall storeys above a basement, a large staircase window near the centre. One-storey wing to the W, probably an addition (see the different brickwork). A brick dated 174- was found in the upper E wall, and the house appears on a map of 1758, together with a matching E wing, demolished *c.* 1900. The front of the house was elegantly remodelled in the later C18, with the addition of broad bowed end bays; two stone bands between ground and first floor, echoed by a bold cornice. Porch with Corinthian columns. The central three windows have moulded surrounds. Wide entrance hall paved in marble, with a fine mid-C18 stair with twisted balusters and carved tread ends, panelling in some of the rooms. The fame of the house rests on its association with William Morris (born 1834) whose family moved here from Woodford in 1848 and lived at Water House until 1856. Edward Lloyd, newspaper publisher, lived there from 1857–85. The borough acquired house and grounds in 1899 and added the balustraded terraces behind the house. The museum was opened in 1950. A perimeter walk remains around the moat, which is crossed by a C19 rustic iron footbridge. The C20 theatre and car park on the island seem incongruous.

VESTRY HOUSE MUSEUM, Vestry Road. *See* Walthamstow Village perambulation.

REGISTRY OFFICE, No. 106 Grove Road. The former parsonage of the demolished St Stephen's church. By *Habershon & Fawckner*, *c.* 1883, a double-gabled house with tall chimneys and trefoil-headed windows.

CENTRAL LIBRARY, High Street. A bold street front of 1907–9 by *J. W. Dunford*, paid for by Andrew Carnegie, in free English Baroque, with channelled stone ground floor and prominent hipped roof with little cupola. Segmental pediments on Ionic columns frame two large arched windows to the first floor, which light a splendid upper room with plaster barrel vault, planned as a public hall with a stage. It is reached by an elaborately carved timber stair (well restored after fire damage in 1982). The ground-floor rooms were used as Lending Library and Reading Room. All this was added in front of an older villa to which a reading room was added in 1894, probably by *Lewis Angell*. This survives, with later mezzanine inserted below the open roof trusses. Extensions behind, with new entrance, 1985.

* An older name, Cricklewoods, links the site to a C14 landowner.

LIBRARY, Wood Street, 1938–9, opened only in 1950, by *F.G. Southgate*, Borough Architect. Low stone-faced building, basement and ground floor only, in a demure Moderne style, with a curved corner. A pantiled roof peeps above the parapet. L-shaped, with Children's Library along Wood Street, main entrance in Forest Road; brick-faced extension beyond.

FRIENDS HALL, Greenleaf Road (adult education centre). 1906. One of the new outer suburban centres established by the Quaker Bedford Institute (*see also* Barclay Hall, East Ham p. 275). Relaxed Free Style in red brick, two storeys with three storey entrance tower in Melville Road, two gables alongside. Broad segment-headed window to the main hall emphasized by a moulded band, but compromised by a crude later porch.

WALTHAMSTOW GREYHOUND STADIUM, Chingford Road. A rare and unusually lavish survival of a popular suburban working-class entertainment of the earlier C20. Long white concrete frontage with stepped Deco parapet, 1932, spiced up by late C20 red tubular railings. Striking at night when the flamboyant neon lighting is visible. The huge tote boards are original, also with Art Deco profiles. Spectator stands N and S of the track with cantilevered roofs, the S one of concrete, the N one clad in corrugated metal, with hospitality suite of the 1980s attached. Low kennels to the E, arranged in a crescent, the end buildings hexagonal with steep-pitched roofs.

POLICE STATION, 360 Forest Road, 1891 by *John Dixon Butler*. A substantial red brick pile, in Butler's imposing yet domestic free Jacobean style, with his typical elongated consoles to the door.

TELEPHONE EXCHANGE, Brookscroft Road. *Office of Works* Baroque; stone aedicules to some of the first-floor windows. Altered top floor.

Former TRAMWAY offices, Chingford Road. Exuberant freestyle with much terracotta, *c.* 1905, when Walthamstow District Council began its electric tramway system. The sheds behind replaced by housing.

LEE BRIDGE WATERWORKS, Lea Bridge Road. The major pumping stations of the East London Waterworks Company on this site have all gone. Beside a cast-iron weir on the Lea, an octagonal water-turbine house of 1885 by *W.B. Bryan*. Remains of 1852 AQUEDUCT from Copper Mill, with ornamental cast-iron bridges, as at Lea Bridge Road.

WATERWORKS INSTALLATIONS in Walthamstow. The creation of 300 acres of reservoirs by the East London Waterworks Company began after an Act of 1853; the earliest, opened 1863 onwards, were the small reservoirs N of Coppermill Lane.

FERRY LANE PUMPING STATION. 1893–4 by *W.B. Bryan*, has a roof with gablets upon a ceramic corbel table.

In COPPERMILL LANE the OLD COPPER MILL (now water company stores) dates from 1806, built to crush linseed for oil, but from 1808 used for copper rolling. Bought by the waterworks in 1860; the Italianate arcaded engine tower was added in 1864. The main building is of brick with giant segmental arches on pilasters with stone capitals. Further reservoirs to the N were built in the C20: Lockwood reservoir (74 acres), 1903; Banbury reservoir (91 acres) 1903, and (in Chingford and Enfield), King George's Reservoir (420 acres) 1913, all under *W.B. Bryan*, engineer. William Girling Reservoir (334 acres), was added in 1951. At the COPPERMILL TREATMENT WORKS, 1970s and later, statue of Aquarius with ewer, from the original Old Ford Works.

WOODFORD or HAGGER LANE PUMPING STATION (The Waterworks), Woodford New Road. By *George Seaton*, 1877 for the East London Waterworks Company. Stock brick with round-headed windows and dentil cornice. It housed two horizontal steam engines.

Colleges and schools

WALTHAM FOREST COLLEGE, Forest Road. Built as SW Essex Technical College and School of Art, 1938 by *John Stuart*, Essex County Architect. Adjoining the Civic Centre, and also grand in scale but sadly leaden in comparison. A very long Neo-Georgian range of brown brick, with dressings of artificial stone. Six-column Ionic portico, the pediment with stiff carved scenes and some flat reliefs within the portico and on the window embrasures. Plain interior with imperial stair.

SIR GEORGE MONOUX COLLEGE, Chingford Road. Long red brick front of 1927 by *Essex County Council* with stone frontispiece and Jacobethan trimmings; a characteristic grammar school type of between the wars. Its style alludes to the C16 origins of the school, founded by Sir George Monoux. It became a comprehensive in 1968, a Sixth Form College from 1986, and had *c.* 1,500 students in 2001. Central barrel-vaulted assembly hall, now library. Classrooms around two courtyards (one with War Memorial of 1949), completed 1933 by a rear block with gym and laboratories. Later extensions behind, rationalized by the addition of The Centre, by *van Heyningen & Haward*, 1990, a neat square block with canteen and common room on the ground floor, with conservatory extension of 2000 overlooking a new courtyard. The upper floor has a conference room added 1997, an attractive clerestory-lit space beneath a steeply pitched open roof. Additions further E by *APT* 2001–3.

HIGH SCHOOL FOR GIRLS, Church Hill. 1911–13 by *C.J. Dawson*. A lively English Baroque front in brick and stone, with wings projecting forward, a segment-headed pediment to the central bay, and a cupola. Entrance with Ionic columns and broken pediment. A bold wooden dentilled cornice pulls the whole composition together. The hall projects at the back. Separate later additions. At the NE corner the former parsonage of St Mary's church, *c.* 1890, now part of the school.

CITY LEARNING CENTRE, Billet Road. By *Austin-Smith:Lord*, 2001. A cheerful, eyecatching structure, mostly timber-clad, on an ingeniously compact plan. Two interlocking polygons, each with a red monopitch-roofed drum rising above shallow sloping roofs. Teaching rooms of different sizes radiate around the drums. It stands in front of MCENTEE TECHNICAL SCHOOL, a long three-storey curtain-walled range of 1957.

HOLY FAMILY TECHNOLOGY COLLEGE, *see* p. 758.

FOREST SCHOOL, *see* p. 763.

BOARD SCHOOLS. The Walthamstow School Board, established 1880, had built thirteen schools by 1903 when elementary schools came under the UDC with *H. Prosser* as architect. A good example of the one-storey earlier type is Wood Street, 1898 by *W.A. Longmore*, surveyor to the Board; larger later examples include: Selwyn Avenue (Highams Park) 1904, Barrett Road 1905, Mission Grove 1906, and Winns Avenue 1907 (*see* further, perambulations).

ST MARY'S SCHOOL, Rectory Road. By *TFP Architects* 1970–2. Paired classrooms around a central hall, sloping clerestory lighting. Clad in white brick with strong use of primary colours.

CHAPEL END JUNIOR SCHOOL, Roberts Road. Red-tiled roofs, polygonal stepped plan. 1970s.

ST PATRICK'S SCHOOL (R.C.), Blackhorse Road. Lively extensions in yellow brick, with silver-clad monopitch roofs at different angles.

Waltham Forest built a number of NURSERY SCHOOLS from the 1970s. A good example is:

LOW HALL NURSERY SCHOOL, Low Hall Lane. Friendly, informal T-shaped cluster, entrance in an angle. Pale brick; big slate roofs with timber gablets. Also INFANT AND NURSERY SCHOOL, Mission Grove and Woodville Road, 1979 by *Michael Foster* of *TFP*. Single storey; brick walls, with space-frame hall roof and well lit interiors.

PERAMBULATIONS

1. Walthamstow Village

From Hoe Street, a little to the N of Walthamstow Central Station, CHURCH HILL leads E to the old centre of the village. Past the crossroads (*see* perambulation below) Church Hill is domestic apart from the SORTING OFFICE, 1965 by the *Ministry of Public Buildings & Works*, and No. 29, ENERGY HOUSE, built as the local authority's electricity showrooms, 1937 by *T.F. Cunningham*, Borough Engineer and Surveyor. Plain Georgian grand manner, with channelled stone ground floor and projecting pedimented centre defined by Tuscan columns and pilasters. Opposite is the attractive group of Girls' School and former parsonage (*see* above).

The quiet area around the church comes as a great surprise, a rural backwater hidden amidst the later C19 suburbs, with an instructive scatter of buildings of pre-Victorian date. N of the church the ALMSHOUSES and former grammar school founded 1527 by the local benefactor George Monoux, City merchant and Lord Mayor (†1544). A long two-storeyed range with a central timber frame and jettied cross-wing which was intended as the residence of schoolmaster, parish clerk and alms priest. Planned with six one-room dwellings to the W, with schoolroom above, and seven rooms to the E. The W range in Elizabethan style, with classical entrance, now looks the earlier part, but is a reconstruction after war damage, 1955 by *Braddell & Laurence*; the rendered E part was rebuilt *c.* 1730.

S of the large, crowded churchyard is CHURCH LANE. Here the ANCIENT HOUSE is a cherished relic of a rural past, a notably 7
complete timber-framed hall house of the C15: the main range with crown-post roof, and jettied and gabled E and W wings with curved braces. The three-bay W wing is a rebuilding of the C16. The house has a long conservation history: its date was recognized in 1934, when it was restored by *C.J. Brewin* with advice from SPAB; weatherboarding was removed from the exterior, revealing the medieval timber frame, which was strengthened by steel ties. A more self-conscious repair in 2001–2 by *Butler & Hegarty*. A tall mullioned window in medieval style was inserted in the main range, and front and rear ones were recreated in the W cross wing. The timber frame of this wing was largely reconstructed, and is structurally independent of the strangely skew brick facing wall of the 1930s along the W flank. Glazing in the pavement reveals the timber sill, well below the present road level. Close by, No. 10, a trim three-bay house of *c.* 1830 with Doric porch and windows within arches. Hidden in Bishop's Close to the S, THE CHESTNUTS, early C19, its stucco regrettably replaced by pebbledash. Four-bay centre with lower pedimented wings linked by a projecting ground storey. One Greek Doric porch remains off centre. Apparently built as a pair, possibly by the Monoux school headmaster for himself and boarders. Returning W along Church Lane, on the N side are the endearing SQUIRE'S ALMSHOUSES of 1795, one storey, brick, but with a central pediment of a size more suitable for a full-scale house. Behind, the former ST MARY'S INFANTS SCHOOL, 1828, now a community centre, a spare five-bay block, slightly projecting centre bays with round-arched windows and shallow stuccoed pediment.

The VESTRY HOUSE MUSEUM was built by the parish as a workhouse in 1730; enlarged 1756, and used as such to the 1830s. A museum since 1931. On a modest and friendly domestic scale: two storeys with segment-headed windows with flush sashes. But on the date plaque (carved by *Samuel Chandler* of Wanstead) a stern warning: 'if any should not work neither should he eat'. The l. side of the originally five-bay front is masked by the mid-C18 extension, built to provide a vestry room. In the long extension at the back a polite C18 doorcase from Church Hill House. Inside, an original closed-string staircase with urn balusters, also early C17 panelling and overmantel on the ground floor from Essex Hall, which stood near

Blackhorse Road, demolished in the 1930s. Originally the workhouse had dormitories on the upper floor and workshops behind. At the back and to the W, reticent top-glazed link to an extension of 2001 by *David Gibson Architects*, with community room and open veranda overlooking a newly planted formal garden.

The very large Corinthian capital outside the Museum is from the great portico of *Smirke's* General Post Office N of St Paul's Cathedral (demolished 1912), donated by a Walthamstow stonemason.

Opposite, in Church Lane, frugal buildings for St Mary's National Boys' school, with plaque dated 1819. Enlarged 1825. One-storey centre, two-storey wings. Now National Spiritualist church. Further on in Vestry Road, former POST OFFICE SORTING OFFICE, 1903, with amazingly lavish orange-terracotta frieze and central shaped pediment. Converted to MOSQUE and ISLAMIC CENTRE, 1995 by *Sayyid Nakhavi*, with halls to seat 2000.

S of the Church to Orford Road and the S part of Hoe Street

S from Vestry Road is ORFORD ROAD, named from its one older house. ORFORD HOUSE, now a club and much altered, is a large early C19 stuccoed villa with three-bay centre, distinguished by a pediment over each side bay. The recessed entrance has Doric columns and entablature with wreaths, a popular early C19 motif. Two canted bays to the garden. Development in this area began from 1850, after the enclosure of Church Common, which was divided up for building from 1853. Orford Road became a shopping street, and until 1941 the centre of civic administration. Nos. 45–47, formerly an ironmongery and oilshop, retain some original fittings. On the N side, the OLD TOWN HALL (now a nursery), built in 1876 for the Walthamstow Local Board by its surveyor, *J. W. Swann*, extended 1890–91. A miniature French chateau; small but stately street front with shallow four-column Doric portico and steep iron-crested slate roof over the centre. The building was added in front of a public hall built by a private company in 1865. The hall was replaced by housing around a courtyard, in a tactful refurbishment and rebuilding by *Cube Architects*, 1994. Also on the N side the former ST MARY'S NATIONAL SCHOOLS, 1866 by *W. Wigginton*, now an Asian centre, simplified Gothic, with a big circular window in the brick gable. Round the corner further E the road becomes domestic, with some plain villas of *c.* 1860.

To the S of Orford Road are streets with a pleasing variety of small cottages, built in ones and twos from 1853; some sport rustic gables, others aspire to shared pediments; they can be sampled in a tour starting in BEULAH ROAD, turning W via GROSVENOR RISE EAST to EDEN ROAD, RANDOLPH

ROAD and WINGFIELD ROAD. This area was laid out in 1862 by *Ebenezer Clarke*, chairman of the Local Board of Health, a philanthropic town-planning exercise in healthy living for the poor.* Further W are slightly grander villas, together with later houses, in GROSVENOR PARK ROAD leading W to Hoe Street, which was built up from 1850 on the Grosvenor Park estate. Two contemporary pubs: the Windmill (1857) and Castle (1866).

HOE STREET has only intermittent interest. Only two remain from several mansions in this area which survived into the mid-C20. On the E side No. 285, CLEVELAND HOUSE (now flats), set back from the road. Much altered, but the tall three-bay centre is early C18. Three storeys and basement, later stucco dressings, and r. extension of 1871. Better preserved, on the W side, is CHESTNUT HOUSE (No. 398; Walthamstow Training Agency). An excellent C18 house, in an early Georgian tradition though rainwater heads give the dates 1745 and 1747. The initials are for Thomas and Catherine Allen, who lived here from 1743–63. The last of a succession of owners (1851–91) was J.F.H. Read, active in promoting local education and music. The large grounds were sold to the Tottenham and Forest Gate Railway Co. in the 1890s.

The house is of 2-3-2 bays, three floors over a now largely hidden basement, the present level perhaps created together with the later stuccoed and pedimented entrance porch. Three advanced centre bays with pediment over the first two storeys and an attic floor above. Window frames have thick glazing bars under segment-headed arches of rubbed brick, and there is a brick string and cornice. The S side is of three bays, with two later canted bay windows, another bay window to the W. Well preserved interior: a broad hall runs through the centre of the building, with pilasters dividing front and back. The stair rises on the r., an elegant showpiece, with three twisted balusters to the tread, carved tread ends, and rail ending in spiral around a fluted newel. Plaster panels on the upper walls have festoons and baskets of fruit and flowers. Good cornices and panelling throughout (and a plaster ceiling l. of the entrance). To the N a low service wing and stable block in matching style. Nice gatepiers, but a dismal setting of temporary buildings to the S.

On the E side of Hoe Street, the long range with beehive motifs was built as the Jubilee Branch of the Stratford Co-operative and Industrial Society, 1911 and 1915 by *W.H. Cockcroft*, free classical with two round-headed gables, the S end with jolly turret and leaded dome at the corner of Orford Road. Also on the E side, TELEPHONE EXCHANGE of 1956, quite cheerful with chequer brick panels to brighten up the concrete grid. (Its Neo-Georgian predecessor of 1937 is to the E in Grosvenor Park Road.) S of Boundary Road (strictly speaking in Leyton) Nos. 368–76, the former EMPRESS CINEMA, 1913, a rendered façade, the centre with four Ionic columns above

* Described in Clarke's *History of Walthamstow*, 1862. Information from Chris Pond.

the entrance (double-height barrel-vaulted auditorium with gallery, and unusually elaborate plasterwork for its date).

2. Forest Road and Shernhall Street, starting from the Town Hall

Much of the N side of Forest Road is taken up by the civic buildings and adjacent College (*see* above). Opposite is No. 590, BROOKSCROFT, one of several C18 houses which survive to demonstrate the popularity of the plain but well-proportioned country villa in this area. Rate books suggests it replaced an older house *c.* 1762. Five bays, the centre three slightly advanced, with a good Doric doorcase. Two storeys, divided by a stone band, with dentilled cornice; above, probably a later addition, is an attic floor with centre pediment containing a lunette window, flanked by dormers cutting into the pediment. At the back the top floor is of full height. C20 W extension. Now flats.

Further E the N side of Forest Road becomes industrial. A detour to the N up FULBOURNE ROAD can take in FOREST WORKS. Buildings of 1935–9 by *Wallis Gilbert & Partners* for Asea and Fuller Electric Ltd, a Swedish and British company established 1905, later Hawker Siddeley. Two-storey staggered front with brick bands between long windows; the three-storey office building, by the same firm, is similar, but given grandeur by a formal stone frontispiece on the end wall: over the entrance a tripartite window and clock below a stepped-back, slightly Deco parapet.

THORPE COMBE HOUSE (formerly North Bank), at the E corner of Forest Road and Shernhall Street, is of similar date and width to Brookscroft, but of three full storeys, with pediment over the three advanced centre bays. Doric porch, restored. Apparently built as a speculation in 1762, together with two other houses on adjacent plots, and let to Richard Manby, a City bookseller. Inside, a mid-C18 staircase with twisted and turned balusters remains, set within an apsed end, and a good Rococo plasterwork in the larger reception room. Later C18 additions and outbuildings were removed when the house was used as a maternity hospital (1919–73); the tall, oddly mannered Neo-Georgian nurses' home on the r. dates from this period.

Of the two adjacent contemporary houses only the substantial WALTHAMSTOW HOUSE survives, much enlarged, immediately to the S. It is approached from Shernhall Street, through iron gates with cannon bollards. Now part of HOLY FAMILY TECHNOLOGY COLLEGE. Its Neo-Georgian extension to the l. dates from occupation by St Mary's Convent and a girls' orphanage (*c.* 1885–1982); further school extensions beyond. The C18 house itself is of several dates, a recurrent pattern in this area, where houses of merchant families were often altered to suit frequent changes of owner. N-facing front of three storeys divided by stone strings; segment-headed windows throughout. The three-bay centre has a sturdy Doric porch approached up steps, and is grandly flanked by a large canted full-height bay at each end. But the canted bays are not identical, and the placing of the chimneys, confirmed by the internal evidence, shows that the W part is an addition; the original house of *c.* 1762 was only of five bays with the entrance one bay E of the present one. The enlargements, including a rear wing, were to accommodate the large family of the owner from 1782, Sir Robert Wigram (†1830), shipowner, director of the East India Company and M.P. He had twenty-three children. His son Sir Robert Fitzwigram occupied the house until 1843 (two other sons lived at Thorpe Combe and Brookscroft, *see* above).

Inside, the original entrance hall is now a cupboard, and the front door leads into a handsome square room; an enriched dentil cornice frames a fine Rococo ceiling with delicate low reliefs of musical instruments around a sunburst. The NE room has another decorative ceiling, defined by rods with floral garlands, extending into the canted bay. At the back, in the original centre of the house, lit by a tall, arched window, is a good staircase, somewhat altered, with carved tread ends and fluted balusters to the upper flight. The large, later W room (shown on a print of 1803) perhaps dining room or ballroom, runs the depth of the house, with a curved end within the canted bay.

Further down SHERNHALL STREET on the E side, the quaint St Gabriel's vicarage, a suburban interwar house with rustic lych-gate porch and stained glass (the church is to the E down Havant Road), and the LORD BROOKE, a lavish pub of *c.* 1900, Old English style with half-timbered gables. Opposite, No. 28 is the former SHALE'S ICE CREAM FACTORY. Also on the W side, more buildings of HOLY FAMILY TECHNOLOGY COLLEGE, partly in gaunt institutional premises built 1875 for St John's R.C. Boys' Industrial Schools. Further S is the striking R.C. church of Our Lady and St George (*see* above).

3. *Hoe Street and High Street starting from Walthamstow Central Station*

CENTRAL STATION (formerly Hoe Street), on the S side of the tracks, is an attractively unspoilt Great Eastern Railway station of 1870. Polychrome brickwork with a touch of Gothic in the window heads. Prominent ridge-and-furrow canopy on cantilevered lattice beams. On the N side is a BUS INTERCHANGE adjoining the Victoria Line exit, *c.* 1968, with light overlapping butterfly roofs on thin hollow-steel posts creating the illusion of exotic cantilevers. (For Hoe Street S of the station *see* perambulation, p. 257). This tour turns N up Hoe Street to the junction with HIGH STREET, mostly rebuilt from *c.* 1958–72, partly as a result of Second World War damage, by the Borough Architect *F.G. Southgate.* The NW side is a cheery piece of post-Festival townscape, with a Clock Tower at the corner of Church Hill, attached to a bank. Stone-faced, with local pride expressed by mosaic decoration with coats of arms. Running uphill from it are shops with a lively wavy canopy of concrete pierced with holes (an echo of Tecton?) and flats above. More flats along Church Hill, with a pattern of angled balconies. The less inventive and later group on the w side of Hoe Street, also with flats over shops, was demolished in 2003–4 for a new library and leisure centre by the *Colman Partnership* planned in 2001.

Further up Hoe Street is the splendidly showy frontage of the
95 former Granada Cinema, 1930 by *Massey & Komisarjevsky*,
their first London work for this chain. Closed 2003. Tripartite frontage with fancifully eclectic Moorish features, tall trefoil arches, spiral columns oddly capped by classical urns, the façade continuing to l. and r. of the main building. Spacious foyer with classical fluted pilasters. (Horseshoe-shaped auditorium, red and gold in Moorish style, seating 3,000.) Little to see further N apart from the landmarks of the Rose and Crown, with tall, shaped gables and a corner turret, and still further N, The Bell, dated 1900, prominent at the start of Chingford Road.

Now along High Street, the main commercial thoroughfare, architecturally scrappy, but famous for its street market extending for most of its narrow half-mile length. The E end used to have quite an impressive sequence of Edwardian public buildings, but the Baths and Palace Music Hall have gone, as has the rock-faced Congregational church of 1871 by *Tarring*, and the Monoux school of 1889. The dignified Library (*see* above) is the only significant survivor. There were once good C18 houses too; the sole remnant is a late Georgian building, The Chequers, three broad storeys with pediment inscribed against a tall parapet. Further on a view N to the formal frontage of the Mission Grove School of 1906; two storeyed, with four-bay centre below a segmental stone pediment.

The s side of the High Street has two big shopping developments of the later C20: Selborne Walk, announced by a brisk zigzag of eleven gables over oriel windows, comfortably in scale with the street, with covered malls behind, and a lumpier brown brick Sainsburys with still bleaker rear and car park. At No. 76, L. Manze & Co. Eel and Pie shop, with tiled Edwardian interior. The W end of the High Street is more pompously urban. At the corner with St James Street, No. 2, a substantial Art Deco period piece of 1935, built as a Montagu Burtons store in the characteristic style of their in-house architect's department. Faced in white faience, windows to the two upper storeys framed by fancy Egyptian detail. The building was planned with billiard hall and social facilities above, now Embassy Snooker and Social Club. Opposite are tall shopping terraces of *c.* 1900, sporting much cream terracotta ornament, with gabled dormers displaying the Warner monogram.

The local landowner, Thomas Courtenay Warner (later M.P., High Sheriff of Essex and Mayor of Walthamstow) began to develop this area in the 1880s. By then the family was living in grandeur at the still-rural Highams (*see* p. 722), a typical example of the local gentry of the area moving eastward as suburban development spread. Just N of the High Street, at the W end of MISSION GROVE, CLOCK HOUSE is the former family mansion, now hemmed in by later building and restored from *c.* 2000 after many alterations. A restrained Regency villa of white Suffolk brick, built in 1813 for an earlier Thomas Warner. Three bays under a shallow hipped roof with broad eaves, the side bays very slightly advanced, with the ground-floor windows set within arches. The building was run briefly as a district supply store for six shops in the area. Courtenay Warner was unusual in undertaking the development of the surrounding streets himself rather than selling off his land. His architect was *John Dunn*. Their modest but well-built mixtures of terraces and cottage flats were intended for letting to respectable artisans. Like their exact contemporary, Rowland Plumbe's Noel Park estate, Wood Green (Haringey), also designed for artisan residents, they show the pared-down influence of Norman Shaw's London work of the 1870s. The houses are of red brick, or yellow brick with red trim, with occasional gables and terracotta detail to break the monotony. PRETORIA AVENUE running N from Mission Grove, is one of the more ambitious streets, with some semi-detached houses with shaped gables, 1888. WARNER ROAD to the E is varied by gables faced with terracotta rosettes. Here too is a BOARD SCHOOL of Walthamstow's usual earlier one-storey type, 1888, enlarged 1903, planned together with the housing. The tall terraces in ST JAMES STREET opposite the station (opened 1870) are treated with more panache, enlivened by shaped gables and classical friezes in terracotta. Between them runs LEUCHA ROAD, 1895, 85
with two-storey cottage flats, especially complete in their details, thanks to their acquisition by the council in the 1960s and careful treatment since as a conservation area.

4. *North of Forest Road, from Blackhorse Road Station*

The undistinguished Victoria Line station at the junction of Forest Road and BLACKHORSE ROAD (a corruption from Black House, a building preceding Clock House) is a tough clerestory-lit box of dark brick, 1968. Fibreglass relief of a black stallion by *David McFall*. Further E, on the S side of Forest Road, the LORD PALMERSTON, a jolly pub with much red terracotta; interior with engraved glass and some original (altered) furnishings.

Those wishing to pursue further Warner developments can explore the area to the N, where building carried on into the 1930s. To the N, the area around WINNS AVENUE was begun in 1898. Here too is a group of SCHOOLS of 1907 by *H. Prosser*: behind sturdy gatepiers, low-gabled ranges with sparing stone carving to copings and keystones. The later Warner housing in this area was laid out to conform with the UDC's town-planning scheme of 1912: between Pennant Terrace and Billet Road winding roads of garden suburb type appear in place of a straight grid of streets, and the details of the house façades become simpler. On Billet Road, ROGER ASCHAM SCHOOL, 1929 by Walthamstow Urban District Council. Old-fashioned brick porch with Baroque pediment to the name plaque above, half-timbered gable behind, with bellcote. The layout is more innovative: two wings in a Y-formation, their big gabled windows facing S to the playground.

To the W of COUNTESS ROAD, the council built its own housing after the Second World War: PRIORY COURT, a striking group by the Borough Architect *F.G. Southgate*. It impressed Pevsner in the 1950s: 'twenty straight six-storeyed blocks, so well grouped that they make an impressive whole of true C20 character, urban yet not inhuman'. The grouping remains; but the buildings were radically transformed from the mid- to late 1990s. They now have gleaming white walls and dominant curved roofs, after refurbishment for Circle 33 by *BPTW* and the *Waltham Forest Borough Architect's Department* with the contractors Wilmott Dixon. A community centre has been added. Further W, less interesting council housing, and much industry which developed from the late C19 between the N part of Blackhorse Road and the River Lea.

FOREST ROAD continues W between the Lea Valley reservoirs (*see* p. 752–3). On the N side, the attractive FERRY BOAT INN, partly C18, two storeys and three bays, with later extensions and bay windows, on the site of an older ferry house at the crossing over the Lea. A toll bridge was built in 1760, replaced in 1915. Close to the inn, an iron bridge of 1904 over the waterworks river.

5. *East Walthamstow: Wood Street and the Forest*

The E fringes of built up Walthamstow merge into Woodford and Snaresbrook (*see* Redbridge), interspersed with the greenery of Epping Forest, which stretches S as far as Whipps Cross Road. Enclosures for gentry houses on the fringe of the Forest took place through the C18; their character can still be seen at the Forest School which occupies a group of such houses. In contrast, a humble suburban area grew around the station from the 1870s.

WOOD STREET, a minor shopping street, runs S from Forest Road to Lea Bridge Road. Half way down is the STATION, opened 1873, now a simple glazed booking hall with space-frame roof. Looming above, ST PATRICK'S COURT, built in the later 1960s as Northwood Tower, twenty-one storeys of council flats, refurbished by *Hunt Thompson* in 1990–2 in an emphatic Postmodern idiom, following their similar transformation of St David's Court in Parkstone Road further N (1989). Concrete-panelled walls were covered by patterned brickwork and the skyline given a strong cornice and broken pediment. In contrast, No. 76 is a relic of the former character of the area: a small, former butcher's shop, timber-framed and weatherboarded. Shop on the r. with butchers' hooks; on the l. a meat store with slatted ventilation screen. Much of the rest is indifferent later C19; minor landmarks are the WHITE SWAN, 1887, with terracotta decoration, overpainted, and WOODSIDE SCHOOL, 1898 by *W.A. Longmore*, three buildings with steep hipped roofs, one retaining a cupola. WARWICK SCHOOL further S in Barrett Road, now a secondary with later additions, is a grander but awkward composition with striped brick centre gable and octagonal-turreted ends, by *H. Prosser*, 1905.

The best building in Wood Street is towards the S end near Lea Bridge Road: CLOCK HOUSE, a stately early C18 house, now deprived of its grounds and sandwiched by C20 wings of flats to E and W by *F.G. Southgate*. Three storeys above a high basement, seven bays of straight-headed windows. Refronted in the later C18 when the central pediment was added. The W-facing garden side (now with only a yard behind) has a later C18 curved central bay and a C19 tented first-floor balcony, boldly detailed with iron columns and pretty valencing, which runs the width of the house, supported on an arcade (a very similar arrangement to Highams, *see* p. 723). Entrance hall with black and white marble floor, and fielded panelling, early C18 staircase with turned balusters. The grounds, now built up, were laid out after 1713 by Sir Jacob Jacobsen and extended E of Wood Street; Woodside Park Avenue follows the line of a formal avenue, a pond at the end remains from more elaborate water features.

WOODFORD NEW ROAD, N of the Lea Bridge Road roundabout, was cut through the Forest in 1828. Just to its E is THE FOREST, an informal cluster consisting of GWYDR LODGE, mid-C18, four irregular bays and two storeys (staircase and panelling inside), IVY COTTAGES, an early C19 pair, and two Victorian pairs built for Forest School.

Development on this fringe of Epping Forest began in the 1740s when three rows of houses were built by Sir John Salter, a Lord Mayor and chairman of the East India Company. The remaining group in COLLEGE PLACE is now FOREST SCHOOL. The school was founded in 1834 with twenty-two pupils, as a private establishment for the sons of the local gentry. The handsome cast-iron Neo-Grecian railings and gateposts with lions' heads fit this date. The intimate, domestic scale of College Place conceals a much-expanded site now catering for 1,200 students. The centrepiece is a neat mid-C18 house of five bays and two storeys, dignified by an advanced three-bay centre with steep central pediment, a lunette window within it. Doric porch on columns, and fanlight over the door. On the l. a range with segment-headed windows in a pattern of 2-3-2, and no doors, apparently a service wing. On the r. a more irregular group, a small three-bay house (the present pedimented entrance is a later addition), then the warden's house, acquired later and extended on a grander scale. The centre house has an C18 front hall; the room on the r. has early C19 joinery and fireplace. The back was altered in the late C18 (as shown on a plan of 1798): a delicate top-lit stair winds up against a curved back wall, and to its l., now opening into later additions, is a circular study with a pretty cornice and fireplace, and window in a bowed W wall. At the back of the service wing is the LIBRARY added for the school, a sober room with three big windows to the N. In 1863–5 it was lined with dark C17 panelling with rusticated pilasters, which came from the chapel of Jesus College Oxford; the connection is explained by the friendship between *G.E. Street*, restorer of the college chapel in 1864, the headmaster, Frederick Barlow Guy, and William Morris who was tutored by Guy before he went to Oxford.

Across an informal quadrangle, connected by a W cloister walk of the 1870s, is the school CHAPEL, built 1857 with funding from William Cotton (*see* Leytonstone) and extended in the same style in 1875, when the architect was *William White*. Quirky, angular Gothic, of brick, with plate-tracery windows and large triangular dormers. Inside, the steep timber roof dominates, a spiky confection of scissor-braced trusses, hammerbeams and king-posts. Deep W gallery with more woodwork from Jesus College. The original chapel is aisleless, the E part opens out, with transepts divided off by columns. Here the Guy family's Anglo-Catholic taste is reflected by the refined angels designed by *White*, carved by *Harry Hems*. Later statues of saints in the nave, less good, not improved by 1960s colouring. Other furnishings were lost in the Second World War. REREDOS, a carved Last Supper, 1955. STAINED GLASS. N transept W: by *William Morris & Co.*, Samuel and Timothy, 1881. Nave N: fragment with head from a lost *Morris* window. Cartoon by *Morris & Co.* for lost E window with David and Jonathan, 1878. Nave S by *E.P. Barraud*, Elijah and St John; another by *Powell & Sons* of Whitefriars, Good Shepherd and St Peter (both artists had sons at the school). The post-war E window is a 1950s period piece by *Francis Skeat*, Christ with two idealized schoolboys. MONUMENT. Frederick Barlow Guy †1890 by *W. Goscombe John*. A fine bronze relief; recumbent figure with St George and St John Baptist.

The DINING HALL on the E side of the quadrangle is of 1886 by *Richard Creed*. Although at the time there were only fifty boys, it is on an Oxbridge collegiate scale, a long hall with Perp windows high up, raised above ground-floor kitchens. Brick outside and in, but dull apart from the fine double-hammerbeam roof. The panelling was added later. At the high end there was originally a *Morris* tapestry below the timber cornice, which is another fragment from Jesus College. Above is the school banner of 1879, designed by *Morris*. The hall backs onto the WARDEN'S LODGINGS which has its main front to the S, three bays wide, with giant pilasters of stone, pompously Victorian in comparison with the adjoining C18 buildings. On the ground floor a single grand reception room. The entrance is through the oddly angled adjacent older house to the W, acquired by the school in the 1870s and adapted for the purpose. It retains a delightful early C19 drawing-room on the first floor. This has a rounded bay and a matching curve at the opposite end. The restrained joinery and ceiling of starfish form are remarkably in the character of *Soane's* work. N of the chapel, former INFIRMARY, 1859, a simple two-storey cottage. The succession of C20 BUILDINGS starts opposite, with the ASTON BUILDING, a well-proportioned, functional classroom block of 1951–3. At the SW corner of the site, hexagonal THEATRE, 1963–7, with *Arup Associates* as engineers; originally its concrete construction was boldly exposed, but unhappily muted by tile-cladding in the 1990s. Timber-lined inside. In the entrance lobby a window made up of fragments of medieval glass (canopy, figure of a saint, grisaille leaves and vinescroll border) from Howden Minster (Yorks East Riding) where F.B. Guy's father was rector. To its N, arts block with a bland Neo-Georgian W façade, *c.* 2000. Behind the chapel, sixth form centre, polygonal music centre, and sports hall of the 1970s onwards. E of the Dining Hall the Junior School, incorporating a plain five-bay C18 house, cricket pavilion with computer centre tucked beneath, and Girls' School, 1978–81, a cluster of hexagons, by *Tooley Foster Partnership*.

Further N on WOODFORD NEW ROAD, the early C19 church of St Peter in the Forest (*see* p. 747) used by the school until it had its own chapel. For the area N of this *see* Highams Park (p. 722) and Woodford (pp. 370–1).

SOURCES AND FURTHER READING

The documentary information in this book is drawn from a mixture of printed sources, planning records, local history collections and archives of individual boroughs, reports by English Heritage and other organizations, and other unpublished material kindly made available by those carrying out individual research (*see also* Acknowledgements p. xvi). The following is only an introductory selection from a vast range of material.

Many books on London give little attention to the parts of the metropolis covered by this volume, confining their attention to the riverside and a few well-known landmarks. The titles mentioned here are chiefly those which include material on East London. For the wider London context the section on Sources and Further Reading in the other London volumes in this series can be consulted, most recently *London 6: Westminster*, by Simon Bradley and Nikolaus Pevsner (2003).

The most detailed London bibliography is the extensive *Bibliography of Printed Works of London History to 1939* edited by H. Creaton (1994). *Capital Histories, a bibliographical study of London* ed. by P.L. Garside (1998) has chapters on different periods discussing studies published from 1975 in the *London Journal* and elsewhere. An invaluable one-volume reference book is the *Encyclopedia of London* ed. B. Weinreb and C. Hibbert (2nd ed. 1992). Recent single volume histories include R. Porter, *London, A Social History* (1994), F. Shepherd, *London, A History* (1998), S. Inwood, *A History of London* (1999), P. Ackroyd, *London, the Biography* (2000). A planner's view is provided by M. Hebbert's excellent *London* (1998). Among the histories of particular periods especially relevant are G. Rudé, *Hanoverian London 1714–1808* (1971), F. Sheppard, *London 1808–70, the infernal wen* (1971); J. White, *London in the Twentieth Century* (2001). The Second World War and the Blitz are covered in numerous books; the best single account is P. Ziegler, *London at War* (1995).

The historic East End has inspired its own histories: Walter Besant, *East London* (1903), and *London North of the Thames*, (1911) remain useful compendia, and Millicent Rose's *The East End of London* (1951, reprinted 1973) is still both readable and informative. Alan Palmer, *The East End, four centuries of London Life* (1989), is a well-referenced and wide-ranging introduction. Outstanding among the many East End studies concerned primarily with people and social history is W.J. Fishman's evocatively illustrated *The Streets of East London* (1979). Short biographies of eminent Eastenders are in H. Finch, *The Tower*

Hamlets Connection, a biographical guide (1996). *East London Papers*, from 1958–73 and its successor, the *London Journal* have been an important forum for current research. C20 developments are discussed in *London, Aspects of Change* (Centre for Urban studies report no. 3, 1964), and more recent developments in T. Butler and M. Rustin, eds, *Rising in the East. The Regeneration of East London* (1996).

Studies especially relevant to East London include *The Peopling of London, fifteen thousand years of settlement from overseas*, ed. N. Merriman (Museum of London, 1993); *London World City 1800–1840*, ed. C. Fox, with an essay on architecture of the period by A. Saint. There is a large campaigning literature on the general character of the C19 East End and its inhabitants, from H. Gavin's *Sanitary Ramblings, Being Sketches and illustrations of Bethnal Green*, 1848, and Mayhew's *London Labour and the London Poor*, 1851 to A. Mearns, *The Bitter Cry of Outcast London*, 1883 (reprinted 1970 with introduction by A.S. Wohl) and Charles Booth's *Life and Labour of the People of London*, 1889 (maps reprinted by the Lon. Topog. Soc. 1984). R. Mudie-Smith, *The Religious Life of London*, 1904 includes discussion of the Tower Hamlets and Newham areas. Among the late C19 and early C20 novels which played an important part in forming impressions of the area were Walter Besant, *All Sorts and Conditions of Men* (1882), Arthur Morrison, *Child of the Jago* (1896) and Jack London, *The People of the Abyss* (1903). For the C20 there is the *New Survey of London Life and Labour* (1934) and D.L. Munby's detailed survey, *Industry and Planning in Stepney* (1951). Harold Clunn, *The Face of London*, 1951, is a mid-C20 snapshot of the capital, including walks through the East End.

Architecture and Housing

John Summerson's classic, *Georgian London* (1945, new edition edited by H.M. Colvin, 2003) was focused on the West End, but has a gazetteer including East End buildings. Recent studies have paid more attention to buildings outside the realm of the great estates, notably Elizabeth McKellar, *The Birth of Modern London* (1999) and Peter Guillery, *The Small House in Eighteenth Century London* (2004). Other studies on this period are D. Cruikshank and P. Wyld, *The Art of Georgian Building* (1975), A. Byrne, *London's Georgian Houses* (1986), *Good and Proper Materials, the Fabric of London since the Great Fire*, ed. A. Saunders (London Topographical Society), 1989, on building materials. C19 working-class housing is discussed by J.N. Tarn: *Five per cent Philanthropy* (1973), and The Peabody Donation Fund, *Victorian Studies* (1966); by A.S. Wohl, *The Eternal Slum: Housing and Social Policy in Victorian London* (1977), and J.A. Yelling, *Slum and slum clearance in Victorian London*, 1986. S. Beattie admirably deals with the early role of the LCC in *A Revolution in London housing, LCC Housing Architects and their work, 1893–1914* (1980) and the next phase of public housing: Mark Swenarton, *Homes Fit for Heroes* (1981). *Home Sweet Home*, Greater London Council

(1976), carries the story onwards. Contemporary records were published by the LCC: *The Housing Question in London 1855–1900* (1900), *Housing* (1928), *Housing 1928–30* (1931), *Housing 1945–9* (1949). A. Cox, *Public Housing, A London archives guide* (1993), is a useful introduction. On the post-war scene: A. Cleeve Barr, *Public Authority Housing* (1958); Nicholas Bullock, *Rebuilding the Post-War World* (2002) includes a chapter on London 1940–49; Lionel Esher, *A Broken Wave, the Rebuilding of England 1940–1980*, (1981), also has a chapter on London. For public housing of the 1950s–70s, there is M. Glendinning and S. Muthesius, *Tower Block* (1994). K. Wedd, *Creative Quarters, the art world in London 1700–2000*, Museum of London (2001), has a chapter on artists in the East End in the later C20. *London Suburbs*, introduction by Andrew Saint (English Heritage 1999), is an introductory chronological account, with short summaries on each borough.

Building Types

A good introduction is E. Harwood and A. Saint, *London* (1991) which discusses a wide variety of subjects arranged by buildings types. Specialized studies include C. Hewett, *Church Carpentry* (1982), for Essex churches, M.H. Port, *Six Hundred New Churches* (1961, new ed. forthcoming), on C19 churches. *The Victorian Church* ed. C. Brooks and A. Saint (1995), has a chapter by A. Saint on London churches, including those in Bethnal Green. *Twentieth Century Architecture* vol.3, published by the Twentieth Century Society, has essays on modern churches (1998). On R.C. churches, D. Evinson, *Catholic Churches of London* (1998), A. Rottman, *London Catholic Churches* (1926). For synagogues, S. Kadish, ed., *Building Jerusalem, Jewish Architecture in Britain* (1996); records of the Survey of the Jewish Built Heritage (www.jewish-heritage-uk.org); and J. Glasman, London Synagogues in the late C19: Design in Context, *London Journal*, 13.1 (1998). F. Gailani, *The Mosques of London* (2000). Especially thorough are the books based on detailed surveys by Royal Commission staff (later English Heritage): *English Hospitals 1660–1948*, ed. H. Richardson (1998), The *Workhouse*, by K. Morrison (1999), *English Shops and Shopping*, by K. Morrison (2003) and *Court Houses* (unpublished typescript). Also published by English Heritage is *London's Town Halls* (1999), a slim volume with essays on both architecture and local government from 1840. John Booker, *Temples of Mammon* (1990) deals with banks. The Theatres Trust has published *Guide to British Theatres, 1700–1950*, ed. J. Earl and M. Sell (2000). On cinemas, Richard Gray, *Cinemas in Britain* (1996) and four works by A. Eyles: *ABC – The first name in entertainment* (1993); *Gaumont British Cinemas* (1996); *The Granada Theatres* (1998); also *Odeon Cinemas* (2002).

M. Girouard, *Victorian Pubs* (1975), and H. Meller, *London cemeteries* (1981), include East London examples. Especially relevant for the East End is D. Weiner, *Architecture and social reform in late Victorian London* (1994), and by the same author, The architecture of Victorian philanthropy, the settlement house as manorial residence, *Art History* 13, no. 2 (1990). On gardens and parks T. Longstaffe-Gowan, *The London Town Garden, 1700–1840*, (2001), J.J. Sexby, *The Municipal Parks, Gardens and Open Spaces of London* (1898), S. Daniels, *Humphry Repton* (1999).

On schools: D. Gregory-Jones, *The London Board Schools*, E.R. Robson, in A. Service, ed., *Edwardian Architecture and its Origins* (1975), R. Ringshall et al., *The Urban School* (1983), A Jackson in *Lon Topog. Record* 25 (1995), M. Seaborne, *The English School* vol. 1 1370–1870 (1971) and vol. 2, with R. Lowe, 1870–1970 (1977). A. Jackson, 'Sermons in Brick': Design and Social Purpose in London Board Schools *Lon. Journal* v. 18, no.1, 1993.

A.W.G. Ball, *The Public Libraries of Greater London* (1977), Roger Bowdler and Steven Brindle, *A Survey of Pre-war Libraries in London* (English Heritage, typescript, 1992).

On transport there are T.C. Barker and M.R. Robbins, *A History of London Transport* (2 vols.) (1963–74); H.P.White, *A Regional History of the Railways of Great Britain*, vol. 3, *Greater London* (2nd ed. 1971), David Lawrence, *Underground Architecture* (1994); D. Leboff, *London's Underground Stations* (1994), J. Glover, *London's Underground* (1996). D. Bennett, *The Architecture of the Jubilee Line Extension* (2003).

On industrial archaeology the pioneer studies were A. Wilson, *London's Industrial Heritage* (1967) and Ashdown, Bussell and Carter's *Industrial Monuments of Greater London* (1969). See also East Midlands and Eastern England volumes in the *Canals of the British Isles* series, M. Denney, *London's Waterways* (1977), Herbert Spencer, *London's Canal* (1976) on the Regent's Canal. R. Sisley, *The London Water Supply* (1899). H.W Dickinson, *Water Supply of Greater London* (1954) and publications of the Metropolitan Water Board. S. Everard, *History of the Gas, Light and Coke Co.* (1949), North Thames Gas Board's *Historical Index of Gas Works* (1957). Farries and Mason, *Industries of London since 1861* (1962). A popular and readable account of the background to the main drainage project is S. Halliday, *The Great Stink of London* (2001). Minutes of *Proceedings of the Institute of Civil Engineers* and other contemporary publications provide further detail. Recent fieldwork is published by the Greater London Industrial Archaeology Society.

Architects, Planners, Sculptors

Well known architects are few in East London compared with elsewhere. The essential reference books are H.M. Colvin, *Biographical Dictionary of English Architects*, 1600–1840 (3rd ed. 1995), *Directory of British Architects 1834–1900* (British Architectural Library 1993 (expanded ed. 2001 up to 1914) and A.S. Gray, *Edwardian Architecture, a biographical dictionary* 1985. The work of C20 architects can be pursued through the indexes and database at the Royal Institute of British Architects and in contemporary periodicals. Especially useful for the C19 onwards are *The Illustrated London News*, *The Builder*, *Building News* (later

Architect and Building News), the *Architectural Review, Architect's Journal and RIBA Journal;* for the C20 can be added: *Architecture Illustrated, Official Architecture and Planning, Concrete Quarterly, Building Design, London Architect* and *Church Building.*

Monographs on architects with work in East London include A. Foyle, *George Smith, surveyor to the Mercers' Company from 1814* (Courtauld Inst. M.A). G. Tyack, *Sir James Pennethorne and the Making of Victorian London* (1992). A. Crawford, *C.R. Ashbee*, 1985, J. Allan, *Lubetkin* (1992), W. Curtis, *Denys Lasdun* (1994), H. Webster, ed, *Modernism without Rhetoric,* on the Smithsons. E. Jamilly, 'Anglo-Jewish Architects and Architecture in the C18 and C19, *Transactions of the Jewish Historical Society of England*, vol. 18 (1958) has short biographies of the major firms. On C20 planning the essential contemporary documents are the *County of London Plan* by J.H. Forshaw and P. Abercrombie (1943) and Abercrombie's complementary *Greater London Plan* (1944), the *London County Council Plan* (1951), its *First Review* (1960), the *Greater London Development Plan* (1965) and the documents associated with the enquiry that followed.

For sculpture standard works are R. Gunnis, *Dictionary of British Sculptors, 1660–1851* (rev. ed. 1968), M. Whinney, *Sculpture in Britain 1530–1830* (rev. by J. Physick, 1988); A. White, A Biographical Dictionary of London Tomb Sculpture 1560–1660, *Walpole Society* vol. LXI (1999), B. Read, *Victorian Sculpture* (1982), S. Beattie, *The New Sculpture* (1983). On public statues J. Blackwood, *London's Immortals* (1989).

Topography

John Stow's *Survey of London* (1603; ed. C.L. Kingsford 1908) initiated detailed topographical descriptions of London, and threw light on the eastern City fringes transformed in his lifetime. John Strype's edition of Stow (1720), includes a tour of the rural parishes beyond the built up suburbs, including Leyton where he was rector. Later topographical works which cover the eastern areas include D. Lysons, *Environs of London*, vol. 4 (1797), Edward Walford, *Old and New London* (1872–8). James Thorne, *Handbook to the Environs of London* (1876, reprinted 1970), is a comprehensive gazetteer to places within twenty miles of the capital giving a revealing snapshot of their character at the time.

On the former parts of Essex, the older works are P. Morant, *History and Antiquities of Essex* (1768), P. Muilman, *A New and Complete History of Essex*, 6 vols. 1770–72, T. Wright, *History and Topography of Essex* (1836), and White's *Directory* (1848). The various editions of Kelly are useful for the C20. See also F. Chancellor, *Ancient Sepulchral Monuments of Essex* (1890); W. Lack, H.M. Stutchfield, P. Whittemore, *The Monumental Brasses of Essex*, 2 vols. (2003).

Essential topographical tools are B. Adams, *London Illustrated, 1604–1851*, 1983, a catalogue of published views, the London Topographical Society's facsimile of and introduction to Gascoyne's 1703 *Survey of Stepney*, the same society's five *'A–Z'* volumes reproducing historic maps from the C16 to the C19 and the facsimiles of old Ordnance Survey maps of London published by Alan Godfrey.

Individual Areas

The titles listed below are only a brief introductory selection. Rich resources are available in the boroughs' local studies centres, which include maps and photographs as well as books and local records. A helpful start can be the old photos reproduced in the recent picture books on local areas published by Alan Sutton and Historical Publications, which often have well-informed captions. Records of the former LCC and GLC are held by London Metropolitan Archives (including County Council minutes, Buildings Act Case Files, and war damage maps; the Essex County Record office has material relating to the areas formerly in Essex. Essential starting points are the relevant volumes of the *Victoria County History.* The VCH *Middlesex* vol. I (1971) includes medieval religious houses on the east fringe of London; vol. II (1998), has an account of Bethnal Green together with the early history of the parish of Stepney. *Essex* vols. V, VI, and VII) cover those parts formerly within that county (see below under boroughs). The general surveys by the *Royal Commission on Historical Monuments* (relatively early and so confined to buildings up to 1714) are *East London*, 1930, covering Tower Hamlets, and Essex vols. II (1921) and III (1922). The official *Lists of buildings of architectural and historic interest*, and their supplements, are now a source of information on a wide range of C20 buildings as well as earlier ones. Background research for much recent listing was carried out by English Heritage, whose London research files (continuing the work undertaken by the Historic Buildings Division within the Greater London Council and its predecessor, the LCC), provide much information unavailable elsewhere. English Heritage also has records of threatened buildings and other reports, which can be consulted at the National Monuments Record, Swindon.

Tower Hamlets

M.J. Power, *The Urban development of East London 1550–1700* (PhD 1971). Isobel Watson, From West Heath to Stepney Green: building development in Mile End Old Town, 1660–1820, *Lon. Topog. Record*, vol. 27 (1995). D. Morris, *Mile End Old Town 1740–1780* (2002). T. Ridge, *Central Stepney Walk* (1998) is a well-informed introduction, as is A.J. Robinson and D.H.B. Chesshyre, *The Green*, 1978, on Bethnal Green. On Poplar *see* Stephen Porter, All Saints Poplar, the making of a parish. *Lon. Journal*, vol. 17 n. 2 (1992). The *Survey of London*'s first activities were focused on the East End, resulting in a volume on the fast vanishing monuments of Bromley-by-Bow (1900) and two early monographs (see below); awareness of later threats drew its team to record *Spitalfields* (1958) and *Poplar* (two volumes, 1994). The Survey's volume on Spitalfields has been supplemented by new archaeological information: C. Thomas, B. Sloane and C. Phillpotts, *Excavations at the Priory Hospital of St Mary Spital*

London (1997), and more briefly, C. Thomas, *Life and Death in London's East End. 2000 years at Spitalfields* (2004). Discoveries at Christ Church are examined in M. Cox, *Life and Death in Spitalfields 1700–1850* (1996). On the medieval foundation of St Katharine see K. Jamieson, *The History of the Royal Hospital of St Katharine by the Tower of London* (1952), J.B. Nichols, *Some Account of the Royal Hospital and Collegiate Church of St Katharine* (1824); C. Tracy, *English Gothic Choir Stalls 1200–1400* (1987).

Churches: Gordon Barnes, *Stepney Churches, an historical account* (1967) is a small but excellent history. On the 1711 churches: M.H. Port, The commissions for building fifty new churches in London, *London Record Society* (1986). Hawksmoor's churches have their own literature, principally: K. Downes' two books, both entitled *Hawksmoor* (1959 and 1970); P. du Prey, *Hawksmoor's London churches, architecture and theology* (2000), V. Hart, *Nicholas Hawksmoor, rebuilding ancient wonders* (2002). Anglican churches in the whole of Tower Hamlets are included in B.F.L. Clarke, *Parish Churches of London* (1966, 1987). English Heritage carried out a comprehensive survey of places of worship in Tower Hamlets in 2003–4. A detailed account of one of them is P. Guillery, *St George's German Lutheran church*, Historic Chapels Trust (2004).

C19 developments: Jean M. Imray, The Mercers' estate in East London, *East London Papers* 9.1 (1966); Mona Paton, Corporate East End landlords, the example of the London hospital and the Mercers' Company, *Lon. Journal* 18.2 (1993). *The Jewish East End 1840–1939* (Proceedings of a Conference, Jewish Historical Society of England, 1981). I. Watson, 'Rebuilding London', Abraham Davis and his brothers 1881–1924, *Lon. Journal* 29.1 (2004). J. White, *Rothschild Buildings, life in an East End Tenement Block* (1980), J.E. Connor and B.J. Critchley, *Palaces for the Poor* and *The Red Cliffs of Stepney* (both 1984); A. Briggs, *Toynbee Hall* (1984). P. Henri, *John Wilton's Music Hall*. C. Poulsen, *Victoria Park* (1976). R. Taylor, *Every Stone tells a Story* (1996) describes Tower Hamlets Cemetery. H. Walker, *East London: Sketches of Christian Work and Workers*, 1896 describes the mission work of the late C19. C20: D.L. Munby, *Industry and Planning in Stepney* (1951) is an invaluable mid-C20 survey. On Lansbury, J. Westergaerd and R. Glass in *London Aspects of Change* (see above), and E. Harwood in *Twentieth Century Architecture* vol. 5 (2001). D. Farson, *Limehouse Days* (1991) is a lively account covering aspects of the C19 and C20.

Boundary Estate is covered in detail in S. Beattie (see above) and R.V. Steffel, The Boundary Street Estate: An Example of Urban Redevelopment by the LCC, 1889–1914, *Town Planning Review*, vol. 47 (1976).

Docklands: *The Buildings of England: London Docklands, an architectural guide*, by Elizabeth Williamson and Nikolaus Pevsner (1998) is an account of the whole LDDC area. Further detail is in *Poplar, Blackwall and the Isle of Dogs: the Parish of All Saints*, Survey of London vols. XLIII, XLIV (1994).

John Pudney, *London's Docks* (1975) and R. Douglas Brown,

The Port of London (1978) are useful general histories. On dock structures: E. Sargent, the Planning and Early Buildings of the West India Docks, *The Mariner's Mirror*, 77 ii (1991); A.W. Skempton, Engineering in the Port of London, 1789–1808 and 1808–1833, *Trans. Newcomen Soc.*, 50 (1979) and 53 (1982); I Greeves, *London Docks 1800–1980, a civil engineering history* (1980); T. Smith, Hydraulic Power in the Port of London, *Industrial Archaeology Review* XIV, 1, (1991). *The Thames Gateway: recording Historic Buildings and landscapes on the Thames estuary*, RCHME, (1995), includes E. Sargent on the development of the Royal Docks; *Dockland: an illustrated history of life and work in East London*, ed. S.K. Al Naib and R.J.M. Carr (1986), includes essays by M. Tucker on warehouses, by P. Calvocoressi on lost buildings, and by I. Greeves on the work of the dock engineer. On more recent history *see* S. Brownill, *Developing London's Docklands: another great planning disaster?* (1990), and the special issue of the *London Journal* on Docklands, vol. 17, 2 (1992) which includes M. Hebbert, One 'planning disaster after another, London Docklands 1970–1992'.

The Essex Boroughs

Much less has been written on the boroughs which were formerly part of Essex. The relevant volumes of the VCH are the best starting point. On post-war Essex schools there is *Essex Education* (Essex County Council), published regularly 1945–65, also *Architectural Design* vol. 20 (May 1950).

BARKING: *VCH Essex* vol. V (1966). On Barking Abbey, A.W. Clapham, *Essex Archaeol. Trans*, xii (1913); London Survey Monograph 11, *Eastbury Manor House, Barking*, 1917; J. Howson, *A brief history of Barking and Dagenham* (6th ed., 1990); T. Clifford, *Barking and Dagenham Buildings Past and Present* (1992); R. Home, *'A Township complete in itself': A Planning History of the Becontree/Dagenham Estate* (1997); the post-war issues of the *Barking Record* and *Dagenham Digest* are a useful source of information on the developments of the 1950s and 1960s.

HAVERING: *VCH Essex* vol. VII (1978). J. Drury, *Treasures of Havering*, (1998), C.T. Perfect, *Ye Olde Village of Hornchurch* (1917), T. Benton, *The changing face of Hornchurch*, (1999), *The Book of the Exhibition of Houses and Cottages, Romford Garden Suburb*, Gidea Park (1911). H. Smith, *History of the Parish of Havering-atte-Bower* (1925).

NEWHAM: VCH *Essex* vol. VI (1973) includes West Ham and East Ham. A. Stokes, *East Ham, from village to County Borough* (1933); S. Pewsey, *East Ham* (1996); London Borough of Newham, *West Ham 1886–1986*; J. Marriot, West Ham London's Industrial Centre, *Lon. Journal*, 13.2 (1987–8), 14.2 (1989). *Focus on Newham* (statistics) (2002).

REDBRIDGE: VCH *Essex* vol.VI (1973) covers Wanstead and Woodford. Both these areas have active historical societies with their own publications. G. Dixon and P. Wilkinson, *The Parish of Wanstead* (1990), K. Myers, ed., *The Gardens of Wanstead, Proceedings of a Study Day held at the Temple, Wanstead Park, 25 September 1999*, London Parks and Gardens Trust (2003). W. Addison, *Wanstead Park*. K. Morrison and A. Robey, *One Hundred Years of Suburbia* (RCHME), 1999 (on Aldersbrook). VCH *Essex* vol. V(1966) covers Ilford. G. Tasker, *Ilford Past and Present* (1901); N. Gunby, *A Potted History of Ilford* (1997).

WALTHAM FOREST: Chingford is covered in VCH Essex vol. v, Leyton and Walthamstow in vol. VI. J. Kennedy, *History of the Parish of Leyton* (1894) remains useful. Publications of Walthamstow Antiquarian Society include M. Batsford, *Timber-framed buildings in Waltham Forest*. C18 houses are discussed in *Some Old Walthamstow Houses* (Walthamstow Historical Society, 1998). The Leyton Society has published *A look at Leyton and Leytonstone*.

Other sources: an increasing amount of material of architectural interest is now available online. The following are relevant to East London:

Survey of the Jewish Built Heritage *(www.jewish-heritage-uk.org)* is a comprehensive survey of Jewish monuments and sites in Britain.

Public Monuments and Sculpture Association *(www.pmsa.org)*: provides access to the database of the East London recording project.

Looking at Buildings *(www.lookingatbuildings.org)* from the Pevsner Architectural Guides has further information on East London's buildings, an architectural glossary and database of architects.

Church Plans Online (*www.churchplansonline.org*) is a database of the Incorporated Church Building Society's records, including plans.

GLOSSARY

Numbers and letters refer to the illustrations (by John Sambrook) on pp. 784–91.

ABACUS: flat slab forming the top of a capital (3a).

ACANTHUS: classical formalized leaf ornament (4b).

ACCUMULATOR TOWER: *see* Hydraulic power.

ACHIEVEMENT: a complete display of armorial bearings.

ACROTERION: plinth for a statue or ornament on the apex or ends of a pediment; more usually, both the plinth and what stands on it (4a).

AEDICULE (*lit.* little building): architectural surround, consisting usually of two columns or pilasters supporting a pediment.

AGGREGATE: *see* Concrete.

AISLE: subsidiary space alongside the body of a building, separated from it by columns, piers, or posts.

ALMONRY: a building from which alms are dispensed to the poor.

AMBULATORY (*lit.* walkway): aisle around the sanctuary (q.v.).

ANGLE ROLL: roll moulding in the angle between two planes (1a).

ANSE DE PANIER: *see* Arch.

ANTAE: simplified pilasters (4a), usually applied to the ends of the enclosing walls of a portico *in antis* (q.v.).

ANTEFIXAE: ornaments projecting at regular intervals above a Greek cornice, originally to conceal the ends of roof tiles (4a).

ANTHEMION: classical ornament like a honeysuckle flower (4b).

APRON: raised panel below a window or wall monument or tablet.

APSE: semicircular or polygonal end of an apartment, especially of a chancel or chapel. In classical architecture sometimes called an *exedra*.

ARABESQUE: non-figurative surface decoration consisting of flowing lines, foliage scrolls etc., based on geometrical patterns. Cf. Grotesque.

ARCADE: series of arches supported by piers or columns. *Blind arcade* or *arcading*: the same applied to the wall surface. *Wall arcade*: in medieval churches, a blind arcade forming a dado below windows. Also a covered shopping street.

ARCH: Shapes *see* 5c. *Basket arch* or *anse de panier* (basket handle): three-centred and depressed, or with a flat centre. *Nodding*: ogee arch curving forward from the wall face. *Parabolic*: shaped like a chain suspended from two level points, but inverted. Special purposes. *Chancel*: dividing chancel from nave or crossing. *Crossing*: spanning piers at a crossing (q.v.). *Relieving or discharging*: incorporated in a wall to relieve superimposed weight (5c). *Skew*: spanning responds not diametrically opposed. *Strainer*: inserted in an opening to resist inward pressure. *Transverse*: spanning a main axis (e.g. of a vaulted space). *See also* Jack arch, Triumphal arch.

ARCHITRAVE: formalized lintel, the lowest member of the classical entablature (3a). Also the moulded frame of a door or window (often borrowing the profile of a classical architrave). For *lugged* and *shouldered* architraves *see* 4b.

ARCUATED: dependent structurally on the arch principle. Cf. Trabeated.

ARK: chest or cupboard housing the

tables of Jewish law in a synagogue.

ARRIS: sharp edge where two surfaces meet at an angle (3a).

ASHLAR: masonry of large blocks wrought to even faces and square edges (6d).

ASTRAGAL: classical moulding of semicircular section (3f).

ASTYLAR: with no columns or similar vertical features.

ATLANTES: *see* Caryatids.

ATRIUM (plural: atria): inner court of a Roman or C20 house; in a multi-storey building, a top lit covered court rising through all storeys. Also an open court in front of a church.

ATTACHED COLUMN: *see* Engaged column.

ATTIC: small top storey within a roof. Also the storey above the main entablature of a classical façade.

AUMBRY: recess or cupboard to hold sacred vessels for the Mass.

BALANCE BEAM: *see* Canals.

BALDACCHINO: free-standing canopy, originally fabric, over an altar. Cf. Ciborium.

BALLFLOWER: globular flower of three petals enclosing a ball (1a). Typical of the Decorated style.

BALUSTER: pillar or pedestal of bellied form. *Balusters*: vertical supports of this or any other form, for a handrail or coping, the whole being called a *balustrade* (6c). *Blind balustrade*: the same applied to the wall surface.

BARGEBOARDS (corruption of 'vergeboards'): boards, often carved or fretted, fixed beneath the eaves of a gable to cover and protect the rafters.

BAROQUE: style originating in Rome *c.*1600 and current in England *c.*1680–1720, characterized by dramatic massing and silhouette and the use of the giant order.

BARROW: burial mound.

BARTIZAN: corbelled turret, square or round, frequently at an angle.

BASCULE: hinged part of a lifting (or bascule) bridge.

BASE: moulded foot of a column or pilaster. For *Attic* base *see* 3b.

BASEMENT: lowest, subordinate storey; hence the lowest part of a classical elevation, below the *piano nobile* (q.v.).

BASILICA: a Roman public hall; hence an aisled building with a clerestory.

BASTION: one of a series of defensive semicircular or polygonal projections from the main wall of a fortress or city.

BATTER: intentional inward inclination of a wall face.

BATTLEMENT: defensive parapet, composed of *merlons* (solid) and *crenels* (embrasures) through which archers could shoot; sometimes called *crenellation*. Also used decoratively.

BAY: division of an elevation or interior space as defined by regular vertical features such as arches, columns, windows etc.

BAY LEAF: classical ornament of overlapping bay leaves (3f).

BAY WINDOW: window of one or more storeys projecting from the face of a building. *Canted*: with a straight front and angled sides. *Bow window*: curved. *Oriel*: rests on corbels or brackets and starts above ground level; also the bay window at the dais end of a medieval great hall.

BEAD-AND-REEL: *see* Enrichments.

BEAKHEAD: Norman ornament with a row of beaked bird or beast heads usually biting into a roll moulding (1a).

BELFAST TRUSS: a lightweight, segmental form of girder (q.v.) made from timber components with a lattice framework.

BELFRY: chamber or stage in a tower where bells are hung.

BELLCOTE: small gabled or roofed housing for the bell(s).

BILLET: Norman ornament of small half-cylindrical or rectangular blocks (1a).

BIMAH: platform in a synagogue, traditionally centrally placed, for the reading of the Torah.

BLIND: *see* Arcade, Baluster, Portico.

BLOCK CAPITAL: *see* 1a.

BLOCKED: columns, etc. interrupted

by regular projecting blocks (*blocking*), as on a Gibbs surround (4b).

BLOCKING COURSE: course of stones, or equivalent, on top of a cornice and crowning the wall.

BOLECTION MOULDING: covering the joint between two different planes (6b).

BOND: the pattern of long sides (*stretchers*) and short ends (*headers*) produced on the face of a wall by laying bricks in a particular way (6e).

BOSS: knob or projection, e.g. at the intersection of ribs in a vault (2c).

BOWTELL: a term in use by the C15 for a form of roll moulding, usually three-quarters of a circle in section (also called *edge roll*).

BOW WINDOW: *see* Bay window.

BOX FRAME: timber-framed construction in which vertical and horizontal wall members support the roof (7). Also concrete construction where the loads are taken on cross walls; also called *cross-wall construction*.

BRACE: subsidiary member of a structural frame, curved or straight. *Bracing* is often arranged decoratively e.g. quatrefoil, herringbone (7). *See also* Roofs.

BRATTISHING: ornamental crest, usually formed of leaves, Tudor flowers or miniature battlements.

BRESSUMER (*lit.* breast-beam): big horizontal beam supporting the wall above, especially in a jettied building (7).

BRICK: *see* Bond, Cogging, Engineering, Gauged, Tumbling.

BRIDGE: *Bowstring*: with arches rising above the roadway which is suspended from them. *Clapper*: one long stone forms the roadway. *Roving*: *see* Canal. *Suspension*: roadway suspended from cables or chains slung between towers or pylons. *Stay-suspension* or *stay-cantilever*: supported by diagonal stays from towers or pylons. *See also* Bascule.

BRISES-SOLEIL: projecting fins or canopies which deflect direct sunlight from windows.

BROACH: *see* Spire and 1c.

BUCRANIUM: ox skull used decoratively in classical friezes.

BULL-NOSED SILL: sill displaying a pronounced convex upper moulding.

BULLSEYE WINDOW: small oval window, set horizontally (cf. Oculus). Also called *œil de bœuf*.

BUTTRESS: vertical member projecting from a wall to stabilize it or to resist the lateral thrust of an arch, roof, or vault (1c, 2c). A *flying buttress* transmits the thrust to a heavy abutment by means of an arch or half-arch (1c).

CABLE OR ROPE MOULDING: originally Norman, like twisted strands of a rope.

CAMPANILE: free-standing bell-tower.

CANALS: *Flash lock*: removable weir or similar device through which boats pass on a flush of water. Predecessor of the *pound lock*: chamber with gates at each end allowing boats to float from one level to another. *Tidal gates*: single pair of lock gates allowing vessels to pass when the tide makes a level. *Balance beam*: beam projecting horizontally for opening and closing lock gates. *Roving bridge*: carrying a towing path from one bank to the other.

CANTILEVER: horizontal projection (e.g. step, canopy) supported by a downward force behind the fulcrum.

CAPITAL: head or crowning feature of a column or pilaster; for classical types *see* 3; for medieval types *see* 1b.

CARTOUCHE: classical tablet with ornate frame (4b).

CARYATIDS: female figures supporting an entablature; their male counterparts are *Atlantes* (*lit.* Atlas figures).

CASEMATE: vaulted chamber, with embrasures for defence, within a castle wall or projecting from it.

CASEMENT: side-hinged window.

CASTELLATED: with battlements (q.v.).

CAST IRON: hard and brittle, cast in a mould to the required shape. *Wrought iron* is ductile, strong in tension, forged into decorative patterns or forged and rolled into e.g. bars, joists, boiler plates; *mild steel* is its modern equivalent, similar but stronger.

CATSLIDE: *See* 8a.

CAVETTO: concave classical moulding of quarter-round section (3f).

CELURE OR CEILURE: enriched area of roof above rood or altar.

CEMENT: *see* Concrete.

CENOTAPH (*lit.* empty tomb): funerary monument which is not a burying place.

CENTRING: wooden support for the building of an arch or vault, removed after completion.

CHAMFER (*lit.* corner-break): surface formed by cutting off a square edge or corner. For types of chamfers and *chamfer stops see* 6a. *See also* Double chamfer.

CHANCEL: part of the E end of a church set apart for the use of the officiating clergy.

CHANTRY CHAPEL: often attached to or within a church, endowed for the celebration of Masses principally for the soul of the founder.

CHEVET (*lit.* head): French term for chancel with ambulatory and radiating chapels.

CHEVRON: V-shape used in series or double series (later) on a Norman moulding (1a). Also (especially when on a single plane) called *zigzag*.

CHOIR: the part of a cathedral, monastic or collegiate church where services are sung.

CIBORIUM: a fixed canopy over an altar, usually vaulted and supported on four columns; cf. Baldacchino. Also a canopied shrine for the reserved sacrament.

CINQUEFOIL: *see* Foil.

CIST: stone-lined or slab-built grave.

CLADDING: external covering or skin applied to a structure, especially a framed one.

CLERESTORY: uppermost storey of the nave of a church, pierced by windows. Also high-level windows in secular buildings.

CLOSER: a brick cut to complete a bond (6e).

CLUSTER BLOCK: *see* Multi-storey.

COADE STONE: ceramic artificial stone made in Lambeth 1769–*c.*1840 by Eleanor Coade (†1821) and her associates.

COB: walling material of clay mixed with straw. Also called *pisé*.

COFFERING: arrangement of sunken panels (coffers), square or polygonal, decorating a ceiling, vault, or arch.

COGGING: a decorative course of bricks laid diagonally (6e). Cf. Dentilation.

COLLAR: *see* Roofs and 7.

COLLEGIATE CHURCH: endowed for the support of a college of priests.

COLONNADE: range of columns supporting an entablature. Cf. Arcade.

COLONNETTE: small medieval column or shaft.

COLOSSAL ORDER: *see* Giant order.

COLUMBARIUM: shelved, niched structure to house multiple burials.

COLUMN: a classical, upright structural member of round section with a shaft, a capital, and usually a base (3a, 4a).

COLUMN FIGURE: carved figure attached to a medieval column or shaft, usually flanking a doorway.

COMMUNION TABLE: unconsecrated table used in Protestant churches for the celebration of Holy Communion.

COMPOSITE: *see* Orders.

COMPOUND PIER: grouped shafts (q.v.), or a solid core surrounded by shafts.

CONCRETE: composition of *cement* (calcined lime and clay), *aggregate* (small stones or rock chippings), sand and water. It can be poured into *formwork* or *shuttering* (temporary frame of timber or metal) on site (*in-situ* concrete), or *pre-cast* as components before construction. *Reinforced*: incorporating steel rods to take the tensile force. *Pre-stressed*: with tensioned steel rods. Finishes include the impression of boards left by formwork (*board-marked* or *shuttered*), and texturing with steel brushes (*brushed*) or hammers (*hammer-dressed*). *See also* Shell.

CONSOLE: bracket of curved outline (4b).

COPING: protective course of masonry or brickwork capping a wall (6d).

CORBEL: projecting block supporting something above. *Corbel course*: continuous course of projecting stones or bricks fulfilling the same function. *Corbel table*: series of corbels to carry a parapet or a wall-plate or wall-post (7). *Corbelling*: brick or masonry courses built out beyond one another to support a chimney-stack, window, etc.

CORINTHIAN: *see* Orders and 3d.

CORNICE: flat-topped ledge with moulded underside, projecting along the top of a building or feature, especially as the highest member of the classical entablature (3a). Also the decorative moulding in the angle between wall and ceiling.

COTTAGE ORNÉ: an artfully rustic small house associated with the Picturesque movement.

COUNTERCHANGING: of joists on a ceiling divided by beams into compartments, when placed in opposite directions in alternate squares.

COURSE: continuous layer of stones, etc. in a wall (6e).

COVE: a broad concave moulding, e.g. to mask the eaves of a roof. *Coved ceiling*: with a pronounced cove joining the walls to a flat central panel smaller than the whole area of the ceiling.

CRADLE ROOF: *see* Wagon roof.

CREDENCE: a shelf within or beside a piscina (q.v.), or a table for the sacramental elements and vessels.

CRENELLATION: parapet with crenels (*see* Battlement).

CRINKLE-CRANKLE WALL: garden wall undulating in a series of serpentine curves.

CROCKETS: leafy hooks. *Crocketing* decorates the edges of Gothic features, such as pinnacles, canopies, etc. *Crocket capital*: *see* 1b.

CROSSING: central space at the junction of the nave, chancel, and transepts. *Crossing tower*: above a crossing.

CROSS-WINDOW: with one mullion and one transom (qq.v.).

CROWN-POST: *see* Roofs and 7.

CROWSTEPS: squared stones set like steps, e.g. on a gable (8a).

CRUCKS (*lit.* crooked): pairs of inclined timbers (*blades*), usually curved, set at bay-lengths; they support the roof timbers and, in timber buildings, also support the walls (8b). *Base*: blades rise from ground level to a tie- or collar-beam which supports the roof timbers. *Full*: blades rise from ground level to the apex of the roof, serving as the main members of a roof truss. *Jointed*: blades formed from more than one timber; the lower member may act as a wall-post; it is usually elbowed at wall-plate level and jointed just above. *Middle*: blades rise from half way up the walls to a tie- or collar-beam. *Raised*: blades rise from half way up the walls to the apex. *Upper*: blades supported on a tie-beam and rising to the apex.

CRYPT: underground or half-underground area, usually below the E end of a church. *Ring crypt*: corridor crypt surrounding the apse of an early medieval church, often associated with chambers for relics. Cf. Undercroft.

CUPOLA (*lit.* dome): especially a small dome on a circular or polygonal base crowning a larger dome, roof, or turret.

CURTAIN WALL: a connecting wall between the towers of a castle. Also a non-load-bearing external wall applied to a C20 framed structure.

CUSP: *see* Tracery and 2b.

CYCLOPEAN MASONRY: large irregular polygonal stones, smooth and finely jointed.

CYMA RECTA and CYMA REVERSA: classical mouldings with double curves (3f). Cf. Ogee.

DADO: the finishing (often with panelling) of the lower part of a wall in a classical interior; in origin a formalized continuous pedestal. *Dado rail*: the moulding along the top of the dado.

DAGGER: *see* Tracery and 2b.

DALLE-DE-VERRE (*lit.* glass-slab): a

late C20 stained-glass technique, setting large, thick pieces of cast glass into a frame of reinforced concrete or epoxy resin.

DEC (DECORATED): English Gothic architecture *c.* 1290 to *c.* 1350. The name is derived from the type of window tracery (q.v.) used during the period.

DEMI- OR HALF-COLUMNS: engaged columns (q.v.) half of whose circumference projects from the wall.

DENTIL: small square block used in series in classical cornices (3c). *Dentilation* is produced by the projection of alternating headers along cornices or stringcourses.

DIAPER: repetitive surface decoration of lozenges or squares flat or in relief. Achieved in brickwork with bricks of two colours.

DIOCLETIAN OR THERMAL WINDOW: semicircular with two mullions, as used in the Baths of Diocletian, Rome (4b).

DISTYLE: having two columns (4a).

DOGTOOTH: E.E. ornament, consisting of a series of small pyramids formed by four stylized canine teeth meeting at a point (1a).

DORIC: *see* Orders and 3a, 3b.

DORMER: window projecting from the slope of a roof (8a).

DOUBLE CHAMFER: a chamfer applied to each of two recessed arches (1a).

DOUBLE PILE: *see* Pile.

DRAGON BEAM: *see* Jetty.

DRAWDOCK: a sloping ramp where boats can unload cargo or be drawn up above high water.

DRESSINGS: the stone or brickwork worked to a finished face about an angle, opening, or other feature.

DRIPSTONE: moulded stone projecting from a wall to protect the lower parts from water. Cf. Hoodmould, Weathering.

DRUM: circular or polygonal stage supporting a dome or cupola. Also one of the stones forming the shaft of a column (3a).

DRY DOCK: a dock so designed that the water can be let out for the repair and maintenance of ships.

DUTCH OR FLEMISH GABLE: *see* 8a.

EASTER SEPULCHRE: tomb-chest used for Easter ceremonial, within or against the N wall of a chancel.

EAVES: overhanging edge of a roof; hence *eaves cornice* in this position.

ECHINUS: ovolo moulding (q.v.) below the abacus of a Greek Doric capital (3a).

EDGE RAIL: *see* Railways.

E.E. (EARLY ENGLISH): English Gothic architecture *c.* 1190–1250.

EGG-AND-DART: *see* Enrichments and 3f.

ELEVATION: any face of a building or side of a room. In a drawing, the same or any part of it, represented in two dimensions.

EMBATTLED: with battlements.

EMBRASURE: small splayed opening in a wall or battlement (q.v.).

ENCAUSTIC TILES: earthenware tiles fired with a pattern and glaze.

EN DELIT: stone cut against the bed.

ENFILADE: reception rooms in a formal series, usually with all doorways on axis.

ENGAGED OR ATTACHED COLUMN: one that partly merges into a wall or pier.

ENGINEERING BRICKS: dense bricks, originally used mostly for railway viaducts etc.

ENRICHMENTS: the carved decoration of certain classical mouldings, e.g. the ovolo (qq.v.) with *egg-and-dart*, the cyma reversa with *waterleaf*, the astragal with *bead-and-reel* (3f).

ENTABLATURE: in classical architecture, collective name for the three horizontal members (architrave, frieze, and cornice) carried by a wall or a column (3a).

ENTASIS: very slight convex deviation from a straight line, used to prevent an optical illusion of concavity.

EPITAPH: inscription on a tomb.

EXEDRA: *see* Apse.

EXTRADOS: outer curved face of an arch or vault.

EYECATCHER: decorative building terminating a vista.

FASCIA: plain horizontal band, e.g. in an architrave (3c, 3d) or on a shopfront.

FENESTRATION: the arrangement of windows in a façade.

FERETORY: site of the chief shrine of a church, behind the high altar.

FESTOON: ornamental garland, suspended from both ends. Cf. Swag.

FIBREGLASS, or glass-reinforced polyester (GRP): synthetic resin reinforced with glass fibre. GRC: glass-reinforced concrete.

FIELD: *see* Panelling and 6b.

FILLET: a narrow flat band running down a medieval shaft or along a roll moulding (1a). It separates larger curved mouldings in classical cornices, fluting or bases (3c).

FINGER JETTY: a narrow peninsula built out into a dock to increase length of quay (q.v.)

FLAMBOYANT: the latest phase of French Gothic architecture, with flowing tracery.

FLASH LOCK: *see* Canals.

FLÈCHE or SPIRELET (*lit.* arrow): slender spire on the centre of a roof.

FLEURON: medieval carved flower or leaf, often rectilinear (1a).

FLUSHWORK: knapped flint used with dressed stone to form patterns.

FLUTING: series of concave grooves (flutes), their common edges sharp (arris) or blunt (fillet) (3).

FOIL (*lit.* leaf): lobe formed by the cusping of a circular or other shape in tracery (2b). *Trefoil* (three), *quatrefoil* (four), *cinquefoil* (five), and *multifoil* express the number of lobes in a shape.

FOLIATE: decorated with leaves.

FORMWORK: *see* Concrete.

FRAMED BUILDING: where the structure is carried by a framework – e.g. of steel, reinforced concrete, timber – instead of by load-bearing walls.

FREESTONE: stone that is cut, or can be cut, in all directions.

FRESCO: *al fresco*: painting on wet plaster. *Fresco secco*: painting on dry plaster.

FRIEZE: the middle member of the classical entablature, sometimes ornamented (3a). *Pulvinated frieze* (*lit.* cushioned): of bold convex profile (3c). Also a horizontal band of ornament.

FRONTISPIECE: in C16 and C17 buildings the central feature of doorway and windows above linked in one composition.

GABLE: For types *see* 8a. *Gablet*: small gable. *Pedimental gable*: treated like a pediment.

GADROONING: classical ribbed ornament like inverted fluting that flows into a lobed edge.

GALILEE: chapel or vestibule usually at the W end of a church enclosing the main portal(s).

GALLERY: a long room or passage; an upper storey above the aisle of a church, looking through arches to the nave; a balcony or mezzanine overlooking the main interior space of a building; or an external walkway.

GALLETING: small stones set in a mortar course.

GAMBREL ROOF: *see* 8a.

GARDEROBE: medieval privy.

GARGOYLE: projecting water spout often carved into human or animal shape.

GAUGED or RUBBED BRICKWORK: soft brick sawn roughly, then rubbed to a precise (gauged) surface. Mostly used for door or window openings (5c).

GAZEBO (jocular Latin, 'I shall gaze'): ornamental lookout tower or raised summer house.

GEOMETRIC: English Gothic architecture *c.* 1250–1310. *See also* Tracery. For another meaning, *see* Stairs.

GIANT or COLOSSAL ORDER: classical order (q.v.) whose height is that of two or more storeys of the building to which it is applied.

GIBBS SURROUND: C18 treatment of an opening (4b), seen particularly in the work of James Gibbs (1682–1754).

GIRDER: a large beam. *Box*: of hollow-box section. *Bowed*: with its top rising in a curve. *Plate*: of I-section, made from iron or steel plates. *Lattice*: with braced framework.

GLAZING BARS: wooden or sometimes metal bars separating and supporting window panes.

GRAFFITI: *see* Sgraffito.

GRANGE: farm owned and run by a religious order.

GRAVING DOCK: a dry dock (q.v.); so called as ships' bottoms were scraped and covered originally with graves (the dregs of tallow) here.

GRC: *see* Fibreglass.

GRISAILLE: monochrome painting on walls or glass.

GROIN: sharp edge at the meeting of two cells of a cross-vault; *see* Vault and 2c.

GROTESQUE (*lit.* grotto-esque): wall decoration adopted from Roman examples in the Renaissance. Its foliage scrolls incorporate figurative elements. Cf. Arabesque.

GROTTO: artificial cavern.

GRP: *see* Fibreglass.

GUILLOCHE: classical ornament of interlaced bands (4b).

GUNLOOP: opening for a firearm.

GUTTAE: stylized drops (3b).

HALF-TIMBERING: archaic term for timber-framing (q.v.). Sometimes used for non-structural decorative timberwork.

HALL CHURCH: medieval church with nave and aisles of approximately equal height.

HAMMERBEAM: *see* Roofs and 7.

HAMPER: in C20 architecture, a visually distinct topmost storey or storeys.

HEADER: *see* Bond and 6e.

HEADSTOP: stop (q.v.) carved with a head (5b).

HELM ROOF: *see* 1C.

HENGE: ritual earthwork.

HERM (*lit.* the god Hermes): male head or bust on a pedestal.

HERRINGBONE WORK: *see* 7ii. Cf. Pitched masonry.

HEXASTYLE: *see* Portico.

HILL-FORT: Iron Age earthwork enclosed by a ditch and bank system.

HIPPED ROOF: *see* 8a.

HOODMOULD: projecting moulding above an arch or lintel to throw off water (2b, 5b). When horizontal often called a *label*. For label stop *see* Stop.

HUSK GARLAND: festoon of stylized nutshells (4b).

HYDRAULIC JIGGER: winch consisting of a hydraulic ram (q.v.) fitted with pulley sheaves, wound with chain or wire rope.

HYDRAULIC POWER: use of water under high pressure to work machinery. *Accumulator tower*: houses a hydraulic accumulator which accommodates fluctuations in the flow through hydraulic mains.

HYDRAULIC RAM: long piston moving in a cylinder under hydraulic pressure.

HYPOCAUST (*lit.* underburning): Roman underfloor heating system.

IMPOST: horizontal moulding at the springing of an arch (5c).

IMPOST BLOCK: block between abacus and capital (1b).

IN ANTIS: *see* Antae, Portico and 4a.

INDENT: shape chiselled out of a stone to receive a brass.

INDUSTRIALIZED OR SYSTEM BUILDING: system of manufactured units assembled on site.

INGLENOOK (*lit.* fire-corner): recess for a hearth with provision for seating.

INTERLACE: decoration in relief simulating woven or entwined stems or bands.

INTRADOS: *see* Soffit.

IONIC: *see* Orders and 3c.

JACK ARCH: shallow segmental vault springing from beams, used for fireproof floors, bridge decks, etc.

JAMB (*lit.* leg): one of the vertical sides of an opening.

JETTY: in a timber-framed building, the projection of an upper storey beyond the storey below, made by the beams and joists of the lower storey oversailing the wall; on their outer ends is placed the sill of the walling for the storey above (7). Buildings can be jettied on several sides, in which case a *dragon beam* is set diagonally at the corner to carry the joists to either side.

JOGGLE: the joining of two stones to prevent them slipping by a notch in one and a projection in the other.

KEEL MOULDING: moulding used from the late C12, in section like the keel of a ship (1a).

KEEP: principal tower of a castle.

KENTISH CUSP: *see* Tracery and 2b.

KEY PATTERN: *see* 4b.

KEYSTONE: central stone in an arch or vault (4b, 5c).

KINGPOST: *see* Roofs and 7.

KNEELER: horizontal projecting stone at the base of each side of a gable to support the inclined coping stones (8a).

LABEL: *see* Hoodmould and 5b.

LABEL STOP: *see* Stop and 5b.

LACED BRICKWORK: vertical strips of brickwork, often in a contrasting colour, linking openings on different floors.

LACING COURSE: horizontal reinforcement in timber or brick to walls of flint, cobble, etc.

LADY CHAPEL: dedicated to the Virgin Mary (Our Lady).

LANCET: slender single-light, pointed-arched window (2a).

LANTERN: circular or polygonal windowed turret crowning a roof or a dome. Also the windowed stage of a crossing tower lighting the church interior.

LANTERN CROSS: churchyard cross with lantern-shaped top.

LAVATORIUM: in a religious house, a washing place adjacent to the refectory.

LEAN-TO: *see* Roofs.

LESENE (*lit.* a mean thing): pilaster without base or capital. Also called *pilaster strip*.

LIERNE: *see* Vault and 2c.

LIGHT: compartment of a window defined by the mullions.

LINENFOLD: Tudor panelling carved with simulations of folded linen. *See also* Parchemin.

LINTEL: horizontal beam or stone bridging an opening.

LOCK: a device to hold back water while allowing a vessel to pass through by the opening and closing of sluices and lock gates (q.v.).

LOCK GATE *Flap gate*: hinged horizontally at the bottom of the lock and lifted by cables. *Mitre gate*: one which meets in a chevron shape. *Sector gates*: in the form of two segments of cylinders closing tangentially.

LOGGIA: gallery, usually arcaded or colonnaded; sometimes freestanding.

LONG-AND-SHORT WORK: quoins consisting of stones placed with the long side alternately upright and horizontal, especially in Saxon building.

LOUVRE: roof opening, often protected by a raised timber structure, to allow the smoke from a central hearth to escape.

LOWSIDE WINDOW: set lower than the others in a chancel side wall, usually towards its W end.

LUCAM: projecting housing for hoist pulley on upper storey of warehouses, mills, etc., for raising goods to loading doors.

LUGGED ARCHITRAVE: *see* 4b.

LUNETTE: semicircular window or blind panel.

LYCHGATE (*lit.* corpse-gate): roofed gateway entrance to a churchyard for the reception of a coffin.

MACHICOLATIONS (*lit.* mashing devices): series of openings between the corbels that support a projecting parapet through which missiles can be dropped. Used decoratively in post-medieval buildings.

MANOMETER OR STANDPIPE TOWER: containing a column of water to regulate pressure in water mains.

MANSARD: *see* 8a.

MATHEMATICAL TILES: facing tiles with the appearance of brick, most often applied to timber-framed walls.

MAUSOLEUM: monumental building or chamber usually intended for the burial of members of one family.

MERLON: *see* Battlement.

METOPES: spaces between the triglyphs in a Doric frieze (3b).

MEZZANINE: low storey between two higher ones.

MILD STEEL: *see* Cast iron.

MISERICORD (*lit.* mercy): shelf on a carved bracket placed on the underside of a hinged choir stall

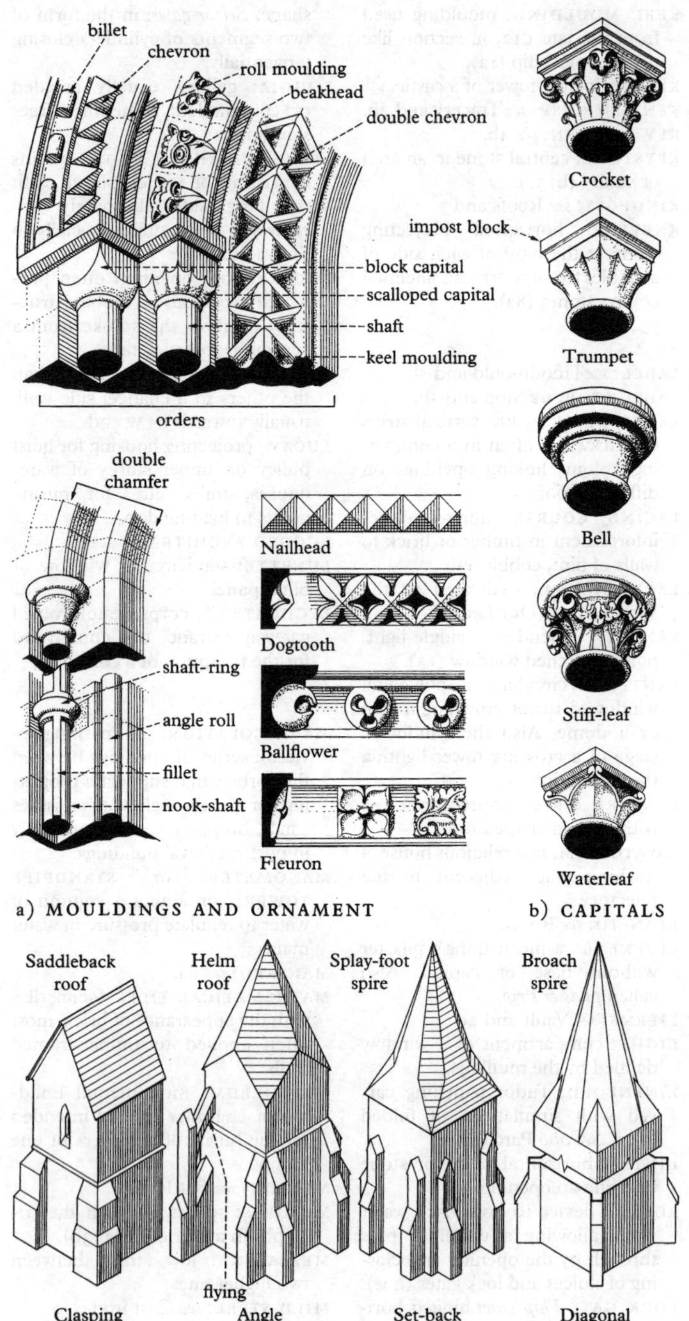

a) MOULDINGS AND ORNAMENT

b) CAPITALS

c) BUTTRESSES, ROOFS AND SPIRES

FIGURE 1: MEDIEVAL

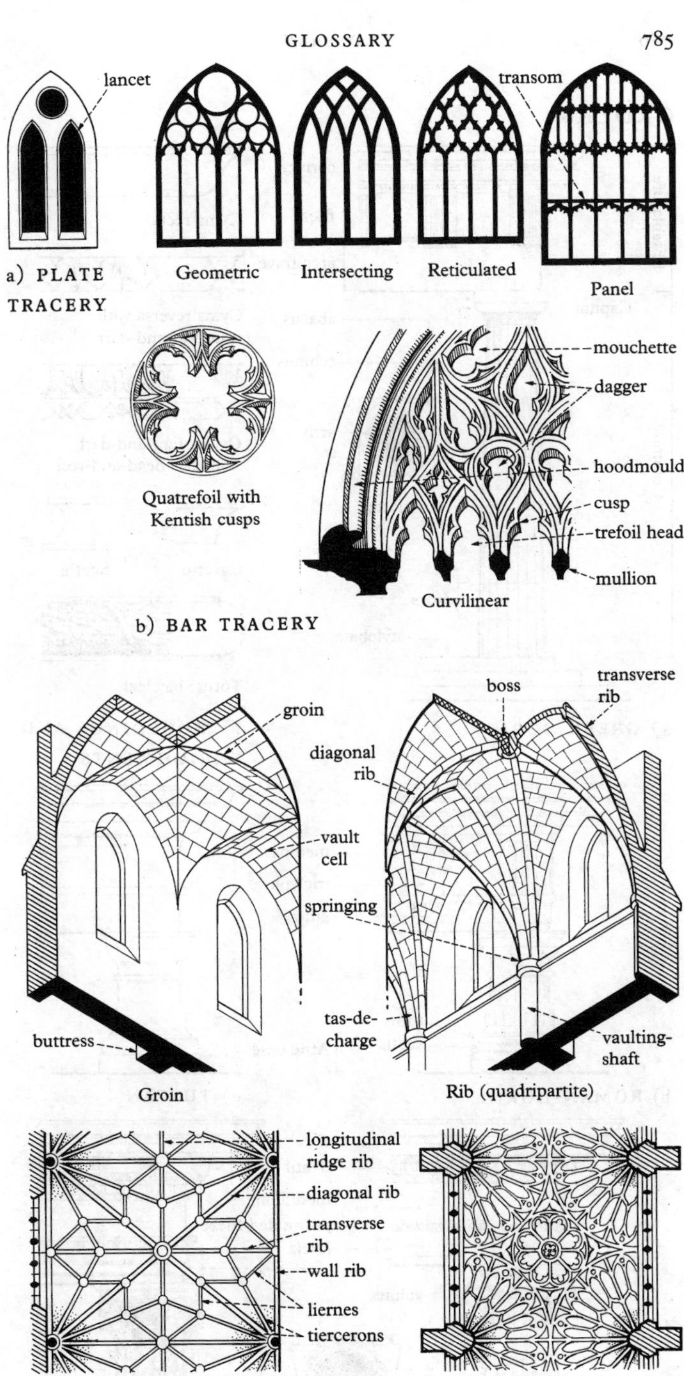
lancet
transom
a) PLATE TRACERY
Geometric
Intersecting
Reticulated
Panel
mouchette
dagger
hoodmould
cusp
trefoil head
mullion
Quatrefoil with Kentish cusps
Curvilinear
b) BAR TRACERY
groin
diagonal rib
vault cell
springing
tas-de-charge
buttress
Groin
boss
transverse rib
vaulting-shaft
Rib (quadripartite)
longitudinal ridge rib
diagonal rib
transverse rib
wall rib
liernes
tiercerons
Lierne
Fan
c) VAULTS

FIGURE 2: MEDIEVAL

ORDERS

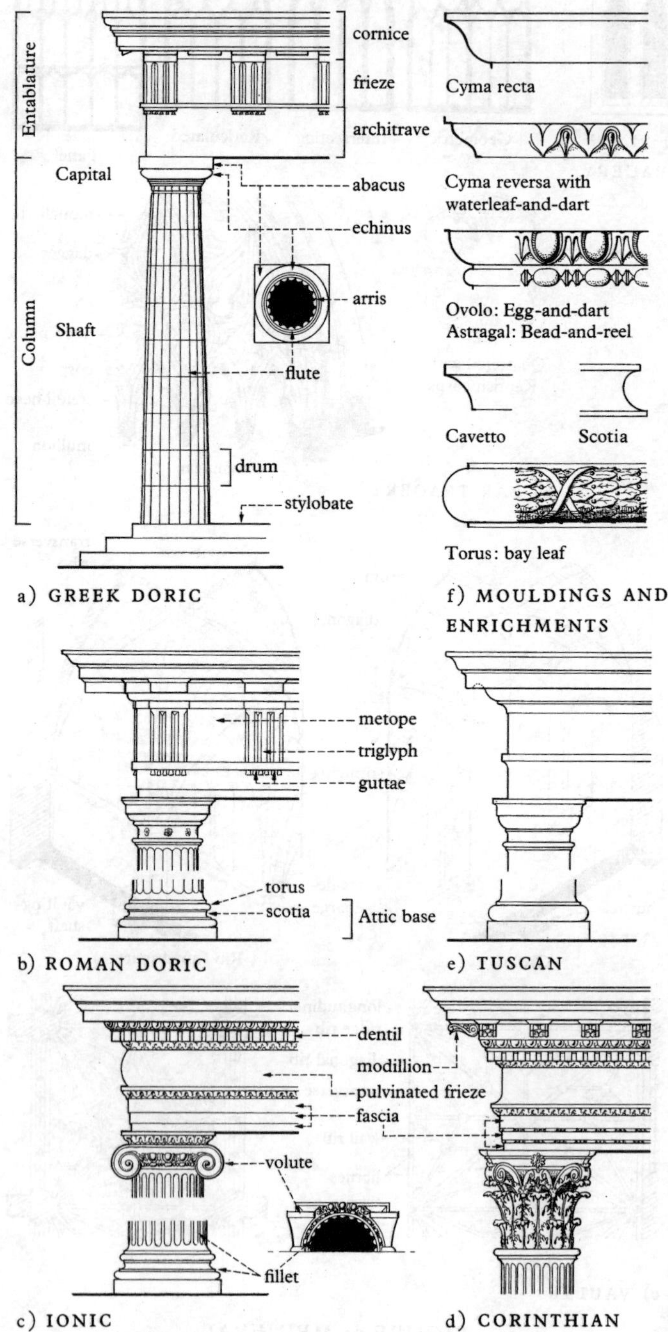
Entablature
cornice
frieze
architrave
Capital
abacus
echinus
arris
Column
Shaft
flute
drum
stylobate
a) GREEK DORIC
Cyma recta
Cyma reversa with waterleaf-and-dart
Ovolo: Egg-and-dart
Astragal: Bead-and-reel
Cavetto
Scotia
Torus: bay leaf
f) MOULDINGS AND ENRICHMENTS
metope
triglyph
guttae
torus
scotia
Attic base
b) ROMAN DORIC
e) TUSCAN
dentil
modillion
pulvinated frieze
fascia
volute
fillet
c) IONIC
d) CORINTHIAN

FIGURE 3: CLASSICAL

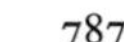

acroterion
tympanum
antefixa
column
anta
naos
naos
pronaos

a) PORTICO

Distyle in antis

Prostyle

Anthemion & Palmette

Guilloche

Key pattern

Rinceau

Husk garland

Vitruvian scroll

Console

Diocletian window

Acanthus

Broken pediment

Lugged architrave

Segmental pediment

Shouldered architrave

Venetian window

console
keystone
cartouche
blocking

Open pediment

Swan-neck pediment

Gibbs surround

b) ORNAMENTS AND FEATURES

FIGURE 4: CLASSICAL

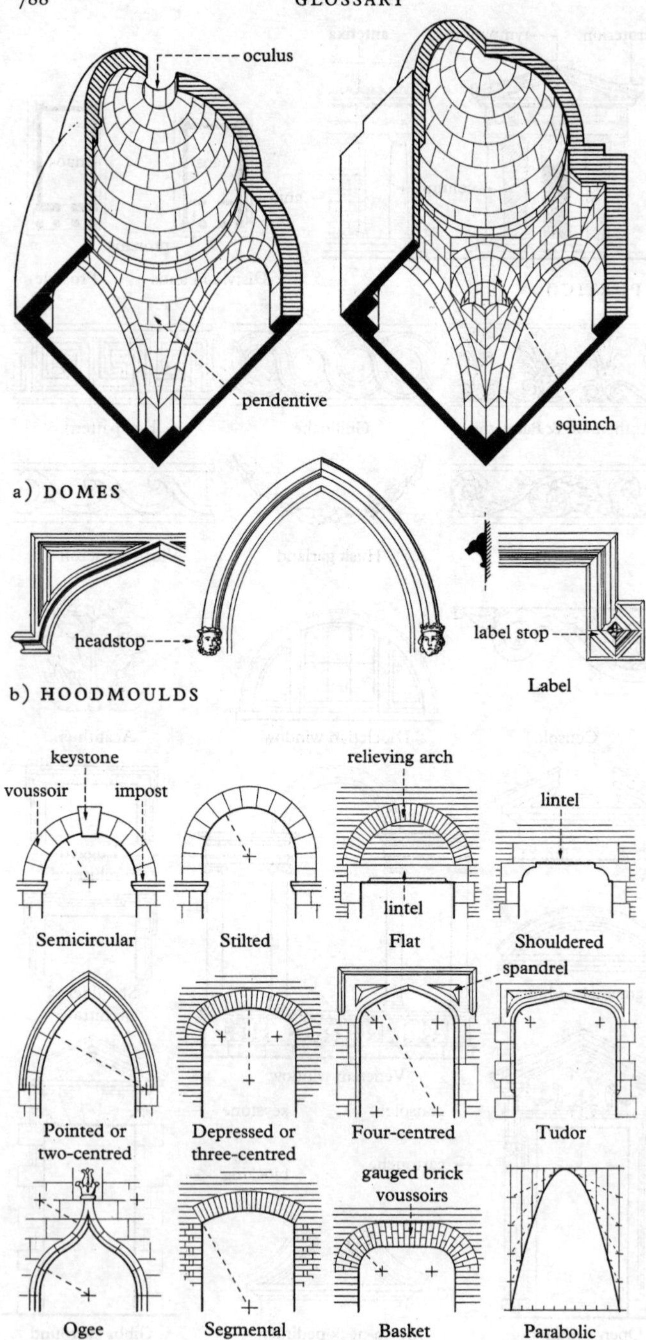

FIGURE 5: CONSTRUCTION

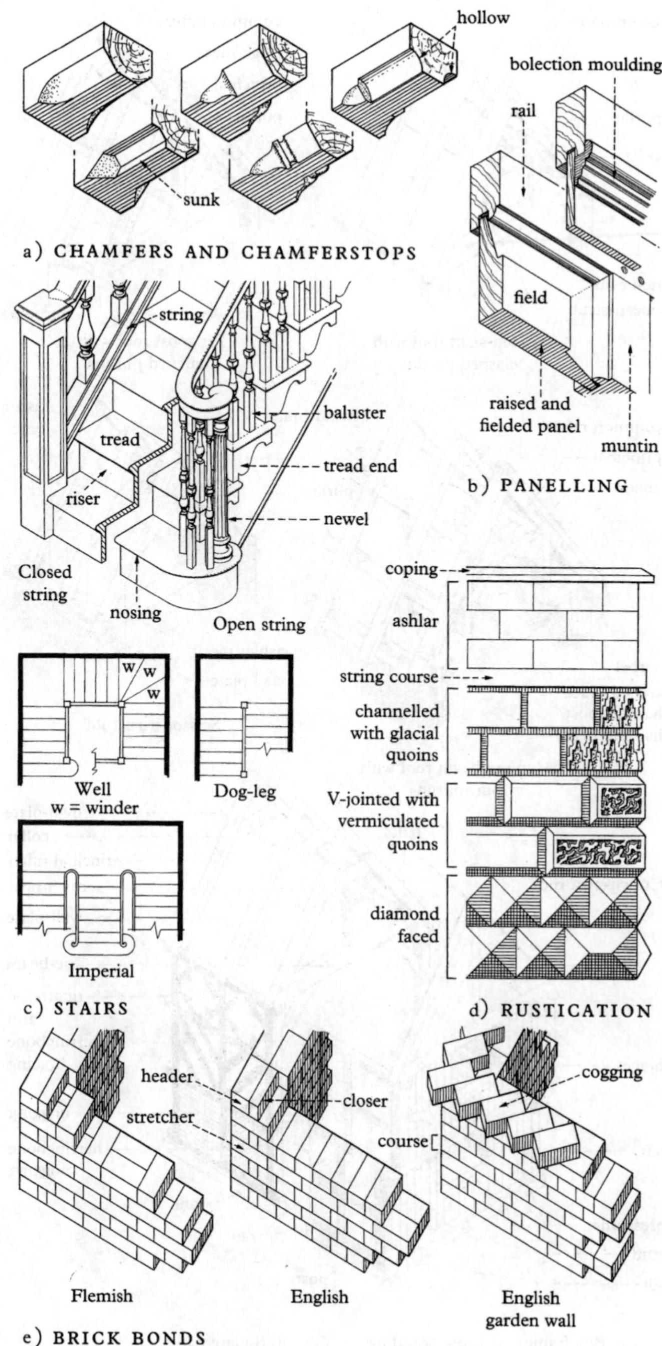

FIGURE 6: CONSTRUCTION

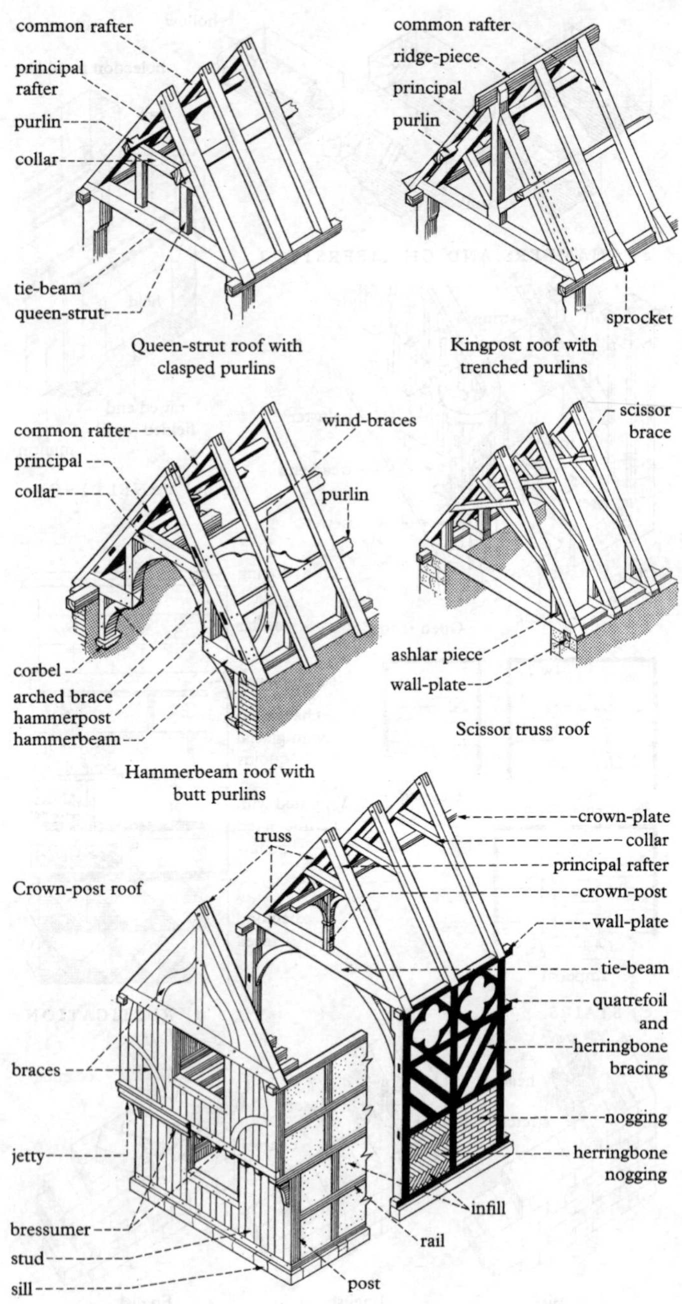

FIGURE 7: ROOFS AND TIMBER-FRAMING

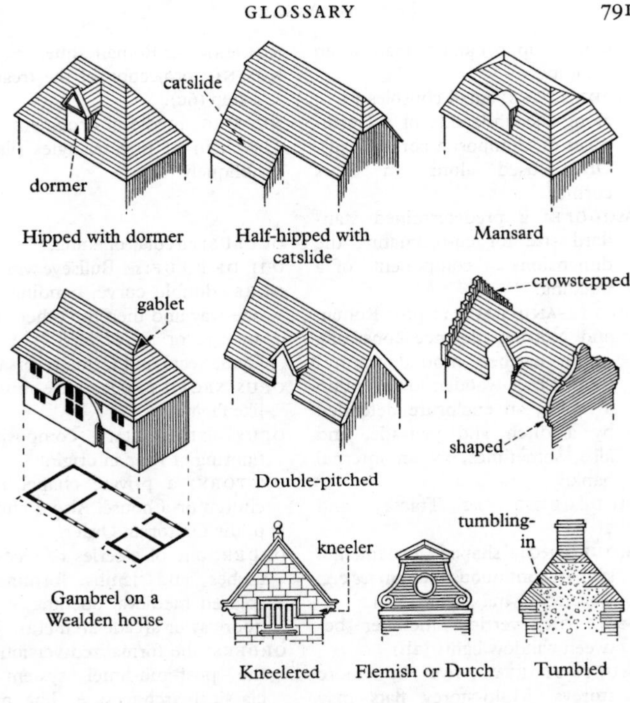

a) ROOF FORMS AND GABLES

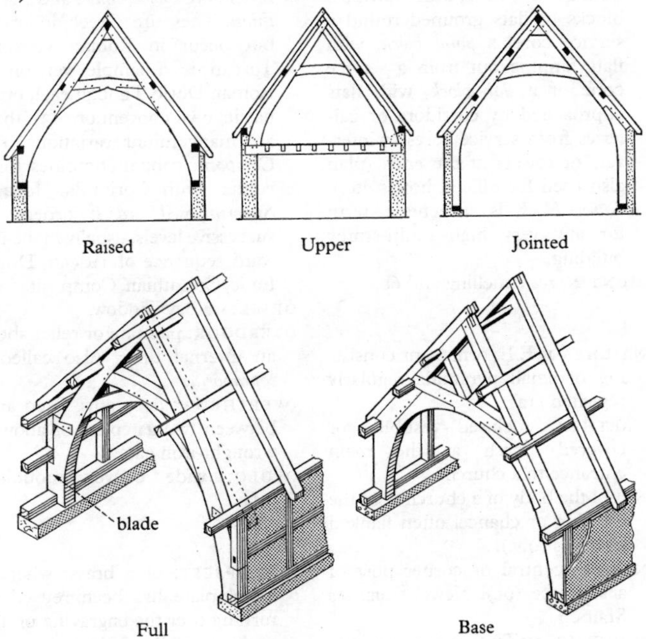

b) CRUCK FRAMES

FIGURE 8: ROOFS AND TIMBER-FRAMING

seat to support an occupant when standing.

MODILLIONS: small consoles (q.v.) along the underside of a Corinthian or Composite cornice (3d). Often used along an eaves cornice.

MODULE: a predetermined standard size for co-ordinating the dimensions of components of a building.

MOTTE-AND-BAILEY: post-Roman and Norman defence consisting of an earthen mound (motte) topped by a wooden tower within a bailey, an enclosure defended by a ditch and palisade, and also, sometimes, by an internal bank.

MOUCHETTE: *see* Tracery and 2b.

MOULDING: shaped ornamental strip of continuous section; *see* e.g. Cavetto, Cyma, Ovolo, Roll.

MULLION: vertical member between window lights (2b).

MULTI-STOREY: five or more storeys. Multi-storey flats may form a *cluster block*, with individual blocks of flats grouped round a service core; a *point block*, with flats fanning out from a service core; or a *slab block*, with flats approached by corridors or galleries from service cores at intervals or towers at the ends (plan also used for offices, hotels etc.). *Tower block* is a generic term for any very high multi-storey building.

MUNTIN: *see* Panelling and 6b.

NAILHEAD: E.E. ornament consisting of small pyramids regularly repeated (1a).

NARTHEX: enclosed vestibule or covered porch at the main entrance to a church.

NAVE: the body of a church W of the crossing or chancel often flanked by aisles (q.v.).

NEWEL: central or corner post of a staircase (6c). Newel stair: *see* Stairs.

NOGGING: *see* Timber-framing (7).

NOOK-SHAFT: shaft set in the angle of a wall or opening (1a).

NORMAN: *see* Romanesque.

NOSING: projection of the tread of a step (6c).

NUTMEG: medieval ornament with a chain of tiny triangles placed obliquely.

OCULUS: circular opening.

ŒIL DE BŒUF: *see* Bullseye window.

OGEE: double curve, bending first one way and then the other, as in an *ogee* or *ogival arch* (5c). Cf. Cyma recta and Cyma reversa.

OPUS SECTILE: decorative mosaic-like facing.

OPUS SIGNINUM: composition flooring of Roman origin.

ORATORY: a private chapel in a church or a house. Also a church of the Oratorian Order.

ORDER: one of a series of recessed arches and jambs forming a splayed medieval opening, e.g. a doorway or arcade arch (1a).

ORDERS: the formalized versions of the post-and-lintel system in classical architecture. The main orders are *Doric*, *Ionic*, and *Corinthian*. They are Greek in origin but occur in Roman versions. Tuscan is a simple version of Roman Doric. Though each order has its own conventions (3), there are many minor variations. The *Composite* capital combines Ionic volutes with Corinthian foliage. *Superimposed orders*: orders on successive levels, usually in the upward sequence of Tuscan, Doric, Ionic, Corinthian, Composite.

ORIEL: *see* Bay window.

OVERDOOR: painting or relief above an internal door. Also called a *sopraporta*.

OVERTHROW: decorative fixed arch between two gatepiers or above a wrought-iron gate.

OVOLO: wide convex moulding (3f).

PALIMPSEST: of a brass: where a metal plate has been reused by turning over the engraving on the back; of a wall painting: where one overlaps and partly obscures an earlier one.

PALLADIAN: following the examples and principles of Andrea Palladio (1508–80).

PALMETTE: classical ornament like a palm shoot (4b).

PANELLING: wooden lining to interior walls, made up of vertical members (*muntins*) and horizontals (*rails*) framing panels: also called *wainscot*. *Raised and fielded*: with the central area of the panel (*field*) raised up (6b).

PANTILE: roof tile of S section.

PARAPET: wall for protection at any sudden drop, e.g. at the wall-head of a castle where it protects the *parapet walk* or wall-walk. Also used to conceal a roof.

PARCLOSE: *see* Screen.

PARGETTING (*lit.* plastering): exterior plaster decoration, either in relief or incised.

PARLOUR: in a religious house, a room where the religious could talk to visitors; in a medieval house, the semi-private living room below the solar (q.v.).

PARTERRE: level space in a garden laid out with low, formal beds.

PATERA (*lit.* plate): round or oval ornament in shallow relief.

PAVILION: ornamental building for occasional use; or projecting subdivision of a larger building, often at an angle or terminating a wing.

PEBBLEDASHING: *see* Rendering.

PEDESTAL: a tall block carrying a classical order, statue, vase, etc.

PEDIMENT: a formalized gable derived from that of a classical temple; also used over doors, windows, etc. For variations *see* 4b.

PENDENTIVE: spandrel between adjacent arches, supporting a drum, dome or vault and consequently formed as part of a hemisphere (5a).

PENTHOUSE: subsidiary structure with a lean-to roof. Also a separately roofed structure on top of a C20–21 multi-storey block.

PERIPTERAL: *see* Peristyle.

PERISTYLE: a colonnade all round the exterior of a classical building, as in a temple which is then said to be *peripteral*.

PERP (PERPENDICULAR): English Gothic architecture *c.* 1335–50 to *c.* 1530. The name is derived from the upright tracery panels then used (*see* Tracery and 2a).

PERRON: external stair to a doorway, usually of double-curved plan.

PEW: loosely, seating for the laity outside the chancel; strictly, an enclosed seat. *Box pew*: with equal high sides and a door.

PIANO NOBILE: principal floor of a classical building above a ground floor or basement and with a lesser storey overhead.

PIAZZA: formal urban open space surrounded by buildings.

PIER: large masonry or brick support, often for an arch. *See also* Compound pier.

PILASTER: flat representation of a classical column in shallow relief. *Pilaster strip*: *see* Lesene.

PILE: row of rooms. *Double pile*: two rows thick.

PILLAR: free-standing upright member of any section, not conforming to one of the orders (q.v.).

PILLAR PISCINA: *see* Piscina.

PILOTIS: C20 French term for pillars or stilts that support a building above an open ground floor.

PISCINA: basin for washing Mass vessels, provided with a drain; set in or against the wall to the S of an altar or free-standing (*pillar piscina*).

PISÉ: *see* Cob.

PITCHED MASONRY: laid on the diagonal, often alternately with opposing courses (*pitched and counterpitched* or *herringbone*).

PLATBAND: flat horizontal moulding between storeys. Cf. stringcourse.

PLATE RAIL: *see* Railways.

PLATEWAY: *see* Railways.

PLINTH: projecting courses at the foot of a wall or column, generally chamfered or moulded at the top.

PODIUM: a continuous raised platform supporting a building; or a large block of two or three storeys beneath a multi-storey block of smaller area.

POINT BLOCK: *see* Multi-storey.

POINTING: exposed mortar jointing of masonry or brickwork. Types include *flush*, *recessed* and *tuck* (with a narrow channel filled with finer, whiter mortar).

POPPYHEAD: carved ornament of leaves and flowers as a finial for a bench end or stall.

PORTAL FRAME: C20 frame comprising two uprights rigidly connected to a beam or pair of rafters.

PORTCULLIS: gate constructed to rise and fall in vertical grooves at the entry to a castle.

PORTICO: a porch with the roof and frequently a pediment supported by a row of columns (4a). A portico *in antis* has columns on the same plane as the front of the building. A *prostyle* porch has columns standing free. Porticoes are described by the number of front columns, e.g. tetrastyle (four), hexastyle (six). The space within the temple is the *naos*, that within the portico the *pronaos*. *Blind portico*: the front features of a portico applied to a wall.

PORTICUS (plural: porticūs): subsidiary cell opening from the main body of a pre-Conquest church.

POST: upright support in a structure (7).

POSTERN: small gateway at the back of a building or to the side of a larger entrance door or gate.

POUND LOCK: *see* Canals.

PRESBYTERY: the part of a church lying E of the choir where the main altar is placed; or a priest's residence.

PRINCIPAL: *see* Roofs and 7.

PRONAOS: *see* Portico and 4a.

PROSTYLE: *see* Portico and 4a.

PULPIT: raised and enclosed platform for the preaching of sermons. *Three-decker*: with reading desk below and clerk's desk below that. *Two-decker*: as above, minus the clerk's desk.

PULPITUM: stone screen in a major church dividing choir from nave.

PULVINATED: *see* Frieze and 3c.

PURLIN: *see* Roofs and 7.

PUTHOLES or PUTLOG HOLES: in the wall to receive putlogs, the horizontal timbers which support scaffolding boards; sometimes not filled after construction is complete.

PUTTO (plural: putti): small naked boy.

QUARRIES: square (or diamond) panes of glass supported by lead strips (*cames*); square floor slabs or tiles.

QUATREFOIL: *see* Foil and 2b.

QUAY: a vertical wall and the level space behind for vessels to load and unload cargo.

QUEEN-STRUT: *see* Roofs and 7.

QUIRK: sharp groove to one side of a convex medieval moulding.

QUOINS: dressed stones at the angles of a building (6d).

RADBURN SYSTEM: vehicle and pedestrian segregation in residential developments, based on that used at Radburn, New Jersey, USA, by Wright and Stein, 1928–30.

RADIATING CHAPELS: projecting radially from an ambulatory or an apse (*see* Chevet).

RAFTER: *see* Roofs and 7.

RAGGLE: groove cut in masonry, especially to receive the edge of a roof-covering.

RAIL: *see* Panelling and 6b; also 7.

RAILWAYS: *Edge rail*: on which flanged wheels can run. *Plate rail*: L-section rail for plain unflanged wheels. *Plateway*: early railway using plate rails.

RAISED AND FIELDED: *see* Panelling and 6b.

RAKE: slope or pitch.

RAMPART: defensive outer wall of stone or earth. *Rampart walk*: path along the inner face.

REBATE: rectangular section cut out of a masonry edge to receive a shutter, door, window, etc.

REBUS: a heraldic pun, e.g. a fiery cock for Cockburn.

REEDING: series of convex mouldings, the reverse of fluting (q.v.). Cf. Gadrooning.

RENDERING: the covering of outside walls with a uniform surface or skin for protection from the weather. *Limewashing*: thin layer of lime plaster. *Pebble-dashing*: where aggregate is thrown at the wet plastered wall for a textured effect. *Roughcast*: plaster mixed with a coarse aggregate such as gravel. *Stucco*: fine lime plaster worked to a smooth surface. *Cement rendering*: a cheaper substitute for stucco, usually with a grainy texture.

REPOUSSÉ: relief designs in metalwork, formed by beating it from the back.

REREDORTER (*lit.* behind the dormitory): latrines in a medieval religious house.

REREDOS: painted and/or sculptured screen behind and above an altar. Cf. Retable.

RESPOND: half-pier or half-column bonded into a wall and carrying one end of an arch. It usually terminates an arcade.

RETABLE: painted or carved panel standing on or at the back of an altar, usually attached to it.

RETROCHOIR: in a major church, the area between the high altar and E chapel.

REVEAL: the plane of a jamb, between the wall and the frame of a door or window.

RIB-VAULT: *see* Vault and 2c.

RINCEAU: classical ornament of leafy scrolls (4b).

RISER: vertical face of a step (6c).

ROACH: a rough-textured form of Portland stone, with small cavities and fossil shells.

ROCK-FACED: masonry cleft to produce a rugged appearance.

ROCOCO: style current *c.* 1720 and *c.* 1760, characterized by a serpentine line and playful, scrolled decoration.

ROLL MOULDING: medieval moulding of part-circular section (1a).

ROMANESQUE: style current in the C11 and C12. In England often called Norman. *See also* Saxo-Norman.

ROOD: crucifix flanked by the Virgin and St John, usually over the entry into the chancel, on a beam (*rood beam*) or painted on the wall. The *rood screen* below often had a walkway (*rood loft*) along the top, reached by a *rood stair* in the side wall.

ROOFS: Shape. For the main external shapes (hipped, mansard, etc.) *see* 8a. *Helm* and *Saddleback*: *see* 1c.
Lean-to: single sloping roof built against a vertical wall; lean-to is also applied to the part of the building beneath.
Construction. *See* 7.
Single-framed roof: with no main trusses. The rafters may be fixed to the wall-plate or ridge, or longitudinal timber may be absent altogether.
Double-framed roof: with longitudinal members, such as purlins, and usually divided into bays by principals and principal rafters.
Other types are named after their main structural components, e.g. *hammerbeam*, *crown-post* (*see* Elements below and 7).
Elements. *See* 7.
Ashlar piece: a short vertical timber connecting inner wall-plate or timber pad to a rafter.
Braces: subsidiary timbers set diagonally to strengthen the frame. *Arched braces*: curved pair forming an arch, connecting wall or post below with tie- or collar-beam above. *Passing braces*: long straight braces passing across other members of the truss. *Scissor-braces*: pair crossing diagonally between pairs of rafters or principals. *Wind-braces*: short, usually curved braces connecting side purlins with principals; sometimes decorated with cusping.
Collar or *collar-beam*: horizontal transverse timber connecting a pair of rafter or cruck blades (q.v.), set between apex and the wall-plate.
Crown-post: a vertical timber set centrally on a tie-beam and supporting a collar purlin braced to it longitudinally. In an open truss lateral braces may rise to the collar-beam; in a closed truss they may descend to the tie-beam.
Hammerbeams: horizontal brackets projecting at wall-plate level like an interrupted tie-beam; the inner ends carry *hammerposts*, vertical timbers which support a purlin

and are braced to a collar-beam above.

Kingpost: vertical timber set centrally on a tie- or collar-beam, rising to the apex of the roof to support a ridge-piece (cf. Strut).

Plate: longitudinal timber set square to the ground. *Wall-plate*: plate along the top of a wall which receives the ends of the rafters; cf. Purlin.

Principals: pair of inclined lateral timbers of a truss. Usually they support side purlins and mark the main bay divisions.

Purlin: horizontal longitudinal timber. *Collar purlin* or *crown plate*: central timber which carries collar-beams and is supported by crown-posts. *Side purlins*: pairs of timbers placed some way up the slope of the roof, which carry common rafters. *Butt* or *tenoned purlins* are tenoned into either side of the principals. *Through purlins* pass through or past the principal; they include *clasped purlins*, which rest on queenposts or are carried in the angle between principals and collar, and *trenched purlins* trenched into the backs of principals.

Queen-strut: paired vertical, or near-vertical, timbers placed symmetrically on a tie-beam to support side purlins.

Rafters: inclined lateral timbers supporting the roof covering. *Common rafters*: regularly spaced uniform rafters placed along the length of a roof or between principals. *Principal rafters*: rafters which also act as principals.

Ridge, ridge-piece: horizontal longitudinal timber at the apex supporting the ends of the rafters.

Sprocket: short timber placed on the back and at the foot of a rafter to form projecting eaves.

Strut: vertical or oblique timber between two members of a truss, not directly supporting longitudinal timbers.

Tie-beam: main horizontal transverse timber which carries the feet of the principals at wall level.

Truss: rigid framework of timbers at bay intervals, carrying the longitudinal roof timbers which support the common rafters.

Closed truss: with the spaces between the timbers filled, to form an internal partition.

See also Cruck, Wagon roof.

ROPE MOULDING: *see* Cable moulding.

ROSE WINDOW: circular window with tracery radiating from the centre. Cf. Wheel window.

ROTUNDA: building or room circular in plan.

ROUGHCAST: *see* Rendering.

ROVING BRIDGE: *see* Canals.

RUBBED BRICKWORK: *see* Gauged brickwork.

RUBBLE: masonry whose stones are wholly or partly in a rough state. *Coursed*: coursed stones with rough faces. *Random*: uncoursed stones in a random pattern. *Snecked*: with courses broken by smaller stones (snecks).

RUSTICATION: *see* 6d. Exaggerated treatment of masonry to give an effect of strength. The joints are usually recessed by V-section chamfering or square-section channelling (*channelled rustication*). *Banded rustication* has only the horizontal joints emphasized. The faces may be flat, but can be *diamond-faced*, like shallow pyramids, *vermiculated*, with a stylized texture like worm-casts, and *glacial* (frost-work), like icicles or stalactites.

SACRISTY: room in a church for sacred vessels and vestments.

SADDLEBACK ROOF: *see* 1c.

SALTIRE CROSS: with diagonal limbs.

SANCTUARY: area around the main altar of a church. Cf. Presbytery.

SANGHA: residence of Buddhist monks or nuns.

SARCOPHAGUS: coffin of stone or other durable material.

SAXO-NORMAN: transitional Romanesque style combining Anglo-Saxon and Norman features, current *c.* 1060–1100.

SCAGLIOLA: composition imitating marble.

SCALLOPED CAPITAL: *see* 1a.

SCOTIA: a hollow classical moulding, especially between tori (q.v.) on a column base (3b, 3f).

SCREEN: in a medieval church, usually at the entry to the chancel; *see* Rood (screen) and Pulpitum. A *parclose screen* separates a chapel from the rest of the church.

SCREENS OR SCREENS PASSAGE: screened-off entrance passage between great hall and service rooms.

SECTION: two-dimensional representation of a building, moulding, etc., revealed by cutting across it.

SEDILIA (singular: sedile): seats for the priests (usually three) on the S side of the chancel.

SET-OFF: *see* Weathering.

SETTS: squared stones, usually of granite, used for paving or flooring.

SGRAFFITO: decoration scratched, often in plaster, to reveal a pattern in another colour beneath. *Graffiti*: scratched drawing or writing.

SHAFT: vertical member of round or polygonal section (1a, 3a). *Shaft-ring*: at the junction of shafts set *en delit* (q.v.) or attached to a pier or wall (1a).

SHELL: thin, self-supporting roofing membrane of timber or concrete.

SHOULDERED ARCHITRAVE: *see* 4b.

SHUTTERING: *see* Concrete.

SILL: horizontal member at the bottom of a window or door frame; or at the base of a timber-framed wall into which posts and studs are tenoned (7).

SLAB BLOCK: *see* Multi-storey.

SLATE-HANGING: covering of overlapping slates on a wall. *Tile-hanging* is similar.

SLYPE: covered way or passage leading E from the cloisters between transept and chapter house.

SNECKED: *see* Rubble.

SOFFIT (*lit.* ceiling): underside of an arch (also called *intrados*), lintel, etc. *Soffit roll*: medieval roll moulding on a soffit.

SOLAR: private upper chamber in a medieval house, accessible from the high end of the great hall.

SOUNDING-BOARD: *see* Tester.

SPANDRELS: roughly triangular spaces between an arch and its containing rectangle, or between adjacent arches (5c). Also non-structural panels under the windows in a curtain-walled building.

SPERE: a fixed structure screening the lower end of the great hall from the screens passage. *Spere-truss*: roof truss incorporated in the spere.

SPIRE: tall pyramidal or conical feature crowning a tower or turret. *Broach*: starting from a square base, then carried into an octagonal section by means of triangular faces; and *splayed-foot*: variation of the broach form, found principally in the south-east, in which the four cardinal faces are splayed out near their base, to cover the corners, while oblique (or intermediate) faces taper away to a point (1c). *Needle spire*: thin spire rising from the centre of a tower roof, well inside the parapet: when of timber and lead often called a *spike*.

SPIRELET: *see* Flèche.

SPLAY: of an opening when it is wider on one face of a wall than the other.

SPRING OR SPRINGING: level at which an arch or vault rises from its supports. *Springers*: the first stones of an arch or vaulting rib above the spring (2c).

SQUINCH: arch or series of arches thrown across an interior angle of a square or rectangular structure to support a circular or polygonal superstructure, especially a dome or spire (5a).

SQUINT: an aperture in a wall or through a pier usually to allow a view of an altar.

STAIRS: *see* 6c. *Dog-leg stair*: parallel flights rising alternately in opposite directions, without an open well. *Flying stair*: cantilevered from the walls of a stairwell, without newels; sometimes called a *Geometric* stair when the inner edge describes a curve. *Newel stair*: ascending round a central supporting newel (q.v.); called a *spiral stair* or *vice* when in a circular shaft, a *winder* when in a rectangular compartment. (Winder also applies to the steps on the turn.) *Well stair*: with flights round a square open well framed by newel posts. *See also* Perron.

STALL: fixed seat in the choir or chancel for the clergy or choir (cf. Pew). Usually with arm rests, and often framed together.

STANCHION: upright structural member, of iron, steel or reinforced concrete.

STANDPIPE TOWER: *see* Manometer.

STEAM ENGINES: *Atmospheric*: worked by the vacuum created when low-pressure steam is condensed in the cylinder, as developed by Thomas Newcomen. *Beam engine*: with a large pivoted beam moved in an oscillating fashion by the piston. It may drive a flywheel or be *non-rotative*. *Watt* and *Cornish*: single-cylinder; *compound*: two cylinders; *triple expansion*: three cylinders.

STEEPLE: tower together with a spire, lantern, or belfry.

STIFF-LEAF: type of E.E. foliage decoration. *Stiff-leaf capital see* 1b.

STOP: plain or decorated terminal to mouldings or chamfers, or at the end of hoodmoulds and labels (*label stop*), or stringcourses (5b, 6a); *see also* Headstop.

STOUP: vessel for holy water, usually near a door.

STRAINER: *see* Arch.

STRAPWORK: late C16 and C17 decoration, like interlaced leather straps.

STRETCHER: *see* Bond and 6e.

STRING: *see* 6c. Sloping member holding the ends of the treads and risers of a staircase. *Closed string*: a broad string covering the ends of the treads and risers. *Open string*: cut into the shape of the treads and risers.

STRING COURSE: horizontal course or moulding projecting from the surface of a wall (6d).

STUCCO: *see* Rendering.

STUDS: subsidiary vertical timbers of a timber-framed wall or partition (7).

STUPA: Buddhist shrine, circular in plan.

STYLOBATE: top of the solid platform on which a colonnade stands (3a).

SUSPENSION BRIDGE: *see* Bridge.

SWAG: like a festoon (q.v.), but representing cloth.

SYSTEM BUILDING: *see* Industrialized building.

TABERNACLE: canopied structure to contain the reserved sacrament or a relic; or architectural frame for an image or statue.

TABLE TOMB: memorial slab raised on free-standing legs.

TERM: pedestal or pilaster tapering downward, usually with the upper part of a human figure growing out of it.

TERRACOTTA: moulded and fired clay ornament or cladding.

TESSELLATED PAVEMENT: mosaic flooring, particularly Roman, made of *tesserae*, i.e. cubes of glass, stone, or brick.

TESTER: flat canopy over a tomb or pulpit, where it is also called a *sounding-board*.

TESTER TOMB: tomb-chest with effigies beneath a tester, either free-standing (tester with four or more columns), or attached to a wall (*half-tester*) with columns on one side only.

TETRASTYLE: *see* Portico.

THERMAL WINDOW: *see* Diocletian window.

THREE-DECKER PULPIT: *see* Pulpit.

TIDAL GATES: *see* Canals.

TIE-BEAM: *see* Roofs and 7.

TIERCERON: *see* Vault and 2c.

TILE-HANGING: *see* Slate-hanging.

TIMBER-FRAMING: *see* 7. Method of construction where the structural frame is built of interlocking timbers. The spaces are filled with non-structural material, e.g. *infill* of wattle and daub, lath and plaster, brickwork (known as *nogging*), etc. and may be covered by plaster, weatherboarding (q.v.), or tiles.

TOMB-CHEST: chest-shaped tomb, usually of stone. Cf. Table tomb, Tester tomb.

TORUS (plural: tori): large convex moulding usually used on a column base (3b, 3f).

TOUCH: soft black marble quarried near Tournai.

TOURELLE: turret corbelled out from the wall.

TOWER BLOCK: *see* Multi-storey.

TRABEATED: depends structurally on the use of the post and lintel. Cf. Arcuated.

TRACERY: openwork pattern of masonry or timber in the upper part of an opening. *Blind tracery* is tracery applied to a solid wall.

Plate tracery, introduced *c.* 1200, is the earliest form, in which shapes are cut through solid masonry (2a).

Bar tracery was introduced into England *c.* 1250. The pattern is formed by intersecting moulded ribwork continued from the mullions. It was especially elaborate during the Decorated period (q.v.). Tracery shapes can include circles, *daggers* (elongated ogee-ended lozenges), *mouchettes* (like daggers but with curved sides) and upright rectangular *panels*. They often have *cusps*, projecting points defining lobes or *foils* (q.v.) within the main shape: *Kentish* or *split-cusps* are forked (2b).

Types of bar tracery (*see* 2b) include *Geometric(al)*: *c.* 1250–1310, chiefly circles, often foiled; *Y-tracery*: *c.* 1300, with mullions branching into a Y-shape; *intersecting*: *c.* 1300, formed by interlocking mullions; *reticulated*: early C14, net-like pattern of ogee-ended lozenges; *curvilinear*: C14, with uninterrupted flowing curves; *panel*: Perp, with straight-sided panels, often cusped at the top and bottom.

TRANSEPT: transverse portion of a church.

TRANSITIONAL: generally used for the phase between Romanesque and Early English (*c.* 1175–*c.* 1200).

TRANSOM: horizontal member separating window lights (2b).

TREAD: horizontal part of a step. The *tread end* may be carved on a staircase (6c).

TREFOIL: *see* Foil.

TRIFORIUM: middle storey of a church treated as an arcaded wall passage or blind arcade, its height corresponding to that of the aisle roof.

TRIGLYPHS (*lit.* three-grooved tablets): stylized beam-ends in the Doric frieze, with metopes between (3b).

TRIUMPHAL ARCH: influential type of Imperial Roman monument.

TROPHY: sculptured or painted group of arms or armour.

TRUMEAU: central stone mullion supporting the tympanum of a wide doorway. *Trumeau figure*: carved figure attached to it (cf. Column figure).

TRUMPET CAPITAL: *see* 1b.

TRUSS: braced framework, spanning between supports. *See also* Roofs and 7.

TUMBLING or TUMBLING-IN: courses of brickwork laid at right-angles to a slope, e.g. of a gable, forming triangles by tapering into horizontal courses (8a).

TUSCAN: *see* Orders and 3e.

TWO-DECKER PULPIT: *see* Pulpit.

TYMPANUM: the surface between a lintel and the arch above it or within a pediment (4a).

UNDERCROFT: usually describes the vaulted room(s), beneath the main room(s) of a medieval house. Cf. Crypt.

VAULT: arched stone roof (sometimes imitated in timber or plaster). For types see 2c.

Tunnel or *barrel vault*: continuous semicircular or pointed arch, often of rubble masonry.

Groin-vault: tunnel vaults intersecting at right angles. *Groins* are the curved lines of the intersections.

Rib-vault: masonry framework of intersecting arches (ribs) supporting *vault cells*, used in Gothic architecture. *Wall rib* or *wall arch*:

between wall and vault cell. *Transverse rib*: spans between two walls to divide a vault into bays. *Quadripartite* rib-vault: each bay has two pairs of diagonal ribs dividing the vault into four triangular cells. *Sexpartite* rib-vault: most often used over paired bays, has an extra pair of ribs springing from between the bays. More elaborate vaults may include *ridge ribs* along the crown of a vault or bisecting the bays; *tiercerons*: extra decorative ribs springing from the corners of a bay; and *liernes*: short decorative ribs in the crown of a vault, not linked to any springing point. A *stellar* or *star* vault has liernes in star formation.

Fan-vault: form of barrel vault used in the Perp period, made up of halved concave masonry cones decorated with blind tracery.

VAULTING SHAFT: shaft leading up to the spring or springing (q.v.) of a vault (2c).

VENETIAN or SERLIAN WINDOW: derived from Serlio (4b). The motif is used for other openings.

VERMICULATION: *see* Rustication and 6d.

VESICA: oval with pointed ends.

VICE: *see* Stair.

VILLA: originally a Roman country house or farm. The term was revived in England in the C18 under the influence of Palladio and used especially for smaller, compact country houses. In the later C19 it was debased to describe any suburban house.

VITRIFIED: bricks or tiles fired to a darkened glassy surface.

VITRUVIAN SCROLL: classical running ornament of curly waves (4b).

VOLUTES: spiral scrolls. They occur on Ionic capitals (3c). *Angle volute*: pair of volutes, turned outwards to meet at the corner of a capital.

VOUSSOIRS: wedge-shaped stones forming an arch (5c).

WAGON ROOF: with the appearance of the inside of a wagon tilt; often ceiled. Also called *cradle roof*.

WAINSCOT: *see* Panelling.

WALL MONUMENT: attached to the wall and often standing on the floor. *Wall tablets* are smaller with the inscription as the major element.

WALL-PLATE: *see* Roofs and 7.

WALL-WALK: *see* Parapet.

WARMING ROOM: room in a religious house where a fire burned for comfort.

WATERHOLDING BASE: early Gothic base with upper and lower mouldings separated by a deep hollow.

WATERLEAF: *see* Enrichments and 3f.

WATERLEAF CAPITAL: Late Romanesque and Transitional type of capital (1b).

WATER WHEELS: described by the way water is fed on to the wheel. *Breastshot*: mid-height, falling and passing beneath. *Overshot*: over the top. *Pitchback*: on the top but falling backwards. *Undershot*: turned by the momentum of the water passing beneath. In a *water turbine*, water is fed under pressure through a vaned wheel within a casing.

WEALDEN HOUSE: type of medieval timber-framed house with a central open hall flanked by bays of two storeys, roofed in line; the end bays are jettied to the front, but the eaves are continuous (8a).

WEATHERBOARDING: wall cladding of overlapping horizontal boards.

WEATHERING or SET-OFF: inclined, projecting surface to keep water away from the wall below.

WEEPERS: figures in niches along the sides of some medieval tombs. Also called mourners.

WHEEL WINDOW: circular, with radiating shafts like spokes. Cf. Rose window.

WROUGHT IRON: *see* Cast iron.

INDEX OF ARCHITECTS, ARTISTS AND PATRONS

The names of architects and artists working in the areas covered by this volume are given in *italic*. Entries for partnerships and group practices are listed after entries for a single surname. Minor differences in title are disregarded.

Indexed here are also the names/titles of families and individuals (not of bodies or commercial firms) recorded in this volume as having owned property or commissioned architectural work. It includes monuments to members of such families and other individuals where they are of particular interest.

Entries for partnerships and group practices are listed after entries for a single surname.

INDEX OF STREETS, BUILDINGS AND LOCALITIES

Principal references are in **bold** type. References in *italic* are to buildings which no longer stand, and to defunct streets or street names. References in roman type within an italic entry are to remaining parts or furnishings of a vanished building.

Buildings whose use has changed may be indexed under both present and former names. Broadways, High Roads and High Streets are indexed together.

Building types indexed together include: Almshouses; Baptist Chapels and Churches, Baths and Swimming Pools; Board Schools; Breweries; Cemeteries etc.; Cinemas; County Courts; Dispensaries; Docks; East End Dwellings Co. housing; Fire Stations; Four per cent Industrial Dwellings Co. housing, Friends Meeting Houses; Gasworks; Health Centres, Clinics and Doctors' Practices; Hospitals and Asylums; Improved Industrial Dwellings Co. housing; Libraries; Magistrates Courts; Methodist Chapels and Churches; Mosques; Parks; Peabody Estates; Police Stations; Post Offices; Presbyterian Churches; Pumping Stations; Reservoirs and Waterworks; Seamen's Missions; Stations; Synagogues; Telephone Exchanges; Temples; Theatres; Town Halls (including Vestry Halls, Board of Works offices, Municipal Buildings and Civic Centres); Unitarian Churches; United Reformed Churches; War Memorials; Workhouses and Industrial Schools.

The following abbreviations are used for the boroughs:

BD: Barking and Dagenham
HV: Havering
NM: Newham
TH: Tower Hamlets
RB: Redbridge
WF: Waltham Forest